This work: "Grammatical theory", was originally published by Language Science Press and is being sold pursuant to a Creative Commons license permitting commercial use. All rights not granted by the work's license are retained by the author or authors.

Cover Image Credit/Copyright Attribution: IIIerlok_Xolms/Shutterstock

Grammatical theory

From transformational grammar to constraint-based approaches
Third revised and extended edition

Stefan Müller

Stefan Müller. 2018. *Grammatical theory: From transformational grammar to constraint-based approaches*. Third revised and extended edition. (Textbooks in Language Sciences 1). Berlin: Language Science Press.

© 2019, Stefan Müller
Published under the Creative Commons Attribution 4.0 Licence (CC BY 4.0):
http://creativecommons.org/licenses/by/4.0/

Translator: Andrew Murphy, Stefan Müller
Typesetting: Stefan Müller
Proofreading: Viola Auermann, Armin Buch, Andreea Calude, Rong Chen, Matthew Czuba, Leonel de Alencar, Christian Döhler, Joseph T. Farquharson, Andreas Hölzl, Gianina Iordăchioaia, Paul Kay, Anne Kilgus, Sandra Kübler, Timm Lichte, Antonio Machicao y Priemer, Michelle Natolo, Stephanie Natolo, Sebastian Nordhoff, Elizabeth Pankratz, Parviz Parsafar, Conor Pyle, Daniela Schröder, Eva Schultze-Berndt, Alec Shaw, Benedikt Singpiel, Anelia Stefanova, Neal Whitman, Viola Wiegand
Open reviewing: Armin Buch, Leonel de Alencar, Andreas Hölzl, Dick Hudson, Gianina Iordăchioaia, Paul Kay, Timm Lichte, Antonio Machicao y Priemer, Andrew McIntyre, Arne Nymos, Sebastian Nordhoff, Neal Whitman
Fonts: Linux Libertine, Arimo, DejaVu Sans Mono
Typesetting software: X${}_{\exists}$LATEX

Language Science Press
Unter den Linden 6
10099 Berlin, Germany

For Max

Contents

Preface	xv

I Background and specific theories   1

1 Introduction and basic terms   3
- 1.1 Why do syntax? 3
- 1.2 Why do it formally? 6
- 1.3 Constituents 6
  - 1.3.1 Constituency tests 7
  - 1.3.2 Some comments on the status of constituent tests 11
- 1.4 Parts of speech 17
- 1.5 Heads 28
- 1.6 Arguments and adjuncts 30
- 1.7 Grammatical functions 35
  - 1.7.1 Subjects 35
  - 1.7.2 The adverbial 40
  - 1.7.3 Predicatives 41
  - 1.7.4 Valence classes 42
- 1.8 A topological model of the German clause 43
  - 1.8.1 The position of the verb 43
  - 1.8.2 The sentence bracket, prefield, middle field and postfield . 44
  - 1.8.3 Assigning elements to fields 45
  - 1.8.4 Recursion 49

2 Phrase structure grammar   53
- 2.1 Symbols and rewrite rules 53
- 2.2 Expanding PSG with features 59
- 2.3 Semantics 60
- 2.4 Phrase structure rules for some aspects of German syntax 63
  - 2.4.1 Noun phrases 63
  - 2.4.2 Prepositional phrases 71
- 2.5 $\overline{\text{X}}$ theory 73

3 Transformational Grammar – Government & Binding   83
- 3.1 General remarks on the representational format 84
  - 3.1.1 Transformations 84

		3.1.2	The hypothesis regarding language acquisition: Principles & Parameters 86

        3.1.3   The T model 87
        3.1.4 $\overline{\text{X}}$ theory 93
        3.1.5   CP and IP in English 96
        3.1.6   The structure of the German clause 101
  3.2 Verb position 102
  3.3 Long-distance dependencies 106
  3.4 Passive 109
        3.4.1   Structural and lexical case 109
        3.4.2   Case assignment and the Case Filter 110
  3.5 Local reordering 114
  3.6 Summary and classification 117
        3.6.1   Explaining language acquisition 118
        3.6.2   Formalization 118

4 Transformational Grammar – Minimalism   127
  4.1 General remarks on the representational format 127
        4.1.1   Basic architecture 128
        4.1.2   Valence, feature checking, and agreement 129
        4.1.3   Phrase structure and $\overline{\text{X}}$ theory 131
        4.1.4   Little *v* 132
        4.1.5   CP, TP, *v*P, VP 134
        4.1.6   Adjuncts 138
  4.2 Verb position 138
  4.3 Long-distance dependencies 139
  4.4 Passive 140
  4.5 Local reordering 142
  4.6 New developments and theoretical variants 143
        4.6.1   Move, Merge, feature-driven movement and functional projections 144
        4.6.2   Labeling 154
        4.6.3   Specifiers, complements, and the remains of $\overline{\text{X}}$ theory 160
        4.6.4   Minimalism, Categorial Grammar, and HPSG 164
        4.6.5   Selection of atomic features vs. selection of complex categories . 172
        4.6.6   Summary 174
  4.7 Summary and classification 174
        4.7.1   Explaining language acquisition 175
        4.7.2   Formalization 175

5 Generalized Phrase Structure Grammar   181
  5.1 General remarks on the representational format 181
        5.1.1   Complex categories, the Head Feature Convention, and $\overline{\text{X}}$ rules . 182
        5.1.2   Local reordering 184
        5.1.3   Metarules 186

		5.1.4 Semantics 188

        5.1.4   Semantics 188
        5.1.5   Adjuncts 189
  5.2   Passive as a metarule 191
  5.3   Verb position 194
  5.4   Long-distance dependencies as the result of local dependencies 195
  5.5   Summary and classification 198
        5.5.1   Valence and morphology 199
        5.5.2   Valence and partial verb phrase fronting 200
        5.5.3   Generative capacity 201

6 Feature descriptions   205
  6.1   Feature descriptions 205
  6.2   Types 208
  6.3   Disjunction 210
  6.4   Structure sharing 211
  6.5   Cyclic structures 213
  6.6   Unification 213
  6.7   Phenomena, models and formal theories 215

7 Lexical Functional Grammar   221
  7.1   General remarks on the representational format 223
        7.1.1   Functional structure 223
        7.1.2   Completeness 226
        7.1.3   Coherence 226
        7.1.4   Restrictions on the c-structure/f-structure relation 227
        7.1.5   Semantics 227
        7.1.6   Adjuncts 230
  7.2   Passive 231
  7.3   Verb position 234
  7.4   Local reordering 235
  7.5   Long-distance dependencies and functional uncertainty 237
  7.6   Summary and classification 241

8 Categorial Grammar   245
  8.1   General remarks on the representational format 246
        8.1.1   Representation of valence information 246
        8.1.2   Semantics 247
        8.1.3   Adjuncts 249
  8.2   Passive 249
  8.3   Verb position 251
  8.4   Local reordering 253
  8.5   Long-distance dependencies 254
        8.5.1   Type Raising 254
        8.5.2   Forward and backward composition 254

Contents

		8.5.3	Analysis of long-distance dependencies 255
	8.6	Summary and classification 257

9 Head-Driven Phrase Structure Grammar   **263**
- 9.1 General remarks on the representational format 266
    - 9.1.1 Representation of valence information 267
    - 9.1.2 Representation of constituent structure 271
    - 9.1.3 Linearization rules 274
    - 9.1.4 Projection of head properties 275
    - 9.1.5 Inheritance hierarchies and generalizations 277
    - 9.1.6 Semantics 280
    - 9.1.7 Adjuncts 283
- 9.2 Passive 285
    - 9.2.1 Valence information and the Case Principle 288
- 9.3 Verb position 290
- 9.4 Local reordering 296
- 9.5 Long-distance dependencies 298
- 9.6 New developments and theoretical variants 303
- 9.7 Summary and classification 304

10 Construction Grammar   **311**
- 10.1 General remarks on the representational format 313
    - 10.1.1 The head-complement construction 314
    - 10.1.2 Representation of valence information 315
    - 10.1.3 Semantics 315
    - 10.1.4 Adjuncts 315
- 10.2 Passive 315
- 10.3 Verb position 320
- 10.4 Local reordering 323
- 10.5 Long-distance dependencies 323
- 10.6 New developments and theoretical variants 324
    - 10.6.1 Berkeley Construction Grammar 324
    - 10.6.2 Sign-Based Construction Grammar 327
    - 10.6.3 Embodied Construction Grammar 338
    - 10.6.4 Fluid Construction Grammar 342
- 10.7 Summary and classification 361

11 Dependency Grammar   **365**
- 11.1 General remarks on the representational format 368
    - 11.1.1 Valence information, nucleus and satellites 368
    - 11.1.2 Adjuncts 370
    - 11.1.3 Linearization 371
    - 11.1.4 Semantics 372
- 11.2 Passive 373

	11.3	Verb position	375
	11.4	Local reordering	376
	11.5	Long-distance dependencies	377
	11.6	New developments and theoretical variants	382
		11.6.1 Tesnière's part of speech classification	382
		11.6.2 Connection, junction, and transfer	383
		11.6.3 Scope	389
	11.7	Summary and classification	390
		11.7.1 Linearization	390
		11.7.2 Dependency Grammar vs. phrase structure grammar	397
12	**Tree Adjoining Grammar**		**415**
	12.1	General remarks on representational format	416
		12.1.1 Representation of valence information	416
		12.1.2 Substitution	416
		12.1.3 Adjunction	417
		12.1.4 Semantics	418
	12.2	Local reordering	420
	12.3	Verb position	425
	12.4	Passive	425
	12.5	Long-distance dependencies	426
	12.6	New developments and theoretical variants	426
		12.6.1 FTAG	427
		12.6.2 V-TAG	430
		12.6.3 The competence-performance distinction and the generative capacity of tree-local MC-LTAG	432
	12.7	Summary and classification	437

II General discussion — 441

13	**The innateness of linguistic knowledge**		**447**
	13.1	Syntactic universals	449
		13.1.1 Head Directionality Parameter	450
		13.1.2 $\overline{\text{X}}$ structures	451
		13.1.3 Grammatical functions such as subject and object	454
		13.1.4 Binding principles	456
		13.1.5 Properties of long-distance dependencies	458
		13.1.6 Grammatical morphemes for tense, mood and aspect	466
		13.1.7 Parts of speech	466
		13.1.8 Recursion and infinitude	467
		13.1.9 Summary	475
	13.2	Speed of language acquisition	475
	13.3	Critical period for acquisition	476

Contents

13.4	Lack of acquisition among non-human primates	477
13.5	Creole and sign languages	478
13.6	Localization in special parts of the brain	479
13.7	Differences between language and general cognition	480
	13.7.1 Williams Syndrome	481
	13.7.2 KE family with FoxP2 mutation	481
13.8	Poverty of the Stimulus	482
	13.8.1 Gold's Theorem	482
	13.8.2 Four case studies	486
	13.8.3 Unsupervised Data-Oriented Parsing (U-DOP)	496
	13.8.4 Negative evidence	503
13.9	Summary	504

14 Generative-enumerative vs. model-theoretic approaches — 507
- 14.1 Graded acceptability — 509
- 14.2 Utterance fragments — 510
- 14.3 A problem for model-theoretic approaches? — 512

15 The competence/performance distinction — 517
- 15.1 The derivational theory of complexity — 519
- 15.2 Incremental processing — 522

16 Language acquisition — 529
- 16.1 Principles & Parameters — 529
- 16.2 Principles and the lexicon — 537
- 16.3 Pattern-based approaches — 537
- 16.4 Selection-based approaches — 544
- 16.5 Summary — 545

17 Generative capacity and grammar formalisms — 547

18 Binary branching, locality, and recursion — 553
- 18.1 Binary branching — 553
- 18.2 Locality — 556
- 18.3 Recursion — 565

19 Empty elements — 567
- 19.1 Views on empty elements — 567
- 19.2 Eliminating empty elements from grammars — 569
- 19.3 Empty elements and semantic interpretation — 574
- 19.4 Evidence for empty elements — 581
- 19.5 Transformations, lexical rules, and empty elements — 581

20 Extraction, scrambling, and passive: one or several descriptive devices? — 587

21 Phrasal vs. lexical analyses — 597
21.1 Some putative advantages of phrasal models — 598
- 21.1.1 Usage-based theories — 598
- 21.1.2 Coercion — 600
- 21.1.3 Aspect as a clause level phenomenon — 602
- 21.1.4 Simplicity and polysemy — 602

21.2 Evidence for lexical approaches — 605
- 21.2.1 Valence and coordination — 605
- 21.2.2 Valence and derivational morphology — 609

21.3 Radical underspecification: the end of argument structure? — 621
- 21.3.1 Neo-Davidsonianism — 621
- 21.3.2 Little v and idiom asymmetries — 623
- 21.3.3 Deverbal nominals — 625
- 21.3.4 Idiosyncratic syntactic selections — 628
- 21.3.5 Expletives — 630
- 21.3.6 An exoskeletal approach — 631
- 21.3.7 Is there an alternative to lexical valence structure? — 636
- 21.3.8 Summary — 636

21.4 Relations between constructions — 637
- 21.4.1 Inheritance hierarchies for constructions — 637
- 21.4.2 Mappings between different levels of representations — 643
- 21.4.3 Is there an alternative to lexical rules? — 645

21.5 Further problems for phrasal approaches — 646
- 21.5.1 Particle verbs and commitment to phrase structure configurations — 646

21.6 Arguments from language acquisition — 647
- 21.6.1 Recognizability of constructions — 647
- 21.6.2 Coordination and discontinuousness — 648

21.7 Arguments from psycho- and neurolinguistics — 653
- 21.7.1 Lexical rules vs. phrasal constructions — 653
- 21.7.2 Light verbs — 656
- 21.7.3 Arguments from neurolinguistics — 657

21.8 Arguments from statistical distribution — 660
- 21.8.1 Unsupervised Data-Oriented Parsing — 661
- 21.8.2 Collostructions — 663

21.9 Conclusion — 664
21.10 Why (phrasal) constructions? — 664
- 21.10.1 Verbless directives — 665
- 21.10.2 Serial verbs — 672
- 21.10.3 Relative and interrogative clauses — 673
- 21.10.4 The N-P-N construction — 675

22 Structure, potential structure and underspecification — 679

23 Universal Grammar and comparative linguistics without UG 685
23.1 Formal tools for capturing generalizations 685
23.2 How to develop linguistic theories that capture cross-linguistic generalizations 689

24 Conclusion 699

Appendix A: Solutions to the exercises 703
A.1 Introduction and basic terms 703
A.2 Phrase structure grammars 704
A.3 Transformational Grammar – Government & Binding 707
A.4 Generalized Phrase Structure Grammar 709
A.5 Feature descriptions 711
A.6 Lexical Functional Grammar 713
A.7 Categorial Grammar 714
A.8 Head-Driven Phrase Structure Grammar 715
A.9 Construction Grammar 716
A.10 Dependency Grammar 717
A.11 Tree Adjoining Grammar 718

References 721

Index 823
Name index 823
Language index 837
Subject index 839

Preface

This book is an extended and revised version of my German book *Grammatiktheorie* (Müller 2013a). It introduces various grammatical theories that play a role in current theorizing or have made contributions in the past which are still relevant today. I explain some foundational assumptions and then apply the respective theories to what can be called the "core grammar" of German. I have decided to stick to the object language that I used in the German version of this book since many of the phenomena that will be dealt with cannot be explained with English as the object language. Furthermore, many theories have been developed by researchers with English as their native language and it is illuminative to see these theories applied to another language. I show how the theories under consideration deal with arguments and adjuncts, active/passive alternations, local reorderings (so-called scrambling), verb position, and fronting of phrases over larger distances (the verb second property of the Germanic languages without English).

The second part deals with foundational questions that are important for developing theories. This includes a discussion of the question of whether we have innate domain specific knowledge of language (UG), the discussion of psycholinguistic evidence concerning the processing of language by humans, a discussion of the status of empty elements and of the question whether we construct and perceive utterances holistically or rather compositionally, that is, whether we use phrasal or lexical constructions. The second part is not intended as a standalone book although the printed version of the book is distributed this way for technical reasons (see below). Rather it contains topics that are discussed again and again when frameworks are compared. So instead of attaching these discussions to the individual chapters they are organized in a separate part of the book.

Unfortunately, linguistics is a scientific field with a considerable amount of terminological chaos. I therefore wrote an introductory chapter that introduces terminology in the way it is used later on in the book. The second chapter introduces phrase structure grammars, which plays a role for many of the theories that are covered in this book. I use these two chapters (excluding the Section 2.3 on interleaving phrase structure grammars and semantics) in introductory courses of our BA curriculum for German studies. Advanced readers may skip these introductory chapters. The following chapters are structured in a way that should make it possible to understand the introduction of the theories without any prior knowledge. The sections regarding new developments and classification are more ambitious: they refer to chapters still to come and also point to other publications that are relevant in the current theoretical discussion but cannot be repeated or summarized in this book. These parts of the book address advanced students and researchers. I use this book for teaching the syntactic aspects of the theories in a seminar for advanced students in our BA. The slides are available on my web page. The second part of the book, the general discussion, is more ambitious and contains the discussion of advanced topics and current research literature.

This book only deals with relatively recent developments. For a historical overview, see for instance Robins (1997); Jungen & Lohnstein (2006). I am aware of the fact that chapters on Integrational Linguistics (Lieb 1983; Eisenberg 2004; Nolda 2007), Optimality Theory (Prince & Smolensky 1993; Grimshaw 1997; G. Müller 2000), Role and Reference Grammar (Van Valin 1993) and Relational Grammar (Perlmutter 1983; 1984) are missing. I will leave these theories for later editions.

The original German book was planned to have 400 pages, but it finally was much bigger: the first German edition has 525 pages and the second German edition has 564 pages. I added a chapter on Dependency Grammar and one on Minimalism to the English version and now the book has 849 pages. I tried to represent the chosen theories appropriately and to cite all important work. Although the list of references is over 85 pages long, I was probably not successful. I apologize for this and any other shortcomings.

Available versions of this book

The canonical version of this book is the PDF document available from the Language Science Press webpage of this book[1]. This page also links to a Print on Demand version. Since the book is very long, we decided to split the book into two volumes. The first volume contains the description of all theories and the second volume contains the general discussion. Both volumes contain the complete list of references and the indices. The second volume starts with page 443. The printed volumes are therefore identical to the parts of the PDF document.

Acknowledgments

I would like to thank David Adger, Jason Baldridge, Felix Bildhauer, Emily M. Bender, Stefan Evert, Gisbert Fanselow, Sandiway Fong, Hans-Martin Gärtner, Kim Gerdes, Adele Goldberg, Bob Levine, Paul Kay, Jakob Maché, Guido Mensching, Laura Michaelis, Geoffrey Pullum, Uli Sauerland, Roland Schäfer, Jan Strunk, Remi van Trijp, Shravan Vasishth, Tom Wasow, and Stephen Wechsler for discussion and Monika Budde, Philippa Cook, Laura Kallmeyer, Tibor Kiss, Gisela Klann-Delius, Jonas Kuhn, Timm Lichte, Anke Lüdeling, Jens Michaelis, Bjarne Ørsnes, Andreas Pankau, Christian Pietsch, Frank Richter, Ivan Sag, and Eva Wittenberg for comments on earlier versions of the German edition of this book and Thomas Groß, Dick Hudson, Sylvain Kahane, Paul Kay, Haitao Liu (刘海涛), Andrew McIntyre, Sebastian Nordhoff, Tim Osborne, Andreas Pankau, and Christoph Schwarze for comments on earlier versions of this book. Thanks to Leonardo Boiko and Sven Verdoolaege for pointing out typos. Special thanks go to Martin Haspelmath for very detailed comments on an earlier version of the English book.

---

[1] http://langsci-press.org/catalog/book/255

This book was the first Language Science Press book that had an open review phase (see below). I thank Dick Hudson, Paul Kay, Antonio Machicao y Priemer, Andrew McIntyre, Sebastian Nordhoff, and one anonymous open reviewer for their comments. Theses comments are documented at the download page of this book. In addition the book went through a stage of community proofreading (see also below). Some of the proofreaders did much more than proofreading, their comments are highly appreciated and I decided to publish these comments as additional open reviews. Armin Buch, Leonel de Alencar, Andreas Hölzl, Gianina Iordăchioaia, Timm Lichte, Antonio Machicao y Priemer, and Neal Whitman deserve special mention here.

I thank Wolfgang Sternefeld and Frank Richter, who wrote a detailed review of the German version of this book (Sternefeld & Richter 2012). They pointed out some mistakes and omissions that were corrected in the second edition of the German book and which are of course not present in the English version.

Thanks to all the students who commented on the book and whose questions lead to improvements. Lisa Deringer, Aleksandra Gabryszak, Simon Lohmiller, Theresa Kallenbach, Steffen Neuschulz, Reka Meszaros-Segner, Lena Terhart and Elodie Winckel deserve special mention.

Since this book is built upon all my experience in the area of grammatical theory, I want to thank all those with whom I ever discussed linguistics during and after talks at conferences, workshops, summer schools or via email. Werner Abraham, John Bateman, Dorothee Beermann, Rens Bod, Miriam Butt, Manfred Bierwisch, Ann Copestake, Holger Diessel, Kerstin Fischer, Dan Flickinger, Peter Gallmann, Petter Haugereid, Lars Hellan, Tibor Kiss, Wolfgang Klein, Hans-Ulrich Krieger, Andrew McIntyre, Detmar Meurers, Gereon Müller, Martin Neef, Manfred Sailer, Anatol Stefanowitsch, Peter Svenonius, Michael Tomasello, Hans Uszkoreit, Gert Webelhuth, Daniel Wiechmann and Arne Zeschel deserve special mention.

I thank Sebastian Nordhoff for a comment regarding the completion of the subject index entry for *recursion*.

Andrew Murphy translated part of Chapter 1 and the Chapters 2–3, 5–10, and 12–23. Many thanks for this!

I also want to thank the 27 community proofreaders (Viola Auermann, Armin Buch, Andreea Calude, Rong Chen, Matthew Czuba, Leonel de Alencar, Christian Döhler, Joseph T. Farquharson, Andreas Hölzl, Gianina Iordăchioaia, Paul Kay, Anne Kilgus, Sandra Kübler, Timm Lichte, Antonio Machicao y Priemer, Michelle Natolo, Stephanie Natolo, Sebastian Nordhoff, Elizabeth Pankratz, Parviz Parsafar, Conor Pyle, Daniela Schröder, Eva Schultze-Berndt, Alec Shaw, Benedikt Singpiel, Anelia Stefanova, Neal Whitman, Viola Wiegand) that each worked on one or more chapters and really improved this book. I got more comments from every one of them than I ever got for a book done with a commercial publisher. Some comments were on content rather than on typos and layout issues. No proofreader employed by a commercial publisher would have spotted these mistakes and inconsistencies since commercial publishers do not have staff that knows all the grammatical theories that are covered in this book.

During the past years, a number of workshops on theory comparison have taken place. I was invited to three of them. I thank Helge Dyvik and Torbjørn Nordgård for inviting me to the fall school for Norwegian PhD students *Languages and Theories in Contrast*, which took place 2005 in Bergen. Guido Mensching and Elisabeth Stark invited me to the workshop *Comparing Languages and Comparing Theories: Generative Grammar and Construction Grammar*, which took place in 2007 at the Freie Universität Berlin and Andreas Pankau invited me to the workshop *Comparing Frameworks* in 2009 in Utrecht. I really enjoyed the discussion with all participants of these events and this book benefited enormously from the interchange.

I thank Peter Gallmann for the discussion of his lecture notes on GB during my time in Jena. The Sections 3.1.3–3.4 have a structure that is similar to the one of his script and take over a lot. Thanks to David Reitter for the LaTeX macros for Combinatorial Categorial Grammar, to Mary Dalrymple and Jonas Kuhn for the LFG macros and example structures, and to Laura Kallmeyer for the LaTeX sources of most of the TAG analyses. Most of the trees have been adapted to the forest package because of compatibility issues with XƎLaTeX, but the original trees and texts were a great source of inspiration and without them the figures in the respective chapters would not be half as pretty as they are now.

I thank Sašo Živanović for implementing the LaTeX package forest. It really simplifies typesetting of trees, dependency graphs, and type hierarchies. I also thank him for individual help via email and on stackexchange. In general, those active on stackexchange could not be thanked enough: most of my questions regarding specific details of the typesetting of this book or the implementation of the LaTeX classes that are used by Language Science Press now have been answered within several minutes. Thank you! Since this book is a true open access book under the CC-BY license, it can also be an open source book. The interested reader finds a copy of the source code at https://github.com/langsci/25. By making the book open source I pass on the knowledge provided by the LaTeX gurus and hope that others benefit from this and learn to typeset their linguistics papers in nicer and/or more efficient ways.

Viola Auermann and Antje Bahlke, Sarah Dietzfelbinger, Lea Helmers, and Chiara Jancke cannot be thanked enough for their work at the copy machines. Viola also helped a lot with proof reading prefinal stages of the translation. I also want to thank my (former) lab members Felix Bildhauer, Philippa Cook, Janna Lipenkova, Jakob Maché, Bjarne Ørsnes and Roland Schäfer, which were mentioned above already for other reasons, for their help with teaching. During the years from 2007 until the publication of the first German edition of this book two of the three tenured positions in German Linguistics were unfilled and I would have not been able to maintain the teaching requirements without their help and would have never finished the *Grammatiktheorie* book.

I thank Tibor Kiss for advice in questions of style. His diplomatic way always was a shining example for me and I hope that this is also reflected in this book.

On the way this book is published

I started to work on my dissertation in 1994 and defended it in 1997. During the whole time the manuscript was available on my web page. After the defense, I had to look for a publisher. I was quite happy to be accepted to the series *Linguistische Arbeiten* by Niemeyer, but at the same time I was shocked about the price, which was 186.00

DM for a paperback book that was written and typeset by me without any help by the publisher (twenty times the price of a paperback novel).² This basically meant that my book was depublished: until 1998 it was available from my web page and after this it was available in libraries only. My Habilitationsschrift was published by CSLI Publications for a much more reasonable price. When I started writing textbooks, I was looking for alternative distribution channels and started to negotiate with no-name print on demand publishers. Brigitte Narr, who runs the Stauffenburg publishing house, convinced me to publish my HPSG textbook with her. The copyrights for the German version of the book remained with me so that I could publish it on my web page. The collaboration was successful so that I also published my second textbook about grammatical theory with Stauffenburg. I think that this book has a broader relevance and should be accessible for non-German-speaking readers as well. I therefore decided to have it translated into English. Since Stauffenburg is focused on books in German, I had to look for another publisher. Fortunately the situation in the publishing sector changed quite dramatically in comparison to 1997: we now have high profile publishers with strict peer review that are entirely open access. I am very glad about the fact that Brigitte Narr sold the rights of my book back to me and that I can now publish the English version with Language Science Press under a CC-BY license.

Language Science Press: scholar-owned high quality linguistic books

In 2012 a group of people found the situation in the publishing business so unbearable that they agreed that it would be worthwhile to start a bigger initiative for publishing linguistics books in platinum open access, that is, free for both readers and authors. I set up a web page and collected supporters, very prominent linguists from all over the world and all subdisciplines and Martin Haspelmath and I then founded Language Science Press. At about the same time the DFG had announced a program for open access monographs and we applied (Müller & Haspelmath 2013) and got funded (two out of 18 applications got funding). The money is used for a coordinator (Dr. Sebastian Nordhoff) and an economist (Debora Siller), two programmers (Carola Fanselow and Dr. Mathias Schenner), who work on the publishing plattform Open Monograph Press (OMP) and on conversion software that produces various formats (ePub, XML, HTML) from our LaTeX code. Svantje Lilienthal works on the documentation of OMP, produces screencasts and does user support for authors, readers and series editors.

OMP is extended by open review facilities and community-building gamification tools (Müller 2012a; Müller & Haspelmath 2013). All Language Science Press books are reviewed by at least two external reviewers. Reviewers and authors may agree to publish these reviews and thereby make the whole process more transparent (see also Pullum (1984) for the suggestion of open reviewing of journal articles). In addition there is an optional second review phase: the open review. This review is completely open to ev-

---

²As a side remark: in the meantime Niemeyer was bought by de Gruyter and closed down. The price of the book is now 139.95 €/ $ 196.00. The price in Euro corresponds to 273.72 DM.

Preface

erybody. The whole community may comment on the document that is published by Language Science Press. After this second review phase, which usually lasts for two months, authors may revise their publication and an improved version will be published. This book was the first book to go through this open review phase. The annotated open review version of this book is still available via the web page of this book.

Currently, Language Science Press has 17 series on various subfields of linguistics with high profile series editors from all continents. We have 18 published and 17 forthcoming books and 146 expressions of interest. Series editors and authors are responsible for delivering manuscripts that are typeset in LaTeX, but they are supported by a web-based typesetting infrastructure that was set up by Language Science Press and by volunteer typesetters from the community. Proofreading is also community-based. Until now 53 people helped improving our books. Their work is documented in the Hall of Fame: http://langsci-press.org/hallOfFame.

If you think that textbooks like this one should be freely available to whoever wants to read them and that publishing scientific results should not be left to profit-oriented publishers, then you can join the Language Science Press community and support us in various ways: you can register with Language Science Press and have your name listed on our supporter page with almost 600 other enthusiasts, you may devote your time and help with proofreading and/or typesetting, or you may donate money for specific books or for Language Science Press in general. We are also looking for institutional supporters like foundations, societies, linguistics departments or university libraries. Detailed information on how to support us is provided at the following webpage: http://langsci-press.org/supportUs. In case of questions, please contact me or the Language Science Press coordinator at contact@langsci-press.org.

Berlin, March 11, 2016   Stefan Müller

Foreword of the second edition

The first edition of this book was published almost exactly two years ago. The book has app. 15,000 downloads and is used for teaching and in research all over the world. This is what every author and every teacher dreams of: distribution of knowledge and accessibility for everybody. The foreword of the first edition ends with a description of Language Science Press in 2016. This is the situation now:[3] We have 324 expressions of interest and 58 published books. Books are published in 20 book series with 263 members of editorial boards from 44 different countries from six continents. We have a total of 175,000 downloads. 138 linguists from all over the world have participated in proofreading. There are currently 296 proofreaders registered with Language Science Press. Language Science Press is a community-based publisher, but there is one person who manages everything: Sebastian Nordhoff. His position has to be paid. We were successful in acquiring financial support by almost 100 academic institutions including Harvard, the MIT, and Berkeley.[4] If you want to support us by just signing the list

---

[3] See http://userblogs.fu-berlin.de/langsci-press/2018/01/18/achievements-2017/ for the details and graphics.
[4] A full list of supporting institutions is available here: http://langsci-press.org/knowledgeunlatched.

of supporters, by publishing with us, by helping as proofreader or by convincing your librarian/institution to support Language Science Press financially, please refer to http://langsci-press.org/supportUs.

After these more general remarks concerning Language Science Press I describe the changes I made for the second edition and I thank those who pointed out mistakes and provided feedback.

I want to thank Wang Lulu for pointing out some typos that she found while translating the book to Chinese. Thanks for both the typos and the translation.

Fritz Hamm noticed that the definition of Intervention (see p. 138) was incomplete and pointed out some inconsistencies in translations of predicates in Section 2.3. I turned some straight lines in Chapter 3 into triangles and added a discussion of different ways to represent movement (see Figure 3.8 on p. 99). I now explain what SpecIP stands for and I added footnote 8 on SpecIP as label in trees. I extended the discussion of Pirahã in Section 13.1.8.2 and added lexical items that show that Pirahã-like modification without recursion can be captured in a straightforward way in Categorial Grammar.

I reorganized the HPSG chapter to be in line with more recent approaches assuming the valence features SPR and COMPS (Sag 1997; Müller 2019b) rather than a single valence feature. I removed the section on the LOCAL feature in Sign-based Construction Grammar (Section 10.6.2.2 in the first edition) since it was build on the wrong assumption that the filler would be identical to the representation in the valence specification. In Sag (2012: 536) only the information in SYN and SEM is shared.

I added the example (60) on page 628 that shows a difference in choice of preposition in a prepositional object in Dutch vs. German. Since the publication of the first English edition of the Grammatical Theory textbook I worked extensively on the phrasal approach to benefactive constructions in LFG (Asudeh, Giorgolo & Toivonen 2014). Section 21.2.2 was revised and adapted to what will be published as Müller (2018a). There is now a brief chapter on complex predicates in TAG and Categorial Grammar/HPSG (Chapter 22), that shows that valence-based approaches allow for an underspecification of structure. Valence is potential structure, while theories like TAG operate with actual structure.

Apart from this I fixed several minor typos, added and updated some references and URLs. Thanks to Philippa Cook, Timm Lichte, and Antonio Machicao y Priemer for pointing out typos. Thanks to Leonel Figueiredo de Alencar, Francis Bond, John Carroll, Alexander Koller, Emily M. Bender, and Glenn C. Slayden for pointers to literature. Sašo Živanović helped adapting version 2.0 of the `forest` package so that it could be used with this large book. I am very graceful for this nice tree typesetting package and all the work that went into it.

The source code of the book and the version history is available on GitHub. Issues can be reported there: https://github.com/langsci/25. The book is also available on paperhive, a platform for collective reading and annotation: https://paperhive.org/documents/remote?type=langsci&id=25. It would be great if you would leave comments there.

Berlin, 21st March 2018   Stefan Müller

Foreword of the third edition

Since more and more researchers and students are using the book now, I get feedback that helps improve it. For the third edition I added references, expanded the discussion of the passive in GB (Section 3.4) a bit and fixed typos.[5]

Chapter 4 contained figures from different chapters of Adger (2003). Adger introduces the DP rather late in the book and I had a mix of NPs and DPs in figures. I fixed this in the new edition. I am so used to talking about NPs that there were references to NP in the general discussion that should have been references to DP. I fixed this as well. I added a figure explaining the architecture in the Phase model of Minimalism and since the figures mention the concept of *numeration*, I added a footnote on numerations. I also added a figure depicting the architecture assumed in Minimalist theories with Phases (right figure in Figure 4.1).

I thank Frank Van Eynde for pointing out eight typos in his review of the first edition. They have been fixed. He also pointed out that the placement of ARG-ST in the feature geometry of signs in HPSG did not correspond to Ginzburg & Sag (2000), where ARG-ST is on the top level rather than under CAT. Note that earlier versions of this book had ARG-ST under CAT and there had never been proper arguments for why it should not be there, which is why many practitioners of HPSG have kept it in that position (Müller 2018a). One reason to keep ARG-ST on the top level is that ARG-ST is appropriate for lexemes only. If ARG-ST is on the sign level, this can be represented in the type hierarchy: lexemes and word have an ARG-ST feature, phrases do not. If ARG-ST is on the CAT level, one would have to distinguish between CAT values that belong to lexemes and words on the one hand and phrasal CAT values on the other hand, which would require two additional subtypes of the type *cat*. The most recent version of the computer implementation done in Stanford by Dan Flickinger has ARG-ST under LOCAL (2019-01-24). So, I was tempted to leave everything as it was in the second edition of the book. However, there is a real argument for not having ARG-ST under CAT. CAT is assumed to be shared in coordinations and CAT contains valence features for subjects and complements. The values of these valence features are determined by a mapping from ARG-ST. In some analyses, extracted elements are not mapped to the valence features and the same is sometimes assumed for omitted elements. To take an example consider (1):

(1) He saw and helped the hikers.

saw and *helped* are coordinated and the members in the valence lists have to be compatible. Now if one coordinates a ditransitive verb with one omitted argument with a strictly transitive verb, this would work under the assumption that the omitted argument is not part of the valence representation. But if ARG-ST is part of CAT, coordination would be made impossible since a three-place argument structure list would be incompatible with a two-place list. Hence I decided to change this in the third edition and represent ARG-ST outside of CAT from now on.

---

[5] A detailed list of issues and fixes can be found in the GitHub repository of this book at https://github.com/langsci/25/.

I changed the section about Sign-Based Construction Grammar (SBCG) again. An argument about nonlocal dependencies and locality was not correct, since Sag (2012: 166) does not share all information between filler and extraction side. The argument is now revised and presented as Section 10.6.2.3. Reviewing Müller (2019c), Bob Borsley pointed out to me that the XARG feature is a way to circumvent locality restrictions that is actually used in SBCG. I added a footnote to the section on locality in SBCG.

A brief discussion of Welke's (2019) analysis of the German clause structure was added to the chapter about Construction Grammar (see Section 10.3).

The analysis of a verb-second sentence in LFG is now part of the LFG chapter (Figure 7.5 on page 242) and not just an exercise in the appendix. A new exercise was designed instead of the old one and the old one was integrated into the main text.

I added a brief discussion of Osborne's (2019) claim that Dependency Grammars are simpler than phrase structure grammars (p. 409).

Geoffrey Pullum pointed out at the HPSG conference in 2019 that the label *constraint-based* may not be the best for the theories that are usually referred to with it. Changing the term in this work would require to change the title of the book. The label *model theoretic* may be more appropriate but some implementational work in HPSG and LFG not considering models may find the term inappropriate. I hence decided to stick to the established term.

I followed the advice by Lisbeth Augustinus and added a preface to Part II of the book that gives the reader some orientation as to what to expect.

I thank Mikhail Knyazev for pointing out to me that the treatment of V to I to C movement in the German literature differs from the lowering that is assumed for English and that some further references are needed in the chapter on Government & Binding.

Working on the Chinese translation of this book, Wang Lulu pointed out some typos and a wrong example sentence in Chinese. Thanks for these comments!

I thank Bob Borsley, Gisbert Fanselow, Hubert Haider and Pavel Logacev for discussion and Ina Baier for a mistake in a CG proof and Jonas Benn for pointing out some typos to me. Thanks to Tabea Reiner for a comment on gradedness. Thanks also to Antonio Machicao y Priemer for yet another set of comments on the second edition and to Elizabeth Pankratz for proofreading parts of what I changed.

Berlin, 15th August 2019   Stefan Müller

Part I

Background and specific theories

1 Introduction and basic terms

The aim of this chapter is to explain why we actually study syntax (Section 1.1) and why it is important to formalize our findings (Section 1.2). Some basic terminology will be introduced in Sections 1.3–1.8: Section 1.3 deals with criteria for dividing up utterances into smaller units. Section 1.4 shows how words can be grouped into classes; that is I will introduce criteria for assigning words to categories such as verb or adjective. Section 1.5 introduces the notion of heads, in Section 1.6 the distinction between arguments and adjuncts is explained, Section 1.7 defines grammatical functions and Section 1.8 introduces the notion of topological fields, which can be used to characterize certain areas of the clause in languages such as German.

Unfortunately, linguistics is a scientific field with a considerable amount of terminological chaos. This is partly due to the fact that terminology originally defined for certain languages (e.g., Latin, English) was later simply adopted for the description of other languages as well. However, this is not always appropriate since languages differ from one another considerably and are constantly changing. Due to the problems caused by this, the terminology started to be used differently or new terms were invented. When new terms are introduced in this book, I will always mention related terminology or differing uses of each term so that readers can relate this to other literature.

1.1 Why do syntax?

Every linguistic expression we utter has a meaning. We are therefore dealing with what has been referred to as form-meaning pairs (de Saussure 1916b). A word such as *tree* in its specific orthographical form or in its corresponding phonetic form is assigned the meaning *tree'*. Larger linguistic units can be built up out of smaller ones: words can be joined together to form phrases and these in turn can form sentences.

The question which now arises is the following: do we need a formal system which can assign a structure to these sentences? Would it not be sufficient to formulate a pairing of form and meaning for complete sentences just as we did for the word *tree* above?

That would, in principle, be possible if a language were just a finite list of word sequences. If we were to assume that there is a maximum length for sentences and a maximum length for words and thus that there can only be a finite number of words, then the number of possible sentences would indeed be finite. However, even if we were to restrict the possible length of a sentence, the number of possible sentences would still be enormous. The question we would then really need to answer is: what is the maximum length of a sentence? For instance, it is possible to extend all the sentences in (1):

1 Introduction and basic terms

(1)   a. This sentence goes on and on and on and on …
       b. [A sentence is a sentence] is a sentence.
       c. that Max thinks that Julius knows that Otto claims that Karl suspects that Richard confirms that Friederike is laughing

In (1b), something is being said about the group of words *a sentence is a sentence*, namely that it is a sentence. One can, of course, claim the same for the whole sentence in (1b) and extend the sentence once again with *is a sentence*. The sentence in (1c) has been formed by combining *that Friederike is laughing* with *that*, *Richard* and *confirms*. The result of this combination is a new sentence *that Richard confirms that Friederike is laughing*. In the same way, this has then been extended with *that*, *Karl* and *suspects*. Thus, one obtains a very complex sentence which embeds a less complex sentence. This partial sentence in turn contains a further partial sentence and so on. (1c) is similar to those sets of Russian nesting dolls, also called *matryoshka*: each doll contains a smaller doll which can be painted differently from the one that contains it. In just the same way, the sentence in (1c) contains parts which are similar to it but which are shorter and involve different nouns and verbs. This can be made clearer by using brackets in the following way:

(2)   that Max thinks [that Julius knows [that Otto claims [that Karl suspects [that Richard confirms [that Friederike is laughing]]]]]

We can build incredibly long and complex sentences in the ways that were demonstrated in (1).[1]

It would be arbitrary to establish some cut-off point up to which such combinations can be considered to belong to our language (Harris 1957: 208; Chomsky 1957: 23). It is also implausible to claim that such complex sentences are stored in our brains as a single complex unit. While evidence from psycholinguistic experiments shows that highly frequent or idiomatic combinations are stored as complex units, this could not be the case for sentences such as those in (1). Furthermore, we are capable of producing utterances that we have never heard before and which have also never been uttered or written down previously. Therefore, these utterances must have some kind of structure, there must be patterns which occur again and again. As humans, we are able to build such complex structures out of simpler ones and, vice-versa, to break down complex utterances into their component parts. Evidence for humans' ability to make use of rules for combining words into larger units has now also been provided by research in neuroscience (Pulvermüller 2010: 170).

---

[1] It is sometimes claimed that we are capable of constructing infinitely long sentences (Nowak, Komarova & Niyogi 2001: 117; Kim & Sells 2008: 3; Dan Everett in O'Neill & Wood (2012) at 25:19; Chesi 2015: 67; Martorell 2018: 2; Wikipedia entry of Biolinguistics, 2018-09-27) or that Chomsky made such claims (Leiss 2003: 341). This is, however, not correct since every sentence has to come to an end at some point. Even in the theory of formal languages developed in the Chomskyan tradition, there are no infinitely long sentences. Rather, certain formal grammars can describe a set containing infinitely many finite sentences (Chomsky 1957: 13). See also Pullum & Scholz (2010) and Section 13.1.8 on the issue of recursion in grammar and for claims about the infinite nature of language.

1.1 Why do syntax?

It becomes particularly evident that we combine linguistic material in a rule-governed way when these rules are violated. Children acquire linguistic rules by generalizing from the input available to them. In doing so, they produce some utterances which they could not have ever heard previously:

(3) Ich festhalte die. (Friederike, 2;6)
 I PART.hold them
 Intended: 'I hold them tight.'

Friederike, who was learning German, was at the stage of acquiring the rule for the position of the finite verb (namely, second position). What she did here, however, was to place the whole verb, including a separable particle *fest* 'tight', in the second position although the particle should be realized at the end of the clause (*Ich halte die fest.*).

If we do not wish to assume that language is merely a list of pairings of form and meaning, then there must be some process whereby the meaning of complex utterances can be obtained from the meanings of the smaller components of those utterances. Syntax reveals something about the way in which the words involved can be combined, something about the structure of an utterance. For instance, knowledge about subject-verb agreement helps with the interpretation of the following sentences in German:

(4) a. Die Frau schläft.
 the woman sleep.3SG
 'The woman sleeps.'

 b. Die Mädchen schlafen.
 the girls sleep.3PL
 'The girls sleep.'

 c. Die Frau kennt die Mädchen.
 the woman know.3SG the girls
 'The woman knows the girls.'

 d. Die Frau kennen die Mädchen.
 the woman know.3PL the girls
 'The girls know the woman.'

The sentences in (4a,b) show that a singular or a plural subject requires a verb with the corresponding inflection. In (4a,b), the verb only requires one argument so the function of *die Frau* 'the woman' and *die Mädchen* 'the girls' is clear. In (4c,d) the verb requires two arguments and *die Frau* 'the woman' and *die Mädchen* 'the girls' could appear in either argument position in German. The sentences could mean that the woman knows somebody or that somebody knows the woman. However, due to the inflection on the verb and knowledge of the syntactic rules of German, the hearer knows that there is only one available reading for (4c) and (4d), respectively.

It is the role of syntax to discover, describe and explain such rules, patterns and structures.

1 Introduction and basic terms

1.2 Why do it formally?

The two following quotations give a motivation for the necessity of describing language formally:

> Precisely constructed models for linguistic structure can play an important role, both negative and positive, in the process of discovery itself. By pushing a precise but inadequate formulation to an unacceptable conclusion, we can often expose the exact source of this inadequacy and, consequently, gain a deeper understanding of the linguistic data. More positively, a formalized theory may automatically provide solutions for many problems other than those for which it was explicitly designed. Obscure and intuition-bound notions can neither lead to absurd conclusions nor provide new and correct ones, and hence they fail to be useful in two important respects. I think that some of those linguists who have questioned the value of precise and technical development of linguistic theory have failed to recognize the productive potential in the method of rigorously stating a proposed theory and applying it strictly to linguistic material with no attempt to avoid unacceptable conclusions by ad hoc adjustments or loose formulation. (Chomsky 1957: 5)

> As is frequently pointed out but cannot be overemphasized, an important goal of formalization in linguistics is to enable subsequent researchers to see the defects of an analysis as clearly as its merits; only then can progress be made efficiently. (Dowty 1979: 322)

If we formalize linguistic descriptions, it is easier to recognize what exactly a particular analysis means. We can establish what predictions it makes and we can rule out alternative analyses. A further advantage of precisely formulated theories is that they can be written down in such a way that computer programs can process them. When a theoretical analysis is implemented as a computationally processable grammar fragment, any inconsistency will become immediately evident. Such implemented grammars can then be used to process large collections of text, so-called corpora, and they can thus establish which sentences a particular grammar cannot yet analyze or which sentences are assigned the wrong structure. For more on using computer implementation in linguistics see Bierwisch (1963: 163), Müller (1999b: Chapter 22) and Bender (2008b) as well as Section 3.6.2.

1.3 Constituents

If we consider the sentence in (5), we have the intuition that certain words form a unit.

(5) Alle Studenten lesen während dieser Zeit Bücher.
    all students read during this time books
    'All the students are reading books at this time.'

For example, the words *alle* 'all' and *Studenten* 'students' form a unit which says something about who is reading. *während* 'during', *dieser* 'this' and *Zeit* 'time' also form a unit which refers to a period of time during which the reading takes place, and *Bücher* 'books' says something about what is being read. The first unit is itself made up of two parts, namely *alle* 'all' and *Studenten* 'students'. The unit *während dieser Zeit* 'during this time' can also be divided into two subcomponents: *während* 'during' and *dieser Zeit* 'this time'. *dieser Zeit* 'this time' is also composed of two parts, just like *alle Studenten* 'all students' is.

Recall that in connection with (1c) above we talked about the sets of Russian nesting dolls (*matryoshkas*). Here, too, when we break down (5) we have smaller units which are components of bigger units. However, in contrast to the Russian dolls, we do not just have one smaller unit contained in a bigger one but rather, we can have several units which are grouped together in a bigger one. The best way to envisage this is to imagine a system of boxes: one big box contains the whole sentence. Inside this box, there are four other boxes, which each contain *alle Studenten* 'all students', *lesen* 'reads', *während dieser Zeit* 'during this time' and *Bücher* 'books', respectively. Figure 1.1 illustrates this.

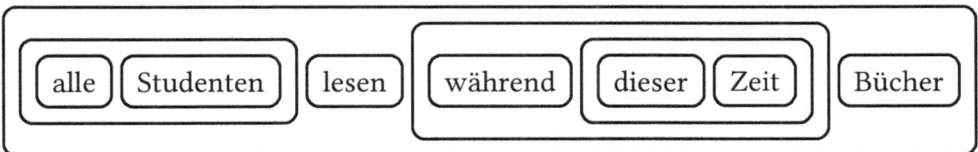

Figure 1.1: Words and phrases in boxes

In the following section, I will introduce various tests which can be used to show how certain words seem to "belong together" more than others. When I speak of a *word sequence*, I generally mean an arbitrary linear sequence of words which do not necessarily need to have any syntactic or semantic relationship, e.g., *Studenten lesen während* 'students read during' in (5). A sequence of words which form a structural entity, on the other hand, is referred to as a *phrase*. Phrases can consist of words as in *this time* or of combinations of words with other phrases as in *during this time*. The parts of a phrase and the phrase itself are called *constituents*. So all elements that are in a box in Figure 1.1 are constituents of the sentence.

Following these preliminary remarks, I will now introduce some tests which will help us to identify whether a particular string of words is a constituent or not.

1.3.1 Constituency tests

There are a number of ways to test the constituent status of a sequence of words. In the following subsections, I will present some of these. In Section 1.3.2, we will see that there are cases when simply applying a test "blindly" leads to unwanted results.

1.3.1.1 Substitution

If it is possible to replace a sequence of words in a sentence with a different sequence of words and the acceptability of the sentence remains unaffected, then this constitutes evidence for the fact that each sequence of words forms a constituent.

1 Introduction and basic terms

In (6), *den Mann* 'the man' can be replaced by the string *eine Frau* 'a woman'. This is an indication that both of these word sequences are constituents.

(6)   a. Er kennt [den Mann].
           he knows   the man
           'He knows the man.'

       b. Er kennt [eine Frau].
           he knows   a   woman
           'He knows a woman.'

Similarly, in (7a), the string *das Buch zu lesen* 'the book to read' can be replaced by *dem Kind das Buch zu geben* 'the woman the book to give'.

(7)   a. Er versucht, [das Buch zu lesen].
           he tries   the book to read
           'He is trying to read the book.'

       b. Er versucht, [dem Kind das Buch zu geben].
           he tries   the   child the book to give
           'He is trying to give the child the book.'

This test is referred to as the *substitution test*.

1.3.1.2 Pronominalization

Everything that can be replaced by a pronoun forms a constituent. In (8), one can for example refer to *der Mann* 'the man' with the pronoun *er* 'he':

(8)   a. [Der Mann] schläft.
           the man   sleeps
           'The man is sleeping.'

       b. Er schläft.
           he sleeps
           'He is sleeping.'

It is also possible to use a pronoun to refer to constituents such as *das Buch zu lesen* 'the book to read' in (7a), as is shown in (9):

(9)   a. Peter versucht, [das Buch zu lesen].
           Peter tries   the book to read
           'Peter is trying to read the book.'

       b. Klaus versucht das auch.
           Klaus tries   that also
           'Klaus is trying to do that as well.'

The pronominalization test is another form of the substitution test.

1.3 Constituents

1.3.1.3 Question formation

A sequence of words that can be elicited by a question forms a constituent:

(10) a. [Der Mann] arbeitet.
    the man works
    'The man is working.'
 b. Wer arbeitet?
    who works
    'Who is working?'

Question formation is a specific case of pronominalization. One uses a particular type of pronoun (an interrogative pronoun) to refer to the word sequence.

Constituents such as *das Buch zu lesen* in (7a) can also be elicited by questions, as (11) shows:

(11) Was versucht er?
    what tries he
    'What does he try?'

1.3.1.4 Permutation test

If a sequence of words can be moved without adversely affecting the acceptability of the sentence in which it occurs, then this is an indication that this word sequence forms a constituent.

In (12), *keiner* 'nobody' and *dieses Kind* 'this child' exhibit different orderings, which suggests that *dieses* 'this' and *Kind* 'child' belong together.

(12) a. dass keiner [dieses Kind] kennt
    that nobody this child knows
 b. dass [dieses Kind] keiner kennt
    that this child nobody knows
    'that nobody knows this child'

On the other hand, it is not plausible to assume that *keiner dieses* 'nobody this' forms a constituent in (12a). If we try to form other possible orderings by trying to move *keiner dieses* 'nobody this' as a whole, we see that this leads to unacceptable results:[2]

(13) a. * dass Kind keiner dieses kennt
    that child nobody this knows

---

[2]I use the following notational conventions for all examples: '*' indicates that a sentence is ungrammatical, '#' denotes that the sentence has a reading which differs from the intended one and finally '§' should be understood as a sentence which is deviant for semantic or information-structural reasons, for example, because the subject must be animate, but is in fact inanimate in the example in question, or because there is a conflict between constituent order and the marking of given information through the use of pronouns.

1 Introduction and basic terms

      b. * dass Kind kennt keiner dieses
          that child knows nobody this

Furthermore, constituents such as *das Buch zu lesen* 'to read the book' in (7a) can be moved:

(14) a. Er hat noch nicht [das Buch zu lesen] versucht.
         he has PART not   the book to read   tried
         'He has not yet tried to read the book.'

      b. Er hat [das Buch zu lesen] noch nicht versucht.
         he has the book to read   PART not   tried

      c. Er hat noch nicht versucht, [das Buch zu lesen].
         he has PART not   tried   the book to read

1.3.1.5 Fronting

Fronting is a further variant of the movement test. In German declarative sentences, only a single constituent may normally precede the finite verb:

(15) a.   [Alle Studenten] lesen   während der vorlesungsfreien Zeit Bücher.
          all   students   read.3PL during   the lecture.free   time books
          'All students read books during the semester break.'

      b.   [Bücher] lesen alle Studenten während der vorlesungsfreien Zeit.
          books   read all   students   during   the lecture.free   time

      c. * [Alle Studenten] [Bücher] lesen während der vorlesungsfreien Zeit.
           all   students   books   read during   the lecture.free   time

      d. * [Bücher] [alle Studenten] lesen während der vorlesungsfreien Zeit.
           books   all   students   read during   the lecture.free   time

The possibility for a sequence of words to be fronted (that is to occur in front of the finite verb) is a strong indicator of constituent status.

1.3.1.6 Coordination

If two sequences of words can be conjoined then this suggests that each sequence forms a constituent.

    In (16), *der Mann* 'the man' and *die Frau* 'the woman' are conjoined and the entire coordination is the subject of the verb *arbeiten* 'to work'. This is a good indication of the fact that *der Mann* and *die Frau* each form a constituent.

(16) [Der Mann] und [die Frau]   arbeiten.
        the man   and the woman work.3PL
        'The man and the woman work.'

The example in (17) shows that phrases with *to*-infinitives can be conjoined:

(17) Er hat versucht, [das Buch zu lesen] und [es dann unauffällig verschwinden zu
     he had tried   the book to read   and it then secretly   disappear   to
     lassen].
     let
     'He tried to read the book and then make it quietly disappear.'

1.3.2 Some comments on the status of constituent tests

It would be ideal if the tests presented here delivered clear-cut results in every case, as the empirical basis on which syntactic theories are built would thereby become much clearer. Unfortunately, this is not the case. There are in fact a number of problems with constituent tests, which I will discuss in what follows.

1.3.2.1 Expletives

There is a particular class of pronouns – so-called *expletives* – which do not denote people, things, or events and are therefore non-referential. An example of this is *es* 'it' in (18).

(18) a. Es regnet.
         it rains
         'It is raining.'
     b. Regnet es?
         rains it
         'Is it raining?'
     c. dass es jetzt regnet
         that it now rains
         'that it is raining now'

As the examples in (18) show, *es* can either precede the verb, or follow it. It can also be separated from the verb by an adverb, which suggests that *es* should be viewed as an independent unit.

Nevertheless, we observe certain problems with the aforementioned tests. Firstly, *es* 'it' is restricted with regard to its movement possibilities, as (19a) and (20b) show.

(19) a. * dass jetzt es regnet
           that now it rains
           Intended: 'that it is raining now'
     b. dass jetzt keiner klatscht
         that now nobody claps
         'that nobody is clapping now'

1 Introduction and basic terms

(20)   a.   Er sah es regnen.
             he saw it.ACC rain

             'He saw that it was raining.'

      b.   * Es sah er regnen.
             it.ACC saw he rain

             Intended: 'he saw that it was raining.'

      c.   Er sah einen Mann klatschen.
             he saw a.ACC man clap

             'He saw a man clapping.'

      d.   Einen Mann sah er klatschen.
             a.ACC man saw he clap

             'A man, he saw clapping.'

Unlike the accusative object *einen Mann* 'a man' in (20c,d), the expletive in (20b) cannot be fronted.

Secondly, substitution and question tests also fail:

(21)   a.   * Der Mann / er regnet.
             the man he rains

      b.   * Wer / was regnet?
             who what rains

Similarly, the coordination test cannot be applied either:

(22)   * Es und der Mann regnet / regnen.
        it and the man rains rain

The failure of these tests can be easily explained: weakly stressed pronouns such as *es* are preferably placed before other arguments, directly after the conjunction (*dass* in (18c)) and directly after the finite verb in (20a) (see Abraham 1995: 570). If an element is placed in front of the expletive, as in (19a), then the sentence is rendered ungrammatical. The reason for the ungrammaticality of (20b) is the general ban on accusative *es* appearing in clause-initial position. Although such cases exist, they are only possible if *es* 'it' is referential (Lenerz 1994: 162; Gärtner & Steinbach 1997: 4).

The fact that we could not apply the substitution and question tests is also no longer mysterious as *es* is not referential in these cases. We can only replace *es* 'it' with another expletive such as *das* 'that'. If we replace the expletive with a referential expression, we derive a different semantic interpretation. It does not make sense to ask about something semantically empty or to refer to it with a pronoun.

It follows from this that not all of the tests must deliver a positive result for a sequence of words to count as a constituent. That is, the tests are therefore not a necessary requirement for constituent status.

1.3.2.2 Movement

The movement test is problematic for languages with relatively free constituent order, since it is not always possible to tell what exactly has been moved. For example, the string *gestern dem Mann* 'yesterday the man' occupies different positions in the following examples:

(23) a. weil   keiner   gestern   dem Mann geholfen hat
       because nobody yesterday the man   helped   has
       'because nobody helped the man yesterday'

   b. weil   gestern   dem Mann keiner   geholfen hat
       because yesterday the man nobody helped   has
       'because nobody helped the man yesterday'

One could therefore assume that *gestern* 'yesterday' and *dem Mann* 'the man', which of course do not form a constituent, have been moved together. An alternative explanation for the ordering variants in (23) is that adverbs can occur in various positions in the clause and that only *dem Mann* 'the man' has been moved in front of *keiner* 'nobody' in (23b). In any case, it is clear that *gestern* and *dem Mann* have no semantic relation and that it is impossible to refer to both of them with a pronoun. Although it may seem at first glance as if this material had been moved as a unit, we have seen that it is in fact not tenable to assume that *gestern dem Mann* 'yesterday the man' forms a constituent.

1.3.2.3 Fronting

As mentioned in the discussion of (15), the position in front of the finite verb is normally occupied by a single constituent. The possibility for a given word sequence to be placed in front of the finite verb is sometimes even used as a clear indicator of constituent status, and even used in the definition of *Satzglied*[3]. An example of this is taken from Bußmann (1983), but is no longer present in Bußmann (1990):[4]

> **Satzglied test** A procedure based on → topicalization used to analyze complex constituents. Since topicalization only allows a single constituent to be moved to the beginning of the sentence, complex sequences of constituents, for example adverb phrases, can be shown to actually consist of one or more constituents. In the example *Ein Taxi quält sich im Schrittempo durch den Verkehr* 'A taxi was struggling at walking speed through the traffic', *im Schrittempo* 'at walking speed' and *durch den Verkehr* 'through the traffic' are each constituents as both can be fronted independently of each other. (Bußmann 1983: 446)

---

[3] *Satzglied* is a special term used in grammars of German, referring to a constituent on the clause level (Eisenberg et al. 2005: 783).

[4] The original formulation is: **Satzgliedtest** [Auch: Konstituententest]. Auf der → Topikalisierung beruhendes Verfahren zur Analyse komplexer Konstituenten. Da bei Topikalisierung jeweils nur eine Konstituente bzw. ein → Satzglied an den Anfang gerückt werden kann, lassen sich komplexe Abfolgen von Konstituenten (z. B. Adverbialphrasen) als ein oder mehrere Satzglieder ausweisen; in *Ein Taxi quält sich im Schrittempo durch den Verkehr* sind *im Schrittempo* und *durch den Verkehr* zwei Satzglieder, da sie beide unabhängig voneinander in Anfangsposition gerückt werden können.

1 Introduction and basic terms

The preceding quote has the following implications:

- Some part of a piece of linguistic material can be fronted independently →
  This material does not form a constituent.

- Linguistic material can be fronted together →
  This material forms a constituent.

It will be shown that both of these prove to be problematic.

The first implication is cast into doubt by the data in (24):

(24)   a. Keine Einigung erreichten Schröder und Chirac über den Abbau der
           no agreement reached Schröder and Chirac about the reduction of.the
           Agrarsubventionen.[5]
           agricultural.subsidies

           'Schröder and Chirac could not reach an agreement on the reduction of agricultural subsidies.'

     b. [Über den Abbau der Agrarsubventionen] erreichten Schröder und
         about the reduction of.the agricultural.subsidies reached Schröder and
         Chirac keine Einigung.
         Chirac no agreement

Although parts of the noun phrase *keine Einigung über den Abbau der Agrarsubventionen* 'no agreement on the reduction of agricultural subsidies' can be fronted individually, we still want to analyze the entire string as a noun phrase when it is not fronted as in (25):

(25)   Schröder und Chirac erreichten [keine Einigung über den Abbau der
       Schröder and Chirac reached no agreement about the reduction of.the
       Agrarsubventionen].
       agricultural.subsidies

The prepositional phrase *über den Abbau der Agrarsubventionen* 'on the reduction of agricultural subsidies' is semantically dependent on *Einigung* 'agreement' cf. (26):

(26)   Sie einigen sich über die Agrarsubventionen.
       they agree REFL about the agricultural.subsidies

       'They agree on the agricultural subsidies.'

This word sequence can also be fronted together:

(27)   [Keine Einigung über den Abbau der Agrarsubventionen] erreichten
       no agreement about the reduction of.the agricultural.subsidies reached
       Schröder und Chirac.
       Schröder and Chirac

In the theoretical literature, it is assumed that *keine Einigung über den Abbau der Agrarsubventionen* forms a constituent which can be "split up" under certain circumstances.

---

[5] tagesschau, 15.10.2002, 20:00.

1.3 Constituents

In such cases, the individual subconstituents can be moved independently of each other (De Kuthy 2002) as we have seen in (25).

The second implication is problematic because of examples such as (28):

(28) a. [Trocken] [durch die Stadt] kommt man am Wochenende auch mit der
    dry through the city comes one at.the weekend also with the
    BVG.⁶
    BVG

   'With the BVG, you can be sure to get around town dry at the weekend.'

   b. [Wenig] [mit Sprachgeschichte] hat der dritte Beitrag in dieser Rubrik
    little with language.history has the third contribution in this section
    zu tun, [...]⁷
    to do

   'The third contribution in this section has little to do with language history.'

In (28), there are multiple constituents preceding the finite verb, which bear no obvious syntactic or semantic relation to each other. Exactly what is meant by a "syntactic or semantic relation" will be fully explained in the following chapters. At this point, I will just point out that in (28a) the adjective *trocken* 'dry' has *man* 'one' as its subject and furthermore says something about the action of 'travelling through the city'. That is, it refers to the action denoted by the verb. As (29b) shows, *durch die Stadt* 'through the city' cannot be combined with the adjective *trocken* 'dry'.

(29) a. Man ist / bleibt trocken.
    one is stays dry

   'One is/stays dry.'

   b. * Man ist / bleibt trocken durch die Stadt.
    one is stays dry through the city

Therefore, the adjective *trocken* 'dry' does not have a syntactic or semantic relationship with the prepositional phrase *durch die Stadt* 'through the city'. Both phrases have in common that they refer to the verb and are dependent on it.

One may simply wish to treat the examples in (28) as exceptions. This approach would, however, not be justified, as I have shown in an extensive empirical study (Müller 2003a).

If one were to classify *trocken durch die Stadt* as a constituent due to it passing the fronting test, then one would have to assume that *trocken durch die Stadt* in (30) is also a constituent. In doing so, we would devalue the term *constituent* as the whole point of constituent tests is to find out which word strings have some semantic or syntactic relationship.⁸

---

⁶taz berlin, 10.07.1998, p. 22.

⁷Zeitschrift für Dialektologie und Linguistik, LXIX, 3/2002, p. 339.

⁸These data can be explained by assuming a silent verbal head preceding the finite verb and thereby ensuring that there is in fact just one constituent in initial position in front of the finite verb (Müller 2005c; 2017a). Nevertheless, this kind of data are problematic for constituent tests since these tests have been specifically designed to tease apart whether strings such as *trocken* and *durch die Stadt* or *wenig* and *mit Sprachgeschichte* in (30) form a constituent.

1 Introduction and basic terms

(30)   a.   Man kommt am Wochenende auch mit der BVG trocken durch die
one comes at.the weekend also with the BVG dry through the
Stadt.
city
'With the BVG, you can be sure to get around town dry at the weekend.'

     b.   Der dritte Beitrag in dieser Rubrik hat wenig mit Sprachgeschichte zu
the third contribution in this section has little with language.history to
tun.
do
'The third contribution in this section has little to do with language history.'

The possibility for a given sequence of words to be fronted is therefore not a sufficient diagnostic for constituent status.

We have also seen that it makes sense to treat expletives as constituents despite the fact that the accusative expletive cannot be fronted (cf. (20a)):

(31)   a.   Er bringt es bis zum Professor.
he brings EXPL until to.the professor
'He makes it to professor.'

     b.   # Es bringt er bis zum Professor.
it brings he until to.the professor

There are other elements that can also not be fronted. Inherent reflexives are a good example of this:

(32)   a.   Karl hat sich nicht erholt.
Karl has REFL not recovered
'Karl hasn't recovered.'

     b.   * Sich hat Karl nicht erholt.
REFL has Karl not recovered

It follows from this that fronting is not a necessary criterion for constituent status. Therefore, the possibility for a given word string to be fronted is neither a necessary nor sufficient condition for constituent status.

1.3.2.4 Coordination

Coordinated structures such as those in (33) also prove to be problematic:

(33)   Deshalb kaufte der Mann einen Esel und die Frau ein Pferd.
therefore bought the man a donkey and the woman a horse
'Therefore, the man bought a donkey and the woman a horse.'

At first glance, *der Mann einen Esel* 'the man a donkey' and *die Frau ein Pferd* 'the woman a horse' in (33) seem to be coordinated. Does this mean that *der Mann einen Esel* and *die Frau ein Pferd* each form a constituent?

As other constituent tests show, this assumption is not plausible. This sequence of words cannot be moved together as a unit:[9]

(34) * Der Mann einen Esel kaufte deshalb.
    the man a donkey bought therefore

Replacing the supposed constituent is also not possible without ellipsis:

(35) a. # Deshalb kaufte er.
       therefore bought he
    b. * Deshalb kaufte ihn.
       therefore bought him

The pronouns do not stand in for the two logical arguments of *kaufen* 'to buy', which are realized by *der Mann* 'the man' and *einen Esel* 'a donkey' in (33), but rather for one in each. There are analyses that have been proposed for examples such as (33) in which two verbs *kauft* 'buys' occur, where only one is overt, however (Crysmann 2008). The example in (33) would therefore correspond to:

(36) Deshalb kaufte der Mann einen Esel und kaufte die Frau ein Pferd.
    therefore bought the man a donkey and bought the woman a horse

This means that although it seems as though *der Mann einen Esel* 'the man a donkey' and *die Frau ein Pferd* 'the woman a horse' are coordinated, it is actually *kauft der Mann einen Esel* 'buys the man a donkey' and *(kauft) die Frau ein Pferd* 'buys the woman a horse' which are conjoined.

We should take the following from the previous discussion: even when a given word sequence passes certain constituent tests, this does not mean that one can automatically infer from this that we are dealing with a constituent. That is, the tests we have seen are not sufficient conditions for constituent status.

Summing up, it has been shown that these tests are neither sufficient nor necessary for attributing constituent status to a given sequence of words. However, as long as one keeps the problematic cases in mind, the previous discussion should be enough to get an initial idea about what should be treated as a constituent.

1.4 Parts of speech

The words in (37) differ not only in their meaning but also in other respects.

(37) Der große Biber schwimmt jetzt.
    the big beaver swims now
    'The big beaver swims now.'

---

[9]The area in front of the finite verb is also referred to as the *Vorfeld* 'prefield' (see Section 1.8). Apparent multiple fronting is possible under certain circumstances in German. See the previous section, especially the discussion of the examples in (28) on page 15. The example in (34) is created in such a way that the subject is present in the prefield, which is not normally possible with verbs such as *kaufen* 'to buy' for reasons which have to do with the information-structural properties of these kinds of fronting constructions. Compare also De Kuthy & Meurers 2003b on subjects in fronted verb phrases and Bildhauer & Cook 2010: 72 on frontings of subjects in apparent multiple frontings.

1 Introduction and basic terms

Each of the words is subject to certain restrictions when forming sentences. It is common practice to group words into classes with other words which share certain salient properties. For example, *der* 'the' is an article, *Biber* 'beaver' is a noun, *schwimmt* 'swims' is a verb and *jetzt* 'now' is an adverb. As can be seen in (38), it is possible to replace all the words in (37) with words from the same word class.

(38) Die kleine Raupe   frisst immer.
      the small caterpillar eats always
      'The small caterpillar is always eating.'

This is not always the case, however. For example, it is not possible to use a verb such as *verschlingt* 'devours' or the second-person form *schwimmst* in (38). This means that the categorization of words into parts of speech is rather coarse and that we will have to say a lot more about the properties of a given word. In this section, I will discuss various word classes/parts of speech and in the following sections I will go into further detail about the various properties which characterize a given word class.

The most important parts of speech are *verbs*, *nouns*, *adjectives*, *prepositions* and *adverbs*. In earlier decades, it was common among researchers working on German (see also Section 11.6.1 on Tesnière's category system) to speak of *action words*, *describing words*, and *naming words*. These descriptions prove problematic, however, as illustrated by the following examples:

(39) a. die *Idee*
         the idea

      b. die *Stunde*
         the hour

      c. das laute *Sprechen*
         the loud speaking
         '(the act of) speaking loudly'

      d. Die *Erörterung* der   Lage   dauerte mehrere Stunden.
         the discussion of.the situation lasted several hours
         'The discussion of the situation lasted several hours.'

(39a) does not describe a concrete entity, (39b) describes a time interval and (39c) and (39d) describe actions. It is clear that *Idee* 'idea', *Stunde* 'hour', *Sprechen* 'speaking' and *Erörterung* 'discussion' differ greatly in terms of their meaning. Nevertheless, these words still behave like *Raupe* 'caterpillar' and *Biber* 'beaver' in many respects and are therefore classed as nouns.

The term *action word* is not used in scientific linguistic work as verbs do not always need to denote actions:

(40) a. Ihm gefällt das Buch.
         him pleases the book
         'He likes the book.'

  b. Das Eis schmilzt.
    the ice melts

    'The ice is melting.'

  c. Es regnet.
    it rains

    'It is raining.'

One would also have to class the noun *Erörterung* 'discussion' as an action word.

 Adjectives do not always describe properties of objects. In the following examples, the opposite is in fact true: the characteristic of being a murderer is expressed as being possible or probable, but not as being true properties of the modified noun.

(41) a. der mutmaßliche Mörder
    the suspected murderer

  b. Soldaten sind potenzielle Mörder.
    soldiers are potential murderers

The adjectives themselves in (41) do not actually provide any information about the characteristics of the entities described. One may also wish to classify *lachende* 'laughing' in (42) as an adjective.

(42) der lachende Mann
   the laughing man

If, however, we are using properties and actions as our criteria for classification, *lachend* 'laughing' should technically be an action word.

 Rather than semantic criteria, it is usually formal criteria which are used to determine word classes. The various forms a word can take are also taken into account. So *lacht* 'laughs', for example, has the forms given in (43).

(43) a. Ich lache.
    I laugh

  b. Du lachst.
    you.SG laugh

  c. Er lacht.
    he laughs

  d. Wir lachen.
    we laugh

  e. Ihr lacht.
    you.PL laugh

  f. Sie lachen.
    they laugh

1 Introduction and basic terms

In German, there are also forms for the preterite, imperative, present subjunctive, past subjunctive and non-finite forms (participles and infinitives with or without *zu* 'to'). All of these forms constitute the inflectional paradigm of a verb. Tense (present, preterite, future), mood (indicative, subjunctive, imperative), person (1st, 2nd, 3rd) and number (singular, plural) all play a role in the inflectional paradigm. Certain forms can coincide in a paradigm, as (43c) and (43e) and (43d) and (43f) show.

Parallel to verbs, nouns also have an inflectional paradigm:

(44)   a. der   Mann
              the.NOM man

       b. des   Mannes
              the.GEN man.GEN

       c. dem   Mann
              the.DAT man

       d. den   Mann
              the.ACC man

       e. die   Männer
              the.NOM men

       f. der   Männer
              the.GEN men

       g. den   Männern
              the.DAT men.DAT

       h. die   Männer
              the.ACC men

We can differentiate between nouns on the basis of gender (feminine, masculine, neuter). The choice of gender is often purely formal in nature and is only partially influenced by biological sex or the fact that we are describing a particular object:

(45)   a. die   Tüte
              the.F bag(F)
              'the bag'

       b. der   Krampf
              the.M cramp(M)
              'cramp'

       c. das   Kind
              the.N child(N)
              'the child'

As well as gender, case (nominative, genitive, dative, accusative) and number are also important for nominal paradigms.

Like nouns, adjectives inflect for gender, case and number. They differ from nouns, however, in that gender marking is variable. Adjectives can be used with all three genders:

(46) a. eine schöne Blume
     a.F beautiful.F flower

   b. ein schöner Strauß
      a beautiful.M bunch

   c. ein schönes Bouquet
      a beautiful.N bouquet

In addition to gender, case and number, we can identify several inflectional classes. Traditionally, we distinguish between strong, mixed and weak inflection of adjectives. The inflectional class that we have to choose is dependent on the form or presence of the article:

(47) a. ein alter Wein
        an old wine

   b. der alte Wein
      the old wine

   c. alter Wein
      old wine

Furthermore, adjectives have comparative and superlative wordforms:

(48) a. klug
        clever

   b. klüg-er
      clever-er

   c. am klüg-sten
      at.the clever-est

This is not always the case. Especially for adjectives which make reference to some end point, a degree of comparison does not make sense. If a particular solution is optimal, for example, then no better one exists. Therefore, it does not make sense to speak of a "more optimal" solution. In a similar vein, it is not possible to be "deader" than dead.

There are some special cases such as color adjectives ending in *-a* in German *lila* 'purple' and *rosa* 'pink'. These inflect optionally (49a), and the uninflected form is also possible:

(49) a. eine lilan-e Blume
        a purple-F flower

   b. eine lila Blume
      a purple flower

1 Introduction and basic terms

In both cases, *lila* is classed an adjective. We can motivate this classification by appealing to the fact that both words occur at the same positions as other adjectives that clearly behave like adjectives with regard to inflection.

The parts of speech discussed thus far can all be differentiated in terms of their inflectional properties. For words which do not inflect, we have to use additional criteria. For example, we can classify words by the syntactic context in which they occur (as we did for the non-inflecting adjectives above). We can identify prepositions, adverbs, conjunctions, interjections and sometimes also particles. Prepositions are words which occur with a noun phrase whose case they determine:

(50) a. in diesen Raum
 in this.ACC room

 b. in diesem Raum
 in this.DAT room

wegen 'because' is often classed as a preposition although it can also occur after the noun and in these cases would technically be a postposition:

(51) des Geldes wegen
 the money.GEN because

 'because of the money'

It is also possible to speak of *adpositions* if one wishes to remain neutral about the exact position of the word.

Unlike prepositions, adverbs do not require a noun phrase.

(52) a. Er schläft in diesem Raum.
 he sleeps in this room

 b. Er schläft dort.
 he sleeps there

Sometimes adverbs are simply treated as a special variant of prepositions (see page 94). The explanation for this is that a prepositional phrase such as *in diesem Raum* 'in this room' shows the same syntactic distribution as the corresponding adverbs. *in* differs from *dort* 'there' in that it needs an additional noun phrase. These differences are parallel to what we have seen with other parts of speech. For instance, the verb *schlafen* 'sleep' requires only a noun phrase, whereas *erkennen* 'recognize' requires two.

(53) a. Er schläft.
 he sleeps

 b. Peter erkennt ihn.
 Peter recognizes him

Conjunctions can be subdivided into subordinating and coordinating conjunctions. Coordinating conjunctions include *und* 'and' and *oder* 'or'. In coordinate structures, two units with the same syntactic properties are combined. They occur adjacent to one another. *dass* 'that' and *weil* 'because' are subordinating conjunctions because the clauses that they introduce can be part of a larger clause and depend on another element of this larger clause.

(54) a. Klaus glaubt, dass er lügt.
Klaus believes that he lies

'Klaus believes that he is lying.'

b. Klaus glaubt ihm nicht, weil er lügt.
Klaus believes him not because he lies

'Klaus doesn't believe him because he is lying.'

Interjections are clause-like expressions such as *Ja!* 'Yes!', *Bitte!* 'Please!' *Hallo!* 'Hello!', *Hurra!* 'Hooray!', *Bravo!* 'Bravo!', *Pst!* 'Psst!', *Plumps!* 'Clonk!'.

If adverbs and prepositions are not assigned to the same class, then adverbs are normally used as a kind of "left over" category in the sense that all non-inflecting words which are neither prepositions, conjunctions nor interjections are classed as adverbs. Sometimes this category for "left overs" is subdivided: only words which can appear in front of the finite verb when used as a constituent are referred to as adverbs. Those words which cannot be fronted are dubbed *particles*. Particles themselves can be subdivided into various classes based on their function, e.g., degree particles and illocutionary particles. Since these functionally defined classes also contain adjectives, I will not make this distinction and simply speak of *adverbs*.

We have already sorted a considerable number of inflectional words into word classes. When one is faced with the task of classifying a particular word, one can use the decision diagram in Figure 1.2 on the next page, which is taken from the Duden grammar of German (Eisenberg et al. 2005: 133).[10]

If a word inflects for tense, then it is a verb. If it displays different case forms, then one has to check if it has a fixed gender. If this is indeed the case, then we know that we are dealing with a noun. Words with variable gender have to be checked to see if they have comparative forms. A positive result will be a clear indication of an adjective. All other words are placed into a residual category, which the Duden refers to as pronouns/article words. Like in the class of non-inflectional elements, the elements in this remnant category are subdivided according to their syntactic behavior. The Duden grammar makes a distinction between pronouns and article words. According to this classification, pronouns are words which can replace a noun phrase such as *der Mann* 'the man', whereas article words normally combine with a noun. In Latin grammars, the notion of 'pronoun' includes both pronouns in the above sense and articles, since the forms with and without the noun are identical. Over the past centuries, the forms have undergone split development to the point where it is now common in contemporary Romance languages to distinguish between words which replace a noun phrase and those which must occur with a noun. Elements which belong to the latter class are also referred to as *determiners*.

---

[10]The Duden is the official document for the German orthography. The Duden grammar does not have an official status but is very influential and is used for educational purposes as well. I will refer to it several times in this introductory chapter.

1 Introduction and basic terms

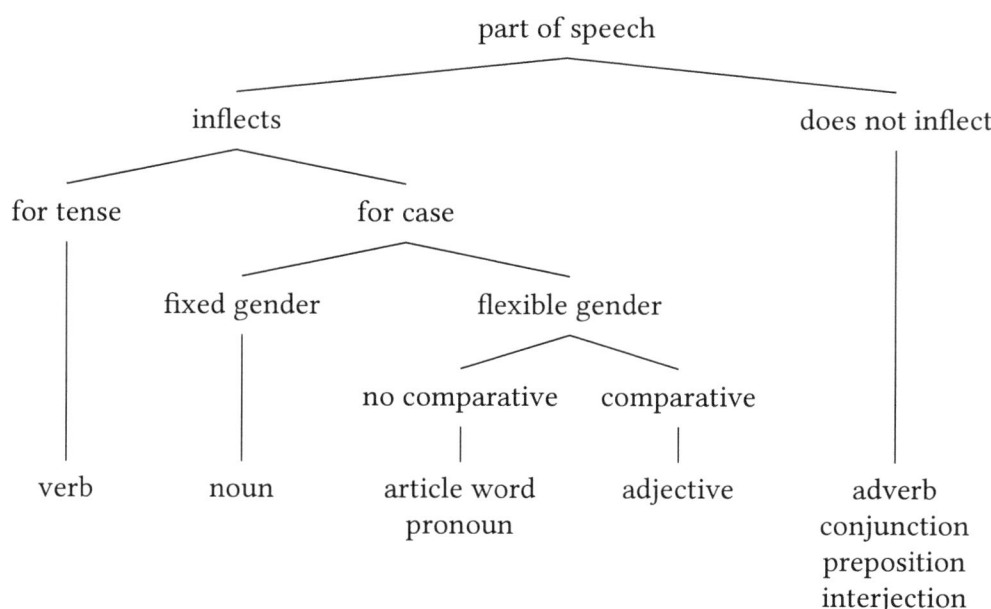

Figure 1.2: Decision tree for determining parts of speech following Eisenberg et al. (2005: 133)

If we follow the decision tree in Figure 1.2, the personal pronouns *ich* 'I', *du* 'you', *er* 'he', *sie* 'her', *es* 'it', *wir* 'we', *ihr* 'you', and *sie* 'they', for example, would be grouped together with the possessive pronouns *mein* 'mine', *dein* 'your', *sein* 'his'/'its', *ihr* 'her'/ 'their', *unser* 'our', and *euer* 'your'. The corresponding reflexive pronouns, *mich* 'myself', *dich* 'yourself', *sich* 'himself'/'herself'/'itself', 'themselves', *uns* 'ourselves', *euch* 'yourself', and the reciprocal pronoun *einander* 'each other' have to be viewed as a special case in German as there are no differing gender forms of *sich* 'himself'/'herself'/'itself' and *einander* 'each other'. Case is not expressed morphologically by reciprocal pronouns. By replacing genitive, dative and accusative pronouns with *einander*, it is possible to see that there must be variants of *einander* 'each other' in these cases, but these variants all share the same form:

(55) a. Sie gedenken seiner / einander.
     they commemorate him.GEN each.other

  b. Sie helfen ihm / einander.
     they help him.DAT each.other

  c. Sie lieben ihn / einander.
     they love him.ACC each.other

So-called pronominal adverbs such as *darauf* 'on there', *darin* 'in there', *worauf* 'on where', *worin* 'in where' also prove problematic. These forms consist of a preposition (e.g., *auf* 'on') and the elements *da* 'there' and *wo* 'where'. As the name suggests, *pronominal adverbs* contain something pronominal and this can only be *da* 'there' and

1.4 Parts of speech

wo 'where'. However, *da* 'there' and *wo* 'where' do not inflect and would therefore, following the decision tree, not be classed as pronouns.

The same is true of relative pronouns such as *wo* 'where' in (56):

(56) a. Ich komme eben aus der Stadt, wo ich Zeuge eines Unglücks gewesen
I come PART from the city where I witness of.an accident been
bin.¹¹
am
'I come from the city where I was witness to an accident.'

b. Studien haben gezeigt, daß mehr Unfälle in Städten passieren, wo die
studies have shown that more accidents in cities happen where the
Zebrastreifen abgebaut werden, weil die Autofahrer unaufmerksam
zebra.crossings removed become because the drivers unattentive
werden.¹²
become
'Studies have shown that there are more accidents in cities where they do away with zebra crossings, because drivers become unattentive.'

c. Zufällig war ich in dem Augenblick zugegen, wo der Steppenwolf
coincidentally was I in the moment present where the Steppenwolf
zum erstenmal unser Haus betrat und bei meiner Tante sich einmietete.¹³
to.the first.time our house entered and by my aunt REFL took.lodgings
'Coincidentally, I was present at the exact moment in which Steppenwolf entered our house for the first time and took lodgings with my aunt.'

If they are uninflected, then they cannot belong to the class of pronouns according to the decision tree above. Eisenberg (2004: 277) notes that *wo* 'where' is a kind of *uninflected relative pronoun* (he uses quotation marks) and remarks that this term runs contrary to the exclusive use of the term pronoun for nominal, that is, inflected, elements. He therefore uses the term *relative adverb* for them (see also Eisenberg et al. (2005: §856, §857)).

There are also usages of the relatives *dessen* 'whose' and *wessen* 'whose' in combination with a noun:

(57) a. der Mann, dessen Schwester ich kenne
the man whose sister I know

b. Ich möchte wissen, wessen Schwester du kennst.
I would.like know whose sister you know
'I would like to know whose sister you know.'

According to the classification in the Duden, these should be covered by the terms *Relativartikelwort* 'relative article word' and *Interrogativartikelwort* 'interrogative article

---

¹¹Drosdowski (1984: 672).
¹²taz berlin, 03.11.1997, p. 23.
¹³Herman Hesse, *Der Steppenwolf*. Berlin und Weimar: Aufbau-Verlag. 1986, p. 6.

word'. They are mostly counted as part of the relative pronouns and question pronouns (see for instance Eisenberg (2004: 229)). Using Eisenberg's terminology, this is unproblematic as he does not make a distinction between articles, pronouns and nouns, but rather assigns them all to the class of nouns. But authors who do make a distinction between articles and pronouns sometimes also speak of interrogative pronouns when discussing words which can function as articles or indeed replace an entire noun phrase.

One should be prepared for the fact that the term *pronoun* is often simply used for words which refer to other entities and, this is important, not in the way that nouns such as *book* and *John* do, but rather dependent on context. The personal pronoun *er* 'he' can, for example, refer to either a table or a man. This usage of the term *pronoun* runs contrary to the decision tree in Figure 1.2 and includes uninflected elements such as *da* 'there' and *wo* 'where'.

Expletive pronouns such as *es* 'it' and *das* 'that', as well as the *sich* 'him'/'her'/'itself' belonging to inherently reflexive verbs, do not make reference to actual objects. They are considered pronouns because of the similarity in form. Even if we were to assume a narrow definition of pronouns, we would still get the wrong results as expletive forms do not vary with regard to case, gender and number. If one does everything by the book, expletives would belong to the class of uninflected elements. If we assume that *es* 'it' as well as the personal pronouns have a nominative and accusative variant with the same form, then they would be placed in with the nominals. We would then have to admit that the assumption that *es* has gender would not make sense. That is we would have to count *es* as a noun by assuming neuter gender, analogous to personal pronouns.

We have not yet discussed how we would deal with the italicized words in (58):

(58) a. das *geliebte* Spielzeug
 the beloved toy

 b. das *schlafende* Kind
 the sleeping child

 c. die Frage des *Sprechens* und *Schreibens* über Gefühle
 the question of.the talking and writing about feelings
 'the question of talking and writing about feelings'

 d. Auf dem Europa-Parteitag fordern die *Grünen* einen ökosozialen
 on the Europe-party.conference demand the Greens a eco-social
 Politikwechsel.
 political.change
 'At the European party conference, the Greens demanded eco-social political change.'

 e. Max lacht *laut*.
 Max laughs loudly

 f. Max würde *wahrscheinlich* lachen.
 Max would probably laugh

geliebte 'beloved' and *schlafende* 'sleeping' are participle forms of *lieben* 'to love' and *schlafen* 'to sleep'. These forms are traditionally treated as part of the verbal paradigm.

In this sense, *geliebte* and *schlafende* are verbs. This is referred to as lexical word class. The term *lexeme* is relevant in this case. All forms in a given inflectional paradigm belong to the relevant lexeme. In the classic sense, this term also includes the regularly derived forms. That is participle forms and nominalized infinitives also belong to a verbal lexeme. Not all linguists share this view, however. Particularly problematic is the fact that we are mixing verbal with nominal and adjectival paradigms. For example, *Sprechens* 'speaking.GEN' is in the genitive case and adjectival participles also inflect for case, number and gender. Furthermore, it is unclear as to why *schlafende* 'sleeping' should be classed as a verbal lexeme and a noun such as *Störung* 'disturbance' is its own lexeme and does not belong to the lexeme *stören* 'to disturb'. I subscribe to the more modern view of grammar and assume that processes in which a word class is changed result in a new lexeme being created. Consequently, *schlafende* 'sleeping' does not belong to the lexeme *schlafen* 'to sleep', but is a form of the lexeme *schlafend*. This lexeme belongs to the word class 'adjective' and inflects accordingly.

As we have seen, it is still controversial as to where to draw the line between inflection and derivation (creation of a new lexeme). Sag, Wasow & Bender (2003: 263–264) view the formation of the present participle (*standing*) and the past participle (*eaten*) in English as derivation as these forms inflect for gender and number in French.

Adjectives such as *Grünen* 'the Greens' in (58d) are nominalized adjectives and are written with a capital like other nouns in German when there is no other noun that can be inferred from the immediate context:

(59) A: Willst du den roten Ball haben?
         want you the red ball have
         'Do you want the red ball?'
    B: Nein, gib mir bitte den grünen.
         no give me please the green
         'No, give me the green one, please.'

In the answer to (59), the noun *Ball* has been omitted. This kind of omission is not present in (58d). One could also assume here that a word class change has taken place. If a word changes its class without combination with a visible affix, we refer to this as *conversion*. Conversion has been treated as a sub-case of derivation by some linguists. The problem is, however, that *Grüne* 'greens' inflects just like an adjective and the gender varies depending on the object it is referring to:

(60) a. Ein Grüner hat vorgeschlagen, ...
       a green.M has suggested
      'A (male) member of the Green Party suggested ...'
    b. Eine Grüne hat vorgeschlagen, ...
       a green.F has suggested
      'A (female) member of the Green Party suggested ...'

We also have the situation where a word has two properties. We can make life easier for ourselves by talking about *nominalized adjectives*. The lexical category of *Grüne* is adjective and its syntactic category is noun.

The word in (58e) can inflect like an adjective and should therefore be classed as an adjective following our tests. Sometimes, these kinds of adjectives are also classed as adverbs. The reason for this is that the uninflected forms of these adjectives behave like adverbs:

(61) Max lacht immer / oft   / laut.
     Max laughs always often loud
     'Max (always/often) laughs (loudly).'

To capture this dual nature of words some researchers distinguish between lexical and syntactic category of words. The lexical category of *laut* 'loud(ly)' is that of an adjective and the syntactic category to which it belongs is 'adverb'. The classification of adjectives such as *laut* 'loud(ly)' in (61) as adverbs is not assumed by all authors. Instead, some speak of adverbial usage of an adjective, that is, one assumes that the syntactic category is still adjective but it can be used in a different way so that it behaves like an adverb (see Eisenberg 2004: Section 7.3, for example). This is parallel to prepositions, which can occur in a variety of syntactic contexts:

(62) a. Peter schläft im   Büro.
        Peter sleeps in.the office
        'Peter sleeps in the office.'
     b. der Tisch im   Büro
        the table in.the office
        'the table in the office'

We have prepositional phrases in both examples in (62); however, in (62a) *im Büro* 'in the office' acts like an adverb in that it modifies the verb *schläft* 'sleeps' and in (62b) *im Büro* modifies the noun *Tisch* 'table'. In the same way, *laut* 'loud' can modify a noun (63) or a verb (61).

(63) die laute Musik
     the loud music

1.5 Heads

The head of a constituent/phrase is the element which determines the most important properties of the constituent/phrase. At the same time, the head also determines the composition of the phrase. That is, the head requires certain other elements to be present in the phrase. The heads in the following examples have been marked in *italics*:

(64) a. *Träumt* dieser   Mann?
        dreams this.NOM man
        'Does this man dream?'

b. *Erwartet* er diesen Mann?
   expects he.NOM this.ACC man

   'Is he expecting this man?'

c. *Hilft* er diesem Mann?
   helps he.NOM this.DAT man

   'Is he helping this man?'

d. *in* diesem Haus
   in this.DAT house

e. ein *Mann*
   a.NOM man

Verbs determine the case of their arguments (subjects and objects). In (64d), the preposition determines which case the noun phrase *diesem Haus* 'this house' bears (dative) and also determines the semantic contribution of the phrase (it describes a location). (64e) is controversial: there are linguists who believe that the determiner is the head (Vennemann & Harlow 1977; Hellan 1986; Abney 1987; Netter 1994; 1998) while others assume that the noun is the head of the phrase (Van Langendonck 1994; Pollard & Sag 1994: 49; Demske 2001; Müller 2007a: Section 6.6.1; Hudson 2004; Bruening 2009).

The combination of a head with another constituent is called a *projection of the head*. A projection which contains all the necessary parts to create a well-formed phrase of that type is a *maximal projection*. A sentence is the maximal projection of a finite verb.

Figure 1.3 shows the structure of (65) in box representation.

(65) Der Mann liest einen Aufsatz.
     the man reads an essay

     'The man is reading an essay.'

Unlike Figure 1.1, the boxes have been labelled here.

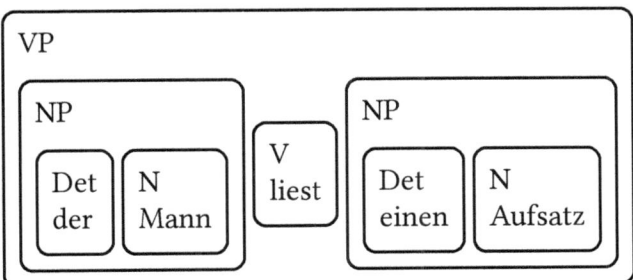

Figure 1.3: Words and phrases in annotated boxes

The annotation includes the category of the most important element in the box. VP stands for *verb phrase* and NP for *noun phrase*. VP and NP are maximal projections of their respective heads.

Anyone who has ever faced the hopeless task of trying to find particular photos of their sister's wedding in a jumbled, unsorted cupboard can vouch for the fact that it is most definitely a good idea to mark the boxes based on their content and also mark the albums based on the kinds of photos they contain.

An interesting point is that the exact content of the box with linguistic material does not play a role when the box is put into a larger box. It is possible, for example, to replace the noun phrase *der Mann* 'the man' with *er* 'he', or indeed the more complex *der Mann aus Stuttgart, der das Seminar zur Entwicklung der Zebrafinken besucht* 'the man from Stuttgart who takes part in the seminar on the development of zebra finches'. However, it is not possible to use *die Männer* 'the men' or *des Mannes* 'of the man' in this position:

(66)   a.   * Die Männer liest einen Aufsatz.
                the men   reads an   essay
   b.   * Des Mannes liest einen Aufsatz.
                of.the man.GEN reads an   essay

The reason for this is that *die Männer* 'the men' is in plural and the verb *liest* 'reads' is in singular. The noun phrase bearing genitive case *des Mannes* can also not occur, only nouns in the nominative case. It is therefore important to mark all boxes with the information that is important for placing these boxes into larger boxes. Figure 1.4 shows our example with more detailed annotation.

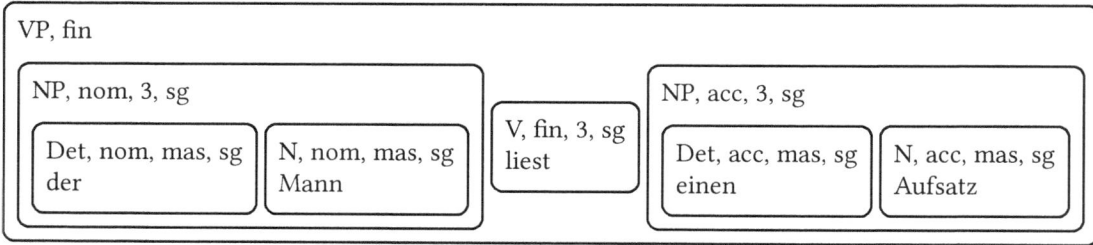

Figure 1.4: Words and word strings in annotated boxes

The features of a head which are relevant for determining in which contexts a phrase can occur are called *head features*. The features are said to be *projected* by the head.

1.6 Arguments and adjuncts

The constituents of a given clause have different relations to their head. It is typical to distinguish between arguments and adjuncts. The syntactic arguments of a head correspond for the most part to their logical arguments. We can represent the meaning of (67a) as (67b) using predicate logic.

(67)   a.   Peter helps Maria.
   b.   *help'(peter', maria')*

1.6 Arguments and adjuncts

The logical representation of (67b) resembles what is expressed in (67a); however, it abstracts away from constituent order and inflection. *Peter* and *Maria* are syntactic arguments of the verb *help* and their respective meanings (*Peter'* and *Maria'*) are arguments of the logical relation expressed by *help'*. One could also say that *help* assigns semantic roles to its arguments. Semantic roles include agent (the person carrying out an action), patient (the affected person or thing), beneficiary (the person who receives something) and experiencer (the person experiencing a psychological state). The subject of *help* is an agent and the direct object is a beneficiary. Arguments which fulfil a semantic role are also called *actants*. This term is also used for inanimate objects.

This kind of relation between a head and its arguments is covered by the terms *selection* and *valence*. Valence is a term borrowed from chemistry. Atoms can combine with other atoms to form molecules with varying levels of stability. The way in which the electron shells are occupied plays an important role for this stability. If an atom combines with others atoms so that its electron shell is fully occupied, then this will lead to a stable connection. Valence tells us something about the number of hydrogen atoms which an atom of a certain element can be combined with. In forming H_2O, oxygen has a valence of 2. We can divide elements into valence classes. Following Mendeleev, elements with a particular valence are listed in the same column in the periodic table.

The concept of valence was applied to linguistics by Tesnière (1959): a head needs certain arguments in order to form a stable compound. Words with the same valence – that is which require the same number and type of arguments – are divided into valence classes. Figure 1.5 shows examples from chemistry as well as linguistics.

Figure 1.5: Combination of hydrogen and oxygen and the combination of a verb with its arguments

We used (67) to explain logical valence. Logical valence can, however, sometimes differ from syntactic valence. This is the case with verbs like *rain*, which require an expletive pronoun as an argument. Inherently reflexive verbs such as *sich erholen* 'to recover' in German are another example.

(68) a. Es regnet.
    it rains
    'It is raining.'

 b. Klaus erholt sich.
    Klaus recovers REFL
    'Klaus is recovering.'

The expletive *es* 'it' with weather verbs and the *sich* of so-called inherent reflexives such as *erholen* 'to recover' have to be present in the sentence. Germanic languages have expletive elements that are used to fill the position preceding the finite verb. These positional expletives are not realized in embedded clauses in German, since embedded clauses have a structure that differs from canonical unembedded declarative clauses, which have the finite verb in second position. (69a) shows that *es* cannot be omitted in *dass*-clauses.

(69) a. * Ich glaube, dass regnet.
          I   think   that rains

        Intended: 'I think that it is raining.'

    b. * Ich glaube, dass Klaus erholt.
          I   believe that Klaus recovers

        Intended: 'I believe that Klaus is recovering.'

Neither the expletive nor the reflexive pronoun contributes anything semantically to the sentence. They must, however, be present to derive a complete, well-formed sentence. They therefore form part of the valence of the verb.

Constituents which do not contribute to the central meaning of their head, but rather provide additional information are called *adjuncts*. An example is the adverb *deeply* in (70):

(70)   John loves Mary deeply.

This says something about the intensity of the relation described by the verb. Further examples of adjuncts are attributive adjectives (71a) and relative clauses (71b):

(71) a. a *beautiful* woman
    b. the man *who Mary loves*

Adjuncts have the following syntactic/semantic properties:

(72) a. Adjuncts do not fulfil a semantic role.
    b. Adjuncts are optional.
    c. Adjuncts can be iterated.

The phrase in (71a) can be extended by adding another adjunct:

(73)   a beautiful clever woman

If one puts processing problems aside for a moment, this kind of extension by adding adjectives could proceed infinitely (see the discussion of (38) on page 65). Arguments, on the other hand, cannot be realized more than once:

(74)   * The man the boy sleeps.

If the entity carrying out the sleeping action has already been mentioned, then it is not possible to have another noun phrase which refers to a sleeping individual. If one wants to express the fact that more than one individual is sleeping, this must be done by means of coordination as in (75):

(75) The man and the boy are sleeping.

One should note that the criteria for identifying adjuncts proposed in (72) is not sufficient, since there are also syntactic arguments that do not fill semantic roles (e.g., *es* 'it' in (68a) and *sich* (REFL) in (68b)) or are optional as *pizza* in (76).

(76) Tony is eating (pizza).

Heads normally determine the syntactic properties of their arguments in a relatively fixed way. A verb is responsible for the case which its arguments bear.

(77) a. Er gedenkt des Opfers.
       he remembers the.GEN victim.GEN
       'He remembers the victim.'

   b. *Er gedenkt dem Opfer.
       he remembers the.DAT victim

   c. Er hilft dem Opfer.
       he helps the.DAT victim
       'He helps the victim.'

   d. *Er hilft des Opfers.
       he helps the.GEN victim.GEN

The verb *governs* the case of its arguments.

The preposition and the case of the noun phrase in the prepositional phrase are both determined by the verb:[14]

(78) a. Er denkt an seine Modelleisenbahn.
       he thinks on his.ACC model.railway
       'He is thinking of his model railway.'

   b. #Er denkt an seiner Modelleisenbahn.
       He thinks on his.DAT model.railway

   c. Er hängt an seiner Modelleisenbahn.
       He hangs on his.DAT model.railway
       'He clings to his model railway.'

   d. *Er hängt an seine Modelleisenbahn.
       he hangs on his.ACC model.railway

The case of noun phrases in modifying prepositional phrases, on the other hand, depends on their meaning. In German, directional prepositional phrases normally require a noun phrase bearing accusative case (79a), whereas local PPs (denoting a fixed location) appear in the dative case (79b):

---

[14]For similar examples, see Eisenberg (1994b: 78).

(79) a. Er geht in die Schule / auf den Weihnachtsmarkt / unter die
he goes in the.ACC school on the.ACC Christmas.market under the.ACC
Brücke.
bridge

'He is going to school/to the Christmas market/under the bridge.'

b. Er schläft in der Schule / auf dem Weihnachtsmarkt / unter der
he sleeps in the.DAT school on the.DAT Christmas.market under the.DAT
Brücke.
bridge

'He is sleeping at school/at the Christmas market/under the bridge.'

An interesting case is the verb *sich befinden* 'to be located', which expresses the location of something. This cannot occur without some information about the location pertaining to the verb:

(80) * Wir befinden uns.
we are.located REFL

The exact form of this information is not fixed – neither the syntactic category nor the preposition inside of prepositional phrases is restricted:

(81) Wir befinden uns hier / unter der Brücke / neben dem Eingang / im Bett.
we are REFL here under the bridge next.to the entrance in bed

'We are here/under the bridge/next to the entrance/in bed.'

Local modifiers such as *hier* 'here' or *unter der Brücke* 'under the bridge' are analyzed with regard to other verbs (e.g., *schlafen* 'sleep') as adjuncts. For verbs such as *sich befinden* 'to be (located)', we will most likely have to assume that information about location forms an obligatory syntactic argument of the verb.

The verb selects a phrase with information about location, but does not place any syntactic restrictions on its type. This specification of location behaves semantically like the other adjuncts we have seen previously. If I just consider the semantic aspects of the combination of a head and adjunct, then I also refer to the adjunct as a *modifier*.[15] Arguments specifying location with verbs such as *sich befinden* 'to be located' are also subsumed under the term *modifier*. Modifiers are normally adjuncts, and therefore optional, whereas in the case of *sich befinden* they seem to be (obligatory) arguments.

In conclusion, we can say that constituents that are required to occur with a certain head are arguments of that head. Furthermore, constituents which fulfil a semantic role with regard to the head are also arguments. These kinds of arguments can, however, sometimes be optional.

---

[15] See Section 1.7.2 for more on the grammatical function of adverbials. The term adverbial is normally used in conjunction with verbs. *modifier* is a more general term, which normally includes attributive adjectives.

Arguments are normally divided into subjects and complements.[16] Not all heads require a subject (see Müller 2007a: Section 3.2). The number of arguments of a head can therefore also correspond to the number of complements of a head.

1.7 Grammatical functions

In some theories, grammatical functions such as subject and object form part of the formal description of language (see Chapter 7 on Lexical Functional Grammar, for example). This is not the case for the majority of the theories discussed here, but these terms are used for the informal description of certain phenomena. For this reason, I will briefly discuss them in what follows.

1.7.1 Subjects

Although I assume that the reader has a clear intuition about what a subject is, it is by no means a trivial matter to arrive at a definition of the word *subject* which can be used cross-linguistically. For German, Reis (1982) suggested the following syntactic properties as definitional for subjects:

- agreement of the finite verb with it
- nominative case in non-copular clauses
- omitted in infinitival clauses (control)
- optional in imperatives

I have already discussed agreement in conjunction with the examples in (4). Reis (1982) argues that the second bullet point is a suitable criterion for German. She formulates a restriction to non-copular clause because there can be more than one nominative argument in sentences with predicate nominals such as (82):

(82) a. Er   ist ein Lügner.
        he.NOM ist a   liar.NOM
        'He is a liar.'
    b. Er   wurde ein Lügner genannt.
        he.NOM was   a   liar.NOM called
        'He was called a liar.'

Following this criterion, arguments in the dative case such as *den Männern* 'the men' cannot be classed as subjects in German:

---

[16]In some schools the term complement is understood to include the subject, that is, the term complement is equivalent to the term argument (see for instance Groß 2003: 342). Some researchers treat some subjects, e.g., those of finite verbs, as complements (Pollard 1996a; Eisenberg 1994a: 376).

1 Introduction and basic terms

(83)   a.   Er hilft den Männern.
           he helps the.DAT men.DAT
           'He is helping the men.'
     b.   Den Männern wurde geholfen.
           the.DAT men.DAT were.3SG helped
           'The men were helped.'

Following the other criteria, datives should also not be classed as subjects – as Reis (1982) has shown. In (83b), *wurde*, which is the 3rd person singular form, does not agree with *den Männern*. The third of the aforementioned criteria deals with infinitive constructions such as those in (84):

(84)   a.   Klaus behauptet, den Männern zu helfen.
           Klaus claims the.DAT men.DAT to help
           'Klaus claims to be helping the men.'
     b.   Klaus behauptet, dass er den Männern hilft.
           Klaus claims that he the.DAT men.DAT helps
           'Klaus claims that he is helping the men.'
     c.   * Die Männer behaupten, geholfen zu werden.
           the men claim helped to become
           Intended: 'The men are claiming to be helped.'
     d.   * Die Männer behaupten, elegant getanzt zu werden.
           the men claim elegantly danced to become
           Intended: 'The men claim that there is elegant dancing.'

In the first sentence, an argument of the verb *helfen* 'to help' has been omitted. If one wishes to express it, then one would have to use the subordinate clause beginning with *dass* 'that' as in (84b). Examples (84c,d) show that infinitives which do not require a nominative argument cannot be embedded under verbs such as *behaupten* 'to claim'. If the dative noun phrase *den Männern* 'the men' were the subject in (83b), we would expect the control construction (84c) to be well-formed. This is, however, not the case. Instead of (84c), it is necessary to use (85):

(85)   Die Männer behaupten, dass ihnen geholfen wird.
       the men.NOM claim that them.DAT helped becomes
       'The men claim that they are being helped.'

In the same way, imperatives are not possible with verbs that do not require a nominative. (86) shows some examples from Reis (1982: 186).

(86)   a.   Fürchte dich nicht!
           be.scared REFL not
           'Don't be scared!'

b. * Graue nicht!
   dread not
   'Don't dread it!'

c. Werd einmal unterstützt und …
   be   once   supported   and
   'Let someone support you for once and …'

d. * Werd einmal geholfen und …
   be   once   helped   and
   'Let someone help you and …'

The verb *sich fürchten* 'to be scared' in (86a) obligatorily requires a nominative argument as its subject (87a). The similar verb *grauen* 'to dread' in (86b) takes a dative argument (87b).

(87) a. Ich   fürchte   mich vor   Spinnen.
        I.NOM be.scared REFL before spiders
        'I am scared of spiders.'

    b. Mir   graut   vor   Spinnen.
        me.DAT scares before spiders
        'I am dreading spiders.'

Interestingly, dative arguments in Icelandic behave differently. Zaenen et al. (1985) discuss various characteristics of subjects in Icelandic and show that it makes sense to describe dative arguments as subjects in passive sentences even if the finite verb does not agree with them (Section 3.1) or they do not bear nominative case. An example of this is infinitive constructions with an omitted dative argument (p. 457):

(88) a. Ég vonast til   að verða hjálpað.
        I hope   for to be   helped
        'I hope that I will be helped.'

    b. Að vera hjálpað í prófinu   er óleyfilegt.
        to be   helped on the.exam is not.allowed
        'It is not allowed for one to be helped during the exam.'

In a number of grammars, clausal arguments such as those in (89) are classed as subjects as they can be replaced by a noun phrase in the nominative (90) (see e.g., Eisenberg 2004: 63, 289).

(89) a. Dass er schon   um sieben kommen wollte, stimmt nicht.
        that he already at seven come   wanted is.true not
        'It's not true that he wanted to come as soon as seven.'

    b. Dass er Maria geheiratet hat, gefällt mir.
        that he Maria married   has pleases me
        'I'm glad that he married Maria.'

(90) a. Das stimmt nicht.
     that is.true not
     'That isn't true.'
  b. Das gefällt mir.
     that pleases me
     'I like that.'

It should be noted that there are different opinions on the question of whether clausal arguments should be treated as subjects or not. As recent publications show, there is still some discussion in Lexical Function Grammar (see Chapter 7) (Dalrymple & Lødrup 2000; Berman 2003b; 2007; Alsina, Mohanan & Mohanan 2005; Forst 2006).

If we can be clear about what we want to view as a subject, then the definition of object is no longer difficult: objects are all other arguments whose form is directly determined by a given head. As well as clausal objects, German has genitive, dative, accusative and prepositional objects:

(91) a. Sie gedenken des Mannes.
     they remember the.GEN man.GEN
     'They remember the man.'
  b. Sie helfen dem Mann.
     they help the.DAT man.DAT
     'They are helping the man.'
  c. Sie kennen den Mann.
     they know the.ACC man.ACC
     'They know the man.'
  d. Sie denken an den Mann.
     they think on the man
     'They are thinking of the man.'

As well as defining objects by their case, it is commonplace to talk of *direct objects* and *indirect objects*. The direct object gets its name from the fact that – unlike the indirect object – the referent of a direct object is directly affected by the action denoted by the verb. With ditransitives such as the German *geben* 'to give', the accusative object is the direct object and the dative is the indirect object.

(92) dass er dem Mann den Aufsatz gibt
     that he.NOM the.DAT man.DAT the.ACC essay.ACC gives
     'that he gives the man the essay'

For trivalent verbs (verbs taking three arguments), we see that the verb can take either an object in the genitive case (93a) or, for verbs with a direct object in the accusative, a second accusative object (93b):

1.7 Grammatical functions

(93) a. dass er den   Mann   des   Mordes   bezichtigte
         that he the.ACC man.ACC the.GEN murder.GEN accused
         'that he accused the man of murder'
    b. dass er den   Mann   den   Vers   lehrte
         that he the.ACC man.ACC the.ACC verse.ACC taught
         'that he taught the man the verse'

These kinds of objects are sometimes also referred to as indirect objects.

Normally, only those objects which are promoted to subject in passives with *werden* 'to be' are classed as direct objects. This is important for theories such as LFG (see Chapter 7) since passivization is defined with reference to grammatical function. With two-place verbal predicates, the dative is not normally classed as a direct object (Cook 2006).

(94) dass er dem   Mann   hilft
     that he the.DAT man.DAT helps
     'that he helps the man'

In many theories, grammatical function does not form a primitive component of the theory, but rather corresponds to positions in a tree structure. The direct object in German is therefore the object which is first combined with the verb in a configuration assumed to be the underlying structure of German sentences. The indirect object is the second object to be combined with the verb. On this view, the dative object of *helfen* 'to help' would have to be viewed as a direct object.

In the following, I will simply refer to the case of objects and avoid using the terms direct object and indirect object.

In the same way as with subjects, we consider whether there are object clauses which are equivalent to a certain case and can fill the respective grammatical function of a direct or indirect object. If we assume that *dass du sprichst* 'that you are speaking' in (95a) is a subject, then the subordinate clause must be a direct object in (95b):

(95) a. Dass du sprichst, wird erwähnt.
         that you speak   is   mentioned
         'The fact that you're speaking is being mentioned.'
    b. Er erwähnt, dass du sprichst.
         he mentions that you speak
         'He mentions that you are speaking.'

In this case, we cannot really view the subordinate clause as the accusative object since it does not bear case. However, we can replace the sentence with an accusative-marked noun phrase:

(96) Er erwähnt diesen   Sachverhalt.
     he mentions this.ACC matter
     'He mentions this matter.'

If we want to avoid this discussion, we can simply call these arguments clausal objects.

1 Introduction and basic terms

1.7.2 The adverbial

Adverbials differ semantically from subjects and objects. They tell us something about the conditions under which an action or process takes place, or the way in which a certain state persists. In the majority of cases, adverbials are adjuncts, but there are – as we have already seen – a number of heads which also require adverbials. Examples of these are verbs such as *to be located* or *to make one's way*. For *to be located*, it is necessary to specify a location and for *to proceed to* a direction is needed. These kinds of adverbials are therefore regarded as arguments of the verb.

The term *adverbial* comes from the fact that adverbials are often adverbs. This is not the only possibility, however. Adjectives, participles, prepositional phrases, noun phrases and even sentences can be adverbials:

(97) a. Er arbeitet sorgfältig.
 he works carefully

 b. Er arbeitet vergleichend.
 he works comparatively
 'He does comparative work.'

 c. Er arbeitet in der Universität.
 he works in the university
 'He works at the university.'

 d. Er arbeitet den ganzen Tag.
 he works the whole day.ACC
 'He works all day.'

 e. Er arbeitet, weil es ihm Spaß macht.
 he works because it him.DAT fun makes
 'He works because he enjoys it.'

Although the noun phrase in (97d) bears accusative case, it is not an accusative object. *den ganzen Tag* 'the whole day' is a so-called temporal accusative. The occurrence of accusative in this case has to do with the syntactic and semantic function of the noun phrase, it is not determined by the verb. These kinds of accusatives can occur with a variety of verbs, even with verbs that do not normally require an accusative object:

(98) a. Er schläft den ganzen Tag.
 he sleeps the whole day
 'He sleeps the whole day.'

 b. Er liest den ganzen Tag diesen schwierigen Aufsatz.
 he reads the.ACC whole.ACC day this.ACC difficult.ACC essay
 'He spends the whole day reading this difficult essay.'

 c. Er gibt den Armen den ganzen Tag Suppe.
 he gives the.DAT poor.DAT the.ACC whole.ACC day soup
 'He spends the whole day giving soup to the poor.'

The case of adverbials does not change under passivization:

(99) a. weil den ganzen Tag gearbeitet wurde
because the.ACC whole.ACC day worked was
'because someone worked all day'

b. * weil der ganze Tag gearbeitet wurde
because the.NOM whole.NOM day worked was

1.7.3 Predicatives

Adjectives like those in (100a,b) as well as noun phrases such as *ein Lügner* 'a liar' in (100c) are counted as predicatives.

(100) a. Klaus ist *klug*.
Klaus is clever

b. Er isst den Fisch *roh*.
he eats the fish raw

c. Er ist *ein Lügner*.
he is a liar

In the copula construction in (100a,c), the adjective *klug* 'clever' and the noun phrase *ein Lügner* 'a liar' is an argument of the copula *sein* 'to be' and the depictive adjective in (100b) is an adjunct to *isst* 'eats'.

For predicative noun phrases, case is not determined by the head but rather by some other element.[17] For example, the accusative in (101a) becomes nominative under passivization (101b):

---

[17] There is some dialectal variation with regard to copula constructions: in Standard German, the case of the noun phrase with *sein* 'to be' is always nominative and does not change when embedded under *lassen* 'to let'. According to Drosdowski (1995: § 1259), in Switzerland the accusative form is common which one finds in examples such as (ii.a).

(i) a. Ich bin dein Tanzpartner.
I am your.NOM dancing.partner

b. Der wüste Kerl ist ihr Komplize.
the wild guy is her.NOM accomplice

c. Laß den wüsten Kerl [...] meinetwegen ihr Komplize sein.
let the.ACC wild.ACC guy for.all.I.care her.NOM accomplice be
'Let's assume that the wild guy is her accomplice, for all I care.' (Grebe & Gipper 1966: § 6925)

d. Baby, laß mich dein Tanzpartner sein.
baby let me.ACC your.NOM dancing.partner be
'Baby, let me be your dancing partner!' (Funny van Dannen, Benno-Ohnesorg-Theater, Berlin, Volksbühne, 11.10.1995)

(ii) a. Er lässt den lieben Gott 'n frommen Mann sein.
he lets the.ACC dear.ACC god a pious.ACC man be
'He is completely lighthearted/unconcerned.'

b. * Er lässt den lieben Gott 'n frommer Mann sein.
he lets the.ACC dear.ACC god a pious.NOM man be

(101)   a. Sie nannte ihn   einen Lügner.
           she called him.ACC a.ACC liar
           'She called him a liar.'
        b. Er   wurde ein   Lügner genannt.
           he.NOM was a.NOM liar   called
           'He was called a liar.'

Only *ihn* 'him' can be described as an object in (101a). In (101b), *ihn* becomes the subject and therefore bears nominative case. *einen Lügner* 'a liar' refers to *ihn* 'him' in (101a) and to *er* 'he' in (101b) and agrees in case with the noun over which it predicates. This is also referred to as *agreement case*.

For other predicative constructions see Eisenberg et al. (2005: § 1206) and Müller (2002a: Chapter 4, Chapter 5) and Müller (2008).

1.7.4 Valence classes

It is possible to divide verbs into subclasses depending on how many arguments they require and on the properties these arguments are required to have. The classic division describes all verbs which have an object which becomes the subject under passivization as *transitive*. Examples of this are verbs such as *love* or *beat*. Intransitive verbs, on the other hand, are verbs which have either no object, or one that does not become the subject in passive sentences. Examples of this type of verb are *schlafen* 'to sleep', *helfen* 'to help', *gedenken* 'to remember'. A subclass of transitive verbs are ditransitive verbs such as *geben* 'to give' and *zeigen* 'to show'.

Unfortunately, this terminology is not always used consistently. Sometimes, two-place verbs with dative and genitive objects are also classed as transitive verbs. In this naming tradition, the terms intransitive, transitive and ditransitive are synonymous with one-place, two-place and three-place verbs.

The fact that this terminological confusion can lead to misunderstandings between even established linguistics is shown by Culicover and Jackendoff's (2005: 59) criticism of Chomsky. Chomsky states that the combination of the English auxiliary *be* + verb with passive morphology can only be used for transitive verbs. Culicover and Jackendoff claim that this cannot be true because there are transitive verbs such as *weigh* and *cost*, which cannot undergo passivization:

(102)   a. This book weighs ten pounds / costs ten dollars.
        b. * Ten pounds are weighed / ten dollar are cost by this book.

Culicover and Jackendoff use *transitive* in the sense of a verb requiring two arguments. If we only view those verbs whose object becomes the subject of a passive clause as transitive, then *weigh* and *cost* no longer count as transitive verbs and Culicover and Jackendoff's criticism no longer holds.[18] That noun phrases such as those in (102) are no

---

[18] Their cricitism also turns out to be unjust even if one views transitives as being two-place predicates. If one claims that a verb must take at least two arguments to be able to undergo passivization, one is not necessarily claiming that all verbs taking two or more arguments have to allow passivization. The property of taking multiple arguments is a condition which must be fulfilled, but it is by no means the only one.

ordinary objects can also be seen by the fact they cannot be replaced by pronouns. It is therefore not possible to ascertain which case they bear since case distinctions are only realized on pronouns in English. If we translate the English examples into German, we find accusative objects:

(103)   a. Das Buch kostete einen Dollar.
           the book costs one.ACC dollar

'The book costs one dollar.'

       b. Das Buch wiegt einen Zentner.
           the book weighs one.ACC centner

'The book weighs one centner.'

In the following, I will use *transitive* in the former sense, that is for verbs with an object that becomes the subject when passivized (e.g., with *werden* in German). When I talk about the class of verbs that includes *helfen* 'to help', which takes a nominative and dative argument, and *schlagen* 'to hit', which takes a nominative and accusative argument, I will use the term *two-place* or *bivalent verb*.

1.8 A topological model of the German clause

In this section, I introduce the concept of so-called *topological fields* (*topologische Felder*). These will be used frequently in later chapters to discuss different parts of the German clause. One can find further, more detailed introductions to topology in Reis (1980), Höhle (1986) and Askedal (1986). Wöllstein (2010) is a textbook about the topological field model.

1.8.1 The position of the verb

It is common practice to divide German sentences into three types pertaining to the position of the finite verb:

- verb-final clauses
- verb-first (initial) clauses
- verb-second (V2) clauses

The following examples illustrate these possibilities:

(104)   a. (Peter hat erzählt,) dass er das Eis gegessen *hat*.
           Peter has told that he the ice.cream eaten has

'Peter said that he has eaten the ice cream.'

       b. *Hat* Peter das Eis gegessen?
           has Peter the ice.cream eaten

'Has Peter eaten the ice cream?'

       c. Peter *hat* das Eis gegessen.
           Peter has the ice.cream eaten

'Peter has eaten the ice cream.'

1 Introduction and basic terms

1.8.2 The sentence bracket, prefield, middle field and postfield

We observe that the finite verb *hat* 'has' is only adjacent to its complement *gegessen* 'eaten' in (104a). In (104b) and (104c), the verb and its complement are separated, that is, discontinuous. We can then divide the German clause into various sub-parts on the basis of these distinctions. In (104b) and (104c), the verb and the auxiliary form a "bracket" around the clause. For this reason, we call this the *sentence bracket* (*Satzklammer*). The finite verbs in (104b) and (104c) form the left bracket and the non-finite verbs form the right bracket. Clauses with verb-final order are usually introduced by conjunctions such as *weil* 'because', *dass* 'that' and *ob* 'whether'. These conjunctions occupy the same position as the finite verb in verb-initial or verb-second clauses. We therefore also assume that these conjunctions form the left bracket in these cases. Using the notion of the sentence bracket, it is possible to divide the structure of the German clause into the prefield (*Vorfeld*), middle field (*Mittelfeld*) and postfield (*Nachfeld*). The prefield describes everything preceding the left sentence bracket, the middle field is the section between the left and right bracket and the postfield describes the position after the right bracket. The Tables 1.1 and 1.2 give some examples of this. The right bracket can contain multiple verbs and is often referred to as a *verbal complex* or *verb cluster*. The assignment of question words and relative pronouns to the prefield will be discussed in the following section.

Table 1.1: Examples of how topological fields can be occupied in declarative main clauses

Prefield	Left b.	Middle field	Right b.	Postfield
Karl	*schläft.*			
Karl	sleeps			
Karl	*hat*		*geschlafen.*	
Karl	has		slept	
Karl	*erkennt*	*Maria.*		
Karl	recognizes	Maria		
Karl	*färbt*	den Mantel	*um*	*den Maria kennt.*
Karl	dies	the coat	PARTICLE	that Maria knows
Karl	*hat*	*Maria*	*erkannt.*	
Karl	has	Maria	recognized	
Karl	*hat*	*Maria als sie aus dem Bus stieg sofort*	*erkannt.*	
Karl	has	Maria when she got.off the bus immediately	recognized	
Karl	*hat*	*Maria sofort*	*erkannt*	*als sie aus dem Bus stieg.*
Karl	has	Maria immediately	recognized	when she got.off the bus
Karl	*hat*	*Maria zu erkennen*	*behauptet.*	
Karl	has	Maria to recognize	claimed	
Karl	*hat*		*behauptet*	*Maria zu erkennen.*
Karl	has		claimed	Maria to know

1.8 A topological model of the German clause

Table 1.2: Examples of how topological fields can be occupied in yes/no questions, imperatives, exclamatives and various verb final sentences including adverbial clauses, interrogative and relative clauses

Prefield	Left b.	Middle field	Right b.	Postfield
	Schläft sleeps	Karl? Karl		
	Schlaf! sleep			
	Iss eat	jetzt deinen Kuchen now your cake	auf! up	
	Hat has	er doch den ganzen Kuchen alleine he after.all the whole cake alone	gegessen! eaten	
	weil because	er den ganzen Kuchen alleine he the whole cake alone	*gegessen hat* eaten has	*ohne es zu bereuen* without it to regret
	weil because	er den ganzen Kuchen alleine he the whole cake	*essen können will* eat can wants.to	*ohne gestört zu werden* without disturbed to be
wer who		den ganzen Kuchen alleine the whole cake alone	*gegessen hat* eaten has	
der who.REL		den ganzen Kuchen alleine the whole cake alone	*gegessen hat* eaten has	
mit wem with whom		*du* you	*geredet hast* spoken have	
mit dem with whom.REL		*du* you	*geredet hast* spoken have	

1.8.3 Assigning elements to fields

As the examples in the Tables 1.1 and 1.2 show, it is not required that all fields are always occupied. Even the left bracket can be empty if one opts to leave out the copula *sein* 'to be' such as in the examples in (105):

(105) a. [...] egal,   was noch passiert, der Norddeutsche Rundfunk
          regardless what still happens   the north.German broadcasting.company
       steht   schon jetzt als Gewinner fest.[19]
       stands already now as winner   PART

   'Regardless of what still may happen, the North German broadcasting company is already the winner.'

---

[19]Spiegel, 12/1999, p. 258.

1 Introduction and basic terms

    b. Interessant, zu erwähnen, daß ihre Seele völlig   in Ordnung war.[20]
       interesting to mention   that her soul completely in order   was
      'It is interesting to note that her soul was entirely fine.'

    c. Ein Treppenwitz der   Musikgeschichte, daß die Kollegen von Rammstein
       an afterwit   of.the history.of.music that the colleagues of   Rammstein
       vor   fünf Jahren noch im   Vorprogramm von Sandow spielten.[21]
       before five years   still in.the pre.programme of   Sandow played
      'One of the little ironies of music history is that five years ago their colleagues of Rammstein were still an opening act for Sandow.'

The examples in (105) correspond to those with the copula in (106):

(106)   a. Egal   ist, was noch passiert, ...
           regardless is   what still   happens
           'It is not important what still may happen ...'

        b. Interessant ist zu erwähnen, dass ihre Seele völlig   in Ordnung war.
           interesting is to mention   that her soul completely in order   was
           'It is interesting to note that her soul was completely fine.'

        c. Ein Treppenwitz der   Musikgeschichte ist, dass die Kollegen   von
           an afterwit   of.the music.history   is   that the colleagues of
           Rammstein vor   fünf Jahren noch im Vorprogramm   von Sandow spielten.
           Rammstein before five years   still in pre.programme of   Sandow played
           'It is one of the little ironies of music history that five years ago their colleagues of Rammstein were still an opening act for Sandow.'

When fields are empty, it is sometimes not clear which fields are occupied by certain constituents. For the examples in (105), one would have to insert the copula to be able to ascertain that a single constituent is in the prefield and, furthermore, which fields are occupied by the other constituents.

In the following example taken from Paul (1919: 13), inserting the copula obtains a different result:

(107)   a. Niemand da?
           nobody   there

        b. Ist niemand da?
           is nobody   there
           'Is nobody there?'

Here we are dealing with a question and *niemand* 'nobody' in (107a) should therefore not be analyzed as in the prefield but rather the middle field.

---

[20] Michail Bulgakow, *Der Meister und Margarita*. München: Deutscher Taschenbuch Verlag. 1997, p. 422.
[21] Flüstern & Schweigen, taz, 12.07.1999, p. 14.

1.8 A topological model of the German clause

In (108), there are elements in the prefield, the left bracket and the middle field. The right bracket is empty.[22]

(108) Er   gibt der Frau   das Buch,   die   er kennt.
       he.M gives the woman(F) the book.(N) that.F he knows
       'He gives the book to the woman that he knows.'

How should we analyze relative clauses such as *die er kennt* 'that he knows'? Do they form part of the middle field or the postfield? This can be tested using a test developed by Bech (1955: 72) (*Rangprobe*): first, we modify the example in (108) so that it is in the perfect. Since non-finite verb forms occupy the right bracket, we can clearly see the border between the middle field and postfield. The examples in (109) show that the relative clause cannot occur in the middle field unless it is part of a complex constituent with the head noun *Frau* 'woman'.

(109) a. Er hat [der Frau]   das Buch gegeben, [die er kennt].
           he has the woman   the book given   that he knows
           'He has given the book to the woman that he knows.'

       b. * Er hat [der Frau]   das Buch, [die er kennt,] gegeben.
             he has the woman   the book   that he knows   given

       c. Er hat [der Frau,   die er kennt,] das Buch gegeben.
           he has the woman that he knows   the book given

This test does not help if the relative clause is realized together with its head noun at the end of the sentence as in (110):

(110) Er gibt das Buch der Frau,   die er kennt.
       he gives the book the woman that he knows
       'He gives the book to the woman that he knows.'

If we put the example in (110) in the perfect, then we observe that the lexical verb can occur before or after the relative clause:

(111) a. Er hat das Buch [der Frau]   gegeben, [die er kennt].
           he has the book the woman   given   that he knows
           'He has given the book to the woman he knows.'

       b. Er hat das Buch [der Frau,   die er kennt,] gegeben.
           he has the book the woman that he knows   given

In (111a), the relative clause has been extraposed. In (111b) it forms part of the noun phrase *der Frau, die er kennt* 'the woman that he knows' and therefore occurs inside the NP in the middle field. It is therefore not possible to rely on this test for (110). We assume that the relative clause in (110) also belongs to the NP since this is the most simple structure. If

---

[22]The sentence requires emphasis on *der* 'the'. *der Frau, die er kennt* 'the woman' is contrasted with another woman or other women.

47

1 Introduction and basic terms

the relative clause were in the postfield, we would have to assume that it has undergone extraposition from its position inside the NP. That is, we would have to assume the NP-structure anyway and then extraposition in addition.

We have a similar problem with interrogative and relative pronouns. Depending on the author, these are assumed to be in the left bracket (Kathol 2001; Dürscheid 2003: 94–95; Eisenberg 2004: 403; Pafel 2011: 57) or the prefield (Eisenberg et al. 2005: §1345; Wöllstein 2010: 29–30, Section 3.1) or even in the middle field (Altmann & Hofman 2004: 75). In Standard German interrogative or relative clauses, both fields are never simultaneously occupied. For this reason, it is not immediately clear to which field an element belongs. Nevertheless, we can draw parallels to main clauses: the pronouns in interrogative and relative clauses can be contained inside complex phrases:

(112) a. der Mann, [mit dem] du gesprochen hast
 the man with whom you spoken have
 'the man you spoke to'

b. Ich möchte wissen, [mit wem] du gesprochen hast.
 I want.to know with whom you spoken have
 'I want to know who you spoke to.'

Normally, only individual words (conjunctions or verbs) can occupy the left bracket,[23] whereas words and phrases can appear in the prefield. It therefore makes sense to assume that interrogative and relative pronouns (and phrases containing them) also occur in this position.

Furthermore, it can be observed that the dependency between the elements in the *Vorfeld* of declarative clauses and the remaining sentence is of the same kind as the dependency between the phrase that contains the relative pronoun and the remaining sentence. For instance, *über dieses Thema* 'about this topic' in (113a) depends on *Vortrag* 'talk', which is deeply embedded in the sentence: *einen Vortrag* 'a talk' is an argument of *zu halten* 'to hold', which in turn is an argument of *gebeten* 'asked'.

(113) a. Über dieses Thema habe ich ihn gebeten, einen Vortrag zu halten.
 about this topic have I him asked a talk to hold
 'I asked him to give a talk about this topic.'

b. das Thema, über das ich ihn gebeten habe, einen Vortrag zu halten
 the topic about which I him asked have a talk to hold
 'the topic about which I asked him to give a talk'

The situation is similar in (113b): the relative phrase *über das* 'about which' is a dependent of *Vortrag* 'talk' which is realized far away from it. Thus, if the relative phrase is assigned to the *Vorfeld*, it is possible to say that such nonlocal frontings always target the *Vorfeld*.

---

[23]Coordination is an exception to this:

(i) Er [kennt und liebt] diese Schallplatte.
 he knows and loves this record
 'He knows and loves this record.'

1.8 A topological model of the German clause

Finally, the Duden grammar (Eisenberg et al. 2005: §1347) provides the following examples from non-standard German (mainly southern dialects):

(114) a. Kommt drauf an, mit wem dass sie zu tun haben.
      comes there.upon PART with whom that you to do have
      'It depends on whom you are dealing with.'

(115) a. Lotti, die wo eine tolle Sekretärin ist, hat ein paar merkwürdige
         Lotti who where a great secretary is has a few strange
         Herren empfangen.
         gentlemen welcomed
         'Lotti, who is a great secretary, welcomed a few strange gentlemen.'
      b. Du bist der beste Sänger, den wo ich kenn.
         you are the best singer who where I know
         'You are the best singer whom I know.'

These examples of interrogative and relative clauses show that the left sentence bracket is filled with a conjunction (*dass* 'that' or *wo* 'where' in the respective dialects). So if one wants to have a model that treats Standard German and the dialectal forms uniformly, it is reasonable to assume that the relative phrases and interrogative phrases are located in the *Vorfeld*.

1.8.4 Recursion

As already noted by Reis (1980: 82), when occupied by a complex constituent, the prefield can be subdivided into further fields including a postfield, for example. The constituents *für lange lange Zeit* 'for a long, long time' in (116b) and *daß du kommst* 'that you are coming' in (116d) are inside the prefield but occur to the right of the right bracket *verschüttet* 'buried' / *gewußt* 'knew', that is they are in the postfield of the prefield.

(116) a. Die Möglichkeit, etwas zu verändern, ist damit verschüttet für lange
         the possibility something to change is there.with buried for long
         lange Zeit.
         long time
         'The possibility to change something will now be gone for a long, long time.'
      b. [Verschüttet für lange lange Zeit] ist damit die Möglichkeit, etwas
         buried for long long time ist there.with the possibility something
         zu verändern.
         to change
      c. Wir haben schon seit langem gewußt, daß du kommst.
         we have PART since long known that you come
         'We have known for a while that you are coming.'
      d. [Gewußt, daß du kommst,] haben wir schon seit langem.
         known that you come have we PART since long

1 Introduction and basic terms

Like constituents in the prefield, elements in the middle field and postfield can also have an internal structure and be divided into subfields accordingly. For example, *daß* 'that' is the left bracket of the subordinate clause *daß du kommst* in (116c), whereas *du* 'you' occupies the middle field and *kommst* 'come' the right bracket.

Comprehension questions

1. How does the head of a phrase differ from non-heads?

2. What is the head in the examples in (117)?

   (117) a. he

   b. Go!

   c. quick

3. How do arguments differ from adjuncts?

4. Identify the heads, arguments and adjuncts in the following sentence (118) and in the subparts of the sentence:

   (118) Er hilft den kleinen Kindern in der Schule.
   he helps the small children in the school

   'He helps small children at school.'

5. How can we define the terms prefield (*Vorfeld*), middle field (*Mittelfeld*), postfield (*Nachfeld*) and the left and right sentence brackets (*Satzklammer*)?

Exercises

1. Identify the sentence brackets, prefield, middle field and postfield in the following sentences. Do the same for the embedded clauses!

   (119) a. Karl isst.
             Karl eats
             'Karl is eating.'

         b. Der Mann liebt eine Frau, den Peter kennt.
             the man loves a woman who Peter knows
             'The man who Peter knows loves a woman.'

         c. Der Mann liebt eine Frau, die Peter kennt.
             the man loves a woman that Peter knows
             'The man loves a woman who Peter knows.'

         d. Die Studenten haben behauptet, nur wegen der Hitze
             the students have claimed only because.of the heat
             einzuschlafen.
             to.fall.asleep
             'The students claimed that they were only falling asleep because of the heat.'

         e. Dass Peter nicht kommt, ärgert Klaus.
             that Peter not comes annoys Klaus
             '(The fact) that Peter isn't coming annoys Klaus.'

         f. Einen Mann küssen, der ihr nicht gefällt, würde sie nie.
             a man kiss that her not pleases would she never
             'She would never kiss a man she doesn't like.'

1 Introduction and basic terms

Further reading

Reis (1980) gives reasons for why field theory is important for the description of the position of constituents in German.

Höhle (1986) discusses fields to the left of the prefield, which are needed for left-dislocation structures such as with *der Mittwoch* in (120), *aber* in (121a) and *denn* in (121b):

(120) Der Mittwoch, der passt mir gut.
　　　the Wednesday that fits me good

　　　'Wednesday, that suits me fine.'

(121)　a. Aber würde denn jemand den Hund füttern morgen　Abend?
　　　　　but would PART anybody the dog feed tomorrow evening

　　　　　'But would anyone feed the dog tomorrow evening?'

　　　b. Denn　dass es regnet, damit　rechnet keiner.
　　　　　because that it rains there.with reckons nobody

　　　　　'Because no-one expects that it will rain.'

Höhle also discusses the historical development of field theory.

2 Phrase structure grammar

This chapter deals with phase structure grammars (PSGs), which play an important role in several of the theories we will encounter in later chapters.

2.1 Symbols and rewrite rules

Words can be assigned to a particular part of speech on the basis of their inflectional properties and syntactic distribution. Thus, *weil* 'because' in (1) is a conjunction, whereas *das* 'the' and *dem* 'the' are articles and therefore classed as determiners. Furthermore, *Buch* 'book' and *Mann* 'man' are nouns and *gibt* 'gives' is a verb.

(1) weil   er das Buch dem Mann gibt
    because he the book the   man   gives

    'because he gives the man the book'

Using the constituency tests we introduced in Section 1.3, we can show that individual words as well as the strings *das Buch* 'the book' and *dem Mann* 'the man', form constituents. These get then assigned certain symbols. Since nouns form an important part of the phrases *das Buch* and *dem Mann*, these are referred to as *noun phrases* or NPs, for short. The pronoun *er* 'he' can occur in the same positions as full NPs and can therefore also be assigned to the category NP.

Phrase structure grammars come with rules specifying which symbols are assigned to certain kinds of words and how these are combined to create more complex units. A simple phrase structure grammar which can be used to analyze (1) is given in (2):[1,2]

(2)   NP → Det N   NP → er   N → Buch
       S → NP NP NP V   Det → das   N → Mann
                                        Det → dem   V → gibt

We can therefore interpret a rule such as NP → Det N as meaning that a noun phrase, that is, something which is assigned the symbol NP, can consist of a determiner (Det) and a noun (N).

---

[1] I ignore the conjunction *weil* 'because' for now. Since the exact analysis of German verb-first and verb-second clauses requires a number of additional assumptions, we will restrict ourselves to verb-final clauses in this chapter.

[2] The rule NP → er may seem odd. We could assume the rule PersPron → er instead but then would have to posit a further rule which would specify that personal pronouns can replace full NPs: NP → PersPron. The rule in (2) combines the two aforementioned rules and states that *er* 'he' can occur in positions where noun phrases can.

2 Phrase structure grammar

We can analyze the sentence in (1) using the grammar in (2) in the following way: first, we take the first word in the sentence and check if there is a rule in which this word occurs on the right-hand side of the rule. If this is the case, then we replace the word with the symbol on the left-hand side of the rule. This happens in lines 2–4, 6–7 and 9 of the derivation in (3). For instance, in line 2 *er* is replaced by NP. If there are two or more symbols which occur together on the right-hand side of a rule, then all these words are replaced with the symbol on the left. This happens in lines 5, 8 and 10. For instance, in line 5 and 8, Det and N are rewritten as NP.

(3)

	words and symbols					rules that are applied
1	er	das	Buch	dem	Mann	gibt	
2	NP	das	Buch	dem	Mann	gibt	NP → er
3	NP	Det	Buch	dem	Mann	gibt	Det → das
4	NP	Det	N	dem	Mann	gibt	N → Buch
5	NP		NP	dem	Mann	gibt	NP → Det N
6	NP		NP	Det	Mann	gibt	Det → dem
7	NP		NP	Det	N	gibt	N → Mann
8	NP		NP		NP	gibt	NP → Det N
9	NP		NP		NP	V	V → gibt
10						S	S → NP NP NP V

In (3), we began with a string of words and it was shown that we can derive the structure of a sentence by applying the rules of a given phrase structure grammar. We could have applied the same steps in reverse order: starting with the sentence symbol S, we would have applied the steps 9–1 and arrived at the string of words. Selecting different rules from the grammar for rewriting symbols, we could use the grammar in (2) to get from S to the string *er dem Mann das Buch gibt* 'he the man the book gives'. We can say that this grammar licenses (or generates) a set of sentences.

The derivation in (3) can also be represented as a tree. This is shown by Figure 2.1. The

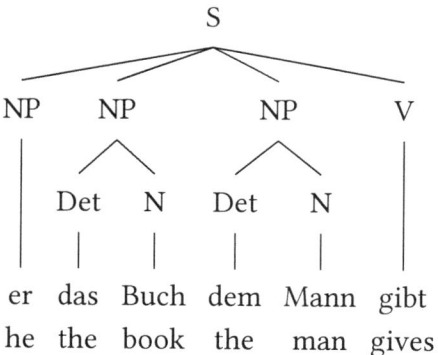

Figure 2.1: Analysis of *er das Buch dem Mann gibt* 'he the book the man gives'

symbols in the tree are called *nodes*. We say that S immediately dominates the NP nodes and the V node. The other nodes in the tree are also dominated, but not immediately dominated, by S. If we want to talk about the relationship between nodes, it is common

2.1 Symbols and rewrite rules

to use kinship terms. In Figure 2.1, S is the *mother node* of the three NP nodes and the V node. The NP node and V are *sisters* since they have the same mother node. If a node has two daughters, then we have a binary branching structure. If there is exactly one daughter, then we have a unary branching structure. Two constituents are said to be *adjacent* if they are directly next to each other.

Phrase structure rules are often omitted in linguistic publications. Instead, authors opt for tree diagrams or the compact equivalent bracket notation such as (4).

(4) [$_S$ [$_{NP}$ er] [$_{NP}$ [$_{Det}$ das] [$_N$ Buch]] [$_{NP}$ [$_{Det}$ dem] [$_N$ Mann]] [$_V$ gibt]]
       he   the   book   the   man   gives

Nevertheless, it is the grammatical rules which are actually important since these represent grammatical knowledge which is independent of specific structures. In this way, we can use the grammar in (2) to parse or generate the sentence in (5), which differs from (1) in the order of objects:

(5)   [weil]   er   dem   Mann das   Buch gibt
     because he.NOM the.DAT man   the.ACC book gives

'because he gives the man the book'

The rules for replacing determiners and nouns are simply applied in a different order than in (1). Rather than replacing the first Det with *das* 'the' and the first noun with *Buch* 'book', the first Det is replaced with *dem* 'the' and the first noun with *Mann*.

At this juncture, I should point out that the grammar in (2) is not the only possible grammar for the example sentence in (1). There is an infinite number of possible grammars which could be used to analyze these kinds of sentences (see exercise 1). Another possible grammar is given in (6):

(6)   NP → Det N   NP → er   N → Buch
     V → NP V   Det → das   N → Mann
                           Det → dem   V → gibt

This grammar licenses binary branching structures as shown in Figure 2.2 on the following page.

Both the grammar in (6) and (2) are too imprecise. If we adopt additional lexical entries for *ich* 'I' and *den* 'the' (accusative) in our grammar, then we would incorrectly license the ungrammatical sentences in (7b–d):[3]

---

[3] With the grammar in (6), we also have the additional problem that we cannot determine when an utterance is complete since the symbol V is used for all combinations of V and NP. Therefore, we can also analyze the sentence in (i) with this grammar:

(i) a. * der Mann erwartet
      the man   expects

   b. * des   Mannes   er   das   Buch dem   Mann gibt
      the.GEN man.GEN he.NOM the.ACC book the.DAT man   gives

The number of arguments required by a verb must be somehow represented in the grammar. In the following chapters, we will see exactly how the selection of arguments by a verb (valence) can be captured in various grammatical theories.

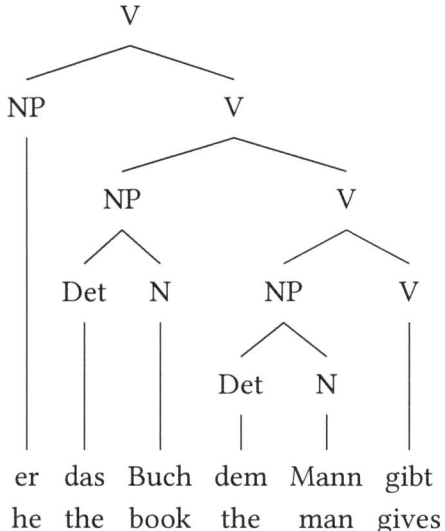

Figure 2.2: Analysis of *er das Buch dem Mann gibt* with a binary branching structure

(7) a. er das Buch dem Mann gibt
 he.NOM the.ACC book the.DAT man gives
 'He gives the book to the man.'
 b. * ich das Buch dem Mann gibt
 I.NOM the.ACC book the.DAT man gives
 c. * er das Buch den Mann gibt
 he.NOM the.ACC book the.ACC man gives
 d. * er den Buch dem Mann gibt
 he.NOM the.M book(N) the man gives

In (7b), subject-verb agreement has been violated, in other words: *ich* 'I' and *gibt* 'gives' do not fit together. (7c) is ungrammatical because the case requirements of the verb have not been satisfied: *gibt* 'gives' requires a dative object. Finally, (7d) is ungrammatical because there is a lack of agreement between the determiner and the noun. It is not possible to combine *den* 'the', which is masculine and bears accusative case, and *Buch* 'book' because *Buch* is neuter gender. For this reason, the gender properties of these two elements are not the same and the elements can therefore not be combined.

In the following, we will consider how we would have to change our grammar to stop it from licensing the sentences in (7b–d). If we want to capture subject-verb agreement, then we have to cover the following six cases in German, as the verb has to agree with the subject in both person (1, 2, 3) and number (sg, pl):

(8) a. Ich schlafe. (1, sg)
 I sleep

b. Du schläfst. (2, sg)
   you sleep

c. Er schläft. (3, sg)
   he sleeps

d. Wir schlafen. (1, pl)
   we sleep

e. Ihr schlaft. (2, pl)
   you sleep

f. Sie schlafen. (3, pl)
   they sleep

It is possible to capture these relations with grammatical rules by increasing the number of symbols we use. Instead of the rule S → NP NP NP V, we can use the following:

(9) S → NP_1_sg NP NP V_1_sg
    S → NP_2_sg NP NP V_2_sg
    S → NP_3_sg NP NP V_3_sg
    S → NP_1_pl NP NP V_1_pl
    S → NP_2_pl NP NP V_2_pl
    S → NP_3_pl NP NP V_3_pl

This would mean that we need six different symbols for noun phrases and verbs respectively, as well as six rules rather than one.

In order to account for case assignment by the verb, we can incorporate case information into the symbols in an analogous way. We would then get rules such as the following:

(10) S → NP_1_sg_nom NP_dat NP_acc V_1_sg_nom_dat_acc
     S → NP_2_sg_nom NP_dat NP_acc V_2_sg_nom_dat_acc
     S → NP_3_sg_nom NP_dat NP_acc V_3_sg_nom_dat_acc
     S → NP_1_pl_nom NP_dat NP_acc V_1_pl_nom_dat_acc
     S → NP_2_pl_nom NP_dat NP_acc V_2_pl_nom_dat_acc
     S → NP_3_pl_nom NP_dat NP_acc V_3_pl_nom_dat_acc

Since it is necessary to differentiate between noun phrases in four cases, we have a total of six symbols for NPs in the nominative and three symbols for NPs with other cases. Since verbs have to match the NPs, that is, we have to differentiate between verbs which select three arguments and those selecting only one or two (11), we have to increase the number of symbols we assume for verbs.

(11) a. Er schläft.
        he sleeps
        'He is sleeping.'

    b. *Er schläft das Buch.
        he sleeps the book

c. Er kennt das Buch.
   he knows the book
   'He knows the book.'

d. * Er kennt.
   he knows

In the rules above, the information about the number of arguments required by a verb is included in the marking 'nom_dat_acc'.

In order to capture the determiner-noun agreement in (12), we have to incorporate information about gender (fem, mas, neu), number (sg, pl), case (nom, gen, dat, acc) and the inflectional classes (strong, weak)[4].

(12) a. der   Mann, die   Frau,   das   Buch   (gender)
         the.M man(M) the.F woman(F) the.N book(N)

      b. das Buch,   die Bücher   (number)
         the book.SG the books.PL

      c. des   Buches,   dem   Buch   (case)
         the.GEN book.GEN the.DAT book

      d. ein Beamter,   der Beamte   (inflectional class)
         a   civil.servant the civil.servant

Instead of the rule NP → Det N, we will have to use rules such as those in (13):[5]

(13) NP_3_sg_nom → Det_fem_sg_nom N_fem_sg_nom
     NP_3_sg_nom → Det_mas_sg_nom N_mas_sg_nom
     NP_3_sg_nom → Det_neu_sg_nom N_neu_sg_nom
     NP_3_pl_nom → Det_fem_pl_nom N_fem_pl_nom
     NP_3_pl_nom → Det_mas_pl_nom N_mas_pl_nom
     NP_3_pl_nom → Det_neu_pl_nom N_neu_pl_nom

     NP_3_sg_nom → Det_fem_sg_nom N_fem_sg_nom
     NP_3_sg_nom → Det_mas_sg_nom N_mas_sg_nom
     NP_3_sg_nom → Det_neu_sg_nom N_neu_sg_nom
     NP_3_pl_nom → Det_fem_pl_nom N_fem_pl_nom
     NP_3_pl_nom → Det_mas_pl_nom N_mas_pl_nom
     NP_3_pl_nom → Det_neu_pl_nom N_neu_pl_nom

(13) shows the rules for nominative noun phrases. We would need analogous rules for genitive, dative, and accusative. We would then require 24 symbols for determiners (3 * 2 * 4), 24 symbols for nouns and 24 rules rather than one. If inflection class is taken into account, the number of symbols and the number of rules doubles.

---

[4] These are inflectional classes for adjectives which are also relevant for some nouns such as *Beamter* 'civil servant', *Verwandter* 'relative', *Gesandter* 'envoy'. For more on adjective classes see page 21.

[5] To keep things simple, these rules do not incorporate information regarding the inflection class.

2.2 Expanding PSG with features

Phrase structure grammars which only use atomic symbols are problematic as they cannot capture certain generalizations. We as linguists can recognize that NP_3_sg_nom stands for a noun phrase because it contains the letters NP. However, in formal terms this symbol is just like any other symbol in the grammar and we cannot capture the commonalities of all the symbols used for NPs. Furthermore, unstructured symbols do not capture the fact that the rules in (13) all have something in common. In formal terms, the only thing that the rules have in common is that there is one symbol on the left-hand side of the rule and two on the right.

We can solve this problem by introducing features which are assigned to category symbols and therefore allow for the values of such features to be included in our rules. For example, we can assume the features person, number and case for the category symbol NP. For determiners and nouns, we would adopt an additional feature for gender and one for inflectional class. (14) shows two rules augmented by the respective values in brackets:[6]

(14) NP(3,sg,nom) → Det(fem,sg,nom) N(fem,sg,nom)
NP(3,sg,nom) → Det(mas,sg,nom) N(mas,sg,nom)

If we were to use variables rather than the values in (14), we would get rule schemata as the one in (15):

(15) NP(3,Num,Case) → Det(Gen,Num,Case) N(Gen,Num,Case)

The values of the variables here are not important. What is important is that they match. For this to work, it is important that the values are ordered; that is, in the category of a determiner, the gender is always first, number second and so on. The value of the person feature (the first position in the NP(3,Num,Case)) is fixed at '3' by the rule. These kind of restrictions on the values can, of course, be determined in the lexicon:

(16) NP(3,sg,nom)   → es
Det(mas,sg,nom) → des

The rules in (10) can be collapsed into a single schema as in (17):

(17) S → NP(Per1,Num1,nom)
NP(Per2,Num2,dat)
NP(Per3,Num3,acc)
V(Per1,Num1,ditransitive)

The identification of Per1 and Num1 on the verb and on the subject ensures that there is subject-verb agreement. For the other NPs, the values of these features are irrelevant. The case of these NPs is explicitly determined.

---

[6]Chapter 6 introduces attribute value structures. In these structure we always have pairs of a feature name and a feature value. In such a setting, the order of values is not important, since every value is uniquely identified by the corresponding feature name. Since we do not have a feature name in schemata like (13), the order of the values is important.

2.3 Semantics

In the introductory chapter and the previous sections, we have been dealing with syntactic aspects of language and the focus will remain very much on syntax for the remainder of this book. It is, however, important to remember that we use language to communicate, that is, to transfer information about certain situations, topics or opinions. If we want to accurately explain our capacity for language, then we also have to explain the meanings that our utterances have. To this end, it is necessary to understand their syntactic structure, but this alone is not enough. Furthermore, theories of language acquisition that only concern themselves with the acquisition of syntactic constructions are also inadequate. The syntax-semantics interface is therefore important and every grammatical theory has to say something about how syntax and semantics interact. In the following, I will show how we can combine phrase structure rules with semantic information. To represent meanings, I will use first-order predicate logic and λ-calculus. Unfortunately, it is not possible to provide a detailed discussion of the basics of logic so that even readers without prior knowledge can follow all the details, but the simple examples discussed here should be enough to provide some initial insights into how syntax and semantics interact and furthermore, how we can develop a linguistic theory to account for this.

To show how the meaning of a sentence is derived from the meaning of its parts, we will consider (18a). We assign the meaning in (18b) to the sentence in (18a).

(18)   a. Max schläft.
         Max sleeps
         'Max is sleeping.'

     b. *schlafen'(max')*

Here, we are assuming *schlafen'* to be the meaning of *schläft* 'sleeps'. We use prime symbols to indicate that we are dealing with word meanings and not actual words. At first glance, it may not seem that we have really gained anything by using *schlafen'* to represent the meaning of (18a), since it is just another form of the verb *schläft* 'sleeps'. It is, however, important to concentrate on a single verb form as inflection is irrelevant when it comes to meaning. We can see this by comparing the examples in (19a) and (19b):

(19)   a. Jeder Junge schläft.
         every boy   sleeps
         'Every boy sleeps.'

     b. Alle Jungen schlafen.
         all boys   sleep
         'All boys sleep.'

To enhance readability I use English translations of the predicates in semantic representations from now on.[7] So the meaning of (18a) is represented as (20) rather then (18b):

---

[7] Note that I do not claim that English is suited as representation language for semantic relations and concepts that can be expressed in other languages.

(20) $sleep'(max')$

When looking at the meaning in (20), we can consider which part of the meaning comes from each word. It seems relatively intuitive that *max'* comes from *Max*, but the trickier question is what exactly *schläft* 'sleeps' contributes in terms of meaning. If we think about what characterizes a 'sleeping' event, we know that there is typically an individual who is sleeping. This information is part of the meaning of the verb *schlafen* 'to sleep'. The verb meaning does not contain information about the sleeping individual, however, as this verb can be used with various subjects:

(21) a. Paul schläft.
   Paul sleeps
   'Paul is sleeping.'

   b. Mio schläft.
   Mio sleeps
   'Mio is sleeping.'

   c. Xaver schläft.
   Xaver sleeps
   'Xaver is sleeping.'

We can therefore abstract away from any specific use of *sleep'* and instead of, for example, *max'* in (20), we use a variable (e.g., x). This x can then be replaced by *paul'*, *mio'* or *xaver'* in a given sentence. To allow us to access these variables in a given meaning, we can write them with a λ in front. Accordingly, *schläft* 'sleeps' will have the following meaning:

(22) $\lambda x\ sleep'(x)$

The step from (20) to (22) is referred to as *lambda abstraction*. The combination of the expression (22) with the meaning of its arguments happens in the following way: we remove the λ and the corresponding variable and then replace all instances of the variable with the meaning of the argument. If we combine (22) and *max'* as in (23), we arrive at the meaning in (20), namely $sleep'(max')$.

(23) $\lambda x\ sleep'(x)\ max'$

The process is called β-reduction or λ-conversion. To show this further, let us consider an example with a transitive verb. The sentence in (24a) has the meaning given in (24b):

(24) a. Max mag Lotte.
   Max likes Lotte
   'Max likes Lotte.'

   b. $like'(max', lotte')$

The λ-abstraction of *mag* 'likes' is shown in (25):

(25) $\lambda y \lambda x\ like'(x, y)$

2 Phrase structure grammar

Note that it is always the first λ that has to be used first. The variable *y* corresponds to the object of *mögen* 'to like'. For languages like English it is assumed that the object forms a verb phrase (VP) together with the verb and this VP is combined with the subject. German differs from English in allowing more freedom in constituent order. The problems that result for form meaning mappings are solved in different ways by different theories. The respective solutions will be addressed in the following chapters.

If we combine the representation in (25) with that of the object *Lotte*, we arrive at (26a), and following β-reduction, (26b):

(26) a. *λyλx like'(x, y)lotte'*
 b. *λx like'(x, lotte')*

This meaning can in turn be combined with the subject and we then get (27a) and (27b) after β-reduction:

(27) a. *λx like'(x, lotte')max'*
 b. *like'(max', lotte')*

After introducing lambda calculus, integrating the composition of meaning into our phrase structure rules is simple. A rule for the combination of a verb with its subject has to be expanded to include positions for the semantic contribution of the verb, the semantic contribution of the subject and then the meaning of the combination of these two (the entire sentence). The complete meaning is the combination of the individual meanings in the correct order. We can therefore take the simple rule in (28a) and turn it into (28b):

(28) a. S → NP(nom) V
 b. S(V′ NP′) → NP(nom, NP′) V(V′)

V′ stands for the meaning of V and NP′ for the meaning of the NP(nom). V′ NP′ stands for the combination of V′ and NP′. When analyzing (18a), the meaning of V′ is *λx sleep'(x)* and the meaning of NP′ is *max'*. The combination of V′ NP′ corresponds to (29a) or after β-reduction to (18b) – repeated here as (29b):

(29) a. *λx sleep'(x)max'*
 b. *sleep'(max')*

For the example with a transitive verb in (24a), the rule in (30) can be proposed:

(30) S(V′ NP2′ NP1′) → NP(nom, NP1′) V(V′) NP(acc, NP2′)

The meaning of the verb (V′) is first combined with the meaning of the object (NP2′) and then with the meaning of the subject (NP1′).

At this point, we can see that there are several distinct semantic rules for the phrase structure rules above. The hypothesis that we should analyze language in this way is called the *rule-to-rule hypothesis* (Bach 1976: 184). A more general process for deriving the meaning of linguistic expression will be presented in Section 5.1.4.

2.4 Phrase structure rules for some aspects of German syntax

Whereas determining the direct constituents of a sentence is relative easy, since we can very much rely on the movement test due to the somewhat flexible order of constituents in German, it is more difficult to identify the parts of the noun phrase. This is the problem we will focus on in this section. To help motivate assumptions about $\overline{\text{X}}$ syntax to be discussed in Section 2.5, we will also discuss prepositional phrases.

2.4.1 Noun phrases

Up to now, we have assumed a relatively simple structure for noun phrases: our rules state that a noun phrase consists of a determiner and a noun. Noun phrases can have a distinctly more complex structure than (31a). This is shown by the following examples in (31):

(31)   a. eine Frau
       a   woman

    b. eine Frau, die wir kennen
       a   woman who we know

    c. eine Frau aus Stuttgart
       a   woman from Stuttgart

    d. eine kluge Frau
       a   smart woman

    e. eine Frau aus Stuttgart, die wir kennen
       a   woman from Stuttgart who we know

    f. eine kluge Frau aus Stuttgart
       a   smart woman from Stuttgart

    g. eine kluge Frau, die wir kennen
       a   smart woman who we know

    h. eine kluge Frau aus Stuttgart, die wir kennen
       a   smart woman from Stuttgart who we know

As well as determiners and nouns, noun phrases can also contain adjectives, prepositional phrases and relative clauses. The additional elements in (31) are adjuncts. They restrict the set of objects which the noun phrase refers to. Whereas (31a) refers to a being which has the property of being a woman, the referent of (31b) must also have the property of being known to us.

    Our previous rules for noun phrases simply combined a noun and a determiner and can therefore only be used to analyze (31a). The question we are facing now is how we can modify this rule or which additional rules we would have to assume in order to

2 Phrase structure grammar

analyze the other noun phrases in (31). In addition to rule (32a), one could propose a rule such as the one in (32b).[8,9]

(32)   a. NP → Det N
          b. NP → Det A N

However, this rule would still not allow us to analyze noun phrases such as (33):

(33)   alle weiteren schlagkräftigen Argumente
        all   further   strong   arguments
    'all other strong arguments'

In order to be able to analyze (33), we require a rule such as (34):

(34)   NP → Det A A N

It is always possible to increase the number of adjectives in a noun phrase and setting an upper limit for adjectives would be entirely arbitrary. Even if we opt for the following abbreviation, there are still problems:

(35)   NP → Det A* N

The asterisk in (35) stands for any number of iterations. Therefore, (35) encompasses rules with no adjectives as well as those with one, two or more.

The problem is that according to the rule in (35) adjectives and nouns do not form a constituent and we can therefore not explain why coordination is still possible in (36):

(36)   alle [[großen Seeelefanten] und [grauen Eichhörnchen]]
        all   big   elephant.seals and grey   squirrels
    'all the big elephant seals and grey squirrels'

If we assume that coordination involves the combination of two or more word strings with the same syntactic properties, then we would have to assume that the adjective and noun form a unit.

The following rules capture the noun phrases with adjectives discussed thus far:

(37)   a. NP → Det $\overline{\text{N}}$
          b. $\overline{\text{N}}$ → A $\overline{\text{N}}$
          c. $\overline{\text{N}}$ → N

These rules state the following: a noun phrase consists of a determiner and a nominal element ($\overline{\text{N}}$). This nominal element can consist of an adjective and a nominal element (37b), or just a noun (37c). Since $\overline{\text{N}}$ is also on the right-hand side of the rule in (37b), we can apply this rule multiple times and therefore account for noun phrases with multiple adjectives such as (33). Figure 2.3 on the next page shows the structure of a noun phrase without an adjective and that of a noun phrase with one or two adjectives. The adjective

---

[8]See Eisenberg (2004: 238) for the assumption of flat structures in noun phrases.
[9]There are, of course, other features such as gender and number, which should be part of all the rules discussed in this section. I have omitted these in the following for ease of exposition.

2.4 Phrase structure rules for some aspects of German syntax

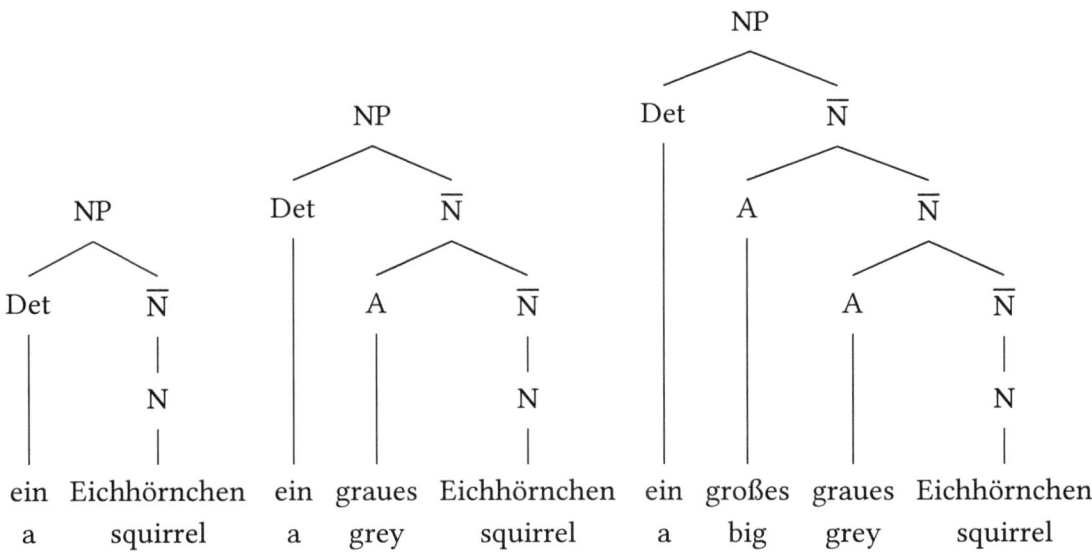

Figure 2.3: Noun phrases with differing numbers of adjectives

grau 'grey' restricts the set of referents for the noun phrase. If we assume an additional adjective such as *groß* 'big', then it only refers to those squirrels who are grey as well as big. These kinds of noun phrases can be used in contexts such as the following:

(38) A: Alle grauen Eichhörnchen sind groß.
    all grey   squirrels   are   big

'All grey squirrels are big.' B: Nein, ich habe ein kleines graues Eichhörnchen
                                  no   I   have a   small   grey   squirrel

gesehen.
seen

'No, I saw a small grey squirrel.'

We observe that this discourse can be continued with *Aber alle kleinen grauen Eichhörnchen sind krank* 'but all small grey squirrels are ill' and a corresponding answer. The possibility to have even more adjectives in noun phrases such as *ein kleines graues Eichhörnchen* 'a small grey squirrel' is accounted for in our rule system in (37). In the rule (37b), $\overline{\text{N}}$ occurs on the left as well as the right-hand side of the rule. This kind of rule is referred to as *recursive*.

We have now developed a nifty little grammar that can be used to analyze noun phrases containing adjectival modifiers. As a result, the combination of an adjective and noun is given constituent status. One may wonder at this point if it would not make sense to also assume that determiners and adjectives form a constituent, as we also have the following kind of noun phrases:

(39) diese schlauen und diese neugierigen Frauen
     these smart   and these curious   women

65

2 Phrase structure grammar

Here, we are dealing with a different structure, however. Two full NPs have been conjoined and part of the first conjunct has been deleted.

(40)   diese schlauen ~~Frauen~~ und diese neugierigen Frauen
       these smart   women   and these curious   women

One can find similar phenomena at the sentence and even word level:

(41)   a. dass Peter dem Mann das Buch ~~gibt~~ und Maria der Frau die Schallplatte
          that Peter the man the book gives and Maria the woman the record
          gibt
          gives
          'that Peters gives the book to the man and Maria the record to the woman'
       b. be- und ent-laden
          PRT and PRT-load
          'load and unload'

Thus far, we have discussed how we can ideally integrate adjectives into our rules for the structure of noun phrases. Other adjuncts such as prepositional phrases or relative clauses can be combined with $\overline{\text{N}}$ in an analogous way to adjectives:

(42)   a. $\overline{\text{N}} \rightarrow \overline{\text{N}}$ PP
       b. $\overline{\text{N}} \rightarrow \overline{\text{N}}$ relative clause

With these rules and those in (37), it is possible – assuming the corresponding rules for PPs and relative clauses – to analyze all the examples in (31).

(37c) states that it is possible for $\overline{\text{N}}$ to consist of a single noun. A further important rule has not yet been discussed: we need another rule to combine nouns such as *Vater* 'father', *Sohn* 'son' or *Bild* 'picture', so-called *relational nouns*, with their arguments. Examples of these can be found in (43a–b). (43c) is an example of a nominalization of a verb with its argument:

(43)   a. der Vater von Peter
          the father of Peter
          'Peter's father'
       b. das Bild   vom   Gleimtunnel
          the picture of.the Gleimtunnel
          'the picture of the Gleimtunnel'
       c. das Kommen des   Installateurs
          the coming of.the plumber
          'the plumber's visit'

The rule that we need to analyze (43a,b) is given in (44):

(44) $\overline{\text{N}} \rightarrow$ N PP

2.4 Phrase structure rules for some aspects of German syntax

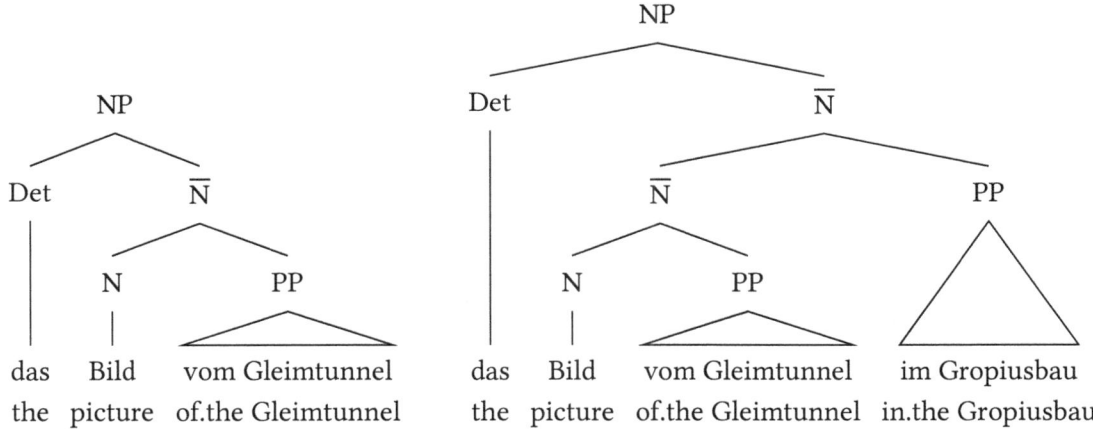

Figure 2.4: Combination of a noun with PP complement *vom Gleimtunnel* to the right with an adjunct PP

Figure 2.4 shows two structures with PP-arguments. The tree on the right also contains an additional PP-adjunct, which is licensed by the rule in (42a).

In addition to the previously discussed NP structures, there are other structures where the determiner or noun is missing. Nouns can be omitted via ellipsis. (45) gives an example of noun phrases, where a noun that does not require a complement has been omitted. The examples in (46) show NPs in which only one determiner and complement of the noun has been realized, but not the noun itself. The underscore marks the position where the noun would normally occur.

(45)   a. eine kluge _
      a   smart

    'a smart one'

  b. eine kluge große _
      a   smart tall

    'a smart tall one'

  c. eine kluge _ aus Hamburg
      a   smart   from Hamburg

    'a smart one from Hamburg'

  d. eine kluge _, die   alle   kennen
      a   smart   who everyone knows

    'a smart one who everyone knows'

(46)   a. (Nein, nicht der Vater von Klaus), der _ von Peter war gemeint.
      no   not the father of   Klaus the   of   Peter was meant

    'No, it wasn't the father of Klaus, but rather the one of Peter that was meant.'

67

b. (Nein, nicht das Bild von der Stadtautobahn), das _ vom Gleimtunnel war
   no   not   the picture of the motorway   the of.the Gleimtunnel was
   beeindruckend.
   impressive

   'No, it wasn't the picture of the motorway, but rather the one of the Gleimtunnel that was impressive.'

c. (Nein, nicht das Kommen des   Tischlers), das _ des   Installateurs ist
   no   not the coming of.the carpenter   the of.the plumber   is
   wichtig.
   important

   'No, it isn't the visit of the carpenter, but rather the visit of the plumber that is important.'

In English, the pronoun *one* must often be used in the corresponding position,[10] but in German the noun is simply omitted. In phrase structure grammars, this can be described by a so-called *epsilon production*. These rules replace a symbol with nothing (47a). The rule in (47b) is an equivalent variant which is responsible for the term *epsilon production*:

(47) a. N →

   b. N → ϵ

The corresponding trees are shown in Figure 2.5. Going back to boxes, the rules in (47)

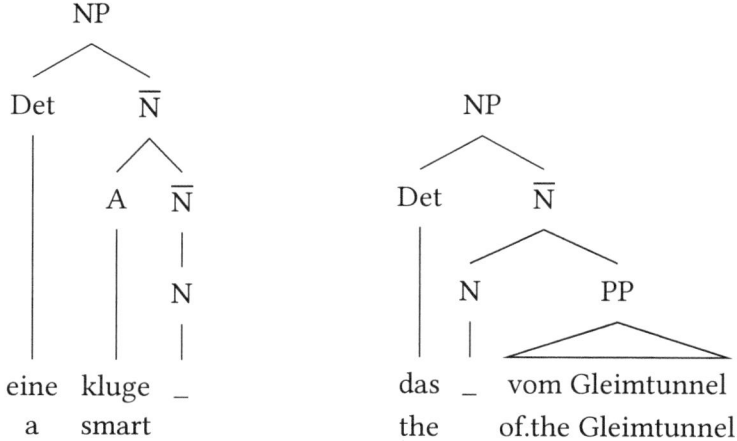

Figure 2.5: Noun phrases without an overt head

correspond to empty boxes with the same labels as the boxes of ordinary nouns. As we have considered previously, the actual content of the boxes is unimportant when considering the question of where we can incorporate them. In this way, the noun phrases in (31) can occur in the same sentences. The empty noun box also behaves like one with

---

[10] See Fillmore et al. (2012: Section 4.12) for English examples without the pronoun *one*.

2.4 Phrase structure rules for some aspects of German syntax

a genuine noun. If we do not open the empty box, we will not be able to ascertain the difference to a filled box.

It is not only possible to omit the noun from noun phrases, but the determiner can also remain unrealized in certain contexts. (48) shows noun phrases in plural:

(48) a. Frauen
   women
 b. Frauen, die wir kennen
   women who we know
 c. kluge Frauen
   smart women
 d. kluge Frauen, die wir kennen
   smart women who we know

The determiner can also be omitted in singular if the noun denotes a mass noun:

(49) a. Getreide
   grain
 b. Getreide, das gerade gemahlen wurde
   grain that just ground was
   'grain that has just been ground'
 c. frisches Getreide
   fresh grain
 d. frisches Getreide, das gerade gemahlen wurde
   fresh grain that just ground was
   'fresh grain that has just been ground'

Finally, both the determiner and the noun can be omitted:

(50) a. Ich helfe klugen.
   I help smart
   'I help smart ones.'
 b. Dort drüben steht frisches, das gerade gemahlen wurde.
   there over stands fresh that just ground was
   'Over there is some fresh (grain) that has just been ground.'

Figure 2.6 on the next page shows the corresponding trees.

It is necessary to add two further comments to the rules we have developed up to this point: up to now, I have always spoken of adjectives. However, it is possible to have very complex adjective phrases in pre-nominal position. These can be adjectives with complements (51a,b) or adjectival participles (51c,d):

(51) a. der seiner Frau treue Mann
   the his.DAT wife faithful man
   'the man faithful to his wife'

2 Phrase structure grammar

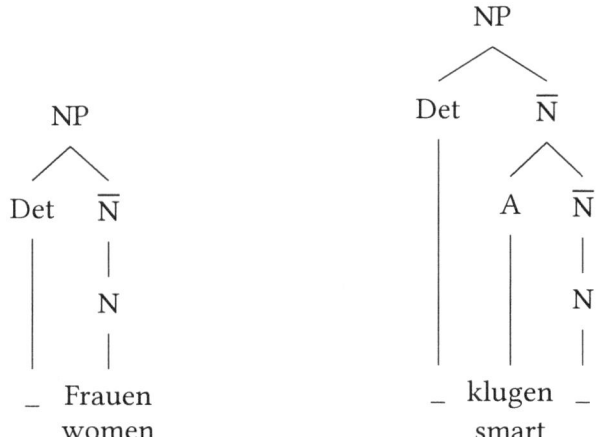

Figure 2.6: Noun phrases without overt determiner

   b. der auf seinen Sohn stolze Mann
      the on his.ACC son proud man
     'the man proud of his son'

   c. der seine Frau liebende Mann
      the his.ACC woman loving man
     'the man who loves his wife'

   d. der von seiner Frau geliebte Mann
      the by his.DAT wife loved man
     'the man loved by his wife'

Taking this into account, the rule (37b) has to be modified in the following way:

(52) $\overline{N} \rightarrow AP\,\overline{N}$

An adjective phrase (AP) can consist of an NP and an adjective, a PP and an adjective or just an adjective:

(53)   a. AP → NP A
     b. AP → PP A
     c. AP → A

There are two imperfections resulting from the rules we have developed thus far. These are the rules for adjectives or nouns without complements in (53c) as well as (37c) – repeated here as (54):

(54) $\overline{N} \rightarrow N$

If we apply these rules, then we will generate unary branching subtrees, that is trees with a mother that only has one daughter. See Figure 2.6 for an example of this. If we

2.4 Phrase structure rules for some aspects of German syntax

maintain the parallel to the boxes, this would mean that there is a box which contains another box which is the one with the relevant content.

In principle, nothing stops us from placing this information directly into the larger box. Instead of the rules in (55), we will simply use the rules in (56):

(55)   a. A → kluge

       b. N → Mann

(56)   a. AP → kluge

       b. N̄ → Mann

(56a) states that *kluge* 'smart' has the same properties as a full adjective phrase, in particular that it cannot be combined with a complement. This is parallel to the categorization of the pronoun *er* 'he' as an N̄P in the grammars (2) and (6).

Assigning N̄ to nouns which do not require a complement has the advantage that we do not have to explain why the analysis in (57b) is possible as well as (57a) despite there not being any difference in meaning.

(57)   a. [$_{NP}$ einige [$_{\overline{N}}$ kluge [$_{\overline{N}}$ [$_{\overline{N}}$ [$_N$ Frauen] und [$_{\overline{N}}$ [$_N$ Männer]]]]]]
           some   smart   women   and   men

      b. [$_{NP}$ einige [$_{\overline{N}}$ kluge [$_{\overline{N}}$ [$_N$ [$_N$ Frauen] und [$_N$ Männer]]]]]
           some   smart   women   and   men

In (57a), two nouns have projected to N̄ and have then been joined by coordination. The result of coordination of two constituents of the same category is always a new constituent with that category. In the case of (57a), this is also N̄. This constituent is then combined with the adjective and the determiner. In (57b), the nouns themselves have been coordinated. The result of this is always another constituent which has the same category as its parts. In this case, this would be N. This N becomes N̄ and is then combined with the adjective. If nouns which do not require complements were categorized as N̄ rather than N, we would not have the problem of spurious ambiguities. The structure in (58) shows the only possible analysis.

(58)   [$_{NP}$ einige [$_{\overline{N}}$ kluge [$_{\overline{N}}$ [$_{\overline{N}}$ Frauen] und [$_{\overline{N}}$ Männer]]]]
        some   smart   women   and   men

2.4.2 Prepositional phrases

Compared to the syntax of noun phrases, the syntax of prepositional phrases (PPs) is relatively straightforward. PPs normally consist of a preposition and a noun phrase whose case is determined by that preposition. We can capture this with the following rule:

(59)   PP → P NP

This rule must, of course, also contain information about the case of the NP. I have omitted this for ease of exposition as I did with the NP-rules and AP-rules above.

2 Phrase structure grammar

The Duden grammar (Eisenberg et al. 2005: §1300) offers examples such as those in (60), which show that certain prepositional phrases serve to further define the semantic contribution of the preposition by indicating some measurement, for example:

(60) a. [[Einen Schritt] vor dem Abgrund] blieb er stehen.
    one step before the abyss remained he stand
    'He stopped one step in front of the abyss.'
  b. [[Kurz] nach dem Start] fiel die Klimaanlage aus.
    shortly after the take.off fell the air.conditioning out
    'Shortly after take off, the air conditioning stopped working.'
  c. [[Schräg] hinter der Scheune] ist ein Weiher.
    diagonally behind the barn is a pond
    'There is a pond diagonally across from the barn.'
  d. [[Mitten] im Urwald] stießen die Forscher auf einen alten Tempel.
    middle in.the jungle stumbled the researchers on an old temple
    'In the middle of the jungle, the researches came across an old temple.'

To analyze the sentences in (60a,b), one could propose the following rules in (61):

(61) a. PP → NP PP
  b. PP → AP PP

These rules combine a PP with an indication of measurement. The resulting constituent is another PP. It is possible to use these rules to analyze prepositional phrases in (60a,b), but it unfortunately also allows us to analyze those in (62):

(62) a. * [PP einen Schritt [PP kurz [PP vor dem Abgrund]]]
      one step shortly before the abyss
  b. * [PP kurz [PP einen Schritt [PP vor dem Abgrund]]]
      shortly one step before the abyss

Both rules in (61) were used to analyze the examples in (62). Since the symbol PP occurs on both the left and right-hand side of the rules, we can apply the rules in any order and as many times as we like.

We can avoid this undesired side-effect by reformulating the previously assumed rules:

(63) a. PP → NP $\overline{\text{P}}$
  b. PP → AP $\overline{\text{P}}$
  c. PP → $\overline{\text{P}}$
  d. $\overline{\text{P}}$ → P NP

Rule (59) becomes (63d). The rule in (63c) states that a PP can consist of $\overline{\text{P}}$. Figure 2.7 on the facing page shows the analysis of (64) using (63c) and (63d) as well as the analysis of an example with an adjective in the first position following the rules in (63b) and (63d):

(64) vor dem Abgrund
    before the abyss
    'in front of the abyss'

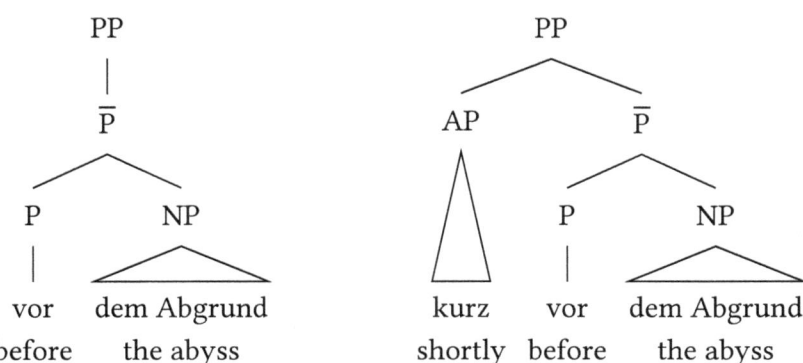

Figure 2.7: Prepositional phrases with and without measurement

At this point, the attentive reader is probably wondering why there is no empty measurement phrase in the left figure of Figure 2.7, which one might expect in analogy to the empty determiner in Figure 2.6. The reason for the empty determiner in Figure 2.6 is that the entire noun phrase without the determiner has a meaning similar to those with a determiner. The meaning normally contributed by the visible determiner has to somehow be incorporated in the structure of the noun phrase. If we did not place this meaning in the empty determiner, this would lead to more complicated assumptions about semantic combination: we only really require the mechanisms presented in Section 2.3 and these are very general in nature. The meaning is contributed by the words themselves and not by any rules. If we were to assume a unary branching rule such as that in the left tree in Figure 2.7 instead of the empty determiner, then this unary branching rule would have to provide the semantics of the determiner. This kind of analysis has also been proposed by some researchers. See Chapter 19 for more on empty elements.

Unlike determiner-less NPs, prepositional phrases without an indication of degree or measurement do not lack any meaning component for composition. It is therefore not necessary to assume an empty indication of measurement, which somehow contributes to the meaning of the entire PP. Hence, the rule in (63c) states that a prepositional phrase consists of $\overline{P}$, that is, a combination of P and NP.

2.5 $\overline{X}$ theory

If we look again at the rules that we have formulated in the previous section, we see that heads are always combined with their complements to form a new constituent (65a,b), which can then be combined with further constituents (65c,d):

(65) a. $\overline{N} \rightarrow N\ PP$
    b. $\overline{P} \rightarrow P\ NP$

2 Phrase structure grammar

    c. NP → Det $\overline{\text{N}}$
    d. PP → NP $\overline{\text{P}}$

Grammarians working on English noticed that parallel structures can be used for phrases which have adjectives or verbs as their head. I discuss adjective phrases at this point and postpone the discussion of verb phrases to Chapter 3. As in German, certain adjectives in English can take complements with the important restriction that adjective phrases with complements cannot realize these pre-nominally in English. (66) gives some examples of adjective phrases:

(66)   a. He is proud.
       b. He is very proud.
       c. He is proud of his son.
       d. He is very proud of his son.

Unlike prepositional phrases, complements of adjectives are normally optional. *proud* can be used with or without a PP. The degree expression *very* is also optional.

The rules which we need for this analysis are given in (67), with the corresponding structures in Figure 2.8.

(67)   a. AP → $\overline{\text{A}}$
       b. AP → AdvP $\overline{\text{A}}$
       c. $\overline{\text{A}}$ → A PP
       d. $\overline{\text{A}}$ → A

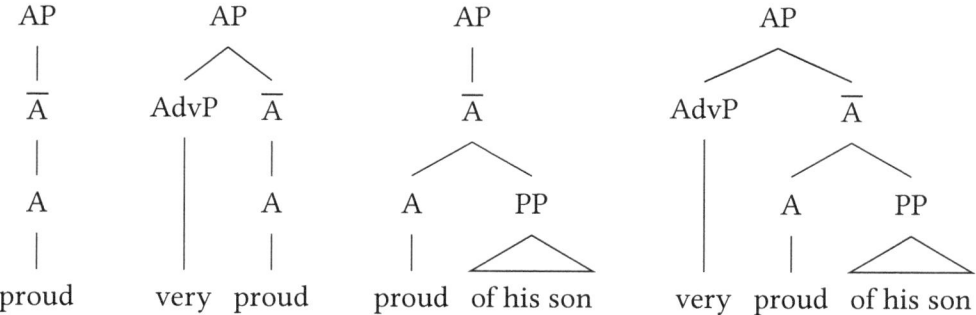

Figure 2.8: English adjective phrases

As was shown in Section 2.2, it is possible to generalize over very specific phrase structure rules and thereby arrive at more general rules. In this way, properties such as person, number and gender are no longer encoded in the category symbols, but rather only simple symbols such as NP, Det and N are used. It is only necessary to specify something about the values of a feature if it is relevant in the context of a given rule. We can take this abstraction a step further: instead of using explicit category symbols such

2.5 X̄ Theory

as N, V, P and A for lexical categories and NP, VP, PP and AP for phrasal categories, one can simply use a variable for the word class in question and speak of X and XP.

This form of abstraction can be found in so-called X̄ theory (or X-bar theory, the term *bar* refers to the line above the symbol), which was developed by Chomsky (1970) and refined by Jackendoff (1977). This form of abstract rules plays an important role in many different theories. For example: Government & Binding (Chapter 3), Generalized Phrase Structure Grammar (Chapter 5) and Lexical Functional Grammar (Chapter 7). In HPSG (Chapter 9), X̄ theory also plays a role, but not all restrictions of the X̄ schema have been adopted.

(68) shows a possible instantiation of X̄ rules, where the category X has been used in place of N, as well as examples of word strings which can be derived by these rules:

(68)

X̄ rule	with specific categories	example strings
X̿ → specifier X̄	N̿ → DET N̄	the [picture of Paris]
X̄ → X̄ adjunct	N̄ → N̄ REL_CLAUSE	[picture of Paris] [that everybody knows]
X̄ → adjunct X̄	N̄ → Ā N̄	beautiful [picture of Paris]
X̄ → X complement*	N̄ → N P̿	picture [of Paris]

Any word class can replace X (e.g., V, A or P). The X without the bar stands for a lexical item in the above rules. If one wants to make the bar level explicit, then it is possible to write X^0. Just as with the rule in (15), where we did not specify the case value of the determiner or the noun but rather simply required that the values on the right-hand side of the rule match, the rules in (68) require that the word class of an element on the right-hand side of the rule (X or X̄) matches that of the element on the left-hand side of the rule (X̄ or X̿).

A lexical element can be combined with all its complements. The '*' in the last rule stands for an unlimited amount of repetitions of the symbol it follows. A special case is zerofold occurrence of complements. There is no PP complement of *Bild* 'picture' present in *das Bild* 'the picture' and thus N becomes N̄. The result of the combination of a lexical element with its complements is a new projection level of X: the projection level 1, which is marked by a bar. X̄ can then be combined with adjuncts. These can occur to the left or right of X̄. The result of this combination is still X̄, that is the projection level is not changed by combining it with an adjunct. Maximal projections are marked by two bars. One can also write XP for a projection of X with two bars. An XP consists of a specifier and X̄. Depending on one's theoretical assumptions, subjects of sentences (Haider 1995; 1997a; Berman 2003a: Section 3.2.2) and determiners in NPs (Chomsky 1970: 210) are specifiers. Furthermore, degree modifiers (Chomsky 1970: 210) in adjective phrases and measurement indicators in prepositional phrases are also counted as specifiers.

Non-head positions can only host maximal projections and therefore complements, adjuncts and specifiers always have two bars. Figure 2.9 on the following page gives an overview of the minimal and maximal structure of phrases.

2 Phrase structure grammar

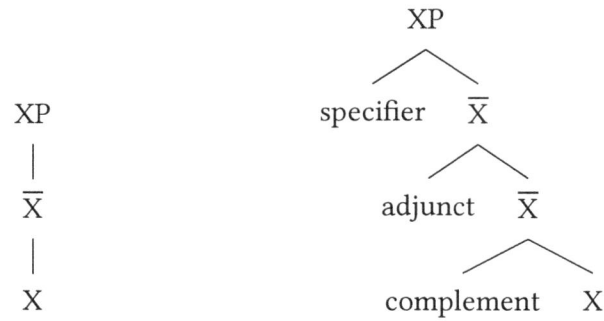

Figure 2.9: Minimal and maximal structure of phrases

Some categories do not have a specifier or have the option of having one. Adjuncts are optional and therefore not all structures have to contain an X̄ with an adjunct daughter. In addition to the branching shown in the right-hand figure, adjuncts to XP and head-adjuncts are sometimes possible. There is only a single rule in (68) for cases in which a head precedes the complements, however an order in which the complement precedes the head is of course also possible. This is shown in Figure 2.9.

Figure 2.10 on the next page shows the analysis of the NP structures *das Bild* 'the picture' and *das schöne Bild von Paris* 'the beautiful picture of Paris'. The NP structures in Figure 2.10 and the tree for *proud* in Figure 2.8 show examples of minimally populated structures. The left tree in Figure 2.10 is also an example of a structure without an adjunct. The right-hand structure in Figure 2.10 is an example for the maximally populated structure: specifier, adjunct, and complement are present.

The analysis given in Figure 2.10 assumes that all non-heads in a rule are phrases. One therefore has to assume that there is a determiner phrase even if the determiner is not combined with other elements. The unary branching of determiners is not elegant but it is consistent.[11] The unary branchings for the NP *Paris* in Figure 2.10 may also seem somewhat odd, but they actually become more plausible when one considers more complex noun phrases:

(69)   a. das Paris der   dreißiger Jahre
           the Paris of.the thirty   years
        '30's Paris'

    b. die Maria aus   Hamburg
           the Maria from Hamburg
        'Maria from Hamburg'

Unary projections are somewhat inelegant but this should not concern us too much here, as we have already seen in the discussion of the lexical entries in (56) that unary branching nodes can be avoided for the most part and that it is indeed desirable to avoid such structures. Otherwise, one gets spurious ambiguities. In the following chapters, we

---

[11]For an alternative version of X̄ theory which does not assume elaborate structure for determiners see Muysken (1982).

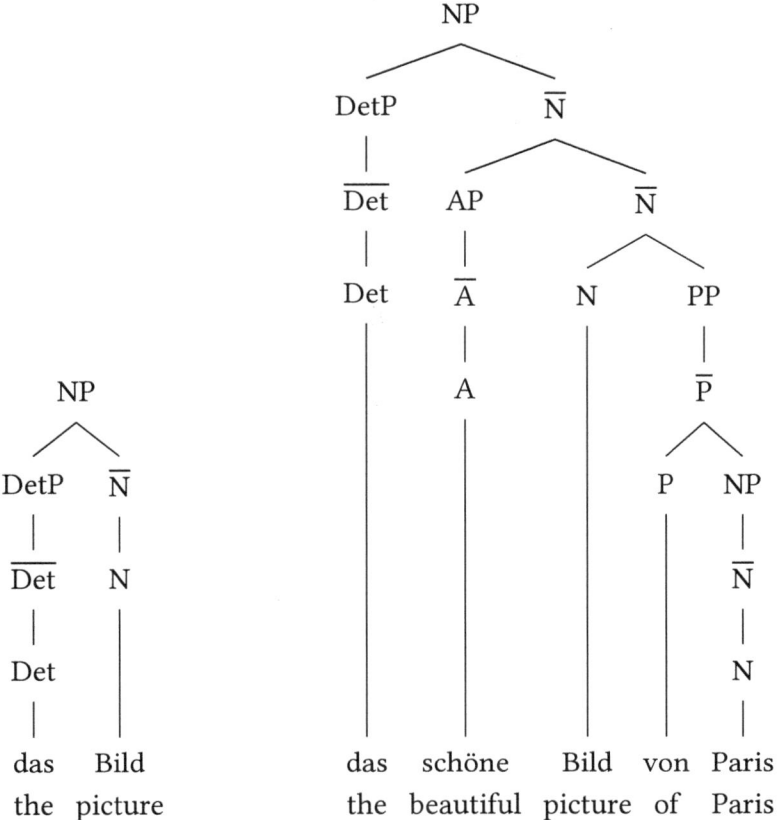

Figure 2.10: X̄ analysis of *das Bild* 'the picture' and *das schöne Bild von Paris* 'the beautiful picture of Paris'

will discuss approaches such as Categorial Grammar and HPSG, which do not assume unary rules for determiners, adjectives and nouns.

Furthermore, other X̄ theoretical assumptions will not be shared by several theories discussed in this book. In particular, the assumption that non-heads always have to be maximal projections will be disregarded. Pullum (1985) and Kornai & Pullum (1990) have shown that the respective theories are not necessarily less restrictive than theories which adopt a strict version of the X̄ theory. See also the discussion in Section 13.1.2.

Comprehension questions

1. Why are phrase structure grammars that use only atomic categories inadequate for the description of natural languages?

2. Assuming the grammar in (6), state which steps (replacing symbols) one has to take to get to the symbol V in the sentence (70).

   (70) er das Buch dem Mann gibt
        he the book the man gives
        'He gives the book to the man.'

   Your answer should resemble the analysis in (3).

3. Give a representation of the meaning of (71) using predicate logic:

   (71) a. Ulrike kennt Hans.
           Ulrike knows Hans

        b. Joshi freut   sich.
           Joshi is.happy REFL
           'Joshi is happy.'

Exercises

1. On page 55, I claimed that there is an infinite number of grammars we could use to analyze (1). Why is this claim correct?

2. Try to come up with some ways in which we can tell which of these possible grammars is or are the best?

3. A fragment for noun phrase syntax was presented in Section 2.4.1. Why is the interaction of the rules in (72) problematic?

(72) a. NP → Det $\overline{\text{N}}$
b. $\overline{\text{N}}$ → N
c. Det → ϵ
d. N → ϵ

4. Why is it not a good idea to mark *books* as NP in the lexicon?

5. Can you think of some reasons why it is not desirable to assume the following rule for nouns such as *books*:

(73) NP → Modifier* books Modifier*

The rule in (73) combines an unlimited number of modifiers with the noun *books* followed by an unlimited number of modifiers. We can use this rule to derive phrases such as those in (74):

(74) a. books
b. interesting books
c. interesting books from Stuttgart

Make reference to coordination data in your answer. Assume that symmetric coordination requires that both coordinated phrases or words have the same syntactic category.

6. Fillmore, Lee-Goldmann & Rhomieux (2012) suggested treating nounless structures like those in (75) as involving a phrasal construction combining the determiner *the* with an adjective.

(75) a. Examine the plight of the very poor.
b. Their outfits range from the flamboyant to the functional.
c. The unimaginable happened.

(76) shows a phrase structure rule that corresponds to their construction:

(76) NP → the Adj

Adj stands for something that can be a single word like *poor* or complex like *very poor*.

Revisit the German data in (45) and (46) and explain why such an analysis and even a more general one as in (77) would not extend to German.

(77) NP → Det Adj

7. Why can $\overline{\text{X}}$ theory not account for German adjective phrases without additional assumptions? (This task is for (native) speakers of German only.)

8. Come up with a phrase structure grammar that can be used to analyze the sentence in (78), but also rules out the sentences in (79).

   (78) a. Der   Mann hilft dem   Kind.
          the.NOM man   helps the.DAT child
          'The man helps the child.'
       b. Er   gibt ihr   das Buch.
          he.NOM gives her.DAT the book
          'He gives her the book.'
       c. Er   wartet auf ein Wunder.
          he.NOM waits on a   miracle
          'He is waiting for a miracle.'

   (79) a. * Der   Mann hilft er.
            the.NOM man   helps he.NOM
       b. * Er   gibt ihr   den   Buch.
            he.NOM gives her.DAT the.M book.N

9. Consider which additional rules would have to be added to the grammar you developed in the previous exercise in order to be able to analyze the following sentences:

   (80) a. Der   Mann hilft dem   Kind jetzt.
          the.NOM man   helps the.DAT child now
          'The man helps the child now.'
       b. Der   Mann hilft dem   Kind neben   dem Bushäuschen.
          the.NOM man   helps the.DAT child next.to the bus.shelter
          'The man helps the child next to the bus shelter.'
       c. Er   gibt ihr   das   Buch jetzt.
          he.NOM gives her.DAT the.ACC book now
          'He gives her the book now.'
       d. Er   gibt ihr   das   Buch neben   dem Bushäuschen.
          he.NOM gives her.DAT the.ACC book next.to the bus.shelter
          'He gives her the book next to the bus shelter.'

e. Er   wartet jetzt auf ein Wunder.
   he.NOM waits now on a   miracle
   'He is waiting for a miracle now.'

f. Er   wartet neben dem   Bushäuschen auf ein Wunder.
   he.NOM waits next.to the.DAT bus.shelter on a   miracle
   'He is waiting for a miracle next to the bus shelter.'

10. Install a Prolog system (e.g., SWI-Prolog[a]) and try out your grammar. SWI-Prolog also comes with an online version where you can input your grammar directly without any installation.[b] Details regarding the notation can be found in the English Wikipedia entry for Definite Clause Grammar (DCG).[c]

---

[a] http://www.swi-prolog.org, 2018-02-20.
[b] https://swish.swi-prolog.org/, 2018-02-20.
[c] https://en.wikipedia.org/wiki/Definite_clause_grammar, 2018-02-20.

Further reading

The expansion of phrase structure grammars to include features was proposed as early as 1963 by Harman (1963).

The phrase structure grammar for noun phrases discussed in this chapter covers a large part of the syntax of noun phrases but cannot explain certain NP structures. Furthermore, it has the problem, which exercise 3 is designed to show. A discussion of these phenomena and a solution in the framework of HPSG can be found in Netter (1998) and Kiss (2005).

The discussion of the integration of semantic information into phrase structure grammars was very short. A detailed discussion of predicate logic and its integration into phrase structure grammars – as well as a discussion of quantifier scope – can be found in Blackburn & Bos (2005).

3 Transformational Grammar – Government & Binding

Transformational Grammar and its subsequent incarnations (such as Government and Binding Theory and Minimalism) were developed by Noam Chomsky at MIT in Boston (Chomsky 1957; 1965; 1975; 1981a; 1986a; 1995b). Manfred Bierwisch (1963) was the first to implement Chomsky's ideas for German. In the 60s, the decisive impulse came from the *Arbeitsstelle Strukturelle Grammatik* 'Workgroup for Structural Grammar', which was part of the Academy of Science of the GDR. See Bierwisch 1992 and Vater 2010 for a historic overview. As well as Bierwisch's work, the following books focusing on German or the Chomskyan research program in general should also be mentioned: Fanselow (1987), Fanselow & Felix (1987), von Stechow & Sternefeld (1988), Grewendorf (1988), Haider (1993), Sternefeld (2006).

The different implementations of Chomskyan theories are often grouped under the heading *Generative Grammar*. This term comes from the fact that phrase structure grammars and the augmented frameworks that were suggested by Chomsky can generate sets of well-formed expressions (see p. 54). It is such a set of sentences that constitutes a language (in the formal sense) and one can test if a sentence forms part of a language by checking if a particular sentence is in the set of sentences generated by a given grammar. In this sense, simple phrase structure grammars and, with corresponding formal assumptions, GPSG, LFG, HPSG and Construction Grammar (CxG) are generative theories. In recent years, a different view of the formal basis of theories such as LFG, HPSG and CxG has emerged such that the aforementioned theories are now *model theoretic* theories rather than generative-enumerative ones[1] (See Chapter 14 for discussion). In 1965, Chomsky defined the term *Generative Grammar* in the following way (see also Chomsky 1995b: 162):

> A grammar of a language purports to be a description of the ideal speaker-hearer's intrinsic competence. If the grammar is, furthermore, perfectly explicit – in other words, if it does not rely on the intelligence of the understanding reader but rather provides an explicit analysis of his contribution – we may call it (somewhat redundantly) a *generative grammar*. (Chomsky 1965: 4)

In this sense, all grammatical theories discussed in this book would be viewed as generative grammars. To differentiate further, sometimes the term *Mainstream Generative Grammar* (MGG) is used (Culicover & Jackendoff 2005: 3) for Chomskyan models. In this

---

[1] Model theoretic approaches are always constraint-based and the terms *model theoretic* and *constraint-based* are sometimes used synonymously.

chapter, I will discuss a well-developed and very influential version of Chomskyan grammar, GB theory. More recent developments following Chomsky's Minimalist Program are dealt with in Chapter 4.

3.1 General remarks on the representational format

This section provides an overview of general assumptions. I introduce the concept of transformations in Section 3.1.1. Section 3.1.2 provides background information about assumptions regarding language acquisition, which shaped the theory considerably, Section 3.1.3 introduces the so-called T model, the basic architecture of GB theory. Section 3.1.4 introduces the $\overline{\text{X}}$ theory in the specific form used in GB and Section 3.1.5 shows how this version of the $\overline{\text{X}}$ theory can be applied to English. The discussion of the analysis of English sentences is an important prerequisite for the understanding of the analysis of German, since many analyses in the GB framework are modeled in parallel to the analyses of English. Section 3.1.6 introduces the analysis of German clauses in a parallel way to what has been done for English in Section 3.1.5.

3.1.1 Transformations

In the previous chapter, I introduced simple phrase structure grammars. Chomsky (1957: Chapter 5) criticized this kind of rewrite grammars since – in his opinion – it is not clear how one can capture the relationship between active and passive sentences or the various ordering possibilities of constituents in a sentence. While it is of course possible to formulate different rules for active and passive sentences in a phrase structure grammar (e.g., one pair of rules for intransitive (1), one for transitive (2) and one for ditransitive verbs (3)), it would not adequately capture the fact that the same phenomenon occurs in the example pairs in (1)–(3):

(1)   a. weil   dort   noch jemand   arbeitet
because there still   somebody works

  'because somebody is still working there'

  b. weil   dort   noch gearbeitet wurde
because there still   worked   was

  'because work was still being done there'

(2)   a. weil   er den Weltmeister   schlägt
because he the world.champion beats

  'because he beats the world champion'

  b. weil   der Weltmeister   geschlagen wurde
because the world.champion beaten   was

  'because the world champion was beaten'

3.1 General remarks on the representational format

(3) a. weil der Mann der Frau den Schlüssel stiehlt
   because the man the woman the key steals
   'because the man is stealing the key from the woman'

   b. weil der Frau der Schlüssel gestohlen wurde
   because the woman the key stolen was
   'because the key was stolen from the woman'

Chomsky (1957: 43) suggests a transformation that creates a connection between active and passive sentences. The transformation that he suggests for English corresponds to (4), which is taken from Klenk (2003: 74):

(4) NP V NP → 3 [$_{AUX}$ be] 2en [$_{PP}$ [$_P$ by] 1]
    1   2 3

This transformational rule maps a tree with the symbols on the left-hand side of the rule onto a tree with the symbols on the right-hand side of the rule. Accordingly, 1, 2 and 3 on the right of the rule correspond to symbols, which are under the numbers on the left-hand side. *en* stands for the morpheme which forms the participle (*seen, been, ...*, but also *loved*). Both trees for (5a,b) are shown in Figure 3.1.

(5) a. John loves Mary.

   b. Mary is loved by John.

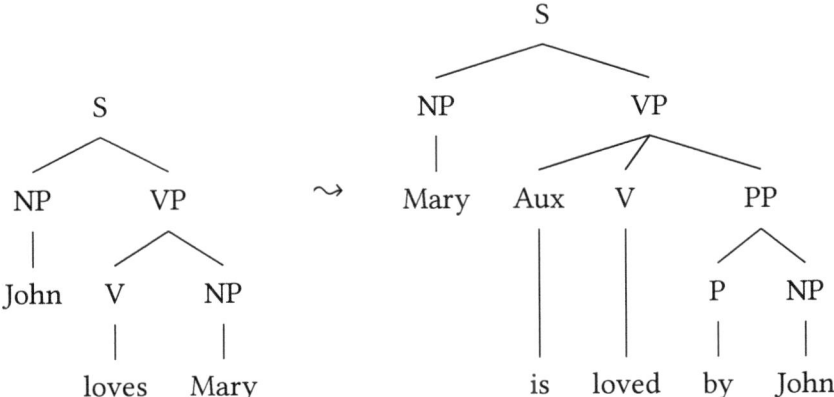

Figure 3.1: Application of passive transformation

The symbols on the left of transformational rules do not necessarily have to be in a local tree, that is, they can be daughters of different mothers as in Figure 3.1.

Rewrite grammars were divided into four complexity classes based on the properties they have. The simplest grammars are assigned to the class 3, whereas the most complex are of Type-0. The so-called context-free grammars we have dealt with thus far are of Type-2. Transformational grammars which allow symbols to be replaced by arbitrary

85

other symbols are of Type-0 (Peters & Ritchie 1973). Research on the complexity of natural languages shows that the highest complexity level (Type-0) is too complex for natural language. It follows from this – assuming that one wants to have a restrictive formal apparatus for the description of grammatical knowledge (Chomsky 1965: 62) – that the form and potential power of transformations has to be restricted.[2] Another criticism of early versions of transformational grammar was that, due to a lack of restrictions, the way in which transformations interact was not clear. Furthermore, there were problems associated with transformations which delete material (see Peters & Ritchie 1973; Klenk 2003: Section 3.1.4). For this reason, new theoretical approaches such as Government & Binding (Chomsky 1981a) were developed. In this model, the form that grammatical rules can take is restricted (see Section 3.1.4). Elements moved by transformations are still represented in their original position, which makes them recoverable at the original position and hence the necessary information is available for semantic interpretation. There are also more general principles, which serve to restrict transformations.

After some initial remarks on the model assumed for language acquisition in GB theory, we will take a closer look at phrase structure rules, transformations and constraints.

3.1.2 The hypothesis regarding language acquisition: Principles & Parameters

Chomsky (1965: Section I.8) assumes that linguistic knowledge must be innate since the language system is, in his opinion, so complex that it would be impossible to learn a language from the given input using more general cognitive principles alone (see also Section 13.8). If it is not possible to learn language solely through interaction with our environment, then at least part of our language ability must be innate. The question of exactly what is innate and if humans actually have an innate capacity for language remains controversial and the various positions on the question have changed over the course of the last decades. Some notable works on this topic are Pinker (1994), Tomasello (1995), Wunderlich (2004), Hauser, Chomsky & Fitch (2002), Chomsky (2007), and Pullum & Scholz (2001) and other papers in the same volume. For more on this discussion, see Chapter 13.

Chomsky (1981a) also assumes that there are general, innate principles which linguistic structure cannot violate. These principles are parametrized, that is, there are options. Parameter settings can differ between languages. An example for a parametrized principle is shown in (6):

(6) Principle: A head occurs before or after its complement(s) depending on the value of the parameter POSITION.

The Principles & Parameters model (P&P model) assumes that a significant part of language acquisition consists of extracting enough information from the linguistic input in order to be able to set parameters. Chomsky (2000: 8) compares the setting of parameters to flipping a switch. For a detailed discussion of the various assumptions about language

---

[2]For more on the power of formal languages, see Chapter 17.

3.1 General remarks on the representational format

acquisition in the P&P-model, see Chapter 21.6. Speakers of English have to learn that heads occur before their complements in their language, whereas a speaker of Japanese has to learn that heads follow their complements. (7) gives the respective examples:

(7) a. be showing pictures of himself

b. zibun -no syasin-o mise-te iru
 REFL from picture showing be

As one can see, the Japanese verb, noun and prepositional phrases are a mirror image of the corresponding phrases in English. (8) provides a summary and shows the parametric value for the position parameter:

(8) | Language | Observation | Parameter: head initial |
|---|---|---|
| English | Heads occur before complements | + |
| Japanese | Heads occur after complements | − |

Investigating languages based on their differences with regard to certain assumed parameters has proven to be a very fruitful line of research in the last few decades and has resulted in an abundance of comparative cross-linguistic studies.

After these introductory comments on language acquisition, the following sections will discuss the basic assumptions of GB theory.

3.1.3 The T model

Chomsky criticized simple PSGs for not being able to adequately capture certain correlations. An example of this is the relationship between active and passive sentences. In phrase structure grammars, one would have to formulate active and passive rules for intransitive, transitive and ditransitive verbs (see the discussion of (1)–(3) above). The fact that the passive can otherwise be consistently described as the suppression of the most prominent argument is not captured by phrase structure rules. Chomsky therefore assumes that there is an underlying structure, the so-called *Deep Structure*, and that other structures are derived from this. The general architecture of the so-called T model is discussed in the following subsections.

3.1.3.1 D-structure and S-structure

During the derivation of new structures, parts of the Deep Structure can be deleted or moved. In this way, one can explain the relationship between active and passive sentences. As the result of this kind of manipulation of structures, also called transformations, one derives a new structure, the *Surface Structure*, from the original Deep Structure. Since the Surface Structure does not actually mirror the actual use of words in a sentence in some versions of the theory, the term *S-structure* is sometimes used instead as to avoid misunderstandings.

(9) *Surface Structure* = S-structure
 Deep Structure = D-structure

Figure 3.2 gives an overview of the GB architecture: phrase structure rules and the lexicon license the D-structure from which the S-structure is derived by means of transformations. S-structure feeds into Phonetic Form (PF) and Logical Form (LF). The model is

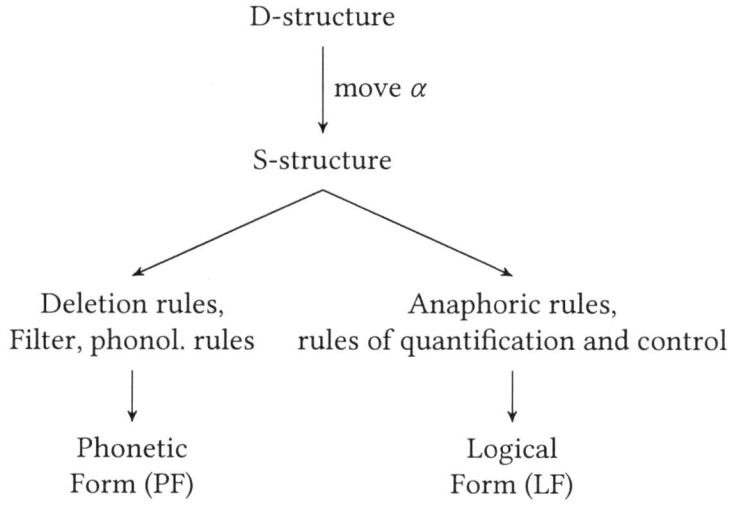

Figure 3.2: The T model

referred to as the *T-model* (or Y-model) because D-structure, S-structure, PF and LF form an upside-down T (or Y). We will look at each of these individual components in more detail.

Using phrase structure rules, one can describe the relationships between individual elements (for instance words and phrases, sometimes also parts of words). The format for these rules is $\overline{X}$ syntax (see Section 2.5). The lexicon, together with the structure licensed by $\overline{X}$ syntax, forms the basis for D-structure. D-structure is then a syntactic representation of the selectional grid (= valence classes) of individual word forms in the lexicon.

The lexicon contains a lexical entry for every word which comprises information about morphophonological structure, syntactic features and selectional properties. This will be explained in more detail in Section 3.1.3.4. Depending on one's exact theoretical assumptions, morphology is viewed as part of the lexicon. Inflectional morphology is, however, mostly consigned to the realm of syntax. The lexicon is an interface for semantic interpretation of individual word forms.

The surface position in which constituents are realized is not necessarily the position they have in D-structure. For example, a sentence with a ditransitive verb has the following ordering variants:

(10) a. [dass] der Mann der Frau das Buch gibt
    that the.NOM man the.DAT woman the.ACC book gives
    'that the man gives the woman the book'

3.1 General remarks on the representational format

b. Gibt der Mann der Frau das Buch?
   gives the.NOM man the.DAT woman the.ACC book

   'Does the man give the woman the book?'

c. Der Mann gibt der Frau das Buch.
   the.NOM man gives the.DAT woman the.ACC book

   'The man gives the woman the book.'

The following transformational rules for the movements above are assumed: (10b) is derived from (10a) by fronting the verb, and (10c) is derived from (10b) by fronting the nominative noun phrase. In GB theory, there is only one very general transformation: Move α = "Move anything anywhere!". The nature of what exactly can be moved where and for which reason is determined by principles. Examples of such principles are the Theta-Criterion and the Case Filter, which will be dealt with below.

The relations between a predicate and its arguments that are determined by the lexical entries have to be accessible for semantic interpretation at all representational levels. For this reason, the base position of a moved element is marked with a trace. This means, for instance, that the position in which the fronted *gibt* 'gives' originated is indicated in (11b). The respective marking is referred to as a *trace* or a *gap*. Such empty elements may be frightening when one encounters them first, but I already motivated the assumption of empty elements in nominal structures in Section 2.4.1 (page 68).

(11) a. [dass] der Mann der Frau das Buch gibt
        that the man the woman the book gives

        'that the man gives the woman the book'

   b. Gibt$_i$ der Mann der Frau das Buch _$_i$?
      gives the man the woman the book

      'Does the man give the woman the book?'

   c. [Der Mann]$_j$ gibt$_i$ _$_j$ der Frau das Buch _$_i$.
      the man gives the woman the book

      'The man gives the woman the book.'

(11c) is derived from (11a) by means of two movements, which is why there are two traces in (11c). The traces are marked with indices so it is possible to distinguish the moved constituents. The corresponding indices are then present on the moved constituents. Sometimes, *e* (for *empty*) or *t* (for *trace*) is used to represent traces.

The S-structure derived from the D-structure is a surface-like structure but should not be equated with the structure of actual utterances.

3.1.3.2 Phonetic Form

Phonological operations are represented at the level of Phonetic Form (PF). PF is responsible for creating the form which is actually pronounced. For example, so-called *wanna*-contraction takes place at PF (Chomsky 1981a: 20–21).

(12) a. The students want to visit Paris.
    b. The students wanna visit Paris.

The contraction in (12) is licensed by the optional rule in (13):

(13) want + to → wanna

3.1.3.3 Logical Form

Logical Form is the syntactic level which mediates between S-structure and the semantic interpretation of a sentence. Some of the phenomena which are dealt with by LF are anaphoric reference of pronouns, quantification and control.

Syntactic factors play a role in resolving anaphoric dependencies. An important component of GB theory is Binding Theory, which seeks to explain what a pronoun can or must refer to and when a reflexive pronoun can or must be used. (14) gives some examples of both personal and reflexive pronouns:

(14) a. Peter kauft einen Tisch. Er gefällt ihm.
    Peter buys   a   table(M) he likes him
    'Peter is buying a table. He likes it/him.'

   b. Peter kauft eine Tasche. Er gefällt ihm.
    Peter buys   a   bag(F)   he likes him
    'Peter is buying a bag. He likes it/him.'

   c. Peter kauft eine Tasche. Er gefällt sich.
    Peter buys   a   bag(F)   he likes himself
    'Peter is buying a bag. He likes himself.'

In the first example, *er* 'he' can refer to either Peter, the table or something/someone else that was previously mentioned in the context. *ihm* 'him' can refer to Peter or someone in the context. Reference to the table is restricted by world knowledge. In the second example, *er* 'he' cannot refer to *Tasche* 'bag' since *Tasche* is feminine and *er* is masculine. *er* 'he' can refer to Peter only if *ihm* 'him' does not refer to Peter. *ihm* would otherwise have to refer to a person in the wider context. This is different in (14c). In (14c), *er* 'he' and *sich* 'himself' must refer to the same object. This is due to the fact that the reference of reflexives such as *sich* is restricted to a particular local domain. Binding Theory attempts to capture these restrictions.

LF is also important for quantifier scope. Sentences such as (15a) have two readings. These are given in (15b) and (15c).

(15) a. Every man loves a woman.
    b. $\forall x \exists y (man(x) \rightarrow (woman(y) \wedge love(x,y)))$
    c. $\exists y \forall x (man(x) \rightarrow (woman(y) \wedge love(x,y)))$

3.1 General remarks on the representational format

The symbol ∀ stands for a *universal quantifier* and ∃ stands for an *existential quantifier*. The first formula corresponds to the reading that for every man, there is a woman who he loves and in fact, these can be different women. Under the second reading, there is exactly one woman such that all men love her. The question of when such an ambiguity arises and which reading is possible when depends on the syntactic properties of the given utterance. LF is the level which is important for the meaning of determiners such as *a* and *every*.

Control Theory is also specified with reference to LF. Control Theory deals with the question of how the semantic role of the infinitive subject in sentences such as (16) is filled.

(16)   a.   Der Professor schlägt dem Studenten vor, die Klausur noch mal zu
             the professor suggests the student   PART the test   once again to
             schreiben.
             write
             'The professor advises the student to take the test again.'

       b.   Der Professor schlägt dem Studenten vor, die Klausur nicht zu bewerten.
             the professor suggests the student   PART the test   not to grade
             'The professor suggests to the student not to grade the test.'

       c.   Der Professor schlägt dem Studenten vor, gemeinsam ins Kino zu gehen.
             the professor suggests the student   PART together into cinema to go
             'The professor suggests to the student to go to the cinema together.'

3.1.3.4 The lexicon

The meaning of words tells us that they have to be combined with certain roles like "acting person" or "affected thing" when creating more complex phrases. For example, the fact that the verb *beat* needs two arguments belongs to its semantic contribution. The semantic representation of the contribution of the verb *beat* in (17a) is given in (17b):

(17)   a.   Judit beats the grandmaster.
       b.   *beat'*(x,y)

Dividing heads into valence classes is also referred to as *subcategorization*: *beat* is subcategorized for a subject and an object. This term comes from the fact that a head is already categorized with regard to its part of speech (verb, noun, adjective, …) and then further subclasses (e.g., intransitive or transitive verb) are formed with regard to valence information. Sometimes the phrase *X subcategorizes for Y* is used, which means *X selects Y*. *beat* is referred to as the predicate since *beat'* is the logical predicate. The subject and object are the arguments of the predicate. There are several terms used to describe the set of selectional requirements such as *argument structure, valence frames, subcategorization frame, thematic grid* and *theta-grid* or *θ-grid*.

3 Transformational Grammar – Government & Binding

Adjuncts modify semantic predicates and when the semantic aspect is emphasized they are also called *modifiers*. Adjuncts are not present in the argument structure of predicates.

Following GB assumptions, arguments occur in specific positions in the clause – in so-called argument positions (e.g., the sister of an X^0 element, see Section 2.5). The Theta-Criterion states that elements in argument positions have to be assigned a semantic role – a so-called theta-role – and each role can be assigned only once (Chomsky 1981a: 36):

Principle 1 (Theta-Criterion)
- *Each theta-role is assigned to exactly one argument position.*

- *Every phrase in an argument position receives exactly one theta-role.*

The arguments of a head are ordered, that is, one can differentiate between higher- and lower-ranked arguments. The highest-ranked argument of verbs and adjectives has a special status. Since GB assumes that it is often (and always in some languages) realized in a position outside of the verb or adjective phrase, it is often referred to as the *external argument*. The remaining arguments occur in positions inside of the verb or adjective phrase. These kind of arguments are dubbed *internal arguments* or *complements*. For simple sentences, this often means that the subject is the external argument.

When discussing types of arguments, one can identify three classes of theta-roles:

- Class 1: agent (acting individual), the cause of an action or feeling (stimulus), holder of a certain property

- Class 2: experiencer (perceiving individual), the person profiting from something (beneficiary) (or the opposite: the person affected by some kind of damage), possessor (owner or soon-to-be owner of something, or the opposite: someone who has lost or is lacking something)

- Class 3: patient (affected person or thing), theme

If a verb has several theta-roles of this kind to assign, Class 1 normally has the highest rank, whereas Class 3 has the lowest. Unfortunately, the assignment of semantic roles to actual arguments of verbs has received a rather inconsistent treatment in the literature. This problem has been discussed by Dowty (1991), who suggests using proto-roles. An argument is assigned the proto-agent role if it has sufficiently many of the properties that were identified by Dowty as prototypical properties of agents (e.g., animacy, volitionality).

The mental lexicon contains *lexical entries* with the specific properties of syntactic words needed to use that word grammatically. Some of these properties are the following:

- form

- meaning (semantics)

3.1 General remarks on the representational format

- grammatical features: syntactic word class + morphosyntactic features
- theta-grid

(18) shows an example of a lexical entry:

(18)

form	*helf-* 'help'
semantics	*helfen'*
grammatical features	verb
theta-grid	
theta-roles	<u>agent</u> beneficiary
grammatical particularities	dative

Assigning semantic roles to specific syntactic requirements (beneficiary = dative) is also called *linking*.

Arguments are ordered according to their ranking: the highest argument is furthest left. In the case of *helfen*, the highest argument is the external argument, which is why the agent is underlined. With so-called unaccusative verbs,[3] the highest argument is not treated as the external argument. It would therefore not be underlined in the corresponding lexical entry.

3.1.4 $\overline{\text{X}}$ theory

In GB, it is assumed that all syntactic structures licensed by the core grammar[4] correspond to the $\overline{\text{X}}$ schema (see Section 2.5).[5] In the following sections, I will comment on the syntactic categories assumed and the basic assumptions with regard to the interpretation of grammatical rules.

3.1.4.1 Syntactic categories

The categories which can be used for the variable X in the $\overline{\text{X}}$ schema are divided into lexical and functional categories. This correlates roughly with the difference between open and closed word classes. The following are lexical categories:

- V = verb
- N = noun
- A = adjective

---

[3] See Perlmutter (1978) for a discussion of unaccusative verbs. The term *ergative verb* is also common, albeit a misnomer. See Burzio (1981; 1986) for the earliest work on unaccusatives in the Chomskyan framework and Grewendorf (1989) for German. Also, see Pullum (1988) on the usage of these terms and for a historical evaluation.

[4] Chomsky (1981a: 7–8) distinguishes between a regular area of language that is determined by a grammar that can be acquired using genetically determined language-specific knowledge and a periphery, to which irregular parts of language such as idioms (e.g., *to pull the wool over sb.'s eyes*) belong. See Section 16.3.

[5] Chomsky (1970: 210) allows for grammatical rules that deviate from the $\overline{\text{X}}$ schema. It is, however, common practice to assume that languages exclusively use $\overline{\text{X}}$ structures.

- P = preposition/postposition
- Adv = adverb

Lexical categories can be represented using binary features and a cross-classification:[6]

Table 3.1: Representation of four lexical categories using two binary features

	−V	+V
−N	P = [−N, −V]	V = [−N, +V]
+N	N = [+N, −V]	A = [+N, +V]

Adverbs are viewed as intransitive prepositions and are therefore captured by the decomposition in the table above.

Using this cross-classification, it is possible to formulate generalizations. One can, for example, simply refer to adjectives and verbs: all lexical categories which are [+V] are either adjectives or verbs. Furthermore, one can say of [+N] categories (nouns and adjectives) that they can bear case.

Apart from this, some authors have tried to associate the head position with the feature values in Table 3.1 (see e.g., Grewendorf 1988: 52; Haftka 1996: 124; G. Müller 2011: 238). With prepositions and nouns, the head precedes the complement in German:

(19) a. *für* Marie
       for Marie

   b. *Bild* von Maria
       picture of Maria

With adjectives and verbs, the head is final:

(20) a. dem König *treu*
       the king loyal
       'Loyal to the king'

   b. der [dem Kind *helfende*] Mann
       the the child helping man
       'the man helping the child'

   c. dem Mann *helfen*
       the man help
       'help the man'

---

[6]See Chomsky (1970: 199) for a cross-classification of N, A and V, and Jackendoff (1977: Section 3.2) for a cross-classification that additionally includes P but has a different feature assignment.

3.1 General remarks on the representational format

This data seems to suggest that the head is final with [+V] categories and initial with [−V] categories. Unfortunately, this generalization runs into the problem that there are also postpositions in German. These are, like prepositions, not verbal, but do occur after the NP they require:

(21) a. des Geldes *wegen*
 the money because
 'because of the money'
 b. die Nacht *über*
 the night during
 'during the night'

Therefore, one must either invent a new category, or abandon the attempt to use binary category features to describe ordering restrictions. If one were to place postpositions in a new category, it would be necessary to assume another binary feature.[7] Since this feature can have either a negative or a positive value, one would then have four additional categories. There are then eight possible feature combinations, some of which would not correspond to any plausible category.

For functional categories, GB does not propose a cross-classification. Usually, the following categories are assumed:

 C Complementizer (subordinating conjunctions such as *dass* 'that')
 I Finiteness (as well as Tense and Mood);
  also Infl in earlier work (inflection),
  T in more recent work (Tense)
 D Determiner (article, demonstrative)

3.1.4.2 Assumptions and rules

In GB, it is assumed that all rules must follow the $\overline{X}$ format discussed in Section 2.5. In other theories, rules which correspond to the $\overline{X}$ format are used along other rules which do not. If the strict version of $\overline{X}$ theory is assumed, this comes with the assumption of

---

[7]Martin Haspelmath has pointed out that one could assume a rule that moves a post-head argument into a pre-head position (see Riemsdijk 1978: 89 for the discussion of a transformational solution). This would be parallel to the realization of prepositional arguments of adjectives in German:

(i) a. auf seinen Sohn stolz
  on his son proud
  'proud of his son'
 b. stolz auf seinen Sohn
  proud of his son

But note that the situation is different with postpositions here, while all adjectives that take prepositional objects allow for both orders, this is not the case for prepositions. Most prepositions do not allow their object to occur before them. It is an idiosyncratic feature of some postpositions that they want to have their argument to the left.

endocentricity: every phrase has a head and every head is part of a phrase (put more technically: every head projects to a phrase).

Furthermore, as with phrase structure grammars, it is assumed that the branches of tree structures cannot cross (*Non-Tangling Condition*). This assumption is made by the majority of theories discussed in this book. There are, however, some variants of TAG, HPSG, Construction Grammar, and Dependency Grammar which allow crossing branches and therefore discontinuous constituents (Becker, Joshi & Rambow 1991; Reape 1994; Bergen & Chang 2005; Heringer 1996: 261; Eroms 2000: Section 9.6.2).

In $\overline{X}$ theory, one normally assumes that there are at most two projection levels (X' and X''). However, there are some versions of Mainstream Generative Grammar and other theories which allow three or more levels (Jackendoff 1977; Uszkoreit 1987). In this chapter, I follow the standard assumption that there are two projection levels, that is, phrases have at least three levels:

- X^0 = head

- X' = intermediate projection ($\overline{X}$, read: X bar)

- XP = highest projection (= X'' = $\overline{\overline{X}}$), also called *maximal projection*

3.1.5 CP and IP in English

Most work in Mainstream Generative Grammar is heavily influenced by previous publications dealing with English. If one wants to understand GB analyses of German and other languages, it is important to first understand the analyses of English and, for this reason, this will be the focus of this section. The CP/IP system is also assumed in LFG grammars of English and thus the following section also provides a foundation for understanding some of the fundamentals of LFG presented in Chapter 7.

In earlier work, the rules in (22a) and (22b) were proposed for English sentences (Chomsky 1981a: 19).

(22)   a.   S → NP VP
        b.   S → NP Infl VP

Infl stands for *Inflection* as inflectional affixes are inserted at this position in the structure. The symbol AUX was also used instead of Infl in earlier work, since auxiliary verbs are treated in the same way as inflectional affixes. Figure 3.3 on the next page shows a sample analysis of a sentence with an auxiliary, which uses the rule in (22b).

Together with its complements, the verb forms a structural unit: the VP. The constituent status of the VP is supported by several constituent tests and further differences between subjects and objects regarding their positional restrictions.

The rules in (22) do not follow the $\overline{X}$ template since there is no symbol on the right-hand side of the rule with the same category as one on the left-hand side, that is, there is no head. In order to integrate rules like (22) into the general theory, Chomsky (1986a: 3) developed a rule system with two layers above the verb phrase (VP), namely the CP/IP

3.1 General remarks on the representational format

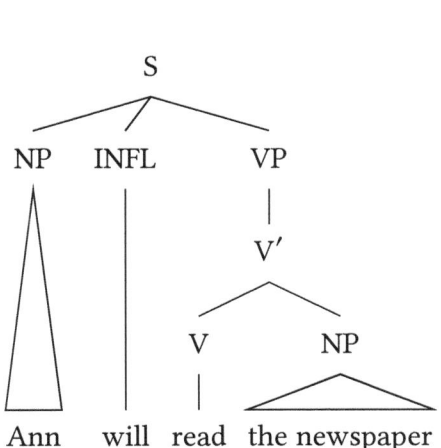

Figure 3.3: Sentence with an auxiliary verb following Chomsky (1981a: 19)

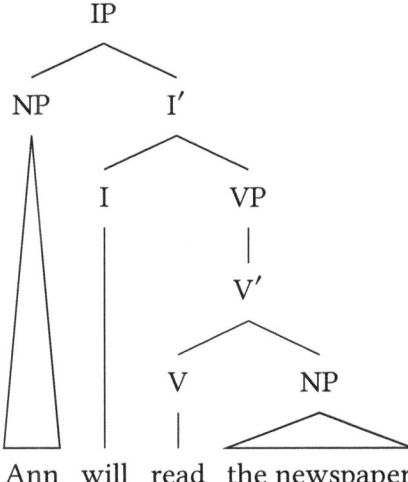

Figure 3.4: Sentence with auxiliary verb in the CP/IP system

system. CP stands for *Complementizer Phrase*. The head of a CP can be a complementizer. Before we look at CPs in more detail, I will discuss an example of an IP in this new system. Figure 3.4 shows an IP with an auxiliary in the I^0 position. As we can see, this corresponds to the structure of the $\overline{X}$ template: I^0 is a head, which takes the VP as its complement and thereby forms I'. The subject is the specifier of the IP. Another way to phrase this is to say that the subject is in the specifier position of the IP. This position is usually referred to as SpecIP.[8]

The sentences in (23) are analyzed as complementizer phrases (CPs), the complementizer is the head:

(23)   a. that Ann will read the newspaper
       b. that Ann reads the newspaper

In sentences such as (23), the CPs do not have a specifier. Figure 3.5 on the next page shows the analysis of (23a).

Yes/no-questions in English such as those in (24) are formed by moving the auxiliary verb in front of the subject.

(24)   Will Ann read the newspaper?

Let us assume that the structure of questions corresponds to the structure of sentences with complementizers. This means that questions are also CPs. Unlike the sentences in (23), however, there is no subordinating conjunction. In the D-structure of questions, the C^0 position is empty and the auxiliary verb is later moved to this position. Figure 3.6

---

[8]Sometimes SpecIP and similar labels are used in trees (for instance by Haegeman (1994), Meinunger (2000) and Lohnstein (2014)). I avoid this in this book since SpecIP, SpecAdvP are not categories like NP or AP or AdvP but positions that items of a certain category can take. See Chapter 2 on the phrase structure rules that license trees.

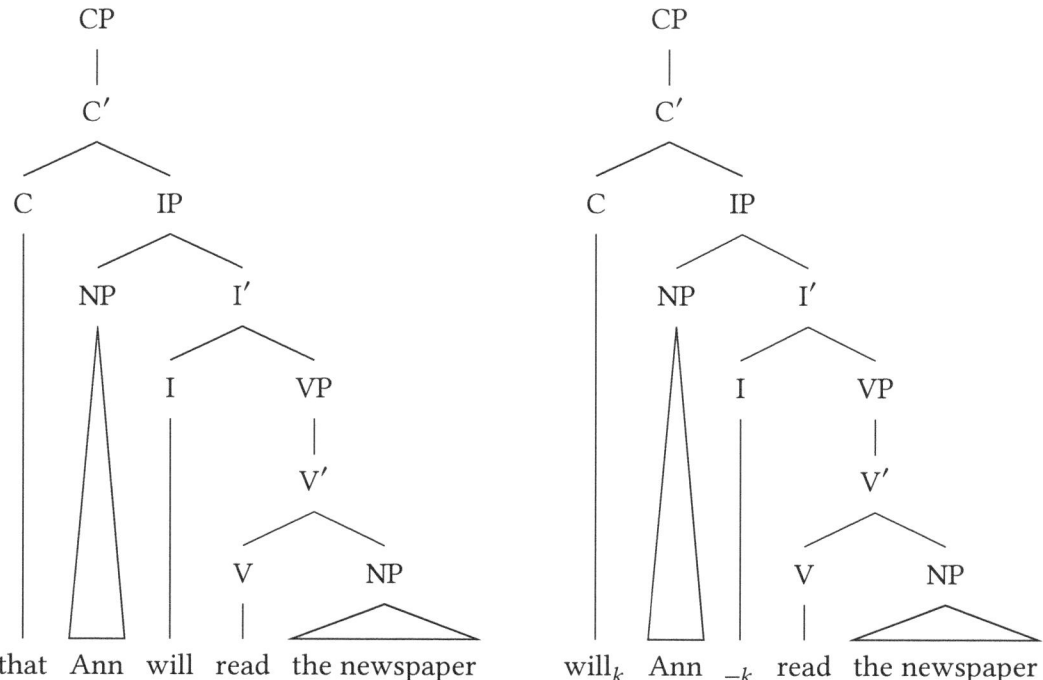

Figure 3.5: Complementizer phrase   Figure 3.6: Polar question

shows an analysis of (24). The original position of the auxiliary is marked by the trace $_k$, which is coindexed with the moved auxiliary.

wh-questions are formed by the additional movement of a constituent in front of the auxiliary; that is into the specifier position of the CP. Figure 3.7 on the facing page shows the analysis of (25):

(25)   What will Ann read?

As before, the movement of the object of *read* is indicated by a trace. This is important when constructing the meaning of the sentence. The verb assigns some semantic role to the element in its object position. Therefore, one has to be able to "reconstruct" the fact that *what* actually originates in this position. This is ensured by coindexation of the trace with *what*.

Several ways to depict traces are used in the literature. Some authors assume a trace instead of the object NP as in Figure 3.8a (Grewendorf 1988: 249, 322; Haegeman 1994: 420). Others have the object NP in the tree and indicate the movement by a trace that is dominated by the NP as in Figure 3.8b (von Stechow & Sternefeld 1988: 376; Grewendorf 1988: 185; Haegeman 1994: 355; Sternefeld 2006: 333). The first proposal directly reflects the assumption that a complete phrase is moved and leaves a trace that represents the thing that is moved. If one thinks about the properties of the trace it is clear that it has the same category as the element that was at this position before movement. Hence the second way to represent the moved category is appropriate as well. Figure 3.8b basically

3.1 General remarks on the representational format

Figure 3.7: *wh*-question

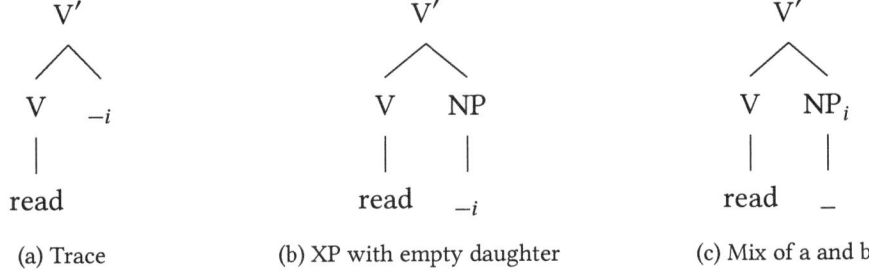

Figure 3.8: Alternative ways of depicting movement: the moved constituent can be represented by a trace or by an XP dominating a trace

says that the object that is moved is an NP but that there is nothing to pronounce. Given what was just said the most appropriate way to represent movement would be the one in Figure 3.8c. This picture is a mix of the two other pictures. The index is associated with the category and not with the empty phonology. In my opinion this best depicts the fact that trace and filler are related. However, I never saw this way of depicting movement in the GB literature and hence I will stick to the more common notation in Figure 3.8b. This way to depict movement is also more similar to the representation that is used by all authors for the movement of words (so-called head-movement). For example the trace $_{-k}$, which stands for a moved I^0 in Figure 3.6 is never depicted as daughter of I′ but always as a daughter of I^0.

99

Until now, I have not yet discussed sentences without auxiliaries such as (23b). In order to analyze this kind of sentences, it is usually assumed that the inflectional affix is present in the I^0 position. An example analysis is given in Figure 3.9. Since the inflectional affix

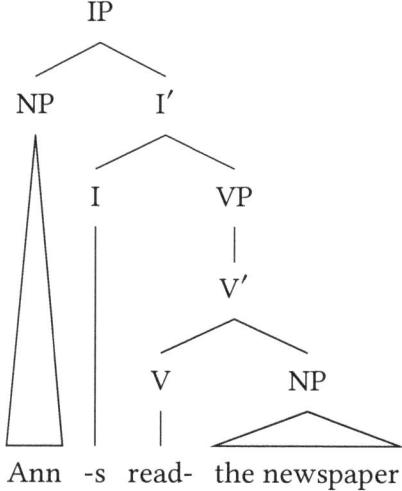

Figure 3.9: Sentence without auxiliary

precedes the verb, some kind of movement operation still needs to take place. There are two suggestions in the literature: one is to assume lowering, that is, the affix moves down to the verb (Pollock 1989: 394; Chomsky 1991; Haegeman 1994: 110, 601; Sportiche et al. 2013). The alternative is to assume that the verb moves up to the affix (Fanselow & Felix 1987: 258–259). Since theories with lowering of inflectional affixes are complicated for languages in which the verb ultimately ends up in C (basically in all Germanic languages except English), I follow Fanselow & Felix's (1987: 258–259) suggestion for English and Grewendorf's (1993: 1289) suggestion for German and assume that the verb moves from V to I in English and from V to I to C in German.[9]

---

[9] Sportiche, Koopman & Stabler (2013) argue for an affix lowering approach by pointing out that approaches assuming that the verb stem moves to I (their T) predict that adverbs appear to the right of the verb rather than to the left:

(i) a. John will carefully study Russian.
    b. John carefully studies Russian.
    c. *John studies carefully Russian.

If the affix -s is in the position of the auxiliary and the verb moves to the affix, one would expect (i.c) to be grammatical rather than (i.b).

A third approach is to assume empty I heads for present and past tense and have these heads select a fully inflected verb. See Carnie (2013: 220–221) for such an approach to English.

For German it was also suggested not to distinguish between I and V at all and treat auxiliaries like normal verbs (see footnote 10 below). In such approaches verbs are inflected as V, no I node is assumed (Haider 1993; 1997a).

3.1 General remarks on the representational format

Following this excursus on the analysis of English sentences, we can now turn to German.

3.1.6 The structure of the German clause

The CP/IP model has been adopted by many scholars for the analysis of German.[10] The categories C, I and V, together with their specifier positions, can be linked to the topological fields as shown in Figure 3.10.

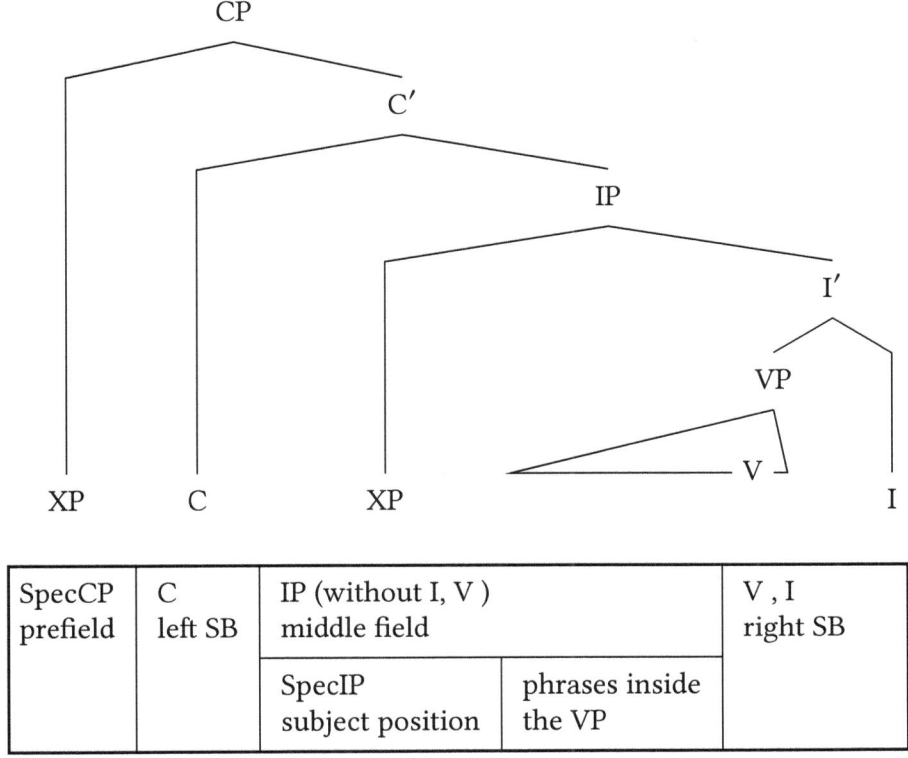

Figure 3.10: CP, IP and VP and the topological model of German

Note that SpecCP and SpecIP are not category symbols. They do not occur in grammars with rewrite rules. Instead, they simply describe positions in the tree.

As shown in Figure 3.10, it is assumed that the highest argument of the verb (the subject in simple sentences) has a special status. It is taken for granted that the subject always occurs outside of the VP, which is why it is referred to as the external argument. The VP itself does not have a specifier. In more recent work, however, the subject is

---

[10] For GB analyses without IP, see Bayer & Kornfilt (1989), Höhle (1991a: 157), Haider (1993; 1997a) and Sternefeld (2006: Section IV.3). Haider assumes that the function of I is integrated into the verb. In LFG, an IP is assumed for English (Bresnan 2001: Section 6.2; Dalrymple 2001: Section 3.2.1), but not for German (Berman 2003a: Section 3.2.3.2). In HPSG, no IP is assumed.

101

generated in the specifier of the VP (Fukui & Speas 1986; Koopman & Sportiche 1991). In some languages, it is assumed that it moves to a position outside of the VP. In other languages such as German, this is the case at least under certain conditions (e.g., definiteness, see Diesing 1992). I am presenting the classical GB analysis here, where the subject is outside the VP. All arguments other than the subject are complements of the V, that are realized within the VP, that is, they are internal arguments. If the verb requires just one complement, then this is the sister of the head V^0 and the daughter of V' according to the $\overline{X}$ schema. The accusative object is the prototypical complement.

Following the $\overline{X}$ template, adjuncts branch off above the complements of V'. The analysis of a VP with an adjunct is shown in Figure 3.11.

(26) weil der Mann morgen den Jungen trifft
 because the man tomorrow the boy meets
 'because the man is meeting the boy tomorrow'

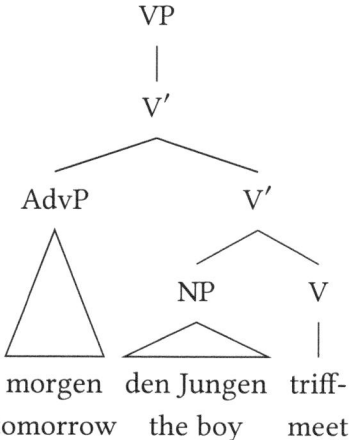

Figure 3.11: Analysis of adjuncts in GB theory

3.2 Verb position

In German, the position of the heads of VP and IP (V^0 and I^0) are to the right of their complements and V^0 and I^0 form part of the right sentence bracket. The subject and all other constituents (complements and adjuncts) all occur to the left of V^0 and I^0 and form the middle field. It is assumed that German – at least in terms of D-structure – is an SOV language (= a language with the base order Subject–Object–Verb). The analysis of German as an SOV language is almost as old as Transformational Grammar itself. It was originally proposed by Bierwisch (1963: 34).[11] Unlike German, Germanic languages like Danish, English and Romance languages like French are SVO languages, whereas Welsh and Arabic are VSO languages. Around 40 % of all languages belong to the SOV languages, around 35 % are SVO (Dryer 2013c).

The assumption of verb-final order as the base order is motivated by the following observations:[12]

1. Verb particles form a close unit with the verb.

    (27) a. weil   er morgen   an-fängt
             because he tomorrow PART-starts
             'because he is starting tomorrow'

          b. Er fängt morgen   an.
             he starts tomorrow PART
             'He is starting tomorrow.'

This unit can only be seen in verb-final structures, which speaks for the fact that this structure reflects the base order.

Verbs which are derived from a noun by back-formation (e.g., *uraufführen* 'to perform something for the first time'), can often not be divided into their component parts and V2 clauses are therefore ruled out (This was first mentioned by Höhle (1991b) in unpublished work. The first published source is Haider (1993: 62)):

    (28) a. weil   sie das Stück heute ur-auf-führen
             because they the play   today PREF-PART-lead
             'because they are performing the play for the first time today'

          b. * Sie   ur-auf-führen   heute das Stück.
               they PREF-PART-lead today the play

          c. * Sie   führen heute das Stück ur-auf.
               they lead   today the play PREF-PART

The examples show that there is only one possible position for this kind of verb. This order is the one that is assumed to be the base order.

---

[11]Bierwisch attributes the assumption of an underlying verb-final order to Fourquet (1957). A German translation of the French manuscript cited by Bierwisch can be found in Fourquet (1970: 117–135). For other proposals, see Bach (1962), Reis (1974), Koster (1975) and Thiersch (1978: Chapter 1). Analyses which assume that German has an underlying SOV pattern were also suggested in GPSG (Jacobs 1986: 110), LFG (Berman 1996: Section 2.1.4) and HPSG (Kiss & Wesche 1991; Oliva 1992; Netter 1992; Kiss 1993; Frank 1994; Kiss 1995; Feldhaus 1997; Meurers 2000; Müller 2005b; 2017a).

[12]For points 1 and 2, see Bierwisch (1963: 34–36). For point 4 see Netter (1992: Section 2.3).

2. Verbs in non-finite clauses and in finite subordinate clauses with a conjunction are always in final position (I am ignoring the possibility of extraposing constituents):

(29) a. Der Clown versucht, Kurt-Martin die Ware zu geben.
the clown tries Kurt-Martin the goods to give

'The clown is trying to give Kurt-Martin the goods.'

b. dass der Clown Kurt-Martin die Ware gibt
that the clown Kurt-Martin the goods gives

'that the clown gives Kurt-Martin the goods'

3. If one compares the position of the verb in German with Danish (Danish is an SVO language like English), then one can clearly see that the verbs in German form a cluster at the end of the sentence, whereas they occur before any objects in Danish (Ørsnes 2009a: 146):

(30) a. dass er ihn gesehen₃ haben₂ muss₁
that he him seen have must

b. at han må₁ have₂ set₃ ham
that he must have seen him

'that he must have seen him'

4. The scope relations of the adverbs in (31) depend on their order: the left-most adverb has scope over the two following elements.[13] This was explained by assuming the following structure:

---

[13] At this point, it should be mentioned that there seem to be exceptions from the rule that modifiers to the left take scope over those to their right. Kasper (1994: 47) discusses examples such as (i), which go back to Bartsch & Vennemann (1972: 137).

(i) a. Peter liest gut wegen der Nachhilfestunden.
Peter reads well because.of the tutoring

b. Peter liest wegen der Nachhilfestunden gut.
Peter reads because.of the tutoring well

'Peter can read well thanks to the tutoring.'

As Koster (1975: Section 6) and Reis (1980: 67) have shown, these are not particularly convincing counterexamples as the right sentence bracket is not filled in these examples and therefore the examples are not necessarily instances of normal reordering inside of the middle field, but could instead involve extraposition of the PP. As noted by Koster and Reis, these examples become ungrammatical if one fills the right bracket and does not extrapose the causal adjunct:

(ii) a. * Hans hat gut wegen der Nachhilfestunden gelesen.
Hans has well because.of the tutoring read

b. Hans hat gut gelesen wegen der Nachhilfestunden.
Hans has well read because.of the tutoring

'Hans has been reading well because of the tutoring.'

However, the following example from Crysmann (2004: 383) shows that, even with the right bracket occupied, one can still have an order where an adjunct to the right has scope over one to the left:

(31) a. dass er [absichtlich [nicht lacht]]
         that he intentionally not   laughs
         'that he is intentionally not laughing'
      b. dass er [nicht [absichtlich   lacht]]
         that he not   intentionally laughs
         'that he is not laughing intentionally'

It is interesting to note that scope relations are not affected by verb position. If one assumes that sentences with verb-second order have the underlying structure in (31), then this fact requires no further explanation. (32) shows the derived S-structure for (31):

(32) a. Er lacht$_i$ [absichtlich [nicht $\_i$]].
         he laughs   intentionally not
         'He is intentionally not laughing.'
      b. Er lacht$_i$ [nicht [absichtlich $\_i$]].
         he laughs   not   intentionally
         'He is not laughing intentionally.'

After motivating and briefly sketching the analysis of verb-final order, I will now look at the CP/IP analysis of German in more detail. C^0 corresponds to the left sentence bracket and can be filled in two different ways: in subordinate clauses introduced by a conjunction, the subordinating conjunction (the complementizer) occupies C^0 as in English. The verb remains in the right sentence bracket, as illustrated by (33).

(33) dass jeder   diesen Mann kennt
      that everybody this   man knows
      'that everybody knows this man'

Figure 3.12 on the following page gives an analysis of (33). In verb-first and verb-second clauses, the finite verb is moved to C^0 via the I^0 position: $V^0 \rightarrow I^0 \rightarrow C^0$ (Grewendorf 1993: 1289). Figure 3.13 on page 107 shows the analysis of (34):

(34) Kennt jeder   diesen Mann?
      knows everybody this   man
      'Does everybody know this man?'

(iii) Da muß es   schon erhebliche Probleme mit der Ausrüstung gegeben haben, da   wegen
       there must EXPL already serious   problems with the equipment given   have since because.of
       schlechten Wetters ein Reinhold Messmer niemals aufgäbe.
       bad   weather a   Reinhold Messmer never   would.give.up
       'There really must have been some serious problems with the equipment because someone like Reinhold Messmer would never give up just because of some bad weather.'

Nevertheless, this does not change anything regarding the fact that the corresponding cases in (31) and (32) have the same scope relations regardless of the position of the verb. The general means of semantic composition may well have to be implemented in the same way as in Crysmann's analysis.

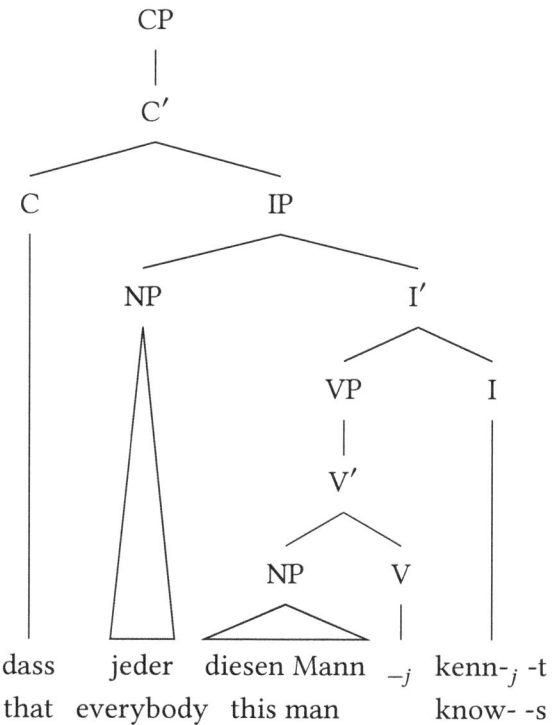

Figure 3.12: Sentence with a complementizer in C⁰

The C⁰ position is empty in the D-structure of (34). Since it is not occupied by a complementizer, the verb can move there.

3.3 Long-distance dependencies

The SpecCP position corresponds to the prefield and can be filled by any XP in declarative clauses in German. In this way, one can derive the sentences in (36) from (35) by moving a constituent in front of the verb:

(35) Gibt der Mann dem Kind jetzt den Mantel?
gives the.NOM man the.DAT child now the.ACC coat
'Is the man going to give the child the coat now?'

(36) a. Der Mann gibt dem Kind jetzt den Mantel.
the.NOM man gives the.DAT child now the.ACC coat
'The man is giving the child the coat now.'
b. Dem Kind gibt der Mann jetzt den Mantel.
the.DAT child gives the.NOM man now the.ACC coat

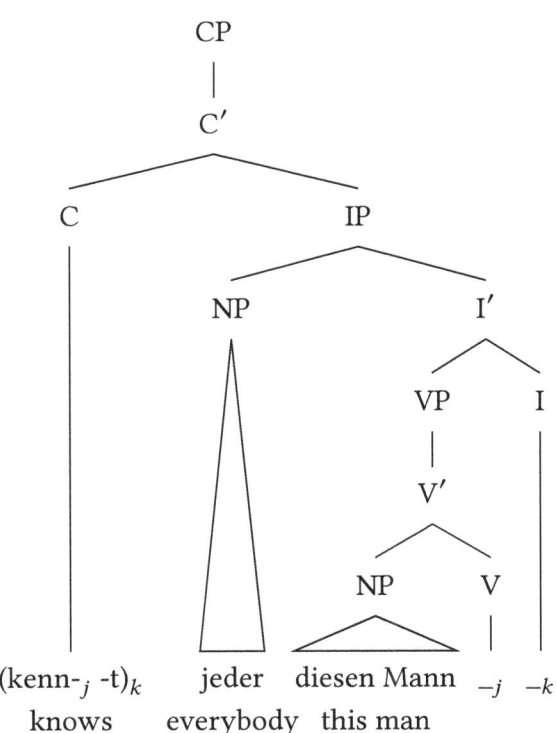

Figure 3.13: Verb position in GB

   c. Den   Mantel gibt der   Mann dem   Kind jetzt.
      the.ACC coat   gives the.NOM man the.DAT child now

   d. Jetzt gibt der   Mann dem   Kind den   Mantel.
      now gives the.NOM man the.DAT child the.ACC coat

Since any constituent can be placed in front of the finite verb, German is treated typologically as one of the verb-second languages (V2). Thus, it is a verb-second language with SOV base order. English, on the other hand, is an SVO language without the V2 property, whereas Danish is a V2 language with SVO as its base order (see Ørsnes 2009a for Danish).

Figure 3.14 on the following page shows the structure derived from Figure 3.13. The crucial factor for deciding which phrase to move is the *information structure* of the sentence. That is, material connected to previously mentioned or otherwise-known information is placed further left (preferably in the prefield) and new information tends to occur to the right. Fronting to the prefield in declarative clauses is often referred to as *topicalization*. But this is rather a misnomer, since the focus (informally: the constituent being asked for) can also occur in the prefield. Furthermore, expletive pronouns can occur there and these are non-referential and as such cannot be linked to preceding or known information, hence expletives can never be topics.

3 Transformational Grammar – Government & Binding

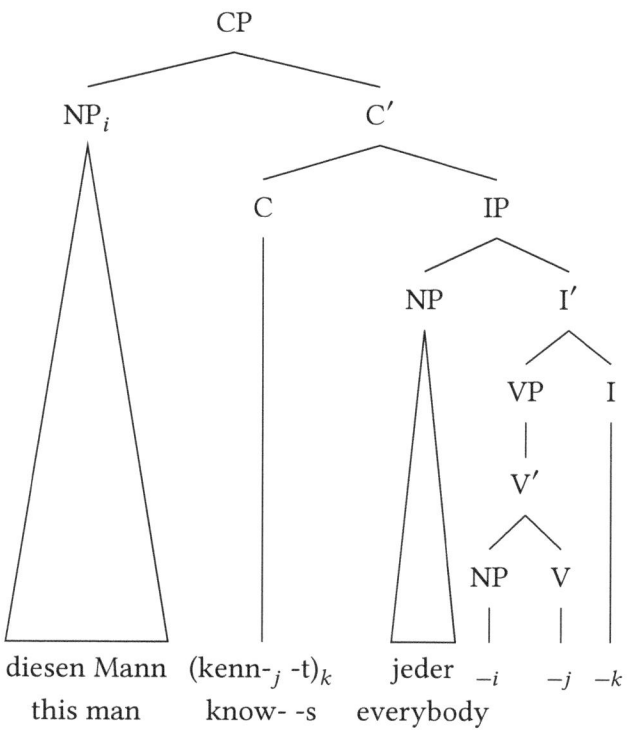

Figure 3.14: Fronting in GB theory

Transformation-based analyses also work for so-called *long-distance dependencies*, that is, dependencies crossing several phrase boundaries:

(37) a. [Um   zwei Millionen Mark]$_i$ soll   er versucht haben, [eine
        around two million   Deutsche.Marks should he tried   have   an
        Versicherung   _$_i$ zu betrügen].[14]
        insurance.company   to deceive

    'He apparently tried to cheat an insurance company out of two million Deutsche Marks.'

  b. „Wer$_i$, glaubt er, daß er _$_i$ ist?" erregte sich ein Politiker vom   Nil.[15]
        who   believes he that he   is   retort REFL a   politician from.the Nile

    ' "Who does he think he is?", a politician from the Nile exclaimed.'

  c. Wen$_i$ glaubst du, daß ich _$_i$ gesehen habe?[16]
        who   believe you that I   seen   have

    'Who do you think I saw?'

---
[14]taz, 04.05.2001, p. 20.
[15]Spiegel, 8/1999, p. 18.
[16]Scherpenisse (1986: 84).

d. [Gegen ihn]$_i$ falle es den Republikanern hingegen schwerer,
  against him fall it the Republicans however more.difficult
 [[Angriffe _$_i$] zu lancieren].[17]
  attacks to launch

 'It is, however, more difficult for the Republicans to launch attacks against him.'

The elements in the prefield in the examples in (37) all originate from more deeply embedded phrases. In GB, it is assumed that long-distance dependencies across sentence boundaries are derived in steps (Grewendorf 1988: 75–79), that is, in the analysis of (37c), the interrogative pronoun is moved to the specifier position of the *dass*-clause and is moved from there to the specifier of the matrix clause. The reason for this is that there are certain restrictions on movement which must be checked locally.

3.4 Passive

Before I turn to the analysis of the passive in Section 3.4.2, the first subsection will elaborate on the differences between structural and lexical case.

3.4.1 Structural and lexical case

The case of many case-marked arguments is dependent on the syntactic environment in which the head of the argument is realized. These arguments are referred to as arguments with *structural case*. Case-marked arguments, which do not bear structural case, are said to have *lexical case*.[18]

The following are examples of structural case:[19]

(38) a. Der Installateur kommt.
  the.NOM plumber comes

 'The plumber is coming.'

 b. Der Mann lässt den Installateur kommen.
  the man lets the.ACC plumber come

 'The man is getting the plumber to come.'

---

[17]taz, 08.02.2008, p. 9.

[18]Furthermore, there is a so-called *agreeing case* (see page 41) and *semantic case*. Agreeing case is found in predicatives. This case also changes depending on the structure involved, but the change is due to the antecedent element changing its case. Semantic case depends on the function of certain phrases (e.g., temporal accusative adverbials). Furthermore, as with lexical case of objects, semantic case does not change depending on the syntactic environment. For the analysis of the passive, which will be discussed in this section, only structural and lexical case will be relevant.

[19]Compare Heinz & Matiasek (1994: 200).
 (38b) is a so-called AcI construction. AcI stands for *Accusativus cum infinitivo*, which means "accusative with infinitive". The logical subject of the embedded verb (*kommen* 'to come' in this case) becomes the accusative object of the matrix verb *lassen* 'to let'. Examples for AcI-verbs are perception verbs such as *hören* 'to hear' and *sehen* 'to see' as well as *lassen* 'to let'.

       c. das Kommen des   Installateurs
          the coming   of.the plumber
          'the plumber's visit'

In the first example, the subject is in the nominative case, whereas *Installateur* 'plumber' is in accusative in the second example and even in the genitive in the third following nominalization. The accusative case of objects is normally structural case. This case becomes nominative under passivization:

(39)   a. Karl schlägt den   Weltmeister.
         Karl beats   the.ACC world.champion
         'Karl beats the world champion.'
     b. Der   Weltmeister   wird geschlagen.
         the.NOM world.champion is   beaten
         'The world champion is being beaten.'

Unlike the accusative, the genitive governed by a verb is a lexical case. The case of a genitive object does not change when the verb is passivized.

(40)   a. Wir gedenken der   Opfer.
         we remember the.GEN victims
     b. Der   Opfer wird gedacht.
         the.GEN victims are   remembered
         'The victims are being remembered.'

(40b) is an example of the so-called *impersonal passive*. Unlike example (39b), where the accusative object became the subject, there is no subject in (40b). See Section 1.7.1.

Similarly, there is no change in case with dative objects:

(41)   a. Der Mann hat ihm   geholfen.
         the man   has him.DAT helped
         'The man has helped him.'
     b. Ihm   wird geholfen.
         him.DAT is   helped
         'He is being helped.'

It still remains controversial as to whether all datives should be treated as lexical or whether some or all of the datives in verbal environments should be treated as instances of structural case. For reasons of space, I will not recount this discussion but instead refer the interested reader to Chapter 14 of Müller (2007a). In what follows, I assume – like Haider (1986a: 20) – that the dative is in fact a lexical case.

3.4.2 Case assignment and the Case Filter

In GB, it is assumed that the subject receives case from (finite) I and that the case of the remaining arguments comes from V (Chomsky 1981a: 50; Haider 1984: 26; Fanselow & Felix 1987: 71–73).

3.4 Passive

Principle 2 (Case Principle)

- *V assigns objective case (accusative) to its complement if it bears structural case.*

- *When finite, INFL assigns case to the subject.*

The Case Filter rules out structures where case has not been assigned to an NP.
Figure 3.15 shows the Case Principle in action with the example in (42a).[20]

(42) a. [dass] der Mann der   Frau   den   Jungen zeigt
         that the man the.DAT woman the.ACC boy   shows

   'that the man shows the boy to the woman'

   b. [dass] der Junge   der   Frau   gezeigt wird
         that the boy.NOM the.DAT woman shown   is

   'that the boy is shown to the woman'

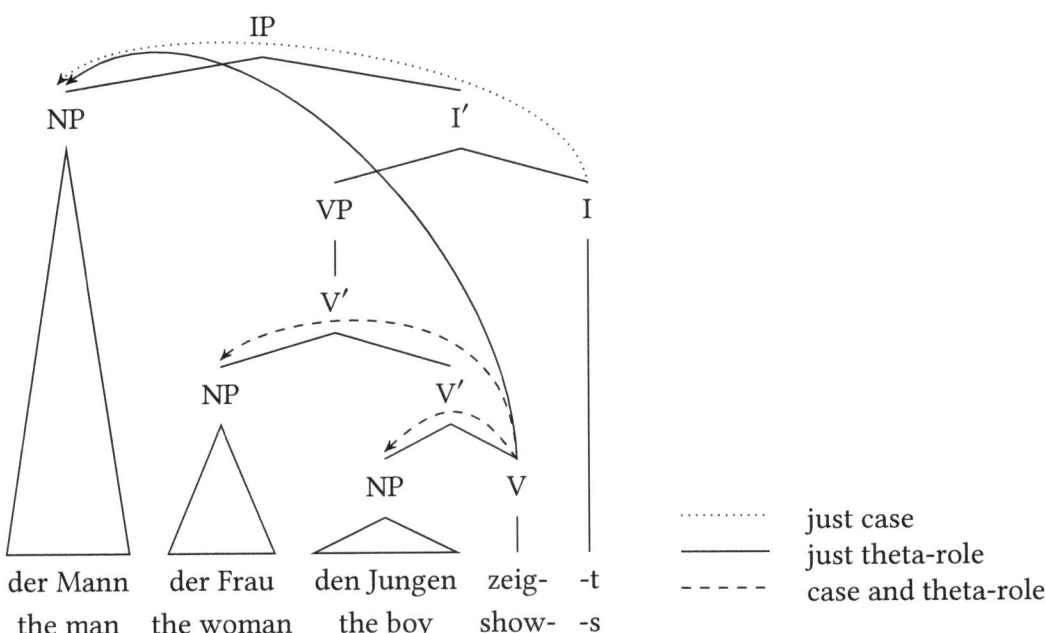

Figure 3.15: Case and theta-role assignment in active clauses

The passive morphology blocks the subject and absorbs the structural accusative. The object that would get accusative in the active receives only a semantic role in its base

---

[20]The figure does not correspond to X̄ theory in its classic form, since *der Frau* 'the woman' is a complement which is combined with V'. In classical X̄ theory, all complements have to be combined with V⁰. This leads to a problem in ditransitive structures since the structures have to be binary (see Larson (1988) for a treatment of double object constructions). Furthermore, in the following figures the verb has been left in V⁰ for reasons of clarity. In order to create a well-formed S-structure, the verb would have to move to its affix in I⁰.

3 Transformational Grammar – Government & Binding

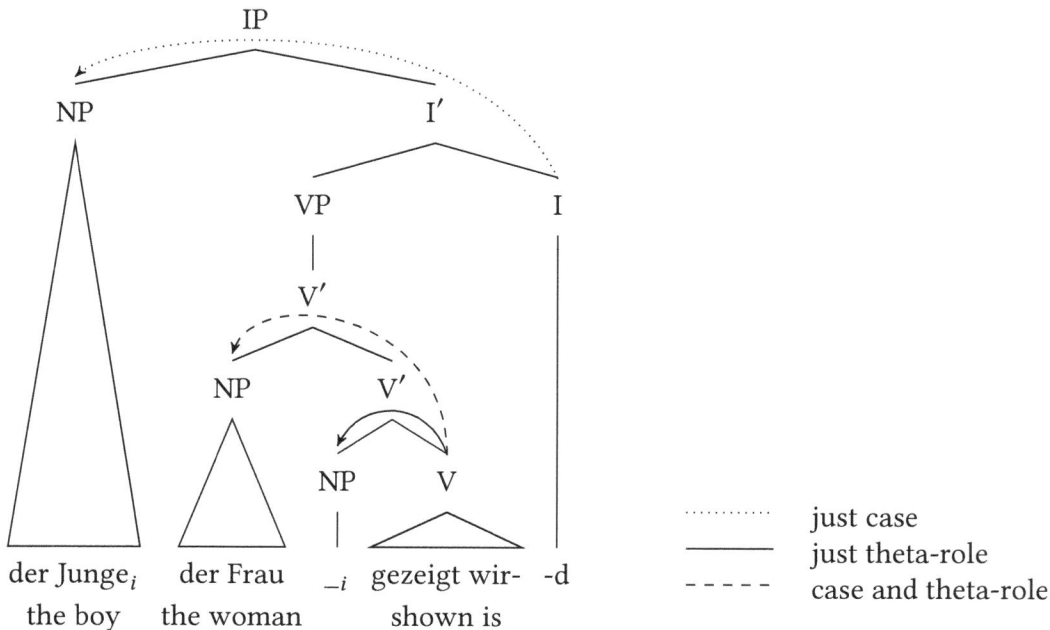

Figure 3.16: Case and theta-role assignment in passive clauses

position in the passive, but it does not get the absorbed case. Therefore, it has to move to a position where case can be assigned to it (Chomsky 1981a: 124). Figure 3.16 shows how this works for example (42b). This movement-based analysis works well for English since the underlying object always has to move:

(43)   a.   The mother gave [the girl] [a cookie].
        b.   [The girl] was given [a cookie] (by the mother).
        c.   * It was given [the girl] [a cookie].

(43c) shows that filling the subject position with an expletive is not possible, so the object really has to move. However, Lenerz (1977: Section 4.4.3) showed that such a movement is not obligatory in German:

(44)   a.   weil   das   Mädchen dem   Jungen den   Ball schenkte
            because the.NOM girl   the.DAT boy   the.ACC ball gave
            'because the girl gave the ball to the boy'
        b.   weil   dem   Jungen der   Ball geschenkt wurde
            because the.DAT boy   the.NOM ball given   was
            'because the ball was given to the boy'
        c.   weil   der   Ball dem   Jungen geschenkt wurde
            because the.NOM ball the.DAT boy   given   was

3.4 Passive

In comparison to (44c), (44b) is the unmarked order. *der Ball* 'the ball' in (44b) occurs in the same position as *den Ball* in (44a), that is, no movement is necessary. Only the case differs. (44c) is, however, somewhat marked in comparison to (44b). So, if one assumed (44c) to be the normal order for passives and (44b) is derived from this by movement of *dem Jungen* 'the boy', (44b) should be more marked than (44c), contrary to the facts. To solve this problem, an analysis involving abstract movement has been proposed for cases such as (44b): the elements stay in their positions, but are connected to the subject position and receive their case information from there. Grewendorf (1993: 1311) assumes that there is an empty expletive pronoun in the subject position of sentences such as (44b) as well as in the subject position of sentences with an impersonal passive such as (45):[21]

(45) weil heute nicht gearbeitet wird
because today not worked is

'because there will be no work done today'

A silent expletive pronoun is something that one cannot see or hear and that does not carry any meaning. For discussion of this kind of empty element, see Section 13.1.3 and Chapter 19.

In the following chapters, I describe alternative treatments of the passive that do without mechanisms such as empty elements that are connected to argument positions and that seek to describe the passive in a more general, cross-linguistically consistent manner as the suppression of the most prominent argument.

A further question which needs to be answered is why the accusative object does not receive case from the verb. This is captured by a constraint, which goes back to Burzio (1986: 178–185) and is therefore referred to as *Burzio's Generalization*.[22]

(46) Burzio's Generalization (modified):

If V does not have an external argument, then it does not assign (structural) accusative case.

---

[21]See Koster (1986: 11–12) for a parallel analysis for Dutch as well as Lohnstein (2014) for a movement-based account of the passive that also involves an empty expletive for the analysis of the impersonal passive.

[22]Burzio's original formulation was equivalent to the following: a verb assigns accusative if and only if it assigns a semantic role to its subject. This claim is problematic from both sides. In (i), the verb does not assign a semantic role to the subject; however there is nevertheless accusative case:

(i) Mich friert.
me.ACC freezes

'I am freezing.'

One therefore has to differentiate between structural and lexical accusative and modify Burzio's Generalization accordingly. The existence of verbs like *begegnen* 'to bump into' is problematic for the other side of the implication. *begegnen* has a subject but still does not assign accusative but rather dative:

(ii) Peter begegnete einem Mann.
Peter met a.DAT man

'Peter met a man.'

See Haider (1999) and Webelhuth (1995: 89) as well as the references cited there for further problems with Burzio's Generalization.

Koster (1986: 12) has pointed out that the passive in English cannot be derived by Case Theory since if one allowed empty expletive subjects for English as well as German and Dutch, then it would be possible to have analyses such as the following in (47) where np is an empty expletive:

(47) np was read the book.

Koster rather assumes that subjects in English are either bound by other elements (that is, non-expletive) or lexically filled, that is, filled by visible material. Therefore, the structure in (47) would be ruled out and it would be ensured that *the book* would have to be placed in front of the finite verb so that the subject position is filled.

3.5 Local reordering

Arguments in the middle field can, in principle, occur in an almost arbitrary order. (48) exemplifies this:

(48) a. [weil]   der Mann der Frau   das Buch gibt
          because the man   the woman the book gives
        'because the man gives the book to the woman'
      b. [weil]   der Mann das Buch der Frau   gibt
          because the man   the book the woman gives
      c. [weil]   das Buch der Mann der Frau   gibt
          because the book the man   the woman gives
      d. [weil]   das Buch der Frau   der Mann gibt
          because the book the woman the man   gives
      e. [weil]   der Frau   der Mann das Buch gibt
          because the woman the man   the book gives
      f. [weil]   der Frau   das Buch der Mann gibt
          because the woman the book the man   gives

In (48b–f), the constituents receive different stress and the number of contexts in which each sentence can be uttered is more restricted than in (48a) (Höhle 1982). The order in (48a) is therefore referred to as the *neutral order* or *unmarked order*.

Two proposals have been made for analyzing these orders: the first suggestion assumes that the five orderings in (48b–f) are derived from a single underlying order by means of Move-α (Frey 1993). As an example, the analysis of (48c) is given in Figure 3.17 on the next page. The object *das Buch* 'the book' is moved to the left and adjoined to the topmost IP.

An argument that has often been used to support this analysis is the fact that scope ambiguities exist in sentences with reorderings which are not present in sentences in the base order. The explanation of such ambiguities comes from the assumption that the scope of quantifiers can be derived from their position in the surface structure as

3.5 Local reordering

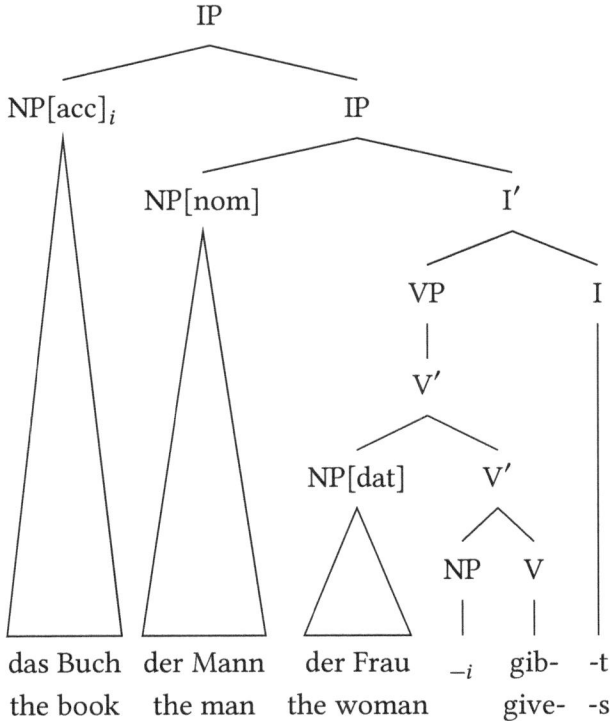

Figure 3.17: Analysis of local reordering as adjunction to IP

well as their position in the deep structure. If the position in both the surface and deep structure are the same, that is, when there has not been any movement, then there is only one reading possible. If movement has taken place, however, then there are two possible readings (Frey 1993: 185):

(49) a. Es ist nicht der Fall, daß er mindestens einem Verleger fast jedes Gedicht
it is not the case that he at.least one publisher almost every poem
anbot.
offered
'It is not the case that he offered at least one publisher almost every poem.'

b. Es ist nicht der Fall, daß er fast jedes Gedicht$_i$ mindestens einem Verleger
it is not the case that he almost every poem at.least one publisher
_$_i$ anbot.
offered
'It is not the case that he offered almost every poem to at least one publisher.'

It turns out that approaches assuming traces run into problems as they predict certain readings for sentences with multiple traces which do not exist (see Kiss 2001: 146 and Fanselow 2001: Section 2.6). For instance in an example such as (50), it should be possible to interpret *mindestens einem Verleger* 'at least one publisher' at the position of _$_i$, which would lead to a reading where *fast jedes Gedicht* 'almost every poem' has scope over *mindestens einem Verleger* 'at least one publisher'. However, this reading does not exist.

(50) Ich glaube, dass mindestens einem Verleger$_i$ fast jedes Gedicht$_j$ nur dieser
I believe that at.least one publisher almost every poem only this
Dichter _$_i$ _$_j$ angeboten hat.
poet offered has

'I think that only this poet offered almost every poem to at least one publisher.'

Sauerland & Elbourne (2002: 308) discuss analogous examples from Japanese, which they credit to Kazuko Yatsushiro. They develop an analysis where the first step is to move the accusative object in front of the subject. Then, the dative object is placed in front of that and then, in a third movement, the accusative is moved once more. The last movement can take place to construct either the S-structure[23] or as a movement to construct the Phonological Form. In the latter case, this movement will not have any semantic effects. While this analysis can predict the correct available readings, it does require a number of additional movement operations with intermediate steps.

The alternative to a movement analysis is so-called *base generation*: the starting structure generated by phrase structure rules is referred to as the *base*. One variant of base generation assumes that the verb is combined with one argument at a time and each θ-role is assigned in the respective head-argument configuration. The order in which arguments are combined with the verb is not specified, which means that all of the orders in (48) can be generated directly without any transformations.[24] Fanselow (2001) suggested such an analysis within the framework of GB.[25] Note that such a base-generation analysis is incompatible with an IP approach that assumes that the subject is realized in the specifier of IP. An IP approach with base-generation of different argument orders would allow the complements to appear in any order within the VP but the subject would be first since it is part of a different phrase. So the orders in (51a,b) could be analyzed, but the ones in (51c–f) could not:

(51) a. dass der Mann der Frau ein Buch gibt
that the.NOM man the.DAT woman a.ACC book gives

b. dass der Mann ein Buch der Frau gibt
that the.NOM man a.ACC book the.DAT woman gives

---

[23]The authors are working in the Minimalist framework. This means there is no longer S-structure strictly speaking. I have simply translated the analysis into the terms used here.

[24]Compare this to the grammar in (6) on page 55. This grammar combines a V and an NP to form a new V. Since nothing is said about the case of the argument in the phrase structure rule, the NPs can be combined with the verb in any order.

[25]The base generation analysis is the natural analysis in the HPSG framework. It has already been developed by Gunji in 1986 for Japanese and will be discussed in more detail in Section 9.4. Sauerland & Elbourne (2002: 313–314) claim that they show that syntax has to be derivational, that is, a sequence of syntactic trees has to be derived. I am of the opinion that this cannot generally be shown to be the case. There is, for example, an analysis by Kiss (2001) which shows that scope phenomena can be explained well by constraint-based approaches.

c. dass der Frau der Mann ein Buch gibt
   that the.DAT woman the.NOM man a.ACC book gives

d. dass der Frau ein Buch der Mann gibt
   that the.DAT woman a.ACC book the.NOM man gives

e. dass ein Buch der Frau der Mann gibt
   that a.ACC book the.DAT woman the.NOM man gives

f. dass ein Buch der Mann der Frau gibt
   that a.ACC book the.NOM man the.DAT woman gives

For the discussion of different approaches to describing constituent position, see Fanselow (1993).

3.6 Summary and classification

Works in GB and some contributions to the Minimalist Program (see Chapter 4) have led to a number of new discoveries in both language-specific and cross-linguistic research. In the following, I will focus on some aspects of German syntax.

The analysis of verb movement developed in Transformational Grammar by Bierwisch (1963: 34), Reis (1974), Koster (1975), Thiersch (1978: Chapter 1) and den Besten (1983) has become the standard analysis in almost all grammar models (possibly with the exception of Construction Grammar and Dependency Grammar).

The work by Lenerz (1977) on constituent order has influenced analyses in other frameworks (the linearization rules in GPSG and HPSG go back to Lenerz' descriptions). Haider's work on constituent order, case and passive (1984; 1985b; 1985a; 1986a; 1990b; 1993) has had a significant influence on LFG and HPSG analyses of German.

The entire configurationality discussion, that is, whether it is better to assume that the subject of finite verbs in German is inside or outside the VP, was important (for instance Haider 1982; Grewendorf 1983; Kratzer 1984; 1996; Webelhuth 1985; Sternefeld 1985b; Scherpenisse 1986; Fanselow 1987; Grewendorf 1988; Dürscheid 1989; Webelhuth 1990; Oppenrieder 1991; Wilder 1991; Haider 1993; Grewendorf 1993; Frey 1993; Lenerz 1994; Meinunger 2000) and German unaccusative verbs received their first detailed discussion in GB circles (Grewendorf 1989; Fanselow 1992a). The works by Fanselow and Frey on constituent order, in particular with regard to information structure, have advanced German syntax quite considerably (Fanselow 1988; 1990; 1993; 2000a; 2001; 2003b,c; 2004a; Frey 2000; 2001; 2004b; 2005). Infinitive constructions, complex predicates and partial fronting have also received detailed and successful treatments in the GB/MP frameworks (Bierwisch 1963; Evers 1975; Haider 1982; 1986b; 1990a; 1991; 1993; Grewendorf 1983; 1987; 1988; den Besten 1985; Sternefeld 1985b; Fanselow 1987; 2002; von Stechow & Sternefeld 1988; Bayer & Kornfilt 1989; G. Müller 1996a; 1998; Vogel & Steinbach 1998). In the area of secondary predication, the work by Winkler (1997) is particularly noteworthy.

This list of works from subdisciplines of grammar is somewhat arbitrary (it corresponds more or less to my own research interests) and is very much focused on German.

There are, of course, a wealth of other articles on other languages and phenomena, which should be recognized without having to be individually listed here.

In the remainder of this section, I will critically discuss two points: the model of language acquisition of the Principles & Parameters framework and the degree of formalization inside Chomskyan linguistics (in particular the last few decades and the consequences this has). Some of these points will be mentioned again in Part II.

3.6.1 Explaining language acquisition

One of the aims of Chomskyan research on grammar is to explain language acquisition. In GB, one assumed a very simple set of rules, which was the same for all languages ($\overline{X}$ theory), as well as general principles that hold for all languages, but which could be parametrized for individual languages or language classes. It was assumed that a parameter was relevant for multiple phenomena. The Principles & Parameters model was particularly fruitful and led to a number of interesting studies in which commonalities and differences between languages were uncovered. From the point of view of language acquisition, the idea of a parameter which is set according to the input has often been cricitized as it cannot be reconciled with observable facts: after setting a parameter, a learner should have immediately mastered certain aspects of that language. Chomsky (1986b: 146) uses the metaphor of switches which can be flipped one way or the other. As it is assumed that various areas of grammar are affected by parameters, setting one parameter should have a significant effect on the rest of the grammar of a given learner. However, the linguistic behavior of children does not change in an abrupt fashion as would be expected (Bloom 1993: 731; Haider 1993: 6; Abney 1996: 3; Ackerman & Webelhuth 1998: Section 9.1; Tomasello 2000; 2003). Furthermore, it has not been possible to prove that there is a correlation between a certain parameter and various grammatical phenomena. For more on this, see Chapter 16.

The Principles & Parameters model nevertheless remains interesting for cross-linguistic research. Every theory has to explain why the verb precedes its objects in English and follows them in Japanese. One can name this difference a parameter and then classify languages accordingly, but whether this is actually relevant for language acquisition is being increasingly called in question.

3.6.2 Formalization

In his 1963 work on Transformational Grammar, Bierwisch writes the following:[26]

> It is very possible that the rules that we formulated generate sentences which are outside of the set of grammatical sentences in an unpredictable way, that is, they

---

[26] Es ist also sehr wohl möglich, daß mit den formulierten Regeln Sätze erzeugt werden können, die auch in einer nicht vorausgesehenen Weise aus der Menge der grammatisch richtigen Sätze herausfallen, die also durch Eigenschaften gegen die Grammatikalität verstoßen, die wir nicht wissentlich aus der Untersuchung ausgeschlossen haben. Das ist der Sinn der Feststellung, daß eine Grammatik eine Hypothese über die Struktur einer Sprache ist. Eine systematische Überprüfung der Implikationen einer für natürliche Sprachen angemessenen Grammatik ist sicherlich eine mit Hand nicht mehr zu bewältigende Aufgabe. Sie könnte vorgenommen werden, indem die Grammatik als Rechenprogramm in einem Elektronenrechner realisiert wird, so daß überprüft werden kann, in welchem Maße das Resultat von der zu beschreibenden Sprache abweicht.

> violate grammaticality due to properties that we did not deliberately exclude in
> our examination. This is meant by the statement that a grammar is a hypothesis
> about the structure of a language. A systematic check of the implications of a
> grammar that is appropriate for natural languages is surely a task that cannot be
> done by hand any more. This task could be solved by implementing the grammar
> as a calculating task on a computer so that it becomes possible to verify to which
> degree the result deviates from the language to be described. (Bierwisch 1963: 163)

Bierwisch's claim is even more valid in light of the empirical progress made in the last decades. For example, Ross (1967) identified restrictions for movement and long-distance dependencies and Perlmutter (1978) discovered unaccusative verbs in the 70s. For German, see Grewendorf (1989) and Fanselow (1992a). Apart from analyses of these phenomena, restrictions on possible constituent positions have been developed (Lenerz 1977), as well as analyses of case assignment (Yip, Maling & Jackendoff 1987; Meurers 1999c; Przepiórkowski 1999b) and theories of verbal complexes and the fronting of parts of phrases (Evers 1975; Grewendorf 1988; Hinrichs & Nakazawa 1994; Kiss 1995; G. Müller 1998; Meurers 1999b; Müller 1999b; 2002a; De Kuthy 2002). All these phenomena interact!

Consider another quote:

> A goal of earlier linguistic work, and one that is still a central goal of the linguistic
> work that goes on in computational linguistics, is to develop grammars that assign
> a reasonable syntactic structure to every sentence of English, or as nearly every
> sentence as possible. This is not a goal that is currently much in fashion in theoretical linguistics. Especially in Government-Binding theory (GB), the development
> of large fragments has long since been abandoned in favor of the pursuit of deep
> principles of grammar. The scope of the problem of identifying the correct parse
> cannot be appreciated by examining behavior on small fragments, however deeply
> analyzed. Large fragments are not just small fragments several times over – there
> is a qualitative change when one begins studying large fragments. As the range of
> constructions that the grammar accommodates increases, the number of undesired
> parses for sentences increases dramatically. (Abney 1996: 20)

So, as Bierwisch and Abney point out, developing a sound theory of a large fragment of a human language is a really demanding task. But what we aim for as theoretical linguists is much more: the aim is to formulate restrictions which ideally hold for all languages or at least for certain language classes. It follows from this, that one has to have an overview of the interaction of various phenomena in not just one but several languages. This task is so complex that individual researchers cannot manage it. This is the point at which computer implementations become helpful as they immediately flag inconsistencies in a theory. After removing these inconsistencies, computer implementations can be used to systematically analyze test data or corpora and thereby check the empirical adequacy of the theory (Müller, 1999b: Chapter 22; 2015b; 2014d; Oepen & Flickinger 1998; Bender 2008b, see Section 1.2).

More than 60 years after the first important published work by Chomsky, it is apparent that there has not been one large-scale implemented grammatical fragment on the basis of Transformational Grammar analyses. Chomsky has certainly contributed to the formalization of linguistics and developed important formal foundations which are still relevant in the theory of formal languages in computer science and in theoretical computational linguistics (Chomsky 1959). However, in 1981, he had already turned his back on rigid formalization:

> I think that we are, in fact, beginning to approach a grasp of certain basic principles of grammar at what may be the appropriate level of abstraction. At the same time, it is necessary to investigate them and determine their empirical adequacy by developing quite specific mechanisms. We should, then, try to distinguish as clearly as we can between discussion that bears on leading ideas and discussion that bears on the choice of specific realizations of them. (Chomsky 1981a: 2–3)

This is made explicit in a letter to *Natural Language and Linguistic Theory*:

> Even in mathematics, the concept of formalization in our sense was not developed until a century ago, when it became important for advancing research and understanding. I know of no reason to suppose that linguistics is so much more advanced than 19th century mathematics or contemporary molecular biology that pursuit of Pullum's injunction would be helpful, but if that can be shown, fine. For the present, there is lively interchange and exciting progress without any sign, to my knowledge, of problems related to the level of formality of ongoing work. (Chomsky 1990: 146)

This departure from rigid formalization has led to there being a large number of publications inside Mainstream Generative Grammar with sometimes incompatible assumptions to the point where it is no longer clear how one can combine the insights of the various publications. An example of this is the fact that the central notion of government has several different definitions (see Aoun & Sportiche 1983 for an overview[27]).

This situation has been cricitized repeatedly since the 80s and sometimes very harshly by proponents of GPSG (Gazdar, Klein, Pullum & Sag 1985: 6; Pullum 1985; 1989a; Pullum 1991: 48; Kornai & Pullum 1990).

The lack of precision and working out of the details[28] and the frequent modification of basic assumptions[29] has led to insights gained by Mainstream Generative Grammar rarely being translated into computer implementations. There are some implementations that are based on Transformational Grammar/GB/MP models or borrow ideas from Mainstream Generative Grammar (Petrick 1965; Zwicky, Friedman, Hall & Walker 1965; Kay 1967; Friedman 1969; Friedman, Bredt, Doran, Pollack & Martner 1971; Plath 1973; Morin 1973; Marcus 1980; Abney & Cole 1986; Kuhns 1986; Correa 1987; Stabler 1987; 1992; 2001; Kolb & Thiersch 1991; Fong 1991; Crocker & Lewin 1992; Lohnstein 1993; Lin 1993; Fordham & Crocker 1994; Nordgård 1994; Veenstra 1998; Fong & Ginsburg 2012),[30] but these

---

[27] A further definition can be found in Aoun & Lightfoot (1984). This is, however, equivalent to an earlier version as shown by Postal & Pullum (1986: 104–106).

[28] See e.g., Kuhns (1986: 550), Crocker & Lewin (1992: 508), Kolb & Thiersch (1991: 262), Kolb (1997: 3) and Freidin (1997: 580), Veenstra (1998: 25, 47), Lappin et al. (2000a: 888) and Stabler (2011a: 397, 399, 400) for the latter.

[29] See e.g., Kolb (1997: 4), Fanselow (2009) and the quote from Stabler on page 177.

[30] See Fordham & Crocker (1994) for a combination of a GB approach with statistical methods.

3.6 Summary and classification

implementations often do not use transformations or differ greatly from the theoretical assumptions of the publications. For example, Marcus (1980: 102–104) and Stabler (1987: 5) use special purpose rules for auxiliary inversion.[31] These rules reverse the order of *John* and *has* for the analysis of sentences such as (52a) so that we get the order in (52b), which is then parsed with the rules for non-inverted structures.

(52) a. Has John scheduled the meeting for Wednesday?
     b. John has scheduled the meeting for Wednesday?

These rules for auxiliary inversion are very specific and explicitly reference the category of the auxiliary. This does not correspond to the analyses proposed in GB in any way. As we have seen in Section 3.1.5, there are no special transformational rules for auxiliary inversion. Auxiliary inversion is carried out by the more general transformation Move-α and the associated restrictive principles. It is not unproblematic that the explicit formulation of the rule refers to the category *auxiliary* as is clear when one views Stabler's GB-inspired phrase structure grammar:

(53) a. s → switch(aux_verb,np), vp.
     b. s([First|L0],L,X0,X) :- aux_verb(First),
        np(L0,L1,X0,X1),
        vp([First|L1],L,X1,X).

The rule in (53a) is translated into the Prolog predicate in (53b). The expression [First|L0] after the s corresponds to the string, which is to be processed. The '|'-operator divides the list into a beginning and a rest. *First* is the first word to be processed and L0 contains all other words. In the analysis of (52a), First is *has* and L0 is *John scheduled the meeting for Wednesday*. In the Prolog clause, it is then checked whether First is an auxiliary (aux_verb(First)) and if this is the case, then it will be tried to prove that the list L0 begins with a noun phrase. Since *John* is an NP, this is successful. L1 is the sublist of L0 which remains after the analysis of L0, that is *scheduled the meeting for Wednesday*. This list is then combined with the auxiliary (First) and now it will be checked whether the resulting list *has scheduled the meeting for Wednesday* begins with a VP. This is the case and the remaining list L is empty. As a result, the sentence has been successfully processed.

The problem with this analysis is that exactly one word is checked in the lexicon. Sentences such as (54) can not be analyzed:[32]

(54) Could or should we pool our capital with that of other co-ops to address the needs of a regional "neighborhood"?[33]

---

[31]Nozohoor-Farshi (1986; 1987) has shown that Marcus' parser can only parse context-free languages. Since natural languages are of a greater complexity (see Chapter 17) and grammars of corresponding complexity are allowed by current versions of Transformational Grammar, Marcus' parser can be neither an adequate implementation of the Chomskyan theory in question nor a piece of software for analyzing natural language in general.

[32]For a discussion that shows that the coordination of lexical elements has to be an option in linguistic theories, see Abeillé (2006).

[33]http://www.cooperativegrocer.coop/articles/index.php?id=595. 2010-03-28.

In this kind of sentence, two modal verbs have been coordinated. They then form an X^0 and – following GB analyses – can be moved together. If one wanted to treat these cases as Stabler does for the simplest case, then we would need to divide the list of words to be processed into two unlimited sub-lists and check whether the first list contains an auxiliary or several coordinated auxiliaries. We would require a recursive predicate aux_verbs which somehow checks whether the sequence *could or should* is a well-formed sequence of auxiliaries. This should not be done by a special predicate but rather by syntactic rules responsible for the coordination of auxiliaries. The alternative to a rule such as (53a) would be the one in (55), which is the one that is used in theories like GPSG (Gazdar et al. 1985: 62), LFG (Falk 1984: 491), some HPSG analyses (Ginzburg & Sag 2000: 36), and Construction Grammar (Fillmore 1999):

(55) s → v(aux+), np, vp.

This rule would have no problems with coordination data like (54) as coordination of multiple auxiliaries would produce an object with the category v(aux+) (for more on coordination see Section 21.6.2). If inversion makes it necessary to stipulate a special rule like (53a), then it is not clear why one could not simply use the transformation-less rule in (55).

In the MITRE system (Zwicky et al. 1965), there was a special grammar for the surface structure, from which the deep structure was derived via reverse application of transformations, that is, instead of using one grammar to create deep structures which are then transformed into other structures, one required two grammars. The deep structures that were determined by the parser were used as input to a transformational component since this was the only way to ensure that the surface structures can actually be derived from the base structure (Kay 2011: 10).

The REQUEST system by Plath (1973) also used a surface grammar and inverse transformations to arrive at the deep structure, which was used for semantic interpretation.

There are other implementations discussed in this chapter that differ from transformation-based analyses. For example, Kolb & Thiersch (1991: 265, Section 4) arrive at the conclusion that a declarative, constraint-based approach to GB is more appropriate than a derivational one. Johnson (1989) suggests a *Parsing as Deduction* approach which reformulates sub-theories of GB ($\overline{X}$ theory, Theta-Theory, Case Theory, …) as logical expressions.[34] These can be used independently of each other in a logical proof. In Johnson's analysis, GB theory is understood as a constraint-based system. More general restrictions are extracted from the restrictions on S- and D-structure which can then be used directly for parsing. This means that transformations are not directly carried out by the parser. As noted by Johnson, the language fragment he models is very small. It contains no description of *wh*-movement, for example (p. 114).

Lin (1993) implemented the parser PrinciParse. It is written in C++ and based on GB and Barriers – the theoretical stage after GB (see Chomsky 1986a). The system contains constraints like the Case Filter, the Theta-Criterion, Subjacency, the Empty Category

---

[34]See Crocker & Lewin (1992: 511) and Fordham & Crocker (1994: 38) for another constraint-based Parsing-as-Deduction approach.

Principle and so on. The Theta-Criterion is implemented with binary features +/-theta, there is no implementation of Logical Form (p. 119). The system organizes the grammar in a network that makes use of the object-oriented organization of C++ programs, that is, default-inheritance is used to represent constraints in super and subclasses (Lin 1993: Section 5). This concept of inheritance is alien to GB theory: it does not play any role in the main publications. The grammar networks license structures corresponding to $\overline{\text{X}}$ theory, but they code the possible relations directly in the network. The network contains categories like IP, Ibar, I, CP, Cbar, C, VP, Vbar, V, PP, PSpec, Pbar, P and so on. This corresponds to simple phrase structure grammars that fully specify the categories in the rules (see Section 2.2) rather than working with abstract schemata like the ones assumed in $\overline{\text{X}}$ theory (see Section 2.5). Furthermore Lin does not assume transformations but uses a GPSG-like feature passing approach to nonlocal dependencies (p. 116, see Section 5.4 on the GPSG approach).

Probably the most detailed implementation in the tradition of GB and Barriers is Stabler's Prolog implementation (1992). Stabler's achievement is certainly impressive, but his book confirms what has been claimed thus far: Stabler has to simply stipulate many things which are not explicitly mentioned in *Barriers* (e.g., using feature-value pairs when formalizing $\overline{\text{X}}$ theory, a practice that was borrowed from GPSG) and some assumptions cannot be properly formalized and are simply ignored (see Briscoe 1997 for details).

GB analyses which fulfill certain requirements can be reformulated so that they no longer make use of transformations. These transformation-less approaches are also called *representational*, whereas the transformation-based approaches are referred to as *derivational*. For representational analyses, there are only surface structures augmented by traces but none of these structures is connected to an underlying structure by means of transformations (see e.g., Koster 1978: 1987: 235; Kolb & Thiersch 1991; Haider 1993: Section 1.4; Frey 1993: 14; Lohnstein 1993: 87–88, 177–178; Fordham & Crocker 1994: 38; Veenstra 1998: 58). These analyses can be implemented in the same way as corresponding HPSG analyses (see Chapter 9) as computer-processable fragments and this has in fact been carried out for example for the analysis of verb position in German.[35] However, such implemented analyses differ from GB analyses with regard to their basic architecture and in small, but important details such as how one deals with the interaction of long-distance dependencies and coordination (Gazdar 1981b). For a critical discussion and classification of movement analyses in Transformational Grammar, see Borsley (2012).

Following this somewhat critical overview, I want to add a comment in order to avoid being misunderstood: I do not demand that all linguistic work shall be completely formalized. There is simply no space for this in a, say, thirty page essay. Furthermore, I do not believe that all linguists should carry out formal work and implement their analyses as computational models. However, there has to be *somebody* who works out the formal

---

[35]This shows that ten Hacken's contrasting of HPSG with GB and LFG (ten Hacken 2007: Section 4.3) and the classification of these frameworks as belonging to different research paradigms is completely mistaken. In his classification, ten Hacken refers mainly to the model-theoretic approach that HPSG assumes. However, LFG also has a model-theoretic formalization (Kaplan 1995). Furthermore, there is also a model-theoretic variant of GB (Rogers 1998). For further discussion, see Chapter 14.

details and these basic theoretical assumptions should be accepted and adopted for a sufficient amount of time by the research community in question.

Comprehension questions

1. Give some examples of functional and lexical categories.

2. How can one represent lexical categories with binary features and what advantages does this have?

Exercises

1. Draw syntactic trees for the following examples:

    (56) a. dass die Frau den Mann liebt
    that the.NOM woman the.ACC man loves
    'that the woman loves the man'
    b. dass der Mann geliebt wird
    that the.NOM man loved is
    'that the man is loved'
    c. Der Mann wird geliebt.
    the.NOM man is loved
    'The man is loved.'
    d. dass der Mann der Frau hilft
    that the.NOM man the.DAT woman helps
    'that the man helps the woman'
    e. Der Mann hilft der Frau.
    the man.NOM helps the.DAT woman
    'The man is helping the woman.'

    For the passive sentences, use the analysis where the subject noun phrase is moved from the object position, that is, the analysis without an empty expletive as the subject.

Further reading

For Sections 3.1–3.5, I used material from Peter Gallmann from 2003 (Gallmann 2003). This has been modified, however, at various points. I am solely responsible for any mistakes or inadequacies. For current materials by Peter Gallmann, see http://www.syntax-theorie.de.

In the book *Syntaktische Analyseperspektiven*, Lohnstein (2014) presents a variant of GB which more or less corresponds to what is discussed in this chapter (CP/IP, movement-based analysis of the passive). The chapters in said book have been written by proponents of various theories and all analyze the same newspaper article. This book is extremely interesting for all those who wish to compare the various theories out there.

Haegeman (1994) is a comprehensive introduction to GB. Those who do read German may consider the textbooks by Fanselow & Felix (1987), von Stechow & Sternefeld (1988) and Grewendorf (1988) since they are also addressing the phenomena that are covered in this book.

In many of his publications, Chomsky discusses alternative, transformationless approaches as "notational variants". This is not appropriate, as analyses without transformations can make different predictions to transformation-based approaches (e.g., with respect to coordination and extraction. See Section 5.5 for a discussion of GPSG in this respect). In Gazdar (1981a), one can find a comparison of GB and GPSG as well as a discussion of the classification of GPSG as a notational variant of Transformational Grammar with contributions from Noam Chomsky, Gerald Gazdar and Henry Thompson.

Borsley (1999b) and Kim & Sells (2008) have parallel textbooks for GB and HPSG in English. For the comparison of Transformational Grammar and LFG, see Bresnan & Kaplan (1982). Kuhn (2007) offers a comparison of modern derivational analyses with constraint-based LFG and HPSG approaches. Borsley (2012) contrasts analyses of long-distance dependencies in HPSG with movement-based analyses as in GB/Minimalism. Borsley discusses four types of data which are problematic for movement-based approaches: extraction without fillers, extraction with multiple gaps (see also the discussion of (57) on p. 171 and of (55) on p. 199 of this book), extractions where fillers and gaps do not match and extraction without gaps.

4 Transformational Grammar – Minimalism

Like the Government & Binding framework that was introduced in the previous chapter, the Minimalist framework was initiated by Noam Chomsky at the MIT in Boston. Chomsky (1993; 1995b) argued that the problem of language evolution should be taken seriously and that the question of how linguistic knowledge could become part of our genetic endowment should be answered. To that end he suggested refocusing the theoretical developments towards models that have to make minimal assumptions regarding the machinery that is needed for linguistic analyses and hence towards models that assume less language specific innate knowledge.

Like GB, Minimalism is wide-spread: theoreticians all over the world are working in this framework, so the following list of researchers and institutions is necessarily incomplete. *Linguistic Inquiry* and *Syntax* are journals that almost exclusively publish Minimalist work and the reader is referred to these journals to get an idea about who is active in this framework. The most prominent researchers in Germany are Artemis Alexiadou, Humboldt University Berlin; Günther Grewendorf (2002), Frankfurt am Main; Joseph Bayer, Konstanz; and Gereon Müller, Leipzig.

While innovations like $\overline{\text{X}}$ theory and the analysis of clause structure in GB are highly influential and can be found in most of the other theories that are discussed in this book, this is less so for the technical work done in the Minimalist framework. It is nevertheless useful to familiarize with the technicalities since Minimalism is a framework in which a lot of work is done and understanding the basic machinery makes it possible to read empirically interesting work in that framework.

While the GB literature of the 1980s and 1990s shared a lot of assumptions, there was an explosion of various approaches in the Minimalist framework that is difficult to keep track of. The presentation that follows is based on David Adger's textbook (Adger 2003).

4.1 General remarks on the representational format

The theories that are developed in the framework of the Minimalist Program build on the work done in the GB framework. So a lot of things that were explained in the previous chapter can be taken over to this chapter. However, there have been some changes in fundamental assumptions. The general parametrized principles were dropped from the theory and instead the relevant distinctions live in features. Languages differ in the values that certain features may have and in addition to this, features may be strong or weak and feature strength is also a property that may vary from language to language.

Strong features make syntactic objects move to higher positions. The reader is familiar with this feature-driven movement already since it was a component of the movement-based analysis of the passive in Section 3.4. In the GB analysis of passive, the object had to move to the specifier position of IP in order to receive case. Such movements that are due to missing feature values are a key component in Minimalist proposals.

4.1.1 Basic architecture

Chomsky assumes that there are just two operations (rules) for combining linguistic objects: External and Internal Merge. External Merge simply combines two elements like *the* and *book* and results in a complex phrase. Internal Merge is used to account for movement of constituents. It applies to one linguistic object and takes some part of this linguistic object and adjoins it to the left of the respective object. The application of External Merge and Internal Merge can apply in any order. For instance, two objects can be combined with External Merge and then one of the combined items is moved to the left by applying Internal Merge. The resulting object can be externally merged with another object and so on. As an example consider the Determiner Phrase (DP) in (1):[1]

(1) the man who we know

To derive this DP the verb *know* is externally merged with its object *who*. After several intermediate merges that will be discussed below, *know who* will be merged with *we* and finally the *who* is moved to the left by Internal Merge, resulting in *who we know*. This relative clause can be externally merged with *man* and so on.

So, Minimalist theories differ from GB in not assuming a Deep Structure that is generated by some $\overline{\text{X}}$ grammar and a Surface Structure that is derived from the Deep Structure by Move-α. Instead, it is assumed that there is a phase in which External and Internal Merge (combination and movement) apply in any order to derive a certain structure that is then said to be spelled out. It is said that the structure is sent to the interfaces: the articulatory-perceptual system (AP) on the one hand and the conceptual-intentional system (CI) on the other side. AP corresponds to the level of Phonological Form (PF) and CI to the level of Logical Form (LF) in GB. The new architecture is depicted in Figure 4.1 on the facing page (left figure). Syntax is assumed to operate on so-called numerations, selections of lexical items that are relevant for a derivation.[2] *Overt syntax* stands for syntactic operations that usually have a visible effect. After overt syntax the syntactic object is sent off to the interfaces and some transformations may take place after this Spell-Out point. Since such transformations do not affect pronunciation, this part of

---

[1] Most researchers working in Minimalism follow Abney (1987) in assuming that the determiner rather than the noun is the head of nominal structures. Hence sequence like (1) are determiner phrases rather than noun phrases.

[2] It is unclear to me how numerations are determined. Since empty elements play a crucial role in the analysis of sentences in Minimalism and since it is not known which empty elements are needed in an actual analysis until the analysis is carried out, there will be infinitely many numerations that potentially could be used in the analysis of a given string. Which numeration is chosen and how numerations could be integrated in psycholinguistically plausible models of human sentence comprehension is unclear to me. Numerations will be ignored in what follows and it will be assumed that lexical items come from the lexicon directly. See Hornstein et al. (2005: Section 2.3.2.6) for more on numerations.

4.1 General remarks on the representational format

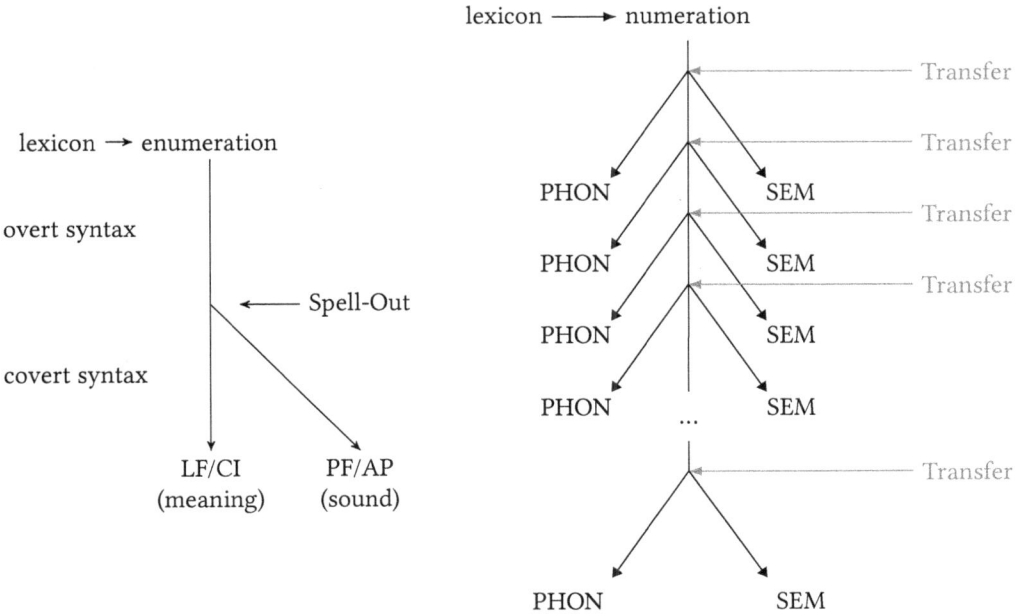

Figure 4.1: Architecture assumed in Minimalist theories before the Phase model (left) and in the Phase model (right) according to Richards (2015: 812, 830)

syntax is called *covert syntax*. Like in GB's LF, the covert syntax can be used to derive certain scope readings.

This architecture was later modified to allow Spell-Out at several points in the derivation (right figure). It is now assumed that there are *phases* in a derivation and that a completed phase is spelled out once it is used in a combination with a head (Chomsky 2008). For instance, a subordinated sentence like *that Peter comes* in (2) is one phase and is sent to the interfaces before the whole sentence is completed.[3]

(2) He believes that Peter comes.

There are different proposals as to what categories form complete phases. Since the concept of phases is not important for the following introduction, I will ignore this concept in the following. See Section 15.1 on the psycholinguistic plausibility of phases in particular and the Minimalist architecture in general.

4.1.2 Valence, feature checking, and agreement

The basic mechanism in Minimalist theories is feature checking. For instance, the noun *letters* may have a P feature, which means that it has to combine with a PP in order to form a complete phrase.

---
[3]Andreas Pankau (p. c. 2015) pointed out to me that there is a fundamental problem with such a conception of phases, since if it is the case that only elements that are in a relation to a head are send off to the interface then the topmost phrase in a derivation would never be sent to the interfaces, since it does not depend on any head.

(3) letters to him

It is assumed that there are interpretable and uninterpretable features. An example of an interpretable feature is the number feature of nouns. The singular/plural distinction is semantically relevant. The category features for part of speech information are purely syntactic and hence cannot be interpreted semantically. Minimalism assumes that all uninterpretable features have to be used up during the derivation of a complex linguistic object. This process of eating up the features is called *checking*. As an example, let us consider the noun *letters* again. The analysis of (3) is depicted in Figure 4.2. The fact

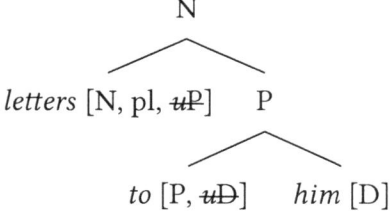

Figure 4.2: Valence representation via uninterpretable features

that the P feature of *letters* is uninterpretable is represented by the little *u* in front of the P. The uninterpretable P feature of *letters* can be checked against the P feature of *to him*. *him* is assumed to be of category D since it can appear in the same places as full nominal phrases, which are assumed to be DPs here. All checked features are said to delete automatically. The deletion is marked by striking the features out in the figures. Strings like (4) are ruled out as complete derivations since the D feature of P is not checked. This situation is shown in Figure 4.3.

(4) * letters to

Figure 4.3: Illegitimate syntactic object due to an uninterpretable feature

If this structure would be used in a larger structure that is spelled out, the derivation would *crash* since the conceptual system could not make sense of the D feature that is still present at the P node.

Selectional features are atomic, that is, the preposition cannot select an DP[*acc*] as in GB and the other theories in this book unless DP[*acc*] is assumed to be atomic. Therefore, an additional mechanism is assumed that can check other features in addition to selectional features. This mechanism is called *Agree*.

4.1 General remarks on the representational format

(5) a. * letters to he
    b. letters to him

The analysis of (5b) is shown in Figure 4.4. There is an interesting difference between the

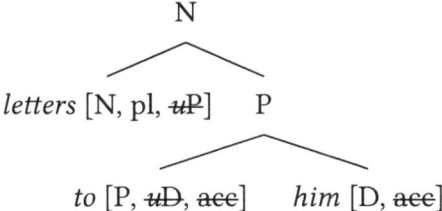

Figure 4.4: Feature checking via Agree

checking of selectional features and the checking of features via Agree. The features that are checked via Agree do not have to be at the top node of the object that is combined with a head. This will play a role later in the analysis of the passive and local reordering.

4.1.3 Phrase structure and $\overline{\text{X}}$ theory

The projections of $\overline{\text{X}}$ structures were given in Figure 2.9 on page 76. According to early versions of the $\overline{\text{X}}$ theory, there could be arbitrarily many complements that were combined with X^0 to form an $\overline{\text{X}}$. Arbitrarily many adjuncts could attach to $\overline{\text{X}}$ and then at most one specifier could be combined with the $\overline{\text{X}}$ yielding an XP. Minimalist theories assume binary branching and hence there is at most one complement, which is the first-merged item. Furthermore, it is not assumed that there is a unique specifier position. Chomsky rather assumes that all items that are not complements are specifiers. That is, he distinguishes between first-merged (complements) and later-merged items (specifiers). Figure 4.5 shows an example with two specifiers. It is also possible to have just a complement and no specifier or to have one or three specifiers. What structures are

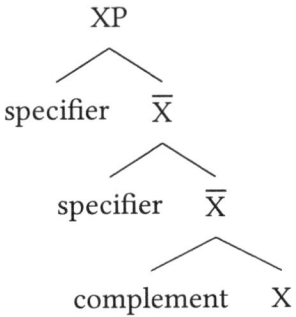

Figure 4.5: Complements and specifiers in Minimalist theories

ultimately licensed depends on the features of the items that are involved in the Merge operations. Whether a phrasal projection counts as an $\overline{X}$ or an XP depends on whether the phrase is used as a complement or specifier of another head or whether it is used as head in further Merge operations. If a phrase is used as specifier or complement its status is fixed to be a phrase (XP), otherwise the projectional status of resulting phrases is left underspecified. Lexical head daughters in Merge operations have the category X and complex head daughters in Merge operations have the category $\overline{X}$. This solves the problem that standard $\overline{X}$ theoretic approaches had with pronouns and proper names: a lot of unary branching structure had to be assumed (See left picture in Figure 2.9). This is not necessary any longer in current Minimalist theories.[4]

4.1.4 Little *v*

In Section 3.4, I used $\overline{X}$ structures in which a ditransitive verb was combined with its accusative object to form a $\overline{V}$, which was then combined with the dative object to form a further $\overline{V}$. Such binary branching structures and also flat structures in which both objects are combined with the verb to form a $\overline{V}$ are rejected by many practitioners of GB and Minimalism since the branching does not correspond to branchings that would be desired for phenomena like the binding of reflexives and negative polarity items. A binding in which *Benjamin* binds *himself* in (6a) is impossible:

(6) a. * Emily showed himself Benjamin in the mirror.
 b. Peter showed himself Benjamin in the mirror.

What is required for the analysis of Binding and NPI phenomena in theories that analyze these phenomena in terms of tree configurations is that the reflexive pronoun is "higher" in the tree than the proper name *Benjamin*. More precisely, the reflexive pronoun *himself* has to c-command *Benjamin*. c-command is defined as follows (Adger 2003: 117):[5]

(7) A node A c-commands B if, and only if A's sister either:
 a. is B, or
 b. contains B

In the trees to the left and in the middle of Figure 4.6 on the next page the c-command relations are not as desired: in the left-most tree both DPs c-command each other and in the middle one *Benjamin* c-commands *himself* rather than the other way round. Hence it is assumed that the structures at the left and in the middle are inappropriate and that there is some additional structure involving the category *v*, which is called *little v* (Adger 2003: Section 4.4). The sister of *himself* is $\overline{V}$ and $\overline{V}$ contains *Benjamin*, hence *himself* c-commands *Benjamin*. Since the sister of *Benjamin* is V and V neither is nor contains *himself*, *Benjamin* does not c-command *himself*.

---

[4]For problems with this approach see Brosziewski (2003: Section 2.1).
[5]c-command also plays a prominent role in GB. In fact, one part of Government & Binding is the Binding Theory, which was not discussed in the previous chapter since binding phenomena do not play a role in this book.

4.1 General remarks on the representational format

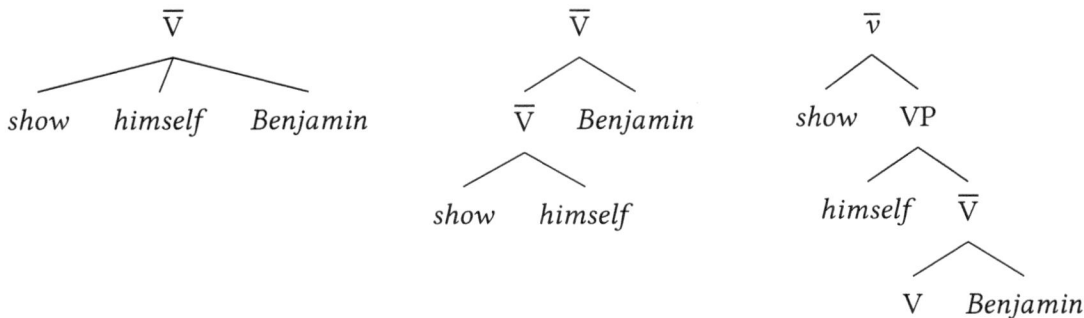

Figure 4.6: Three possible analyses of ditransitives

The analysis of ditransitives involving an additional verbal head goes back to Larson (1988). Hale & Keyser (1993: 70) assume that this verbal head contributes a causative semantics. The structure in Figure 4.7 is derived by assuming that the verb *show* starts out in the V position and then moves to the *v* position. *show* is assumed to mean *see* and in the position of little *v* it picks up the causative meaning, which results in a *cause-see'* meaning (Adger 2003: 133).

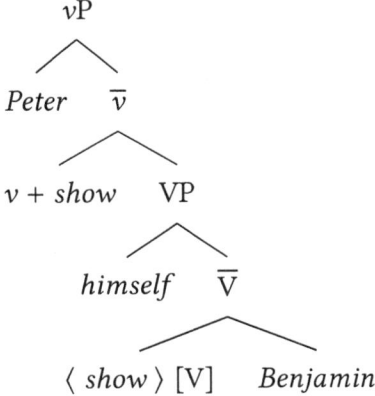

Figure 4.7: Analysis of ditransitives involving movement to little *v*

While the verb shell analysis with an empty verbal head was originally invented by Larson (1988) for the analysis of ditransitive verbs, it is now also used for the analysis of strictly transitive and even intransitive verbs.

Adger (2003: Section 4.5) argues that semantic roles are assigned uniformly in certain tree configurations:

(8)   a. DP daughter of *v*P → interpreted as agent
        b. DP daughter of VP → interpreted as theme
        c. PP daughter of $\bar{v}$ → interpreted as goal

4 Transformational Grammar – Minimalism

Adger assumes that such uniformly assigned semantic roles help in the process of language acquisition and from this, it follows that little *v* should also play a role in the analysis of examples with strictly transitive and intransitive verbs. The Figures 4.8 and 4.9 show the analysis of sentences containing the verbs *burn* and *laugh*, respectively.[6]

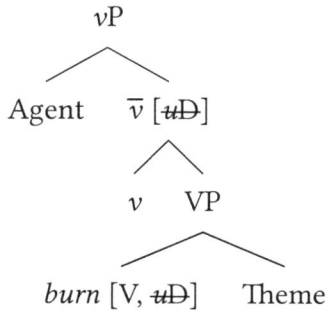

Figure 4.8: Analysis of strictly transitives involving little *v*

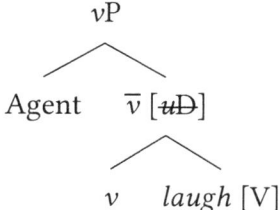

Figure 4.9: Analysis of intransitives involving little *v*

Adger (2003: 164) assumes that intransitive and transitive verbs move from V to little *v* as well. This will be reflected in the following figures.

4.1.5 CP, TP, *v*P, VP

Section 3.1.5 dealt with the CP/IP system in GB. In the course of the development of Minimalism, the Inflectional Phrase was split into several functional projections (Chomsky 1989) of which only the Tense Phrase is assumed in current Minimalist analyses. So, the TP of Minimalism corresponds to IP in the GB analysis. Apart from this change, the core ideas of the CP/IP analysis have been transferred to the Minimalist analysis of English. This subsection will first discuss special features that are assumed to trigger movement (Subsection 4.1.5.1) and then case assignment (Subsection 4.1.5.2).

---

[6]If all intransitive verbs of this type are supposed to have agents as subjects, a very broad conception of agent has to be assumed that also subsumes the subject of verbs like *sleep*. Usually sleeping is not an activity that is performed intentionally.

4.1 General remarks on the representational format

4.1.5.1 Features as triggers for movement: The EPP feature on T

In GB approaches, the modals and auxiliaries were analyzed as members of the category I and the subjects as specifiers of IP. In the previous section, I showed how subjects are analyzed as specifiers of *v*P. Now, if one assumes that a modal verb combines with such a *v*P, the subject follows the modal, which does not correspond to the order that is observable in English. This problem is solved by assuming a strong uninterpretable D feature at T. Since the feature is strong, a suitable D has to move to the specifier of T and check the D locally. Figure 4.10 shows the TP that plays a role in the analysis of (9):

(9) Anna will read the book.

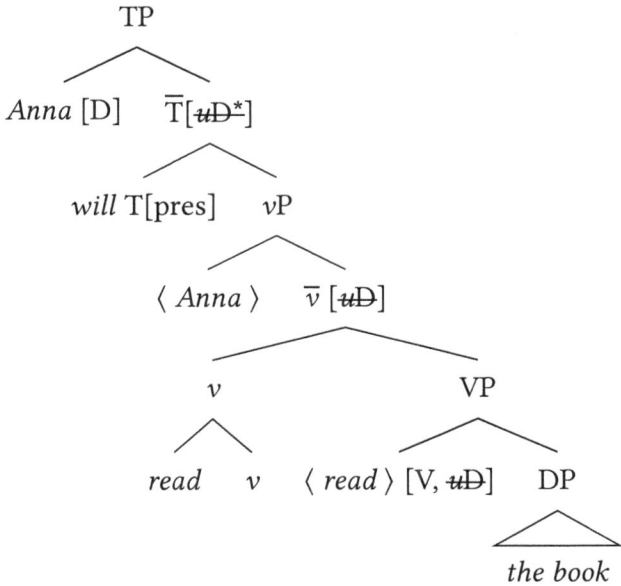

Figure 4.10: Analysis of *Anna will read the book.* involving a modal and movement of the subject from *v* to T

The Determiner Phrase (DP) *the book* is the object of *read* and checks the D feature of *read*. little *v* selects for the subject *Anna*. Since T has a strong D feature (marked by an asterisk '*'), *Anna* must not remain inside of the *v*P but moves on to the specifier position of TP.

Full sentences are CPs. For the analysis of (9), an empty C head is assumed that is combined with the TP. The empty C contributes a clause type feature Decl. The full analysis of (9) is shown in Figure 4.11.

The analysis of the question in (10) involves an unvalued clause-type feature on T for the sentence type *question*.

(10) What will Anna read?

135

4 Transformational Grammar – Minimalism

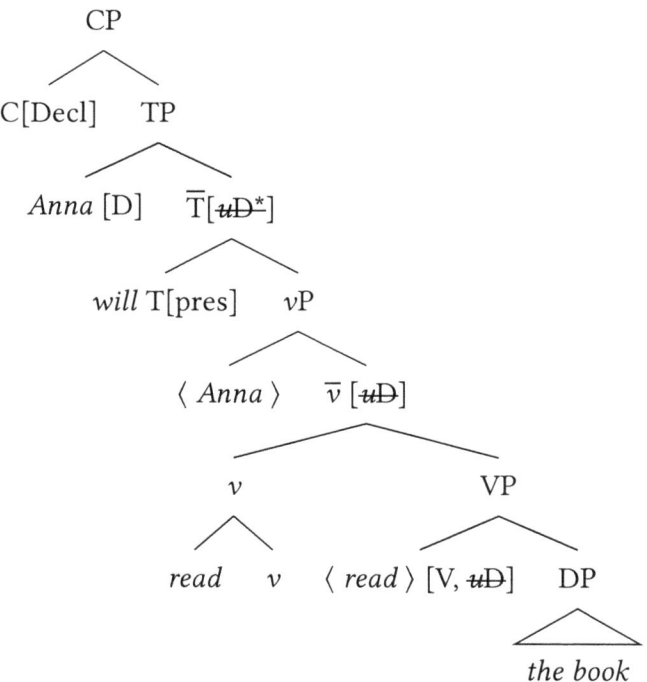

Figure 4.11: Analysis of *Anna will read the book.* as CP with an empty C with the clause-type feature Decl

The empty complementizer C has a Q feature that can value the clause-type feature on T. Since clause-type features on T that have the value Q are stipulated to be strong, the T element has to move to C to check the feature locally. In addition, the *wh* element is moved. This movement is enforced by a strong *wh* feature on C. The analysis of (10) is given in Figure 4.12 on the next page.

4.1.5.2 Case assignment

In the GB analysis that was presented in Chapter 3, nominative was assigned by (finite) I and the other cases by the verb (see Section 3.4.2). The assignment of nominative is taken over to Minimalist analyses, so it is assumed that nominative is assigned by (finite) T. However, in the Minimalist theory under consideration, there is not a single verb projection, but there are two verbal projections: *v*P and VP. Now, one could assume that V assigns accusative to its complement or that *v* assigns accusative to the complement of the verb it dominates. Adger (2003: Section 6.3.2, Section 6.4) assumes the latter approach, since it is compatible with the analysis of so-called unaccusative verbs and the passive. Figure 4.13 on the facing page shows the TP for (11):

(11) Anna reads the book.

The two DPs *Anna* and *the book* start out with unvalued uninterpretable case features: [*u*case:]. The features get valued by T and *v*. It is assumed that only one feature is

136

4.1 General remarks on the representational format

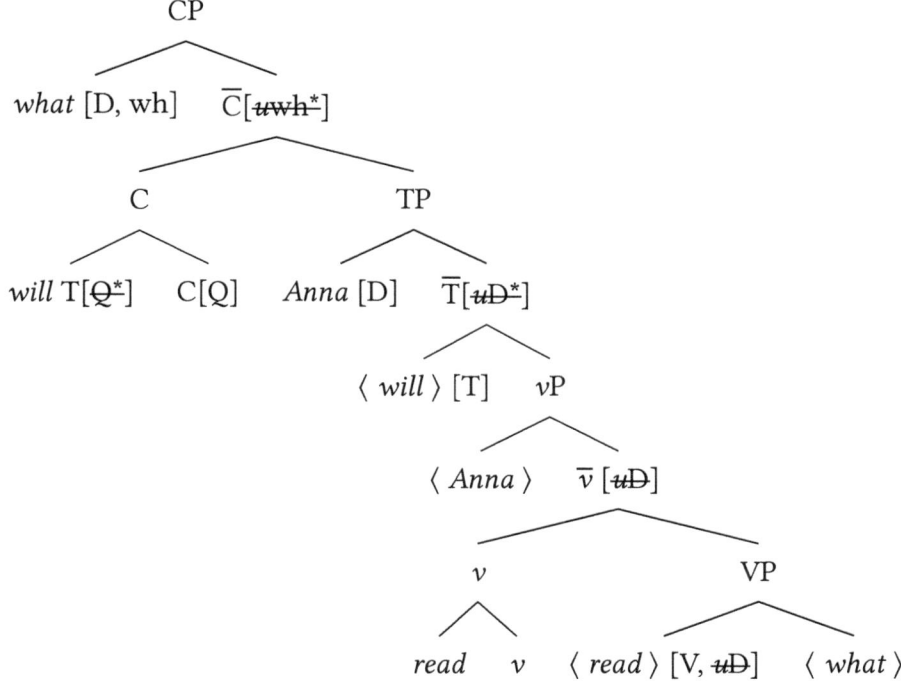

Figure 4.12: Analysis of *What will Anna read?* with an empty C with a strong *wh* feature

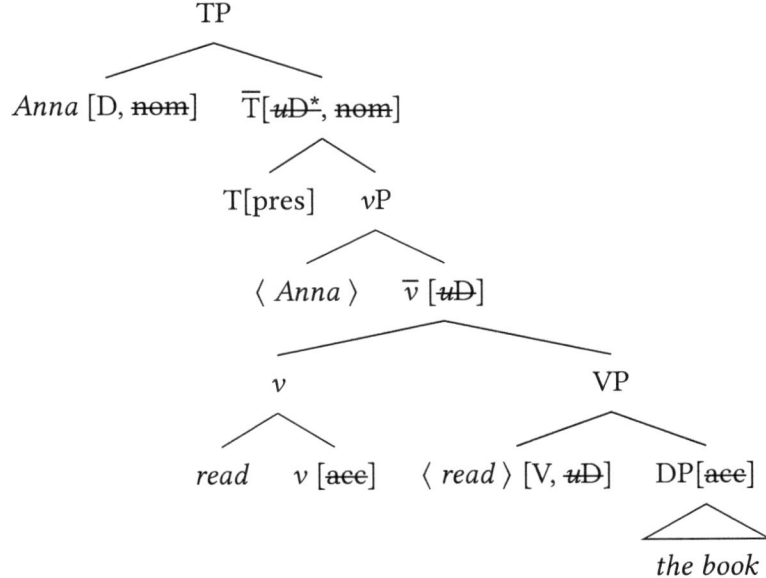

Figure 4.13: Case assignment by T and *v* in the TP for of *Anna reads the book.*

checked by Merge, so this would be the D feature on T, leaving the case feature for the other available checking mechanism: Agree. Agree can be used to check features in sister nodes, but also features further away in the tree. The places that are possible candidates for Agree relations have to stand in a certain relation to each other. The first node has to c-command the node it Agrees with. c-command roughly means: one node up and then arbitrarily many nodes down. So *v* c-commands VP, V, the DP *the book*, and all the nodes within this DP. Since Agree can value features of c-commanded nodes, the accusative on *v* can value the case feature of the DP *the book*.

The non-locality that is build into Agree raises a problem: why is it that (12) is ungrammatical?

(12)   * Him likes she.

The accusative of *v* could be checked with its subject and the nominative of T with the object of *likes*. Both DPs stand in the necessary c-command relations to T and *v*. This problem is solved by requiring that all Agree relations have to involve the closest possible element. Adger (2003: 218) formulates this constraint as follows:

(13)   Locality of matching: Agree holds between a feature F on X and a matching feature F on Y if and only if there is no intervening Z[F].

Intervention is defined as in (14):

(14)   Intervention: In a structure [X ... Z ... Y], Z intervenes between X and Y iff X c-commands Z and Z c-commands Y.

So, since T may Agree with *Anna* it must not Agree with *the book*. Hence nominative assignment to *she* in (12) is impossible and (12) is correctly ruled out.

4.1.6 Adjuncts

Adger (2003: Section 4.2.3) assumes that adjuncts attach to XP and form a new XP. He calls this operation *Adjoin*. Since this operation does not consume any features it is different from External Merge and hence a new operation would be introduced into the theory, contradicting Chomsky's claim that human languages use only Merge as a structure building operation. There are proposals to treat adjuncts as elements in special adverbial phrases with empty heads (see Section 4.6.1) that are also assumed to be part of a hierarchy of functional projections. Personally, I prefer Adger's solution that corresponds to what is done in many other frameworks: there is a special rule or operation for the combination of adjuncts and heads (see for instance Section 9.1.7 on the HPSG schema for head adjunct combinations).

4.2 Verb position

The analysis of verb first sentences in German is straightforward, given the machinery that was introduced in the previous section. The basic idea is the same as in GB: the finite verb moves from V to *v* to T and then to C. The movement to T is forced by a strong tense feature on T and the movement of the T complex to C is enforced by a clause-type feature on T that is valued as a strong Interrogative feature (Int) or a strong Declarative feature (Decl) by C. The analysis of the interrogative clause in (15) is shown in Figure 4.14.

(15)   Kennt jeder   diesen Mann?
       knows everybody this   man
       'Does everybody know this man?'

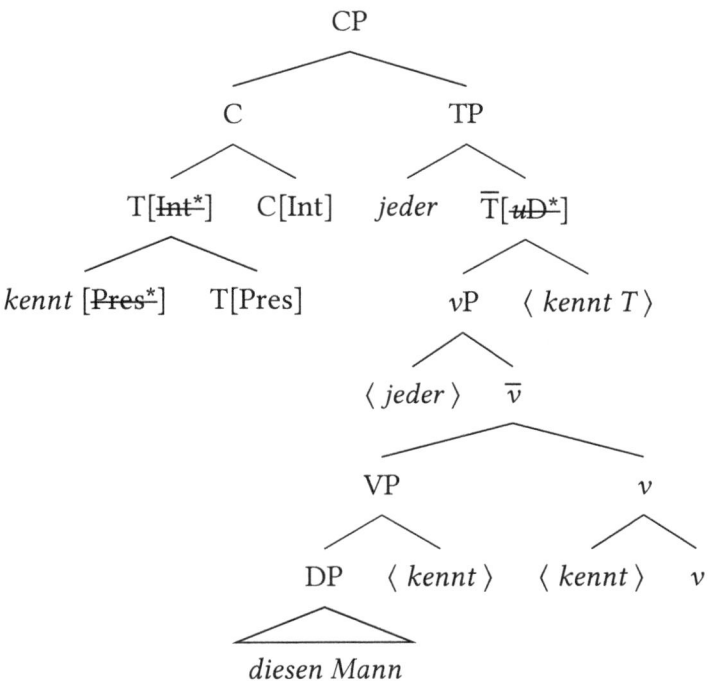

Figure 4.14: Analysis of *Kennt jeder diesen Mann?* 'Does everybody know this man?' following the analysis of Adger (2003)

4.3 Long-distance dependencies

Having explained the placement of the verb in initial position, the analysis of V2 sentences does not come with a surprise: Adger (2003: 331) assumes a feature that triggers the movement of a constituent to a specifier position of C. Adger calls this feature top, but this is a misnomer since the initial position in German declarative sentences is not restricted to topics (maybe he would assume an alternative C head with a foc feature). Figure 4.15 on the following page shows the analysis of (16):

139

(16) Diesen Mann kennt jeder.
      this   man   knows everybody
      'Everbody knows this man.'

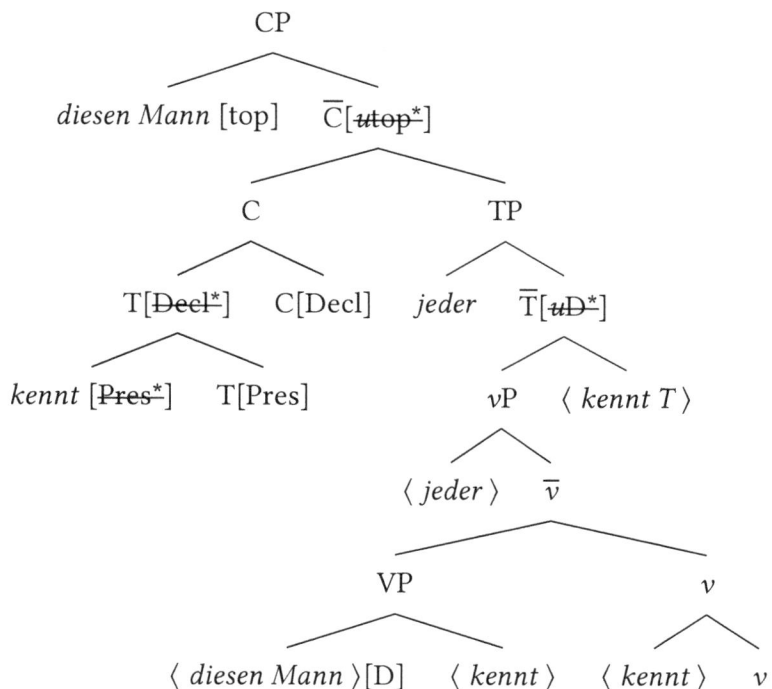

Figure 4.15: Analysis of *Diesen Mann kennt jeder.* 'This man, everybody knows.' following the analysis of Adger (2003: 331)

As in the verb-initial clause in Figure 4.14 a feature on C triggers verb movement. This time it is a Decl feature since we are dealing with a declarative clause. The top feature triggers movement of *diesen Mann* 'this man' to the specifier position of C.

4.4 Passive

Adger (2003) suggests an analysis for the passive in English, which I adapted here to German. Like in the GB analysis that was discussed in Section 3.4 it is assumed that the verb does not assign accusative to the object of *schlagen* 'to beat'. In Minimalist terms, this means that little *v* does not have an acc feature that has to be checked. This special version of little *v* is assumed to play a role in the analysis of sentences of so-called unaccusative verbs (Perlmutter 1978). Unaccusative verbs are a subclass of intransitive verbs that have many interesting properties. For instance, they can be used as adjectival participles although this is usually not possible with intransitive verbs:

140

4.4 Passive

(17)   a.   * der getanzte Mann
             the danced   man

       b.   der gestorbene Mann
             the died   man
             'the dead man'

The explanation of this difference is that adjectival participles predicate over what is the object in active sentences:

(18)   a.   dass der Mann das Buch gelesen hat
             that the man   the book read   has
             'that the man read the book'

       b.   das gelesene Buch
             the read   book

Now the assumption is that the argument of *gestorben* 'died' behaves like an object, while the argument of *getanzt* 'danced' behaves like a subject. If adjectival passives predicate over the object it is explained why (17b) is possible, while (17a) is not.

Adger (2003: 140) assumes the structure in Figure 4.16 for *v*Ps with unaccusative verbs. It is assumed that this unaccusative variant of little *v* plays a role in the analysis of the

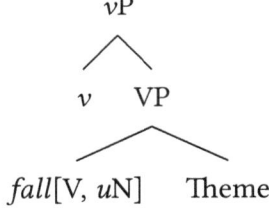

Figure 4.16: Structure of *v*P with unaccusative verbs like *fall, collapse, wilt* according to Adger (2003: 140)

passive. Unaccusative verbs are similar to passivized verbs in that they do have a subject that somehow also has object properties. The special version of little *v* is selected by the Passive head *werden* 'be', which forms a Passive Phrase (abbreviated as PassP). See Figure 4.17 for the analysis of the example in (19):

(19)   dass er geschlagen wurde
        that he beaten   was
        'that he was beaten'

The Pass head requires the Infl feature of little *v* to have the value Pass, which results in participle morphology at spellout. Hence the form that is used is *geschlagen* 'beaten'. The auxiliary moves to T to check the strong Infl feature at T and since the Infl feature is past, the past form of *werden* 'be', namely *wurde* 'was', is used at spellout. T has a nom

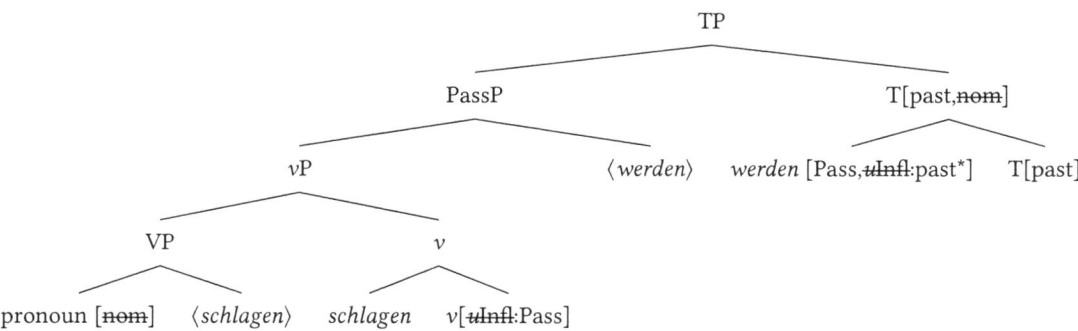

Figure 4.17: Minimalist analysis of the passive without movement but with nonlocal case assignment via Agree

feature that has to be checked. Interestingly, the Minimalist approach does not require the object of *schlagen* to move to the specifier position of T in order to assign case, since case assignment is done via Agree. Hence in principle, the pronominal argument of *schlagen* could stay in its object position and nevertheless get nominative from T. This would solve the problem of the GB analysis that was pointed out by Lenerz (1977: Section 4.4.3). See page 112 for Lenerz' examples and discussion of the problem. However, Adger (2003: 332) assumes that German has a strong EPP feature on T. If this assumption is upheld, all problems of the GB account will carry over to the Minimalist analysis: all objects have to move to T even when there is no reordering taking place. Furthermore, impersonal passives of the kind in (20) would be problematic, since there is no noun phrase that could be moved to T in order to check the EPP feature:

(20) weil   getanzt wurde
     because danced was
     'because there was dancing there'

4.5 Local reordering

Adger (2003) does not treat local reordering. But there are several other suggestions in the literature. Since all reorderings in Minimalist theories are feature-driven, there must be an item that has a feature that triggers reorderings like those in (21b):

(21) a. [weil]   jeder   diesen Mann kennt
        because everyone   this   man knows
        'because everyone knows this man'
     b. [weil]   diesen Mann jeder   kennt
        because this   man everyone knows

There have been various suggestions involving functional projections like Topic Phrase (Laenzlinger 2004: 222) or AgrS and AgrO (Meinunger 2000: Chapter 4) that offer places to move to. G. Müller (2014a: Section 3.5) offers a leaner solution, though. In his approach, the object simply moves to a second specifier position of little *v*. The analysis is depicted in Figure 4.18.[7]

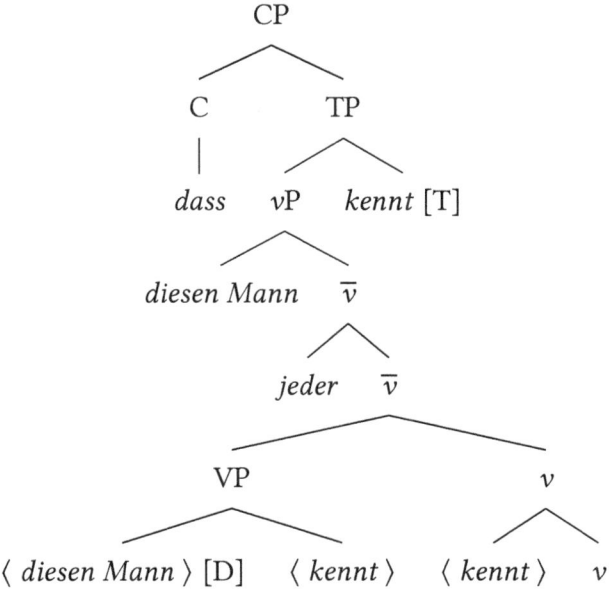

Figure 4.18: Analysis of *dass diesen Mann jeder kennt* 'that everybody knows this man' as movement of the object to a specifier position of *v*

An option that was suggested by Laenzlinger (2004: 229–230) is to assume several Object Phrases for objects that may appear in any order. The objects move to the specifier positions of these projections and since the order of the Object Phrases is not restricted, both orders in (22) can be analyzed:

(22)   a. dass Hans diesen Brief meinem Onkel gibt
            that Hans this   letter my   uncle gives

        'that Hans gives this letter to my uncle'

    b. dass Hans meinem Onkel diesen Brief gibt
            that Hans my   uncle this letter gives

        'that Hans gives to my uncle this letter'

4.6 New developments and theoretical variants

At the start of the 90s, Chomsky suggested a major rethink of the basic theoretical assumptions of GB and only keeping those parts of the theory which are absolutely nec-

---

[7]G. Müller assumes optional features on *v* and V that trigger local reorderings (p. 48). These are not given in the figure.

essary. In the *Minimalist Program*, Chomsky gives the central motivations for the far-reaching revisions of GB theory (Chomsky 1993; 1995b). Until the beginning of the 90s, it was assumed that Case Theory, the Theta-Criterion, $\overline{\text{X}}$ theory, Subjacency, Binding Theory, Control Theory etc. all belonged to the innate faculty for language (Richards 2015: 804). This, of courses, begs the question of how this very specific linguistic knowledge made its way into our genome. The Minimalist Program follows up on this point and attempts to explain properties of language through more general cognitive principles and to reduce the amount of innate language-specific knowledge postulated. The distinction between Deep Structure and Surface Structure, for example, was abandoned. Move still exists as an operation, but can be used directly to build sub-structures rather than after a complete D-structure has been created. Languages differ with regard to whether this movement is visible or not.

Although Chomsky's Minimalist Program should be viewed as a successor to GB, advocates of Minimalism often emphasize the fact that Minimalism is not a theory as such, but rather a research program (Chomsky 2007: 4; 2013: 6). The actual analyses suggested by Chomsky (1995b) when introducing the research program have been reviewed by theoreticians and have sometimes come in for serious criticism (Kolb 1997; Johnson & Lappin 1997; 1999; Lappin, Levine & Johnson 2000a,b; 2001; Seuren 2004; Pinker & Jackendoff 2005), however, one should say that some criticisms overshoot the mark.

There are various strains of Minimalism. In the following sections, I will discuss some of the central ideas and explain which aspects are regarded problematic.

4.6.1 Move, Merge, feature-driven movement and functional projections

Johnson, Lappin and Kolb have criticized the computational aspects of Chomsky's system. Chomsky suggested incorporating principles of economy into the theory. In certain cases, the grammatical system can create an arbitrary number of structures, but only the most economical, that is, the one which requires the least effort to produce, will be accepted as grammatical (transderivational economy). This assumption does not necessarily have to be taken too seriously and, in reality, does not play a role in many works in the Minimalist framework (although see Richards (2015) for recent approaches with derivations which are compared in terms of economy). Nevertheless, there are other aspects of Chomsky's theory which can be found in many recent works. For example, Chomsky has proposed reducing the number of basic, structure building operations which license structures to two: Move and Merge (that is, Internal and External Merge). Move corresponds to the operation Move-α, which was already discussed in Chapter 3, and Merge is the combination of (two) linguistic objects.

It is generally assumed that exactly two objects can be combined (Chomsky 1995b: 226). For Move, it is assumed that there must be a reason for a given movement operation. The reason for movement is assumed to be that an element can check some feature in the position it is moved to. This idea was already presented in the analysis of the passive in Section 3.4: the accusative object does not bear case in passive sentences and therefore has to be moved to a position where it can receive case. This kind of approach is also used in newer analyses for a range of other phenomena. For example, it is assumed that there are phrases whose heads have the categories focus and topic. The corresponding functional heads are always empty in languages like German and English. Nevertheless, the assumption of these heads is motivated by the fact that other languages possess markers which signal the topic or focus of a sentence morphologically. This argumentation is only possible if one also assumes that the inventory of categories is the same for all languages. Then, the existence of a category in one language would suggest the existence of the same category in all other languages. This assumption of a shared universal component (Universal Grammar, UG) with detailed language-specific knowledge is, however, controversial and is shared by few linguists outside of the Chomskyan tradition. Even for those working in Chomskyan linguistics, there have been questions raised about whether it is permissible to argue in this way since if it is only the ability to create recursive structures that is responsible for the human-specific ability to use language (faculty of language in the narrow sense) – as Hauser, Chomsky & Fitch (2002) assume –, then the individual syntactic categories are not part of UG and data from other languages cannot be used to motivate the assumption of invisible categories in another language.

4.6.1.1 Functional projections and modularization of linguistic knowledge

The assumption that movement must be licensed by feature checking has led to an inflation of the number of (silent) functional heads.[8] Rizzi (1997: 297) suggests the structure in Figure 4.19 on the next page (see also Grewendorf 2002: 85, 240; 2009).

The functional categories Force, Top, Foc and Fin correspond to clause type, topic, focus and finiteness. It is assumed that movement always targets a specifier position. Topics and focused elements are always moved to the specifier position of the corresponding phrase. Topics can precede or follow focused elements, which is why there are two topic projections: one above and one below FocP. Topic phrases are recursive, that is, an arbitrary number of TopPs can appear at the positions of TopP in the figure. Following Grewendorf (2002: 70), topic and focus phrases are only realized if they are required for particular information structural reasons, such as movement.[9] Chomsky (1995b: 147) follows Pollock (1989) in assuming that all languages have functional projections for subject and object agreement as well as negation (AgrS, AgrO, Neg).[10] Sternefeld (1995:

---

[8]The assumption of such heads is not necessary since features can be "bundled" and then they can be checked together. For an approach in this vein, which is in essence similar to what theories such as HPSG assume, see Sternefeld (2006: Section II.3.3.4, Section II.4.2).

In so-called cartographic approaches, it is assumed that every morphosyntactic feature corresponds to an independent syntactic head (Cinque & Rizzi 2010: 54, 61). For an explicitly formalized proposal in which exactly one feature is consumed during a combination operation see Stabler (2001: 335). Stabler's *Minimalist Grammars* are discussed in more detail in Section 4.6.4.

[9]There are differing opinions as to whether functional projections are optional or not. Some authors assume that the complete hierarchy of functional projections is always present but functional heads can remain empty (e.g., Cinque 1999: 106 and Cinque & Rizzi 2010: 55).

[10]See Chomsky (1995b: Section 4.10.1), however.

4 Transformational Grammar – Minimalism

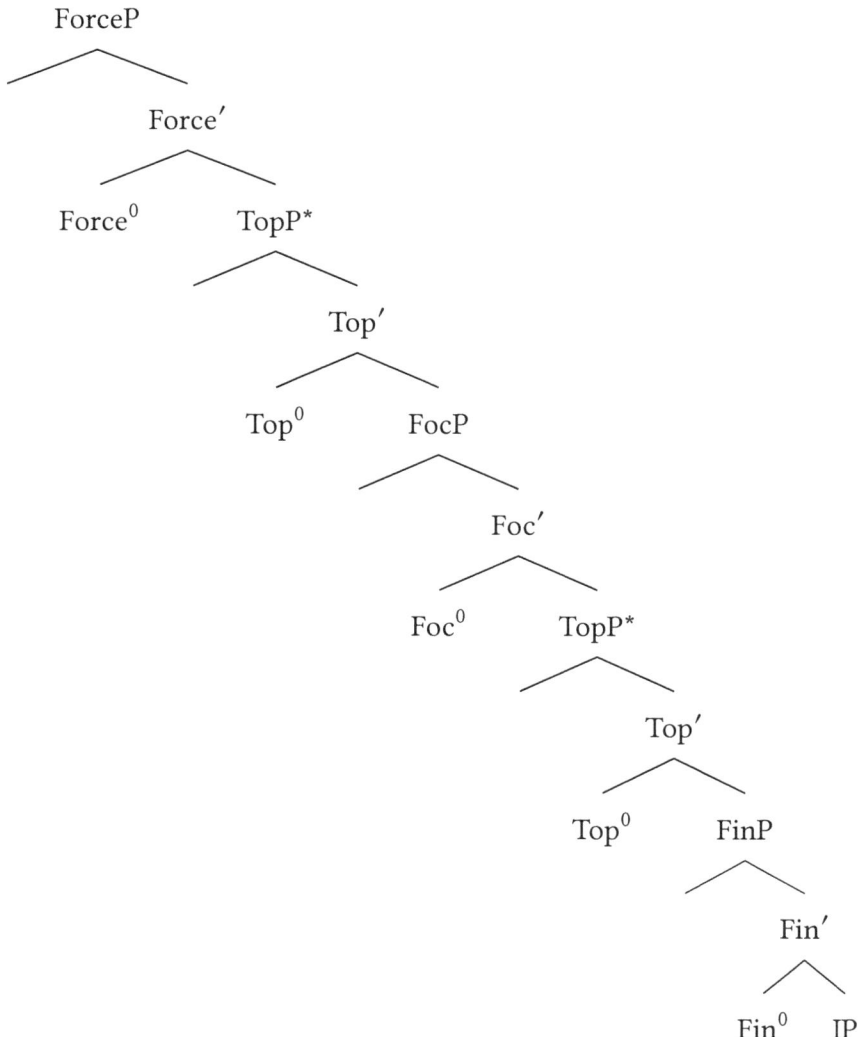

Figure 4.19: Syntactic structure of sentences following Rizzi (1997: 297)

78), von Stechow (1996: 103) and Meinunger (2000: 100–101, 124) differentiate between two agreement positions for direct and indirect objects (AgrO, AgrIO). As well as AgrS, AgrO and Neg, Beghelli & Stowell (1997) assume the functional heads Share and Dist in order to explain scope phenomena in English as feature-driven movements at LF. For a treatment of scope phenomena without empty elements or movement, see Section 19.3. Błaszczak & Gärtner (2005: 13) assume the categories −PolP, +PolP and %PolP for their discussion of polarity.

Webelhuth (1995: 76) gives an overview of the functional projections that had been proposed up to 1995 and offers references for AgrA, AgrN, AgrV, Aux, Clitic Voices, Gender, Honorific, μ, Number, Person, Predicate, Tense, Z.

In addition to AdvP, NegP, AgrP, FinP, TopP and ForceP, Wiklund, Hrafnbjargarson, Bentzen & Hróarsdóttir (2007) postulate an OuterTopP. Poletto (2000: 31) suggests both

4.6 New developments and theoretical variants

a HearerP and a SpeakerP for the position of clitics in Italian. Bosse & Bruening (2011: 75) assume a BenefactiveP

Cinque (1999: 106) adopts the 32 functional heads in Table 4.1 in his work. He assumes

Table 4.1: Functional heads following Cinque (1999: 106)

1. $\text{Mood}_{\text{Speech Act}}$	2. $\text{Mood}_{\text{Evaluative}}$	3. $\text{Mood}_{\text{Evidential}}$	4. $\text{Mood}_{\text{Epistemic}}$
5. T(Past)	6. T(Future)	7. $\text{Mood}_{\text{Irrealis}}$	8. $\text{Mod}_{\text{Necessity}}$
9. $\text{Mod}_{\text{Possibility}}$	10. $\text{Mod}_{\text{Volitional}}$	11. $\text{Mod}_{\text{Obligation}}$	12. $\text{Mod}_{\text{Ability/permission}}$
13. $\text{Asp}_{\text{Habitual}}$	14. $\text{Asp}_{\text{Repetitive(I)}}$	15. $\text{Asp}_{\text{Frequentative(I)}}$	16. $\text{Asp}_{\text{Celerative(I)}}$
17. T(Anterior)	18. $\text{Asp}_{\text{Terminative}}$	19. $\text{Asp}_{\text{Continuative}}$	20. $\text{Asp}_{\text{Perfect(?)}}$
21. $\text{Asp}_{\text{Retrospective}}$	22. $\text{Asp}_{\text{Proximative}}$	23. $\text{Asp}_{\text{Durative}}$	24. $\text{Asp}_{\text{Generic/progressive}}$
25. $\text{Asp}_{\text{Prospective}}$	26. $\text{Asp}_{\text{SgCompletive(I)}}$	27. $\text{Asp}_{\text{PlCompletive}}$	28. $\text{Asp}_{\text{Voice}}$
29. $\text{Asp}_{\text{Celerative(II)}}$	30. $\text{Asp}_{\text{SgCompletive(II)}}$	31. $\text{Asp}_{\text{Repetitive(II)}}$	32. $\text{Asp}_{\text{Frequentative(II)}}$

that all sentences contain a structure with all these functional heads. The specifier positions of these heads can be occupied by adverbs or remain empty. Cinque claims that these functional heads and the corresponding structures form part of Universal Grammar, that is, knowledge of these structures is innate (page 107).[11] Laenzlinger (2004) follows Cinque in proposing this sequence of functional heads for German. He also follows Kayne (1994), who assumes that all syntactic structures have the order specifier head complement cross-linguistically, even if the surface order of the constituents seems to contradict this.

The constituent orders that are visible in the end are derived by leftward-movement.[12] Figure 4.20 on page 149 shows the analysis of a verb-final clause where the functional

---

[11]Table 4.1 shows only the functional heads in the clausal domain. Cinque (1994: 96, 99) also accounts for the order of adjectives with a cascade of projections: Quality, Size, Shape, Color, Nationality. These categories and their ordering are also assumed to belong to UG (p. 100).

Cinque (1994: 96) claims that a maximum of seven attributive adjectives are possible and explains this with the fact that there are a limited number of functional projections in the nominal domain. As was shown on page 65, with a fitting context it is possible to use several adjectives of the same kind, which is why some of Cinque's functional projections would have to be subject to iteration.

[12]This also counts for extraposition, that is, the movement of constituents into the postfield in German. Whereas this would normally be analyzed as rightward-movement, Kayne (1994: Chapter 9) analyzes it as movement of everything else to the left. Kayne assumes that (i.b) is derived from (i.a) by moving part of the DP:

(i) a. just walked into the room [$_{\text{DP}}$ someone who we don't know].
   b. Someone$_i$ just walked into the room [$_{\text{DP}}$ _$_i$ who we don't know].

(i.a) must have to be some kind of derived intermediate representation, otherwise English would not be SV(O) underlyingly but rather V(O)S. (i.a) is therefore derived from (ii) by fronting the VP *just walked into the room*.

(ii) Someone who we don't know just walked into the room

Such analyses have the downside that they cannot be easily combined with performance models (see Chapter 15).

adverbial heads have been omitted.[13] Subjects and objects are generated as arguments inside of vP and VP, respectively. The subject is moved to the specifier of the subject phrase and the object is moved to the specifier of the object phrase. The verbal projection (VP_k) is moved in front of the auxiliary into the specifier position of the phrase containing the auxiliary. The only function of SubjP and ObjP is to provide a landing site for the respective movements. For a sentence in which the object precedes the subject, Laenzlinger assumes that the object moves to the specifier of a topic phrase. Figure 4.20 contains only a ModP and an AspP, although Laenzlinger assumes that all the heads proposed by Cinque are present in the structure of all German clauses. For ditransitive verbs, Laenzlinger assumes multiple object phrases (page 230). A similar analysis with movement of object and subject from verb-initial VPs to Agr positions was suggested by Zwart (1994) for Dutch.

For general criticism of Kayne's model, see Haider (2000). Haider shows that a Kayne-like theory makes incorrect predictions for German (for instance regarding the position of selected adverbials and secondary predicates and regarding verbal complex formation) and therefore fails to live up to its billing as a theory which can explain all languages. Haider (1997a: Section 4) has shown that the assumption of an empty Neg head, as assumed by Pollock (1989), Haegeman (1995) and others, leads to problems. See Bobaljik (1999) for problems with the argumentation for Cinque's cascade of adverb-projections.

Furthermore, it has to be pointed out that SubjP and ObjP, TraP (Transitive Phrase) and IntraP (Intransitive Phrase) (Karimi-Doostan 2005: 1745) and TopP (topic phrase), DistP (quantifier phrase), AspP (aspect phrase) (Kiss 2003: 22; Karimi 2005: 35), PathP and PlaceP (Svenonius 2004: 246) encode information about grammatical function, valence, information structure and semantics in the category symbols.[14] In a sense, this is a misuse of category symbols, but such a misuse of information structural and semantic categories is necessary since syntax, semantics, and information structure are tightly connected and since it is assumed that the semantics interprets the syntax, that is, it is assumed that semantics comes after syntax (see Figure 3.2 and Figure 4.1). By using semantically and pragmatically relevant categories in syntax, there is no longer a clean distinction between the levels of morphology, syntax, semantics and pragmatics: everything has been 'syntactified'. Rizzi (2014) himself talks about syntactification. He points out that there are fundamental problems with the T-model and its current variants in Minimalism and concludes that a syntactification in terms of Rizzi-style functional heads or a proliferation of T heads with respective features (see also Borsley 2006; Borsley & Müller 2019) is the only way to save this architecture. Felix Bildhauer (p. c. 2012) has pointed out to me that approaches which assume a cascade of functional projections where the individual aspects of meaning are represented by nodes are actually very close to phrasal approaches in Construction Grammar (see Adger 2013: 470 also for a similar view). One

---

[13]These structures do not correspond to $\overline{\text{X}}$ theory as it was presented in Section 2.5. In some cases, heads have been combined with complements to form an XP rather than an X′. For more on $\overline{\text{X}}$ theory in the Minimalist Program, see Section 4.6.3.

[14]For further examples and references, see Newmeyer (2004a: 194; 2005: 82). Newmeyer references also works which stipulate a projection for each semantic role, e.g., Agent, Reciprocal, Benefactive, Instrumental, Causative, Comitative, and Reversive Phrase.

4.6 New developments and theoretical variants

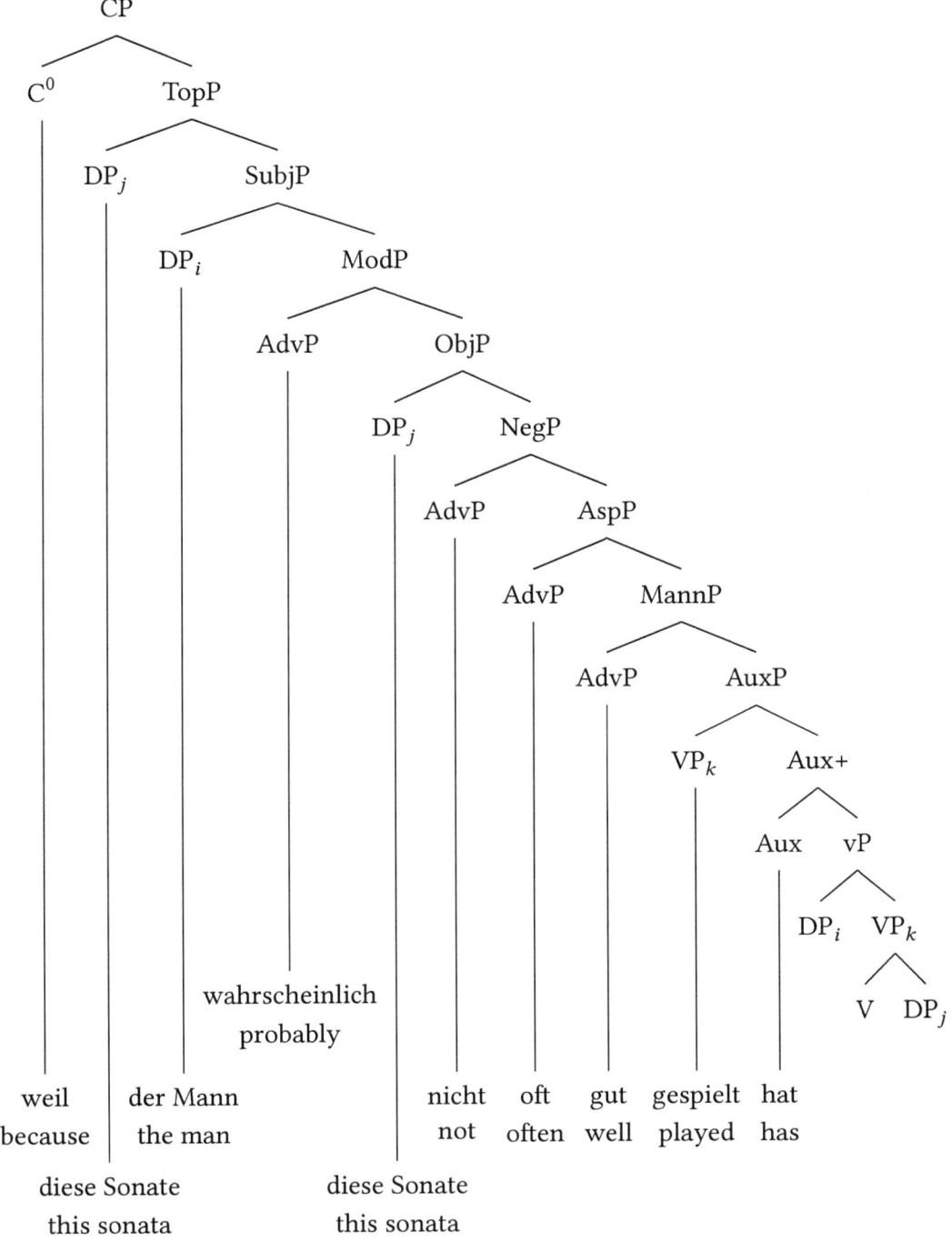

Figure 4.20: Analysis of sentence structure with leftward remnant movement and functional heads following Laenzlinger (2004: 224)

simply lists configurations and these are assigned a meaning (or features which are interpreted post-syntactically, see Cinque & Rizzi (2010: 62) for the interpretation of TopP, for example).

4.6.1.2 Feature checking in specifier positions

If one takes the theory of feature checking in Specifier-Head relations to its logical conclusion, then one arrives at an analysis such as the one suggested by Radford (1997: 452). Radford assumes that prepositions are embedded in an Agreement Phrase in addition to the structure in (23), which is usually assumed, and that the preposition adjoins to the head of the Agreement Phrase and the argument of the preposition is moved to the specifier position of the Agreement Phrase.

(23) [_PP_ P DP]

The problem here is that the object now precedes the preposition. In order to rectify this, Radford assumes a functional projection p (read *little p*) with an empty head to which the preposition then adjoins. This analysis is shown in Figure 4.21. This machinery is

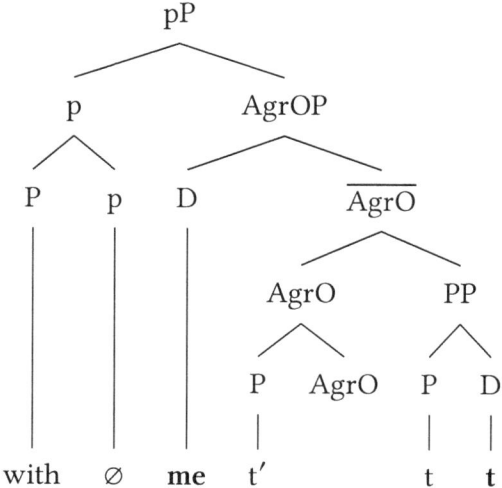

Figure 4.21: PP analysis following Radford with case assignment in specifier position and little p

only necessary in order to retain the assumption that feature checking takes place in specifier-head relations. If one were to allow the preposition to determine the case of its object locally, then all this theoretical apparatus would not be necessary and it would be possible to retain the well-established structure in (23).

Sternefeld (2006: 549–550) is critical of this analysis and compares it to Swiss cheese (being full of holes). The comparison to Swiss cheese is perhaps even too positive since, unlike Swiss cheese, the ratio of substance to holes in the analysis is extreme (2 words vs.

4.6 New developments and theoretical variants

5 empty elements). We have already seen an analysis of noun phrases on page 70, where the structure of an NP, which only consisted of an adjective *klugen* 'clever', contained more empty elements than overt ones. The difference to the PP analysis discussed here is that empty elements are only postulated in positions where overt determiners and nouns actually occur. The little p projection, on the other hand, is motivated entirely theory-internally. There is no theory-external motivation for any of the additional assumptions made for the analysis in Figure 4.21 (see Sternefeld 2006: 549–550).

A variant of this analysis has been proposed by Hornstein, Nunes & Grohmann (2005: 124). The authors do without little p, which makes the structure less complex. They assume the structure in (24), which corresponds to the AgrOP-subtree in Figure 4.21.

(24) $[_{\text{AgrP}} \text{DP}_k \, [_{\text{Agr}'} \, P_i + \text{Agr} \, [_{\text{PP}} \, t_i \, t_k \,]]]$

The authors assume that the movement of the DP to SpecAgrP happens invisibly, that is, covert. This solves Radford's problem and makes the assumption of pP redundant.

The authors motivate this analysis by pointing out agreement phenomena in Hungarian: Hungarian postpositions agree with the preceding noun phrase in person and number. That is, the authors argue that English prepositional and Hungarian postpositional phrases have the same structure derived by movement, albeit the movement is covert in English.

In this way, it is possible to reduce the number and complexity of basic operations and, in this sense, the analysis is minimal. These structures are, however, still incredibly complex. No other kind of theory discussed in this book needs the amount of inflated structure to analyze the combination of a preposition with a noun phrase. The structure in (24) cannot be motivated by reference to data from English and it is therefore impossible to acquire it from the linguistic input. A theory which assumes this kind of structures would have to postulate a Universal Grammar with the information that features can only be checked in (certain) specifier positions (see Chapters 13 and 16 for more on Universal Grammar and language acquisition). For general remarks on (covert) movement see Haider (2014: Section 2.3).

4.6.1.3 Locality of selection and functional projections

Another problem arises from the use of functional heads to encode linear order. In the classic CP/IP-system and all other theories discussed here, a category stands for a class of objects with the same distribution, that is, NP (or DP) stands for pronouns and complex noun phrases. Heads select phrases with a certain category. In the CP/IP-system, I selects a VP and an DP/NP, whereas C selects an IP. In newer analyses, this kind of selectional mechanism does not work as easily. Since movement has taken place in (25b), we are dealing with a TopP or FocP in *das Buch dem Mann zu geben* 'the book the man to give'. Therefore, *um* cannot simply select an non-finite IP, but rather has to disjunctively be able to select a TopP, FocP or IP. It has to be ensured that TopPs and FocPs are marked with regard to the form of the verb contained inside them, since *um* can only be combined with *zu*-infinitives.

(25) a. um dem Mann das Buch zu geben
     for the man the book to give
   'to give the man the book'

   b. um das Buch dem Mann zu geben
      for the book the man to give
   'to give the book to the man'

The category system, selectional mechanisms and projection of features would therefore have to be made considerably more complicated when compared to a system which simply base generates the orders or a system in which a constituent is moved out of the IP, thereby creating a new IP.

Proposals that follow Cinque (1999) are problematic for similar reasons: Cinque assumes the category AdverbP for the combination of an adverb and a VP. There is an empty functional head, which takes the verbal projection as its complement and the adverb surfaces in the specifier of this projection. In these systems, adverb phrases have to pass on inflectional properties of the verb since verbs with particular inflectional properties (finiteness, infinitives with *zu*, infinitives without *zu*, participles) have to be selected by higher heads (see page 183 and Section 9.1.4). There is of course the alternative to use Agree for this, but then all selection would be nonlocal and after all selection is not agreement. For further, more serious problems with this analysis like modification of adverbs by adverbs in connection with partial fronting and restrictions on non-phrasality of preverbal adverbials in English, see Haider (1997a: Section 5).

A special case of the adverb problem is the negation problem: Ernst (1992) studied the syntax of negation more carefully and pointed out that negation can attach to several different verbal projections (26a,b), to adjectives (26c) and adverbs (26d).

(26) a. Ken could not have heard the news.
   b. Ken could have not heard the news.
   c. a [not unapproachable] figure
   d. [Not always] has she seasoned the meat.

If all of these projections are simply NegPs without any further properties (about verb form, adjective part of speech, adverb part of speech), it would be impossible to account for their different syntactic distributions. Negation is clearly just a special case of the more general problem, since adverbs may attach to adjectives forming adjectival phrases in the traditional sense and not adverb phrases in Chinque's sense. For instance, the adverb *oft* 'often' in (27) modifies *lachender* 'laughing' forming the adjectival phrase *oft lachender*, which behaves like the unmodified adjectival participle *lachender*: it modifies *Mann* 'man' and it precedes it.

(27) a. ein lachender Mann
     a   laughing man
   'a laughing man'

b. ein oft lachender Mann
   a often laughing man
   'a man that laughs often'

Of course one could imagine solutions to the last three problems that use the Agree relation to enforce selectional constraints nonlocally, but such accounts would violate locality of selection (see Ernst 1992: 110 and the discussion in Section 18.2 of this book) and would be much more complicated than accounts that assume a direct selection of dependents.

Related to the locality issues that were discussed in the previous paragraph is the assumption of special functional projections for the placement of clitics: if one uses SpeakerP so that a clitic for first person singular can be moved to the correct specifier positions and a HearerP so that the clitic for second person can be moved to the correct position (Poletto 2000: 31), then what one has are special projections which need to encode in addition all features that are relevant for clauses (alternatively one could of course assume nonlocal Agree to be responsible for distributional facts). In addition to these features, the category labels contain information that allows higher heads to select clauses containing clitics. In other approaches and earlier variants of transformational grammar, selection was assumed to be strictly local so that higher heads only have access to those properties of embedded categories that are directly relevant for selection (Abraham 2005: 223; Sag 2007) and not information about whether an argument of a head within the clause is the speaker or the hearer or whether some arguments in the clause are realized as clitics. Locality will be discussed further in Section 18.2.

4.6.1.4 Feature-driven movement

Finally, there is a conceptual problem with feature-driven movement, which has been pointed out by Gisbert Fanselow: Frey (2004b: 27) assumes a KontrP (contrastive phrase) and Frey (2004a) a TopP (topic phrase) (see Rizzi (1997) for TopP and FocP (focus phrase) in Italian and Haftka (1995), Grewendorf (2002: 85, 240); 2009, Abraham (2003: 19), Laenzlinger (2004: 224) and Hinterhölzel (2004: 18) for analyses of German with TopP and/or FocP). Constituents have to move to the specifier of these functional heads depending on their information structural status. Fanselow (2003a) has shown that such movement-based theories for the ordering of elements in the middle field are not compatible with current assumptions of the Minimalist Program. The reason for this is that sometimes movement takes place in order to create space for other elements (altruistic movement). If the information structure of a sentence requires that the closest object to a verb is neither focused nor part of the focus, then the object closest to the verb should not receive the main stress in the clause. This can be achieved by deaccentuation, that is, by moving the accent to another constituent or even, as shown in (28b), by moving the object to a different position from the one in which it receives structural stress.

(28) a. dass die Polizei gestern Linguisten verhaftete
       that the police yesterday linguists arrested
       'that the police arrested linguists yesterday'

b. dass die Polizei Linguisten gestern verhaftete
   that the police linguists yesterday arrested
   'that the police arrested linguists yesterday'

In Spanish, partial focus can be achieved not by special intonation, but rather only by altruistic movement in order to move the object out of the focus. See also Bildhauer & Cook (2010: p. 72) for a discussion of "altruistic" multiple frontings in German.

It is therefore not possible to assume that elements are moved to a particular position in the tree in order to check some feature motivated by information structural properties. Since feature checking is a prerequisite for movement in current minimalist theory, one would have to postulate a special feature, which only has the function of triggering altruistic movement. Fanselow (2003a: Section 4; 2006: 8) has also shown that the ordering constraints that one assumes for topic, focus and sentence adverbs can be adequately described by a theory which assumes firstly, that arguments are combined (in minimalist terminology: *merged*) with their head one after the other and secondly, that adjuncts can be adjoined to any projection level. The position of sentence adverbs directly before the focused portion of the sentence receives a semantic explanation: since sentence adverbs behave like focus-sensitive operators, they have to directly precede elements that they refer to. It follows from this that elements which do not belong to the focus of an utterance (topics) have to occur in front of the sentence adverb. It is therefore not necessary to assume a special topic position to explain local reorderings in the middle field. This analysis is also pursued in LFG and HPSG. The respective analyses are discussed in more detail in the corresponding chapters.

4.6.2 Labeling

In the Minimalist Program, Chomsky tries to keep combinatorial operations and mechanisms as simple as possible. He motivates this with the assumption that the existence of a UG with less language-specific knowledge is more plausible from a evolutionary point of view than a UG which contains a high degree of language-specific knowledge (Chomsky 2008: 135).

For this reason, he removes the projection levels of $\overline{X}$ theory, traces, indices and "similar descriptive technology" (Chomsky 2008: 138). All that remains is Merge and Move, that is, Internal and External Merge. Internal and External Merge combine two syntactic objects α and β into a larger syntactic object which is represented as a set $\{\alpha, \beta\}$. α and β can be either lexical items or internally complex syntactic objects. Internal Merge moves a part of an object to its periphery.[15] The result of internally merging an element is a set $\{\alpha, \beta\}$ where α was a part of β. External Merge also produces a set with two elements. However, two independent objects are merged. The objects that are created by Merge have a certain category (a set of features). For instance, if one combines the elements α and β, one gets $\{l, \{\alpha, \beta\}\}$, where l is the category of the resulting object.

---

[15] To be more specific, part of a syntactic object is copied and the copy is placed at the edge of the entire object. The original of this copy is no longer relevant for pronunciation (*Copy Theory of Movement*).

4.6 New developments and theoretical variants

This category is also called a *label*. Since it is assumed that all constituents are headed, the category that is assigned to { α, β } has to be either the category of α or the category of β. Chomsky (2008: 145) discusses the following two rules for the determination of the label of a set.

(29)   a. In { H, α }, H an LI, H is the label.

         b. If α is internally merged to β, forming { α, β } then the label of β is the label of { α, β }.

As Chomsky notes, these rules are not unproblematic since the label is not uniquely determined in all cases. An example is the combination of two lexical elements. If both H and α in (29a) are lexical items (LI), then both H and α can be the label of the resulting structure. Chomsky notices that this could result in deviant structures, but claims that this concern is unproblematic and ignores it. Chomsky offered a treatment of the combination of two lexical items in his 2013 paper. The solution to the problem is to assume that all combinations of lexical elements consist of a functional element and a root (Marantz 1997; Borer 2005). Roots are not considered as labels per definition[16] and hence the category of the functional element determines the category of the combination (Chomsky 2013: 47). Such an analysis can only be rejected: the goal of the Minimalist Program is to simplify the theoretical proposals to such an extent that the models of language acquisition and language evolution become plausible, but in order to simplify basic concepts it is stipulated that a noun cannot simply be a noun but needs a functional element to tell the noun what category it has. Given that the whole point of Chomsky's Bare Phrase Structure (Chomsky 1995a) was the elimination of the unary branching structures in $\overline{\text{X}}$ theory, it is unclear why they are reintroduced now through the backdoor, only more complex with an additional empty element.[17] Theories like Categorial Grammar and HPSG can combine lexical items directly without assuming any auxiliary projections or empty elements. See also Rauh (2016) for a comparison of the treatment of syntactic categories in earlier versions of Transformational Grammar, HPSG, Construction Grammar, Role and Reference Grammar and root-based Neo-Constructivist proposals like the one assumed by Chomsky (2013). Rauh concludes that the direct connection of syntactic and semantic information is needed and that the Neo-Constructivism of Marantz and Borer has to be rejected. For further criticism of Neo-Constructivist approaches see Wechsler (2008a) and Müller & Wechsler (2014a: Sections 6.1 and 7).

The combination of a pronoun with a verbal projection poses a problem that is related to what has been said above. In the analysis of *He left*, the pronoun *he* is a lexical element

---

[16]Another category that is excluded as label per definition is *Conj*, which stands for conjunction (Chomsky 2013: 45–46). This is a stipulation that is needed to get coordination to work. See below.

[17]The old $\overline{\text{X}}$ rule in (i.a) corresponds to the binary combination in (i.b).

(i)   a. N′ → N

         b. N → N-func root

In (i.a) a lexical noun is projected to an N′ and in (i.b), a root is combined with a functional nominal head into a nominal category.

and hence would be responsible for the label of *He left*, since *left* is an internally complex verbal projection in Minimalist theories. The result would be a nominal label rather than a verbal one. To circumvent this problem, Chomsky (2013: 46) assumes that *he* has a complex internal structure: 'perhaps D-pro', that is, *he* is (perhaps) composed out of an invisible determiner and a pronoun.

The case in which two non-LIs are externally merged (for instance a nominal and a verbal phrase) is not discussed in Chomsky (2008). Chomsky (2013: 43–44) suggests that a phrase XP is irrelevant for the labeling of { XP, YP } if XP is moved (or rather copied in the Copy Theory of Movement) in a further step. Chomsky assumes that one of two phrases in an { XP, YP } combination has to move, since otherwise labeling would be impossible (p. 12).[18] The following coordination example will illustrate this: Chomsky assumes that the expression *Z and W* is analyzed as follows: first, Z and W are merged. This expression is combined with Conj (30a) and in the next step Z is raised (30b).

(30) a. [$_\alpha$ Conj [$_\beta$ Z W]]
      b. [$_\gamma$ Z [$_\alpha$ Conj [$_\beta$ Z W]]]

Since Z in β is only a copy, it does not count for labeling and β can get the label of W. It is stipulated for the combination of Z and α that Conj cannot be the label and hence the label of the complete structure is Z.[19]

A special case that is discussed by Chomsky is the Internal Merge of an LI α with a non LI β. According to rule (29a) the label would be α. According to (29b), the label would be β (see also Donati (2006)). Chomsky discusses the combination of the pronoun *what* with *you wrote* as an example.

(31) what [C [you wrote *t*]]

If the label is determined according to (29b), one then has a syntactic object that would be called a CP in the GB framework; since this CP is, moreover, interrogative, it can function as the complement of *wonder* as in (32a). If the label is determined according to

---

[18] His explanation is contradictory: on p. 11 Chomsky assumes that a label of a combination of two entities with the same category is this category. But in his treatment of coordination, he assumes that one of the conjuncts has to be raised, since otherwise the complete structure could not be labeled.

[19] As Bob Borsley (p.c. 2013) pointed out to me, this makes wrong predictions for coordinations of two singular noun phrases with *and*, since the result of the coordination is a plural DP and not a singular one like the first conjunct. Theories like HPSG can capture this by grouping features in bundles that can be shared in coordinated structures (syntactic features and nonlocal features, see Pollard & Sag (1994: 202)).

Furthermore the whole account cannot explain why (i.b) is ruled out.

(i) a. both Kim and Lee
     b. * both Kim or Lee

The information about the conjunction has to be part of the representation for *or Lee* in order to be able to contrast it with *and Lee*.

A further problem is that the label of α should be the label of W since Conj does not count for label determination. This would lead to a situation in which we have to choose between Z and W to determine the label of γ. Following Chomsky's logic, either Z or W would have to move on to make it possible to label γ. Chomsky (2013) mentions this problem in footnote 40, but does not provide a solution.

(29a), one gets an object that can function as the accusative object of *read* in (32b), that is, something that corresponds to a DP in GB terminology.

(32) a. I wonder what you wrote.
  b. I read what you wrote.

what you wrote in (32b) is a so-called free relative clause.

Chomsky's approach to free relative clauses is interesting but is unable to describe the phenomenon in full breadth. The problem is that the phrase that contains the relative pronoun may be complex (contrary to Donati's claims, see also Citko (2008: 930–932) for a rejection of Donati's claim).[20] (33) provides an English example from Bresnan & Grimshaw (1978: 333). German examples from Bausewein (1990: 155) and Müller (1999a: 78) are given in (34).

(33) I'll read [whichever book] you give me.

(34) a. Ihr könnt beginnen, [mit *wem*] ihr wollt.[21]
  you can start with whom you want
  'You can start with whoever you like.'

  b. [*Wessen* Birne] noch halbwegs in der Fassung steckt, pflegt solcherlei
  whose bulb/head yet halfway in the socket is uses such
  Erloschene zu meiden;[22]
  extinct to avoid
  'Those who still have their wits half way about them tend to avoid such vacant characters;'

  c. [*Wessen* Schuhe] „danach" besprenkelt sind, hat keinen Baum gefunden und
  whose shoes after.that speckled are has no tree found and
  war nicht zu einem Bogen in der Lage.[23]
  was not to a bow in the position
  'Those whose shoes are spattered afterwards couldn't find a tree and were incapable of peeing in an arc.'

Since *wessen Schuhe* 'whose shoes' is not a lexical item, rule (29b) has to be applied, provided no additional rules are assumed to deal with such cases. This means that the whole free relative clause *wessen Schuhe danach besprenkelt sind* is labeled as CP. For the free relatives in (33) and (34) the labeling as a CP is an unwanted result, since they function as subjects or objects of the matrix predicates and hence should be labelled DP. However, since *wessen Schuhe* is a complex phrase and not a lexical item, (29a) does not apply and hence there is no analysis of the free relative clause as a DP. Therefore,

---

[20] Chomsky (2013: 47) admits that there are many open questions as far as the labeling in free relative clauses is concerned and hence admits that there remain many open questions with labeling as such.
[21] Bausewein (1990: 155).
[22] Thomas Gsella, taz, 12.02.1997, p. 20.
[23] taz, taz mag, 08./09.08.1998, p. XII.

it seems one must return to something like the GB analysis proposed by Groos & van Riemsdijk (1981), at least for the German examples. Gross and van Riemsdijk assume that free relatives consist of an empty noun that is modified by the relative clause like a normal noun. In such an approach, the complexity of the relative phrase is irrelevant. It is only the empty head that is relevant for labeling the whole phrase.[24] However, once empty heads are countenanced in the analysis, the application of (29a) to (31) is undesirable since the application would result in two analyses for (32b): one with the empty nominal head and one in which (31) is labeled as DP directly. One might argue that in the case of several possible derivations, the most economical one wins, but the assumption of transderivational constraints leads to undesired consequences (Pullum 2013: Section 5).

Chomsky (2013) abandons the labeling condition in (29b) and replaces it with general labeling rules that hold for both internal and external Merge of two phrases. He distinguishes two cases. In the first case, labeling becomes possible since one of the two phrases of the set { XP, YP } is moved away. This case was already discussed above. Chomsky writes about the other case: *X and Y are identical in a relevant respect, provid-*

---

[24]Assuming an empty head is problematic since it may be used as an argument only in those cases in which it is modified by an adjunct, namely the relative clause (Müller 1999a: 97). See also Ott (2011: 187) for a later rediscovery of this problem. It can be solved in HPSG by assuming a unary projection that projects the appropriate category from a relative clause. I also use the unary projection to analyze so-called *nonmatching* free relative clauses (Müller 1999a). In constructions with nonmatching free relative clauses, the relative clause fills an argument slot that does not correspond to the properties of the relative phrase (Bausewein 1990). Bausewein discusses the following example, in which the relative phrase is a PP but the free relative fills the accusative slot of *kocht* 'cooks'.

   (i) Sie kocht, worauf   sie Appetit hat.
        she cooks where.on she appetite has
        'She cooks what she feels like eating.'

See Müller (1999a: 60–62) for corpus examples.

Minimalist theories do not employ unary projections. Ott (2011) develops an analysis in which the category of the relative phrase is projected, but he does not have a solution for nonmatching free relative clauses (p. 187). The same is true for Citko's analysis, in which an internally merged XP can provide the label.

Many other proposals for labeling or, rather, non-labeling exist. For instance, some Minimalists want to eliminate labeling altogether and argue for a label-free syntax. As was pointed out by Osborne, Putnam & Groß (2011), such analyses bring Minimalism closer to Dependency Grammar. It is unclear how any of these models could deal with non-matching free relative clauses. Groß & Osborne (2009: Section 5.3.3) provide an analysis of free relatives in their version of Dependency Grammar, but deny the existence of nonmatching ones (p. 78). They suggest an analysis in which the relative phrase is the root/label of the free relative clause and hence they have the same problem as Minimalist proposals have with non-matching free relative clauses. As Groß & Osborne (2009: 73) and Osborne et al. (2011: 327) state: empty heads are usually not assumed in (their version of) Dependency Grammar. Neither are unary branching projections. This seems to make it impossible to state that free relative clauses with a relative phrase YP can function as XP, provided XP is a category that is higher in the obliqueness hierarchy of Keenan & Comrie (1977), a generalization that was discovered by Bausewein (1990) (see also Müller 1999a: 60–62 and Vogel 2001: 4). In order to be able to express the relevant facts, an element or a label has to exist that is different from the label of *worauf* in (i).

ing the same label, which can be taken as the label of the SO (p. 11). He sketches an analysis of interrogative clauses on p. 13 in which the interrogative phrase has a Q feature and the remaining sentence from which the Q phrase was extracted has a Q feature as well. Since the two constituents share this property, the label of the complete clause will be Q. This kind of labeling will "perhaps" also be used for labeling normal sentences consisting of a subject and a verb phrase agreeing in person and number. These features would be responsible for the label of the sentence. The exact details are not worked out, but almost certainly will be more complex than (29b).

A property that is inherent in both Chomsky (2005) and Chomsky (2013) is that the label is exclusively determined from one of the merged objects. As Bob Borsley pointed out to me, this is problematic for interrogative/relative phrases like (35).

(35)   with whom

The phrase in (35) is both a prepositional phrase (because the first word is a preposition) and an interrogative/relative phrase (because the second word is an interrogative/relative word). So, what is needed for the correct labeling of PPs like the one in (35) is a well-defined way of percolating different properties from daughters to the mother node.[25]

For further problems concerning labeling and massive overgeneration by recent formulations of Merge see Fabregas et al. (2016).

Summarizing, one can say that labeling, which was introduced to simplify the theory and reduce the amount of language specific innate knowledge that has to be assumed, can only be made to function with a considerable amount of stipulations. For instance, the combination of lexical elements requires the assumption of empty functional heads, whose only purpose is determining the syntactic category of a certain lexical element. If this corresponded to linguistic reality, knowledge about labeling, the respective functional categories, and information about those categories that have to be ignored for the labeling would have to be part of innate language specific knowledge and nothing would be gained. One would be left with bizarre analyses with an enormous degree of complexity without having made progress in the Minimalist direction. Furthermore, there are empirical problems and a large number of unsolved cases.

---

[25]HPSG solves this problem by distinguishing head features including part of speech information and nonlocal features containing information about extraction and interrogative/relative elements. Head features are projected from the head, the nonlocal features of a mother node are the union of the nonlocal features of the daughters minus those that are bound off by certain heads or in certain configurations.

Citko (2008: 926) suggests an analysis in which both daughters can contribute to the mother node. The result is a complex label like { P, { D, N } }. This is a highly complex data structure and Citko does not provide any information on how the relevant information that it contains is accessed. Is an object with the label { P, { D, N } } a P, a D or an N? One could say that P has priority since it is in the least embedded set, but D and N are in one set. What about conflicting features? How does a preposition that selects for a DP decide whether { D, N } is a D or an N? In any case it is clear that a formalization will involve recursive relations that dig out elements of subsets in order to access their features. This adds to the overall complexity of the proposal and is clearly dispreferred over the HPSG solution, which uses one part of speech value per linguistic object.

4 Transformational Grammar – Minimalism

The conclusion is that the label of a binary combination should not be determined in the ways suggested by Chomsky (2008; 2013). An alternative option for computing the label is to use the functor of a functor argument structure as the label (Berwick & Epstein 1995: 145). This is the approach taken by Categorial Grammar (Ajdukiewicz 1935; Steedman 2000) and in Stabler's Minimalist Grammars (2011b).[26] Stabler's formalization of Merge will be discussed in Section 4.6.4.

4.6.3 Specifiers, complements, and the remains of $\overline{X}$ theory

Chomsky (2008: 146) assumes that every head has exactly one complement but an arbitrary number of specifiers. In standard $\overline{X}$ theory, the restriction that there can be at most one complement followed from the general $\overline{X}$ schema and the assumption that structures are at most binary branching: in standard $\overline{X}$ theory a lexical head was combined with all its complements to form an X′. If there are at most two daughters in a phrase, it follows that there can be only one complement (Sentences with ditransitive verbs have been analyzed with an empty head licensing an additional argument; see Larson (1988) for the suggestion of an empty verbal head and Müller & Wechsler (2014a: Sections 6.1 and 7) for a critical assessment of approaches involving little *v*). In standard $\overline{X}$ theory there was just one specifier. This restriction has now been abandoned. Chomsky writes that the distinction between specifier and complement can now be derived from the order in which elements are merged with their head: elements that are *first-merged* are complements and all others – those which are *later-merged* – are specifiers.

Such an approach is problematic for sentences with monovalent verbs: according to Chomsky's proposal, subjects of monovalent verbs would not be specifiers but complements.[27] This problem will be discussed in more detail in Section 4.6.4.

---

[26] For the Categorial Grammar approach to work, it is necessary to assign the category x/x to an adjunct, where x stands for the category of the head to which the adjunct attaches. For instance, an adjective combines with a nominal object to form a nominal object. Therefore its category is n/n rather than adj.

Similarly, Stabler's approach does not extend to adjuncts unless he is willing to assign the category noun to attributive adjectives. One way out of this problem is to assume a special combination operation for adjuncts and their heads (see Frey & Gärtner 2002: Section 3.2). Such a combination operation is equivalent to the Head-Adjunct Schema of HPSG.

[27] Pauline Jacobson (p.c. 2013) pointed out that the problem with intransitive verbs could be solved by assuming that the last-merged element is the specifier and all non-last-merged elements are complements. This would solve the problems with intransitive verbs and with the coordination of verbs in (36) but it would not solve the problem of coordination in head-final languages as in (39). Furthermore, current Minimalist approaches make use of multiple specifiers and this would be incompatible with the Jacobsonian proposal unless one would be willing to state more complicated restrictions on the status of non-first-merged elements.

Apart from this, theories assuming that syntactic objects merged with word groups are specifiers do not allow for analyses in which two lexical verbs are directly coordinated, as in (36):[28]

(36) He [knows and loves] this record.

For example, in an analysis suggested by Steedman (1991: 264), *and* (being the head) is first merged with *loves* and then the result is merged with *knows*. The result of this combination is a complex object that has the same syntactic properties as the combined parts: the result is a complex verb that needs a subject and an object. After the combination of the conjunction with the two verbs, the result has to be combined with *this record* and *he*. *this record* behaves in all relevant respects like a complement. Following Chomsky's definition, however, it should be a specifier, since it is combined with the third application of Merge. The consequences are unclear. Chomsky assumes that Merge does not specify constituent order. According to him, the linearization happens at the level of Phonological Form (PF). The restrictions that hold there are not described in his recent papers. However, if the categorization as complement or specifier plays a role for linearization as in Kayne's work (2011: 2, 12) and in Stabler's proposal (see Section 4.6.4), *this record* would have to be serialized before *knows and loves*, contrary to the facts. This means that a Categorial Grammar-like analysis of coordination is not viable and the only remaining option would seem to assume that *knows* is combined with an object and then two VPs are coordinated. Kayne (1994: 61, 67) follows Wexler & Culicover (1980: 303) in suggesting such an analysis and assumes that the object in the first VP is deleted. However, Borsley (2005: 471) shows that such an analysis makes wrong predictions, since (37a) would be derived from (37b) although these sentences differ in meaning.[29]

(37) a. Hobbs whistled and hummed the same tune.
      b. Hobbs whistled the same tune and hummed the same tune.

---

[28]Chomsky (2013: 46) suggests the coordination analysis in (30): according to this analysis, the verbs would be merged directly and one of the verbs would be moved around the conjunction in a later step of the derivation. As was mentioned in the previous section, such analyses do not contribute to the goal of making minimal assumptions about innate language specific knowledge since it is absolutely unclear how such an analysis of coordination would be acquired by language learners. Hence, I will not consider this coordination analysis here.

Another innovation of Chomsky's 2013 paper is that he eliminates the concept of specifier. He writes in footnote 27 on page 43: *There is a large and instructive literature on problems with Specifiers, but if the reasoning here is correct, they do not exist and the problems are unformulable.* This is correct, but this also means that everything that was explained with reference to the notion of specifier in the Minimalist framework until now does not have an explanation any longer. If one follows Chomsky's suggestion, a large part of the linguistic research of the past years becomes worthless and has to be redone.

Chomsky did not commit himself to a particular view on linearization in his earlier work, but somehow one has to ensure that the entities that were called specifier are realized in a position in which constituents are realized that used to be called specifier. This means that the following remarks will be relevant even under current Chomskyan assumptions.

[29]See also Bartsch & Vennemann (1972: 102), Jackendoff (1977: 192–193), Dowty (1979: 143), den Besten (1983: 104–105), Klein (1985: 8–9) and Eisenberg (1994b) for similar observations and criticism of similar proposals in earlier versions of Transformational Grammar.

Since semantic interpretation cannot see processes such as deletion that happen at the level of Phonological Form (Chomsky 1995b: Chapter 3), the differences in meaning cannot be explained by an analysis that deletes material.

In a further variant of the VP coordination analysis, there is a trace that is related to *this record*. This would be a *Right-Node-Raising* analysis. Borsley (2005) has shown that such analyses are problematic. Among the problematic examples that he discusses is the following pair (see also Bresnan 1974: 615).

(38) a. He tried to persuade and convince him.

b. * He tried to persuade, but couldn't convince, him.

The second example is ungrammatical if *him* is not stressed. In contrast, (38a) is well-formed even with unstressed *him*. So, if (38a) were an instance of Right-Node-Raising, the contrast would be unexpected. Borsley therefore excludes a Right-Node-Raising analysis.

The third possibility to analyze sentences like (36) assumes discontinuous constituents and uses material twice: the two VPs *knows this record* and *loves this record* are coordinated with the first VP being discontinuous. (See Crysmann (2001) and Beavers & Sag (2004) for such proposals in the framework of HPSG.) However, discontinuous constituents are not usually assumed in the Minimalist framework (see for instance Kayne (1994: 67)). Furthermore, Abeillé (2006) showed that there is evidence for structures in which lexical elements are coordinated directly. This means that one needs analyses like the CG analysis discussed above, which would result in the problems with the specifier/complement status just discussed.

Furthermore, Abeillé has pointed out that NP/DP coordinations in head-final languages like Korean and Japanese present difficulties for Merge-based analyses. (39) shows a Japanese example.

(39) Robin-to Kim
Robin-and Kim
'Kim and Robin'

In the first step *Robin* is merged with *to*. In a second step *Kim* is merged. Since *Kim* is a specifier, one would expect that *Kim* is serialized before the head as it is the case for other specifiers in head-final languages.

Chomsky tries to get rid of the unary branching structures of standard $\overline{X}$ theory, which were needed to project lexical items like pronouns and determiners into full phrases, referring to work by Muysken (1982). Muysken used the binary features MIN and MAX to classify syntactic objects as minimal (words or word-like complex objects) or maximal (syntactic objects that stand for complete phrases). Such a feature system can be used to describe pronouns and determiners as [+MIN, +MAX]. Verbs like *give*, however, are classified as [+MIN, −MAX]. They have to project in order to reach the [+MAX]-level. If specifiers and complements are required to be [+MAX], then determiners and pronouns fulfill this requirement without having to project from X^0 via X' to the XP-level.

4.6 New developments and theoretical variants

In Chomsky's system, the MIN/MAX distinction is captured with respect to the completeness of heads (complete = phrase) and to the property of being a lexical item. However, there is a small but important difference between Muysken's and Chomsky's proposal: the predictions with regard to the coordination data that was discussed above. Within the category system of $\overline{\text{X}}$ theory, it is possible to combine two X^0s to get a new, complex X^0. This new object has basically the same syntactic properties that simple X^0s have (see Jackendoff 1977: 51 and Gazdar, Klein, Pullum & Sag 1985). In Muysken's system, the coordination rule (or the lexical item for the conjunction) can be formulated such that the coordination of two +MIN items is a +MIN item. In Chomsky's system an analogous rule cannot be defined, since the coordination of two lexical items is not a lexical item any longer.

Like Chomsky in his recent Minimalist work, Categorial Grammar (Ajdukiewicz 1935) and HPSG (Pollard and Sag 1987; 1994: 39–40) do not (strictly) adhere to $\overline{\text{X}}$ theory. Both theories assign the symbol NP to pronouns (for CG see Steedman & Baldridge (2006: p. 615), see Steedman (2000: Section 4.4) for the incorporation of lexical type raising in order to accommodate quantification). The phrase *likes Mary* and the word *sleeps* have the same category in Categorial Grammar (s\np). In both theories it is not necessary to project a noun like *tree* from N^0 to $\overline{\text{N}}$ in order to be able to combine it with a determiner or an adjunct. Determiners and monovalent verbs in controlled infinitives are not projected from an X^0 level to the XP level in many HPSG analyses, since the valence properties of the respective linguistic objects (an empty SUBCAT or COMPS list) are sufficient to determine their combinatoric potential and hence their distribution (Müller 1996d; Müller 1999b). If the property of being minimal is needed for the description of a phenomenon, the binary feature LEX is used in HPSG (Pollard and Sag 1987: 172; 1994: 22). However, this feature is not needed for the distinction between specifiers and complements. This distinction is governed by principles that map elements of an argument structure list (ARG-ST) onto valence lists that are the value of the SPECIFIER and the COMPLEMENTS feature (abbreviated as SPR and COMPS respectively).[30] Roughly speaking, the specifier in a verbal projection is the least oblique argument of the verb for configurational languages like English. Since the argument structure list is ordered according to the obliqueness hierarchy of Keenan & Comrie (1977), the first element of this list is the least oblique argument of a verb and this argument is mapped to the SPR list. The element in the SPR list is realized to the left of the verb in SVO languages like English. The elements in the COMPS list are realized to the right of their head. Approaches like the one by Ginzburg & Sag (2000: 34, 364) that assume that head-complement phrases combine a word with its arguments have the same problem with coordinations like (36) since the head of the VP is not a word.[31] However, this restriction for the head can be replaced by one that refers

---

[30]Some authors assume a three-way distinction between subjects, specifiers, and complements.

[31]As mentioned above, a multidomination approach with discontinuous constituents is a possible solution for the analysis of (36) (see Crysmann 2001 and Beavers & Sag 2004). However, the coordination of lexical items has to be possible in principle as Abeillé (2006) has argued. Note also that the HPSG approach to coordination cannot be taken over to the MP. The reason is that the HPSG proposals involve special grammar rules for coordination and MP comes with the claim that there is only Merge. Hence the additional introduction of combinatorial rules is not an option within the MP.

to the LEX feature rather than to the property of being a word or lexical item.

Pollard & Sag as well as Sag & Ginzburg assume flat structures for English. Since one of the daughters is marked as lexical, it follows that the rule does not combine a head with a subset of its complements and then apply a second time to combine the result with further complements. Therefore, a structure like (40a) is excluded, since *gave John* is not a word and hence cannot be used as the head daughter in the rule.

(40)   a. [[gave John] a book]
         b. [gave John a book]

Instead of (40a), only analyses like (40b) are admitted; that is, the head is combined with all its arguments all in one go. The alternative is to assume binary branching structures (Müller 2015a; Müller & Ørsnes 2015: Section 1.2.2). In such an approach, the head complement schema does not restrict the word/phrase status of the head daughter. The binary branching structures in HPSG correspond to External Merge in the MP.

In the previous two sections, certain shortcomings of Chomsky's labeling definition and problems with the coordination of lexical items were discussed. In the following section, I discuss Stabler's definition of Merge in Minimalist Grammar, which is explicit about labeling and in one version does not have the problems discussed above. I will show that his formalization corresponds rather directly to HPSG representations.

4.6.4 Minimalism, Categorial Grammar, and HPSG

In this section, I will relate Minimalism, Categorial Grammar and HPSG to one another. Readers who are not yet familiar with Categorial Grammar and HPSG should skim this section or consult the Chapters 6, 8 and 9 and return here afterwards.

In Section 4.6.2, it was shown that Chomsky's papers leave many crucial details about labeling unspecified. Stabler's work is relatively close to recent Minimalist approaches, but is worked out much more precisely (see also Stabler (2011a: 397, 399, 400) on formalization of post GB approaches). Stabler (2001) shows how Kayne's theory of remnant movement can be formalized and implemented. Stabler refers to his particular way of formalizing Minimalist theories as *Minimalist Grammars* (MG). There are a number of interesting results with regard to the weak capacity of Minimalist Grammars and variants thereof (Michaelis 2001). It has been shown, for instance, that the number of possible languages one could create with MGs includes the set of those which can be created by Tree Adjoining Grammars (see Chapter 12). This means that it is possible to assign a greater number of word strings to structures with MGs, however, the structures derived by MGs are not necessarily always the same as the structures created by TAGs. For more on the generative capacity of grammars, see Chapter 17.

Although Stabler's work can be regarded as a formalization of Chomsky's Minimalist ideas, Stabler's approach differs from Chomsky's in certain matters of detail. Stabler assumes that the results of the two Merge operations are not sets but pairs. The head in a pair is marked by a pointer ('<' or '>'). Bracketed expressions like $\{\alpha, \{\alpha, \beta\}\}$ (discussed in Section 4.6.2) are replaced by trees like the one in (41).

4.6 New developments and theoretical variants

(41)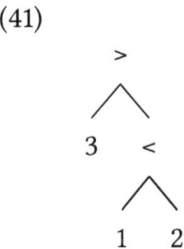

1 is the head in (41), 2 is the complement and 3 the specifier. The pointer points to the part of the structure that contains the head. The daughters in a tree are ordered, that is, 3 is serialized before 1 and 1 before 2.

Stabler (2011a: 402) defines External Merge as follows:

(42) $\text{em}(t_1[=f], t_2[f]) = \begin{cases} \begin{array}{c} < \\ \wedge \\ t_1 \ \ t_2 \end{array} & \text{if } t_1 \text{ has exactly 1 node} \\ \\ \begin{array}{c} > \\ \wedge \\ t_2 \ \ t_1 \end{array} & \text{otherwise} \end{cases}$

=f is a selection feature and f the corresponding category. When $t_1[=f]$ and $t_2[f]$ are combined, the result is a tree in which the selection feature of t_1 and the respective category feature of t_2 are deleted. The upper tree in (42) represents the combination of a (lexical) head with its complement. t_1 is positioned before t_2. The condition that t_1 has to have exactly one node corresponds to Chomsky's assumption that the first Merge is a Merge with a complement and that all further applications of Merge are Merges with specifiers (Chomsky 2008: 146).

Stabler defines Internal Merge as follows:[32]

(43) $\text{im}(t_1[+f]) =$

$$\begin{array}{c} > \\ \wedge \\ t_2^> \quad t_1\{t_2[-f]^> \mapsto \epsilon\} \end{array}$$

t_1 is a tree with a subtree t_2 which has the feature f with the value '−'. This subtree is deleted ($t_2[-f]^> \mapsto \epsilon$) and a copy of the deleted subtree without the −f feature ($t_2^>$) is positioned in specifier position. The element in specifier position has to be a maximal projection. This requirement is visualized by the raised '>'.

Stabler provides an example derivation for the sentence in (44).

(44) who Marie praises

---

[32] In addition to what is shown in (43), Stabler's definition contains a variant of the *Shortest Move Constraint* (SMC), which is irrelevant for the discussion at hand and hence will be omitted.

praises is a two-place verb with two =D features. This encodes the selection of two determiner phrases. *who* and *Marie* are two Ds and they fill the object and subject position of the verb. The resulting verbal projection *Marie praises who* is embedded under an empty complementizer which is specified as +WH and hence provides the position for the movement of *who*, which is placed in the specifier position of CP by the application of Internal Merge. The −WH feature of *who* is deleted and the result of the application of Internal Merge is *who Marie praises*.

This analysis has a problem that was pointed out by Stabler himself in unpublished work cited by Veenstra (1998: 124): it makes incorrect predictions in the case of monovalent verbs. If a verb is combined with an DP, the definition of External Merge in (42) treats this DP as a complement[33] and serializes it to the right of the head. Instead of analyses of sentences like (45a) one gets analyses of strings like (45b).

(45)   a.   Max sleeps.
      b.   * Sleeps Max.

To solve this problem, Stabler assumes that monovalent verbs are combined with a nonovert object (see Veenstra (1998: 61, 124) who, quoting Stabler's unpublished work, also adopts this solution). With such an empty object, the resulting structure contains the empty object as a complement. The empty object is serialized to the right of the verb and *Max* is the specifier and hence serialized to the left of the verb as in (46).

(46)   Max sleeps _.

Of course, any analysis of this kind is both stipulative and entirely ad hoc, being motivated only by the wish to have uniform structures. Moreover, it exemplifies precisely one of the methodological deficiencies of Transformational Generative Grammar discussed at length by Culicover & Jackendoff (2005: Section 2.1.2): the excessive appeal to uniformity.

An alternative is to assume an empty verbal head that takes *sleeps* as complement and *Max* as subject. Such an analysis is often assumed for ditransitive verbs in Minimalist theories which assume Larsonian verb shells (Larson 1988). Larsonian analyses usually assume that there is an empty verbal head that is called little *v* and that contributes a causative meaning. As was discussed in Section 4.1.4, Adger (2003) adopts a little *v*-based analysis for intransitive verbs. Omitting the TP projection, his analysis is provided in Figure 4.22 on the next page. Adger argues that the analysis of sentences with unergative verbs involves a little *v* that selects an agent, while the analysis of unaccusative verbs involves a little *v* that does not select an N head. For unaccusatives, he assumes that the verb selects a theme. He states that little *v* does not necessarily have a causative meaning but introduces the agent. But note that in the example at hand the subject of *sleep* is neither causing an event, nor is it necessarily deliberately doing something. So it is rather an undergoer than an agent. This means that the assumption of the empty *v* head is made for purely theory-internal reasons without any semantic motivation in the

---

[33]Compare also Chomsky's definition of specifier and complement in Section 4.6.3.

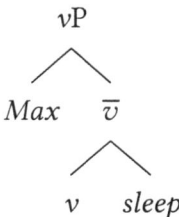

Figure 4.22: Little *v*-based analysis of *Max sleeps*

case of intransitives. If the causative contribution of little *v* in ditransitive constructions is assumed, this would mean that one needs two little *v*s, one with and one without a causative meaning. In addition to the lack of theory-external motivation for little *v*, there are also empirical problems for such analyses (for instance with coordination data). The reader is referred to Müller & Wechsler (2014a: Sections 6.1 and 7) for further details.

Apart from the two operations that were defined in (42) and (43), there are no other operations in MG.[34] Apart from the problems with monovalent verbs, this results in the problem that was discussed in Section 4.6.3: there is no analysis with a direct combination of verbs for (36) – repeated here as (47).

(47) He [knows and loves] this record.

The reason is that the combination of *knows, and* and *loves* consists of three nodes and the Merge of *knows and loves* with *this record* would make *this record* the specifier of the structure. Therefore *this record* would be serialized before *knows and loves*, contrary to the facts. Since the set of languages that can be generated with MGs contains the languages that can be generated with certain TAGs and with Combinatorial Categorial Grammar (Michaelis 2001), the existence of a Categorial Grammar analysis implies that the coordination examples can be derived in MGs somehow. But for linguists, the fact that it is possible to generate a certain string at all (the weak capacity of a grammar) is of less significance. It is the actual structures that are licensed by the grammar that are important (the strong capacity).

4.6.4.1 Directional Minimalist Grammars and Categorial Grammar

Apart from reintroducing X^0 categories, the coordination problem can be solved by changing the definition of Merge in a way that allows heads to specify the direction of combination with their arguments: Stabler (2011b: p. 635) suggests marking the position of an argument relative to its head together with the selection feature and gives the following redefinition of External Merge.

---

[34]For extensions see Frey & Gärtner (2002: Section 3.2).

4 Transformational Grammar – Minimalism

(48) $\text{em}(t_1[\alpha], t_2[x]) = \begin{cases} \begin{array}{c} < \\ \wedge \\ t_1 \ \ t_2 \end{array} & \text{if } \alpha \text{ is =x} \\ \begin{array}{c} > \\ \wedge \\ t_2 \ \ t_1 \end{array} & \text{if } \alpha \text{ is x=} \end{cases}$

The position of the equal sign specifies on which side of the head an argument has to be realized. This corresponds to forward and backward Application in Categorial Grammar (see Section 8.1.1). Stabler calls this form of grammar Directional MG (DMG). This variant of MG avoids the problem with monovalent verbs and the coordination data is unproblematic as well if one assumes that the conjunction is a head with a variable category that selects for elements of the same category to the left and to the right of itself. *know* and *love* would both select an object to the right and a subject to the left and this requirement would be transferred to *knows and loves*.[35] See Steedman (1991: 264) for the details of the CG analysis and Bouma & van Noord (1998: 52) for an earlier HPSG proposal involving directionality features along the lines suggested by Stabler for his DMGs.

4.6.4.2 Minimalist Grammars and Head-Driven Phrase Structure Grammar

The notation for marking the head of a structure with '>' and '<' corresponds directly to the HPSG representation of heads. Since HPSG is a sign-based theory, information about all relevant linguistic levels is represented in descriptions (phonology, morphology, syntax, semantics, information structure). (49) gives an example: the lexical item for the word *grammar*.

(49) $\begin{bmatrix} word \\ \text{PHON} & \langle \text{'gramər} \rangle \\ \text{SYNSEM}|\text{LOC} & \begin{bmatrix} loc \\ \text{CAT} & \begin{bmatrix} cat \\ \text{HEAD} & noun \\ \text{SPR} & \langle \text{DET} \rangle \end{bmatrix} \\ \text{CONT} & \ldots \begin{bmatrix} grammar \\ \text{INST} & X \end{bmatrix} \end{bmatrix} \end{bmatrix}$

The part of speech of *grammar* is *noun*. In order to form a complete phrase, it requires a determiner. This is represented by giving the SPR feature the value ⟨ DET ⟩. Semantic information is listed under CONT. For details see Chapter 9.

---

[35] Note however, that this transfer makes it necessary to select complex categories, a fact that I overlooked in Müller (2013c). The selection of simplex features vs. complex categories will be discussed in Section 4.6.5.

4.6 New developments and theoretical variants

Since we are dealing with syntactic aspects exclusively, only a subset of the used features is relevant: valence information and information about part of speech and certain morphosyntactic properties that are relevant for the external distribution of a phrase is represented in a feature description under the path SYNSEM|LOC|CAT. The features that are particularly interesting here are the so-called head features. Head features are shared between a lexical head and its maximal projection. The head features are located inside CAT and are grouped together under the path HEAD. Complex hierarchical structure is also modelled with feature value pairs. The constituents of a complex linguistic object are usually represented as parts of the representation of the complete object. For instance, there is a feature HEAD-DAUGHTER the value of which is a feature structure that models a linguistic object that contains the head of a phrase. The Head Feature Principle (50) refers to this daughter and ensures that the head features of the head daughter are identical with the head features of the mother node, that is, they are identical to the head features of the complete object.

(50) $\textit{headed-phrase} \Rightarrow \begin{bmatrix} \text{SYNSEM}|\text{LOC}|\text{CAT}|\text{HEAD} \; \boxed{1} \\ \text{HEAD-DTR}|\text{SYNSEM}|\text{LOC}|\text{CAT}|\text{HEAD} \; \boxed{1} \end{bmatrix}$

Identity is represented by boxes with the same number.

Ginzburg & Sag (2000: 30) represent all daughters of a linguistic object in a list that is given as the value of the DAUGHTERS attribute. The value of the feature HEAD-DAUGHTER is identified with one of the elements of the DAUGHTERS list:

(51) a. $\begin{bmatrix} \text{HEAD-DTR} \; \boxed{1} \\ \text{DTRS} \quad \langle \boxed{1} \; \alpha, \beta \rangle \end{bmatrix}$

b. $\begin{bmatrix} \text{HEAD-DTR} \; \boxed{1} \\ \text{DTRS} \quad \langle \alpha, \boxed{1} \; \beta \rangle \end{bmatrix}$

α and β are shorthands for descriptions of linguistic objects. The important point about the two descriptions in (51) is that the head daughter is identical to one of the two daughters, which is indicated by the $\boxed{1}$ in front of α and β, respectively. In the first feature description, the first daughter is the head and in the second description, the second daughter is the head. Because of the Head Feature Principle, the syntactic properties of the whole phrase are determined by the head daughter. That is, the syntactic properties of the head daughter correspond to the label in Chomsky's definition. This notation corresponds exactly to the one that is used by Stabler: (51a) is equivalent to (52a) and (51b) is equivalent to (52b).

(52) a.   b.

An alternative structuring of this basic information, discussed by Pollard & Sag (1994: Chapter 9), uses the two features HEAD-DAUGHTER and NON-HEAD-DAUGHTERS rather than HEAD-DAUGHTER and DAUGHTERS. This gives rise to feature descriptions like (53a), which corresponds directly to Chomsky's set-based representations, discussed in Section 4.6.2 and repeated here as (53b).

(53) a. $\begin{bmatrix} \text{HEAD-DTR} & \alpha \\ \text{NON-HEAD-DTRS} & \langle \beta \rangle \end{bmatrix}$

b. $\{\alpha, \{\alpha, \beta\}\}$

The representation in (53a) does not contain information about linear precedence of α and β. Linear precedence of constituents is constrained by linear precedence rules, which are represented independently from constraints regarding (immediate) dominance.

The definition of Internal Merge in (43) corresponds to the Head-Filler Schema in HPSG (Pollard & Sag 1994: 164). Stabler's derivational rule deletes the subtree $t_2[-f]^>$. HPSG is monotonic, that is, nothing is deleted in structures that are licensed by a grammar. Instead of deleting t_2 inside of a larger structure, structures containing an empty element (NB – not a tree) are licensed directly.[36] Both in Stabler's definition and in the HPSG schema, t_2 is realized as filler in the structure. In Stabler's definition of Internal Merge, the category of the head daughter is not mentioned, but Pollard & Sag (1994: 164) restrict the head daughter to be a finite verbal projection. Chomsky (2007: 17) assumes that all operations but External Merge operate on phase level. Chomsky assumes that CP and v*P are phases. If this constraint is incorporated into the definition in (43), the restrictions on the label of t_1 would have to be extended accordingly. In HPSG, sentences like (54) have been treated as VPs, not as CPs and hence Pollard & Sag's requirement that the head daughter in the Head Filler Schema be verbal corresponds to Chomsky's restriction.

(54) Bagels, I like.

Hence, despite minor presentational differences, we may conclude that the formalization of Internal Merge and that of the Head-Filler Schema are very similar.

An important difference between HPSG and Stabler's definition is that 'movement' is not feature driven in HPSG. This is an important advantage since feature-driven movement cannot deal with instances of so-called altruistic movement (Fanselow 2003a), that is, movement of a constituent that happens in order to make room for another constituent in a certain position (see Section 4.6.1.4).

A further difference between general $\overline{\text{X}}$ theory and Stabler's formalization of Internal Merge on the one hand and HPSG on the other is that in the latter case there is no restriction regarding the completeness (or valence 'saturation') of the filler daughter. Whether the filler daughter has to be a maximal projection (English) or not (German),

---

[36] See Bouma, Malouf & Sag (2001) for a traceless analysis of extraction in HPSG and Müller (2017a: Chapter 7) and Chapter 19 of this book for a general discussion of empty elements.

follows from restrictions that are enforced locally when the trace is combined with its head. This makes it possible to analyze sentences like (55) without remnant movement.[37]

(55) Gelesen$_i$ hat$_j$ das Buch keiner $\_i$ $\_j$.
read has the book nobody

In contrast, Stabler is forced to assume an analysis like the one in (56b) (see also G. Müller (1998) for a remnant movement analysis). In a first step, *das Buch* is moved out of the VP (56a) and in a second step, the emptied VP is fronted as in (56b).

(56) a. Hat [das Buch]$_j$ [keiner [$_{VP}$ $\_j$ gelesen]].
b. [$_{VP}$ $\_j$ Gelesen]$_i$ hat [das Buch]$_j$ [keiner $\_i$].

Haider (1993: 281), De Kuthy & Meurers (2001: Section 2) and Fanselow (2002) showed that this kind of remnant movement analysis is problematic for German. The only phenomenon that Fanselow identified as requiring a remnant movement analysis is the problem of multiple fronting (see Müller (2003a) for an extensive discussion of relevant data). Müller (2005b,c; 2017a) develops an alternative analysis of these multiple frontings which uses an empty verbal head in the *Vorfeld*, but does not assume that adjuncts or arguments like *das Buch* in (56b) are extracted from the *Vorfeld* constituent. Instead of the remnant movement analysis, the mechanism of argument composition from Categorial Grammar (Geach 1970; Hinrichs & Nakazawa 1994) is used to ensure the proper realization of arguments in the sentence. Chomsky (2007: 20) already uses argument composition as part of his analysis of TPs and CPs. Hence both remnant movement and argument composition are assumed in recent Minimalist proposals. The HPSG alternative, however, would appear to need less theoretical apparatus and hence has to be preferred for reasons of parsimony.

Finally, it should be mentioned that all transformational accounts have problems with Across the Board extraction like (57a) and (57) in which one element corresponds to several gaps.

(57) a. Bagels, I like and Ellison hates.[38]
b. The man who$_i$ [Mary loves $\_i$] and [Sally hates $\_i$] computed my tax.

This problem was solved for GPSG by Gazdar (1981b) and the solution carries over to HPSG. The Minimalist community tried to address these problems by introducing operations like sideward movement (Nunes 2004) where constituents can be inserted into sister trees. So in the example in (57a), *Bagels* is copied from the object position of *hates* into the object position of *like* and then these two copies are related to the fronted element. Kobele criticized such solutions since they overgenerate massively and need complicated filters. What he suggests instead is the introduction of a GPSG-style SLASH mechanism into Minimalist theories (Kobele 2008).

---

[37] See also Müller & Ørsnes (2013b) for an analysis of object shift in Danish that can account for verb fronting without remnant movement. The analysis does not have any of the problems that remnant movement analyses have.
[38] Pollard & Sag (1994: 205).

Furthermore, movement paradoxes (Bresnan 2001: Chapter 2) can be avoided by not sharing all information between filler and gap, a solution that is not available for transformational accounts, which usually assume identity of filler and gap or – as under the Copy Theory of Movement – assume that a derivation contains multiple copies of one object only one of which is spelled out. See also Borsley (2012) for further puzzles for, and problems of, movement-based approaches.

A further difference between MG and HPSG is that the Head-Filler Schema is not the only schema for analyzing long-distance dependencies. As was noted in footnote 12 on page 147, there is dislocation to the right (extraposition) as well as fronting. Although these should certainly be analyzed as long-distance dependencies, they differ from other long-distance dependencies in various respects (see Section 13.1.5). For analyses of extraposition in the HPSG framework, see Keller (1995), Bouma (1996), and Müller (1999b).

Apart from the schema for long-distance dependencies, there are of course other schemata in HPSG which are not present in MG or Minimalism. These are schemata which describe constructions without heads or are necessary to capture the distributional properties of parts of constructions, which cannot be easily captured in lexical analyses (e.g., the distribution of *wh*- and relative pronouns). See Section 21.10.

Chomsky (2010) has compared a Merge-based analysis of auxiliary inversion to a HPSG analysis and critiqued that the HPSG analysis uses ten schemata rather than one (Merge). Ginzburg & Sag (2000) distinguish three types of construction with moved auxiliaries: inverted sentences such as those with fronted adverbial and with *wh*-questions (58a,b), inverted exclamatives (58c) and polar interrogatives (58d):

(58) a. Under no circumstances *did she think they would do that.*
 b. Whose book *are you reading*?
 c. Am I tired!
 d. Did Kim leave?

Fillmore (1999) captures various different usage contexts in his Construction Grammar analysis of auxiliary inversion and shows that there are semantic and pragmatic differences between the various contexts. Every theory must be able to account for these. Furthermore, one does not necessarily require ten schemata. It is possible to determine this – as Categorial Grammar does – in the lexical entry for the auxiliary or on an empty head (see Chapter 21 for a more general discussion of lexical and phrasal analyses). Regardless of this, every theory has to somehow account for these ten differences. If one wishes to argue that this has nothing to do with syntax, then somehow this has to be modelled in the semantic component. This means that there is no reason to prefer one theory over another at this point.

4.6.5 Selection of atomic features vs. selection of complex categories

Berwick & Epstein (1995) pointed out that Minimalist theories are very similar to Categorial Grammar and I have discussed the similarities between Minimalist theories and

4.6 New developments and theoretical variants

HPSG in Müller (2013c) and in the previous subsections. However, I overlooked one crucial difference between the usual assumptions about selection in Minimalist proposals on the one hand and Categorial Grammar, Dependency Grammar, LFG, HPSG, TAG, and Construction Grammar on the other hand: what is selected in the former type of theory is a single feature, while the latter theories select for feature bundles. This seems to be a small difference, but the consequences are rather severe. Stabler's definition of External Merge that was given on page 165 removes the selection feature (=f) and the corresponding feature of the selected element (f). In some publications and in the introduction in this book, the selection features are called uninterpretable features and are marked with a *u*. The uninterpretable features have to be checked and then they are removed from the linguistic object as in Stabler's definition. The fact that they have been checked is represented by striking them out. It is said that all uninterpretable features have to be checked before a syntactic object is send to the interfaces (semantics and pronunciation). If uninterpretable features are not checked, the derivation crashes. Adger (2003: Section 3.6) explicitly discusses the consequences of these assumptions: a selecting head checks a feature of the selected object. It is not possible to check features of elements that are contained in the object that a head combines with. Only features at the topmost node, the so-called root node, can be checked with external merge. The only way features inside complex objects can be checked is by means of movement. This means that a head may not combine with a partially saturated linguistic object, that is, with a linguistic object that has an unchecked selection feature. I will discuss this design decision with reference to an example provided by Adger (2003: 95). The noun *letters* selects for a P and Ps select for an N. The analysis of (59a) is depicted left in Figure 4.23.

(59) a. letters to Peter
     b. * letters to

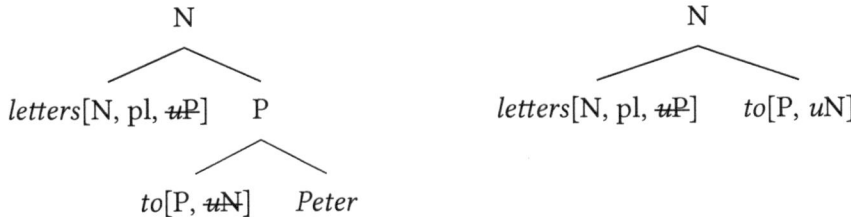

Figure 4.23: The analysis of *letters to Peter* according to Adger (2003: 95)

The string in (59b) is ruled out since the uninterpretable N feature of the preposition *to* is not checked. So this integrates the constraint that all dependent elements have to be maximal into the core mechanism. This makes it impossible to analyze examples like (60) in the most straightforward way, namely as involving a complex preposition and a noun that is lacking a determiner:

(60) vom   Bus
     from.the bus

In theories in which complex descriptions can be used to describe dependants, the dependent may be partly saturated. So for instance in HPSG, fused prepositions like *vom* 'from.the' can select an $\overline{\text{N}}$, which is a nominal projection lacking a specifier:

(61) N[SPR ⟨ DET ⟩]

The description in (61) is an abbreviation for an internally structured set of feature-value pairs (see Section 9.1.1). The example here is given for the illustration of the differences only, since there may be ways of accounting for such cases in a single-feature-Merge system. For instance, one could assume a DP analysis and have the complex preposition select a complete NP (something of category N with no uninterpretable features). Alternatively, one can assume that there is indeed a full PP with all the structure that is usually assumed and the fusion of preposition and determiner happens during pronunciation. The first suggestion eliminates the option of assuming an NP analysis as it was suggested by Bruening (2009) in the Minimalist framework.

Apart from this illustrative example with a fused preposition, there are other cases in which one may want to combine unsaturated linguistic objects. I already discussed coordination examples above. Another example is the verbal complex in languages like German, Dutch, and Japanese. Of course there are analyses of these languages that do not assume a verbal complex (G. Müller 1998; Wurmbrand 2003a), but these are not without problems. Some of the problems were discussed in the previous section as well.

Summing up this brief subsection, it has to be said that the feature checking mechanism that is built into the conception of Merge is more restrictive than the selection that is used in Categorial Grammar, Lexical Functional Grammar, HPSG, Construction Grammar, and TAG. In my opinion, it is too restrictive.

4.6.6 Summary

In sum, one can say that the computational mechanisms of the Minimalist Program (e.g., transderivational constraints and labeling), as well as the theory of feature-driven movement are problematic and the assumption of empty functional categories is sometimes ad hoc. If one does not wish to assume that these categories are shared by all languages, then proposing two mechanisms (Merge and Move) does not represent a simplification of grammar since every single functional category which must be stipulated constitutes a complication of the entire system.

The labeling mechanism is not yet worked out in detail, does not account for the phenomena it was claimed to provide accounts for, and hence should be replaced by the head/functor-based labeling that is used in Categorial Grammar and HPSG.

4.7 Summary and classification

This section is similar to Section 3.6. I first comment on language acquisition and then on formalization.

4.7.1 Explaining language acquisition

Chomsky (2008: 135) counts theories in the MP as Principle & Parameter analyses and identifies MP parameters as being in the lexicon. Also, see Hornstein (2013: 396). UG is defined as possibly containing non-language-specific components, which are genetically determined (Chomsky 2007: 7). UG consists of unbounded Merge and the condition that expressions derived by a grammar must fulfill the restrictions imposed by the phonological and conceptual-intentional interfaces. In addition, a specific repertoire of features is assumed to be part of UG (Chomsky 2007: 6–7). The exact nature of these features has not been explained in detail and, as a result, the power of UG is somewhat vague. However, there is a fortunate convergence between various linguistic camps as Chomsky does not assume that the swathes of functional projections which we encountered in Section 4.6.1 also form part of UG (however, authors like Cinque & Rizzi (2010) do assume that a hierarchy of functional projections is part of UG). Since there are still parameters, the same arguments used against GB approaches to language acquisition that were mentioned in Section 3.6.1 are still relevant for theories of language acquisition in the Minimalist Program. See Chapter 16 for an in-depth discussion of approaches to language acquisition and the Principles & Parameters model as well as input-based approaches.

Chomsky's main goal in the Minimalist Program is to simplify the theoretical assumptions regarding formal properties of language and the computational mechanisms that are used so much as to make it plausible that they or relevant parts of them are part of our genetic endowment. But if we recapitulate what was assumed in this chapter, it is difficult to believe that Minimalist theories achieve this goal. To derive a simple sentence with an intransitive verb, one needs several empty heads and movements. Features can be strong or weak, Agree operates nonlocally in trees across several phrase boundaries. And in order to make correct predictions, it has to be made sure that Agree can only see the closest possible element (13)–(14). This is a huge machinery in comparison to a Categorial Grammar that just combines adjacent things. Categorial Grammars can be acquired from input (see Section 13.8.3), while it is really hard to imagine how the fact that there are features that trigger movement when they are strong, but do not trigger it when they are weak, should be acquired from data alone.

4.7.2 Formalization

Section 3.6.2 commented on the lack of formalization in transformational grammar up until the 1990s. The general attitude towards formalization did not change in the minimalist era and hence there are very few formalizations and implementations of Minimalist theories.

Stabler (2001) shows how it is possible to formalize and implement Kayne's theory of remnant movement. In Stabler's implementation[39], there are no transderivational

---
[39] His system is available at: http://linguistics.ucla.edu/people/stabler/coding.html. 2018-02-20.

constraints, no numerations[40], he does not assume Agree (see Fong 2014: 132) etc. The following is also true of Stabler's implementation of Minimalist Grammars and GB systems: there are no large grammars. Stabler's grammars are small, meant as a proof of concept and purely syntactic. There is no morphology[41], no treatment of multiple agreement (Stabler 2011b: Section 27.4.3) and above all no semantics. PF and LF processes are not modelled.[42] The grammars and the computational system developed by Sandiway Fong are of similar size and faithfulness to the theory (Fong & Ginsburg 2012; Fong 2014): the grammar fragments are small, encode syntactic aspects such as labeling directly in the phrase structure (Fong & Ginsburg 2012: Section 4) and therefore, fall behind $\overline{\text{X}}$ theory. Furthermore, they do not contain any morphology. Spell-Out is not implemented, so in the end it is not possible to parse or generate any utterances.[43] Herring's (2016) dissertation is a promising beginning. Herring developed a system that can be used for

---

[40] There is a numeration lexicon in Veenstra (1998: Chapter 9). This lexicon consists of a set of numerations, which contain functional heads, which can be used in sentences of a certain kind. For example, Veenstra assumes numerations for sentences with bivalent verbs and subjects in initial position, for embedded sentences with monovalent verbs, for *wh*-questions with monovalent verbs, and for polar interrogatives with monovalent verbs. An element from this set of numerations corresponds to a particular configuration and a phrasal construction in the spirit of Construction Grammar. Veenstra's analysis is not a formalization of the concept of the numeration that one finds in Minimalist works. Normally, it is assumed that a numeration contains all the lexical entries which are needed for the derivation of a sentence. As (i) shows, complex sentences can consist of combinations of sentences with various different sentence types:

(i) Der Mann, der   behauptet hat, dass Maria gelacht hat, steht   neben der Palme,   die   im letzten
     the man   who claimed   has that Maria laughed has stands next.to the palm.tree which in last
     Jahr gepflanzt wurde.
     year planted   was

     'The man who claimed Maria laughed is standing next to the palm tree that was planted last year.'

In (i), there are two relative clauses with verbs of differing valence, an embedded sentence with a monovalent verb and the matrix clause. Under a traditional understanding of numerations, Veenstra would have to assume an infinite numeration lexicon containing all possible combinations of sentence types.

[41] The test sentences have the form as in (i).

(i) a. the king will -s eat
     b. the king have -s eat -en
     c. the king be -s eat -ing
     d. the king -s will -s have been eat -ing the pie

[42] See Sauerland & Elbourne (2002) for suggestions of PF and LF-movement and the deletion of parts of copies (p. 285). The implementation of this would be far from trivial.

[43] The claim by Berwick, Pietroski, Yankama & Chomsky (2011: 1221) in reference to Fong's work is just plain wrong: *But since we have sometimes adverted to computational considerations, as with the ability to "check" features of a head/label, this raises a legitimate concern about whether our framework is computationally realizable. So it is worth noting that the copy conception of movement, along with the locally oriented "search and labeling" procedure described above, can be implemented computationally as an efficient parser; see Fong, 2014, for details.* If one has a piece of software which cannot parse a single sentence, then one cannot claim that it is efficient since one does not know whether the missing parts of the program could make it extremely inefficient. Furthermore, one cannot compare the software to other programs. As has already been discussed, labeling is not carried out by Fong as was described in Chomsky's work, but instead he uses a phrase structure grammar of the kind described in Chapter 2.

4.7.1 Explaining language acquisition

Chomsky (2008: 135) counts theories in the MP as Principle & Parameter analyses and identifies MP parameters as being in the lexicon. Also, see Hornstein (2013: 396). UG is defined as possibly containing non-language-specific components, which are genetically determined (Chomsky 2007: 7). UG consists of unbounded Merge and the condition that expressions derived by a grammar must fulfill the restrictions imposed by the phonological and conceptual-intentional interfaces. In addition, a specific repertoire of features is assumed to be part of UG (Chomsky 2007: 6–7). The exact nature of these features has not been explained in detail and, as a result, the power of UG is somewhat vague. However, there is a fortunate convergence between various linguistic camps as Chomsky does not assume that the swathes of functional projections which we encountered in Section 4.6.1 also form part of UG (however, authors like Cinque & Rizzi (2010) do assume that a hierarchy of functional projections is part of UG). Since there are still parameters, the same arguments used against GB approaches to language acquisition that were mentioned in Section 3.6.1 are still relevant for theories of language acquisition in the Minimalist Program. See Chapter 16 for an in-depth discussion of approaches to language acquisition and the Principles & Parameters model as well as input-based approaches.

Chomsky's main goal in the Minimalist Program is to simplify the theoretical assumptions regarding formal properties of language and the computational mechanisms that are used so much as to make it plausible that they or relevant parts of them are part of our genetic endowment. But if we recapitulate what was assumed in this chapter, it is difficult to believe that Minimalist theories achieve this goal. To derive a simple sentence with an intransitive verb, one needs several empty heads and movements. Features can be strong or weak, Agree operates nonlocally in trees across several phrase boundaries. And in order to make correct predictions, it has to be made sure that Agree can only see the closest possible element (13)–(14). This is a huge machinery in comparison to a Categorial Grammar that just combines adjacent things. Categorial Grammars can be acquired from input (see Section 13.8.3), while it is really hard to imagine how the fact that there are features that trigger movement when they are strong, but do not trigger it when they are weak, should be acquired from data alone.

4.7.2 Formalization

Section 3.6.2 commented on the lack of formalization in transformational grammar up until the 1990s. The general attitude towards formalization did not change in the minimalist era and hence there are very few formalizations and implementations of Minimalist theories.

Stabler (2001) shows how it is possible to formalize and implement Kayne's theory of remnant movement. In Stabler's implementation[39], there are no transderivational

---

[39] His system is available at: http://linguistics.ucla.edu/people/stabler/coding.html. 2018-02-20.

constraints, no numerations[40], he does not assume Agree (see Fong 2014: 132) etc. The following is also true of Stabler's implementation of Minimalist Grammars and GB systems: there are no large grammars. Stabler's grammars are small, meant as a proof of concept and purely syntactic. There is no morphology[41], no treatment of multiple agreement (Stabler 2011b: Section 27.4.3) and above all no semantics. PF and LF processes are not modelled.[42] The grammars and the computational system developed by Sandiway Fong are of similar size and faithfulness to the theory (Fong & Ginsburg 2012; Fong 2014): the grammar fragments are small, encode syntactic aspects such as labeling directly in the phrase structure (Fong & Ginsburg 2012: Section 4) and therefore, fall behind $\overline{\text{X}}$ theory. Furthermore, they do not contain any morphology. Spell-Out is not implemented, so in the end it is not possible to parse or generate any utterances.[43] Herring's (2016) dissertation is a promising beginning. Herring developed a system that can be used for

---

[40] There is a numeration lexicon in Veenstra (1998: Chapter 9). This lexicon consists of a set of numerations, which contain functional heads, which can be used in sentences of a certain kind. For example, Veenstra assumes numerations for sentences with bivalent verbs and subjects in initial position, for embeded sentences with monovalent verbs, for *wh*-questions with monovalent verbs, and for polar interrogatives with monovalent verbs. An element from this set of numerations corresponds to a particular configuration and a phrasal construction in the spirit of Construction Grammar. Veenstra's analysis is not a formalization of the concept of the numeration that one finds in Minimalist works. Normally, it is assumed that a numeration contains all the lexical entries which are needed for the derivation of a sentence. As (i) shows, complex sentences can consist of combinations of sentences with various different sentence types:

(i) Der Mann, der behauptet hat, dass Maria gelacht hat, steht neben der Palme, die im letzten
    the man who claimed has that Maria laughed has stands next.to the palm.tree which in last
    Jahr gepflanzt wurde.
    year planted was
    'The man who claimed Maria laughed is standing next to the palm tree that was planted last year.'

In (i), there are two relative clauses with verbs of differing valence, an embedded sentence with a monovalent verb and the matrix clause. Under a traditional understanding of numerations, Veenstra would have to assume an infinite numeration lexicon containing all possible combinations of sentence types.

[41] The test sentences have the form as in (i).

(i) a. the king will -s eat
    b. the king have -s eat -en
    c. the king be -s eat -ing
    d. the king -s will -s have been eat -ing the pie

[42] See Sauerland & Elbourne (2002) for suggestions of PF and LF-movement and the deletion of parts of copies (p. 285). The implementation of this would be far from trivial.

[43] The claim by Berwick, Pietroski, Yankama & Chomsky (2011: 1221) in reference to Fong's work is just plain wrong: *But since we have sometimes adverted to computational considerations, as with the ability to "check" features of a head/label, this raises a legitimate concern about whether our framework is computationally realizable. So it is worth noting that the copy conception of movement, along with the locally oriented "search and labeling" procedure described above, can be implemented computationally as an efficient parser; see Fong, 2011, for details.* If one has a piece of software which cannot parse a single sentence, then one cannot claim that it is efficient since one does not know whether the missing parts of the program could make it extremely inefficient. Furthermore, one cannot compare the software to other programs. As has already been discussed, labeling is not carried out by Fong as was described in Chomsky's work, but instead he uses a phrase structure grammar of the kind described in Chapter 2.

grammar development in the Minimalist Program. In the version described in his thesis the system could generate but was unable to parse sentences (p. 138, 143). PF phenomena were not modeled (p. 142–143) and the two example fragments are small and come without a semantics (p. 143).

The benchmark here has been set by implementations of grammars in constraint-based theories; for example, the HPSG grammars of German (Müller & Kasper 2000), English (Flickinger, Copestake & Sag 2000) and Japanese (Siegel 2000) that were developed in the 90s as part of Verbmobil (Wahlster 2000) for the analysis of spoken language or the LFG or CCG systems with large coverage. These grammars can analyze up to 83 % of utterances in spoken language (for Verbmobil from the domains of appointment scheduling and trip planning) or written language. Linguistic knowledge is used to generate and analyze linguistic structures. In one direction, one arrives at a semantic representation of a string of words and in the other one can create a string of words from a given semantic representation. A morphological analysis is indispensable for analyzing naturally occurring data from languages with elaborated morphological marking systems. In the remainder of this book, the grammars and computational systems developed in other theories will be discussed at the beginning of the respective chapters.

The reason for the lack of larger fragments inside of GB/MP could have to do with the fact that the basic assumptions of Minimalist community change relatively quickly:

> In Minimalism, the triggering head is often called a *probe*, the moving element is called a *goal*, and there are various proposals about the relations among the features that trigger syntactic effects. Chomsky (1995b: p. 229) begins with the assumption that features represent requirements which are checked and deleted when the requirement is met. The first assumption is modified almost immediately so that only a proper subset of the features, namely the 'formal', 'uninterpretable' features are deleted by checking operations in a successful derivation (Collins, 1997; Chomsky 1995b: §4.5). Another idea is that certain features, in particular the features of certain functional categories, may be initially unvalued, becoming valued by entering into appropriate structural configurations with other elements (Chomsky 2008; Hiraiwa, 2005). And some recent work adopts the view that features are never deleted (Chomsky 2007: p. 11). These issues remain unsolved. (Stabler 2011a: 397)

In order to fully develop a grammar fragment, one needs at least three years (compare the time span between the publication of *Barriers* (1986) and Stabler's implementation (1992)). Particularly large grammars require the knowledge of several researchers working in international cooperation over the space of years or even decades. This process is disrupted if fundamental assumptions are repeatedly changed at short intervals.

Further reading

This chapter heavily draws on Adger (2003). Other textbooks on Minimalism are Radford (1997), Grewendorf (2002), and Hornstein, Nunes & Grohmann (2005).

Kuhn (2007) offers a comparison of modern derivational analyses with constraint-based LFG and HPSG approaches. Borsley (2012) contrasts analyses of long-distance dependencies in HPSG with movement-based analyses as in GB/Minimalism. Borsley discusses four types of data which are problematic for movement-based approaches: extraction without fillers, extraction with multiple gaps, extractions where fillers and gaps do not match and extraction without gaps.

The discussion of labeling, abandonment of $\overline{\text{X}}$ theory and a comparison between Stabler's Minimalist Grammars and HPSG from Sections 4.6.2–4.6.4 can be found in Müller (2013c).

Intonational Phrasing, Discontinuity, and the Scope of Negation by Błaszczak & Gärtner (2005) is recommended for the more advanced reader. The authors compare analyses of negated quantifiers with wide scope in the framework of Minimalism (following Kayne) as well as Categorial Grammar (following Steedman).

Sternefeld (2006) is a good, detailed introduction to syntax (839 pages) which develops a Transformational Grammar analysis of German which (modulo transformations) almost matches what is assumed in HPSG (feature descriptions for arguments ordered in a valence list according to a hierarchy). Sternefeld's structures are minimal since he does not assume any functional projections if they cannot be motivated for the language under discussion. Sternefeld is critical regarding certain aspects which some other analyses take for granted. Sternefeld views his book explicitly as a textbook from which one can learn how to argue coherently when creating theories. For this reason, this book is not just recommended for students and PhD students.

Sternefeld & Richter (2012) discuss the situation in theoretical linguistics with particular focus on the theories described in this and the previous chapter. I can certainly understand the frustration of the authors with regard to the vagueness of analyses, argumentation style, empirical base of research, rhetorical clichés, immunization attempts and general respect for scientific standards: a current example of this is the article *Problems of Projection* by Chomsky (2013).[a] I, however, do not share the general, pessimistic tone of this article. In my opinion, the patient's condition is critical, but he is not dead yet. As a reviewer of the Sternefeld and Richter paper pointed out, the situation in linguistics has changed so much that now having a dissertation from MIT does not necessarily guarantee you a position (footnote 16) later on. One could view a reorientation of certain scientists with regard to certain empirical questions, adequate handling of data (Fanselow

2004b; 2009: 137) and improved communication between theoretical camps as a way out of this crisis.

Since the 90s, it is possible to identify an increased empirical focus (especially in Germany), which manifests itself, for example, in the work of linguistic Collaborative Research Centers (SFBs) or the yearly *Linguistic Evidence* conference. As noted by the reviewer cited above, in the future, it will not be enough to focus on Chomsky's problems in determining the syntactic categories in sentences such as *He left* (see Section 4.6.2). Linguistic dissertations will have to have an empirical section, which shows that the author actually understands something about language. Furthermore, dissertations, and of course other publications, should give an indication that the author has not just considered theories from a particular framework but is also aware of the broad range of relevant descriptive and theoretical literature.

---

[a]Vagueness: in this article, *perhaps* occurs 19 times, *may* 17 as well as various *if*s. Consistency: the assumptions made are inconsistent. See footnote 18 on page 156 of this book. Argumentation style: the term specifier is abolished and it is claimed that the problems associated with this term can no longer be formulated. Therefore, they are now not of this world. See footnote 28 on page 161 of this book. Immunization: Chomsky writes the following regarding the Empty Category Principle: *apparent exceptions do not call for abandoning the generalization as far as it reaches, but for seeking deeper reasons to explain where and why it holds* p. 9. This claim is most certainly correct, but one wonders how much evidence one needs in a specific case in order to disregard a given analysis. In particular regarding the essay *Problems of Projection*, one has to wonder why this essay was even published only five years after *On phases*. The evidence against the original approach is overwhelming and several points are taken up by Chomsky (2013) himself. If Chomsky were to apply his own standards (for a quote of his from 1957, see page 6) as well as general scientific methods (Occam's Razor), the consequence would surely be a return to head-based analyses of labeling.

For detailed comments on this essay, see Sections 4.6.2 and 4.6.3.

As I have shown in Section 4.6.4 and in Müller (2013c) and will also show in the following chapters and the discussion chapters in particular, there are most certainly similarities between the various analyses on the market and they do converge in certain respects. The way of getting out of the current crisis lies with the empirically-grounded and theoretically broad education and training of following generations.

In short: both teachers and students should read the medical record by Sternefeld and Richter. I implore the students not to abandon their studies straight after reading it, but rather to postpone this decision at least until after they have read the remaining chapters of this book.

5 Generalized Phrase Structure Grammar

Generalized Phrase Structure Grammar (GPSG) was developed as an answer to Transformational Grammar at the end of the 1970s. The book by Gazdar, Klein, Pullum & Sag (1985) is the main publication in this framework. Hans Uszkoreit has developed a largish GPSG fragment for German (1987). Analyses in GPSG were so precise that it was possible to use them as the basis for computational implementations. The following is a possibly incomplete list of languages with implemented GPSG fragments:

- German (Weisweber 1987; Weisweber & Preuss 1992; Naumann 1987; 1988; Volk 1988)

- English (Evans 1985; Phillips & Thompson 1985; Phillips 1992; Grover, Carroll & Briscoe 1993)

- French (Emirkanian, Da Sylva & Bouchard 1996)

- Persian (Bahrani, Sameti & Manshadi 2011)

As was discussed in Section 3.1.1, Chomsky (1957) argued that simple phrase structure grammars are not well-suited to describe relations between linguistic structures and claimed that one needs transformations to explain them. These assumptions remained unchallenged for two decades (with the exception of publications by Harman (1963) and Freidin (1975)) until alternative theories such as LFG and GPSG emerged, which addressed Chomsky's criticisms and developed non-transformational explanations of phenomena for which there were previously only transformational analyses or simply none at all. The analysis of local reordering of arguments, passives and long-distance dependencies are some of the most important phenomena that have been discussed in this framework. Following some introductory remarks on the representational format of GPSG in Section 5.1, I will present the GPSG analyses of these phenomena in some more detail.

5.1 General remarks on the representational format

This section has five parts. The general assumptions regarding features and the representation of complex categories is explained in Section 5.1.1, the assumptions regarding the linearization of daughters in a phrase structure rule is explained in Section 5.1.2. Section 5.1.3 introduces metarules, Section 5.1.4 deals with semantics, and Section 5.1.5 with adjuncts.

5.1.1 Complex categories, the Head Feature Convention, and $\overline{\text{X}}$ rules

In Section 2.2, we augmented our phrase structure grammars with features. GPSG goes one step further and describes categories as sets of feature-value pairs. The category in (1a) can be represented as in (1b):

(1) a. NP(3,sg,nom)
  b. { CAT n, BAR 2, PER 3, NUM sg, CASE nom }

It is clear that (1b) corresponds to (1a). (1a) differs from (1b) with regard to the fact that the information about part of speech and the $\overline{\text{X}}$ level (in the symbol NP) are prominent, whereas in (1b) these are treated just like the information about case, number or person.

Lexical entries have a feature SUBCAT. The value is a number which says something about the kind of grammatical rules in which the word can be used. (2) shows examples for grammatical rules and lists some verbs which can occur in these rules.[1]

(2) V2 → H[5]   (*kommen* 'come', *schlafen* 'sleep')
  V2 → H[6], N2[CASE acc]   (*kennen* 'know', *suchen* 'search')
  V2 → H[7], N2[CASE dat]   (*helfen* 'help', *vertrauen* 'trust')
  V2 → H[8], N2[CASE dat], N2[CASE acc] (*geben* 'give', *zeigen* 'show')
  V2 → H[9], V3[+dass]   (*wissen* 'know', *glauben* 'believe')

These rules license VPs, that is, the combination of a verb with its complements, but not with its subject. The numbers following the category symbols (V or N) indicate the $\overline{\text{X}}$ projection level. For Uszkoreit, the maximum number of projections of a verbal projection is three rather than two as is often assumed.

The H on the right side of the rule stands for *head*. The *Head Feature Convention* (HFC) ensures that certain features of the mother node are also present on the node marked with H (for details see Gazdar, Klein, Pullum & Sag 1985: Section 5.4 and Uszkoreit 1987: 67):

Principle 1 (Head Feature Convention)
The mother node and the head daughter must bear the same head features unless indicated otherwise.

In (2), examples for verbs which can be used in the rules are given in brackets. As with ordinary phrase structure grammars, one also requires corresponding lexical entries for verbs in GPSG. Two examples are provided in (3):

(3) V[5, VFORM *inf*] → einzuschlafen
  V[6, VFORM *inf*] → aufzuessen

The first rule states that *einzuschlafen* 'to fall asleep' has a SUBCAT value of 5 and the second indicates that *aufzuessen* 'to finish eating' has a SUBCAT value of 6. It follows, then, that *einzuschlafen* can only be used in the first rule (2) and *aufzuessen* can only be

---
[1] The analyses discussed in the following are taken from Uszkoreit (1987).

5.1 General remarks on the representational format

used in the second. Furthermore, (3) contains information about the form of the verb (*inf* stands for infinitives with *zu* 'to').

If we analyze the sentence in (4) with the second rule in (2) and the second rule in (3), then we arrive at the structure in Figure 5.1.

(4) Karl hat versucht, [den Kuchen aufzuessen].
    Karl has tried   the cake   to.eat.up

'Karl tried to finish eating the cake.'

den Kuchen   aufzuessen
the cake   to.eat.up

Figure 5.1: Projection of head features in GPSG

The rules in (2) say nothing about the order of the daughters which is why the verb (H[6]) can also be in final position. This aspect will be discussed in more detail in Section 5.1.2. With regard to the HFC, it is important to bear in mind that information about the infinitive verb form is also present on the mother node. Unlike simple phrase structure rules such as those discussed in Chapter 2, this follows automatically from the Head Feature Convention in GPSG. In (3), the value of VFORM is given and the HFC ensures that the corresponding information is represented on the mother node when the rules in (2) are applied. For the phrase in (4), we arrive at the category V2[VFORM *inf*] and this ensures that this phrase only occurs in the contexts it is supposed to:

(5)   a.   [Den Kuchen aufzuessen] hat er nicht gewagt.
              the cake   to.eat.up   has he not   dared

             'He did not dare to finish eating the cake.'

   b.   * [Den Kuchen aufzuessen] darf   er nicht.
               the cake   to.eat.up   be.allowed.to he not

             Intended: 'He is not allowed to finish eating the cake.'

   c.   * [Den Kuchen aufessen] hat er nicht gewagt.
               the cake   eat.up   has he not   dared

             Intended: 'He did not dare to finish eating the cake.'

   d.   [Den Kuchen aufessen] darf   er nicht.
              the cake   eaten.up   be.allowed.to he not

             'He is not allowed to finish eating the cake.'

gewagt 'dared' selects for a verb or verb phrase with an infinitive with *zu* 'to' but not a bare infinitive, while *darf* 'be allowed to' takes a bare infinitive.

This works in an analogous way for noun phrases: there are rules for nouns which do not take an argument as well as for nouns with certain arguments. Examples of rules for nouns which either require no argument or two PPs are given in (6) (Gazdar, Klein, Pullum & Sag 1985: 127):

(6)   N1 → H[30]   (*Haus* 'house', *Blume* 'flower')
       N1 → H[31], PP[*mit*], PP[*über*]   (*Gespräch* 'talk', *Streit* 'argument')

The rule for the combination of $\overline{\text{N}}$ and a determiner is as follows:

(7)   N2 → Det, H1

N2 stands for NP, that is, for a projection of a noun phrase on bar level two, whereas H1 stands for a projection of the head daughter on the bar level one. The Head Feature Convention ensures that the head daughter is also a nominal projection, since all features on the head daughter apart from the $\overline{\text{X}}$ level are identified with those of the whole NP. When analyzing (8), the second rule in (6) licenses the $\overline{\text{N}}$ *Gesprächs mit Maria über Klaus*. The fact that *Gesprächs* 'conversation' is in the genitive is represented in the lexical item of *Gesprächs* and since *Gesprächs* is the head, it is also present at $\overline{\text{N}}$, following the Head Feature Convention.

(8)   des   Gespräch-s   mit Maria über Klaus
        the.GEN conversation-GEN with Maria about Klaus
        'the conversation with Maria about Klaus'

For the combination of $\overline{\text{N}}$ with the determiner, we apply the rule in (7). The category of the head determines the word class of the element on the left-hand side of the rule, which is why the rule in (7) corresponds to the classical $\overline{\text{X}}$ rules that we encountered in (65c) on page 74. Since *Gesprächs mit Maria über Klaus* is the head daughter, the information about the genitive of $\overline{\text{N}}$ is also present at the NP node.

5.1.2 Local reordering

The first phenomenon to be discussed is local reordering of arguments. As was already discussed in Section 3.5, arguments in the middle field can occur in an almost arbitrary order. (9) gives some examples:

(9)   a.   [weil]   der   Mann der   Frau   das   Buch gibt
          because the.NOM man   the.DAT woman the.ACC book gives
          'because the man gives the book to the woman'
    b.   [weil]   der   Mann das   Buch der   Frau   gibt
          because the.NOM man   the.ACC book the.DAT woman gives
    c.   [weil]   das   Buch der   Mann der   Frau   gibt
          because the.ACC book the.NOM man   the.DAT woman gives

5.1 General remarks on the representational format

d. [weil] das Buch der Frau der Mann gibt
   because the.ACC book the.DAT woman the.NOM man gives

e. [weil] der Frau der Mann das Buch gibt
   because the.DAT woman the.NOM man the.ACC book gives

f. [weil] der Frau das Buch der Mann gibt
   because the.DAT woman the.ACC book the.NOM man gives

In the phrase structure grammars in Chapter 2, we used features to ensure that verbs occur with the correct number of arguments. The following rule in (10) was used for the sentence in (9a):

(10)   S → NP[nom] NP[dat] NP[acc] V_nom_dat_acc

If one wishes to analyze the other orders in (9), then one requires an additional five rules, that is, six in total:

(11)   S → NP[nom] NP[dat] NP[acc] V_nom_dat_acc
       S → NP[nom] NP[acc] NP[dat] V_nom_dat_acc
       S → NP[acc] NP[nom] NP[dat] V_nom_dat_acc
       S → NP[acc] NP[dat] NP[nom] V_nom_dat_acc
       S → NP[dat] NP[nom] NP[acc] V_nom_dat_acc
       S → NP[dat] NP[acc] NP[nom] V_nom_dat_acc

In addition, it is necessary to postulate another six rules for the orders with verb-initial order:

(12)   S → V_nom_dat_acc NP[nom] NP[dat] NP[acc]
       S → V_nom_dat_acc NP[nom] NP[acc] NP[dat]
       S → V_nom_dat_acc NP[acc] NP[nom] NP[dat]
       S → V_nom_dat_acc NP[acc] NP[dat] NP[nom]
       S → V_nom_dat_acc NP[dat] NP[nom] NP[acc]
       S → V_nom_dat_acc NP[dat] NP[acc] NP[nom]

Furthermore, one would also need parallel rules for transitive and intransitive verbs with all possible valences. Obviously, the commonalities of these rules and the generalizations regarding them are not captured. The point is that we have the same number of arguments, they can be realized in any order and the verb can be placed in initial or final position. As linguists, we find it desirable to capture this property of the German language and represent it beyond phrase structure rules. In Transformational Grammar, the relationship between the orders is captured by means of movement: the Deep Structure corresponds to verb-final order with a certain order of arguments and the surface order is derived by means of Move-α. Since GPSG is a non-transformational theory, this kind of explanation is not possible. Instead, GPSG imposes restrictions on *immediate dominance* (ID), which differ from those which refer to *linear precedence* (LP): rules such as (13) are to be understood as dominance rules, which do not have anything to say about the order of the daughters (Pullum 1982).

(13) S → V, NP[nom], NP[acc], NP[dat]

The rule in (13) simply states that S dominates all other nodes. Due to the abandonment of ordering restrictions for the right-hand side of the rule, we only need one rule rather than twelve.

Nevertheless, without any kind of restrictions on the right-hand side of the rule, there would be far too much freedom. For example, the following order would be permissible:

(14) * Der Frau   der   Mann gibt ein   Buch.
        the woman.DAT the.NOM man gives the.ACC book

Such orders are ruled out by so-called *Linear Precedence Rules* or LP-rules. LP-constraints are restrictions on local trees, that is, trees with a depth of one. It is, for example, possible to state something about the order of V, NP[nom], NP[acc] and NP[dat] in Figure 5.2 using linearization rules.

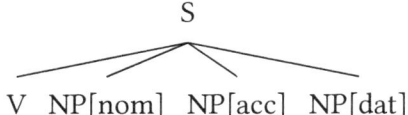

Figure 5.2: Example of a local tree

The following linearization rules serve to exclude orders such as those in (14):

(15) V[+MC] < X
      X   < V[−MC]

MC stands for *main clause*. The LP-rules ensure that in main clauses (+MC), the verb precedes all other constituents and follows them in subordinate clauses (−MC). There is a restriction that says that all verbs with the MC-value '+' also have to be (+FIN). This will rule out infinitive forms in initial position.

These LP rules do not permit orders with an occupied prefield or postfield in a local tree. This is intended. We will see how fronting can be accounted for in Section 5.4.

5.1.3 Metarules

We have previously encountered linearization rules for sentences with subjects, however our rules have the form in (16), that is, they do not include subjects:

(16) V2 → H[7], N2[CASE dat]
      V2 → H[8], N2[CASE dat], N2[CASE acc]

These rules can be used to analyze the verb phrases *dem Mann das Buch zu geben* 'to give the man the book' and *das Buch dem Mann zu geben* 'to give the book to the man' as they appear in (17), but we cannot analyze sentences like (9), since the subject does not occur on the right-hand side of the rules in (16).

5.1 General remarks on the representational format

(17) a. Er verspricht, [dem Mann das Buch zu geben].
 he promises the.DAT man the.ACC book to give

 'He promises to give the man the book.'

 b. Er verspricht, [das Buch dem Mann zu geben].
 he promises the.ACC book the.DAT man to give

 'He promises to give the book to the man.'

A rule with the format of (18) does not make much sense for a GPSG analysis of German since it cannot derive all the orders in (9) as the subject can occur between the elements of the VP as in (9c).

(18) S → N2 V2

With the rule in (18), it is possible to analyze (9a) as in Figure 5.3 and it would also be possible to analyze (9b) with a different ordering of the NPs inside the VP. The remaining examples in (9) cannot be captured by the rule in (18), however. This has to do with the

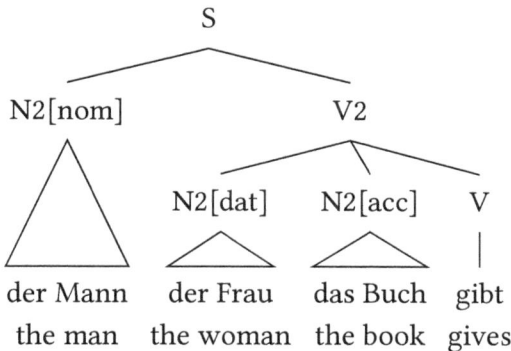

Figure 5.3: VP analysis for German (not appropriate in the GPSG framework)

fact that only elements in the same local tree, that is, elements which occur on the right-hand side of a rule, can be reordered. While we can reorder the parts of the VP and thereby derive (9b), it is not possible to place the subject at a lower position between the objects. Instead, a metarule can be used to analyze sentences where the subject occurs between other arguments of the verb. This rule relates phrase structure rules to other phrase structure rules. A metarule can be understood as a kind of instruction that creates another rule for each rule with a certain form and these newly created rules will in turn license local trees.

For the example at hand, we can formulate a metarule which says the following: if there is a rule with the form "V2 consists of something" in the grammar, then there also has to be another rule "V3 consists of whatever V2 consists + an NP in the nominative". In formal terms, this looks as follows:

(19) V2 → W ↦
 V3 → W, N2[CASE nom]

W is a variable which stands for an arbitrary number of categories (W = *whatever*). The metarule creates the following rule in (20) from the rules in (16):

(20) V3 → H[7], N2[CASE dat], N2[CASE nom]
      V3 → H[8], N2[CASE dat], N2[CASE acc], N2[CASE nom]

Now, the subject and other arguments both occur in the right-hand side of the rule and can therefore be freely ordered as long as no LP rules are violated.

5.1.4 Semantics

The semantics adopted by Gazdar, Klein, Pullum & Sag (1985: Chapter 9–10) goes back to Richard Montague (1974). Unlike a semantic theory which stipulates the combinatorial possibilities for each rule (see Section 2.3), GPSG uses more general rules. This is possible due to the fact that the expressions to be combined each have a semantic type. It is customary to distinguish between entities (*e*) and truth values (*t*). Entities refer to an object in the world (or in a possible world), whereas entire sentences are either true or false, that is, they have a truth value. It is possible to create more complex types from the types *e* and *t*. Generally, the following holds: if *a* and *b* are types, then ⟨ *a, b* ⟩ is also a type. Examples of complex types are ⟨ *e, t* ⟩ and ⟨ *e*, ⟨ *e, t* ⟩⟩. We can define the following combinatorial rule for this kind of typed expressions:

(21) If α is of type ⟨ *b, a* ⟩ and β of type *b*, then $\alpha(\beta)$ is of type *a*.

This type of combination is also called *functional application*. With the rule in (21), it is possible that the type ⟨ *e*, ⟨ *e, t* ⟩⟩ corresponds to an expression which still has to be combined with two expressions of type *e* in order to result in an expression of *t*. The first combination step with *e* will yield ⟨ *e, t* ⟩ and the second step of combination with a further *e* will give us *t*. This is similar to what we saw with λ-expressions on page 62: $\lambda y \lambda x$ *like'*(x, y) has to combine with a y and an x. The result in this example was *mögen'*(*max'*, *lotte'*), that is, an expression that is either true or false in the relevant world.

In Gazdar et al. (1985), an additional type is assumed for worlds in which an expression is true or false. For reasons of simplicity, I will omit this here. The types that we need for sentences, NPs and N's, determiners and VPs are given in (22):

(22) a. TYP(S) = *t*
      b. TYP(NP) = ⟨ ⟨ *e, t* ⟩, *t* ⟩
      c. TYP(N') = ⟨ *e, t* ⟩
      d. TYP(Det) = ⟨ TYP(N'), TYP(NP) ⟩
      e. TYP(VP) = ⟨ *e, t* ⟩

A sentence is of type *t* since it is either true or false. A VP needs an expression of type *e* to yield a sentence of type *t*. The type of the NP may seem strange at first glance, however, it is possible to understand it if one considers the meaning of NPs with quantifiers. For sentences such as (23a), a representation such as (23b) is normally assumed:

(23) a. All children laugh.
      b. $\forall x$ *child'*(x) → *laugh'*(x)

5.1 General remarks on the representational format

The symbol ∀ stands for the universal quantifier. The formula can be read as follows. For every object, for which it is the case that it has the property of being a child, it is also the case that it is laughing. If we consider the contribution made by the NP, then we see that the universal quantifier, the restriction to children and the logical implication come from the NP:

(24) $\forall x \; child'(x) \rightarrow P(x)$

This means that an NP is something that must be combined with an expression which has exactly one open slot corresponding to the x in (24). This is formulated in (22b): an NP corresponds to a semantic expression which needs something of type $\langle e, t \rangle$ to form an expression which is either true or false (that is, of type t).

An N′ stands for a nominal expression for the kind $\lambda x \; child(x)$. This means if there is a specific individual which one can insert in place of the x, then we arrive at an expression that is either true or false. For a given situation, it is the case that either John has the property of being a child or he does not. An N′ has the same type as a VP.

TYP(N′) and TYP(NP) in (22d) stand for the types given in (22c) and (22b), that is, a determiner is semantically something which has to be combined with the meaning of N′ to give the meaning of an NP.

Gazdar, Klein, Pullum & Sag (1985: 209) point out a redundancy in the semantic specification of grammars which follow the rule-to-rule hypothesis (see Section 2.3) since, instead of giving rule-by-rule instructions with regard to combinations, it suffices in many cases simply to say that the functor is applied to the argument. If we use types such as those in (22), it is also clear which constituent is the functor and which is the argument. In this way, a noun cannot be applied to a determiner, but rather only the reverse is possible. The combination in (25a) yields a well-formed result, whereas (25b) is ruled out.

(25) a. Det′(N′)
     b. N′(Det′)

The general combinatorial principle is then as follows:

(26) Use functional application for the combination of the semantic contribution of the daughters to yield a well-formed expression corresponding to the type of the mother node.

The authors of the GPSG book assume that this principle can be applied to the vast majority of GPSG rules so that only a few special cases have to be dealt with by explicit rules.

5.1.5 Adjuncts

For nominal structures in English, Gazdar et al. (1985: 126) assume the $\overline{X}$ analysis and, as we have seen in Section 2.4.1, this analysis is applicable to nominal structures in German. Nevertheless, there is a problem regarding the treatment of adjuncts in the verbal domain if one assumes flat branching structures, since adjuncts can freely occur between arguments:

(27) a. weil   der Mann der Frau   das Buch *gestern*   gab
       because the man the woman the book yesterday gave
       'because the man gave the book to the woman yesterday'
    b. weil   der Mann der Frau   *gestern*   das Buch gab
       because the man the woman yesterday   the book gave
    c. weil   der Mann *gestern*   der Frau   das Buch gab
       because the man yesterday   the woman the book gave
    d. weil   *gestern*   der Mann der Frau   das Buch gab
       because yesterday the man the woman the book gave

For (27), one requires the following rule:

(28)   V3 → H[8], N2[CASE dat], N2[CASE acc], N2[CASE nom], AdvP

Of course, adjuncts can also occur between the arguments of verbs from other valence classes:

(29) weil   (oft)   die Frau   (oft)   dem Mann (oft)   hilft
     because often the woman often the man   often helps
     'because the woman often helps the man'

Furthermore, adjuncts can occur between the arguments of a VP:

(30) Der Mann hat versucht, der Frau   heimlich das Buch zu geben.
     the man   has tried   the woman secretly the book to give
     'The man tried to secretly give the book to the woman.'

In order to analyze these sentences, we can use a metarule which adds an adjunct to the right-hand side of a V2 (Uszkoreit 1987: 146).

(31)   V2 → W ↦
       V2 → W, AdvP

By means of the subject introducing metarule in (19), the V3-rule in (28) is derived from a V2-rule. Since there can be several adjuncts in one sentence, a metarule such as (31) must be allowed to apply multiple times. The recursive application of metarules is often ruled out in the literature due to reasons of generative capacity (see Chapter 17) (Thompson 1982; Uszkoreit 1987: 146). If one uses the Kleene star, then it is possible to formulate the adjunct metarule in such as way that it does not have to apply recursively (Uszkoreit 1987: 146):

(32)   V2 → W ↦
       V2 → W, AdvP*

If one adopts the rule in (32), then it is not immediately clear how the semantic contribution of the adjuncts can be determined.[2] For the rule in (31), one can combine the semantic contribution of the AdvP with the semantic contribution of the V2 in the input rule. This is of course also possible if the metarule is applied multiple times. If this metarule is applied to (33a), for example, the V2-node in (33a) contains the semantic contribution of the first adverb.

(33)   a.   V2 → V, NP, AdvP
        b.   V2 → V, NP, AdvP, AdvP

The V2-node in (33b) receives the semantic representation of the adverb applied to the V2-node in (33a).

Weisweber & Preuss (1992) have shown that it is possible to use metarules such as (31) if one does not use metarules to compute a set of phrase structure rules, but rather directly applies the metarules during the analysis of a sentence. Since sentences are always of finite length and the metarule introduces an additional AdvP to the right-hand side of the newly licensed rule, the metarule can only be applied a finite number of times.

5.2 Passive as a metarule

The German passive can be described in an entirely theory-neutral way as follows:[3]

- The subject is suppressed.
- If there is an accusative object, this becomes the subject.

This is true for all verb classes which can form the passive. It does not make a difference whether the verbs takes one, two or three arguments:

(34)   a.   weil   er   noch gearbeitet hat
            because he.NOM still   worked   has

            'because he has still worked'

       b.   weil   noch gearbeitet wurde
            because still   worked   was

            'because there was still working there'

---

[2] In LFG, an adjunct is entered into a set in the functional structure (see Section 7.1.6). This also works with the use of the Kleene Star notation. From the f-structure, it is possible to compute the semantic denotation with corresponding scope by making reference to the c-structure. In HPSG, Kasper (1994) has made a proposal which corresponds to the GPSG proposal with regard to flat branching structures and an arbitrary number of adjuncts. In HPSG, however, one can make use of so-called relational constraints. These are similar to small programs which can create relations between values inside complex structures. Using such relational constraints, it is then possible to compute the meaning of an unrestricted number of adjuncts in a flat branching structure.

[3] This characterization does not hold for other languages. For instance, Icelandic allows for dative subjects. See Zaenen, Maling & Thráinsson (1985).

(35) a. weil   er   an Maria gedacht hat
       because he.NOM on Maria thought has
       'because he thought of Maria'
   b. weil   an Maria gedacht wurde
       because on Maria thought was
       'because Maria was thought of'

(36) a. weil   sie   ihn   geschlagen hat
       because she.NOM him.ACC beaten   has
       'because she has beaten him'
   b. weil   er   geschlagen wurde
       because he.NOM beaten   was
       'because he was beaten'

(37) a. weil   er   ihm   den   Aufsatz gegeben hat
       because he.NOM him.DAT the.ACC essay   given   has
       'because he has given him the essay'
   b. weil   ihm   der   Aufsatz gegeben wurde
       because him.DAT the.NOM essay   given   was
       'because he was given the essay'

In a simple phrase structure grammar, we would have to list two separate rules for each pair of sentences making reference to the valence class of the verb in question. The characteristics of the passive discussed above would therefore not be explicitly stated in the set of rules. In GPSG, it is possible to explain the relation between active and passive rules using a metarule: for each active rule, a corresponding passive rule with suppressed subject is licensed. The link between active and passive clauses can therefore be captured in this way.

An important difference to Transformational Grammar/GB is that we are not creating a relation between two trees, but rather between active and passive rules. The two rules license two unrelated structures, that is, the structure of (38b) is not derived from the structure of (38a).

(38) a. weil   sie   ihn   geschlagen hat
       because she.NOM him.ACC beaten   has
       'because she has beaten him'
   b. weil   er   geschlagen wurde
       because he.NOM beaten   was
       'because he was beaten'

The generalization with regard to active/passive is captured nevertheless.

In what follows, I will discuss the analysis of the passive given in Gazdar, Klein, Pullum & Sag (1985) in some more detail. The authors suggest the following metarule for English (p. 59):[4]

(39) VP → W, NP ↦
      VP[PAS] → W, (PP[*by*])

This rule states that verbs which take an object can occur in a passive VP without this object. Furthermore, a *by*-PP can be added. If we apply this metarule to the rules in (40), then this will yield the rules listed in (41):

(40) VP → H[2], NP
      VP → H[3], NP, PP[*to*]

(41) VP[PAS] → H[2], (PP[*by*])
      VP[PAS] → H[3], PP[*to*], (PP[*by*])

It is possible to use the rules in (40) to analyze verb phrases in active sentences:

(42) a. [$_S$ The man [$_{VP}$ devoured the carcass]].
      b. [$_S$ The man [$_{VP}$ handed the sword to Tracy]].

The combination of a VP with the subject is licensed by an additional rule (S → NP, VP).

With the rules in (41), one can analyze the VPs in the corresponding passive sentences in (43):

(43) a. [$_S$ The carcass was [$_{VP[PAS]}$ devoured (by the man)]].
      b. [$_S$ The sword was [$_{VP[PAS]}$ handed to Tracy (by the man)]].

At first glance, this analysis may seem odd as an object is replaced inside the VP by a PP which would be the subject in an active clause. Although this analysis makes correct predictions with regard to the syntactic well-formedness of structures, it seems unclear how one can account for the semantic relations. It is possible, however, to use a lexical rule that licenses the passive participle and manipulates the semantics of the output lexical item in such a way that the *by*-PP is correctly integrated semantically (Gazdar et al. 1985: 219).

We arrive at a problem, however, if we try to apply this analysis to German since the impersonal passive cannot be derived by simply suppressing an object. The V2-rules for verbs such as *arbeiten* 'work' and *denken* 'think' as used for the analysis of (34a) and (35a) have the following form:

(44) V2 → H[5]
      V2 → H[13], PP[*an*]

---

[4]See Weisweber & Preuss (1992: 1114) for a parallel rule for German which refers to accusative case on the left-hand side of the metarule.

There is no NP on the right-hand side of these rules which could be turned into a *von*-PP. If the passive is to be analyzed as suppressing an NP argument in a rule, then it should follow from the existence of the impersonal passive that the passive metarule has to be applied to rules which license finite clauses, since information about whether there is a subject or not is only present in rules for finite clauses.[5] In this kind of system, the rules for finite sentences (V3) are the basic rules and the rules for V2 would be derived from these.

It would only make sense to have a metarule which applies to V3 for German since English does not have V3 rules which contain both the subject and its object on the right-hand side of the rule.[6] For English, it is assumed that a sentence consists of a subject and a VP (see Gazdar et al. 1985: 139). This means that we arrive at two very different analyses for the passive in English and German, which do not capture the descriptive insight that the passive is the suppression of the subject and the subsequent promotion of the object in the same way. The central difference between German and English seems to be that English obligatorily requires a subject,[7] which is why English does not have an impersonal passive. This is a property independent of passives, which affects the possibility of having a passive structure, however.

The problem with the GPSG analysis is the fact that valence is encoded in phrase structure rules and that subjects are not present in the rules for verb phrases. In the following chapters, we will encounter approaches from LFG, Categorial Grammar, HPSG, Construction Grammar, and Dependency Grammar which encode valence separately from phrase structure rules and therefore do not have a principled problem with impersonal passive.

See Jacobson (1987b: 394–396) for more problematic aspects of the passive analysis in GPSG and for the insight that a lexical representation of valence – as assumed in Categorial Grammar, GB, LFG and HPSG – allows for a lexical analysis of the phenomenon, which is however unformulable in GPSG for principled reasons having to do with the fundamental assumptions regarding valence representations.

5.3 Verb position

Uszkoreit (1987) analyzed verb-initial and verb-final order as linearization variants of a flat tree. The details of this analysis have already been discussed in Section 5.1.2.

An alternative suggestion in a version of GPSG comes from Jacobs (1986: 110): Jacobs's analysis is a rendering of the verb movement analysis in GB. He assumes that there is an

---

[5] GPSG differs from GB in that infinitive verbal projections do not contain nodes for empty subjects. This is also true for all other theories discussed in this book with the exception of Tree-Adjoining Grammar.

[6] Gazdar et al. (1985: 62) suggest a metarule similar to our subject introduction metarule on page 187. The rule that is licensed by their metarule is used to analyze the position of auxiliaries in English and only licenses sequences of the form AUX NP VP. In such structures, subjects and objects are not in the same local tree either.

[7] Under certain conditions, the subject can also be omitted in English. For more on imperatives and other subject-less examples, see page 534.

5.4 Long-distance dependencies as the result of local dependencies

One of the main innovations of GPSG is its treatment of long-distance dependencies as a sequence of local dependencies (Gazdar 1981b). This approach will be explained taking constituent fronting to the prefield in German as an example. Until now, we have only seen the GPSG analysis for verb-initial and verb-final position: the sequences in (45) are simply linearization variants.

(45) a. [dass] der Mann der Frau das Buch gibt
      that the man the woman the book gives
      'that the man gives the book to the woman'

  b. Gibt der Mann der Frau das Buch?
      gives the man the woman the book
      'Does the man give the book to the woman?'

What we want is to derive the verb-second order in the examples in (46) from V1 order in (45b).

(46) a. Der Mann gibt der Frau das Buch.
      the man gives the woman the book
      'The man gives the woman the book.'

  b. Der Frau gibt der Mann das Buch.
      the woman gives the man the book
      'The man gives the woman the book.'

For this, the metarule in (47) has to be used. This metarule removes an arbitrary category X from the set of categories on the right-hand side of the rule and represents it on the left-hand side with a slash ('/'):[8]

(47) V3 → W, X ↦
      V3/X → W

This rule creates the rules in (49) from (48):

(48) V3 → H[8], N2[CASE dat], N2[CASE acc], N2[CASE nom]

(49) V3/N2[CASE nom] → H[8], N2[CASE dat], N2[CASE acc]
      V3/N2[CASE dat] → H[8], N2[CASE acc], N2[CASE nom]
      V3/N2[CASE acc] → H[8], N2[CASE dat], N2[CASE nom]

---

[8] An alternative to Uszkoreit's trace-less analysis (1987: 77), which is explained here, consists of using a trace for the extracted element as in GB.

The rule in (50) connects a sentence with verb-initial order with a constituent which is missing in the sentence:

(50)   V3[+FIN] → X[+TOP], V3[+MC]/X

In (50), X stands for an arbitrary category which is marked as missing in V3 by the '/'. X is referred to as a *filler*.

The interesting cases of values for X with regard to our examples are given in (51):

(51)   V3[+FIN] → N2[+TOP, CASE nom], V3[+MC]/N2[CASE nom]
       V3[+FIN] → N2[+TOP, CASE dat], V3[+MC]/N2[CASE dat]
       V3[+FIN] → N2[+TOP, CASE acc], V3[+MC]/N2[CASE acc]

(51) does not show actual rules. Instead, (51) shows examples for insertions of specific categories into the X-position, that is, different instantiations of the rule.

The following linearization rule ensures that a constituent marked by [+TOP] in (50) precedes the rest of the sentence:

(52)   [+TOP] < X

TOP stands for *topicalized*. As was mentioned on page 107, the prefield is not restricted to topics. Focused elements and expletives can also occur in the prefield, which is why the feature name is not ideal. However, it is possible to replace it with something else, for instance *prefield*. This would not affect the analysis. X in (52) stands for an arbitrary category. This is a new X and it is independent from the one in (50).

Figure 5.4 shows the interaction of the rules for the analysis of (53).[9]

(53)   Dem   Mann gibt er   das   Buch.
       the.DAT man gives he.NOM the.ACC book

   'He gives the man the book.'

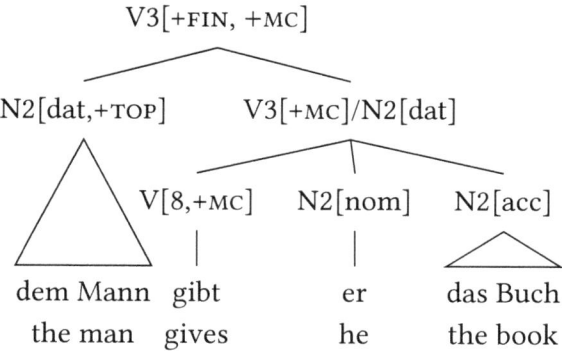

Figure 5.4: Analysis of fronting in GPSG

---

[9]The FIN feature has been omitted on some of the nodes since it is redundant: +MC-verbs always require the FIN value '+'.

5.4 Long-distance dependencies as the result of local dependencies

The metarule in (47) licenses a rule which adds a dative object into slash. This rule now licenses the subtree for *gibt er das Buch* 'gives he the book'. The linearization rule V[+MC] < X orders the verb to the very left inside of the local tree for V3. In the next step, the constituent following the slash is bound off. Following the LP-rule [+TOP] < X, the bound constituent must be ordered to the left of the V3 node.

The analysis given in Figure 5.4 may seem too complex since the noun phrases in (53) all depend on the same verb. It is possible to invent a system of linearization rules which would allow one to analyze (53) with an entirely flat structure. One would nevertheless still need an analysis for sentences such as those in (37) on page 108 – repeated here as (54) for convenience:

(54) a. [Um zwei Millionen Mark]$_i$ soll er versucht haben, [eine
around two million Deutsche.Marks should he tried have an
Versicherung _$_i$ zu betrügen].[10]
insurance.company to deceive

'He apparently tried to cheat an insurance company out of two million Deutsche Marks.'

b. „Wer$_i$ glaubt er, daß er _$_i$ ist?" erregte sich ein Politiker vom Nil.[11]
who believes he that he is retort REFL a politician from.the Nile

' "Who does he think he is?", a politician from the Nile exclaimed.'

c. Wen$_i$ glaubst du, daß ich _$_i$ gesehen habe?[12]
who believe you that I seen have

'Who do you think I saw?'

d. [Gegen ihn]$_i$ falle es den Republikanern hingegen schwerer,
against him fall it the Republicans however more.difficult
[[Angriffe _$_i$] zu lancieren].[13]
attacks to launch

'It is, however, more difficult for the Republicans to launch attacks against him.'

The sentences in (54) cannot be explained by local reordering as the elements in the prefield are not dependent on the highest verb, but instead originate in the lower clause. Since only elements from the same local tree can be reordered, the sentences in (54) cannot be analyzed without postulating some kind of additional mechanism for long-distance dependencies.[14]

---

[10] taz, 04.05.2001, p. 20.
[11] Spiegel, 8/1999, p. 18.
[12] Scherpenisse (1986: 84).
[13] taz, 08.02.2008, p. 9.
[14] One could imagine analyses that assume the special mechanism for nonlocal dependencies only for sentences that really involve dependencies that are nonlocal. This was done in HPSG by Kathol (1995) and Wetta (2011) and by Groß & Osborne (2009) in Dependency Grammar. I discuss the Dependency Grammar analyses in detail in Section 11.7.1 and show that analyses that treat simple V2 sentences as ordering variants of non-V2 sentences have problems with the scope of fronted adjuncts, with coordination of simple sentences and sentences with nonlocal dependencies and with so-called multiple frontings.

5 Generalized Phrase Structure Grammar

Before I conclude this chapter, I will discuss yet another example of fronting, namely one of the more complex examples in (54). The analysis of (54c) consists of several steps: the introduction, percolation and finally binding off of information about the long-distance dependency. This is shown in Figure 5.5. Simplifying somewhat, I assume that

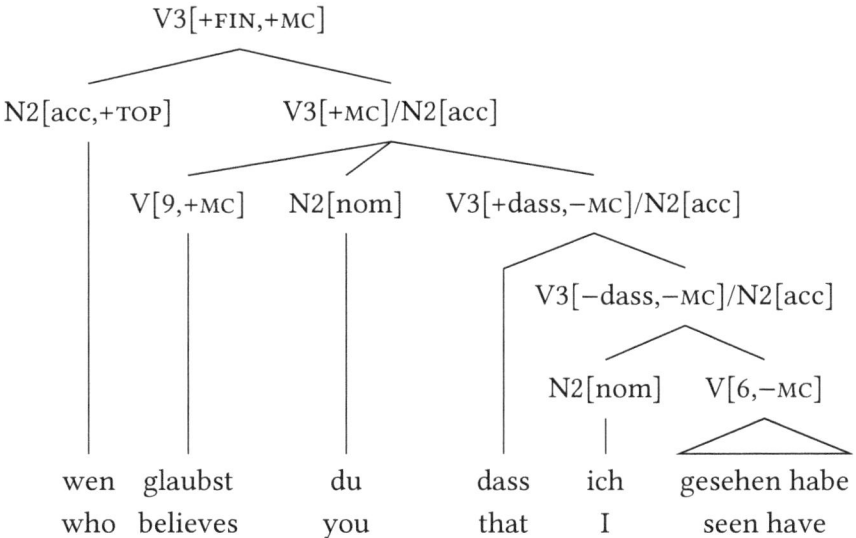

Figure 5.5: Analysis of long-distance dependencies in GPSG

gesehen habe 'have seen' behaves like a normal transitive verb.[15] A phrase structure rule licensed by the metarule in (47) licenses the combination of *ich* 'I' and *gesehen habe* 'has seen' and represents the missing accusative object on the V3 node. The complementizer *dass* 'that' is combined with *ich gesehen habe* 'I have seen' and the information about the fact that an accusative NP is missing is percolated up the tree. This percolation is controlled by the so-called *Foot Feature Principle*, which states that all foot features of all the daughters are also present on the mother node. Since the SLASH feature is a foot feature, the categories following the '/' percolate up the tree if they are not bound off in the local tree. In the final step, the V3/N2[acc] is combined with the missing N2[acc]. The result is a complete finite declarative clause of the highest projection level.

5.5 Summary and classification

Some twenty years after Chomsky's criticism of phrase structure grammars, the first large grammar fragment in the GPSG framework appeared and offered analyses of phenomena which could not be described by simple phrase structure rules. Although works in GPSG essentially build on Harman's 1963 idea of a transformation-less grammar, they also go far beyond this. A special achievement of GPSG is, in particular, the treatment of

---

[15] See Nerbonne (1986b) and Johnson (1986), for analyses of verbal complexes in GPSG.

long-distance dependencies as worked out by Gazdar (1981b). By using the SLASH-mechanism, it was possible to explain the simultaneous extraction of elements from conjuncts (Across the Board Extraction, Ross 1967). The following examples from Gazdar (1981b: 173) show that gaps in conjuncts must be identical, that is, a filler of a certain category must correspond to a gap in every conjunct:

(55) a. The kennel which Mary made and Fido sleeps in has been stolen.
(= S/NP & S/NP)

b. The kennel in which Mary keeps drugs and Fido sleeps has been stolen.
(= S/PP & S/PP)

c. * The kennel (in) which Mary made and Fido sleeps has been stolen.
(= S/NP & S/PP)

GPSG can plausibly handle this with mechanisms for the transmission of information about gaps. In symmetric coordination, the SLASH elements in each conjunct have to be identical. On the one hand, a transformational approach is not straightforwardly possible since one normally assumes in such analyses that there is a tree and something is moved to another position in the tree thereby leaving a trace. However, in coordinate structures, the filler would correspond to two or more traces and it cannot be explained how the filler could originate in more than one place.

While the analysis of Across the Board extraction is a true highlight of GPSG, there are some problematic aspects that I want to address in the following: the interaction between valence and morphology, the representation of valence and partial verb phrase fronting, and the expressive power of the GPSG formalism.

5.5.1 Valence and morphology

The encoding of valence in GPSG is problematic for several reasons. For example, morphological processes take into account the valence properties of words. Adjectival derivation with the suffix -*bar* '-able' is only productive with transitive verbs, that is, with verbs with an accusative object which can undergo passivization:

(56) a. lös-bar   (nominative, accusative)
       solv-able

b. vergleich-bar   (nominative, accusative, PP[mit])
   compar-able

c. * schlaf-bar   (nominative)
   sleep-able

d. * helf-bar   (nominative, dative)
   help-able

A rule for derivations with -*bar*- '-able' must therefore make reference to valence information. This is not possible in GPSG grammars since every lexical entry is only assigned a number which says something about the rules in which this entry can be used. For -*bar*-

derivations, one would have to list in the derivational rule all the numbers which correspond to rules with accusative objects, which of course does not adequately describe the phenomenon. Furthermore, the valence of the resulting adjective also depends on the valence of the verb. For example, a verb such as *vergleichen* 'compare' requires a *mit* (with)-PP and *vergleichbar* 'comparable' does too (Riehemann 1993: 7, 54; 1998: 68). In the following chapters, we will encounter models which assume that lexical entries contain information as to whether a verb selects for an accusative object or not. In such models, morphological rules which need to access the valence properties of linguistic objects can be adequately formulated.

The issue of interaction of valence and derivational morphology will be taken up in Section 21.2.2 again, where approaches in LFG and Construction Grammar are discussed that share assumptions about the encoding of valence with GPSG.

5.5.2 Valence and partial verb phrase fronting

Nerbonne (1986b) and Johnson (1986) investigate fronting of partial VPs in the GPSG framework. (57) gives some examples: in (57a) the bare verb is fronted and its arguments are realized in the middle field, in (57b) one of the objects is fronted together with the verb and in (57c) both objects are fronted with the verb.

(57)   a.   Erzählen wird er seiner Tochter ein Märchen können.
           tell   will he his   daughter a   fairy.tale can

       b.   Ein Märchen erzählen wird er seiner Tochter können.
           a   fairy.tale tell   will he his   daughter can

       c.   Seiner Tochter ein Märchen erzählen wird er können.
           his   daughter a   fairy.tale tell   will he can

         'He will be able to tell his daughter a fairy tale.'

The problem with sentences such as those in (57) is that the valence requirements of the verb *erzählen* 'to tell' are realized in various positions in the sentence. For fronted constituents, one requires a rule which allows a ditransitive to be realized without its arguments or with one or two objects. Furthermore, it has to be ensured that the arguments that are missing in the prefield are realized in the remainder of the clause. It is not legitimate to omit obligatory arguments or realize arguments with other properties like a different case, as the examples in (58) show:

(58)   a.   Verschlungen hat er   es   nicht.
           devoured   has he.NOM it.ACC not
         'He did not devour it.'

       b.   * Verschlungen hat er   nicht.
             devoured   has he.NOM not

       c.   * Verschlungen hat er   ihm   nicht.
             devoured   has he.NOM him.DAT not

5.5 Summary and classification

The obvious generalization is that the fronted and unfronted arguments must add up to the total set belonging to the verb. This is scarcely possible with the rule-based valence representation in GPSG. In theories such as Categorial Grammar (see Chapter 8), it is possible to formulate elegant analyses of (58) (Geach 1970). Nerbonne and Johnson both suggest analyses for sentences such as (58) which ultimately amount to changing the representation of valence information in the direction of Categorial Grammar.

Before I turn to the expressive power of the GPSG formalism, I want to note that the problems that we discussed in the previous subsections are both related to the representation of valence in GPSG. We already run into valence-related problems when discussing the passive in Section 5.2: since subjects and objects are introduced in phrase structure rules and since there are some languages in which subject and object are not in the same local tree, there seems to be no way to describe the passive as the suppression of the subject in GPSG.

5.5.3 Generative capacity

In GPSG, the system of linearization, dominance and metarules is normally restricted by conditions we will not discuss here in such a way that one could create a phrase structure grammar of the kind we saw in Chapter 2 from the specification of a GPSG grammar. Such grammars are also called context-free grammars. In the mid-80s, it was shown that context-free grammars are not able to describe natural language in general, that is it could be shown that there are languages that need more powerful grammar formalisms than context-free grammars (Shieber 1985; Culy 1985; see Pullum (1986) for a historical overview). The so-called *generative capacity* of grammar formalisms is discussed in Chapter 17.

Following the emergence of constraint-based models such as HPSG (see Chapter 9) and unification-based variants of Categorial Grammar (see Chapter 8 and Uszkoreit 1986a), most authors previously working in GPSG turned to other frameworks. The GPSG analysis of long-distance dependencies and the distinction between immediate dominance and linear precedence are still used in HPSG and variants of Construction Grammar to this day. See also Section 12.2 for a Tree Adjoining Grammar variant that separates dominance from precedence.

Comprehension questions

1. What does it mean for a grammar to be in an ID/LP format?

2. How are linear variants of constituents in the middle field handled by GPSG?

3. Think of some phenomena which have been described by transformations and consider how GPSG has analyzed these data using other means.

Exercises

1. Write a small GPSG grammar which can analyze the following sentences:

   (59) a. [dass] der   Mann ihn   liest
             that the.NOM man him.ACC reads
           'that the man reads it'
        b. [dass] ihn   der   Mann liest
             that him.ACC the.NOM man reads
           'that the man reads it'
        c. Der   Mann liest ihn.
           the.NOM man reads him.ACC
           'The man reads it.'

   Include all arguments in a single rule without using the metarule for introducing subjects.

Further reading

The main publication in GPSG is Gazdar, Klein, Pullum & Sag (1985). This book has been critically discussed by Jacobson (1987b). Some problematic analyses are contrasted with alternatives from Categorial Grammar and reference is made to the heavily Categorial Grammar influenced work of Pollard (1984), which counts as one of the predecessors of HPSG. Some of Jacobson's suggestions can be found in later works in HPSG.

Grammars of German can be found in Uszkoreit (1987) and Busemann (1992). Gazdar (1981b) developed an analysis of long-distance dependencies, which is still used today in theories such as HPSG.

A history of the genesis of GPSG can be found in Pullum (1989b).

6 Feature descriptions

In the previous chapter, we talked about sets of feature-value pairs, which can be used to describe linguistic objects. In this chapter, we will introduce feature descriptions which play a role in theories such as LFG, HPSG, Construction Grammar, versions of Categorial Grammar and TAG (and even some formalizations of Minimalist theories (Veenstra 1998)). This chapter will therefore lay some of the groundwork for the chapters to follow.

Feature structures are complex entities which can model properties of a linguistic object. Linguists mostly work with feature descriptions which describe only parts of a given feature structure. The difference between models and descriptions will be explained in more detail in Section 6.7.

Alternative terms for feature structures are:

- feature-value structure
- attribute-value structure

Other terms for feature description are the following:

- *attribute-value matrix* (AVM)
- *feature matrix*

In what follows, I will restrict the discussion to the absolutely necessary details in order to keep the formal part of the book as short as possible. I refer the interested reader to Shieber (1986), Pollard & Sag (1987: Chapter 2), Johnson (1988), Carpenter (1992), King (1994) and Richter (2004). Shieber's book is an accessible introduction to Unification Grammars. The works by King and Richter, which introduce important foundations for HPSG, would most probably not be accessible for those without a good grounding in mathematics. However, it is important to know that these works exist and that the corresponding linguistic theory is build on a solid foundation.

6.1 Feature descriptions

When describing linguistic signs, we have to say something about their properties. For a noun, we can say that it has case, gender, number and person features. For a word such as *Mannes* 'man', we can say that these features have the values *genitive*, *masculine*, *singular* and *3*. If we were to write these as a list of feature-value pairs, we would arrive at the following feature description:

6 Feature descriptions

(1) Feature-value pair for *Mannes*:
$$\begin{bmatrix} \text{CASE} & \textit{genitive} \\ \text{GENDER} & \textit{masculine} \\ \text{NUMBER} & \textit{singular} \\ \text{PERSON} & \textit{3} \end{bmatrix}$$

It is possible to describe a variety of different things using feature descriptions. For example, we can describe a person as in (2):

(2) $\begin{bmatrix} \text{FIRSTNAME} & \textit{max} \\ \text{LASTNAME} & \textit{meier} \\ \text{DATE-OF-BIRTH} & \textit{10.10.1985} \end{bmatrix}$

People are related to other people – a fact that can also be expressed in feature-value pairs. For example, the fact that Max Meier has a father called Peter Meier can be captured by expanding (2) as follows:

(3) $\begin{bmatrix} \text{FIRSTNAME} & \textit{max} \\ \text{LASTNAME} & \textit{meier} \\ \text{DATE-OF-BIRTH} & \textit{10.10.1985} \\ \text{FATHER} & \begin{bmatrix} \text{FIRSTNAME} & \textit{peter} \\ \text{LASTNAME} & \textit{meier} \\ \text{DATE-OF-BIRTH} & \textit{10.05.1960} \\ \text{FATHER} & \ldots \\ \text{MOTHER} & \ldots \end{bmatrix} \\ \text{MOTHER} & \ldots \end{bmatrix}$

The value of the FATHER feature is another feature description containing the same features as (2).

In feature descriptions, a *path* is a sequence of features which immediately follow each other. The *value of a path* is the feature description at the end of the path. Therefore, the value of FATHER|DATE-OF-BIRTH is *10.05.1960*.

One can think of many different features that could be included in representations such as (3). One may wonder how to integrate information about offspring into (3).

An obvious solution would be to add features for DAUGHTER and SON:

(4) $\begin{bmatrix} \text{FIRSTNAME} & \textit{max} \\ \text{LASTNAME} & \textit{meier} \\ \text{DATE-OF-BIRTH} & \textit{10.10.1985} \\ \text{FATHER} & \ldots \\ \text{MOTHER} & \ldots \\ \text{DAUGHTER} & \ldots \end{bmatrix}$

This solution is not satisfactory as it is not immediately clear how one could describe a person with several daughters. Should one really introduce features such as DAUGHTER-1 or DAUGHTER-3?

(5) $\begin{bmatrix} \text{FIRSTNAME} & \textit{max} \\ \text{LASTNAME} & \textit{meier} \\ \text{DATE-OF-BIRTH} & \textit{10.10.1985} \\ \text{FATHER} & \dots \\ \text{MOTHER} & \dots \\ \text{DAUGHTER-1} & \dots \\ \text{DAUGHTER-2} & \dots \\ \text{DAUGHTER-3} & \dots \end{bmatrix}$

How many features do we want to assume? Where is the limit? What would the value of DAUGHTER-32 be?

For this case, it makes much more sense to use a list. Lists are indicated with angle brackets. Any number of elements can occur between these brackets. A special case is when no element occurs between the brackets. A list with no elements is also called *empty list*. In the following example, Max Meier has a daughter called Clara, who herself has no daughter.

(6)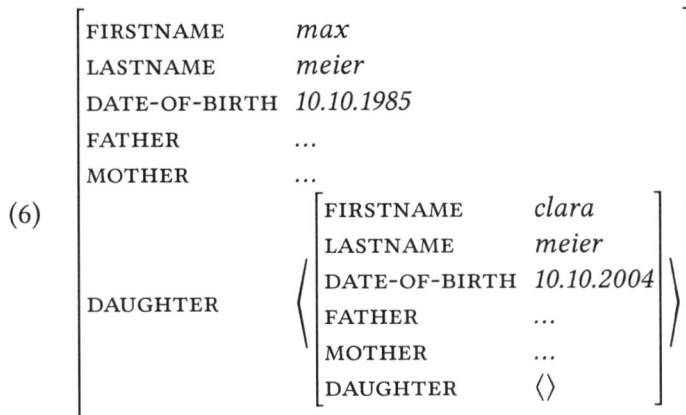

Now, we are left with the question of sons. Should we add another list for sons? Do we want to differentiate between sons and daughters? It is certainly the case that the gender of the children is an important property, but these are properties of the objects themselves, since every person has a gender. The description in (7) therefore offers a more adequate representation.

At this point, one could ask why the parents are not included in a list as well. In fact, we find similar questions also in linguistic works: how is information best organized for the job at hand? One could argue for the representation of descriptions of the parents under separate features, by pointing out that with such a representation it is possible to make certain claims about a mother or father without having to necessarily search for the respective descriptions in a list.

If the order of the elements is irrelevant, then we could use sets rather than lists. Sets are written inside curly brackets.[1]

---

[1] The definition of a set requires many technicalities. In this book, I would use sets only for collecting semantic information. This can be done equally well using lists, which is why I do not introduce sets here and instead use lists.

6 Feature descriptions

(7) $\begin{bmatrix} \text{FIRSTNAME} & max \\ \text{LASTNAME} & meier \\ \text{DATE-OF-BIRTH} & 10.10.1985 \\ \textbf{GENDER} & \textbf{\textit{male}} \\ \text{FATHER} & \ldots \\ \text{MOTHER} & \ldots \\ \text{CHILDREN} & \left\langle \begin{bmatrix} \text{FIRSTNAME} & clara \\ \text{LASTNAME} & meier \\ \text{DATE-OF-BIRTH} & 10.10.2004 \\ \textbf{GENDER} & \textbf{\textit{female}} \\ \text{FATHER} & \ldots \\ \text{MOTHER} & \ldots \\ \text{CHILDREN} & \langle \rangle \end{bmatrix} \right\rangle \end{bmatrix}$

6.2 Types

In the previous section, we introduced feature descriptions consisting of feature-value pairs and showed that it makes sense to allow for complex values for features. In this section, feature descriptions will be augmented to include types. Feature descriptions which are assigned a type are also called *typed feature descriptions*. Types say something about which features can or must belong to a particular structure. The description previously discussed describes an object of the type *person*.

(8) $\begin{bmatrix} person \\ \text{FIRSTNAME} & max \\ \text{LASTNAME} & meier \\ \text{DATE-OF-BIRTH} & 10.10.1985 \\ \text{GENDER} & male \\ \text{FATHER} & \ldots \\ \text{MOTHER} & \ldots \\ \text{CHILDREN} & \langle \ldots, \ldots \rangle \end{bmatrix}$

Types are written in *italics*.

The specification of a type determines which properties a modelled object has. It is then only possible for a theory to say something about these properties. Properties such as OPERATING VOLTAGE are not relevant for objects of the type *person*. If we know the type of a given object, then we also know that this object must have certain properties even if we do not yet know their exact values. In this way, (9) is still a description of Max Meier even though it does not contain any information about Max' date of birth:

(9) $\begin{bmatrix} person \\ \text{FIRSTNAME} & max \\ \text{LASTNAME} & meier \\ \text{GENDER} & male \end{bmatrix}$

208

We know, however, that Max Meier must have been born on some day since this is a description of the type *person*. The question *What is Max' date of birth?* makes sense for a structure such as (9) in a way that the question *Which operating voltage does Max have?* does not. If we know that an object is of the type *person*, then we have the following basic structure:

(10) $\begin{bmatrix} person \\ \text{FIRSTNAME} & firstname \\ \text{LASTNAME} & lastname \\ \text{DATE-OF-BIRTH} & date \\ \text{GENDER} & gender \\ \text{FATHER} & person \\ \text{MOTHER} & person \\ \text{CHILDREN} & list\ of\ person \end{bmatrix}$

In (10) and (9), the values of features such as FIRSTNAME are in italics. These values are also types. They are different from types such as *person*, however, as no features belong to them. These kinds of types are called *atomic*.

Types are organized into hierarchies. It is possible to define the subtypes *woman* and *man* for *person*. These would determine the gender of a given object. (11) shows the feature structure for the type *woman*, which is analogous to that of *man*.

(11) $\begin{bmatrix} female\ person \\ \text{FIRSTNAME} & firstname \\ \text{LASTNAME} & lastname \\ \text{DATE-OF-BIRTH} & date \\ \text{GENDER} & female \\ \text{FATHER} & person \\ \text{MOTHER} & person \\ \text{CHILDREN} & list\ of\ person \end{bmatrix}$

At this point, we could ask ourselves if we really need the feature GENDER. The necessary information is already represented in the type *woman*. The question if specific information is represented by special features or whether it is stored in a type without a corresponding individual feature will surface again in the discussion of linguistic analyses. Both alternatives differ mostly in the fact that the information which is modelled by types is not immediately accessible for structure sharing, which is discussed in Section 6.4.

Type hierarchies play an important role in capturing linguistic generalizations, which is why type hierarchies and the inheritance of constraints and information will be explained with reference to a further example in what follows. One can think of type hierarchies as an effective way of organizing information. In an encyclopedia, the individual entries are linked in such a way that the entries for monkey and mouse will each contain a pointer to mammal. The description found under mammal does therefore not have to be repeated for the subordinate concepts. In the same way, if one wishes to

6 Feature descriptions

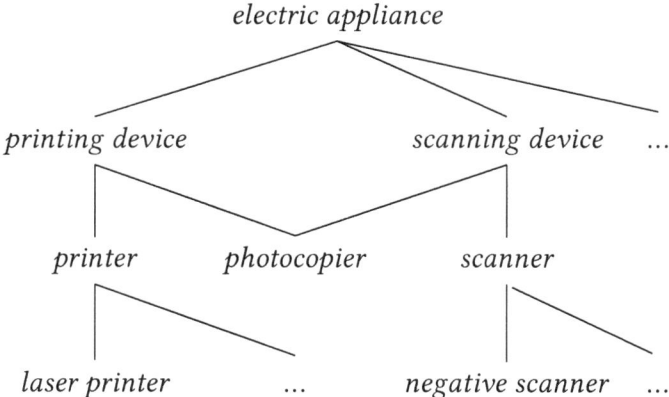

Figure 6.1: Non-linguistic example of multiple inheritance

describe various electric appliances, one can use the hierarchy in Figure 6.1. The most general type *electrical device* is the highest in Figure 6.1. Electrical devices have certain properties, e.g., a power supply with a certain power consumption. All subtypes of *electrical device* "inherit" this property. In this way, *printing device* and *scanning device* also have a power supply with a specific power consumption. A *printing device* can produce information and a *scanning device* can read in information. A *photocopier* can both produce information and read it. Photocopiers have both the properties of scanning and printing devices. This is expressed by the connection between the two superordinate types and *photocopier* in Figure 6.1. If a type is at the same time the subtype of several superordinate types, then we speak of *multiple inheritance*. If devices can print, but not scan, they are of type *printer*. This type can have further more specific subtypes, which in turn may have particular properties, e.g., *laser printer*. New features can be added to subtypes, but it is also possible to make values of inherited features more specific. For example, the material that can be scanned with a *negative scanner* is far more restricted than that of the supertype *scanner*, since negative scanners can only scan negatives.

The objects that are modeled always have a maximally specific type. In the example above, this means that we can have objects of the type *laser printer* and *negative scanner* but not of the type *printing device*. This is due to the fact that *printing device* is not maximally specific since this type has two subtypes.

Type hierarchies with multiple inheritance are an important means for expressing linguistic generalizations (Flickinger, Pollard & Wasow 1985; Flickinger 1987; Sag 1997). Types of words or phrases which occur at the very top of these hierarchies correspond to constraints on linguistic objects, which are valid for linguistic objects in all languages. Subtypes of such general types can be specific to certain languages or language classes.

6.3 Disjunction

Disjunctions can be used if one wishes to express the fact that a particular object can have various different properties. If one were to organize a class reunion twenty years after leaving school and could not recall the exact names of some former classmates, it would be possible to search the web for "Julia (Warbanow or Barbanow)". In feature descriptions, this "or" is expressed by a '∨'.

(12) $\begin{bmatrix} \textit{person} \\ \text{FIRSTNAME} \quad \textit{julia} \\ \text{LASTNAME} \quad \textit{warbanow} \lor \textit{barbanow} \end{bmatrix}$

Some internet search engines do not allow for searches with 'or'. In these cases, one has to carry out two distinct search operations: one for "Julia Warbanow" and then another for "Julia Barbanow". This corresponds to the two following disjunctively connected descriptions:

(13) $\begin{bmatrix} \textit{person} \\ \text{FIRSTNAME} \quad \textit{julia} \\ \text{LASTNAME} \quad \textit{warbanow} \end{bmatrix} \lor \begin{bmatrix} \textit{person} \\ \text{FIRSTNAME} \quad \textit{julia} \\ \text{LASTNAME} \quad \textit{barbanow} \end{bmatrix}$

Since we have type hierarchies as a means of expression, we can sometimes do without disjunctive specification of values and instead state the supertype: for *printer* ∨ *photocopier*, one can simply write *printing device* if one assumes the type hierarchy in Figure 6.1 on the preceding page.

6.4 Structure sharing

Structure sharing is an important part of the formalism. It serves to express the notion that certain parts of a structure are identical. A linguistic example for the identity of values is agreement. In sentences such as (14), the number value of the noun phrase has to be identical to that of the verb:

(14)   a.   Der Mann schläft.
             the man   sleeps
             'The man is sleeping.'

       b.   Die Männer schlafen.
             the men   sleep
             'The men are sleeping.'

       c.   * Der Mann schlafen.
               the man   sleep
             Intended: 'The man are sleeping.'

The identity of values is indicated by boxes containing numbers. The boxes can also be viewed as variables.

When describing objects we can make claims about equal values or claims about identical values. A claim about the identity of values is stronger. Let us take the following feature description containing information about the children that Max's father and mother have as an example:

6 Feature descriptions

(15)
$$\begin{bmatrix} person \\ \text{FIRSTNAME} & max \\ \text{LASTNAME} & meier \\ \text{DATE-OF-BIRTH} & 10.10.1985 \\ \text{FATHER} & \begin{bmatrix} person \\ \text{FIRSTNAME} & peter \\ \text{LASTNAME} & meier \\ \text{CHILDREN} & \left\langle \begin{bmatrix} person \\ \text{FIRSTNAME} & klaus \end{bmatrix}, \ldots \right\rangle \end{bmatrix} \\ \text{MOTHER} & \begin{bmatrix} person \\ \text{FIRSTNAME} & anna \\ \text{LASTNAME} & meier \\ \text{CHILDREN} & \left\langle \begin{bmatrix} person \\ \text{FIRSTNAME} & klaus \end{bmatrix}, \ldots \right\rangle \end{bmatrix} \end{bmatrix}$$

Notice that under the paths FATHER|CHILDREN and MOTHER|CHILDREN, we find a list containing a description of a person with the first name Klaus. The question of whether the feature description is of one or two children of Peter and Anna cannot be answered. It is certainly possible that we are dealing with two different children from previous partnerships who both happen to be called Klaus.

By using structure sharing, it is possible to specify the identity of the two values as in (16). In (16), Klaus is a single child that belongs to both parents. Everything inside

(16)
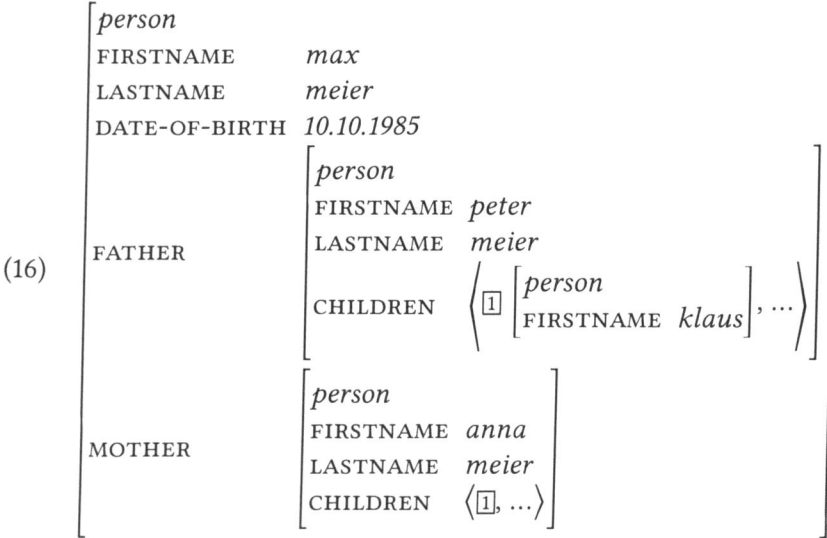

the brackets which immediately follow ① is equally present in both positions. One can think of ① as a pointer or reference to a structure which has only been described once.

One question still remains open: what about Max? Max is also a child of his parents and should therefore also occur in a list of the children of his parents. There are two points in (16) where there are three dots. These ellipsis marks stand for information about the other children of Peter and Anna Meier. Our world knowledge tells us that both of them must have the same child namely Max Meier himself. In the following section, we will see how this can be expressed in formal terms.

6.5 Cyclic structures

We have introduced structure sharing in order to be able to express the fact that Max's parents both have a son Klaus together. It would not be enough to list Max in the child-lists of his parents separately. We want to capture the fact that it is the same Max which appears in each of these lists and furthermore, we have to ensure that the child being described is identical to the entire object being described. Otherwise, the description would permit a situation where Max's parents could have a second child also called Max. The description given in (17) can capture all facts correctly.

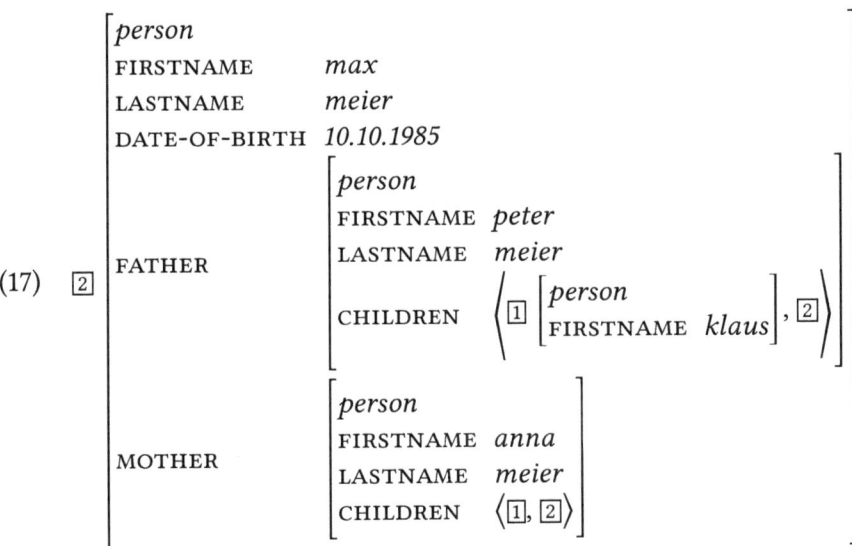

Structures such as those described in (17) are called cyclic because one ends up going in a circle if one follows a particular path: e.g., the path FATHER|CHILDREN|...|FATHER|CHILDREN|...[2] can be potentially repeated an infinite number of times.

6.6 Unification

Grammatical rules are written exactly like lexical entries in HPSG and Construction Grammar and are done so with the help of feature descriptions. For a word or a larger

---

[2]The dots here stand for the path to ② in the list which is the value of CHILDREN. See Exercise 3.

6 Feature descriptions

phrasal entity to be usable as daughter in a phrase licensed by some grammatical rule, the word or phrase must have properties which are compatible with the description of the daughters in the grammatical rule. If this kind of compatibility exists, then we can say that the respective items are *unifiable*.[3] If one unifies two descriptions, the result is a description which contains information from both descriptions but no additional information.

The way unification works can be demonstrated with feature descriptions describing people. One can imagine that Bettina Kant goes to the private detective Max Müller and wants to find a specific person. Normally, those who go to a detective's office only come with a partial description of the person they are looking for, e.g., the gender, hair color or date of birth. Perhaps even the registration number of the car belonging to the person is known.

It is then expected of the detective that he or she provides information fitting the description. If we are looking for a blonde female named Meier (18a), then we do not want to get descriptions of a male red-head (18b). The descriptions in (18) are incompatible and cannot be unified:

(18) a. $\begin{bmatrix} person \\ \text{LASTNAME} & meier \\ \text{GENDER} & female \\ \text{HAIRCOLOR} & blonde \end{bmatrix}$

b. $\begin{bmatrix} person \\ \text{LASTNAME} & meier \\ \text{GENDER} & male \\ \text{HAIRCOLOR} & red \end{bmatrix}$

The description in (19) would be a possible result for a search for a blonde, female individual called Meier:

(19) $\begin{bmatrix} person \\ \text{FIRSTNAME} & katharina \\ \text{LASTNAME} & meier \\ \text{GENDER} & female \\ \text{DATE-OF-BIRTH} & 15.10.1965 \\ \text{HAIRCOLOR} & blonde \end{bmatrix}$

---

[3]The term *unification* should be used with care. It is only appropriate if certain assumptions with regard to the formal basis of linguistic theories are made. Informally, the term is often used in formalisms where unification is not technically defined. In HPSG, it mostly means that the constraints of two descriptions lead to a single description. What one wants to say here, intuitively, is that the objects described have to satisfy the constraints of both descriptions at the same time (*constraint satisfaction*). Since the term *unification* is so broadly-used, it will also be used in this section. The term will not play a role in the remaining discussions of theories with the exception of explicitly unification-based approaches. In contrast, the concept of constraint satisfaction presented here is very important for the comprehension of the following chapters.

Katharina Meier could also have other properties unknown to the detective. The important thing is that the properties known to the detective match those that the client is looking for. Furthermore, it is important that the detective uses reliable information and does not make up any information about the sought object. The unification of the search in (18a) and the information accessible to the detective in (19) is in fact (19) and not (20), for example:

(20) $\begin{bmatrix} person \\ \text{FIRSTNAME} & katharina \\ \text{LASTNAME} & meier \\ \text{GENDER} & female \\ \text{DATE-OF-BIRTH} & 15.10.1965 \\ \text{HAIRCOLOR} & blond \\ \text{CHILDREN} & \langle \rangle \end{bmatrix}$

(20) contains information about children, which is neither contained in (18a) nor in (19). It could indeed be the case that Katharina Meier has no children, but there are perhaps several people called Katharina Meier with otherwise identical properties. With this invented information, we might exclude one or more possible candidates.

It is possible that our detective Max Müller does not have any information about hair color in his files. His files could contain the following information:

(21) $\begin{bmatrix} person \\ \text{FIRSTNAME} & katharina \\ \text{LASTNAME} & meier \\ \text{GENDER} & female \\ \text{DATE-OF-BIRTH} & 15.10.1965 \end{bmatrix}$

These data are compatible with the search criteria. If we were to unify the descriptions in (18a) and (21), we would get (19). If we assume that the detective has done a good job, then Bettina Kant now knows that the person she is looking for has the properties of her original search plus the newly discovered properties.

6.7 Phenomena, models and formal theories

In the previous sections, we introduced feature descriptions with types. These feature descriptions describe typed feature structures, which are models of observable linguistic structures. In the definitions of types, one determines which properties of linguistic objects should be described. The type hierarchy together with type definitions is also referred to as a *signature*. As a grammarian, one typically uses types in feature descriptions. These descriptions contain constraints which must hold for linguistic objects. If no constraints are given, all values that are compatible with the specification in the signature are possible values. For example, one can omit the case description of a linguistic object such as *Frau* 'woman' since *Frau* can – as shown in (22) – appear in all four cases:

6 Feature descriptions

(22) a. Die Frau schläft. (nominative)
the.NOM woman sleeps

b. Wir gedenken der Frau. (genitive)
we commemorate the.GEN woman

c. Er hilft der Frau. (dative)
he helps the.DAT woman

d. Er liebt die Frau. (accusative)
he loves the.ACC woman

In a given model, there are only fully specified representations, that is, the model contains four forms of *Frau*, each with a different case. For masculine nouns such as *Mann* 'man', one would have to say something about case in the description since the genitive-singular form *Mann-es* differs from other singular forms, which can be seen by adding *Mann* into the examples in (22). (23) shows the feature descriptions for *Frau* 'woman' and *Mann* 'man':

(23) a. Frau 'woman':
$$[\text{GENDER } \textit{fem}]$$

b. Mann 'man':
$$\begin{bmatrix} \text{GENDER} & \textit{mas} \\ \text{CASE} & \textit{nominative} \lor \textit{dative} \lor \textit{accusative} \end{bmatrix}$$

Unlike (23b), (23a) does not contain a case feature since we do not need to say anything special about case in the description of *Frau*. Since all nominal objects require a case feature, it becomes clear that the structures for *Frau* must actually also have a case feature. The value of the case feature is of the type *case*. *case* is a general type which subsumes the subtypes *nominative*, *genitive*, *dative* and *accusative*. Concrete linguistic objects always have exactly one of these maximally specified types as their case value. The feature structures belonging to (23) are given in Figure 6.2 and Figure 6.3.

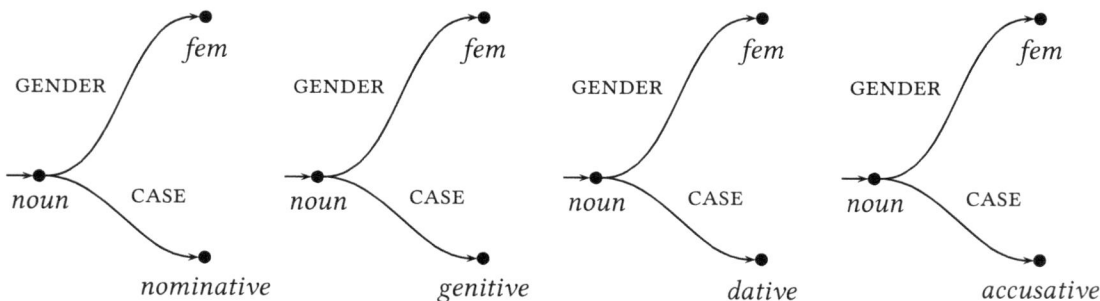

Figure 6.2: Feature structures for the description of *Frau* 'woman' in (23a)

In these representations, each node has a certain type (*noun*, *fem*, *nominative*, ...) and the types in feature structures are always maximally specific, that is, they do not have any further subtypes. There is always an entry node (*noun* in the example above) and

6.7 Phenomena, models and formal theories

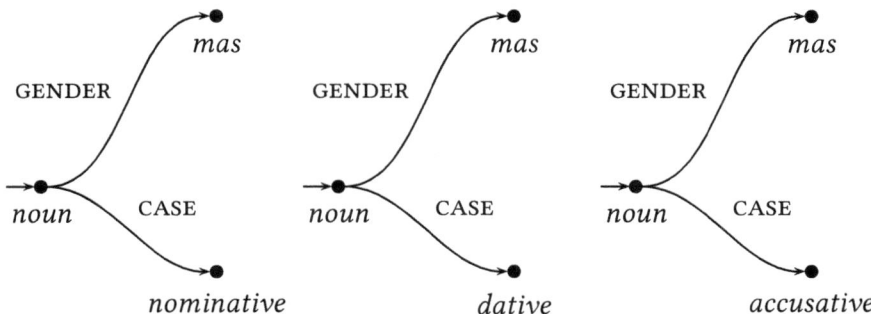

Figure 6.3: Feature structures for the description of *Mann* 'man' in (23b)

the other nodes are connected with arrows that are annotated with the feature labels (GENDER, CASE).

If we return to the example with people from the previous sections, we can capture the difference between a model and a description as follows: if we have a model of people that includes first name, last name, date of birth, gender and hair color, then it follows that every object we model also has a birthday. We can, however, decide to omit these details from our descriptions if they do not play a role for stating constraints or formulating searches.

The connection between linguistic phenomena, the model and the formal theory is shown in Figure 6.4. The model is designed to model linguistic phenomena. Further-

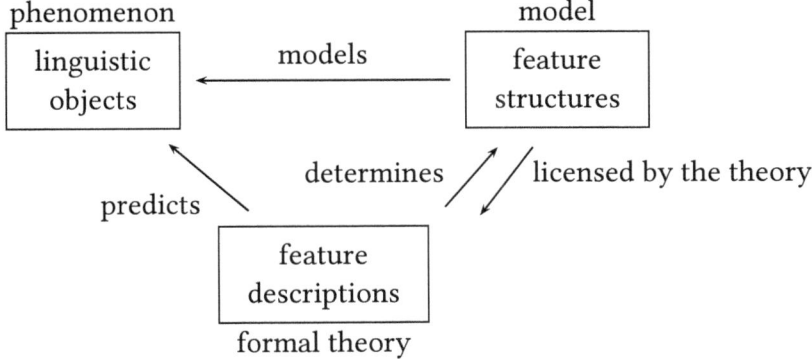

Figure 6.4: Phenomenon, model and formal theory

more, it must be licensed by our theory. The theory determines the model and makes predictions with regard to possible phenomena.

217

6 Feature descriptions

Comprehension questions

1. What are the reasons for using types?

2. What is inheritance? What is special about multiple inheritance?

3. Are the following structures compatible, that is, can they be used to describe the same object?

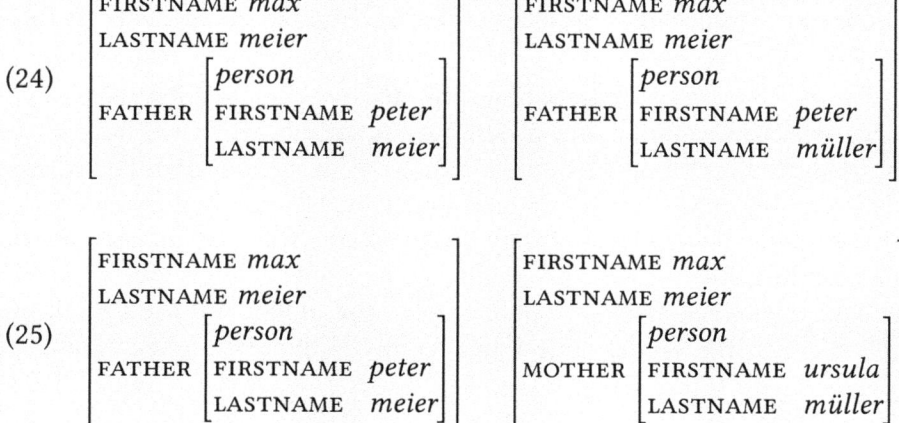

Exercises

1. Think about how one could describe musical instruments using feature descriptions.

2. Come up with a type hierarchy for the word classes (*det, comp, noun, verb, adj, prep*). Think about the ways in which one can organize the type hierachy so that one can express the generalizations that where captured by the binary features in Table 3.1 on page 94.

3. In this chapter, we introduced lists. This may look like an extension of the formalism, but it is not as it is possible to convert the list notation into a notation which only requires feature-value pairs. Think about how one could do this.

4. (Additional exercise) The relation *append* will play a role in Chapter 9. This relation serves to combine two lists to form a third. Relational constraints such as *append* do in fact constitute an expansion of the formalism. Using relational constraints, it is possible to relate any number of feature values to other values, that is, one can write programs which compute a particular value depending on other values. This poses the question as to whether one needs such powerful descriptive tools in a linguistic theory and if we do allow them, what kind of complexity we afford them. A theory which can do without relational constraints should be preferred over one that uses relational constraints (see Müller 2007a: Chapter 20 for a comparison of theories).

For the concatenation of lists, there is a possible implementation in feature structures without recourse to relational constraints. Find out how this can be done. Give your sources and document how you went about finding the solution.

Further reading

This chapter was designed to give the reader an easy-to-follow introduction to typed feature structures. The mathematical properties of the structures, type hierarchies and the combinatorial possibilities of such structures could not be discussed in detail here, but knowledge of at least part of these properties is important for work in computational linguistics and in developing one's own analyses. For more information, I refer the interested reader to the following publications: Shieber (1986) is a short introduction to the theory of Unification Grammar. It offers a relatively general overview followed by the discussion of important grammar types such as DCG, LFG, GPSG, HPSG, PATR-II. Johnson (1988) describes the formalism of untyped feature structures in a mathematically precise way. Carpenter (1992) goes into the detail about the mathematical aspects of typed feature structures. The formalism developed by King (1999) for HPSG-grammars forms the basis for the formalism by Richter (2004), which currently counts as the standard formalism for HPSG.

7 Lexical Functional Grammar

Lexical Functional Grammar (LFG) was developed in the 80s by Joan Bresnan and Ron Kaplan (Bresnan & Kaplan 1982). LFG forms part of so-called West-Coast linguistics: unlike MIT, where Chomsky works and teaches, the institutes of researchers such as Joan Bresnan and Ron Kaplan are on the west coast of the USA (Joan Bresnan in Stanford and Ron Kaplan at Xerox in Palo Alto and now at the language technology firm Nuance Communications in the Bay Area in California).

Bresnan & Kaplan (1982) view LFG explicitly as a psycholinguistically plausible alternative to transformation-based approaches. For a discussion of the requirements regarding the psycholinguistic plausibility of linguistics theories, see Chapter 15.

The more in-depth works on German are Berman (1996; 2003a) and Cook (2001).

LFG has well-designed formal foundations (Kaplan & Bresnan 1982; Kaplan 1995), and hence first implementations were available rather quickly (Frey & Reyle 1983b,a; Yasukawa 1984; Block & Hunze 1986; Eisele & Dörre 1986; Wada & Asher 1986; Delmonte 1990; Her, Higinbotham & Pentheroudakis 1991; Kohl 1992; Kohl, Gardent, Plainfossé, Reape & Momma 1992; Kaplan & Maxwell III 1996; Mayo 1997; 1999; Boullier & Sagot 2005a,b; Clément 2009; Clément & Kinyon 2001).

The following is a list of languages with implemented LFG fragments, probably incomplete:

- Arabic (Attia 2008),

- Arrernte (Dras, Lareau, Börschinger, Dale, Motazedi, Rambow, Turpin & Ulinski 2012),

- Bengali (Sengupta & Chaudhuri 1997),

- Danish (Ørsnes 2002; Ørsnes & Wedekind 2003; 2004),

- English (Her, Higinbotham & Pentheroudakis 1991; Butt, Dipper, Frank & King 1999; Riezler, King, Kaplan, Crouch, Maxwell III & Johnson 2002; King & Maxwell III 2007),

- French (Zweigenbaum 1991; Frank 1996; Frank & Zaenen 2002; Butt, Dipper, Frank & King 1999; Clément & Kinyon 2001; Boullier, Sagot & Clément 2005; Schwarze & de Alencar 2016; de Alencar 2017),

- Georgian (Meurer 2009),

- German (Rohrer 1996; Berman 1996; Kuhn & Rohrer 1997; Butt, Dipper, et al. 1999; Dipper 2003; Rohrer & Forst 2006; Forst 2006; Frank 2006; Forst & Rohrer 2009),

- Hungarian (Laczkó et al. 2010),
- Indonesian (Arka, Andrews, Dalrymple, Mistica & Simpson 2009),
- Italian (Delmonte 1990; Mayo 1999; Quaglia 2014),
- Irish (Sulger 2009; 2010),
- Japanese (Her, Higinbotham & Pentheroudakis 1991; Masuichi & Ohkuma 2003; Umemoto 2006),
- Korean (Her, Higinbotham & Pentheroudakis 1991),
- Malagasy (Randriamasimanana 2006; Dalrymple, Liakata & Mackie 2006),
- Mandarin Chinese (Her, Higinbotham & Pentheroudakis 1991; Fang & King 2007),
- Murrinh-Patha (Seiss & Nordlinger 2012),
- Norwegian (Dyvik, Meurer & Rosén 2005),
- Polish (Patejuk & Przepiórkowski 2012),
- Portuguese (de Alencar 2004; 2013; 2015),
- Spanish (Mayo 1999),
- Tigrinya (Kifle 2012),
- Turkish (Çetinoğlu & Oflazer 2006),
- Hungarian (Laczkó, Rákosi & Tóth 2010; Rákosi, Laczkó & Csernyi 2011),
- Urdu/Hindi (Butt, King & Roth 2007; Bögel, Butt & Sulger 2008),
- Welsh (Mittendorf & Sadler 2005) and
- Wolof (Dione 2014; 2013).

Many of theses grammars were developed in the ParGram consortium[1] (Butt, King, Niño & Segond 1999; Butt, Dyvik, King, Masuichi & Rohrer 2002). Apart from these grammars there is a small fragment of Northern Sotho, which is currently being expanded (Faaß 2010).

Many of the LFG systems combine linguistically motivated grammars with a statistical component. Such a component can help to find preferred readings of a sentence first, it can increase the efficiency of processing and make the complete processing robust (for instance Kaplan et al. 2004; Riezler et al. 2002). Josef van Genabith's group in Dublin is working on the induction of LFG grammars from corpora (e.g., Johnson et al. 1999; O'Donovan et al. 2005; Cahill et al. 2005; Chrupala & van Genabith 2006; Guo et al. 2007; Cahill et al. 2008; Schluter & van Genabith 2009).

---
[1] http://pargram.b.uib.no/research-groups/. 2018-02-20.

Some of the systems can be tested online:

- http://iness.uib.no/xle-web/xle-web

- http://www.xlfg.org/

7.1 General remarks on the representational format

LFG assumes multiple levels of representation.[2] The most important are c-structure and f-structure. c-structure is the constituent structure and it is licensed by a phrase structure grammar. This phrase structure grammar uses $\overline{\text{X}}$ structures for languages for which this is appropriate. f-structure stands for functional structure. Functional structure contains information about the predicates involved and about the grammatical functions (subject, object, …) which occur in a constituent. Mappings mediate between these representational levels.

7.1.1 Functional structure

In LFG, grammatical functions such as subject and object play a very important role. Unlike in most other theories discussed in this book, they are primitives of the theory. A sentence such as (1a) will be assigned a functional structure as in (1b):

(1) a. David devoured a sandwich.

  b. $\begin{bmatrix} \text{PRED} & \text{'DEVOUR}\langle\text{SUBJ, OBJ}\rangle\text{'} \\ \text{SUBJ} & \begin{bmatrix} \text{PRED} & \text{'DAVID'} \end{bmatrix} \\ \text{OBJ} & \begin{bmatrix} \text{SPEC} & \text{A} \\ \text{PRED} & \text{'SANDWICH'} \end{bmatrix} \end{bmatrix}$

All lexical items that have a meaning (e.g., nouns, verbs, adjectives) contribute a PRED feature with a corresponding value. The grammatical functions governed by a head (government = subcategorization) are determined in the specification of PRED.[3] Corresponding functions are called *governable grammatical functions*. Examples of this are shown in Table 7.1 on the next page (Dalrymple 2006). The PRED specification corresponds to the theta grid in GB theory. The valence of a head is specified by the PRED value.

The non-governable grammatical functions are given in Table 7.2 on the following page. Topic and focus are information-structural terms. There are a number of works on their exact definition, which differ to varying degrees (Kruijff-Korbayová & Steedman

---

[2]The English examples and their analyses discussed in this section are taken from Dalrymple (2001) and Dalrymple (2006).

[3]In the structure in (1b), the SUBJ and OBJ in the list following *devour* are identical to the values of SUBJ and OBJ in the structure. For reasons of presentation, this will not be explicitly indicated in this structure and following structures.

Table 7.1: Governable grammatical functions

SUBJ:	subject
OBJ:	object
COMP:	sentential complement or closed (non-predicative) infinitival complement
XCOMP:	open (predicative) complement, often infinitival, the SUBJ function is externally controlled
OBJ_θ:	secondary OBJ functions that are related to a special, language specific set of grammatical roles; English has OBJ_{THEME} only.
OBL_θ:	a group of thematically restricted oblique functions, as for instance OBL_{GOAL} or OBL_{AGENT}. These often correspond to adpositional phrases in c-structure.

Table 7.2: Non-governable grammatical functions

ADJ:	adjuncts
TOPIC:	the topic of an utterance
FOCUS:	the focus of an utterance

2003: 253–254), but broadly speaking, one can say that the focus of an utterance constitutes new information and that the topic is old or given information. Bresnan (2001: 97) uses the following question tests in order to determine topic and focus:

(2) Q: What did you name your cat?
    A: Rosie I named her. (*Rosie* = FOCUS)

(3) Q: What did you name your pets?
    A: My dog, I named Harold. My cat, I named Rosie. (*my dog*, *my cat* = TOPIC)

f-structures are characterized using functional descriptions, for example, one can refer to a value of the feature TENSE in the functional structure f using the following expression:

(4) (f TENSE)

It is possible to say something about the value which this feature should have in the feature description. The following descriptions express the fact that in the structure f, the feature TENSE must have the value PAST.

(5) (f TENSE) = PAST

The value of a feature may also be a specific f-structure. The expression in (6) ensures that the SUBJ feature in f is the f-structure g:

7.1 General remarks on the representational format

(6) $(f\ \text{SUBJ}) = g$

For the analysis of (7a), we get the constraints in (7b):

(7) a. David sneezed.
   b. $(f\ \text{PRED}) = \text{'SNEEZE}\langle\text{SUBJ}\rangle\text{'}$
   $(f\ \text{TENSE}) = \text{PAST}$
   $(f\ \text{SUBJ}) = g$
   $(g\ \text{PRED}) = \text{'DAVID'}$

The description in (7b) describes the following structure:

(8) $f:\begin{bmatrix} \text{PRED} & \text{'SNEEZE}\langle\text{SUBJ}\rangle\text{'} \\ \text{TENSE} & \text{PAST} \\ \text{SUBJ} & g:\begin{bmatrix}\text{PRED 'DAVID'}\end{bmatrix} \end{bmatrix}$

But (7b) also describes many other structures which contain further features. We are only interested in minimal structures that contain the information provided in the description.

(9) shows how a node in the c-structure can be connected to the f-structure for the entire sentence:

(9)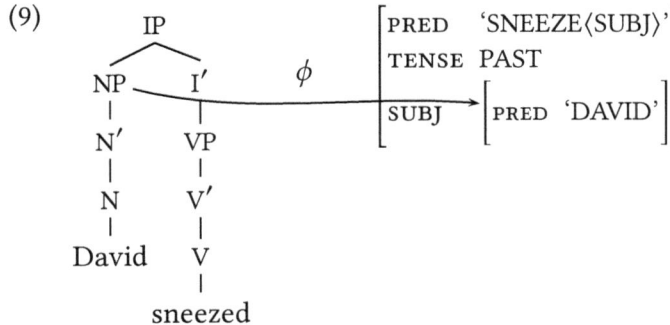

The function ϕ from the NP-node to the f-structure corresponding to the NP is depicted with an arrow marked ϕ.

A phrase and its head always correspond to the same f-structure:

(10)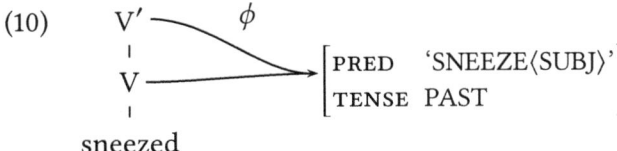

In LFG grammars of English, the CP/IP system is assumed as in GB theory (see Section 3.1.5). IP, I' and I (and also VP) are mapped onto the same f-structure.

(11) a. David is yawning.

7 Lexical Functional Grammar

b.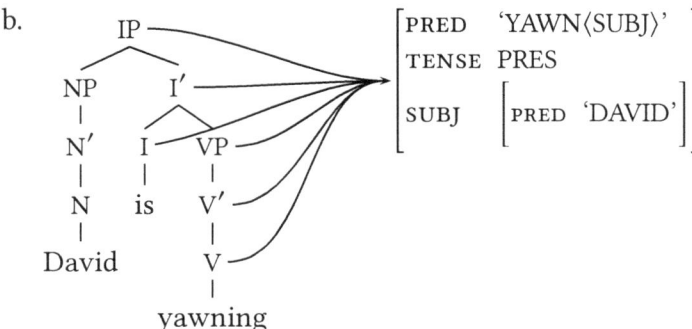

f-structures have to fulfill two well-formedness conditions: they have to be both *complete* and *coherent*. Both these conditions will be discussed in the following sections.

7.1.2 Completeness

Every head adds a constraint of the PRED value of the corresponding f-structure. In determining completeness, one has to check that the elements required in the PRED value are actually realized. In (12b), OBJ is missing a value, which is why (12a) is ruled out by the theory.

(12) a. * David devoured.

b. $\begin{bmatrix} \text{PRED} & \text{'DEVOUR}\langle\text{SUBJ,OBJ}\rangle\text{'} \\ \text{SUBJ} & [\text{PRED 'DAVID'}] \end{bmatrix}$

7.1.3 Coherence

The Coherence Condition requires that all argument functions in a given f-structure have to be selected in the value of the local PRED attribute. (13a) is ruled out because COMP does not appear under the arguments of *devour*.

(13) a. * David devoured a sandwich that Peter sleeps.

b. $\begin{bmatrix} \text{PRED} & \text{'DEVOUR}\langle\text{SUBJ,OBJ}\rangle\text{'} \\ \text{SUBJ} & [\text{ PRED 'DAVID' }] \\ \text{OBJ} & \begin{bmatrix} \text{SPEC} & \text{A} \\ \text{PRED} & \text{'SANDWICH'} \end{bmatrix} \\ \text{COMP} & \begin{bmatrix} \text{PRED} & \text{'SLEEP}\langle\text{SUBJ}\rangle\text{'} \\ \text{SUBJ} & [\text{PRED 'PETER'}] \end{bmatrix} \end{bmatrix}$

The constraints on completeness and coherence together ensure that all and only those arguments required in the PRED specification are actually realized. Both of those constraints taken together correspond to the Theta-Criterion in GB theory (see page 92).[4]

---

[4]For the differences between predicate-argument structures in LFG and the Deep Structure oriented Theta Criterion, see Bresnan & Kaplan (1982: xxvi–xxviii).

7.1.4 Restrictions on the c-structure/f-structure relation

Symbols in c-structures are assigned restrictions for f-structures. The following symbols are used: '↑' refers to the f-structure of the immediately dominating node and '↓' refers to the f-structure of the c-structure node bearing the annotation. A common annotation is '↑ = ↓'. This constraint states that the f-structure of the mother node is identical to that of the annotated category:

(14) V' → V
              ↑ = ↓
      f-structure of the mother = own f-structure

The annotation '↑ = ↓' is below the head of a structure.

Phrases which are licensed by the annotated c-structure in (14) can be visualized as follows:

(15) V' ──→ [ ]
      |
      V ─╯

(16) shows a V' rule with an object:

(16) V' →   V   NP
           ↑ = ↓   (↑ OBJ) = ↓

The annotation on the NP signals that the OBJ value in the f-structure of the mother (↑ OBJ) is identical to the f-structure of the NP node, that is, to everything that is contributed from the material below the NP node (↓). This is shown in the figure in (17):

(17) V' ──────→ [OBJ ──→ [ ]]
      ╱╲
     V   NP ─╯

In the equation (↑ OBJ) = ↓, the arrows '↑' and '↓' correspond to feature structures. '↑' and '↓' stand for the f and g in equations such as (6).

(18) is an example with an intransitive verb and (19) is the corresponding visualization:

(18) *sneezed* V   (↑ PRED) = 'SNEEZE⟨SUBJ⟩'
                    (↑ TENSE) = PAST

(19)   V ──────→ [PRED   'SNEEZE⟨SUBJ⟩']
        | [TENSE PAST   ]
      sneezed

7.1.5 Semantics

Following Dalrymple (2006: 90–92), *glue semantics* is the dominant approach to semantic interpretation in LFG (Dalrymple, Lamping & Saraswat 1993; Dalrymple 2001: Chapter 8). There are, however, other variants where Kamp's discourse representation structures (Kamp & Reyle 1993) are used (Frey & Reyle 1983b,a).

7 Lexical Functional Grammar

In the following, glue semantics will be presented in more detail.[5] Under a glue-based approach, it is assumed that f-structure is the level of syntactic representation which is crucial for the semantic interpretation of a phrase, that is, unlike GB theory, it is not the position of arguments in the tree which play a role in the composition of meaning, but rather functional relations such as SUBJ and OBJ. Glue semantics assumes that each substructure of the f-structure corresponds to a semantic resource connected to a meaning and furthermore, that the meaning of a given f-structure comes from the sum of these parts. The way the meaning is assembled is regulated by certain instructions for the combination of semantic resources. These instructions are given as a set of logic premises written in linear logic as *glue language*. The computation of the meaning of an utterance corresponds to a logical conclusion.

This conclusion is reached on the basis of logical premises contributed by the words in an expression or possibly even by a syntactic construction itself. The requirements on how the meaning of the parts can be combined to yield the full meaning are expressed in linear logic, a resource-based logic. Linear logic is different from classic logic in that it does not allow that premises of conclusions are not used at all or more than once in a derivation. Hence, in linear logic, premises are resources which have to be used. This corresponds directly to the use of words in an expression: words contribute to the entire meaning exactly once. It is not possible to ignore them or to use their meaning more than once. A sentence such as *Peter knocked twice.* does not mean the same as *Peter knocked.* The meaning of *twice* must be included in the full meaning of the sentences. Similarly, the sentence cannot mean the same as *Peter knocked twice twice.*, since the semantic contribution of a given word cannot be used twice.

The syntactic structure for the sentence in (20a) together with its semantic representation is given in (20b):

(20)   a. David yawned.

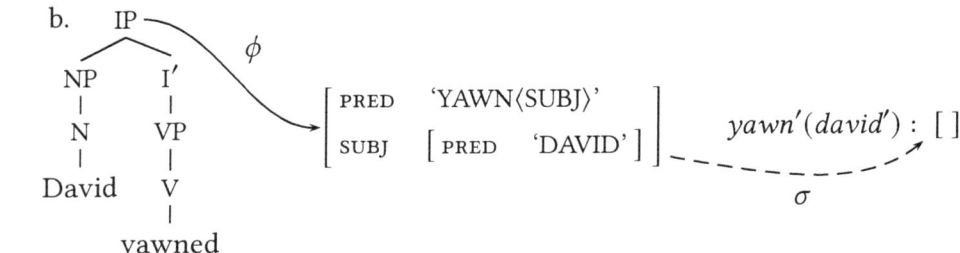

The semantic structure of this sentence is connected to the f-structure via the correspondence function σ (depicted here as a dashed line). The semantic representation is derived from the lexical information for the verb *yawned*, which is given in (21).

(21) $\lambda x.yawn'(x) : (\uparrow \text{SUBJ})_\sigma \multimap \uparrow_\sigma$

This formula is referred to as the *meaning constructor*. Its job is to combine the meaning of *yawned* – a one place predicate $\lambda x.yawn'(x)$ – with the formula $(\uparrow \text{SUBJ})_\sigma \multimap \uparrow_\sigma$ in

---
[5]The following discussion heavily draws from the corresponding section of Dalrymple (2006). (It is a translation of my translation of the original material into German.)

7.1 General remarks on the representational format

linear logic. Here, the connective ⊸ is the *linear implication* symbol of linear logic. The symbol contains the meaning that *if* a semantic resource (↑ SUBJ)$_\sigma$ for the meaning of the subject is available, *then* a semantic resource for ↑$_\sigma$ must be created which will stand for the entire meaning of the sentence. Unlike the implication operator of classic logic, the linear implication must consume and produce semantic resources: the formula (↑ SUBJ)$_\sigma$ ⊸ ↑$_\sigma$ states that if a semantic resource (↑ SUBJ)$_\sigma$ is found, it is consumed and the semantic resource ↑$_\sigma$ is produced.

Furthermore, it is assumed that a proper name such as *David* contributes its own semantic structure as a semantic resource. In an utterance such as *David yawned*, this resource is consumed by the verb *yawned*, which requires a resource for its SUBJ in order to produce the resource for the entire sentence. This corresponds to the intuition that a verb in any given sentence requires the meaning of its arguments in order for the entire sentence to be understood.

The f-structure of *David yawned* with the instantiated meaning construction contributed by *David* and *yawned* is given in (22):

(22) $y : \begin{bmatrix} \text{PRED} & \text{'YAWN⟨SUBJ⟩'} \\ \text{SUBJ} & d : [\text{PRED} \quad \text{'DAVID'}] \end{bmatrix}$

   [David] $david' : d_\sigma$
   [yawn] $\lambda x. yawn'(x) : d_\sigma \multimap y_\sigma$

The left side of the meaning constructor marked by **[David]** is the meaning of the proper name *David*, *david'* to be precise. The left-hand side of the meaning constructor **[yawn]** is the meaning of the intransitive verb – a one-place predicate $\lambda x. yawn'(x)$.

Furthermore, one must still postulate further rules to determine the exact relation between the right-hand side (the glue) of the meaning constructors in (22) and the left-hand side (the meaning). For simple, non-implicational meaning constructors such as **[David]** in (22), the meaning on the left is the same as the meaning of the semantic structure on the right. Meaning constructors such as **[yawn]** have a λ-expression on the left, which has to be combined with another expression via functional application (see Section 2.3). The linear implication on the right-hand side must be applied in parallel. This combined process is shown in (23).

(23) $\dfrac{x : f_\sigma \qquad P : f_\sigma \multimap g_\sigma}{P(x) : g_\sigma}$

The right-hand side of the rule corresponds to a logical conclusion following the *modus ponens* rule. With these correspondences between expressions in linear logic and the meanings themselves, we can proceed as shown in (24), which is based on Dalrymple (2006: 92). After combining the respective meanings of *yawned* and *David* and then carrying out β-reduction, we arrive at the desired result of $yawn'(david')$ as the meaning of *David yawned*.

(24) $david' : d_\sigma$ The meaning $david'$ is associated with the semantic structure of SUBJ d_σ.

$\lambda x.yawn'(x) : d_\sigma \multimap y_\sigma$ If we find the semantic resource for the SUBJ d_σ on the glue side, this resource is consumed and the semantic resource for the entire sentence y_σ is produced. On the meaning side, we apply the function $\lambda x.yawn'(x)$ to the meaning associated with d_σ.

$yawn'(david') : y_\sigma$ We have created the semantic structure y_σ for the entire sentence, associated with the meaning of $yawn'(david')$.

Glue analyses of quantification, modification and other phenomena have been investigated in a volume on glue semantics (Dalrymple 1999). Particularly problematic for these approaches are cases where there appear to be too many or too few resources for the production of utterances. These kinds of cases have been discussed by Asudeh (2004).

7.1.6 Adjuncts

Adjuncts are not selected by their head. The grammatical function ADJ is a non-governable grammatical function. Unlike arguments, where every grammatical function can only be realized once, a sentence can contain multiple adjuncts. The value of ADJ in the f-structure is therefore not a simple structure as with the other grammatical functions, but rather a set. For example, the f structure for the sentence in (25a) contains an ADJ set with two elements: one for *yesterday* and one for *at noon*.

(25) a. David devoured a sandwich at noon yesterday.

b. $\begin{bmatrix} \text{PRED} & \text{'DEVOUR}\langle\text{SUBJ,OBJ}\rangle\text{'} \\ \text{SUBJ} & [\text{PRED 'DAVID'}] \\ \text{OBJ} & \begin{bmatrix} \text{SPEC} & \text{A} \\ \text{PRED} & \text{'SANDWICH'} \end{bmatrix} \\ \text{ADJ} & \left\{ [\text{PRED 'YESTERDAY'}], \begin{bmatrix} \text{PRED} & \text{'AT}\langle\text{OBJ}\rangle\text{'} \\ \text{OBJ} & [\text{PRED 'NOON'}] \end{bmatrix} \right\} \end{bmatrix}$

The annotation on the c-structure rule for adjuncts requires that the f-structure of the adjuncts be part of the ADJ set of the mother's f-structure:

(26) V′ →   V′   PP
              ↑ = ↓   ↓ ∈ (↑ ADJ)

The representation of adjuncts in a set is not sufficient to characterize the meaning of an utterance containing scope-bearing adjuncts (as for instance the negation in sentences like (31) on page 105). In order to determine scopal relations, one has to refer to the linear order of the adjuncts, that is, the c-structure. For linearization restrictions in LFG, see Zaenen & Kaplan (1995).

7.2 Passive

Bresnan & Mchombo (1995) argue that one should view words as "atoms" of which syntactic structure is comprised (*lexical integrity*[6]).

Syntactic rules cannot create new words or make reference to the internal structure of words. Every terminal node (each "leaf" of the tree) is a word. It follows from this that analyses such as the GB analysis of Pollock (1989) in Figure 7.1 on the next page for the French example in (27) are ruled out (the figure is taken from Kuhn 2007: 617):

(27) Marie ne parlerait pas
 Marie NEG speak.COND.3SG NEG
 'Marie would not speak.'

In Pollock's analysis, the various morphemes are in specific positions in the tree and are combined only after certain movements have been carried out.

The assumption of lexical integrity is made by all theories discussed in this book with the exception of GB and Minimalism. However, formally, this is not a must as it is also possible to connect morphemes to complex syntactic structures in theories such as Categorial Grammar, GPSG, HPSG, CxG, DG and TAG (Müller 2018c: Section 4). As far as I know, this kind of analysis has never been proposed.

Bresnan noticed that, as well as passivized verbs, there are passivized adjectives which show the same morphological idiosyncrasies as the corresponding participles (Bresnan 1982b: 21; Bresnan 2001: 31). Some examples are given in (28):

(28) a. a well-written novel (write – written)
 b. a recently given talk (give – given)
 c. my broken heart (break – broken)
 d. an uninhabited island (inhabit – inhabited)
 e. split wood (split – split)

If one assumes lexical integrity, then adjectives would have to be derived in the lexicon. If the verbal passive were not a lexical process, but rather a phrase-structural one, then the form identity would remain unexplained.

In LFG, grammatical functions are primitives, that is, they are not derived from a position in the tree (e.g., Subject = SpecIP). Words (fully inflected word-forms) determine the

---

[6]See Anderson (1992: 84) for more on lexical integrity.

7 Lexical Functional Grammar

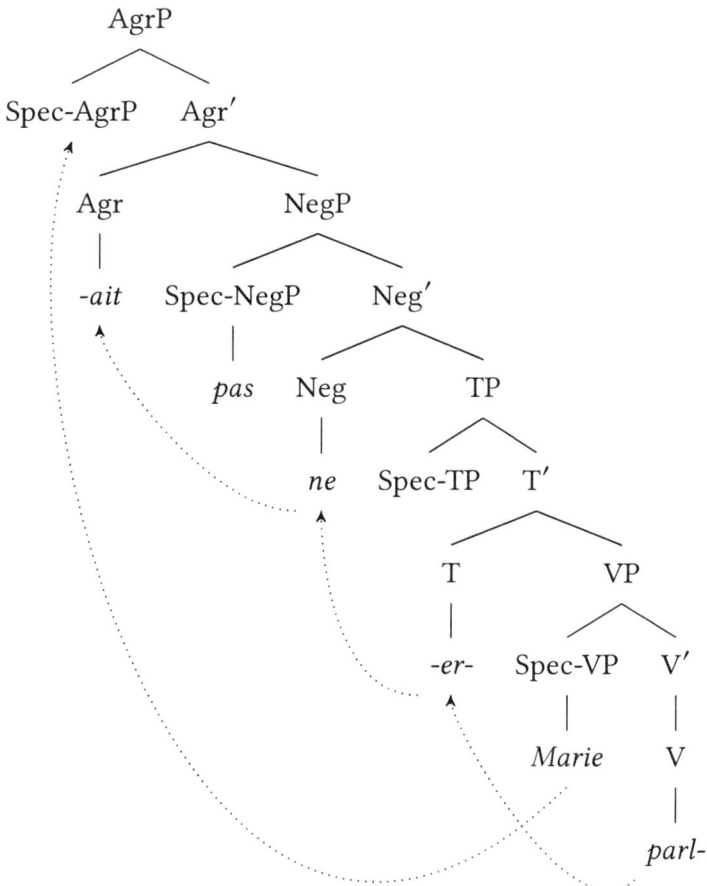

Figure 7.1: Pollock's analysis of *Marie ne parlerait pas* 'Marie would not speak.' according to Kuhn (2007: 617)

grammatical function of their arguments. Furthermore, there is a hierarchy of grammatical functions. During participle formation in morphology, the highest verbal argument is suppressed. The next highest argument moves up and is not realized as the OBJECT but rather as the SUBJECT. This was explicitly encoded in earlier work (Bresnan 1982b: 8):

(29) Passivization rule:
(SUBJ) ↦ ∅/(OBL)
(OBJ) ↦ (SUBJ)

The first rule states that the subject is either not realized (∅) or it is realized as an oblique element (the *by*-PP in English). The second rule states that if there is an accusative object, this becomes the subject.

In later work, the assignment of grammatical functions was taken over by Lexical Mapping Theory (Bresnan & Kanerva 1989). It is assumed that thematic roles are ordered in a universally valid hierarchy (Bresnan & Kanerva 1989; Bresnan 2001: 307): agent >

beneficiary > experiencer/goal > instrument > patient/theme > locative. Patient-like roles are marked as unrestricted ([−r]) in a corresponding representation, the so-called a-structure. Secondary patient-like roles are marked as *objective* ([+o]) and all other roles are marked as non-objective ([−o]). For the transitive verb *schlagen* 'to beat', we have the following:

(30)   Agent   Patient
       a-structure   *schlagen* 'beat'   ⟨ x   y ⟩
                                                [−o]   [−r]

The mapping of a-structure to f-structure is governed by the following restrictions:

(31)   a. Subject-Mapping-Principle: The most prominent role marked with [−o] is mapped to SUBJ if it is initial in the a-structure. Otherwise, the role marked with [−r] is mapped to SUBJ.

       b. The argument roles are connected to grammatical functions as shown in the following table. Non-specified values for o and r are to be understood as '+':

                [−r]   [+r]
       [−o]   SUBJ OBL_θ
       [+o]   OBJ OBJ_θ

       c. Function-Argument Biuniqueness: Every a-structure role must be associated to exactly one function and vice versa.

For the argument structure in (30), the principle in (31a) ensures that the agent x receives the grammatical function SUBJ. (31b) adds an o-feature with the value '+' so that the patient y is associated with OBJ:

(32)   Agent   Patient
       a-structure   *schlagen* 'beat'   ⟨ x   y ⟩
                                                [−o]   [−r]
                                                SUBJ   OBJ

Under passivization, the most prominent role is suppressed so that only the [−r] marked patient role remains. Following (31a), this role will then be mapped to the subject.

(33)   Agent   Patient
       a-structure   *schlagen* 'beat'   ⟨ x   y ⟩
                                                [−o]   [−r]
                                                ∅   SUBJ

Unlike the objects of transitive verbs, the objects of verbs such as *helfen* 'help' are marked as [+o] (Berman 1999). The lexical case of the objects is given in the a-structure, since this case (dative) is linked to a semantic role (Zaenen, Maling & Thráinsson 1985: 465). The corresponding semantic roles are obligatorily mapped to the grammatical function OBJ_θ.

(34) a-structure   *helfen* 'help'
$$\frac{\begin{array}{cc} \text{Agent} & \text{Beneficiary} \\ \langle\, x & y \,\rangle \\ [-o] & [+o]/\text{DAT} \end{array}}{\begin{array}{cc} \text{SUBJ} & \text{OBJ}_\theta \end{array}}$$

Passivization will yield the following:

(35) a-structure   *helfen* 'help'
$$\frac{\begin{array}{cc} \text{Agent} & \text{Beneficiary} \\ \langle\, x & y \,\rangle \\ [-o] & [+o]/\text{DAT} \end{array}}{\begin{array}{cc} \varnothing & \text{OBJ}_\theta \end{array}}$$

Since there is neither a [−o] nor a [−r] argument, no argument is connected to the subject function. The result is an association of arguments and grammatical functions that corresponds to the one found in impersonal passives.

These mapping principles may seem complex at first glance, but they play a role in analyzing an entire range of phenomena, e.g., the analysis of unaccusative verbs (Bresnan & Zaenen 1990). For the analysis of the passive, we can now say that the passive suppresses the highest [−o] role. Mentioning an eventual object in the passive rule is no longer necessary.

7.3 Verb position

There are two possibilities for the analysis of verb placement in German.

- a trace in verb-final position (as in GB) (see Choi 1999, Berman 1996: Section 2.1.4) and

- so-called *extended head domains* (see Berman 2003a).

In the analysis of extended head domains, the verb is simply omitted from the verb phrase. The following preliminary variant of the VP rule is used:[7]

(36)   VP → NP* (V)

All components of the VP are optional as indicated by the brackets and by the Kleene star. The Kleene star stands for arbitrarily many occurrences of a symbol. This also includes zero occurrences. As in GB analyses, the verb in verb-first clauses is in C. No I projection is assumed – as in a number of GB works (Haider 1993; 1995; 1997a; Sternefeld 2006: Section IV.3), since it is difficult to motivate its existence for German (Berman 2003a: Section 3.2.2). The verb contributes its f-structure information from the C position. Figure 7.2 on the facing page contains a simplified version of the analysis proposed by Berman (2003a: 41).

---

[7]See Bresnan (2001: 110), Zaenen & Kaplan (2002: 413) and Dalrymple (2006: 84) for corresponding rules with optional constituents on the right-hand side of the rule. Zaenen & Kaplan (2002: 413) suggest a rule that is similar to (36) for German.

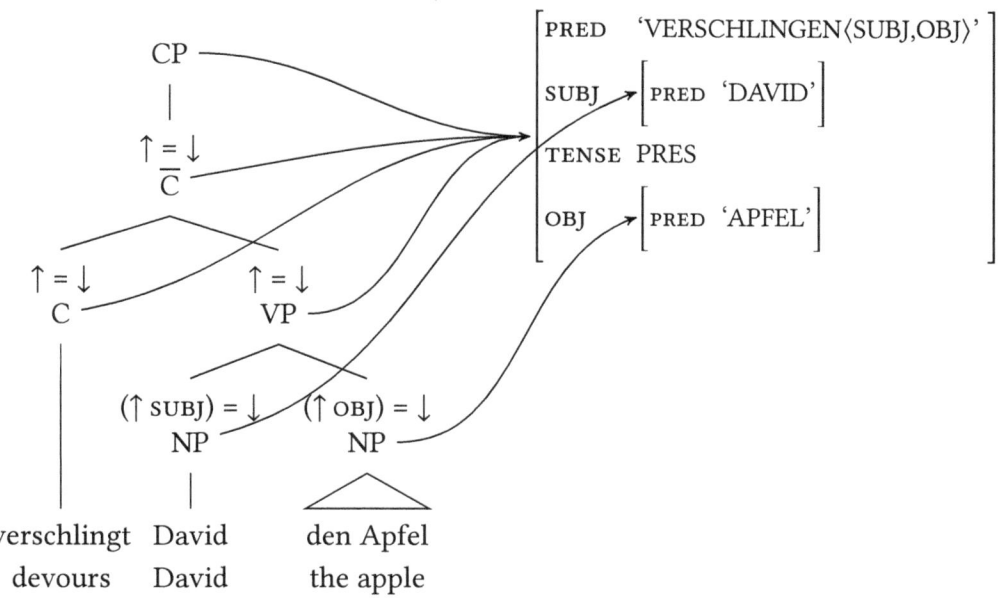

Figure 7.2: Analysis of verb placement following Berman (2003a: 41)

After what we learned about phrase structure rules in Chapters 2 and 5, it may seem strange to allow VPs without V. This is not a problem in LFG, however, since for the analysis of a given sentence, it only has to be ensured that all the necessary parts (and only these) are present. This is ensured by the constraints on completeness and coherence. Where exactly the information comes from is not important. In Figure 7.2, the verb information does not come from the VP, but rather from the C node. C′ is licensed by a special rule:

(37) C′ →   C   VP
              ↑ = ↓ ↑ = ↓

In LFG rules, there is normally only one element annotated with '↑ = ↓', namely the head. In (37), there are two such elements, which is why both equally contribute to the f-structure of the mother. The head domain of V has been extended to C. The information about SUBJ and OBJ comes from the VP and the information about PRED from C.

7.4 Local reordering

Two possibilities for treating local reordering have been discussed in the literature:[8]

- movement of arguments from a base configuration as in GB (see Choi 1999)
- direct licensing by phrase structure rules (see Berman 1996: Section 2.1.3.1; 2003a)

---

[8]Kaplan (1995: 20–21) shows how one can write grammars in the ID/LP format in LFG. A GPSG-like analysis of German constituent order has not been proposed in the LFG framework.

7 Lexical Functional Grammar

If one assumes that traces are relevant for the semantic interpretation of a given structure, then the first option has the same problems as movement-based GB analyses. These have already been discussed in Section 3.5.

In what follows, I will present the analysis proposed by Berman (1996: Section 2.1.3) in a somewhat simplified form. Case and grammatical functions of verbal arguments are determined in the lexicon (Berman 1996: 22). (38) shows the lexical entry for the verb *verschlingen* 'devour':[9,10]

(38) *verschlingt*   V   (↑ PRED) = 'VERSCHLINGEN⟨SUBJ, OBJ⟩'
       (↑ SUBJ AGR CAS) = NOM
       (↑ OBJ AGR CAS) = ACC
       (↑ TENSE) = PRES

---

[9]The four cases in German can be represented using two binary features (GOV, OBL) (Berman 1996: 22). Nominative corresponds to GOV− and OBL− and accusative to GOV+ and OBL−. This kind of encoding allows one to leave case partially underspecified. If one does not provided a value for GOV, then an element with OBL− is compatible with both nominative and accusative. Since this underspecification is not needed in the following discussion, I will omit this feature decomposition and insert the case values directly.

[10]Alternative analyses derive the grammatical function of an NP from its case (Berman 2003a: 37 for German; Bresnan 2001: 187, 201 for German and Russian).

 (i) (↓ CASE) = ACC ⇒ (↑ OBJ) = ↓

Karttunen (1989: Section 2.1) makes a similar suggestion for Finnish in the framework of Categorial Grammar. Such analyses are not entirely unproblematic as case cannot always be reliably paired with grammatical functions. In German, as well as temporal accusatives (ii.a), there are also verbs with two accusative objects (ii.b–c) and predicative accusatives (ii.d).

(ii) a. Er arbeitete den ganzen Tag.
    he worked the.ACC whole.ACC day

  b. Er lehrte ihn den Ententanz.
    he taught him.ACC the.ACC duck.dance

  c. Das kostet ihn einen Taler.
    that costs him.ACC a.ACC taler

  d. Sie nannte ihn einen Lügner.
    she called him.ACC a.ACC liar

All of these accusatives can occur in long-distance dependencies (see Section 7.5):

(iii) Wen glaubst du, dass ich getroffen habe.
   who believe you that I met have
   'Who do you think I met?'

wen is not the object of *glauben* 'believe' and as such cannot be included in the f-structure of *glauben* 'believe'. One would have to reformulate the implication in (i) as a disjunction of all possible grammatical functions of the accusative and in addition account for the fact that accusatives can come from a more deeply embedded f-structure.

 Bresnan (2001: 202) assumes that nonlocal dependencies crossing a clause involve a gap in German. With such a gap one can assume that case is only assigned locally within the verbal projection. In any case one would have to distinguish several types of frontings in German and the specification of case/grammatical function interaction would be much more complicate than (i).

Berman proposes an analysis that does not combine the verb with all its arguments and adjuncts at the same time, as was the case in GPSG. Instead, she chooses the other extreme and assumes that the verb is not combined with an adjunct or an argument, but rather forms a VP directly. The rule for this is shown in (39):

(39) VP →   (V)
              ↑ = ↓

At first sight, this may seem odd since a V such as *verschlingen* 'devour' does not have the same distribution as a verb with its arguments. However, one should recall that the constraints pertaining to coherence and completeness of f-structures play an important role so that the theory does not make incorrect predictions.

Since the verb can occur in initial position, it is marked as optional in the rule in (39) (see Section 7.3).

The following rule can be used additionally to combine the verb with its subject or object.

(40) VP →   NP   VP
              (↑ SUBJ |OBJ |OBJ$_\theta$) = ↓   ↑ = ↓

The '|' here stands for a disjunction, that is, the NP can either be the subject or the object of the superordinate f-structure. Since VP occurs both on the left and right-hand side of the rule in (40), it can be applied multiple times. The rule is not complete, however. For instance, one has to account for prepositional objects, for clausal arguments, for adjectival arguments and for adjuncts. See footnote 12 on page 241.

Figure 7.3 on the next page shows the analysis for (41a).

(41) a. [dass] David den Apfel verschlingt
           that David the apple devours
         'that David is devouring the apple'
      b. [dass] den Apfel David verschlingt
           that the apple David devours

The analysis of (41b) is shown in Figure 7.4 on the following page. The analysis of (41b) differs from the one of (41a) only in the order of the replacement of the NP node by the subject or object.

One further fact must be discussed: in the rule (39), the verb is optional. If it is omitted, the VP is empty. In this way, the VP rule in (40) can have an empty VP on the right-hand side of the rule. This VP is also simply omitted even though the VP symbol in the right-hand side of rule (40) is not marked as optional. That is, the corresponding symbol then also becomes optional as a result of taking the rest of the grammar into consideration as well as possible interactions with other rules.

7.5 Long-distance dependencies and functional uncertainty

We have seen that LFG can explain phenomena such as passivization, local reordering as well as verb placement without transformations. In Chapter 5 on GPSG, we already

7 Lexical Functional Grammar

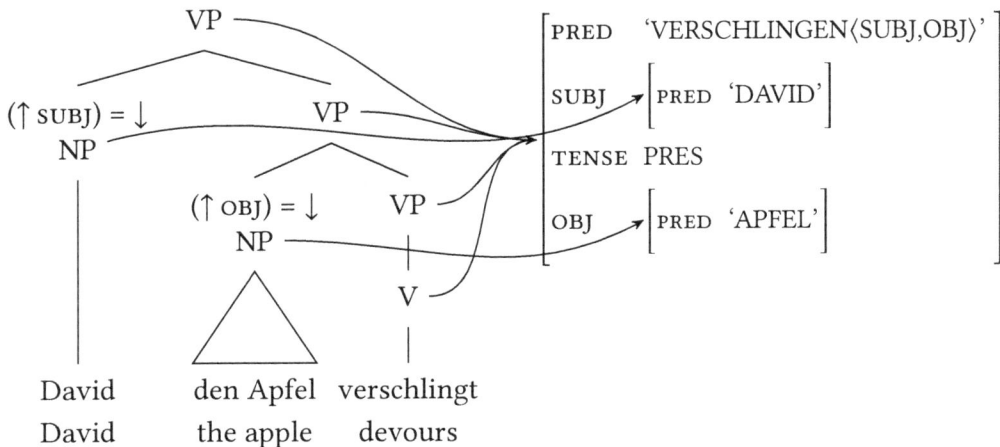

Figure 7.3: Analysis of SOV order following Berman (1996)

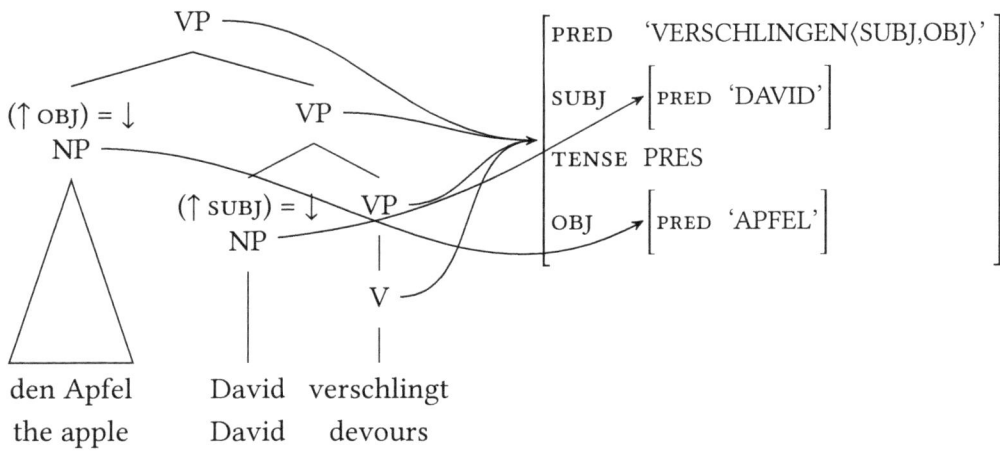

Figure 7.4: Analysis of OSV order following Berman (1996)

saw that the development of a transformation-less analysis for long-distance dependencies constitutes a real achievement. In LFG, Kaplan & Zaenen (1989) proposed another transformation-less analysis of long-distance dependencies, which we will consider in further detail in what follows.

In example (42), the displaced constituent *Chris* is characterized by two functions:

(42) Chris, we think that David saw.

For one, it has an argument function which is normally realized in a different position (the OBJ function of *saw* in the above example) and additionally it has a discourse function: a certain emphasis of the information-structural status in this construction (TOPIC in the matrix clause). In LFG, TOPIC and FOCUS are assumed to be grammaticalized discourse functions (furthermore, SUBJ is classified as the default discourse function). Only grammaticalized discourse functions are represented on the level of f-structure, that is,

7.5 Long-distance dependencies and functional uncertainty

those that are created by a fixed syntactic mechanism and that interact with the rest of the syntax.

Unlike argument functions, the discourse functions TOPIC and FOCUS are not lexically subcategorized and are therefore not subject to the completeness and coherence conditions. The values of discourse function features like TOPIC and FOCUS are identified with an f-structure that bears an argument function. (43) gives the f-structure for the sentence in (42):

(43)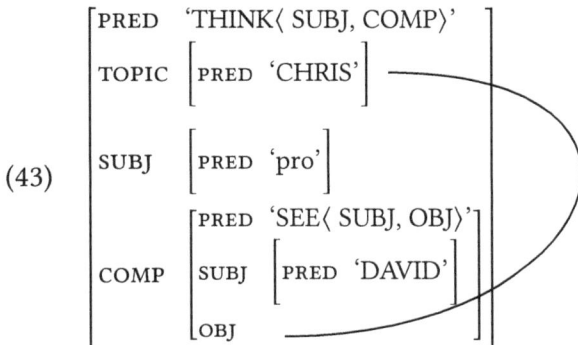

The connecting line means that the value of TOPIC is identical to the value of COMP|OBJ. In Chapter 6 on feature descriptions, I used boxes for structure sharing rather than connecting lines, since boxes are more common across frameworks. It is possible to formulate the structure sharing in (43) as an f-structure constraint as in (44):

(44)   (↑ TOPIC) = (↑ COMP OBJ)

Fronting operations such as (42) are possible from various levels of embedding: for instance, (45a) shows an example with less embedding. The object is located in the same f-structure as the topic. However, the object in (42) comes from a clause embedded under *think*.

The f-structure corresponding to (45a) is given in (45b):

(45)   a. Chris, we saw.
       b.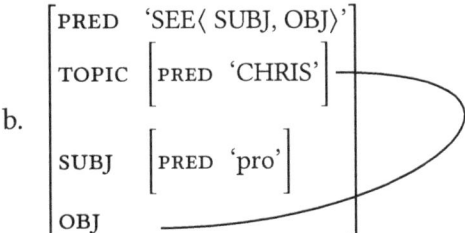

The identity restriction for TOPIC and object can be formulated in this case as in (46):

(46)   (↑ TOPIC) = (↑ OBJ)

Example (47a) shows a case of even deeper embedding than in (42) and (47b,c) show the corresponding f-structure and the respective restriction.

(47) a. Chris, we think Anna claims that David saw.

b.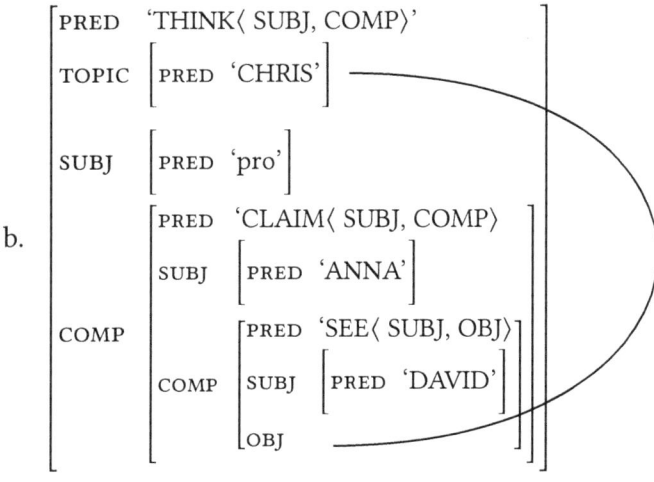

c. (↑ TOPIC) = (↑ COMP COMP OBJ)

The restrictions in (44), (46) and (47c) are c-structure constraints. The combination of a c-structure with (44) is given in (48):

(48) CP →   XP   C′
              (↑ TOPIC) = ↓   ↑ = ↓
              (↑ TOPIC) = (↑ COMP OBJ)

(48) states that the first constituent contributes to the TOPIC value in the f-structure of the mother and furthermore that this topic value has to be identical to that of the object in the complement clause. We have also seen examples of other embeddings of various depths. We therefore need restrictions of the following kind as in (49):

(49) a. (↑ TOPIC) = (↑ OBJ)
     b. (↑ TOPIC) = (↑ COMP OBJ)
     c. (↑ TOPIC) = (↑ COMP COMP OBJ)
     d. ...

The generalization emerging from these equations is given in (50):

(50) (↑ TOPIC) = (↑ COMP* OBJ)

Here, '*' stands for an unrestricted number of occurrences of COMP. This means of leaving the possible identification of discourse and grammatical function open is known as *functional uncertainty*, see Kaplan & Zaenen (1989).

As was shown in the discussion of examples (2) and (3) on page 224, it is not the case that only a TOPIC can be placed in the specifier position of CP in English as FOCUS can occur there too. One can use disjunctions in LFG equations and express the corresponding condition as follows:

(51) (↑ TOPIC|FOCUS) = (↑ COMP* OBJ)

One can introduce a special symbol for TOPIC|FOCUS, which stands for a disjunction of discourse functions: DF. (51) can then be abbreviated as in (52):

(52)   (↑ DF) = (↑ COMP* OBJ)

The final version of the c-structure rule for fronting in English will therefore have the form of (53):[11]

(53)   CP   →   XP   C′
                    (↑ DF) = ↓   ↑ = ↓
                    (↑ DF) = (↑ COMP* OBJ)

In German, as well as objects, nearly any other constituent (e.g., subjects, sentential complements, adjuncts) can be fronted. The c-structure rule for this is shown in (54):[12]

(54)   CP   →   XP   C′
                    (↑ DF) = ↓   ↑ = ↓
                    (↑ DF) = (↑ COMP* GF)

Here, GF is an abbreviation for a disjunction of grammatical functions which can occur in the prefield. Figure 7.5 shows the analysis of the sentence in (55):

(55)   Den   Apfel verschlingt David.
       the.ACC apple devours   David.NOM
       'David is devouring the apple.'

Neither the finite verb nor the object *den Apfel* 'the apple' is realized within the VP. The finite verb is realized in C and contributes its f-structure information as a co-head to the VP to the VP f-structure. The NP in the prefield adds information to the f-structure of the sentence under TOPIC, which is one of the options to resolve DF, and the TOPIC value is identified with the OBJ grammatical function via the functional uncertainty equation (↑ DF) = (↑ COMP* GF).

7.6 Summary and classification

LFG is a constraint-based theory and utilizes feature descriptions and PSG rules. Grammatical functions are treated as primitives of the theory, which sets LFG apart from most of the other theories covered in this book. They are not defined structurally (as in GB). LFG is a lexicalist theory. Like GPSG, LFG can do without transformations. Processes affecting argument structure such as passivization are analyzed by means of lexical rules.

---

[11]Note that the two disjunctions that are abbreviated by the respective occurrences of DF are independent in principle. This is unwanted. We want to talk about either a topic or a focus not about a topic and a focus in the mother f-structure. So additional machinery is needed to ensure that both occurrences of DF refer to the same discourse function.

[12]Berman (1996) uses the symbol ZP for symbols in the prefield rather than XP in (54). She formulates various phrase structure rules for ZPs, which replace ZP with NP, PP, AP and various adjuncts. Following Berman, ZPs can also be combined with the verb in the middle field. For reasons of exposition, I refrained from using ZP symbols in the formulation of the VP rule (40) in Section 7.4 and instead used NP directly.

7 Lexical Functional Grammar

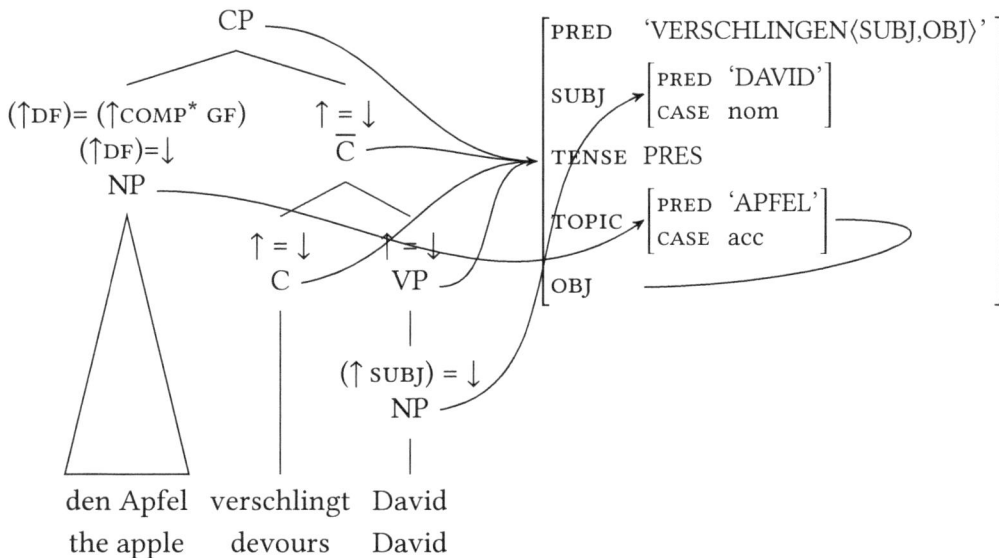

Figure 7.5: Analysis of verb second

Whereas GPSG treated long-distance dependencies using the percolation of information in trees, LFG uses functional uncertainty: a part of the f-structure is identified with another f-structure that can be embedded to an arbitrary depth. Coherence and completeness ensure that the long-distance dependency can be correctly resolved, that is, it ensures that a fronted object is not assigned to an f-structure which already contains an object or one in which no object may occur.

While LFG does contain a phrase-structural component, this plays a significantly less important role compared to other models of grammar. There are rules in which all constituents are optional and it has even been proposed for some languages that there are rules where the part of speech of the constituents is not specified (see Section 13.1.2). In these kinds of grammars, f-structure, coherence and completeness work together to ensure that the grammar only allows well-formed structures.

LFG differs from other theories such as HPSG and variants of Construction Grammar in that feature structures are untyped. Generalizations can therefore not be represented in type hierarchies. Until a few years ago, the hierarchical organization of knowledge in inheritance hierarchies did not form part of theoretical analyses. In computer implementations, there were macros but these were viewed as abbreviations without any theoretical status. It is possible to organize macros into hierarchies and macros were discussed explicitly in Dalrymple, Kaplan & King (2004) with reference to capturing linguistic generalizations. Asudeh, Dalrymple & Toivonen (2008) suggest using macros not only for the organization of lexical items but also for capturing generalizations regarding c-structure annotations. Because of these developments, there was a greater convergence between LFG and other theories such as HPSG and CxG.

Williams (1984) compares analyses in LFG with GB. He shows that many analyses are

7.6 Summary and classification

in fact transferable: the function that f-structure has in LFG is handled by the Theta-Criterion and Case Theory in GB. LFG can explicitly differentiate between subjects and non-subjects. In GB, on the other hand, a clear distinction is made between external and internal arguments (see Williams 1984: Section 1.2). In some variants of GB, as well as in HPSG and CxG, the argument with subject properties (if there is one) is marked explicitly (Haider 1986a; Heinz & Matiasek 1994; Müller 2003b; Michaelis & Ruppenhofer 2001). This special argument is referred to as the *designated argument*. In infinitival constructions, subjects are often not expressed inside the infinitival phrase. Nevertheless, the unexpressed subject is usually coreferential with an argument of the matrix verb:

(56) a. Er versucht, [das Buch zu lesen].
     he tries   the book to read
    'He is trying to read the book.'
   b. Er zwingt ihn, [das Buch zu lesen].
     he forces him the book to read
    'He is forcing him to read the book.'

This is a fact that every theory needs to be able to capture, that is, every theory must be able to differentiate between subjects and non-subjects.

For a comparison of GB/Minimalism and LFG/HPSG, see Kuhn (2007).

Comprehension questions

1. What do the terms *coherence* and *completeness* mean?

2. What are extended head domains?

3. What does lexical integrity mean?

Exercises

1. Give the lexical entry for *kannte* 'knew'.

2. How could one analyze the following sentence?

   (57) Dem   Kind hilft Sandy.
        the.DAT child helps Sandy.NOM
        'Sandy helps the child.'

   Provide the necessary c-structure rules. What kind of f-structure is licensed? Draw a syntactic tree with corresponding references to the f-structure. For fronted constituents, simply write NP rather than expanding the XP node. The c-structure rule for the NP can also be omitted and a triangle can be drawn in the tree.

Further reading

Section 7.1 was based extensively on the textbook and introductory article of Dalrymple (2001; 2006). Additionally, I have drawn from teaching materials of Jonas Kuhn from 2007. Bresnan (2001) is a comprehensive textbook in English for the advanced reader. Some of the more in-depth analyses of German in LFG are Berman (1996; 2003a). Schwarze & de Alencar (2016) is an introduction to LFG that uses French examples. The authors demonstrate how the XLE system can be used for the development of a French LFG grammar. The textbook also discusses the Finite State Morphology component that comes with the XLE system.

Levelt (1989) developed a model of language production based on LFG. Pinker (1984) – one of the best-known researchers on language acquisition – used LFG as the model for his theory of acquisition. For another theory on first and second language acquisition that uses LFG, see Pienemann (2005).

8 Categorial Grammar

Categorial Grammar is the second oldest of the approaches discussed in this book. It was developed in the 30s by the Polish logician Kazimierz Ajdukiewicz (Ajdukiewicz 1935). Since syntactic and semantic descriptions are tightly connected and all syntactic combinations correspond to semantic ones, Categorial Grammar is popular amongst logicians and semanticists. Some stellar works in the field of semantics making use of Categorial Grammar are those of Richard Montague (1974). Other important works come from David Dowty in Columbus, Ohio (1979), Michael Moortgat in Utrecht (1989), Glyn Morrill in Barcelona (1994), Bob Carpenter in New York (1998) and Mark Steedman in Edinburgh (1991; 1997; 2000). A large fragment for German using Montague Grammar has been developed by von Stechow (1979). The 2569-page grammar of the *Institut für Deutsche Sprache* in Mannheim (Eroms, Stickel & Zifonun 1997) contains Categorial Grammar analyses in the relevant chapters. Fanselow (1981) worked on morphology in the framework of Montague Grammar. Uszkoreit (1986a), Karttunen (1986; 1989) and Calder, Klein & Zeevat (1988) developed combinations of unification-based approaches and Categorial Grammar.

The basic operations for combining linguistic objects are rather simple and well-understood so that it is no surprise that there are many systems for the development and processing of Categorial Grammars (Yampol & Karttunen 1990; Carpenter 1994; Bouma & van Noord 1994; Lloré 1995; König 1999; Moot 2002; White & Baldridge 2003; Baldridge, Chatterjee, Palmer & Wing 2007; Morrill 2012; 2017). An important contribution has been made by Mark Steedman's group (see for instance Clark, Hockenmaier & Steedman 2002; Clark & Curran 2007).

Implemented fragments exist for the following languages:

- German (Uszkoreit 1986a; König 1999; Vierhuff, Hildebrandt & Eikmeyer 2003; Vancoppenolle, Tabbert, Bouma & Stede 2011)

- English (Villavicencio 2002; Baldridge 2002; Beavers 2003; 2004)

- Finish (Karttunen 1989)

- French (Baschung, Bes, Corluy & Guillotin 1987)

- Dutch (Bouma & van Noord 1994; Baldridge 2002)

- Tagalog (Baldridge 2002)

- Turkish (Hoffman 1995; Baldridge 2002)

8 *Categorial Grammar*

In addition, Baldridge, Chatterjee, Palmer & Wing (2007: 15) mention an implementation for Classical Arabic.

Some of the systems for the processing of Categorial Grammars have been augmented by probabilistic components so that the processing is robust (Osborne & Briscoe 1997; Clark, Hockenmaier & Steedman 2002). Some systems can derive lexical items from corpora, and Briscoe (2000) and Villavicencio (2002) use statistical information in their UG-based language acquisition models.

8.1 General remarks on the representational format

In what follows I introduce some basic assumptions of Categorial Grammar. After these introductory remarks, I will discuss specific analyses that were developed by Steedman (1997) in the framework of Combinatory Categorial Grammar. There are other variants of Categorial Grammar as for instance type-logical CG, the variety espoused by Morrill (1994), Dowty (1997), Moortgat (2011), and others, which cannot be discussed here.

8.1.1 Representation of valence information

In Categorial Grammar, complex categories replace the SUBCAT feature that is used in GPSG to ensure that a head can only be used with suitable grammatical rules. Simple phrase structure rules can be replaced with complex categories as follows:

(1) Rule   Category in the lexicon
     vp → v(ditrans) np np   (vp/np)/np
     vp → v(trans) np   vp/np
     vp → v(np_and_pp) np pp(to)   (vp/pp)/np

vp/np stands for something that needs an np in order for it to form a vp.

In Categorial Grammar, there are only a few very abstract rules. One of these is forward application, also referred to as the multiplication rule:

(2) forward application:
     X/Y ∗ Y = X

This rule combines an X looking for a Y with a Y and requires that Y occurs to the right of X/Y. The result of this combination is an X that no longer requires a Y. X/Y is called the *functor* and Y is the *argument* of the functor.

As in GB theory, valence is encoded only once in Categorial Grammar, in the lexicon. In GPSG, valence information was present in grammatical rules and in the SUBCAT feature of the lexical entry.

Figure 8.1 on the next page shows how a lexical entry for a transitive verb is combined with its object. A derivation in CG is basically a binary branching tree; it is, however, mostly represented as follows: an arrow under a pair of categories indicates that these have been combined via a combinatorial rule. The direction of this arrow indicates the direction of this combination. The result is given beneath the arrow. Figure 8.2 on the facing page shows the tree corresponding to Figure 8.1.

8.1 General remarks on the representational format

$$\frac{chased}{vp/np} \quad \frac{Mary}{np}$$
$$\overline{}\!>$$
$$vp$$

Figure 8.1: Combination of a verb and its object (preliminary)

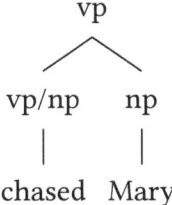

Figure 8.2: Derivation in Figure 8.1 as a tree diagram

One usually assumes left associativity for '/'; that is, (vp/pp)/np = vp/pp/np.

If we look at the lexical entries in (1), it becomes apparent that the category v does not appear. The lexicon only determines what the product of combination of a lexical entry with its arguments is. The symbol for vp can also be eliminated: an (English) vp is something that requires an NP to its left in order to form a complete sentence. This can be represented as s\np. Using the rule for backward application, it is possible to compute derivations such as the one in Figure 8.3.

(3) Backward application:
Y ∗ X\Y = X

$$\frac{the}{np/n} \quad \frac{cat}{n} \quad \frac{chased}{(s\backslash np)/np} \quad \frac{Mary}{np}$$

Figure 8.3: Analysis of a sentence with a transitive verb

In Categorial Grammar, there is no explicit difference made between phrases and words: an intransitive verb is described in the same way as a verb phrase with an object: s\np. Equally, proper nouns are complete noun phrases, which are assigned the symbol np.

8.1.2 Semantics

As already mentioned, Categorial Grammar is particularly popular among semanticists as syntactic combinations always result in parallel semantic combinations and even for complex combinations such as those we will discuss in more detail in the following sections, there is a precise definition of meaning composition. In the following, we will take a closer look at the representational format discussed in Steedman (1997: Section 2.1.2).

8 Categorial Grammar

Steedman proposes the following lexical entry for the verb *eats*:[1]

(4) eats := (s: *eat'*(x, y)\np$_{3S}$:x)/np:y

In (4), the meaning of each category is given after the colon. Since nothing is known about the meaning of the arguments in the lexical entry of *eat*, the meaning is represented by the variables *x* and *y*. When the verb combines with an NP, the denotation of the NP is inserted. An example is given in (5):[2]

(5) $$\frac{(s : eat'(x,y) \backslash np_{3S} : x)/np : y \quad np : apples'}{s : eat'(x, apples') \backslash np_{3S} : x} >$$

When combining a functor with an argument, it must be ensured that the argument fits the functor, that is, it must be unifiable with it (for more on unification see Section 6.6). The unification of np:y with np: *apples'* results in np: *apples'* since *apples'* is more specific than the variable y. Apart from its occurrence in the term np:y, y occurs in the description of the verb in another position (s: *eat'*(x, y)\np$_{3S}$:x) and therefore also receives the value *apples'* there. Thus, the result of this combination is s: *eat'*(x, *apples'*)\np$_{3S}$:x as shown in (5).

Steedman notes that this notation becomes less readable with more complex derivations and instead uses the more standard λ-notation:

(6) eats := (s\np$_{3S}$)/np: $\lambda y.\lambda x.eat'(x, y)$

Lambdas are used to allow access to open positions in complex semantic representations (see Section 2.3). A semantic representation such as $\lambda y.\lambda x.eat'(x, y)$ can be combined with the representation of *apples* by removing the first lambda expression and inserting the denotation of *apples* in all the positions where the corresponding variable (in this case, y) appears (see Section 2.3 for more on this point):

(7) $\lambda y.\lambda x.eat'(x, y)$ *apples'*
     $\lambda x.eat'(x, apples')$

This removal of lambda expressions is called β-reduction.

If we use the notation in (6), the combinatorial rules must be modified as follows:

(8) X/Y:f * Y:a = X: f a
     Y:a   * X\Y:f = X: f a

In such rules, the semantic contribution of the argument (a) is written after the semantic denotation of the functor (f). The open positions in the denotation of the functor are represented using lambdas. The argument can be combined with the first lambda expression using β-reduction.

Figure 8.4 on the facing page shows the derivation of a simple sentence with a transitive verb. After forward and backward application, β-reduction is immediately applied.

---

[1] I have adapted his notation to correspond to the one used in this book.
[2] The assumption that *apples* means *apples'* and not *apples'*(z) minus the quantifier contribution is a simplification here.

$$
\begin{array}{ccc}
\underline{Jacob} & \underline{eats} & \underline{apples} \\
np : jacob' & (s\backslash np)/np : \lambda y.\lambda x.eat'(x,y) & np : apples'
\end{array}
$$

$$
\cfrac{\cfrac{s\backslash np : \lambda y.\lambda x.eat'(x,y) \; apples'}{= \lambda x.eat'(x, apples')}>}{s : \lambda x.eat'(x, apples') \; jacob'}<
$$
$$
= eat'(jacob', apples')
$$

Figure 8.4: Meaning composition in Categorial Grammar

8.1.3 Adjuncts

As noted in Section 1.6, adjuncts are optional. In phrase structure grammars, this can be captured, for example, by rules that have a certain element (for instance a VP) on the left-hand side of the rule and the same element and an adjunct on the right-hand side of the rule. Since the symbol on the left is the same as the one on the right, this rule can be applied arbitrarily many times. (9) shows some examples of this:

(9)   a. VP → VP PP
       b. Noun → Noun PP

One can analyze an arbitrary amount of PPs following a VP or noun using these rules.

In Categorial Grammar, adjuncts have the following general form: X\X or X/X. Adjectives are modifiers, which must occur before the noun. They have the category n/n. Modifiers occurring after nouns (prepositional phrases and relative clauses) have the category n\n instead.[3] For VP-modifiers, X is replaced by the symbol for the VP (s\np) and this yields the relatively complex expression (s\np)\(s\np). Adverbials in English are VP-modifiers and have this category. Prepositions that can be used in a PP modifying a verb require an NP in order to form a complete PP and therefore have the category ((s\np)\(s\np))/np. Figure 8.5 on the next page gives an example of an adverb (*quickly*) and a preposition (*round*). Note that the result of the combination of *round* and *the garden* corresponds to the category of the adverb ((s\np)\(s\np)). In GB theory, adverbs and prepositions were also placed into a single class (see page 94). This overarching class was then divided into subclasses based on the valence of the elements in question.

8.2 Passive

In Categorial Grammar, the passive is analyzed by means of lexical rule (Dowty 1978: 412; Dowty 2003: Section 3.4). (10) shows the rule in Dowty (2003: 49).

(10)   Syntax: $\alpha \in (s\backslash np)/np \rightarrow \text{PST-PART}(\alpha) \in \text{PstP}/np_{by}$
         Semantics: $\alpha' \qquad\qquad\quad \rightarrow \lambda y \lambda x \alpha'(y)(x)$

---

[3]In Categorial Grammar, there is no category symbol like $\overline{X}$ for intermediate projections of $\overline{X}$ theory. So rather than assuming $\overline{N}/\overline{N}$, CG uses n/n. See Exercise 2.

8 Categorial Grammar

The	small	cat	chased	Mary	quickly	round	the	garden
np/n	n/n	n	$(s\backslash np)/np$	np	$(s\backslash np)\backslash(s\backslash np)$	$(s\backslash np)\backslash(s\backslash np)/np$	np/n	n

$$\text{derivation combining to } s$$

Figure 8.5: Example of an analysis with adjuncts in Categorial Grammar

Here, PstP stands for past participle and np_{by} is an abbreviation for a verb phrase modifier of the form vp\vp or rather (s\np)\(s\np). The rule says the following: if a word belongs to the set of words with the category (s\np)/np, then the word with past participle morphology also belongs in the set of words with the category $PstP/np_{by}$.

(11a) shows the lexical entry for the transitive verb *touch* and (11b) the result of rule application:

(11) a. touch: (s\np)/np
      b. touched: $PstP/np_{by}$

The auxiliary *was* has the category (s\np)/PstP and the preposition *by* has the category np_{by}/np, or its unabbreviated form ((s\np)\(s\np))/np. In this way, (12) can be analyzed as in Figure 8.6.

(12) John was touched by Mary.

John	was	touched	by	Mary.
np	$(s\backslash np)/PstP$	$PstP/np_{by}$ —LR	np_{by}/np	np

Figure 8.6: Analysis of the passive using a lexical rule

The question as to how to analyze the pair of sentences in (13) still remains unanswered.[4]

(13) a. He gave the book to Mary.
      b. The book was given to Mary.

gave has the category ((s\np)/pp)/np, that is, the verb must first combine with an NP (*the book*) and a PP (*to Mary*) before it can be combined with the subject. The problem

---
[4]Thanks to Roland Schäfer (p. m., 2009) for pointing out these data to me.

is that the rule in (10) cannot be applied to *gave* with a *to*-PP since the pp argument is sandwiched between both np arguments in ((s\np)/pp)/np. One would have to generalize the rule in (10) somehow by introducing new technical means[5] or assume additional rules for cases such as (13b).

8.3 Verb position

Steedman (2000: 159) proposed an analysis with variable branching for Dutch, that is, there are two lexical entries for *at* 'eat': an initial one with its arguments to the right, and another occupying final position with its arguments to its left.

(14) a. *at* 'eat' in verb-final position: $(s_{+SUB}\backslash np)\backslash np$
       b. *at* 'eat' in verb-initial position: $(s_{-SUB}/np)/np$

Steedman uses the feature SUB to differentiate between subordinate and non-subordinate sentences. Both lexical items are related via lexical rules.

One should note here that the NPs are combined with the verb in different orders. The normal order is:

(15) a. in verb-final position: $(s_{+SUB}\backslash np[nom])\backslash np[acc]$
       b. in verb-initial position: $(s_{-SUB}/np[acc])/np[nom]$

The corresponding derivations for German sentences with a bivalent verb are shown in Figures 8.7 and 8.8.

$$\frac{\frac{er}{np[nom]} \quad \frac{\frac{ihn}{np[acc]} \quad \frac{isst}{(s_{+SUB}\backslash np[nom])\backslash np[acc]}}{s_{+SUB}\backslash np[nom]}<}{s_{+SUB}}<$$

Figure 8.7: Analysis of verb-final sentences following Steedman

$$\frac{\frac{\frac{isst}{((s_{-SUB}/np[acc])/np[nom]} \quad \frac{er}{np[nom]}}{s_{-SUB}/np[acc]}> \quad \frac{ihn}{np[acc]}}{s_{-SUB}}>$$

Figure 8.8: Analysis of verb-initial sentences following Steedman

In Figure 8.7, the verb is first combined with an accusative object, whereas in Figure 8.8, the verb is first combined with the subject. For criticism of these kinds of analyses with variable branching, see Netter (1992) and Müller (2005b; 2017a).

---
[5]Baldridge (p. M. 2010) suggests using regular expressions in a general lexical rule for passive.

8 Categorial Grammar

Jacobs (1991) developed an analysis which corresponds to the verb movement analysis in GB. He assumes verb-final structures, that is, there is a lexical entry for verbs where arguments are selected to the left of the verb. A transitive verb would therefore have the entry in (16a). Additionally, there is a trace in verb-final position that requires the arguments of the verb and the verb itself in initial position. (16b) shows what the verb trace looks like for a transitive verb in initial position:

(16)   a. Verb in final position:
          (s\np[nom])\np[acc]

     b. Verb trace for the analysis of verb-first:
          ((s\((s\np[nom])\np[acc]))\np[nom])\np[acc]

The entry for the verb trace is very complex. It is probably simpler to examine the analysis in Figure 8.9.

Figure 8.9: Analysis of verb-initial sentences following Jacobs (1991)

The trace is the head in the entire analysis: it is first combined with the accusative object and then with the subject. In a final step, it is combined with the transitive verb in initial-position.[6] A problem with this kind of analysis is that the verb *isst* 'eats', as well as *er* 'he' and *ihn* 'him'/'it', are arguments of the verb trace in (17).

(17) Morgen   [isst [er [ihn _]]]
     tomorrow eats he him

     'He will eat it/him tomorrow.'

Since adjuncts can occur before, after or between arguments of the verb in German, one would expect that *morgen* 'tomorrow' can occur before the verb *isst*, since *isst* is just a normal argument of the verbal trace in final position. As adjuncts do not change the categorial status of a projection, the phrase *morgen isst er ihn* 'tomorrow he eats him' should be able to occur in the same positions as *isst er ihn*. This is not the case, however. If we replace *isst er ihn* by *morgen isst er ihn* in (18a), the result is (18b), which is ungrammatical.

(18)   a. Deshalb isst er ihn.
          therefore eats he him

          'Therefore he eats it/him.'

     b. *Deshalb morgen isst er ihn.
          therefore tomorrow eats he him

---

[6]See Netter (1992) for a similar analysis in HPSG.

An approach which avoids this problem comes from Kiss & Wesche (1991) (see Section 9.3). Here, the authors assume that there is a verb in initial position which selects a projection of the verb trace. If adverbials are only combined with verbs in final-position, then a direct combination of *morgen* 'tomorrow' and *isst er ihn* 'eats he it' is ruled out. If one assumes that the verb in first-position is the functor, then it is possible to capture the parallels between complementizers and verbs in initial position (Höhle 1997): finite verbs in initial position differ from complementizers only in requiring a projection of a verb trace, whereas complementizers require projections of overt verbs:

(19) a. dass [er ihn isst]
    that he it eats
  b. Isst [er ihn _]
    eats he it

This description of verb position in German captures the central insights of the GB analysis in Section 3.2.

8.4 Local reordering

Up to now, we have seen combinations of functors and arguments where the arguments were either to the left or to the right of the functor. The saturation of arguments always took place in a fixed order: the argument furthest to the right was combined first with the functor, e.g., (s\np)/pp first combined with the PP, and the result of this combination was combined with the NP.

There are a number of possibilities to analyze ordering variants in German: Uszkoreit (1986b) suggests accounting for possible orders lexically; that is, that each possible order corresponds to a lexical item. One would therefore have at least six lexical items for a ditransitive verb. Briscoe (2000: 257) and Villavicencio (2002: 96–98) propose a variant of this analysis where the order of arguments is modified in the syntax: a syntactic rule can, for example, change the order (S/PRT)/NP into (S/NP)/PRT.

A different approach is suggested by Steedman & Baldridge (2006). They discuss various options for ordering arguments attested in the languages of the world. This includes languages in which the order of combination is free, as well as languages where the direction of combination is free. Steedman and Baldridge introduce the following convention for representing categories: elements in curly brackets can be discharged in any order. '|' in place of '\' or '/' serves to indicate that the direction of combination is free. Some prototypical examples are shown in (20):

(20) English   (S\NP)/NP   S(VO)
      Latin   S{|NP[nom], |NP[acc] } free order
      Tagalog   S{/NP[nom], /NP[acc] } free order, verb-initial
      Japanese S{\NP[nom], \NP[acc] } free order, verb-final

Hoffman (1995: Section 3.1) has proposed an analysis analogous to that of Japanese for Turkish and this could also be used in conjunction with an analysis of verb position for German. This would correspond to the GB/MP analysis of Fanselow (2001) or the HPSG analysis presented in Section 9.4.

8 Categorial Grammar

8.5 Long-distance dependencies

Steedman (1989: Section 1.2.4) proposes an analysis of long-distance dependencies without movement or empty elements. For examples such as (21), he assumes that the category of *Harry must have been eating* or *Harry devours* is s/np.

(21) a. These apples, Harry must have been eating.
 b. apples which Harry devours

The fronted NP *these apples* and the relative pronoun *which* are both functors in the analysis of (21) which take s/np as their argument. Using the machinery introduced up to now, we cannot assign the category s/np to the strings *Harry must have been eating* and *Harry devours* in (21) although it is intuitively the case that *Harry devours* is a sentence missing an NP. We still require two further extensions of Categorial Grammar: type raising and forward and backward composition. Both of these operations will be introduced in the following sections.

8.5.1 Type Raising

The category np can be transformed into the category (s/(s\np)) by *type raising*. If we combine this category with (s\np), then we get the same result as if we had combined np and (s\np) with the forward application rule in (2). (22a) shows the combination of an NP with a VP (a sentence missing an NP to its left). The combination of the type-raised NP with the VP is given in (22b).

(22) a. np * s\np = s
 b. s/(s\np) * s\np = s

In (22a), a verb or verb phrase selects an NP to its left (s\np). In (22b), an NP having undergone type raising selects a verb or verb phrase to its right which requires an NP to its left (s\np).

Type raising simply reverses the direction of selection: the VP in (22a) is the functor and the NP is the argument, whereas in (22b), it is the type raised NP which acts as the functor, and the VP is the argument. In each case, the result of the combination is the same. This change of selectional direction may just seem like a trick at first glance, but as we will see, this trick can be extremely useful. First, however, we will introduce forward and backward composition.

8.5.2 Forward and backward composition

(23) shows the rules for forward and backward composition.

(23) a. Forward composition (> B)
 X/Y * Y/Z = X/Z
 b. Backward composition (< B)
 Y\Z * X\Y = X\Z

8.5 Long-distance dependencies

These rules will be explained using forward composition as an example. (23a) can be understood as follows: X/Y more or less means; if I find a Y, then I am a complete X. In the combinatorial rule, X/Y is combined with Y/Z. Y/Z stands for a Y that is not yet complete and is still missing a Z. The requirement that Y must find a Z in order to be complete is postponed: we pretend that Y is complete and use it anyway, but we still bear in mind that something is actually still missing. Hence, if we combine X/Y with Y/Z, we get something which becomes an X when combined with a Z.

8.5.3 Analysis of long-distance dependencies

By using forward composition, we can assign *Harry must have been eating* the category s/np. Figure 8.10 shows how this works. *must* is a verb which requires an unmarked

These apples	*Harry*	*must*	*have*	*been*	*eating*
np	s/(s\np) >T	(s\np)/vp	vp/vp-en	vp-en/vp-ing	vp-ing/np

$\qquad\qquad\qquad\quad$ s/vp $\longrightarrow$B

$\qquad\qquad\qquad\qquad\qquad\quad$ s/vp-en $\longrightarrow$B

$\qquad\qquad\qquad\qquad\qquad\qquad\qquad$ s/vp-ing $\longrightarrow$B

$\qquad\qquad\qquad\qquad\qquad\qquad\qquad\qquad\quad$ s/np $\longrightarrow$B

Figure 8.10: Application of forward composition to VP-chains

infinitive form, *have* requires a participle and *been* must combine with a present participle. In the above figure, the arrow with a small 'T' stands for type raising, whereas the arrows with a 'B' indicate composition. The direction of composition is shown by the direction of the arrow.

For the analysis of (21a), we are still missing one small detail, a rule that turns the NP at the beginning of the sentence into a functor which can be combined with s/np. Normal type raising cannot handle this because it would produce s/(s\np) when s/(s/np) is required.

Steedman (1989: 217) suggests the rule in (24):

(24) Topicalization (↑):
 X ⇒ st/(s/X)
 where X ∈ { np, pp, vp, ap, s′ }

st stands for a particular type of sentence (s), namely one with topicalization (t). The ⇒ expresses that one can type raise any X into an st/(s/X).

If we replace X with np, we can turn *these apples* into st/(s/np) and complete the analysis of (21a) as shown in Figure 8.11 on the next page. The mechanism presented here will of course also work for dependencies that cross sentence boundaries. Figure 8.12 on the following page shows the analysis for (25):

(25) Apples, I believe that Harry eats.

8 Categorial Grammar

```
  These apples        Harry         must          have         been         eating
 ──────────── >↑    ────────── >T  ─────────    ─────────    ──────────   ─────────
   st/(s/np)          s/(s\np)     (s\np)/vp    vp/vp-en    vp-en/vp-ing  vp-ing/np
                     ──────────────────────── >B
                              s/vp
                     ─────────────────────────────────── >B
                                  s/vp-en
                     ──────────────────────────────────────────────── >B
                                        s/vp-ing
                     ───────────────────────────────────────────────────────────── >B
                                                s/np
                     ────────────────────────────────────────────────────────────────── >
                                                  st
```

Figure 8.11: Analysis of long-distance dependencies in Categorial Grammar

```
   Apples         I        believe       that       Harry        eats
 ────────── >↑  ────── >T  ─────────    ──────    ────────── >T  ─────────
  st/(s/np)     s/(s\np)   (s\np)/s'    s'/s      s/(s\np)       (s\np)/np
                ──────────────────── >B                          ──────── >B
                       s/s'                                        s/np
                ─────────────────────────── >B
                           s/s
                ───────────────────────────────────────────────────────── >B
                                        s/np
                ────────────────────────────────────────────────────────────── >
                                           st
```

Figure 8.12: Analysis of long-distance dependencies across sentence boundaries

Using the previously described tools, it is, however, only possible to describe extractions where the fronted element in the sentence would have occurred at the right edge of the phrase without fronting. This means it is not possible to analyze sentences where the middle argument of a ditransitive verb has been extracted (Steedman 1985: 532). Pollard (1988: 406) provides the derivation in Figure 8.13 for (26).

(26) Fido we put downstairs.

```
       Fido                  we          put         downstairs
 ─────────────────── >↑↑   ────── >T   ─────────────     pp
 (st/pp)/((s/pp)/np)       s/(s\np)    ((s\np)/pp)/np
                          ─────────────────────── >BB
                                  (s/pp)/np
                          ───────────────────────────────── >
                                        st/pp
                          ──────────────────────────────────── >
                                           st
```

Figure 8.13: Analysis of long-distance dependencies across sentence boundaries

In this analysis, it is not possible to combine *we* and *put* using the rule in (23a) since (s\np) is not directly accessible: breaking down ((s\np)/pp)/np into functor and argument gives us ((s\np)/pp) and np. In order to deal with such cases, we need another variant of composition:

256

(27) Forward composition for n=2 (> BB)
X/Y * (Y/Z1)/Z2 = (X/Z1)/Z2

With this addition, it is now possible to combine the type-raised *we* with *put*. The result is (s/pp)/np. The topicalization rule in (24), however, requires an element to the right of st with the form (s/X). This is not the case in Figure 8.13. For the NP *Fido*, we need a functor category which allows that the argument itself is complex. The rule which is needed for the case in (26) is given in (28).

(28) Topicalization for n=2 (↑↑):
X2 ⇒ (st/X1)/((s/X1)/X2)
where X1 and X2 ∈ { NP, PP, VP, AP, S′ }

If we assume that verbs can have up to four arguments (z. B. *buy*: buyer, seller, goods, price), then it would be necessary to assume a further rule for composition as well as another topicalization rule. Furthermore, one requires a topicalization rule for subject extraction (Pollard 1988: 405). Steedman has developed a notation which provides a compact notation of the previously discussed rules, but if one considers what exactly these representations stand for, one still arrives at the same number of rules that have been discussed here.

8.6 Summary and classification

The operations of Combinatory Categorial Grammar, which go beyond those of standard Categorial Grammar, allow for so much flexibility that it is even possible to assign a category to sequences of words that would not normally be treated as a constituent. This is an advantage for the analysis of coordination (see Section 21.6.2) and furthermore, Steedman (1991) has argued that intonation data support the constituent status of these strings. See also Section 15.2 for a direct model of incremental language processing in Categorial Grammar. In phrase structure grammars, it is possible to use GPSG mechanisms to pass information about relative pronouns contained in a phrase up the tree. These techniques are not used in CG and this leads to a large number of recategorization rules for topicalization and furthermore leads to inadequate analyses of pied-piping constructions in relative clauses. As the topicalization analysis was already discussed in Section 8.5, I will briefly elaborate on relative clauses here.

Steedman & Baldridge (2006: 614) present an analysis of long-distance dependencies using the following relative clause in (29):

(29) the man that Manny says Anna married

The relative pronoun is the object of *married* but occurs outside the clause *Anna married*.
Steedman assumes the lexical entry in (30) for relative pronouns:

(30) (n\n)/(s/np)

8 Categorial Grammar

This means the following: if there is a sentence missing an NP to the right of a relative pronoun, then the relative pronoun can form an N-modifier (n\n) with this sentence. The relative pronoun is the head (functor) in this analysis.

Utilizing both additional operations of type raising and composition, the examples with relative clauses can be analyzed as shown in Figure 8.14. The lexical entry for the

$$
\cfrac{
  \cfrac{that}{(n\backslash n)/(s/np)} \quad
  \cfrac{
    \cfrac{
      \cfrac{Manny}{s/(s\backslash np)}^{>T} \quad \cfrac{says}{(s\backslash np)/s}
    }{s/s}^{>B} \quad
    \cfrac{
      \cfrac{Anna}{s/(s\backslash np)}^{>T} \quad \cfrac{married}{(s\backslash np)/np}
    }{s/np}^{>B}
  }{s/np}^{>B}
}{n\backslash n}^{>}
$$

Figure 8.14: Categorial Grammar analysis of a relative clause with long-distance dependency

verbs corresponds to what was discussed in the preceding sections: *married* is a normal transitive verb and *says* is a verb that requires a sentential complement and forms a VP (s\np) with it. This VP yields a sentence when combined with an NP. The noun phrases in Figure 8.14 have been type raised. Using forward composition, it is possible to combine *Anna* and *married* to yield s/np. This is the desired result: a sentence missing an NP to its right. *Manny* and *says* and then *Manny says* and *Anna married* can also be combined via forward composition and we then have the category s/np for *Manny says Anna married*. This category can be combined with the relative pronoun using forward application and we then arrive at n\n, which is exactly the category for postnominal modifiers.

However, the assumption that the relative pronoun constitutes the head is problematic since one has to then go to some lengths to explain pied-piping constructions such as those in (31).

(31) a. Here's the minister [[in [the middle [of [whose sermon]]]] the dog barked].[7]
  b. Reports [the height of the lettering on the covers of which] the government prescribes should be abolished.[8]

In (31), the relative pronoun is embedded in a phrase that has been extracted from the rest of the relative clause. The relative pronoun in (31a) is the determiner of *sermon*. Depending on the analysis, *whose* is the head of the phrase *whose sermon*. The NP is embedded under *of* and the phrase *of whose sermon* depends on *middle*. The entire NP *the middle of the sermon* is a complement of the preposition *in*. It would be quite a stretch to claim that *whose* is the head of the relative clause in (31a). The relative pronoun in (31b) is even more deeply embedded. Steedman (1997: 50) gives the following lexical entries for *who*, *whom* and *which*:

---

[7]Pollard & Sag (1994: 212).
[8]Ross (1967: 109).

8.6 Summary and classification

(32) a. ((n\n)/(s\np))\(np/np)   (complex subject-relative phrase)
    b. ((n\n)/(s/pp))\(pp/np)   (complex extracted PP-relative phrase)
    c. ((n\n)/(s/np))\(np/np)   (complex extracted NP-relative phrase)

Using (32b) and (32c), it is possible to analyze (33a) and (33b):

(33) a. a report the cover of which Keats (expects that Chapman) will design
    b. a subject on which Keats (expects that Chapman) will speak

In the analysis of (33b), *which* requires a preposition to its left (pp/np) so it can form the category (n\n)/(s/pp). This category needs a sentence lacking a PP to its right in order to form a post-nominal modifier (n\n). In the analysis of (33a), *the cover of* becomes np/np by means of composition and *which* with the lexical entry (32c) can combine with *the cover of* to its left. The result is the category (n\n)/(s/np), that is, something that requires a sentence missing an NP.

Ross' examples (31b) can also be analyzed as follows (32c):

(34) reports [the height of the lettering on the covers of]$_{np/np}$ which]$_{(n\n)/(s/np)}$ the government prescribes

The complex expression *the height of the lettering on the covers of* becomes np/np after composition and the rest of the analysis proceeds as that of (33a).

In addition to entries such as those in (32), we also need further entries to analyze sentences such as (35), where the relative phrase has been extracted from the middle of the clause (see Pollard 1988: 410):

(35) Fido is the dog which we put downstairs.

The problem here is similar to what we saw with topicalization: *we put* does not have the cateory s/np but rather (s/pp)/np and as such, cannot be directly combined with the relative pronoun in (30).

Morrill (1995: 204) discusses the lexical entry in (32b) for the relative pronoun in (36):

(36) about which John talked

In the lexical entry (32b), *which* requires something to the left of it, which requires a noun phrase in order to form a complete prepositional phrase; that is, *which* selects a preposition. Morrill noted that there is a need to postulate further lexical items for cases like (37) in which the relative pronoun occurs in the middle of the fronted phrase.

(37) the contract [the loss of which after so much wrangling] John would finally have to pay for

These and other cases could be handled by additional lexical stipulations. Morrill instead proposes additional types of the combination of functors and arguments, which allow a functor B ↑ A to enclose its argument A and produce B, or a functor A ↓ B to enclose its argument to then yield B (p. 190). Even with these additional operations, he still needs the two lexical items in (38) for the derivation of a pied-piping construction with an argument NP or a PP:

259

(38) a. (NP ↑ NP) ↓ (N\N)/(S/NP)
    b. (PP ↑ NP) ↓ (N\N)/(S/PP)

These lexical items are still not enough, however, as (38b) contains a PP but this PP corresponds to an argument PP, which is required for (36). To analyze (31a), which involves a PP adjunct, we need to assume the category (s\np)/(s\np) for the prepositional phrase *in the middle of whose sermon*. We, therefore, also require at least three additional items for relative pronouns.

By introducing new operations, Morrill manages to reduce the number of lexical entries for *which*; however, the fact remains that he has to mention the categories which can occur in pied-piping constructions in the lexical entry of the relative pronoun.

Furthermore, the observation that relative clauses consist of a phrase with a relative pronoun plus a sentence missing a relative phrase is lost. This insight can be kept if one assumes a GPSG-style analysis where information about whether there is a relative pronoun in the relative phrase can be passed up to the highest node of the relative phrase. The relative clause can then be analyzed as the combination of a sentence with a gap and an appropriately marked relative phrase. For the discussion of such analyses in the framework of GB theory and HPSG/CxG, see Section 21.10.3.

Comprehension questions

1. Identify the functors and arguments in Figures 8.1 and 8.3.

2. Which combination operations do you know?

3. What is composition used for?

Exercises

1. Analyze the following sentence:

    (39) The children in the room laugh loudly.

2. Analyze the noun phrase in (40):

    (40) the picture of Mary

    Compare the resulting analysis with the structure given in Figure 2.4 on page 67 and think about which categories of $\overline{\text{X}}$ syntax the categories in Categorial Grammar correspond to.

Further reading

Mark Steedman discusses a variant of Categorial Grammar, *Combinatory Categorial Grammar*, in a series of books and articles: Steedman (1991; 2000); Steedman & Baldridge (2006).

Lobin (2003) compares Categorial Grammar with Dependency Grammar and Pickering & Barry (1993) suggest a combination of Dependency Grammar and Categorial Grammar, which they call Dependency Categorial Grammar.

Briscoe (2000) and Villavicencio (2002) discuss UG-based acquisition models in the framework of Categorial Grammar.

9 Head-Driven Phrase Structure Grammar

Head-Driven Phrase Structure Grammar (HPSG) was developed by Carl Pollard and Ivan Sag in the mid-80's in Stanford and in the Hewlett-Packard research laboratories in Palo Alto (Pollard & Sag 1987; 1994). Like LFG, HPSG is part of so-called West Coast linguistics. Another similarity to LFG is that HPSG aims to provide a theory of competence which is compatible with performance (Sag & Wasow 2011; 2015, see also Chapter 15).

The formal properties of the description language for HPSG grammars are well-understood and there are many systems for processing such grammars (Dörre & Seiffert 1991; Dörre & Dorna 1993; Popowich & Vogel 1991; Uszkoreit, Backofen, Busemann, Diagne, Hinkelman, Kasper, Kiefer, Krieger, Netter, Neumann, Oepen & Spackman 1994; Erbach 1995; Schütz 1996; Schmidt, Theofilidis, Rieder & Declerck 1996; Schmidt, Rieder & Theofilidis 1996; Uszkoreit, Backofen, Calder, Capstick, Dini, Dörre, Erbach, Estival, Manandhar, Mineur & Oepen 1996; Müller 1996c; 2004d; Carpenter & Penn 1996; Penn & Carpenter 1999; Götz, Meurers & Gerdemann 1997; Copestake 2002; Callmeier 2000; Dahllöf 2003; Meurers, Penn & Richter 2002; Penn 2019; Müller 2007d; Sato 2008; Kaufmann 2009; Slayden 2012; Packard 2015).[1] Currently, the LKB system by Ann Copestake and the TRALE system, that was developed by Gerald Penn (Meurers, Penn & Richter 2002; Penn 2019), have the most users. The DELPH-IN consortium – whose grammar fragments are based on the LKB – and various TRALE users have developed many small and some large grammar fragments of various languages. The following is a list of implementations in different systems:

- Arabic (Haddar, Boukedi & Zalila 2010; Hahn 2011; Masum, Islam, Rahman & Ahmed 2012; Boukedi & Haddar 2014; Loukam, Balla & Laskri 2015; Arad Greshler, Herzig Sheinfux, Melnik & Wintner 2015),

- Bengali (Paul 2004; Islam, Hasan & Rahman 2012),

- Bulgarian (Simov, Osenova, Simov & Kouylekov 2004; Osenova 2010a,b; 2011),

- Cantonese (Fan, Song & Bond 2015),

- Danish (Ørsnes 1995; 2009b; Neville & Paggio 2004; Müller 2009c; Müller & Ørsnes 2011; Müller 2012b; Müller & Ørsnes 2015),

---

[1] Uszkoreit et al. (1996) and Bolc et al. (1996) compare systems that were available or were developed at the beginnings of the 1990s. Melnik (2007) compares LKB and TRALE. See also Müller (2015b: Section 5.1).

- Dutch (van Noord & Bouma 1994; Bouma, van Noord & Malouf 2001; Fokkens 2011),

- German (Kiss 1991; Netter 1993; 1996; Meurers 1994; Hinrichs et al. 1997; Kordoni 1999; Tseng 2000; Geißler & Kiss 1994; Keller 1994; Müller 1996c; 1999b; Müller & Kasper 2000; Crysmann 2003; 2005b,c; Müller 2007a; Kaufmann & Pfister 2007; 2008; Kaufmann 2009; Fokkens 2011),

- English (Copestake & Flickinger 2000; Flickinger, Copestake & Sag 2000; Flickinger 2000; Dahllöf 2002; 2003; De Kuthy & Meurers 2003a; Meurers, De Kuthy & Metcalf 2003; De Kuthy, Metcalf & Meurers 2004; Müller & Machicao y Priemer 2019; Müller 2018a),

- Esperanto (Li 1996),

- French (Tseng 2003),

- Ga (Kropp Dakubu, Hellan & Beermann 2007; Hellan 2007),

- Georgian (Abzianidze 2011),

- Greek (Kordoni & Neu 2005),

- Hausa (Crysmann 2005a; 2009; 2011; 2012; 2016),

- Hebrew (Melnik 2007; Haugereid, Melnik & Wintner 2013; Arad Greshler, Herzig Sheinfux, Melnik & Wintner 2015),

- Indonesian (Moeljadi, Bond & Song 2015)

- Japanese (Siegel 2000; Siegel & Bender 2002; Bender & Siegel 2005; Siegel, Bender & Bond 2016),

- Korean (Kim & Yang 2003; 2004; 2006; 2009; Kim, Sells & Yang 2007; Song, Kim, Bond & Yang 2010; Kim, Yang, Song & Bond 2011),

- Maltese (Müller 2009b),

- Mandarin Chinese (Liu 1997; Ng 1997; Müller & Lipenkova 2009; 2013; Yang & Flickinger 2014; Fan, Song & Bond 2015),

- Norwegian (Hellan & Haugereid 2003; Beermann & Hellan 2004; Hellan & Beermann 2006; Haugereid 2017),

- Persian (Müller 2010b; Müller & Ghayoomi 2010),

- Polish (Przepiórkowski, Kupść, Marciniak & Mykowiecka 2002; Mykowiecka, Marciniak, Przepiórkowski & Kupść 2003),

- Portuguese (Branco & Costa 2008a,b; 2010),

- Russian (Avgustinova & Zhang 2009),
- Sahaptin (Drellishak 2009),
- Spanish (Pineda & Meza 2005a,b; Bildhauer 2008; Marimon 2013),
- Sign Language (German, French, British, Greek!) (Sáfár & Marshall 2002; Marshall & Sáfár 2004; Sáfár & Glauert 2010),
- South African Sign Language (Bungeroth 2002),
- Turkish (Fokkens, Poulson & Bender 2009),
- Wambaya (Bender 2008a,c; 2010).
- Yiddish (Müller & Ørsnes 2011),

The first implemented HPSG grammar was a grammar of English developed in the Hewlett-Packard labs in Palo Alto (Flickinger, Pollard & Wasow 1985; Flickinger 1987). Grammars for German were developed in Heidelberg, Stuttgart and Saarbrücken in the LILOG project. Subsequently, grammars for German, English and Japanese were developed in Heidelberg, Saarbrücken and Stanford in the Verbmobil project. Verbmobil was the largest ever AI project in Germany. It was a machine translation project for spoken language in the domains of trip planning and appointment scheduling (Wahlster 2000).

Currently there are two larger groups that are working on the development of grammars: the DELPH-IN consortium (Deep Linguistic Processing with HPSG)[2] and the group that developed out of the network CoGETI (Constraintbasierte Grammatik: Empirie, Theorie und Implementierung). Many of the grammar fragments that are listed above were developed by members of DELPH-IN and some were derived from the Grammar Matrix which was developed for the LKB to provide grammar writers with a typologically motivated initial grammar that corresponds to the properties of the language under development (Bender, Flickinger & Oepen 2002). The CoreGram project[3] is a similar project that was started at the Freie Universität Berlin and which is now being run at the Humboldt-Universität zu Berlin. It is developing grammars for German, Danish, Persian, Maltese, Mandarin Chinese, Spanish, French, Welsh, and Yiddish that share a common core. Constraints that hold for all languages are represented in one place and used by all grammars. Furthermore there are constraints that hold for certain language classes and again they are represented together and used by the respective grammars. So while the Grammar Matrix is used to derive grammars that individual grammar writers can use, adapt and modify to suit their needs, CoreGram really develops grammars for various languages that are used simultaneously and have to stay in sync. A description of the CoreGram can be found in Müller (2013b; 2015b).

There are systems that combine linguistically motivated analyses with statistics components (Brew 1995; Miyao et al. 2005; Miyao & Tsujii 2008) or learn grammars or lexica from corpora (Fouvry 2003; Cramer & Zhang 2009).

---

[2] http://www.delph-in.net/. 2018-02-20.
[3] https://hpsg.hu-berlin.de/Projects/CoreGram.html. 15.08.2019.

The following URLs point to pages on which grammars can be tested:

- http://www.delph-in.net/erg/
- https://hpsg.hu-berlin.de/Demos/

9.1 General remarks on the representational format

HPSG has the following characteristics: it is a lexicon-based theory, that is, the majority of linguistic constraints are situated in the descriptions of words or roots. HPSG is sign-based in the sense of Saussure (1916a): the form and meaning of linguistic signs are always represented together. Typed feature structures are used to model all relevant information.[4] Hence, HPSG belongs to the class of model-theoretic grammars (King 1999; see also Chapter 14 of this book). The feature structures can be described with feature descriptions such as in (1). Lexical entries, phrases and principles are always modeled and described with the same formal means. Generalizations about word classes or rule schemata are captured with inheritance hierarchies (see Section 6.2). Phonology, syntax and semantics are represented in a single structure. There are no separate levels of representation such as PF or LF in Government & Binding Theory. (1) shows an excerpt from the representation of a word such as *Grammatik* 'grammar'.

(1) Lexical item for the word *Grammatik* 'grammar':

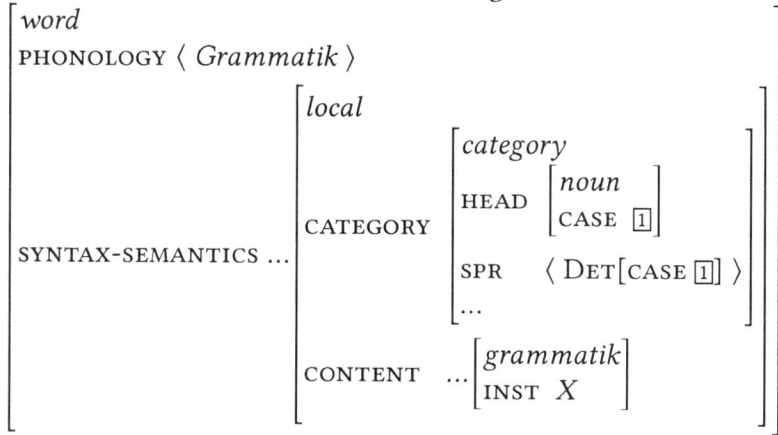

One can see that this feature description contains information about the phonology, syntactic category and semantic content of the word *Grammatik* 'grammar'. To keep things simple, the value of PHONOLOGY (PHON) is mostly given as an orthographic representation. In fully fleshed-out theories, the PHON value is a complex structure that contains information about metrical grids and weak or strong accents. See Bird & Klein (1994), Orgun (1996), Höhle (1999), Walther (1999), Crysmann (2002: Chapter 6), and Bildhauer

---

[4]Readers who read this book non-sequentially and who are unfamiliar with typed feature descriptions and typed feature structures should consult Chapter 6 first.

9.1 General remarks on the representational format

(2008) for phonology in the framework of HPSG. The details of the description in (1) will be explained in the following sections.

HPSG has adopted various insights from other theories and newer analyses have been influenced by developments in other theoretical frameworks. Functor-argument structures, the treatment of valence information and function composition have been adopted from Categorial Grammar. Function composition plays an important role in the analysis of verbal complexes in languages like German and Korean. The Immediate Dominance/Linear Precedence format (ID/LP format, see Section 5.1.2) as well as the Slash mechanism for long-distance dependencies (see Section 5.4) both come from GPSG. The analysis assumed here for verb position in German is inspired by the one that was developed in the framework of Government & Binding (see Section 3.2). Starting in 1995, HPSG also incorporated insights from Construction Grammar (Sag 1997, see also Section 10.6.2 on Sign-Based Construction Grammar, which is a HPSG variant).

9.1.1 Representation of valence information

The phrase structure grammars discussed in Chapter 2 have the disadvantage that one requires a great number of different rules for the various valence types. (2) shows some examples of this kind of rules and the corresponding verbs.

(2)   S → NP[*nom*], V   *X schläft* 'X is sleeping'
       S → NP[*nom*], NP[*acc*], V   *X Y erwartet* 'X expects Y'
       S → NP[*nom*], PP[*über*], V   *X über Y spricht* 'X talks about Y'
       S → NP[*nom*], NP[*dat*], NP[*acc*], V   *X Y Z gibt* 'X gives Z to Y'
       S → NP[*nom*], NP[*dat*], PP[*mit*], V   *X Y mit Z dient* 'X serves Y with Z'

In order for the grammar not to create any incorrect sentences, one has to ensure that verbs are only used with appropriate rules.

(3)   a. * dass Peter das Buch schläft
          that Peter the book sleeps

      b. * dass Peter erwartet
          that Peter expects

      c. * dass Peter über den Mann erwartet
          that Peter about the man expects

Therefore, verbs (and heads in general) have to be divided into valence classes. These valence classes have to then be assigned to grammatical rules. One must therefore further specify the rule for transitive verbs in (2) as follows:

(4)   S → NP[*nom*], NP[*acc*], V[*nom_acc*]

Here, valence has been encoded twice. First, we have said something in the rules about what kind of elements can or must occur, and then we have stated in the lexicon which valence class the verb belongs to. In Section 5.5, it was pointed out that morphological processes need to refer to valence information. Hence, it is desirable to remove redundant valence information from grammatical rules. For this reason, HPSG – like Categorial Grammar – includes descriptions of the arguments of a head in the lexical entry of that head. There are the features SPECIFIER (SPR) and COMPLEMENTS (COMPS), whose values are lists containing descriptions of the elements that must combine with a head in order to yield a complete phrase. (5) gives some examples for the verbs in (2):

(5)   verb   COMPS
       schlafen 'to sleep'   ⟨ NP[*nom*] ⟩
       erwarten 'to expect'   ⟨ NP[*nom*], NP[*acc*] ⟩
       sprechen 'to speak'   ⟨ NP[*nom*], PP[*über*] ⟩
       geben 'to give'   ⟨ NP[*nom*], NP[*dat*], NP[*acc*] ⟩
       dienen 'to serve'   ⟨ NP[*nom*], NP[*dat*], PP[*mit*] ⟩

The table and the following figures use COMPS as a valence feature. Former versions of HPSG (Pollard & Sag 1987) used the feature SUBCAT instead, which stands for subcategorization. It is often said that a head subcategorizes for certain arguments. See page 91 for more on the term *subcategorization*. Depending on the language, subjects are treated differently from other arguments (see for example Chomsky (1981a: 26–28), Hoekstra (1987: 33)). The subject in SVO languages like English has properties that differ from those of objects. For example, the subject is said to be an extraction island. This is not the case for SOV languages like German and hence it is usually assumed that all arguments of finite verbs are treated alike (Pollard 1996a; Eisenberg 1994a: 376). Therefore the subject is included in the lists above. I will return to English shortly.

Figure 9.1 shows the analysis for (6a) and the analysis for (6b) is in Figure 9.2 on the next page:

(6)   a.   [dass] Peter schläft
             that   Peter sleeps

       b.   [dass] Peter Maria erwartet
             that   Peter Maria expects

       'that Peter expects Maria'

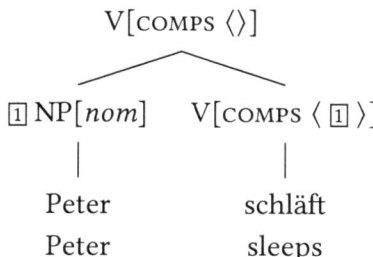

Figure 9.1: Analysis of *Peter schläft* 'Peter sleeps' in *dass Peter schläft* 'that Peter sleeps'

In Figures 9.1 and 9.2, one element of the COMPS list is combined with its head in each local tree. The elements that are combined with the selecting head are then no longer present

9.1 General remarks on the representational format

in the COMPS list of the mother node. V[COMPS ⟨ ⟩] corresponds to a complete phrase (VP or S). The boxes with numbers show the structure sharing (see Section 6.4). Structure sharing is the most important means of expression in HPSG. It plays a central role for phenomena such as valence, agreement and long-distance dependencies. In the examples above, 1 indicates that the description in the COMPS list is identical to another daughter in the tree. The descriptions contained in valence lists are usually partial descriptions, that is, not all properties of the argument are exhaustively described. Therefore, it is possible that a verb such as *schläft* 'sleeps' can be combined with various kinds of linguistic objects: the subject can be a pronoun, a proper name or a complex noun phrase, it only matters that the linguistic object in question is complete (has an empty SPR list and an empty COMPS list) and bears the correct case.[5]

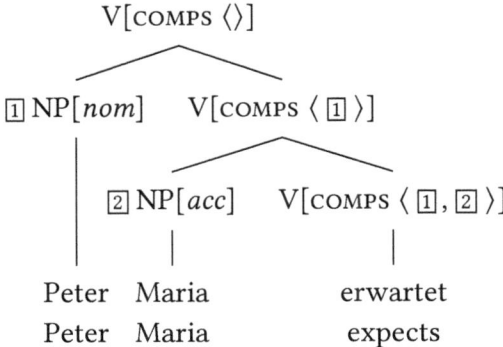

Figure 9.2: Analysis of *Peter Maria erwartet* 'Peter expects Maria.'

As mentioned above researchers working on German usually assume that subjects and objects should be treated similarly since they do not differ in fundamental ways as they do in SVO languages like English. Hence, for German, all arguments are represented in the same list. However, for SVO languages it proved useful to assume a special valence feature for preverbal dependents (Borsley 1987; Pollard & Sag 1994: Chapter 9). The arguments can be split in subjects, that are represented in the SPR list, and other arguments (complements), which are represented in the COMPS list. The equivalent of our table for German is given as (7):

(7) | verb | SPR | COMPS | ARG-ST |
| --- | --- | --- | --- |
| sleep | ⟨ NP[*nom*] ⟩ | ⟨ ⟩ | ⟨ NP[*nom*] ⟩ |
| expect | ⟨ NP[*nom*] ⟩ | ⟨ NP[*acc*] ⟩ | ⟨ NP[*nom*], NP[*acc*] ⟩ |
| speak | ⟨ NP[*nom*] ⟩ | ⟨ PP[*about*] ⟩ | ⟨ NP[*nom*], PP[*about*] ⟩ |
| give | ⟨ NP[*nom*] ⟩ | ⟨ NP[*acc*], NP[*acc*] ⟩ | ⟨ NP[*nom*], NP[*acc*], NP[*acc*] ⟩ |
| serve | ⟨ NP[*nom*] ⟩ | ⟨ NP[*acc*], PP[*with*] ⟩ | ⟨ NP[*nom*], NP[*acc*], PP[*with*] ⟩ |

The analysis of (8) is shown in Figure 9.3.

(8) Kim talks about the summer.

---

[5]Furthermore, it must agree with the verb. This is not shown here.

9 Head-Driven Phrase Structure Grammar

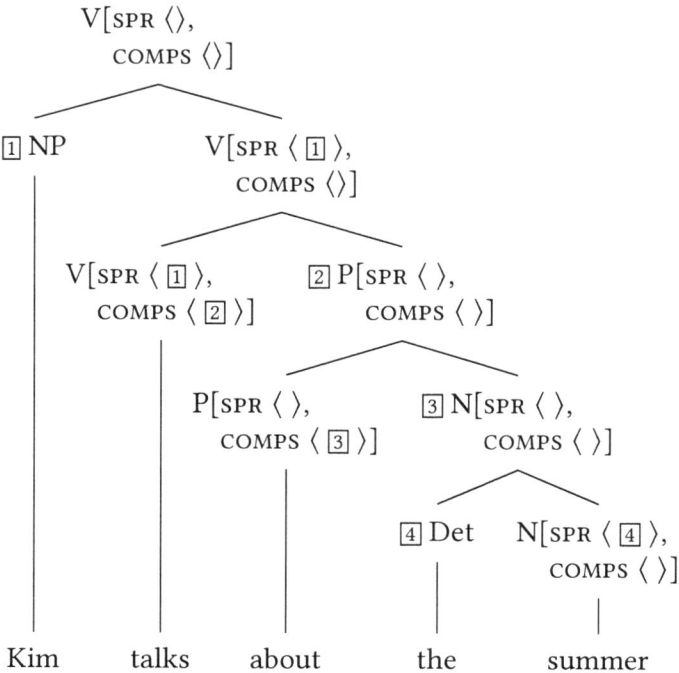

Figure 9.3: Analysis of *Kim talks about the summer*.

A head is combined with all its complements first and then with its specifier.[6] So, *talks* is combined with *about the summer* and the resulting VP is combined with its subject *Kim*. The SPR list works like the COMPS list: if an element is combined with its head, it is not contained in the SPR list of the mother. Figure 9.3 also shows the analysis of an NP: nouns select a determiner via SPR. The combination of *the* and *summer* is complete as far as specifiers are concerned and hence the SPR list at the node for *the summer* is the empty list. Nominal elements with empty SPR list and COMPS list will be abbreviated as NP. Similarly fully saturated linguistic objects with Ps as heads are PPs.

(7) provides the SPR and COMPS values of some example verbs. In addition it also provides the ARG-ST value. ARG-ST stands for *argument structure* and is a list of all arguments of a head. This argument structure list plays a crucial role in establishing the connection between syntax (valence) and semantics. The term for this is *linking*. We will deal with linking in more detail in Section 9.1.6.

After this brief discussion of English constituent structure, I will turn to German again and ignore the SPR feature. The value of SPR in all the verbal structures that are discussed in the following is the empty list.

---

[6] I present the analyses in a bottom-up way here but it is very important that HPSG does not make any statements about the order in which linguistic objects are combined. This is crucial when it comes to psycholinguistic plausibility of linguistic theories. See Chapter 15 for discussion.

270

9.1.2 Representation of constituent structure

As already noted, feature descriptions in HPSG serve as the sole descriptive inventory of morphological rules, lexical entries and syntactic rules. The trees we have seen thus far are only visualizations of the constituent structure and do not have any theoretical status. There are also no rewrite rules in HPSG.[7] The job of phrase structure rules is handled by feature descriptions. Information about dominance is represented using DTR features (head daughter and non-head daughter), information about precedence is implicitly contained in PHON. (9) shows the representation of PHON values in a feature description corresponding to the tree in Figure 9.4.

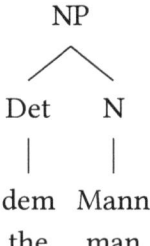

Figure 9.4: Analysis of *dem Mann* 'the man'

(9) $\begin{bmatrix} \text{PHON} & \langle \textit{dem Mann} \rangle \\ \text{HEAD-DTR} & [\text{PHON} \langle \textit{Mann} \rangle] \\ \text{NON-HEAD-DTRS} & \langle [\text{PHON} \langle \textit{dem} \rangle] \rangle \end{bmatrix}$

In (9), there is exactly one head daughter (HEAD-DTR). The head daughter is always the daughter containing the head. In a structure with the daughters *das* 'the' and *Bild von Maria* 'picture of Maria', the latter would be the head daughter. In principle, there can be multiple non-head daughters. If we were to assume a flat structure for a sentence with a ditransitive verb, as in Figure 2.1 on page 54, we would have three non-head daughters. It also makes sense to assume binary branching structures without heads (see Müller 2007a: Chapter 11 for an analysis of relative clauses). In such structures we would also have more than one non-head daughter, namely exactly two.

Before it is shown how it is ensured that only those head-complement structures are licensed in which the argument matches the requirements of the head, I will present the general structure of feature descriptions in HPSG. The structure presented at the start of this chapter is repeated in (10) with all the details relevant to the present discussion:

---

[7] However, phrase structure rules are used in some computer implementations of HPSG in order to improve the efficiency of processing.

(10)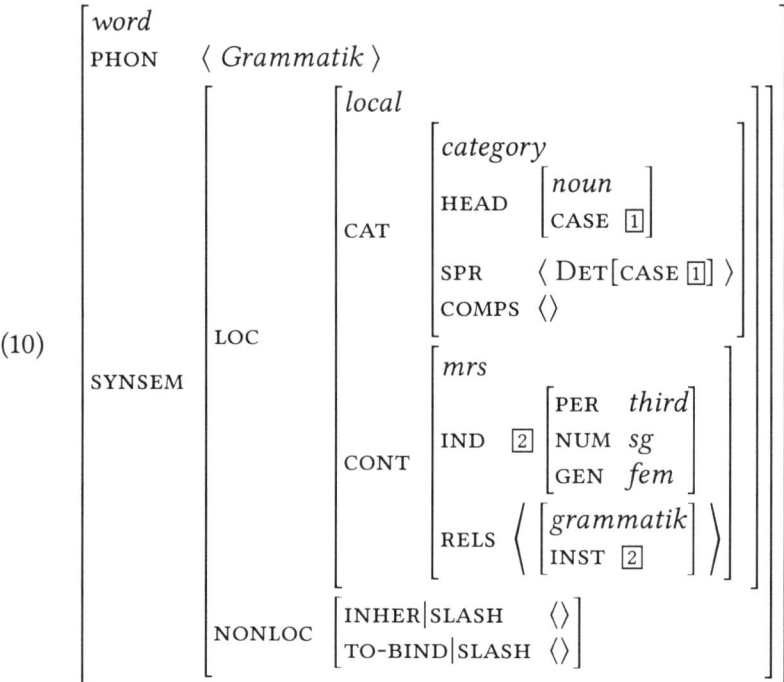

In the outer layer, there are the features PHON and SYNSEM. As previously mentioned, PHON contains the phonological representation of a linguistic object. The value of SYNSEM is a feature structure which contains syntactic and semantic information that can be selected by other heads. The daughters of phrasal signs are represented outside of SYNSEM. This ensures that there is a certain degree of locality involved in selection: a head cannot access the internal structure of the elements which it selects (Pollard & Sag 1987: 143–145; 1994: 23). See also Sections 10.6.2.1 and 18.2 for a discussion of locality. Inside SYNSEM, there is information relevant in local contexts (LOCAL, abbreviated to LOC) as well as information important for long-distance dependencies (NONLOCAL or NONLOC for short). Locally relevant information includes syntactic (CATEGORY or CAT), and semantic (CONTENT or CONT) information. Syntactic information encompasses information that determines the central characteristics of a phrase, that is, the head information. This is represented under HEAD. Further details of this will be discussed in Section 9.1.4. Among other things, the part of speech of a linguistic object belongs to the head properties of a phrase. As well as HEAD, SPR and COMPS belongs to the information contained inside CAT. The semantic content of a sign is present under CONT. The type of the CONT value is *mrs*, which stands for *Minimal Recursion Semantics* (Copestake, Flickinger, Pollard & Sag 2005). An MRS structure is comprised of an index and a list of relations which restrict this index. Of the NONLOCAL features, only SLASH is given here. There are further features for dealing with relative and interrogative clauses (Pollard & Sag 1994; Sag 1997; Ginzburg & Sag 2000; Holler 2005), which will not be discussed here.

As can be seen, the description of the word *Grammatik* 'grammar' becomes relatively complicated. In theory, it would be possible to list all properties of a given object directly in a single list of feature-value pairs. This would, however, have the disadvantage that the identity of groups of feature-value pairs could not be expressed as easily. Using the feature geometry in (10), one can express the fact that the CAT values of both conjuncts in symmetric coordinations such as those in (11) are identical.

(11) a. [der Mann] und [die Frau]
  the man and the woman

 b. Er [kennt] und [liebt] diese Schallplatte.
  he.NOM knows and loves this.ACC record

 c. Er ist [dumm] und [arrogant].
  he is dumb and arrogant

(11b) should be compared with the examples in (12). In (12a), the verbs select for an accusative and a dative object, respectively and in (12b), the verbs select for an accusative and a prepositional object:

(12) a. * Er kennt und hilft dieser Frau / diese Frau.
  he.NOM knows and helps this.DAT woman this.ACC woman

  Intended: 'He knows and helps this woman.'

 b. * weil er auf Maria kennt und wartet
  because he for Maria knows and waits

  Intended: 'because he knows Maria and waits for her'

While the English translation of (12a) is fine, since both *knows* and *helps* take an accusative, (12a) is out, since *kennt* 'knows' takes an accusative and *hilft* 'helps' a dative object. Similarly, (12b) is out since *kennt* 'knows' selects an accusative object and *wartet* 'waits' selects for a prepositional phrase containing the preposition *auf* 'for'.

If valence and the part of speech information were not represented in one common sub-structure, we would have to state separately that utterances such as (11) require that both conjuncts have the same valence and part of speech.

After this general introduction of the feature geometry that is assumed here, we can now turn to the Head-Complement Schema:

Schema 1 (Head-Complement Schema (binary branching, preliminary version))

head-complement-phrase ⇒
$$\begin{bmatrix} \text{SYNSEM}|\text{LOC}|\text{CAT}|\text{COMPS } \boxed{1} \\ \text{HEAD-DTR}|\text{SYNSEM}|\text{LOC}|\text{CAT}|\text{COMPS } \boxed{1} \oplus \langle \boxed{2} \rangle \\ \text{NON-HEAD-DTRS } \langle\, [\, \text{SYNSEM } \boxed{2}\,]\, \rangle \end{bmatrix}$$

Schema 1 states the properties a linguistic object of the type *head-complement-phrase* must have. The arrow in Schema 1 stands for a logical implication and not for the arrow of rewrite rules as we know it from phrase structure grammars. '⊕' (*append*) is a relation which combines two lists. (13) shows possible splits of a list that contains two elements:

(13) ⟨ x, y ⟩ = ⟨ x ⟩ ⊕ ⟨ y ⟩ or
  ⟨ ⟩ ⊕ ⟨ x, y ⟩ or
  ⟨ x, y ⟩ ⊕ ⟨ ⟩

The list ⟨ x, y ⟩ can be subdivided into two lists each containing one element, or alternatively into the empty list and ⟨ x, y ⟩.

Schema 1 can be read as follows: if an object is of the type *head-complement-phrase* then it must have the properties on the right-hand side of the implication. In concrete terms, this means that these objects always have a valence list which corresponds to ①, that they have a head daughter with a valence list that can be divided into two sublists ① and ⟨ ② ⟩ and also that they have a non-head daughter whose syntactic and semantic properties (SYNSEM value) are compatible with the last element of the COMPS list of the head daughter (②). (14) provides the corresponding feature description for the example in (6a).

(14) $\begin{bmatrix} \textit{head-complement-phrase} \\ \text{PHON} \ \langle \textit{Peter schläft} \rangle \\ \text{SYNSEM}|\text{LOC}|\text{CAT}|\text{COMPS} \ \langle\rangle \\ \text{HEAD-DTR} \begin{bmatrix} \text{PHON} \ \langle \textit{schläft} \rangle \\ \text{SYNSEM}|\text{LOC}|\text{CAT}|\text{COMPS} \ \langle \boxed{1}\ \text{NP}[\textit{nom}] \rangle \end{bmatrix} \\ \text{NON-HEAD-DTRS} \ \left\langle \begin{bmatrix} \text{PHON} \ \langle \textit{Peter} \rangle \\ \text{SYNSEM} \ \boxed{1} \end{bmatrix} \right\rangle \end{bmatrix}$

NP[*nom*] is an abbreviation for a complex feature description. Schema 1 divides the COMPS list of the head daughter into a single-element list and what is left. Since *schläft* 'sleeps' only has one element in its COMPS list, what remains is the empty list. This remainder is also the COMPS value of the mother.

9.1.3 Linearization rules

Dominance schemata do not say anything about the order of the daughters. As in GPSG, linearization rules are specified separately. Linearization rules can make reference to the properties of daughters, their function in a schema (head, complement, adjunct, …) or both. If we assume a feature INITIAL for all heads, then heads which precede their complements would have the INITIAL value '+' and heads following their complements would have the value '−'. The linearization rules in (15) ensure that ungrammatical orders such as (16b,d) are ruled out.[8]

(15) a. Head[INITIAL +] < Complement
      b. Complement < Head[INITIAL−]

Prepositions have an INITIAL value '+' and therefore have to precede arguments. Verbs in final position bear the value '−' and have to follow their arguments.

---

[8] Noun phrases pose a problem for (15): determiners have been treated as argument until now and were included in the COMPS list of the head noun. Determiners occur to the left of noun, whereas all other arguments of the noun are to the right. This problem can be solved either by refining linearization rules (Müller 1999b: 164–165) or by introducing a special valence feature for determiners (Pollard & Sag 1994: Section 9.4). For an approach using such a feature, see Section 9.1.1.

(16) a. [in [den Schrank]]
    in the cupboard

b. * [[den Schrank] in]
    the cupboard in

c. dass [er [ihn umfüllt]]
    that he it decants

d. * dass [er [umfüllt ihn]]
    that he decants it

9.1.4 Projection of head properties

As was explained in Section 1.5 certain properties of heads are important for the distribution of the whole phrase. For instance, the verb form belongs to the features that are important for the distribution of verbal projections. Certain verbs require a verbal argument with a particular form:

(17) a. [Dem Mann helfen] will er nicht.
    the man help wants he not
    'He doesn't want to help the man.'

b. [Dem Mann geholfen] hat er nicht.
    the man helped has he not
    'He hasn't helped the man.'

c. * [Dem Mann geholfen] will er nicht.
    the man helped wants he not

d. * [Dem Mann helfen] hat er nicht.
    the man help has he not

wollen 'to want' always requires an infinitive without *zu* 'to', while *haben* 'have' on the other hand requires a verb in participle form. *glauben* 'believe' can occur with a finite clause, but not with an infinitive without *zu*:

(18) a. Ich glaube, Peter kommt morgen.
    I believe Peter comes tomorrow
    'I think Peter is coming tomorrow.'

b. * Ich glaube, Peter morgen kommen.
    I believe Peter tomorrow come

c. * Ich glaube, morgen kommen.
    I believe tomorrow come

This shows that projections of verbs must not only contain information about the part of speech but also information about the verb form. Figure 9.5 on the next page shows this on the basis of the finite verb *gibt* 'gives'.

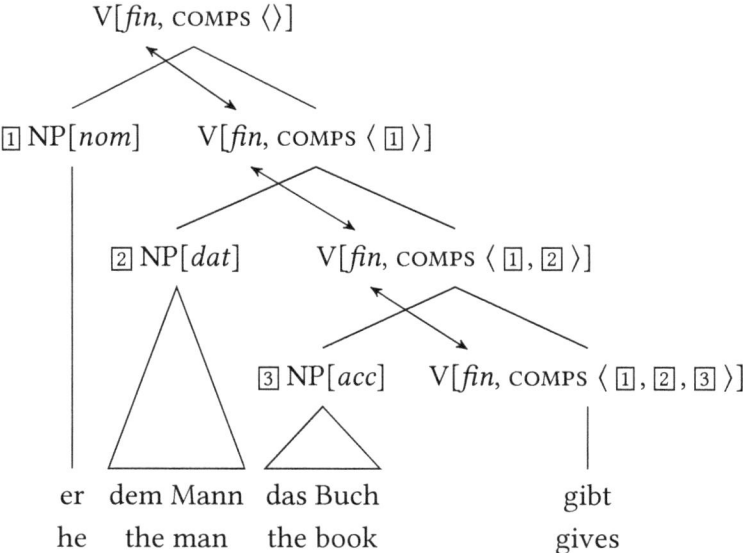

Figure 9.5: Projection of the head features of the verb

GPSG has the Head Feature Convention that ensures that head features on the mother node are identical to those on the node of the head daughter. In HPSG, there is a similar principle. Unlike GPSG, head features are explicitly contained as a group of features in the feature structures. They are listed under the path SYNSEM|LOC|CAT|HEAD. (19) shows the lexical item for *gibt* 'gives':

(19) *gibt* 'gives':
$$\begin{bmatrix} word \\ \text{PHON } \langle\, gibt\,\rangle \\ \text{SYNSEM|LOC|CAT} \begin{bmatrix} \text{HEAD} \begin{bmatrix} verb \\ \text{VFORM } fin \end{bmatrix} \\ \text{COMPS } \langle\, \text{NP}[nom], \text{NP}[dat], \text{NP}[acc]\,\rangle \end{bmatrix} \end{bmatrix}$$

The *Head Feature Principle* takes the following form:

Principle 1 (*Head Feature Principle*)
The HEAD *value of any headed phrase is structure-shared with the* HEAD *value of the head daughter.*

Figure 9.6 on the facing page is a variant of Figure 9.5 with the structure sharing made explicit.

The following section will deal with how this principle is formalized as well as how it can be integrated into the architecture of HPSG.

9.1 General remarks on the representational format

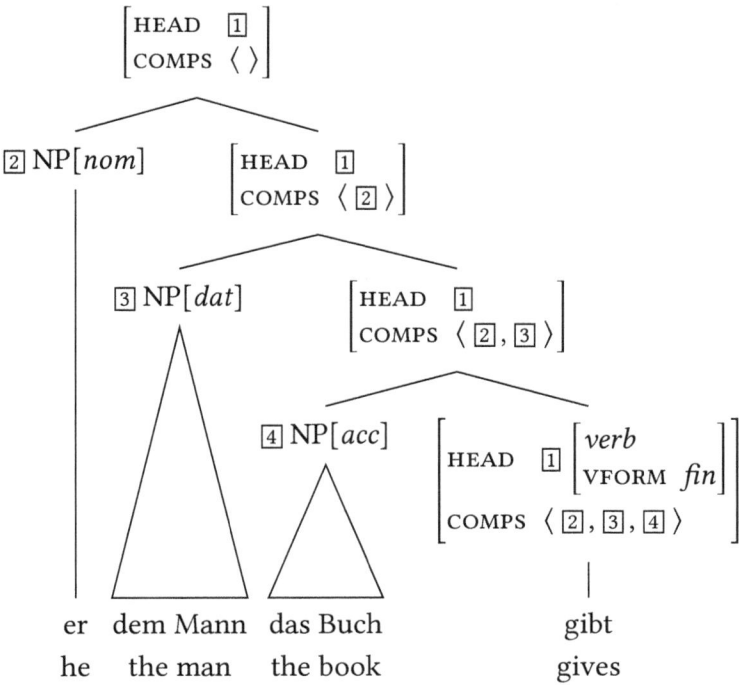

Figure 9.6: Projection of head features of a verb with structure sharing

9.1.5 Inheritance hierarchies and generalizations

Up to now, we have seen one example of a dominance schema and more will follow in the coming sections, e.g., schemata for head-adjunct structures as well as for the binding off of long-distance dependencies. The Head Feature Principle is a general principle which must be met by all structures licensed by these schemata. As mentioned above, it must be met by all structures with a head. Formally, this can be captured by categorizing syntactic structures into those with and those without heads and assigning the type *headed-phrase* to those with a head. The type *head-complement-phrase* – the type which the description in Schema 1 on page 273 has – is a subtype of *headed-phrase*. Objects of a certain type x always have all properties that objects have that are supertypes of x. Recall the example from Section 6.2: an object of the type *female person* has all the properties of the type *person*. Furthermore, objects of type *female person* have additional, more specific properties not shared by other subtypes of *person*.

If one formulates a restriction on a supertype, this automatically affects all of its subtypes. The Head Feature Principle hence can be formalized as follows:

(20) *headed-phrase* ⇒ $\begin{bmatrix} \text{SYNSEM}|\text{LOC}|\text{CAT}|\text{HEAD} & \boxed{1} \\ \text{HEAD-DTR}|\text{SYNSEM}|\text{LOC}|\text{CAT}|\text{HEAD} & \boxed{1} \end{bmatrix}$

The arrow corresponds to a logical implication, as mentioned above. Therefore, (20) can be read as follows: if a structure is of type *headed-phrase*, then it must hold that the value of SYNSEM|LOC|CAT|HEAD is identical to the value of HEAD-DTR|SYNSEM|LOC|CAT|HEAD.

An extract from the type hierarchy under *sign* is given in Figure 9.7.

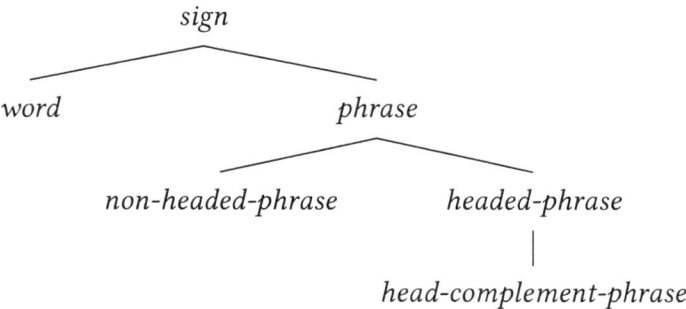

Figure 9.7: Type hierarchy for *sign*: all subtypes of *headed-phrase* inherit constraints

word and *phrase* are subclasses of linguistic signs. Phrases can be divided into phrases with heads (*headed-phrase*) and those without (*non-headed-phrase*). There are also subtypes for phrases of type *non-headed-phrase* and *headed-phrase*. We have already discussed *head-complement-phrase*, and other subtypes of *headed-phrase* will be discussed in the later sections. As well as *word* and *phrase*, there are the types *root* and *stem*, which play an important role for the structure of the lexicon and the morphological component. Due to space considerations, it is not possible to further discuss these types here, but see Chapter 23.

The description in (21) shows the Head-Complement Schema from page 273 together with the restrictions that the type *head-complement-phrase* inherits from *headed-phrase*.

(21) Head-Complement Schema + Head Feature Principle:
$$\begin{bmatrix} \textit{head-complement-phrase} \\ \text{SYNSEM|LOC|CAT} \begin{bmatrix} \text{HEAD} & \boxed{1} \\ \text{COMPS} & \boxed{2} \end{bmatrix} \\ \text{HEAD-DTR|SYNSEM|LOC|CAT} \begin{bmatrix} \text{HEAD} & \boxed{1} \\ \text{COMPS} & \boxed{2} \oplus \langle \boxed{3} \rangle \end{bmatrix} \\ \text{NON-HEAD-DTRS} \ \langle \ [\ \text{SYNSEM}\ \boxed{3}\ ]\ \rangle \end{bmatrix}$$

(22) gives a description of a structure licensed by Schema 1. As well as valence information, the head information is specified in (22) and it is also apparent how the Head Feature Principle ensures the projection of features: the head value of the entire structure (□) corresponds to the head value of the verb *gibt* 'gives'.

9.1 General remarks on the representational format

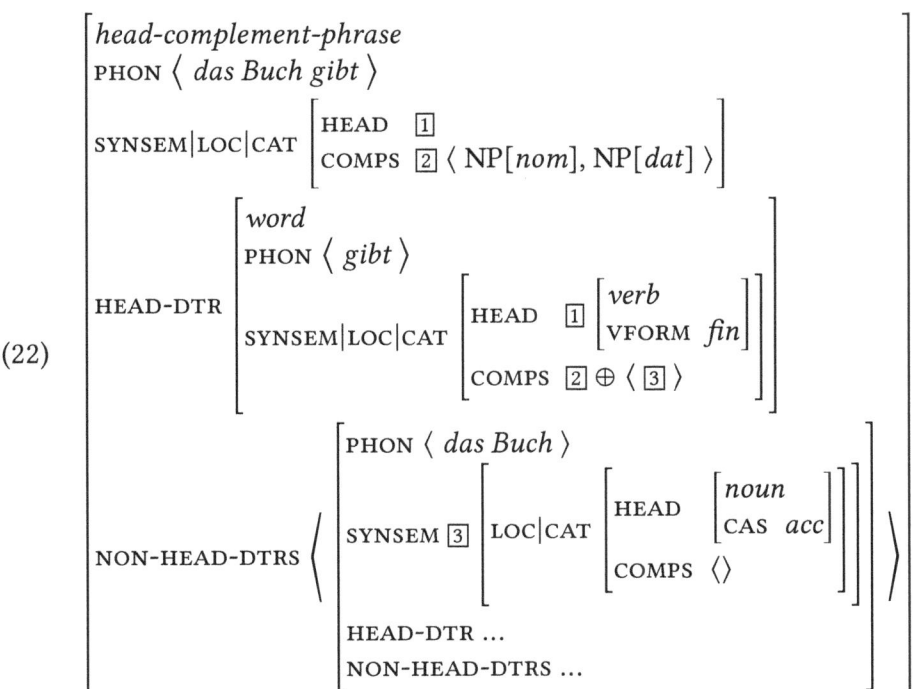

For the entire clause *er das Buch dem Mann gibt* 'he the book to the man gives', we arrive at a structure (already shown in Figure 9.6) described by (23):

$$(23) \quad \begin{bmatrix} \text{SYNSEM}|\text{LOC}|\text{CAT} \begin{bmatrix} \text{HEAD} & \begin{bmatrix} \textit{verb} \\ \text{VFORM } \textit{fin} \end{bmatrix} \\ \text{SPR} & \langle\rangle \\ \text{COMPS} & \langle\rangle \end{bmatrix} \end{bmatrix}$$

This description corresponds to the sentence symbol S in the phrase structure grammar on page 53, however (23) additionally contains information about the form of the verb.

Using dominance schemata as an example, we have shown how generalizations about linguistic objects can be captured, however, we also want to be able to capture generalizations in other areas of the theory: like Categorial Grammar, the HPSG lexicon contains a very large amount of information. Lexical entries (roots and words) can also be divided into classes, which can then be assigned types. In this way, it is possible to capture what all verbs, intransitive verbs and transitive verbs, have in common. See Figure 23.1 on page 688.

Now that some fundamental concepts of HPSG have been introduced, the following section will show how the semantic contribution of words is represented and how the meaning of a phrase can be determined compositionally.

9.1.6 Semantics

An important difference between theories such as GB, LFG and TAG, on the one hand, and HPSG and CxG on the other is that the semantic content of a linguistic object is modeled in a feature structure just like all its other properties. As previously mentioned, semantic information is found under the path SYNSEM|LOC|CONT. (24) gives an example of the CONT value for *Buch* 'book'. The representation is based on Minimal Recursion Semantics (MRS):[9]

$$(24) \begin{bmatrix} mrs \\ \text{IND} \quad \boxed{1} \begin{bmatrix} \text{PER} & 3 \\ \text{NUM} & sg \\ \text{GEN} & neu \end{bmatrix} \\ \text{RELS} \quad \left\langle \begin{bmatrix} buch \\ \text{INST} & \boxed{1} \end{bmatrix} \right\rangle \end{bmatrix}$$

IND stands for index and RELS is a list of relations. Features such as person, number and gender are part of a nominal index. These are important in determining reference or coreference. For example, *sie* 'she' in (25) can refer to *Frau* 'woman' but not to *Buch* 'book'. On the other hand, *es* 'it' cannot refer to *Frau* 'woman'.

(25) Die Frau$_i$ kauft ein Buch$_j$. Sie$_i$ liest es$_j$.
the woman buys a book she reads it

'The woman buys a book. She reads it.'

In general, pronouns have to agree in person, number and gender with the element they refer to. Indices are then identified accordingly. In HPSG, this is done by means of structure sharing. It is also common to speak of *coindexation*. (26) provides some examples of coindexation of reflexive pronouns:

(26) a. Ich$_i$ sehe mich$_i$.
I see myself

b. Du$_i$ siehst dich$_i$.
you see yourself

c. Er$_i$ sieht sich$_i$.
he sees himself

d. Wir$_i$ sehen uns$_i$.
we see ourselves

e. Ihr$_i$ seht euch$_i$.
you see yourselves

f. Sie$_i$ sehen sich$_i$.
they see themselves

---

[9]Pollard & Sag (1994) and Ginzburg & Sag (2000) make use of Situation Semantics (Barwise & Perry 1983; Cooper, Mukai & Perry 1990; Devlin 1992). An alternative approach which has already been used in HPSG is Lexical Resource Semantics (Richter & Sailer 2004). For an early underspecification analysis in HPSG, see Nerbonne (1993).

9.1 General remarks on the representational format

The question of which instances of coindexation are possible and which are necessary is determined by Binding Theory. Pollard & Sag (1992; 1994) have shown that Binding Theory in HPSG does not have many of the problems that arise when implementing binding in GB with reference to tree configurations. There are, however, a number of open questions for Binding Theory in HPSG (Müller 1999b: Section 20.4).

(27) shows the CONT value for the verb *geben* 'give':

$$
(27) \quad \begin{bmatrix} mrs \\ \text{IND} \quad \boxed{1} \; event \\ \text{RELS} \; \left\langle \begin{bmatrix} geben \\ \text{EVENT} \quad \boxed{1} \\ \text{AGENT} \quad index \\ \text{GOAL} \quad index \\ \text{THEME} \quad index \end{bmatrix} \right\rangle \end{bmatrix}
$$

It is assumed that verbs have an event variable of the type *event*, which is represented under IND just as with indices for nominal objects. Until now, we did not assign elements in the valence list to argument roles in the semantic representation. This connection is referred to as *linking*. (28) shows how linking works in HPSG. The referential indices of the argument noun phrases are structure-shared with one of the semantic roles of the relation contributed by the head.

(28) Lexical entry for the lexeme *geben* 'give':

$$
\begin{bmatrix} \text{CONT} \quad \begin{bmatrix} mrs \\ \text{IND} \quad \boxed{4} \; event \\ \text{RELS} \; \left\langle \begin{bmatrix} geben \\ \text{EVENT} \quad \boxed{4} \\ \text{AGENT} \quad \boxed{1} \\ \text{GOAL} \quad \boxed{2} \\ \text{THEME} \quad \boxed{3} \end{bmatrix} \right\rangle \end{bmatrix} \\ \text{ARG-ST} \; \left\langle \text{NP}[nom]_{\boxed{1}}, \text{NP}[dat]_{\boxed{2}}, \text{NP}[acc]_{\boxed{3}} \right\rangle \end{bmatrix}
$$

The list that contains all the arguments of a head is called *argument structure list* and it is represented as value of the ARG-ST feature. This list plays a very important role in HPSG grammars: case is assigned there, the Binding Theory operates on ARG-ST and the linking between syntax and semantics takes place on ARG-ST as well.

For finite verbs, the value of ARG-ST is identical to the value of COMPS in German. As was explained in Section 9.1.1, the first element of the ARG-ST list is the subject in languages like English and it is represented in the SPR list (Sag, Wasow & Bender 2003: Section 4.3, 7.3.1; Müller 2019b). All other elements from ARG-ST are contained in the COMPS list. So there are language specific ways to represent the valence but there is one common representation that is the same for all argument structure representations. This makes it possible to capture cross-linguistic generalizations.

Since we use general terms such as AGENT and PATIENT for argument roles, it is possible to state generalizations about valence classes and the realization of argument roles.

For example, one can divide verbs into verbs taking an agent, verbs with an agent and theme, verbs with agent and patient etc. These various valence/linking patterns can be represented in type hierarchies and these classes can be assigned to the specific lexical entries, that is, one can have them inherit constraints from the respective types. A type constraint for verbs with agent, theme and goal takes the form of (29):

$$
(29) \quad \begin{bmatrix} \text{CONT} \begin{bmatrix} \textit{mrs} \\ \text{IND} \quad \boxed{4} \; \textit{event} \\ \text{RELS} \; \left\langle \begin{bmatrix} \textit{agent-goal-theme-rel} \\ \text{EVENT} \quad \boxed{4} \\ \text{AGENT} \quad \boxed{1} \\ \text{GOAL} \quad \boxed{2} \\ \text{THEME} \quad \boxed{3} \end{bmatrix} \right\rangle \end{bmatrix} \\ \text{ARG-ST} \; \left\langle \; []_{\boxed{1}}, \; []_{\boxed{2}}, \; []_{\boxed{3}} \; \right\rangle \end{bmatrix}
$$

$[]_{\boxed{1}}$ stands for an object of unspecified syntactic category with the index $\boxed{1}$. The type for the relation *geben′* is a subtype of *agent-goal-theme-rel*. The lexical entry for the word *geben* 'give' or rather the root *geb-* has the linking pattern in (29). For more on theories of linking in HPSG, see Davis (1996), Wechsler (1991) und Davis & Koenig (2000).

Up to now, we have only seen how the meaning of lexical entries can be represented. The Semantics Principle determines the computation of the semantic contribution of phrases: the index of the entire expression corresponds to the index of the head daughter, and the RELS value of the entire sign corresponds to the concatenation of the RELS values of the daughters plus any relations introduced by the dominance schema. The last point is important because the assumption that schemata can add something to meaning can capture the fact that there are some cases where the entire meaning of a phrase is more than simply the sum of its parts. Pertinent examples are often discussed as part of Construction Grammar. Semantic composition in HPSG is organized such that meaning components that are due to certain patterns can be integrated into the complete meaning of an utterance. For examples, see Section 21.10.

The connection between the semantic contribution of the verb and its arguments is established in the lexical entry. As such, we ensure that the argument roles of the verb are assigned to the correct argument in the sentence. This is, however, not the only thing that the semantics is responsible for. It has to be able to generate the various readings associated with quantifier scope ambiguities (see page 90) as well as deal with semantic embedding of predicates under other predicates. All these requirements are fulfilled by MRS. Due to space considerations, we cannot go into detail here. The reader is referred to the article by Copestake, Flickinger, Pollard & Sag (2005) and to Section 19.3 in the discussion chapter.

9.1.7 Adjuncts

Analogous to the selection of arguments by heads via COMPS, adjuncts can also select their heads using a feature (MODIFIED). Adjectives, prepositional phrases that modify nouns, and relative clauses select an almost complete nominal projection, that is, a noun that only still needs to be combined with a determiner to yield a complete NP. (30) shows a description of the respective *synsem* object. The symbol $\overline{\text{N}}$, which is familiar from $\overline{\text{X}}$ theory (see Section 2.5), is used as abbreviation for this feature description.

(30) AVM that is abbreviated as $\overline{\text{N}}$:

$$\left[\text{CAT} \begin{bmatrix} \text{HEAD} & \textit{noun} \\ \text{SPR} & \langle \text{DET} \rangle \\ \text{COMPS} & \langle \rangle \end{bmatrix} \right]$$

(31) shows part of the lexical item for *interessantes* 'interesting':[10]

(31) CAT value for *interessantes* 'interesting':

$$\begin{bmatrix} \text{HEAD} & \begin{bmatrix} \textit{adj} \\ \text{MOD} & \overline{\text{N}} \end{bmatrix} \\ \text{COMPS} & \langle \rangle \end{bmatrix}$$

interessantes is an adjective that does not take any arguments and therefore has an empty COMPS list. Adjectives such as *treu* 'loyal' have a dative NP in their COMPS list.

(32) ein dem König treues Mädchen
    a   the.DAT king loyal girl

'a girl loyal to the king'

The CAT value is given in (33):

(33) CAT value for *treues* 'loyal':

$$\begin{bmatrix} \text{HEAD} & \begin{bmatrix} \textit{adj} \\ \text{MOD} & \overline{\text{N}} \end{bmatrix} \\ \text{COMPS} & \langle \text{NP}[\textit{dat}] \rangle \end{bmatrix}$$

dem König treues 'loyal to the king' forms an adjective phrase, which modifies *Mädchen*.

Unlike the selectional feature COMPS that belongs to the features under CAT, MOD is a head feature. The reason for this is that the feature that selects the modifying head has to be present on the maximal projection of the adjunct. The $\overline{\text{N}}$-modifying property of the adjective phrase *dem König treues* 'loyal to the king' has to be included in the representation of the entire AP just as it is present in the lexical entry for adjectives in

---

[10] In what follows, I am also omitting the SPR feature, whose value would be the empty list.

(31) at the lexical level. The adjectival phrase *dem König treues* has the same syntactic properties as the basic adjective *interessantes* 'interesting':

(34) CAT value für *dem König treues* 'loyal to the king':
$$\begin{bmatrix} \text{HEAD} & \begin{bmatrix} adj \\ \text{MOD} & \overline{\text{N}} \end{bmatrix} \\ \text{COMPS} & \langle\rangle \end{bmatrix}$$

Since MOD is a head feature, the Head Feature Principle (see page 276) ensures that the MOD value of the entire projection is identical to the MOD value of the lexical entry for *treues* 'loyal'.

As an alternative to the selection of the head by the modifier, one could assume a description of all possible adjuncts on the head itself. This was suggested by Pollard & Sag (1987: 161). Pollard & Sag (1994: Section 1.9) revised the earlier analysis since the semantics of modification could not be captured.[11]

Figure 9.8 demonstrates selection in head-adjunct structures.

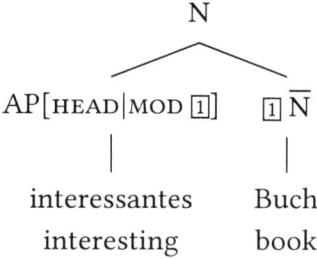

interessantes   Buch
interesting   book

Figure 9.8: Head-adjunct structure (selection)

Head-adjunct structures are licensed by the Schema 2.

Schema 2 (Head-Adjunct Schema)

head-adjunct-phrase ⇒
$$\begin{bmatrix} \text{HEAD-DTR}|\text{SYNSEM} & \boxed{1} \\ \text{NON-HEAD-DTRS} & \left\langle \begin{bmatrix} \text{SYNSEM}|\text{LOC}|\text{CAT} & \begin{bmatrix} \text{HEAD}|\text{MOD} & \boxed{1} \\ \text{SPR} & \langle\rangle \\ \text{COMPS} & \langle\rangle \end{bmatrix} \end{bmatrix} \right\rangle \end{bmatrix}$$

The value of the selectional feature on the adjunct ($\boxed{1}$) is identified with the SYNSEM value of the head daughter, thereby ensuring that the head daughter has the properties

---

[11] See Bouma, Malouf & Sag (2001), however. Bouma, Malouf & Sag (2001) pursue a hybrid analysis where there are adjuncts which select heads and also adjuncts that are selected by a head. Minimal Recursion Semantics is the semantic theory underlying this analysis. Using this semantics, the problems arising for Pollard & Sag (1987) with regard to the semantics of modifiers are avoided.

specified by the adjunct. The COMPS value of the non-head daughter is the empty list, which is why only completely saturated adjuncts are allowed in head-adjunct structures. Phrases such as (35b) are therefore correctly ruled out:

(35)   a.   die Wurst in der Speisekammer
             the sausage in the pantry

       b. * die Wurst in
             the sausage in

Example (35a) requires some further explanation. The preposition *in* (as used in (35a)) has the following CAT value:

(36)   CAT value of *in*:
$$\begin{bmatrix} \text{HEAD} & \begin{bmatrix} prep \\ \text{MOD} & \overline{N} \end{bmatrix} \\ \text{COMPS} & \langle \text{NP}[dat] \rangle \end{bmatrix}$$

After combining *in* with the nominal phrase *der Speisekammer* 'the pantry' one gets:

(37)   CAT value for *in der Speisekammer* 'in the pantry':
$$\begin{bmatrix} \text{HEAD} & \begin{bmatrix} prep \\ \text{MOD} & \overline{N} \end{bmatrix} \\ \text{COMPS} & \langle \, \rangle \end{bmatrix}$$

This representation corresponds to that of the adjective *interessantes* 'interesting' and can – ignoring the position of the PP – also be used in the same way: the PP modifies a $\overline{N}$.

Heads that can only be used as arguments but do not modify anything have a MOD value of *none*. They can therefore not occur in the position of the non-head daughter in head-adjunct structures since the MOD value of the non-head daughter has to be compatible with the SYNSEM value of the head daughter.

9.2 Passive

HPSG follows Bresnan's argumentation (see Section 7.2) and takes care of the passive in the lexicon.[12] A lexical rule takes the verb stem as its input and licenses the participle form and the most prominent argument (the so-called designated argument) is

---

[12] Some exceptions to this are analyses influenced by Construction Grammar such as Tseng (2007) and Haugereid (2007). These approaches are problematic, however, as they cannot account for Bresnan's adjectival passives. For other problems with Haugereid's analysis, see Müller (2007b) and Section 21.3.6.

suppressed.[13] Since grammatical functions are not part of theory in HPSG, we do not require any mapping principles that map objects to subjects. Nevertheless, one still has to explain the change of case under passivization. If one fully specifies the case of a particular argument in the lexical entries, one has to ensure that the accusative argument of a transitive verb is realized as nominative in the passive. (38) shows what the respective lexical rule would look like:

(38) Lexical rule for personal passives adapted from Kiss (1992):

$$\begin{bmatrix} stem \\ \text{PHON } \boxed{1} \\ \text{SYNSEM|LOC|CAT|HEAD } verb \\ \text{ARG-ST } \langle \text{NP}[nom], \text{NP}[acc]_{\boxed{2}} \rangle \oplus \boxed{3} \end{bmatrix} \mapsto$$

$$\begin{bmatrix} word \\ \text{PHON } f(\boxed{1}) \\ \text{SYNSEM|LOC|CAT|HEAD|VFORM } passive\text{-}part \\ \text{ARG-ST } \langle \text{NP}[nom]_{\boxed{2}} \rangle \oplus \boxed{3} \end{bmatrix}$$

This lexical rule takes a verb stem[14] as its input, which requires a nominative argument, an accusative argument and possibly further arguments (if $\boxed{3}$ is not the empty list) and licenses a lexical entry that requires a nominative argument and possibly the arguments in $\boxed{3}$.[15] The output of the lexical rule specifies the VFORM value of the output word. This is important as the auxiliary and the main verb must go together. For example, it is not possible to use the perfect participle instead of the passive participle since these differ in their valence in Kiss' approach:

---

[13]For more on the designated argument, see Haider (1986a). HPSG analyses of the passive in German have been considerably influenced by Haider. Haider uses the designated argument to model the difference between so-called unaccusative and unergative verbs (Perlmutter 1978): unaccusative verbs differ from unergatives and transitives in that they do not have a designated argument. We cannot go into the literature on unaccusativity here. The reader is referred to the original works by Haider and the chapter on the passive in Müller (2007a).

[14]The term *stem* includes roots (*helf-* 'help-'), products of derivation (*besing-* 'to sing about') and compounds. The lexical rule can therefore also be applied to stems like *helf-* and derived forms such as *besing-*.

[15]This rule assumes that arguments of ditransitive verbs are in the order nominative, accusative, dative. Throughout this chapter, I assume a nominative, dative, accusative order, which corresponds to the unmarked order of arguments in the German clause. Kiss (2001) argued that a representation of the unmarked order is needed to account for scope facts in German. Furthermore, the order of the arguments corresponds to the order one would assume for English, which has the advantage that cross-linguistic generalizations can be captured. In earlier work I assumed that the order is nominative, accusative, dative since this order encodes a prominence hierarchy that is relevant in a lot of areas in German grammar. Examples are: ellipsis (Klein 1985), Topic Drop (Fries 1988), free relatives (Bausewein 1990; Pittner 1995; Müller 1999a), depictive secondary predicates (Müller 2004b; 2002a; 2008), Binding Theory (Grewendorf 1985; Pollard & Sag: 1992; 1994: Chapter 6). This order also corresponds to the Obliqueness Hierarchy suggested by Keenan & Comrie (1977) and Pullum (1977). In order to capture this hierarchy, a special list with nominative, accusative, dative order would have to be assumed.

The version of the passive lexical rule that will be suggested below is compatible with both orders of arguments.

(39) a. Der Mann hat den Weltmeister geschlagen.
     the man has the world.champion beaten
     'The man has beaten the world champion.'

  b. * Der Mann wird den Weltmeister geschlagen.
       the man is   the world.champion beaten

  c. Der Weltmeister wird geschlagen.
     the world.champion is beaten
     'The world champion is (being) beaten.'

There are a few conventions for the interpretation of lexical rules: all information that is not mentioned in the output sign is taken over from the input sign. Thus, the meaning of the verb is not mentioned in the passive rule, which makes sense as the passive rule is a meaning preserving rule. The CONT values of the input and output are not mentioned in the rule and hence are identical. It is important here that the linking information its retained. As an example consider the application of the rule to the verb stem *schlag-* 'beat':

(40) a. Input *schlag-* 'beat':
$$\begin{bmatrix} \text{PHON} \ \langle \textit{schlag} \rangle \\ \text{SYNSEM}|\text{LOC} \begin{bmatrix} \text{CAT} & [\text{HEAD} \ \textit{verb}] \\ \text{CONT} & \begin{bmatrix} \text{IND} & \boxed{3} \ \textit{event} \\ \text{RELS} & \left\langle \begin{bmatrix} \textit{schlagen} \\ \text{EVENT} & \boxed{3} \\ \text{AGENT} & \boxed{1} \\ \text{PATIENT} & \boxed{2} \end{bmatrix} \right\rangle \end{bmatrix} \end{bmatrix} \\ \text{ARG-ST} \ \langle \text{NP}[\textit{nom}]_{\boxed{1}}, \text{NP}[\textit{acc}]_{\boxed{2}} \rangle \end{bmatrix}$$

b. Output *geschlagen* 'beaten':
$$\begin{bmatrix} \text{PHON} \ \langle \textit{geschlagen} \rangle \\ \text{SYNSEM}|\text{LOC} \begin{bmatrix} \text{CAT} & \begin{bmatrix} \text{HEAD} & \begin{bmatrix} \textit{verb} \\ \text{VFORM} \ \textit{passive-part} \end{bmatrix} \end{bmatrix} \\ \text{CONT} & \begin{bmatrix} \text{IND} & \boxed{3} \ \textit{event} \\ \text{RELS} & \left\langle \begin{bmatrix} \textit{schlagen} \\ \text{EVENT} & \boxed{3} \\ \text{AGENT} & \boxed{1} \\ \text{PATIENT} & \boxed{2} \end{bmatrix} \right\rangle \end{bmatrix} \end{bmatrix} \\ \text{ARG-ST} \ \langle \text{NP}[\textit{nom}]_{\boxed{2}} \rangle \end{bmatrix}$$

The agent role is connected to the subject of *schlag-*. After passivization, the subject is suppressed and the argument connected to the patient role of *schlag-* becomes the subject of the participle. Argument linking is not affected by this and thus the nominative argument is correctly assigned to the patient role.

As Meurers (2001) has shown, lexical rules can also be captured with feature descriptions. (41) shows the feature description representation of (38).

(41) $\begin{bmatrix} acc\text{-}passive\text{-}lexical\text{-}rule \\ \text{PHON } f(\boxed{1}) \\ \text{SYNSEM}|\text{LOC}|\text{CAT}|\text{HEAD}|\text{VFORM } passive\text{-}part \\ \text{ARG-ST } \langle \text{NP}[nom]_{\boxed{2}} \rangle \oplus \boxed{3} \\ \text{LEX-DTR } \begin{bmatrix} stem \\ \text{PHON } \boxed{1} \\ \text{SYNSEM}|\text{LOC}|\text{CAT}|\text{HEAD } verb \\ \text{ARG-ST } \langle \text{NP}[nom], \text{NP}[acc]_{\boxed{2}} \rangle \oplus \boxed{3} \end{bmatrix} \end{bmatrix}$

What is on the left-hand side of the rule in (38), is contained in the value of LEX-DTR in (41). Since this kind of lexical rule is fully integrated into the formalism, feature structures corresponding to these lexical rules also have their own type. If the result of the application of a given rule is an inflected word, then the type of the lexical rule (*acc-passive-lexical-rule* in our example) is a subtype of *word*. Since lexical rules have a type, it is possible to state generalizations over lexical rules.

The lexical rules discussed thus far work well for the personal passive. For the impersonal passive, however, we would require a second lexical rule. Furthermore, we would have two different lexical items for the passive and the perfect, although the forms are always identical in German. In the following, I will discuss the basic assumptions that are needed for a theory of the passive that can sufficiently explain both personal and impersonal passives and thereby only require one lexical item for the participle form.

9.2.1 Valence information and the Case Principle

In Section 3.4.1, the difference between structural and lexical case was motivated. In the HPSG literature, it is assumed following Haider (1986a) that the dative is a lexical case. For arguments marked with a lexical case, their case value is directly specified in the description of the argument. Arguments with structural case are also specified in the lexicon as taking structural case, but the actual case value is not provided. In order for the grammar not to make any false predictions, it has to be ensured that the structural cases receive a unique value dependent on their environment. This is handled by the Case Principle:[16]

---

[16] The Case Principle has been simplified here. Cases of so-called 'raising' require special treatment. For more details, see Meurers (1999c), Przepiórkowski (1999a) and Müller (2007a: Chapter 14, Chapter 17). The Case Principle given in these publications is very similar to the one proposed by Yip, Maling & Jackendoff (1987) and can therefore also explain the case systems of the languages discussed in their work, notably the complicated case system of Icelandic.

9.2 Passive

Principle 2 (Case Principle (simplified))

- *The first element with structural case in the argument structure list receives nominative.*
- *All other elements in the list with structural case receive accusative.*
- *In nominal environments, elements with structural case are assigned genitive.*

(42) shows prototypical valence lists for finite verbs:

(42) a. *schläft* 'sleeps':   ARG-ST $\langle \text{NP}[str]_j \rangle$

  b. *unterstützt* 'supports': ARG-ST $\langle \text{NP}[str]_j, \text{NP}[str]_k \rangle$

  c. *hilft* 'helps':   ARG-ST $\langle \text{NP}[str]_j, \text{NP}[ldat]_k \rangle$

  d. *schenkt* 'gives':   ARG-ST $\langle \text{NP}[str]_j, \text{NP}[ldat]_k, \text{NP}[str]_l \rangle$

str stands for *structural* and *ldat* for lexical dative. The Case Principle ensures that the subjects of the verbs listed above have to be realized in the nominative and also that objects with structural case are assigned accusative.

With the difference between structural and lexical case, it is possible to formulate a passive-lexical rule that can account for both the personal and the impersonal passive:

(43) Lexical rule for personal and impersonal passive (simplified):

$$\begin{bmatrix} stem \\ \text{PHON } \boxed{1} \\ \text{SYNSEM}|\text{LOC}|\text{CAT}|\text{HEAD } verb \\ \text{ARG-ST } \langle \text{NP}[str] \rangle \oplus \boxed{2} \end{bmatrix} \mapsto$$

$$\begin{bmatrix} word \\ \text{PHON } f(\boxed{1}) \\ \text{SYNSEM}|\text{LOC}|\text{CAT}|\text{HEAD}|\text{VFORM } ppp \\ \text{ARG-ST } \boxed{2} \end{bmatrix}$$

This lexical rule does exactly what we expect it to do from a pretheoretical perspective on the passive: it suppresses the most prominent argument with structural case, that is, the argument that corresponds to the subject in the active clause.

(44) a. *geschlafen* 'slept':   ARG-ST $\langle \, \rangle$

  b. *unterstützt* 'supported': ARG-ST $\langle \text{NP}[str]_k \rangle$

  c. *geholfen* 'helped':   ARG-ST $\langle \text{NP}[ldat]_k \rangle$

  d. *geschenkt* 'given':   ARG-ST $\langle \text{NP}[ldat]_k, \text{NP}[str]_l \rangle$

The standard analysis of verb auxiliary constructions in German assumes that the main verb and the auxiliary forms a verbal complex (Hinrichs & Nakazawa 1994; Pollard 1994; Müller 1999b; 2002a; Meurers 2000; Kathol 2000). The arguments of the embedded verb are taken over by the auxiliary. For the analysis of the passive this means that the auxiliary has an ARG-ST that starts with the elements shown in (44). (44) differs from (42) in that a different NP is in first position. If this NP has structural case, it will receive nominative case. If there is no NP with structural case, as in (44c), the case remains as it was, that is, lexically specified.

We cannot go into the analysis of the perfect here. It should be noted, however, that the same lexical item for the participle is used for (45).

(45) a. Er hat den Weltmeister geschlagen.
he has the world.champion beaten

'He has beaten the world champion.'

b. Der Weltmeister wurde geschlagen.
the world.champion was beaten

'The world champion was beaten.'

It is the auxiliary that determines which arguments are realized (Haider 1986a; Müller 2007a: Chapter 17). The lexical rule in (43) licenses a form that can be used both in passive and perfect. Therefore, the VFORM value is of *ppp*, which stands for *perfect passive participle*.

One should note that this analysis of the passive works without movement of constituents. The problems with the GB analysis do not arise here. Reordering of arguments (see Section 9.4) is independent of passivization. The accusative object is not mentioned at all unlike in GPSG, Categorial Grammar or Bresnan's LFG analysis from before the introduction of Lexical Mapping Theory (see page 232). The passive can be analyzed directly as the suppression of the subject. Everything else follows from interaction with other principles of grammar.

9.3 Verb position

The analysis of verb position that I will present here is based on the GB-analysis. In HPSG, there are a number of different approaches to describe the verb position, however in my opinion, the HPSG variant of the GB analysis is the only adequate one (Müller 2005b,c; 2017a). The analysis of (46) can be summarized as follows: in the verb-initial clauses, there is a trace in verb-final position. There is a special form of the verb in initial position that selects a projection of the verb trace. This special lexical item is licensed by a lexical rule. The connection between the verb and the trace is treated like long-distance dependencies in GPSG via identification of information in the tree or feature structure (structure sharing).

(46) Kennt$_k$ jeder diesen Mann _$_k$?
knows everyone this man

'Does everyone know this man?'

Figure 9.9 on the next page gives an overview of this. The verb trace in final position behaves just like the verb both syntactically and semantically. The information about the missing word is represented as the value of the feature DOUBLE SLASH (abbreviated:

9.3 Verb position

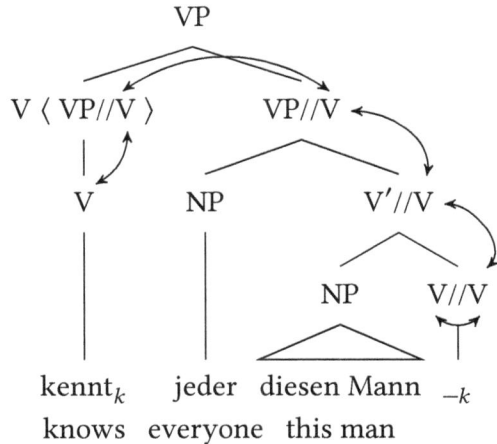

Figure 9.9: Analysis of verb position in HPSG

DSL). This is a head feature and is therefore passed up to the maximal projection (VP). The verb in initial position has a VP in its COMPS list which is missing a verb (VP//V). This is the same verb that was the input for the lexical rule and that would normally occur in final position. In Figure 9.9, there are two maximal verb projections: *jeder diesen Mann* $_{-k}$ with the trace as the head and *kennt jeder diesen Mann* $_{-k}$ with *kennt* as the head.

This analysis will be explained in more detail in what follows. For the trace in Figure 9.9, one could assume the lexical entry in (47).

(47) Verb trace for *kennt* 'knows':

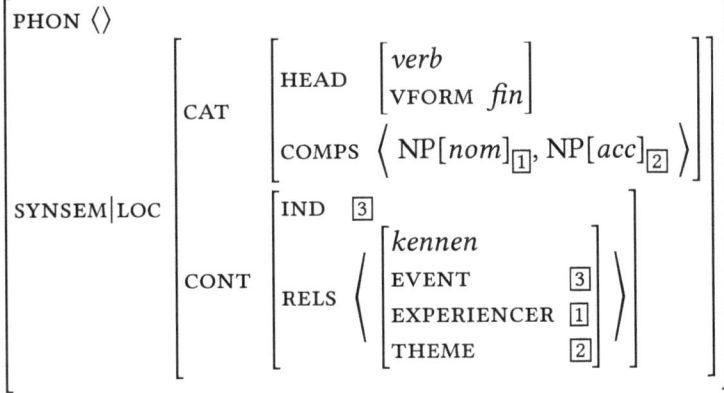

This lexical entry differs from the normal verb *kennt* only in its PHON value. The syntactic aspects of an analysis with this trace are represented in Figure 9.10 on the following page.

The combination of the trace with *diesen Mann* 'this man' and *jeder* 'everbody' follows the rules and principles that we have encountered thus far. This begs the immediate question as to what licenses the verb *kennt* in Figure 9.10 and what status it has.

291

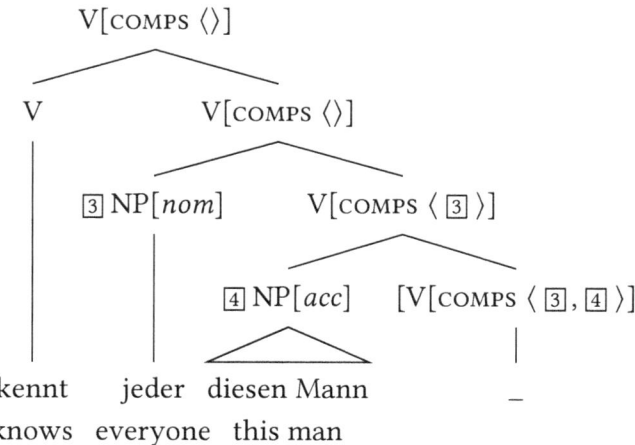

Figure 9.10: Analysis of *Kennt jeder diesen Mann?* 'Does everyone know this man?'

If we want to capture the fact that the finite verb in initial position behaves like a complementizer (Höhle 1997), then it makes sense to give head status to *kennt* in Figure 9.10 and have *kennt* select a saturated, verb-final verbal projection. Finite verbs in initial position differ from complementizers in that they require a projection of a verb trace, whereas complementizers need projections of overt verbs:

(48) a. dass [jeder   diesen Mann kennt]
        that everybody this   man   knows
        'that everybody knows this man'

    b. Kennt [jeder   diesen Mann _]
        knows everybody this   man
        'Does everybody know this man?'

It is normally not the case that *kennen* 'know' selects a complete sentence and nothing else as would be necessary for the analysis of *kennt* as the head in (48b). Furthermore, we must ensure that the verbal projection with which *kennt* is combined contains the verb trace belonging to *kennt*. If it could contain a trace belonging to *gibt* 'gives', for example, we would be able to analyze sentences such as (49b):

(49) a. Gibt [der Mann der Frau   das Buch $_{-gibt}$]?
        gives the man the woman the book
        'Does the man give the woman the book?'

    b. *Kennt [der Mann der Frau   das Buch $_{-gibt}$]?
        knows the man the woman the book

In the preceding discussion, the dependency between the fronted verb and the verb trace was expressed by coindexation. In HPSG, identity is always enforced by structure sharing. The verb in initial position must therefore require that the trace has exactly those properties of the verb that the verb would have had, were it in final position. The information that must be shared is therefore all locally relevant syntactic and semantic information, that is, all information under LOCAL. Since PHON is not part of the LOCAL features, it is not shared and this is why the PHON values of the trace and verb can differ. Up to now, one crucial detail has been missing in the analysis: the LOCAL value of the trace cannot be directly structure-shared with a requirement of the initial verb since the verb *kennt* can only select the properties of the projection of the trace and the COMPS list of the selected projection is the empty list. This leads us to the problem that was pointed out in the discussion of (49b). It must therefore be ensured that all information about the verb trace is available on the highest node of its projection. This can be achieved by introducing a head feature whose value is identical to the LOCAL value of the trace. This feature is referred to as DSL. As was already mentioned above, DSL stands for *double slash*. It is called so because it has a similar function to the SLASH feature, which we will encounter in the following section.[17] (50) shows the modified entry for the verb trace:

(50) Verb trace of *kennt* (preliminary version):

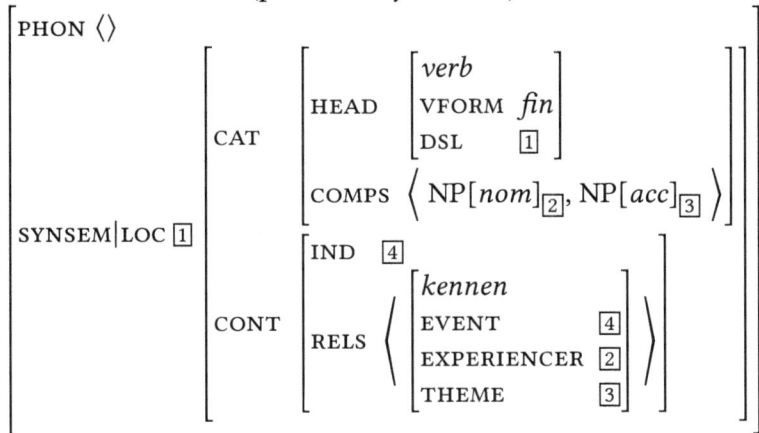

Through sharing of the LOCAL value and the DSL value in (50), the syntactic and semantic information of the verb trace is present at its maximal projection, and the verb in initial position can check whether the projection of the trace is compatible.[18]

---

[17]The feature DSL was proposed by Jacobson (1987a) in the framework of Categorial Grammar to describe head movement in English inversions. Borsley (1989) adopted this idea and translated it into HPSG terms, thereby showing how head movement in a HPSG variant of the CP/IP system can be modeled using DSL. The introduction of the DSL feature to describe head movement processes in HPSG is motivated by the fact that, unlike long-distance dependencies as will be discussed in Section 9.5, this kind of movement is local.

The suggestion to percolate information about the verb trace as part of the head information comes from Oliva (1992).

[18]Note that the description in (50) is cyclic since the tag 1 is used inside itself. See Section 6.5 on cyclic feature descriptions. This cyclic description is the most direct way to express that a linguistic object with certain local properties is missing and to pass this information on along the head path as the value of the DSL feature. This will be even clearer when we look at the final version of the verb trace in (52) on page 295.

The special lexical item for verb-initial position is licensed by the following lexical rule:[19]

(51) Lexical rule for verbs in initial position:

$$
\begin{bmatrix} \text{SYNSEM}|\text{LOC} & \boxed{1} & \begin{bmatrix} \text{CAT}|\text{HEAD} & \begin{bmatrix} \textit{verb} \\ \text{VFORM} & \textit{fin} \\ \text{INITIAL} & - \end{bmatrix} \end{bmatrix} \end{bmatrix} \mapsto
$$

$$
\begin{bmatrix} \text{SYNSEM}|\text{LOC}|\text{CAT} & \begin{bmatrix} \text{HEAD} & \begin{bmatrix} \textit{verb} \\ \text{VFORM} & \textit{fin} \\ \text{INITIAL} & + \\ \text{DSL} & \textit{none} \end{bmatrix} \\ \text{COMPS} & \left\langle \begin{bmatrix} \text{LOC}|\text{CAT} & \begin{bmatrix} \text{HEAD} & \begin{bmatrix} \textit{verb} \\ \text{DSL} & \boxed{1} \end{bmatrix} \\ \text{COMPS} & \langle\rangle \end{bmatrix} \end{bmatrix} \right\rangle \end{bmatrix} \end{bmatrix}
$$

The verb licensed by this lexical rule selects a maximal projection of the verb trace which has the same local properties as the input verb. This is achieved by the coindexation of the LOCAL values of the input verb and the DSL values of the selected verb projection. Only finite verbs in final position (INITIAL−) can be the input for this rule. The output is a verb in initial-position (INITIAL+). The corresponding extended analysis is given in Figure 9.11 on the next page. V1-LR stands for the verb-initial lexical rule. The lexical rule in (51) licenses a verb that selects a VP (boxed{1} in Figure 9.11). The DSL value of this VP corresponds to the LOCAL value of the verb that is the input of the lexical rule. Part of the DSL value is also the valence information represented in Figure 9.11 (boxed{2}). Since DSL is a head feature, the DSL value of the VP is identical to that of the verb trace and since the LOCAL value of the verb trace is identified with the DSL value, the COMPS information of the verb *kennen* is also available at the trace. The combination of the trace with its arguments proceeds exactly as with an ordinary verb.

It would be unsatisfactory if we had to assume a special trace for every verb. Fortunately, this is not necessary as a general trace as in (52) will suffice for the analysis of sentences with verb movement.

---

[19] The lexical rule analysis cannot explain sentences such as (i):

(i) Karl kennt und liebt diese Schallplatte.
Karl knows and loves this record

This has to do with the fact that the lexical rule cannot be applied to the result of coordination, which constitutes a complex syntactic object. If we apply the lexical rule individually to each verb, then we arrive at variants of the verbs which would each select verb traces for *kennen* 'to know' and *lieben* 'to love'. Since the CAT values of the conjuncts are identified with each other in coordinations, coordinations involving the V1 variants of *kennt* and *liebt* would be ruled out since the DSL values of the selected VPs contain the meaning of the respective verbs and are hence not compatible (Müller 2005b: 13). Instead of a lexical rule, one must assume a unary syntactic rule that applies to the phrase *kennt und liebt* 'knows and loves'. As we have seen, lexical rules in the HPSG formalization assumed here correspond to unary rules such that the difference between (51) and a corresponding syntactic rule is mostly a difference in representation.

9.3 Verb position

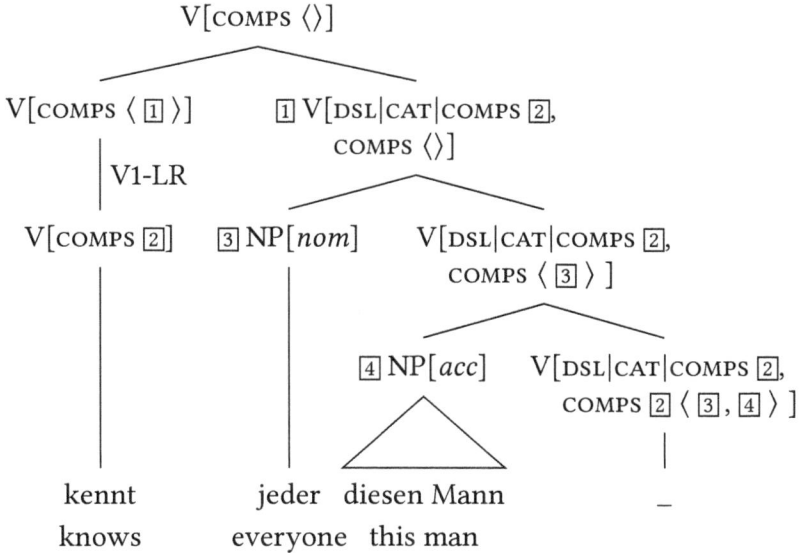

Figure 9.11: Visualization of the analysis of *Kennt jeder diesen Mann?* 'Does everyone know this man?'

(52) General verb trace following Meurers (2000: 206–208):
$$\begin{bmatrix} \text{PHON} \; \langle \rangle \\ \text{SYNSEM}|\text{LOC} \; \boxed{1} \; \begin{bmatrix} \text{CAT}|\text{HEAD}|\text{DSL} \; \boxed{1} \end{bmatrix} \end{bmatrix}$$

This may seem surprising at first glance, but if we look closer at the interaction of the lexical rule (51) and the percolation of the DSL feature in the tree, then it becomes clear that the DSL value of the verb projection and therefore the LOCAL value of the verb trace is determined by the LOCAL value of the input verb. In Figure 9.11, *kennt* is the input for the verb movement lexical rule. The relevant structure sharing ensures that, in the analysis of (46), the LOCAL value of the verb trace corresponds exactly to what is given in (50).

The most important points of the analysis of verb position are summarized below:

- A lexical rule licenses a special lexical item for each finite verb.
- This lexical item occupies the initial position and requires as its argument a complete projection of a verb trace.
- The projection of the verb trace must have a DSL value corresponding to the LOCAL value of the input verb of the lexical rule.
- Since DSL is a head feature, the selected DSL value is also present on the trace.
- As the DSL value of the trace is identical to its LOCAL value, the LOCAL value of the trace is identical to the LOCAL value of the input verb in the lexical rule.

After discussing the analysis of verb-first sentences, we will now turn to local reordering.

295

9.4 Local reordering

There are several possibilities for the analysis of constituent order in the middle field: one can assume completely flat structures as in GPSG (Kasper 1994; Bouma & van Noord 1998), or instead assume binary branching structures and allow for arguments to be saturated in any order. A compromise was proposed by Kathol (2001) and Müller (1999b; 2002a; 2004d): binary branching structures with a special list that contains the arguments and adjuncts belonging to one head. The arguments and adjuncts are allowed to be freely ordered inside such lists. See Reape (1994) and Section 11.7.2.2 of this book for the formal details of these approaches. Both the completely flat analysis and the compromise have proved to be on the wrong track (see Müller 2005b; 2014c and Müller 2007a: Section 9.5.1) and therefore, I will only discuss the analysis with binary branching structures.

Figure 9.12 shows the analysis of (53a).

(53) a. [weil] jeder diesen Mann kennt
     because everyone this man knows

 b. [weil] diesen Mann jeder kennt
     because this man everyone knows

'because everyone knows this man'

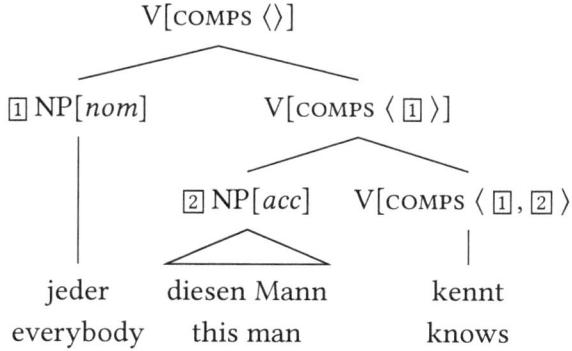

Figure 9.12: Analysis of constituent order in HPSG: unmarked order

The arguments of the verb are combined with the verb starting with the last element of the COMPS list, as explained in Section 9.1.2. The analysis of the marked order is shown in Figure 9.13 on the next page. Both trees differ only in the order in which the elements are taken off from the COMPS list: in Figure 9.12, the last element of the COMPS list is discharged first and in Figure 9.13 the first one is.

The following schema is a revised version of the Head-Complement Schema:

Schema 3 (Head-Complement Schema (binary branching))

head-complement-phrase ⇒
$$\begin{bmatrix} \text{SYNSEM}|\text{LOC}|\text{CAT}|\text{COMPS } \boxed{1} \oplus \boxed{3} \\ \text{HEAD-DTR}|\text{SYNSEM}|\text{LOC}|\text{CAT}|\text{COMPS } \boxed{1} \oplus \langle \boxed{2} \rangle \oplus \boxed{3} \\ \text{NON-HEAD-DTRS } \langle\, [\, \text{SYNSEM } \boxed{2}\,]\, \rangle \end{bmatrix}$$

9.4 Local reordering

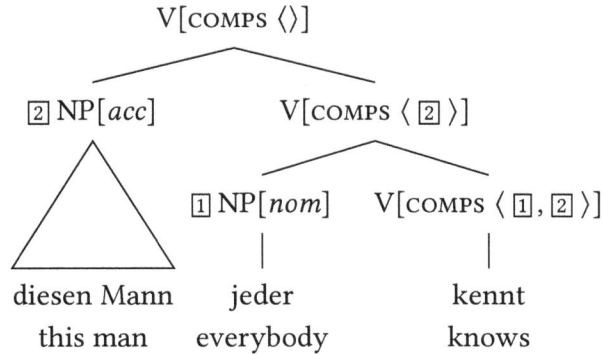

Figure 9.13: Analysis of constituent order in HPSG: marked order

Whereas in the first version of the Head-Complement Schema it was always the last element from the COMPS list that was combined with the head, the COMPS list is divided into three parts using *append*: a list of arbitrary length (1), a list consisting of exactly one element (⟨ 2 ⟩) and a further list of arbitrary length (3). The lists 1 and 3 are combined and the result is the COMPS value of the mother node.

Languages with fixed constituent order (such as English) differ from languages such as German in that they discharge the arguments starting from one side (for more on the subject in English, see Section 9.1.1), whereas languages with free constituent order can combine arguments with the verb in any order. In languages with fixed constituent order, either 1 or 3 is always the empty list. Since German structures are not restricted with regard to 1 or 3, that is 1 and 3 can either be the empty list or contain elements, the intuition is captured that there are less restrictions in languages with free constituent order than in languages with fixed order. We can compare this to the Kayneian analysis from Section 4.6.1, where it was assumed that all languages are derived from the base order [specifier [head complement]] (see Figure 4.20 on page 149 for Laenzlinger's analysis of German as an SVO-language (Laenzlinger 2004)). In these kinds of analyses, languages such as English constitute the most basic case and languages with free ordering require some considerable theoretical effort to get the order right. In comparison to that, the analysis proposed here requires more theoretical restrictions if the language has more restrictions on permutations of its constituents. The complexity of the licensed structures does not differ considerably from language to language under an HPSG approach. Languages differ only in the type of branching they have.[20, 21]

The analysis presented here utilizing the combination of arguments in any order is similar to that of Fanselow (2001) in the framework of GB/MP as well as the Categorial

---

[20]This does not exclude that the structures in question have different properties as far as their processability by humans is concerned. See Gibson (1998); Hawkins (1999) and Chapter 15.

[21]Haider (1997b: 18) has pointed out that the branching type of VX languages differs from those of XV languages in analyses of the kind that is proposed here. This affects the c-command relations and therefore has implications for Binding Theory in GB/MP. However, the direction of branching is irrelevant for HPSG analyses as Binding Principles are defined using o-command (Pollard & Sag 1994: Chapter 6) and o-command makes reference to the Obliqueness Hierarchy, that is, the order of elements in the COMPS list rather than the order in which these elements are combined with the head.

Grammar analyses of Hoffman (1995: Section 3.1) and Steedman & Baldridge (2006). Gunji proposed similar HPSG analyses for Japanese as early as 1986. See also Kim (2016: 16) for such an analysis of Korean.

9.5 Long-distance dependencies

The analysis of long-distance dependencies utilizes techniques that were originally developed in GPSG: information about missing constituents is passed up the tree (or feature structure).[22] There is a trace at the position where the fronted element would normally occur. Figure 9.14 shows the analysis of (54).

(54) [Diesen Mann]$_j$ kennt$_i$ $\_j$ jeder $\_i$.
     this   man   knows   everyone

'Everyone knows this man.'

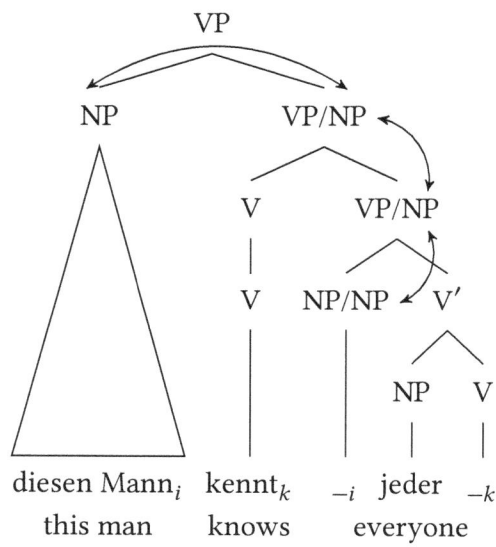

Figure 9.14: Analysis of long-distance dependencies in HPSG

In principle, one could also assume that the object is extracted from its unmarked position (see Section 3.5 on the unmarked position). The extraction trace would then follow the subject:

---

[22]In HPSG, nothing is actually 'passed up' in a literal sense in feature structures or trees. This could be seen as one of the most important differences between deterministic (e.g., HPSG) and derivational theories like transformational grammars (see Section 15.1). Nevertheless, it makes sense for expository purposes to explain the analysis as if the structure were built bottom-up, but linguistic knowledge is independent of the direction of processing. In recent computer implementations, structure building is mostly carried out bottom-up but there were other systems which worked top-down. The only thing that is important in the analysis of nonlocal dependencies is that the information about the missing element on all intermediate nodes is identical to the information in the filler and the gap.

(55) [Diesen Mann]_j kennt_i jeder _j _i.
    this man knows everyone
    'Everyone knows this man.'

Fanselow (2004c) argues that certain phrases can be placed in the Vorfeld without having a special pragmatic function. For instance, (expletive) subjects in active sentences (56a), temporal adverbials (56b), sentence adverbials (56c), dative objects of psychological verbs (56d) and objects in passives (56e) can be placed in the Vorfeld, even though they are neither topic nor focus.

(56) a. Es regnet.
        it rains
        'It rains.'

   b. Am Sonntag hat ein Eisbär einen Mann gefressen.
      on Sunday has a polar.bear a man eaten
      'On Sunday, a polar bear ate a man.'

   c. Vielleicht hat der Schauspieler seinen Text vergessen.
      perhaps has the actor his text forgotten
      'Perhaps, the actor has forgotton his text.'

   d. Einem Schauspieler ist der Text entfallen.
      a.DAT actor is the.NOM text forgotten
      'An actor forgot the text.'

   e. Einem Kind wurde das Fahrrad gestohlen.
      a.DAT child was the.NOM bike stolen
      'A bike was stolen from a child.'

Fanselow argues that information structural effects can be due to reordering in the Mittelfeld. So by ordering the accusative object as in (57), one can reach certain effects:

(57) Kennt diesen Mann jeder?
     knows this man everybody
     'Does everybody know this man?'

If one assumes that there are frontings to the *Vorfeld* that do not have information structural constraints attached to them and that information structural constraints are associated with reorderings in the Mittelfeld, then the assumption that the initial element in the Mittelfeld is fronted explains why the examples in (56) are not information structurally marked. The elements in the Vorfeld are unmarked in the initial position in the Mittelfeld as well:

(58) a. Regnet es?
        rains it
        'Does it rain?'

b. Hat am Sonntag ein Eisbär einen Mann gefressen?
   has on Sunday a polar.bear a man eaten
   'Did a polar bear eat a man on Sunday?'

c. Hat vielleicht der Schauspieler seinen Text vergessen?
   has perhaps the actor his text forgotten
   'Has the actor perhaps forgotton his text?'

d. Ist einem Schauspieler der Text entfallen?
   is a.DAT actor the.NOM text forgotten
   'Did an actor forget the text?'

e. Wurde einem Kind das Fahrrad gestohlen?
   was a.DAT child the.NOM bike stolen
   'Was a bike stolen from a child?'

So, I assume that the trace of a fronted argument that would not be Mittelfeld-initial in the unmarked order is combined with the head last, as described in Section 9.4. Of course, the same applies to all extracted arguments that would be Mittelfeld-initial in the unmarked order anyway: the traces are combined last with the head as for instance in (59):

(59) [Jeder]$_j$ kennt$_i$ _$_j$ diesen Mann _$_i$.
     everybody knows this man
     'Everyone knows this man.'

After this rough characterization of the basic idea, we now turn to the technical details: unlike verb movement, which was discussed in Section 9.3, constituent movement is nonlocal, which is why the two movement types are modeled with different features (SLASH vs. DSL). DSL is a head feature and, like all other head features, projects to the highest node of a projection (for more on the Head Feature Principle, see page 276). SLASH, on the other hand, is a feature that belongs to the NONLOC features represented under SYNSEM|NONLOC. The value of the NONLOC feature is a structure with the features INHERITED (or INHER for short) and TO-BIND. The value of INHER is a structure containing information about elements involved in a long-distance dependency. (60) gives the structure assumed by Pollard & Sag (1994: 163):[23]

(60) $\begin{bmatrix} nonloc \\ \text{QUE} & \textit{list of npros} \\ \text{REL} & \textit{list of indices} \\ \text{SLASH} & \textit{list of local structures} \end{bmatrix}$

QUE is important for the analysis of interrogative clauses as is REL for the analysis of relative clauses. Since these will not feature in this book, they will be omitted in what follows. The value of SLASH is a list of *local* objects.

---

[23]Pollard & Sag assume that the values of QUE, REL, and SLASH are sets rather than lists. The math behind sets is rather complicated, which is why I assume lists here.

As with the analysis of verb movement, it is assumed that there is a trace in the position where the accusative object would normally occur and that this trace shares the properties of that object. The verb can therefore satisfy its valence requirements locally. Information about whether there has been combination with a trace and not with a genuine argument is represented inside the complex sign and passed upward in the tree. The long-distance dependency can then be resolved by an element in the prefield higher in the tree.

Long-distance dependencies are introduced by the trace, which has a feature corresponding to the LOCAL value of the required argument in its SLASH list. (61) shows the description of the trace as is required for the analysis of (54):

(61) Trace of the accusative object of *kennen* (preliminary):

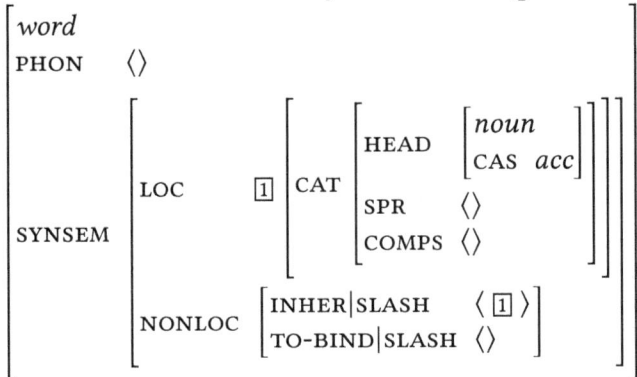

Since traces do not have internal structure (no daughters), they are of type *word*. The trace has the same properties as the accusative object. The fact that the accusative object is not present at the position occupied by the trace is represented by the value of SLASH.

The following principle is responsible for ensuring that NONLOC information is passed up the tree.

Principle 3 (Nonlocal Feature Principle)
In a headed phrase, for each nonlocal feature, the INHERITED *value of the mother is a list that is the concatenation of the* INHERITED *values of the daughters minus the elements in the* TO-BIND *list of the head daughter.*

The Head-Filler Schema (Schema 4) licenses the highest node in Figure 9.15 on the next page. The schema combines a finite, verb-initial clause (INITIAL+) that has an element in SLASH with a non-head daughter whose LOCAL value is identical to the SLASH element. In this structure, no arguments are saturated. Nothing can be extracted from the filler daughter itself, which is ensured by the specification of the SLASH value of the non-head daughter. Figure 9.15 shows a more detailed variant of the analysis of fronting to the prefield. The verb movement trace for *kennt* 'knows' is combined with a nominative NP and an extraction trace. The extraction trace stands for the accusative object in our example. The accusative object is described in the COMPS list of the verb (4). Following the mechanism for verb movement, the valence information that was originally contained

9 Head-Driven Phrase Structure Grammar

Schema 4 (Head-Filler Schema)

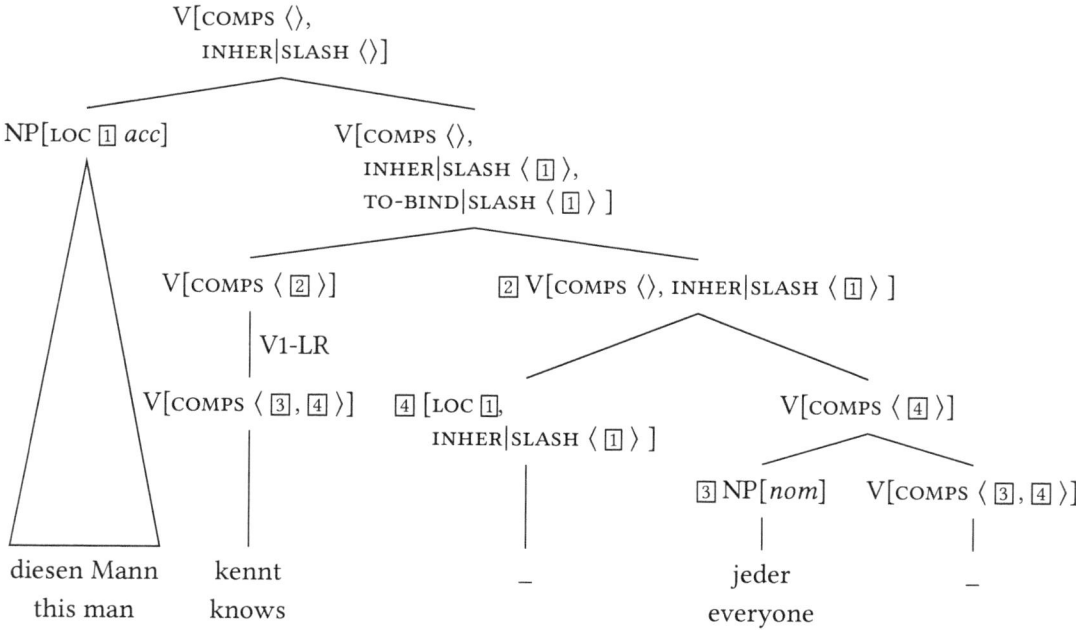

Figure 9.15: Analysis of *Diesen Mann kennt jeder.* 'Everyone knows this man.' combined with the verb movement analysis for verb-initial order

in the entry for *kennt* (⟨ 3 , 4 ⟩) is present on the verb trace. The combination of the projection of the verb trace with the extraction trace works in exactly the same way as for non-fronted arguments. The SLASH value of the extraction trace is passed up the tree and bound off by the Head-Filler Schema.

(61) provides the lexical entry for a trace that can function as the accusative object of *kennen* 'to know'. As with the analysis of verb movement, it is not necessary to have numerous extraction traces with differing properties listed in the lexicon. A more general entry such as the one in (62) will suffice:

(62) Extraction trace:
$$\begin{bmatrix} word \\ \text{PHON} \quad \langle\rangle \\ \text{SYNSEM} \begin{bmatrix} \text{LOC} & \boxed{1} \\ \text{NONLOC} & \begin{bmatrix} \text{INHER}|\text{SLASH} & \langle \boxed{1} \rangle \\ \text{TO-BIND}|\text{SLASH} & \langle\rangle \end{bmatrix} \end{bmatrix} \end{bmatrix}$$

This has to do with the fact that the head can satisfactorily determine the LOCAL properties of its arguments and therefore also the local properties of the traces that it combines with. The identification of the object in the COMPS list of the head with the SYNSEM value of the trace coupled with the identification of the information in SLASH with information about the fronted element serves to ensure that the only elements that can be realized in the prefield are those that fit the description in the COMPS list of the head. The same holds for fronted adjuncts: since the LOCAL value of the constituent in the prefield is identified with the LOCAL value of the trace via the SLASH feature, there is then sufficient information available about the properties of the trace.

The central points of the preceding analysis can be summarized as follows: information about the local properties of a trace is contained in the trace itself and then present on all nodes dominating it until one reaches the filler. This analysis can offer an explanation for so-called extraction path marking languages where certain elements show inflection depending on whether they are combined with a constituent out of which something has been extracted in a long-distance dependency. Bouma, Malouf & Sag (2001) cite Irish, Chamorro, Palauan, Icelandic, Kikuyu, Ewe, Thompson Salish, Moore, French, Spanish, and Yiddish as examples of such languages and provide corresponding references. Since information is passed on step-by-step in HPSG analyses, all nodes intervening in a long-distance dependency can access the elements in that dependency.

9.6 New developments and theoretical variants

The schemata that were presented in this chapter combine adjacent constituents. The assumption of adjacency can be dropped and discontinuous constituents maybe permitted. Variants of HPSG that allow for discontinuous constituents are usually referred to as *Linearization-based HPSG*. The first formalization was developed by Mike Reape

(1991; 1992; 1994). Proponents of linearization approaches are for instance Kathol (1995; 2000); Donohue & Sag (1999); Richter & Sailer (1999b); Crysmann (2008); Beavers & Sag (2004); Sato (2006); Wetta (2011). I also suggested linearization-based analyses (Müller 1999b; 2002a) and implemented a large-scale grammar fragment based on Reape's ideas (Müller 1996c). Linearization-based approaches to the German sentence structure are similar to the GPSG approach in that it is assumed that verb and arguments and adjuncts are members of the same linearization domain and hence may be realized in any order. For instance, the verb may precede arguments and adjuncts or follow them. Hence, no empty element for the verb in final position is necessary. While this allows for grammars without empty elements for the analysis of the verb position, it is unclear how examples with apparent multiple frontings can be accounted for, while such data can be captured directly in the proposal suggested in this chapter. The whole issue is discussed in more detail in Müller (2017a). I will not explain Reape's formalization here, but defer its discussion until Section 11.7.2.2, where the discontinuous, non-projective structures of some Dependency Grammars are compared to linearization-based HPSG approaches. Apparent multiple frontings and the problems they pose for simple linearization-based approaches are discussed in Section 11.7.1.

9.7 Summary and classification

In HPSG, feature descriptions are used to model all properties of linguistic objects: roots, words, lexical rules and dominance schemata are all described using the same formal tools. Unlike GPSG and LFG, there are no separate phrase structure rules. Thus, although HPSG stands for Head-Driven Phrase Structure Grammar, it is not a phrase structure grammar. In HPSG implementations, a phrase structure backbone is often used to increase the efficiency of processing. However, this is not part of the theory and linguistically not necessary.

HPSG differs from Categorial Grammar in that it assumes considerably more features and also in that the way in which features are grouped plays an important role for the theory.

Long-distance dependencies are not analyzed using function composition as in Categorial Grammar, but instead as in GPSG by appealing to the percolation of information in the tree. In this way, it is possible to analyze pied-piping constructions such as those discussed in Section 8.6 with just one lexical item per relative pronoun, whose relevant local properties are identical to those of the demonstrative pronoun. The relative clause in (63) would be analyzed as a finite clause from which a PP has been extracted:

(63)   der Mann, [$_{RS}$ [$_{PP}$ an den] [$_{S/PP}$ wir gedacht haben]]
         the man   on who   we thought have
         'the man we thought of'

For relative clauses, it is required that the first daughter contains a relative pronoun. This can, as shown in the English examples on page 258, be in fact very deeply embedded. Information about the fact that *an den* 'of whom' contains a relative pronoun is provided

in the lexical entry for the relative pronoun *den* by specifying the value of NONLOC|
INHER|REL. The Nonlocal Feature Principle passes this information on upwards so that
the information about the relative pronoun is contained in the representation of the
phrase *an den*. This information is bound off when the relative clause is put together
(Pollard & Sag 1994: Chapter 5; Sag 1997). It is possible to use the same lexical entry for
den in the analyses of both (63) and (64) as – unlike in Categorial Grammar – the relative
pronoun does not have to know anything about the contexts in which it can be used.

(64) der Mann, [RS [NP den] [S/NP wir kennen]]
 the man that we know
 'the man that we know'

Any theory that wants to maintain the analysis sketched here will have to have some
mechanism to make information available about the relative pronoun in a complex
phrase. If we have such a mechanism in our theory – as is the case in LFG and HPSG –
then we can also use it for the analysis of long-distance dependencies. Theories such as
LFG and HPSG are therefore more parsimonious with their descriptive tools than other
theories when it comes to the analysis of relative phrases.

In the first decade of HPSG history (Pollard & Sag 1987; 1994; Nerbonne, Netter &
Pollard 1994), despite the differences already mentioned here, HPSG was still very similar to Categorial Grammar in that it was a strongly lexicalized theory. The syntactic
make-up and semantic content of a phrase was determined by the head (hence the term
head-driven). In cases where head-driven analyses were not straight-forwardly possible,
because no head could be identified in the phrase in question, then it was commonplace
to assume empty heads. An example of this is the analysis of relative clauses in Pollard
& Sag (1994: Chapter 5). Since an empty head can be assigned any syntactic valence and
an arbitrary semantics (for discussion of this point, see Chapter 19), one has not really
explained anything as one needs very good reasons for assuming an empty head, for
example that this empty position can be realized in other contexts. This is, however,
not the case for empty heads that are only proposed in order to save theoretical assumptions. Therefore, Sag (1997) developed an analysis of relative clauses without any empty
elements. As in the analyses sketched for (63) and (64), the relative phrases are combined directly with the partial clause in order to form the relative clause. For the various
observable types of relative clauses in English, Sag proposes different dominance rules.
His analysis constitutes a departure from strong lexicalism: in Pollard & Sag (1994), there
are six dominance schemata, whereas there are 23 in Ginzburg & Sag (2000).

The tendency to a differentiation of phrasal schemata can also be observed in the
proceedings of recent conferences. The proposals range from the elimination of empty
elements to radically phrasal analyses (Haugereid 2007; 2009).[24]

Even if this tendency towards phrasal analyses may result in some problematic analyses, it is indeed the case that there are areas of grammar where phrasal analyses are required (see Section 21.10). For HPSG, this means that it is no longer entirely head-driven
and is therefore neither Head-Driven nor Phrase Structure Grammar.

---

[24]For discussion, see Müller (2007b) and Section 21.3.6.

HPSG makes use of typed feature descriptions to describe linguistic objects. Generalizations can be expressed by means of hierarchies with multiple inheritance. Inheritance also plays an important role in Construction Grammar. In theories such as GPSG, Categorial Grammar and TAG, it does not form part of theoretical explanations. In implementations, macros (abbreviations) are often used for co-occurring feature-value pairs (Dalrymple, Kaplan & King 2004). Depending on the architecture assumed, such macros are not suitable for the description of phrases since, in theories such as GPSG and LFG, phrase structure rules are represented differently from other feature-value pairs (however, see Asudeh, Dalrymple & Toivonen (2008; 2013) for macros and inheritance used for c-structure annotations). Furthermore, there are further differences between types and macros, which are of a more formal nature: in a typed system, it is possible under certain conditions to infer the type of a particular structure from the presence of certain features and of certain values. With macros, this is not the case as they are only abbreviations. The consequences for linguistic analyses made by this differences are, however, minimal.

HPSG differs from GB theory and later variants in that it does not assume transformations. In the 80s, representational variants of GB were proposed, that is, it was assumed that there was no D-structure from which an S-structure is created by simultaneous marking of the original position of moved elements. Instead, one assumed the S-structure with traces straight away and the assumption that there were further movements in the mapping of S-structure to Logical Form was also abandoned (Koster 1978; Haider 1993: Section 1.4; Frey 1993: 14). This view corresponds to the view in HPSG and many of the analyses in one framework can be translated into the other.

In GB theory, the terms subject and object do not play a direct role: one can use these terms descriptively, but subjects and objects are not marked by features or similar devices. Nevertheless it is possible to make the distinction since subjects and objects are usually realized in different positions in the trees (the subject in specifier position of IP and the object as the complement of the verb). In HPSG, subject and object are also not primitives of the theory. Since valence lists (or ARG-ST lists) are ordered, however, this means that it is possible to associate the ARG-ST elements to grammatical functions: if there is a subject, this occurs in the first position of the valence list and objects follow.[25] For the analysis of (65b) in a transformation-based grammar, the aim is to connect the base order in (65a) and the derived order in (65b). Once one has recreated the base order, then it is clear what is the subject and what is the object. Therefore, transformations applied to the base structure in (65a) have to be reversed.

(65)   a.   [weil]   jeder   diesen Mann kennt
               because everyone this   man   knows
               'because everyone knows this man'
       b.   [weil]   diesen Mann jeder   kennt
               because this   man   everyone knows

---

[25]When forming complex predicates, an object can occur in first position. See Müller (2002a: 157) for the long passive with verbs such as *erlauben* 'allow'. In general, the following holds: the subject is the first argument with structural case.

9.7 Summary and classification

In HPSG and also in other transformation-less models, the aim is to assign arguments in the order in (65b) to descriptions in the valence list. The valence list (or ARG-ST in newer approaches) corresponds in a sense to Deep Structure in GB. The difference is that the head itself is not included in the argument structure, whereas this is the case with D-structure.

Bender (2008c) has shown how one can analyze phenomena from non-configurational languages such as Wambaya by referring to the argument structure of a head. In Wambaya, words that would normally be counted as constituents in English or German can occur discontinuously, that is an adjective that semantically belongs to a noun phrase and shares the same case, number and gender values with other parts of the noun phrase can occur in a position in the sentence that is not adjacent to the remaining noun phrase. Nordlinger (1998) has analyzed the relevant data in LFG. In her analysis, the various parts of the constituent refer to the f-structure of the sentence and thus indirectly ensure that all parts of the noun phrase have the same case. Bender adopts a variant of HPSG where valence information is not removed from the valence list after an argument has been combined with its head, but rather this information remains in the valence list and is passed up towards the maximal projection of the head (Meurers 1999c; Przepiórkowski 1999b; Müller 2007a: Section 17.4). Similar proposals were made in GB by Higginbotham (1985: 560) and Winkler (1997). By projecting the complete valence information, it remains accessible in the entire sentence and discontinuous constituents can refer to it (e.g., via MOD) and the respective constraints can be formulated.[26] In this analysis, the argument structure in HPSG corresponds to f-structure in LFG. The extended head domains of LFG, where multiple heads can share the same f-structure, can also be modeled in HPSG. To this end, one can utilize function composition as it was presented in the chapter on Categorial Grammar (see Chapter 8.5.2). The exact way in which this is translated into HPSG cannot be explained here due to space restrictions. The reader is referred to the original works by Hinrichs & Nakazawa (1994) and the explanation in Müller (2007a: Chapter 15).

Valence information plays an important role in HPSG. The lexical item of a verb in principle predetermines the set of structures in which the item can occur. Using lexical rules, it is possible to relate one lexical item to other lexical items. These can be used in other sets of structures. So one can see the functionality of lexical rules in establishing a relation between sets of possible structures. Lexical rules correspond to transformations in Transformational Grammar. This point is discussed in more detail in Section 19.5. The effect of lexical rules can also be achieved with empty elements. This will also be the matter of discussion in Section 19.5.

In GPSG, metarules were used to license rules that created additional valence patterns for lexical heads. In principle, metarules could also be applied to rules without a lexical head. This is explicitly ruled out by Flickinger (1983) and Gazdar et al. (1985: 59) using a special constraint. Flickinger, Pollard & Wasow (1985: 265) pointed out that this kind of

---

[26] See also Müller (2008) for an analysis of depictive predicates in German and English that makes reference to the list of realized or unrealized arguments of a head, respectively. This analysis is also explained in Section 18.2.

constraint is unnecessary if one uses lexical rules rather than metarules since the former can only be applied to lexical heads.

For a comparison of HPSG and Stabler's Minimalist Grammars, see Section 4.6.4.

Comprehension questions

1. What status do syntactic trees have in HPSG?

2. How does case assignment take place in the analysis of example (66)?

    (66) Dem   Mann wurde ein   Buch geschenkt.
         the.DAT man was   a.NOM book given
         'The man was given a book.'

3. What is *linking* and how is it accounted for in HPSG?

Exercises

1. Give a feature description for (67) ignoring *dass*.

    (67) [dass] Max lacht
         that   Max laughs

2. The analysis of the combination of a noun with a modifying adjective in Section 9.1.7 was just a sketch of an analysis. It is, for example, not explained how one can ensure that the adjective and noun agree in case. Consider how it would be possible to expand such an analysis so that the adjective-noun combination in (68a) can be analyzed, but not the one in (68b):

    (68) a. eines interessanten   Mannes
              an.GEN interesting.GEN man.GEN

          b. *eines interessanter   Mannes
              an.GEN interesting.NOM man.GEN

Further reading

Here, the presentation of the individual parts of the theory was – as with other theories – kept relatively short. For a more comprehensive introduction to HPSG, including motivation of the feature geometry, see Müller (2007a). In particular, the analysis of the passive was sketched in brief here. The entire story including the analysis of unaccusative verbs, adjectival participles, modal infinitives as well as diverse passive variants and the long passive can be found in Müller (2002a: Chapter 3) and Müller (2007a: Chapter 17).

Overviews of HPSG can be found in Levine & Meurers (2006), Przepiórkowski & Kupść (2006), Bildhauer (2014) and Müller (2015a).

Müller (2014b) and Müller & Machicao y Priemer (2019) are two papers in collections comparing frameworks. The first one is in German and contains an analysis of a newspaper text.[a] The second one is in English and contains a general description of the framework and a detailed analysis of the sentence in (69):[b]

(69) After Mary introduced herself to the audience, she turned to a man that she had met before.

The books are similar to this one in that the respective authors describe a shared set of phenomena within their favorite theories but the difference is that the descriptions come straight from the horse's mouth. Especially the newspaper text is interesting since for some theories it was the first time for them to be applied to real live data. As a result of this one sees phenomena covered that are rarely treated in the rest of the literature.

---

[a] See https://hpsg.hu-berlin.de/~stefan/Pub/artenvielfalt.html for the example sentences and some interactive analyses of the examples.

[b] See https://hpsg.hu-berlin.de/~stefan/Pub/current-approaches-hpsg.html for an interactive analysis of the example.

10 Construction Grammar

Like LFG and HPSG, *Construction Grammar* (CxG) forms part of West Coast linguistics. It has been influenced considerably by Charles Fillmore, Paul Kay and George Lakoff (all three at Berkeley) and Adele Goldberg (who completed her PhD in Berkeley and is now in Princeton) (Fillmore 1988; Fillmore, Kay & O'Connor 1988; Kay & Fillmore 1999; Kay 2002; 2005; Goldberg 1995; 2006).

Fillmore, Kay, Jackendoff and others have pointed out the fact that, to a large extent, languages consist of complex units that cannot straightforwardly be described with the tools that we have seen thus far. In frameworks such as GB, an explicit distinction is made between core grammar and the periphery (Chomsky 1981a: 8), whereby the periphery is mostly disregarded as uninteresting when formulating a theory of Universal Grammar. The criticism leveled at such practices by CxG is justified since what counts as the 'periphery' sometimes seems completely arbitrary (Müller 2014d) and no progress is made by excluding large parts of the language from the theory just because they are irregular to a certain extent.

In Construction Grammar, idiomatic expressions are often discussed with regard to their interaction with regular areas of grammar. Kay & Fillmore (1999) studied the *What's X doing Y?*-construction in their classic essay. (1) contains some examples of this construction:

(1) a. What is this scratch doing on the table?
    b. What do you think your name is doing in my book?

The examples show that we are clearly not dealing with the normal meaning of the verb *do*. As well as the semantic bleaching here, there are particular morphosyntactic properties that have to be satisfied in this construction. The verb *do* must always be present and also in the form of the present participle. Kay and Fillmore develop an analysis explaining this construction and also capturing some of the similarities between the WXDY-construction and the rest of the grammar.

There are a number of variants of Construction Grammar:

- Berkeley Construction Grammar (Fillmore 1988; Kay & Fillmore 1999; Fried 2015)
- Goldbergian/Lakovian Construction Grammar (Lakoff 1987; Goldberg 1995; 2006)
- Cognitive Grammar (Langacker 1987; 2000; 2008; Dąbrowska 2004)
- Radical Construction Grammar (Croft 2001)
- Embodied Construction Grammar (Bergen & Chang 2005)

- Fluid Construction Grammar (Steels & De Beule 2006; Steels 2011)
- Sign-Based Construction Grammar (Sag 2010; 2012)

The aim of Construction Grammar is to both describe and theoretically explore language in its entirety. In practice, however, irregularities in language are often given far more importance than the phenomena described as 'core grammar' in GB. Construction Grammar analyses usually analyze phenomena as phrasal patterns. These phrasal patterns are represented in inheritance hierarchies (e.g., Croft 2001; Goldberg 2003b). An example for the assumption of a phrasal construction is Goldberg's analysis of resultative constructions. Goldberg (1995) and Goldberg & Jackendoff (2004) argue for the construction status of resultatives. In their view, there is no head in (2) that determines the number of arguments.

(2) Willy watered the plants flat.

The number of arguments is determined by the construction instead, that is, by a rule or schema saying that the subject, verb, object and a predicative element must occur together and that the entire complex has a particular meaning. This view is fundamentally different from analyses in GB, Categorial Grammar, LFG[1] and HPSG. In the aforementioned theories, it is commonly assumed that arguments are always selected by lexical heads and not independently licensed by phrasal rules. See Simpson (1983), Neeleman (1994), Wunderlich (1997), Wechsler (1997), and Müller (2002a) for corresponding work in LFG, GB, Wunderlich's Lexical Decomposition Grammar and HPSG.

Like the theories discussed in Chapters 5–9, CxG is also a non-transformational theory. Furthermore, no empty elements are assumed in most variants of the theory and the assumption of lexical integrity is maintained as in LFG and HPSG. It can be shown that these assumptions are incompatible with phrasal analyses of resultative constructions (see Section 21.2.2 and Müller 2006; 2007b). This point will not be explained further here. Instead, I will discuss the work of Fillmore and Kay to prepare the reader to be able to read the original articles and subsequent publications. Although the literature on Construction Grammar is now relatively vast, there is very little work on the basic formal assumptions or analyses that have been formalized precisely. Examples of more formal works are Kay & Fillmore (1999), Kay (2002), Michaelis & Ruppenhofer (2001), and Goldberg (2003b). Another formal proposal was developed by Jean-Pierre Koenig (1999) (formerly Berkeley). This work is couched in the framework of HPSG, but it has been heavily influenced by CxG. Fillmore and Kay's revisions of their earlier work took place in close collaboration with Ivan Sag. The result was a variant of HPSG known as Sign-Based Construction Grammar (SBCG) (Sag 2010; 2012). See Section 10.6.2 for further discussion.

John Bryant, Nancy Chang, Eva Mok have developed a system for the implementation of Embodied Construction Grammar[2]. Luc Steels is working on the simulation of language evolution and language acquisition (Steels 2003). Steels works experimentally

---

[1] See Alsina (1996) and Asudeh, Dalrymple & Toivonen (2008; 2013), however. For more discussion of this point, see Sections 21.1.3 and 21.2.2.
[2] See http://www.icsi.berkeley.edu/~jbryant/old-analyzer.html and Bryant (2003).

modeling virtual communities of interacting agents. Apart from this he uses robots that interact in language games (Steels 2015). In personal communication (p. c. 2007) Steels stated that it is a long way to go until robots finally will be able to learn to speak but the current state of the art is already impressive. Steels can use robots that have a visual system (camera and image processing) and use visual information paired with audio information in simulations of language acquisition. The implementation of Fluid Construction Grammar is documented in Steels (2011) and Steels (2012). The second book contains parts about German, in which the implementation of German declarative clauses and *w* interrogative clauses is explained with respect to topological fields (Micelli 2012). The FCG system, various publications and example analyses are available at: http://www.fcg-net.org/. Jurafsky (1996) developed a Construction Grammar for English that was paired with a probabilistic component. He showed that many performance phenomena discussed in the literature (see Chapter 15 on the Competence/Performance Distinction) can be explained with recourse to probabilities of phrasal constructions and valence properties of words. Bannard, Lieven & Tomasello (2009) use a probabilistic context-free grammar to model grammatical knowledge of two and three year old children.

Lichte & Kallmeyer (2017) show that their version of Tree-Adjoining Grammar can be seen as a formalization of several tenets of Construction Grammar. See for example the analysis of idioms explained in Figure 18.6 on page 562.

10.1 General remarks on the representational format

In this section, I will discuss the mechanisms of Berkeley Construction Grammar (BCG). As I pointed out in Müller (2006), there are fundamental problems with the formalization of BCG. The details will be given in Section 10.6.1. While the framework was developed further into Sign-Based Construction Grammar (see Section 10.6.2) by its creators Kay and Fillmore, there are still authors working in the original framework (for instance Fried 2013). I will therefore present the basic mechanisms here to make it possible to understand the original ideas and put them into a broader context.

As we saw in Section 9.1.2, dominance relations in HPSG are modeled like other properties of linguistic objects using feature-value pairs. In general, CxG uses feature-value pairs to describe linguistic objects, but dominance relations are represented by boxes (Kay & Fillmore 1999; Goldberg 2003b):

(3) $\begin{array}{|l|} \hline \text{phon} \langle \textit{the man} \rangle \\ \hline \begin{array}{|l|l|} \hline \text{phon} \langle \textit{the} \rangle & \text{phon} \langle \textit{man} \rangle \\ \hline \end{array} \\ \hline \end{array}$

The structure can be written using feature-value pairs as follows:

(4) $\begin{bmatrix} \text{PHON} & \langle \textit{the man} \rangle \\ \text{DTRS} & \langle\, [\, \text{PHON} \langle \textit{the} \rangle \,],\, [\, \text{PHON} \langle \textit{man} \rangle \,] \,\rangle \end{bmatrix}$

10 Construction Grammar

10.1.1 The head-complement construction

Kay & Fillmore (1999) assume the following construction for the combination of heads with their complements:

(5) Head plus Complements Construction (HC)

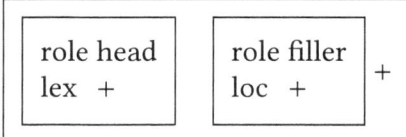

A head is combined with at least one complement (the '+' following the box stands for at least one sign that fits the description in that box). LOC+ means that this element must be realized locally. The value of ROLE tells us something about the role that a particular element plays in a construction. Unfortunately, here the term *filler* is used somewhat differently than in GPSG and HPSG. Fillers are not necessarily elements that stand in a long-distance dependency to a gap. Instead, a *filler* is a term for a constituent that fills the argument slot of a head.

The verb phrase construction is a sub-construction of the head-complement construction:

(6) Verb phrase Construction:

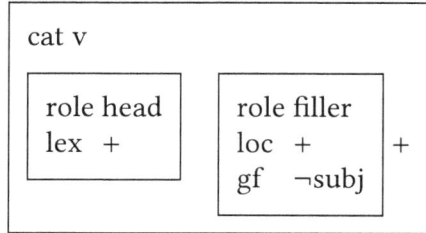

The syntactic category of the entire construction is V. Its complements cannot have the grammatical function subject.

The VP construction is a particular type of head-complement construction. The fact that it has much in common with the more general head-complement construction is represented as follows:

(7) Verb phrase Construction with inheritance statement:

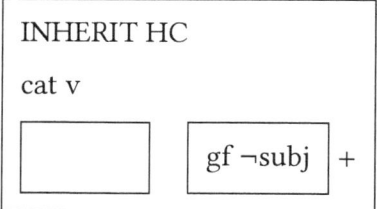

This representation differs from the one in HPSG, aside from the box notation, only in the fact that feature descriptions are not typed and as such it must be explicitly stated in the representation from which superordinate construction inheritance takes place. HPSG – in addition to the schemata – has separate type hierarchies specifying the inheritance relation between types.

10.1.2 Representation of valence information

In Kay and Fillmore, valence information is represented in a set (VAL). The Valence Principle states that local filler-daughters have to be identified with an element in the valence set of the mother.³ The Subset Principle states that the set values of the head-daughter are subsets of the corresponding sets of the mother. This is the exact opposite approach to the one taken in Categorial Grammar and HPSG. In HPSG grammars, valence lists at the mother nodes are shorter, whereas in Berkeley CxG at least as many elements are present on the mother node as on the head-daughter.

10.1.3 Semantics

Semantics in CxG is handled exactly the same way as in HPSG: semantic information is contained in the same feature structure as syntactic information. The relation between syntax and semantics is captured by using the same variable in the syntactic and semantic description. (8) contains a feature description for the verb *arrive*:

(8) Lexical entry for *arrive* following Kay & Fillmore (1999: 11):

$$\begin{bmatrix} \text{cat} & \text{v} \\ \text{sem} & \left\{ \begin{bmatrix} ^{\text{I}} \text{ FRAME } & \text{ARRIVE} \\ \text{ARGS} & \{A\} \end{bmatrix} \right\} \\ \text{val} & \{\,[\,\text{SEM}\,\{A\}\,]\,\} \end{bmatrix}$$

Kay & Fillmore (1999: 9) refer to their semantic representations as a notational variant of the Minimal Recursion Semantics of Copestake, Flickinger, Pollard & Sag (2005). In later works, Kay (2005) explicitly uses MRS. As the fundamentals of MRS have already been discussed in Section 9.1.6, I will not repeat them here. For more on MRS, see Section 19.3.

10.1.4 Adjuncts

For the combination of heads and modifiers, Kay and Fillmore assume further phrasal constructions that are similar to the verb phrase constructions discussed above and create a relation between a head and a modifier. Kay and Fillmore assume that adjuncts also contribute something to the VAL value of the mother node. In principle, VAL is nothing more than the set of all non-head daughters in a tree.

10.2 Passive

The passive has been described in CxG by means of so-called linking constructions, which are combined with lexical entries in inheritance hierarchies. In the base lexicon, it is only listed which semantic roles a verb fulfils and the way in which these are realized is determined by the respective linking constructions with which the basic lexical entry is combined. Figure 10.1 gives an example of a relevant inheritance hierarchy. There is

---

³Sets in BCG work differently from those used in HPSG. A discussion of this is deferred to Section 10.6.1.

10 Construction Grammar

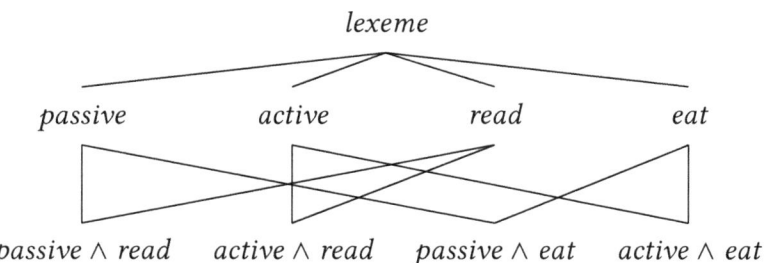

Figure 10.1: Passive and linking constructions

a linking construction for both active and passive as well as lexical entries for *read* and *eat*. There is then a cross-classification resulting in an active and a passive variant of each verb.

The idea behind this analysis goes back to work by Fillmore and Kay between 1995 and 1997[4], but variants of this analysis were first published in Koenig (1999: Chapter 3) and Michaelis & Ruppenhofer (2001: Chapter 4). Parallel proposals have been made in TAG (Candito 1996; Clément & Kinyon 2003: 188; Kallmeyer & Osswald 2012: 171–172) and HPSG (Koenig 1999; Davis & Koenig 2000; Kordoni 2001).

Michaelis & Ruppenhofer (2001: 55–57) provide the following linking constructions:[5]

(9)   a. *Transitive Construction*:
$$\begin{bmatrix} \text{SYN} & \begin{bmatrix} \text{CAT} & v \\ \text{VOICE} & active \end{bmatrix} \\ \text{VAL} & \left\{ \begin{bmatrix} \text{ROLE} & \begin{bmatrix} \text{GF} & obj \\ \text{DA} & - \end{bmatrix} \end{bmatrix} \right\} \end{bmatrix}$$

   b. the *Subject Construction*:
$$\begin{bmatrix} \text{SYN} & \begin{bmatrix} \text{CAT} & v \end{bmatrix} \\ \text{VAL} & \left\{ \begin{bmatrix} \text{ROLE} & \begin{bmatrix} \text{GF} & subj \end{bmatrix} \end{bmatrix} \right\} \end{bmatrix}$$

   c. the *Passive Construction*:
$$\begin{bmatrix} \text{SYN} & \begin{bmatrix} \text{CAT} & v \\ \text{FORM} & PastPart \end{bmatrix} \\ \text{VAL} & \left\{ \begin{bmatrix} \text{ROLE} & \begin{bmatrix} \text{GF} & obl \\ \text{DA} & + \end{bmatrix} \\ \text{SYN} & \text{P[von]}/zero \end{bmatrix} \right\} \end{bmatrix}$$

---

[4] http://www.icsi.berkeley.edu/~kay/bcg/ConGram.html. 2018-02-20.

[5] In the original version of the transitive construction in (9a), there is a feature θ that has the value DA−, however, DA is a feature itself and − is the value. I have corrected this in (9a) accordingly.

In the following structures, GF stands for *grammatical function* and DA for *distinguished argument*. The distinguished argument usually corresponds to the subject in an active clause.

10.2 Passive

The structure in (9a) says that the valence set of a linguistic object that is described by the transitive construction has to contain an element that has the grammatical function *object* and whose DA value is '−'. The DA value of the argument that would be the subject in an active clause is '+' and '−' for all other arguments. The subject construction states that an element of the valence set must have the grammatical function *subject*. In the passive construction, there has to be an element with the grammatical function *oblique* that also has the DA value '+'. In the passive construction the element with the DA value '+' is realized either as a *by*-PP or not at all (*zero*).

The interaction of the constructions in (9) will be explained on the basis of the verb *schlagen* 'to beat':

(10) Lexical entry for *schlag-* 'beat':
$$\begin{bmatrix} \text{SYN} & [\text{CAT} \;\; v] \\ \text{VAL} & \left\{ \begin{bmatrix} \text{ROLE} & \begin{bmatrix} \theta & agent \\ \text{DA} & + \end{bmatrix} \end{bmatrix}, \begin{bmatrix} \text{ROLE} & [\theta \;\; patient] \end{bmatrix} \right\} \end{bmatrix}$$

If we combine this lexical entry with the transitive and subject constructions, we arrive at (11a) following Fillmore, Kay, Michaelis, and Ruppenhofer, whereas combining it with the subject and passive construction yields (11b):[6]

(11) a. *schlag-* + Subject and Transitive Construction:
$$\begin{bmatrix} \text{SYN} & \begin{bmatrix} \text{CAT} & v \\ \text{VOICE} & active \end{bmatrix} \\ \text{VAL} & \left\{ \begin{bmatrix} \text{ROLE} & \begin{bmatrix} \theta & agent \\ \text{GF} & subj \\ \text{DA} & + \end{bmatrix} \end{bmatrix}, \begin{bmatrix} \text{ROLE} & \begin{bmatrix} \theta & patient \\ \text{GF} & obj \\ \text{DA} & - \end{bmatrix} \end{bmatrix} \right\} \end{bmatrix}$$

b. *schlag-* + Subject and Passive Construction:
$$\begin{bmatrix} \text{SYN} & \begin{bmatrix} \text{CAT} & v \\ \text{FORM} & PastPart \end{bmatrix} \\ \text{VAL} & \left\{ \begin{bmatrix} \text{ROLE} & \begin{bmatrix} \theta & agent \\ \text{GF} & obl \\ \text{DA} & + \end{bmatrix} \\ \text{SYN} & \text{P}[von]/zero \end{bmatrix}, \begin{bmatrix} \text{ROLE} & \begin{bmatrix} \theta & patient \\ \text{GF} & subj \end{bmatrix} \end{bmatrix} \right\} \end{bmatrix}$$

Using the entries in (11), it is possible to analyze the sentences in (12):

(12) a. Er schlägt den Weltmeister.
     he beats   the world.champion
     'He is beating the world champion.'

---

[6]This assumes a particular understanding of set unification. For criticism of this, see Section 10.6.1.

10 Construction Grammar

      b. Der Weltmeister wird (von ihm) geschlagen.
         the world.champion is by him beaten
      'The world champion is being beaten (by him).'

This analysis is formally inconsistent as set unification cannot be formalized in such a way that the aforementioned constructions can be unified (Müller 2006; Müller 2007a: Section 7.5.2, see also Section 10.6.1 below). It is, however, possible to fix this analysis by using the HPSG formalization of sets (Pollard & Sag 1987; Pollard & Moshier 1990). The Subject, Transitive and Passive Constructions must then be modified such that they can say something about what an element in VAL looks like, rather than specifying the VAL value of a singleton set.

(13) The *Subject Construction* with Pollard & Moschier's definition of sets:
$$\begin{bmatrix} \text{SYN}|\text{CAT } v \\ \text{VAL } \boxed{1} \end{bmatrix} \wedge \left\{ \begin{bmatrix} \text{ROLE} \begin{bmatrix} \text{GF } subj \end{bmatrix} \end{bmatrix} \right\} \subset \boxed{1}$$

The restriction in (13) states that the valence set of a head has to contain an element that has the grammatical function *subj*. By these means, it is possible to suppress arguments (by specifying SYN as *zero*), but it is not possible to add any additional arguments to the fixed set of arguments of *schlagen* 'to beat'.[7] For the analysis of Middle Constructions such as (14), inheritance-based approaches do not work as there is no satisfactory way to add the reflexive pronoun to the valence set:[8]

(14) Das Buch liest sich gut.
     the book reads REFL good

     'The book reads well / is easy to read.'

If we want to introduce additional arguments, we require auxiliary features. An analysis using auxiliary features has been suggested by Koenig (1999). Since there are many argument structure changing processes that interact in various ways and are linked to particular semantic side-effects, it is inevitable that one ends up assuming a large number of syntactic and semantic auxiliary features. The interaction between the various linking constructions becomes so complex that this analysis also becomes cognitively implausible and has to be viewed as technically unusable. For a more detailed discussion of this point, see Müller (2007a: Section 7.5.2).

---

[7]Rather than requiring that *schlagen* 'to beat' has exactly two arguments as in HPSG, one could also assume that the constraint on the main lexical item would be of the kind in (11a). One would then require that *schlagen* has at least the two members in its valence set. This would complicate everything considerably and furthermore it would not be clear that the subject referred to in (13) would be one of the arguments that are referred to in the description of the lexical item for *schlagen* in (11a).

[8]One technically possible solution would be the following: one could assume that verbs that occur in middle constructions always have a description of a reflexive pronoun in their valence set. The Transitive Construction would then have to specify the SYN value of the reflexive pronoun as *zero* so that the additional reflexive pronoun is not realized in the Transitive Construction. The middle construction would suppress the subject, but realizes the object and the reflexive.

    This solution cannot be applied to the recursive processes we will encounter in a moment such as causativization in Turkish, unless one wishes to assume infinite valence sets.

10.2 Passive

The following empirical problem is much more serious: some processes like passivization, impersonalization and causativization can be applied in combination or even allow for multiple application, but if the grammatical function of a particular argument is determined once and for all by unification, additional unifications cannot change the initial assignment. We will first look at languages which allow for a combination of passivization and impersonalization, such as Lithuanian (Timberlake 1982: Section 5), Irish (Noonan 1994), and Turkish (Özkaragöz 1986; Knecht 1985: Section 2.3.3). I will use Özkaragöz's Turkish examples in (15) for illustration (1986: 77):

(15)   a. Bu şato-da   boğ-ul-un-ur.
           this château-LOC strangle-PASS-PASS-AOR
           'One is strangled (by one) in this château.'

        b. Bu oda-da   döv-ül-ün-ür.
           this room-LOC hit-PASS-PASS-AOR
           'One is beaten (by one) in this room.'

        c. Harp-te vur-ul-un-ur.
           war-LOC shoot-PASS-PASS-AOR
           'One is shot (by one) in war.'

-In, *-n*, and *-Il* are allomorphs of the passive/impersonal morpheme.[9]

Approaches that assume that the personal passive is the unification of some general structure with some passive-specific structure will not be able to capture double passivization or passivization + impersonalization since they have committed themselves to a certain structure too early. The problem for nontransformational approaches that state syntactic structure for the passive is that such a structure, once stated, cannot be modified. That is, we said that the underlying object is the subject in the passive sentence. But in order to get the double passivization/passivization + impersonalization, we have to suppress this argument as well. What is needed is some sort of process (or description) that takes a representation and relates it to another representation with a suppressed subject. This representation is related to a third representation which again suppresses the subject resulting in an impersonal sentence. In order to do this one needs different strata as in Relational Grammar (Timberlake 1982; Özkaragöz 1986), metarules (Gazdar, Klein, Pullum & Sag 1985), lexical rules (Dowty, 1978: 412; 2003: Section 3.4; Bresnan 1982b; Pollard & Sag 1987; Blevins 2003; Müller 2003b), transformations (Chomsky 1957), or just a morpheme-based morphological analysis that results in items with different valence properties when the passivization morpheme is combined with a head (Chomsky 1981a).

The second set of problematic data that will be discussed comes from causativization in Turkish (Lewis 1967: 146):

---

[9] According to Özkaragöz, the data is best captured by an analysis that assumes that the passive applies to a passivized transitive verb and hence results in an impersonal passive. The cited authors discussed their data as instances of double passivization, but it was argued by Blevins (2003) that these and similar examples from other languages are impersonal constructions that can be combined with personal passives.

(16) öl-dür-t-tür-t-
'to cause someone to cause someone to cause someone to kill someone'
(kill = cause someone to die)

The causative morpheme -*t* is combined four times with the verb (*tür* is an allomorph of the causative morpheme). This argument structure-changing process cannot be modeled in an inheritance hierarchy since if we were to say that a word can inherit from the causative construction three times, we would still not have anything different to what we would have if the inheritance via the causative construction had applied only once. For this kind of phenomenon, we would require rules that relate a linguistic object to another, more complex object, that is, lexical rules (unary branching rules which change the phonology of a linguistic sign) or binary rules that combine a particular sign with a derivational morpheme. These rules can semantically embed the original sign (that is, add *cause* to *kill*).

The problem of repeated combination with causativization affixes is an instance of a more general problem: derivational morphology cannot be handled by inheritance as was already pointed out by Krieger & Nerbonne (1993) with respect to cases like *preprepreversion*.

If we assume that argument alternations such as passive, causativization and the Middle Construction should be described with the same means across languages, then evidence from Lithuanian and Turkish form an argument against inheritance-based analyses of the passive (Müller 2006; 2007b; Müller & Wechsler 2014a). See also Section 21.2.2 for the discussion of an inheritance-based approach to passive in LFG and Section 21.4.2 for the discussion of an inheritance-based approach in Simpler Syntax.

10.3 Verb position

At present, I only know of two publications in the framework of CxG dealing with German clause structure: Micelli (2012) and Welke (2019). Micelli (2012) describes a computer implementation of a German grammar in Fluid Construction Grammar. This fragment is restricted to declarative V2-clauses and *wh*-questions. In her analysis, the middle field forms a constituent comprising exactly two constituents (the direct and indirect object).[10] The right sentence bracket and the postfield are empty. Long-distance dependencies are not discussed. It is only possible for arguments of the verb in the left sentence bracket to occur in the prefield. Micelli's work is an interesting starting point, but one will have to wait and see how the analysis will be modified when the grammar fragment is expanded.

Welke (2019: 283) assumes argument structure constructions like the one in (17):

(17) $\boxed{\text{Nom}_{1/Ag} - \text{Akk}_{2/Pat}}$

Welke states that arguments of a verb come in a fixed order in what he calls the primary perspectivization. So in (17), nominative comes before accusative. In addition to

---

[10] Note that none of the constituent tests that were discussed in Section 1.3 justifies such an analysis and that no other theory in this book assumes the *Mittelfeld* to be a constituent.

the primary perspectivization, there may be a secondary perspectivization that allows for alternative orders like accusative before nominative. He deals with the verb position in Section 7.3: his proposal assumes that certain positions are reserved for verbs in argument structure constructions like (17). He gives the following extended schemata that include argument structure information and information about the verb position:

(18) a. $\boxed{-\ \text{Arg Arg Arg}}$

b. $\boxed{\text{Arg} - \text{Arg Arg}}$

c. $\boxed{\text{Arg Arg Arg} -}$

(18a) is the schema for verb-initial clauses, (18b) the schema for verb-second clauses and (18c) the schema for verb-final clauses. These schemata stand for argument structure constructions with exactly three arguments, but of course there are others with fewer or more arguments. Welke (2019: Section 7.4) notes that modifiers can be placed anywhere between the arguments in German. He assumes that there is a fusion process that can insert a modifier into argument structure constructions. Welke notes that inserting modifiers into constructions like (18) causes problems with the verb-second property of German since a pattern Modifier Arg Verb Arg Arg is V3 rather than V2. He hence concludes that a generalized construction consisting of verb(s), arguments and modifiers is needed: a construction that corresponds to the topological fields model of the German clause (Welke 2019: Section 7.5). Details about the integration of the semantics of the adjuncts, about the interaction of the topological fields schemata with argument structure constructions and about the analysis of nonlocal dependencies are not provided.

So, it must be said that neither Micelli's analysis nor Welke's provides fully worked out proposals of the phenomena discussed in this book and hence I will not discuss them any further, but instead explore some of the possibilities for analyzing German sentence structure that are at least possible in principle in a CxG framework. Since there are neither empty elements nor transformations, the GB and HPSG analyses from Chapter 3 and 9 as well as their variants in Categorial Grammar are ruled out. The following options remain:

- an analysis similar to LFG with an optional verb
- an entirely flat analysis as proposed in GPSG
- an analysis with binary branching but variable verb position like that of Steedman (2000: 159)

Different variants of CxG make different assumptions about how abstract constructions can be. In Categorial Grammar, we have very general combinatorial rules which combine possibly complex signs without adding any meaning of their own (see rule (2) on page 246 for example). (19) shows an example in which the abstract rule of forward application was used:

(19) [[[[Gibt] der Mann] der Frau] das Buch]
       give the man the woman the book

'Does the man give the woman the book?'

If we do not want these kinds of abstract combinatorial rules, then this analysis must be excluded.

The LFG analysis in Section 7.3 is probably also unacceptable on a CxG view, as it is assumed in this analysis that *der Mann der Frau das Buch* forms a VP, although only three NPs have been combined. CxG has nothing like the theory of extended head domains that was presented in Section 7.3.

Thus, both variants with binary-branching structures are ruled out and only the analysis with flat branching structures remains. Sign-based CxG, which is a variant of HPSG (Sag 2010: 486), as well as Embodied Construction Grammar (Bergen & Chang 2005: 156) allow for a separation of immediate dominance and linear order so that it would be possible to formulate a construction which would correspond to the dominance rule in (20) for transitive verbs:[11]

(20) S → V, NP, NP

Here, we have the problem that adjuncts in German can occur between any of the arguments. In GPSG, adjuncts are introduced by metarules. In formal variants of CxG, lexical rules, but not metarules, are used.[12] If one does not wish to expand the formalism to include metarules, then there are three options remaining:

- Adjuncts are introduced in the lexicon (van Noord & Bouma 1994; Bouma, Malouf & Sag 2001) and treated as arguments in the syntax,
- Constructions always have slots available for an arbitrary number of adjuncts, or
- Constructions can be discontinuous.

Kasper (1994) has proposed an analysis of the first type in HPSG: adjuncts and arguments are combined with the head in a flat structure. This corresponds to the dominance rule in (21), where the position of adjuncts is not stated by the dominance rule.

(21) S → V, NP, NP, Adj*

If we want to say something about the meaning of the entire construction, then one has to combine the original construction (transitive, in the above example) with the semantics contributed by each of the adjuncts. These computations are not trivial and require relational constraints (small computer programs), which should be avoided if there are conceptually simpler solutions for describing a particular phenomenon.

---

[11]In principle, this is also Micelli's analysis, but she assumed that the middle field forms a separate constituent.

[12]Goldberg (2014: 116) mentions metarule-like devices and refers to Cappelle (2006). The difference between metarules and their CxG variant as envisioned by Cappelle and Goldberg is that in CxG, two constructions are related without one construction being basic and the other one derived. Rather, there exists a mutual relation between two constructions.

The alternative would be to use discontinuous constructions. Analyses with discontinuous constituents have been proposed in both HPSG (Reape 1994) and Embodied Construction Grammar (Bergen & Chang 2005). If we apply Bergen and Chang's analysis to German, the italicized words in (22) would be part of a ditransitive construction.

(22) *Gibt der Mann* morgen *der Frau* unter der Brücke *das Geld*?
 gives the man tomorrow the woman under the bridge the money

 'Is the man going to give the woman the money under the bridge tomorrow?'

The construction has been realized discontinuously and the adjuncts are inserted into the gaps. In this kind of approach, one still has to explain how the scope of quantifiers and adjuncts is determined. While this may be possible, the solution is not obvious and has not been worked out in any of the CxG approaches to date. For further discussions of approaches that allow for discontinuous constituents see Section 11.7.2.2.

10.4 Local reordering

If we assume flat branching structures, then it is possible to use the GPSG analysis for the order of arguments. However, Kay (2002) assumes a phrasal construction for so-called Heavy-NP-Shift in English, which means that there is a new rule for the reordering of heavy NPs in English rather than one rule and two different ways to linearize the daughters.

In CxG, it is often argued that the usage contexts of certain orders differ and we therefore must be dealing with different constructions. Accordingly, one would have to assume six constructions to capture the ordering variants of sentences with ditransitive verbs in final position (see also page 185). An alternative would be to assume that the ordering variants all have a similar structure and that the information-structural properties are dependent on the position of constituents in the respective structure (see De Kuthy 2000 for German and Bildhauer 2008 for Spanish).

10.5 Long-distance dependencies

Kay & Fillmore (1999: Section 3.10) discuss long-distance dependencies in their article. Since the number of arguments is not specified in the verb phrase construction, it is possible that an argument of the verb is not locally present. Like the LFG and GPSG analyses in previous chapters, there are no empty elements assumed for the analysis of long-distance dependencies. In the *Left Isolation Construction* that licenses the entire sentence, there is a left daughter and a right daughter. The left daughter corresponds to whatever was extracted from the right daughter. The connection between the fronted element and the position where it is missing is achieved by the operator VAL. VAL provides all elements of the valence set of a linguistic object as well as all elements in the valence set of these elements and so on. It is thereby possible to have unrestricted access to an argument or adjunct daughter of any depth of embedding, and then identify the

10 Construction Grammar

fronted constituent with an open valence slot.[13] This approach corresponds to the LFG analysis of Kaplan & Zaenen (1989) based on functional uncertainty.

10.6 New developments and theoretical variants

Berkeley Construction Grammar was already discussed in the main part of this chapter. The discussion of the formal underpinnings was deferred until the theoretical variants section, since it is more advanced. I made some comments on set unification in Müller (2006: 858), but the longer discussion is only available in Müller (2007a: Section 7.5.2), which is in German. Therefore, I include Section 10.6.1 here, which discusses the formal underpinnings of Berkeley Construction Grammar in more detail and shows that they are not suited for what they were intended to do.

Section 10.6.2 discusses Sign-Based Construction Grammar, which was developed in joint work by Charles Fillmore, Paul Kay and Ivan Sag. It embodies ideas from BCG without having its formal flaws. Section 10.6.3 deals with Embodied Construction Grammar, which is based on work by Charles Fillmore, Paul Kay and George Lakoff. Section 10.6.4 deals with Fluid Construction Grammar.

10.6.1 Berkeley Construction Grammar

Section 10.2 discussed the valence representation in BCG and linking constructions for active and passive. Kay & Fillmore (1999) represent valence information in sets and I deferred the discussion of the formal properties of sets in BCG to this section. Fillmore and Kay's assumptions regarding set unification differ fundamentally from those that are made in HPSG. Kay and Fillmore assume that the unification of the set { a } with the set { b }, where a and b do not unify, results in the union of the two sets, that is { a, b }. Due to this special understanding of sets it is possible to increase the number of elements in a set by means of unification. The unification of two sets that contain compatible elements is the disjunction of sets that contain the respective unifications of the compatible elements. This sounds complicated, but we are only interested in a specific case: the unification of an arbitrary set with a singleton set:

(23) { NP[*nom*], NP[*acc*] } ∧ { NP[*nom*] } = { NP[*nom*], NP[*acc*] }

According to Fillmore & Kay the unification of a set with another set that contains a compatible element does not result in an increase of the number of list elements. (24) illustrates another possible case:

(24) { NP, NP[*acc*] } ∧ { NP[*nom*] } = { NP[*nom*], NP[*acc*] }

---

[13] Note again, that there are problems with the formalization of this proposal in Kay & Fillmore's paper. The formalization of VAL, which was provided by Andreas Kathol, seems to presuppose a formalization of sets as the one that is used in HPSG, but the rest of Fillmore & Kay's paper assumes a different formalization, which is inconsistent. See Section 10.6.1.

10.6 New developments and theoretical variants

The first NP in (24) is underspecified with respect to its case. The case of the NP in the second set is specified as nominative. NP[*nom*] does not unify with NP[*acc*] but with NP.

This particular conception of unification has consequences. Unification is usually defined as follows:

(25) The unification of two structures FS_1 and FS_2 is the structure FS_3 that is subsumed by both FS_1 and FS_2 where there is no other structure that subsumes FS_1 and FS_2 and is subsumed by FS_3.

A structure FS_1 is said to subsume FS_3 iff FS_3 contains all feature value pairs and structure sharings from FS_1. FS_3 may contain additional feature value pairs or structure sharings. The consequence is that the subsumption relations in (26b,c) have to hold if unification of valence sets works as in (26a):

(26) Properties of the set unification according to Kay & Fillmore (1999):
 a. { NP[*nom*] } ∧ { NP[*acc*] } = { NP[*nom*], NP[*acc*] }
 b. { NP[*nom*] } ⊵ { NP[*nom*], NP[*acc*] }
 c. { NP[*acc*] } ⊵ { NP[*nom*], NP[*acc*] }

(26b) means that a feature structure with a valence set that contains just one NP[*nom*] is more general than a feature structure that contains both an NP[*nom*] and an NP[*acc*]. Therefore the set of transitive verbs is a subset of the intransitive verbs. This is rather unintuitive, but compatible with Fillmore & Kay's system for the licensing of arguments. However, there are problems with the interaction of valence specifications and linking constructions, which we turn to now.

We have seen the result of combining lexical items with linking constructions in (11a) and (11b), but the question of how these results are derived has not been addressed so far. Kay (2002) suggests an automatic computation of all compatible combinations of maximally specific constructions. Such a procedure could be used to compute the lexical representations we saw in Section 10.2 and these could be then used to analyze the well-formed sentences in (12).

However, problems would result for ungrammatical sentences like (27b). *grauen* 'to dread' is a subjectless verb. If one would simply combine all compatible linking constructions with *grauen*, the Kay & Fillmoreian conception of set unification would cause the introduction of a subject into the valence set of *grauen*. (27b) would be licensed by the grammar:

(27) a. Dem Student graut vor der Prüfung.
 the.DAT student dreads before the exam
 'The student dreads the exam.'
 b. * Ich graue dem Student vor der Prüfung.
 I dread the.DAT student before the exam

One could solve this problem by specifying an element with the grammatical function *subject* in the lexical entry of *grauen* 'to dread'. In addition, it would have to be stipulated that this subject can only be realized as an overt or covert expletive (The covert expletive would be SYN *zero*). For the covert expletive, this means it has neither a form nor a meaning. Such expletive pronouns without phonological realization are usually frowned upon in Construction Grammar and analyses that can do without such abstract entities are to be preferred.

Kay & Fillmore (1999) represent the semantic contribution of signs as sets as well. This excludes the possibility of preventing the unwanted unification of linking constructions by referring to semantic constraints since we have the same effect as we have with valence sets: if the semantic descriptions are incompatible, the set is extended. This means that in an automatic unification computation all verbs are compatible with the Transitive Construction in (9a) and this would license analyses for (28) in addition to those of (27b).

(28)   a.   * Der Mann schläft das Buch.
            the man sleeps the book

       b.   * Der Mann denkt an die Frau das Buch.
            the man thinks at the woman the book

An intransitive verb was unified with the Transitive Construction in the analysis of (28a) and in (28b) a verb that takes a prepositional object was combined with the Transitive Construction. This means that representations like (11) cannot be computed automatically as was intended by Kay (2002). Therefore one would have to specify subconstructions for all argument structure possibilities for every verb (active, passive, middle, …). This does not capture the fact that speakers can form passives after acquiring new verbs without having to learn about the fact that the newly learned verb forms one.

Michaelis & Ruppenhofer (2001) do not use sets for the representation of semantic information. Therefore they could use constraints regarding the meaning of verbs in the Transitive Construction. To this end, one needs to represent semantic relations with feature descriptions as it was done in Section 9.1.6. Adopting such a representation, it is possible to talk about two-place relations in an abstract way. See for instance the discussion of (29) on page 282. However, the unification with the Subject Construction cannot be blocked with reference to semantics since there exist so-called raising verbs that take a subject without assigning a semantic role to it. As is evidenced by subject verb agreement, *du* 'you' is the subject in (29), but the subject does not get a semantic role. The referent of *du* is not the one who *seems*.

(29)   Du scheinst gleich einzuschlafen.
        you seem.2SG soon in.to.sleep

        'You seem like you will fall asleep soon.'

This means that one is forced to either assume an empty expletive subject for verbs like *grauen* or to specify explicitly which verbs may inherit from the subject construction and which may not.

In addition to (29), there exist object raising constructions with accusative objects that can be promoted to subject in passives. The subject in the passive construction does not get a semantic role from the finite verb:

(30) a. Richard lacht ihn an.
    Richard laughs him towards
    'Richard smiles at him.'
  b. Richard fischt den Teich leer.
    Richard fishes the pond empty

The objects in (30) are semantic arguments of *an* 'towards' and *leer* 'empty', respectively, but not semantic arguments of the verbs *lacht* 'laughs' and *fischt* 'fishes', respectively. If one wants to explain these active forms and the corresponding passive forms via the linking constructions in (9), one cannot refer to semantic properties of the verb. Therefore, one is forced to postulate specific lexical entries for all possible verb forms in active and passive sentences.

10.6.2 Sign-Based Construction Grammar

In more recent work by Fillmore, Kay, Michaelis and Sag, the Kay & Fillmore formalization of the description of valence using the Kay & Fillmore version of sets was abandoned in favor of the HPSG formalization (Kay 2005; Michaelis 2006; Sag 2012; Sag, Boas & Kay 2012: 10–11). Sign-Based Construction Grammar was developed from the Berkeley variant of CxG. Sign-Based Construction Grammar is a variant of HPSG (Sag 2010: 486) and as such uses the formal apparatus of HPSG (typed feature structures). Valence and saturation are treated in exactly the same way as in standard HPSG. Changes in valence are also analyzed as in HPSG using lexical rules (Sag, Boas & Kay 2012: Section 2.3). The analysis of long-distance dependencies was adopted from HPSG (or rather GPSG). Minimal Recursion Semantics (MRS; Copestake, Flickinger, Pollard & Sag 2005) is used for the description of semantic content. The only difference to works in standard HPSG is the organization of the features in feature structures. A new feature geometry was introduced to rule out constructions that describe daughters of daughters and therefore have a much larger locality domain in contrast to rules in phrase structure grammars, LFG, and GPSG. I do not view this new feature geometry as particularly sensible as it can be easily circumvented and serves to complicate the theory. This will be discussed in Section 10.6.2.1. Another change was the omission of valence features, which is discussed in Section 10.6.2.4.

10.6.2.1 Locality and MOTHER

Sag, Wasow & Bender (2003: 475–489) and Sag (2007; 2012) suggest using a MOTHER feature in addition to daughter features. The Head-Complement Construction would then have the form in (31):

(31) Head-Complement Construction following Sag, Wasow & Bender (2003: 481):
head-comp-cx ⇒
$$\begin{bmatrix} \text{MOTHER}|\text{SYN}|\text{VAL}|\text{COMPS} \langle \rangle \\ \text{HEAD-DTR } \boxed{0} \begin{bmatrix} word \\ \text{SYN}|\text{VAL}|\text{COMPS } \boxed{A} \end{bmatrix} \\ \text{DTRS } \langle \boxed{0} \rangle \oplus \boxed{A} \text{ nelist} \end{bmatrix}$$

The value of COMPS is then a list of the complements of a head (see Section 9.1.1). Unlike in standard HPSG, it is not *synsem* objects that are selected with valence lists, but rather signs. The analysis of the phrase *ate a pizza* takes the form in (32).[14]

(32)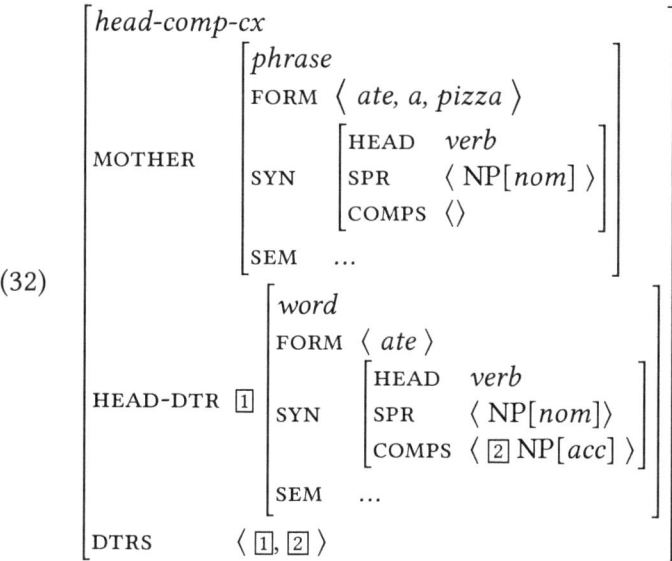

The difference to HPSG in the version of Pollard & Sag (1994) is that for Sag, Wasow & Bender, signs do not have daughters and this makes the selection of daughters impossible. As a result, the SYNSEM feature becomes superfluous (selection of the PHON value and of the value of the newly introduced FORM feature is allowed in Sag, Wasow & Bender (2003) and Sag (2012)). The information about the linguistic objects that contribute to a complex sign is only represented in the very outside of the structure. The sign represented under MOTHER is of the type *phrase* but does not contain any information about the daughters. The object described in (32) is of course also of another type than the phrasal or lexical signs that can occur as its daughters. We therefore need the following extension so that the grammar will work (Sag, Wasow & Bender 2003: 478):[15]

---

[14] SBCG uses a FORM feature in addition to the PHON feature, which is used for phonological information as in earlier versions of HPSG (Sag 2012: Section 3.1, Section 3.6). The FORM feature is usually provided in example analyses.

[15] A less formal version of this constraint is given as the Sign Principle by Sag (2012: 105): "Every sign must be listemically or constructionally licensed, where: a sign is listemically licensed only if it satisfies some listeme, and a sign is constructionally licensed if it is the mother of some well-formed construct."

10.6 New developments and theoretical variants

(33) Φ is a Well-Formed Structure according to a grammar G if and only if:
1. there is a construction C in G, and
2. there is a feature structure I that is an instantiation of C, such that Φ is the value of the MOTHER feature of I.

For comparison, a description is given in (34) with the feature geometry that was assumed in Section 9.1.1.

(34)

In (34), the features HEAD-DTR and NON-HEAD-DTRS belong to those features that phrases of type *head-complement-phrase* have. In (32), however, the phrase corresponds only to the value of the MOTHER feature and therefore has no daughters represented in the sign itself. Using the feature geometry in (34), it is in principle possible to formulate restrictions on the daughters of the object in the NON-HEAD-DTRS list, which would be completely ruled out under the assumption of the feature geometry in (32) and the restriction in (33).

There are several arguments against this feature geometry, which will be discussed in the following subsections. The first one is an empirical one: there may be idioms that span clauses. The second argument concerns the status of the meta statement in (33) and the third one computational complexity.

10.6.2.1.1 Idioms that cross constituent boundaries

In Müller (2007a: Chapter 12) I conjectured that the locality restrictions may be too strong since there may be idioms that require one to make reference to daughters of daughters for their description. Richter & Sailer (2009) discuss the following idioms as examples:

(35) a. nicht wissen, wo   X_Dat der Kopf steht
      not know   where X   the head stands
    'to not know where x's head is at'

329

b. glauben, X_Acc tritt ein Pferd
   believe X   kicks a horse
   'be utterly surprised'

c. aussehen, als hätten X_Dat die Hühner das Brot weggefressen
   look   as.if had   X   the chicken the bread away.eaten
   'to look confused/puzzled'

d. look as if butter wouldn't melt [in X's mouth]
   'to look absolutely innocent'

In sentences containing the idioms in (35a–c), the X-constituent has to be a pronoun that refers to the subject of the matrix clause. If this is not the case, the sentences become ungrammatical or lose their idiomatic meaning.

(36) a. Ich glaube, mich / # dich   tritt ein Pferd.
        I   believe me.ACC you.ACC kicks a horse

     b. Jonas glaubt, ihn tritt ein Pferd.[16]
        Jonas believes him kicks a horse
        'Jonas is utterly surprised.'

     c. # Jonas glaubt, dich tritt ein Pferd.
        Jonas believes you kicks a horse
        'Jonas believes that a horse kicks you.'

In order to enforce this co-reference, a restriction has to be able to refer to both the subject of *glauben* 'believe' and the object of *treten* 'kick' at the same time. In SBCG, there is the possibility of referring to the subject since the relevant information is also available on maximal projections (the value of a special feature (XARG) is identical to the subject of a head). In (35a–c), we are dealing with accusative and dative objects. Instead of only making information about one argument accessible, one could represent the complete argument structure on the maximal projection (as is done in some versions of HPSG, see page 307 and pages 562–564). This would remove locality of selection, however, since if all heads project their argument structure, then it is possible to determine the properties of arguments of arguments by looking at the elements present in the argument structure. Thus, the argument structure of *wissen* 'to know' in (37) would contain the description of a *dass* clause.

(37) Peter weiß, dass Klaus kommt.
     Peter knows that Klaus comes
     'Peter knows that Klaus is coming.'

Since the description of the *dass* clause contains the argument structure of *dass*, it is possible to access the argument of *dass*. *wissen* 'to know' can therefore access *Klaus kommt*. As such, *wissen* also has access to the argument structure of *kommt* 'to come',

---

[16] http://www.machandel-verlag.de/der-katzenschatz.html, 2015-07-06.

10.6 New developments and theoretical variants

which is why *Klaus* is also accessible to *wissen*. However, the purpose of the new, more restrictive feature geometry was to rule out such nonlocal access to arguments.

An alternative to projecting the complete argument structure was suggested by Kay et al. (2015: Section 6): instead of assuming that the subject is the XARG in idiomatic constructions like those in (35), they assume that the accusative or dative argument is the XARG. This is an interesting proposal that could be used to fix the cases under discussion, but the question is whether it scales up if interaction with other phenomena are considered. For instance, Bender & Flickinger (1999) use XARG in their account of question tags in English. So, if English idioms can be found that require a non-subject XARG in embedded sentences while also admitting the idiom parts in the embedded sentence to occur as full clause with question tag, we would have conflicting demands and would have to assume different XARGs for root and embedded clauses, which would make this version of the lexical theory rather unattractive, since we would need two lexical items for the respective verb.

(35d) is especially interesting, since here the X that refers to material outside the idiom is in an adjunct. If such cases existed, the XARG mechanism would be clearly insufficient since XARG is not projected from adjuncts. However, as Kay et al. (2015) point out the X does not necessarily have to be a pronoun that is coreferent with an element in a matrix clause. They provide the following example:

(38) Justin Bieber—Once upon a time ∅ butter wouldn't melt in little Justin's mouth. Now internationally famous for being a weapons-grade petulant brat ...

So, whether examples of the respective kind can be found is an open question.

Returning to our *horse* examples, Richter & Sailer (2009: 313) argue that the idiomatic reading is only available if the accusative pronouns is fronted and the embedded clause is V2. The examples in (39) do not have the idiomatic reading:

(39) a. Ich glaube, dass mich ein Pferd tritt.
       I believe that me a horse kicks
       'I believe that a horse kicks me.'

   b. Ich glaube, ein Pferd tritt mich.
      I believe a horse kicks me
      'I believe that a horse kicks me.'

Richter & Sailer assume a structure for *X_Acc tritt ein Pferd* in (35b) that contains, among others, the constraints in (40).

The feature geometry in (40) differs somewhat from what was presented in Chapter 9 but that is not of interest here. It is only of importance that the semantic contribution of the entire phrase is *surprised'*($x_{\boxed{2}}$). The following is said about the internal structure of the phrase: it consists of a filler-daughter (an extracted element) and also of a head daughter corresponding to a sentence from which something has been extracted. The head daughter means 'a horse kicks $x_{\boxed{2}}$' and has an internal head somewhere whose argument structure list contains an indefinite NP with the word *Pferd* 'horse' as its head.

331

(40)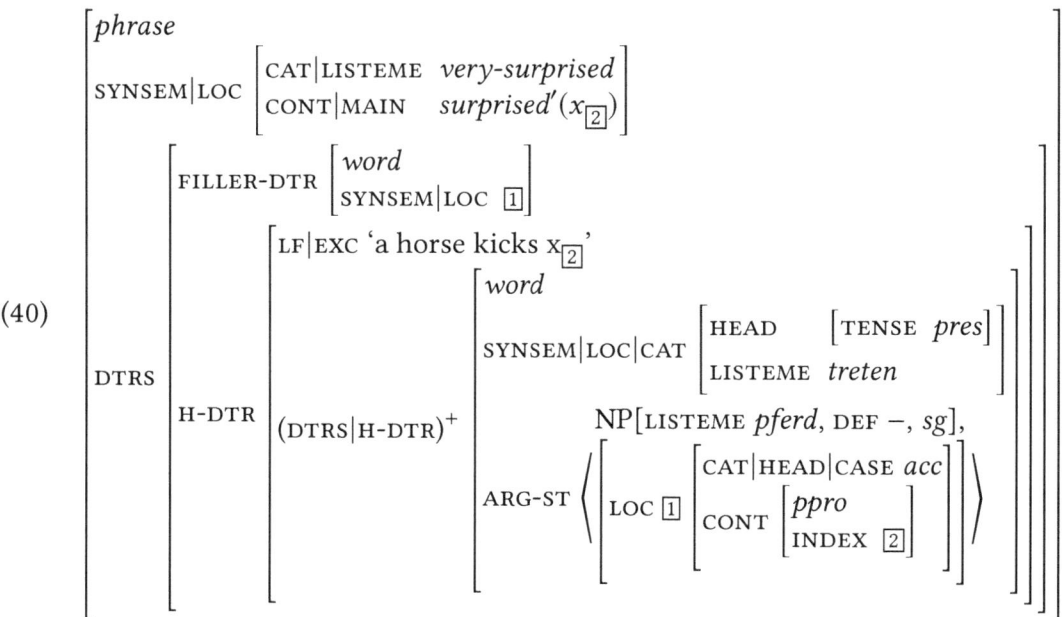

The second element in the argument structure is a pronominal NP in the accusative whose LOCAL value is identical to that of the filler (1). The entire meaning of this part of the sentence is $surprised'(x_{2})$, whereby 2 is identical to the referential index of the pronoun. In addition to the constraints in (40), there are additional ones that ensure that the partial clause appears with the relevant form of *glauben* 'to believe' or *denken* 'to think'. The exact details are not that important here. What is important is that one can specify constraints on complex syntactic elements, that is, it must be possible to refer to daughters of daughters. This is possible with the classical HPSG feature geometry, but not with the feature geometry of SBCG. For a more general discussion of locality, see Section 18.2.

The restrictions on *Pferd* clauses in (40) are too strict, however, since there are variants of the idiom that do not have the accusative pronoun in the *Vorfeld*:

(41) a. ich glaub es   tritt mich ein Pferd wenn ich einen derartigen Unsinn
         I   believe EXPL kicks me   a   horse when I   a   such   nonsense
         lese.[17]
         read

      'I am utterly surprised when I read such nonsense.'

   b. omg dieser xBluuR der nn ist wieder da   ey nein ich glaub es   tritt
      omg this   XBluuR he   is again there no   I   believe EXPL kicks
      mich ein Pferd!![18]
      me   a   horse

      'OMG, this xBluuR, the nn, he is here again, no, I am utterly surprised.'

---

[17] http://www.welt.de/wirtschaft/article116297208/Die-verlogene-Kritik-an-den-Steuerparadiesen.html, commentary section, 2018-02-20.

[18] http://forum.gta-life.de/index.php?user/3501-malcolm/, 10.12.2015.

c. ich glaub jetzt tritt mich ein pferd[19]
   I believe now kicks me a horse
   'I am utterly surprised now.'

In (42a–b) the *Vorfeld* is filled by an expletive and in (42c) an adverb fills the *Vorfeld* position. While these forms of the idiom are really rare, they do exist and should be allowed for by the description of the idiom. So, one would have to make sure that *ein Pferd* 'a horse' is not fronted, but this can be done in the lexical item of *tritt* 'kicks'. This shows that the cases at hand cannot be used to argue for models that allow for the representation of (underspecified) trees of depth greater one, but I still believe that such idioms can be found. Of course this is an open empirical question.

What is not an open empirical question though is whether humans store chunks with complex internal structure or not. It is clear that we do and much Construction Grammar literature emphasizes this. Constructional HPSG can represent such chunks, but SBCG cannot since linguistic signs do not have daughters. So here Constructional HPSG and TAG are the theories that can represent complex chunks of linguistic material with its internal structure, while other theories like GB, Minimalism, CG, LFG and DG can not.

10.6.2.1.2 Complicated licensing of constructions

In addition to these empirical problems, there is a conceptual problem with (33): (33) is not part of the formalism of typed feature structures but rather a meta-statement. Therefore, grammars which use (33) cannot be described with the normal formalism. The formalization given in Richter (2004) cannot be directly applied to SBCG, which means that the formal foundations of SBCG still have to be worked out.[20] Furthermore, the original problem that (33) was designed to solve is not solved by introducing the new feature geometry and the meta statement. Instead, the problem is just moved to another level since we now need a theory about what is a permissible meta-statement and what is not. As such, a grammarian could add a further clause to the meta statement stating that Φ is only a well-formed structure if it is true of the daughters of a relevant construction C that they are the MOTHER value of a construction C′. It would be possible to formulate constraints in the meta-statement about the construction C′ or individual values inside the corresponding feature structures. In this way, locality would have been abandoned since it is possible to refer to daughters of daughters. By assuming (33), the theoretical inventory has been increased without any explanatory gain.

10.6.2.1.3 Computational complexity

One motivation behind restrictions on locality was to reduce the computational complexity of the formalism (Ivan Sag, p. c. 2011, See Chapter 17 on computational complexity and

---

[19] http://www.castingshow-news.de/menowin-frhlich-soll-er-zum-islam-konvertieren-7228/, 2018-02-20.
[20] A note of caution is necessary since there were misunderstandings in the past regarding the degree of formalizations of SBCG: in comparison to most other theories discussed in this book, SBCG is well-formalized. For instance it is easy to come up with a computer implementation of SBCG fragments. I implemented one in the TRALE system myself. The reader is referred to Richter (2004) to get an idea what kind of deeper formalization is talked about here.

generative power). However, the locality restrictions of SBCG can be circumvented easily by structure sharing (Müller 2013a: Section 9.6.1). To see this consider a construction with the following form:[21]

(42) $\begin{bmatrix} \text{MOTHER} & \begin{bmatrix} \textit{sign} \\ \text{PHON} & \textit{phonological-object} \\ \text{FORM} & \textit{morphological-object} \\ \text{SYN} & \textit{syntactic information} \\ \text{SEM} & \textit{semantic information} \\ \text{NASTY} & \boxed{1} \end{bmatrix} \\ \text{DTRS} & \boxed{1} \textit{ list of signs} \end{bmatrix}$

The feature NASTY in the MOTHER sign refers to the value of DTRS and hence all the internal structure of the sign that is licensed by the constructional schema in (42) is available. Of course one could rule out such things by stipulation – if one considered it to be empirically adequate, but then one could as well continue to use the feature geometry of Constructional HPSG (Sag 1997) and stipulate constraints like "Do not look into the daughters." An example of such a constraint given in prose is the Locality Principle of Pollard & Sag (1987: 143–144).

10.6.2.2 Selection of PHON and FORM values

The feature geometry of constructional HPSG has the PHON value outside of SYNSEM. Therefore verbs can select for syntactic and semantic properties of their arguments but not for their phonology. For example, they can require that an object has accusative case but not that it starts with a vowel. SBCG allows for the selection of phonological information (the feature is called FORM here) and one example of such a selection is the indefinite article in English, which has to be either *a* or *an* depending on whether the noun or nominal projection it is combined with starts with a vowel or not (Flickinger, Mail to the HPSG mailing list, 01.03.2016):

(43)   a. an institute

       b. a house

The distinction can be modeled by assuming a selection feature for determiners.[22] An alternative would be of course to capture all phonological phenomena by formulating constraints on phonology on the phrasal level (see Bird & Klein 1994 and Walther 1999 for phonology in HPSG).

---

[21]Bob Borsley (p.c. 2019) pointed out to me that a feature like NASTY in (42) is actually used in SBCG: the XARG feature makes available one argument (usually the subject) at a complete projection even though the respective element may be contained within it (Sag 2012: 84). XARG can be used to refer to a daughter within a complex structure for example to establish agreement in question tag formation (Bender & Flickinger 1999).

[22]In Standard HPSG there is mutual selection between the determiner and the noun. The noun selects the determiner via SPR and the determiner selects the noun via a feature called SPECIFIED. This feature is similar to the MOD feature, which was explained in Section 9.1.7.

Note also that the treatment of raising in SBCG admits nonlocal selection of phonology values, since the analysis of raising in SBCG assumes that the element on the valence list of the embedded verb is identical to an element in the ARG-ST list of the matrix verb (Sag 2012: 159). Hence, both verbs in (44) can see the phonology of the subject:

(44) Kim can eat apples.

In principle there could be languages in which the form of the downstairs verb depends on the presence of an initial consonant in phonology of the subject. English allows for long chains of raising verbs and one could imagine languages in which all the verbs on the way are sensitive to the phonology of the subject. Such languages probably do not exist.

Now, is this a problem? Not for me, but if one develops a general setup in a way to exclude everything that is not attested in the languages of the world (as for instance the selection of arguments of arguments of arguments), then it is a problem that heads can see the phonology of elements that are far away.

There are two possible conclusions for practitioners of SBCG: either the MOTHER feature could be given up since one agrees that theories that do not make wrong predictions are sufficiently constrained and one does not have to explicitly state what cannot occur in languages or one would have to react to the problem with nonlocally selected phonology values and therefore assume a SYNSEM or LOCAL feature that bundles information that is relevant in raising and does not include the phonology. This supports the argument I made on MOTHER in the previous subsection.

10.6.2.3 The LOCAL feature and information shared in nonlocal dependencies

Similarly, elements of the ARG-ST list contain information about FORM. In nonlocal dependencies, this information is shared in the GAP list (SLASH list in other versions of HPSG) and is available all the way to the filler. In other versions of HPSG only LOCAL information is shared and elements in valence lists do not have a PHON feature. If the sign that is contained in the GAP list were identified with the filler, the information about phonological properties of the filler would be available at the extraction side and SBCG could be used to model languages in which the phonology of a filler is relevant for a head from which it is extracted. So for instance, *likes* could see the phonology of *bagels* in (45):

(45) Bagels, I think that Peter likes.

It would be possible to state constraints saying that the filler has to contain a vowel or two vowels or that it ends with a consonant. In addition, all elements on the extraction path (*that* and *think*) can see the phonology of the filler as well. While there are languages that mark the extraction path, I doubt that there are languages that have phonological effects across long distances. This problem can be and has been solved by assuming that the filler is not shared with the information in the GAP list, but that parts of the filler are shared with parts in the GAP list: Sag (2012: 166) assumes that SYN, SEM and STORE information are identified individually. Originally, the feature geometry of

HPSG was motivated by the wish to structure-share information. Everything within LO-CAL was shared between filler and extraction side. This kind of motivation is given up in SBCG.

Note also that not sharing the complete filler with the gap means that the FORM value of the element in the ARG-ST list at the extraction side is not constrained. Without any constraint the theory would be compatible with infinitely many models, since the FORM value could be anything. For example, the FORM value of an extracted adjective could be ⟨ *Donald Duck* ⟩ or ⟨ *Dunald Dock* ⟩ or any arbitrary chaotic sequence of letters/phonemes. To exclude this, one can stipulate the FORM values of extracted elements to be the empty list, but this leaves one with the unintuitive situation that the element in GAP has an empty FORM list while the corresponding filler has a different, filled one.

10.6.2.4 The VALENCE list

Another change from Constructional HPSG to SBCG involves the use of a single valence feature rather then three features SPR, SUBJ and COMPS that were suggested by Borsley (1987) to solve problems in earlier HPSG versions that used a single valence feature (SUBCAT). Borseley's suggestion was taken up by Pollard & Sag (1994: Chapter 9) and has been used in some version or other in other HPSG versions since then.

Sag (2012: 85) assumes that VPs are described by the following feature description:

(46) $\begin{bmatrix} \text{SYN} & [\text{VAL} \ \langle \text{NP} \rangle] \end{bmatrix}$

The problem with such an approach is that VPs differ from other phrasal projections in having an element on their VALENCE list. APs, NPs, and (some) PPs have an empty VALENCE list. In other versions of HPSG the complements are represented on the COMPS list and generalizations about phrases with fully saturated COMPS lists can be expressed directly. One such generalization is that projections with an empty COMPS list (NPs, PPs, VPs, adverbs, CPs) can be extraposed in German (Müller 1999b: Section 13.1.2).

Note also that reducing the number of valence features does not necessarily reduce the number of constructions in the grammar. While classical HPSG has a Specifier-Head Schema and a Head-Complement Schema, SBCG has two Head-Complement Constructions: one with a mother with a singleton COMPS list and one with a mother with an empty COMPS list (Sag 2012: 152). That two seperate constructions are needed is due to the assumption of flat structures.

10.6.2.5 The HEAD feature and the HEAD feature principle

While Sag et al. (2003) still assume a HEAD feature, Sag (2012) eliminated it. Rather than having one place in a feature structure where all information is stated that is always shared between a lexical head and its projection, the features that were represented under HEAD are now simply represented under CAT. Sag (2012) got rid of the Head Feature Principle (see p. 276) and stated identity of information explicitly within constructions. Structure sharing is not stated with boxed numbers anymore but with capital letters instead. An exclamation mark can be used to specify information that is not shared (Sag

2012: 125). While the use of letters instead of numbers is just a presentational variant, the exclamation mark is a non-trivial extension. (47) provides an example: the constraints on the type *pred-hd-comp-cxt*:

(47) Predicational Head-Complement Construction following Sag (2012: 152):
pred-hd-comp-cxt ⇒
$$\begin{bmatrix} \text{MOTHER}|\text{SYN X ! [VAL} \langle Y \rangle] \\ \text{HEAD-DTR Z:} \begin{bmatrix} \textit{word} \\ \text{SYN X: } [\text{VAL } \langle Y \rangle \oplus L] \end{bmatrix} \\ \text{DTRS } \langle Z \rangle \oplus L\text{:}\textit{nelist} \end{bmatrix}$$

The X stands for all syntactic properties of the head daughter. These are identified with the value of SYN of the mother with the exception of the VAL value, which is specified to be a list with the element Y. It is interesting to note that the !-notation is not without problems: Sag (2012: 145) states that the version of SBCG that he presents is "purely monotonic (non-default)", but if the SYN value of the mother is not identical because of overwriting of VAL, it is unclear how the type of SYN can be constrained. ! can be understood as explicitly sharing all features that are not mentioned after the !. Note though, that the type has to be shared as well. This is not trivial since structure sharing cannot be applied here since structure sharing the type would also identify all features belonging to the respective value. So one would need a relation that singles out a type of a structure and identifies this type with the value of another structure. Note also that information from features behind the ! can make the type of the complete structure more specific. Does this affect the shared structure (e.g., HEAD-DTR|SYN in (47))? What if the type of the complete structure is incompatible with the features in this structure? What seems to be a harmless notational device in fact involves some non-trivial machinery in the background. Keeping the Head Feature Principle makes this additional machinery unnecessary.

10.6.2.6 Conclusion

Due to the conceptual problems with meta-statements and the relatively simple ways of getting around locality restrictions, the reorganization of features (MOTHER vs. SYN-SEM) does not bring with it any advantages. Since the grammar becomes more complex due to the meta-constraint, we should reject this change.[23] Other changes in the fea-

---

[23]In Müller (2013a: 253) I claimed that SBCG uses a higher number of features in comparison to other variants of HPSG because of the assumption of the MOTHER feature. As Van Eynde (2015) points out this is not true for more recent variants of HPSG since they have the SYNSEM feature, which is not needed if MOTHER is assumed. (Van Eynde refers to the LOCAL feature, but the LOCAL feature was eliminated because it was considered superfluous because of the lexical analysis of extraction. If one simply omits the MOTHER feature from SBCG one is back to the 1987 version of HPSG (Pollard & Sag 1987), which also used a SYN and a SEM feature. What would be missing would be the locality of selection (Sag 2012: 149) that was enforced to some extent by the SYNSEM feature. Note that the locality of selection that is enforced by SYNSEM can be circumvented by the use of relational constraints as well (see Frank Richter and Manfred Sailer's work on collocations (Richter & Sailer 1999a; Soehn & Sailer 2008)). So in principle, we end up with style guides in this area of grammar as well.

10 Construction Grammar

ture geometry (elimination of the LOCAL feature and use of a single valence feature) are problematic as well. However, if we do reject the revised feature geometry and revert to the feature geometry that was used before, then Sign-Based Construction Grammar and Constructional HPSG (Sag 1997) are (almost) indistinguishable.

10.6.3 Embodied Construction Grammar

Embodied Construction Grammar was developed by Bergen & Chang (2005) and there are some implementations of fragments of German that use this format (Porzel et al. 2006). In the following, I will briefly present the formalism using an example construction. (48) gives the DetNoun construction:[24]

(48)
```
Construction DetNoun
    subcase of RefExp
    constructional
    d:Determiner
    c:CommonNoun
    self.case      ↔ d.case
    self.number    ↔ c.number
    d.gender       ↔ c.gender
    d.case         ↔ c.case
    d.number       ↔ c.number
form
    d.f before c.f
meaning
    self.m         ↔ c.m
```

This representational form is reminiscent of PATR-II grammars (Shieber, Uszkoreit, Pereira, Robinson & Tyson 1983): as in PATR-II, the daughters of a construction are given names. As such, (48) contains the daughters c and d. d is a determiner and c is a common noun. It is possible to refer to the construction itself via the object **self**. Constructions (and also their daughters) are feature-value descriptions. Structure sharing is represented by path equations. For example, d.gender ↔ c.gender states that the value of the gender feature of the determiner is identical to the gender feature of the noun. As well as restrictions on features, there are restrictions on the form. d.f **before** c.f states that the form contribution of the determiner must occur before that of the noun. Bergen & Chang (2005) differentiate between immediate (**meets**) and non-immediate precedence (**before**). Part of the information represented under f is the orthographic form (f.orth). The inheritance relation is given explicitly in the construction as in Kay & Fillmore (1999).

The construction in (48) can be represented in a similar way to the format used in Chapter 6: (49) shows how this is done. The structure in (49) corresponds to a construc-

---

[24]For a similar construction, see Bergen & Chang (2005: 162).

10.6 New developments and theoretical variants

(49)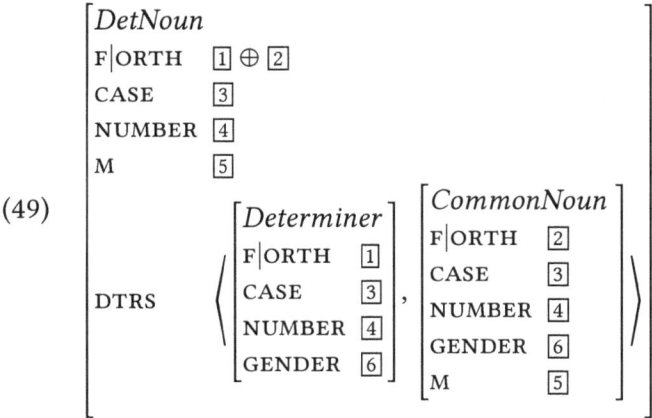

tion where the determiner directly precedes the noun because the form contribution of the determiner has been combined with that of the noun. This strict adjacency constraint makes sense as the claim that the determiner must precede the noun is not restrictive enough since sequences such as (50b) would be allowed:

(50) a. [dass] die Frauen Türen öffnen
 that the women doors open
 'that the woman open doors'
 b. * die Türen öffnen Frauen

If discontinuous phrases are permitted, *die Türen* 'the doors' can be analyzed with the DetNoun Construction although another noun phrase intervenes between the determiner and the noun (Müller 1999b: 424; 1999d). The order in (50b) can be ruled out by linearization constraints or constraints on the continuity of arguments. If we want the construction to require that the determiner and noun be adjacent, then we would simply use **meets** instead of **before** in the specification of the construction.

This discussion has shown that (49) is more restrictive than (48). There are, however, contexts in which one could imagine using discontinuous constituents such as the deviant one in (50b). For example, discontinuous constituents have been proposed for verbal complexes, particle verbs and certain coordination data (Wells 1947). Examples for analyses with discontinuous constituents in the framework of HPSG are Reape (1994), Kathol (1995), Kathol (2000), Crysmann (2008), and Beavers & Sag (2004).[25] These analyses, which are discussed in Section 11.7.2.2 in more detail, differ from those previously presented in that they use a feature DOMAIN instead of or in addition to the daughters features. The value of the DOMAIN feature is a list containing the head and the elements dependent on it. The elements do not have to necessarily be adjacent in the utterance, that is, discontinuous constituents are permitted. Which elements are entered into this

---

[25] Crysmann, Beaver and Sag deal with coordination phenomena. For an analysis of coordination in TAG that also makes use of discontinuous constituents, see Sarkar & Joshi (1996) and Section 21.6.2.

list in which way is governed by the constraints that are part of the linguistic theory. This differs from the simple **before** statement in ECG in that it is much more flexible and in that one can also restrict the area in which a given element can be ordered since elements can be freely ordered inside their domain only.

There is a further difference between the representation in (48) and the general HPSG schemata: in the ECG variant, linearization requirements are linked to constructions. In HPSG and GPSG, it is assumed that linearization rules hold generally, that is, if we were to assume the rules in (51), we would not have to state for each rule explicitly that shorter NPs tend to precede longer ones and that animate nouns tend to occur before inanimate ones.

(51)   a.   S → NP[nom], NP[acc], V
        b.   S → NP[nom], NP[dat], V
        c.   S → NP[nom], NP[dat], NP[acc], V
        d.   S → NP[nom], NP[acc], PP, V

It is possible to capture these generalizations in ECG if one specifies linearization constraints for more general constructions and more specific constructions inherit them from these. As an example, consider the Active-Ditransitive Construction discussed by Bergen & Chang (2005: 170):

(52)
> **Construction** Active-Ditransitive
>   **subcase of** Pred-Expr
>   **constructional**
>   agent:Ref-Expr
>   action:Verb
>   recipient:Ref-Expr
>   theme:Ref-Expr
>   ...
> **form**
>   agent.f **before** action.f
>   action.f **meets** recipient.f
>   recipient.f **meets** theme.f
> **meaning**
>   ...

These restrictions allow the sentences in (53a,b) and rule out those in (53c):

(53)   a.   Mary tossed me a drink.
        b.   Mary happily tossed me a drink.
        c.   * Mary tossed happily me a drink.

The restriction agent.f **before** action.f forces an order where the subject occurs before the verb but also allows for adverbs to occur between the subject and the verb. The other

10.6 New developments and theoretical variants

constraints on form determine the order of the verb and its object: the recipient must be adjacent to the verb and the theme must be adjacent to the recipient. The requirement that an agent in the active must occur before the verb is not specific to ditransitive constructions. This restriction could therefore be factored out as follows:

(54)   **Construction** Active-Agent-Verb
      subcase of Pred-Expr
      constructional
      agent:Ref-Expr
      action:Verb
    form
      agent.f **before** action.f

The Active-Ditransitive Construction in (52) would then inherit the relevant information from (54).

In addition to the descriptive means used in (48), there is the evokes operator (Bergen & Chang 2005: 151–152). An interesting example is the representation of the term hypotenuse: this concept can only be explained by making reference to a right-angled triangle (Langacker 1987: Chapter 5). Chang (2008: 67) gives the following formalization:

(55)   **Schema** hypotenuse
      subcase of line-segment
      evokes right-triangle **as** rt
    constraints
      self ↔ rt.long-side

This states that a hypotenuse is a particular line segment, namely the longest side of a right-angled triangle. The concept of a right-angled triangle is activated by means of the evokes operator. Evokes creates an instance of an object of a certain type (in the example, *rt* of type *right-triangle*). It is then possible to refer to the properties of this object in a schema or in a construction.

The feature description in (56) is provided in the notation from Chapter 6. It is the equivalent to (55).

$$(56) \quad \boxed{1} \begin{bmatrix} \textit{hypotenuse} \\ \text{EVOKES} \quad \left\langle \begin{bmatrix} \textit{right-triangle} \\ \text{LONG-SIDE} \;\; \boxed{1} \end{bmatrix} \right\rangle \end{bmatrix}$$

The type *hypotenuse* is a subtype of *line-segment*. The value of EVOKES is a list since a schema or construction can evoke more than one concept. The only element in this list in (56) is an object of type *right-triangle*. The value of the feature LONG-SIDE is identified with the entire structure. This essentially means the following: I, as a hypotenuse, am the long side of a right-angled triangle.

Before turning to FCG in the next subsection, we can conclude that ECG and HPSG are notational variants.

10.6.4 Fluid Construction Grammar

Van Trijp (2013; 2014) claims that SBCG and HPSG are fundamentally different from Fluid Construction Grammar (FCG).[26] He claims that the former approaches are generative ones while the latter is a cognitive-functional one. I think that it is not legitimate to draw these distinctions on the basis of what is done in FCG.[27] I will comment on this at various places in this section. I first deal with the representations that are used in FCG, talk about argument structure constructions, the combination operations fusion and merging that are used in FCG and then provide a detailed comparison of FCG and SBCG/HPSG.

10.6.4.1 General remarks on the representational format

Fluid Construction Grammar (FCG, Steels 2011) is similar to HPSG in that it uses attribute value matrices to represent linguistic objects. However, these AVMs are untyped as in LFG. Since there are no types, there are no inheritance hierarchies that can be used to capture generalizations, but one can use macros to reach similar effects. Constructions can refer to more general constructions (van Trijp 2013: 105). Every AVM comes with a name and can be depicted as follows:

(57) $\begin{bmatrix} \textit{unit-name} \\ [\text{FEATURE}_1 \quad \textit{value}_1] \\ \ldots \\ [\text{FEATURE}_n \quad \textit{value}_n] \end{bmatrix}$

Linguistic objects have a form and a meaning pole. The two poles could be organized into a single feature description by using a SYN and a SEM feature, but in FCG papers the two poles are presented separately and connected via a double arrow. (58) is an example:

(58) The name *Kim* according to van Trijp (2013: 99):

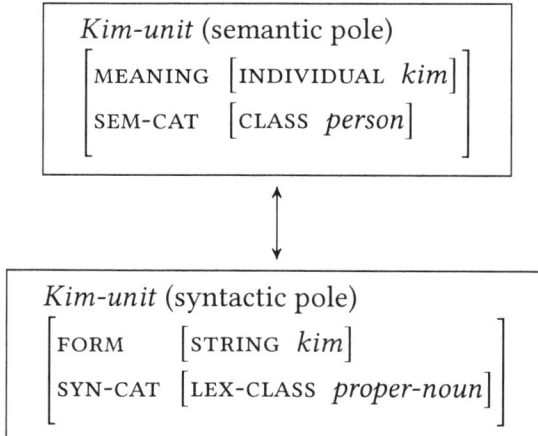

---

[26] A reply to van Trijp based on the discussion in this section is published as Müller (2017b).

[27] Steels (2013: 153) emphasizes the point that FCG is a technical tool for implementing constructionist ideas rather than a theoretical framework of its own. However, authors working with the FCG system publish linguistic papers that share a certain formal background and certain linguistic assumptions. So this section addresses some of the key assumptions made and some of the mechanisms used.

10.6 New developments and theoretical variants

Depending on the mode in which the lexical items are used, the syntactic pole or the semantic pole is used first. The first processing step is a matching phase in which it is checked whether the semantic pole (for generation) or the syntactic pole (for parsing) matches the structure that was build so far. After this test for unification, the actual unification, which is called merging, is carried out. After this step, the respective other pole (syntax for generation and semantics for parsing) is merged. This is illustrated in Figure 10.2.

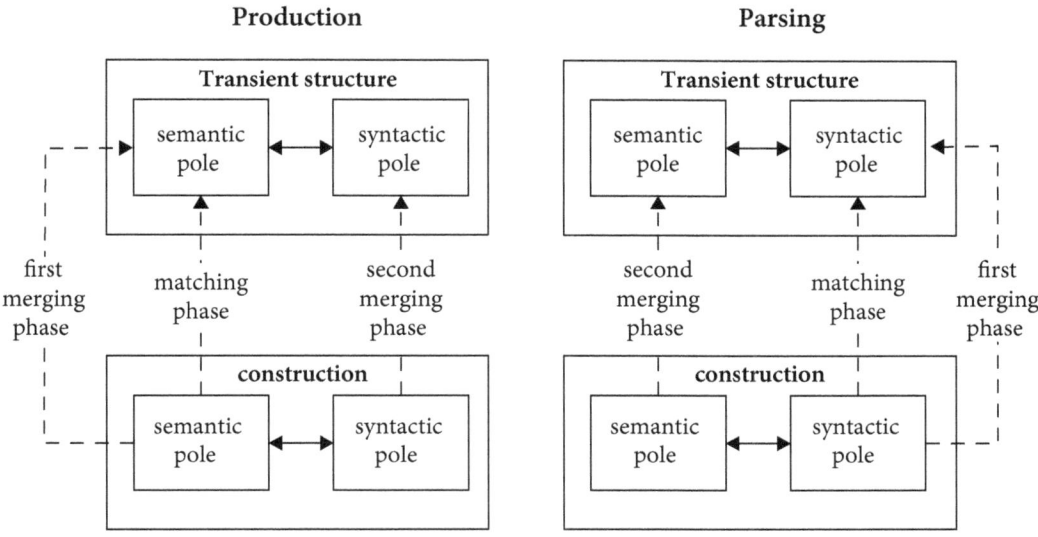

Figure 10.2: Generation and parsing in FCG (van Trijp 2013: 99)

10.6.4.2 Argument Structure Constructions

Fluid Construction Grammar assumes a phrasal approach to argument structure, that is, it is assumed that lexical items enter into phrasal configurations that contribute independent meaning (van Trijp 2011). The FCG approach is one version of implementing Goldberg's plugging approach to argument structure constructions (Goldberg 1995). Van Trijp suggests that every lexical item comes with a representation of potential argument roles like Agent, Patient, Recipient, and Goal. Phrasal argument structure constructions are combined with the respective lexical items and realize a subset of the argument roles, that is they assign them to grammatical functions. Figure 10.3 shows an example: the verb *sent* has the semantic roles Agent, Patient, Recipient, and Goal (upper left of the figure). Depending on the argument structure construction that is chosen, a subset of these roles is selected for realization.[28] The figures show the relation between sender,

---

[28]It is interesting to note here that van Trijp (2011: 141) actually suggests a lexical account since every lexical item is connected to various phrasal constructions via coapplication links. So every such pair of a lexical item and a phrasal construction corresponds to a lexical item in Lexicalized Tree Adjoining Grammar (LTAG). See also Müller & Wechsler (2014a: 25) on Goldberg's assumption that every lexical item is associated with phrasal constructions.

Note that such coapplication links are needed since without them the approach cannot account for cases in which two or more argument roles can only be realized together but not in isolation or in any other combination with other listed roles.

343

10 Construction Grammar

sent, and sendee and more the more abstract semantic roles and the relation between these roles and grammatical functions for the sentences in (59):

(59)   a. He sent her the letter.
        b. He sent the letter.
        c. The letter was sent to her.

While in (59a) the agent, the patient and the recipient are mapped to grammatical functions, only the agent and the patient are mapped to grammatical functions in (59b). The recipient is left out. (59c) shows an argument realization in which the sendee is realized as a *to* phrase. According to van Trijp this semantic role is not a recipient but a goal.

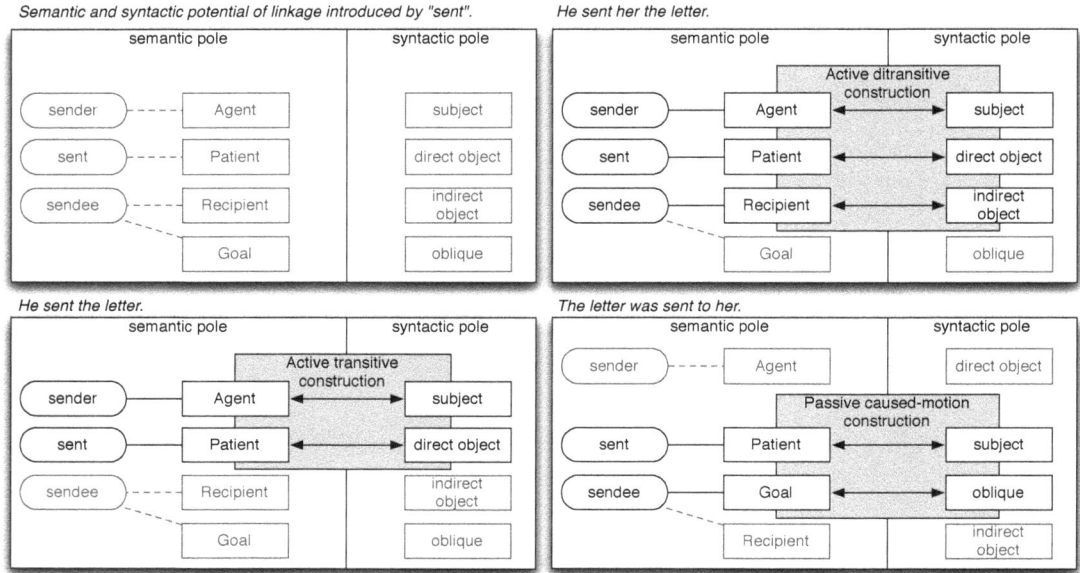

Figure 10.3: Lexical items and phrasal constructions. Figure from van Trijp (2011: 122)

Note that under such an approach, it is necessary to have a passive variant of every active construction. For languages that allow for the combination of passive and impersonal constructions, one would be forced to assume a transitive-passive-impersonal construction. As was argued in Müller (2006: Section 2.6) free datives (commodi/incommodi) in German can be added to almost any construction. They interact with the dative passive and hence should be treated as arguments. So, for the resultative construction one would need an active variant, a passive variant, a variant with dative argument, a variant with dative argument and dative passive, and a middle variant. While it is technically possible to list all these patterns and it is imaginable that we store all this information in our brains, the question is whether such listings really reflect our linguistic knowledge. If a new construction comes into existence, lets say an active sentence pattern with a nominative and two datives in German, wouldn't we expect that this pattern can be used in the passive? While proposals that establish relations between active and passive constructions would predict this, alternative proposals that just list the attested possibilities do not.

The issue of how such generalizations should be captured was discussed in connection with the organization of the lexicon in HPSG (Flickinger 1987; Meurers 2001). In the lexical world, one could simply categorize all verbs according to their valence and say that *loves* is a transitive verb and the passive variant *loved* is an intransitive verb. Similarly *gives* would be categorized as a ditransitive verb and *given* as a two-place verb. Obviously this misses the point that *loved* and *given* share something: they both are related to their active form in a systematic way. This kind of generalization is captured by lexical rules that relate two lexical items. The respective generalizations that are captured by lexical rules are called a horizontal generalizations as compared to vertical generalizations, which describe relations between subtypes and supertypes in an inheritance hierarchy.

The issue is independent of the lexical organization of knowledge, it can be applied to phrasal representations as well. Phrasal constructions can be organized in hierarchies (vertical), but the relation between certain variants is not covered by this. The analog to the lexical rules in a lexical approach are GPSG-like metarules in a phrasal approach. So what seems to be missing in FCG is something that relates phrasal patterns, e.g., allostructions (Cappelle 2006; Goldberg 2014: 116, see also footnote 12).

10.6.4.3 Fusion, matching and merging

As was pointed out by Dowty (1989: 89–90), checking for semantic compatibility is not sufficient when deciding whether a verb may enter (or be fused with) a certain construction. The example is the contrast between *dine*, *eat*, and *devour*. While the thing that is eaten may not be realized with *dine*, its realization is optional with *eat* and obligatory with *devour*. So the lexical items have to come with some information about this.

Van Trijp (2011) and Steels & van Trijp (2011) make an interesting suggestion that could help here: every verb comes with a list of potential roles and argument structure constructions can pick subsets of these roles (see Figure 10.3). This is called *matching*: introducing new argument roles is not allowed. This would make it possible to account for *dine*: one could say that there is something that is eaten, but that no Theme role is made available for linking to the grammatical functions. This would be a misuse of thematic roles for syntactic purposes though since *dine* is semantically a two-place predicate. To account for the extension of argument roles as it is observed in the Caused-Motion Construction (Goldberg 1995: Chapter 7), Steels & van Trijp (2011) suggest a process called *merging*. Merging is seen as a repair strategy: if an utterance involves an intransitive verb and some other material, the utterance cannot be processed with matching alone. For example, when processing Goldberg's example in (60), *he sneezed* could be parsed, but *the foam* and *off the cappuccino* would be unintegrated (see Chapter 21 for an extended discussion of such constructions).

(60) He sneezed the foam off the cappuccino.[29]

---

[29] Goldberg (2006: 42).

So, Steels & van Trijp (2011: 319–320) suggest that only if regular constructions cannot apply, merging is allowed. The problem with this is that human language is highly ambiguous and in the case at hand this could result in situations in which there is a reading for an utterance, so that the repair strategy would never kick in. Consider (61):[30]

(61) Schlag den Mann tot!
 beat the man dead

 'Beat the man to death!' or 'Beat the dead man!'

(61) has two readings: the resultative reading in which *tot* 'dead' expresses the result of the beating and another reading in which *tot* is a depictive predicate. The second reading is dispreferred, since the activity of beating dead people is uncommon, but the structure is parallel to other sentences with depictive predicates:

(62) Iss den Fisch roh!
 eat the fish raw

The depictive reading can be forced by coordinating *tot* with a predicate that is not a plausible result predicate:

(63) Schlag ihn tot oder lebendig!
 beat him dead or alive

 'Beat him when he is dead or while he is alive!'

So, the problem is that (61) has a reading which does not require the invocation of the repair mechanism: *schlug* 'beat' is used with the transitive construction and *tot* is an adjunct (see Winkler 1997). However, the more likely analysis of (61) is the one with the resultative analysis, in which the valence frame is extended by an oblique element. So this means that one has to allow the application of merging independent of other analyses that might be possible. As Steels & van Trijp (2011: 320) note, if merging is allowed to apply freely, utterances like (64a) will be allowed and of course (64b) as well.

(64) a. * She sneezed her boyfriend.
 b. * She dined a steak.

In (64) *sneeze* and *dined* are used in the transitive construction.

The way out of this dilemma is to establish information in lexical items that specifies in which syntactic environments a verb can be used. This information can be weighted and for instance the probability of *dine* to be used transitively would be extremely low. Steels and van Trijp would connect their lexical items to phrasal constructions via so-called coapplication links and the strength of the respective link would be very low for

---

[30] I apologize for these examples .... An English example that shows that there may be ambiguity between the depictive and the resultative construction is the following one that is due to Haider (2016):

 (i) They cooked the chicken dry.

I use the German example below since the resultative reading is strongly preferred over the depictive one.

dine and the transitive construction and reasonably high for *sneeze* and the Caused-Motion Construction. This would explain the phenomena (and in a usage-based way), but it would be a lexical approach, as it is common in CG, HPSG, SBCG, and DG.

10.6.4.4 Long-distance dependencies

Van Trijp (2014) compares the SLASH-based approaches that are used in GPSG, HPSG, and SBCG with the approach that he suggests within the framework of FCG. He claims that there are fundamental differences between SBCG and FCG and assigns SBCG to the class of generative grammars, while placing FCG in the class of cognitive-functional approaches. He claims that his cognitive-functional approach is superior in terms of completeness, explanatory adequacy, and theoretical parsimony (p. 2). What van Trijp (2014) suggests is basically an analysis that was suggested by Reape (2000) in unpublished work (see Reape (1994) for a published version of an linearization-based approach and Kathol (2000); Müller (1996c; 1999b; 2002a) for linearization-based approaches that despite of being linearization-based assume the SLASH approach for nonlocal dependencies). Van Trijp develops a model of grammar that allows for discontinuous constituents and just treats the serialization of the object in sentences like (65) as an alternative linearization option.

(65)   a. This book, I read.
       b. What did the boy hit?

Van Trijp's analysis involves several units that do not normally exist in phrase structure grammars, but can be modeled via adjacency constraints or which represent relations between items which are part of lexical representations in HPSG/SBCG anyway. An example is the subject-verb anchor that connects the subject and the verb to represent the fact that these two items play an important functional role. Figure 10.4 shows the analysis of (66).

(66)   What did the boy hit?

As can be seen in the figure, van Trijp also refers to information structural terms like topic and focus. It should be noted here that the analysis of information structure has quite some history in the framework of HPSG (Engdahl & Vallduví 1996; Kuhn 1995; 1996; Günther et al. 1999; Wilcock 2001; 2005; De Kuthy 2002; Paggio 2005; Bildhauer 2008; Bildhauer & Cook 2010). The fact that information structure is not talked about in syntax papers like Sag (2012) does not entail that information structure is ignored or should be ignored in theories like HPSG and SBCG. So much for completeness. The same holds of course for explanatory adequacy. This leaves us with theoretical parsimony, but before I comment on this, I want to discuss van Trijp's analysis in a little bit more detail in order to show that many of his claims are empirically problematic and that his theory therefore cannot be explanatory since empirical correctness is a precondition for explanatory adequacy.

10 Construction Grammar

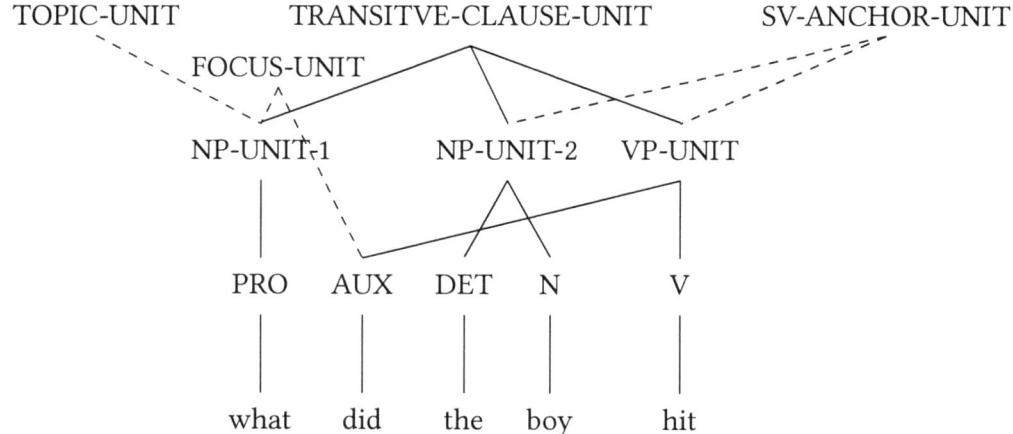

Figure 10.4: The analysis of *What did the boy hit?* according to van Trijp (2014: 265)

Van Trijp claims that sentences with nonlocal dependency constructions in English start with a topic.[31] Bresnan's sentences in (2) and (3) were discussed on page 224 (Bresnan 2001: 97) and are repeated below for convenience:

(67) Q: What did you name your cat?
A: Rosie I named her. (*Rosie* = focus)

(68) Q: What did you name your pets?
A: My dog, I named Harold. My cat, I named Rosie. (*my dog*, *my cat* = topic)

These sentences show that the pre-subject position is not unambiguously a topic or a focus position. So, a statement saying that the fronted element is a topic is empirically not correct. If this position is to be associated with an information structural function, this association has to be a disjunction admitting both topics and focused constituents.

A further problematic aspect of van Trijp's analysis is that he assumes that the auxiliary *do* is an object marker (p. 10, 22) or a non-subject marker (p. 23). It is true that *do* support is not necessary in subject questions like (69a), but only in (69b), but this does not imply that all items that are followed by *do* are objects.

(69) a. Who saw the man?
b. Who did John see?

First, *do* can be used to emphasize the verb:

(70) Who *did* see the man?

Second, all types of other grammatical functions can precede the verb:

---

[31]Van Trijp (2014: 256) uses the following definitions for topic and focus: "Topicality is defined in terms of aboutness: the topic of an utterance is what the utterance is 'about'. Focality is defined in terms of salience: focus is used for highlighting the most important information given the current communicative setting."

(71) a. Where did you see the man? (adverbial)
 b. How tall is the man? (predicative)
 c. What did John consider Peter? (predicative)
 d. What does this book cost? (adverbial)
 e. About what did you talk? (prepositional object)

And finally, even a subject can appear in front of *do* if it is extracted from another clause:

(72) Who does he think saw this man? (subject)

There is a further empirical problem: approaches that assume that a filler is related to its origin can explain scope ambiguities that only arise when an element is extracted. Compare for instance the sentence in (73a) with the sentences in (73b, c): although the order of *oft* 'often' and *nicht* 'not' in (73a) and (73c) is the same, (73a) is ambiguous but (73c) is not.

(73) a. Oft liest er das Buch nicht.
  often reads he the book not

  'It is often that he does not read the book.' or 'It is not the case that he reads the book often.'

 b. dass er das Buch nicht oft liest
  that he the book not often reads

  'that it is not the case that he reads the book often'

 c. dass er das Buch oft nicht liest
  that he the book often not reads

  'that it is often that he does not read the book'

(73a) has the two readings that correspond to (73b) and (73c). A purely linearization-based approach probably has difficulties to explain this. A SLASH-based approach can assume that (73a) has a gap (or some similar means for the introduction of nonlocal dependencies) at the position of *oft* in (73b) or (73c). The gap information is taken into account in the semantic composition at the site of the gap. This automatically accounts for the observed readings.

Another empirical problem that has to be solved is the existence of extraction path marking languages. Bouma, Malouf & Sag (2001) list a number of languages in which elements vary depending on the existence or absence of a gap in a constituent they attach to. For instance, Irish has complementizers that have one form if the clause they attach to has an element extracted and another form if it does not. SLASH-based proposals can account for this in a straight-forward way: the fact that a constituent is missing in a phrase is represented in the SLASH value of the trace and this information is percolated up the tree. So even complex structures contain the information that there is a constituent missing inside them. Complementizers that are combined with sentences therefore can select sentences with SLASH values that correspond to the form of the complementizer. Van Trijp's answer to this challenge is that all languages are different (van Trijp 2014:

263) and that the evidence from one language does not necessarily mean that the analysis for that language is also appropriate for another language. While I agree with this view in principle (see Section 13.1), I do think that extraction is a rather fundamental property of languages and that nonlocal dependencies should be analyzed in parallel for those languages that have it.

10.6.4.5 Coordination

One of the success stories of non-transformational grammar is the SLASH-based analysis of nonlocal dependencies by Gazdar (1981b). This analysis made it possible for the first time to explain Ross's Across the Board Extraction (Ross 1967). The examples were already discussed on page 199 and are repeated here for convenience:

(74) a. The kennel which Mary made and Fido sleeps in has been stolen.
(= S/NP & S/NP)
b. The kennel in which Mary keeps drugs and Fido sleeps has been stolen.
(= S/PP & S/PP)
c. * The kennel (in) which Mary made and Fido sleeps has been stolen.
(= S/NP & S/PP)

The generalization is that two (or more) constituents can be coordinated if they have identical syntactic categories and identical SLASH values. This explains why *which* and *in which* in (74a,b) can fill two positions in the respective clauses. Now, theories that do not use a SLASH feature for the percolation of information about missing elements have to find different ways to make sure that all argument slots are filled and that the correct correspondence between extracted elements and the respective argument role is established. Note that this is not straightforward in models like the one suggested by van Trijp, since he has to allow the preposition *in* to be combined with some material to the left of it that is simultaneously also the object of *made*. Usually an NP cannot simply be used by two different heads as their argument. As an example consider (75a):

(75) a. * John said about the cheese that I like.
b. John said about the cheese that I like it.

If it would be possible to use material several times, a structure for (75a) would be possible in which *the cheese* is the object of the preposition *about* and of the verb *like*. This sentence, however, is totally out: the pronoun *it* has to be used to fill the object slot.

10.6.4.6 Discontinuous constituents and performance models

Van Trijp points out that SBCG does not have a performance model and contrasts this with FCG. On page 252 he states:

> So parsing starts by segmenting the utterance into discrete forms, which are then categorized into words by morphological and lexical constructions, and which can then be grouped together as phrases (see Steels, 2011b, for a detailed account of

10.6 New developments and theoretical variants

lexico-phrasal processing in FCG). So the parser will find similar constituents for all four utterances, as shown in examples (21–24). Since auxiliary-*do* in example (24) falls outside the immediate domain of the VP, it is not yet recognized as a member of the VP.

All of these phrases are disconnected, which means that the grammar still has to identify the relations between the phrases. (van Trijp 2014: 252)

In his (21)–(24), van Trijp provides several tree fragments that contain NPs for subject and object and states that these have to be combined in order to analyze the sentences he discusses. This is empirically inadequate: if FCG does not make the competence/performance distinction, then the way utterances are analyzed should reflect the way humans process language (and this is what is usually claimed about FCG). However, all we know about human language processing points towards an incremental processing, that is, we process information as soon as it is available. We start to process the first word taking into account all of the relevant aspects (phonology, stress, part of speech, semantics, information structure) and come up with an hypothesis about how the utterance could proceed. As soon as we have two words processed (in fact even earlier: integration already happens during the processing of words) we integrate the second word into what we know already and continue to follow our hypothesis, or revise it, or simply fail. See Section 15.2 for details on processing and the discussion of experiments that show that processing is incremental. So, we have to say that van Trijp's analysis fails on empirical grounds: his modeling of performance aspects is not adequate.

The parsing scheme that van Trijp describes is pretty much similar to those of computational HPSG parsers, but these usually come without any claims about human performance. Modeling human performance is rather complex since a lot of factors play a role. It is therefore reasonable to separate competence and performance and continue to work the way it is done in HPSG and FCG. This does not mean that performance aspects should not be modeled, in fact psycholinguistic models using HPSG have been developed in the past (Konieczny 1996), but developing both a grammar with large coverage and the performance model that combines with it demands a lot of resources.

10.6.4.7 Discontinuity vs. Subject-Head and Head-Filler Schema

I now turn to parsimony: van Trijp uses a subject-verb anchor construction that combines the subject and the main verb. Because of examples like (76) it must be possible to have discontinuous subject-verb constructions:[32]

(76) Peter often reads books.

---

[32]Unless modals and tense auxiliaries are treated as main verbs (which they should not in English), constructions with modals seem to be another case where the subject and the main verb are not adjacent:

(i) a. Peter will read the book.
    b. Peter has read the book.

But if such constructions can be discontinuous one has to make sure that (77b) cannot be an instantiation of the subject-verb construction:

(77)   a.   The boy I think left.
          b.   * I the boy think left.

Here it is required to have some adjacency between the subject and the verb it belongs to, modulo some intervening adverbials. This is modelled quite nicely in phrase structure grammars that have a VP node. Whatever the internal structure of such a VP node may be, it has to be adjacent to the subject in sentences like (76) and (77a) above. The dislocated element has to be adjacent to the complex consisting of subject and VP. This is what the Filler-Head Schema does in HPSG and SBCG. Van Trijp criticizes SBCG for having to stipulate such a schema, but I cannot see how his grammar can be complete without a statement that ensures the right order of elements in sentences with fronted elements.

Van Trijp stated that FCG differs from what he calls generative approaches in that it does not want to characterize only the well-formed utterances of a language. According to him, the parsing direction is much more liberal in accepting input than other theories. So it could well be that he is happy to find a structure for (77b). Note though that this is incompatible with other claims made by van Trijp: he argued that FCG is superior to other theories in that it comes with a performance model (or rather in not separating competence from performance at all). But then (77b) should be rejected both on competence and performance grounds. It is just unacceptable and speakers reject it for whatever reasons. Any sufficiently worked out theory of language has to account for this.

10.6.4.8 Restricting discontinuity

There is a further problem related to discontinuity. If one does not restrict continuity, then constituent orders like (78b) are admitted by the grammar:

(78)   a.   Deshalb klärt, dass Peter kommt, ob Klaus spielt.
              therefore resolves that Peter comes whether Klaus plays

          'Therefore that Peter comes resolves whether Klaus will play.'

          b.   * Deshalb klärt dass ob Peter Klaus kommt spielt.
              therefore resolves that whether Peter Klaus comes plays

The interesting thing about the word salad in (78b) is that the constituent order within the *dass* clause and within the *ob* clause is correct. That is, the complementizer precedes the subject, which in turn precedes the verb. The problem is that the constituents of the two clauses are mixed.

In a model that permits discontinuous constituents, one cannot require that all parts of an argument have to be arranged after all parts that belong to another argument since discontinuity is used to account for nonlocal dependencies. So, it must be possible to have *Klaus* before other arguments (or parts of other arguments) since *Klaus* can be extracted. An example of mixing parts of phrases is given in (79):

(79) Dieses Buch hat der Mann mir versprochen, seiner Frau zu geben, der gestern
this book has the man me promised his wife to give who yesterday
hier aufgetreten ist.
here performed is

'The man who performed here yesterday promised me to give this book to his wife.'

We see that material that refers to *der Mann* 'the man', namely the relative clause *der gestern hier aufgetreten ist* 'who performed here yesterday', appears to the right. And the object of *geben* 'to give', which would normally be part of the phrase *dieses Buch seiner Frau zu geben* 'this book his wife to give' appears to the left. So, in general it is possible to mix parts of phrases, but this is possible in a very restricted way only. Some dependencies extend all the way to the left of certain units (fronting) and others all the way to the right (extraposition). Extraposition is clause-bound, while extraction is not. In approaches like GPSG, HPSG and SBCG, the facts are covered by assuming that constituents for a complete clause are continuous apart from constituents that are fronted or extraposed. The fronted and extraposed constituents are represented in SLASH and EXTRA (Keller 1995; Müller 1999b: Section 13.2; Crysmann 2013), respectively, rather than in valence features, so that it is possible to require of constituents that have all their valents saturated to be continuous (Müller 1999c: 294).

Summing up the discussion of parsimony, it has to be said that van Trijp has to provide the details on how continuity is ensured. The formalization of this is not trivial and only after this is done can FCG be compared with the SLASH-based approach.

In addition to all the points discussed so far, there is a logical flaw in van Trijp's argumentation. He states that:

> whereas the filler-gap analysis cannot explain WHY *do*-support does not occur in *wh*-questions where the subject is assigned questioning focus, this follows naturally from the interaction of different linguistic perspectives in this paper's approach. (van Trijp 2014: 263)

The issue here is whether a filler-gap analysis or an analysis with discontinuous constituents is suited better for explaining the data. A correct argumentation against the filler-gap analysis would require a proof that information structural or other functional constraints cannot be combined with this analysis. This proof was not provided and in fact I think it cannot be provided since there are approaches that integrate information structure. Simply pointing out that a theory is incomplete does not falsify a theory. This point was already made in my review of Boas (2003) and in a reply to Boas (2014). See Müller (2005a: 655–656), Müller (2007a: Chapter 20), and Müller & Wechsler (2014b: Footnote 15).

The conclusion about the FCG analysis of nonlocal dependencies is that there are some empirical flaws that can be easily fixed or assumptions that can simply be dropped (role of *do* as object marker, claim that the initial position in English fronting construction is the topic), some empirical shortcomings (coordination, admittance of illformed

10 Construction Grammar

utterances with discontinuous constituents), some empirical problems when the analysis is extended to other languages (scope of adjuncts in German), and the parsimony of the analyses is not really comparable since the restrictions on continuity are not really worked out (or at least not published). If the formalization of restrictions on continuity in FCG turns out to be even half as complex as the formalization that is necessary for accounts of nonlocal dependencies (extraction and extraposition) in linearization-based HPSG that Reape (2000) suggested,[33] the SLASH-based analysis would be favorable.

In any case, I do not see how nonlocal dependencies could be used to drive a wedge between SBCG and FCG. If there are functional considerations that have to be taken into account, they should be modeled in both frameworks. In general, FCG should be more restrictive than SBCG since FCG claims to integrate a performance model, so both competence and performance constraints should be operative. I will come back to the competence/performance distinction in the following section, which is a more general comparison of SBCG and FCG.

10.6.4.9 Comparison to Sign-Based Construction Grammar/HPSG

According to van Trijp (2013), there are the differences shown in Table 10.1. These differences will be discussed in the following subsections.

Table 10.1: Differences between SBCG and FCG according to van Trijp (2013: 112)

Scientific model	Theoretical physics (abstract calculus)	Evolutionary theory (complex adaptive system)
Linguistic approach	Generative (competence model)	Cognitive-functional (parsing and production)
Formalization	Mathematical (amenable for implementation)	Computational (implemented)
Constructions	Static type constraints	Dynamic mappings
Constructicon	Signature and grammar	Open-ended inventory
Processing	Assumption of processing-independence	Bidirectional processing model

10.6.4.9.1 Competence/performance distinction

As for the linguistic approach, the use of the term *generative* is confusing. What van Trijp means – and also explains in the paper – is the idea that one should separate competence and performance. We will deal with both the generative-enumerative vs. constraint-based view and with the competence/performance distinction in more detail

---

[33] See Kathol & Pollard (1995) for a linearization-based account of extraposition. This account is implemented in the Babel System (Müller 1996c). See (Müller 1999c) on restricting discontinuity. Linearization-based approaches were argued to not be able to account for apparent multiple frontings in German (Müller 2005c; 2017a) and hence linearization-based approaches were replaced by more traditional variants that allow for continuous constituents only.

in the Chapters 14 and 15, respectively. Concerning the cognitive-functional approach, van Trijp writes:

> The goal of a cognitive-functional grammar, on the other hand, is to explain how speakers express their conceptualizations of the world through language (= *production*) and how listeners analyze utterances into meanings (= *parsing*). Cognitive-functional grammars therefore implement both a competence and a processing model. (van Trijp 2013: 90)

It is true that HPSG and SBCG make a competence/performance distinction (Sag & Wasow 2011). HPSG theories are theories about the structure of utterances that are motivated by distributional evidence. These theories do not contain any hypothesis regarding brain activation, planning of utterances, processing of utterances (garden path effects) and similar things. In fact, none of the theories that are discussed in this book contains an explicit theory that explains all these things. I think that it is perfectly legitimate to work in this way: it is legitimate to study the structure of words without studying their semantics and pragmatics, it is legitimate to study phonology without caring about syntax, it is legitimate to deal with specific semantic problems without caring about phonology and so on, provided there are ways to integrate the results of such research into a bigger picture. In comparison, it is wrong to develop models like those developed in current versions of Minimalism (called Biolinguistics), where it is assumed that utterances are derived in phases (NPs, CPs, depending on the variant of the theory) and then shipped to the interfaces (spell out and semantic interpretation). This is not what humans do (see Chapter 15).[34] But if we are neutral with respect towards such issues, we are fine. In fact, there is psycholinguistic work that couples HPSG grammars to performance models (Konieczny 1996) and similar work exists for TAG (Shieber & Johnson 1993; Demberg & Keller 2008).

Finally, there is also work in Construction Grammar that abstracts away from performance considerations. For instance, Adele Goldberg's book from 1995 does not contain a worked out theory of performance facts. It contains boxes in which grammatical functions are related to semantic roles. So this basically is a competence theory as well. Of course there are statements about how this is connected to psycholinguistic findings, but this is also true for theories like HPSG, SBCG and Simpler Syntax (Jackendoff 2011: 600) that explicitly make the competence/performance distinction.

10.6.4.9.2 Mathematical formalization vs. implementation

The difference between mathematical and computational formalization is a rather strange distinction to make. I think that a formal and precise description is a prerequisite for implementation (see the discussion in Section 3.6.2 and Section 4.7.2). Apart from this, a computer implementation of SBCG is trivial, given the systems that we have for processing HPSG grammars. In order to show this, I want to address one issue that van Trijp discusses. He claims that SBCG cannot be directly implemented. On issues of complexity of constraint solving systems he quotes (Levine & Meurers 2006: Section 4.2.2):

---

[34] Attempts to integrate current Minimalist theories with psycholinguistic findings (Phillips 2003) are incompatible with core principles of Minimalism like the *No Tampering Condition* of Chomsky (2008).

> Actual implementations of HPSG typically handle the problem by guiding the linguistic processor using a (rule-based) phrase structure backbone, but the disadvantage of this approach is that the "organization and formulation of the grammar is different from that of the linguistic theory" (Levine & Meurers 2006: Section 4.2.2). (van Trijp 2013: 108)

He concludes:

> Applying all these observations to the operationalization of SBCG, we can conclude that an SBCG grammar is certainly amenable for computational implementation because of its formal explicitness. There are at least two computational platforms available, mostly used for implementing HPSG-based grammars, whose basic tenets are compatible with the foundations of SBCG: LKB (Copestake 2002) and TRALE (Richter 2006). However, none of these platforms supports a 'direct' implementation of an SBCG grammar as a general constraint system, so SBCG's performance-independence hypothesis remains conjecture until proven otherwise.

There are two issues that should be kept apart here: efficiency and faithfulness to the theory. First, as Levine and Meurers point out, there were many constraint solving systems at the beginning of the 90's. So there are computer systems that can and have been used to implement and process HPSG grammars. This is very valuable since they can be used for direct verification of specific theoretical proposals. As was discussed by Levine and Meurers, trying to solve constraints without any guidance is not the most efficient way to deal with the parsing/generation problem. Therefore, additional control-structure was added. This control structure is used for instance in a parser to determine the syntactic structure of a phrase and other constraints will apply as soon as there is sufficient information available for them to apply. For instance, the assignment of structural case happens once the arguments of a head are realized. Now, is it bad to have a phrase structure backbone? One can write down phrase structure grammars that use phrase structure rules that have nothing to do with what HPSG grammars usually do. The systems TRALE (Meurers, Penn & Richter 2002; Penn 2019) and LKB will process them. But one is not forced to do this. For instance, the grammars that I developed for the CoreGram project (Müller 2013b; 2015b) are very close to the linguistic theory. To see that this is really the case, let us look at the Head-Argument Schema. The Head-Argument Schema is basically the type *head-argument-phrase* with certain type constraints that are partly inherited from its supertypes. The type with all the constraints was given on page 278 and is repeated here as (80):

(80) (syntactic) constraints on *head-complement-phrase*:

$$\begin{bmatrix} \textit{head-complement-phrase} \\ \text{SYNSEM}|\text{LOC}|\text{CAT} \begin{bmatrix} \text{HEAD} & \boxed{1} \\ \text{COMPS} & \boxed{2} \end{bmatrix} \\ \text{HEAD-DTR}|\text{SYNSEM}|\text{LOC}|\text{CAT} \begin{bmatrix} \text{HEAD} & \boxed{1} \\ \text{COMPS} & \boxed{2} \oplus \langle \boxed{3} \rangle \end{bmatrix} \\ \text{NON-HEAD-DTRS} \langle [\text{SYNSEM } \boxed{3}] \rangle \end{bmatrix}$$

This can be translated into phrase structure grammar rules in a straight-forward way:

(81) a. $\begin{bmatrix} \textit{head-complement-phrase} \\ \text{SYNSEM}|\text{LOC}|\text{CAT} \begin{bmatrix} \text{HEAD} & \boxed{1} \\ \text{COMPS} & \boxed{2} \end{bmatrix} \\ \text{HEAD-DTR } \boxed{4} \, |\text{SYNSEM}|\text{LOC}|\text{CAT} \begin{bmatrix} \text{HEAD} & \boxed{1} \\ \text{COMPS} & \boxed{2} \oplus \langle \boxed{3} \rangle \end{bmatrix} \\ \text{NON-HEAD-DTRS } \langle \boxed{5} \, [\text{ SYNSEM } \boxed{3}] \rangle \end{bmatrix} \rightarrow \boxed{4}, \boxed{5}$

b. $\begin{bmatrix} \textit{head-complement-phrase} \\ \text{SYNSEM}|\text{LOC}|\text{CAT} \begin{bmatrix} \text{HEAD} & \boxed{1} \\ \text{COMPS} & \boxed{2} \end{bmatrix} \\ \text{HEAD-DTR } \boxed{4} \, |\text{SYNSEM}|\text{LOC}|\text{CAT} \begin{bmatrix} \text{HEAD} & \boxed{1} \\ \text{COMPS} & \boxed{2} \oplus \langle \boxed{3} \rangle \end{bmatrix} \\ \text{NON-HEAD-DTRS } \langle \boxed{5} \, [\text{ SYNSEM } \boxed{3}] \rangle \end{bmatrix} \rightarrow \boxed{5}, \boxed{4}$

The left hand side of the rule is the mother node of the tree, that is, the sign that is licensed by the schema provided that the daughters are present. The right hand side in (81a) consists of the head daughter ④ followed by the non-head daughter ⑤. We have the opposite order in (81b), that is, the head daughter follows the non-head daughter. The two orders correspond to the two orders that are permitted by LP-rules: the head precedes its argument if it is marked INITIAL+ and it follows it if it is marked INITIAL−.

The following code shows how (81b) is implemented in TRALE:

```
arg_h rule (head_complement_phrase,
            synsem:loc:cat:head:initial:minus,
            head_dtr:HeadDtr,
            non_head_dtrs:[NonHeadDtr])
===>
cat> NonHeadDtr,
cat> HeadDtr.
```

A rule starts with an identifier that is needed for technical reasons like displaying intermediate structures in the parsing process in debugging tools. A description of the mother node follows and after the arrow we find a list of daughters, each introduced by the operator cat>.[35] Structure sharing is indicated by values with capital letters. The above TRALE rule is a computer-readable variant of (81b) additionally including the explicit specification of the value of INITIAL.

Now, the translation of a parallel schema using a MOTHER feature like (82a) into a phrase structure rule is almost as simple:

---

[35] Other operators are possible in TRALE. For instance, sem_head can be used to guide the generator. This is control information that has nothing to do with linguistic theory and not necessarily with the way humans process natural language. There is also a cats operator, which precedes lists of daughters. This can be used to implement phrase structures with more than one non-head daughter.

10 Construction Grammar

(82) a.
$$\begin{bmatrix} \textit{head-complement-cx} \\ \text{MOTHER|SYNSEM|LOC|CAT} \begin{bmatrix} \text{HEAD} & \boxed{1} \\ \text{COMPS} & \boxed{2} \end{bmatrix} \\ \text{HEAD-DTR|SYNSEM|LOC|CAT} \begin{bmatrix} \text{HEAD} & \boxed{1} \\ \text{COMPS} & \boxed{2} \oplus \langle \boxed{3} \rangle \end{bmatrix} \\ \text{NON-HEAD-DTRS} \; \langle \; [\; \text{SYNSEM} \; \boxed{3} \;] \; \rangle \end{bmatrix}$$

b. $\boxed{6} \to \boxed{4}, \boxed{5}$ where
$$\begin{bmatrix} \textit{head-complement-cx} \\ \text{MOTHER} \; \boxed{6} \; |\text{SYNSEM|LOC|CAT} \begin{bmatrix} \text{HEAD} & \boxed{1} \\ \text{COMPS} & \boxed{2} \end{bmatrix} \\ \text{HEAD-DTR} \; \boxed{4} \; |\text{SYNSEM|LOC|CAT} \begin{bmatrix} \text{HEAD} & \boxed{1} \\ \text{COMPS} & \boxed{2} \oplus \langle \boxed{3} \rangle \end{bmatrix} \\ \text{NON-HEAD-DTRS} \; \langle \; \boxed{5} \; [\; \text{SYNSEM} \; \boxed{3} \;] \; \rangle \end{bmatrix}$$

(82b) is only one of the two phrase structure rules that correspond to (82a), but since the other one only differs from (82b) in the ordering of $\boxed{4}$ and $\boxed{5}$, it is not given here.

For grammars in which the order of the elements corresponds to the observable order of the daughters in a DTRS list, the connection to phrase structure rules is even simpler:

(83) $\boxed{1} \to \boxed{2}$ where $\begin{bmatrix} \textit{construction} \\ \text{MOTHER} & \boxed{1} \\ \text{DTRS} & \boxed{2} \end{bmatrix}$

The value of DTRS is a list and hence $\boxed{2}$ stands for the list of daughters on the right hand side of the phrase structure rule as well. The type *construction* is a supertype of all constructions and hence (83) can be used to analyze all phrases that are licensed by the grammar. In fact, (83) is one way to put the meta constraint in (33).

So, this shows that the version of SBCG that has been developed by Sag (2012) has a straightforward implementation in TRALE.[36] The question remains whether "SBCG's performance-independence hypothesis remains conjecture until proven otherwise" as van Trijp sees it. The answer is: it is not a conjecture since any of the old constraint-solving systems of the nineties could be used to process SBCG. The question of whether this is efficient is an engineering problem that is entirely irrelevant for theoretical linguistics. Theoretical linguistics is concerned with human languages and how they are processed by humans. So whether some processing system that does not make any claims about human language processing is efficient or not is absolutely irrelevant. Phrase structure-based backbones are therefore irrelevant as well, provided they refer to the grammar as described in theoretical work.

Now, this begs the question whether there is a contradiction in my claims. On page 333 I pointed out that SBCG is lacking a formalization in Richter's framework (Richter 2004).

---

[36] A toy fragment of English using a MOTHER feature and phrase structure rules with specifications of the kind given above can be downloaded at https://hpsg.hu-berlin.de/Fragments/SBCG-TRALE/.

10.6 New developments and theoretical variants

Richter and also Levine & Meurers (2006) pointed out that there are problems with certain theoretically possible expressions and it is these expressions that mathematical linguists care about. So the goal is to be sure that any HPSG grammar has a meaning and that it is clear what it is. Therefore, this goal is much more foundational than writing a single grammar for a particular fragment of a language. There is no such foundational work for FCG since FCG is a specific toolkit that has been used to implement a set of grammars.

10.6.4.9.3 Static constraints vs. dynamic mappings and signature + grammar vs. open-endedness

On very interesting feature of Fluid Construction Grammar is its fluidity, that is there are certain constraints that can be adapted if there is pressure, the inventory of the theory is open-ended, so categories and features can be added if need be.

Again, this is not a fundamental difference between HPSG/SBCG and FCG. An HPSG grammar fragment of a specific language is a declarative representation of linguistic knowledge and as such it of course just represents a certain fragment and does not contain any information how this set of constraints evolved or how it is acquired by speakers. For this we need specific theories about language evolution/language change/language acquisition. This is parallel to what was said about the competence/performance distinction, in order to account for language evolution we would have to have several HPSG grammars and say something about how one developed from the other. This will involve weighted constraints, it will involve recategorization of linguistic items and lots more.[37] So basically HPSG has to be extended, has to be paired with a model about language evolution in the very same way as FCG is.

10.6.4.9.4 Theoretical physics vs. Darwinian evolutionary theory

Van Trijp compares SBCG and FCG and claims that SBCG follows the model of theoretical physics – like Chomsky does –, while FCG adopts a Darwinian model of science – like Croft does –, the difference being that SBCG makes certain assumptions that are true of all languages, while FCG does not make any a priori assumptions. The fundamental assumptions made in both theories are that the objects that we model are best described by feature value pairs (a triviality). FCG assumes that there is always a syntactic and a semantic pole (fundamental assumption in the system) and researchers working in HPSG/SBCG assume that if languages have certain phenomena, they will be analyzed in similar ways. For instance, if a language has nonlocal dependencies, these will be analyzed via the SLASH mechanism. However, this does not entail that one believes that

---

[37]There are systems that use weighted constraints. We had a simple version of this in the German HPSG grammar that was developed in Verbmobil project (Müller & Kasper 2000) already. Further theoretical approaches to integrate weighted constraints are Brew (1995) and more recently Guzmán Naranjo (2015). Usually such weighted constraints are not part of theoretical papers, but there are exceptions as for instance the paper by Briscoe and Copestake about lexical rules (Briscoe & Copestake 1999).

grammars of all languages have a SLASH feature. And in fact, there may even be languages that do not have valence features (Koenig & Michelson 2010), which may be a problem for FCG since it relies on the SYN-pole for the matching phase. So as far as SBCG is concerned, there is considerable freedom to choose features that are relevant in an analysis, and of course additional features and types can be assumed in case a language is found that provides evidence for this. The only example of a constraint provided by van Trijp that is possibly too strong is the locality constraint imposed by the MOTHER feature. The idea about this feature is that everything that is of relevance in a more nonlocal context has to be passed up explicitly. This is done for nonlocal dependencies (via SLASH) and for instance also for information concerning the form of a preposition inside of a PP (via PFORM or more recently via FORM). Certain verbs require prepositional objects and restrict the form of the preposition. For instance, *wait* has to make sure that its prepositional object has the preposition *for* in it. Since this information is usually available only at the preposition, it has to be passed up to the PP level in order to be directly selectable by the governing verb.

(84) I am waiting for my man.

So, assuming strict locality of selection requires that all phenomena that cannot be treated locally have to be analyzed by passing information up. Assuming strict locality is a design decision that does not have any empirical consequences, as far as it does not rule out any language or construction in principle. It just requires that information has to be passed up that needs to be accessed at higher nodes. As I have shown in Section 10.6.2, the locality constraint is easily circumvented even within SBCG and it makes the analysis of idioms unnecessarily complicated and unintuitive, so I suggest dropping the MOTHER feature. But even if MOTHER is kept, it is not justified to draw a distinction between SBCG and FCG along the lines suggested by van Trijp.

Independent of the MOTHER issue, the work done in the CoreGram project (Müller 2013b; 2015b) shows that one can derive generalizations in a bottom-up fashion rather than imposing constraints on grammars in a top-down way. The latter paper discusses Croft's methodological considerations and shows how methodological pitfalls are circumvented in the project. HPSG/SBCG research differs from work in Chomskyan frameworks in not trying to show that all languages are like English or Romance or German or whatever, rather languages are treated on their own as it is common in the Construction Grammar community. This does not imply that there is no interest in generalizations and universals or near universals or tendencies, but again the style of working and the rhetoric in HPSG/SBCG is usually different from the ones in Mainstream Generative Grammar. Therefore, I think that the purported difference between SBCG and FCG does not exist.

10.6.4.9.5 Permissiveness of the theories

Van Trijp claims that HPSG/SBCG is a "generative grammar" since its aim is to account for and admit only grammatical sentences. FCG on the other hand is more permissive and tries to get the most out of the input even if it is fragmentary or ungrammatical (see also Steels 2013: 166). While it is an engineering decision to be able to parse ungrammatical input – and there are most certainly systems for the robust processing of HPSG grammars (Kiefer, Krieger & Nederhof 2000; Copestake 2007), it is also clear that humans cannot parse everything. There are strong constraints whose violations cause measurable effects in the brain. This is something that a model of language (that includes competence and performance factors or does not make the difference at all) has to explain. The question is what the cause of deviance is: is it processing complexity? Is it a category mismatch? A clash in information structure? So, if FCG permits structures that are not accepted by human native speakers and that do not make any sense whatsoever, additional constraints have to be added. If they are not added, the respective FCG theory is not an adequate theory of the language under consideration. Again, there is no difference between HPSG/SBCG and FCG.

10.6.4.9.6 A note on engineering

A problematic property of work done in FCG is that linguistic and engineering aspects are mixed.[38] Certain bookkeeping features that are needed only for technical reasons appear in linguistic papers, technical assumptions that are made to get a parser running are mixed with linguistic constraints. Bit vector encodings that are used to represent case information are part of papers about interesting case systems. There is certainly nothing wrong with bit vector encodings. They are used in HPSG implementations as well (Reape 1991: 55; Müller 1996c: 269), but this is not mixed into the theoretical papers.

It was a big breakthrough in the 80's when theoretical linguists and computational linguists started working together and developed declarative formalisms that were independent of specific parsers and processing systems. This made it possible to take over insights from a lot of linguists who were not concerned with the actual implementation but took care of finding linguistic generalizations and specifying constraints. Since this separation is given up in FCG, it will remain an engineering project without much appeal to the general linguist.

10.7 Summary and classification

There are currently three formalized variants of Construction Grammar: Sign-Based Construction Grammar, Embodied Construction Grammar, and Fluid Construction Grammar. The first two variants can be viewed as notational variants of (Constructional) HPSG (for SBCG with regard to this point, see Sag (2007: 411) and Sag (2010: 486)), or put differently, sister theories of HPSG. This is also true to a large extend for FCG, although van Trijp (2013) spends 25 pages working out the alleged differences. As I have

---

[38]This is not a problem if all FCG papers are read as papers documenting the FCG-system (see Footnote 27 on page 342) since then it would be necessary to include these technical details. If the FCG papers are to be read as theoretical linguistics papers that document a certain Construction Grammar analysis, the Lisp statements and the implementational details are simply an obstacle.

shown in Section 10.6.4, HPSG and FCG are rather similar and I would say that these theories are sister theories as well.

Due to the origins of all three theories, respective analyses can differ quite considerably: HPSG is a strongly lexicalized theory, where phrasal dominance schemata have only been increasingly more used in the last ten years under the influence of Ivan Sag. The phrasal dominance schemata that Ivan Sag uses in his work are basically refinements of schemata that were present in earlier versions of HPSG. Crucially, all phenomena that interact with valence receive a lexical analysis (Sag, Boas & Kay 2012: Section 2.3). In CxG, on the other hand, predominantly phrasal analyses are adopted due to the influence of Adele Goldberg.

As already emphasized in Chapter 9, these are only tendencies that do not apply to all researchers working in the theories in question.

Exercises

1. Find three examples of utterances whose meaning cannot be derived from the meaning of the individual words. Consider how one could analyze these examples in Categorial Grammar (yes, Categorial Grammar).

Further reading

There are two volumes on Construction Grammar in German: Fischer & Stefanowitsch (2006) and Stefanowitsch & Fischer (2008). Deppermann (2006) discusses Construction Grammar from the point of view of conversational analysis. The 37(3) volume of the *Zeitschrift für germanistische Linguistik* from 2009 was also devoted to Construction Grammar. Goldberg (2003a) and Michaelis (2006) are overview articles in English. Goldberg's books constitute important contributions to Construction Grammar (1995; 2006; 2009). Goldberg (1995) has argued against lexical analyses such as those common in GB, LFG, CG, HPSG, and DG. These arguments can be invalidated, however, as will be shown in Section 21.7.1. Sag (1997), Borsley (2006), Jacobs (2008) and Müller & Lipenkova (2009) give examples of constructions that require a phrasal analysis if one wishes to avoid postulating empty elements. Jackendoff (2008) discusses the noun-preposition-noun construction that can only be properly analyzed as a phrasal construction (see Section 21.10). The discussion on whether argument structure constructions should be analyzed phrasally or lexically (Goldberg 1995; 2006; Müller 2006) culminated in a series of papers (Goldberg 2013a) and a target article by Müller & Wechsler (2014a) with several responses in the same volume.

Tomasello's publications on language acquisition (Tomasello 2000; 2003; 2005; 2006c) constitute a Construction Grammar alternative to the Principle & Parameters theory of acquisition as it does not have many of the problems that P&P analyses have (for more on language acquisition, see Chapter 16). For more on language acquisition and Construction Grammar, see Behrens (2009).

Dąbrowska (2004) looks at psycholinguistic constraints for possible grammatical theories.

11 Dependency Grammar

Dependency Grammar (DG) is the oldest framework described in this book. According to Hudson (2019), the basic assumptions made today in Dependency Grammar were already present in the work of the Hungarian Sámuel Brassai in 1873 (see Imrényi 2013), the Russian Aleksej Dmitrievsky in 1877 and the German Franz Kern (1884). The most influential version of DG was developed by the French linguist Lucien Tesnière (1893–1954). His foundational work *Eléments de syntaxe structurale* 'Elements of structural syntax' was basically finished in 1938 only three years after Ajdukiewicz's paper on Categorial Grammar (1935), but the publication was delayed until 1959, five years after his death. Since valence is central in Dependency Grammar, it is sometimes also referred to as Valence Grammar. Tesnière's ideas are wide-spread nowadays. The conceptions of valence and dependency are present in almost all of the current theories (Ágel & Fischer 2010: 262–263, 284).

Although there is some work on English (Anderson 1971; Hudson 1984), Dependency Grammar is most popular in central Europe and especially so in Germany (Engel 1996: 56–57). Ágel & Fischer (2010: 250) identified a possible reason for this: Tesnière's original work was not available in English until very recently (Tesnière 2015), but there has been a German translation for more than 35 years now (Tesnière 1980). Since Dependency Grammar focuses on dependency relations rather than linearization of constituents, it is often felt to be more appropriate for languages with freer constituent order, which is one reason for its popularity among researchers working on Slavic languages: the New Prague School represented by Sgall, Hajičová and Panevova developed Dependency Grammar further, beginning in the 1960s (see Hajičová & Sgall 2003 for an overview). Igor A. Mel'čuk and A. K. Žolkovskij started in the 1960s in the Soviet Union to work on a model called Meaning–Text Theory, which was also used in machine translation projects (Mel'čuk 1964; 1981; 1988; Kahane 2003). Mel'čuk left the Soviet Union towards Canada in the 1970s and now works in Montréal.

Dependency Grammar is very wide-spread in Germany and among scholars of German linguistics worldwide. It is used very successfully for teaching German as a foreign language (Helbig & Buscha 1969; 1998). Helbig and Buscha, who worked in Leipzig, East Germany, started to compile valence dictionaries (Helbig & Schenkel 1969) and later researchers working at the Institut für Deutsche Sprache (Institute for German Language) in Mannheim began similar lexicographic projects (Schumacher et al. 2004).

The following enumeration is a probably incomplete list of linguists who are/were based in Germany: Vilmos Ágel (2000), Kassel; Klaus Baumgärtner (1965; 1970), Leipzig later Stuttgart; Ulrich Engel (1977; 2014), IDS Mannheim; Hans-Werner Eroms (1985; 1987; 2000), Passau; Heinz Happ, Tübingen; Peter Hellwig (1978; 2003), Heidelberg; Jürgen Heringer (1996), Augsburg; Jürgen Kunze (1968; 1975), Berlin; Henning Lobin (1993), Gießen; Klaus Schubert (1987), Hildesheim; Heinz Josef Weber (1997), Trier; Klaus Welke (1988; 2011), Humboldt University Berlin; Edeltraud Werner (1993), Halle-Wittenberg.

Although work has been done in many countries and continuously over the decades since 1959, a periodical international conference was established as late as 2011.[1,2]

From early on, Dependency Grammar was used in computational projects. Mel'čuk worked on machine translation in the Soviet Union (Mel'čuk 1964) and David G. Hays worked on machine translation in the United States (Hays & Ziehe 1960). Jürgen Kunze, based in East Berlin at the German Academy of Sciences, where he had a chair for computational linguistics, also started to work on machine translation in the 1960s. A book that describes the formal background of the linguistic work was published as Kunze (1975). Various researchers worked in the Collaborative Research Center 100 *Electronic linguistic research* (SFB 100, Elektronische Sprachforschung) from 1973–1986 in Saarbrücken. The main topic of this SFB was machine translation as well. There were projects on Russian to German, French to German, English to German, and Esperanto to German translation. For work from Saarbrücken in this context see Klein (1971), Rothkegel (1976), and Weissgerber (1983). Muraki et al. (1985) used Dependency Grammar in a project that analyzed Japanese and generated English. Richard Hudson started to work in a dependency grammar-based framework called Word Grammar in the 1980s (Hudson 1984; 2007) and Sleator and Temperly have been working on Link Grammar since the 1990s (Sleator & Temperley 1991; Grinberg et al. 1995). Fred Karlsson's Constraint Grammars (1990) are developed for many languages (bigger fragments are available for Danish, Portuguese, Spanish, English, Swedish, Norwegian, French, German, Esperanto, Italian, and Dutch) and are used for school teaching, corpus annotation and machine translation. An online demo is available at the project website.[3]

In recent years, Dependency Grammar became more and more popular among computational linguists. The reason for this is that there are many annotated corpora (tree banks) that contain dependency information.[4] Statistical parsers are trained on such tree banks (Yamada & Matsumoto 2003; Attardi 2006; Nivre 2003; Kübler et al. 2009; Bohnet 2010). Many of the parsers work for multiple languages since the general approach is language independent. It is easier to annotate dependencies consistently since there are fewer possibilities to do so. While syntacticians working in constituency-based models may assume binary branching or flat models, high or low attachment of adjuncts, empty elements or no empty elements and argue fiercely about this, it is fairly clear what the dependencies in an utterance are. Therefore it is easy to annotate consistently and train statistical parsers on such annotated data.

Apart from statistical modeling, there are also so-called deep processing systems, that is, systems that rely on a hand-crafted, linguistically motivated grammar. I already mentioned Mel'čuk's work in the context of machine translation; Hays & Ziehe (1960) had

---

[1] http://depling.org/. 2018-02-20.
[2] A conference on Meaning–Text Theory has taken place biannually since 2003.
[3] http://beta.visl.sdu.dk/constraint_grammar. 2018-02-20.
[4] According to Kay (2000), the first treebank ever was developed by Hays and did annotate dependencies.

a parser for Russian; Starosta & Nomura (1986) developed a parser that was used with an English grammar, Jäppinen, Lehtola & Valkonen (1986) developed a parser that was demoed with Finnish, Hellwig (1986; 2003; 2006) implemented grammars of German in the framework of Dependency Unification Grammar, Hudson (1989) developed a Word Grammar for English, Covington (1990) developed a parser for Russian and Latin, which can parse discontinuous constituents, and Menzel (1998) implemented a robust parser of a Dependency Grammar of German. Other work on computational parsing to be mentioned is Kettunen (1986); Lehtola (1986); Menzel & Schröder (1998b). The following is a list of languages for which Dependency Grammar fragments exist:

- Danish (Bick 2001; Bick & Nygaard 2007)
- English (Muraki et al. 1985; Starosta & Nomura 1986; Lavoie & Rambow 1997; Hudson 1989; Sleator & Temperley 1991; Voutilainen et al. 1992; Iordanskaja et al. 1992; Coch 1996)
- Esperanto (Bick 2009)
- Estonian (Müürisep 1999; Müürisep, Puolakainen, Muischnek, Koit, Roosmaa & Uibo 2003)
- Faroese (Trosterud 2009)
- Finnish (Nelimarkka, Jäppinen & Lehtola 1984; Jäppinen, Lehtola & Valkonen 1986)
- French (Iordanskaja et al. 1992; Coch 1996; Bick 2010)
- German (Hellwig 1986; Coch 1996; Heinecke et al. 1998; Menzel & Schröder 1998a; Hellwig 2003; 2006; Gerdes & Kahane 2001)
- Irish (Dhonnchadha & van Genabith 2006)
- Japanese (Muraki, Ichiyama & Fukumochi 1985)
- Latin (Covington 1990)
- Mandarin Chinese (Liu & Huang 2006; Liu 2009)
- Norwegian (Hagen, Johannessen & Nøklestad 2000),
- Old Icelandic (Maas 1977)
- Portuguese (Bick 2003)
- Russian (Hays & Ziehe 1960; Mel'čuk 1964; Covington 1990)
- Spanish (Coch 1996; Bick 2006)
- Swahili (Hurskainen 2006)

The Constraint Grammar webpage[5] additionally lists grammars for Basque, Catalan, English, Finnish, German, Italian, Sami, and Swedish.

11.1 General remarks on the representational format

11.1.1 Valence information, nucleus and satellites

The central concept of Dependency Grammar is valence (see Section 1.6). The central metaphor for this is the formation of stable molecules, which is explained in chemistry with reference to layers of electrons. A difference between chemical compounds and linguistic structures is that the chemical compounding is not directed, that is, it would not make sense to claim that oxygen is more important than hydrogen in forming water. In contrast to this, the verb is more important than the nominal phrases it combines with to form a complete clause. In languages like English and German, the verb determines the form of its dependents, for instance their case.

One way to depict dependencies is shown in Figure 11.1. The highest node is the verb *reads*. Its valence is a nominative NP (the subject) and an accusative NP (an object). This is

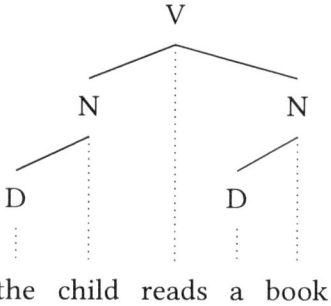

Figure 11.1: Analysis of *The child reads a book*.

depicted by the dependency links between the node representing the verb and the nodes representing the respective nouns. The nouns themselves require a determiner, which again is shown by the dependency links to *the* and *a* respectively. Note that the analysis presented here corresponds to the NP analysis that is assumed in HPSG for instance, that is, the noun selects its specifier (see Section 9.1.1). It should be noted, though, that the discussion whether an NP or a DP analysis is appropriate also took place within the Dependency Grammar community (Hudson 1984: 90; Van Langendonck 1994; Hudson 2004). See Engel (1977) for an analysis with the N as head and Welke (2011: 31) for an analysis with the determiner as head.

The verb is the head of the clause and the nouns are called *dependents*. Alternative terms for head and dependent are *nucleus* and *satellite*, respectively.

---

[5]http://beta.visl.sdu.dk/constraint_grammar_languages.html, 2018-02-20.

11.1 General remarks on the representational format

An alternative way to depict the dependencies, which is used in the Dependency Grammar variant Word Grammar (Hudson 2007), is provided in Figure 11.2. This graph displays the grammatical functions rather than information about part of speech, but apart from this it is equivalent to the representation in Figure 11.1. The highest node in Figure 11.1 is labeled with the ROOT arrow in Figure 11.2. Downward links are indicated by the direction of the arrows.

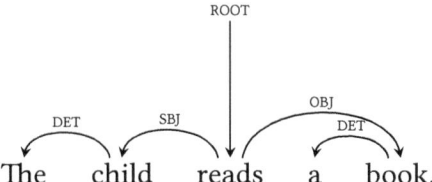

Figure 11.2: Alternative presentation of the analysis of *The child reads a book.*

A third form of representing the same dependencies provided in Figure 11.3 has the tree format again. This tree results if we pull the root node in Figure 11.2 upwards. Since we

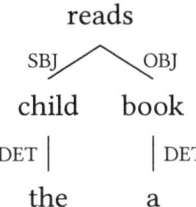

Figure 11.3: Alternative presentation of the analysis of *The child reads a book.*

have a clear visualization of the dependency relation that represents the nucleus above the dependents, we do not need to use arrows to encode this information. However, some variants of Dependency Grammar – for instance Word Grammar – use mutual dependencies. So for instance, some theories assume that *his* depends on *child* and *child* depends on *his* in the analysis of *his child*. If mutual dependencies have to be depicted, either arrows have to be used for all dependencies or some dependencies are represented by downward lines in hierarchical trees and other dependencies by arrows.

Of course part of speech information can be added to the Figures 11.2 and 11.3, grammatical function labels could be added to Figure 11.1, and word order can be added to Figure 11.3.

The above figures depict the dependency relation that holds between a head and the respective dependents. This can be written down more formally as an *n*-ary rule that is similar to phrase structure rules that were discussed in Chapter 2 (Gaifman 1965: 305; Hays 1964: 513; Baumgärtner 1970: 61; Heringer 1996: Section 4.1). For instance Baumgärtner suggests the general rule format in (1):

(1) $\chi \rightarrow \varphi_1 \ldots \varphi_i * \varphi_{i+2} \ldots \varphi_n$, where $0 < i \leq n$

The asterisk in (1) corresponds to the word of the category χ. In our example, χ would be V, the position of the '*' would be taken by *reads*, and φ_1 and φ_3 would be N. Together with the rule in (2b) for the determiner-noun combination, the rule in (2a) would license the dependency tree in Figure 11.1.

(2)   a. $V \rightarrow N * N$
       b. $N \rightarrow D *$

Alternatively, several binary rules can be assumed that combine a head with its subject, direct object, or indirect object (Kahane 2009). Dependency rules will be discussed in more detail in Section 11.7.2, where dependency grammars are compared with phrase structure grammars.

11.1.2 Adjuncts

Another metaphor that was used by Tesnière is the drama metaphor. The core participants of an event are the *actants* and apart from this there is the background, the stage, the general setting. The actants are the arguments in other theories and the stage-describing entities are called *circumstants*. These circumstants are modifiers and usually analyzed as adjuncts in the other theories described in this book. As far as the representation of dependencies is concerned, there is not much of a difference between arguments and adjuncts in Dependency Grammar. Figure 11.4 shows the analysis of (3):

(3)   The child often reads the book slowly.

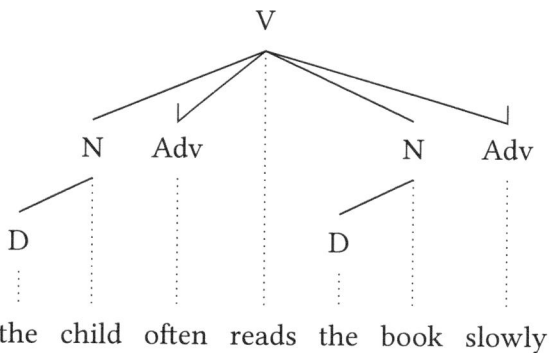

Figure 11.4: Analysis of *The child often reads the book slowly.*

The dependency annotation uses a technical device suggested by Engel (1977) to depict different dependency relations: adjuncts are marked with an additional line upwards from the adjunct node (see also Eroms 2000). An alternative way to specify the argument/adjunct, or rather the actant/circumstant distinction, is of course an explicit specification of the status as argument or adjunct. So one can use explicit labels for adjuncts and arguments as it was done for grammatical functions in the preceding. German grammars and valence dictionaries often use the labels E and A for *Ergänzung* and *Angabe*, respectively.

11.1.3 Linearization

So far we have seen dependency graphs that had connections to words that were linearized in a certain order. The order of the dependents, however, is in principle not determined by the dependency and therefore a Dependency Grammar has to contain additional statements that take care of the proper linearization of linguistic objects (stems, morphemes, words). Engel (2014: 50) assumes the dependency graph in Figure 11.5 for the sentences in (4).[6]

(4) a. Gestern war ich bei Tom.
yesterday was I with Tom
'I was with Tom yesterday.'

b. Ich war gestern bei Tom.
I was yesterday with Tom

c. Bei Tom war ich gestern.
with Tom was I yesterday

d. Ich war bei Tom gestern.
I was with Tom yesterday

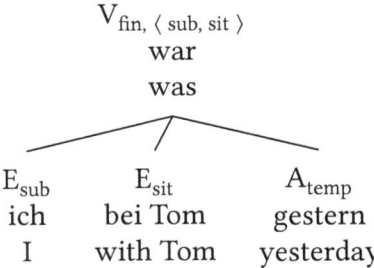

Figure 11.5: Dependency graph for several orders of *ich*, *war*, *bei Tom*, and *gestern* 'I was with Tom yesterday.' according to Engel (2014: 50)

According to Engel (2014: 50), the correct order is enforced by surface syntactic rules as for instance the rules that states that there is always exactly one element in the Vorfeld in declarative main clauses and that the finite verb is in second position.[7,8] Furthermore,

---

[6]Engel uses E_{sub} for the subject and E_{acc}, E_{dat}, and E_{gen} for the objects with respective cases.
[7]"Die korrekte Stellung ergibt sich dann zum Teil aus oberflächensyntaktischen Regeln (zum Beispiel: im Vorfeld des Konstativsatzes steht immer genau ein Element; das finite Verb steht an zweiter Stelle) [...]"
[8]Engel (1970: 81) provides counterexamples to the claim that there is exactly one element in the *Vorfeld*. Related examples will be discussed in Section 11.7.1.

there are linearization rules that concern pragmatic properties, as for instance given information before new information. Another rule ensures that weak pronouns are placed into the Vorfeld or at the beginning of the Mittelfeld. This conception of linear order is problematic both for empirical and conceptual reasons and we will turn to it again in Section 11.7.1. It should be noted here that approaches that deal with dependency alone admit discontinuous realizations of heads and their dependents. Without any further constraints, Dependency Grammars would share a problem that was already discussed on page 339 in Section 10.6.3 on Embodied Construction Grammar and in Section 10.6.4.4 with respect to Fluid Construction Grammar: one argument could interrupt another argument as in Figure 11.6. In order to exclude such linearizations in languages in which

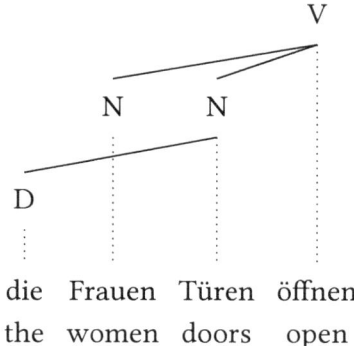

Figure 11.6: Unwanted analysis of *dass die Frauen Türen öffnen* 'that the women open doors'

they are impossible, it is sometimes assumed that analyses have to be projective, that is crossing branches like those in Figure 11.6 are not allowed. This basically reintroduces the concept of constituency into the framework, since this means that all dependents of a head have to be realized close to the head unless special mechanisms for liberation are used (see for instance Section 11.5 on nonlocal dependencies).[9] Some authors explicitly use a phrase structure component to be able to formulate restrictions on serializations of constituents (Gerdes & Kahane 2001; Hellwig 2003).

11.1.4 Semantics

Tesnière already distinguished the participants of a verb in a way that was later common in theories of semantic roles. He suggested that the first actant is the agent, the second one a patient and the third a benefactive (Tesnière 2015: Chapter 106). Given that Dependency Grammar is a lexical framework, all lexical approaches to argument linking can

---

[9] While this results in units that are also assumed in phrase structure grammars, there is a difference: the units have category labels in phrase structure grammars (for instance NP), which is not the case in Dependency Grammars. In Dependency Grammars, one just refers to the label of the head (for instance the N that belongs to *child* in Figure 11.4) or one refers to the head word directly (for instance, the word *child* in Figure 11.3). So there are fewer nodes in Dependency Grammar representations (but see the discussion in Section 11.7.2.3).

be adopted. However, argument linking and semantic role assignment are just a small part of the problem that has to be solved when natural language expressions have to be assigned a meaning. Issues regarding the scope of adjuncts and quantifiers have to be solved and it is clear that dependency graphs representing dependencies without taking into account linear order are not sufficient. An unordered dependency graph assigns grammatical functions to a dependent of a head and hence it is similar in many respects to an LFG f-structure.[10] For a sentence like (25a) on page 230, repeated here as (5), one gets the f-structure in (25b) on page 230. This f-structure contains a subject (*David*), an object (*a sandwich*), and an adjunct set with two elements (*at noon* and *yesterday*).

(5) David devoured a sandwich at noon yesterday.

This is exactly what is encoded in an unordered dependency graph. Because of this parallel it comes as no surprise that Bröker (2003: 308) suggested to use glue semantics (Dalrymple, Lamping & Saraswat 1993; Dalrymple 2001: Chapter 8) for Dependency Grammar as well. Glue semantics was already introduced in Section 7.1.5.

There are some variants of Dependency Grammar that have explicit treatments of semantics. One example is Meaning–Text Theory (Mel'čuk 1988). Word Grammar is another one (Hudson 1991: Chapter 7; 2007: Chapter 5). The notations of these theories cannot be introduced here. It should be noted though that theories like Hudson's Word Grammar are rather rigid about linear order and do not assume that all the sentences in (4) have the same dependency structure (see Section 11.5). Word Grammar is closer to phrase structure grammar and therefore can have a semantics that interacts with constituent order in the way it is known from constituent-based theories.

11.2 Passive

Dependency Grammar is a lexical theory and valence is the central concept. For this reason, it is not surprising that the analysis of the passive is a lexical one. That is, it is assumed that there is a passive participle that has a different valence requirement than the active verb (Hudson 1990: Chapter 12; Eroms 2000: Section 10.3; Engel 2014: 53–54).

Our standard example in (6) is analyzed as shown in Figure 11.7 on the next page.

(6) [dass] der Weltmeister geschlagen wird
 that the world.champion beaten is
 'that the world champion is (being) beaten'

This figure is an intuitive depiction of what is going on in passive constructions. A formalization would probably amount to a lexical rule for the personal passive. See Hellwig (2003: 629–630) for an explicit suggestion of a lexical rule for the analysis of the passive in English.

---

[10]Tim Osborne (p. c. 2015) reminds me that this is not true in all cases: for instance non-predicative prepositions are not reflected in f-structures, but of course they are present in dependency graphs.

11 Dependency Grammar

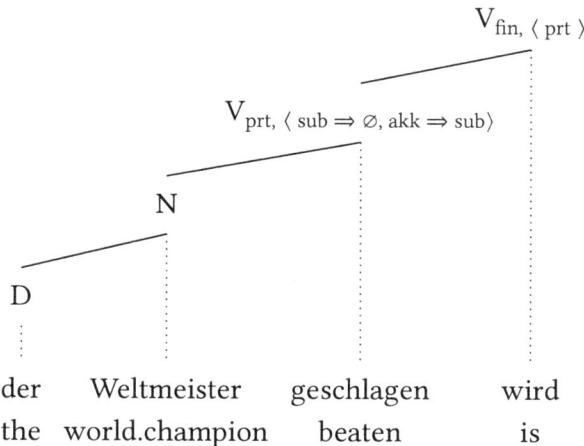

Figure 11.7: Analysis of [*dass*] *der Weltmeister geschlagen wird* 'that the world champion is (being) beaten' parallel to the analyses provided by Engel (2014: 53–54)

Note that *der Weltmeister* 'the world champion' is not an argument of the passive auxiliary *wird* 'is' in Engel's analysis. This means that subject–verb agreement cannot be determined locally and some elaborated mechanism has to be developed for ensuring agreement.[11] Hudson (1990), Eroms (2000: Section 5.3) and Groß & Osborne (2009) assume that subjects depend on auxiliaries rather than on the main verb. This requires

---

[11]This problem would get even more pressing for cases of the so-called remote passive:

(i) a. weil   der   Wagen zu reparieren versucht wurde
       because the.SG.NOM car   to repair   tried   was
       'because it was tried to repair the car'

   b. weil   die   Wagen zu reparieren versucht wurden
       because the.PL.NOM cars   to repair   tried   were
       'because it was tried to repair the cars'

Here the object of *zu reparieren*, which is the object of a verb which is embedded two levels deep, agrees with the auxiliaries *wurde* 'was' and *wurden* 'were'. However, the question how to analyze these remote passives is open in Engel's system anyway and the solution of this problem would probably involve the mechanism applied in HPSG: the arguments of *zu reparieren* are raised to the governing verb *versucht*, passive applies to this verb and turns the object into a subject which is then raised by the auxiliary. This explains the agreement between the underlying object of *zu reparieren* 'to repair' and *wurde* 'was'. Hudson (1997), working in the framework of Word Grammar, suggests an analysis of verbal complementation in German that involves what he calls *generalized raising*. He assumes that both subjects and complements may be raised to the governing head. Note that such an analysis involving generalized raising would make an analysis of sentences like (i) straightforward, since the object would depend on the same head as the subject, namely on *hat* 'has' and hence can be placed before the subject.

(ii) Gestern   hat sich der Spieler verletzt.
     yesterday has self the player injured
     'The player injured himself yesterday.'

For a discussion of Groß & Osborne's account of (ii) see page 594.

some argument transfer as it is common in Categorial Grammar (see Section 8.5.2) and HPSG (Hinrichs & Nakazawa 1994). The adapted analysis that treats the subject of the participle as a subject of the auxiliary is given in Figure 11.8.

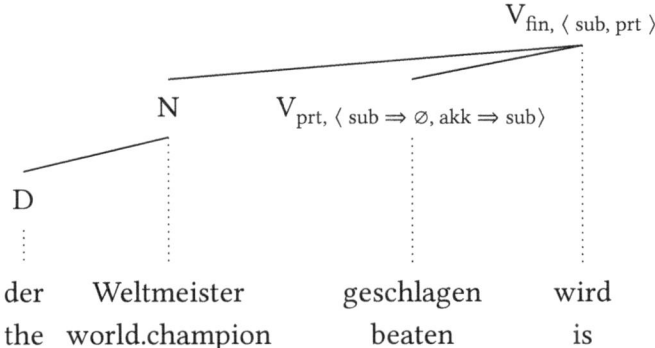

Figure 11.8: Analysis of [*dass*] *der Weltmeister geschlagen wird* 'that the world champion is (being) beaten' with the subject as dependent of the auxiliary

11.3 Verb position

In many Dependency Grammar publications on German, linearization issues are not dealt with and authors just focus on the dependency relations. The dependency relations between a verb and its arguments are basically the same in verb-initial and verb-final sentences. If we compare the dependency graphs of the sentences in (7) given in the Figures 11.9 and 11.10, we see that only the position of the verb is different, but the dependency relations are the same, as it should be.[12]

(7) a. [dass] jeder diesen Mann kennt
       that everybody this man knows
    'that everybody knows this man'

---

[12]Eroms (2000) uses the part of speech Pron for pronouns like *jeder* 'everybody'. If information about part of speech plays a role in selection, this makes necessary a disjunctive specification of all valence frames of heads that govern nominal expressions, since they can either combine with an NP with internal structure or with a pronoun. By assigning pronouns the category N, such a disjunctive specification is avoided. A pronoun differs from a noun in its valence (it is fully saturated, while a noun needs a determiner), but not in its part of speech. Eroms & Heringer (2003: 259) use the symbol N_pro for pronouns. If the pro-part is to be understood as a special property of items with the part of speech N, this is compatible with what I have said above: heads could then select for Ns. If N_pro and N are assumed to be distinct atomic symbols, the problem remains.

Using N rather than Pron as part of speech for pronouns is standard in other versions of Dependency Grammar, as for instance Word Grammar (Hudson 1990: 167; Hudson 2007: 190). See also footnote 2 on page 53 on the distinction of pronouns and NPs in phrase structure grammars.

11 Dependency Grammar

b. Kennt jeder diesen Mann?
   knows everybody this man
   'Does everybody know this man?'

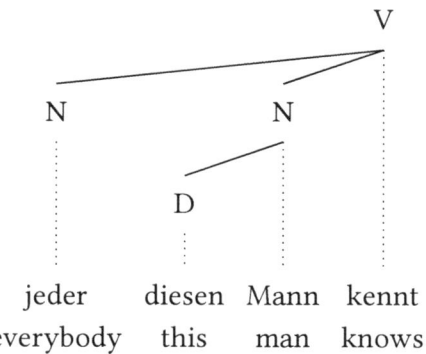

Figure 11.9: Analysis of [*dass*] *jeder diesen Mann kennt* 'that everybody knows this man'

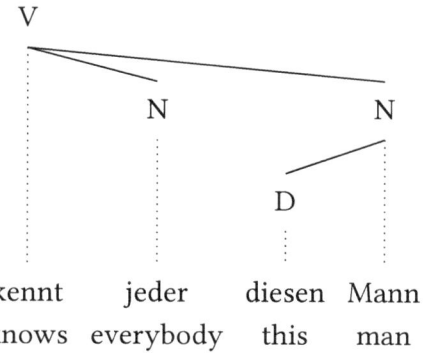

Figure 11.10: Analysis of *Kennt jeder diesen Mann?* 'Does everybody know this man?'

The correct ordering of the verb with respect to its arguments and adjuncts is ensured by linearization constraints that refer to the respective topological fields. See Section 11.1.3 and Section 11.7.1 for further details on linearization.

11.4 Local reordering

The situation regarding local reordering is the same. The dependency relations of the sentence in (8b) are shown in Figure 11.11 on the next page. The analysis of the sentence with normal order in (8a) has already been given in Figure 11.9.

(8) a. [dass] jeder diesen Mann kennt
       that everybody this man knows
       'that everybody knows this man'

b. [dass] diesen Mann jeder kennt
   that this man everybody knows
   'that everybody knows this man'

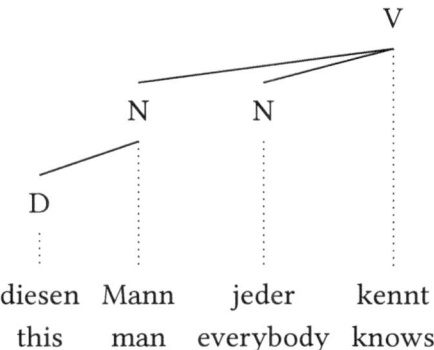

Figure 11.11: Analysis of [*dass*] *diesen Mann jeder kennt* 'that everybody knows this man'

11.5 Long-distance dependencies

There are several possibilities to analyze nonlocal dependencies in Dependency Grammar. The easiest one is the one we have already seen in the previous sections. Many analyses just focus on the dependency relations and assume that the order with the verb in second position is just one of the possible linearization variants (Eroms 2000: Section 9.6.2; Groß & Osborne 2009). Figure 11.12 shows the analysis of (9):

(9) [Diesen Mann] kennt jeder.
    this man knows everybody
    'Everyone knows this man.'

Now, this is the simplest case, so let us look at the example in (10), which really involves a *nonlocal* dependency:

(10) Wen$_i$ glaubst du, daß ich $\_i$ gesehen habe?[13]
     who.ACC believe.2SG you.NOM that I.NOM seen have
     'Who do you think I saw?'

The dependency relations are depicted in Figure 11.13 on the following page. This graph differs from most graphs we have seen before in not being projective. This means that there are crossing lines: the connection between V$_{prt}$ and the N for *wen* 'who' crosses the lines connecting *glaubst* 'believe' and *du* 'you' with their category symbols. Depending on the version of Dependency Grammar assumed, this is seen as a problem or it is not.

---
[13]Scherpenisse (1986: 84).

377

11 Dependency Grammar

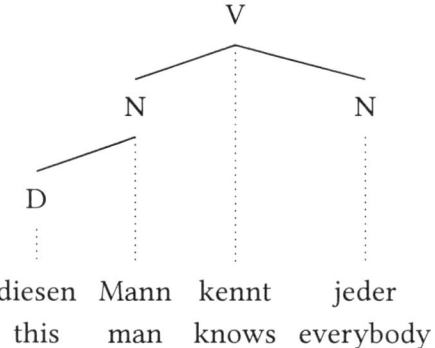

Figure 11.12: Analysis of *Diesen Mann kennt jeder.* 'This man, everybody knows.' without special treatment of fronting

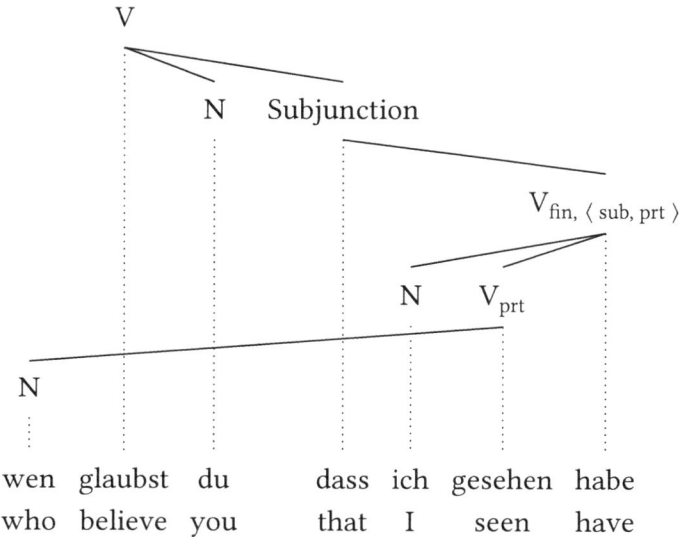

Figure 11.13: Non-projective analysis of *Wen glaubst du, dass ich gesehen habe?* 'Who do you think I saw?'

Let us explore the two options: if discontinuity of the type shown in Figure 11.13 is allowed for as in Heringer's and Eroms' grammars (Heringer 1996: 261; Eroms 2000: Section 9.6.2),[14] there has to be something in the grammar that excludes discontinuities that are ungrammatical. For instance, an analysis of (11) as in Figure 11.14 on the next page should be excluded.

(11) * Wen   glaubst   ich   du,   dass gesehen habe?
     who.ACC believe.2SG I.NOM you.NOM that seen   have
     Intended: 'Who do you think I saw?'

---

[14] However, the authors mention the possibility of raising an extracted element to a higher node. See for instance Eroms & Heringer (2003: 260).

11.5 Long-distance dependencies

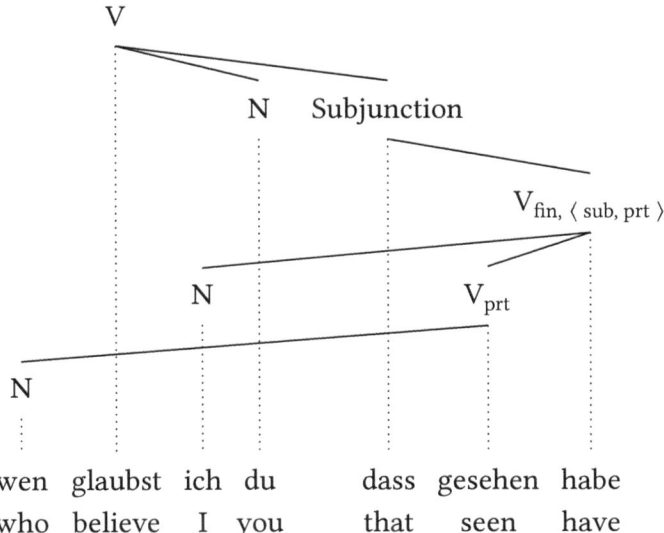

Figure 11.14: Unwanted dependency graph of * *Wen glaubst ich du, dass gesehen habe?* 'Who do you think I saw?'

Note that the order of elements in (11) is compatible with statements that refer to topological fields as suggested by Engel (2014: 50): there is a *Vorfeld* filled by *wen* 'who', there is a left sentence bracket filled by *glaubst* 'believe', and there is a *Mittelfeld* filled by *ich* 'I', *du* 'you' and the clausal argument. Having pronouns like *ich* and *du* in the *Mittelfeld* is perfectly normal. The problem is that these two pronouns come from different clauses: *du* belongs to the matrix verb *glaubst* 'believe' while *ich* 'I' depends on *gesehen* 'seen' *habe* 'have'. What has to be covered by a theory is the fact that fronting and extraposition target the left-most and right-most positions of a clause, respectively. This can be modeled in constituency-based approaches in a straightforward way, as has been shown in the previous chapters.

As an alternative to discontinuous constituents, one could assume additional mechanisms that promote the dependency of an embedded head to a higher head in the structure. Such an analysis was suggested by Kunze (1968), Hudson (1997; 2000), Kahane (1997), Kahane et al. (1998), and Groß & Osborne (2009). In what follows, I use the analysis by Groß & Osborne (2009) as an example for such analyses. Groß & Osborne depict the reorganized dependencies with a dashed line as in Figure 11.15.[15,16] The origin of the dependency (V_{prt}) is marked with a *g* and the dependent is connected to the node to which it has risen (the topmost V) by a dashed line. Instead of realizing the accusative dependent of *gesehen* 'seen' locally, information about the missing element is transferred to a higher node and realized there.

---

[15] Eroms & Heringer (2003: 260) make a similar suggestion but do not provide any formal details.

[16] Note that Groß & Osborne (2009) do not assume a uniform analysis of simple and complex V2 sentences. That is, for cases that can be explained as local reordering they assume an analysis without rising. Their analysis of (9) is the one depicted in Figure 11.12. This leads to problems which will be discussed in Section 11.7.1.

379

11 Dependency Grammar

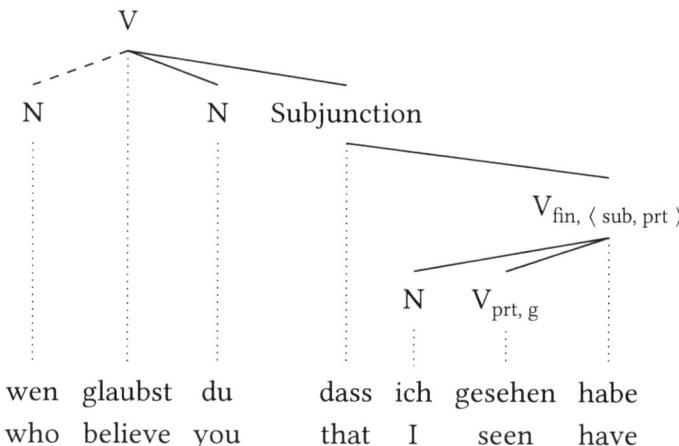

Figure 11.15: Projective analysis of *Wen glaubst du, dass ich gesehen habe?* 'Who do you think I saw?' involving rising

The analysis of Groß & Osborne (2009) is not very precise. There is a *g* and there is a dashed line, but sentences may involve multiple nonlocal dependencies. In (12) for instance, there is a nonlocal dependency in the relative clauses *den wir alle begrüßt haben* 'who we all greeted have' and *die noch niemand hier gesehen hat* 'who yet nobody here seen has': the relative pronouns are fronted inside the relative clauses. The phrase *dem Mann, den wir alle kennen* 'the man who we all know' is the fronted dative object of *gegeben* 'given' and *die noch niemand hier gesehen hat* 'who yet nobody here seen has' is extraposed from the NP headed by *Frau* 'woman'.

(12) Dem Mann, den wir alle begrüßt haben, hat die Frau das Buch gegeben, die
the man who we all greeted have has the woman the book given who
noch niemand hier gesehen hat.
yet nobody here seen has

'The woman who nobody ever saw here gave the book to the man, who all of us greeted.'

So this means that the connections (dependencies) between the head and the dislocated element have to be made explicit. This is what Hudson (1997; 2000) does in his Word Grammar analysis of nonlocal dependencies: in addition to dependencies that relate a word to its subject, object and so on, he assumes further dependencies for extracted elements. For example, *wen* 'who' in (10) – repeated here as (13) for convenience – is the object of *gesehen* 'seen' and the extractee of *glaubst* 'believe' and *dass* 'that':

(13) Wen glaubst du, dass ich gesehen habe?
who believe you that I seen have

'Who do you believe that I saw?'

380

11.5 Long-distance dependencies

Hudson states that the use of multiple dependencies in Word Grammar corresponds to structure sharing in HPSG (Hudson 1997: 15). Nonlocal dependencies are modeled as a series of local dependencies as it is done in GPSG and HPSG. This is important since it allows one to capture extraction path marking effects (Bouma, Malouf & Sag 2001: 1–2, Section 3.2): for instance, there are languages that use a special form of the complementizer for sentences from which an element is extracted. Figure 11.16 shows the analysis of (13) in Word Grammar. The links above the words are the usual dependency

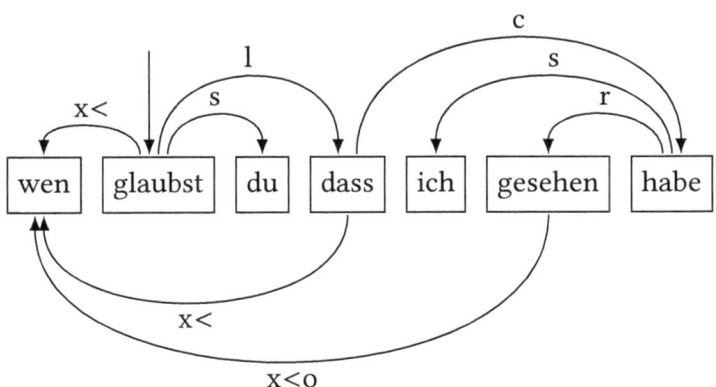

Figure 11.16: Projective analysis of *Wen glaubst du, dass ich gesehen habe?* 'Who do you think I saw?' in Word Grammar involving multiple dependencies

links for subjects (s) and objects (o) and other arguments (r is an abbreviation for *sharer*, which refers to verbal complements, l stands for *clausal complement*) and the links below the words are links for extractees (x<). The link from *gesehen* 'seen' to *wen* 'who' is special since it is both an object link and an extraction link (x<o). This link is an explicit statement which corresponds to both the little *g* and the N that is marked by the dashed line in Figure 11.15. In addition to what is there in Figure 11.15, Figure 11.16 also has an extraction link from *dass* 'that' to *wen* 'who'. One could use the graphic representation of Engel, Eroms, and Gross & Osborne to display the Word Grammar dependencies: one would simply add dashed lines from the V_{prt} node and from the Subjunction node to the N node dominating *wen* 'who'.

While this looks simple, I want to add that Word Grammar employs further principles that have to be fulfilled by well-formed structures. In the following I explain the *No-tangling Principle*, the *No-dangling Principle* and the *Sentence-root Principle*.

Principle 1 (The No-tangling Principle) *Dependency arrows must not tangle.*

Principle 2 (The No-dangling Principle) *Every word must have a parent.*

Principle 3 (The Sentence-root Principle) *In every non-compound sentence there is just one word whose parent is not a word but a contextual element.*

The No-tangling Principle ensures that there are no crossing dependency lines, that is, it ensures that structures are projective (Hudson 2000: 23). Since non-local dependency relations are established via the specific dependency mechanism, one wants to rule out the non-projective analysis. This principle also rules out (14b), where *green* depends on *peas* but is not adjacent to *peas*. Since *on* selects *peas* the arrow from *on* to *peas* would cross the one from *peas* to *green*.

(14)   a.   He lives on green peas.
       b.   * He lives green on peas.

The No-dangling Principle makes sure that there are no isolated word groups that are not connected to the main part of the structure. Without this principle (14b) could be analyzed with the isolated word *green* (Hudson 2000: 23).

The Sentence-root Principle is needed to rule out structures with more than one highest element. *glaubst* 'believe' is the root in Figure 11.16. There is no other word that dominates it and selects for it. The principle makes sure that there is no other root. So the principle rules out situations in which all elements in a phrase are roots, since otherwise the No-dangling Principle would lose its force as it could be fulfilled trivially (Hudson 2000: 25).

I added this rather complicated set of principles here in order to get a fair comparison with phrase structure-based proposals. If continuity is assumed for phrases in general, the three principles do not have to be stipulated. So, for example, LFG and HPSG do not need these three principles.

Note that Hudson (1997: 16) assumes that the element in the *Vorfeld* is extracted even for simple sentences like (9). I will show in Section 11.7.1 why I think that this analysis has to be preferred over analyses assuming that simple sentences like (9) are just order variants of corresponding verb-initial or verb-final sentences.

11.6 New developments and theoretical variants

This section mainly deals with Tesnière's variant of Dependency Grammar. Section 11.6.1 deals with Tesnière's part of speech system and Section 11.6.2 describes the modes of combinations of linguistics objects assumed by Tesnière.

11.6.1 Tesnière's part of speech classification

As mentioned in the introduction, Tesnière is a central figure in the history of Dependency Grammar as it was him who developed the first formal model (Tesnière 1959; 1980; 2015). There are many versions of Dependency Grammar today and most of them use the part of speech labels that are used in other theories as well (N, P, A, V, Adv, Conj, …). Tesnière had a system of four major categories: noun, verb, adjective, and adverb. The labels for these categories were derived from the endings that are used in Esperanto, that is, they are O, I, A, and E, respectively. These categories were defined semantically as

11.6 New developments and theoretical variants

Table 11.1: Semantically motivated part of speech classification by Tesnière

	substance	process
concrete	noun	verb
abstract	adjective	adverb

specified in Table 11.1.[17] Tesnière assumed these categories to be universal and suggested that there are constraints in which way these categories may depend on others.

According to Tesnière, nouns and adverbs may depend on verbs, adjectives may depend on nouns, and adverbs may depend on adjectives or adverbs. This situation is depicted in the general dependency graph in Figure 11.17. The '*' means that there can be an arbitrary number of dependencies between Es. It is of course easy to find examples

Figure 11.17: Universal configuration for dependencies according to Tesnière
(I = verb, O = noun, A = adjective, E = adverb)

in which adjectives depend on verbs and sentences (verbs) depend on nouns. Such cases are handled via so-called *transfers* in Tesnière's system. Furthermore, conjunctions, determiners, and prepositions are missing from this set of categories. For the combination of these elements with their dependents Tesnière used special combinatoric relations: junction and transfer. We will deal with these in the following subsection.

11.6.2 Connection, junction, and transfer

Tesnière (1959) suggested three basic relations between nodes: connection, junction, and transfer. Connection is the simple relation between a head and its dependents that we have already covered in the previous sections. Junction is a special relation that plays a

---

[17]As Weber (1997: 77) points out this categorization is not without problems: in what sense is *Angst* 'fear' a substance? Why should *glauben* 'believe' be a concrete process? See also Klein (1971: Section 3.4) for the discussion of *schlagen* 'to beat' and *Schlag* 'the beat' and similar cases. Even if one assumes that *Schlag* is derived from the concrete process *schlag-* by a transfer into the category O, the assumption that such Os stand for concrete substances is questionable.

11 Dependency Grammar

role in the analysis of coordination and transfer is a tool that allows one to change the category of a lexical item or a phrase.

11.6.2.1 Junction

Figure 11.18 illustrates the junction relation: the two conjuncts *John* and *Mary* are connected with the conjunction *and*. It is interesting to note that both of the conjuncts are connected to the head *laugh*.

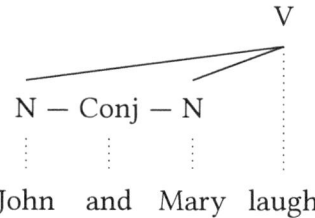

Figure 11.18: Analysis of coordination using the special relation *junction*

In the case of two coordinated nouns we get dependency graphs like the one in Figure 11.19. Both nouns are connected to the dominating verb and both nouns dominate

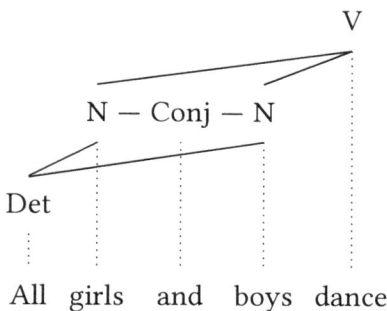

Figure 11.19: Analysis of coordination using the special relation *junction*

the same determiner.

An alternative to such a special treatment of coordination would be to treat the conjunction as the head and the conjuncts as its dependents.[18] The only problem of such a proposal would be the category of the conjunction. It cannot be Conj since the governing verb does not select a Conj, but an N. The trick that could be applied here is basically the same trick as in Categorial Grammar (see Section 21.6.2): the category of the conjunction in Categorial Grammar is (X\X)/X. We have a functor that takes two arguments of the same category and the result of the combination is an object that has the same category as the two arguments. Translating this approach to Dependency Grammar, one would

---

[18] I did not use Tesnière's category labels here to spare the reader the work of translating I to V and O to N.

get an analysis as the one depicted in Figure 11.20 rather than the ones in Figure 11.18 and Figure 11.19. The figure for *all girls and boys* looks rather strange since both the

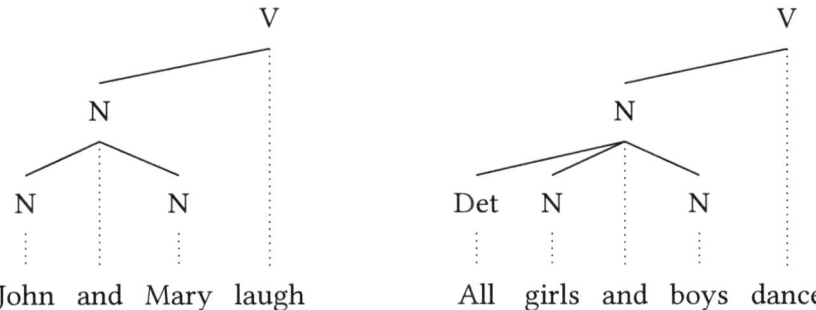

Figure 11.20: Analysis of coordination without *junction* and the conjunction as head

determiner and the two conjuncts depend on the conjunction, but since the two Ns are selecting a Det, the same is true for the result of the coordination. In Categorial Grammar notation, the category of the conjunction would be ((NP\Det)\(NP\Det))/(NP\Det) since X is instantiated by the nouns which would have the category (NP\Det) in an analysis in which the noun is the head and the determiner is the dependent.

Note that both approaches have to come up with an explanation of subject–verb agreement. Tesnière's original analysis assumes two dependencies between the verb and the individual conjuncts.[19] As the conjuncts are singular and the verb is plural, agreement cannot be modeled in tandem with dependency relations in this approach. If the second analysis finds ways of specifying the agreement properties of the coordination in the conjunction, the agreement facts can be accounted for without problems.

The alternative to a headed approach as depicted in Figure 11.20 is an unheaded one. Several authors working in phrase structure-based frameworks suggested analyses of coordination without a head. Such analyses are also assumed in Dependency Grammar (Hudson 1988; Kahane 1997). Hudson (1988) and others who make similar assumptions assume a phrase structure component for coordination: the two nouns and the conjunction are combined to form a larger object which has properties which do not correspond to the properties of any of the combined words.

Similarly, the junction-based analysis of coordination poses problems for the interpretation of the representations. If semantic role assignment happens in parallel to dependency relations, there would be a problem with graphs like the one in Figure 11.18, since the semantic role of *laugh* cannot be filled by *John* and *Mary* simultaneously. Rather it is filled by one entity, namely the one that refers to the set containing John and Mary. This semantic representation would belong to the phrase *John and Mary* and the natural candidate for being the topmost entity in this coordination is *and*, as it embeds the meaning of *John* and the meaning of *Mary*: and'(John', Mary').

---

[19]Eroms (2000: 467) notes the agreement problem and describes the facts. In his analysis, he connects the first conjunct to the governing head, although it seems to be more appropriate to assume an internally structured coordination structure and then connect the highest conjunction.

11 Dependency Grammar

Such junctions are also assumed for the coordination of verbs. This is, however, not without problems, since adjuncts can have scope over the conjunct that is closest to them or over the whole coordination. An example is the following sentence from Levine (2003: 217):

(15) Robin came in, found a chair, sat down, and whipped off her logging boots in exactly thirty seconds flat.

The adjunct *in exactly thirty seconds flat* can refer either to *whipped off her logging boots* as in (16a) or scope over all three conjuncts together as in (16b):

(16) a. Robin came in, found a chair, sat down, and [[pulled off her logging boots] in exactly thirty seconds flat].
 b. Robin [[came in, found a chair, sat down, and pulled off her logging boots] in exactly thirty seconds flat].

The Tesnièreian analysis in Figure 11.21 corresponds to (17), while an analysis that treats the conjunction as the head as in Figure 11.22 on the next page corresponds to (16b).

(17) Robin came in in exactly thirty seconds flat and Robin found a chair in exactly thirty seconds flat and Robin pulled off her logging boots in exactly thirty seconds flat.

The reading in (17) results when an adjunct refers to each conjunct individually rather then referring to a cumulative event that is expressed by a verb phrase as in (16b).

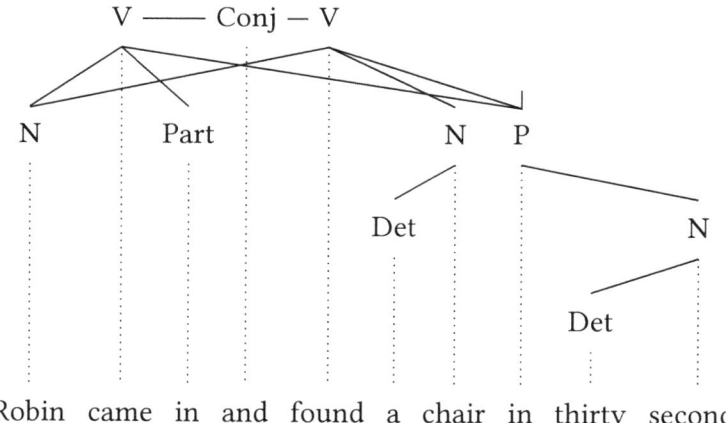

Figure 11.21: Analysis of verb coordination involving the junction relation

Levine (2003: 217) discusses these sentences in connection to the HPSG analysis of extraction by Bouma, Malouf & Sag (2001). Bouma, Malouf & Sag suggest an analysis in which adjuncts are introduced lexically as dependents of a certain head. Since adjuncts are introduced lexically, the coordination structures basically have the same structure as

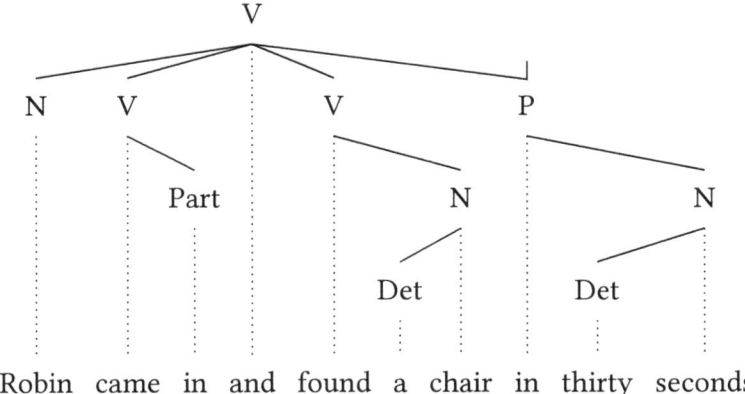

Figure 11.22: Analysis of verb coordination involving the connection relation

the ones assumed in a Tesnièreian analysis. It may be possible to come up with a way to get the semantic composition right even though the syntax does not correspond to the semantic dependencies (see Chaves 2009 for suggestions), but it is clear that it is simpler to derive the semantics from a syntactic structure which corresponds to what is going on in semantics.

11.6.2.2 Transfer

Transfers are used in Tesnière's system for the combination of words or phrases with a head of one of the major categories (for instance nouns) with words in minor categories (for instance prepositions). In addition, transfers can transfer a word or phrase into another category without any other word participating.

Figure 11.23 shows an example of a transfer. The preposition *in* causes a category change: while *Traumboot* 'dream boat' is an O (noun), the combination of the preposition and the noun is an E. The example shows that Tesnière used the grammatical category to encode grammatical functions. In theories like HPSG there is a clear distinction: there is information about part of speech on the one hand and the function of elements as modifiers and predicates on the other hand. The modifier function is encoded by the selectional feature MOD, which is independent of the part of speech. It is therefore possible to have modifying and non-modifying adjectives, modifying and non-modifying prepositional phrases, modifying and non-modifying noun phrases and so on. For the example at hand, one would assume a preposition with directional semantics that selects for an NP. The preposition is the head of a PP with a filled MOD value.

Another area in which transfer is used is morphology. For instance, the derivation of French *frappant* 'striking' by suffixation of *-ant* to the verb stem *frapp* is shown in Figure 11.24. Such transfers can be subsumed under the general connection relation if the affix is treated as the head. Morphologists working in realizational morphology and construction morphology argue against such morpheme-based analyses since they involve

11 Dependency Grammar

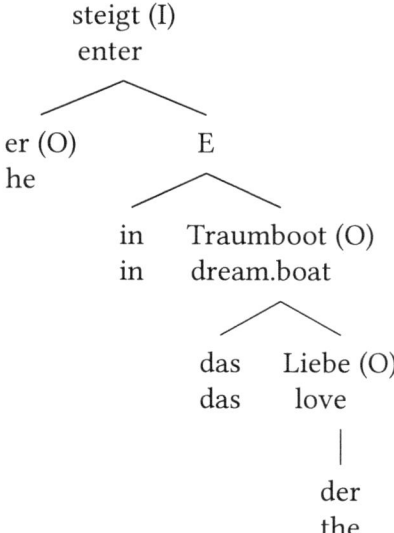

Figure 11.23: Transfer with an example adapted from Weber (1997: 83)

Figure 11.24: Transfer in morphology and its reconceptualization as normal dependency

a lot of empty elements for conversions as for instance the conversion of the verb *play* into the noun *play* (see Figure 11.25). Consequently, lexical rules are assumed for deriva-

Figure 11.25: Conversion as transfer from I (verb) to O (substantive) and as dependency with an empty element of the category N as head

tions and conversions in theories like HPSG. HPSG lexical rules are basically equivalent

388

11.6 New developments and theoretical variants

to unary branching rules (see the discussion of (41) on page 288 and Section 19.5). The affixes are integrated into the lexical rules or into realization functions that specify the morphological form of the item that is licensed by the lexical rule.

Concluding it can be said that transfer corresponds to

- binary-branching phrase structure rules, if a word or phrase is combined with another word,

- unary phrase structure rules or binary branching phrase structure rules together with an empty head if a phrase is converted to another category without any additional element present or

- a (unary) lexical rule if a word or stem is mapped to a word or a stem.

For further discussion of the relation between Tesnière's transfer rules and constituency rules see Kahane & Osborne (2015: Section 4.9.1–4.9.2). Kahane & Osborne point out that transfer rules can be used to model exocentric constructions, that is, constructions in which there is no single part that could be identified as the head. For more on headless constructions see Section 11.7.2.4.

11.6.3 Scope

As Kahane & Osborne (2015: lix) point out, Tesnière uses so-called polygraphs to represent scopal relations. So, since *that you saw yesterday* in (18) refers to *red cars* rather than *cars* alone, this is represented by a line that starts at the connection between *red* and *cars* rather than on one of the individual elements (Tesnière 2015: 150, Stemma 149).

(18) red cars that you saw yesterday

Tesnière's analysis is depicted in the left representation in Figure 11.26. It is worth noting that this representation corresponds to the phrase structure tree on the right of Figure 11.26. The combination B between *red* and *cars* corresponds to the B node in the right-

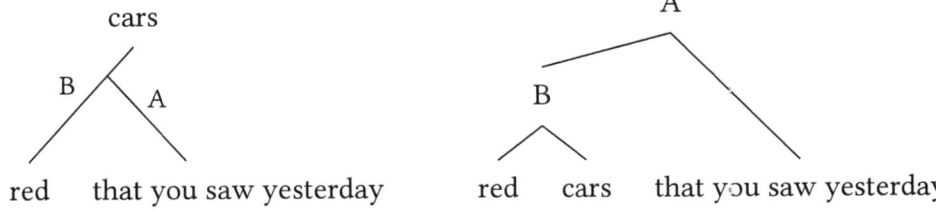

Figure 11.26: Tesnière's way of representing scope and the comparison with phrase structure-based analyses by Kahane & Osborne (2015: lix)

hand figure and the combination A of *red cars* and *that you saw yesterday* corresponds to the A node. So, what is made explicit and is assigned a name in phrase structure grammars remains nameless in Tesnière's analysis, but due to the assumption of polygraphs,

11 Dependency Grammar

it is possible to refer to the combinations. See also the discussion of Figure 11.46, which shows additional nodes that Hudson assumes in order to model semantic relations.

11.7 Summary and classification

Proponents of Dependency Grammar emphasize the point that Dependency Grammar is much simpler than phrase structure grammars, since there are fewer nodes and the general concept is more easy to grasp (see for instance Osborne 2014: Section 3.2, Section 7). This is indeed true: Dependency Grammar is well-suited for teaching grammar in introductory classes. However, as Sternefeld & Richter (2012: 285) point out in a rather general discussion, simple syntax has the price of complex semantics and vice versa. So, in addition to the dependency structure that is described in Dependency Syntax, one needs other levels. One level is the level of semantics and another one is linearization. As far as linearization is concerned, Dependency Grammar has two options: assuming continuous constituents, that is, projective structures, or allowing for discontinuous constituents. These options will be discussed in the following subsections. Section 11.7.2 compares dependency grammars with phrase structure grammars and shows that projective Dependency Grammars can be translated into phrase structure grammars. It also shows that non-projective structures can be modeled in theories like HPSG. The integration of semantics is discussed in Section 11.7.2.3 and it will become clear that once other levels are taken into account, Dependency Grammars are not necessarily simpler than phrase structure grammars.

11.7.1 Linearization

We have seen several approaches to linearization in this chapter. Many just assume a dependency graph and some linearization according to the topological fields model. As has been argued in Section 11.5, allowing discontinuous serialization of a head and its dependents opens up Pandora's box. I have discussed the analysis of nonlocal dependencies by Kunze (1968), Hudson (1997; 2000), Kahane, Nasr & Rambow (1998), and Groß & Osborne (2009). With the exception of Hudson those authors assume that dependents of a head rise to a dominating head only in those cases in which a discontinuity would arise otherwise. However, there seems to be a reason to assume that fronting should be treated by special mechanisms even in cases that allow for continuous serialization. For instance, the ambiguity or lack of ambiguity of the examples in (19) cannot be explained in a straightforward way:

(19)   a. Oft   liest er das Buch nicht.
             often reads he the book not

          'It is often that he does not read the book.' or
          'It is not the case that he reads the book often.'

b. dass er das Buch nicht oft liest
   that he the book not often reads

   'It is not the case that he reads the book often.'

c. dass er das Buch oft nicht liest
   that he the book often not reads

   'It is often that he does not read the book.'

The point about the three examples is that only (19a) is ambiguous. Even though (19c) has the same order as far as *oft* 'often' and *nicht* 'not' are concerned, the sentence is not ambiguous. So it is the fronting of an adjunct that is the reason for the ambiguity. The dependency graph for (19a) is shown in Figure 11.27. Of course the dependencies

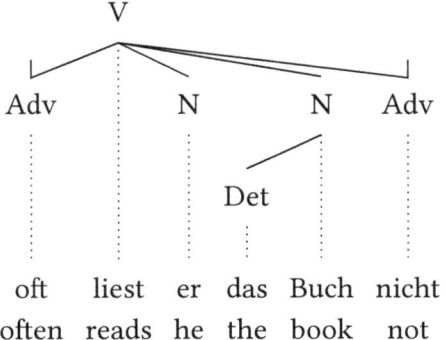

Figure 11.27: Dependency graph for *Oft liest er das Buch nicht.* 'He does not read the book often.'

for (19b) and (19c) do not differ. The graphs would be the same, only differing in serialization. Therefore, differences in scope could not be derived from the dependencies and complicated statements like (20) would be necessary:

(20) If a dependent is linearized in the *Vorfeld* it can both scope over and under all other adjuncts of the head it is a dependent of.

Eroms (1985: 320) proposes an analysis of negation in which the negation is treated as the head; that is, the sentence in (21) has the structure in Figure 11.28.[20]

(21) Er kommt nicht.
    he comes not

    'He does not come.'

This analysis is equivalent to analyses in the Minimalist Program assuming a NegP and it has the same problem: the category of the whole object is Adv, but it should be V. This is a problem since higher predicates may select for a V rather than an Adv.[21]

---

[20]But see Eroms (2000: Section 11.2.3).
[21]See for instance the analysis of embedded sentences like (23) below.

11 Dependency Grammar

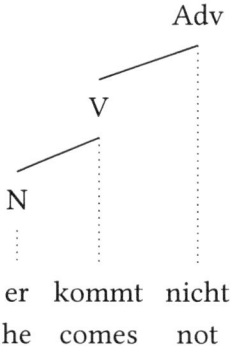

er kommt nicht
he comes not

Figure 11.28: Analysis of negation according to Eroms (1985: 320)

The same is true for constituent negation or other scope bearing elements. For example, the analysis of (22) would have to be the one in Figure 11.29.

(22) der angebliche Mörder
      the alleged   murderer

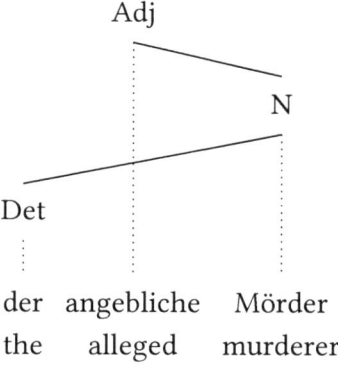

der angebliche Mörder
the alleged   murderer

Figure 11.29: Analysis that would result if one considered all scope-bearing adjuncts to be heads

This structure would have the additional problem of being non-projective. Eroms does treat the determiner differently from what is assumed here, so this type of non-projectivity may not be a problem for him. However, the head analysis of negation would result in non-projectivity in so-called coherent constructions in German. The sentence in (23) has two readings: in the first reading, the negation scopes over *singen* 'sing' and in the second one over *singen darf* 'sing may'.

(23) dass er nicht singen darf
      that he not   sing   may
      'that he is not allowed to sing' or 'that he is allowed not to sing'

392

11.7 Summary and classification

The reading in which *nicht* 'not' scopes over the whole verbal complex would result in the non-projective structure that is given in Figure 11.30. Eroms also considers an

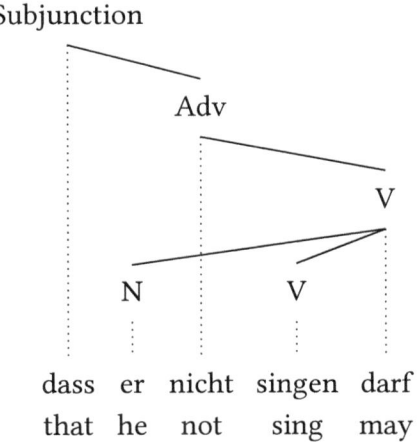

Figure 11.30: Analysis that results if one assumes the negation to be a head

analysis in which the negation is a word part ('Wortteiläquivalent'). This does, however, not help here since first the negation and the verb are not adjacent in V2 contexts like (19a) and even in verb-final contexts like (23). Eroms would have to assume that the object to which the negation attaches is the whole verbal complex *singen darf* 'sing may', that is, a complex object consisting of two words.

This leaves us with the analysis provided in Figure 11.27 and hence with a problem since we have one structure with two possible adjunct realizations that correspond to different readings. This is not predicted by an analysis that treats the two possible linearizations simply as alternative orderings.

Thomas Groß (p. c. 2013) suggested an analysis in which *oft* does not depend on the verb but on the negation. This corresponds to constituent negation in phrase structure approaches. The dependency graph is shown on the left-hand side in Figure 11.31. The figure on the right-hand side shows the graph for the corresponding verb-final sentence. The reading corresponding to constituent negation can be illustrated with contrastive expressions. While in (24a) it is only *oft* 'often' which is negated, it is *oft gelesen* 'often read' that is in the scope of negation in (24b).

(24) a. Er hat das Buch nicht oft gelesen, sondern selten.
    he has the book not often read but seldom
    'He did not read the book often, but seldom.'

  b. Er hat das Buch nicht oft gelesen, sondern selten gekauft.
    he has the book not often read but seldom bought
    'He did not read the book often but rather bought it seldom.'

These two readings correspond to the two phrase structure trees in Figure 11.32. Note that in an HPSG analysis, the adverb *oft* would be the head of the phrase *nicht oft* 'not

11 Dependency Grammar

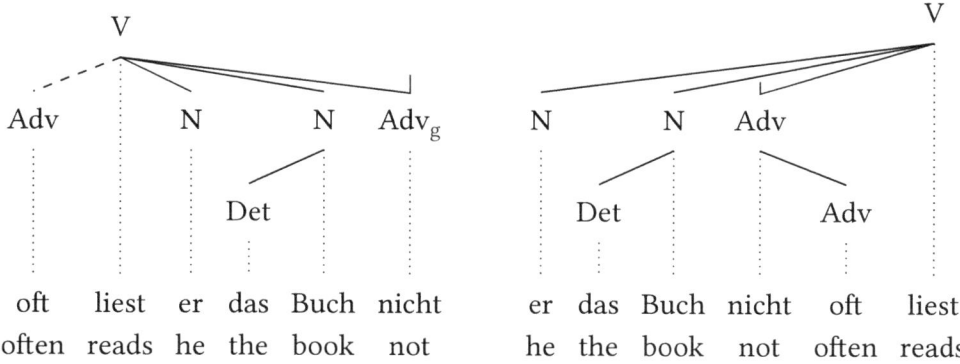

Figure 11.31: Dependency graph for *Oft liest er das Buch nicht.* 'He does not read the book often.' according to Groß and verb-final variant

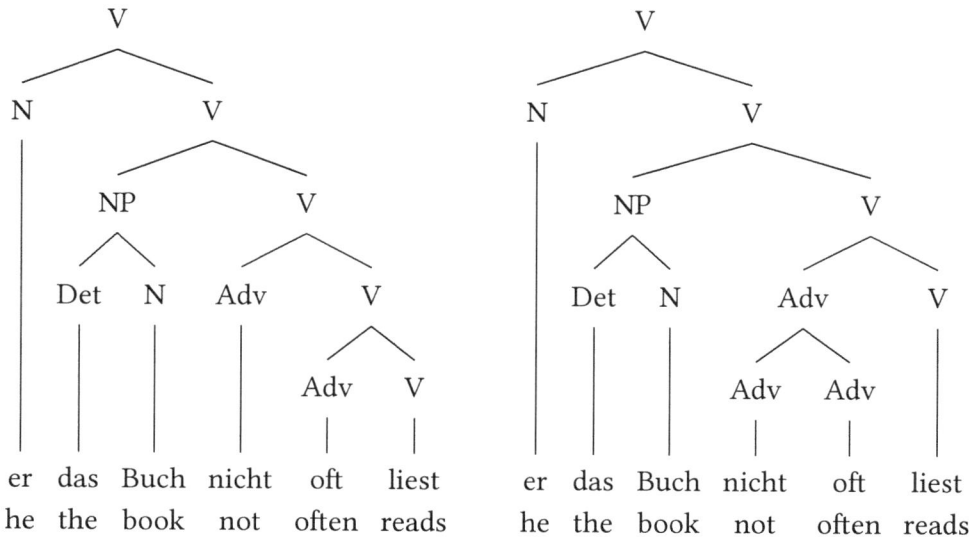

Figure 11.32: Possible syntactic analyses for *er das Buch nicht oft liest* 'he does not read the book often'

often'. This is different from the Dependency Grammar analysis suggested by Groß. Furthermore, the Dependency Grammar analysis has two structures: a flat one with all adverbs depending on the same verb and one in which *oft* depends on the negation. The phrase structure-based analysis has three structures: one with the order *oft* before *nicht*, one with the order *nicht* before *oft* and the one with direct combination of *nicht* and *oft*. The point about the example in (19a) is that one of the first two structures is missing in the Dependency Grammar representations. This probably does not make it impossible to derive the semantics, but it is more difficult than it is in constituent-based approaches.

Furthermore, note that models that directly relate dependency graphs to topological fields will not be able to account for sentences like (25).

394

11.7 Summary and classification

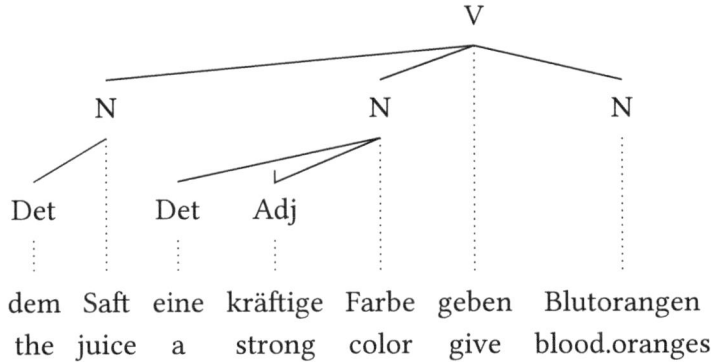

Figure 11.33: Dependency graph for *Dem Saft eine kräftige Farbe geben Blutorangen.* 'Blood oranges give the juice a strong color.'

(25) Dem Saft eine kräftige Farbe geben Blutorangen.[22]
 the juice a strong color give blood.oranges
 'Blood oranges give a strong color to the juice.'

The dependency graph of this sentence is given in Figure 11.33.

Such apparent multiple frontings are not restricted to NPs. Various types of dependents can be placed in the *Vorfeld*. An extensive discussion of the data is provided in Müller (2003a). Additional data have been collected in a research project on multiple frontings and information structure (Bildhauer 2011). Any theory based on dependencies alone and not allowing for empty elements is forced to give up the restriction commonly assumed in the analysis of V2 languages, namely that the verb is in second position. In comparison, analyses like GB and those HPSG variants that assume an empty verbal head can assume that a projection of such a verbal head occupies the *Vorfeld*. This explains why the material in the *Vorfeld* behaves like a verbal projection containing a visible verb: such *Vorfelds* are internally structured topologically. They may have a filled *Nachfeld* and even a particle that fills the right sentence bracket. See Müller (2005c; 2017a) for further data, discussion, and a detailed analysis. The equivalent of the analysis in Gross & Osborne's framework (2009) would be something like the graph that is shown in Figure 11.34, but note that Groß & Osborne (2009: 73) explicitly reject empty elements, and in any case an empty element which is stipulated just to get the multiple fronting cases right would be entirely ad hoc.[23] It is important to note that the issue is not solved by simply dropping the V2 constraint and allowing dependents of the finite verb to be realized to its left, since the fronted constituents do not necessarily depend on the finite verb as the examples in (26) show:

---

[22] Bildhauer & Cook (2010) found this example in the *Deutsches Referenzkorpus* (DeReKo), hosted at Institut für Deutsche Sprache, Mannheim: http://www.ids-mannheim.de/kl/projekte/korpora, 2018-02-20.

[23] I stipulated such an empty element in a linearization-based variant of HPSG allowing for discontinuous constituents (Müller 2002b), but later modified this analysis so that only continuous constituents are allowed, verb position is treated as head-movement and multiple frontings involve the same empty verbal head as is used in the verb movement analysis (Müller 2005c; 2017a).

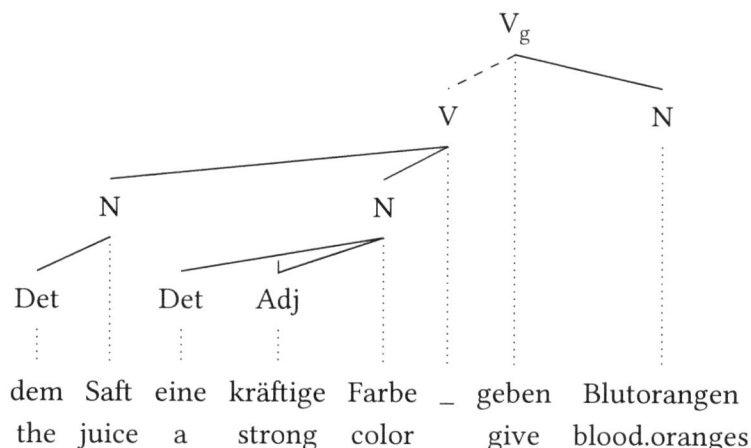

Figure 11.34: Dependency graph for *Dem Saft eine kräftige Farbe geben Blutorangen.* 'Blood oranges give the juice a strong color.' with an empty verbal head for the *Vorfeld*

(26) a. [Gezielt]   [Mitglieder] [im   Seniorenbereich]   wollen die Kendoka
         specifically members   in.the senior.citizens.sector want.to the Kendoka
         allerdings nicht werben.[24]
         however   not   recruit

    'However, the Kendoka do not intend to target the senior citizens sector with their member recruitment strategy.'

  b. [Kurz]   [die Bestzeit] hatte der Berliner Andreas Klöden [...] gehalten.[25]
     briefly the best.time had   the Berliner Andreas Klöden   held

    'Andreas Klöden from Berlin had briefly held the record time.'

And although the respective structures are marked, such multiple frontings can even cross clause boundaries:

(27) Der   Maria einen Ring glaube ich nicht, daß er je   schenken wird.[26]
      the.DAT Maria a.ACC ring believe I   not   that he ever give   will

      'I don't think that he would ever give Maria a ring.'

If such dependencies are permitted it is really difficult to constrain them. The details cannot be discussed here, but the reader is referred to Müller (2005c; 2017a).

Note also that Engel's statement regarding the linear order in German sentences (2014: 50) referring to one element in front of the finite verb (see footnote 7) is very imprecise. One can only guess what is intended by the word *element*. One interpretation is that it

---

[24] taz, 07.07.1999, p. 18. Quoted from Müller (2002b).
[25] Märkische Oderzeitung, 28./29.07.2001, p. 28.
[26] Fanselow (1993: 67).

11.7 Summary and classification

is a continuous constituent in the classical sense of constituency-based grammars. An alternative would be that there is a continuous realization of a head and some but not necessarily all of its dependents. This alternative would allow an analysis of extraposition with discontinuous constituents of (28) as it is depicted in Figure 11.35.

(28) Ein junger Kerl stand da,   mit   langen blonden Haaren, die sein Gesicht
     a   young guy stood there with   long   blond   hair   that his face
     einrahmten, [...]²⁷
     framed

'A young guy was standing there with long blond hair that framed his face'

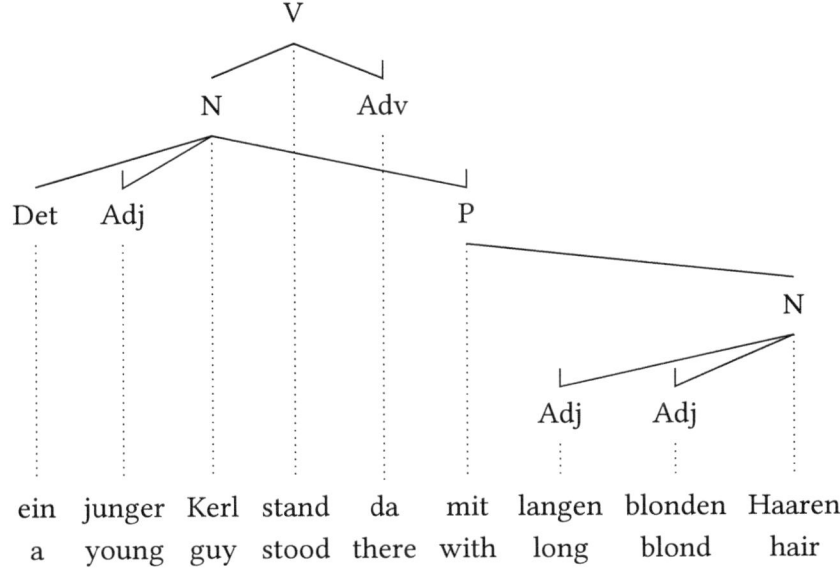

Figure 11.35: Dependency graph for *Ein junger Kerl stand da, mit langen blonden Haaren.* 'A young guy was standing there with long blond hair.' with a discontinuous constituent in the *Vorfeld*

A formalization of such an analysis is not trivial, since one has to be precise about what exactly can be realized discontinuously and which parts of a dependency must be realized continuously. Kathol & Pollard (1995) developed such an analysis of extraposition in the framework of HPSG. See also Müller (1999b: Section 13.3). I discuss the basic mechanisms for such linearization analyses in HPSG in the following section.

11.7.2 Dependency Grammar vs. phrase structure grammar

This section deals with the relation between Dependency Grammars and phrase structure grammars. I first show that projective Dependency Grammars can be translated

---
²⁷Charles Bukowski, *Der Mann mit der Ledertasche*. München: Deutscher Taschenbuch Verlag, 1994, p. 201, translation by Hans Hermann.

into phrase structure grammars (Section 11.7.2.1). I will then deal with non-projective DGs and show how they can be captured in linearization-based HPSG (Section 11.7.2.2). Section 11.7.2.3 argues for the additional nodes that are assumed in phrase structure-based theories and Section 11.7.2.4 discusses headless constructions, which pose a problem for all Dependency Grammar accounts.

11.7.2.1 Translating projective Dependency Grammars into phrase structure grammars

As noted by Gaifman (1965), Covington (1990: 234), Oliva (2003) and Hellwig (2006: 1093), certain projective headed phrase structure grammars can be turned into Dependency Grammars by moving the head one level up to replace the dominating node. So in an NP structure, the N is shifted into the position of the NP and all other connections remain the same. Figure 11.36 illustrates. Of course this procedure cannot be applied to all phrase

Figure 11.36: *a book* in a phrase structure and a Dependency Grammar analysis

structure grammars directly since some involve more elaborate structure. For instance, the rule S → NP, VP cannot be translated into a dependency rule, since NP and VP are both complex categories.

In what follows, I want to show how the dependency graph in Figure 11.1 can be recast as headed phrase structure rules that license a similar tree, namely the one in Figure 11.37. I did not use the labels NP and VP to keep the two figures maximally similar. The P part of NP and VP refers to the saturation of a projection and is often ignored in figures. See Chapter 9 on HPSG, for example. The grammar that licenses the tree is given in (29), again ignoring valence information.

(29)   N → D N   N → child   D → the   D → a
       V → N V N   N → book   V → reads

If one replaces the N and V in the right-hand side of the two left-most rules in (29) with the respective lexical items and then removes the rules that license the words, one arrives at the lexicalized variant of the grammar given in (30):

(30)   N → D book   D → the
       N → D child   D → a
       V → N reads N

11.7 Summary and classification

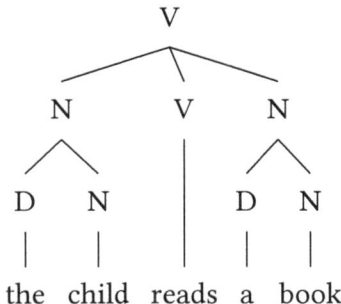

Figure 11.37: Analysis of *The child reads a book.* in a phrase structure with flat rules

Lexicalized means that every partial tree licensed by a grammar rule contains a lexical element. The grammar in (30) licenses exactly the tree in Figure 11.1.[28]

One important difference between classical phrase structure grammars and Dependency Grammars is that the phrase structure rules impose a certain order on the daughters. That is, the V rule in (30) implies that the first nominal projection, the verb, and the second nominal projection have to appear in the order stated in the rule. Of course this ordering constraint can be relaxed as it is done in GPSG. This would basically permit any order of the daughters at the right hand side of rules. This leaves us with the integration of adjuncts. Since adjuncts depend on the head as well (see Figure 11.4), a rule could be assumed that allows arbitrarily many adjuncts in addition to the arguments. So the V rule in (30) would be changed to the one in (31):[29]

(31) V → N reads N Adv*

Such generalized phrase structures would give us the equivalent of projective Dependency Grammars.[30] However, as we have seen, some researchers allow for crossing

---

[28] As mentioned on page 369, Gaifman (1965: 305), Hays (1964: 513), Baumgärtner (1970: 57) and Heringer (1996: 37) suggest a general rule format for dependency rules that has a special marker ('*' and '~', respectively) in place of the lexical words in (30). Heringer's rules have the form in (31):

(i) X[Y1, Y2, ~, Y3]

X is the category of the head, Y1, Y2, and Y3 are dependents of the head and '~' is the position into which the head is inserted.

[29] See page 190 for a similar rule in GPSG and see Kasper (1994) for an HPSG analysis of German that assumes entirely flat structures and integrates an arbitrary number of adjuncts. Dahl (1980) argues that one needs "higher nodes" ($\overline{\text{N}}$ nodes and VP nodes in other terminology) for adjunct attachment for semantic reasons. I think this is not correct since – as Kasper showed – relational constraints could be used to determine complex semantic representations. I agree though that assuming these nodes makes things a lot easier. See also footnote 36.

[30] Sylvain Kahane (p. c. 2015) states that binarity is important for Dependency Grammars, since there is one rule for the subject, one for the object and so on (as for instance in Kahane 2009, which is an implementation of Dependency Grammar in the HPSG formalism). However, I do not see any reason to disallow for flat structures. For instance, Ginzburg & Sag (2000: 364) assumed a flat rule for subject auxiliary inversion in HPSG. In such a flat rule the specifier/subject and the other complements are combined with the verb in one go. This would also work for more than two valence features that correspond to grammatical functions like subject, direct object, indirect object. See also footnote 28 on flat rules.

edges, that is, for discontinuous constituents. In what follows, I show how such Dependency Grammars can be formalized in HPSG.

11.7.2.2 Non-projective Dependency Grammars and phrase structure grammars with discontinuous constituents

The equivalent to non-projective dependency graphs are discontinuous constituents in phrase structure grammars. In what follows I want to provide one example of a phrase structure-based theory that permits discontinuous structures. Since, as I will show, discontinuities can be modeled as well, the difference between phrase structure grammars and Dependency Grammars boils down to the question of whether units of words are given a label (for instance NP) or not.

The technique that is used to model discontinuous constituents in frameworks like HPSG goes back to Mike Reape's work on German (1991; 1992; 1994). Reape uses a list called DOMAIN to represent the daughters of a sign in the order in which they appear at the surface of an utterance. (32) shows an example in which the DOM value of a headed-phrase is computed from the DOM value of the head and the list of non-head daughters.

(32) $\textit{headed-phrase} \Rightarrow \begin{bmatrix} \text{HEAD-DTR}|\text{DOM} & \boxed{1} \\ \text{NON-HEAD-DTRS} & \boxed{2} \\ \text{DOM} & \boxed{1} \bigcirc \boxed{2} \end{bmatrix}$

The symbol '$\bigcirc$' stands for the *shuffle* relation. *shuffle* relates three lists A, B and C iff C contains all elements from A and B and the order of the elements in A and the order of the elements of B is preserved in C. (33) shows the combination of two sets with two elements each:

(33) $\langle a, b \rangle \bigcirc \langle c, d \rangle = \langle a, b, c, d \rangle \vee$
$\langle a, c, b, d \rangle \vee$
$\langle a, c, d, b \rangle \vee$
$\langle c, a, b, d \rangle \vee$
$\langle c, a, d, b \rangle \vee$
$\langle c, d, a, b \rangle$

The result is a disjunction of six lists. *a* is ordered before *b* and *c* before *d* in all of these lists, since this is also the case in the two lists $\langle a, b \rangle$ and $\langle c, d \rangle$ that have been combined. But apart from this, *b* can be placed before, between or after *c* and *d*. Every word comes with a domain value that is a list that contains the word itself:

(34) Domain contribution of single words, here *gibt* 'gives':

$\boxed{1} \begin{bmatrix} \text{PHON} & \langle \textit{gibt} \rangle \\ \text{SYNSEM} & \ldots \\ \text{DOM} & \langle \boxed{1} \rangle \end{bmatrix}$

11.7 Summary and classification

The description in (34) may seem strange at first glance, since it is cyclic, but it can be understood as a statement saying that *gibt* contributes itself to the items that occur in linearization domains.

The constraint in (35) is responsible for the determination of the PHON values of phrases:

(35) $phrase \Rightarrow \begin{bmatrix} \text{PHON} \quad \boxed{1} \oplus ... \oplus \boxed{n} \\ \text{DOM} \quad \left\langle \begin{bmatrix} sign \\ \text{PHON} \ \boxed{1} \end{bmatrix}, ..., \begin{bmatrix} sign \\ \text{PHON} \ \boxed{n} \end{bmatrix} \right\rangle \end{bmatrix}$

It states that the PHON value of a sign is the concatenation of the PHON values of its DOMAIN elements. Since the order of the DOMAIN elements corresponds to their surface order, this is the obvious way to determine the PHON value of the whole linguistic object.

Figure 11.38 shows how this machinery can be used to license binary branching structures with discontinuous constituents. Words or word sequences that are separated by

Figure 11.38: Analysis of *dass der Frau ein Mann das Buch gibt* 'that a man gives the woman the book' with binary branching structures and discontinuous constituents

commas stand for separate domain objects, that is, ⟨ *das, Buch* ⟩ contains the two objects *das* and *Buch* and ⟨ *das Buch, gibt* ⟩ contains the two objects *das Buch* and *gibt*. The important point to note here is that the arguments are combined with the head in the order accusative, dative, nominative, although the elements in the constituent order domain are realized in the order dative, nominative, accusative rather than nominative, dative, accusative, as one would expect. This is possible since the formulation of the computation of the DOM value using the shuffle operator allows for discontinuous constituents. The node for *der Frau das Buch gibt* 'the woman the book gives' is discontinuous: *ein Mann* 'a man' is inserted into the domain between *der Frau* 'the woman' and *das Buch*

11 Dependency Grammar

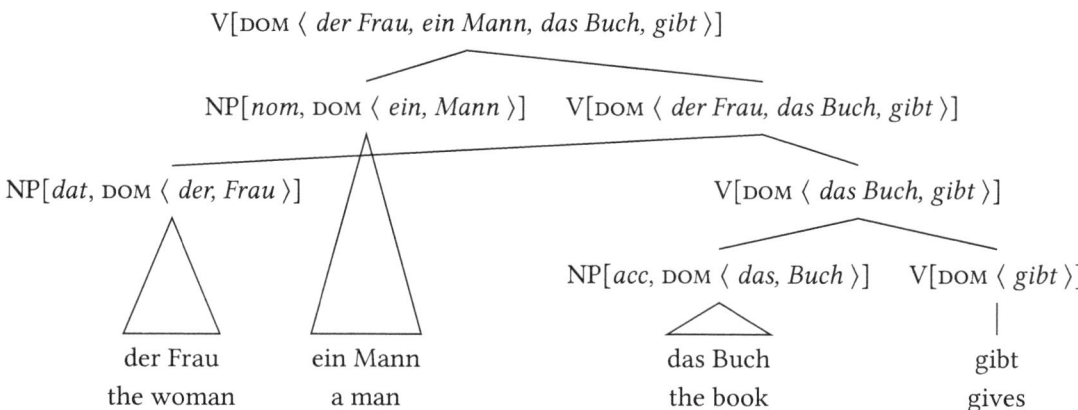

Figure 11.39: Analysis of *dass der Frau ein Mann das Buch gibt* 'that a man gives the woman the book' with binary branching structures and discontinuous constituents showing the discontinuity

'the book'. This is more obvious in Figure 11.39, which has a serialization of NPs that corresponds to their order.

Such binary branching structures were assumed for the analysis of German by Kathol (1995; 2000) and Müller (1995; 1996c; 1999b; 2002a), but as we have seen throughout this chapter, Dependency Grammar assumes flat representations (but see Footnote 30 on page 399). Schema 1 licenses structures in which all arguments of a head are realized in one go.[31]

Schema 1 (Head-Complement Schema (flat structure))
head-complement-phrase ⇒
$$\begin{bmatrix} \text{SYNSEM|LOC|CAT|COMPS} \langle\rangle \\ \text{HEAD-DTR|SYNSEM|LOC|CAT|COMPS} \boxed{1} \\ \text{NON-HEAD-DTRS} \boxed{1} \end{bmatrix}$$

To keep the presentation simple, I assume that the COMPS list contains descriptions of complete signs. Therefore the whole list can be identified with the list of non-head daughters.[32] The computation of the DOM value can be constrained in the following way:

(36) *headed-phrase* ⇒ $\begin{bmatrix} \text{HEAD-DTR} & \boxed{1} \\ \text{NON-HEAD-DTRS} & \langle \boxed{2}, ..., \boxed{n} \rangle \\ \text{DOM} & \langle \boxed{1} \rangle \bigcirc \langle \boxed{2} \rangle \bigcirc ... \bigcirc \langle \boxed{n} \rangle \end{bmatrix}$

---

[31] I assume here that all arguments are contained in the COMPS list of a lexical head, but nothing hinges on that. One could also assume several valence features and nevertheless get a flat structure. For instance, Borsley (1989: 339) suggests a schema for auxiliary inversion in English and verb-initial sentences in Welsh that refers to both the valence feature for subjects and for complements and realizes all elements in a flat structure.

[32] Without this assumption one would need a relational constraint that maps a list with descriptions of type *synsem* onto a list with descriptions of type *sign*. See Meurers (1999c: 198) for details.

This constraint says that the value of DOM is a list which is the result of shuffling singleton lists each containing one daughter as elements. The result of such a shuffle operation is a disjunction of all possible permutations of the daughters. This seems to be overkill for something that GPSG already gained by abstracting away from the order of the elements on the right hand side of a phrase structure rule. Note, however, that this machinery can be used to reach even freer orders: by referring to the DOM values of the daughters rather than the daughters themselves, it is possible to insert individual words into the DOM list.

(37) *headed-phrase* ⇒ $\begin{bmatrix} \text{HEAD-DTR}|\text{DOM} & \boxed{1} \\ \text{NON-HEAD-DTRS} & \langle\,[\,\text{DOM}\,\boxed{2}\,]\,\ldots\,[\,\text{DOM}\,\boxed{n}\,]\,\rangle \\ \text{DOM} & \langle\,\boxed{1}\,\rangle \bigcirc \langle\,\boxed{2}\,\rangle \bigcirc \ldots \bigcirc \langle\,\boxed{n}\,\rangle \end{bmatrix}$

Using this constraint we have DOM values that basically contain all the words in an utterance in any permutation. What we are left with is a pure Dependency Grammar without any constraints on projectivity. With such a grammar we could analyze the non-projecting structure of Figure 11.6 on page 372 and much more. The analysis in terms of domain union is shown in Figure 11.40. It is clear that such discontinuity is

Figure 11.40: Unwanted analysis of *dass die Frauen Türen öffnen* 'that the women open doors' using Reape-style constituent order domains

unwanted and hence one has to have restrictions that enforce continuity. One possible restriction is to require projectivity and hence equivalence to phrase structure grammars in the sense that was discussed above.

There is some dispute going on about the question of whether constituency/dependency is primary/necessary to analyze natural language: while Hudson (1980) and Engel (1996) claim that dependency is sufficient, a claim that is shared by dependency grammarians (according to Engel 1996), Leiss (2003) claims that it is not. In order to settle the issue, let us take a look at some examples:

(38) Dass Peter kommt, klärt nicht, ob Klaus spielt.
that Peter comes resolves not whether Klaus plays

'That Peter comes does not resolve the question of whether Klaus will play.'

If we know the meaning of the utterance, we can assign a dependency graph to it. Let us assume that the meaning of (38) is something like (39):

11 Dependency Grammar

(39) ¬ *resolve'(that'(come'(Peter')), whether'(play'(Klaus')))*

With this semantic information, we can of course construct a dependency graph for (38). The reason is that the dependency relation is reflected in a bi-unique way in the semantic representation in (39). The respective graph is given in Figure 11.41. But note that this

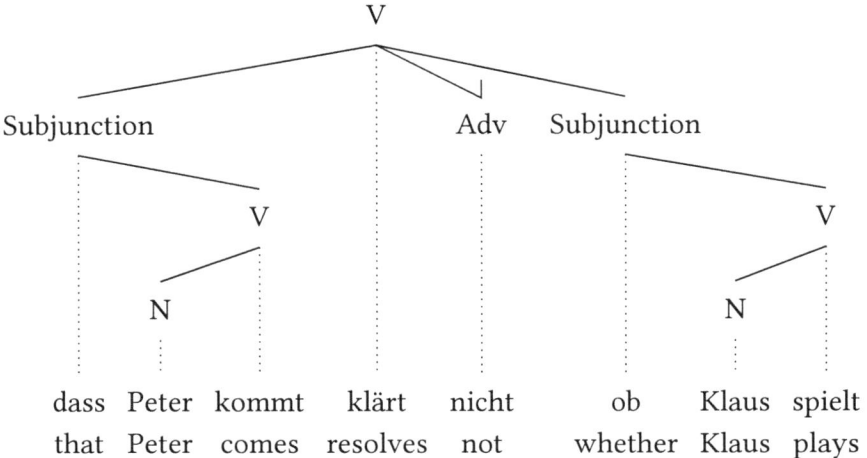

Figure 11.41: The dependency graph of *Dass Peter kommt, klärt nicht, ob Klaus spielt.* 'That Peter comes does not resolve the question of whether Klaus plays.' can be derived from the semantic representation.

does not hold in the general case. Take for instance the example in (40):

(40) Dass Peter kommt, klärt   nicht, ob   Klaus kommt.
      that Peter comes resolves not   whether Klaus plays

'That Peter comes does not resolve the question of whether Klaus comes.'

Here the word *kommt* appears twice. Without any notion of constituency or restrictions regarding adjacency, linear order and continuity, we cannot assign a dependency graph unambiguously. For instance, the graph in Figure 11.42 is perfectly compatible with the meaning of this sentence: *dass* dominates *kommt* and *kommt* dominates *Peter*, while *ob* dominates *kommt* and *kommt* dominates *Klaus*. I used the wrong *kommt* in the dependency chains, but this is an issue of linearization and is independent of dependency. As soon as one takes linearization information into account, the dependency graph in Figure 11.42 is ruled out since *ob* 'whether' does not precede its verbal dependent *kommt* 'comes'. But this explanation does not work for the example in Figure 11.6. Here, all dependents are linearized correctly; it is just the discontinuity of *die* and *Türen* that is inappropriate. If it is required that *die* and *Türen* are continuous, we have basically let constituents back in (see Footnote 9 on page 372).

Similarly, non-projective analyses without any constraints regarding continuity would permit the word salad in (41b):

11.7 Summary and classification

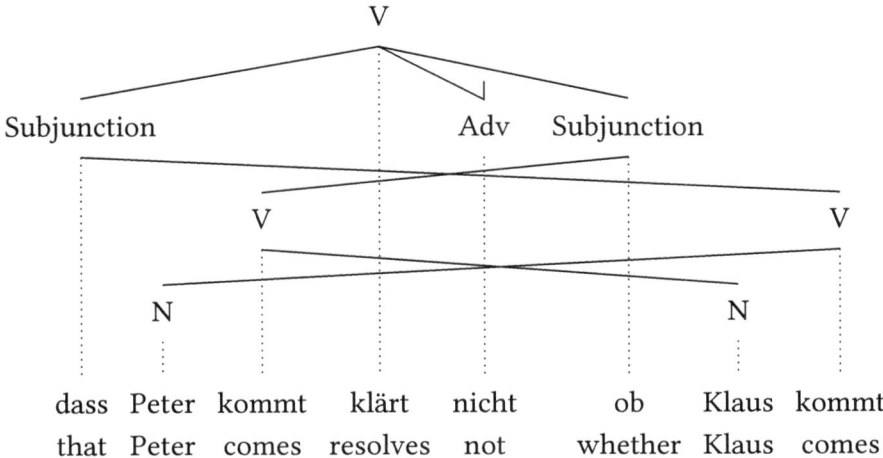

Figure 11.42: The dependency graph of *Dass Peter kommt, klärt nicht, ob Klaus kommt.* 'That Peter comes does not resolve the question of whether Klaus comes.' is not unambiguously determined by semantics.

(41) a. Deshalb klärt, dass Peter kommt, ob Klaus spielt.
       therefore resolves that Peter comes whether Klaus plays

   b. *Deshalb klärt dass ob Peter Klaus kommt spielt.
       therefore resolves that whether Peter Klaus comes plays

(41b) is a variant of (41a) in which the elements of the two clausal arguments are in correct order with respect to each other, but both clauses are discontinuous in such a way that the elements of each clause alternate. The dependency graph is shown in Figure 11.43. As was explained in Section 10.6.4.4 on the analysis of nonlocal dependencies in Fluid Construction Grammar, a grammar of languages like English and German has to constrain the clauses in such a way that they are continuous with the exception of extractions to the left. A similar statement can be found in Hudson (1980: 192). Hudson also states that an item can be fronted in English, provided all of its dependents are fronted with it (p. 184). This "item with all its dependents" is the constituent in constituent-based grammars. The difference is that this object is not given an explicit name and is not assumed to be a separate entity containing the head and its dependents in most Dependency Grammars.[33]

Summing up what has been covered in this section so far, I have shown what a phrase structure grammar that corresponds to a certain Dependency Grammar looks like. I have also shown how discontinuous constituents can be allowed for. However, there are issues that remained unaddressed so far: not all properties that a certain phrase has are identical to its lexical head and the differences have to be represented somewhere. I will discuss this in the following subsection.

---

[33] See however Hellwig (2003) for an explicit proposal that assumes that there is a linguistic object that represents the whole constituent rather than just the lexical head.

11 Dependency Grammar

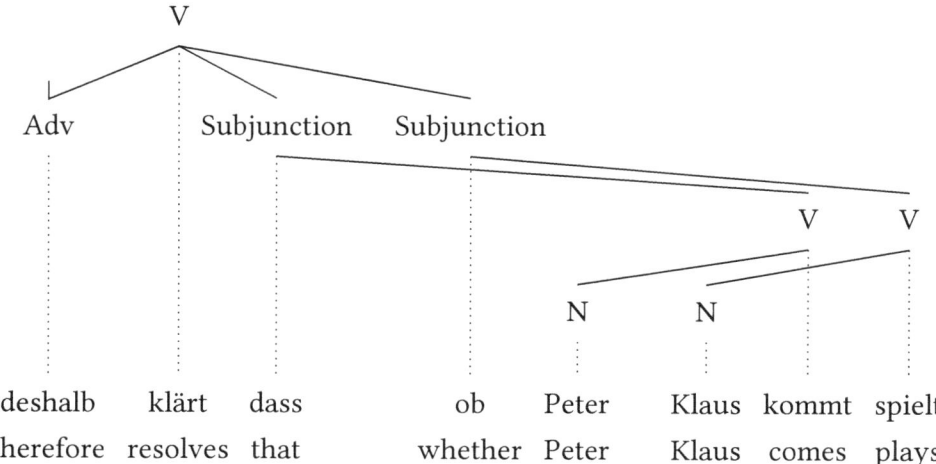

Figure 11.43: The dependency graph of the word salad *Deshalb klärt dass ob Peter Klaus kommt spielt*. 'Therefore resolves that whether Peter Klaus comes plays' which is admitted by non-projective Dependency Grammars that do not restrict discontinuity

11.7.2.3 Features that are not identical between heads and projections

As Oliva (2003) points out, the equivalence of Dependency Grammar and HPSG only holds up as far as HEAD values are concerned. That is, the node labels in dependency graphs correspond to the HEAD values in an HPSG. There are, however, additional features like CONT for the semantics and SLASH for nonlocal dependencies. These values usually differ between a lexical head and its phrasal projections. For illustration, let us have a look at the phrase *a book*. The semantics of the lexical material and the complete phrase is given in (42):[34]

(42)   a.   *a*: $\lambda P \lambda Q \exists x (P(x) \wedge Q(x))$

       b.   *book*: $\lambda y \, (book'(y))$

       c.   *a book*: $\lambda Q \exists x (book'(x) \wedge Q(x))$

Now, the problem for the Dependency Grammar notation is that there is no NP node that could be associated with the semantics of *a book* (see Figure 11.36 on page 398), the only thing present in the tree is a node for the lexical N: the node for *book*.[35] This is not a big

---

[34] For lambda expressions see Section 2.3.

[35] Hudson (2003: 391–392) is explicit about this: "In dependency analysis, the dependents modify the head word's meaning, so the latter carries the meaning of the whole phrase. For example, in *long books about linguistics*, the word *books* means 'long books about linguistics' thanks to the modifying effect of the dependents." For a concrete implementation of this idea see Figure 11.44.

An alternative is to assume different representational levels as in Meaning–Text Theory (Mel'čuk 1981). In fact the CONT value in HPSG is also a different representational level. However, this representational level is in sync with the other structure that is build.

problem, however: the lexical properties can be represented as part of the highest node as the value of a separate feature. The N node in a dependency graph would then have a CONT value that corresponds to the semantic contribution of the complete phrase and a LEX-CONT value that corresponds to the contribution of the lexical head of the phrase. So for *a book* we would get the following representation:

(43) $\begin{bmatrix} \text{CONT} & \lambda Q \exists x (book'(x) \wedge Q(x)) \\ \text{LEXICAL-CONT} & \lambda y\, (book'(y)) \end{bmatrix}$

With this kind of representation one could maintain analyses in which the semantic contribution of a head together with its dependents is a function of the semantic contribution of the parts.

Now, there are probably further features in which lexical heads differ from their projections. One such feature would be SLASH, which is used for nonlocal dependencies in HPSG and could be used to establish the relation between the risen element and the head in an approach à la Groß & Osborne (2009). Of course we can apply the same trick again. We would then have a feature LEXICAL-SLASH. But this could be improved and the features of the lexical item could be grouped under one path. The general skeleton would then be (44):

(44) $\begin{bmatrix} \text{CONT} & \\ \text{SLASH} & \\ \text{LEXICAL} & \begin{bmatrix} \text{CONT} \\ \text{SLASH} \end{bmatrix} \end{bmatrix}$

But if we rename LEXICAL to HEAD-DTR, we basically get the HPSG representation.

Hellwig (2003: 602) states that his special version of Dependency Grammar, which he calls Dependency Unification Grammar, assumes that governing heads select complete nodes with all their daughters. These nodes may differ in their properties from their head (p. 604). They are in fact constituents. So this very explicit and formalized variant of Dependency Grammar is very close to HPSG, as Hellwig states himself (p. 603).

Hudson's Word Grammar (2017) is also explicitly worked out and, as will be shown, it is rather similar to HPSG. The representation in Figure 11.44 is a detailed description of what the abbreviated version in Figure 11.45 stands for. What is shown in the first-diagram is that a combination of two nodes results in a new node.[36] For instance, the combination of *playing* and *outside* yields *playing'*, the combination of *small* and *children* yields *children'*, and the combination of *children'* and *playing'* yields *playing"*. The combination of *were* and *playing"* results in *were'* and the combination of *children"* and *were'* yields *were"*. The only thing left to explain is why there is a node for *children* that is not the result of the combination of two nodes, namely *children"*. The line with the triangle at the bottom stands for default inheritance. That is, the upper node inherits all

---

[36] By assuming these additional nodes Hudson addresses earlier criticism by Dahl (1980), who pointed out that *ordinary* in *ordinary French house* does not refer to *house* but to *French house*. So there has to be a representation for *French house* somewhere. At least at the semantic level. Hudson's additional nodes and classical $\overline{\text{N}}$ nodes solve this problem as well.

11 Dependency Grammar

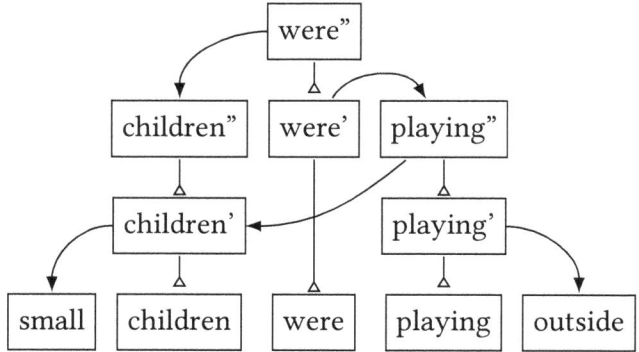

Figure 11.44: Analysis of *Small children were playing outside.* according to Hudson (2017: 105)

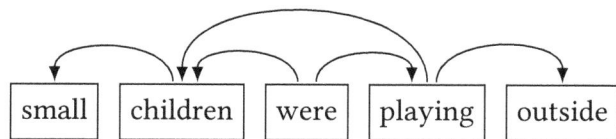

Figure 11.45: Abbreviated analysis of *Small children were playing outside.* according to Hudson (2017: 105)

properties from the lower node by default. Defaults can be overridden, that is, information at the upper node may differ from information at the dominated node. This makes it possible to handle semantics compositionally: nodes that are the result of the combination of two nodes have a semantics that is the combination of the meaning of the two combined nodes. Turning to *children* again, *children′* has the property that it must be adjacent to *playing*, but since the structure is a raising structure in which *children* is raised to the subject of *were*, this property is overwritten in a new instance of *children*, namely *children″*.

The interesting point now is that we get almost a normal phrase structure tree if we replace the words in the diagram in Figure 11.44 by syntactic categories. The result of the replacement is shown in Figure 11.46. The only thing unusual in this graph (marked by dashed lines) is that N′ is combined with V[*ing*]′ and the mother of N′, namely N″, is combined with V[*fin*]′. As explained above, this is due to the analysis of raising in Word Grammar, which involves multiple dependencies between a raised item and its heads. There are two N nodes (N′ and N″) in Figure 11.46 and two instances of *children* in Figure 11.44. Apart from this, the structure corresponds to what an HPSG grammar would license. The nodes in Hudson's diagram which are connected with lines with triangles at the bottom are related to their children using default inheritance. This too is rather similar to those versions of HPSG that use default inheritance. For instance, Ginzburg & Sag (2000: 33) use a Generalized Head Feature Principle that projects all properties of the head daughter to the mother by default.

The conclusion of this section is that the only principled difference between phrase structure grammars and Dependency Grammar is the question of how much intermedi-

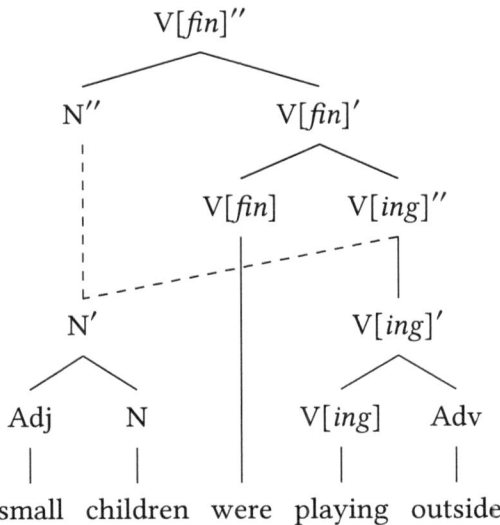

Figure 11.46: Analysis of *Small children are playing outside.* with category symbols

ate structure is assumed: is there a VP without the subject? Are there intermediate nodes for adjunct attachment? It is difficult to decide these questions in the absence of fully worked out proposals that include semantic representations. Those proposals that are worked out – like Hudson's and Hellwig's – assume intermediate representations, which makes these approaches rather similar to phrase structure-based approaches. If one compares the structures of these fully worked out variants of Dependency Grammar with phrase structure grammars, it becomes clear that the claim that Dependency Grammars are simpler is unwarranted. This claim holds for compacted schematic representations like Figure 11.45 but it does not hold for fully worked out analyses.

The simplicity claim is repeatedly made in Timothy Osborne's work (for example in Osborne & Groß 2016: 132; Osborne 2018b: 2). In a reply to Osborne (2018b), I mentioned some of the phenomena discussed above and pointed out that they are not captured by simple dependency structures (Müller 2019a) and argued that additional structure is needed in order to account for these phenomena. Somewhat ironically, Osborne (2019) worked out analyses in his reply that introduced a new concept (the Colocant) and additional structure to capture semantic groupings. By doing so, he proved the point made above and in Müller (2019a).

11.7.2.4 Non-headed constructions

Hudson (1980: Section 4.E) discusses headless constructions like those in (45):

(45) a. the rich
      b. the biggest
      c. the longer the stem
      d. (with) his hat over his eyes

He argues that the terms *adjective* and *noun* should be accompanied by the term *substantive*, which subsumes both terms. Then he suggests that *if a rule needs to cover the constructions traditionally referred to as noun-phrases, with or without heads, it just refers to 'nouns', and this will automatically allow the constructions to have either substantives or adjectives as heads.* (p. 195) The question that has to be asked here, however, is what the internal dependency structure of substantive phrases like *the rich* would be. The only way to connect the items seems to be to assume that the determiner is dependent on the adjective. But this would allow for two structures of phrases like *the rich man*: one in which the determiner depends on the adjective and one in which it depends on the noun. So underspecification of part of speech does not seem to solve the problem. Of course all problems with non-headed constructions can be solved by assuming empty elements.[37] This has been done in HPSG in the analysis of relative clauses (Pollard & Sag 1994: Chapter 5). English and German relative clauses consist of a phrase that contains a relative word and a sentence in which the relative phrase is missing. Pollard & Sag assume an empty relativizer that selects for the relative phrase and the clause with a gap (Pollard & Sag 1994: 216–217). Similar analyses can be found in Dependency Grammar (Eroms 2000: 291).[38] Now, the alternative to empty elements are phrasal constructions.[39] Sag (1997) working on relative clauses in English suggested a phrasal analysis of relative clauses in which the relative phrase and the clause from which it is extracted form a new phrase. A similar analysis was assumed by Müller (1996c) and is documented in Müller (1999b: Chapter 10). As was discussed in Section 8.6 it is neither plausible to assume the relative pronoun or some other element in the relative phrase to be the head of the entire relative clause, nor is it plausible to assume the verb to be the head of the entire relative clause (pace Sag), since relative clauses modify $\overline{N}$s, something that projections of (finite) verbs usually do not do. So assuming an empty head or a phrasal schema seems to be the only option.

Chapter 21 is devoted to the discussion of whether certain phenomena should be analyzed as involving phrase structural configurations or whether lexical analyses are better suited in general or for modeling some phenomena. I argue there that all phenomena in-

---

[37] See Section 2.4.1 for the assumption of an empty head in a phrase structure grammar for noun phrases.

[38] The Dependency Grammar representations usually have a *d-* element as the head of the relative clause. However, since the relative pronoun is also present in the clause and since the *d-* is not pronounced twice, assuming an additional *d-* head is basically assuming an empty head.

Another option is to assume that words may have multiple functions: so, a relative pronoun may be both a head and a dependent simultaneously (Tesnière 2015: Chapter 246, §8–11; Kahane & Osborne 2015: xlvi; Kahane 2009: 129–130). At least the analysis of Kahane is an instance of the Categorial Grammar analysis that was discussed in Section 8.6 and it suffers from the same problems: if the relative pronoun is a head that selects for a clause that is missing the relative pronoun, it is not easy to see how this analysis extends to cases of pied-piping like (i) in which the extracted element is a complete phrase containing the relative pronoun rather than just the pronoun itself.

(i) die Frau, von deren Schwester ich ein Bild gesehen habe
 the woman of whose sister I a picture seen have
 'the woman of whose sister I saw a picture'

[39] See Chapter 19 on empty elements in general and Subsection 21.10.3 on relative clauses in particular.

teracting with valence should be treated lexically. But there are other phenomena as well and Dependency Grammar is forced to assume lexical analyses for all linguistic phenomena. There always has to be some element on which others depend. It has been argued by Jackendoff (2008) that it does not make sense to assume that one of the elements in N-P-N constructions like those in (46) is the head.

(46) a. day by day, paragraph by paragraph, country by country
  b. dollar for dollar, student for student, point for point
  c. face to face, bumper to bumper
  d. term paper after term paper, picture after picture
  e. book upon book, argument upon argument

Of course there is a way to model all the phenomena that would be modeled by a phrasal construction in frameworks like GPSG, CxG, HPSG, or Simpler Syntax: an empty head. Figure 11.47 shows the analysis of *student after student*. The lexical item for the empty N

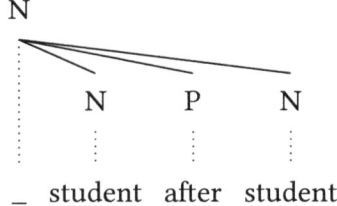

Figure 11.47: Dependency Grammar analysis of the N-P-N Construction with empty head

would be very special, since there are no similar non-empty lexical nouns, that is, there is no noun that selects for two bare Ns and a P.

Bargmann (2015) pointed out an additional aspect of the N-P-N construction, which makes things more complicated. The pattern is not restricted to two nouns. There can be arbitrarily many of them:

(47) Day after day after day went by, but I never found the courage to talk to her.

So rather than an N-P-N pattern Bargmann suggests the pattern in (48), where '+' stands for at least one repetition of a sequence.

(48) N (P N)+

Now, such patterns would be really difficult to model in selection-based approaches, since one would have to assume that an empty head or a noun selects for an arbitrary number of pairs of the same preposition and noun or nominal phrase. Of course one could assume that P and N form some sort of constituent, but still one would have to make sure that the right preposition is used and that the noun or nominal projection has the right phonology. Another possibility would be to assume that the second N in N-P-N can be an N-P-N and thereby allow recursion in the pattern. But if one follows this approach it is getting really difficult to check the constraint that the involved Ns should have the same or at least similar phonologies.

One way out of these problems would of course be to assume that there are special combinatorial mechanisms that assign a new category to one or several elements. This would basically be an unheaded phrase structure rule and this is what Tesnière suggested: transfer rules (see Section 11.6.2.2). But this is of course an extension of pure Dependency Grammar towards a mixed model.

See Section 21.10 for the discussion of further cases which are probably problematic for purely selection-based grammars.

Exercises

Provide the dependency graphs for the following three sentences:

(49)   a. Ich habe einen Mann getroffen, der blonde Haare hat.
           I have a man met who blond hair has
        'I have met a man who has blond hair.'

       b. Einen Mann getroffen, der blonde Haare hat, habe ich noch nie.
           a man met who blond hair has have I yet never
        'I have never met a man who has blond hair.'

       c. Dass er morgen kommen wird, freut uns.
           that he tomorrow come will pleases us
        'That he will come tomorrow pleases us.'

You may use non-projective dependencies. For the analysis of relative clauses authors usually propose an abstract entity that functions as a dependent of the modified noun and as a head of the verb in the relative clause.

Further reading

In the section on further reading in Chapter 3, I referred to the book called *Syntaktische Analyseperspektiven* 'Syntactic perspectives on analyses'. The chapters in this book have been written by proponents of various theories and all analyze the same newspaper article. The book also contains a chapter by Engel (2014), assuming his version of Dependency Grammar, namely *Dependent Verb Grammar*.

Ágel, Eichinger, Eroms, Hellwig, Heringer & Lobin (2003; 2006) published a handbook on dependency and valence that discusses all aspects related to Dependency Grammar in any imaginable way. Many of the papers have been cited in this chapter. Papers comparing Dependency Grammar with other theories are especially relevant in the context of this book: Lobin (2003) compares Dependency Grammar and Categorial Grammar, Oliva (2003) deals with the representation of valence and dependency in HPSG, and Bangalore, Joshi & Rambow (2003) describe how valence and dependency are covered in TAG. Hellwig (2006) compares rule-based grammars with Dependency Grammars with special consideration given to parsing by computer programs.

Osborne & Groß (2012) compare Dependency Grammar with Construction Grammar and Osborne, Putnam & Groß (2011) argue that certain variants of Minimalism are in fact reinventions of dependency-based analyses.

The original work on Dependency Grammar by Tesnière (1959) is also available in parts in German (Tesnière 1980) and in full in English (Tesnière 2015).

12 Tree Adjoining Grammar

Tree Adjoining Grammar (TAG) was developed by Aravind Joshi at the University of Pennsylvania in the USA (Joshi, Levy & Takahashi 1975). Several important dissertations in TAG have been supervised by Aravind Joshi and Anthony Kroch at the University of Pennsylvania (e.g., Rambow 1994). Other research centers with a focus on TAG are Paris 7 (Anne Abeillé), Columbia University in the USA (Owen Rambow) and Düsseldorf, Germany (Laura Kallmeyer). Rambow (1994) and Gerdes (2002b) are more detailed studies of German.[1]

TAG and its variants with relevant extensions are of interest because it is assumed that this grammatical formalism can – with regard to its expressive power – relatively accurately represent what humans do when they produce or comprehend natural language. The expressive power of Generalized Phrase Structure Grammar was deliberately constrained so that it corresponds to context-free phrase structure grammars (Type-2 languages) and it has in fact been demonstrated that this is not enough (Shieber 1985; Culy 1985).[2] Grammatical theories such as HPSG and CxG can generate/describe so-called Type-0 languages and are thereby far above the level of complexity presently assumed for natural languages. The assumption is that this complexity lies somewhere between context-free and context-sensitive (Type-1) languages. This class is thus referred to as *mildly context-sensitive*. Certain TAG-variants are inside of this language class and it is assumed that they can produce exactly those structures that occur in natural languages. For more on complexity, see Section 12.6.3 and Chapter 17.

There are various systems for the processing of TAG grammars (Doran, Hockey, Sarkar, Srinivas & Xia 2000; Parmentier, Kallmeyer, Maier, Lichte & Dellert 2008; Kallmeyer, Lichte, Maier, Parmentier, Dellert & Evang 2008; Koller 2017). Smaller and larger TAG fragments have been developed for the following languages:

- Arabic (Fraj, Zribi & Ahmed 2008),
- German (Rambow 1994; Gerdes 2002a; Kallmeyer & Yoon 2004; Lichte 2007),
- English (XTAG Research Group 2001; Frank 2002; Kroch & Joshi 1987),
- French (Abeillé 1988; Candito 1996; 1998; 1999; Crabbé 2005),
- Italian (Candito 1998; 1999),

---

[1]Since my knowledge of French leaves something to be desired, I just refer to the literature in French here without being able to comment on the content.

[2]See Pullum (1986) for a historical overview of the complexity debate and G. Müller (2011) for argumentation for the non-context-free nature of German, which follows parallel to Culy with regard to the N-P-N construction (see Section 21.10.4).

12 Tree Adjoining Grammar

- Korean (Han, Yoon, Kim & Palmer 2000; Kallmeyer & Yoon 2004),
- Vietnamese (Le, Nguyen & Roussanaly 2008)

Candito (1996) has developed a system for the representation of meta grammars which allows the uniform specification of crosslinguistic generalizations. This system was used by some of the projects mentioned above for the derivation of grammars for specific languages. For instance Kinyon, Rambow, Scheffler, Yoon & Joshi (2006) derive the verb second languages from a common meta grammar. Among those grammars for verb second languages is a grammar of Yiddish for which there was no TAG grammar until 2006.

Resnik (1992) combines TAG with a statistics component.

12.1 General remarks on representational format

12.1.1 Representation of valence information

Figure 12.1 shows so-called elementary trees. These are present in the lexicon and can be combined to create larger trees. Nodes for the insertion of arguments are specially

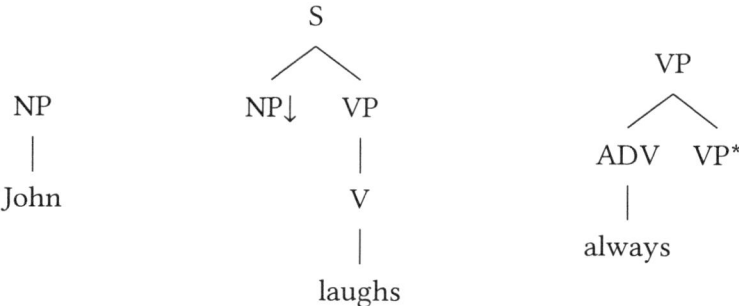

Figure 12.1: Elementary trees

marked (NP↓ in the tree for *laughs*). Nodes for the insertion of adjuncts into a tree are also marked (VP* in the tree for *always*). Grammars where elementary trees always contain at least one word are referred to as *Lexicalized Tree Adjoining Grammar* (LTAG, Schabes, Abeillé & Joshi (1988)).

12.1.2 Substitution

Figure 12.2 on the next page shows the substitution of nodes. Other subtrees have to be inserted into substitution nodes such as the NP node in the tree for *laughs*. The tree for *John* is inserted there in the example derivation.

12.1 General remarks on representational format

Figure 12.2: Substitution

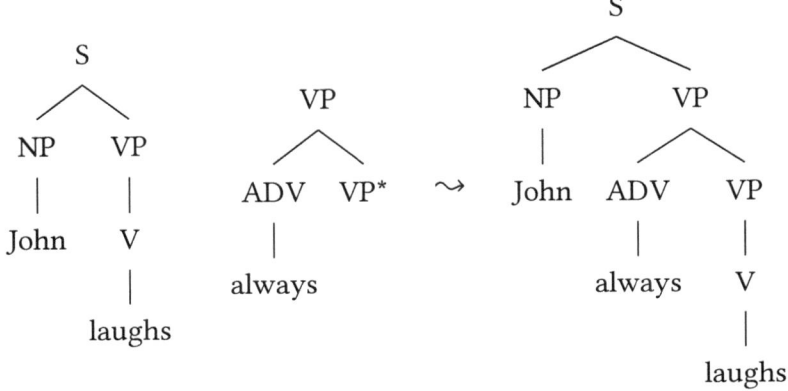

Figure 12.3: Adjunction

12.1.3 Adjunction

Figure 12.3 shows an example of how the adjunction tree for *always* can be used.

Adjunction trees can be inserted into other trees. Upon insertion, the target node (bearing the same category as the node marked with '*') is replaced by the adjunction tree.

TAG differs considerably from the simple phrase structure grammars we encountered in Chapter 2 in that the trees extend over a larger domain: for example, there is an NP node in the tree for *laughs* that is not a sister of the verb. In a phrase structure grammar (and of course in GB and GPSG since these theories are more or less directly built on phrase structure grammars), it is only ever possible to describe subtrees with a depth of one level. For the tree for *laughs*, the relevant rules would be those in (1):

(1) S   → NP VP
    VP → V
    V → laughs

In this context, it is common to speak of *locality domains*. The extension of the locality domain is of particular importance for the analysis of idioms (see Section 18.2).

TAG differs from other grammatical theories in that it is possible for structures to be broken up again. In this way, it is possible to use adjunction to insert any amount of material into a given tree and thereby cause originally adjacent constituents to end up being arbitrarily far away from each other in the final tree. As we will see in Section 12.5, this property is important for the analysis of long-distance dependencies without movement.

12.1.4 Semantics

There are different approaches to the syntax-semantics interface in TAG. One possibility is to assign a semantic representation to every node in the tree. The alternative is to assign each elementary tree exactly one semantic representation. The semantics construction does not make reference to syntactic structure but rather the way the structure is combined. This kind of approach has been proposed by Candito & Kahane (1998) and then by Kallmeyer & Joshi (2003), who build on it. The basic mechanisms will be briefly presented in what follows.

In the literature on TAG, a distinction is made between derived trees and derivation trees. Derived trees correspond to constituent structure (the trees for *John laughs* and *John always laughs* in Figures 12.2 and 12.3). The derivation tree contains the derivational history, that is, information about how the elementary trees were combined. The elements in a derivation tree represent predicate-argument dependencies, which is why it is possible to derive a semantic derivation tree from them. This will be shown on the basis of the sentence in (2):

(2) Max likes Anouk.

The elementary tree for (2) and the derived tree are given in Figure 12.4 on the next page. The nodes in trees are numbered from top to bottom and from left to right. The result of this numbering of nodes for *likes* is shown in Figure 12.5 on the facing page. The topmost node in the tree for *likes* is S and has the position 0. Beneath S, there is an NP and a VP node. These nodes are again numbered starting at 1. NP has the position 1 and VP the position 2. The VP node has in turn two daughters: V and the object NP. V receives number 1 and the object NP 2. This makes it possible to combine these numbers and then it is possible to unambiguously access individual elements in the tree. The position for the subject NP is 1 since this is a daughter of S and occurs in first position. The object NP has the numeric sequence 2.2 since it is below the VP (the second daughter of S = 2) and occurs in second position (the second daughter of VP = 2).

With these tree positions, the derivation tree for (2) can be represented as in Figure 12.6 on the next page. The derivation tree expresses the fact that the elementary tree for *likes* was combined with two arguments that were inserted into the substitution positions 1

12.1 General remarks on representational format

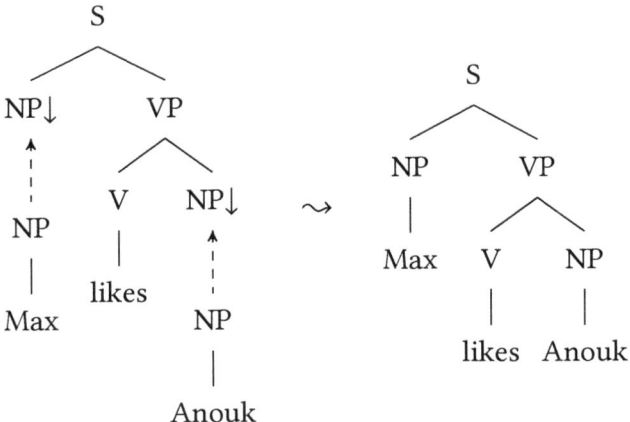

Figure 12.4: Elementary trees and derived tree for *Max likes Anouk*.

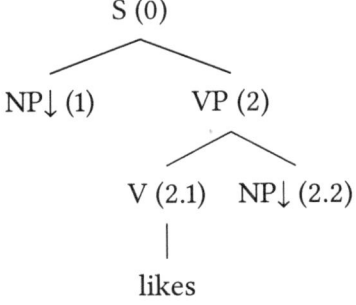

Figure 12.5: Node positions in the elementary tree for *likes*

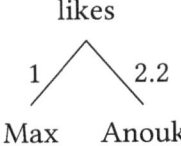

Figure 12.6: Derivation tree for *Max likes Anouk*.

and 2.2. The derivation tree also contains information about what exactly was placed into these nodes.

Kallmeyer & Joshi (2003) use a variant of *Minimal Recursion Semantics* as their semantic representational formalism (Copestake, Flickinger, Pollard & Sag 2005). I will use a considerably simplified representation here, as I did in Section 9.1.6 on semantics in HPSG. For the elementary trees *Max*, *likes* and *Anouk*, we can assume the semantic representations in (3).

(3) Semantic representations for elementary trees:

max(x)	like(x_1, x_2)	anouk(y)
arg: –	arg: $\langle x_1, 1 \rangle$, $\langle x_2, 2.2 \rangle$	arg: –

In a substitution operation, a variable is assigned a value. If, for example, the elementary tree for *Max* is inserted into the subject position of the tree for *likes*, then x_1 is identified with x. In the same way, x_2 is identified with y if the tree for *Anouk* is inserted into the object position. The result of these combinations is the representation in (4):

(4) Combination of the meaning of elementary trees:

like(x, y)
max(x)
anouk(y)
arg: –

Kallmeyer & Joshi (2003) show how an extension of TAG, Multi-Component LTAG, can handle quantifier scope and discuss complex cases with embedded verbs. Interested readers are referred to the original article.

12.2 Local reordering

In TAG, there is a family of trees for each word. In order to account for ordering variants, one can assume that there are six trees corresponding to a ditransitive verb and that each of these corresponds to a different ordering of the arguments. Trees are connected to one another via lexical rules. This lexical rule-based analysis is parallel to the one developed by Uszkoreit (1986b) in Categorial Grammar.

Alternatively, one could assume a format for TAG structures similar to what we referred to as the ID/LP format in the chapter on GPSG. Joshi (1987b) defines an elementary structure as a pair that consists of a dominance structure and linearization constraints. Unlike GPSG, linearization rules do not hold for all dominance rules but rather for a particular dominance structure. This is parallel to what we saw in Section 10.6.3 on Embodied-CxG. Figure 12.7 on the facing page shows a dominance tree with numbered nodes. If we combine this dominance structure with the linearization rules in (5), we arrive at the exact order that we would get with ordinary phrase structure rules, namely NP_1 V NP_2.

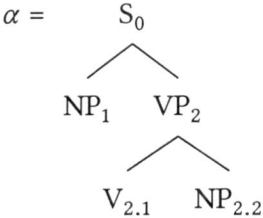

Figure 12.7: Dominance structure with numbered nodes

(5) $LP_1^\alpha = \{\, 1 < 2,\ 2.1 < 2.2 \,\}$

If one specifies the linearization restrictions as in (6), all the orders in (7) are permitted, since the empty set means that we do not state any restrictions at all.

(6) $LP_2^\alpha = \{\,\}$

(7)   a. NP_1 V NP_2
     b. NP_2 V NP_1
     c. NP_1 NP_2 V
     d. NP_2 NP_1 V
     e. V NP_1 NP_2
     f. V NP_2 NP_1

This means that it is possible to derive all orders that were derived in GPSG with flat sentence rules despite the fact that there is a constituent in the tree that consists of NP and VP. Since the dominance rules include a larger locality domain, such grammars are called LD/LP grammars (local dominance/linear precedence) rather than ID/LP grammars (immediate dominance/linear precedence) (Joshi, Vijay-Shanker & Weir 1990).

Simple variants of TAG such as those presented in Section 12.1 cannot deal with reordering if the arguments of different verbs are scrambled as in (8).

(8) weil   ihm   das   Buch jemand   zu lesen versprochen hat[3]
    because him.DAT the.ACC book somebody.NOM to read promised   has
    'because somebody promised him to read the book'

In (8), *das Buch* 'the book' is the object of *zu lesen* 'to read', and *ihm* 'him' and *jemand* 'somebody' are dependent on *versprochen* and *hat*, respectively. These cases can be analyzed by LD/LP-TAG developed by Joshi (1987b) and Free Order TAG (FO-TAG) (Becker, Joshi & Rambow 1991: 21) since both of these TAG variants allow for crossing edges.

Since certain restrictions cannot be expressed in FO-TAG (Rambow 1994: 48–50), so-called Multi-Component TAG was developed. Joshi, Becker & Rambow (2000) illustrate

---

[3] For more on this kind of examples, see Bech (1955).

the problem that simple LTAG grammars have with sentences such as (8) using examples such as (9):[4]

(9) a. ... daß der   Detektiv dem   Klienten [den   Verdächtigen des
         that the.NOM detective the.DAT client   the.ACC suspect   the.GEN
    Verbrechens zu überführen] versprach
    crime   to indict   promised
    'that the detective promised the client to indict the suspect of the crime'

   b. ... daß des   Verbrechens$_k$ der   Detektiv den   Verdächtigen$_j$
         that the.GEN crime   the.NOM detective the.ACC suspect
    dem   Klienten [$_{-j}$ $_{-k}$ zu überführen] versprach
    the.DAT client   to indict   promised

In LTAG, the elementary trees for the relevant verbs look as shown in Figure 12.8. The

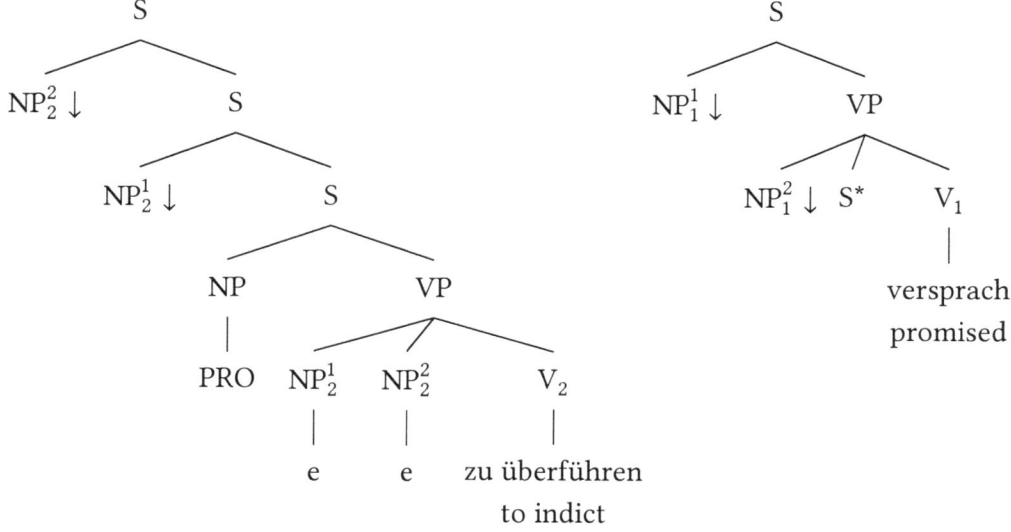

Figure 12.8: Elementary trees of an infinitive and a control verb

verbs are numbered according to their level of embedding. The NP arguments of a verb bear the same index as that verb and each has a superscript number that distinguishes it from the other arguments. The trees are very similar to those in GB. In particular, it is assumed that the subject occurs outside the VP. For non-finite verbs, it is assumed that the subject is realized by PRO. PRO is, like *e*, a phonologically empty pronominal category that also comes from GB. The left tree in Figure 12.8 contains traces in the normal position of the arguments and the relevant NP slots in higher trees positions. An interesting difference to other theories is that these traces only exist in the tree. They are not represented as individual entries in the lexicon as the lexicon only contains words and the corresponding trees.

---

[4]The authors use *versprochen hat* 'has promised' rather than *versprach* 'promised', which sounds better but does not correspond to the trees they use.

The tree for *versprach* 'promised' can be inserted into any S node in the tree for *zu überführen* 'to indict' and results in trees such as those in the Figures 12.9 and 12.10.

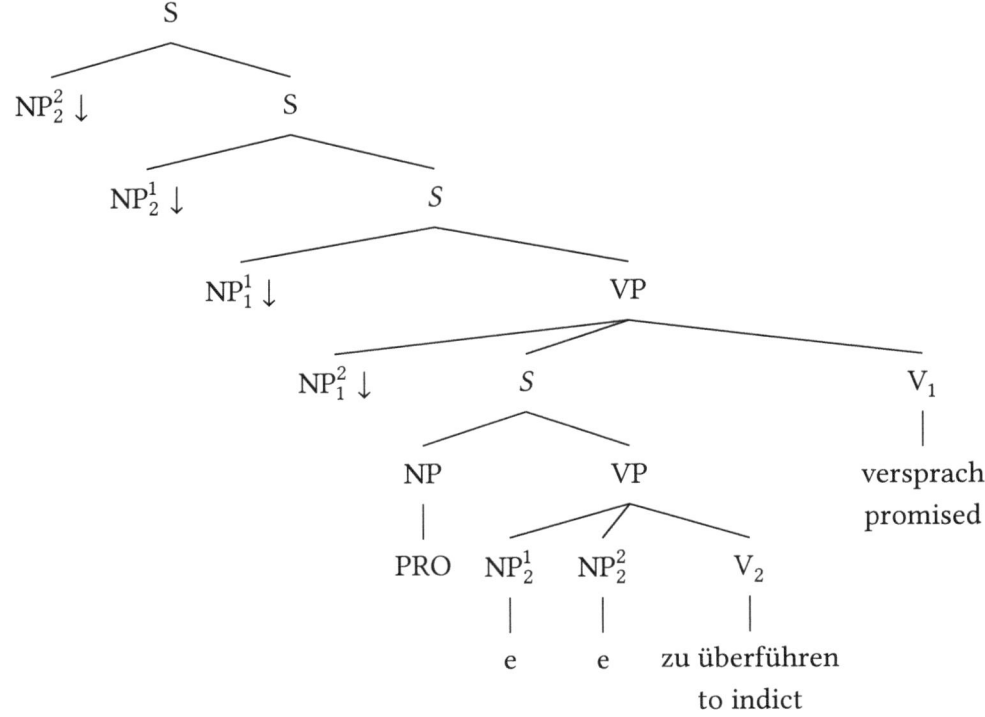

Figure 12.9: Analysis of the order NP_2^2 NP_2^1 NP_1^1 NP_1^2 V_2V_1: adjunction to the lowest S node

In Figure 12.9, the tree for *versprach* is inserted directly above the PRO NP and in Figure 12.10 above NP_2^1.

It is clear that it is not possible to derive a tree in this way where an argument of *überführen* 'to indict' occurs between the arguments of *versprach* 'promised'. Joshi, Becker & Rambow (2000) therefore suggest an extension of the LTAG formalism. In MC-TAG, the grammar does not consist of elementary trees but rather finite sets of elementary trees. In every derivational step, a set is selected and the elements of that set are simultaneously added to the tree. Figure 12.11 on the following page shows an elementary tree for *versprach* 'promised' consisting of multiple components. This tree contains a trace of NP_1^1 that was moved to the left. The bottom-left S node and the top-right S node are connected by a dashed line that indicates the dominance relation. However, immediate dominance is not required. Therefore, it is possible to insert the two subtrees into another tree separately from each other and thereby analyze the order in Figure 12.12 on page 425, for example.

Other variants of TAG that allow for other constituent orders are V-TAG (Rambow 1994) and TT-MC-TAG (Lichte 2007).

12 Tree Adjoining Grammar

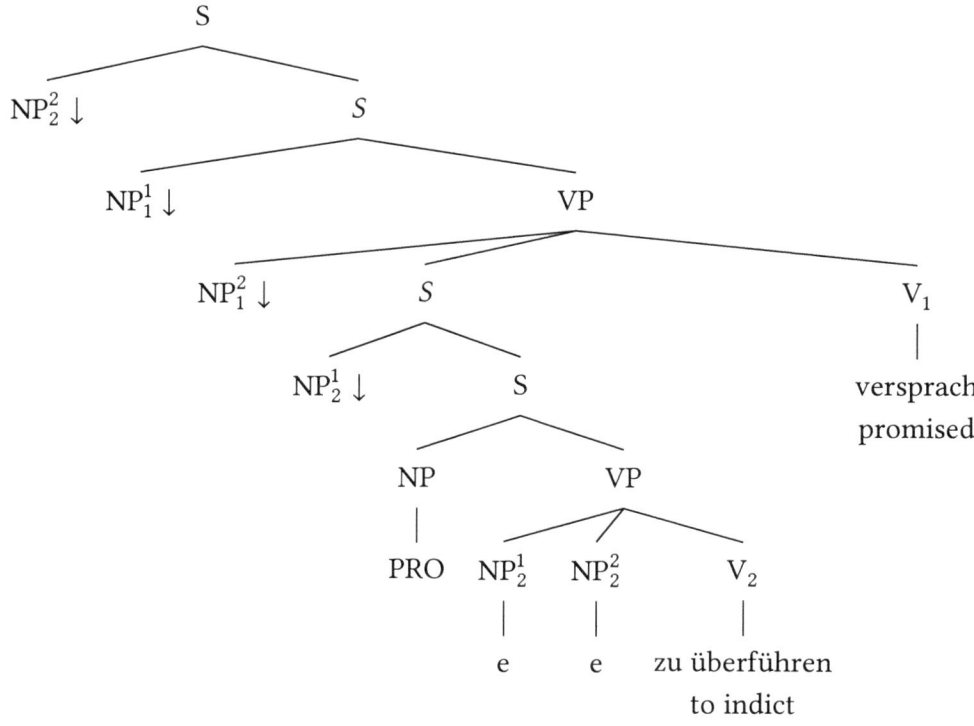

Figure 12.10: Analysis of the order $NP_2^2\ NP_1^1\ NP_1^2\ NP_2^1\ V_2V_1$: adjunction to the S node between NP_2^2 and NP_2^1

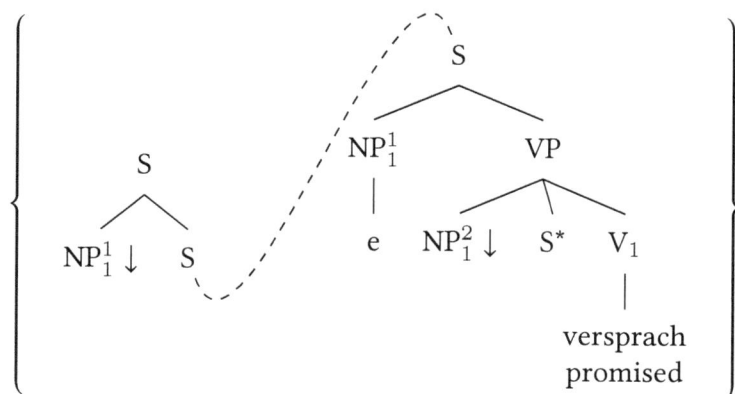

Figure 12.11: Elementary tree set for *versprach* consisting of multiple components

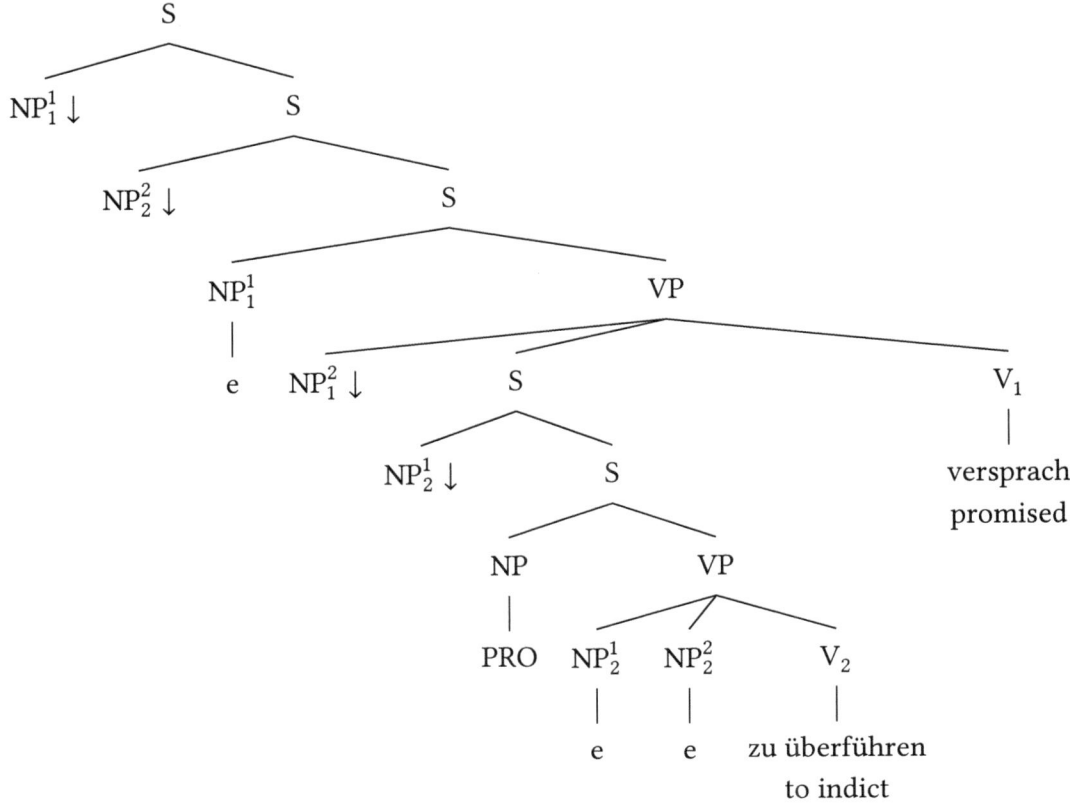

Figure 12.12: Analysis of the order $NP_1^1\ NP_2^2\ NP_1^2\ NP_2^1\ V_2V_1$: adjunction to the S node between NP_2^2 and NP_2^1

12.3 Verb position

The position of the verb can be analyzed in a parallel way to the GPSG analysis: the verb can be realized in initial or in final position in a given linearization domain. Since the verb position has an effect on the clause type and hence on semantics, a lexical rule-based analysis would be also viable: a tree with the finite verb in initial position is licensed by a lexical rule that takes a tree with the verb in final position as input. This would be similar to the analyses in GB, Minimalism, and HPSG.

12.4 Passive

There is a possible analysis for the passive that is analogous to the transformations in Transformational Grammar: one assumes lexical rules that license a lexical item with a passive tree for every lexical item with an active tree (Kroch & Joshi 1985: 50–51).

Kroch & Joshi (1985: 55) propose an alternative to this transformation-like approach that more adequately handles so-called raising constructions. Their analysis assumes that arguments of verbs are represented in subcategorization lists. Verbs are entered into trees that match their subcategorization list. Kroch and Joshi formulate a lexical rule that corresponds to the HPSG lexical rule that was discussed on page 286, that is, an accusative object is explicitly mentioned in the input of the lexical rule. Kroch and Joshi then suggest a complex analysis of the impersonal passive which uses a semantic null role for a non-realized object of intransitive verbs (p. 56). Such an analysis with abstract auxiliary entities can be avoided easily: one can instead use the HPSG analysis going back to Haider (1986a), which was presented in Section 9.2.

There are also proposals in TAG that use inheritance to deal with valence changing processes in general and the passive in particular (Candito 1996 and Kinyon, Rambow, Scheffler, Yoon & Joshi 2006 following Candito). As we saw in Section 10.2 of the Chapter on Construction Grammar, inheritance is not a suitable descriptive tool for valence changing processes. This is because these kinds of processes interact syntactically and semantically in a number of ways and can also be applied multiple times (Müller 2006; 2007b; 2007a: Section 7.5.2; 2013c; 2014a). See also Section 21.4 of this book.

12.5 Long-distance dependencies

The analysis of long-distance dependencies in TAG is handled with the standard apparatus: simple trees are inserted into the middle of other trees. Figure 12.13 on the facing page shows an example of the analysis of (10):

(10) Who$_i$ did John tell Sam that Bill likes _$_i$?

The tree for *WH COMP NP likes* _$_i$ belongs to the tree family of *likes* and is therefore present in the lexicon. The tree for *tell* is adjoined to this tree, that is, this tree is inserted in the middle of the tree for *who that Bill likes* _$_i$. Such an insertion operation can be applied multiple times so that sentences such as (11) where *who* is moved across multiple sentence boundaries can be analyzed:

(11) Who$_i$ did John tell Sam that Mary said that Bill likes _$_i$?

There is another important detail: although the tree for (12) has the category S, (12) is not a grammatical sentence of English.

(12) * who that Bill likes

This has to be captured somehow. In TAG, the marking OA ensures that a tree counts as incomplete. If a tree contains a node with marking OA, then an obligatory adjunction operation must take place at the relevant position.

12.6 New developments and theoretical variants

In Section 12.2, we introduced Multi-Component-TAG. There are a large number of TAG variants with different formal properties. Rambow (1994:) gives an overview of the variants existing in 1994. In the following, I will discuss two interesting variants of TAG:

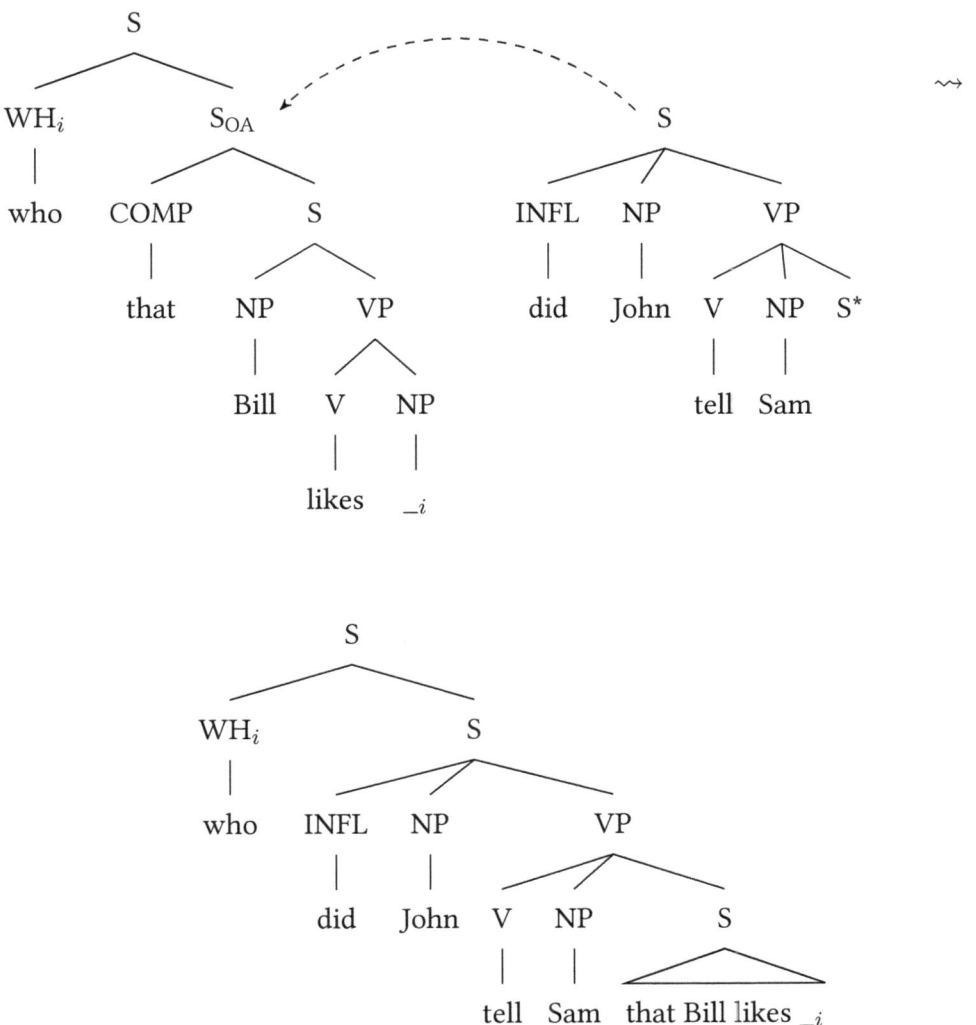

Figure 12.13: Analysis of long-distance dependencies in TAG

Feature Structure-Based TAG (FTAG, Vijay-Shanker & Joshi 1988) and Vector-TAG (V-TAG, Rambow 1994).

12.6.1 FTAG

In FTAG, nodes are not atomic (N, NP, VP or S), but instead consist of feature descriptions. With the exception of substitution nodes, each node has a top structure and a bottom structure. The top structure says something about what kind of properties a given tree has inside a larger structure, and the bottom structure says something about the properties of the structure below the node. Substitution nodes only have a top structure. Figure 12.14 on the next page shows an example tree for *laughs*. A noun phrase can be combined with the tree for *laughs* in Figure 12.14. Its top structure is identified with

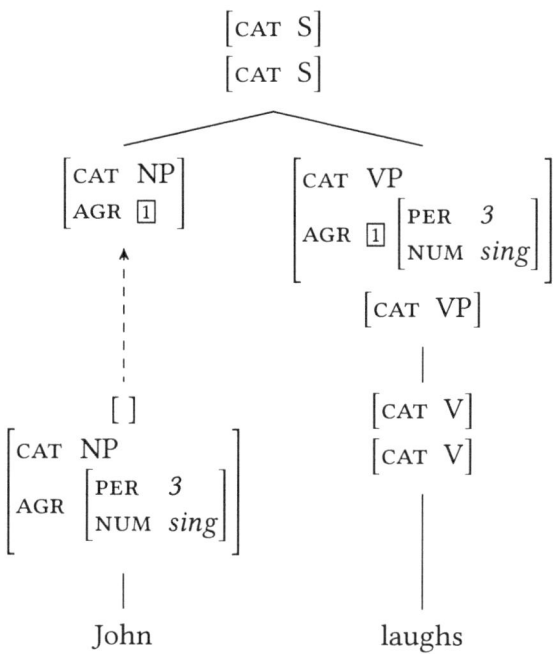

Figure 12.14: Elementary trees for *John* and *laughs* in FTAG

the NP node in the tree for *laughs*. The result of this combination is shown in Figure 12.15 on the facing page.

In a complete tree, all top structures are identified with the corresponding bottom structures. This way, only sentences where the subject is in third person singular can be analyzed with the given tree for *laughs*, that is, those in which the verb's agreement features match those of the subject.

For adjunction, the top structure of the tree that is being inserted must be unifiable with the top structure of the adjunction site, and the bottom structure of the node marked '*' in the inserted tree (the so-called foot node) must be unifiable with the adjunction site.

The elementary trees discussed so far only consisted of nodes where the top part matched the bottom part. FTAG allows for an interesting variant of specifying nodes that makes adjunction obligatory in order for the entire derivation to be well-formed. Figure 12.16 on the next page shows a tree for *laughing* that contains two VP nodes with incompatible MODE values. In order for this subtree to be used in a complete structure, another tree has to be added so that the two parts of the VP node are separated. This happens by means of an auxiliary tree as shown in Figure 12.16. The highest VP node of the auxiliary tree is unified with the upper VP node of *laughing*. The node of the auxiliary tree marked with '*' is unified with the lower VP node of *laughing*. The result of this is given in Figure 12.17 on page 430.

If a tree is used as a final derivation, the top structures are identified with the bottom structures. Thus, the AGR value of the highest VP node is identified with that of the lower one in the tree in Figure 12.17. As such, only NPs that have the same AGR value as the auxiliary can be inserted into the NP slot.

12.6 New developments and theoretical variants

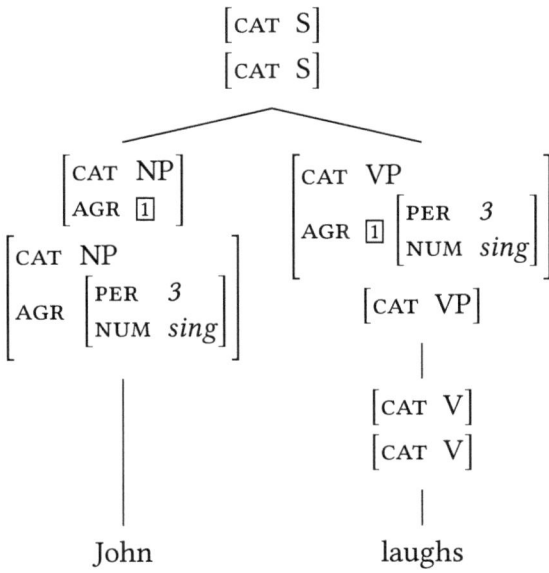

Figure 12.15: Combination of the trees for *John* and *laughs* in FTAG

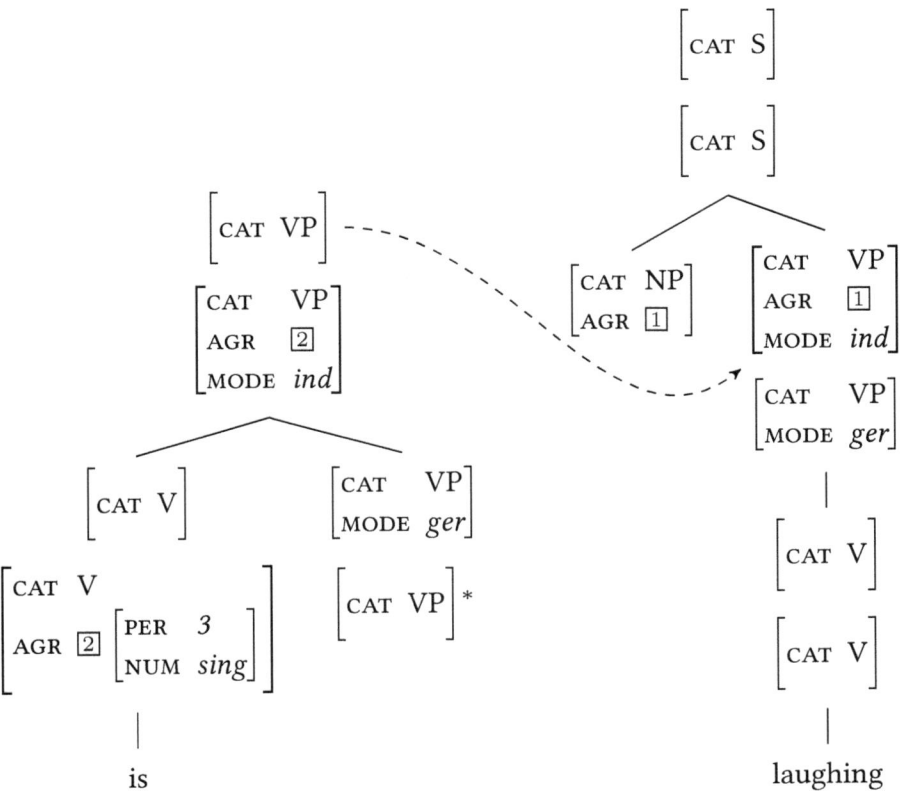

Figure 12.16: Obligatory adjunction in FTAG

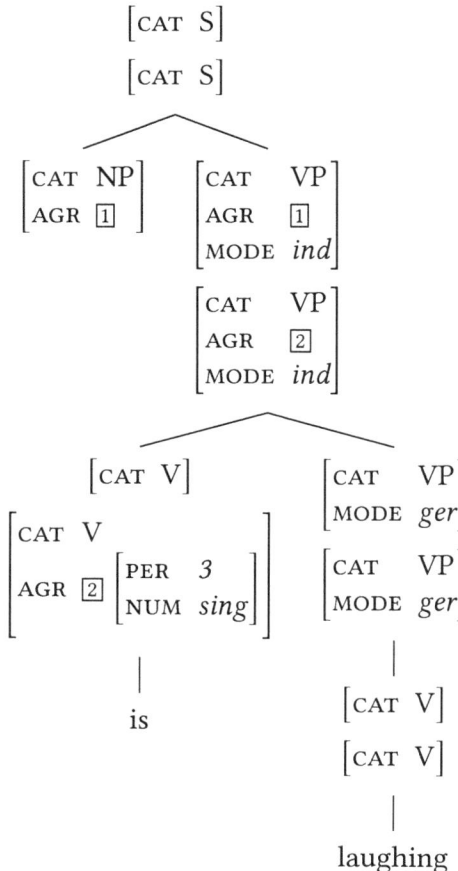

Figure 12.17: Result of obligatory adjunction in FTAG

This example shows that, instead of the marking for obligatory adjunction that we saw in the section on long-distance dependencies, the same effect can be achieved by using incompatible feature specifications on the top and bottom structures. If there are incompatible top and bottom structures in a tree, then it cannot be a final derivation tree and therefore this means that at least one adjunction operation must still take place in order to yield a well-formed tree.

12.6.2 V-TAG

V-TAG is a variant of TAG proposed by Owen Rambow (1994) that also assumes feature structures on nodes. In addition, like MC-TAG, it assumes that elementary trees consist of multiple components. Figure 12.18 on the next page shows the elementary lexical set for the ditransitive verb *geben* 'give'. The lexicon set consists of a tree for the verb, an empty element of the category VP and three trees where a VP has been combined with an NP. As in MC-TAG, dominance relations are also indicated. The dominance constraints in Figure 12.18 ensure that all lower VP nodes dominate the highest VP node

12.6 New developments and theoretical variants

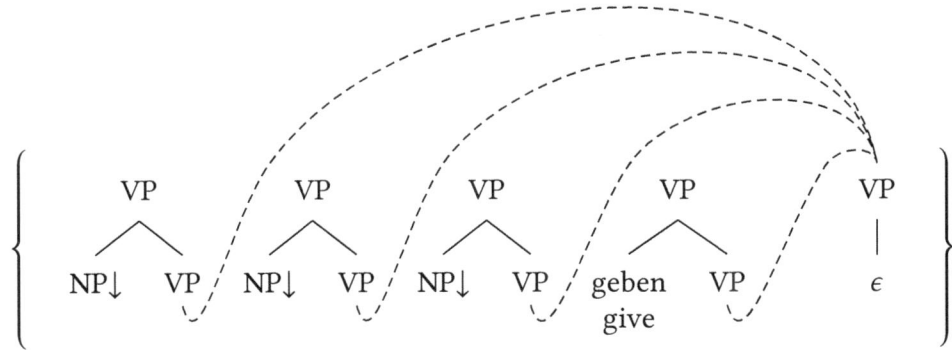

Figure 12.18: Lexicon set for *geben* 'to give' in V-TAG according to Rambow (1994: 6)

of the tree further to the right. The order of the arguments of the verb as well as the position of the verb is not given. The only thing required is that lower VP in the NP trees and lower VP in the *geben* tree dominate the empty VP node. With this lexicon set, it is possible to derive all permutations of the arguments. Rambow also shows how such lexical entries can be used to analyze sentences with verbal complexes. Figure 12.19 shows a verbal complex formed from *zu reparieren* 'to repair' and *versprochen* 'promised' and the relevant dominance constraints. Both of the first NP trees have to dominate

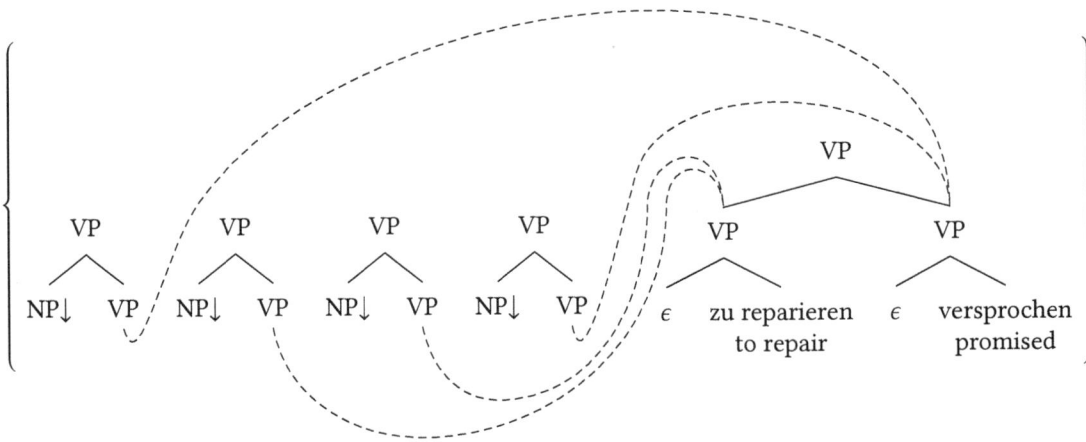

Figure 12.19: Analysis of the verbal complex *zu reparieren versprochen* in V-TAG

versprochen and the third and fourth NP tree have to dominate *zu reparieren*. The order of the NP trees is not restricted and thus all permutations of NPs can be derived.

The interesting thing here is that this approach is similar to the one proposed by Berman (1996: Section 2.1.3) in LFG (see Section 7.4): in Berman's analysis, the verb projects directly to form a VP and the arguments are then adjoined.

431

12 Tree Adjoining Grammar

A difference to other analyses discussed in this book is that there is always an empty element in the derived trees regardless of verb position.

12.6.3 The competence-performance distinction and the generative capacity of tree-local MC-LTAG

In many of the theories discussed in this book, a distinction is made between competence and performance (Chomsky 1965: Section I.1). Competence theories are supposed to describe linguistic knowledge, whereas a performance theory should explain how linguistic knowledge is used and why we make mistakes during speech production and comprehension, etc. See Chapter 15 for further discussion.

Joshi, Becker & Rambow (2000) discuss examples of center self embedding of relative clauses as those in (13b), and follow Chomsky & Miller (1963: 286) in the assumption that the fact that this kind of embedding is only possible up to three levels should not be described by grammar, but is rather due to processing problems with the hearer independent of their principle abilities with regard to grammar.

(13)   a. dass der Hund bellt, der die Katze jagt, die die Maus gefangen hat
        that the dog barks that the cat chases that the mouse caught has
      'that the dog that chases the cat that caught the mouse barks'

    b. dass der Hund, [$_1$ der die Katze, [$_2$ die die Maus gefangen hat, $_2$] jagt $_1$]
       that the dog that the cat that the mouse caught has chases
      bellt
      barks

What is interesting in this context is that it is possible to construct examples of center embedding so that they are easier to process for the hearer. In this way, it is possible to increase the number of center embeddings possible to process by one and therefore to show that all grammars that formulate a restriction that there may be at most two center-embedded relative clauses are incorrect. The following example from Hans Uszkoreit is easier to process since all embedded relative clauses are isolated and the verbs are separated by material from the higher clause.

(14)   Die Bänke, [$_1$ auf denen damals die Alten des Dorfes, [$_2$ die allen
      the benches on which back.then the old.people of.the village that all
     Kindern, [$_3$ die vorbeikamen $_3$], freundliche Blicke zuwarfen $_2$], lange Stunden
     children that came.by friendly glances gave long hours
     schweigend nebeneinander saßen $_1$], mussten im letzten Jahr einem
     silent next.to.each.other sat must in.the last year a
     Parkplatz weichen.
     car.park give.way.to

'The benches on which the older residents of the village, who used to give friendly glances to all the children who came by, used to sit silently next to one another had to give way to a car park last year.'

For other factors that play a role in processing, see Gibson (1998).

Joshi et al. (2000) discuss verbal complexes with reordered arguments. The general pattern that they discuss has the form shown in (15):

(15) $\sigma(\text{NP}_1\ \text{NP}_2\ ...\ \text{NP}_n)\ V_n V_{n-1}\ ...\ V_1$

Here, σ stands for any permutation of noun phrases and V_1 is the finite verb. The authors investigate the properties of Lexicalized Tree Adjoining Grammar (LTAG) with regard to this pattern and notice that LTAG cannot analyze the order in (16) if the semantics is supposed to come out correctly.

(16) $\text{NP}_2\ \text{NP}_3\ \text{NP}_1\ V_3 V_2 V_1$

Since (17) is possible in German, LTAG is not sufficient to analyze all languages.

(17) dass ihm$_2$ das Buch$_3$ niemand$_1$ zu lesen$_3$ versprechen$_2$ darf$_1$
 that him the book nobody   to read   promise   be.allowed.to
 'that nobody is allowed to promise him to read the book'

Therefore, they propose the extension of TAG discussed in Section 12.2; so-called *tree-local multi-component LTAG* (Tree-local MC-LTAG or TL-MCTAG). They show that TL-MCTAG can analyze (17) but not (18) with the correct semantics. They claim that these orders are not possible in German and argue that in this case, unlike the relative clause examples, one has both options, that is, the unavailability of such patterns can be explained as a performance phenomenon or as a competence phenomenon.

(18) $\text{NP}_2\ \text{NP}_4\ \text{NP}_3\ \text{NP}_1\ V_4 V_3 V_2 V_1$

If we treat this as a performance phenomenon, then we are making reference to the complexity of the construction and the resulting processing problems for the hearer. The fact that these orders do not occur in corpora can be explained with reference to the principle of cooperativeness. Speakers normally want to be understood and therefore formulate their sentences in such a way that the hearer can understand them. Verbal complexes in German with more than four verbs are hardly ever found since it is possible to simplify very complex sentences with multiple verbs in the right sentence bracket by extraposing material and therefore avoiding ambiguity (see Netter 1991: 5 and Müller 2007a: 262).

The alternative to a performance explanation would involve using a grammatical formalism which is just powerful enough to allow embedding of two verbs and reordering of their arguments, but rules out embedding of three verbs and reordering of the arguments. Joshi et al. (2000) opt for this solution and therefore attribute the impossibility of the order of arguments in (18) to competence.

In HPSG (and also in Categorial Grammar and in some GB analyses), verbal complexes are analyzed by means of argument composition (Hinrichs & Nakazawa 1989a; 1994). Under this approach, a verbal complex behaves exactly like a simplex verb and the arguments of the verbs involved can be placed in any order. The grammar does not contain any restriction on the number of verbs that can be combined, nor any constraints that ban embedding below a certain level. In the following, I will show that many reorderings are ruled out by communication rules that apply even with cases of simple two-place verbs. The conclusion is that the impossibility of embedding four or more verbs should in fact be explained as a performance issue.

Before I present arguments against a competence-based exclusion of (18), I will make a more general comment: corpora cannot help us here since one does not find any instances of verbs with four or more embeddings. Bech (1955) provides an extensive collection of material, but had to construct the examples with four embedded verbs. Meurers (1999b: 94–95) gives constructed examples with five verbs that contain multiple auxiliaries or modal verbs. These examples are barely processable and are not relevant for the discussion here since the verbs in (18) have to select their own arguments. There are therefore not that many verbs left when constructing examples. It is possible to only use subject control verbs with an additional object (e.g., *versprechen* 'to promise'), object control verbs (e.g., *zwingen* 'to force') or AcI verbs (e.g., *sehen* 'to see' or *lassen* 'to let') to construct examples. When constructing examples, it is important make sure that all the nouns involved differ as much as possible with regard to their case and their selectional restrictions (e.g., animate/inanimate) since these are features that a hearer/reader could use to possibly assign reordered arguments to their heads. If we want to have patterns such as (18) with four NPs each with a different case, then we have to choose a verb that governs the genitive. There are only a very small number of such verbs in German. Although the example constructed by Joshi et al. (2000) in (9b) fulfills these requirements, it is still very marked. It therefore becomes clear that the possibility of finding a corresponding example in a newspaper article is extremely small. This is due to the fact that there are very few situations in which such an utterance would be imaginable. Additionally, all control verbs (with the exception of *helfen* 'to help') require an infinitive with *zu* 'to' and can also be realized incoherently, that is, with an extraposed infinitival complement without verbal complex formation. As mentioned above, a cooperative speaker/author would use a less complex construction and this reduces the probability that these kinds of sentences arise even further.

Notice that tree-local MC-LTAG does not constrain the number of verbs in a sentence. The formalism allows for an arbitrary number of verbs. It is therefore necessary to assume, as in other grammatical theories, that performance constraints are responsible for the fact that we never find examples of verbal complexes with five or more verbs. Tree-local MC-LAG makes predictions about the possibility of arguments to be reordered. I consider it wrong to make constraints regarding mobility of arguments dependent on the power of the grammatical formalism since the restrictions that one finds are independent of verbal complexes and can be found with simplex verbs taking just two arguments. The problem with reordering is that it still has to be possible to assign the noun phrases to the verbs they belong to. If this assignment leads to ambiguity that cannot be resolved by case, selectional restrictions, contextual knowledge or intonation, then the unmarked constituent order is chosen. Hoberg (1981: 68) shows this very nicely with examples similar to the following:[5]

---

[5]Instead of *das* 'the', Hoberg uses the possessive pronoun *ihr* 'her'. This makes the sentences more semantically plausible, but one then gets interference from the linearization requirements for bound pronouns. I have therefore replaced the pronouns with the definite article.

12.6 New developments and theoretical variants

(19) a. Hanna hat immer schon gewußt, daß das Kind sie verlassen will.
Hanna has always already known that the child she leave wants

'Hanna has always known that the child wants to leave her.'

b. # Hanna hat immer schon gewußt, daß sie das Kind verlassen will.
Hanna has always already known that she the child leave wants

Preferred reading: 'Hanna has always known that she wants to leave the child.'

c. Hanna hat immer schon gewußt, daß sie der Mann verlassen
Hanna has always already known that she the.NOM man leave
will.
wants.to

'Hanna has always known that the man wants to leave her.'

It is not possible to reorder (19a) to (19b) without creating a strong preference for another reading. This is due to the fact that neither *sie* 'she' nor *das Kind* 'the child' are unambiguously marked as nominative or accusative. (19b) therefore has to be interpreted as Hanna being the one that wants something, namely to leave the child. This reordering is possible, however, if at least one of the arguments is unambiguously marked for case as in (19c).

For noun phrases with feminine count nouns, the forms for nominative and accusative as well as genitive and dative are the same. For mass nouns, it is even worse. If they are used without an article, all cases are the same for feminine nouns (e.g., *Milch* 'milk') and also for masculines and neuters with exception of the genitive. In the following example from Wegener (1985: 45) it is hardly possible to switch the dative and accusative object, whereas this is possible if the nouns are used with articles as in (20c,d):

(20) a. Sie mischt Wein Wasser bei.
she mixes wine water into

'She mixes water into the wine.'

b. Sie mischt Wasser Wein bei.
she mixes water wine into

'She mixes wine into the water.'

c. Sie mischt dem Wein das Wasser bei.
she mixes the.DAT wine the.ACC water into

'She mixes the water into the wine.'

d. Sie mischt das Wasser dem Wein bei.
she mixes the.ACC water the.DAT wine into

'She mixes the water into the wine.'

The two nouns can only be switched if the meaning of the sentence is clear from the context (e.g., through explicit negation of the opposite) and if the sentence carries a certain intonation.

The problem with verbal complexes is now that with four noun phrases, two of them almost always have the same case if one does not wish to resort to the few verbs governing the genitive. A not particularly nice-sounding example of morphologically unambiguously marked case is (21):

(21) weil   er   den   Mann dem   Jungen des   Freundes gedenken
     because he.NOM the.ACC man   the.DAT boy   of.the.GEN friend   remember
     helfen lassen will
     help   let   wants

   'because he wants to let the man help the boy remember his friend'

Another strategy is to choose verbs that select animate and inanimate objects so that animacy of the arguments can aid interpretation. I have constructed such an example where the most deeply embedded predicate is not a verb but rather an adjective. The predicate *leer fischen* 'to fish empty' is a resultative construction that should be analyzed parallel to verbal complexes (Müller 2002a: Chapter 5).

(22) weil   niemand$_1$ [den   Mann]$_2$ [der   Frau]$_3$ [diesen Teich]$_4$ leer$_4$
     because nobody.NOM the.ACC man   the.DAT woman   this.ACC pond   empty
     fischen$_3$ helfen$_2$ sah$_1$
     fish   help   saw

   'because nobody saw the man help the woman fish the pond empty'

If one reads the sentences with the relevant pauses, it is comprehensible. Case is unambiguously marked on the animate noun phrases and our word knowledge helps us to interpret *diesen Teich* 'this pond' as the argument of *leer* 'empty'.

The sentence in (22) would correctly be analyzed by an appropriately written tree-local MC-LTAG and also by argument composition analyses for verbal complexes and resultative constructions. The sentence in (23) is a variant of (22) that corresponds exactly to the pattern of (18):

(23) weil   [der   Frau]$_2$ [diesen Teich]$_4$ [den   Mann]$_3$ niemand$_1$ leer$_4$
     because the.DAT woman   this.ACC pond   the.ACC man   nobody.NOM empty
     fischen$_3$ helfen$_2$ sah$_1$
     fish   help   saw

   'because nobody saw the man help the woman fish the pond empty'

(23) is more marked than (22), but this is always the case with local reordering (Gisbert Fanselow, p. c. 2006). This sentence should not be ruled out by the grammar. Its markedness is more due to the same factors that were responsible for the markedness of reordering of arguments of simplex verbs. Tree-local MC-LTAG can not correctly analyze sentences such as (23), which shows that this TAG variant is not sufficient for analyzing natural language.

There are varying opinions among TAG researchers as to what should be counted as competence and what should be counted as performance. For instance, Rambow (1994:

15) argues that one should not exclude reorderings that cannot be processed by means of competence grammar or the grammatical formalism. In Chapter 6, he presents a theory of performance that can explain why the reordering of arguments of various verbs in the middle field is harder to process. One should therefore opt for TAG variants such as V-TAG or TT-MC-TAG (Lichte 2007) that are powerful enough to analyze the diverse reorderings and then also use a performance model that makes it possible to explain the gradual differences in acceptability.

An alternative to looking for a grammatical formalism with minimal expressive power is to not restrict the grammatical formalism at all with regard to its expressive power and instead develop as restrictive linguistic theories as possible. For further discussion of this point, see Chapter 17.

12.7 Summary and classification

In sum, we have seen the following: LTAG is lexicalized, that is, there is at least one lexical element in every tree. There are not any trees that correspond to the rule S → NP VP since no words are mentioned in this rule. Instead, there are always complex trees that contain the subject NP and the VP. Inside the VP, there can be as much structure as is necessary to ensure that the verb is contained in the tree. As well as the head, elementary trees in LTAG always contain the arguments of the head. For transitive verbs, this means that both the subject and the object have to be components of the elementary tree. This is also true of the trees used to analyze long-distance dependencies. As shown in Figure 12.13, the object must be part of the tree. The fact that the object can be separated from the verb by multiple sentence boundaries is not represented in the elementary tree, that is, recursive parts of grammar are not contained in elementary trees. The relevant effects are achieved by adjunction, that is, by insertion of material into elementary trees. The elementary tree for extraction in Figure 12.13 differs from the elementary tree for *likes* given in Figure 12.4 for the use in normal SVO clauses. Every minimal construction, in which *likes* can occur (subject extraction, topicalization, subject relative clauses, object relative clauses, passive, ...) needs its own elementary tree (Kallmeyer & Joshi 2003: 10). The different elementary trees can be connected using lexical rules. These lexical rules map a particular tree treated as underlying to other trees. In this way, it is possible to derive a passive tree from an active tree. These lexical rules are parallel to transformations in Transformational Grammar, however, one should bear in mind that there is always a lexical element in the tree, which makes the entire grammar more restrictive than grammars with free transformations.

An interesting difference to GB and variants of LFG, CG, and HPSG that assume empty elements is that the variants of TAG presented here[6] do not contain empty elements in the lexicon. They can be used in trees but trees are listed as a whole in the lexicon.

---

[6] See Rambow (1994) and Kallmeyer (2005: 194), however, for TAG analyses with an empty element in the lexicon.

Elementary trees can be of any size, which makes TAG interesting for the analysis of idioms (see Section 18.2). Since recursion is factored out, trees can contain elements that appear very far away from each other in the derived tree (extended domains of locality).

Kasper, Kiefer, Netter & Vijay-Shanker (1995) show that it is possible to transfer HPSG grammars that fulfill certain requirements into TAG grammars. This is interesting as in this way one arrives at a grammar whose complexity behavior is known. Whereas HPSG grammars are generally in the Type-0 area, TAG grammars can, depending on the variant, fall into the realm of Type-2 languages (context-free) or even in the larger set of the mildly context-sensitive grammars (Joshi 1985). Yoshinaga, Miyao, Torisawa & Tsujii (2001) have developed a procedure for translating FB-LTAG grammars into HPSG grammars.

Comprehension questions

1. How are long-distance dependencies analyzed in TAG? Does one need empty elements for this?

2. Is it possible to analyze the reordering of arguments of multiple verbs using standard TAG processes?

Exercises

1. Analyze the following string in LTAG:

   (24)   der dem   König treue Diener
          the the.DAT king loyal servant
          'the servant loyal to the king'

Further reading

Some important articles are Joshi, Levy & Takahashi (1975), Joshi (1987a), and Joshi & Schabes (1997). Many works discuss formal properties of TAG and are therefore not particularly accessible for linguistically interested readers. Kroch & Joshi (1985) give a good overview of linguistic analyses. An overview of linguistic and computational linguistic works in TAG can be found in the volume edited by Abeillé and Rambow from 2000. Rambow (1994) compares his TAG variant (V-TAG) to Karttunen's *Radical Lexicalism* approach, Uszkoreit's GPSG, Combinatorial Categorial Grammar, HPSG and Dependency Grammar.

Shieber & Johnson (1993) discuss psycholinguistically plausible processing models and show that it is possible to do incremental parsing with TAG. They also present a further variant of TAG: synchronous TAG. In this TAG variant, there is a syntactic tree and a semantic tree connected to it. When building syntactic structure, the semantic structure is always built in parallel. This structure built in parallel corresponds to the level of Logical Form derived from S-Structure using transformations in GB.

Rambow (1994: Chapter 6) presents an automaton-based performance theory. He applies it to German and shows that the processing difficulties that arise when reordering arguments of multiple verbs can be explained.

Kallmeyer & Romero (2008) show how it is possible to derive MRS representations directly via a derivation tree using FTAG. In each top node, there is a reference to the semantic content of the entire structure and each bottom node makes reference to the semantic content below the node. In this way, it becomes possible to insert an adjective (e.g., *mutmaßlichen* 'suspected') into an NP tree *alle Mörder* 'all murderers' so that the adjective has scope over the nominal part of the NP (*Mörder* 'murderers'): for adjunction of the adjective to the N node, the adjective can access the semantic content of the noun. The top node of *mutmaßlichen* is then the top node of the combination *mutmaßlichen Mörder* 'suspected murderers' and this ensures that the meaning of *mutmaßlichen Mörder* is correctly embedded under the universal quantifier.

Part II

General discussion

Preface for Part II

This book is very long. For technical reasons it is split into two parts in the print version. The first part contains the introduction to all the theories and the second part is a collection of topics that are relevant for more than one theory, so it would be inappropriate to discuss them within one of the chapters of Part I. While Part I has a more introductory character and can be used for teaching BA and MA students, the material in Part II is for more advanced readers. I never used it for teaching; it may be a good resource for classes on these topics nevertheless. In what follows, I give a brief overview of the chapters of Part II.

Chapter 13 concerns the assumption of innate domain-specific knowledge, some sort of Universal Grammar. This is probably the hottest debate in linguistics and the side one takes in this debate has severe consequences for the theories that one considers acceptable. In Mainstream Generative Grammar (MGG), lots of invisible elements are postulated and in some versions of MGG, it is claimed that these are present in the grammars of all languages of the world, even though there is no direct evidence for these categories in some of the languages. Usually the motivation for assuming an empty element is that there is another language with visible material in the respective position. Whether one considers such an argumentation as legitimate crucially depends on whether one believes in innate domain-specific knowledge. Chapter 13 tries to summarize the discussion and to show that for all claims regarding the existence of Universal Grammar there are counterclaims. Hauser, Chomsky & Fitch (2002) greatly revised Chomsky's assumptions regarding UG. According to them, UG contains rather few and abstract constraints, but nevertheless UG lives on in the theories developed today and in the way arguments for them are made. Hence, a chapter like Chapter 13 is important to understand the discussions and the alternatives to the theories developed in MGG.

Chapter 14 deals with the difference of generative-enumerative and model-theoretic approaches. Generative-enumerative approaches (basically phrase-structure grammars and MGG variants of it) enumerate a set of strings considered to be well-formed with respect to a grammar and possibly a set of transformations. The model-theoretic view does not say anything about sets but rather deals with formulating well-formedness conditions for utterances. While this seems to be very similar at first glance, there are interesting differences in various respects. Chapter 14 deals with utterance fragments and graded acceptability and discusses alleged problems for model-theoretic approaches.

Chapter 15 introduces the competence/performance distinction. Some researchers reject this distinction completely (most of the researchers working within CxG), others assume it and try to develop models that are performance-compatible (HPSG, LFG, CG, TAG) and others develop models that are highly implausible from a performance point of view (lots of Minimalist work). Chapter 15 introduces the concepts, discusses whether it makes sense to distinguish competence and performance (I think it does) and examines what is required for performance-compatible competence models.

It is often argued that theory X must be wrong since it does not explain how language can be acquired. Interestingly, these accusations go both ways: Construction Grammarians criticize Minimalists for assuming half of their theory to be hard coded in our genetic material and Minimalists claim that constructionist theories do not have an explanation for there being recursive structures. Chapter 16 discusses the major approaches to acquisition and explains where they differ and what shortcomings exist.

Chapter 17 deals with the generative capacity of grammar formalisms. The generative capacity played an important role in the history of generative grammar. Early versions turned out to be too powerful, resulting in quite radical changes of the framework in the 1970s and 1980s. One key advantage of GPSG was that it was much more restrictive than the transformational approaches that were around at the time. As it turned out, it was too restrictive to model language as such since there were languages that could be shown to require more powerful machinery. This lead to the development of HPSG. The HPSG formalism has Turing power, which is the worst complexity a formalism can have. Somewhat ironically, most proponents of HPSG do not care about this at all. Chapter 17 explains why.

Chapter 18 is a brief chapter including the discussion of three topics that come up again and again: binary branching vs. flat structures, locality and recursion. Some researchers argue (without proof) that all theories should assume binary branching structures because otherwise the grammars are not acquirable, while others argue for the opposite view, again often with acquisition arguments (Section 18.1). Locality is an issue that is important both in Minimalism and in other theories like HPSG and LFG. However, there are differences in what is understood by locality. Section 18.2 deals with these issues. Languages usually have recursive structures. So frameworks have to have ways to account for this. All the frameworks discussed in this book do account for recursion despite claims to the contrary. This is topic of Section 18.3.

Chapter 19 deals with empty elements. While some theories have more invisible units in their trees than visible ones (see Figure 4.21 on page 150), there are frameworks that do not assume any empty elements, referring to acquisition again. The chapter shows that certain grammars with empty elements can be converted into grammars without empty elements. I show that empty elements are not required for semantic reasons; underspecification can be used instead. The chapter shows how important the assumptions about UG (Chapter 13) are: if empty elements correspond to visible material that in certain situations occupies the place of the empty element, then there are chances for them to be acquired from data. If the empty elements are stipulated with reference to material in other languages, there is a real acquisition problem. A final section shows that (some) empty elements can be replaced by lexical rules (or templates), which correspond to a certain type of transformation. This relativizes the debate that arose around stipulating such theoretical entities.

When it comes to mechanisms that are used in different frameworks, there is a further difference between (some variants of) GB/Minimalism and the other theories. Some theories in the transformational frameworks assume that extraction, scrambling and passive are dealt with using the same descriptive tool: movement. Other theories use lexical rules, different phrasal schemata and SLASH propagation techniques. Chapter 20 shows that phenomena like the so-called remote passive that seem to require movement can be dealt with without movement. The chapter repeats an example from the GB chapter that showed that the movement-based analysis of the German passive is problematic, since nothing moves in German sentences. Passive is a phenomenon that is independent of movement; it is just English that is SVO and requires a subject before the verb. Since German does not require subjects, nothing has to be reordered. Dependency Grammar proposals assuming the same descriptive tool for the three phenomena are discussed as well, their shortcomings are pointed out and it is concluded that the three phenomena are independent or at least have to be distinguishable in terms of their treatment in a theory.

Chapter 21 discusses a further highly controversial issue: the question of whether language consists of phrasal patterns or whether there are abstract combinatorial rules that combine lexical items that contain rich information. Again, questions of language acquisition play a role here. This chapter is rather long but it reflects the complexity of the discussion in the literature. Many arguments for and against phrasal constructions are evaluated and it is shown that grammars have to be able to account for phrasal patterns, but that so-called argument structure constructions are better treated lexically. This discussion connects nicely to the GPSG-HPSG transition in the 1980s where researchers switched from a phrasal model to a lexical one in the spirit of Categorial Grammar.

The brief Chapter 22 is related to the topic of Chapter 21 but it compares the TAG, LFG and HPSG approaches to complex predicates and points out that there are problems with a certain treatment of complex predicates in TAG. TAG is very similar in spirit to phrasal Construction Grammar approaches: the elementary trees of TAG are phrasal patterns. It is shown that lexical models like HPSG have an advantage over the phrasal TAG approach since they specify lexical potential of items, which is not necessarily the same as actual realization of dependents. It is pointed out that the LFG analysis of complex predicates allowing for overrides of lexical information at phrasal nodes lies somewhere in the middle between TAG and HPSG.

Chapter 23 showcases a way to develop linguistic theories that capture cross-linguistic generalizations. It differs from the general top-down approach in Minimalism, where it is assumed that certain constraints hold for all languages. Instead, constraints that hold for known languages are collected in sets in a bottom-up way. The most general set contains all constraints that hold for all known languages. This approach is independent of the assumption of an innate UG and hence compatible with both CxG and Minimalism. The chapter also contains some speculations on how to integrate universal constraints in an Cinque-like UG way in case there turns out to be an empirical basis for this.

Chapter 24 draws some conclusions as to what an appropriate framework for describing languages should look like.

13 The innateness of linguistic knowledge

If we try and compare the theories presented in this book, we notice that there are a number of similarities.[1] In all of the frameworks, there are variants of theories that use feature-value pairs to describe linguistic objects. The syntactic structures assumed are sometimes similar. Nevertheless, there are some differences that have often led to fierce debates between members of the various schools. Theories differ with regard to whether they assume transformations, empty elements, phrasal or lexical analyses, binary branching or flat structures.

Every theory has to not only describe natural language, but also explain it. It is possible to formulate an infinite number of grammars that license structures for a given language (see Exercise 1 on page 78). These grammars are *observationally adequate*. A grammar achieves *descriptive adequacy* if it corresponds to observations and the intuitions of native speakers.[2] A linguistic theory is descriptively adequate if it can be used to formulate a descriptively adequate grammar for every natural language. However, grammars achieving descriptive adequacy do not always necessarily reach *explanatory adequacy*. Grammars that achieve explanatory adequacy are those that are compatible with acquisition data, that is, grammars that could plausibly be acquired by human speakers (Chomsky 1965: 24–25).

Chomsky (1965: 25) assumes that children already have domain-specific knowledge about what grammars could, in principle, look like and then extract information about what a given grammar actually looks like from the linguistic input. The most prominent

---

[1] The terms *theory* and *framework* may require clarification. A framework is a common set of assumptions and tools that is used when theories are formulated. In this book, I discussed theories of German. These theories were developed in certain frameworks (GB, GPSG, HPSG, LFG, …) and of course there are other theories of other languages that share the same fundamental assumptions. These theories differ from the theories of German presented here but are formulated in the same framework. Haspelmath (2010b) argues for framework-free grammatical theory. If grammatical theories used incompatible tools, it would be difficult to compare languages. So assuming transformations for English nonlocal dependencies and a SLASH mechanism for German would make comparison impossible. I agree with Haspelmath that the availability of formal tools may lead to biases, but in the end the facts have to be described somehow. If nothing is shared between theories, we end up with isolated theories formulated in one man frameworks. If there *is* shared vocabulary and if there are standards for doing framework-free grammatical theory, then the framework is framework-free grammatical theory. See Müller (2015b) and Chapter 23 of this book for further discussion.

[2] This term is not particularly useful as subjective factors play a role. Not everybody finds grammatical theories intuitively correct where it is assumed that every observed order in the languages of the world has to be derived from a common Specifier-Head-Complement configuration, and also only by movement to the left (see Section 4.6.1 for the discussion of such proposals).

variant of acquisition theory in Mainstream Generative Grammar (MGG) is the Principles & Parameters theory, which claims that parametrized principles restrict the grammatical structures possible and children just have to set parameters during language acquisition (see Section 3.1.2).

Over the years, the innateness hypothesis, also known as nativism, has undergone a number of modifications. In particular, assumptions about exactly what forms part of the innate linguistic knowledge, so-called Universal Grammar (UG), have often been subject to change.

Nativism is often rejected by proponents of Construction Grammar, Cognitive Grammar and by many other researchers working in other theories. Other explanations are offered for the facts normally used to argue for the innateness of grammatical categories, syntactic structures or relations between linguistic objects in syntactic structures. Another point of criticism is that the actual complexity of analyses is blurred by the fact that many of the stipulations are simply assumed to be part of UG. The following is a caricature of a certain kind of argumentation in GB/Minimalism analyses:

1. I have developed an analysis for the phenomenon P in the language S.

2. The analysis is elegant/conceptually simple/mine[3].

3. There is no possibility to learn the relevant structures or principles.

4. Therefore, the assumptions A_1 through A_n that are made in this analysis must be part of the innate knowledge of speakers.

By attributing arbitrary assumptions to UG, it is possible to keep the rest of the analysis very simple.

The following section will briefly review some of the arguments for language-specific innate knowledge. We will see that none of these arguments are uncontroversial. In the following chapters, I will discuss fundamental questions about the architecture of grammar, the distinction between competence and performance and how to model performance phenomena, the theory of language acquisition as well as other controversial questions, e.g., whether it is desirable to postulate empty elements in linguistic representations and whether language should be explained primarily based on the properties of words or rather phrasal patterns.

Before we turn to these hotly debated topics, I want to discuss the one that is most fiercely debated, namely the question of innate linguistic knowledge. In the literature, one finds the following arguments for innate knowledge:

- the existence of syntactic universals,

- the speed of acquisition,

- the fact that there is a 'critical period' for language acquisition,

---

[3]Also, see https://www.youtube.com/watch?v=U6zWjUhfj-M. 2018-02-20.

- the fact that all children learn a language, but primates do not,
- the fact that children spontaneously regularize pidgin languages,
- the localization of language processing in particular parts of the brain,
- the alleged dissociation of language and general cognition:
  - Williams Syndrome,
  - the KE family with FoxP2 mutation and
- the Poverty of the Stimulus Argument.

Pinker (1994) offers a nice overview of these arguments. Tomasello (1995) provides a critical review of this book. The individual points will be discussed in what follows.

13.1 Syntactic universals

The existence of syntactic universals has been taken as an argument for the innateness of linguistic knowledge (e.g., Chomsky 1998: 33; Pinker 1994: 237–238). There are varying claims in the literature with regard to what is universal and language-specific. The most prominent candidates for universals are:[4]

- the Head Directionality Parameter
- $\overline{\text{X}}$ structures
- grammatical functions such as subject or object
- binding principles
- properties of long-distance dependencies
- grammatical morphemes for tense, mood and aspect
- parts of speech
- recursion or self-embedding

These supposed universals will each be discussed briefly in what follows. One should emphasize that there is by no means a consensus that these are universal and that the observed properties actually require postulating innate linguistic knowledge.

---

[4] Frans Plank has an archive of universals in Konstanz (Plank & Filimonova 2000): https://typo.uni-konstanz.de/archive/intro/. On 2015-12-23, it contained 2029 entries. The entries are annotated with regard to their quality, and it turns out that many of the universals are statistical universals, that is, they hold for the overwhelming majority of languages, but there are some exceptions. Some of the universals are marked as almost absolute, that is, very few exceptions are known. 1153 were marked as absolute or absolute with a question mark. 1021 of these are marked as absolute without a question mark. Many of the universals captured are implicational universals, that is, they have the form: if a language has the property X, then it also has the property Y. The universals listed in the archive are, in part, very specific and refer to the diachronic development of particular grammatical properties. For example, the fourth entry states that: *If the exponent of vocative is a prefix, then this prefix has arisen from 1st person possessor or a 2nd person subject.*

13 The innateness of linguistic knowledge

13.1.1 Head Directionality Parameter

The Head Directionality Parameter was already introduced in Section 3.1.2. The examples in (7) on page 87, repeated below as (1), show that the structures in Japanese are the mirror image of the English structures:

(1)   a. be showing pictures of himself
       b. zibun   -no syasin-o mise-te   iru
           himself of picture   showing be

In order to capture these facts, a parameter was proposed that is responsible for the position of the head relative to its arguments (e.g., Chomsky 1986b: 146; 1988: 70).

By assuming a Head Directionality Parameter, Radford (1990: 60–61; 1997: 19–22), Pinker (1994: 234, 238), Baker (2003: 350) and other authors claim, either explicitly or implicitly, that there is a correlation between the direction of government of verbs and that of adpositions, that is, languages with verb-final order have postpositions and languages with VO order have prepositions. This claim can be illustrated with the language pair English/Japanese and the examples in (1): the *no* occurs after the pronoun in the prepositional phrase, the noun *syasin-o* 'picture' follows the PP belonging to it, the main verb follows its object and the auxiliary *iru* occurs after the main verb *mise-te*. The individual phrases are the exact mirror image of the respective phrases in English.

A single counterexample is enough to disprove a universal claim and in fact, it is possible to find a language that has verb-final order but nevertheless has prepositions. Persian is such a language. An example is given in (2):

(2)   man ketâb-â-ro   be Sepide dâd-am.
       I   book-PL-RÂ to Sepide gave-1SG
       'I gave the books to Sepide.'

In Section 3.1.4, it was shown that German cannot be easily described with this parameter: German is a verb-final language but has both prepositions and postpositions. The World Atlas of Language Structures lists 41 languages with VO order and postpositions and 14 languages with OV order and prepositions (Dryer 2013b,a).[5] An earlier study by Dryer (1992) done with a smaller sample of languages also points out that there are exceptions to what the Head Directionality Parameter would predict.

Furthermore, Gibson & Wexler (1994: 422) point out that a single parameter for the position of heads would not be enough since complementizers in both English and German/Dutch occur before their complements; however, English is a VO language, whereas German and Dutch count as OV languages.

If one wishes to determine the direction of government based on syntactic categories (Gibson & Wexler 1994: 422, Chomsky 2005: 15), then one has to assume that the syntactic categories in question belong to the inventory of Universal Grammar (see Section 13.1.7, for more on this). Difficulties with prepositions and postpositions also arise for this kind of assumption as these are normally assigned to the same category (P). If we were to

---

[5]http://wals.info/combinations/83A_85A#2/15.0/153.0, 2018-02-20.

introduce special categories for both prepositions and postpositions, then a four-way division of parts of speech like the one on page 94 would no longer be possible. One would instead require an additional binary feature and one would thereby automatically predict eight categories although only five (the four commonly assumed plus an extra one) are actually needed.

One can see that the relation between direction of government that Pinker formulated as a universal claim is in fact correct but rather as a tendency than as a strict rule, that is, there are many languages where there is a correlation between the use of prepositions or postpositions and the position the verb (Dryer 1992: 83).[6]

In many languages, adpositions have evolved from verbs. In Chinese grammar, it is commonplace to refer to a particular class of words as coverbs. These are words that can be used both as prepositions and as verbs. If we view languages historically, then we can find explanations for these tendencies that do not have to make reference to innate linguistic knowledge (see Evans & Levinson 2009a: 445).

Furthermore, it is possible to explain the correlations with reference to processing preferences: in languages with the same direction of government, the distance between the verb and the pre-/postposition is less (Figure 13.1a–b) than in languages with differing directions of government (Figure 13.1c–d). From the point of view of processing, languages with the same direction of government should be preferred since they allow the hearer to better identify the parts of the verb phrase (Newmeyer (2004a: 219–221) cites Hawkins (2004: 32) with a relevant general processing preference, see also Dryer (1992: 131)). This tendency can thus be explained as the grammaticalization of a performance preference (see Chapter 15 for the distinction between competence and performance) and recourse to innate language-specific knowledge is not necessary.

13.1.2 $\overline{\text{X}}$ structures

It is often assumed that all languages have syntactic structures that correspond to the $\overline{\text{X}}$ schema (see Section 2.5) (Pinker 1994: 238; Meisel 1995: 11, 14; Pinker & Jackendoff 2005: 216). There are, however, languages such as Dyirbal (Australia) where it does not seem to make sense to assume hierarchical structure for sentences. Thus, Bresnan (2001: 110) assumes that Tagalog, Hungarian, Malayalam, Warlpiri, Jiwarli, Wambaya, Jakaltek and other corresponding languages do not have a VP node, but rather a rule taking the form of (3):

(3)   S → C*

Here, C* stands for an arbitrary number of constituents and there is no head in the structure. Other examples for structures without heads will be discussed in Section 21.10.

---

[6]Pinker (1994: 234) uses the word *usually* in his formulation. He thereby implies that there are exceptions and that the correlation between the ordering of adpositions and the direction of government of verbs is actually a tendency rather than a universally applicable rule. However, in the pages that follow, he argues that the Head Directionality Parameter forms part of innate linguistic knowledge. Travis (1984: 55) discusses data from Mandarin Chinese that do not correspond to the correlations she assumes. She then proposes treating the Head Directionality Parameter as a kind of Default Parameter that can be overridden by other constraints in the language.

13 The innateness of linguistic knowledge

Figure 13.1: Distance between verb and preposition for various head orders according to Newmeyer (2004a: 221)

$\overline{\text{X}}$ structure was introduced to restrict the form of possible rules. The assumption was that these restrictions reduce the class of grammars one can formulate and thus – according to the assumption – make the grammars easier to acquire. But as Kornai & Pullum (1990) have shown, the assumption of $\overline{\text{X}}$ structures does not lead to a restriction with regard to the number of possible grammars if one allows for empty heads. In GB, a number of null heads were used and in the Minimalist Program, there has been a significant increase of these. For example, the rule in (3) can be reformulated as follows:

(4) $V' \rightarrow V^0 \ C^*$

Here, V^0 is an empty head. Since specifiers are optional, V' can be projected to VP and we arrive at a structure corresponding to the $\overline{\text{X}}$ schema.

Apart from the problem with languages with very free constituent order, there are further problems with adjunction structures: Chomsky's analysis of adjective structure in $\overline{\text{X}}$ theory (Chomsky 1970: 210; see also Section 2.5 of this book, in particular Figure 2.8 on page 74) is not straightforwardly applicable to German since, unlike English, adjective phrases in German are head-final and degree modifiers must directly precede the adjective:

(5) a. der auf seinen Sohn sehr stolze Mann
        the of his   son   very proud man
        'the man very proud of his son'

452

b. * der sehr auf seinen Sohn stolze Mann
   the very of his son proud man

c. * der auf seinen Sohn stolze sehr Mann
   the of his son proud very man

Following the $\overline{\text{X}}$ schema, *auf seinen Sohn* has to be combined with *stolze* and only then can the resulting $\overline{\text{A}}$ projection be combined with its specifier (see Figure 2.8 on page 74 for the structure of adjective phrases in English). It is therefore only possible to derive orders such as (5b) or (5c). Neither of these is possible in German. It is only possible to rescue the $\overline{\text{X}}$ schema if one assumes that German is exactly like English and, for some reason, the complements of adjectives must be moved to the left. If we allow this kind of repair approaches, then of course any language can be described using the $\overline{\text{X}}$ schema. The result would be that one would have to postulate a vast number of movement rules for many languages and this would be extremely complex and difficult to motivate from a psycholinguistic perspective. See Chapter 15 for grammars compatible with performance.

A further problem for $\overline{\text{X}}$ theory in its strictest form as presented in Section 2.5 is posed by so-called hydra clauses (Perlmutter & Ross 1970; Link 1984; Kiss 2005):

(6) a. [[der Kater] und [die Katze]], die einander lieben
       the tomcat and the cat that each.other love
       'the tomcat and the (female) cat that love each other'

    b. [[The boy] and [the girl]] who dated each other are friends of mine.

Since the relative clauses in (6) refer to a group of referents, they can only attach to the result of the coordination. The entire coordination is an NP, however, and adjuncts should actually be attached at the $\overline{\text{X}}$ level. The reverse case of relative clauses in German and English is posed by adjectives in Persian: Samvelian (2007) argues for an analysis where adjectives are combined with nouns directly, and only the combination of nouns and adjectives is then combined with a PP argument.

The discussion of German and English shows that the introduction of specifiers and adjuncts cannot be restricted to particular projection levels, and the preceding discussion of non-configurational languages has shown that the assumption of intermediate levels does not make sense for every language.

It should also be noted that Chomsky himself assumed in 1970 that languages can deviate from the $\overline{\text{X}}$ schema (1970: 210).

If one is willing to encode all information about combination in the lexicon, then one could get by with very abstract combinatorial rules that would hold universally. An example of this kind of combinatorial rules is the multiplication rules of Categorial Grammar (see Chapter 8) as well as Merge in the Minimalist Program (see Section 4). The rules in question simply state that two linguistic objects are combined. These kinds of combination of course exist in every language. With completely lexicalized grammars, however, it is only possible to describe languages if one allows for null heads and makes certain ad hoc assumptions. This will be discussed in Section 21.10.

13 The innateness of linguistic knowledge

13.1.3 Grammatical functions such as subject and object

Bresnan & Kaplan (1982: xxv), Pinker (1994: 236–237), Baker (2003: 349) and others assume that all languages have subjects and objects. In order to determine what exactly this claim means, we have to explore the terms themselves. For most European languages, it is easy to say what a subject and an object is (see Section 1.7); however, it has been argued that it is not possible for all languages or that it does not make sense to use these terms at all (Croft 2001: Chapter 4; Evans & Levinson 2009a: Section 4).

In theories such as LFG – the one in which Pinker worked – grammatical functions play a primary role. The fact that it is still controversial whether one should view sentences as subjects, objects or as specially defined sentential arguments (xcomp) (Dalrymple & Lødrup 2000; Berman 2003b; 2007; Alsina, Mohanan & Mohanan 2005; Forst 2006) serves to show that there is at least some leeway for argumentation when it comes to assigning grammatical functions to arguments. It is therefore likely that one can find an assignment of grammatical functions to the arguments of a functor in all languages.

Unlike LFG, grammatical functions are irrelevant in GB (see Williams 1984; Sternefeld 1985a) and Categorial Grammar. In GB, grammatical functions can only be determined indirectly by making reference to tree positions. Thus, in the approach discussed in Chapter 3, the subject is the phrase in the specifier position of IP.

In later versions of Chomskyan linguistics, there are functional nodes that seem to correspond to grammatical functions (AgrS, AgrO, AgrIO, see page 145). However, Chomsky (1995b: Section 4.10.1) remarks that these functional categories were only assumed for theory internal reasons and should be removed from the inventory of categories that are assumed to be part of UG. See Haider (1997a) and Sternefeld (2006: 509–510) for a description of German that does without functional projections that cannot be motivated in the language in question.

The position taken by HPSG is somewhere in the middle: a special valence feature is used for subjects (in grammars of German, there is a head feature that contains a representation of the subject for non-finite verb forms). However, the value of the subj feature is derived from more general theoretical considerations: in German, the least oblique element with structural case is the subject (Müller 2002a: 153; 2007a: 311).

In GB theory (Extended Projection Principle, EPP, Chomsky (1982: 10)) and also in LFG (Subject Condition), there are principles ensuring that every sentence must have a subject. It is usually assumed that these principles hold universally.[7]

As previously mentioned, there are no grammatical functions in GB, but there are structural positions that correspond to grammatical functions. The position corresponding to the subject is the specifier of IP. The EPP states that there must be an element in SpecIP. If we assume universality of this principle, then every language must have an element in this position. As we have already seen, there is a counterexample to this universal claim: German. German has an impersonal passive (7a) and there are also subjectless verbs (7b,c) and adjectives (7d–f).[8]

---

[7]However, Chomsky (1981a: 27) allows for languages not to have a subject. He assumes that this is handled by a parameter. Bresnan (2001: 311) formulates the Subject Condition, but mentions in a footnote that it might be necessary to parameterize this condition so that it only holds for certain languages.

[8]For further discussion of subjectless verbs in German, see Haider (1993: Sections 6.2.1, 6.5), Fanselow (2000b), Nerbonne (1986a: 912) and Müller (2007a: Section 3.2).

(7) a. dass noch gearbeitet wird
       that still worked   is
       'that people are still working'

    b. Ihm   graut vor der Prüfung.
       him.DAT dreads before the exam
       'He dreads the exam.'

    c. Mich   friert.
       me.ACC freezes
       'I am freezing.'

    d. weil   schulfrei   ist
       because school.free is
       'because there is no school today'

    e. weil   ihm   schlecht ist
       because him.DAT ill   is
       'because he is not feeling well'

    f. Für dich ist immer offen.⁹
       for you is always open
       'We are always open for you.'

Most of the predicates that can be used without subjects can also be used with an expletive subject. An example is given in (8):

(8) dass es   ihm vor   der Prüfung graut
    that EXPL him before the exam   dreads
    'He dreads the exam.'

However, there are verbs such as *liegen* 'lie' in example (9a) from Reis (1982: 185) that cannot occur with an *es* 'it'.

(9) a. Mir   liegt an diesem Plan.
        me.DAT lies on this   plan
        'This plan matters a lot to me.'

    b. * Mir   liegt es an diesem Plan.
         me.DAT lies it on this   plan

Nevertheless, the applicability of the EPP and the Subject Condition is sometimes also assumed for German. Grewendorf (1993: 1311) assumes that there is an empty expletive that fills the subject position of subjectless constructions.

Berman (1999: 11; 2003a: Chapter 4), working in LFG, assumes that verbal morphology can fulfill the subject role in German and therefore even in sentences where no subject is overtly present, the position for the subject is filled in the f-structure. A constraint stating that all f-structures without a PRED value must be third person singular applies to the f-structure of the unexpressed subject. The agreement information in the finite

---
⁹Haider (1986a: 18).

verb has to match the information in the f-structure of the unexpressed subject and hence the verbal inflection in subjectless constructions is restricted to be 3rd person singular (Berman 1999).

As we saw on page 166, some researchers working in the Minimalist Program even assume that there is an object in every sentence (Stabler quoted in Veenstra (1998: 61, 124)). Objects of monovalent verbs are assumed to be empty elements.

If we allow these kinds of tools, then it is of course easy to maintain the existence of many universals: we claim that a language X has the property Y and then assume that the structural items are invisible and have no meaning. These analyses can only be justified theory-internally with the goal of uniformity (see Culicover & Jackendoff 2005: Section 2.1.2).[10]

13.1.4 Binding principles

The principles governing the binding of pronouns are also assumed to be part of UG (Chomsky 1998: 33; Crain, Thornton & Khlentzos 2009: 146; Rizzi 2009b: 468). Binding Theory in GB theory has three principles: principle A states that reflexives such as *sich* or *himself* refer to an element (antecedent) inside of a certain local domain (binding domain). Simplyfying a bit, one could say that a reflexive has to refer to a co-argument.

(10) Klaus$_i$ sagt, dass Peter$_j$ sich$_{*i/j}$ rasiert hat.
Klaus says that Peter himself shaved has

Principle B holds for personal pronouns and states that these cannot refer to elements inside of their binding domain.

(11) Klaus$_i$ sagt, dass Peter$_j$ ihn$_{i/*j}$ rasiert hat.
Klaus says that Peter him shaved has

Principle C determines what referential expressions can refer to. According to Principle C, an expression A_1 cannot refer to another expression A_2 if A_2 c-commands A_1. c-command is defined with reference to the structure of the utterance. There are various definitions of c-command; a simple version states that A c-commands B if there is a path in the constituent structure that goes upwards from A to the next branching node and then only downwards to B.

For the example in (12a), this means that *Max* and *er* 'he' cannot refer to the same individual since *er* c-commands *Max*.

(12) a. Er sagt, dass Max Brause getrunken hat.
he says that Max soda drunk has
'He said that Max drank soda.'

b. Max sagt, dass er Brause getrunken hat.
Max said that he soda drunk has
'Max said that he drank soda.'

---
[10] For arguments from language acquisition, see Chapter 16.

c. Als er hereinkam, trank Max Brause.
   as he came.in drank Max soda
   'As he came in, Max was drinking soda.'

This is possible in (12b), however, as there is no such c-command relation. For *er* 'he', it must only be the case that it does not refer to another argument of the verb *getrunken* 'drunk' and this is indeed the case in (12b). Similarly, there is no c-command relation between *er* 'he' and *Max* in (12c) since the pronoun *er* is inside a complex structure. *er* 'he' and *Max* can therefore refer to the the same or different individuals in (12b) and (12c).

Crain, Thornton & Khlentzos (2009: 147) point out that (12b,c) and the corresponding English examples are ambiguous, whereas (12a) is not, due to Principle C. This means that one reading is not available. In order to acquire the correct binding principles, the learner would need information about which meanings expressions do not have. The authors note that children already master Principle C at age three and they conclude from this that Principle C is a plausible candidate for innate linguistic knowledge. (This is a classic kind of argumentation. For Poverty of the Stimulus arguments, see Section 13.8 and for more on negative evidence, see Section 13.8.4).

Evans & Levinson (2009b: 483) note that Principle C is a strong cross-linguistic tendency but it nevertheless has some exceptions. As an example, they mention both reciprocal expressions in Abaza, where affixes that correspond to *each other* occur in subject position rather than object position as well as Guugu Yimidhirr, where pronouns in a superordinate clause can be coreferent with full NPs in a subordinate clause.

Furthermore, Fanselow (1992b: 351) refers to the examples in (13) that show that Principle C is a poor candidate for a syntactic principle.

(13) a. Mord ist ein Verbrechen.
     murder is a crime

   b. Ein gutes Gespräch hilft Probleme überwinden.
      a good conversation helps problems overcome
      'A good conversation helps to overcome problems.'

(13a) expresses that it is a crime when somebody kills someone else, and (13b) refers to conversations with another person rather than talking to oneself. In these sentences, the nominalizations *Mord* 'murder' and *Gespräch* 'conversation' are used without any arguments of the original verbs. So there aren't any arguments that stand in a syntactic command relation to one another. Nevertheless the arguments of the nominalized verbs cannot be coreferential. Therefore it seems that there is a principle at work that says that the argument slots of a predicate must be interpreted as non-coreferential as long as the identity of the arguments is not explicitly expressed by linguistic means.

In sum, one can say that there are still a number of unsolved problems with Binding Theory. The HPSG variants of Principles A–C in English cannot even be applied to German (Müller 1999b: Chapter 20). Working in LFG, Dalrymple (1993) proposes a variant of Binding Theory where the binding properties of pronominal expressions are determined in the lexicon. In this way, the language-specific properties of pronouns can be accounted for.

13.1.5 Properties of long-distance dependencies

The long-distance dependencies discussed in the preceding chapters are subject to some kind of restrictions. For example, nothing can be extracted out of sentences that are part of a noun phrase in English. Ross (1967: 70) calls the relevant constraint the *Complex NP Constraint*. In later work, the attempt was made to group this, and other constraints such as the *Right Roof Constraint* also formulated by Ross (1967: Section 5.1.2), into a single, more general constraint, namely the Subjacency Principle (Chomsky 1973: 271; 1986a: 40; Baltin 1981; 2017). Subjacency was assumed to hold universally. The Subjacency Constraint states that movement operations can cross at most one bounding node, whereby what exactly counts as a bounding node depends on the language in question (Baltin 1981: 262; 2017; Rizzi 1982: 57; Chomsky 1986a: 38–40).[11]

Currently, there are varying opinions in the GB/Minimalism tradition with regard to the question of whether subjacency should be considered as part of innate linguistic knowledge. Hauser, Chomsky & Fitch (2002) assume that subjacency does not form part of language-specific abilities, at least not in the strictest sense, but rather is a linguistically relevant constraint in the broader sense that the constraints in question can be derived from more general cognitive ones (see p. 465). Since subjacency still plays a role as a UG principle in other contemporary works (Newmeyer 2005: 15, 74–75; 2004a: 184; Baltin 2017[12]; Baker 2009; Freidin 2009; Rizzi 2009b,a), the Subjacency Principle will be discussed here in some further detail.

It is possible to distinguish two types of movement: movement to the left (normally called extraction) and movement to the right (normally referred to as extraposition). Both movement types constitute long-distance dependencies. In the following section, I will discuss some of the restrictions on extraposition. Extraction will be discussed in Section 13.1.5.2 following it.

13.1.5.1 Extraposition

Baltin (1981) and Chomsky (1986a: 40) claim that the extraposed relative clauses in (14) have to be interpreted with reference to the embedding NP, that is, the sentences are not

---

[11]Newmeyer (2004b: 539–540) points out a conceptual problem following from the language-specific determination of bounding nodes: it is argued that subjacency is an innate language-specific principle since it is so abstract that it is impossible for speakers to learn it. However, if parameterization requires that a speaker chooses from a set of categories in the linguistic input, then the corresponding constraints must be derivable from the input at least to the degree that it is possible to determine the categories involved. This raises the question as to whether the original claim of the impossibility of acquisition is actually justified. See Section 13.8 on the *Poverty of the Stimulus* and Section 16.1 on parameter-based theories of language acquisition.
    Note also that a parameter that has as the value a part of speech requires the respective part of speech values to be part of UG.

[12]However, see Baltin (2004: 552).

equivalent to those where the relative clause would occur in the position marked with t, but rather they correspond to examples where it would occur in the position of the t'.

(14) a. [$_{NP}$ Many books [$_{PP}$ with [stories t]] t'] were sold [that I wanted to read].

b. [$_{NP}$ Many proofs [$_{PP}$ of [the theorem t]] t'] appeared [that I wanted to think about].

Here, it is assumed that NP, PP, VP and AP are bounding nodes for rightward movement (at least in English) and the interpretation in question here is thereby ruled out by the Subjacency Principle (Baltin 1981: 262).

If we construct a German example parallel to (14a) and replace the embedding noun so that it is ruled out or dispreferred as a referent, then we arrive at (15):

(15) weil viele Schallplatten mit Geschichten verkauft wurden, die ich noch
because many records with stories sold were that I still
lesen wollte
read wanted

'because many records with stories were sold that I wanted to read'

This sentence can be uttered in a situation where somebody in a record store sees particular records and remembers that he had wanted to read the fairy tales on those records. Since one does not read records, adjunction to the superordinate noun is implausible and thus adjunction to *Geschichten* 'stories' is preferred. By carefully choosing the nouns, it is possible to construct examples such as (16) that show that extraposition can take place across multiple NP nodes:[13]

(16) a. Karl hat mir [ein Bild [einer Frau _$_i$]] gegeben, [die schon lange tot
Karl has me a picture a woman given that PART long dead
ist]$_i$.
is

'Karl gave me a picture of a woman that has been dead some time.'

b. Karl hat mir [eine Fälschung [des Bildes [einer Frau _$_i$]]] gegeben, [die
Karl has me a forgery of.the picture of.a woman given that
schon lange tot ist]$_i$.
PART long dead is

'Karl gave me a forgery of the picture of a woman that has been dead for some time.'

c. Karl hat mir [eine Kopie [einer Fälschung [des Bildes [einer Frau _$_i$]]]]
Karl has me a copy of.a forgery of.the picture of.a woman
gegeben, [die schon lange tot ist]$_i$.
given that PART long dead is

'Karl gave me a copy of a forgery of the picture of a woman that has been dead for some time.'

---

[13] See Müller (1999b: 211) and Müller (2004c; 2007c: Section 3). For parallel examples from Dutch, see Koster (1978: 52).

13 The innateness of linguistic knowledge

This kind of embedding could continue further if one were to not eventually run out of nouns that allow for semantically plausible embedding. NP is viewed as a bounding node in German (Grewendorf 1988: 81; 2002: 17–18; Haider 2001: 285). These examples show that it is possible for rightward extraposed relative clauses to cross any number of bounding nodes.

Koster (1978: 52–54) discusses some possible explanations for the data in (16), where it is assumed that relative clauses move to the NP/PP border and are then moved on further from there (this movement requires so-called escape hatches or escape routes). He argues that these approaches will also work for the very sentences that should be ruled out by subjacency, that is, for examples such as (14). This means that either data such as (14) can be explained by subjacency and the sentences in (16) are counterexamples, or there are escape hatches and the examples in (14) are irrelevant, deviant sentences that cannot be explained by subjacency.

In the examples in (16), a relative clause was extraposed in each case. These relative clauses are treated as adjuncts and there are analyses that assume that extraposed adjuncts are not moved but rather base-generated in their position, and coreference/coindexation is achieved by special mechanisms (Kiss 2005). For proponents of these kinds of analyses, the examples in (16) would be irrelevant to the subjacency discussion as the Subjacency Principle only constrains movement. However, extraposition across phrase boundaries is not limited to relative clauses; sentential complements can also be extraposed:

(17) a. Ich habe [von [der Vermutung $_{-i}$]] gehört, [dass es Zahlen gibt, die
I have from the conjecture heard that EXPL numbers gives that
die folgenden Bedingungen erfüllen]$_i$.
the following requirements fulfill

'I have heard of the conjecture that there are numbers that fulfill the following requirements.'

b. Ich habe [von [einem Beweis [der Vermutung $_{-i}$]]] gehört, [dass es
I have from a proof of.the conjecture heard that EXPL
Zahlen gibt, die die folgenden Bedingungen erfüllen]$_i$.
numbers give that the following requirements fulfill

'I have heard of the proof of the conjecture that there are numbers that fulfill the following requirements.'

c. Ich habe [von [dem Versuch [eines Beweises [der Vermutung $_{-i}$]]]] gehört,
I have from the attempt of.a proof of.the conjecture heard
[dass es Zahlen gibt, die die folgenden Bedingungen erfüllen]$_i$.
that EXPL numbers gives that the following requirements fulfill

'I have heard of the attempt to prove the conjecture that there are numbers that fulfill the following requirements.'

Since there are nouns that select *zu* infinitives or prepositional phrases and since these can be extraposed like the sentences above, it must be ensured that the syntactic category of the postposed element corresponds to the category required by the noun. This means that there has to be some kind of relation between the governing noun and the extraposed element. For this reason, the examples in (17) have to be analyzed as instances of extraposition and provide counter evidence to the claims discussed above.

If one wishes to discuss the possibility of recursive embedding, then one is forced to refer to constructed examples as the likelihood of stumbling across groups of sentences such as those in (16) and (17) is very remote. It is, however, possible to find some individual cases of deep embedding: (18) gives some examples of relative clause extraposition and complement extraposition taken from the Tiger corpus[14] (Müller 2007c: 78–79; Meurers & Müller 2009: Section 2.1).

(18) a. Der 43jährige will nach eigener Darstellung damit [NP den Weg [PP für
the 43.year.old wants after own depiction there.with the way for
[NP eine Diskussion [PP über [NP den künftigen Kurs [NP der stärksten
a discussion about the future course of.the strongest
Oppositionsgruppierung]]]]]] freimachen, [die aber mit 10,4 Prozent
opposition.group free.make that however with 10.4 percent
der Stimmen bei der Wahl im Oktober weit hinter den Erwartungen
of.the votes at the election in October far behind the expectations
zurückgeblieben war]. (s27639)
stayed.back was

'In his own words, the 43-year old wanted to clear the way for a discussion about the future course of the strongest opposition group that had, however, performed well below expectations gaining only 10.4 percent of the votes at the election in October.'

b. [...] die Erfindung der Guillotine könnte [NP die Folge [NP eines
the invention of.the guillotine could the result of.a
verzweifelten Versuches des gleichnamigen Doktors] gewesen sein, [seine
desperate attempt the same.name doctor have been his
Patienten ein für allemal von Kopfschmerzen infolge schlechter Kissen
patients once for all.time of headaches because.of bad pillows
zu befreien]. (s16977)
to free

'The invention of the guillotine could have been the result of a desperate attempt of the eponymous doctor to rid his patients once and for all of headaches from bad pillows.'

It is also possible to construct sentences for English that violate the Subjacency Condition. Uszkoreit (1990: 2333) provides the following example:

(19) [NP Only letters [PP from [NP those people $_{-i}$]]] remained unanswered [that had received our earlier reply]$_i$.

---

[14]See Brants et al. (2004) for more information on the Tiger corpus.

Jan Strunk (p. c. 2008) has found examples for extraposition of both restrictive and non-restrictive relative clauses across multiple phrase boundaries:

(20)   a. For example, we understand that Ariva buses have won [$_{NP}$ a number [$_{PP}$ of [$_{NP}$ contracts [$_{PP}$ for [$_{NP}$ routes in London $_{-i}$]]]]] recently, [which will not be run by low floor accessible buses]$_i$.[15]

         b. I picked up [$_{NP}$ a copy of [$_{NP}$ a book $_{-i}$]] today, by a law professor, about law, [that is not assigned or in any way required to read]$_i$.[16]

         c. We drafted [$_{NP}$ a list of [$_{NP}$ basic demands $_{-i}$]] that night [that had to be unconditionally met or we would stop making and delivering pizza and go on strike]$_i$.[17]

(20a) is also published in Strunk & Snider (2013: 111). Further attested examples from German and English can be found in this paper.

The preceding discussion has shown that subjacency constraints on rightward movement do not hold for English or German and thus cannot be viewed as universal. One could simply claim that NP and PP are not bounding nodes in English or German. Then, these extraposition data would no longer be problematic for theories assuming subjacency. However, subjacency constraints are also assumed for leftward movement. This is discussed in more detail in the following section.

13.1.5.2 Extraction

Under certain conditions, leftward movement is not possible from certain constituents (Ross 1967). These constituents are referred to as islands for extraction. Ross (1967: Section 4.1) formulated the *Complex NP Constraint* (CNPC) that states that extraction is not possible from complex noun phrases. An example of extraction from a relative clause inside a noun phrase is the following:

(21)   * Who$_i$ did he just read [$_{NP}$ the report [$_S$ that was about $_{-i}$]?

Although (21) would be a semantically plausible question, the sentence is still ungrammatical. This is explained by the fact that the question pronoun has been extracted across the sentence boundary of a relative clause and then across the NP boundary and has therefore crossed two bounding nodes. It is assumed that the CNPC holds for all languages. This is not the case, however, as the corresponding structures are possible in Danish (Erteschik-Shir & Lappin 1979: 55), Norwegian, Swedish, Japanese, Korean, Tamil and Akan (see Hawkins (1999: 245, 262) and references therein). Since the restrictions of the CNPC are integrated into the Subjacency Principle, it follows that the Subjacency Principle cannot be universally applicable unless one claims that NP is not a bounding node in the problematic languages. However, it seems indeed to be the case that the majority of languages do not allow extraction from complex noun phrases. Hawkins

---

[15]http://www.publications.parliament.uk/pa/cm199899/cmselect/cmenvtra/32ii/32115.htm, 2018-02-20.
[16]http://greyhame.org/archives/date/2005/09/, 2008-09-27.
[17]http://portland.indymedia.org/en/2005/07/321809.shtml, 2018-02-20.

13.1 Syntactic universals

explains this on the basis of the processing difficulties associated with the structures in question (Section 4.1). He explains the difference between languages that allow this kind of extraction and languages that do not with reference to the differing processing load for structures that stem from the interaction of extraction with other grammatical properties such as verb position and other conventionalized grammatical structures in the respective languages (Section 4.2).

Unlike extraction from complex noun phrases, extraction across a single sentence boundary (22) is not ruled out by the Subjacency Principle.

(22)   Who$_i$ did she think that he saw $\_{_i}$?

Movement across multiple sentence boundaries, as discussed in previous chapters, is explained by so-called cyclic movement in transformational theories: a question pronoun is moved to a specifier position and can then be moved further to the next highest specifier. Each of these movement steps is subject to the Subjacency Principle. The Subjacency Principle rules out long-distance movement in one fell swoop.

The Subjacency Principle cannot explain why extraction from sentences embedded under verbs that specify the kind of utterance (23a) or factive verbs (23b) is deviant (Erteschik-Shir & Lappin 1979: 68–69).

(23)   a. ?? Who$_i$ did she mumble that he saw $\_{_i}$?
       b. ?? Who$_i$ did she realize that he saw $\_{_i}$?

The structure of these sentences seems to be the same as (22). In entirely syntactic approaches, it was also attempted to explain these differences as subjacency violations or as a violation of Ross' constraints. It has therefore been assumed (Stowell 1981: 401–402) that the sentences in (23) have a structure different from those in (22). Stowell treats these sentential arguments of manner of speaking verbs as adjuncts. Since adjunct clauses are islands for extraction by assumption, this would explain why (23a) is marked. The adjunct analysis is compatible with the fact that these sentential arguments can be omitted:

(24)   a. She shouted that he left.
       b. She shouted.

Ambridge & Goldberg (2008: 352) have pointed out that treating such clauses as adjuncts is not justified as they are only possible with a very restricted class of verbs, namely verbs of saying and thinking. This property is a property of arguments and not of adjuncts. Adjuncts such as place modifiers are possible with a wide number of verb classes. Furthermore, the meaning changes if the sentential argument is omitted as in (24b): whereas (24a) requires that some information is communicated, this does not have to be the case with (24b). It is also possible to replace the sentential argument with an NP as in (25), which one would certainly not want to treat as an adjunct.

(25)   She shouted the remark/the question/something I could not understand.

The possibility of classifying sentential arguments as adjuncts cannot be extended to factive verbs as their sentential argument is not optional (Ambridge & Goldberg 2008: 352):

(26) a. She realized that he left.
      b. ?? She realized.

Kiparsky & Kiparsky (1970) suggest an analysis of factive verbs that assumes a complex noun phrase with a nominal head. An optional *fact* Deletion-Transformation removes the head noun and the determiner of the NP in sentences such as (27a) to derive sentences such as (27b) (page 159).

(27) a. She realized [$_{NP}$ the fact [$_S$ that he left]].
      b. She realized [$_{NP}$ [$_S$ that he left]].

The impossibility of extraction out of such sentences can be explained by assuming that two boundary nodes were crossed, which was assumed to be impossible (on the island status of this construction, see Kiparsky & Kiparsky 1970: Section 4). This analysis predicts that extraction from complement clauses of factive verbs should be just as bad as extraction from overt NP arguments since the structure for both is the same. According to Ambridge & Goldberg (2008: 353), this is, however, not the case:

(28) a. * Who did she realize the fact that he saw $_{-i}$?
      b. ?? Who did she realize that he saw $_{-i}$?

Together with Erteschik-Shir (1981), Erteschik-Shir & Lappin (1979), Takami (1988) and Van Valin (1998), Goldberg (2006: Section 7.2) assumes that the gap must be in a part of the utterance that can potentially form the focus of an utterance (see Cook (2001), De Kuthy (2002) and Fanselow (2003c) for German). This means that this part must not be presupposed.[18] If one considers what this means for the data from the subjacency discussion, then one notices that in each case extraction has taken place out of presupposed material:

(29) a. Complex NP
          She didn't see the report that was about him. → The report was about him.
      b. Complement of a verb of thinking or saying
          She didn't whisper that he left. → He left.
      c. Factive verb
          She didn't realize that he left. → He left.

---

[18]Information is presupposed if it is true regardless of whether the utterance is negated or not. Thus, it follows from both (i.a) and (i.b) that there is a king of France.

(i) a. The King of France is bald.
     b. The King of France is not bald.

Goldberg assumes that constituents that belong to backgrounded information are islands (*Backgrounded constructions are islands* (BCI)). Ambridge & Goldberg (2008) have tested this semantic/pragmatic analysis experimentally and compared it to a purely syntactic approach. They were able to confirm that information structural properties play a significant role for the extractability of elements. Along with Erteschik-Shir (1973: Section 3.H), Ambridge & Goldberg (2008: 375) assume that languages differ with regard to how much constituents have to belong to background knowledge in order to rule out extraction. In any case we should not rule out extraction from adjuncts for all languages as there are languages such as Danish where it is possible to extract from relative clauses.[19] Erteschik-Shir (1973: 61) provides the following examples, among others:

(30) a. Det$_i$ er der mange [der kan lide _$_i$].
       that are there many that can like

     'There are many who like that.' (lit.: 'That, there are many who like.')

  b. Det hus$_i$ kender jeg en mand [som har købt _$_i$].
       that house know I a man that has bought

     'I know a man that has bought that house.' (lit.: 'This house, I know a man that has bought.')

And as the following example from McCawley (1981: 108) shows, extraction out of relative clauses is possible even in English:

(31) Then you look at what happens in languages you know and languages that$_i$ you have a friend [who knows _$_i$]. (Charles Ferguson, lecture at university of Chicago, 1971)

Rizzi's parameterization of the subjacency restriction has been abandoned in many works, and the relevant effects have been ascribed to differences in other areas of grammar (Adams 1984; Chung & McCloskey 1983; Grimshaw 1986; Kluender 1992).

We have seen in this subsection that there are reasons other than syntactic properties of structure as to why leftward movement might be blocked. In addition to information structural properties, processing considerations also play a role (Grosu 1973; Ellefson & Christiansen 2000; Gibson 1998; Kluender & Kutas 1993; Hawkins 1999; Sag, Hofmeister & Snider 2007). The length of constituents involved, the distance between filler and gap, definiteness, complexity of syntactic structure and interference effects between similar discourse referents in the space between the filler and gap are all important factors for the acceptability of utterances. Since languages differ with regard to their syntactic structure, varying effects of performance, such as the ones found for extraposition and extraction, are to be expected.

---

[19]Discussing the question of whether UG-based approaches are falsifiable, Crain, Khlentzos & Thornton (2010: 2669) claim that it is not possible to extract from relative clauses and the existence of such languages would call into question the very concept of UG. ("If a child acquiring any language could learn to extract linguistic expressions from a relative clause, then this would seriously cast doubt on one of the basic tenets of UG.") They thereby contradict Evans and Levinson as well as Tomasello, who claim that UG approaches are not falsifiable. If the argumentation of Crain, Khlentzos and Thornton were correct, then (30) and (31) would falsify UG and that would be the end of the discussion.

In sum, we can say that subjacency constraints do not hold for extraposition in either German or English and furthermore that one can better explain constraints on extraction with reference to information structure and processing phenomena than with the Subjacency Principle. Assuming subjacency as a syntactic constraint in a universal competence grammar is therefore unnecessary to explain the facts.

13.1.6 Grammatical morphemes for tense, mood and aspect

Pinker (1994: 238) is correct in claiming that there are morphemes for tense, mood, aspect, case and negation in many languages. However, there is a great deal of variation with regard to which of these grammatical properties a language has and how they are expressed.

For examples of differences in the tense system see Dahl & Velupillai (2013a,b). Mandarin Chinese is a clear case: it has next to no morphology. The fact that the same morphemes occur in one form or another in almost every language can be attributed to the fact that certain things need to be expressed repeatedly and then things which are constantly repeated become grammaticalized.

13.1.7 Parts of speech

In Section 4.6, so-called cartographic approaches were mentioned, some of which assume over thirty functional categories (see Table 4.1 on page 147 for Cinque's functional heads) and assume that these categories form part of UG together with corresponding fixed syntactic structures. Cinque & Rizzi (2010: 55, 57) even assume over 400 functional categories that are claimed to play a role in the grammars of all languages.[20] Also, specific parts of speech such as Infl (inflection) and Comp (complementizer) are referred to when formulating principles that are assumed to be universal (Baltin 1981: 262; 2017; Rizzi 1982; Chomsky 1986a: 38; Hornstein 2013: 397).

Chomsky (1988: 68; 1991; 1995b: 131), Pinker (1994: 284, 286), Briscoe (2000: 270) and Wunderlich (2004: 621) make comparatively fewer assumptions about the innate inventory of parts of speech: Chomsky assumes that all lexical categories (verbs, nouns, adjectives and adpositions) belong to UG and languages have these at their disposal. Pinker, Briscoe and Wunderlich assume that all languages have nouns and verbs. Again critics of UG raised the question as to whether these syntactic categories can be found in other languages in the form known to us from languages such as German and English.

Braine (1987: 72) argues that parts of speech such as verb and noun should be viewed as derived from fundamental concepts like argument and predicate (see also Wunderlich (2008: 257)). This means that there is an independent explanation for the presence of these categories that is not based on innate language-specific knowledge.

Evans & Levinson (2009a: Section 2.2.4) discuss the typological literature and give examples of languages which lack adverbs and adjectives. The authors cite Straits Salish as a language in which there may be no difference between verbs and nouns (see also Evans & Levinson 2009b: 481). They remark that it does make sense to assume the

---

[20]The question of whether these categories form part of UG is left open.

additional word classes ideophone, positional, coverb, classifier for the analysis of non Indo-European languages on top of the four or five normally used.[21] This situation is not a problem for UG-based theories if one assumes that languages can choose from an inventory of possibilities (a toolkit) but do not have to exhaust it (Jackendoff 2002: 263; Newmeyer 2005: 11; Fitch, Hauser & Chomsky 2005: 204; Chomsky 2007: 6–7; Cinque & Rizzi 2010: 55, 58, 65). However, if we condone this view, then there is a certain arbitrariness. It is possible to assume any parts of speech that one requires for the analysis of at least one language, attribute them to UG and then claim that most (or maybe even all) languages do not make use of the entire set of parts of speech. This is what is suggested by Villavicencio (2002: 157), working in the framework of Categorial Grammar, for the categories S, NP, N, PP and PRT. This kind of assumption is not falsifiable (see Riemsdijk 1978: 148; Evans & Levinson 2009a: 436; Tomasello 2009: 471 for a discussion of similar cases and a more general discussion).

Whereas Evans and Levinson assume that one needs additional categories, Haspelmath (2009: 458) and Croft (2009: 453) go so far as to deny the existence of cross-linguistic parts of speech. I consider this to be too extreme and believe that a better research strategy is to try and find commonalities between languages.[22] One should, however, expect to find languages that do not fit into our Indo-European-biased conceptions of grammar.

13.1.8 Recursion and infinitude

In an article in *Science*, Hauser, Chomsky & Fitch (2002) put forward the hypothesis that the only domain-specific universal is recursion, "providing the capacity to generate an infinite range of expressions from a finite set of elements" (see (37b) on page 64 for an example of a recursive phrase structure rule).[23] This assumption is controversial and there have been both formal and empirical objections to it.

13.1.8.1 Formal problems

The claim that our linguistic capabilities are infinite is widespread and can already be found in Humboldt's work:[24]

---

[21] For the opposite view, see Jackendoff & Pinker (2009: 465).

[22] Compare Chomsky (1999: 2): "In the absence of compelling evidence to the contrary, assume languages to be uniform, with variety restricted to easily detectable properties of utterances."

[23] In a discussion article in *Cognition*, Fitch, Hauser & Chomsky (2005) clarify that their claim that recursion is the only language-specific and human-specific property is a hypothesis and it could be the case that are not any language-specific/species-specific properties at all. Then, a particular combination of abilities and properties would be specific to humans (p. 182–201). An alternative they consider is that innate language-specific knowledge has a complexity corresponding to what was assumed in earlier versions of Mainstream Generative Grammar (p. 182). Chomsky (2007: 7) notes that Merge could be a non language-specific operation but still attributes it to UG.

[24] The process of language is not simply one where an individual instantiation is created; at the same time it must allow for an indefinite set of such instantiations and must above all allow the expression of the conditions imposed by thought. Language faces an infinite and truly unbounded subject matter, the epitome of everything one can think of. Therefore, it must make infinite use of finite means and this is possible through the identity of the power that is responsible for the production of thought and language.

13 The innateness of linguistic knowledge

> Das Verfahren der Sprache ist aber nicht bloß ein solches, wodurch eine einzelne Erscheinung zustande kommt; es muss derselben zugleich die Möglichkeit eröffnen, eine unbestimmbare Menge solcher Erscheinungen und unter allen, ihr von dem Gedanken gestellten Bedingungen hervorzubringen. Denn sie steht ganz eigentlich einem unendlichen und wahrhaft grenzenlosen Gebiete, dem Inbegriff alles Denkbaren gegenüber. Sie muss daher von endlichen Mitteln einen unendlichen Gebrauch machen, und vermag dies durch die Identität der gedanken- und spracheerzeugenden Kraft. (Humboldt 1988: 108)

If we just look at the data, we can see that there is an upper bound for the length of utterances. This has to do with the fact that extremely long instances cannot be processed and that speakers have to sleep or will eventually die at some point. If we set a generous maximal sentence length at 100,000 morphemes and then assume a morpheme inventory of X then one can form less than $X^{100,000}$ utterances. We arrive at the number $X^{100,000}$ if we use each of the morphemes at each of the 100,000 positions. Since not all of these sequences will be well-formed, then there are actually less than $X^{100,000}$ possible utterances (see also Weydt 1972 for a similar but more elaborate argument). This number is incredibly large, but still finite. The same is true of thought: we do not have infinitely many possible thoughts (if *infinitely* is used in the mathematical sense of the word), despite claims by Humboldt and Chomsky (2008: 137) to the contrary.[25]

In the literature, one sometimes finds the claim that it is possible to produce infinitely long sentences (see for instance Nowak, Komarova & Niyogi (2001: 117) and Kim & Sells

---

[25] Weydt (1972) discusses Chomsky's statements regarding the existence of infinitely many sentences and whether it is legitimate for Chomsky to refer to Humboldt. Chomsky's quote in *Current Issues in Linguistic Theory* (Chomsky 1964a: 17) leaves out the sentence *Denn sie steht ganz eigentlich einem unendlichen und wahrhaft grenzenlosen Gebiete, dem Inbegriff alles Denkbaren gegenüber.* Weydt (1972: 266) argues that Humboldt, Bühler and Martinet claimed that there are infinitely many thoughts that can be expressed. Weydt claims that it does not follow that sentences may be arbitrarily long. Instead he suggests that there is no upper bound on the length of texts. This claim is interesting, but I guess texts are just the next bigger unit and the argument that Weydt put forward against languages without an upper bound for sentence length also applies to texts. A text can be generated by the rather simplified rule in (i) that combines an utterance U with a text T resulting in a larger text T:

(i) T → T U

U can be a sentence or another phrase that can be part of a text. If one is ready to admit that there is no upper bound on the length of texts, it follows that there cannot be an upper bound on the length of sentences either, since one can construct long sentences by joining all phrases of a text with *and*. Such long sentences that are the product of conjoining short sentences are different in nature from very long sentences that are admitted under the Chomskyan view in that they do not include center-self embeddings of an arbitrary depth (see Section 15), but nevertheless the number of sentences that can be produced from arbitrarily long texts is infinite.

As for arbitrarily long texts there is an interesting problem: Let us assume that a person produces sentences and keeps adding them to an existing text. This enterprise will be interrupted when the human being dies. One could say that another person could take up the text extension until this one dies and so on. Again the question is whether one can understand the meaning and the structure of a text that is several million pages long. 42. If this is not enough of a problem, one may ask oneself whether the language of the person who keeps adding to the text in the year 2731 is still the same that the person who started the text spoke in 2015. If the answer to this question is no, then the text is not a document containing sentences from one language L but a mix from several languages and hence irrelevant for the debate.

(2008: 3) and Dan Everett in O'Neill & Wood (2012) at 25:19). This is most certainly not the case. It is also not the case that the rewrite grammars we encountered in Chapter 2 allow for the creation of infinite sentences as the set of symbols of the right-hand side of the rule has to be finite by definition. While it is possible to derive an infinite number of sentences, the sentences themselves cannot be infinite, since it is always one symbol that is replaced by finitely many other symbols and hence no infinite symbol sequence may result.

Chomsky (1965: Section I.1) follows de Saussure (1916b) and draws a distinction between competence and performance: competence is the knowledge about what kind of linguistic structures are well-formed, and performance is the application of this knowledge (see Section 12.6.3 and Chapter 15). Our restricted brain capacity as well as other constraints are responsible for the fact that we cannot deal with an arbitrary amount of embedding and that we cannot produce utterances longer than 100,000 morphemes. The separation between competence and performance makes sense and allows us to formulate rules for the analysis of sentences such as (32):

(32) a. Richard is sleeping.
      b. Karl suspects that Richard is sleeping.
      c. Otto claims that Karl suspects that Richard is sleeping.
      d. Julius believes that Otto claims that Karl suspects that Richard is sleeping.
      e. Max knows that Julius believes that Otto claims that Karl suspects that Richard is sleeping.

The rule takes the following form: combine a noun phrase with a verb of a certain class and a clause. By applying this rule successively, it is possible to form strings of arbitrary length. Pullum & Scholz (2010) point out that one has to keep two things apart: the question of whether language is a recursive system and whether it is just the case that the best models that we can devise for a particular language happen to be recursive. For more on this point and on processing in the brain, see Luuk & Luuk (2011). When constructing strings of words using the system above, it cannot be shown that (a particular) language is infinite, even if this is often claimed to be the case (Bierwisch 1966: 105–106; Pinker 1994: 86; Hauser, Chomsky & Fitch 2002: 1571; Müller 2007a: 1; Hornstein, Nunes & Grohmann 2005: 7; Kim & Sells 2008: 3).

The "proof" of this infinitude of language is led as an indirect proof parallel to the proof that shows that there is no largest natural number (Bierwisch 1966: 105–106; Pinker 1994: 86). In the domain of natural numbers, this works as follows: assume x is the largest natural number. Then form $x + 1$ and, since this is by definition a natural number, we have now found a natural number that is greater than x. We have therefore shown that the assumption that x is the highest number leads to a contradiction and thus that there cannot be such a thing as the largest natural number.

When transferring this proof into the domain of natural language, the question arises as to whether one would still want to class a string of 1,000,000,000 words as part of the language we want to describe. If we do not want this, then this proof will not work.

If we view language as a biological construct, then one has to accept the fact that it is finite. Otherwise, one is forced to assume that it is infinite, but that an infinitely large part of the biologically real object is not biologically real (Postal 2009: 111). Luuk & Luuk (2011) refer to languages as physically uncountable but finite sets of strings. They point out that a distinction must be made between the ability to imagine extending a sentence indefinitely and the ability to take a sentence from a non-countable set of strings and really extend it. We possess the first ability but not the second.

One possibility to provide arguments for the infinitude of languages is to claim that only generative grammars, which create sets of well-formed utterances, are suited to modeling language and that we need recursive rules to capture the data, which is why mental representations have a recursive procedure that generates infinite numbers of expressions (Chomsky, 1956: 115; 2002: 86–87), which then implies that languages consist of infinitely many expressions. There are two mistakes in this argument that have been pointed out by Pullum & Scholz (2010): even if one assumes generative grammars, it can still be the case that a context-sensitive grammar can still only generate a finite set even with recursive rules. Pullum & Scholz (2010: 120–121) give an interesting example from András Kornai.

The more important mistake is that it is not necessary to assume that grammars generate sets. There are three explicitly formalized alternatives of which only the third is mentioned here, namely the model-theoretic and therefore constraint-based approaches (see Chapter 14). Johnson & Postal's Arc Pair Grammar (1980), LFG in the formalization of Kaplan (1995), GPSG in the reformalization of Rogers (1997) and HPSG with the assumptions of King (1999), Pollard (1999) and Richter (2007) are examples of model-theoretic approaches. In constraint-based theories, one would analyze an example like (32) saying that certain attitude verbs select a nominative NP and a *that* clause and that these can only occur in a certain local configuration where a particular relation holds between the elements involved. One of these relations is subject-verb agreement. In this way, one can represent expressions such as (32) and does not have to say anything about how many sentences can be embedded. This means that constraint-based theories are compatible with both answers to the question of whether there is a finite or infinite number of structures. Using competence grammars formulated in the relevant way, it is possible to develop performance models that explain why certain strings – for instance very long ones – are unacceptable (see Chapter 15).

13.1.8.2 Empirical problems

It is sometimes claimed that all natural languages are recursive and that sentences of an arbitrary length are possible in all languages (Hornstein, Nunes & Grohmann 2005: 7 for an overview, and see Pullum & Scholz (2010: Section 2) for further references). When one speaks of recursion, what is often meant are structures with self-embedding as we saw in the analysis of (32) (Fitch 2010). However, it is possible that there are languages that do not allow self-embedding. Everett (2005) claims that Pirahã is such a language (however, see Nevins, Pesetsky & Rodrigues (2009) and Everett (2009; 2012). A more recent corpus study of Pirahã can be found in Futrell, Stearns, Everett, Piantadosi & Gibson (2016).). A further example of a language without recursion, which is sometimes cited with reference to Hale (1976), is Warlpiri. Hale's rules for the combination of a sentence with a relative clause are recursive, however (page 85). This recursion is made explicit on page 98.[26] Pullum & Scholz (2010: 131) discuss Hixkaryána, an Amazonian language from the Caribbean language family that is not related to Pirahã. This language does have embedding, but the embedded material has a different form to that of the matrix clause. It could be the case that these embeddings cannot be carried out indefinitely. In Hixkaryána, there is also no possibility to coordinate phrases or clauses (Derbyshire (1979: 45) cited by Pullum & Scholz (2010: 131)), which is why this possibility of forming recursive sentence embedding does not exist in this language either. Other languages without self-embedding seem to be Akkadian, Dyirbal and Proto-Uralic.

There is of course a trivial sense in which all languages are recursive: they follow a rule that says that a particular number of symbols can be combined to form another symbol.[27]

(33) X → X ... X

In this sense, all natural languages are recursive and the combination of simple symbols to more complex ones is a basic property of language (Hockett 1960: 6). The fact that the debate about Pirahã is so fierce could go to show that this is not the kind of recursion that is meant. Also, see Fitch (2010).

It is also assumed that the combinatorial rules of Categorial Grammar hold universally. It is possible to use these rules to combine a functor with its arguments (X/Y * Y = X). These rules are almost as abstract as the rules in (33). The difference is that one of the elements has to be the functor. There are also corresponding constraints in the Minimalist Program such as selectional features (see Section 4.6.4) and restrictions on the assignment of semantic roles. However, whether or not a Categorial Grammar licenses recursive structures does not depend on the very general combinatorial schemata, but rather on the lexical entries. Using the lexical entries in (34), it is only possible to analyze the four sentences in (35) and certainly not to build recursive structures. (See Chomsky (2014) for a similar discussion of a hypothetical "trincated English".)

(34) a. the: np/n
      b. woman: n
      c. cat: n
      d. sees: (s\np)/np

---

[26]However, he does note on page 78 that relative clauses are separated from the sentence containing the head noun by a pause. Relative clauses in Warlpiri are always peripheral, that is, they occur to the left or right of a sentence with the noun they refer to. Similar constructions can be found in German:

(i) Es   war einmal ein Mann. Der hatte sieben Söhne.
     there was once a   man   he had   seven sons
     'There once was a man. He had seven sons.'

It could be the case that we are dealing with linking of sentences at text level and not recursion at sentence level.

[27]Chomsky (2005: 11) assumes that Merge combines n objects. A special instance of this is binary Merge.

(35) a. The woman sees the cat.
　　 b. The cat sees the woman.
　　 c. The woman sees the woman.
　　 d. The cat sees the cat.

If we expand the lexicon to include modifiers of the category n/n or conjunctions of the category (X\X)/X, then we arrive at a recursive grammar. For example, if we add the two lexical items in (36), the grammar licenses sentences like (37):

(36) a. ugly: n/n
　　 b. fat: n/n

(37) a. The woman sees the fat cat.
　　 b. The woman sees the ugly fat cat.

The grammar allows for the combination of arbitrarily many instances of *fat* (or any other adjectives in the lexicon) with nouns, since the result of combining an n/n with an n is an n. There is no upper limit on such combinations.

Concerning Pirahã, Everett (2012: 560) stated: "The upper limit of a Piraha sentence is a lexical frame with modifiers—the verb, its arguments, and one modifier for each of these. And up to two (one at each edge of the sentence) additional sentence-level or verb-level prepositional adjuncts" and "there can at most be one modifier per word. You cannot say in Pirahã 'many big dirty Brazil-nuts'. You would need to say 'There are big Brazil-nuts. There are many. They are dirty'.". The restriction to have just one modifier per noun can be incorporated easily into the lexical items for nominal modifiers. One has to assume a feature that distinguishes words from non-words. The result of combining two linguistic objects would be WORD− and words would be WORD+. The lexical item for modifiers like *big* would be as in (38):

(38) *big* with Pirahã-like restriction on word modification:
　　 n/n[WORD+]

The combination of *big* and *Brazil-nuts* is n[WORD−]. Since this is incompatible with n[WORD+] and since all noun modifiers require an n[WORD+], no further modification is possible. So although the combination rule of Categorial Grammar would allow the creation of structures of unbounded complexity, the Pirahã lexicon rules out the respective combinations. Under such a view the issue could be regarded as settled: all langugaes are assumed to combine linguistics objects. The combinations are licensed by the combinatorial rules of Categorial Grammar, by abstract rules like in HPSG or by their respective equivalents in Minimalism (Merge). Since these rules can apply to their own output they are recursive.

Concluding this subsection, it can be said that the existence of languages like Pirahã are not problematic for the assumption that all languages use rules to combine functors with arguments. However, it is problematic for claims stating that all languages allow for the creation of sentences with unbounded length and that recursive structures (NPs containing NPs, Ss containing Ss, ...) can be found in all languages.

Fitch, Hauser & Chomsky (2005: 203) note that the existence of languages that do not license recursive structures is not a problem for UG-based theories as not all the possibilities in UG have to be utilized by an individual language. Similar claims were made with respect to part of speech and other morpho-syntactic properties. It was argued that UG is a toolbox and languages can choose which building blocks they use. As Evans & Levinson (2009a: 436, 443) and Tomasello (2009: 471) noticed, the toolbox approach is problematic as one can posit any number of properties belonging to UG and then decide on a language by language basis whether they play a role or not. An extreme variant of this approach would be that grammars of all languages become part of UG (perhaps with different symbols such as $NP_{Spanish}$, NP_{German}). This variant of a UG-based theory of the human capacity for language would be truly unfalsifiable

In the first edition of this book (Müller 2016a), I followed the view of Evans & Klein and Tomasello, but I want to revise my view here. The criticism applies to things like part of speech (Section 13.1.7) since it is true that the claim that 400 and more parts of speech are part of our genetic endowment Cinque & Rizzi (2010: 55, 57) cannot really be falsified, but the situation is different here. All grammar formalisms that were covered in this book are capable of analyzing recursive structures (see Section 18.3). If Pirahã lacks recursive structures one could use a grammar formalism with lower generative capacity (see Chapter 17 on generative capacity) to model the grammar of Pirahã. Parts of the development of theoretical linguistics were driven by the desire to find formalisms of the right computational complexity to describe human languages. GPSG (with certain assumptions) was equivalent to context-sensitive grammars. When Shieber (1985) and Culy (1985) discovered data from Swiss German and Bambara it was clear that context free grammars are not sufficiently powerful to describe all known languages. Hence, GPSG was not powerful enough and researchers moved on to more powerful formalisms like HPSG. Other frameworks like CCG, TAG, and Minimalist Grammars were shown to be powerful enough to handle so-called *mildly context-sensitive grammars*, which are needed for Swiss German and Bambara. Now, we are working on languages like English using grammar formalisms that can deal with mildly context-sensitive grammars even though English may be context free (Pullum & Rawlins 2007). This is similar to the situation with Pirahã: even though English does not have cross-serial dependencies like Swiss German, linguists use tools that could license them. Even though Pirahã does not have recursive structures, linguists use tools that could license them. In general there are two possibilities: one can have very general combinatory rules and rich specifications in the lexicon or one can have very specific combinatory rules and less information in the lexicon.[28] If one assumes that the basic combinatory rules are abstract (Minimalism, HPSG, TAG, CG), the difference between Pirahã and English is represented in the lexicon only. Pirahã uses the combinatory potential differently. In this sense, Chomsky (2014) is right

---

[28] Personally, I argue for a middle way: Structures like Jackendoff's N-P-N constructions (2008) are analyzed by concrete phrasal constructions. Verb-argument combinations of the kind discussed in the first part of this book are analyzed with abstract combinatory schemata. See Müller (2013c) and Chapter 21.

13 The innateness of linguistic knowledge

in saying that the existence of Pirahã is irrelevant to the discussion of what languages can do. Chomsky also notes that Pirahã people are able to learn other languages that have recursive structures. So in principle, they can understand and produce more complex structures in much the same way as children of English parents are able to learn Swiss German.

So the claim that all languages are infinite and make use of self-embedding recursive structures is probably falsified by languages like Pirahã, but using recursive rules for the description of all languages is probably a good decision. But even if we assume that recursive rules play a role in the analysis of all natural languages, would this mean that the respective rules and capacities are part of our genetic, language-specific endowment? This question is dealt with in the next subsection.

13.1.8.3 Recursion in other areas of cognition

There are also phenomena in domains outside of language that can be described with recursive rules: Hauser, Chomsky & Fitch (2002: 1571) mention navigation, family relations and counting systems.[29] One could perhaps argue that the relevant abilities are acquired late and that higher mathematics is a matter of individual accomplishments that do not have anything to do with the cognitive capacities of the majority, but even children at the age of 3 years and 9 months are already able to produce recursive structures: In 2008, there were newspaper reports about an indigenous Brazilian tribe that was photographed from a plane. I showed this picture to my son and told him that Native Americans shot at the plane with a bow and arrow. He then asked me what kind of plane it was. I told him that you cannot see that because the people who took the photograph were sitting in the plane. He then answered that you would then need another plane if you wanted to take a photo that contained both the plane and the Native Americans. He was pleased with his idea and said "And then another one. And then another one. One after the other". He was therefore very much able to imagine the consequence of embeddings.

Culicover & Jackendoff (2005: 113–114) discuss visual perception and music as recursive systems that are independent of language. Jackendoff (2011) extends the discussion of visual perception and music and adds the domains of planning (with the example of making coffee) and wordless comic strips. Chomsky (2007: 7–8) claims that examples from visual perception are irrelevant but then admits that the ability to build up recursive structures could belong to general cognitive abilities (p. 8). He still attributes this ability to UG. He views UG as a subset of the Faculty of Language, that is, as a subset of non domain-specific abilities (Faculty of Language in the Broad Sense = FLB) and the

---

[29]Pinker & Jackendoff (2005: 230) note, however, that navigation differs from the kind of recursive system described by Chomsky and that recursion is not part of counting systems in all cultures. They assume that those cultures that have developed infinite counting systems could do this because of their linguistic capabilities. This is also assumed by Fitch, Hauser & Chomsky (2005: 203). The latter authors claim that all forms of recursion in other domains depend on language. For more on this point, see Chomsky (2007: 7–8). Luuk & Luuk (2011) note that natural numbers are defined recursively, but the mathematical definition does not necessarily play a role for the kinds of arithmetic operations carried out by humans.

domain-specific abilities (Faculty of Language in the Narrow Sense = FLN) required for language.

13.1.9 Summary

In sum, we can say that there are no linguistic universals for which there is a consensus that one has to assume domain-specific innate knowledge to explain them. At the 2008 meeting of the *Deutsche Gesellschaft für Sprachwissenschaft*, Wolfgang Klein promised € 100 to anyone who could name a non-trivial property that all languages share (see Klein 2009). This begs the question of what is meant by 'trivial'. It seems clear that all languages share predicate-argument structures and dependency relations in some sense (Hudson 2010b; Longobardi & Roberts 2010: 2701) and, all languages have complex expressions whose meaning can be determined compositionally (Manfred Krifka was promised 20 € for coming up with compositionality). However, as has been noted at various points, universality by no means implies innateness (Bates 1984: 189; Newmeyer 2005: 205): Newmeyer gives the example that words for sun and moon probably exist in all languages. This has to do with the fact that these celestial bodies play an important role in everyone's lives and thus one needs words to refer to them. It cannot be concluded from this that the corresponding concepts have to be innate. Similarly, a word that is used to express a relation between two objects (e.g., *catch*) has to be connected to the words describing both of these objects (*I, elephant*) in a transparent way. However, this does not necessarily entail that this property of language is innate.

Even if we can find structural properties shared by all languages, this is still not proof of innate linguistic knowledge, as these similarities could be traced back to other factors. It is argued that all languages must be made in such a way as to be acquirable with the paucity of resource available to small children (Hurford 2002: Section 10.7.2; Behrens 2009: 433). It follows from this that, in the relevant phases of its development, our brain is a constraining factor. Languages have to fit into our brains and since our brains are similar, languages are also similar in certain respects (see Kluender 1992: 251).

13.2 Speed of language acquisition

It is often argued that children learn language extraordinarily quickly and this can only be explained by assuming that they already possess knowledge about language that does not have to be acquired (e.g., Chomsky 1976b: 144; Hornstein 2013: 395). In order for this argument to hold up to closer scrutiny, it must be demonstrated that other areas of knowledge with a comparable degree of complexity require longer to acquire (Sampson 1989: 214–218). This has not yet been shown. Language acquisition spans several years and it is not possible to simply state that language is acquired following *brief exposure*. Chomsky compares languages to physics and points out that it is considerably more difficult for us to acquire knowledge about physics. Sampson (1989: 215) notes, however, that the knowledge about physics one acquires at school or university is not a basis for comparison and one should instead consider the acquisition of everyday knowledge

13 The innateness of linguistic knowledge

about the physical world around us. For example, the kind of knowledge we need when we want to pour liquids into a container, skip with a skipping rope or the knowledge we have about the ballistic properties of objects. The complexity in comparing these domains of knowledge in order to be able to make claims about language acquisition may turn out to be far from trivial. For an in-depth discussion of this aspect, see Sampson (1989: 214–218). Müller & Riemer (1998: 1) point out that children at the age of six can understand 23,700 words and use over 5000. It follows from this that, in the space of four and a half years, they learn on average 14 new words every day. This is indeed an impressive feat, but cannot be used as an argument for innate linguistic knowledge as all theories of acquisition assume that words have to be learned from data rather than being predetermined by a genetically-determined Universal Grammar. In any case the assumption of genetic encoding would be highly implausible for newly created words such as *fax, iPod, e-mail, Tamagotchi*.

Furthermore, the claim that first language acquisition is effortless and rapid when compared to second language acquisition is a myth as has been shown by estimations by Klein (1986: 9): if we assume that children hear linguistic utterances for five hours a day (as a conservative estimate), then in the first five years of their lives, they have 9100 hours of linguistic training. But at the age of five, they have still not acquired all complex constructions. In comparison, second-language learners, assuming the necessary motivation, can learn the grammar of a language rather well in a six-week crash course with twelve hours a day (500 hours in total).

13.3 Critical period for acquisition

Among ducks, there is a critical phase in which their behavior towards parent figures is influenced significantly. Normally, baby ducks follow their mother. If, however, a human is present rather than the mother during a particular time span, the ducks will follow the human. After the critical period, this influence on their behavior can no longer be identified (Lorenz 1970). This kind of critical period can also be identified in other animals and in other areas of cognition, for example the acquisition of visual abilities among primates. Certain abilities are acquired in a given time frame, whereby the presence of the relevant input is important for determining the start of this time frame.

Lenneberg (1964) claims that language acquisition is only possible up to the age of twelve and concludes from the fact that children can learn language much better than adults that this is also due to a critical period and that language acquisition must have similar properties to the behavior of ducks and hence, the predisposition for language acquisition must be innate (Lenneberg 1967: Chapter 4).

The assumptions about the length of the critical period for language acquisition vary considerably. It is possible to find suggestions for 5, 6, 12 and even 15 years (Hakuta et al. 2003: 31). Meisel (2013: 79) talks about "different points of development between 4 and 16 years". An alternative assumption to a critical period would be to assume that the ability to acquire languages decreases continuously over time. Johnson & Newport (1989) tried to determine a critical period for second-language acquisition and they claim that a second language is learned significantly worse from the age of 15. Elman, Bates, Johnson, Karmiloff-Smith, Parisi & Plunkett (1996: 187–188) have, however, pointed out that there is a different curve for Johnson and Newport's data that fits the individual data better. The alternative curve shows no abrupt change but rather a steady decrease in the ability to learn language and therefore offers no proof of an effect created by a critical period.

Hakuta, Bialystok & Wiley (2003) evaluate data from a questionnaire of 2,016,317 Spanish speakers and 324,444 speakers of Mandarin Chinese that immigrated to the United States. They investigated which correlations there were between age, the point at immigration, the general level of education of the speakers and the level of English they acquired. They could not identify a critical point in time after which language acquisition was severely restricted. Instead, there is a steady decline in the ability to learn as age increases. This can also be observed in other domains: for example, learning to drive at an older age is much harder.

Summing up, it seems to be relatively clear that a critical period cannot be proven to exist for second-language acquisition. Sometimes, it is assumed anyway that second-language acquisition is not driven by an innate UG, but is in fact a learning process that accesses knowledge already acquired during the critical period (Lenneberg 1967: 176). One would therefore have to show that there is a critical period for first-language acquisition. This is, however, not straightforward as, for ethical reasons, one cannot experimentally manipulate the point at which the input is available. We cannot, say, take 20 children and let them grow up without linguistic input to the age of 3, 4, 5, 6, … or 15 and then compare the results. This kind of research is dependent on thankfully very rare cases of neglect. For example, Curtiss (1977) studied a girl called Genie. At the time, Genie was 13 years old and had grown up in isolation. She is a so-called feral child. As Curtiss showed, she was no longer able to learn certain linguistic rules. For an objective comparison, one would need other test subjects that had not grown up in complete isolation and in inhumane conditions. The only possibility of gaining relevant experimental data is to study deaf subjects that did not receive any input from a sign language up to a certain age. Johnson & Newport (1989: 63) carried out relevant experiments with learners of American Sign Language. It was also shown here that there is a linear decline in the ability to learn, however nothing like a sudden drop after a certain age or even a complete loss of the ability to acquire language.

13.4 Lack of acquisition among non-human primates

The fact that non-human primates cannot learn natural language is viewed as evidence for the genetic determination of our linguistic ability. All scientists agree on the fact that there are genetically-determined differences between humans and primates and that these are relevant for linguistic ability. Friederici (2009) offers an overview of the literature that claims that in chimpanzees and macaques (and small children), the connections between parts of the brain are not as developed as in adult humans. The connected regions of the brain are together responsible for the processing of lexical-semantic knowledge and could constitute an important prerequisite for the development of language (p. 179).

The question is, however, whether we differ from other primates in having special cognitive capabilities that are specific to language or whether our capability to acquire languages is due to domain-general differences in cognition. Fanselow (1992b: Section 2) speaks of a human-specific formal competence that does not necessarily have to be specific to language, however. Similarly, Chomsky (2007: 7–8) has considered whether Merge (the only structure-building operation, in his opinion), does not belong to language-specific innate abilities, but rather to general human-specific competence (see, however, Section 13.1.8, in particular footnote 29).

One can ascertain that non-human primates do not understand particular pointing gestures. Humans like to imitate things. Other primates also imitate, however, not for social reasons (Tomasello 2006b: 9–10). According to Tomasello et al. (2005: 676), only humans have the ability and motivation to carry out coordinated activities with common goals and socially-coordinated action plans. Primates do understand intentional actions, however, only humans act with a common goal in mind (*shared intentionality*). Only humans use and understand hand gestures (Tomasello et al. 2005: 685, 724, 726). Language is collaborative to a high degree: symbols are used to refer to objects and sometimes also to the speaker or hearer. In order to be able to use this kind of communication system, one has to be able to put oneself in the shoes of the interlocutor and develop common expectations and goals (Tomasello et al. 2005: 683). Non-human primates could thus lack the social and cognitive prerequisites for language, that is, the difference between humans and other primates does not have to be explained by innate linguistic knowledge (Tomasello 2003: Section 8.1.2; Tomasello et al. 2005).

13.5 Creole and sign languages

When speakers that do not share a common language wish to communicate with each other, they develop so-called pidgin languages. These are languages that use parts of the vocabularies of the languages involved but have a very rudimentary grammar. It has been noted that children of pidgin speakers regularize these languages. The next generation of speakers creates a new language with an independent grammar. These languages are referred to as *creole languages*. One hypothesis is that the form of languages that develop from creolization is restricted by an innate UG (Bickerton 1984b). It is assumed that the parameter setting of creole languages corresponds to the default values of parameters (Bickerton 1984a: 217; 1984b: 178), that is, parameters already have values at birth and these correspond to the values that creole languages have. These default values would have to be modified when learning other languages.[30] Bickerton claims that creole languages contain elements that language learners could not have acquired from the input, that is from the pidgin languages. His argumentation is a variant of the classic Poverty of the Stimulus Argument that will be discussed in more detail in Section 13.8.

---

[30]For problems that can arise from the assumption of defaults values, see Meisel (1995: 17). Bickerton (1997: 56, fn. 13) distances himself from the claim that creole languages have the default values of parameters.

Bickerton's claims have been criticized as it cannot be verified whether children had input in the individual languages of the adults (Samarin 1984: 207; Seuren 1984: 209). All that can be said considering this lack of evidence is that there are a number of demographic facts that suggest that this was the case for at least some creole languages (Arends 2008). This means that children did not only have the strings from the pidgin languages as an input but also sentences from the individual languages spoken by parents and others around them. Many creolists assume that adults contribute specific grammatical forms to the emerging language. For example, in the case of Hawaiian Creole English one can observe that there are influences from the mother tongues of the speakers involved: Japanese speakers use SOV order as well as SVO and Philippinos use VOS order as well as SVO order. In total, there is quite a lot of variation in the language that can be traced back to the various native languages of the individual speakers.

It is also possible to explain the effects observed for creolization without the assumption of innate language-specific knowledge: the fact that children regularize language can be attributed to a phenomenon independent of language. In experiments, participants were shown two light bulbs and the test subjects had to predict which of the light bulbs would be turned on next. If one of the bulbs was switched on 70% of the time, the participants also picked this one 70% of the time (although they would have actually had a higher success rate if they had always chosen the bulb turned on with 70% probability). This behavior is known as *Probability Matching*. If we add another light bulb to this scenario and then turn this lamp on in 70% of cases and the other two each 15% of the time, then participants choose the more frequently lit one 80–90% of the time, that is, they regularize in the direction of the most frequent occurrence (Gardner 1957; Weir 1964).

Children regularize more than adults (Hudson & Newport 1999; Hudson Kam & Newport 2005), a fact that can be traced back to their limited brain capacity ("less is more"-hypothesis, Newport 1990; Elman 1993).

Like creolization, a similar situation can be found in certain social contexts with the acquisition of sign language: Singleton & Newport (2004) have shown that a child (Simon) that learned American Sign Language (ASL) makes considerably less mistakes than his parents. The parents first learned ASL at the age of 15 or 16 and performed particular obligatory movements only 70% of the time. Simon made these movements 90% of the time. He regularized the input from his parents, whereby the consistent use of form-meaning pairs plays an important role, that is, he does not simply use Probability Matching, but learns selectively. Singleton & Newport (2004: 401) suspect that these kinds of regularizations also play a role for the emergence of creole and sign languages. However, the relevant statistical data that one would need to confirm this hypothesis are not available.

13.6 Localization in special parts of the brain

By measuring brain activity during speech production/processing and also by investigating patients with brain damage, one can identify special parts of the brain (Broca's area and Wernicke's area) that play an important role for language production and processing (see Friederici (2009) for a current overview). Chomsky talks about there being a center of language and even calls this (metaphorically) an *organ* (Chomsky 1977: 164; Chomsky 2005: 1; Chomsky 2008: 133). This localization was seen as evidence for the innate basis for our linguistic knowledge (see also Pinker 1994: 297–314).

However, it is the case that if these parts are damaged, other areas of the brain can take over the relevant functions. If the damage occurs in early childhood, language can also be learned without these special areas of the brain (for sources, see Dąbrowska 2004: Section 4.1).

Apart from that, it can also be observed that a particular area of the brain is activated when reading. If the conclusion about the localization of processing in a particular part of the brain leading to the innateness of linguistic knowledge were valid, then the activation of certain areas of the brain during reading should also lead us to conclude that the ability to read is innate (Elman et al. 1996: 242; Bishop 2002: 57). This is, however, not assumed (see also Fitch, Hauser & Chomsky 2005: 196).

It should also be noted that language processing affects several areas of the brain and not just Broca's and Wernicke's areas (Fisher & Marcus 2005: 11; Friederici 2009). On the other hand, Broca's and Wernicke's areas are also active during non-linguistic tasks such as imitation, motoric coordination and processing of music (Maess et al. 2001). For an overview and further sources, see Fisher & Marcus (2005).

Musso et al. (2003) investigated brain activity during second-language acquisition. They gave German native speakers data from Italian and Japanese and noticed that there was activation in Broca's area. They then compared this to artificial languages that used Italian and Japanese words but did not correspond to the principles of Universal Grammar as assumed by the authors. An example of the processes assumed in their artificial language is the formation of questions by reversing of word order as shown in (39).

(39) a. This is a statement.
 b. Statement a is this?

The authors then observed that different areas of the brain were activated when learning this artificial language. This is an interesting result, but does not show that we have innate linguistic knowledge. It only shows that the areas that are active when processing our native languages are also active when we learn other languages and that playing around with words such as reversing the order of words in a sentence affects other areas of the brain.

A detailed discussion of localization of languages in particular parts of the brain can be found in Dąbrowska (2004: Chapter 4).

13.7 Differences between language and general cognition

Researchers who believe that there is no such thing as innate linguistic knowledge assume that language can be acquired with general cognitive means. If it can be shown that humans with severely impaired cognition can still acquire normal linguistic abilities or that there are people of normal intelligence whose linguistic ability is restricted, then one can show that language and general cognition are independent.

13.7.1 Williams Syndrome

There are people with a relatively low IQ, who can nevertheless produce grammatical utterances. Among these are people with Williams Syndrome (see Bellugi, Lichtenberger, Jones, Lai & George (2000) for a discussion of the abilities of people with Williams Syndrome). Yamada (1981) takes the existence of such cases as evidence for a separate module of grammar, independent of the remaining intelligence.

IQ is determined by dividing a score in an intelligence test (the mental age) by chronological age. The teenagers that were studied all had a mental age corresponding to that of a four to six year-old child. Yet children at this age already boast impressive linguistic ability that comes close to that of adults in many respects. Gosch, Städing & Pankau (1994: 295) have shown that children with Williams Syndrome do show a linguistic deficit and that their language ability corresponds to what would be expected from their mental age. For problems of sufferers of Williams Syndrome in the area of morphosyntax, see Karmiloff-Smith et al. (1997). The discussion about Williams Syndrome is summarized nicely in Karmiloff-Smith (1998).

13.7.2 KE family with FoxP2 mutation

There is a British family – the so-called KE family – that has problems with language. The members of this family who suffer from these linguistic problems have a genetic defect. Fisher et al. (1998) and Lai et al. (2001) discovered that this is due to a mutation of the FoxP2 gene (FoxP2 stands for *Forkhead-Box P2*). Gopnik & Cargo (1991) conclude from the fact that deficits in the realm of morphology are inherited with genetic defects that there must be a gene that is responsible for a particular module of grammar (morphology). Vargha-Khadem et al. (1995: 930) have demonstrated, however, that the KE family did not just have problems with morphosyntax: the affected family members have intellectual and linguistic problems together with motoric problems with facial muscles. Due to the considerably restricted motion in their facial muscles, it would make sense to assume that their linguistic difficulties also stem from motory problems (Tomasello 2003: 285). The linguistic problems in the KE family are not just limited to production problems, however, but also comprehension problems (Bishop 2002: 58). Nevertheless, one cannot associate linguistic deficiencies directly with FoxP2 as there are a number of other abilities that are affected by the FoxP2 mutation: as well as hindering pronunciation, morphology and syntax, it also has an effect on non-verbal IQ and motory problems with the facial muscles, dealing with non-linguistic tasks, too (Vargha-Khadem et al. 1995).

Furthermore, FoxP2 also occurs in other body tissues: it is also responsible for the development of the lungs, the heart, the intestine and various regions of the brain (Marcus & Fisher 2003). Marcus & Fisher (2003: 260–261) point out that FoxP2 is probably not directly responsible for the development of organs or areas of organs but rather regulates a cascade of different genes. FoxP2 can therefore not be referred to as the language gene, it is just a gene that interacts with other genes in complex ways. It is, among other things, important for our language ability, however, in the same way that it does not make sense to call FoxP2 a language gene, nobody would connect a hereditary muscle disorder with a 'walking gene' just because this myopathy prevents upright walking

(Bishop 2002: 58). A similar argument can be found in Karmiloff-Smith (1998: 392): there is a genetic defect that leads some people to begin to lose their hearing from the age of ten and become completely deaf by age thirty. This genetic defect causes changes in the hairs inside the ear that one requires for hearing. In this case, one would also not want to talk about a 'hearing gene'.

Fitch, Hauser & Chomsky (2005: 190) are also of the opinion that FoxP2 cannot be responsible for linguistic knowledge. For an overview of this topic, see Bishop (2002) and Dąbrowska (2004: Section 6.4.2.2) and for genetic questions in general, see Fisher & Marcus (2005).

13.8 Poverty of the Stimulus

An important argument for the innateness of the linguistic knowledge is the so-called Poverty of the Stimulus Argument (PSA) (Chomsky 1980: 34). Different versions of it can be found in the literature and have been carefully discussed by Pullum & Scholz (2002). After discussing these variants, they summarize the logical structure of the argument as follows (p. 18):

(40)   a. Human children learn their first language either by data-driven learning or by learning supported by innate knowledge (a disjunctive premise by assumption)

       b. If children learn their first language by data-driven learning, then they could not acquire anything for which they did not have the necessary evidence (the definition of data-driven learning)

       c. However, children do in fact learn things that they do not seem to have decisive evidence for (empirical prerequisite)

       d. Therefore, children do not learn their first language by data-driven learning. (*modus tollens* of b and c)

       e. Conclusion: children learn language through a learning process supported by innate knowledge. (disjunctive syllogism of a and d)

Pullum and Scholz then discuss four phenomena that have been claimed to constitute evidence for there being innate linguistic knowledge. These are plurals as initial parts of compounds in English (Gordon 1985), sequences of auxiliaries in English (Kimball 1973), anaphoric *one* in English (Baker 1978) and the position of auxiliaries in English (Chomsky 1971: 29–33). Before I turn to these cases in Section 13.8.2, I will discuss a variant of the PSA that refers to the formal properties of phrase structure grammars.

13.8.1 Gold's Theorem

In theories of formal languages, a language is viewed as a set containing all the expressions belonging to a particular language. This kind of set can be captured using various

13.8 Poverty of the Stimulus

complex rewrite grammars. A kind of rewrite grammar – so-called context-free grammars – was presented in Chapter 2. In context-free grammars, there is always exactly one symbol on the left-hand side of the rule (a so-called non-terminal symbol) and there can be more of these on the right-hand side of the rule. On the right side there can be symbols (so-called non-terminal symbols) or words/morphemes of the language in question (so-called terminal symbols). The words in a grammar are also referred to as vocabulary (V). Part of a formal grammar is a start symbol, which is usually S. In the literature, this has been criticized since not all expressions are sentences (see Deppermann 2006: 44). It is, however, not necessary to assume this. It is possible to use Utterance as the start symbol and define rules that derive S, NP, VP or whatever else one wishes to class as an utterance from Utterance.[31]

Beginning with the start symbol, one can keep applying phrase structure rules in a grammar until one arrives at sequences that only contain words (terminal symbols). The set of all sequences that one can generate are the expressions that belong to the language that is licensed by the grammar. This set is a subset of all sequences of words or morphemes that can be created by arbitrary combination. The set that contains all possible sequences is referred to as V^*.

Gold (1967) has shown that in an environment E, it is not possible to solve the identification problem for any language from particular languages classes, given a finite amount of linguistic input, without additional knowledge. Gold is concerned with the identification of a language from a given class of languages. A language L counts as identified if at a given point in time t_n, a learner can determine that L is the language in question and does not change this hypothesis. This point in time is not determined in advance, however, identification has to take place at some point. Gold calls this *identification in the limit*. The environments are arbitrary infinite sequences of sentences $\langle a_1, a_2, a_3, ...\rangle$, whereby each sentence in the language must occur at least once in this sequence. In order to show that the identification problem cannot be solved for even very simple language classes, Gold considers the class of languages that contain all possible sequences of words from the vocabulary V expect for one sequence: let V be the vocabulary and $x_1, x_2, x_3, ...$ the sequences of words from this vocabulary. The set of all strings from this vocabulary is V^*. For the class of languages in (41), which consist of all possible sequences of elements in V with the exception of one sequence, it is possible to state a process of how one could learn these languages from a text.

(41) $L_1 = V^* - x_1, L_2 = V^* - x_2, L_3 = V^* - x_3, ...$

After every input, one can guess that the language is $V^* - \sigma$, where σ stands for the alphabetically first sequence with the shortest length that has not yet been seen. If the sequence in question occurs later, then this hypothesis is revised accordingly. In this way, one will eventually arrive at the correct language.

---

[31] On page 279, I discussed a description that corresponds to the S symbol in phrase structure grammars. If one omits the specification of head features in this description, then one gets a description of all complete phrases, that is, also *the man* or *now*. See also Ginzburg & Sag (2000: Section 8.1.4) for a unary branching rule that projects an utterance fragment to a sentential category incorporating the utterance context. See Nykiel & Kim (2019) for further details and references on ellipsis in HPSG.

If we expand the set of languages from which we have to choose by V^*, then our learning process will no longer work since, if V^* is the target language, then the guessing will perpetually yield incorrect results. If there were a procedure capable of learning this language class, then it would have to correctly identify V^* after a certain number of inputs. Let us assume that this input is x_k. How can the learning procedure tell us at this point that the language we are looking for is not $V^* - x_j$ for $j \neq k$? If x_k causes one to guess the wrong grammar V^*, then every input that comes after that will be compatible with both the correct ($V^* - x_j$) and incorrect (V^*) result. Since we only have positive data, no input allows us to distinguish between either of the hypotheses and provide the information that we have found a superset of the language we are looking for. Gold has shown that none of the classes of grammars assumed in the theory of formal languages (for example, regular, context-free and context-sensitive languages) can be identified after a finite amount of steps given the input of a text with example utterances. This is true for all classes of languages that contain all finite languages and at least one infinite language. The situation is different if positive and negative data are used for learning instead of text.

The conclusion that has been drawn from Gold's results is that, for language acquisition, one requires knowledge that helps to avoid particular hypotheses from the start. Pullum (2003) criticizes the use of Gold's findings as evidence for the fact that linguistic knowledge must be innate. He lists a number of assumptions that have to be made in order for Gold's results to be relevant for the acquisition of natural languages. He then shows that each of these is not uncontroversial.

1. Natural languages could belong to the class of text-learnable languages as opposed to the class of context-free grammars mentioned above.

2. Learners could have information about which sequences of words are not grammatical (see p. 453–454 of Gold's essay for a similar conjecture). As has been shown since then, children do have direct negative evidence and there is also indirect negative evidence (see Section 13.8.4).

3. It is not clear whether learners really restrict themselves to exactly one grammar. Feldman (1972) has developed a learning procedure that eliminates all incorrect grammars at some point and is infinitely many times correct but it does not have to always choose one correct grammar and stick to the corresponding hypothesis. Using this procedure, it is possible to learn all recursively enumerable languages, that is, all languages for which there is a generative grammar. Pullum notes that even Feldman's learning procedure could prove to be too restrictive. It could take an entire lifetime for a learner to reach the correct grammar and they could have incorrect yet increasingly better hypotheses along the way.

4. Learners could work in terms of improvements. If one allows for a certain degree of tolerance, then acquisition is easier and it even becomes possible to learn the class of recursively enumerable languages (Wharton 1974).

5. Language acquisition does not necessarily constitute the acquisition of knowledge about a particular set of sequences, that is, the acquisition of a generative grammar capable of creating this set. The situation is completely different if grammars are viewed as a set of constraints that partially describe linguistic structures, but not necessarily a unique set of linguistic structures (for more on this point, see Section 6.7 and Chapter 14).

Furthermore, Pullum notes that it is also possible to learn the class of context-sensitive grammars with Gold's procedure with positive input only in a finite number of steps if there is an upper bound k for the number of rules, where k is an arbitrary number. It is possible to make k so big that the cognitive abilities of the human brain would not be able to use a grammar with more rules than this. Since it is normally assumed that natural languages can be described by context-sensitive grammars, it can therefore be shown that the syntax of natural languages in Gold's sense can be learned from texts (see also Scholz & Pullum 2002: 195–196).

Johnson (2004) adds that there is another important point that has been overlooked in the discussion about language acquisition. Gold's problem of identifiability is different from the problem of language acquisition that has played an important role in the nativism debate. In order to make the difference clear, Johnson differentiates between identifiability (in the Goldian sense) and learnability in the sense of language acquisition. Identifiability for a language class C means that there must be a function f that for each environment E for each language L in C permanently converges on hypothesis L as the target language in a finite amount of time.

Johnson proposes the following as the definition of *learnability* (p. 585): *A class C of natural languages is learnable iff, given almost any normal human child and almost any normal linguistic environment for any language L in C, the child will acquire L (or something sufficiently similar to L) as a native language between the ages of one and five.* Johnson adds the caveat that this definition does not correspond to any theory of learnability in psycholinguistics, but rather it is a hint in the direction of a realistic conception of acquisition.

Johnson notes that in most interpretations of Gold's theorem, identifiability and learnability are viewed as one and the same and shows that this is not logically correct: the main difference between the two depends on the use of two quantifiers. Identifiability of *one* language L from a class C requires that the learner converges on L in *every* environment after a finite amount of time. This time can differ greatly from environment to environment. There is not even an upper bound for the time in question. It is straightforward to construct a sequence of environments $E_1, E_2, \ldots$ for L, so that a learner in the environment E_i will not guess L earlier than the time t_i. Unlike identifiability, learnability means that there is a point in time after which in every normal environment, *every* normal child has converged on the correct language. This means that children acquire their language after a particular time span. Johnson quotes Morgan (1989: 352) claiming that children learn their native language after they have heard approximately 4,280,000 sentences. If we assume that the concept of learnability has a finite upper-bound for available time, then very few language classes can be identified in the limit. Johnson has shown this as follows: let C be a class of languages containing L and L', where L and L'

have some elements in common. It is possible to construct a text such that the first *n* sentences are contained both in *L* and in *L′*. If the learner has *L* as its working hypothesis then continue the text with sentences from *L′*, if he has *L′* as his hypothesis, then continue with sentences from *L*. In each case, the learner has entertained a false hypothesis after *n* steps. This means that identifiability is not a plausible model for language acquisition.

Aside from the fact that identifiability is psychologically unrealistic, it is not compatible with learnability (Johnson 2004: 586). For identifiability, only one learner has to be found (the function *f* mentioned above), learnability, however, quantifies over (almost) all normal children. If one keeps all factors constant, then it is easier to show the identifiability of a language class rather than its learnability. On the one hand, identifiability quantifies universally over all environments, regardless of whether these may seem odd or of how many repetitions these may contain. Learnability, on the other hand, has (almost) universal quantification exclusively over normal environments. Therefore, learnability refers to fewer environments than identifiability, such that there are less possibilities for problematic texts that could occur as an input and render a language unlearnable. Furthermore, learnability is defined in such a way that the learner does not have to learn *L* exactly, but rather learn something sufficiently similar to *L*. With respect to this aspect, learnability is a weaker property of a language class than identifiability. Therefore, learnability does not follow from identifiability nor the reverse.

Finally, Gold is dealing with the acquisition of syntactic knowledge without taking semantic knowledge into consideration. However, children possess a vast amount of information from the context that they employ when acquiring a language (Tomasello et al. 2005). As pointed out by Klein (1986: 44), humans do not learn anything if they are placed in a room and sentences in Mandarin Chinese are played to them. Language is acquired in a social and cultural context.

In sum, one should note that the existence of innate linguistic knowledge cannot be derived from mathematical findings about the learnability of languages.

13.8.2 Four case studies

Pullum & Scholz (2002) have investigated four prominent instances of the Poverty of the Stimulus Argument in more detail. These will be discussed in what follows. Pullum and Scholz's article appeared in a discussion volume. Arguments against their article are addressed by Scholz & Pullum (2002) in the same volume. Further PoS arguments from Chomsky (1986b) and from literature in German have been disproved by Eisenberg (1992).

13.8.2.1 Plurals in noun-noun compounding

Gordon (1985) claims that compounds in English only allow irregular plurals in compounds, that is, *mice-eater* but ostensibly not **rats-eater*. Gordon claims that compounds with irregular plurals as first element are so rare that children could not have learned the fact that such compounds are possible purely from data.

13.8 Poverty of the Stimulus

On pages 25–26, Pullum & Scholz discuss data from English that show that regular plurals can indeed occur as the first element of a compound (*chemicals-maker, forms-reader, generics-maker, securities-dealer, drinks trolley, rules committee, publications catalogue*).[32] This shows that what could have allegedly not been learned from data is in fact not linguistically adequate and one therefore does not have to explain its acquisition.

13.8.2.2 Position of auxiliaries

The second study deals with the position of modal and auxiliary verbs. Kimball (1973: 73–75) discusses the data in (42) and the rule in (43) that is similar to one of the rules suggested by Chomsky (1957: 39) and is designed to capture the following data:

(42)   a. It rains.

        b. It may rain.

        c. It may have rained.

        d. It may be raining.

        e. It has rained.

        f. It has been raining.

        g. It is raining.

        h. It may have been raining.

(43)   Aux → T(M)(have+en)(be+ing)

T stands for tense, M for a modal verb and *en* stands for the participle morpheme (*-en* in *been/seen/...* and *-ed* in *rained*). The brackets here indicate the optionality of the expressions. Kimball notes that it is only possible to formulate this rule if (42h) is well-formed. If this were not the case, then one would have to reorganize the material in rules such that the three cases (M)(have+en), (M)(be+ing) and (have+en)(be+ing) would be covered. Kimball assumes that children master the complex rule since they know that sentences such as (42h) are well-formed and since they know the order in which modal and auxiliary verbs must occur. Kimball assumes that children do not have positive evidence for the order in (42h) and concludes from this that the knowledge about the rule in (43) must be innate.

Pullum and Scholz note two problems with this Poverty of the Stimulus Argument: first, they have found hundreds of examples, among them some from children's stories, so that the Kimball's claim that sentences such as (42h) are "vanishingly rare" should be called into question. For PSA arguments, one should at least specify how many occurrences there are allowed to be if one still wants to claim that nothing can be learned from them (Pullum & Scholz 2002: 29).

The second problem is that it does not make sense to assume that the rule in (42h) plays a role in our linguistic knowledge. Empirical findings have shown that this rule is not descriptively adequate. If the rule in (43) is not descriptively adequate, then it cannot

---

[32] Also, see Abney (1996: 7) for examples from the Wall Street Journal.

achieve explanatory adequacy and therefore, one no longer has to explain how it can be acquired.

Instead of a rule such as (43), all theories discussed here currently assume that auxiliary or modal verbs embed a phrase, that is, one does not have an Aux node containing all auxiliary and modal verbs, but rather a structure for (42h) that looks as follows:

(44)   It [may [have [been raining]]].

Here, the auxiliary or modal verb always selects the embedded phrase. The acquisition problem now looks completely different: a speaker has to learn the form of the head verb in the verbal projection selected by the auxiliary or modal verb. If this information has been learned, then it is irrelevant how complex the embedded verbal projections are: *may* can be combined with a non-finite lexical verb (42b) or a non-finite auxiliary (42c,d).

13.8.2.3 Reference of *one*

The third case study investigated by Pullum and Scholz deals with the pronoun *one* in English. Baker (1978: 413–425, 327–340) claims that children cannot learn that *one* can refer to constituents larger than a single word as in (45).

(45)   a. I would like to tell you another funny story, but I've already told you the only *one* I know.
       b. The old man from France was more erudite than the young *one*.

Baker (416–417) claims that *one* can never refer to single nouns inside of NPs and supports this with examples such as (46):

(46)   * The student of chemistry was more thoroughly prepared than the one of physics.

According to Baker, learners would require negative data in order to acquire this knowledge about ungrammaticality. Since learners – following his argumentation – never have access to negative evidence, they cannot possibly have learned the relevant knowledge and must therefore already possess it.

Pullum & Scholz (2002: 33) point out that there are acceptable examples with the same structure as the examples in (46):

(47)   a. I'd rather teach linguistics to a student of mathematics than to one of any discipline in the humanities.
       b. An advocate of Linux got into a heated discussion with one of Windows NT and the rest of the evening was nerd talk.

This means that there is nothing to learn with regard to the well-formedness of the structure in (46). Furthermore, the available data for acquiring the fact that *one* can refer to larger constituents is not as hopeless as Baker (p. 416) claims: there are examples that only allow an interpretation where *one* refers to a larger string of words. Pullum and Scholz offer examples from various corpora. They also provide examples from the CHILDES corpus, a corpus that contains communication with children (MacWhinney 1995). The following example is from a daytime TV show:

(48)   A: "Do you think you will ever remarry again? I don't."
      B: "Maybe I will, someday. But he'd have to be somebody very special. Sensitive and supportive, giving. Hey, wait a minute, where do they make guys like this?"
      A: "I don't know. I've never seen one up close."

Here, it is clear that *one* cannot refer to *guys* since A has certainly already seen *guys*. Instead, it refers to *guys like this*, that is, men who are sensitive and supportive.

Once again, the question arises here as to how many instances a learner has to hear for it to count as evidence in the eyes of proponents of the PSA.

13.8.2.4 Position of auxiliaries in polar questions

The fourth PoS argument discussed by Pullum and Scholz comes from Chomsky and pertains to the position of the auxiliary in polar interrogatives in English. As shown on page 97, it was assumed in GB theory that a polar question is derived by movement of the auxiliary from the I position to the initial position C of the sentence. In early versions of Transformational Grammar, the exact analyses were different, but the main point was that the highest auxiliary is moved to the beginning of the clause. Chomsky (1971: 29–33) discusses the sentences in (49) and claims that children know that they have to move the highest auxiliary verb even without having positive evidence for this.[33] If, for example, they entertained the hypothesis that one simply places the first auxiliary at the beginning of the sentence, then this hypothesis would deliver the correct result (49b) for (49a), but not for (49c) since the polar question should be (49d) and not (49e).

(49)   a.   The dog in the corner is hungry.
       b.   Is the dog in the corner hungry?
       c.   The dog that is in the corner is hungry.
       d.   Is the dog that is in the corner hungry?
       e.   * Is the dog that in the corner is hungry?

Chomsky claims that children do not have any evidence for the fact that the hypothesis that one simply fronts the linearly first auxiliary is wrong, which is why they could pursue this hypothesis in a data-driven learning process. He even goes so far as to claim that speakers of English only rarely or even never produce examples such as (49d) (Chomsky in Piattelli-Palmarini (1980: 114–115)). With the help of corpus data and plausibly constructed examples, Pullum (1996) has shown that this claim is clearly wrong. Pullum (1996) provides examples from the Wall Street Journal and Pullum & Scholz (2002) discuss the relevant examples in more detail and add to them with examples from the CHILDES corpus showing that adult speakers cannot only produce the relevant kinds of

---

[33]Examples with auxiliary inversion are used in more recent PoS arguments too, for example in Berwick, Pietroski, Yankama & Chomsky (2011) and Chomsky (2013: 39). Work by Bod (2009b) is not discussed by the authors. For more on Bod's approach, see Section 13.8.3.

sentences, but also that these occur in the child's input.[34] Examples from CHILDES that disprove the hypothesis that the first auxiliary has to be fronted are given in (50):[35]

(50) a. Is the ball you were speaking of in the box with the bowling pin?
 b. Where's this little boy who's full of smiles?
 c. While you're sleeping, shall I make the breakfast?

Pullum and Scholz point out that *wh*-questions such as (50b) are also relevant if one assumes that these are derived from polar questions (see page 97 in this book) and if one wishes to show how the child can learn the structure-dependent hypothesis. This can be explained with the examples in (51): the base form from which (51a) is derived is (51b). If we were to front the first auxiliary in (51b), we would produce (51c).

(51) a. Where's the application Mark promised to fill out?[36]
 b. the application Mark [$_{AUX}$ PAST] promised to fill out [$_{AUX}$ is] there
 c. * Where did the application Mark promised to fill out is?

Evidence for the fact that (51c) is not correct can, however, also be found in language addressed to children. Pullum and Scholz provide the examples in (52):[37]

(52) a. Where's the little blue crib that was in the house before?
 b. Where's the other dolly that was in here?
 c. Where's the other doll that goes in there?

These questions have the form *Where's NP?*, where NP contains a relative clause.

In (50c), there is another clause preceding the actual interrogative, an adjunct clause containing an auxiliary as well. This sentence therefore provides evidence for falsehood of the hypothesis that the linearly first auxiliary must be fronted (Sampson 1989: 223).

In total, there are a number of attested sentence types in the input of children that would allow them to choose between the two hypotheses. Once again, the question arises as to how much evidence should be viewed as sufficient.

Pullum und Scholz's article has been criticized by Lasnik & Uriagereka (2002) and Legate & Yang (2002). Lasnik and Uriagereka argue that the acquisition problem is much bigger than presented by Pullum and Scholz since a learner without any knowledge about the language he was going to acquire could not just have the hypothesis in (53) that were discussed already but also the additional hypotheses in (54):

(53) a. Place the first auxiliary at the front of the clause.
 b. Place the first auxiliary in matrix-Infl at the front of the clause.

---

[34]For more on this point, see Sampson (1989: 223). Sampson cites part of a poem by William Blake, that is studied in English schools, as well as a children's encyclopedia. These examples surely do not play a role in acquisition of auxiliary position since this order is learned at the age of 3;2, that is, it has already been learned by the time children reach school age.

[35]See Lewis & Elman (2001). Researchers on language acquisition agree that the frequency of this kind of examples in communication with children is in fact very low. See Ambridge et al. (2008: 223).

[36]From the transcription of a TV program in the CHILDES corpus.

[37]These sentences are taken from NINA05.CHA in DATABASE/ENG/SUPPES/.

13.8 Poverty of the Stimulus

(54)   a.   Place any auxiliary at the front of the clause.

       b.   Place any finite auxiliary at the front of the clause.

Both hypotheses in (54) would be permitted by the sentences in (55):

(55)   a.   Is the dog in the corner hungry?

       b.   Is the dog that is in the corner hungry?

They would, however, also allow sentences such as (56):

(56)   * Is the dog that in the corner is hungry?

The question that must now be addressed is why all hypotheses that allow (56) should be discarded since the learners do not have any information in their natural-linguistic input about the fact that (56) is not possible. They are lacking negative evidence. If (55b) is present as positive evidence, then this by no means implies that the hypothesis in (53b) has to be the correct one. Lasnik and Uriagereka present the following hypotheses that would also be compatible with (55b):

(57)   a.   Place the first auxiliary in initial position (that follows a change in intonation).

       b.   Place the first auxiliary in initial position (that follows the first complete constituent).

       c.   Place the first auxiliary in initial position (that follows the first parsed semantic unit).

These hypotheses do not hold for sentences such as (58) that contain a conjunction:

(58)   Will those who are coming and those who are not coming raise their hands?

The hypotheses in (57) would also allow for sentences such as (59):

(59)   * Are those who are coming and those who not coming will raise their hands?

Speakers hearing sentences such as (58) can reject the hypotheses (57) and thereby rule out (59), however, it is still possible to think of analogous implausible hypotheses that are compatible with all data previously discussed.

Legate & Yang (2002) take up the challenge of Pullum and Scholz and explicitly state how many occurrences one needs to acquire a particular phenomenon. They write the following:

> Suppose we have two independent problems of acquisition, P_1 and P_2, each of which involves a binary decision. For P_1, let F_1 be the frequency of the data that can settle P_1 one way or another, and for P_2, F_2. Suppose further that children successfully acquire P_1 and P_2 at roughly the same developmental stage. Then, under any theory that makes quantitative predictions of language development, we expect F_1 and F_2 to be roughly the same. Conversely, if F_1 and F_2 turn out significantly different, then P_1 and P_2 must represent qualitatively different learning problems.
>
> Now let P_1 be the auxiliary inversion problem. The two choices are the structure-dependent hypothesis (3b-i) and the first auxiliary hypothesis (3a-i). (Legate & Yang 2002: 155)

The position of auxiliaries in English is learned by children at the age of 3;2. According to Legate and Yang, another acquisition phenomenon that is learned at the age of 3;2 is needed for comparison. The authors focus on subject drop[38], that is learned at 36 months (two months earlier than auxiliary inversion). According to the authors, acquisition problems involve a binary decision: in the first case, one has to choose between the two hypotheses in (53). In the second case, the learner has to determine whether a language uses overt subjects. The authors assume that the use of expletives such as *there* serves as evidence for learners that the language they are learning is not one with optional subjects. They then count the sentences in the CHILDES corpus that contain *there*-subjects and estimate F_2 at 1.2 % of the sentences heard by the learner. Since, in their opinion, we are dealing with equally difficult phenomena here, sentences such as (49d) and (52) should constitute 1.2 % of the input in order for auxiliary inversion to be learnable.

The authors then searched in the Nina and Adam corpora (both part of CHILDES) and note that 0.068 to 0.045 % of utterances have the form of (52) and none have the form of (49d). They conclude that this number is not sufficient as positive evidence.

Legate and Yang are right in pointing out that Pullum and Scholz's data from the Wall Street Journal are not necessarily relevant for language acquisition and also in pointing out that examples with complex subject noun phrases do not occur in the data or at least to a negligible degree. There are, however, three serious problems with their argumentation: first, there is no correlation between the occurrence of expletive subjects and the property of being a pro-drop language: Galician (Raposo & Uriagereka 1990: Section 2.5) is a pro-drop language with subject expletive pronouns, in Italian there is an existential expletive *ci*,[39] even though Italian counts as a pro-drop language, Franks (1995) lists Upper and Lower Sorbian as pro-drop languages that have expletives in subject position. Since therefore expletive pronouns have nothing to do with the pro-drop parameter, their frequency is irrelevant for the acquisition of a parameter value. If there were a correlation between the possibility of omitting subjects and the occurrence of subject expletives, then Norwegian and Danish children should learn that there has to be a subject in their languages earlier than children learning English since expletives occur a higher percentage of the time in Danish and Norwegian (Scholz & Pullum 2002: 220). In Danish, the constructions corresponding to *there*-constructions in English are twice as frequent. It is still unclear whether there are actually differences in rate of acquisition (Pullum 2009: 246).

Second, in constructing their Poverty of the Stimulus argument, Legate and Yang assume that there is innate linguistic knowledge (the pro-drop parameter). Therefore their argument is circular since it is supposed to show that the assumption of innate linguistic knowledge is indispensable (Scholz & Pullum 2002: 220).

The third problem in Legate and Yang's argumentation is that they assume that a transformational analysis is the only possibility. This becomes clear from the following citation (Legate & Yang 2002: 153):

---

[38]This phenomenon is also called *pro-drop*. For a detailed discussion of the pro-drop parameter see Section 16.1.

[39]However, *ci* is not treated as an expletive by all authors. See Remberger (2009) for an overview.

13.8 Poverty of the Stimulus

The correct operation for question formation is, of course, structure dependent: it involves parsing the sentence into structurally organized phrases, and fronting the auxiliary that follows the subject NP, which can be arbitrarily long:

(4)   a. Is [the woman who is singing] e happy?
        b. Has [the man that is reading a book] e eaten supper?

The analysis put forward by Chomsky (see page 97) is a transformation-based one, that is, a learner has to learn exactly what Legate and Yang describe: the auxiliary must move in front of the subject noun phrase. There are, however, alternative analyses that do not require transformations or equivalent mechanisms. If our linguistic knowledge does not contain any information about transformations, then their claim about what has to be learned is wrong. For example, one can assume, as in Categorial Grammar, that auxiliaries form a word class with particular distributional properties. One possible placement for them is initial positions as observed in questions, the alternative is after the subject (Villavicencio 2002: 104). There would then be the need to acquire information about whether the subject is realized to the left or to the right of its head. As an alternative to this lexicon-based analysis, one could pursue a Construction Grammar (Fillmore 1988: 44; 1999; Kay & Fillmore 1999: 18), Cognitive Grammar (Dąbrowska 2004: Chapter 9), or HPSG (Ginzburg & Sag 2000; Sag 2013) approach. In these frameworks, there are simply two[40] schemata for the two sequences that assign different meanings according to the order of verb and subject. The acquisition problem is then that the learners have to identify the corresponding phrasal patterns in the input. They have to realize that Aux NP VP is a well-formed structure in English that has interrogative semantics. The relevant theories of acquisition in the Construction Grammar-oriented literature have been very well worked out (see Section 16.3 and 16.4). Construction-based theories of acquisition are also supported by the fact that one can see that there are frequency effects, that is, auxiliary inversion is first produced by children for just a few auxiliaries and only in later phases of development is it then extended to all auxiliaries. If speakers have learned that auxiliary constructions have the pattern Aux NP VP, then the coordination data provided by Lasnik and Uriagereka in (58) no longer pose a problem since, if we only assign the first conjunct to the NP in the pattern Aux NP VP, then the rest of the coordinate structure (*and those who are not coming*) remains unanalyzed and cannot be incorporated into the entire sentence. The hearer is thereby forced to revise his assumption that *will those who are coming* corresponds to the sequence Aux NP in Aux NP VP and instead to use the entire NP *those who are coming and those who are not coming*. For acquisition, it is therefore enough to simply learn the pattern Aux NP VP first for some and then eventually for all auxiliaries in English. This has also been shown by Lewis & Elman (2001), who trained a neural network exclusively with data that did not contain NPs with relative clauses in auxiliary constructions. Relative clauses were, however, present in other structures. The complexity of the training material was increased bit by

---

[40] Fillmore (1999) assumes subtypes of the Subject Auxiliary Inversion Construction since this kind of inversion does not only occur in questions.

bit just as is the case for the linguistic input that children receive (Elman 1993).[41] The neural network can predict the next symbol after a sequence of words. For sentences with interrogative word order, the predictions are correct. Even the relative pronoun in (60) is predicted despite the sequence Aux Det N Relp never occurring in the training material.

(60) Is the boy who is smoking crazy?

Furthermore, the system signals an error if the network is presented with the ungrammatical sentence (61):

(61) * Is the boy who smoking is crazy?

A present participle is not expected after the relative pronoun, but rather a finite verb. The constructed neural network is of course not yet an adequate model of what is going on in our heads during acquisition and speech production.[42] The experiment shows, however, that the input that the learner receives contains rich statistical information that can be used when acquiring language. Lewis and Elman point out that the statistical information about the distribution of words in the input is not the only information that speakers have. In addition to information about distribution, they are also exposed to information about the context and can make use of phonological similarities in words.

In connection to the ungrammatical sentences in (61), it has been claimed that the fact that such sentences can never be produced shows that children already know that grammatical operations are structure-dependent and this is why they do not entertain the hypothesis that it is simply the linearly first verb that is moved (Crain & Nakayama 1987). The claim simply cannot be verified since children do not normally form the relevant complex utterances. It is therefore only possible to experimentally illicit utterances where they could make the relevant mistakes. Crain & Nakayama (1987) have carried out such experiments. Their study has been criticized by Ambridge, Rowland & Pine (2008) since these authors could show that children do really make mistakes when fronting auxiliaries. The authors put the difference to the results of the first study by Crain and Nakayama down to unfortunate choice of auxiliary in Crain and Nakayama's study. Due to the use of the auxiliary *is*, the ungrammatical examples had pairs of words that never or only very rarely occur next to each other (*who running* in (62a)).

(62) a. The boy who is running fast can jump high. →
       * Is the boy who running fast can jump high?
    b. The boy who can run fast can jump high. →
       * Can the boy who run fast can jump high?

---

[41]There are cultural differences. In some cultures, adults do not talk to children that have not attained full linguistic competence (Ochs 1982; Ochs & Schieffelin 1985) (also see Section 13.8.4). Children have to therefore learn the language from their environment, that is, the sentences that they hear reflect the full complexity of the language.

[42]See Hurford (2002: 324) and Jackendoff (2007: Section 6.2) for problems that arise for certain kinds of neural networks and Pulvermüller (2003; 2010) for an alternative architecture that does not have these problems.

If one uses the auxiliary *can*, this problem disappears since *who* and *run* certainly do appear together. This then leads to the children actually making mistakes that they should not have, as the incorrect utterances actually violate a constraint that is supposed to be part of innate linguistic knowledge.

Estigarribia (2009) investigated English polar questions in particular. He shows that not even half of the polar questions in children's input have the form Aux NP VP (p. 74). Instead, parents communicated with their children in a simplified form and used sentences such as:

(63)   a. That your tablet?

        b. He talking?

        c. That taste pretty good?

Estigarribia divides the various patterns into complexity classes of the following kind: FRAG (*fragmentary*), SPRED (*subject predicate*) and AUX-IN (*auxiliary inversion*). (64) shows corresponding examples:

(64)   a. coming tomorrow?   (FRAG)

        b. you coming tomorrow?   (SPRED)

        c. Are you coming tomorrow?   (AUX-IN)

What we see is that the complexity increases from class to class. Estigarribia suggests a system of language acquisition where simpler classes are acquired before more complex ones and the latter ones develop from peripheral modifications of more simple classes (p. 76). He assumes that question forms are learned from right to left (*right to left elaboration*), that is, (64a) is learned first, then the pattern in (64b) containing a subject in addition to the material in (64a), and then in a third step, the pattern (64c) in which an additional auxiliary occurs (p. 82). In this kind of learning procedure, no auxiliary inversion is involved. This view is compatible with constraint-based analyses such as that of Ginzburg & Sag (2000). A similar approach to acquisition by Freudenthal, Pine, Aguado-Orea & Gobet (2007) will be discussed in Section 16.3.

A further interesting study has been carried out by Bod (2009b). He shows that it is possible to learn auxiliary inversion assuming trees with any kind of branching even if there is no auxiliary inversion with complex noun phrases present in the input. The procedure he uses as well as the results he gains are very interesting and will be discussed in Section 13.8.3 in more detail.

In conclusion, we can say that children do make mistakes with regard to the position of auxiliaries that they probably should not make if the relevant knowledge were innate. Information about the statistical distribution of words in the input is enough to learn the structures of complex sentences without actually having this kind of complex sentences in the input.

13.8.2.5 Summary

Pullum & Scholz (2002: 19) show what an Argument from Poverty of the Stimulus (APS) would have to look like if it were constructed correctly:

(65) APS specification schema:
   a. ACQUIRENDUM CHARACTERIZATION: describe in detail what is alleged to be known.
   b. LACUNA SPECIFICATION: identify a set of sentences such that if the learner had access to them, the claim of data-driven learning of the acquirendum would be supported.
   c. INDISPENSABILITY ARGUMENT: give reason to think that if learning were data-driven, then the acquirendum could not be learned without access to sentences in the lacuna.
   d. INACCESSIBILITY EVIDENCE: support the claim that tokens of sentences in the lacuna were not available to the learner during the acquisition process.
   e. ACQUISITION EVIDENCE: give reason to believe that the acquirendum does in fact become known to learners during childhood.

As the four case studies have shown, there can be reasons for rejecting the acquirendum. If the acquirendum does not have to be acquired, than there is no longer any evidence for innate linguistic knowledge. The acquirendum must at least be descriptively adequate. This is an empirical question that can be answered by linguists. In three of the four PoS arguments discussed by Pullum and Scholz, there were parts which were not descriptively adequate. In previous sections, we already encountered other PoS arguments that involve claims regarding linguistic data that cannot be upheld empirically (for example, the Subjacency Principle). For the remaining points in (65), interdisciplinary work is required: the specification of the lacuna falls into the theory of formal language (the specification of a set of utterances), the argument of indispensability is a mathematical task from the realm of learning theory, the evidence for inaccessibility is an empirical question that can be approached by using corpora, and finally the evidence for acquisition is a question for experimental developmental psychologists (Pullum & Scholz 2002: 19–20).

Pullum & Scholz (2002: 46) point out an interesting paradox with regard to (65c): without results from mathematical theories of learning, one cannot achieve (65c). If one wishes to provide a valid Poverty of the Stimulus Argument, then this should automatically lead to improvements in theories of learning, that is, it is possible to learn more than was previously assumed.

13.8.3 Unsupervised Data-Oriented Parsing (U-DOP)

Bod (2009b) has developed a procedure that does not require any information about word classes or relations between words contained in utterances. The only assumption that one has to make is that there is some kind of structure. The procedure consists of three steps:

1. Compute all possible (binary-branching) trees (without category symbols) for a set of given sentences.

2. Divide these trees into sub-trees.

3. Compute the ideal tree for each sentence.

13.8 Poverty of the Stimulus

This process will be explained using the sentences in (66):

(66)   a. Watch the dog.
        b. The dog barks.

The trees that are assigned to these utterances only use the category symbol X since the categories for the relevant phrases are not (yet) known. In order to keep the example readable, the words themselves will not be given the category X, although one can of course do this. Figure 13.2 shows the trees for (66). In the next step, the trees are divided

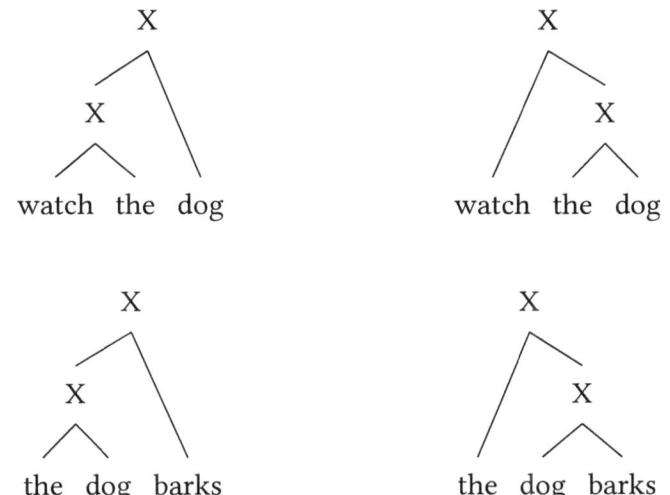

Figure 13.2: Possible binary-branching structures for *Watch the dog* and *The dog barks*.

into subtrees. The trees in Figure 13.2 have the subtrees that can be seen in Figure 13.3 on the following page. In the third step, we now have to compute the best tree for each utterance. For *The dog barks.*, there are two trees in the set of the subtrees that correspond exactly to this utterance. But it is also possible to build structures out of subtrees. There are therefore multiple derivations possible for *The dog barks.* all of which use the trees in Figure 13.3: one the one hand, trivial derivations that use the entire tree, and on the other, derivations that build trees from smaller subtrees. Figure 13.4 gives an impression of how this construction of subtrees happens. If we now want to decide which of the analyses in (67) is the best, then we have to compute the probability of each tree.

(67)   a. [[the dog] barks]
        b. [the [dog barks]]

The probability of a tree is the sum of the probabilities of all its analyses. There are two analyses for (67b), which can be found in Figure 13.4. The probability of the first analysis of (67b) corresponds to the probability of choosing exactly the complete tree for [the [dog barks]] from the set of all subtrees. Since there are twelve subtrees, the probability of choosing that one is 1/12. The probability of the second analysis is the product of the probabilities of the subtrees that are combined and is therefore 1/12 × 1/12 = 1/144. The

13 The innateness of linguistic knowledge

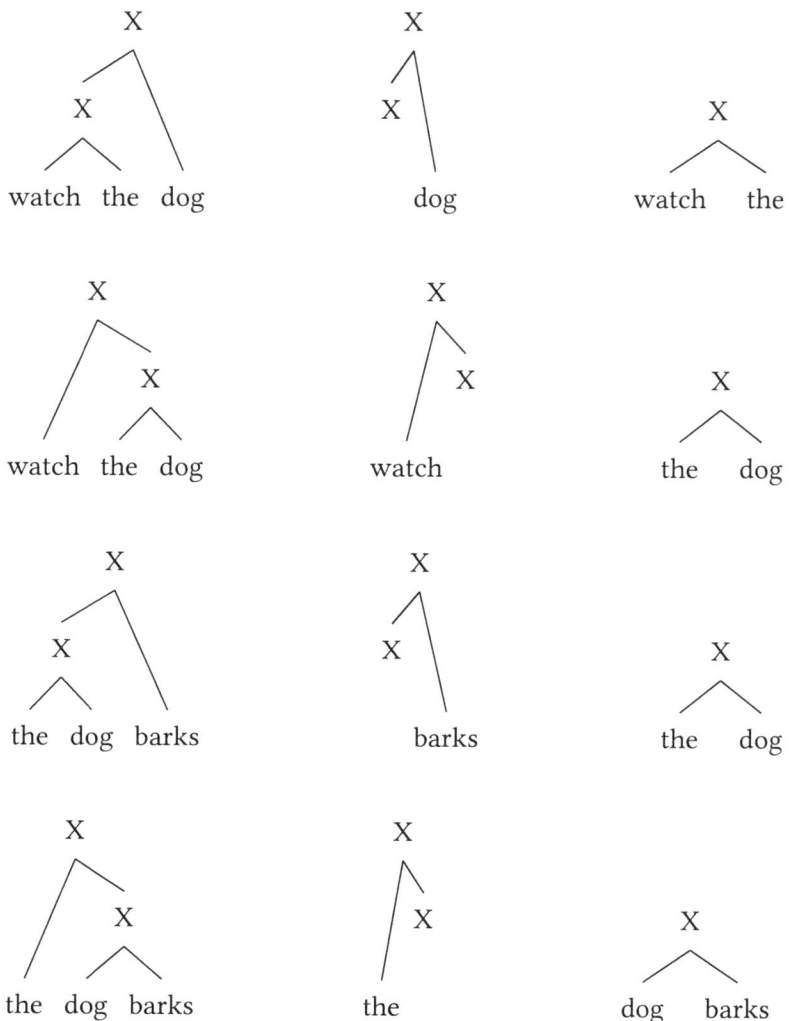

Figure 13.3: Subtrees for the trees in Figure 13.2

probability of the analysis in (67b) is therefore 1/12 + (1/12 × 1/12) = 13/144. One can then calculate the probability of the tree in (67a) in the same way. The only difference here is that the tree for [the dog] occurs twice in the set of subtrees. Its probability is therefore 2/12. The probability of the tree [[the dog] barks] is therefore: 1/12 + (1/12 × 2/12) = 14/144. We have thus extracted knowledge about plausible structures from the corpus. This knowledge can also be applied whenever one hears a new utterance for which there is no complete tree. It is then possible to use already known subtrees to calculate the probabilities of possible analyses of the new utterance. Bod's model can also be combined with weights: those sentences that were heard longer ago by the speaker, will receive a lower weight. One can thereby also account for the fact that children do not have all sentences that they have ever heard available simultaneously. This extension makes the UDOP model more plausible for language acquisition.

13.8 Poverty of the Stimulus

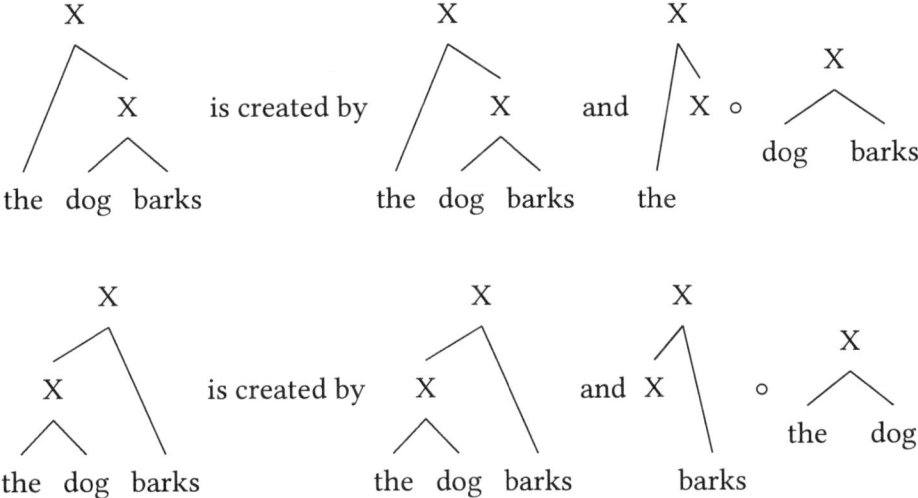

Figure 13.4: Analysis of *The dog barks* using subtrees from Figure 13.3

In the example above, we did not assign categories to the words. If we were to do this, then we would get the tree in Figure 13.5 as a possible subtree. These kinds of

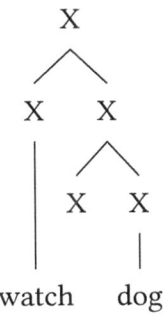

Figure 13.5: Discontinuous partial tree

discontinuous subtrees are important if one wants to capture dependencies between elements that occur in different subtrees of a given tree. Some examples are the following sentences:

(68) a. BA carried *more* people *than* cargo in 2005.
      b. *What's* this scratch *doing* on the table?
      c. Most software *companies* in Vietnam *are* small sized.

It is then also possible to learn auxiliary inversion in English with these kinds of discontinuous trees. All one needs are tree structures for the two sentences in (69) in order to prefer the correct sentence (70a) over the incorrect one (70b).

499

13 The innateness of linguistic knowledge

(69) a. The man who is eating is hungry.
     b. Is the boy hungry?

(70) a. Is the man who is eating hungry?
     b. *Is the man who eating is hungry?

U-DOP can learn the structures for (69) in Figure 13.6 from the sentences in (71):

(71) a. The man who is eating mumbled.
     b. The man is hungry.
     c. The man mumbled.
     d. The boy is eating.

Note that these sentences do not contain any instance of the structure in (70a). With

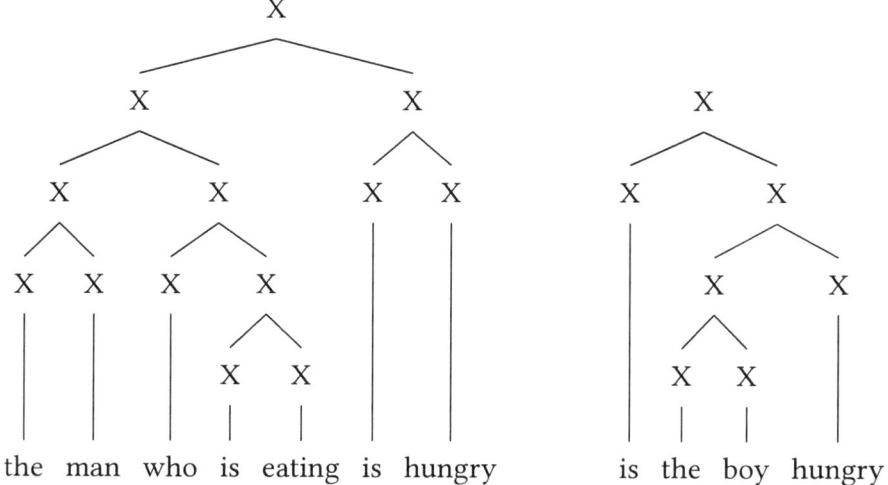

Figure 13.6: Structures that U-DOP learned from the examples in (69) and (71)

the structures learned here, it is possible to show that the shortest possible derivation for the position of the auxiliary is also the correct one: the correct order *Is the man who is eating hungry?* only requires that the fragments in Figure 13.7 on the next page are combined, whereas the structure for *Is the man who eating is hungry?* requires at least four subtrees from Figure 13.6 to be combined with each other. This is shown by Figure 13.8 on the facing page.

The motivation for always taking the derivation that consists of the least subparts is that one maximizes similarity to already known material.

The tree for (72) containing one auxiliary too many can also be created from Figure 13.6 with just two subtrees (with the tree [$_X$ is$_X$ X] and the entire tree for *The man who is eating is hungry*).

13.8 Poverty of the Stimulus

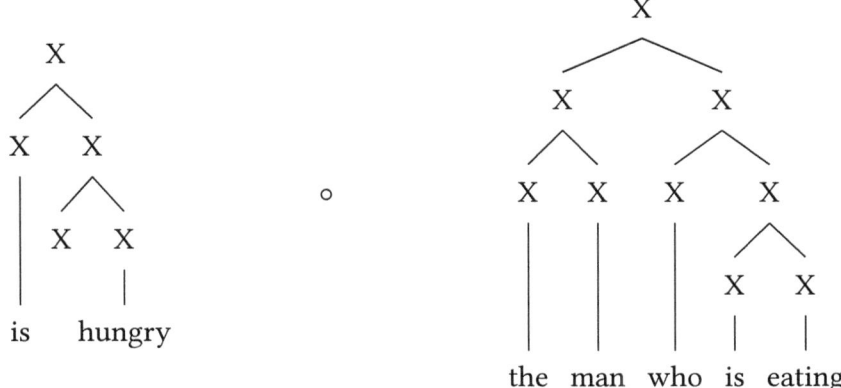

Figure 13.7: Derivation of the correct structure for combination with an auxiliary using two subtrees from Figure 13.6

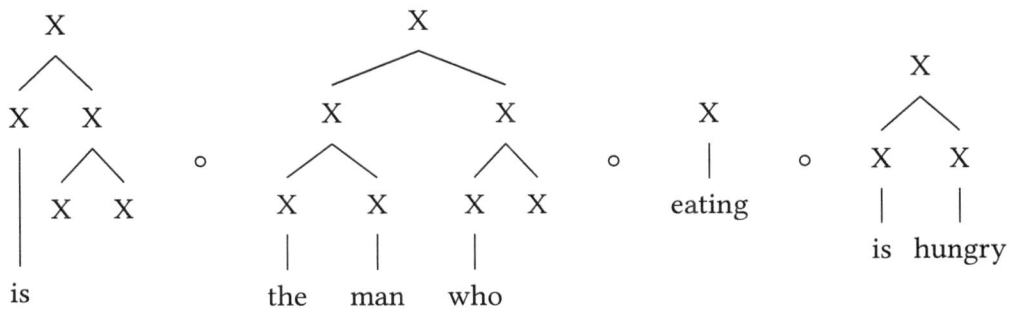

Figure 13.8: Derivation of the incorrect structure for the combination with an auxiliary using two subtrees from Figure 13.6

(72) * Is the man who is eating is hungry?

Interestingly, children do produce this kind of incorrect sentences (Crain & Nakayama 1987: 530; Ambridge, Rowland & Pine 2008). However, if we consider the probabilities of the subtrees in addition to the the number of combined subparts, we get the correct result, namely (70a) and not (72). This is due to the fact that *the man who is eating* occurs in the corpus twice, in (70a) and in (71a). Thus, the probability of *the man who is eating* is just as high as the probability of *the man who is eating is hungry* and thus derivation in Figure 13.7 is preferred over the one for (72). This works for the constructed examples here, however one can imagine that in a realistic corpus, sequences of the form *the man who is eating* are more frequent than sequences with further words since *the man who is eating* can also occur in other contexts. Bod has applied this process to corpora of adult language (English, German and Chinese) as well as applying it to the Eve corpus from the CHILDES database in order to see whether analogy formation constitutes a plausible model for human acquisition of language. He was able to show that what we demonstrated for the sentences above also works for a larger corpus of naturally occurring language: although there were no examples for movement of an auxiliary across a complex NP in the Eve corpus, it is possible to learn by analogy that the auxiliary from a complex NP cannot be fronted.

It is therefore possible to learn syntactic structures from a corpus without any prior knowledge about parts of speech or abstract properties of language. The only assumption that Bod makes is that there are (binary-branching) structures. The assumption of binarity is not really necessary. But if one includes flat branching structures into the computation, the set of trees will become considerably bigger. Therefore, Bod only used binary-branching structures in his experiments. In his trees, X consists of two other X's or a word. We are therefore dealing with recursive structures. Therefore, Bod's work proposes a theory of the acquisition of syntactic structures that only requires recursion, something that is viewed by Hauser, Chomsky & Fitch (2002) as a basic property of language.

As shown in Section 13.1.8, there is evidence that recursion is not restricted to language and thus one can conclude that it is not necessary to assume innate linguistic knowledge in order to be able to learn syntactic structures from the given input.

Nevertheless, it is important to point out something here: what Bod shows is that syntactic structures can be learned. The information about the parts of speech of each word involved which are not yet included in his structures can also be derived using statistical methods (Redington et al. 1998; Clark 2000).[43] In all probability, the structures that can be learned correspond to structures that surface-oriented linguistic theories would also assume. However, not all aspects of the linguistic analysis are acquired. In Bod's model, only occurrences of words in structures are evaluated. Nothing is said about whether words stand in a particular regular relationship to one another or not (for example, a lexical rule connecting a passive participle and perfect participle). Furthermore, nothing is said about how the meaning of expressions arise (are they rather holistic in the sense of Construction Grammar or projected from the lexicon?). These are questions that still concern theoretical linguists (see Chapter 21) and cannot straightforwardly be derived from the statistic distribution of words and the structures computed from them (see Section 21.8.1 for more on this point).

A second comment is also needed: we have seen that statistical information can be used to derive the structure of complex linguistic expressions. This now begs the question of how this relates to Chomsky's earlier argumentation against statistical approaches (Chomsky 1957: 16). Abney (1996: Section 4.2) discusses this in detail. The problem with his earlier argumentation is that Chomsky referred to Markov models. These are statistical versions of finite automatons. Finite automatons can only describe type 3 languages and are therefore not appropriate for analyzing natural language. However, Chomsky's criticism cannot be applied to statistical methods in general.

---

[43] Computational linguistic algorithms for determining parts of speech often look at an entire corpus. But children are always dealing with just a particular part of it. The corresponding learning process must then also include a curve of forgetting. See Braine (1987: 67).

13.8.4 Negative evidence

In a number of works that assume innate linguistic knowledge, it is claimed that children do not have access to negative evidence, that is, nobody tells them that sentences such as (49e) – repeated here as (73) – are ungrammatical (Brown & Hanlon 1970: 42–52; Marcus 1993).

(73)   * Is the dog that in the corner is hungry?

It is indeed correct that adults do not wake up their children with the ungrammatical sentence of the day, however, children do in fact have access to negative evidence of various sorts. For example, Chouinard & Clark (2003) have shown that English and French speaking parents correct the utterances of their children that are not well-formed. For example, they repeat utterances where the verb was inflected incorrectly. Children can deduce from the fact that the utterance was repeated and from what was changed in the repetition that they made a mistake and Chouinard and Clark also showed that they actually do this. The authors looked at data from five children whose parents all had an academic qualification. They discuss the parent-child relationship in other cultures, too (see Ochs (1982); Ochs & Schieffelin (1985) and Marcus (1993: 71) for an overview) and refer to studies of America families with lower socio-economic status (page 660).

A further form of negative evidence is indirect negative evidence, which Chomsky (1981a: 9) also assumes could play a role in acquisition. Goldberg (1995: Section 5.2) gives the utterance in (74a) as an example:[44]

(74)   a.   Look! The magician made the bird disappear.
       b.   * The magician disappeared the bird.

The child can conclude from the fact that adults use a more involved causative construction with *make* that the verb *disappear*, unlike other verbs such as *melt*, cannot be used transitively. An immediately instructive example for the role played by indirect negative evidence comes from morphology. There are certain productive rules that can however still not be applied if there is a word that blocks the application of the rule. An example is the *-er* nominalization suffix in German. By adding an *-er* to a verb stem, one can derive a noun that refers to someone who carries out a particular action (often habitually) (*Raucher* 'smoker', *Maler* 'painter', *Sänger* 'singer', *Tänzer* 'dancer'). However, *Stehler* 'stealer' is very unusual. The formation of *Stehler* is blocked by the existence of *Dieb* 'thief'. Language learners therefore have to infer from the non-existence of *Stehler* that the nominalization rule does not apply to *stehlen* 'to steal'.

Similarly, a speaker with a grammar of English that does not have any restrictions on the position of manner adverbs would expect that both orders in (75) are possible (Scholz & Pullum 2002: 206):

(75)   a.   call the police immediately
       b.   * call immediately the police

---

[44] Also, see Tomasello (2006a: 277).

Learners can conclude indirectly from the fact that verb phrases such as (75b) (almost) never occur in the input that these are probably not part of the language. This can be modeled using the relevant statistical learning algorithms.

The examples for the existence of negative evidence provided so far are more arguments from plausibility. Stefanowitsch (2008) has combined corpus linguistic studies on the statistical distribution with acceptability experiments and has shown that negative evidence gained from expected frequencies correlates with acceptability judgments of speakers. This process will be discussed now briefly: Stefanowitsch assumes the following principle:

(76) Form expectations about the frequency of co-occurrence of linguistic features or elements on the basis of their individual frequency of occurrence and check these expectations against the actual frequency of co-occurrence. (Stefanowitsch 2008: 518)

Stefanowitsch works with the part of the *International Corpus of English* that contains British English (ICE-GB). In this corpus, the verb *say* occurs 3,333 times and sentences with ditransitive verbs (Subj Verb Obj Obj) occur 1,824 times. The entire total of verbs in the corpus is 136,551. If all verbs occurred in all kinds of sentences with the same frequencies, then we would expect *say* to occur 44.52 times (X / 1,824 = 3,333 / 136,551 and hence X = 1,824 × 3,333 / 136,551) in the ditransitive construction. But the number of actual occurrences is actually 0 since, unlike (77b), sentences such as (77a) are not used by speakers of English.

(77) a. * Dad said Sue something nice.
     b. Dad said something nice to Sue.

Stefanowitsch shows that the non-occurrence of *say* in the ditransitive sentence pattern is significant. Furthermore, he investigated how acceptability judgments compare to the frequent occurrence or non-occurrence of verbs in certain constructions. In a first experiment, he was able to show that the frequent non-occurrence of elements in particular constructions correlates with the acceptability judgments of speakers, whereas this is not the case for the frequent occurrence of a verb in a construction.

In sum, we can say that indirect negative evidence can be derived from linguistic input and that it seems to play an important role in language acquisition.

13.9 Summary

It follows from all this that not a single one of the arguments in favor of innate linguistic knowledge remains uncontroversial. This of course does not rule out there still being innate linguistic knowledge but those who wish to incorporate this assumption into their theories have to take more care than was previously the case to prove that what they assume to be innate is actually part of our linguistic knowledge and that it cannot be learned from the linguistic input alone.

Comprehension questions

1. Which arguments are there for the assumption of innate linguistic knowledge?

Further reading

Pinker's book (1994) is the best written book arguing for nativist models of language.

Elman, Bates, Johnson, Karmiloff-Smith, Parisi & Plunkett (1996) discuss all the arguments that have been proposed in favor of innate linguistic knowledge and show that the relevant phenomena can be explained differently. The authors adopt a connectionist view. They work with neuronal networks, which are assumed to model what is happening in our brains relatively accurately. The book also contains chapters about the basics of genetics and the structure of the brain, going into detail about why a direct encoding of linguistic knowledge in our genome is implausible.

Certain approaches using neuronal networks have been criticized because they cannot capture certain aspects of human abilities such as recursion or the multiple usage of the same words in an utterance. Pulvermüller (2010) discusses an architecture that has memory and uses this to analyze recursive structures. In his overview article, certain works are cited that show that the existence of more abstract rules or schemata of the kind theoretical linguists take for granted can be demonstrated on the neuronal level. Pulvermüller does not, however, assume that linguistic knowledge is innate (p. 173).

Pullum and Scholz have dealt with the Poverty-of-the-Stimulus argument in detail (Pullum & Scholz 2002; Scholz & Pullum 2002).

Goldberg (2006) and Tomasello (2003) are the most prominent proponents of Construction Grammar, a theory that explicitly tries to do without the assumption of innate linguistic knowledge.

14 Generative-enumerative vs. model-theoretic approaches

Generative-enumerative approaches assume that a grammar generates a set of sequences of symbols (strings of words). This is where the term Generative Grammar comes from. Thus, it is possible to use the grammar on page 53, repeated here as (1), to derive the string *er das Buch dem Mann gibt* 'he the book the man gives'.

(1) NP → D, N   NP → er   N → Buch
    S → NP, NP, NP, V   D → das   N → Mann
                      D → dem   V → gibt

Beginning with the start symbol (S), symbols are replaced until one reaches a sequence of symbols only containing words. The set of all strings derived in this way is the language described by the grammar.

The following are classed as generative-enumerative approaches:

- all phrase structure grammars
- Transformational Grammars in almost all variants
- GPSG in the formalism of Gazdar, Klein, Pullum & Sag (1985)
- many variants of Categorial Grammar
- many variants of TAG
- Chomsky's Minimalist Grammars

LFG was also originally designed to be a generative grammar.

The opposite of such theories of grammar are model-theoretic or constraint-based approaches (MTA). MTAs formulate well-formedness conditions on the expressions that the grammar describes. In Section 6.7, we already discussed a model-theoretic approach for theories that use feature structures to model phenomena. To illustrate this point, I will discuss another HPSG example: (2) shows the lexical item for *kennst* 'know'. In the description of (2), it is ensured that the PHON value of the relevant linguistic sign is ⟨ *kennst* ⟩, that is, this value of PHON is constrained. There are parallel restrictions for the features given in (2): the SYNSEM value is given. In SYNSEM, there are restrictions on the LOC and NONLOC value. In CAT, there are individual restrictions for HEAD and COMPS. The value of COMPS is a list with descriptions of dependent elements. The descriptions are given as abbreviations here, which actually stand for complex feature descriptions

(2) Lexical item for *kennst*:

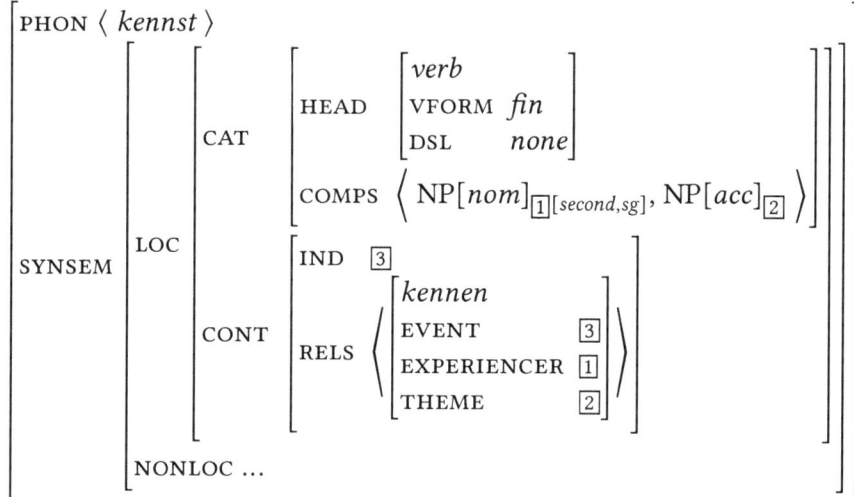

that also consist of feature-value pairs. For the first argument of *kennst*, a HEAD value of type *noun* is required, the PER value in the semantic index has to be *second* and the NUM value has to be *sg*. The structure sharings in (2) are a special kind of constraint. Values that are not specified in the descriptions of lexical entries can vary in accordance with the feature geometry given by the type system. In (2), neither the SLASH value of the nominative NP nor the one of the accusative NP is fixed. This means that SLASH can either be an empty or non-empty list.

The constraints in lexical items such as (2) interact with further constraints that hold for the signs of type *phrase*. For instance, in head-argument structures, the non-head daughter must correspond to an element from the COMPS list of the head daughter.

Generative-enumerative and model-theoretic approaches view the same problem from different sides: the generative side only allows what can be generated by a given set of rules, whereas the model-theoretic approach allows everything that is not ruled out by constraints.[1]

Pullum & Scholz (2001: 19–20) and Pullum (2007) list the following model-theoretic approaches:[2]

- the non-procedural variant of Transformational Grammar of Lakoff, that formulates constraints on potential tree sequences,

- Johnson and Postal's formalization of Relational Grammar (1980),

---

[1] Compare this to an old joke: in dictatorships, everything that is not allowed is banned, in democracies, everything that is not banned is allowed and in France, everything that is banned is allowed. Generative-enumerative approaches correspond to the dictatorships, model-theoretic approaches are the democracies and France is something that has no correlate in linguistics.

[2] See Pullum (2007) for a historical overview of Model Theoretic Syntax (MTS) and for further references.

- GPSG in the variants developed by Gazdar et al. (1988), Blackburn et al. (1993) and Rogers (1997),
- LFG in the formalization of Kaplan (1995)[3] and
- HPSG in the formalization of King (1999).

Categorial Grammars (Bouma & van Noord 1994), TAG (Rogers 1994) and Minimalist approaches (Veenstra 1998) can be formulated in model-theoretic terms.

Pullum & Scholz (2001) point out various differences between these points of view. In the following sections, I will focus on two of these differences.[4] Section 14.3 deals with ten Hacken's objection to the model-theoretic view.

14.1 Graded acceptability

Generative-enumerative approaches differ from model-theoretic approaches in how they deal with the varying degrees of acceptability of utterances. In generative-enumerative approaches, a particular string is either included in the set of well-formed expressions or it is not. This means that it is not straightforwardly possible to say something about the degree of deviance: the first sentence in (3) is judged grammatical and the following three are equally ungrammatical.

(3) a. Du kennst diesen Aufsatz.
    you know.2SG this.ACC essay

  b. *Du kennen diesen Aufsatz.
    you know.3PL this.ACC essay

  c. *Du kennen dieser Aufsatz.
    you know.3PL this.NOM essay

  d. *Du kennen Aufsatz dieser.
    you know.3PL essay this.NOM

At this point, critics of this view raise the objection that it is in fact possible to determine degrees of wellformedness in (3b–d): in (3b), there is no agreement between the subject and the verb, in (3c), *dieser Aufsatz* 'this essay' has the wrong case in addition, and in (3d), *Aufsatz* 'essay' and *dieser* 'this' occur in the wrong order. Furthermore, the sentence in (4) violates grammatical rules of German, but is nevertheless still interpretable.

---

[3] According to Pullum (2013: Section 3.2), there seems to be a problem for model-theoretic formalizations of so-called *constraining equations*.

[4] The reader should take note here: there are differing views with regard to how generative-enumerative and MTS models are best formalized and not all of the assumptions discussed here are compatible with every formalism. The following sections mirror the important points in the general discussion.

(4) Studenten stürmen mit Flugblättern und Megafon die Mensa und rufen alle
    students storm   with flyers   and megaphone the canteen and call all
    auf zur Vollversammlung in der Glashalle *zum kommen. Vielen* bleibt das
    up to plenary.meeting in the glass.hall to.the come   many.DAT stays the
    Essen im   Mund stecken und *kommen sofort   mit*.[5]
    food in.the mouth stick and come   immediately with

'Students stormed into the university canteen with flyers and a megaphone calling for everyone to come to a plenary meeting in the glass hall. For many, the food stuck in their throats and they immediately joined them.'

Chomsky (1975: Chapter 5; 1964b) tried to use a string distance function to determine the relative acceptability of utterances. This function compares the string of an ungrammatical expression with that of a grammatical expression and assigns an ungrammaticality score of 1, 2 or 3 according to certain criteria. This treatment is not adequate, however, as there are much more fine-grained differences in acceptability and the string distance function also makes incorrect predictions. For examples of this and technical problems with calculating the function, see Pullum & Scholz (2001: 29).

In model-theoretic approaches, grammar is understood as a system of well-formedness conditions. An expression becomes worse, the more well-formedness conditions it violates (Pullum & Scholz 2001: 26–27). In (3b), the person and number requirements of the lexical item for the verb *kennst* are violated. In addition, the case requirements for the object have not been fulfilled in (3c). There is a further violation of a linearization rule for the noun phrase in (3d).

Well-formedness conditions can be weighted in such a way as to explain why certain violations lead to more severe deviations than others (Sorace & Keller 2005). Furthermore, performance factors also play a role when judging sentences (for more on the distinction between performance and competence, see Chapter 15). As we will see in Chapter 15, constraint-based approaches work very well as performance-compatible grammar models. If we combine the relevant grammatical theory with performance models, we will arrive at explanations for graded acceptability differences owing to performance factors.

14.2 Utterance fragments

Pullum & Scholz (2001: Section 3.2) point out that generative-enumerative theories do not assign structure to fragments. For instance, neither the string *and of the* nor the string *the of and* would receive a structure since none of these sequences is well-formed as an utterance and they are therefore not elements of the set of sequences generated by the grammar. However, *and of the* can occur as part of the coordination of PPs in sentences such as (5) and would therefore have some structure in these cases, for example the one given in Figure 14.1 on the next page.

---

[5]Streikzeitung der Universität Bremen, 04.12.2003, p. 2. The emphasis is mine.

(5) That cat is afraid of the dog and of the parrot.

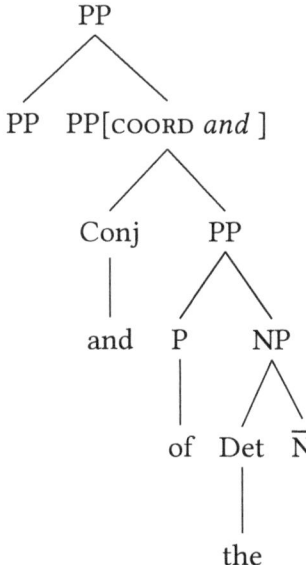

Figure 14.1: Structure of the fragment *and of the* following Pullum & Scholz (2001: 32)

As a result of the interaction of various constraints in a constraint-based grammar, it emerges that *the* is part of an NP and this NP is an argument of *of* and furthermore *and* is combined with the relevant *of*-PP. In symmetric coordination, the first conjunct has the same syntactic properties as the second, which is why the partial structure of *and of the* allows one to draw conclusions about the category of the conjunct despite it not being part of the string.

Ewan Klein noted that Categorial Grammar and Minimalist Grammars, which build up more complex expressions from simpler ones, can sometimes create this kind of fragments (Pullum 2013: 507). This is certainly the case for Categorial Grammars with composition rules, which allow one to combine any sequence of words to form a constituent. If one views derivations as logical proofs, as is common in some variants of Categorial Grammar, then the actual derivation is irrelevant. What matters is whether a proof can be found or not. However, if one is interested in the derived structures, then the argument brought forward by Pullum and Scholz is still valid. For some variants of Categorial Grammar that motivate the combination of constituents based on their prosodic and information-structural properties (Steedman 1991: Section 3), the problem persists since fragments have a structure independent of the structure of the entire utterance and independent of their information-structural properties within this complete structure. This structure of the fragment can be such that it is not possible to analyze it with type-raising rules and composition rules.

In any case, this argument holds for Minimalist theories since it is not possible to have a combination of *the* with a nominal constituent if this constituent was not already built up from lexical material by Merge.

14 Generative-enumerative vs. model-theoretic approaches

14.3 A problem for model-theoretic approaches?

Ten Hacken (2007: 237–238) discusses the formal assumptions of HPSG. In HPSG, feature descriptions are used to describe feature structures. Feature structures must contain all the features belonging to a structure of a certain type. Additionally, the features have to have a maximally-specific value (see Section 6.7). Ten Hacken discusses gender properties of the English noun *cousin*. In English, gender is important in order to ensure the correct binding of pronouns (see page 280 for German):

(6)   a. The man$_i$ sleeps. He$_i$ snores.

      b. The woman$_i$ sleeps. He$_{*i}$ snores.

While *he* in (6a) can refer to *man*, *woman* is not a possible antecedent. Ten Hacken's problem is that *cousin* is not marked with respect to gender. Thus, it is possible to use it to refer to both male and female relatives. As was explained in the discussion of the case value of *Frau* 'woman' in Section 6.7, it is possible for a value in a description to remain unspecified. Thus, in the relevant feature structures, any appropriate and maximally specific value is possible. The case of *Frau* can therefore be nominative, genitive, dative or accusative in an actual feature structure. Similarly, there are two possible genders for *cousin* corresponding to the usages in (7).

(7)   a. I have a cousin$_i$. He$_i$ is very smart.

      b. I have a cousin$_i$. She$_i$ is very smart.

Ten Hacken refers to examples such as (8) and claims that these are problematic:

(8)   a. Niels has two cousins.

      b. How many cousins does Niels have?

In plural usage, it is not possible to assume that *cousins* is feminine or masculine since the set of relatives can contain either women or men. It is interesting to note that (9a) is possible in English, whereas German is forced to use (9b) to express the same meaning.

(9)   a. Niels and Odette are cousins.

      b. Niels und Odette sind Cousin   und Cousine.
         Niels and Odette are   cousin.M and cousin.F

Ten Hacken concludes that the gender value has to remain unspecified and this shows, in his opinion, that model-theoretic analyses are unsuited to describing language.

If we consider what exactly ten Hacken noticed, then it becomes apparent how one can account for this in a model-theoretic approach: Ten Hacken claims that it does not make sense to specify a gender value for the plural form of *cousin*. In a model-theoretic approach, this can be captured in two ways. One can either assume that there are no gender features for referential indices in the plural, or that one can add a gender value that plural nouns can have.

The first approach is supported by the fact that there are no inflectional differences between the plural forms of pronouns with regard to gender. There is therefore no reason to distinguish genders in the plural.

(10) a. Niels and Odette are cousins. They are very smart.

b. The cousins/brothers/sisters are standing over there. They are very smart.

No distinctions are found in plural when it comes to nominal inflection (*brothers, sisters, books*). In German, this is different. There are differences with both nominal inflection and the reference of (some) noun phrases with regard to the sexus of the referent. Examples of this are the previously mentioned examples *Cousin* 'male cousin' and *Cousine* 'female cousin' as well as forms with the suffix *-in* as in *Kindergärtnerin* 'female nursery teacher'. However, gender is normally a grammatical notion that has nothing to do with sexus. An example is the neuter noun *Mitglied* 'member', which can refer to both female and male persons.

The question that one has to ask when discussing Ten Hacken's problem is the following: does gender play a role for pronominal binding in German? If this is not the case, then the gender feature is only relevant within the morphology component, and here the gender value is determined for each noun in the lexicon. For the binding of personal pronouns, there is no gender difference in German.

(11) Die Schwestern / Brüder   / Vereinsmitglieder / Geschwister stehen dort.
      the sisters.F   brothers.M club.members.N   siblings   stand there
      Sie lächeln.
      they smile.

'The sisters/brothers/club members/siblings are standing there. They are smiling.'

Nevertheless, there are adverbials in German that agree in gender with the noun to which they refer (Höhle 1983: Chapter 6):

(12) a. Die Fenster   wurden eins   nach dem anderen geschlossen.
         the windows.N were   one.N after the other   closed

         'The windows were closed one after the other.'

      b. Die Türen   wurden eine   nach der anderen geschlossen.
         the doors.F were   one.F after the other   closed

         'The doors were closed one after the other.'

      c. Die Riegel wurden einer nach dem anderen zugeschoben.
         the bolts.M were   one.M after the other closed

         'The bolts were closed one after the other.'

For animate nouns, it is possible to diverge from the gender of the noun in question and use a form of the adverbial that corresponds to the biological sex:

(13) a. Die Mitglieder des   Politbüros wurden eines / einer nach dem anderen
         the members.N of.the politburo were   one.N one.M after the   other
         aus   dem Saal getragen.
         out.of the hall carried

         'The members of the politburo were carried out of the hall one after the other.'

b. Die Mitglieder des Frauentanzklubs verließen eines / eine nach dem
the members.N of.the women's.dance.club left one.N one.F after the.N
/ der anderen im Schutze der Dunkelheit den Keller.
the.F other in.the protection of.the dark the basement
'The members of the women's dance club left the basement one after the other under cover of darkness.'

This deviation from gender in favor of sexus can also be seen with binding of personal and relative pronouns with nouns such as *Weib* 'woman' (pej.) and *Mädchen* 'girl':

(14) a. „Farbe bringt die meiste Knete!" verriet ein 14jähriges türkisches *Mädchen*,
color brings the most money revealed a 14-year.old Turkish girl.N
die die Mauerstückchen am Nachmittag am Checkpoint Charlie an
who.F the wall.pieces in.the afternoon at Checkpoint Charlie at
Japaner und US-Bürger verkauft.⁶
Japanese and US-citizens sells

' "Color gets the most money" said a 14-year old Turkish girl who sells pieces of the wall to Japanese and American citizens at Checkpoint Charlie.'

b. Es ist ein junges *Mädchen, die* auf der Suche nach CDs bei Bolzes
it is a young girl.N who.F on the search for CDs at Bolzes
reinschaut.⁷
stops.by

'It is a young girl looking for CDs that stops by Bolzes.'

For examples from Goethe, Kafka and Thomas Mann, see Müller (1999b: 417–418).

For inanimate nouns such as those in (12), agreement is obligatory. For the analysis of German, one therefore does in fact require a gender feature in the plural. In English, this is not the case since there are no parallel examples with pronouns inflecting for gender. One can therefore either assume that plural indices do not have a gender feature or that the gender value is *none*. In the latter case, the feature would have a value and hence fulfill the formal requirements. (15) shows the first solution: plural indices are modeled by feature structures of type *pl-ind* and the GENDER feature is just not appropriate for such objects.

(15) a. singular index:
$$\begin{bmatrix} sg\text{-}ind \\ \text{PER} & per \\ \text{NUM} & sg \\ \text{GEN} & gender \end{bmatrix}$$

b. plural index:
$$\begin{bmatrix} pl\text{-}ind \\ \text{PER} & per \\ \text{NUM} & pl \end{bmatrix}$$

---

⁶taz, 14.06.1990, p. 6.
⁷taz, 13.03.1996, p. 11.

14.3 A problem for model-theoretic approaches?

The second solution requires the type hierarchy in Figure 14.2 for the subtypes of *gender*. With such a type hierarchy *none* is a possible value of the GEN feature and no problem will arise.

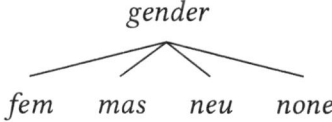

Figure 14.2: Type hierarchy for one of the solutions of ten Hacken's problem

In general, it is clear that cases such as the one constructed by ten Hacken will never be a problem since there are either values that make sense, or there are contexts for which there is no value that makes sense and one therefore does not require the features.

So, while ten Hacken's problem is a non-issue, there are certain problems of a more technical nature. I have pointed out one such technical problem in Müller (1999b: Section 14.4). I show that spurious ambiguities arise for a particular analysis of verbal complexes in German when one resolves the values of a binary feature (FLIP). I also show how this problem can be avoided by the complicated stipulation of a value in certain contexts.

15 The competence/performance distinction

The distinction between competence and performance (Chomsky 1965: Section 1.1), which is assumed by several theories of grammar, was already discussed in Section 12.6.3 about the analysis of scrambling and verbal complexes in TAG. Theories of competence are intended to describe linguistic knowledge and performance theories are assigned the task of explaining how linguistic knowledge is used as well as why mistakes are made in speech production and comprehension. A classic example in the competence/performance discussion are cases of center self-embedding. Chomsky & Miller (1963: 286) discuss the following example with recursively embedded relative clauses:

(1) (the rat (the cat (the dog chased) killed) ate the malt)

(2b) is a corresponding example in German:

(2) a. dass der Hund bellt, der die Katze jagt, die die Maus kennt, die
    that the dog.M barks that.M the cat chases that.F the mouse knows who
    im   Keller lebt
    in.the basement lives
    'that the dog that chases the cat that knows the mouse who is living in the basement is barking'

   b. dass er Hund, [₁ der die Katze, [₂ die die Maus, [₃ die im Keller
      that the dog   that the cat   that the mouse   who in.the basement
      lebt, ₃] kennt, ₂] jagt   ₁] bellt
      lives   knows   chases   barks

The examples in (1) and (2b) are entirely incomprehensible for most people. If one rearranges the material somewhat, it is possible to process the sentences and assign a meaning to them.[1] For sentences such as (2b), it is often assumed that they fall within

---

[1]The sentence in (2a) can be continued following the pattern that was used to create the sentence. For instance by adding *die unter der Treppe lebte, die meine Freunde repariert haben* 'who lived under the staircase which my friends repaired'. This shows that a restriction of the number of elements that depend on one head to seven (Leiss 2003: 322) does not restrict the set of the sentences that are generated or licensed by a grammar to be finite. There are at most two dependents of each head in (2a). The extraposition of the relative clauses allows the hearer to group material into processable and reducible chunks, which reduces the cognitive burden during processing.

This means that the restriction to seven dependents does not cause a finitization of recursion ("Verendlichung von Rekursivität") as was claimed by Leiss (2003: 322). Leiss argued that Miller could not use his insights regarding short term memory, since he worked within Transformational Grammar rather than in Dependency Grammar. The discussion shows that dependency plays an important role, but that linear order is also important for processing.

our grammatical competence, that is, we possess the knowledge required to assign a structure to the sentence, although the processing of utterances such as (2b) exceeds language-independent abilities of our brain. In order to successfully process (2b), we would have to retain the first five noun phrases and corresponding hypotheses about the further progression of the sentence in our heads and could only begin to combine syntactic material when the verbs appear. Our brains become overwhelmed by this task. These problems do not arise when analyzing (2a) as it is possible to immediately begin to integrate the noun phrases into a larger unit.

Nevertheless, center self-embedding of relative clauses can also be constructed in such a way that our brains can handle them. Hans Uszkoreit (p. c. 2009) gives the following example:

(3) Die Bänke, [₁ auf denen damals die Alten des Dorfes, [₂ die allen
    the benches on which back.then the old.people of.the village that all
    Kindern, [₃ die vorbeikamen ₃], freundliche Blicke zuwarfen ₂], lange Stunden
    children that came.by friendly glances gave long hours
    schweigend nebeneinander saßen ₁], mussten im letzten Jahr einem
    silent next.to.each.other sat must in.the last year a
    Parkplatz weichen.
    car.park give.way.to

'The benches on which the older residents of the village, who used to give friendly glances to all the children who came by, used to sit silently next to one another for hours had to give way to a car park last year.'

Therefore, one does not wish to include in the description of our grammatical knowledge that relative clauses are not allowed to be included inside each other as in (2b) as this would also rule out (3).

We can easily accept the fact that our brains are not able to process structures past a certain degree of complexity and also that corresponding utterances then become unacceptable. The contrast in the following examples is far more fascinating:[2]

(4) a. # The patient [who the nurse [who the clinic had hired] admitted] met Jack.
    b. * The patient who the nurse who the clinic had hired met Jack.

Although (4a) is syntactically well-formed and (4b) is not, Gibson & Thomas (1999) were able to show that (4b) is rated better by speakers than (4a). It does not occur to some people that an entire VP is missing. There are a number of explanations for this fact, all of which in some way make the claim that previously heard words are forgotten as soon as new words are heard and a particular degree of complexity is exceeded (Frazier 1985: 178; Gibson & Thomas 1999).

Instead of developing grammatical theories that treat (2b) and (4a) as unacceptable and (3) and (4b) as acceptable, descriptions have been developed that equally allow (2b),

---

[2] See Gibson & Thomas (1999: 227). Frazier (1985: 178) attributes the discovery of this kind of sentences to Janet Fodor.

(3), and (4a) (competence models) and then additionally investigate the way utterances are processed in order to find out what kinds of structures our brains can handle and what kinds of structures it cannot. The result of this research is then a performance model (see Gibson (1998), for example). This does not rule out that there are language-specific differences affecting language processing. For example, Vasishth, Suckow, Lewis & Kern (2010) have shown that the effects that arise in center self-embedding structures in German are different from those that arise in the corresponding English cases such as (4): due to the frequent occurrence of verb-final structures in German, speakers of German were able to better store predictions about the anticipated verbs into their working memory (p. 558).

Theories in the framework of Categorial Grammar, GB, LFG, GPSG and HPSG are theories about our linguistic competence.[3] If we want to develop a grammatical theory that directly reflects our cognitive abilities, then there should also be a corresponding performance model to go with a particular competence model. In the following two sections, I will recount some arguments from Sag & Wasow (2011) in favor of constraint-based theories such as GPSG, LFG and HPSG.

15.1 The derivational theory of complexity

The first point discussed by Sag & Wasow (2011) is the Derivational Theory of Complexity. In the early days of Transformational Grammar, it was assumed that transformations were cognitively real, that is, it is possible to measure the consumption of resources that transformations have. A sentence that requires more transformations than the analysis of another sentence should therefore also be more difficult for humans to process. The corresponding theory was dubbed the *Derivational Theory of Complexity* (DTC) and initial experiments seemed to confirm it (Miller & McKean 1964; Savin & Perchonock 1965; Clifton & Odom 1966), so that in 1968 Chomsky still assumed that the Derivational

---

[3]For an approach where the parser is equated with UG, see Abney & Cole (1986: Section 3.4). For a performance-oriented variant of Minimalism, see Phillips (2003).

In Construction Grammar, the question of whether a distinction between competence and performance would be justified at all is controversially discussed (see Section 10.6.4.9.1). Fanselow, Schlesewsky, Cavar & Kliegl (1999) also suggest a model – albeit for different reasons – where grammatical properties considerably affect processing properties. The aforementioned authors work in the framework of Optimality Theory and show that the OT constraints that they assume can explain parsing preferences. OT is not a grammatical theory on its own but rather a meta theory. It is assumed that there is a component GEN that creates a set of candidates. A further component EVAL then chooses the most optimal candidate from this set of candidates. GEN contains a generative grammar of the kind that we have seen in this book. Normally, a GP/MP variant or also LFG is assumed as the base grammar. If one assumes a transformational theory, then one automatically has a problem with the Derivational Theory of Complexity that we will encounter in the following section. If one wishes to develop OT parsing models, then one has to make reference to representational variants of GB as the aforementioned authors seem to.

Theory of Complexity was in fact correct (Chomsky 1976a: 249–250).[4] Some years later, however, most psycholinguists rejected the DTC. For discussion of several experiments that testify against the DTC, see Fodor, Bever & Garrett (1974: 320–328). One set of phenomena where the DTC makes incorrect predictions for respective analyses is that of elliptical constructions, for example (Fodor, Bever & Garrett 1974: 324): in elliptical constructions, particular parts of the utterance are left out or replaced by auxiliaries. In transformation-based approaches, it was assumed that (5b) is derived from (5a) by means of deletion of *swims* and (5c) is derived from (5b) by inserting *do*.[5]

(5)   a. John swims faster than Bob swims.

       b. John swims faster than Bob.

       c. John swims faster than Bob does.

The DTC predicts that (5b) should require more time to process than (5a), since the analysis of (5b) first requires to build up the structure in (5a) and then delete *swims*. This prediction was not confirmed.

Similarly, no difference could be identified for the pairs in (6) and (7) even though one of the sentences, given the relevant theoretical assumptions, requires more transformations for the derivation from a base structure (Fodor, Bever & Garrett 1974: 324).

(6)   a. John phoned up the girl.

       b. John phoned the girl up.

(7)   a. The bus driver was nervous after the wreck.

       b. The bus driver was fired after the wreck.

In (6), we are dealing with local reordering of the particle and the object. (7b) contains a passive clause that should be derived from an active clause under Transformational Grammar assumptions. If we compare this sentence with an equally long sentence with

---

[4]In the Transformational Grammar literature, transformations were later viewed as a metaphor (Lohnstein 2014: 170, also in Chomsky 2001: Footnote 4), that is, it was no longer assumed to have psycholinguistic reality. In *Derivation by phase* and *On phases*, Chomsky refers once again to processing aspects such as computational and memory load (Chomsky 2001: 11, 12, 15; 2007: 3, 12; 2008: 138, 145, 146, 155). See also Marantz (2005: 440) and Richards (2015). Trinh (2011: 17) cites Chomsky (p.c.) with the following quote: "As speaking involves cognitive effort, Pronunciation Economy might be derived from the general principle of minimizing computation."

A structure building operation that begins with words and is followed by transformations/internal merge and further combinations, as recently assumed by theories in the Minimalist Program, is psycholinguistically implausible for sentence parsing. See Labelle (2007) and Section 15.2 for more on incremental processing.

Chomsky (2007: 6) (written later than *On phases*) seems to adopt a constraint-based view. He writes that "a Merge-based system involves parallel operations" and compares the analysis of an utterance with a proof and explicitly mentions the competence/performance distinction.

[5]Similar analyses are assumed today in the Minimalist Program. For example, Trinh (2011: 63) assumes that VP ellipsis is deletion at Phonological Form (PF). This means that a complete structure is built which is then not pronounced. Since he talks about cognitive efforts and computation with respect to the activity of speaking (p. 17), it follows that he regards the structures he is assuming as cognitively real.

15.1 The derivational theory of complexity

an adjective, like (7a), the passive clause should be more difficult to process. This is, however, not the case.

It is necessary to add two qualifications to Sag & Wasow's claims: if one has experimental data that show that the DTC makes incorrect predictions for a particular analysis, this does not necessarily mean that the DTC has been disproved. One could also try to find a different analysis for the phenomenon in question. For example, instead of a transformation that deletes material, one could assume empty elements for the analysis of elliptical structures that are inserted directly into the structure without deleting any material (see page 68 for the assumption of an empty nominal head in structures with noun ellipsis in German). Data such as (5) would then be irrelevant to the discussion.[6] However, reordering such as (6b) and the passive in (7b) are the kinds of phenomena that are typically explained using transformations.

The second qualification pertains to analyses for which there is a representational variant: it is often said that transformations are simply metaphors (Jackendoff 2000: 22–23; 2007: 5, 20): for example, we have seen that extractions with a transformational grammar yield structures that are similar to those assumed in HPSG. Figure 15.1 shows cyclic movement in GB theory compared to the corresponding HPSG analysis.

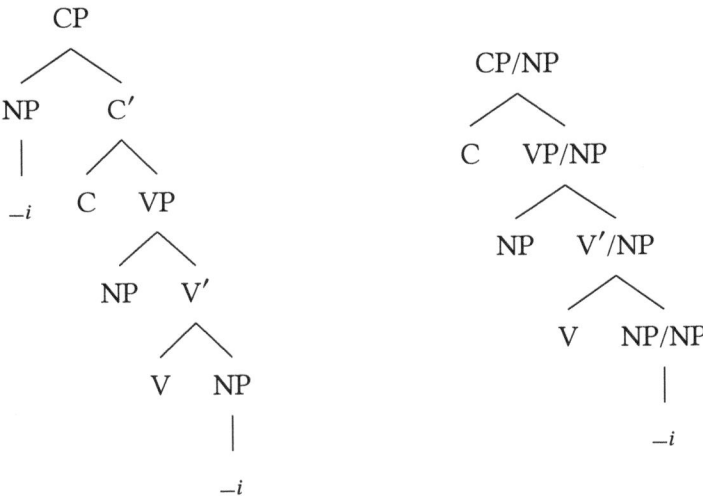

Figure 15.1: Cyclic movement vs. feature percolation

In GB, an element is moved to the specifier position of CP (SpecCP) and can then be moved from there to the next higher SpecCP position.

(8) a. Chris$_i$, we think [$_{CP}$ _$_i$ Anna claims [$_{CP}$ _$_i$ that David saw _$_i$]]. (GB)
    b. Chris$_i$, we think [$_{CP/NP}$ Anna claims [$_{CP/NP}$ that David saw _$_i$]]. (HPSG)

In HPSG, the same effect is achieved by structure sharing. Information about a long-distance dependency is not located in the specifier node but rather in the mother node

---

[6]Culicover & Jackendoff (2005: Chapters 1 and 7) argue in favor of analyzing ellipsis as a semantic or pragmatic phenomenon rather than a syntactic one anyway.

of the projection itself. In Section 19.2, I will discuss various ways of eliminating empty elements from grammars. If we apply these techniques to structures such as the GB structure in Figure 15.1, then we arrive at structures where information about missing elements is integrated into the mother node (CP) and the position in SpecCP is unfilled. This roughly corresponds to the HPSG structure in Figure 15.1.[7] It follows from this that there are classes of phenomena that can be spoken about in terms of transformations without expecting empirical differences with regard to performance when compared to transformation-less approaches. However, it is important to note that we are dealing with an S-structure in the left-hand tree in Figure 15.1. As soon as one assumes that this is derived by moving constituents out of other structures, this equivalence of approaches disappears.

15.2 Incremental processing

The next important point mentioned by Sag & Wasow (2011) is the fact that both comprehension and production of language take places incrementally. As soon as we hear or read even the beginning of a word, we begin to assign meaning and to create structure. In the same way, we sometimes start talking before we have finished planning the entire utterance. This is shown by interruptions and self-correction in spontaneous speech (Clark & Wasow 1998; Clark & Fox Tree 2002). When it comes to processing spoken speech, Tanenhaus et al. (1996) have shown that we access a word as soon as we have heard a part of it (see also Marslen-Wilson 1975). The authors of the study carried out an experiment where participants were instructed to pick up particular objects on a grid and reorganize them. Using eye-tracking measurements, Tanenhaus and colleagues could then show that the participants could identify the object in question earlier if the sound sequence at the beginning of the word was unambiguous than in cases where the initial sounds occurred in multiple words. An example for this is a configuration with a candle and candy: *candy* and *candle* both begin with *can* such that speakers could not yet decide upon hearing this sequence which lexical entry should be accessed. Therefore, there was a slight delay in accessing the lexical entry when compared to words where the objects in question did not contain the same segment at the start of the word (Tanenhaus et al. 1995: 1633).

If complex noun phrases were used in the instructions (*Touch the starred yellow square*), the participants' gaze fell on the object in question 250ms after it was unambiguously identifiable. This means that if there was only a single object with stars on it, then they looked at it after they heard *starred*. In cases where there were starred yellow blocks as well as squares, they looked at the square only after they had processed the word *square* (Tanenhaus et al. 1995: 1632). The planning and execution of a gaze lasts 200ms. From this, one can conclude that hearers combine words directly and as soon as enough information is available, they create sufficient structure in order to capture the (potential) meaning of an expression and react accordingly. This finding is incompatible with models that assume that one must have heard a complete noun phrase or even a complete

---

[7] In Figure 15.1, additionally the unary branching of C′ to CP was omitted in the tree on the right so that C combines directly with VP/NP to form CP/NP.

utterance of even more complexity before it is possible to conclude anything about the meaning of a phrase/utterance. In particular, analyses in the Minimalist Program which assume that only entire phrases or so-called phases[8] are interpreted (see Chomsky 1999 and also Marantz 2005: 441, who explicitly contrasts the MP to Categorial Grammar) must therefore be rejected as inadequate from a psycholinguistic perspective.[9, 10]

With contrastive emphasis of individual adjectives in complex noun phrases (e.g., *the BIG blue triangle*), hearers assumed that there must be a corresponding counterpart to the reference object, e.g., a small blue triangle. The eye-tracking studies carried out by Tanenhaus et al. (1996) have shown that taking this kind of information into account results in objects being identified more quickly.

Similarly, Arnold et al. (2004) have shown, also using eye-tracking studies, that hearers tend to direct their gaze to previously unmentioned objects if the interlocutor interrupts their speech with *um* or *uh*. This can be traced back to the assumption that hearers assume that describing previously unmentioned objects is more complex than referring to objects already under discussion. The speaker can create more time for himself by using *um* or *uh*.

Examples such as those above constitute evidence for approaches that assume that when processing language, information from all available channels is used and that this information is also used as soon as it is available and not only after the structure of the entire utterance or complete phrase has been constructed. The results of experimental research therefore show that the hypothesis of a strictly modular organization of linguistic knowledge must be rejected. Proponents of this hypothesis assume that the output of one module constitutes the input of another without a given module having access to the inner states of another module or the processes taking place inside it. For example, the morphology module could provide the input for syntax and then this would be processed later by the semantic module. One kind of evidence for this kind of organization of linguistic knowledge that is often cited are so-called *garden path sentences* such as (9):

(9) a. The horse raced past the barn fell.
    b. The boat floated down the river sank.

The vast majority of English speakers struggle to process these sentences since their parser is led down a garden path as it builds up a complete structure for (10a) or (10b) only then to realize that there is another verb that cannot be integrated into this structure.

---

[8]Usually, only CP and vP are assumed to be phases.

[9]Sternefeld (2006: 729–730) points out that in theories in the Minimalist Program, the common assumption of uninterpretable features is entirely unjustified. Chomsky assumes that there are features that have to be deleted in the course of a derivation since they are only relevant for syntax. If they are not checked, the derivation crashes at the interface to semantics. It follows from this that NPs should not be interpretable under the assumptions of these theories since they contain a number of features that are irrelevant for the semantics and have to therefore be deleted (see Section 4.1.2 of this book and Richards 2015). As we have seen, these kinds of theories are incompatible with the facts.

[10]It is sometimes claimed that current Minimalist theories are better suited to explain production (generation) than perception (parsing). But these models are as implausible for generation as they are for parsing. The reason is that it is assumed that there is a syntax component that generates structures that are then shipped to the interfaces. This is not what happens in generation though. Usually speakers know what they want to say (at least partly), that is, they start with semantics.

(10) a. The horse raced past the barn.
b. The boat floated down the river.

However, the actual structure of (9) contains a reduced relative clause (*raced past the barn* or *floated down the river*). That is the sentences in (9a) are semantically equivalent to the sentences in (11):

(11) a. The horse that was raced past the barn fell.
b. The boat that was floated down the river sank.

The failure of the parser in these cases was explained by assuming that syntactic processing such as constructing a sentence from NP and VP take place independently of the processing of other constraints. As Crain & Steedman (1985) and others have shown, yet there are data that make this explanation seem less plausible: if (9a) is uttered in a relevant context, the parser is not misled. In (12), there are multiple horses under discussion and each NP is clearly identified by a relative clause. The hearer is therefore prepared for a relative clause and can process the reduced relative clause without being led down the garden path, so to speak.

(12) The horse that they raced around the track held up fine. The horse that was raced down the road faltered a bit. And the horse raced past the barn fell.

By exchanging lexical material, it is also possible to modify (9a) in such way as to ensure that processing is unproblematic without having to add additional context. It is necessary to choose the material so that the interpretation of the noun as the subject of verb in the reduced relative clause is ruled out. Accordingly, *evidence* in (13) refers to an inanimate noun. It is therefore not a possible agent of *examined*. A hypothesis with *evidence* as the agent of *examined* is therefore never created when processing this sentence (Sag & Wasow 2011).

(13) The evidence examined by the judge turned out to be unreliable.

Since processing proceeds incrementally, it is sometimes assumed that realistic grammars should be obliged to immediately assign a constituent structure to previously heard material (Ades & Steedman 1982; Hausser 1992). Proponents of this view would assume a structure for the following sentence where every word forms a constituent with the preceding material:

(14) [[[[[[[[[[[[Das britische] Finanzministerium] stellt] dem] angeschlagenen]
 the British treasury provides the crippled
Bankensystem] des] Landes] mindestens] 200] Milliarden] Pfund] zur]
banking.system of.the country at.least 200 billion pounds to
Verfügung].
use

'The British Treasury is making at least 200 billion pounds available to the crippled banking system.'

Pulman (1985), Stabler (1991) and Shieber & Johnson (1993: 301–308) have shown, however, that it is possible to build semantic structures incrementally, using the kind of phrase structure grammars we encountered in Chapter 2. This means that a partial semantic representation for the string *das britische* 'the British' can be computed without having to assume that the two words form a constituent in (14). Therefore, one does not necessarily need a grammar that licenses the immediate combination of words directly. Furthermore, Shieber & Johnson (1993) point out that from a purely technical point of view, synchronous processing is more costly than asynchronous processing since synchronous processing requires additional mechanisms for synchronization whereas asynchronous processing processes information as soon as it becomes available (p. 297–298). Shieber and Johnson do not clarify whether this also applies to synchronous/asynchronous processing of syntactic and semantic information. See Shieber & Johnson (1993) for incremental processing and for a comparison of Steedman's Categorial Grammar and TAG.

What kind of conclusions can we draw from the data we have previously discussed? Are there further data that can help to determine the kinds of properties a theory of grammar should have in order to count as psycholinguistically plausible? Sag, Wasow & Bender (2003) and Sag & Wasow (2011; 2015) list the following properties that a performance-compatible competence grammar should have:[11]

- surface-oriented

- model-theoretic and therefore constraint-based

- sign-based organization

- strictly lexicalist

- representational underspecification of semantic information

Approaches such as CG, GPSG, LFG, HPSG, CxG and TAG are surface-oriented since they do not assume a base structure from which other structures are derived via transformations. Transformational approaches, however, require additional assumptions.[12] This will be briefly illustrated in what follows. In Section 3.1.5, we encountered the following analysis of English interrogatives:

(15)   [$_{CP}$ What$_i$ [$_{C'}$ will$_k$ [$_{IP}$ Ann [$_{I'}$ _$_k$ [$_{VP}$ read _$_i$]]]]].

---

[11] Also, see Jackendoff (2007) for reflections on a performance model for a constraint-based, surface-oriented linguistic theory.

[12] An exception among transformational approaches is Phillips (2003). Phillips assumes that structures relevant for phenomena such as ellipsis, coordination and fronting are built up incrementally. These constituents are then reordered in later steps by transformations. For example, in the analysis of (i), the string *Wallace saw Gromit in* forms a constituent where *in* is dominated by a node with the label P(P). This node is then turned into a PP in a subsequent step (p. 43–44).

  (i) Wallace saw Gromit in the kitchen.

While this approach is a transformation-based approach, the kind of transformation here is very idiosyncratic and incompatible with other variants of the theory. In particular, the modification of constituents contradicts the assumption of Structure Preservation when applying transformations as well as the *No Tampering Condition* of Chomsky (2008). Furthermore, the conditions under which an incomplete string such as *Wallace saw Gromit in* forms a constituent are not entirely clear.

This structure is derived from (16a) by two transformations (two applications of Move-α):

(16)   a.   Ann will read what?
        b.   * Will Ann read what

The first transformation creates the order in (16b) from (16a), and the second creates (15) from (16b).

When a hearer processes the sentence in (15), he begins to build structure as soon as he hears the first word. Transformations can, however, only be carried out when the entire utterance has been heard. One can, of course, assume that hearers process surface structures. However, since – as we have seen – they begin to access semantic knowledge early into an utterance, this begs the question of what we need a deep structure for at all.

In analyses such as those of (15), deep structure is superfluous since the relevant information can be reconstructed from the traces. Corresponding variants of GB have been proposed in the literature (see page 123). They are compatible with the requirement of being surface-oriented. Chomsky (1981a: 181; 1986a: 49) and Lasnik & Saito (1992: 59–60) propose analyses where traces can be deleted. In these analyses, the deep structure cannot be directly reconstructed from the surface structure and one requires transformations in order to relate the two. If we assume that transformations are applied 'online' during the analysis of utterances, then this would mean that the hearer would have to keep a structure derived from previously heard material as well as a list of possible transformations during processing in his working memory. In constraint-based grammars, entertaining hypotheses about potential upcoming transformation steps is not necessary since there is only a single surface structure that is processed directly. At present, it is still unclear whether it is actually possible to distinguish between these models empirically. But for Minimalist models with a large number of movements (see Figure 4.20 on page 149, for example), it should be clear that they are unrealistic since storage space is required to manage the hypotheses regarding such movements and we know that such short-term memory is very limited in humans.

Frazier & Clifton (1996: 27) assume that a transformation-based competence grammar yields a grammar with pre-compiled rules or rather templates that is then used for parsing. Therefore, theorems derived from UG are used for parsing and not axioms of UG directly. Johnson (1989) also suggests a parsing system that applies constraints from different sub-theories of GB as early as possible. This means that while he does assume the levels of representation D-Structure, S-Structure, LF and PF, he specifies the relevant constraints ($\overline{X}$ theory, Theta-Theory, Case Theory, ...) as logical conditions that can be reorganized, then be evaluated in a different but logically equivalent order and be used for structure building.[13] Chomsky (2007: 6) also compares human parsing to working through a proof, where each step of the proof can be carried out in different orders. This view does not assume the psychological reality of levels of grammatical representation when processing language, but simply assumes that principles and structures play

---

[13] Stabler (1992: Section 15.7) also considers a constraint-based view, but arrives at the conclusion that parsing and other linguistic tasks should use the structural levels of the competence theory. This would again pose problems for the DTC.

a role when it comes to language acquisition. As we have seen, the question of whether we need UG to explain language acquisition was not yet decided in favor of UG-based approaches. Instead, all available evidence seems to point in the opposite direction. However, even if innate linguistic knowledge does exist, the question arises as to why one would want to represent this as several structures linked via transformations when it is clear that these do not play a role for humans (especially language learners) when processing language. Approaches that can represent this knowledge using fewer technical means, e.g., without transformations, are therefore preferable. For more on this point, see Kuhn (2007: 615).

The requirement for constraint-based grammars is supported by incremental processing and also by the ability to deduce what will follow from previously heard material. Stabler (1991) has pointed out that Steedman's argumentation with regard to incrementally processable grammars is incorrect, and instead argues for maintaining a modular view of grammar. Stabler has developed a constraint-based grammar where syntactic and semantic knowledge can be accessed at any time. He formulates both syntactic structures and the semantic representations attached to them as conjoined constraints and then presents a processing system that processes structures based on the availability of parts of syntactic and semantic knowledge. Stabler rejects models of performance that assume that one must first apply all syntactic constraints before the semantic ones can be applied. If one abandons this strict view of modularity, then we arrive at something like (17):

(17) $(Syn_1 \wedge Syn_2 \wedge ... \wedge Syn_n) \wedge (Sem_1 \wedge Sem_2 \wedge ... \wedge Sem_n)$

Syn_1–Syn_n stand for syntactic rules or constraints and Sem_1–Sem_n stand for semantic rules or constraints. If one so desires, the expressions in brackets can be referred to as modules. Since it is possible to randomly reorder conjoined expressions, one can imagine performance models that first apply some rules from the syntax module and then, when enough information is present, respective rules from the semantic module. The order of processing could therefore be as in (18), for example:

(18) $Syn_2 \wedge Sem_1 \wedge Syn_1 \wedge ... \wedge Syn_n \wedge Sem_2 \wedge ... \wedge Sem_n$

If one subscribes to this view of modularity, then theories such as HPSG or CxG also have a modular structure. In the representation assumed in the HPSG variant of Pollard & Sag (1987) and Sign-Based CxG (see Section 10.6.2), the value of SYN would correspond to the syntax module, the value of SEM to the semantic module and the value of PHON to the phonology module. If one were to remove the respective other parts of the lexical entries/dominance schemata, then one would be left with the part of the theory corresponding exactly to the level of representation in question.[14] Jackendoff (2000) argues

---

[14]In current theories in the Minimalist Program, an increasing amount of morphological, syntactic, semantic and information-structural information is being included in analyses (see Section 4.6.1). While there are suggestions for using feature-value pairs (Sauerland & Elbourne 2002: 290–291), a strict structuring of information as in GPSG, LFG, HPSG, CxG and variants of CG and TAG is not present. This means that there are the levels for syntax, Phonological Form and Logical Form, but the information relevant for these levels is an unstructured part of syntax, smeared all over syntactic trees.

for this form of modularity with the relevant interfaces between the modules for phonology, syntax, semantics and further modules from other areas of cognition. Exactly what there is to be gained from assuming these modules and how these could be proved empirically remains somewhat unclear to me. For skepticism with regard to the very concept of modules, see Jackendoff (2000: 22,27). For more on interfaces and modularization in theories such as LFG and HPSG, see Kuhn (2007).

Furthermore, Sag & Wasow (2015: 53–54) argue that listeners often leave semantic interpretation underspecified until enough information is present either in the utterance itself or the context. They do not commit to a certain reading early and run into garden paths or backtrack to other readings. This is modeled appropriately by theories that use a variant of underspecified semantics. For a concrete example of underspecification in semantics see Section 19.3.

In conclusion, we can say that surface-oriented, model-theoretic and strongly lexicalist grammatical theories such as CG, LFG, GPSG, HPSG, CxG and the corresponding GB/MP variants (paired with appropriate semantic representations) can plausibly be combined with processing models, while this is not the case for the overwhelming majority of GB/MP theories.

16 Language acquisition

Linguists and philosophers are fascinated by the human ability to acquire language. Assuming the relevant input during childhood, language acquisition normally takes place completely effortlessly. Chomsky (1965: 24–25) put forward the requirement that a grammatical theory must provide a plausible model of language acquisition. Only then could it actually explain anything and would otherwise remain descriptive at best. In this section, we will discuss theories of acquisition from a number of theoretical standpoints.

16.1 Principles & Parameters

A very influential explanation of language acquisition is Chomsky's Principles & Parameters model (1981a). Chomsky assumes that there is an innate Universal Grammar that contains knowledge that is equally relevant for all languages. Languages can then vary in particular ways. For every difference between languages in the area of core grammar, there is a feature with a specific value. Normally, the value of a parameter is binary, that is, the value is either '+' or '−'. Depending on the setting of a parameter, a language will have certain properties, that is, setting a parameter determines whether a language belongs to a particular class of languages. Parameters are assumed to influence multiple properties of a grammar simultaneously (Chomsky 1981a: 6). For example, Rizzi (1986) claims that the pro-drop parameter affects whether referential subjects can be omitted, the absence of expletives, subject extraction from clauses with complementizers (*that*-t contexts) and interrogatives and finally the possibility of realizing the subject postverbally in VO-languages (see Chomsky 1981a: Section 4.3; Meisel 1995: 12). It has been noted that there are counter-examples to all the correlations assumed.[1] Another example of a parameter is the Head Directionality Parameter discussed in Section 13.1.1. As was shown, there are languages where heads govern in different directions. In his overview article, Haider (2001) still mentions the parametrized Subjacency Principle but notes that subjacency is no longer assumed as a principle in newer versions of the theory (see Section 13.1.5.2 for more on subjacency).

Snyder (2001) discovered a correlation of various phenomena with productive root compounding as it is manifested for instance in compounding of two nouns. He argues

---

[1] See Haider (1994) and Haider (2001: Section 2.2) for an overview. Haider assumes that there is at least a correlation between the absence of expletive subjects and pro-drop. However, Galician is a pro-drop language with expletive subject pronouns (Raposo & Uriagereka 1990: Section 2.5). Franks (1995: 314) cites Upper and Lower Sorbian as pro-drop languages with expletive subjects. Scholz & Pullum (2002: 218) point out that there is an expletive pronoun *ci* in modern Italian although Italian is classed as a pro-drop language.

that the acquisition of complex predicate formation is connected to the acquisition of compound structures and that there is a parameter that is responsible for this type of compounding and simultaneously for the following set of phenomena:

(1) a. John painted the house red. (resultative)
    b. Mary picked the book up/picked up the book. (verb-particle)
    c. Fred made Jeff leave. (*make*-causative)
    d. Fred saw Jeff leave. (perceptual report)
    e. Bob put the book on the table. (*put*-locative)
    f. Alice sent the letter to Sue. (*to*-dative)
    g. Alice sent Sue the letter. (double-object dative)

Snyder examined languages from various language groups: Afroasiatic, Austroasiatic, Austronesian, Finno-Ugric, Indo-European (Germanic, Romance, Slavic), Japanese-Korean, Niger-Kordofanian (Bantu), and Sino-Tibetan, as well as American Sign Language and the language isolate Basque. The languages that were examined either had all of these phenomena or none. This was tested with native speakers of the respective languages. In addition the claim that these phenomena are acquired once noun-noun compounds are used productively was tested for English using CHILDES data. The result was positive with the exception of the double object construction, for which an explanation was provided. The correlation of the phenomena in (1) is interesting and was interpreted as proof of the existence of a parameter that correlates several phenomena in a language. However, Son (2007) and Son & Svenonius (2008) showed that Snyder's claims for Japanese were wrong and that there are further languages like Korean, Hebrew, Czech, Malayalam, Javanese in which some of the phenomena show no correlations.

Gibson & Wexler (1994) discuss the acquisition of constituent order and assume three parameters that concern the position of the verb relative to the subject (SV vs. VS) and relative to the object (VO vs. OV) as well as the V2-property. There is no consensus in the literature about which parameters determine the make-up of languages (see Newmeyer 2005: Section 3.2 and Haspelmath 2008 for an overview and critical discussion). Fodor (1998a: 346–347) assumes that there are 20 to 30 parameters, Gibson & Wexler (1994: 408) mention the number 40, Baker (2003: 349) talks of 10 to 20 and Roberts & Holmberg (2005: 541) of 50 to 100. There is no consensus in the literature as to which parameters one should assume, how they interact and what they predict. However, it is nevertheless possible to contemplate how a grammar of an individual language could be derived from a UG with parameters that need to be set. Chomsky's original idea (1986b: Section 3.5.1) was that the child sets the value of a parameter based on the language input as soon as the relevant evidence is present from the input (see also Gibson & Wexler 1994; Nowak, Komarova & Niyogi 2001). At a given point in time, the learner has a grammar with certain parameter settings that correspond to the input seen so far. In order to fully acquire a grammar, all parameters must be assigned a value. In theory, thirty utterances should be enough to acquire a grammar with thirty parameters if these utterances provide unambiguous evidence for a particular parameter value.

This approach has often been criticized. If setting a parameter leads to a learner using a different grammar, one would expect sudden changes in linguistic behavior. This is, however, not the case (Bloom 1993: 731). Fodor (1998a: 343–344) also notes the following three problems: 1) Parameters can affect things that are not visible from the perceptible constituent order. 2) Many sentences are ambiguous with regard to the setting of a particular parameter, that is, there are sometimes multiple combinations of parameters compatible with one utterance. Therefore, the respective utterances cannot be used to set any parameters (Berwick & Niyogi 1996; Fodor 1998b). 3) There is a problem with the interaction of parameters. Normally multiple parameters play a role in an utterance such that it can be difficult to determine which parameter contributes what and thus how the values should be determined.

Points 1) and 2) can be explained using the constituent order parameters of Gibson & Wexler: imagine a child hears sentences such as the English and the German examples in (2):

(2) a. Daddy drinks juice.
     b. Papa trinkt Saft.
        daddy drinks juice

These sentences look exactly the same, even though radically different structures are assumed for each. According to the theories under discussion, the English sentence has the structure shown in Figure 3.9 on page 100 given in abbreviated form in (3a). The German sentence, on the other hand, has the structure in Figure 3.14 on page 108 corresponding to (3b):

(3) a. $[_{IP}$ [Daddy $[_{I'}$ $_{-k}$ $[_{VP}$ drinks$_k$ juice]]].
     b. $[_{CP}$ Papa$_i$ $[_{C'}$ trinkt$_k$ $[_{IP}$ $_{-i}$ $[_{I'}$ $[_{VP}$ Saft $_{-k}$] $_{-k}$]]]].

English has the basic constituent order SVO. The verb forms a constituent with the object (VP) and this is combined with the subject. The parameter setting must therefore be SV, VO and −V2. German, on the other had, is analyzed as a verb-final and verb-second language and the parameter values would therefore have to be SV, OV and +V2. If we consider the sentences in (2), we see that both sentences do not differ from one another with regard to the order of the verb and its arguments.

Fodor (1998a,b) concludes from this that one first has to build a structure in order to see what grammatical class the grammar licensing the structure belongs to since one first needs the structure in (3b) in order to be able to see that the verb in the partial constituent occurs after its argument in the VP (Saft $_{-k}$). The question is now how one achieves this structure. A UG with 30 parameters corresponds to 2^{30} = 1,073,741,824 fully instantiated grammars. It is an unrealistic assumption that children try out these grammars successively or simultaneously.

Gibson & Wexler (1994) discuss a number of solutions for this problem: parameters have a default value and the learner can only change a parameter value if a sentence that could previously not be analyzed can then be analyzed with the new parameter setting (*Greediness Constraint*). In this kind of procedure, only one parameter can be changed at a time (*Single Value Constraint*), which aims at ruling out great leaps leading to extremely different grammars (see Berwick & Niyogi 1996: 612–613, however). This reduces the processing demands, however with 40 parameters, the worst case could still be that one has to test 40 parameter values separately, that is, try to parse a sentence with

40 different grammars. This processing feat is still unrealistic, which is why Gibson & Wexler (1994: 442) additionally assume that one hypothesis is tested per input sentence. A further modification of the model is the assumption that certain parameters only begin to play a role during the maturation of the child. At a given point in time, there could be only a few accessible parameters that also need to be set. After setting these parameters, new parameters could become available.

In their article, Gibson & Wexler show that the interaction between input and parameter setting is in no way trivial. In their example scenario with three parameters, a situation can arise in which a learner sets a parameter in order to analyze a new sentence, however setting this parameter leads to the fact that the target grammar cannot be acquired because only one value can be changed at a time and changes can only be made if more sentences can be analyzed than before. The learner reaches a so-called local maximum in these problematic cases.[2] Gibson & Wexler then suggest assigning a default value to particular parameters, whereby the default value is the one that will cause the learner to avoid problematic situations. For the V2 parameter, they assume '−' as the default value.

Berwick & Niyogi (1996) show that Gibson & Wexler calculated the problematic conditions incorrectly and that, if one shares their assumptions, it is even more frequently possible to arrive at parameter combinations from which it is not possible to reach the target grammar by changing individual parameter values. They show that one of the problematic cases not addressed by Gibson & Wexler is −V2 (p. 609) and that the assumption of a default value for a parameter does not solve the problem as both '+' and '−' can lead to problematic combinations of parameters.[3] In their article, Berwick and Niyogi show that learners in the example scenario above (with three parameters) learn the target grammar faster if one abandons the Greediness or else the Single Value Constraint. They suggest a process that simply randomly changes one parameter if a sentence cannot be analyzed (*Random Step*, p. 615–616). The authors note that this approach does not share the problems with the local maxima that Gibson & Wexler had in their example and that it also reaches its goal faster than theirs. However, the fact that *Random Step* converges more quickly has to do with the quality of the parameter space (p. 618). Since there is no consensus about parameters in the literature, it is not possible to assess how the entire system works.

Yang (2004: 453) has criticized the classic Principles & Parameters model since abrupt switching between grammars after setting a parameter cannot be observed. Instead, he proposes the following learning mechanism:

(4) For an input sentence, *s*, the child: (i) with probability P_i selects a grammar G_i, (ii) analyzes *s* with G_i, (iii) if successful, reward G_i by increasing P_i, otherwise punish G_i by decreasing P_i.

---

[2]If one imagines the acquisition process as climbing a hill, then the Greediness Constraint ensures that one can only go uphill. It could be the case, however, that one begins to climb the wrong hill and can no longer get back down.

[3]Kohl (1999; 2000) has investigated this acquisition model in a case with twelve parameters. Of the 4096 possible grammars, 2336 (57%) are unlearnable if one assumes the best initial values for the parameters.

Yang discusses the example of the pro-drop and topic drop parameters. In pro-drop languages (e.g., Italian), it is possible to omit the subject and in topic drop languages (e.g., Mandarin Chinese), it possible to omit both the subject and the object if it is a topic. Yang compares English-speaking and Chinese-speaking children noting that English children omit both subjects and objects in an early linguistic stage. He claims that the reason for this is that English-speaking children start off using the Chinese grammar.

The pro-drop parameter is one of the most widely discussed parameters in the context of Principles & Parameters theory and it will therefore be discussed in more detail here. It is assumed that speakers of English have to learn that all sentences in English require a subject, whereas speakers of Italian learn that subjects can be omitted. One can observe that children learning both English and Italian omit subjects (German children too in fact). Objects are also omitted notably more often than subjects. There are two possible explanations for this: a competence-based one and a performance-based one. In competence-based approaches, it is assumed that children use a grammar that allows them to omit subjects and then only later acquire the correct grammar (by setting parameters or increasing the rule apparatus). In performance-based approaches, by contrast, the omission of subjects is traced back to the fact that children are not yet capable of planning and producing long utterances due to their limited brain capacity. Since the cognitive demands are greatest at the beginning of an utterance, this leads to subjects beings increasingly left out. Valian (1991) investigated these various hypotheses and showed that the frequency with which children learning English and Italian respectively omit subjects is not the same. Subjects are omitted more often than objects. She therefore concludes that competence-based explanations are not empirically adequate. The omission of subjects should then be viewed more as a performance phenomenon (see also Bloom 1993). Another argument for the influence of performance factors is the fact that articles of subjects are left out more often than articles of objects (31% vs. 18%, see Gerken 1991: 440). As Bloom notes, no subject article-drop parameter has been proposed so far. If we explain this phenomenon as a performance phenomenon, then it is also plausible to assume that the omittance of complete subjects is due to performance issues.

Gerken (1991) shows that the metrical properties of utterances also play a role: in experiments where children had to repeat sentences, they omitted the subject/article of the subject more often than the object/article of the object. Here, it made a difference whether the intonation pattern was iambic (weak-strong) or trochaic (strong-weak). It can even be observed with individual words that children leave out weak syllables at the beginning of words more often than at the end of the word. Thus, it is more probable that "giRAFFE" is reduced to "RAFFE" than "MONkey" to "MON". Gerken assumes the following for the metrical structure of utterances:

1. A metrical foot contains one and only one strong syllable.

2. Create maximally binary left-to-right feet.

3. Metrical structure is independent of syntactic structure.

Subject pronouns in English are sentence-initial and form a iambic foot with the following strongly emphasized verb as in (5a). Object pronouns, however, can form the weak syllable of a trochaic foot as in (5b).

(5) a. she KISSED + the DOG
 b. the DOG + KISSED her
 c. PETE + KISSED the + DOG

Furthermore, articles in iambic feet as in the object of (5a) and the subject of (5b) are omitted more often than in trochaic feet such as with the object of (5c).

It follows from this that there are multiple factors that influence the omission of elements and that one cannot simply take the behavior of children as evidence for switching between two grammars.

Apart from what has been discussed so far, the pro-drop parameter is of interest for another reason: there is a problem when it comes to setting parameters. The standard explanation is that learners identify that a subject must occur in all English sentences, which is suggested by the appearance of expletive pronouns in the input.

As discussed on page 529, there is no relation between the pro-drop property and the presence of expletives in a language. Since the pro-drop property does not correlate with any of the other putative properties either, only the existence of subject-less sentences in the input constitutes decisive evidence for setting a parameter. The problem is that there are grammatical utterances where there is no visible subject. Examples of this are imperatives such as (6), declaratives with a dropped subject as in (7a) and even declarative sentences without an expletive such as the example in (7b) found by Valian (1991: 32) in the New York Times.

(6) a. Give me the teddy bear!
 b. Show me your toy!

(7) a. She'll be a big hit. Sings like a dream.
 b. Seems like she always has something twin-related perking.

The following title of a Nirvana song also comes from the same year as Valian's article:

(8) Smells like Teen Spirit.

Teen Spirit refers to a deodorant and *smell* is a verb that, both in German and English, requires a referential subject but can also be used with an expletive *it* as subject. The usage that Kurt Cobain had in mind cannot be reconstructed[4], independent of the intended meaning, however, the subject in (8) is missing. Imperatives do occur in the input children have and are therefore relevant for acquisition. Valian (1991: 33) says the following about them:

---

[4]See http://de.wikipedia.org/wiki/Smells_Like_Teen_Spirit. 2018-02-20.

> What is acceptable in the adult community forms part of the child's input, and is also part of what children must master. The utterances that I have termed "acceptable" are not grammatical in English (since English does not have pro subjects, and also cannot be characterized as a simple VP). They lack subjects and therefore violate the extended projection principle (Chomsky 1981a), which we are assuming.
>
> Children are exposed to fully grammatical utterances without subjects, in the form of imperatives. They are also exposed to acceptable utterances which are not fully grammatical, such as [(7a)], as well as forms like, "Want lunch now?" The American child must grow into an adult who not only knows that overt subjects are grammatically required, but also knows when subjects can acceptably be omitted. The child must not only acquire the correct grammar, but also master the discourse conditions that allow relaxation of the grammar. (Valian 1991: 33)

This passage turns the relations on their head: we cannot conclude from the fact that a particular grammatical theory is not compatible with certain data, that these data should not be described by this theory, instead we should modify the incompatible grammar or, if this is not possible, we should reject it. Since utterances with imperatives are entirely regular, there is no reason to categorize them as utterances that do not follow grammatical rules. The quotation above represents a situation where a learner has to acquire two grammars: one that corresponds to the innate grammar and a second that partially suppresses the rules of innate grammar and also adds some additional rules.

The question we can pose at this point is: how does a child distinguish which of the data it hears are relevant for which of the two grammars?

Fodor (1998a: 347) pursues a different analysis that does not suffer from many of the aforementioned problems. Rather than assuming that learners try to find a correct grammar among a billion others, she instead assumes that children work with a single grammar that contains all possibilities. She suggests using parts of trees (*treelets*) rather than parameters. These treelets can also be underspecified and in extreme cases, a treelet can consist of a single feature (Fodor 1998b: 6). A language learner can deduce whether a language has a given property from the usage of a particular treelet. As an example, she provides a VP treelet consisting of a verb and a prepositional phrase. This treelet must be used for the analysis of the VP occurring in *Look at the frog*. Similarly, the analysis of an interrogative clause with a fronted *who* would make use of a treelet with a *wh*-NP in the specifier of a complementizer phrase (see Figure 3.7 on page 99). In Fodor's version of Principles and Parameters Theory, this treelet would be the parameter that licenses *wh*-movement in (overt) syntax. Fodor assumes that there are defaults that allow a learner to parse a sentence even when no or very few parameters have been set. This allows one to learn from utterances that one would have not otherwise been able to use since there would have been multiple possible analyses for them. Assuming a default can lead to misanalyses, however: due to a default value, a second parameter could be set because an utterance was analyzed with a treelet t_1 and t_3, for example, but t_1 was not suited to the particular language in question and the utterance should have instead been analyzed with the non-default treelet t_2 and the treelet t_{17}. In this acquisition model, there must therefore be the possibility to correct wrong decisions in the parameter setting process.

16 Language acquisition

Fodor therefore assumes that there is a frequency-based degree of activation for parameters (p. 365): treelets that are often used in analyses have a high degree of activation, whereas those used less often have a lower degree of activation. In this way, it is not necessary to assume a particular parameter value while excluding others.

Furthermore, Fodor proposes that parameters should be structured hierarchically, that is, only if a parameter has a particular value does it then make sense to think about specific other parameter values.

Fodor's analysis is – as she herself notes (Fodor 2001: 385) – compatible with theories such as HPSG and TAG. Pollard & Sag (1987: 147) characterize UG as the conjunction of all universally applicable principles:

(9) $UG = P_1 \wedge P_2 \wedge \ldots \wedge P_n$

As well as principles that hold universally, there are other principles that are specific to a particular language or a class of languages. Pollard & Sag give the example of the constituent ordering principle that only holds for English. English can be characterized as follows if one assumes that P_{n+1}–P_m are language-specific principles, L_1–L_p a complete list of lexical entries and R_1–R_q a list of dominance schemata relevant for English.

(10) English = $P_1 \wedge P_2 \wedge \ldots \wedge P_m \wedge (L_1 \vee \ldots \vee L_p \vee R_1 \vee \ldots \vee R_q)$

In Pollard & Sag's conception, only those properties of language that equally hold for all languages are part of UG. Pollard & Sag do not count the dominance schemata as part of this. However, one can indeed also describe UG as follows:

(11) $UG = P_1 \wedge P_2 \wedge \ldots \wedge P_n \wedge (R_{en\text{-}1} \vee \ldots \vee R_{en\text{-}q} \vee R_{de\text{-}1} \vee \ldots \vee R_{de\text{-}r} \vee \ldots)$

P_1–P_n are, as before, universally applicable principles and $R_{en\text{-}1}$–$R_{en\text{-}q}$ are the (core) dominance schemata of English and $R_{de\text{-}1}$–$R_{de\text{-}r}$ are the dominance schemata in German. The dominance schemata in (11) are combined by means of disjunctions, that is, not every disjunct needs to have a realization in a specific language. Principles can make reference to particular properties of lexical entries and rule out certain phrasal configurations. If a language only contains heads that are marked for final-position in the lexicon, then grammatical rules that require a head in initial position as their daughter can never be combined with these heads or their projections. Furthermore, theories with a type system are compatible with Fodor's approach to language acquisition because constraints can easily be underspecified. As such, constraints in UG do not have to make reference to all properties of grammatical rules: principles can refer to feature values, the language-specific values themselves do not have to already be contained in UG. Similarly, a supertype describing multiple dominance schemata that have similar but language-specific instantiations can also be part of UG, however the language-specific details remain open and are then deduced by the learner upon parsing (see Ackerman & Webelhuth 1998: Section 9.2). The differences in activation assumed by Fodor can be captured by weighting the constraints: the dominance schemata $R_{en\text{-}1}$–$R_{en\text{-}q}$ etc. are sets of feature-value pairs as well as path equations. As explained in Chapter 15, weights can be added to such constraints and also to sets of constraints. In Fodor's acquisition model, given a German input, the weights for the rules of English would be reduced and those for the German rules would be increased. Note that in Pollard & Sag's acquisition scenario, there are no triggers for parameter setting unlike in Fodor's model. Furthermore, properties that were previously disjunctively specified as part of UG will now be acquired directly. Using the treelet t_{17} (or rather a possibly underspecified dominance schema), it is not the case that the value '+' is set for a parameter P_5 but rather the activation potential of t_{17} is increased such that t_{17} will be prioritized for future analyses.

16.2 Principles and the lexicon

A variant of the UG-driven theory of language acquisition would be to assume that principles are so general that they hold for all languages and individual languages simply differ with regard to their lexicon. Principles then refer to properties of combined entities. Parameters therefore migrate from principles into the lexicon (Chomsky 1999: 2). See Mensching & Remberger (2011) for a study of Romance languages in this model and Son & Svenonius (2008: 395) for an analysis of Snyder's examples that were discussed in the previous subsection.

At this point, one can observe an interesting convergence in these approaches: most of the theories discussed here assume a very general structure for the combination of heads with their arguments. For example, in Categorial Grammar and the Minimalist Program, these are always binary functor-argument combinations. The way in which constituents can be ordered in a particular language depends on the lexical properties of the combined elements.

The question that is being discussed controversially at present is whether the spectrum of lexical properties is determined by UG (Chomsky 2007: 6–7) and whether all areas of the language can be described with the same general combinatorial possibilities (see Section 21.10 on phrasal constructions).

In Section 16.1, I have shown what theories of acquisition assuming innate language specific knowledge can look like and also that variants of such acquisition theories are compatible with all the theories of grammar we have discussed. During this discussion, one should bear in mind the question of whether it makes sense at all to assume that English children use parts of a Chinese grammar during some stages of their acquisition process (as suggested by Yang 2004: 453), or whether the relevant phenomena can be explained in different ways. In the following, I will present some alternative approaches that do not presuppose innate language specific knowledge, but instead assume that language can simply be acquired from the input. The following section will deal with pattern-based approaches and Section 16.4 will discuss the lexically-oriented variant of input-based language acquisition.

16.3 Pattern-based approaches

Chomsky (1981a: 7–8) proposed that languages can be divided into a core area and a periphery. The core contains all regular aspects of language. The core grammar of a language is seen as an instantiation of UG. Idioms and other irregular parts of language are

16 Language acquisition

then part of the periphery. Critics of the Principles & Parameters model have pointed out that idiomatic and irregular constructions constitute a relatively large part of our language and that the distinction, both fluid and somewhat arbitrary, is only motivated theory-internally (Jackendoff 1997: Chapter 7; Culicover 1999; Ginzburg & Sag 2000: 5; Newmeyer 2005: 48; Kuhn 2007: 619). For example, it is possible to note that there are interactions between various idioms and syntax (Nunberg, Sag & Wasow 1994). Most idioms in German with a verbal component allow the verb to be moved to initial position (12b), some allow that parts of idioms can be fronted (12c) and some can undergo passivization (12d).

(12)   a. dass er ihm den Garaus macht
         that he him the GARAUS makes
         'that he finishes him off (kills him)'

     b. Er macht ihm den Garaus.
         he makes him the GARAUS
         'He finishes him off.'

     c. In Amerika sagte man der Kamera nach, die größte Kleinbildkamera der Welt zu sein. Sie war laut Schleiffer am Ende der Sargnagel der Mühlheimer Kameraproduktion.
Den Garaus machte ihr die Diskussion um die Standardisierung des
the GARAUS made her the discussion around the standardization of.the
16-Millimeter-Filmformats, an dessen Ende die DIN-Norm 19022 (Patrone
16-millimeter-film.format at whose end the DIN-norm 19022 cartridge
mit Spule für 16-Millimeter-Film) stand, die im März 1963 zur Norm
with coil for 16-millimeter-film stood that in March 1963 to.the norm
wurde.[5]
became

'In America, one says that this camera was the biggest compact camera in the world. According to Schleiffer, it was the last nail in the coffin for camera production in Mühlheim. What finished it off was the discussion about standardizing the 16 millimeter format, which resulted in the DIN-Norm 19022 (cartridge with coil for 16 millimeter film) that became the norm in March 1963.'

     d. in Heidelberg wird „parasitären Elementen" unter den Professoren *der*
in Heidelberg are parasitic elements among the professors the
Garaus gemacht[6]
GARAUS made

'In Heidelberg, "parasitic elements" among professors are being killed off.'

It is assumed that the periphery and lexicon are not components of UG (Chomsky 1986b: 150–151; Fodor 1998a: 343) but rather are acquired using other learning methods – namely inductively directly from the input. The question posed by critics is now why these

---

[5]Frankfurter Rundschau, 28.06.1997, p. 2.
[6]Mannheimer Morgen, 28.06.1999, Sport; Schrauben allein genügen nicht.

methods should not work for regular aspects of the language as well (Abney 1996: 20; Goldberg 2003a: 222; Newmeyer 2005: 100; Tomasello 2006c: 36; 2006b: 20): the areas of the so-called 'core' are by definition more regular then components of the periphery, which is why they should be easier to learn.

Tomasello (2000; 2003) has pointed out that a Principles & Parameters model of language acquisition is not compatible with the observable facts. The Principles and Parameters Theory predicts that children should no longer make mistakes in a particular area of grammar once they have set a particular parameter correctly (see Chomsky 1986b: 146, Radford 1990: 21–22 and Lightfoot 1997: 175). Furthermore, it is assumed that a parameter is responsible for very different areas of grammar (see the discussion of the pro-drop parameter in Section 16.1). When a parameter value is set, then there should be sudden developments with regard to a number of phenomena (Lightfoot 1997: 174). This is, however, not the case. Instead, children acquire language from utterances in their input and begin to generalize from a certain age. Depending on the input, they can re-order certain auxiliaries and not others, although movement of auxiliaries is obligatory in English.[7] One argument put forward against these kinds of input-based theories is that children produce utterances that cannot be observed to a significant frequency in the input. One much discussed phenomenon of this kind are so called *root infinitives* (RI) or *optional infinitives* (OI) (Wexler 1998). These are infinitive forms that can be used in non-embedded clauses (*root sentences*) instead of a finite verb. Optional infinitives are those where children use both a finite (13a) and non-finite (13b) form (Wexler 1998: 59):

(13) a. Mary likes ice cream.

b. Mary like ice cream.

Wijnen, Kempen & Gillis (2001: 656) showed that Dutch children use the order object infinitive 90 % of the time during the two-word phase although these orders occur in less than 10 % of their mother's utterances that contained a verb. Compound verb forms, e.g., with a modal in initial position as in (14) that contain another instance of this pattern only occurred in 30 % of the input containing a verb (Wijnen, Kempen & Gillis 2001: 647).

(14) Willst du Brei essen?
want you porridge eat

'Do you want to eat porridge?'

At first glance, there seems to be a discrepancy between the input and the child's utterances. However, this deviation could also be explained by an utterance-final bias in learning (Wijnen et al. 2001; Freudenthal, Pine & Gobet 2006). A number of factors can be made responsible for the salience of verbs at the end of an utterance: 1) restrictions of the infant brain. It has been shown that humans (both children and adults) forget words during the course of an utterance, that is, the activation potential decreases. Since the cognitive capabilities of small children are restricted, it is clear why elements at the end of an utterance have an important status. 2) Easier segmentation at the end of an

---

[7] Here, Yang's suggestion to combine grammars with a particular probability does not help since one would have to assume that the child uses different grammars for different auxiliaries, which is highly unlikely.

utterance. At the end of an utterance, part of the segmentation problem for hearers disappears: the hearer first has to divide a sequence of phonemes into individual words before he can understand them and combine them to create larger syntactic entities. This segmentation is easier at the end of an utterance since the word boundary is already given by the end of the utterance. Furthermore according to Wijnen, Kempen & Gillis (2001: 637), utterance-final words have an above average length and do bear a pitch accent. This effect occurs more often in language directed at children.

Freudenthal, Pine, Aguado-Orea & Gobet (2007) have modeled language acquisition for English, German, Dutch, and Spanish. The computer model could reproduce differences between these languages based on input. At first glance, it is surprising that there are even differences between German and Dutch and between English and Spanish with regard to the use of infinitives as German and Dutch have a very similar syntax (SOV+V2). Similarly, English and Spanish are both languages with SVO order. Nevertheless, children learning English make OI mistakes, whereas this is hardly ever the case for children learning Spanish.

Freudenthal, Pine, Aguado-Orea & Gobet (2007) trace the differences in error frequencies back to the distributional differences in each language: the authors note that 75 % of verb-final utterances[8] in English consist of compound verbs (finite verb + dependent verb, e.g., *Can he go?*), whereas this is only the case 30 % of the time in Dutch.

German also differs from Dutch with regard to the number of utterance-final infinitives. Dutch has a progressive form that does not exist in Standard German:

(15) Wat ben je aan het doen?
 what are you on it do.INF
 'What are you doing?'

Furthermore, verbs such as *zitten* 'to sit', *lopen* 'to run' and *staan* 'to stand' can be used in conjunction with the infinitive to describe events happening in that moment:

(16) Zit je te spelen?
 sit you to play
 'Are you sitting and playing?'

Furthermore, there is a future form in Dutch that is formed with *ga* 'go'. These factors contribute to the fact that Dutch has 20 % more utterance-final infinitives than German.

Spanish differs from English in that it has object clitics:

(17) (Yo) Lo quiero.
 I it want
 'I want it.'

Short pronouns such as *lo* in (17) are realized in front of the finite verb so that the verb appears in final position. In English, the object follows the verb, however. Furthermore,

---

[8]For English, the authors only count utterances with a subject in third person singular since it is only in these cases that a morphological difference between the finite and infinitive form becomes clear.

there are a greater number of compound verb forms in the English input (70 %) than in Spanish (25 %). This is due to the higher frequency of the progressive in English and the presence of *do*-support in question formation.

The relevant differences in the distribution of infinitives are captured correctly by the proposed acquisition model, whereas alternative approaches that assume that children possess an adult grammar but use infinitives instead of the finite forms cannot explain the gradual nature of this phenomenon.

Freudenthal, Pine & Gobet (2009) could even show that input-based learning is superior to other explanations for the distribution of NPs and infinitives. They can explain why this order is often used with a modal meaning (e.g., *to want*) in German and Dutch (Ingram & Thompson 1996). In these languages, infinitives occur with modal verbs in the corresponding interrogative clauses. Alternative approaches that assume that the linguistic structures in question correspond to those of adults and only differ from them in that a modal verb is not pronounced cannot explain why not all utterances of object and verb done by children learning German and Dutch do have a modal meaning. Furthermore, the main difference to English cannot be accounted for: in English, the number of modal meanings is considerably less. Input-based models predict this exactly since English can use the dummy verb *do* to form questions:

(18)   a. Did he help you?

       b. Can he help you?

If larger entities are acquired from the end of an utterance, then there would be both a modal and non-modal context for *he help you*. Since German and Dutch normally do not use the auxiliary *tun* 'do', the relevant endings of utterances are always associated with modals contexts. One can thereby explain why infinitival expressions have a modal meaning significantly more often in German and Dutch than in English.

Following this discussion of the arguments against input-based theories of acquisition, I will turn to Tomasello's pattern-based approach. According to Tomasello (2003: Section 4.2.1), a child hears a sentence such as (19) and realizes that particular slots can be filled freely (see also Dąbrowska (2001) for analogous suggestions in the framework of Cognitive Grammar).

(19)   a. Do you want more juice/milk?

       b. Mommy is gone.

From these utterances, it is possible to derive so-called pivot schemata such as those in (20) into which words can then be inserted:

(20)   a. more ___ → more juice/milk

       b. ___ gone → mommy/juice gone

In this stage of development (22 months), children do not generalize using these schemata, these schemata are instead construction islands and do not yet have any syntax (Tomasello et al. 1997). The ability to use previously unknown verbs with a subject and an object in an SVO order is acquired slowly between the age of three and four (Tomasello 2003: 128–129). More abstract syntactic and semantic relations only emerge with time: when confronted with multiple instantiations of the transitive construction, the child is then able to generalize:

(21) a. [s [NP The man/the woman] sees [NP the dog/the rabbit/it]].

   b. [s [NP The man/the woman] likes [NP the dog/the rabbit/it]].

   c. [s [NP The man/the woman] kicks [NP the dog/the rabbit/it]].

According to Tomasello (2003: 107), this abstraction takes the form [Sbj TrVerb Obj]. Tomasello's approach is immediately plausible since one can recognize how abstraction works: it is a generalization about reoccurring patterns. Each pattern is then assigned a semantic contribution. These generalizations can be captured in inheritance hierarchies (see page 209) (Croft 2001: 26). The problem with this kind of approach, however, is that it cannot explain the interaction between different areas of phenomena in the language: it is possible to represent simple patterns such as the use of transitive verbs in (21), but transitive verbs interact with other areas of the grammar such as negation. If one wishes to connect the construction one assumes for the negation of transitive verbs with the transitive construction, then one arrives at a problem since this is not possible in inheritance hierarchies.

(22) The woman did not kick the dog.

The problem is that the transitive construction has a particular semantic contribution but that negated transitive construction has the opposite meaning. The values of SEM features would therefore be contradictory. There are technical tricks to avoid this problem, however, since there are a vast number of these kinds of interactions between syntax and semantics, this kind of technical solution will result in something highly implausible from a cognitive perspective (Müller 2006; 2007b,a; 2010b; Müller & Wechsler 2014a). For discussion of Croft's analysis, see Section 21.4.1.

At this point, proponents of pattern-based analyses might try and argue that these kinds of problems are only the result of a poor/inadequate formalization and would rather do without a formalization (Goldberg 2009: Section 5). However, this does not help here as the problem is not the formalization itself, rather the formalization allows one to see the problem more clearly.

An alternative to an approach built entirely on inheritance is a TAG-like approach that allows one to insert syntactic material into phrasal constructions. Such a proposal was discussed in Section 10.6.3. Bergen & Chang (2005: 170) working in Embodied Construction Grammar suggest an Active-Ditransitive Construction with the form [RefExpr Verb RefExpr RefExpr], where RefExpr stands for a referential expression and the first RefExpr and the verb may be non-adjacent. In this way, it is possible to analyze (23a,b), while ruling out (23c):

(23) a. Mary tossed me a drink.

   b. Mary happily tossed me a drink.

   c. *Mary tossed happily me a drink.

16.3 Pattern-based approaches

While the compulsory adjacency of the verb and the object correctly predicts that (23c) is ruled out, the respective constraint also rules out coordinate structures such as (24):

(24) Mary tossed me a juice and Peter a water.

Part of the meaning of this sentence corresponds to what the ditransitive construction contributes to *Mary tossed Peter a water*. There is, however, a gap between *tossed* and *Peter*. Similarly, one can create examples where there is a gap between both objects of a ditransitive construction:

(25) He showed me and bought for Mary the book that was recommended in the Guardian last week.

In (25), *me* is not adjacent to *the book* .... It is not my aim here to request a coordination analysis. Coordination is a very complex phenomenon for which most theories do not have a straightforward analysis (see Section 21.6.2). Instead, I would simply like to point out that the fact that constructions can be realized discontinuously poses a problem for approaches that claim that language acquisition is exclusively pattern-based. The point is the following: in order to understand coordination data in a language, a speaker must learn that a verb which has its arguments somewhere in the sentence has a particular meaning together with these arguments. The actual pattern [Sbj V Obj1 Obj2] can, however, be interrupted in all positions. In addition to the coordination examples, there is also the possibility of moving elements out of the pattern either to the left or the right. In sum, we can say that language learners have to learn that there is a relation between functors and their arguments. This is all that is left of pattern-based approaches but this insight is also covered by the selection-based approaches that we will discuss in the following section.

A defender of pattern-based approaches could perhaps object that there is a relevant construction for (25) that combines all material. This means that one would have a construction with the form [Sbj V Obj1 Conj V PP Obj2]. It would then have to be determined experimentally or with corpus studies whether this actually makes sense. The generalization that linguists have found is that categories with the same syntactic properties can be coordinated (N, $\overline{\text{N}}$, NP, V, $\overline{\text{V}}$, VP, ...). For the coordination of verbs or verbal projections, it must hold that the coordinated phrases require the same arguments:

(26) a. Er [arbeitet] und [liest viele Bücher].
          he works   and reads many books

      b. Er [kennt und liebt] diese Schallplatte.
          he knows and loves this record

      c. Er [zeigt dem Jungen] und [gibt der Frau] die Punk-Rock-CD.
          he shows the boy   and gives the woman the punk rock CD

      d. Er [liebt diese Schallplatte] und [schenkt ihr ein Buch].
          he loves this record   and gives   her a   book

In an approach containing only patterns, one would have to assume an incredibly large number of constructions and so far we are only considering coordinations that consist

16 Language acquisition

of exactly two conjuncts. However, the phenomenon discussed above is not only restricted to coordination of two elements. If we do not wish to abandon the distinction between competence and performance (see Chapter 15), then the number of conjuncts is not constrained at all (by the competence grammar):

(27) Er [kennt, liebt und verborgt] diese Schallplatte.
 he knows loves and lends.out this record

It is therefore extremely unlikely that learners have patterns for all possible cases in their input. It is much more likely that they draw the same kind of generalizations as linguists from the data occurring in their input: words and phrases with the same syntactic properties can be coordinated. If this turns out to be true, then all that is left for pattern-based approaches is the assumption of discontinuously realized constructions and thus a dependency between parts of constructions that states that they do not have to be immediately adjacent to one another. The acquisition problem is then the same as for selection-based approaches that will be the topic of the following section: what ultimately has to be learned are dependencies between elements or valences (see Behrens (2009: 439), the author reaches the same conclusion following different considerations).

16.4 Selection-based approaches

I will call the alternative to pattern-based approaches *selection-based*. A selection-based approach has been proposed by Green (2011).

The generalizations about the pattern in (21) pertain to the valence class of the verb. In Categorial Grammar, the pattern [Sbj TrVerb Obj] corresponds to the lexical entry (s\np)/np (for the derivation of a sentence with this kind of lexical entry, see Figure 8.3 on page 247). A TAG tree for *likes* was given on page 419. Here, one can see quite clearly that lexical entries determine the structure of sentences in these models. Unlike pattern-based approaches, these analyses allow enough room for semantic embedding: the lexical entries in Categorial Grammar can be combined with adjuncts, and elementary trees in TAG also allow for adjunction to the relevant nodes.

Now, we face the question of how the jump from a pivot schema to a lexical entry with an argument structure takes place. In Tomasello's approach, there is no break between them. Pivot schemata are phrasal patterns and [Sbj TrVerb Obj] is also a phrasal pattern. Both schemata have open slots into which certain elements can be inserted. In selection-based approaches, the situation is similar: the elements that are fixed in the pivot schema are functors in the selection-based approach. Green (2011) proposes a theory of acquisition in HPSG that can do without UG. For the two-word phase, she assumes that *where's* is the head of an utterance such as (28) and that *where's* selects *Robin* as its argument.

(28) Where's Robin?

This means that, rather than assuming that there is a phrasal pattern *Where's* X? with an empty slot X for a person or thing, she assumes that there is a lexical entry *where's*, which contains the information that it needs to be combined with another constituent.

What needs to be acquired is the same in each case: there is particular material that has to be combined with other material in order to yield a complete utterance.

In her article, Green shows how long-distance dependencies and the position of English auxiliaries can be acquired in later stages of development. The acquisition of grammar proceeds in a monotone fashion, that is, knowledge is added – for example, knowledge about the fact that material can be realized outside of the local context – and previous knowledge does not have to be revised. In her model, mistakes in the acquisition process are in fact mistakes in the assignment of lexical entries to valence classes. These mistakes have to be correctable.

In sum, one can say that all of Tomasello's insights can be applied directly to selection-based approaches and the problems with pattern-based approaches do not surface with selection-based approaches. It is important to point out explicitly once again here that the selection-based approach discussed here also is a construction-based approach. Constructions are just lexical and not phrasal. The important point is that, in both approaches, words and also more complex phrases are pairs of form and meaning and can be acquired as such.

In Chapter 21, we will discuss pattern-based approaches further and we will also explore areas of the grammar where phrasal patterns should be assumed.

16.5 Summary

We should take from the preceding discussion that models of language acquisition that assume that a grammar is chosen from a large set of grammars by setting binary parameters are in fact inadequate. All theories that make reference to parameters have in common that they are purely hypothetical since there is no non-trivial set of parameters that all proponents of the model equally agree on. In fact there is not even a trivial one.

In a number of experiments, Tomasello and his colleagues have shown that, in its original form, the Principles & Parameters model makes incorrect predictions and that language acquisition is much more pattern-based than assumed by proponents of P&P analyses. Syntactic competence develops starting from verb islands. Depending on the frequency of the input, certain verbal constructions can be mastered even though the same construction has not yet been acquired with less frequent verbs.

The interaction with other areas of grammar still remains problematic for pattern-based approaches: in a number of publications, it has been shown that the interaction of phenomena that one can observe in complex utterances can in fact not be explained with phrasal patterns since embedding cannot be captured in an inheritance hierarchy. This problem is not shared by selection-based approaches. All experimental results and insights of Tomasello can, however, be successfully extended to selection-based approaches.

Further reading

Meisel (1995) gives a very good overview of theories of acquisition in the Principles & Parameters model.

Adele Goldberg and Michael Tomasello are the most prominent proponents of Construction Grammar, a theory that explicitly tries to do without the assumption of innate linguistic knowledge. They published many papers and books about topics related to Construction Grammar and acquisition. The most important books probably are Goldberg (2006) and Tomasello (2003).

An overview of different theories of acquisition in German can be found in Klann-Delius (2008) an English overview is Ambridge & Lieven (2011).

17 Generative capacity and grammar formalisms

In several of the preceding chapters, the complexity hierarchy for formal languages was mentioned. The simplest languages are so-called regular languages (Type-3), they are followed by those described as context-free grammars (Type-2), then those grammars which are context-sensitive (Type-1) and finally we have unrestricted grammars (Type-0) that create recursively enumerable languages, which are the most complicated class. In creating theories, a conscious effort was made to use formal means that correspond to what one can actually observe in natural language. This led to the abandonment of unrestricted Transformational Grammar since this has generative power of Type-0 (see page 86). GPSG was deliberately designed in such a way as to be able to analyze just the context-free languages and not more. In the mid-80s, it was shown that natural languages have a higher complexity than context-free languages (Shieber 1985; Culy 1985). It is now assumed that so-called *mildly context-sensitive* grammars are sufficient for analyzing natural languages. Researchers working on TAG are working on developing variants of TAG that fall into exactly this category. Similarly, it was shown for different variants of Stabler's *Minimalist Grammars* (see Section 4.6.4 and Stabler 2001; 2011b) that they have a mildly context-sensitive capacity (Michaelis 2001). Peter Hellwig's Dependency Unification Grammar is also mildly context-sensitive (Hellwig 2003: 595). LFG and HPSG, as well as Chomsky's theory in *Aspects*, fall into the class of Type-0 languages (Berwick 1982; Johnson 1988). The question at this point is whether it is an ideal goal to find a descriptive language that has exactly the same power as the object it describes. Carl Pollard (1996b) once said that it would be odd to claim that certain theories in physics were not adequate simply because they make use of tools from mathematics that are too powerful.[1] It is not the descriptive language that should constrain the theory but rather the theory contains the restrictions that must hold for the objects in question. This is the view that Chomsky (1981b: 277, 280) takes. Also, see Berwick (1982: Section 4), Kaplan & Bresnan (1982: Section 8) on LFG and Johnson (1988: Section 3.5) on the *Off-Line Parsability Constraint* in LFG and attribute-value grammars in general.

There is of course a technical reason to look for a grammar with the lowest level of complexity possible: we know that it is easier for computers to process grammars with

---

[1] If physicists required the formalism to constrain the theory:
Editor: Professor Einstein, I'm afraid we can't accept this manuscript of yours on general relativity.
Einstein: Why? Are the equations wrong?
Editor: No, but we noticed that your differential equations are expressed in the first-order language of set theory. This is a totally unconstrained formalism! Why, you could have written down ANY set of differential equations! (Pollard 1996b)

lower complexity than more complex grammars. To get an idea about the complexity of a task, the so-called 'worst case' for the relevant computations is determined, that is, it is determined how long a program needs for an input of a certain length in the least favorable case to get a result for a grammar from a certain class. This begs the question if the worst case is actually relevant. For example, some grammars that allow discontinuous constituents perform less favorably in the worst case than normal phrase structure grammars that only allow for combinations of continuous strings (Reape 1991: Section 8). As I have shown in Müller (2004d), a parser that builds up larger units starting from words (a bottom-up parser) is far less efficient when processing a grammar assuming a verb movement analysis than is the case for a bottom-up parser that allows for discontinuous constituents. This has to do with the fact that verb traces do not contribute any phonological material and a parser cannot locate them without further machinery. It is therefore assumed that a verb trace exists in every position in the string and in most cases these traces do not contribute to an analysis of the complete input. Since the verb trace is not specified with regard to its valence information, it can be combined with any material in the sentence, which results in an enormous computational load. On the other hand, if one allows discontinuous constituents, then one can do without verb traces and the computational load is thereby reduced. In the end, the analysis using discontinuous constituents was eventually discarded for linguistic reasons (Müller 2005b,c; 2007a; 2017a), however, the investigation of the parsing behavior of both grammars is still interesting as it shows that worst case properties are not always informative.

I will discuss another example of the fact that language-specific restrictions can restrict the complexity of a grammar: Gärtner & Michaelis (2007: Section 3.2) assume that Stabler's Minimalist Grammars (see Section 4.6.4) with extensions for late adjunction and extraposition are actually more powerful than mildly context-sensitive. If one bans extraction from adjuncts (Frey & Gärtner 2002: 46) and also assumes the Shortest Move Constraint (see footnote 32 on page 165), then one arrives at a grammar that is mildly context-sensitive (Gärtner & Michaelis 2007: 178). The same is true of grammars with the Shortest Move Constraint and a constraint for extraction from specifiers.

Whether extraction takes place from a specifier or not depends on the organization of the particular grammar in question. In some grammars, all arguments are specifiers (Kratzer 1996: 120–123, also see Figure 18.4 on page 559). A ban on extraction from specifiers would imply that extraction out of arguments would be impossible. This is, of course, not true in general. Normally, subjects are treated as specifiers (also by Frey & Gärtner 2002: 44). It is often claimed that subjects are islands for extraction (see Grewendorf 1989: 35, 41; G. Müller 1996b: 220; 1998: 32, 163; Sabel 1999: 98; Fanselow 2001: 422). Several authors have noted, however, that extraction from subjects is possible in German (see Dürscheid 1989: 25; Haider 1993: 173; Pafel 1993; Fortmann 1996: 27; Suchsland 1997: 320; Vogel & Steinbach 1998: 87; Ballweg 1997: 2066; Müller 1999b: 100–101; De Kuthy 2002: 7). The following data are attested examples:

(1) a. [Von den übrigbleibenden Elementen]$_i$ scheinen [die Determinantien $_{-i}$] die
of the left.over elements seem the determinants the
wenigsten Klassifizierungsprobleme aufzuwerfen.[2]
fewest classification.problems to.throw.up

'Of the remaining elements, the determinants seem to pose the fewest problems for classification.'

b. [Von den Gefangenen]$_i$ hatte eigentlich [keine $_{-i}$] die Nacht der Bomben
of the prisoners had actually none the night of.the bombs
überleben sollen.[3]
survive should

'None of the prisoners should have actually survived the night of the bombings.'

c. [Von der HVA]$_i$ hielten sich [etwa 120 Leute $_{-i}$] dort in ihren Gebäuden
of the HVA held REFL around 120 people there in their buildings
auf.[4]
PRT

'Around 120 people from the HVA stayed there inside their buildings.'

d. [Aus dem „Englischen Theater"]$_i$ stehen [zwei Modelle $_{-i}$] in den Vitrinen.[5]
from the English theater stand two models in the cabinets

'Two models from the 'English Theater' are in the cabinets.'

e. [Aus der Fraktion]$_i$ stimmten ihm [viele $_{-i}$] zu darin, dass die
from the faction agreed him many PRT there.in that the
Kaufkraft der Bürger gepäppelt werden müsse, nicht die gute Laune
buying.power of.the citizens boosted become must not the good mood
der Wirtschaft.[6]
of.the economy

'Many of the fraction agreed with him that it is the buying power of citizens that needed to be increased, not the good spirits of the economy.'

f. [Vom Erzbischof Carl Theodor Freiherr von Dalberg]$_i$ gibt es
from archbishop Carl Theodor Freiherr from Dalberg gives it
beispielsweise [ein Bild $_{-i}$] im Stadtarchiv.[7]
for.example a picture in.the city.archives

'For example, there is a picture of archbishop Carl Theodor Freiherr of Dalberg in the city archives.'

---

[2] In the main text of Engel (1970: 102).
[3] Bernhard Schlink, *Der Vorleser*, Diogenes Taschenbuch 22953, Zürich: Diogenes Verlag, 1997, p. 102.
[4] Spiegel, 3/1999, p. 42.
[5] Frankfurter Rundschau, quoted from De Kuthy (2001: 52).
[6] taz, 16.10.2003, p. 5.
[7] Frankfurter Rundschau, quoted from De Kuthy (2002: 7).

g. [Gegen die wegen Ehebruchs zum Tod durch Steinigen verurteilte
   against the because.of adultery to.the death by stoning sentenced
   Amina Lawal]$_i$ hat gestern in Nigeria [der zweite Berufungsprozess _$_i$]
   Amina Lawal has yesterday in Nigeria the second appeal.process
   begonnen.[8]
   begun

   'The second appeal process began yesterday against Amina Lawal, who was sentenced to death by stoning for adultery.'

h. [Gegen diese Kahlschlagspolitik]$_i$ finden derzeit bundesweit
   against this clear.cutting.politics happen at.the.moment statewide
   [Proteste und Streiks _$_i$] statt.[9]
   protests and strikes PRT

   'At the moment, there are state-wide protests and strikes against this destructive politics.'

i. [Von den beiden, die hinzugestoßen sind], hat [einer _$_i$] eine Hacke, der
   of the both that joined are has one a pickaxe the
   andere einen Handkarren.[10]
   other a handcart

   'Of the two that joined, one had a pickaxe and the other a handcart.'

j. ein Plan, [gegen den]$_i$ sich nun [ein Proteststurm _$_i$] erhebt[11]
   a plan against which REFL now a storm.of.protests rises

   'a plan against which a storm of protests has now risen'

k. Dagegen$_i$ jedoch regt sich jetzt [Widerstand _$_i$]: [...][12]
   against however rises REFL now resistance

   'Resistance to this is now rising, however:'

l. [Aus der Radprofiszene]$_i$ kennt ihn [keiner _$_i$] mehr.[13]
   from the cycling.professional.scene knows him nobody anymore

   'Nobody from the professional cycling scene acts like they know him anymore.'

m. [Über das chinesische Programm der Deutschen Welle] tobt dieser Tage
   about the Chinese program of.the Deutsche Welle rages these days
   [ein heftiger Streit _$_i$].[14]
   a hefty controversy

   'Recently, there has been considerable controversy about the Chinese program by the Deutsche Welle.'

---

[8]taz, 28.08.2003, p. 2.
[9]Streikaufruf, Universität Bremen, 03.12.2003, p. 1.
[10]Haruki Murakami, *Hard-boiled Wonderland und das Ende der Welt*, suhrkamp taschenbuch, 3197, 2000, Translation by Annelie Ortmanns and Jürgen Stalph, p. 414.
[11]taz, 30.12.2004, p. 6.
[12]taz, 02.09.2005, p. 18.
[13]taz, 04.07.2005, p. 5.
[14]taz, 21.10.2008, p. 12.

This means that a ban on extraction from specifiers cannot hold for German. As such, it cannot be true for all languages.

We have a situation that is similar to the one with discontinuous constituents: since it is not possible to integrate the ban on extraction discussed here into the grammar formalism, it is more powerful than what is required for describing natural language. However, the restrictions in actual grammars – in this case, the restrictions on extraction from specifiers in the relevant languages – ensure that the respective language-specific grammars have a mildly context-sensitive capacity.

18 Binary branching, locality, and recursion

This chapter discusses three points: section 18.1 deals with the question of whether all linguistic structures should be binary branching or not. Section 18.2 discusses the question what information should be available for selection, that is, whether governing heads can access the internal structure of selected elements or whether everything should be restricted to local selection. Finally, Section 18.3 discusses recursion and how/whether it is captured in the different grammar theories that are discussed in this book.

18.1 Binary branching

We have seen that the question of the kind of branching structures assumed has received differing treatments in various theories. Classical $\overline{\text{X}}$ theory assumes that a verb is combined with all its complements. In later variants of GB, all structures are strictly binary branching. Other frameworks do not treat the question of branching in a uniform way: there are proposals that assume binary branching structures and others that opt for flat structures.

Haegeman (1994: Section 2.5) uses learnability arguments (rate of acquisition, see Section 13.2 on this point). She discusses the example in (1) and claims that language learners have to choose one of eight structures if flat-branching structures can occur in natural language. If, on the other hand, there are only binary-branching structures, then the sentence in (1) cannot have the structures in Figure 18.1 to start with, and therefore a learner would not have to rule out the corresponding hypotheses.

(1) Mummy must leave now.

However, Haegeman (1994: 88) provides evidence for the fact that (1) has the structure in (2):

(2) [Mummy [must [leave now]]]

The relevant tests showing this include elliptical constructions, that is, the fact that it is possible to refer to the constituents in (2) with pronouns. This means that there is actually evidence for the structure of (1) that is assumed by linguists and we therefore do not have to assume that it is just hard-wired in our brains that only binary-branching structures are allowed. Haegeman (1994: 143) mentions a consequence of the binary branching hypothesis: if all structures are binary-branching, then it is not possible to straightforwardly account for sentences with ditransitive verbs in $\overline{\text{X}}$ theory. In $\overline{\text{X}}$ theory,

18 Binary branching, locality, and recursion

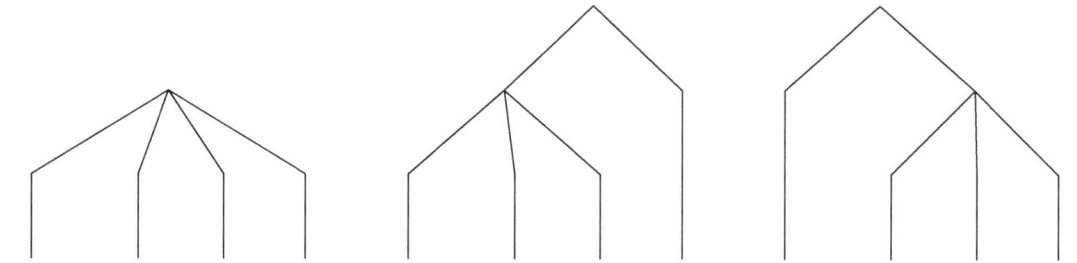

Figure 18.1: Structures with partial flat-branching

it is assumed that a head is combined with all its complements at once (see Section 2.5). So in order to account for ditransitive verbs in X̄ theory, an empty element (little *v*) has to be assumed (see Section 4.1.4).

It should have become clear in the discussion of the arguments for the Poverty of the Stimulus in Section 13.8 that the assumption that only binary-branching structures are possible is part of our innate linguistic knowledge is nothing more than pure speculation. Haegeman offers no kind of evidence for this assumption. As shown in the discussions of the various theories we have seen, it is possible to capture the data with flat structures. For example, it is possible to assume that, in English, the verb is combined with its complements in a flat structure (Pollard & Sag 1994: 39). There are sometimes theory-internal reasons for deciding for one kind of branching or another, but these are not always applicable to other theories. For example, Binding Theory in GB theory is formulated with reference to dominance relations in trees (Chomsky 1981a: 188). If one assumes that syntactic structure plays a crucial role for the binding of pronouns (see page 90), then it is possible to make assumptions about syntactic structure based on the observable binding relations (so also Section 4.1.4). Binding data have, however, received a very different treatment in various theories. In LFG, constraints on f-structure are used for Binding Theory (Dalrymple 1993), whereas Binding Theory in HPSG operates on argument structure lists (valence information that are ordered in a particular way, see Section 9.1.1).

The opposite of Haegeman's position is the argumentation for flat structures put forward by Croft (2001: Section 1.6.2). In his Radical Construction Grammar FAQ, Croft observes that a phrasal construction such as the one in (3a) can be translated into a Categorial Grammar lexical entry like (3b).

(3) a. [_VP V NP]
    b. VP/NP

He claims that a disadvantage of Categorial Grammar is that it only allows for binary-branching structures and yet there exist constructions with more than two parts (p. 49). The exact reason why this is a problem is not explained, however. He even acknowledges himself that it is possible to represent constructions with more than two arguments in Categorial Grammar. For a ditransitive verb, the entry in Categorial Grammar of English would take the form of (4):

18.1 Binary branching

(4) ((s\np)/np)/np

If we consider the elementary trees for TAG in Figure 18.2, it becomes clear that it is equally possible to incorporate semantic information into a flat tree and a binary-branching tree. The binary-branching tree corresponds to a Categorial Grammar deriva-

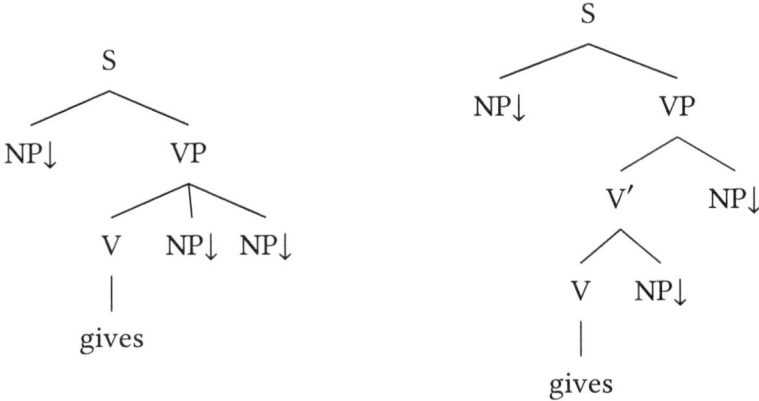

Figure 18.2: Flat and binary-branching elementary trees

tion. In both analyses in Figure 18.2, a meaning is assigned to a head that occurs with a certain number of arguments. Ultimately, the exact structure required depends on the kinds of restrictions on structures that one wishes to formulate. In this book, such restrictions are not discussed, but as explained above some theories model binding relations with reference to tree structures. Reflexive pronouns must be bound within a particular local domain inside the tree. In theories such as LFG and HPSG, these binding restrictions are formulated without any reference to trees. This means that evidence from binding data for one of the structures in Figure 18.2 (or for other tree structures) constitutes nothing more than theory-internal evidence.

Another reason to assume trees with more structure is the possibility to insert adjuncts on any node. In Chapter 9, an HPSG analysis for German that assumes binary-branching structures was proposed. With this analysis, it is possible to attach an adjunct to any node and thereby explain the free ordering of adjuncts in the middle field:

(5) a. [weil] der Mann der Frau das Buch *gestern* gab
because the man the woman the book yesterday gave
'because the man gave the woman the book yesterday'

b. [weil] der Mann der Frau *gestern* das Buch gab
because the man the woman yesterday the book gave

c. [weil] der Mann *gestern* der Frau das Buch gab
because the man yesterday the woman the book gave

d. [weil] *gestern* der Mann der Frau das Buch gab
because yesterday the man the woman the book gave

This analysis is not the only one possible, however. One could also assume an entirely flat structure where arguments and adjuncts are dominated by one node. Kasper (1994) suggests this kind of analysis in HPSG (see also Section 5.1.5 for GPSG analyses that make use of metarules for the introduction of adjuncts). Kasper requires complex relational constraints that create syntactic relations between elements in the tree and also compute the semantic contribution of the entire constituent using the meaning of both the verb and the adjuncts. The analysis with binary-branching structures is simpler than those with complex relational constraints and – in the absence of theory-external evidence for flat structures – should be preferred to the analysis with flat structures. At this point, one could object that adjuncts in English cannot occur in all positions between arguments and therefore the binary-branching Categorial Grammar analysis and the TAG analysis in Figure 18.2 are wrong. This is not correct, however, as it is the specification of adjuncts with regard to the adjunction site that is crucial in Categorial Grammar. An adverb has the category (s\np)\(s\np) or (s\np)/(s\np) and can therefore only be combined with constituents that correspond to the VP node in Figure 18.2. In the same way, an elementary tree for an adverb in TAG can only attach to the VP node (see Figure 12.3 on page 417). For the treatment of adjuncts in English, binary-branching structures therefore do not make any incorrect predictions.

18.2 Locality

The question of local accessibility of information has been treated in various ways by the theories discussed in this book. In the majority of theories, one tries to make information about the inner workings of phrases inaccessible for adjacent or higher heads, that is, *glaubt* 'believe' in (6) selects a sentential argument but it cannot "look inside" this sentential argument.

(6)   a. Karl glaubt, dass morgen seine Schwester kommt.
           Karl believes that tomorrow his sister comes
           'Karl believes that his sister is coming tomorrow.'
    b. Karl glaubt, dass seine Schwester morgen kommt.
           Karl believes that his sister tomorrow comes

Thus for example, *glauben* cannot enforce that the subject of the verb has to begin with a consonant or that the complementizer has to be combined with a verbal projection starting with an adjunct. In Section 1.5, we saw that it is a good idea to classify constituents in terms of their distribution and independent of their internal structure. If we are talking about an NP box, then it is not important what this NP box actually contains. It is only of importance that a given head wants to be combined with an NP with a particular case marking. This is called *locality of selection*.

Various linguistic theories have tried to implement locality of selection. The simplest form of this implementation is shown by phrase structure grammars of the kind discussed in Chapter 2. The rule in (17) on page 59, repeated here as (7), states that a ditransitive verb can occur with three noun phrases, each with the relevant case:

(7) S → NP(Per1,Num1,nom)
     NP(Per2,Num2,dat)
     NP(Per3,Num3,acc)
     V(Per1,Num1,ditransitive)

Since the symbols for NPs do not have any further internal structure, the verb cannot require that there has to be a relative clause in an NP, for example. The internal properties of the NP are not visible to the outside. We have already seen in the discussion in Chapter 2, however, that certain properties of phrases have to be outwardly visible. This was the information that was written on the boxes themselves. For noun phrases, at least information about person, number and case are required in order to correctly capture their relation to a head. The gender value is important in German as well, since adverbial phrases such as *einer nach dem anderen* 'one after the other' have to agree in gender with the noun they refer to (see example (12) on page 513). Apart from that, information about the length of the noun phrases is required, in order to determine their order in a clause. Heavy constituents are normally ordered after lighter ones, and are also often extraposed (cf. Behaghel's *Gesetz der wachsenden Glieder* 'Law of increasing constituents' (1909: 139; 1930: 86)).

Theories that strive to be as restrictive as possible with respect to locality therefore have to develop mechanisms that allow one to only access information that is required to explain the distribution of constituents. This is often achieved by projecting certain properties to the mother node of a phrase. In $\overline{\text{X}}$ theory, the part of speech a head belongs to is passed up to the maximal projection: if the head is an N, for example, then the maximal projection is an NP. In GPSG, HPSG and variants of CxG, there are Head Feature Principles responsible for the projection of features. Head Feature Principles ensure that an entire group of features, so-called head features, are present on the maximal projection of a head. Furthermore, every theory has to be capable of representing the fact that a constituent can lack one of its parts and this part is then realized via a long-distance dependency in another position in the clause. As previously discussed on page 303, there are languages in which complementizers inflect depending on whether their complement is missing a constituent or not. This means that this property must be somehow accessible. In GPSG, HPSG and variants of CxG, there are additional groups of features that are present at every node between a filler and a gap in a long-distance dependency. In LFG, there is f-structure instead. Using Functional Uncertainty, one can look for the position in the f-structure where a particular constituent is missing. In GB theory, movement proceeds cyclically, that is, an element is moved into the specifier of CP and can be moved from there into the next highest CP. It is assumed in GB theory that heads can look inside their arguments, at least they can see the elements in the specifier position. If complementizers can access the relevant specifier positions, then they can determine whether something is missing from an embedded phrase or not. In GB theory, there was also an analysis of case assignment in infinitive constructions in which the case-assigning verb governs into the embedded phrase and assigns case to the element in SpecIP. Figure 18.3 shows the relevant structure taken from Haegeman (1994: 170). Since the Case Principle is formulated in such a way that only finite I can assign

18 Binary branching, locality, and recursion

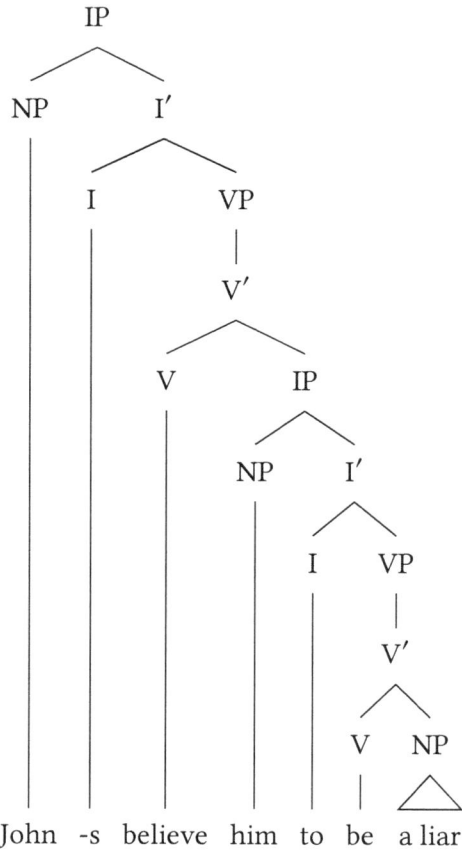

Figure 18.3: Analysis of the AcI construction with *Exceptional Case Marking*

case to the subject (cf. page 111), *him* does not receive case from I. Instead, it is assumed that the verb *believe* assigns case to the subject of the embedded infinitive.

Verbs that can assign case across phrase boundaries are referred to as ECM verbs, where ECM stands for *Exceptional Case Marking*. As the name suggests, this instance of case assignment into a phrase was viewed as an exception. In newer versions of the theory (e.g., Kratzer 1996: 120–123), all case assignment is to specifier positions. For example, the Voice head in Figure 18.4 on the facing page assigns accusative to the DP in the specifier of VP. Since the Voice head governs into the VP, case assignment to a run-of-the-mill object in this theory is an instance of exceptional case assignment as well. The same is true in Adger's version of Minimalism, which was discussed in Chapter 4: Adger (2010) argues that his theory is more restrictive than LFG or HPSG since it is only one feature that can be selected by a head, whereas in LFG and HPSG complex feature bundles are selected. However, the strength of this kind of locality constraint is weakened by the operation Agree, which allows for nonlocal feature checking. As in Kratzer's proposal, case is assigned nonlocally by little *v* to the object inside the VP (see Section 4.1.5.2).

Adger discusses PP arguments of verbs like *depend* and notes that these verbs need specific PPs, that is, the form of the preposition in the PP has to be selectable. While

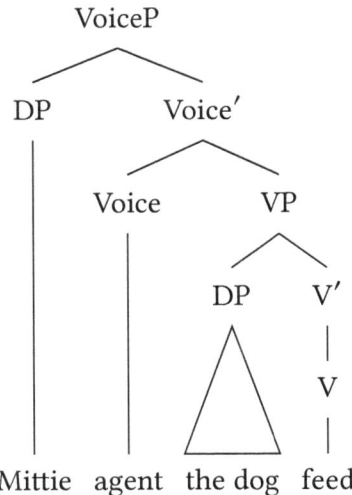

Figure 18.4: Analysis of structures with a transitive verb following Kratzer

this is trivial in Dependency Grammar, where the preposition is selected right away, the respective information is projected in theories like HPSG and is then selectable at the PP node. However, this requires that the governing verb can determine at least two properties of the selected element: its part of speech and the form of the preposition. This is not possible in Adger's system and he left this for further research. Of course it would be possible to assume an onP (a phrasal projection of *on* that has the category 'on'). Similar solutions have been proposed in Minimalist theories (see Section 4.6.1 on functional projections), but such a solution would obviously miss the generalization that all prepositional phrases have something in common, which would not be covered in a system with atomic categories that are word specific.

In theories such as LFG and HPSG, case assignment takes place locally in constructions such as those in (8):

(8)   a. John believes him to be a liar.

     b. Ich halte ihn für einen Lügner.
        I   hold him for a.ACC liar

        'I take him to be a liar.'

     c. Er scheint ein   Lügner zu sein.
        he seems   a.NOM liar   to be

        'He seems to be a liar.'

     d. Er fischt den   Teich leer.
        he fishes the.ACC pond empty

        'He fishes (in) the pond (until it is) empty.'

Although *him*, *ihn* 'him', *er* 'he' and *den Teich* 'the pond' are not semantic arguments of the finite verbs, they are syntactic arguments (they are raised) and can therefore be assigned case locally. See Bresnan (1982a: 348–349 and Section 8.2) and Pollard & Sag

(1994: Section 3.5) for an analysis of raising in LFG and HPSG respectively. See Meurers (1999c), Przepiórkowski (1999b), and Müller (2007a: Section 17.4) for case assignment in HPSG and for its interaction with raising.

There are various phenomena that are incompatible with strict locality and require the projection of at least some information. For example, there are question tags in English that must match the subject of the clause with which they are combined:

(9)   a. She is very smart, isn't she / * he?

       b. They are very smart, aren't they?

Bender & Flickinger (1999), Flickinger & Bender (2003) therefore propose making information about agreement or the referential index of the subject available on the sentence node.[1] In Sag (2007), all information about phonology, syntax and semantics of the subject is represented as the value of a feature XARG (EXTERNAL ARGUMENT). Here, *external argument* does not stand for what it does in GB theory, but should be understood in a more general sense. For example, it makes the possessive pronoun accessible on the node of the entire NP. Sag (2007) argues that this is needed to force coreference in English idioms:

(10)   a. He$_i$ lost [his$_i$ / *her$_j$ marbles].

       b. They$_i$ kept/lost [their$_i$ / *our$_j$ cool].

The use of the XARG feature looks like an exact parallel to accessing the specifier position as we saw in the discussion of GB. However, Sag proposes that complements of prepositions in Polish are also made accessible by XARG since there are data suggesting that higher heads can access elements inside PPs (Przepiórkowski 1999a: Section 5.4.1.2).

In Section 10.6.2 about Sign-based Construction Grammar, we already saw that a theory that only makes the reference to one argument available on the highest node of a projection cannot provide an analysis for idioms of the kind given in (11). This is because the subject is made available with verbal heads, however, it is the object that needs to be accessed in sentences such as (11). This means that one has to be able to formulate constraints affecting larger portions of syntactic structure.

(11)   a. Ich glaube, mich / # dich tritt ein Pferd.[2]
           I believes me   you kicks a   horse
           'I am utterly surprised.'

       b. Jonas glaubt, ihn tritt ein Pferd.[3]
           Jonas believes him kicks a   horse
           'Jonas is utterly surprised.'

       c. # Jonas glaubt, dich tritt ein Pferd.
           Jonas believes you kicks a   horse
           'Jonas believes that a horse kicks you.'

---

[1] See also Sag & Pollard (1991: 89).
[2] Richter & Sailer (2009: 311).
[3] http://www.machandel-verlag.de/der-katzenschatz.html, 2015-07-06.

18.2 Locality

Theories of grammar with extended locality domains do not have any problems with this kind of data.[4] An example for this kind of theory is TAG. In TAG, one can specify trees of exactly the right size (Abeillé 1988; Abeillé & Schabes 1989). All the material that is fixed in an idiom is simply determined in the elementary tree. Figure 18.5 shows the tree for *kick the bucket* as it is used in (12a).

(12) a. The cowboys kicked the bucket.
 b. Cowboys often kick the bucket.
 c. He kicked the proverbial bucket.

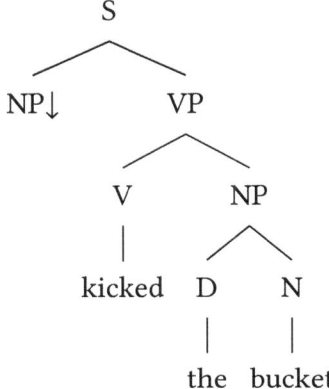

Figure 18.5: Elementary tree for *kick the bucket*

Since TAG trees can be split up by adjunction, it is possible to insert elements between the parts of an idiom as in (12b,c) and thus explain the flexibility of idioms with regard to adjunction and embedding.[5] Depending on whether the lexical rules for the passive and long-distance dependencies can be applied, the idiom can occur in the relevant variants.

---

[4]Or more carefully put: they do not have any serious problems since the treatment of idioms in all their many aspects is by no means trivial (Sailer 2000).

[5]Interestingly, variants of Embodied CxG are strikingly similar to TAG. The Ditransitive Construction that was discussed on page 340 allows for additional material to occur between the subject and the verb.

The problems that arise for the semantics construction are also similar. Abeillé & Schabes (1989: 9) assume that the semantics of *John kicked the proverbial bucket* is computed from the parts *John'*, *kick-the-bucket'* and *proverbial'*, that is, the added modifiers always have scope over the entire idiom. This is not adequate for all idioms (Fischer & Keil 1996):

(i) Er band ihr einen großen Bären auf.
 he tied her a big bear on
 'He pulled (a lot of) wool over her eyes.'

In the idiom in (i), *Bär* 'bear' actually means 'lie' and the adjective has to be interpreted accordingly. The relevant tree should therefore contain nodes that contribute semantic information and also say something about the composition of these features.

In the same way, when computing the semantics of noun phrases in TAG and Embodied Construction Grammar, one should bear in mind that the adjective that is combined with a discontinuous NP Construction (see page 338) or an NP tree can have narrow scope over the noun (*all alleged murderers*).

561

18 Binary branching, locality, and recursion

In cases where the entire idiom or parts of the idiom are fixed, it is possible to rule out adjunction to the nodes of the idiom tree. Figure 18.6 shows a pertinent example from Abeillé & Schabes (1989: 7). The ban on adjunction is marked by a subscript NA.

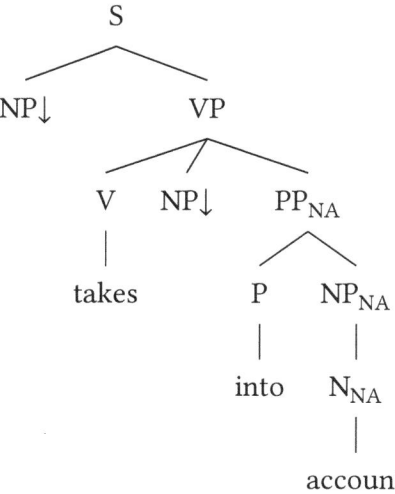

Figure 18.6: Elementary tree for *take into account*

The question that also arises for other theories is whether the efforts that have been made to enforce locality should be abandoned altogether. In our box model in Section 1.5, this would mean that all boxes were transparent. Since plastic boxes do not allow all of the light through, objects contained in multiple boxes cannot be seen as clearly as those in the topmost box (the path of Functional Uncertainty is longer). This is parallel to a suggestion made by Kay & Fillmore (1999) in CxG. Kay and Fillmore explicitly represent all the information about the internal structure of a phrase on the mother node and therefore have no locality restrictions at all in their theory. In principle, one can motivate this kind of theory in parallel to the argumentation in Chapter 17. The argument there made reference to the complexity of the grammatical formalism: the kind of complexity that the language of description has is unimportant, it is only important what one does with it. In the same way, one can say that regardless of what kind of information is in principle accessible, it is not accessed if this is not permitted. This was the approach taken by Pollard & Sag (1987: 143–145).

It is also possible to assume a world in which all the boxes contain transparent areas where it is possible to see parts of their contents. This is more or less the LFG world: the information about all levels of embedding contained in the f-structure is visible to both the inside and the outside. We have already discussed Nordlinger's (1998) LFG analysis of Wambaya on page 307. In Wambaya, words that form part of a noun phrase can be distributed throughout the clause. For example, an adjective that refers to a noun can occur in a separate position from it. Nordlinger models this by assuming that an adjective can make reference to an argument in the f-structure and then agrees with it in terms of

18.2 Locality

case, number and gender. Bender (2008c) has shown that this analysis can be transferred to HPSG: instead of no longer representing an argument on the mother node after it has been combined with a head, simply marking the argument as realized allows us to keep it in the representation (Meurers 1999c; Przepiórkowski 1999b; Müller 2007a: Section 17.4). Detmar Meurers compares both of these HPSG approaches to different ways of working through a shopping list: in the standard approach taken by Pollard & Sag (1994), one tears away parts of the shopping list once the relevant item has been found. In the other case, the relevant item on the list is crossed out. At the end of the shopping trip, one ends up with a list of what has been bought as well as the items themselves.

I have proposed the crossing-out analysis for depictive predicates in German and English (Müller 2004a; 2008). Depictive predicates say something about the state of a person or object during the event expressed by a verb:

(13) a. Er sah sie nackt.[6]
    he saw her naked
  b. He saw her naked.

In (13), the depictive adjective can either refer to the subject or the object. However, there is a strong preference for readings where the antecedent noun precedes the depictive predicate (Lötscher 1985: 208). Figure 18.7 on the next page shows analyses for the sentences in (14):

(14) a. dass er$_i$ die Äpfel$_j$ ungewaschen$_{i/j}$ isst
    that he the apples unwashed eats
    'that he eats the apples unwashed'
  b. dass er$_i$ ungewaschen$_{i/*j}$ die Äpfel$_j$ isst
    that he unwashed the apples eats
    'that he eats the apples (while he is) unwashed'

Arguments that have been realized are still represented on the upper nodes, however, they are crossed-out and thereby marked as "realized". In German, this preference for the antecedent noun can be captured by assuming a restriction that states that the antecedent noun must not yet have been realized.

It is commonly assumed for English that adjuncts are combined with a VP.

(15) a. John [[$_{VP}$ ate the apples$_i$] unwashed$_i$].
  b. You can't [[$_{VP}$ give them$_i$ injections] unconscious$_i$].[7]

In approaches where the arguments of the verb are accessible at the VP node, it is possible to establish a relation between the depictive predicate and an argument although the antecedent noun is inside the VP. English differs from German in that depictives can refer to both realized (*them* in (15b)) and unrealized (*you* in (15b)) arguments.

---

[6]Haider (1985a: 94).
[7]Simpson (2005a: 17).

18 Binary branching, locality, and recursion

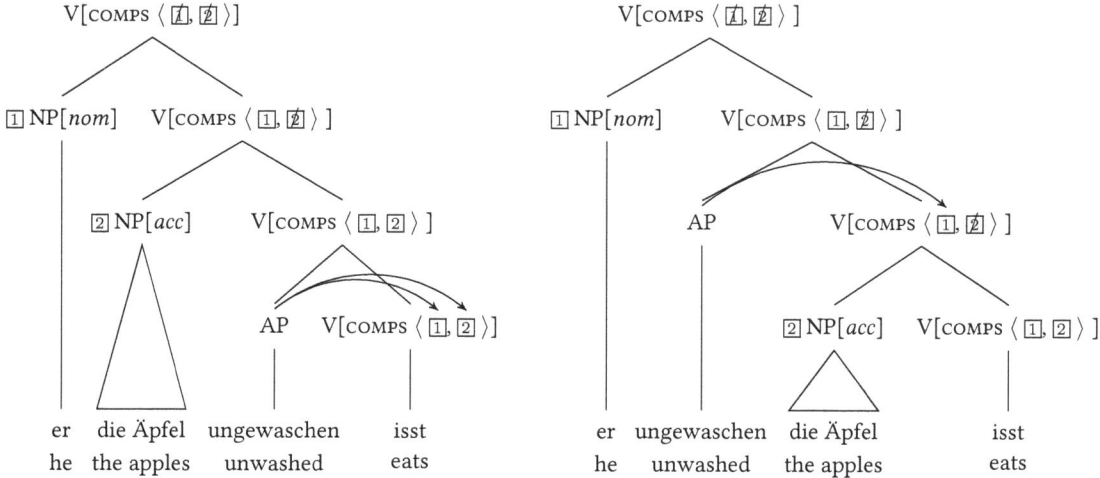

Figure 18.7: Analysis of *dass er die Äpfel ungewaschen isst* 'that he the apples unwashed eats' and *dass er ungewaschen die Äpfel isst* 'that he unwashed the apples eat'

Higginbotham (1985: 560) and Winkler (1997) have proposed corresponding non-cancellation approaches in GB theory. There are also parallel suggestions in Minimalist theories: checked features are not deleted, but instead marked as already checked (Stabler 2011b: 14). However, these features are still viewed as inaccessible.

Depending on how detailed the projected information is, it can be possible to see adjuncts and argument in embedded structures as well as their phonological, syntactic and semantic properties. In the CxG variant proposed by Kay and Fillmore, all information is available. In LFG, information about grammatical function, case and similar properties is accessible. However, the part of speech is not contained in the f-structure. If the part of speech does not stand in a one-to-one relation to grammatical function, it cannot be restricted using selection via f-structure. Nor is phonological information represented completely in the f-structure. If the analysis of idioms requires nonlocal access to phonological information or part of speech, then this has to be explicitly encoded in the f-structure (see Bresnan (1982b: 46–50) for more on idioms).

In the HPSG variant that I adopt, only information about arguments is projected. Since arguments are always represented by descriptions of type *synsem*, no information about their phonological realization is present. However, there are daughters in the structure so that it is still possible to formulate restrictions for idioms as in TAG or Construction Grammar (see Richter & Sailer (2009) for an analysis of the 'horse' example in (11a)). This may seem somewhat like overkill: although we already have the tree structure, we are still projecting information about arguments that have already been realized (unfortunately these also contain information about their arguments and so on). At this point, one could be inclined to prefer TAG or LFG since these theories only make use of one extension of locality: TAG uses trees of arbitrary or rather exactly the necessary size and LFG makes reference to a complete f-structure. However, things are not quite that simple: if one wants to create a relation to an argument when adjoining a depictive predicate in TAG, then one requires a list of possible antecedents. Syntactic factors (e.g., reference to dative vs. accusative noun phrases, to argument vs. adjuncts, coordination of verbs vs. nouns) play a role in determining the referent noun, this cannot be reduced to semantic relations. Similarly, there are considerably different restrictions for different kinds of idioms and these cannot all be formulated in terms of restrictions on f-structure since f-structure does not contain information about parts of speech.

One should bear in mind that some phenomena require reference to larger portions of structure. The majority of phenomena can be treated in terms of head domains and extended head domains, however, there are idioms that go beyond the sentence level. Every theory has to account for this somehow.

18.3 Recursion

Every theory in this book can deal with self-embedding in language as it was discussed on page 4. The example (2) is repeated here as (16):

(16) that Max thinks [that Julia knows [that Otto claims [that Karl suspects [that Richard confirms [that Friederike is laughing]]]]]

Most theories capture this directly with recursive phrase structure rules or dominance schemata. TAG is special with regard to recursion since recursion is factored out of the trees. The corresponding effects are created by an adjunction operation that allows any amount of material to be inserted into trees. It is sometimes claimed that Construction Grammar cannot capture the existence of recursive structure in natural language (e.g., Leiss 2009: 269). This impression is understandable since many analyses are extremely surface-oriented. For example, one often talks of a [Sbj TrVerb Obj] construction. However, the grammars in question also become recursive as soon as they contain a sentence embedding or relative clause construction. A sentence embedding construction could have the form [Sbj that-Verb that-S], where a that-Verb is one that can take a sentential complement and that-S stands for the respective complement. A *that*-clause can then be inserted into the that-S slot. Since this *that*-clause can also be the result of the application of this construction, the grammar is able to produce recursive structures such as those in (17):

(17) Otto claims [$_{that-S}$ that Karl suspects [$_{that-S}$ that Richard sleeps]].

In (17), both *Karl suspects that Richard sleeps* and the entire clause are instances of the [Sbj that-Verb that-S] construction. The entire clause therefore contains an embedded subpart that is licensed by the same construction as the clause itself. (17) also contains a constituent of the category *that*-S that is embedded inside of *that*-S. For more on recursion and self-embedding in Construction Grammar, see Verhagen (2010).

Similarly, every Construction Grammar that allows a noun to combine with a genitive noun phrase also allows for recursive structures. The construction in question could have the form [Det N NP[gen]] or [N NP[gen]]. The [Det N NP[gen]] construction licenses structures such as (18):

(18)　[NP des Kragens [NP des　　Mantels [NP der　　Vorsitzenden]]]
　　　　　the collar　　　of.the coat　　　　of.the chairwoman
　　　'the collar of the coat of the chairwoman'

Jurafsky (1996) and Bannard, Lieven & Tomasello (2009) use probabilistic context-free grammars (PCFG) for a Construction Grammar parser with a focus on psycholinguistic plausibility and modeling of acquisition. Context-free grammars have no problems with self-embedding structures like those in (18) and thus this kind of Construction Grammar itself does not encounter any problems with self-embedding.

Goldberg (1995: 192) assumes that the resultative construction for English has the following form:

(19)　[SUBJ [V OBJ OBL]]

This corresponds to a complex structure as assumed for elementary trees in TAG. LTAG differs from Goldberg's approach in that every structure requires a lexical anchor, that is, for example (19), the verb would have to be fixed in LTAG. But in Goldberg's analysis, verbs can be inserted into independently existing constructions (see Section 21.1). In TAG publications, it is often emphasized that elementary trees do not contain any recursion. The entire grammar is recursive however, since additional elements can be added to the tree using adjunction and – as (17) and (18) show – insertion into substitution nodes can also create recursive structures.

19 Empty elements

This chapter deals with empty elements, I first discuss the general attitude of various research traditions towards empty elements and then show how they can be eliminated from grammars (Section 19.2). Section 19.3 discusses empty elements that have been suggested in order to facilitate semantic interpretation. Section 19.4 discusses possible motivation for empty elements with a special focus on cross-linguistic comparison and the final Section 19.5 shows that certain accounts with transformations, lexical rules, and empty elements can be translated into each other.

19.1 Views on empty elements

One point that is particularly controversial among proponents of the theories discussed in this book is the question of whether one should assume empty elements or not. The discussion of empty elements is quite old: there was already some investigation in 1961 with reference to phrase structure grammars (Bar-Hillel, Perles & Shamir 1961). The discussion of the status of empty elements has carried on ever since (see Löbner 1986; Wunderlich 1987; 1989; von Stechow 1989; Haider 1997a; Sag 2000; Bouma, Malouf & Sag 2001; Levine & Hukari 2006; Müller 2014c; Arnold & Spencer 2015, for example). There are sometimes empirical differences between analyses that assume empty elements and those that do not (Arnold & Spencer 2015), but often this is not the case. Since empty elements often feature prominently in the argumentation for or against particular theories, I will discuss how they have been used in somewhat more detail here.

In GB theory, empty elements were assumed for traces of movement (verb movement and fronting of phrases) as well as for deleted elements in elliptical constructions. Starting with the analysis of Larson (1988), more and more empty heads have been introduced to ensure uniformity of structures and certain semantic interpretations (binding and scope, see Section 4.1.4 on little *v*). Other examples of an empty element that was introduced in order to maintain particular generalizations are the empty expletives of Coopmans (1989: 734) and Postal (2004: Chapter 1). These fill the subject position in inversion structures in English, where the position preceding the verb is occupied by a PP and not by an overt subject NP. Similarly, Safir (1985: Section 4) assumes that impersonal passives in German contain empty expletive subjects. Grewendorf (1993: 1311) assumes that the subject position in impersonal passives and passives without subject movement is in fact occupied by an empty expletive. Also, see Newmeyer (2005: 91) and Lohnstein (2014: 180) for this assumption with regard to the passive in German. Sternefeld (2006: Section II.3.3.3) assumes that there is an empty expletive subject in impersonal passives and subjectless sentences such as (1).

19 Empty elements

(1) a. Mir graut.
    me.DAT scares
    'I am scared.'

b. Mich dürstet.
    me.ACC is.thirsty
    'I am thirsty.'

On page 166, we discussed Stabler's proposal for the analysis of sentences with intransitive verbs. Since, following Chomsky (2008: 146), the element that first merges with a head is the complement, intransitive verbs pose a problem for the theory. This problem is solved by Stabler by assuming that intransitive verbs are combined with an empty object (Veenstra 1998: 61, 124). Since these silent elements do not contribute to the meaning of an expression, we are also dealing with empty expletive pronouns.

In other theories, there are researchers that reject empty elements as well as those who assume them. In Categorial Grammar, Steedman suggests an analysis of nonlocal dependencies that does without empty elements (see Section 8.5), but as Pollard (1988) has shown, Steedman's analysis requires various kinds of type raising for NPs or a correspondingly high number of complex lexical items for relative pronouns (see Section 8.5.3). On the other hand, König (1999) uses traces. In GPSG, there is the traceless analysis of extraction by Uszkoreit (1987: 76–77) that we discussed in Section 5.4, but there is also the analysis of Gazdar, Klein, Pullum & Sag (1985: 143) that uses traces. In LFG, there are both analyses with traces (Bresnan 2001: 67) and those without (see Kaplan & Zaenen (1989); Dalrymple et al. (2001) and Section 7.3 and Section 7.5). Many of the phrasal analyses in HPSG are born out of the wish to avoid empty elements (see Section 21.10). An example for this is the relative clause analysis by Sag (1997) that replaces the empty relativizer in Pollard & Sag (1994) with a corresponding phrasal rule. On the other hand we have Bender (2000) and Sag, Wasow & Bender (2003: 464), who assume a silent copula, Borsley (1999a; 2009; 2013), who argues for empty elements in the grammar of Welsh and Alqurashi & Borsley (2013), who suggest an empty relativizer for Arabic. Another attempt to eliminate empty elements from HPSG was to handle long-distance dependencies not by traces but rather in the lexicon (Bouma, Malouf & Sag 2001). As Levine & Hukari (2006) could show, however, theories of extraction that introduce long-distance dependencies lexically have problems with the semantic interpretation of coordinate structures. For a suggestion of how to solve these problems, see Chaves (2009). There are many TAG analyses without silent elements in the lexicon (see Section 12.5 and Kroch (1987), for example), however there are variants of TAG such as that of Kallmeyer (2005: 194), where a trace is assumed for the reordering of constituents in sentences with a verbal complex. Rambow (1994: 10–11) assumes an empty head in every verb phrase (see Section 12.6.2 on V-TAG).[1] In Dependency Grammar, Mel'čuk (1988: 15, 303; 2003: 219), Starosta (1988: 253), Eroms (2000: 471–472), Hudson (2007: Section 3.7; 2010a: 166) and Engel (2014) assume empty elements for determiners, nouns, ellipsis, imperatives,

---

[1] Note that empty elements in TAG are slightly different from empty elements in other theories. In TAG the empty elements are usually part of elementary trees, that is, they are not lexical items that are combined with other material.

copulas, controlled infinitives, and for coordinate structures, but Groß & Osborne (2009: 73) reject empty elements (with the exception of ellipsis, Osborne 2018a).

No empty elements are assumed in Construction Grammar (Michaelis & Ruppenhofer 2001: 49–50; Goldberg 2003a: 219; Goldberg 2006: 10), the related Simpler Syntax (Culicover & Jackendoff 2005) as well as in Cognitive Grammar.[2] The argumentation against empty elements runs along the following lines:

1. There is no evidence for invisible objects.

2. There is no innate linguistic knowledge.

3. Therefore, knowledge about empty elements cannot be learned, which is why they cannot be assumed as part of our grammar.

This begs the question of whether all the premises on which the conclusion is based actually hold. If we consider an elliptical construction such as (2), then it is clear that a noun has been omitted:

(2) Ich nehme den roten Ball und du den blauen.
 I take the.ACC red.ACC ball and you the.ACC blue.ACC

 'I'll take the red ball and you take the blue one.'

Despite there being no noun in *den blauen* 'the blue', this group of words behaves both syntactically and semantically just like a noun phrase. (2) is of course not necessarily evidence for there being empty elements, because one could simply say that *den blauen* is a noun phrase consisting only of an article and an adjective (Wunderlich 1987).

Similar to the fact that it is understood that a noun is missing in (2), speakers of English know that something is missing after *like*:

(3) Bagels, I like.

Every theory of grammar has to somehow account for these facts. It must be represented in some way that *like* in (3) behaves just like a verb phrase that is missing something. One possibility is to use traces. Bar-Hillel, Perles & Shamir (1961: 153, Lemma 4.1) have shown that it is possible to turn phrase structure grammars with empty elements into those without any. In many cases, the same techniques can be applied to the theories presented here and we will therefore discuss the point in more detail in the following section.

19.2 Eliminating empty elements from grammars

It is possible to turn a grammar with empty elements (also called *epsilon*) into a grammar without these by removing all categories that can be rewritten by an epsilon in every rule that uses such categories and then add the respective rules without the empty elements to the grammar. The following example has an epsilon rule for np. One therefore has to replace all rules containing the symbol np with new rules without this np symbol. (5) shows the result of this conversion of the grammar in (4):

---

[2]However, Fillmore (1988: 51) did not rule them out.

19 Empty elements

(4) v̄ → np, v
    v̄ → np, pp, v
    np → ε

(5) v̄ → np, v
    v̄ → v
    v̄ → np, pp, v
    v̄ → pp, v

This can also lead to cases where all elements on the right-hand side of a rule are removed. Thus, what one has done is actually create a new empty category and then one has to apply the respective replacement processes again. We will see an example of this in a moment. Looking at the pair of grammars in (4)–(5), it is clear that the number of rules has increased in (5) compared to (4) despite the grammars licensing the same sequences of symbols. The fact that an NP argument can be omitted is not expressed directly in (5) but instead is implicitly contained in two rules.

If one applies this procedure to the HPSG grammar in Chapter 9, then the trace does not have a specific category such as NP. The trace simply has to be compatible with a non-head daughter. As the examples in (6) show, adjuncts, arguments and parts of verbal complexes can be extracted.

(6) a. Er$_i$ liest t$_i$ die Berichte.
       he reads   the reports

   b. Oft$_i$ liest er die Berichte t$_i$ nicht.
      often reads he the reports   not
      'Often, he does not read the reports.'

   c. Lesen$_i$ wird er die Berichte t$_i$ müssen.
      read   will he the reports   must
      'He will have to read the reports.'

The relevant elements are combined with their head in a specific schema (Head-Argument Schema, Head-Adjunct Schema, Predicate Complex Schema). See Chapter 9 for the first two schemata; the Predicate Complex Schema is motivated in detail in Müller (2002a: Chapter 2; 2007a: Chapter 15). If one wishes to do without traces, then one needs further additional schemata for the fronting of adjuncts, of arguments and of parts of predicate complexes. The combination of a head with a trace is given in Figure 19.1 on the facing page. The trace-less analysis is shown in Figure 19.2 on the next page. In Figure 19.1, the element in the COMPS list of *kennen* is identified with the SYNSEM value of the trace 4. The lexical entry of the trace prescribes that the LOCAL value of the trace should be identical to the element in the INHER|SLASH list.

The Non-Local Feature Principle (page 301) ensures that the SLASH information is present on the mother node. Since an argument position gets saturated in Head-Argument structures, the accusative object is no longer contained in the COMPS list of the mother node.

19.2 Eliminating empty elements from grammars

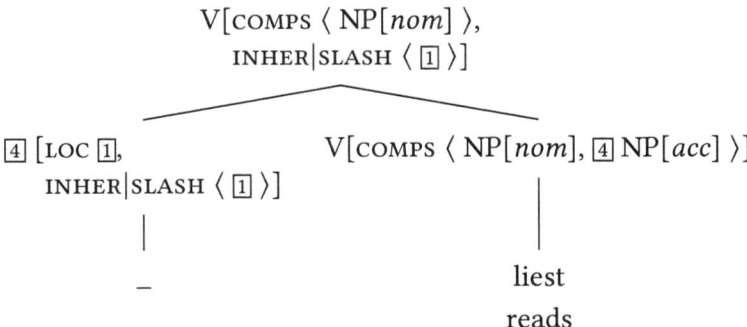

Figure 19.1: Introduction of information about long-distance dependencies with a trace

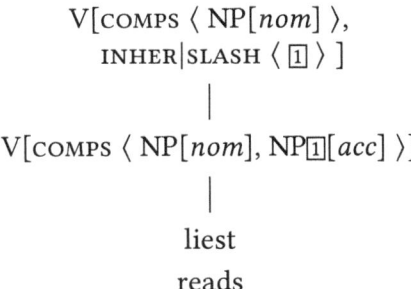

Figure 19.2: Introduction of information about long-distance dependencies using a unary projection

Figure 19.2 shows the parallel trace-less structure. The effect that one gets by combining a trace in argument position in Head-Argument structures is represented directly on the mother node in Figure 19.2: the LOCAL value of the accusative object was identified with the element in INHER|SLASH on the mother node and the accusative object does not occur in the valence list any more.

The grammar presented in Chapter 9 contains another empty element: a verb trace. This would then also have to be eliminated.

(7) a. Er$_i$ liest$_j$ t$_i$ die Berichte t$_j$.
     he reads the reports

   b. Oft$_i$ liest$_j$ er die Berichte t$_i$ nicht t$_j$.
      often reads he the reports not
      'Often, he does not read the reports.'

   c. Lesen$_i$ wird$_j$ er die Berichte t$_i$ müssen t$_j$.
      read will he the reports must
      'He will have to read the reports.'

Figure 19.3 on the following page shows the combination of a verb trace with an accusative object. The verb trace is specified such that the DSL value is identical to the

571

19 Empty elements

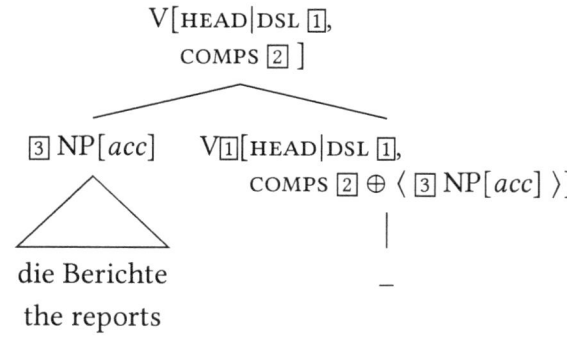

Figure 19.3: Analysis of verb position with verb trace

LOCAL value of the trace (see p. 295). Since DSL is a head feature, the corresponding value is also present on the mother node. Figure 19.4 shows the structures that we get by omitting the empty node. This structure may look odd at first sight since a noun phrase is

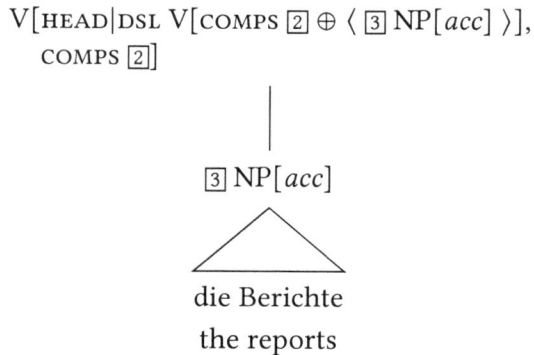

Figure 19.4: Analysis of verb position using a unary projection

projected to a verb (see page 235 for similar verb-less structures in LFG). The information about the fact that a verb is missing in the structure is equally contained in this structure as in the structure with the verb trace. It is the DSL value that is decisive for the contexts in which the structure in Figure 19.4 can appear. This is identical to the value in Figure 19.3 and contains the information that a verb that requires an accusative object is missing in the structure in question. Until now, we have seen that extraction traces can be removed from the grammar by stipulating three additional rules. Similarly, three new rules are needed for the verb trace. Unfortunately, it does not stop here as the traces for extraction and head movement can also interact. For example, the NP in the tree in Figure 19.4 could be an extraction trace. Therefore, the combination of traces can result in more empty elements that then also have to be eliminated. Since we have three schemata, we will have three new empty elements if we combine the non-head daughter with an extraction trace and the head daughter with a verb trace. (8) shows these cases:

(8) a. Er$_i$ [schläft$_j$ t$_i$ t$_j$]. (Extraction trace (argument) + verb trace)
he sleeps

'He is sleeping.'

b. Jetzt$_i$ [schlaf$_j$ t$_i$ t$_j$]! (Extraction trace (adjunct) + verb trace)
now sleep

'Go to sleep now!'

c. Geschlafen$_i$ [wird$_j$ t$_i$ t$_j$]! (Extraction trace (complex) + verb trace)
slept is

'Now is time to sleep!'

These three new traces can occur as non-head daughters in the Head-Argument Schema and thus one would require three new schemata for Head-Argument structures. Using these schemata, it then becomes possible to analyze the sentences in (8).

Six further schemata are required for the examples in (9) and (10) since the three new traces can each occur as heads in Head-Argument structures (9) and Head-Adjunct structures (10):

(9) a. Den Aufsatz$_i$ liest$_j$ [er t$_i$ t$_j$].
the essay reads he

'He is reading the essay.'

b. Oft$_i$ liest$_j$ er [ihn t$_i$ t$_j$].
often reads he it

'He often reads it.'

c. Lesen$_i$ wird$_j$ er [ihn t$_i$ t$_j$].
read will he it

'He will read it.'

(10) a. Den Aufsatz$_i$ liest$_j$ er [nicht t$_i$ t$_j$].
the essay reads he not

'He isn't reading the essay.'

b. Oft$_i$ liest$_j$ er ihn [nicht t$_i$ t$_j$].
often reads he it not

'He often doesn't read it'

c. Lesen$_i$ wird$_j$ er ihn [nicht t$_i$ t$_j$].
reads will he it not

'He won't read it.'

Eliminating two empty elements therefore comes at the price of twelve new rules. These rules are not particularly transparent and it is not immediately obvious why the mother node describes a linguistic object that follows general grammatical laws. For example, there are no heads in the structures following the pattern in Figure 19.4. Since there is no empirical difference between the theoretical variant with twelve additional schemata

19 Empty elements

and the variant with two empty elements, one should prefer the theory that makes fewer assumptions (Occam's Razor) and that is the theory with two empty elements.

One might think that the problem discussed here is just a problem specific to HPSG not shared by trace-less analyses such as the LFG approach that was discussed in Section 7.5. If we take a closer look at the rule proposed by Dalrymple (2006: 84), we see that the situation in LFG grammars is entirely parallel. The brackets around the category symbols mark their optionality. The asterisk following the PP means that any number of PPs (zero or more) can occur in this position.

(11) V′ → (V) (NP) PP*

This means that (11) is a shorthand for rules such as those in (12):

(12)   a. V′ → V
       b. V′ → V NP
       c. V′ → V NP PP
       d. V′ → V NP PP PP
       e. ...
       f. V′ → NP
       g. V′ → NP PP
       h. V′ → NP PP PP
       i. ...

Since all the elements on the right-hand side of the rule are optional, the rule in (11) also stands for (13):

(13) V′ → ϵ

Thus, one does in fact have an empty element in the grammar although the empty element is not explicitly listed in the lexicon. This follows from the optionality of all elements on the right-hand side of a rule. The rule in (12f) corresponds to the schema licensed by the structure in Figure 19.4. In the licensed LFG structure, there is also no head present. Furthermore, one has a large number of rules that correspond to exactly the schemata that we get when we eliminate empty elements from an HPSG grammar. This fact is, however, hidden in the representational format of the LFG rules. The rule schemata of LFG allow for handy abbreviations of sometimes huge sets of rules (even infinite sets when using '*').

Pollard (1988) has shown that Steedman's trace-less analysis of long-distance dependencies is not without its problems. As discussed in Section 8.5.3, a vast number of recategorization rules or lexical entries for relative pronouns are required.

19.3 Empty elements and semantic interpretation

In this section, I discuss an analysis that assumes empty elements in order to allow for different readings of particular sentences. I then show how one can use so-called underspecification approaches to do without empty elements.

19.3 Empty elements and semantic interpretation

Sentences such as (14) are interesting since they have multiple readings (see Dowty 1979: Section 5.6) and it is not obvious how these can be derived.

(14) dass Max alle Fenster wieder öffnete
that Max all windows again opened
'that Max opened all the windows again'

There is a difference between a repetitive and a restitutive reading: for the repetitive reading of (14), Max has to have opened every window at least once before, whereas the restitutive reading only requires that all windows were open at some point, that is, they could have been opened by someone else.

These different readings are explained by decomposing the predicate *open'* into at least two sub-predicates. Egg (1999) suggests the decomposition into CAUSE and *open'*:

(15) CAUSE(x, *open'*(y))

This means that there is a CAUSE operator that has scope over the relation *open'*. Using this kind of decomposition, it is possible to capture the varying scope of *wieder* 'again': in one of the readings, *wieder* scopes over CAUSE and it scopes over *open'* but below CAUSE in the other. If we assume that *öffnen* has the meaning in (15), then we still have to explain how the adverb can modify elements of a word's meaning, that is, how *wieder* 'again' can refer to *open'*. Von Stechow (1996: 93) developed the analysis in Figure 19.5 on the following page. AgrS and AgrO are functional heads proposed for subject and object agreement in languages like Basque and have been adopted for German (see Section 4.6). Noun phrases have to be moved from the VoiceP into the specifier position of the AgrS and AgrO heads in order to receive case. T stands for Tense and corresponds to Infl in the GB theory (see Section 3.1.5 and Section 4.1.5). What is important is that there is the Voice head and the separate representation of *offen* 'open' as the head of its own phrase. In the figure, everything below Voice' corresponds to the verb *öffnen*. By assuming a separate Voice head that contributes causative meaning, it becomes possible to derive both readings in syntax: in the reading with narrow scope of *wieder* 'again', the adverb is adjoined to the XP and has scope over open(x). In the reading with wide scope, the adverb attaches to VoiceP or some higher phrase and therefore has scope over CAUSE(BECOME(open(x))).

Jäger & Blutner (2003) point out that this analysis predicts that sentences such as (16) only have the repetitive reading, that is, the reading where *wieder* 'again' has scope over CAUSE.

(16) dass Max wieder alle Fenster öffnete
that Max again all windows opened

This is because *wieder* precedes *alle Fenster* and therefore all heads that are inside VoiceP. Thus, *wieder* can only be combined with AgrOP or higher phrases and therefore has (too) wide scope. (16) does permit a restitutive reading, however: all windows were open at an earlier point in time and Max reestablishes this state.

Egg (1999) develops an analysis for these *wieder* cases using Constraint Language for Lambda-Structures (CLLS). CLLS is an underspecification formalism, that is, no logical

19 Empty elements

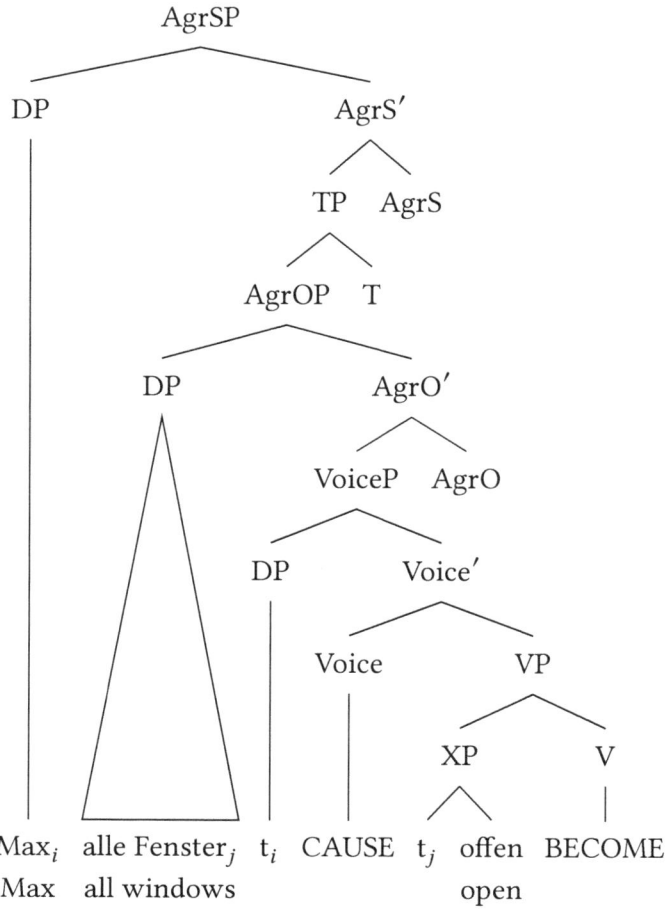

Figure 19.5: Decomposition in syntactic structures

formulae are given but instead expressions that describe logical formulae. Using this kind of expressions, it is possible to leave scope relations underspecified. I have already mentioned Minimal Recursion Semantics (MRS) (Copestake, Flickinger, Pollard & Sag 2005) in several chapters of this book. As well as CLLS, MRS together with Underspecified Discourse Representation Theory (Reyle 1993; Frank & Reyle 1995) and Hole Semantics (Bos 1996; Blackburn & Bos 2005) all belong to the class of underspecification formalisms. See Baldridge & Kruijff (2002) for an underspecification analysis in Categorial Grammar and Nerbonne (1993) for an early underspecification analysis in HPSG. In the following, I will reproduce Egg's analysis in an MRS-like notation.

Before we turn to (14) and (16), let us consider the simpler sentence in (17):

(17)   dass Max alle Fenster   öffnete
       that Max all   windows opened
       'that Max opened all the windows'

This sentence can mean that in a particular situation, it is true of all windows that Max opened them. A less readily accessible reading is the one in which Max causes all of the windows to be open. It is possible to force this reading if one rules out the first reading through contextual information (Egg 1999):

(18) Erst war nur die Hälfte der Fenster im Bus auf, aber dann öffnete Max
 first was only the half of.the windows in.the bus open but then opened Max
 alle Fenster.
 all windows
 'At first, only half of the windows in the bus were open, but then Max opened all of the windows.'

Both readings under discussion here differ with regard to the scope of the universal quantifier. The reading where Max opens all the windows himself corresponds to wide scope in (19a). The reading where some windows could have already been open corresponds to (19b):

(19) a. $\forall x \ window'(x) \rightarrow \text{CAUSE}(max', open'(x))$
 b. $\text{CAUSE}(max', \forall x \ window'(x) \rightarrow open'(x))$

Using underspecification, both of these readings can be represented in one dominance graph such as the one given in Figure 19.6. Each relation in Figure 19.6 has a name that

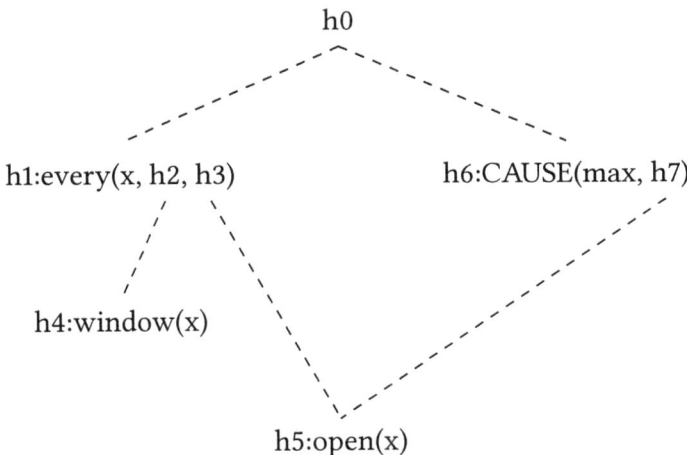

Figure 19.6: Dominance graph for *Max alle Fenster öffnete*

one can use to refer to the relation or "grasp" it. These names are referred to as *handle*. The dominance graph states that *h0* dominates both *h1* and *h6* and that *h2* dominates *h4*, *h3* dominates *h5*, and *h7* dominates *h5*. The exact scopal relations are underspecified: the universal quantifier can have scope over CAUSE or CAUSE can have scope over the universal quantifier. Figures 19.7 and 19.8 show the variants of the graph with resolved scope. The underspecified graph in Figure 19.6 does not say anything about the relation

19 Empty elements

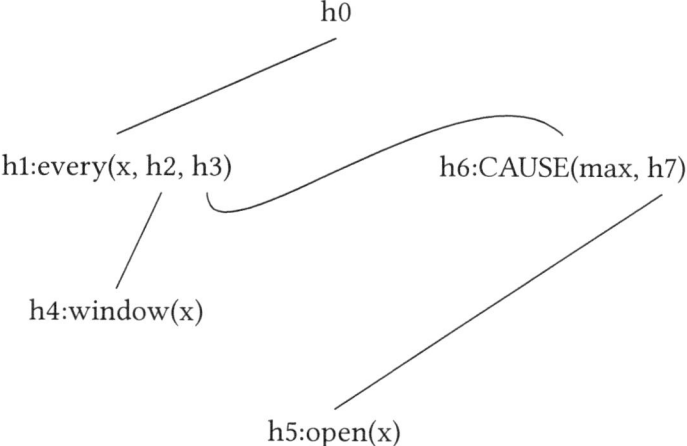

Figure 19.7: Dominance graph for the reading ∀ x window(x) → CAUSE(max,open(x)).

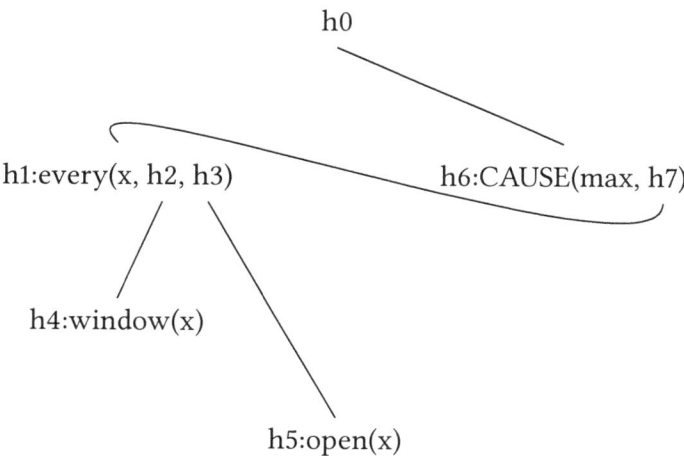

Figure 19.8: Graph for te reading CAUSE(max, ∀ x window(x) → open(x)).

between *h*3 and *h*6. The only thing it says is that *h*3 somehow has to dominate *h*5. In Figure 19.7 every (*h*3) dominates CAUSE (*h*6) and CAUSE dominates open (*h*5). So, *every′* dominates *open′* indirectly. In Figure 19.8, CAUSE dominates *every′* and *every′* dominates *open′*. Again the constraints of Figure 19.6 are fulfilled, but *h*7 dominates *h*5 only indirectly.

The fact that the quantifier dominates *h*4 is determined by the lexical entry of the quantifier. The fact that the quantifier dominates *h*5 does not have to be made explicit in the analysis since the quantifier binds a variable in the relation belonging to *h*5, namely x. The dominance relation between *h*7 and *h*5 is always determined in the lexicon since CAUSE and *open′* both belong to the semantic contribution of a single lexical entry.

The exact syntactic theory that one adopts for this analysis is, in the end, not of great importance. I have chosen HPSG here. As Figure 19.9 on the facing page shows, the

19.3 Empty elements and semantic interpretation

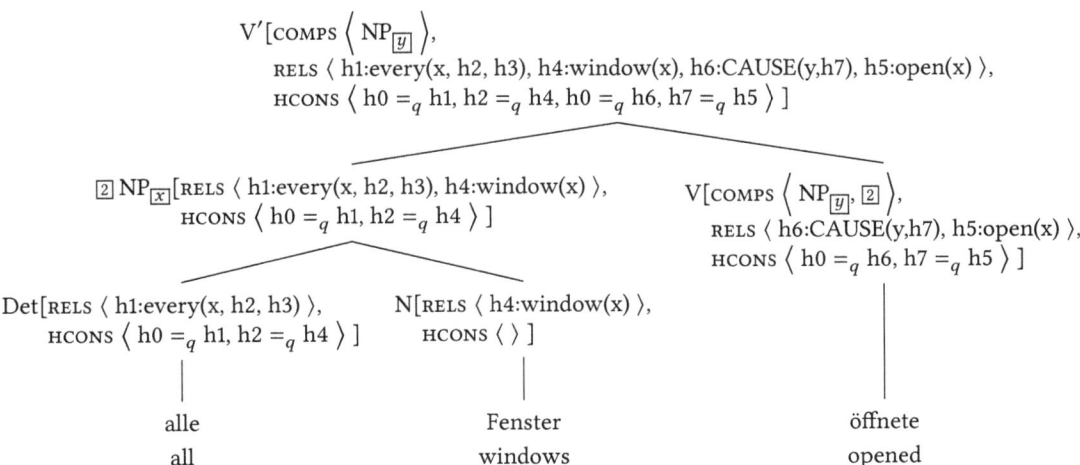

Figure 19.9: MRS analysis of *alle Fenster öffnete*

analysis of *alle Fenster öffnet* contains a simple structure with a verb and an object. This structure does not differ from the one that would be assumed for *alle Kinder kennt* 'all children know', involving the semantically simplex verb *kennen* 'to know'. The only difference comes from the meaning of the individual words involved. As shown in Section 9.1.6, relations between individual words are passed on upwards. The same happens with scopal restrictions. These are also represented in lists. HCONS stands for *handle constraints*. $=_q$ in h0 $=_q$ h6 stand for the equality *modulo* quantifier scope.

Egg lists the following readings for the sentence in (16) – repeated here as (20):

(20) dass Max wieder alle Fenster öffnete
 that Max again all windows opened

 'that Max opened all the windows again'

1. Max opened every window and he had already done that at least once for each window (*again*′(∀(CAUSE(open))); repetitive)

2. Max caused every window to be open and he had done that at least once before (*again*′(CAUSE(∀(open))); repetitive)

3. At some earlier point in time, all windows were simultaneously open and Max re-established this state (CAUSE(*again*′(∀(open))); restitutive)

These readings correspond to the dominance graph in Figure 19.10 on the next page. Figure 19.11 on the following page shows the graph for (14) – repeated here as (21):

(21) dass Max alle Fenster wieder öffnete
 that Max all windows again opened

To derive these dominance graphs from the ones without *wieder* 'again', all one has to do is add the expression h8:again(h9) and the dominance requirements that demand

19 Empty elements

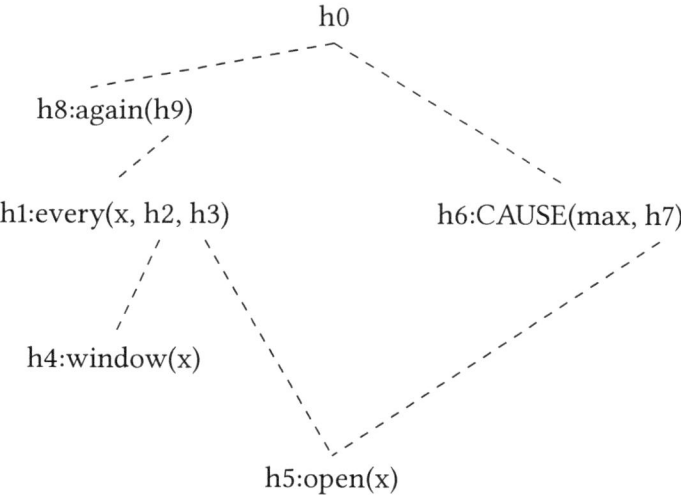

Figure 19.10: Dominance graph for *Max wieder alle Fenster öffnete* 'that Max opened all the windows again'

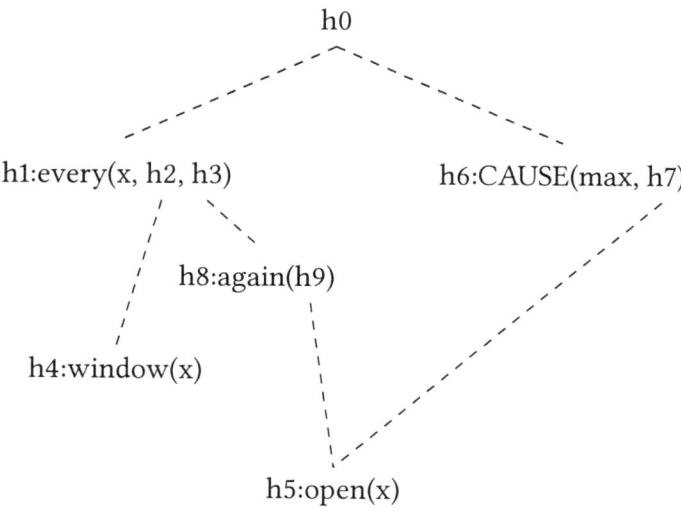

Figure 19.11: Dominance graph for *Max alle Fenster wieder öffnete* 'that Max opened all the windows again'

that *h9* dominates quantifiers occurring to the right of *wieder* and that it is dominated by quantifiers to the left of *wieder*.

It is therefore unproblematic to derive the relevant readings for modification by *wieder* without empty elements for CAUSE and BECOME. The meaning of the word *öffnen* is decomposed in a similar way but the decomposed meaning is assigned to a single element, the verb. By underspecification of the scopal relations in the lexicon, the relevant readings can then be derived.

19.4 Evidence for empty elements

As previously discussed, grammarians agree that both linguists and speakers notice when there is a constituent missing from a string of words. For cases where it can be shown that analyses with or without traces are indistinguishable empirically, then one can assume empty elements. Nevertheless, the learnability argument put forward by Construction Grammarians has some validity: if one assumes that there is no or little innate linguistic knowledge, then it is not possible to motivate empty elements with data from other languages. This means that just because Basque shows object agreement, this does not mean that one can assume an empty head for object agreement (AgrO) in a grammar of German as for instance von Stechow (1996) and Meinunger (2000) do. Since there is no object agreement in German, there would be no way for the child to learn the fact that there is an AgrO head. Knowledge about AgrO must therefore be innate. Since the assumption of innate linguistic knowledge is controversial (see Chapter 13), any theory that uses cross-linguistic data to motivate the use of empty elements is on shaky ground.

Cross-linguistic considerations can only be drawn upon if there are no empirical differences between multiple alternative analyses compatible and motivated by the language under consideration. In this case, one should follow Occam's Razor and choose the analysis which is compatible with analyses of other languages (see Müller 2015b and Chapter 23.2).

19.5 Transformations, lexical rules, and empty elements

In the discussion of the passive in the framework of TAG, it became clear that lexical rules correspond to particular transformations, namely those which have some relation to a lexical item (lexically governed transformations, Dowty 1978; for the discussion of transformations and lexical rules, see Bresnan (1978) and Bresnan & Kaplan (1982)). In the respective variants of TAG, lexical rules establish a relation between a lexical item for an active tree with a lexical item of a passive tree. Both the active and passive tree can be extended by adjunction.

In theories such as Categorial Grammar, the situation is similar: since the direction in which a functor expects to find its argument is fixed for languages such as English, the lexical item stands for an entire tree. Only the attachment of adjuncts is not yet specified in lexical items. The positions in the tree where the adjuncts can occur depend on the properties of the adjuncts. In Section 8.4, we have seen suggestions for treatments of languages with free constituent order. If the direction of combination is not fixed in the lexicon, then the lexical item can occur in a number of trees. If we compare lexical rules that can be applied to this kind of lexical items with transformations, we see that lexical rules create relations between different sets of trees.

In HPSG analyses, this works in a similar way: lexical rules relate lexical items with differing valence properties to each other. In HPSG grammars of English, there is normally a schema that licenses a VP containing the verb and all its complements as well as a schema that connects the subject to the VP (Pollard & Sag 1994: 39). In the lexical items for finite verbs, it is already determined what the tree will look like in the end. As in Categorial Grammar, adjuncts in HPSG can be combined with various intermediate projections. Depending on the dominance schemata used in a particular grammar, the lexical item will determine the constituent structure in which it can occur or allow for multiple structures. In the grammar of German proposed in Chapter 9, it is possible to analyze six different sequences with a lexical item for a ditransitive verb, that is, the lexical item can – putting adjuncts aside – occur in six different structures with verb-final order. Two sequences can be analyzed with the passive lexical item, which only has two arguments. As in Categorial Grammar, sets of licensed structures are related to other sets of licensed structures. In HPSG theorizing and also in Construction Grammar, there have been attempts to replace lexical rules with other mechanisms since their "status is dubious and their interaction with other analyses is controversial" (Bouma, Malouf & Sag 2001: 19). Bouma, Malouf, et al. (2001) propose an analysis for extraction that, rather than connecting lexical items with differing valence lists, establishes a relation between a subset of a particular list in a lexical item and another list in the same lexical item. The results of the two alternative analyses are shown in (22) and (23), respectively:

(22) a. $\begin{bmatrix} \text{COMPS} & \langle \text{NP}[nom], \text{NP}[acc] \rangle \\ \text{SLASH} & \langle \rangle \end{bmatrix}$

b. $\begin{bmatrix} \text{COMPS} & \langle \text{NP}[nom] \rangle \\ \text{SLASH} & \langle \text{NP}[acc] \rangle \end{bmatrix}$

In (22), (22a) is the basic entry and (22b) is related to (22a) via a lexical rule. The alternative analysis would only involve specifying the appropriate value of the ARG-ST feature[3] and the COMPS and SLASH value is then derived from the ARG-ST value using the relevant constraints. (23) shows two of the licensed lexical items.

(23) a. $\begin{bmatrix} \text{ARG-ST} & \langle \text{NP}[nom], \text{NP}[acc] \rangle \\ \text{COMPS} & \langle \text{NP}[nom], \text{NP}[acc] \rangle \\ \text{SLASH} & \langle \rangle \end{bmatrix}$

b. $\begin{bmatrix} \text{ARG-ST} & \langle \text{NP}[nom], \text{NP}[acc] \rangle \\ \text{COMPS} & \langle \text{NP}[nom] \rangle \\ \text{SLASH} & \langle \text{NP}[acc] \rangle \end{bmatrix}$

If we want to eliminate lexical rules entirely in this way, then we would require an additional feature for each change.[4] Since there are many interacting valence-changing processes, things only work out with the stipulation of a large number of auxiliary features. The consequences of assuming such analyses have been discussed in detail in Müller (2007a: Section 7.5.2.2). The problems that arise are parallel for inheritance-based

---

[3] ARG-ST stands for *Argument Structure*. The value of ARG-ST is a list containing all the arguments of a head. For more on ARG-ST, see Section 9.1.1.

[4] Alternatively, one could assume a very complex relation that connects ARG-ST and COMPS. But this would then have to deliver the result of an interaction of a number of phenomena and the interaction of these phenomena would not be captured in a transparent way.

19.5 Transformations, lexical rules, and empty elements

approaches for argument structure-changing processes: they also require auxiliary features since it is not possible to model embedding and multiple changes of valence information with inheritance. See Section 10.2.

Furthermore, the claim that the status of lexical rules is dubious must be rejected: there are worked-out formalizations of lexical rules (Meurers 2001; Copestake & Briscoe 1992; Lascarides & Copestake 1999) and their interaction with other analyses is not controversial. Most HPSG implementations make use of lexical rules and the interaction of a number of rules and constraints can be easily verified by experiments with implemented fragments.

Jackendoff (1975) presents two possible conceptions of lexical rules: in one variant, the lexicon contains all words in a given language and there are just redundancy rules saying something about how certain properties of lexical entries behave with regard to properties of other lexical entries. For example, *les-* 'read-' and *lesbar* 'readable' would both have equal status in the lexicon. In the other way of thinking of lexical rules, there are a few basic lexical entries and the others are derived from these using lexical rules. The stem *les-* 'read-' would be the basic entry and *lesbar* would be derived from it. In HPSG, the second of the two variants is more often assumed. This is equivalent to the assumption of unary rules. In Figure 9.9 on page 291, this has been shown accordingly: the verb *kennt* 'knows' is mapped by a lexical rule to a verb that selects the projection of an empty verbal head. With this conception of lexical rules, it is possible to remove lexical rules from the grammar by assuming binary-branching structures with an empty head rather than unary rules. For example, in HPSG analyses of resultative constructions such as (24), lexical rules have been proposed (Verspoor 1997; Wechsler 1997; Wechsler & Noh 2001; Müller 2002a: Chapter 5).

(24) [dass] Peter den Teich leer   fischt
       that Peter the pond empty fishes

'that Peter fishes the pond empty'

In my own analysis, a lexical rule connects a verb used intransitively to a verb that selects an accusative object and a predicate. Figure 19.12 on the next page shows the corresponding tree. If we consider what (24) means, then we notice that the fishing act causes the pond to become empty. This causation is not contained in any of the basic lexical items for the words in (24). In order for this information to be present in the semantic representation of the entire expression, it has to be added by means of a lexical rule. The lexical rule says: if a verb is used with an additional predicate and accusative object, then the entire construction has a causative meaning.

Figure 19.13 on page 585 shows how a lexical rule can be replaced by an empty head. The empty head requires the intransitive verb and additionally an adjective, an accusative object and a subject. The subject of *fischt* 'fishes' must of course be identical to the subject that is selected by the combination of *fischt* and the empty head. This is not shown in the figure. It is possible, however, to establish this identity (see Hinrichs & Nakazawa 1994). The causative semantics is contributed by the empty head in this analysis. The trick that is being implemented here is exactly what was done in Section 19.2, just in the opposite direction: in the previous section, binary-branching structures with an empty

19 Empty elements

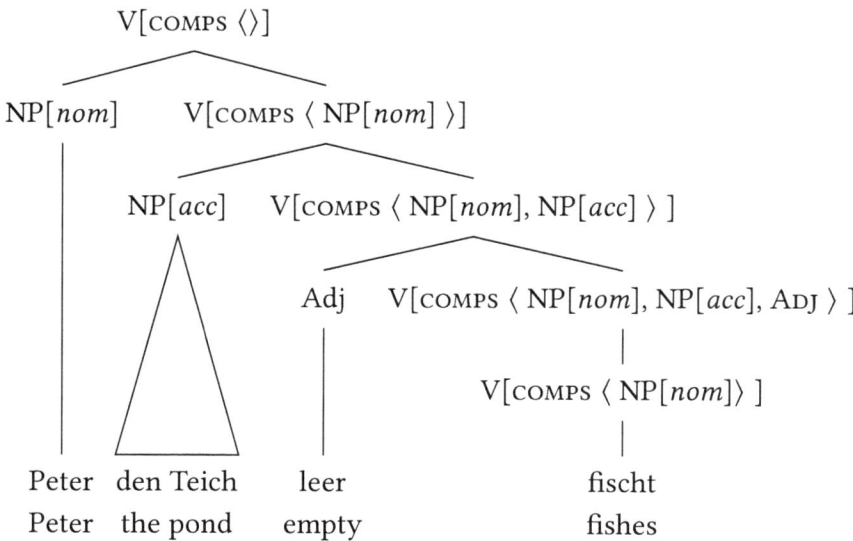

Figure 19.12: Analysis of the resultative construction with a lexical rule

daughter were replaced by unary-branching structures. In this section, we have replaced unary-branching structures with binary-branching structures with an empty daughter.[5]

We have therefore seen that certain transformations can be replaced by lexical rules and also that lexical rules can be replaced by empty heads. The following chapter deals with the question of whether phenomena like extraction, scrambling, and passive should be described with the same tool as in GB/Minimalism or with different tools as in LFG and HPSG.

---

[5]Here, we are discussing lexical rules, but this transformation trick can also be applied to other unary rules. Semanticists often use such rules for type shifting. For example, a rule that turns a referential NP such as *a trickster* in (i.a) into a predicative one (i.b) (Partee 1987).

(i) a. A trickster laughs.
    b. He is a trickster.

These changes can be achieved by a unary rule that is applied to an NP or with a special empty head that takes an NP as its argument. In current Minimalist approaches, empty heads are used (Ramchand 2005: 370), in Categorial Grammar and HPSG unary-branching rules are more common (Flickinger 2008: 91–92; Müller 2009c; 2012b).

19.5 Transformations, lexical rules, and empty elements

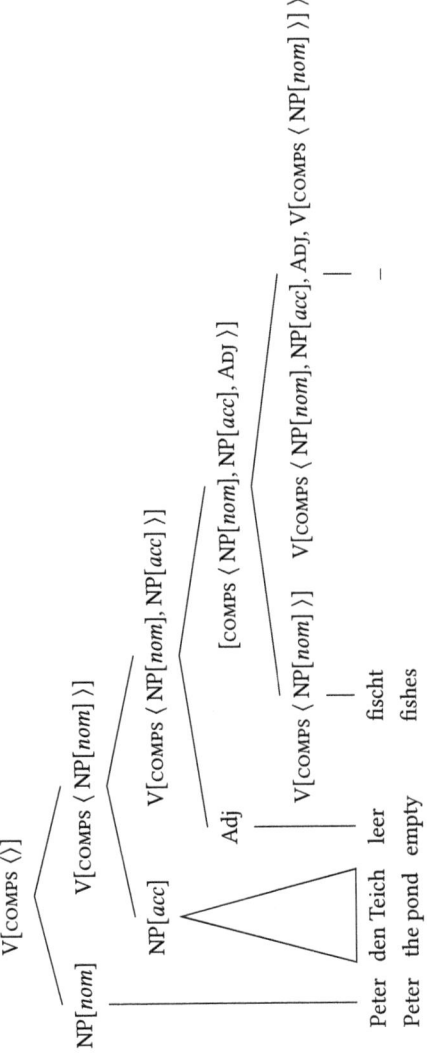

Figure 19.13: Analysis of the resultative construction with an empty head

20 Extraction, scrambling, and passive: one or several descriptive devices?

An anonymous reviewer suggested discussing one issue in which transformational theories differ from theories like LFG and HPSG. The reviewer claimed that Transformational Grammars use just one tool for the description of active/passive alternations, scrambling, and extraction, while theories like LFG and HPSG use different techniques for all three phenomena. If this claim were correct and if the analyses made correct predictions, the respective GB/Minimalism theories would be better than their competitors, since the general aim in science is to develop theories that need a minimal set of assumptions. I already commented on the analysis of passive in GB in Section 3.4, but I want to extend this discussion here and include a Minimalist analysis and one from Dependency Grammar.

The task of any passive analysis is to explain the difference in argument realization in examples like (1):

(1) a. She beats him.
    b. He was beaten.

In these examples about chess, the accusative object of *beat* is realized as the nominative in (1b). In addition, it can be observed that the position of the elements is different: while *him* is realized postverbally in object position in (1a), it is realized preverbally in (1b). In GB this is explained by a movement analysis. It is assumed that the object does not get case in passive constructions and hence has to move into the subject position where case is assigned by the finite verb. This analysis is also assumed in Minimalist work as in David Adger's textbook (2003), for instance. Figure 20.1 on the next page shows his analysis of (2):

(2) Jason was killed.

TP stands for Tense Phrase and corresponds to the IP that was discussed in Chapter 3. PassP is a functional head for passives. *v*P is a special category for the analysis of verb phrases that was originally introduced for the analysis of ditransitives (Larson 1988) and VP is the normal VP that consists of verb and object. In Adger's analysis, the verb *kill* moves from the verb position in VP to the head position of *v*, the passive auxiliary *be* moves from the head position of PassP to the head position of the Tense Phrase. Features like Infl are 'checked' in combination with such movements. The exact implementation of these checking and valuing operations does not matter here. What is important is that *Jason* moves from the object position to a position that was formerly known as the

20 Extraction, scrambling, and passive: one or several descriptive devices?

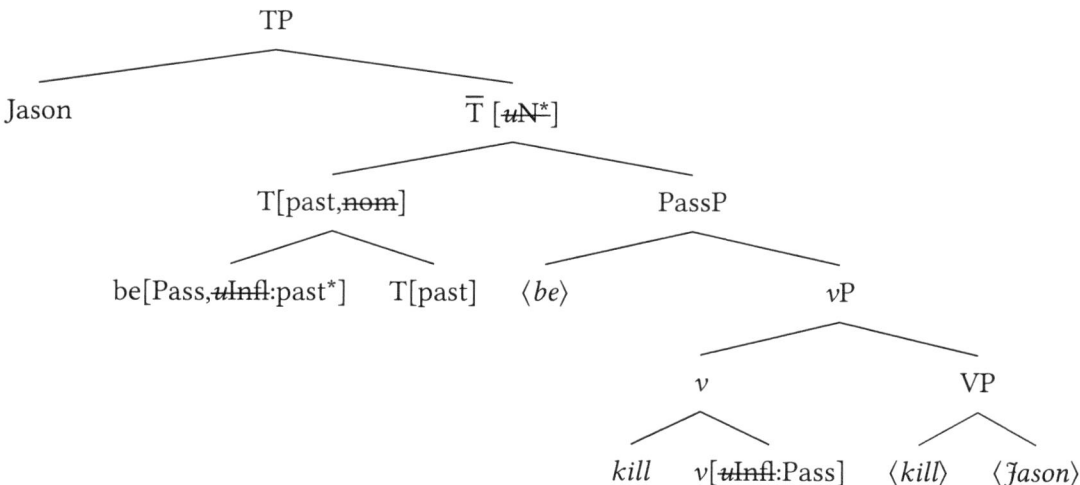

Figure 20.1: Adger's Minimalist movement-based analysis of the passive (p. 231)

specifier position of T (see Footnote 28 on page 161 on the notion of specifier). All these analyses assume that the participle cannot assign accusative to its object and that the object has to move to another position to get case or check features. How exactly one can formally represents the fact that the participle cannot assign case is hardly ever made explicit in the GB literature. The following is a list of statements that can be found in the literature:

(3)   a. We shall assume that a passivized verb loses the ability to assign structural ACCUSATIVE case to its complement. (Haegeman 1994: 183)

       b. das Objekt des Aktivsatzes wird zum Subjekt des Passivsatzes, weil die passivische Verbform keinen Akkusativ-Kasus regieren kann (Akk-Kasus-Absorption). (Lohnstein 2014: 172)

In addition, it is sometimes said that the external theta-role is absorbed by the verb morphology (Jaeggli 1986; Haegeman 1994: 183). Now, what would it entail if we made this explicit? There is some lexical item for verbs like *beat*. The active form has the ability to assign accusative to its object, but the passive form does not. Since this is a property that is shared by all transitive verbs (by definition of the term transitive verb), this is some regularity that has to be captured. One way to capture this is the assumption of a special passive morpheme that suppresses the agent and changes something in the case specification of the stem it attaches too. How this works in detail was never made explicit. Let us compare this morpheme-based analysis with lexical rule-based analyses: as was explained in Section 19.5, empty heads can be used instead of lexical rules in those cases in which the phonological form of the input and the output do not differ. So for example, lexical rules that license additional arguments as in resultative constructions, for instance, can be replaced by an empty head. However, as was explained in Section 9.2, lexical rules are also used to model morphology. This is also true for Construction Grammar (see Gert Booij's work on Construction Morphology (2010), which is in many ways similar to Riehemann's work in HPSG (1993; 1998)). In the case of the passive lexical rule, the participle morphology is combined with the stem and the subject is suppressed in the corresponding valence list. This is exactly what is described in the GB/MP literature. The respective lexical rule for the analysis of *ge-lieb-t* 'loved' is depicted in Figure 20.2 to the left. The morpheme-based analysis is shown to the right. To keep things simple, I

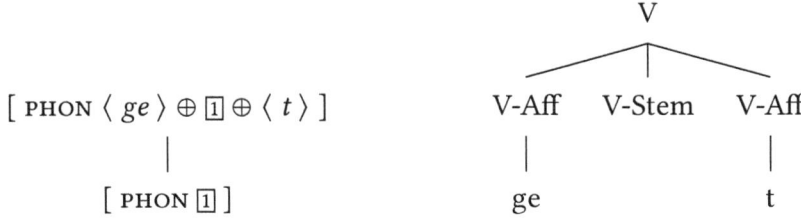

Figure 20.2: Lexical rule-based/constructionist vs. morpheme-based analysis

assume a flat analysis, but those who insist on binary branching structures would have to come up with a way of deciding whether the *ge-* or the *-t* is combined first with the stem and in which way selection and percolation of features takes place. Independent of how morphology is done, the fact that the inflected form (the top node in both figures) has different properties than the verb stem has to be represented somehow. In the morpheme-based world, the morpheme is responsible for suppressing the agent and changing the case assignment properties, in the lexical rule/construction world this is done by the respective lexical rule. There is no difference in terms of needed tools and necessary stipulations.

The situation in Minimalist theories is a little bit different. For instance, (Adger 2003: 229, 231) writes the following:

> Passives are akin to unaccusatives, in that they do not assign accusative case to their object, and they do not appear to have a thematic subject. [...] Moreover, the idea that the function of this auxiliary is to select an unaccusative little *v*P simultaneously explains the lack of accusative case and the lack of a thematic subject. (Adger 2003: 229, 231)

So this is an explicit statement. The relation between a stem and a passive participle form that was assumed in GB analyses is now a verb stem that is combined with two different versions of little *v*. Which *v* is chosen is determined by the governing head, a functional Perf head or a Pass head. This can be depicted as in Figure 20.3 on the next page. When *kill* is used in the perfect or the passive, it is spelled out as *killed*. If it is used in the active with a 3rd person singular subject it is spelled out as *kills*. This can be compared with a lexical analysis, for instance the one assumed in HPSG. The analysis is shown in Figure 20.4 on the following page. The left figure shows a lexical item that is licensed by a lexical rule that is applied to the stem *kill-*. The stem has two elements in its argument structure list and for the active forms the complete argument structure list

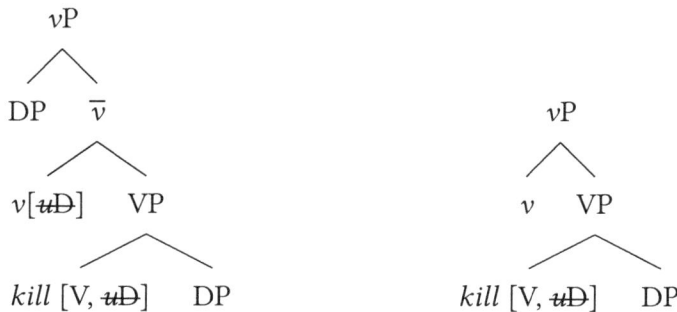

Figure 20.3: Analysis of the passive and the perfect and the passive in a Minimalist theory involving two different versions of little *v*

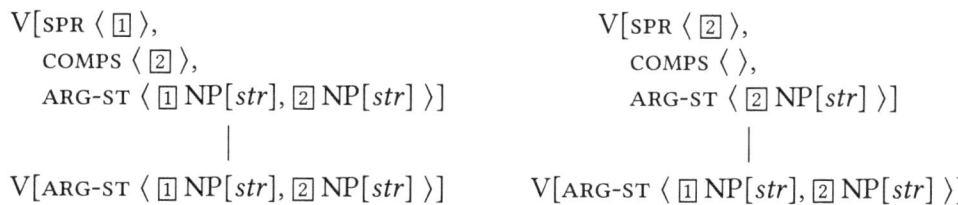

Figure 20.4: Lexical rule-based analysis of the perfect and the passive in HPSG

is shared between the licensed lexical item and the stem. The first element of the ARG-ST list is mapped to SPR and the other elements to COMPS (in English). Passive is depicted in the right figure: the first element of the ARG-ST with structural case is suppressed and since the element that was the second element in the ARG-ST list of the stem ([2]) is now the first element, this item is mapped to SPR. See Section 9.2 for passive in HPSG and Section 9.1.1 for comments on ARG-ST and the differences between German and English.

The discussion of Figures 20.3 and 20.4 are a further illustration of a point made in Section 19.5: lexical rules can be replaced by empty heads and vice versa. While HPSG says there are stems that are related to inflected forms and corresponding to the inflection the arguments are realized in a certain way, Minimalist theories assume two variants of little *v* that differ in their selection of arguments. Now, the question is: are there empirical differences between the two approaches? I think there are differences if one considers the question of language acquisition. What children can acquire from data is that there are various inflected forms and that they are related somehow. What remains questionable is whether they really would be able to detect empty little *v*s. One could claim of course that children operate with chunks of structures such as the ones in Figure 20.3. But then a verb would be just a chunk consisting of little *v* and V and having some open slots. This would be indistinguishable from what the HPSG analysis assumes.

As far as the "lexical rules as additional tool" aspect is concerned, the discussion is closed, but note that the standard GB/Minimalism analyses differ in another way from LFG and HPSG analyses, since they assume that passive has something to do with movement, that is, they assume that the same mechanisms are used that are used for nonlocal dependencies.[1] This works for languages like English in which the object has to be realized in postverbal position in the active and in preverbal position in the passive, but it fails for languages like German in which the order of constituents is more free. Lenerz (1977: Section 4.4.3) discussed the examples in (44) on page 112 – which are repeated here as (4) for convenience:

(4) a. weil das Mädchen dem Jungen den Ball schenkt
because the girl.NOM the.DAT boy the.ACC Ball gives
'because the girl gives the ball to the boy'

b. weil dem Jungen der Ball geschenkt wurde
because the.DAT boy the.NOM ball given was

c. weil der Ball dem Jungen geschenkt wurde
because the.NOM ball the.DAT boy given was
'because the ball was given to the boy'

While both orders in (4b) and (4c) are possible, the one with dative–nominative order in (4b) is the unmarked one. There is a strong linearization preference in German demanding that animate NPs be serialized before inanimate ones (Hoberg 1981: 46). This linearization rule is unaffected by passivization. Theories that assume that passive is movement either have to assume that the passive of (4a) is (4c) and (4b) is derived from (4c) by a further reordering operation (which would be implausible since usually one assumes that more marked constructions require more transformations), or they would have to come up with other explanations for the fact that the subject of the passive sentence has the same position as the object in active sentences. As was already explained in Section 3.4, one such explanation is to assume an empty expletive subject that is placed in the position where nominative is assigned and to somehow connect this expletive element to the subject in object position. While this somehow works, it should be clear that the price for rescuing a movement-based analysis of passive is rather high: one has to assume an empty expletive element, that is, something that neither has a form nor a meaning. The existence of such an object could not be inferred from the input unless it is assumed that the structures in which it is assumed are given. Thus, a rather rich UG would have to be assumed.

The question one needs to ask here is: why does the movement-based analysis have these problems and why does the valence-based analysis not have them? The cause of the problem is that the analysis of the passive mixes two things: the fact that SVO languages like English encode subjecthood positionally, and the fact that the subject is suppressed in passives. If these two things are separated the problem disappears. The fact that the object of the active sentence in (1a) is realized as the subject in (1b) is explained

---

[1] There is another option in Minimalist theories. Since Agree can check features nonlocally, T can assign nominative to an embedded element. So, in principle the object may get nominative in the VP without moving to T. However, Adger (2003: 368) assumes that German has a strong EPP feature on T, so that the underlying object has to move to the specifier of T. This is basically the old GB analysis of passive in German with all its conceptual problems and disadvantages.

by the assumption that the first NP on the argument structure list with structural case is realized as subject and mapped to the respective valence feature: SPR in English. Such mappings can be language specific (see Section 9.1.1 and Müller (2019b) where I discuss Icelandic, which is an SVO language with subjects with lexical case).

In what follows, I discuss another set of examples that are sometimes seen as evidence for a movement-based analysis. The examples in (5) are instances of the so-called remote passive (Höhle 1978: 175–176).[2]

(5) a. daß er auch von mir zu überreden versucht wurde[3]
that he.NOM also from me to persuade tried got
'that an attempt to persuade him was also made by me'

b. weil der Wagen oft zu reparieren versucht wurde
because the car.NOM often to repair tried was
'because many attempts were made to repair the car'

What is interesting about these examples is that the subject is the underlying object of a deeply embedded verb. This seems to suggest that the object is extracted out of the verb phrase. So the analysis of (5b) would be (6):

(6) weil [$_{IP}$ der Wagen$_i$ [$_{VP}$ oft [$_{VP}$ [$_{VP}$ _$_i$ zu reparieren] versucht] wurde]
because the car.NOM often to repair tried was

While this is a straight-forward explanation of the fact that (5b) is grammatical, another explanation is possible as well. In the HPSG analysis of German (and Dutch) it is assumed that verbs like those in (5b) form a verbal complex, that is, *zu reparieren versucht wurde* 'to repair tried was' forms one unit. When two or more verbs form a complex, the highest verb attracts the arguments from the verb it embeds (Hinrichs & Nakazawa 1989b; 1994; Bouma & van Noord 1998). A verb like *versuchen* 'to try' selects a subject, an infinitive with *zu* 'to' and all complements that are selected by this infinitive. In the analysis of (7), *versuchen* 'to try' selects for its subject, the object of *reparieren* 'to repair' and for the verb *zu reparieren* 'to repair'.

(7) weil er den Wagen zu reparieren versuchen will
because he.NOM the.ACC car to repair try wants
'because he wants to try to repair the car'

Now if the passive lexical rule applies to *versuch-*, it suppresses the first argument of *versuch-* with structural case, which is the subject of *versuch-*. The next argument of *versuch-* is the object of *zu reparieren*. Since this element is the first NP with structural case, it gets nominative as in (5b). So, this shows that there is an analysis of the remote passive that does not rely on movement. Since movement-based analyses were shown to be problematic and since there are no data that cannot be explained without movement, analyses without movement have to be preferred.

---

[2]See Müller (2002a: Section 3.1.4.1) and Wurmbrand (2003b) for corpus examples.
[3]Oppenrieder (1991: 212).

This leaves us with movement-based accounts of local reordering (scrambling). The reviewer suggested that scrambling, passive, and nonlocal extraction may be analyzed with the same mechanism. It was long thought that scope facts made the assumption of movement-based analyses of scrambling necessary, but it was pointed out by Kiss (2001: 146) and Fanselow (2001: Section 2.6) that the reverse is true: movement-based accounts of scrambling make wrong predictions with regard to available quantifier scopings. I discussed the respective examples in Section 3.5 already and will not repeat the discussion here. The conclusion that has to be drawn from this is that passive, scrambling, and long distance extraction are three different phenomena that should be treated differently. The solution for the analysis of the passive that is adopted in HPSG is based on an analysis by Haider (1986a), who worked within the GB framework. The "scrambling-as-base generation" approach to local reordering that was used in HPSG right from the beginning (Gunji 1986) is also adopted by some practitioners of GB/Minimalism, e.g., Fanselow (2001).

Having discussed the analyses in GB/Minimalism, I now turn to Dependency Grammar. Groß & Osborne (2009) suggest that *w*-fronting, topicalization, scrambling, extraposition, splitting, and also the remote passive should be analyzed by what they call *rising*. The concept was already explained in Section 11.5. The Figures 20.5 and 20.6 show examples for the fronting and the scrambling of an object. Groß and Osborne assume

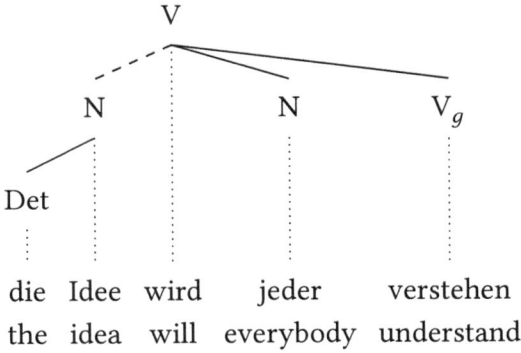

Figure 20.5: Analysis of *Die Idee wird jeder verstehen.* 'Everybody will understand the idea.' involving rising

that the object depends on the main verb in sentences with auxiliary verbs, while the subject depends on the auxiliary. Therefore, the object *die Idee* 'the idea' and the object *sich* 'himself' have to rise to the next higher verb in order to keep the structures projective. Figure 20.7 on the next page shows the analysis of the remote passive. The object of *zu reparieren* 'to repair' rises to the auxiliary *wurde* 'was'.

Groß and Osborne use the same mechanism for all these phenomena, but it should be clear that there have to be differences in the exact implementation. Groß and Osborne say that English does not have scrambling, while German does. If this is to be captured, there must be a way to distinguish the two phenomena, since if this were not possible, one would predict that English has scrambling as well, since both German and English

20 *Extraction, scrambling, and passive: one or several descriptive devices?*

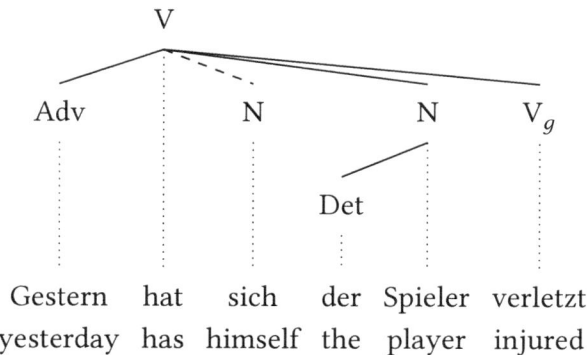

Figure 20.6: Analysis of *Gestern hat sich der Spieler verletzt.* 'Yesterday, the player injured himself.' involving rising of the object of the main verb *verletzt* 'injured'

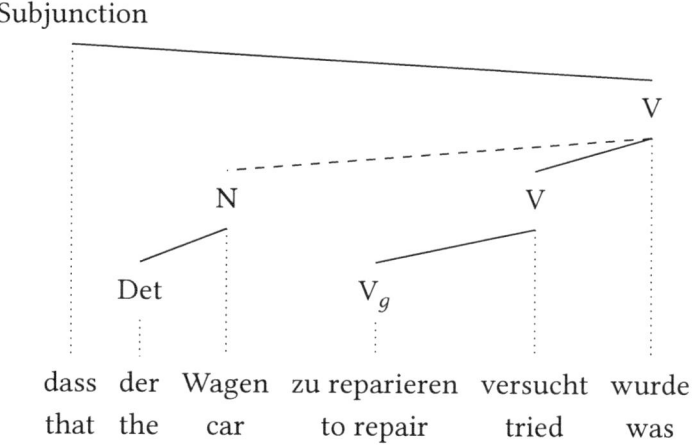

Figure 20.7: Analysis of the remote passive *dass der Wagen zu reparieren versucht wurde* 'that it was tried to repair the car' involving rising

allow long distance fronting. Groß & Osborne (2009: 58) assume that object nouns that rise must take the nominative. But if the kind of rising that they assume for remote passives is identical to the one that they assume for scrambling, they would predict that *den Wagen* gets nominative in (8) as well:

(8) dass den Wagen niemand repariert hat
    that the.ACC car nobody.NOM repaired has
    'that nobody repaired the car'

Since *den Wagen* 'the car' and *repariert* 'repaired' are not adjacent, *den Wagen* has to rise to the next higher head in order to allow for a projective realization of elements. So in order to assign case properly, one has to take into account the arguments that are governed by the head to which a certain element rises. Since the auxiliary *hat* 'has' already governs a nominative, the NP *den Wagen* has to be realized in the accusative. An analysis that assumes that both the accusative and nominative depend on *hat* 'has' in (8) is basically the verbal complex analysis assumed in HPSG and some GB variants.

Note, however, that this does not extend to nonlocal dependencies. Case is assigned locally by verbs or verbal complexes, but not to elements that come from far away. The long distance extraction of NPs is more common in southern variants of German and there are only a few verbs that do not take a nominative argument themselves. The examples below involve *dünken* 'to think', which governs an accusative and a sentential object and *scheinen* 'to seem', which governs a dative and a sentential object. If (9a) is analyzed with *den Wagen* rising to *dünkt*, one might expect that *den Wagen* 'the car' gets nominative since there is no other element in the nominative. However, (8b) is entirely out.

(9) a. Den Wagen dünkt mich, dass er repariert.
      the.ACC car thinks me.ACC that he.NOM repairs
      'I think that he repairs the car'

   b. *Der Wagen dünkt mich, dass er repariert.
      the.NOM car thinks me.ACC that he.NOM repairs

Similarly there is no agreement between the fronted element and the verb to which it attaches:

(10) a. Mir scheint, dass die Wagen ihm gefallen.
       me.DAT.1PL seems.3SG that the cars.3PL him please.3PL
       'He seems to me to like the cars.'

    b. Die Wagen scheint mir, dass ihm gefallen.
       the cars.3PL seem.3SG me.DAT that him please.3PL
       'The cars, he seems to me to like.'

    c. *Die Wagen scheinen mir, dass ihm gefällt.
       the cars.3PL seem.3PL me.DAT that him pleases.3SG

    d. *Die Wagen scheinen mir, dass ihm gefallen.
       the cars.3PL seem.3PL me.DAT that him please.3PL

This shows that scrambling/remote passive and extraction should not be dealt with by the same mechanism or if they are dealt with by the same mechanism one has to make sure that there are specialized variants of the mechanism that take the differences into account. I think what Groß and Osborne did is simply recode the attachment relations of phrase structure grammars. *die Idee* 'the idea' has some relation to *wird jeder verstehen* 'will everybody understand' in Figure 20.5, as it does in GB, LFG, GPSG, HPSG, and other similar frameworks. In HPSG, *die Idee* 'the idea' is the filler in a filler-head configuration. The remote passive and local reorderings of arguments of auxiliaries, modal verbs, and other verbs that behave similarly are explained by verbal complex formation where all non-verbal arguments depend on the highest verb (Hinrichs & Nakazawa 1994).

20 Extraction, scrambling, and passive: one or several descriptive devices?

Concluding this chapter, it can be said that local reorderings and long-distance dependencies are two different things that should be described with different tools (or there should be further constraints that differ for the respective phenomena when the same tool is used). Similarly, movement-based analyses of the passive are problematic since passive does not necessarily imply reordering.

21 Phrasal vs. lexical analyses

coauthored with Stephen Wechsler

This section deals with a rather crucial aspect when it comes to the comparison of the theories described in this book: valence and the question whether sentence structure, or rather syntactic structure in general, is determined by lexical information or whether syntactic structures have an independent existence (and meaning) and lexical items are just inserted into them. Roughly speaking, frameworks like GB/Minimalism, LFG, CG, HPSG, and DG are lexical, while GPSG and Construction Grammar (Goldberg 1995; 2003a; Tomasello 2003; 2006b; Croft 2001) are phrasal approaches. This categorization reflects tendencies, but there are non-lexical approaches in Minimalism (Borer's exoskeletal approach, 2003) and LFG (Alsina 1996; Asudeh et al. 2008; 2013) and there are lexical approaches in Construction Grammar (Sign-Based Construction Grammar, see Section 10.6.2). The phrasal approach is wide-spread also in frameworks like Cognitive Grammar (Dąbrowska 2001; Langacker 2009: 169) and Simpler Syntax (Culicover & Jackendoff 2005; Jackendoff 2008) that could not be discussed in this book.

The question is whether the meaning of an utterance like (1a) is contributed by the verb *give* and the structure needed for the NPs occurring together with the verb does not contribute any meaning or whether there is a phrasal pattern [X Verb Y Z] that contributes some "ditransitive meaning" whatever this may be.[1]

(1)   a. Peter gives Mary the book.
       b. Peter fishes the pond empty.

Similarly, there is the question of how the constituents in (1b) are licensed. This sentence is interesting since it has a resultative meaning that is not part of the meaning of the verb *fish*: Peter's fishing causes the pond to become empty. Nor is this additional meaning part of the meaning of any other item in the sentence. On the lexical account, there is a lexical rule that licenses a lexical item that selects for *Peter*, *the pond*, and *empty*. This lexical item also contributes the resultative meaning. On the phrasal approach, it is

---

[1]Note that the prototypical meaning is a transfer of possession in which Y receives Z from X, but the reverse holds in (i.b):

(i)   a. Er   gibt ihr   den   Ball.
           he.NOM gives her.DAT the.ACC ball
     b. Er   stiehlt ihr   den   Ball.
           he.NOM steals   her.DAT the.ACC ball
        'He steals the ball from her.'

assumed that there is a pattern [Subj V Obj Obl]. This pattern contributes the resultative meaning, while the verb that is inserted into this pattern just contributes its prototypical meaning, e.g., the meaning that *fish* would have in an intransitive construction. I call such phrasal approaches *plugging approaches*, since lexical items are plugged into ready-made structures that do most of the work.

In what follows I will examine these proposals in more detail and argue that the lexical approaches to valence are the correct ones. The discussion will be based on earlier work of mine (Müller 2006; 2007b; 2010b) and work that I did together with Steve Wechsler (Müller & Wechsler 2014a,b). Some of the sections in Müller & Wechsler (2014a) started out as translations of Müller (2013a), but the material was reorganized and refocused due to intensive discussion with Steve Wechsler. So rather than using a translation of Section 11.11 of Müller (2013a), I use parts of Müller & Wechsler (2014a) here and add some subsections that had to be left out of the article due to space restrictions (Subsections 21.3.6 and 21.7.3). Because there have been misunderstandings in the past (e.g., Boas (2014), see Müller & Wechsler (2014b)), a disclaimer is necessary here: this section is not an argument against Construction Grammar. As was mentioned above Sign-Based Construction Grammar is a lexical variant of Construction Grammar and hence compatible with what I believe to be correct. This section is also not against phrasal constructions in general, since there are phenomena that seem to be best captured with phrasal constructions. These are discussed in detail in Subsection 21.10. What I will argue against in the following subsections is a special kind of phrasal construction, namely phrasal argument structure constructions (phrasal ASCs). I believe that all phenomena that have to do with valence and valence alternations should be treated lexically.

21.1 Some putative advantages of phrasal models

In this section we examine certain claims to purported advantages of phrasal versions of Construction Grammar over lexical rules. Then in the following section, we will turn to positive arguments for lexical rules.

21.1.1 Usage-based theories

For many practitioners of Construction Grammar, their approach to syntax is deeply rooted in the ontological strictures of *usage-based* theories of language (Langacker 1987; Goldberg 1995; Croft 2001; Tomasello 2003). Usage-based theorists oppose the notion of "linguistic rules conceived of as algebraic procedures for combining symbols that do not themselves contribute to meaning" (Tomasello 2003: 99). All linguistic entities are symbolic of things in the realm of denotations; "all have communicative significance because they all derive directly from language use" (*ibid*). Although the formatives of language may be rather abstract, they can never be divorced from their functional origin as a tool of communication. The usage-based view of constructions is summed up well in the following quote:

> The most important point is that constructions are nothing more or less than patterns of usage, which may therefore become relatively abstract if these patterns

21.1 Some putative advantages of phrasal models

> include many different kinds of specific linguistic symbols. But never are they empty rules devoid of semantic content or communicative function. (Tomasello 2003: 100)

Thus constructions are said to differ from grammatical rules in two ways: they must carry meaning; and they reflect the actual "patterns of usage" fairly directly.

Consider first the constraint that every element of the grammar must carry meaning, which we call the *semiotic dictum*. Do lexical or phrasal theories hew the most closely to this dictum? Categorial Grammar, the paradigm of a lexical theory (see Chapter 8), is a strong contender: it consists of meaningful words, with only a few very general combinatorial rules such as X/Y * Y = X. Given the rule-to-rule assumption, those combinatorial rules specify the meaning of the whole as a function of the parts. Whether such a rule counts as meaningful in itself in Tomasello's sense is not clear.

What does seem clear is that the combinatorial rules of Construction Grammar, such as Goldberg's Correspondence Principle for combining a verb with a construction (1995: 50), have the same status as those combinatorial rules:

(2) The Correspondence Principle: each participant that is lexically profiled and expressed must be fused with a profiled argument role of the construction. If a verb has three profiled participant roles, then one of them may be fused with a non-profiled argument role of a construction. (Goldberg 1995: 50)

Both verbs and constructions are specified for participant roles, some of which are *profiled*. Argument profiling for verbs is "lexically determined and highly conventionalized" (Goldberg 1995: 46). Profiled argument roles of a construction are mapped to direct grammatical functions, i. e., SUBJ, OBJ, or OBJ2. By the Correspondence Principle the lexically profiled argument roles must be direct, unless there are three of them, in which case one may be indirect.[2] With respect to the semiotic dictum, the Correspondence Principle has the same status as the Categorial Grammar combinatorial rules: a meaningless algebraic rule that specifies the way to combine meaningful items.

Turning now to the lexicalist syntax we favor, some elements abide by the semiotic dictum while others do not. Phrase structure rules for intransitive and transitive VPs (or the respective HPSG ID schema) do not. Lexical valence structures clearly carry meaning since they are associated with particular verbs. In an English ditransitive, the first object expresses the role of "intended recipient" of the referent of the second object. Hence *He carved her a toy* entails that he carved a toy with the intention that she receive it. So the lexical rule that adds a benefactive recipient argument to a verb adds meaning. Alternatively, a phrasal ditransitive construction might contribute that "recipient" meaning.[3] Which structures have meaning is an empirical question for us.

In Construction Grammar, however, meaning is assumed for all constructions *a priori*. But while the ditransitive construction plausibly contributes meaning, no truth-

---

[2]We assume that the second sentence of (2) provides for exceptions to the first sentence.

[3]In Section 21.2.1 we argue that the recipient should be added in the lexical argument structure, not through a phrasal construction. See Wechsler (1991: 111–113; 1995: 88–89) for an analysis of English ditransitives with elements of both constructional and lexical approaches. It is based on Kiparsky's notion of a *thematically restricted positional linker* (1987; 1988).

conditional meaning has yet been discovered for either the intransitive or bivalent transitive constructions. Clearly the constructionist's evidence for the meaningfulness of *certain* constructions such as the ditransitive does not constitute evidence that *all* phrasal constructions have meaning. So the lexical and phrasal approaches seem to come out the same, as far as the semiotic dictum is concerned.

Now consider the second usage-based dictum, that the elements of the grammar directly reflect patterns of usage, which we call *the transparency dictum*. The Construction Grammar literature often presents their constructions informally in ways that suggest that they represent surface constituent order patterns: the transitive construction is "[X VERB Y]" (Tomasello) or "[Subj V Obj]" (Goldberg 1995; 2006)[4]; the passive construction is "X *was* VERB*ed by* Y" (Tomasello 2003: 100) or "Subj aux Vpp (PPby)" (Goldberg 2006: 5). But a theory in which constructions consist of surface patterns was considered in detail and rejected by Müller (2006: Section 2), and does not accurately reflect Goldberg's actual theory.[5] The more detailed discussions present *argument structure constructions*, which are more abstract and rather like the lexicalists' grammatical elements (or perhaps an LFG f-structure): the transitive construction resembles a transitive valence structure (minus the verb itself); the passive construction resembles the passive lexical rule.

With respect to fulfilling the desiderata of usage-based theorists, we do not find any significant difference between the non-lexical and lexical approaches.

21.1.2 Coercion

Researchers working with plugging proposals usually take coercion as an indication of the usefulness of phrasal constructions. For instance, Anatol Stefanowitsch (Lecture in the lecture series *Algorithmen und Muster -- Strukturen in der Sprache*, 2009) discussed the example in (3):

(3) Das Tor zur Welt Hrnglb öffnete sich ohne Vorwarnung und verschlang [sie] ... die Welt Hrnglb wird von Magiern erschaffen, die Träume zu Realität formen können, aber nicht in der Lage sind zu träumen. Haltet aus, Freunde. Und ihr da draußen, bitte träumt ihnen ein Tor.[6]

The crucial part is *bitte träumt ihnen ein Tor* 'Dream a gate for them'. In this fantasy context the word *träumen*, which is intransitive, is forced into the ditransitive construction and therefore gets a certain meaning. This forcing of a verb corresponds to overwriting or rather extending properties of the verb by the phrasal construction.

---

[4]Goldberg et al. (2004: 300) report about a language acquisition experiment that involves an SOV pattern. The SOV order is mentioned explicitly and seen as part of the construction.

[5]This applies to argument structure constructions only. In some of her papers Goldberg assumes that very specific phrase structural configurations are part of the constructions. For instance in her paper on complex predicates in Persian (Goldberg 2003b) she assigns V^0 and $\overline{V}$ categories. See Müller (2010b: Section 4.9) for a critique of that analysis.

[6]http://www.elbenwaldforum.de/showflat.php?Cat=&Board=Tolkiens_Werke&Number=1457418&page=3&view=collapsed&sb=5&o=&fpart=16, 2010-02-27.

'The gate to the world Hrnglb opened without warning and swallowed them. The world Hrnglb is created by magicians that can form reality from dreams but cannot dream themselves. Hold out, friends! And you out there, please, dream a gate for them.'

21.1 Some putative advantages of phrasal models

In cases in which the plugging proposals assume that information is overwritten or extended, lexical approaches assume mediating lexical rules. Briscoe & Copestake (1999: Section 4) have worked out a lexical approach in detail.[7] They discuss the ditransitive sentences in (4), which either correspond to the prototypical ditransitive construction (4a) or deviate from it in various ways.

(4) a. Mary gave Joe a present.
 b. Joe painted Sally a picture.
 c. Mary promised Joe a new car.
 d. He tipped Bill two pounds.
 e. The medicine brought him relief.
 f. The music lent the party a festive air.
 g. Jo gave Bob a punch.
 h. He blew his wife a kiss.
 i. She smiled herself an upgrade.[8]

For the non-canonical examples they assume lexical rules that relate transitive (*paint*) and intransitive (*smile*) verbs to ditransitive ones and contribute the respective semantic information or the respective metaphorical extension. The example in (4i) is rather similar to the *träumen* example discussed above and is also analyzed with a lexical rule (page 509). Briscoe and Copestake note that this lexical rule is much more restricted in its productivity than the other lexical rules they suggest. They take this as motivation for developing a representational format in which lexical items (including those that are derived by lexical rules) are associated with probabilities, so that differences in productivity of various patterns can be captured.

Looking narrowly at such cases, it is hard to see any rational grounds for choosing between the phrasal analysis and the lexical rule. But if we broaden our view, the lexical rule approach can be seen to have a much wider application. Coercion is a very general pragmatic process, occurring in many contexts where no construction seems to be responsible (Nunberg 1995). Nunberg cites many cases such as the restaurant waiter asking *Who is the ham sandwich?* (Nunberg 1995: 115). Copestake & Briscoe (1992: 116) discuss the conversion of terms for animals to mass nouns (see also Copestake & Briscoe (1995: 36–43)). Example (5) is about a substance, not about a cute bunny.

(5) After several lorries had run over the body, there was rabbit splattered all over the road.

The authors suggest a lexical rule that maps a count noun onto a mass noun. This analysis is also assumed by Fillmore (1999: 114–115). Such coercion can occur without any syntactic context: one can answer the question *What's that stuff on the road?* or *What are you eating?* with the one-word utterance *Rabbit*. Some coercion happens to affect

---

[7]Kay (2005), working in the framework of CxG, also suggests unary constructions.
[8]Douglas Adams. 1979. *The Hitchhiker' s Guide to the Galaxy*, Harmony Books. Quoted from Goldberg (2003a: 220).

601

21 Phrasal vs. lexical analyses

the complement structure of a verb, but this is simply a special case of a more general phenomenon that has been analyzed by rules of systematic polysemy.

21.1.3 Aspect as a clause level phenomenon

Alsina (1996), working in the framework of LFG, argues for a phrasal analysis of resultative constructions based on the aspectual properties of sentences, since aspect is normally viewed as a property that is determined by the sentence syntax. Intransitive verbs such as *bark* refer to activities, a resultative construction with the same verb, however, stands for an accomplishment (an extended change of state). Alsina supports this with the following data:

(6) a. (*) The dog barked in five minutes.
     b. The dog barked the neighbors awake in five minutes.

The latter sentence means that the *barking* event was completed after five minutes. A reading referring to the time span of the event is not available for (6a). If (6a) is grammatical at all, then a claim is being made about the time frame in which the event begun.

If we now consider examples such as (7c), however, we see that Alsina's argumentation is not cogent since the resultative meaning is already present at the word-level in nominalizations. As the examples in (7) show, this contrast can be observed in nominal constructions and is therefore independent of the sentence syntax:

(7) a. weil   sie   die Nordsee   in fünf Jahren leer   fischten
         because they the North.Sea in five years   empty fished
         'because they fished the North Sea (until it was) empty in five years'
     b. # weil   sie   in fünf Jahren fischten
         because they in five years   fished
     c. das Leerfischen   der   Nordsee   in fünf Jahren
         the empty.fishing of.the North.Sea in five years
     d. # das Fischen in fünf Jahren
         the fishing in five years

In a lexical approach there is a verb stem selecting for two NPs and a resultative predicate. This stem has the appropriate meaning and can be inflected or undergo derivation und successive inflection. In both cases we get words that contain the resultative semantics and hence are compatible with respective adverbials.

21.1.4 Simplicity and polysemy

Much of the intuitive appeal of the plugging approach stems from its apparent simplicity relative to the use of lexical rules. But the claim to greater simplicity for Construction Grammar is based on misunderstandings of both lexical rules and Construction Grammar (specifically of Goldberg's (1995; 2006) version). It draws the distinction in the

21.1 Some putative advantages of phrasal models

wrong place and misses the real differences between these approaches. This argument from simplicity is often repeated and so it is important to understand why it is incorrect.

Tomasello (2003) presents the argument as follows. Discussing first the lexical rules approach, Tomasello (2003: 160) writes that

> One implication of this view is that a verb must have listed in the lexicon a different meaning for virtually every different construction in which it participates [...]. For example, while the prototypical meaning of *cough* involves only one participant, the cougher, we may say such things as *He coughed her his cold*, in which there are three core participants. In the lexical rules approach, in order to produce this utterance the child's lexicon must have as an entry a ditransitive meaning for the verb *cough*. (Tomasello 2003: 160)

Tomasello (2003: 160) then contrasts a Construction Grammar approach, citing Fillmore et al. (1988), Goldberg (1995), and Croft (2001). He concludes as follows:

> The main point is that if we grant that constructions may have meaning of their own, in relative independence of the lexical items involved, then we do not need to populate the lexicon with all kinds of implausible meanings for each of the verbs we use in everyday life. The construction grammar approach in which constructions have meanings is therefore both much simpler and much more plausible than the lexical rules approach. (Tomasello 2003: 161)

This reflects a misunderstanding of lexical rules, as they are normally understood. There is no implausible sense populating the lexicon. The lexical rule approach to *He coughed her his cold* states that when the word *coughed* appears with two objects, the whole complex has a certain meaning (see Müller 2006: 876). Furthermore we explicitly distinguish between listed elements (lexical entries) and derived ones. The general term subsuming both is *lexical item*.

The simplicity argument also relies on a misunderstanding of a theory Tomasello advocates, namely the theory due to Goldberg (1995; 2006). For his argument to go through, Tomasello must tacitly assume that verbs can combine freely with constructions, that is, that the grammar does not place extrinsic constraints on such combinations. If it is necessary to also stipulate which verbs can appear in which constructions, then the claim to greater simplicity collapses: each variant lexical item with its "implausible meaning" under the lexical rule approach corresponds to a verb-plus-construction combination under the phrasal approach.

Passages such as the following may suggest that verbs and constructions are assumed to combine freely:[9]

> Constructions are combined freely to form actual expressions as long as they can be construed as not being in conflict (invoking the notion of construal is intended

---

[9]The context of these quotes makes clear that the verb and the argument structure construction are considered constructions. See Goldberg (2006: 21, ex. (2)).

603

to allow for processes of accommodation or coercion). [...] Allowing constructions to combine freely as long as there are no conflicts, allows for the infinitely creative potential of language. [...] That is, a speaker is free to creatively combine constructions as long as constructions exist in the language that can be combined suitably to categorize the target message, given that there is no conflict among the constructions. (Goldberg 2006: 22)

But in fact Goldberg does not assume free combination, but rather that a verb is "conventionally associated with a construction" (Goldberg 1995: 50): verbs specify their participant roles and which of those are obligatory direct arguments (*profiled*, in Goldberg's terminology). In fact, Goldberg herself (2006: 211) argues against Borer's putative assumption of free combination (2003) on the grounds that Borer is unable to account for the difference between *dine* (intransitive), *eat* (optionally transitive), and *devour* (obligatorily transitive).[10] Despite Tomasello's comment above, Construction Grammar is no simpler than the lexical rules.

The resultative construction is often used to illustrate the simplicity argument. For example, Goldberg (1995: Chapter 7) assumes that the same lexical item for the verb *sneeze* is used in (8a) and (8b). It is simply inserted into different constructions:

(8) a. He sneezed.

 b. He sneezed the napkin off the table.

The meaning of (8a) corresponds more or less to the verb meaning, since the verb is used in the Intransitive Construction. But the Caused-Motion Construction in (8b) contributes additional semantic information concerning the causation and movement: his sneezing caused the napkin to move off the table. *sneeze* is plugged into the Caused-Motion Construction, which licenses the subject of *sneeze* and additionally provides two slots: one for the theme (*napkin*) and one for the goal (*off the table*). The lexical approach is essentially parallel, except that the lexical rule can feed further lexical processes like passivization (*The napkin was sneezed off the table*), and conversion to nouns or adjectives (see Sections 21.2.2 and 21.6).

In a nuanced comparison of the two approaches, Goldberg (1995: 139–140) considers again the added recipient argument in *Mary kicked Joe the ball*, where *kick* is lexically a 2-place verb. She notes that on the constructional view, "the composite fused structure involving both verb and construction is stored in memory". The verb itself retains its original meaning as a 2-place verb, so that "we avoid implausible verb senses such as 'to cause to receive by kicking'." The idea seems to be that the lexical approach, in contrast, must countenance such implausible verb senses since a lexical rule adds a third argument.

But the lexical and constructional approaches are actually indistinguishable on this point. The lexical rule does not produce a verb with the "implausible sense" in (9a). Instead it produces the sense in (9b):

---

[10]Goldberg's critique cites a 2001 presentation by Borer with the same title as Borer (2003). See Section 21.3.4 for more discussion of this issue. As far as we know, the *dine / eat / devour* minimal triplet originally came from Dowty (1989: 89–90).

(9) a. cause-to-receive-by-kicking(x, y, z)
    b. cause(kick(x, y),receive(z,y))

The same sort of "composite fused structure" is assumed under either view. With respect to the semantic structure, the number and plausibility of senses, and the polyadicity of the semantic relations, the two theories are identical. They mainly differ in the way this representation fits into the larger theory of syntax. They also differ in another respect: on the lexical view, the derived three-argument valence structure is associated with the phonological string *kicked*. Next, we present evidence for this claim.

21.2 Evidence for lexical approaches

21.2.1 Valence and coordination

On the lexical account, the verb *paint* in (4b), for example, is lexically a 2-argument verb, while the unary branching node immediately dominating it is effectively a 3-argument verb. On the constructional view there is no such predicate seeking three arguments that dominates only the verb. Coordination provides evidence for the lexical account.

A generalization about coordination is that two constituents which have compatible syntactic properties can be coordinated and that the result of the coordination is an object that has the syntactic properties of each of the conjuncts. This is reflected by the Categorial Grammar analysis which assumes the category (X\X)/X for the conjunction: the conjunction takes an X to the right, an X to the left and the result is an X.

For example, in (10a) we have a case of the coordination of two lexical verbs. The coordination *know and like* behaves like the coordinated simplex verbs: it takes a subject and an object. Similarly, two sentences with a missing object are coordinated in (10b) and the result is a sentence with a missing object.

(10) a. I know and like this record.
     b. Bagels, I like and Ellison hates.

The German examples in (11) show that the case requirement of the involved verbs has to be respected. In (11b,c) the coordinated verbs require accusative and dative respectively and since the case requirements are incompatible with unambiguously case marked nouns both of these examples are out.

(11) a. Ich kenne und unterstütze diesen Mann.
         I   know and support   this.ACC man
     b. * Ich kenne und helfe diesen Mann.
         I   know and help this.ACC man
     c. * Ich kenne und helfe diesem Mann.
         I   know and help this.DAT man

Interestingly, it is possible to coordinate basic ditransitive verbs with verbs that have additional arguments licensed by the lexical rule. (12) provides examples in English and German ((12b) is quoted from Müller (2013a: 420)):

(12) a. She then offered and made me a wonderful espresso – nice.[11]

b. ich hab ihr jetzt diese Ladung Muffins mit den Herzchen drauf
   I have her now this load Muffins with the little.heart there.on
   gebacken und gegeben.[12]
   baked and given

   'I have now baked and given her this load of muffins with the little heart on top.'

These sentences show that both verbs are 3-argument verbs at the V^0 level, since they involve V^0 coordination:

(13) [$_{V^0}$ offered and made] [$_{NP}$ me] [$_{NP}$ a wonderful espresso]

This is expected under the lexical rule analysis but not the non-lexical constructional one.[13]

Summarizing the coordination argument: coordinated verbs generally must have compatible syntactic properties like valence properties. This means that in (12b), for example, *gebacken* 'baked' and *gegeben* 'given' have the same valence properties. On the lexical approach the creation verb *gebacken*, together with a lexical rule, licenses a ditransitive verb. It can therefore be coordinated with *gegeben*. On the phrasal approach however, the verb *gebacken* has two argument roles and is not compatible with the verb *gegeben*, which has three argument roles. In the phrasal model, *gebacken* can only realize three arguments when it enters the ditransitive phrasal construction or argument structure construction. But in sentences like (12) it is not *gebacken* alone that enters the phrasal syntax, but rather the combination of *gebacken* and *gegeben*. On this view, the verbs are incompatible as far as the semantic roles are concerned.

To fix this under the phrasal approach, one could posit a mechanism such that the semantic roles that are required for the coordinate phrase *baked and given* are shared by each of its conjunct verbs and that they are therefore compatible. But this would amount to saying that there are several verb senses for *baked*, something that the anti-lexicalists claim to avoid, as discussed in the next section.

---

[11]http://www.thespinroom.com.au/?p=102, 2012-07-07.

[12]http://www.musiker-board.de/diverses-ot/35977-die-liebe-637-print.html, 2012-06-08.

[13]One might wonder whether these sentences could be instances of Right Node Raising (RNR) out of coordinated VPs (Bresnan 1974; Abbott 1976):

(i) She [offered ___] and [made me ___] a wonderful espresso.

But this cannot be correct. Under such an analysis the first verb has been used without a benefactive or recipient object. But *me* is interpreted as the recipient of both the offering and making. Secondly, the second object can be an unstressed pronoun (*She offered and made me it*), which is not possible in RNR. Note that *offered and made* cannot be a pseudo-coordination meaning 'offered to make'. This is possible only with stem forms of certain verbs such as *try*.

21.2 Evidence for lexical approaches

A reviewer of Theoretical Linguistics correctly observes that a version of the (phrasal) ASC approach could work in the exactly same way as our lexical analysis. Our ditransitive lexical rule would simply be rechristened as a "ditransitive ASC". This construction would combine with *baked*, thus adding the third argument, prior to its coordination with *gave*. As long as the ASC approach is a non-distinct notational variant of the lexical rule approach then of course it works in exactly the same way. But the literature on the ASC approach represents it as a radical alternative to lexical rules, in which constructions are combined through inheritance hierarchies, instead of allowing lexical rules to alter the argument structure of a verb prior to its syntactic combination with the other words and phrases.

The reviewer also remarked that examples like (14) show that the benefactive argument has to be introduced on the phrasal level.

(14) I designed and built him a house.

Both *designed* and *built* are bivalent verbs and *him* is the benefactive that extends both *designed* and *built*. However, we assume that sentences like (14) can be analyzed as coordination of two verbal items that are licensed by the lexical rule that introduces the benefactive argument. That is, the benefactive is introduced before the coordination.

The coordination facts illustrate a more general point. The output of a lexical rule such as the one that would apply in the analysis of *gebacken* in (12b) is just a word (an X^0), so it has the same syntactic distribution as an underived word with the same category and valence feature. This important generalization follows from the lexical account while on the phrasal view, it is mysterious at best. The point can be shown with any of the lexical rules that the anti-lexicalists are so keen to eliminate in favor of phrasal constructions. For example, active and passive verbs can be coordinated, as long as they have the same valence properties, as in this Swedish example:

(15) Golfklubben begärde och beviljade-s marklov för banbygget efter
golf.club.DEF requested and granted-PASS ground.permit for track.build.DEF after
en hel del förhandlingar och kompromisser med Länsstyrelsen och
a whole part negotiations and compromises with county.board.DEF and
Naturvårdsverket.[14]
nature.protection.agency.DEF

'The golf club requested and was granted a ground permit for fairlane construction after a lot of negotiations and compromises with the County Board and the Environmental Protection Agency.'

(English works the same way, as shown by the grammatical translation line.) The passive of the ditransitive verb *bevilja* 'grant' retains one object, so it is effectively transitive and can be coordinated with the active transitive *begära* 'request'.

Moreover, the English passive verb form, being a participle, can feed a second lexical rule deriving adjectives from verbs. All categories of English participles can be converted to adjectives (Bresnan, 1982b, 2001: Chapter 3):

---
[14] http://www.lyckselegolf.se/klubben/kort-historik/, 25.04.2018.

(16) a. active present participles (cf. The leaf is falling): *the falling leaf*
    b. active past participles (cf. The leaf has fallen): *the fallen leaf*
    c. passive participles (cf. The toy is being broken (by the child).): *the broken toy*

That the derived forms are adjectives, not verbs, is shown by a host of properties, including negative *un-* prefixation: *unbroken* means 'not broken', just as *unkind* means 'not kind', while the *un-* appearing on verbs indicates, not negation, but action reversal, as in *untie* (Bresnan, 1982b: 21, 2001: Chapter 3). Predicate adjectives preserve the subject of predication of the verb and for prenominal adjectives the rule is simply that the role that would be assigned to the subject goes to the modified noun instead (*The toy remained (un-)broken.*; *the broken toy*). Being an A^0, such a form can be coordinated with another A^0, as in the following:

(17) a. The suspect should be considered [armed and dangerous].
    b. any [old, rotting, or broken] toys

In (17b), three adjectives are coordinated, one underived (*old*), one derived from a present participle (*rotting*), and one from a passive participle (*broken*). Such coordination is completely mundane on a lexical theory. Each A^0 conjunct has a valence feature (in HPSG it would be the SPR feature for predicates or the MOD feature for the prenominal modifiers), which is shared with the mother node of the coordinate structure. But the point of the phrasal (or ASC) theory is to deny that words have such valence features.

The claim that lexical derivation of valence structure is distinct from phrasal combination is further supported with evidence from deverbal nominalization (Wechsler 2008a). To derive nouns from verbs, *-ing* suffixation productively applies to all inflectable verbs (*the shooting of the prisoner*), while morphological productivity is severely limited for various other suffixes such as *-(a)tion* (**the shootation of the prisoner*). So forms such as *destruction* and *distribution* must be retrieved from memory while *-ing* nouns such as *looting* or *growing* could be (and in the case of rare verbs or neologisms, must be) derived from the verb or the root through the application of a rule (Zucchi 1993). This difference explains why *-ing* nominals always retain the argument structure of the cognate verb, while other forms show some variation. A famous example is the lack of the agent argument for the noun *growth* versus its retention by the noun *growing*: **John's growth of tomatoes* versus *John's growing of tomatoes* (Chomsky 1970).[15]

But what sort of rule derives the *-ing* nouns, a lexical rule or a phrasal one? In Marantz's (1997) phrasal analysis, a phrasal construction (notated as *v*P) is responsible for assigning the agent role of *-ing* nouns such as *growing*. For him, none of the words directly selects an agent via its argument structure. The *-ing* forms are permitted to appear in the *v*P construction, which licenses the possessive agent. Non-*ing* nouns such as *destruction* and *growth* do not appear in *v*P. Whether they allow expression of the agent depends on semantic and pragmatic properties of the word: *destruction* involves external causation so it does allow an agent, while *growth* involves internal causation so it does not allow an agent.

---

[15] See Section 21.3.3 for further discussion.

21.2 Evidence for lexical approaches

However, a problem for Marantz is that these two types of nouns can coordinate and share dependents (example (18a) is from Wechsler (2008a: Section 7)):

(18) a. With nothing left after the soldier's [destruction and looting] of their home, they reboarded their coach and set out for the port of Calais.[16]

b. The [cultivation, growing or distribution] of medical marijuana within the County shall at all times occur within a secure, locked, and fully enclosed structure, including a ceiling, roof or top, and shall meet the following requirements.[17]

On the phrasal analysis, the nouns *looting* and *growing* occur in one type of syntactic environment (namely *v*P), while forms *destruction*, *cultivation*, and *distribution* occur in a different syntactic environment. This places contradictory demands on the structure of coordinations like those in (18). As far as we know, neither this problem nor the others raised by Wechsler (2008a) have even been addressed by advocates of the phrasal theory of argument structure.

Consider one last example. In an influential phrasal analysis, Hale and Keyser (1993) derived denominal verbs like *to saddle* through noun incorporation out of a structure akin to [PUT a saddle ON x]. Again, verbs with this putative derivation routinely coordinate and share dependents with verbs of other types:

(19) Realizing the dire results of such a capture and that he was the only one to prevent it, he quickly [saddled and mounted] his trusted horse and with a grim determination began a journey that would become legendary.[18]

As in all of these X^0 coordination cases, under the phrasal analysis the two verbs place contradictory demands on a single phrase structure.

A lexical valence structure is an abstraction or generalization over various occurrences of the verb in syntactic contexts. To be sure, one key use of that valence structure is simply to indicate what sort of phrases the verb must (or can) combine with, and the result of semantic composition; if that were the whole story then the phrasal theory would be viable. But it is not. As it turns out, this lexical valence structure, once abstracted, can alternatively be used in other ways: among other possibilities, the verb (crucially including its valence structure) can be coordinated with other verbs that have similar valence structures; or it can serve as the input to lexical rules specifying a new word bearing a systematic relation to the input word. The coordination and lexical derivation facts follow from the lexical view, while the phrasal theory at best leaves these facts as mysterious and at worst leads to irreconcilable contradictions for the phrase structure.

21.2.2 Valence and derivational morphology

Goldberg & Jackendoff (2004), Alsina (1996), and Asudeh, Dalrymple & Toivonen (2008; 2013) suggest analyzing resultative constructions and/or caused-motion constructions

---
[16] http://www.amazon.com/review/R3IG4M3Q6YYNFT, 2018-02-20
[17] http://www.scribd.com/doc/64013640/Tulare-County-medical-cannabis-cultivation-ordinance, 05.03.2016
[18] http://www.jouetthouse.org/index.php?option=com_content&view=article&id=56&Itemid=63, 21.07.2012

609

as phrasal constructions.[19] As was argued in Müller (2006) this is incompatible with the assumption of lexical integrity. Lexical integrity means that word formation happens before syntax and that the morphological structure is inaccessible to syntactic processes (Bresnan & Mchombo 1995).[20] Let us consider a concrete example, such as (20):

(20) a. Er tanzt die Schuhe blutig / in Stücke.
       he dances the shoes bloody into pieces
    b. die in Stücke / blutig getanzten Schuhe
       the into pieces bloody danced shoes
    c. * die getanzten Schuhe
         the danced shoes

The shoes are not a semantic argument of *tanzt*. Nevertheless the referent of the NP that is realized as accusative NP in (20a) is the element the adjectival participle in (20b) predicates over. Adjectival participles like the one in (20b) are derived from a passive participle of a verb that governs an accusative object. If the accusative object is licensed phrasally by configurations like the one in (20a), then it is not possible to explain why the participle *getanzten* can be formed despite the absence of an accusative object in the valence specification of the verb. See Müller (2006: Section 5) for further examples of the interaction of resultatives and morphology. The conclusion drawn by Dowty (1978: 412) and Bresnan (1982b: 21) in the late 70s and early 80s is that phenomena which feed morphology should be treated lexically. The natural analysis in frameworks like HPSG, CG, CxG, and LFG is therefore one that assumes a lexical rule for the licensing of resultative constructions. See Verspoor (1997), Wechsler (1997), Wechsler & Noh (2001), Wunderlich (1992: 45; 1997: 120–126), Kaufmann & Wunderlich (1998), Müller (2002a: Chapter 5), Kay (2005), and Simpson (1983) for lexical proposals in some of these frameworks. The lexical approach assumes that the lexical item for the mono-valent *tanz-* is related to another lexical item for *tanz-* that selects an object and a result predicate in addition to the subject selected by the mono-valent variant. Inflection and adjective derivation apply to this derived stem and the respective results can be used in (20a) or (20b).

This argument for a lexical treatment of resultative constructions is similar to the one that was discussed in connection with the GPSG representation of valence in Section 5.5: morphological processes have to be able to see the valence of the element they apply to.

---

[19] Asudeh & Toivonen (2014: Section 2.3) argue that their account is not constructional. If a construction is a form-meaning pair, their account is constructional, since a certain c-structure is paired with a semantic contribution. Asudeh & Toivonen (2014: Section 2.2) compare their approach with approaches in Constructional HPSG (Sag 1997) and Sign-Based Construction Grammar (see Section 10.6.2), which they term constructional. The only difference between these approaches and the approach by Asudeh, Dalrymple & Toivonen is that the constructions in the HPSG-based theories are modeled using types and hence have a name.

[20] Asudeh et al. (2013: 14) claim that the Swedish Directed Motion Construction does not interact with derivational morphology. However, the parallel German construction does interact with derivational morphology. The absence of this interaction in Swedish can be explained by other factors of Swedish grammar and given this I believe it to be more appropriate to assume an analysis that captures both the German and the Swedish data in the same way.

21.2 Evidence for lexical approaches

This is not the case if arguments are introduced by phrasal configurations after the level of morphology.

Asudeh, Dalrymple & Toivonen's papers are about the concept of lexical integrity and about constructions. Asudeh & Toivonen (2014) replied to our target article and pointed out (again) that their template approach makes it possible to specify the functional structure of words and phrases alike. In the original paper they discussed the Swedish word *vägen*, which is the definite form of *väg* 'way'. They showed that the f-structure is parallel to the f-structure for the English phrase *the way*. In our reply (2014b), we gave in too early, I believe. Since the point is not about being able to provide the f-structure of words, the point is about morphology, that is – in LFG terms – about deriving the f-structure by a morphological analysis. More generally speaking, one wants to derive all properties of the involved words, that is, their valence, their meaning, and the linking of this meaning to their dependents. What we used in our argument based on the sentences in (20) was parallel to what Bresnan (1982b: 21; 2001: 31) used in her classical argument for a lexical treatment of the passive. So either Bresnan's argument (and ours) is invalid or both arguments are valid and there is a problem for Asudeh, Dalrymple & Toivonen's approach and for phrasal approaches in general. I want to give another example that was already discussed in Müller (2006: 869) but was omitted in Müller & Wechsler (2014a) due to space limitations. I will first point out why this example is problematic for phrasal approaches and then explain why it is not sufficient to be able to assign certain f-structures to words: in (21a), we are dealing with a resultative construction. According to the plugging approach, the resultative meaning is contributed by a phrasal construction into which the verb *fischt* is inserted. There is no lexical item that requires a resultative predicate as its argument. If no such lexical item exists, then it is unclear how the relation between (21a) and (21b) can be established:

(21) a. [dass] jemand   die Nordsee   leer   fischt
        that somebody the North.Sea empty fishes
    'that somebody fishes the North Sea empty'

    b. wegen   der   *Leerfischung*   der   Nordsee[21]
       because of.the empty.fishing   of.the North.Sea
    'because of the fishing that resulted in the North Sea being empty'

As Figure 21.1 on the following page shows, both the arguments selected by the heads and the structures are completely different. In (21b), the element that is the subject of the related construction in (21a) is not realized. As is normally the case in nominalizations, it is possible to realize it in a PP with the preposition *durch* 'by':

(22) wegen   der   Leerfischung   der   Nordsee   durch die Anrainerstaaten
     because of.the empty.fishing   of.the North.Sea by   the neighboring.states
    'because of the fishing by the neighboring states that resulted in the North Sea being empty'

---

[21] taz, 20.06.1996, p. 6.

21 Phrasal vs. lexical analyses

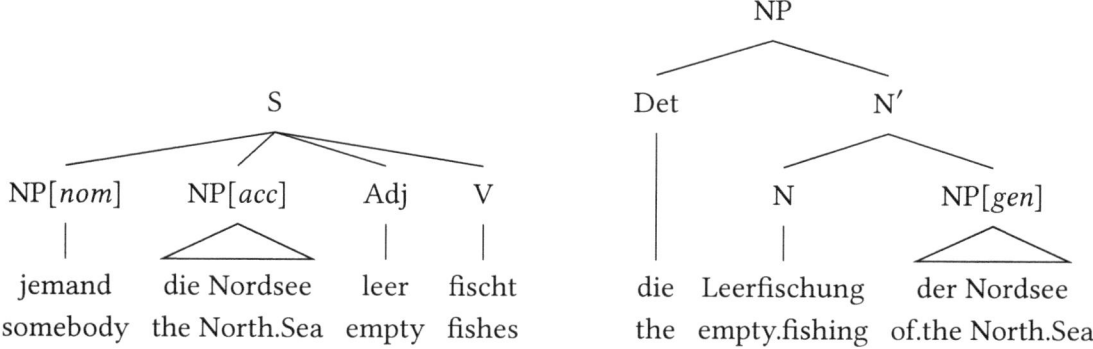

Figure 21.1: Resultative construction and nominalization

If one assumes that the resultative meaning comes from a particular configuration in which a verb is realized, there would be no explanation for (21b) since no verb is involved in the analysis of this example. One could of course assume that a verb stem is inserted into a construction both in (21a) and (21b). The inflectional morpheme *-t* and the derivational morpheme *-ung* as well as an empty nominal inflectional morpheme would then be independent syntactic components of the analysis. However, since Goldberg (2003b: 119) and Asudeh et al. (2013) assume lexical integrity, only entire words can be inserted into syntactic constructions and hence the analysis of the nominalization of resultative constructions sketched here is not an option for them.

One might be tempted to try and account for the similarities between the phrases in (21) using inheritance. One would specify a general resultative construction standing in an inheritance relation to the resultative construction with a verbal head and the nominalization construction. I have discussed this proposal in more detail in Müller (2006: Section 5.3). It does not work as one needs embedding for derivational morphology and this cannot be modeled in inheritance hierarchies (Krieger & Nerbonne (1993), see also Müller (2006) for a detailed discussion).

It would also be possible to assume that both constructions in (23), for which structures such as those in Figure 21.1 would have to be assumed, are connected via metarules.[22,23]

(23)   a.   [Sbj Obj Obl V]
        b.   [Det [[Adj V -ung]] NP[*gen*]]

The construction in (23b) corresponds to Figure 21.2.[24] The genitive NP is an argument

---

[22] Goldberg (p. c. 2007, 2009) suggests connecting certain constructions using GPSG-like metarules. Deppermann (2006: 51), who has a more Croftian view of CxG, rules this out. He argues for active/passive alternations that the passive construction has other information structural properties. Note also that GPSG metarules relate phrase structure rules, that is, local trees. The structure in Figure 21.2, however, is highly complex.

[23] The structure in (23b) violates a strict interpretation of lexical integrity as is commonly assumed in LFG. Booij (2005; 2009), working in Construction Grammar, subscribes to a somewhat weaker version, however.

[24] I do not assume zero affixes for inflection. The respective affix in Figure 21.2 is there to show that there is structure. Alternatively one could assume a unary branching rule/construction as is common in HPSG/Construction Morphology.

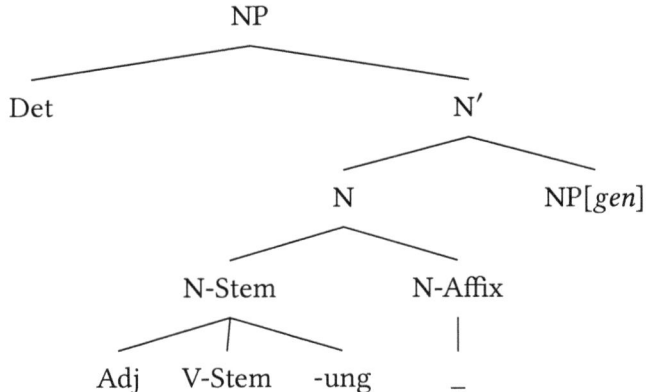

Figure 21.2: Resultative construction and nominalization

of the adjective. It has to be linked semantically to the subject slot of the adjective. Alternatively, one could assume that the construction only has the form [Adj V -*ung*], that is, that it does not include the genitive NP. But then one could also assume that the verbal variant of the resultative construction has the form [OBL V] and that Sbj and Obj are only represented in the valence lists. This would almost be a lexical analysis, however.

Turning to lexical integrity again, I want to point out that all that Asudeh & Toivonen can do is assign some f-structure to the N in Figure 21.2. What is needed, however, is a principled account of how this f-structure comes about and how it is related to the resultative construction on the sentence level.

My argument regarding -*ung*-nominalization from Müller (2006: Section 5.1) was also taken up by Bruening (2018). I noted that *Leerfischung* should not be analyzed as a compound of *leer* and *Fischung* with *Fischung* being the result of combining -*ung* with the intransitive verb lexeme *fisch*- but rather that -*ung* should apply to a version of *fisch*- that selects for a result predicate and its subject and that this version of *Fischung* is then combined with the result predicate it selects for. Bruening argued against my analysis claiming that all arguments of nouns are optional and that my analysis would predict that there is a noun *Fischung* with a resultative meaning but without the resultative predicate. As I pointed out in Müller (2006: 869), a noun *Fischung* does exist but it refers to parts of a boat, not to an event nominalization. Bruening concludes that a syntactic approach is needed and that -*ung* applies to the combination of *leer* and *fisch*-.

Now, while it is generally true that arguments of nouns can be omitted there are situations in which the argument cannot be ommitted without changing the meaning. Sebastian Nordhoff (p. c. 2017) found the following examples:

(24) a. Bartträger
   beard.carrier
   'bearded man'

   b. Spaßmacher
   joke.maker
   'jester'

c. Arbeitgeber
   work.giver
   'employer'

d. Unfallbauer
   crash.builder
   'crasher'

e. Abibauer
   secondary.school.leaving.examination.builder
   'secondary school leaving examination taker'

f. Traumfänger
   dream.catcher
   'dreamcatcher'

g. Zeitschinder
   time.grinder
   'temporizer'

h. Pläneschmieder
   plans.forger
   'contriver'

For example, a *Bartträger* is somebody who has a beard. If one omitted the first part of the compound, one would get a *Träger* 'carrier'; a relation to the original sense cannot be established. Similarly a *Spaßmacher* is literally a 'joke.maker'. Without the first part of the compound this would be *Macher*, which translates as *doer* or *action man*. What the examples above have in common is the following: the verbal parts are frequent and in the most frequent uses of the verb the object is concrete. In the compounds above the first part is unusual in that it is abstract. If the first element of the compound is omitted, we get the default reading of the verb, something that is incompatible with the meaning of the verb in the complete compound.

The contrast between *Leerfischung* and #*Fischung* can be explained in a similar way: the default reading of *fisch-* is the one without resultative meaning. Without the realized predicate we get the derivation product *Fischung*, which does not exist (with the relevant meaning).

So, in a lexical analysis of resultatives we have to make sure that the resultative predicate is not optional and this is what my analysis does. It says that *fisch-* needs a resultative predicate. It does not say that it *optionally* takes a result predicate. What is needed is a careful formulation of a theory of what can be dropped that ensures that no arguments are omitted that are crucial for recognizing the sense of a certain construction/collocation. The nominalization rules have to be set up accordingly.[25] I do not see

---

[25] Note that this also applies to lexical theories of idioms of the kind suggested by Sag (2007) and Kay, Sag & Flickinger (2015). If one analyses idioms like *kick the habit* and *kick the bucket* with a special lexical item for *kick*, one has to make sure that the object of *kick* is not omitted since the idioms are not recognizable without the object.

any problems for the analyses of resultatives and particle verbs that I suggested in Müller (2002a; 2003c).

Before I turn to approaches with radical underspecification of argument structure in the next section, I want to comment on a more recent paper by Asudeh, Giorgolo & Toivonen (2014). The authors discuss the phrasal introduction of cognate objects and benefactives. (25a) is an example of the latter construction.

(25) a. The performer sang the children a song.

b. The children were sung a song.

According to the authors, the noun phrase *the children* is not an argument of *sing* but contributed by the c-structure rule that optionally licenses a benefactive.

(26) V' → V DP DP
↑ = ↓ (↑ OBJ) = ↓ (↑ OBJ$_\theta$) = ↓
(@BENEFACTIVE)

Whenever this rule is called, the template BENEFACTIVE can add a benefactive role and the respective semantics, provided this is compatible with the verb that is inserted into the structure. The authors show how the mappings for the passive example in (25b) work, but they do not provide the c-structure rule that licenses such examples. Unless one assumes that arguments in (26) can be optional (see below), one would need a c-structure rule for passive VPs and this rule has to license a benefactive as well.[26] So it would be:

(27) V' → V[pass] DP
↑ = ↓ (↑ OBJ$_\theta$) = ↓
(@BENEFACTIVE)

Note that a benefactive cannot be added to just any verb: Adding a benefactive to an intransitive verb as in (28a) is out and the passive that would correspond to (28a) is ungrammatical as well, as (28b) shows:

(28) a. * He laughed the children.

b. * The children were laughed.

The benefactive template would account for the ungrammaticality of (28) since it requires an ARG$_2$ to be present and the intransitive *laugh* does not have an ARG$_2$, but this account would not extend to other verbs. For example, the template would admit the sentences in (29b–c) since *give* with prepositional object has an ARG$_2$ (Kibort 2008: 317).

(29) a. He gave it to Mary.

b. * He gave Peter it to Mary.

c. * Peter was given it to Mary.

---

[26] See for instance Bergen & Chang (2005) and van Trijp (2011) for Construction Grammar analyses that assume active and passive variants of phrasal constructions. See Cappelle (2006) on allostructions in general.

give could combine with the *to* PP semantically and would then be equivalent to a transitive verb as far as resources are concerned (looking for an ARG$_1$ and an ARG$_2$). The benefactive template would map the ARG$_2$ to ARG$_3$ and hence (29b) would be licensed. Similar examples can be constructed with other verbs that take prepositional objects, for instance *accuse sb. of something*. Since there are verbs that take a benefactive and a PP object as shown by (30), (29b) cannot be ruled out with reference to non-existing c-structure rules.

(30) I buy him a coat for hundred dollar.

So, if the c-structure is to play a role in argument structure constructions at all, one could not just claim that all c-structure rules optionally introduce a benefactive argument. Therefore there is something special about the two rules in (26) and (27). The problem is that there is no relation between these rules. They are independent statements saying that there can be a benefactive in the active and that there can be one in the passive. This is what Chomsky (1957: 43) criticized in 1957 with respect to simple phrase structure grammar and this was the reason for the introduction of transformations. Bresnan-style LFG captured the generalizations by lexical rules (Bresnan 1978; 1982b) and later by lexical rules in combination with Lexical Mapping Theory (Toivonen 2013). But if elements are added outside the lexical representations, the representations where these elements are added have to be related too. One could say that our knowledge about formal tools has changed since 1957. We now can use inheritance hierarchies to capture generalizations. So one can assume a type (or a template) that is the supertype of all those c-structure rules that introduce a benefactive. But since not all rules allow for the introduction of a benefactive element, this basically amounts to saying: c-structure rule A, B, and C allow for the introduction of a benefactive. In comparison lexical rule-based approaches have one statement introducing the benefactive. The lexical rule states what verbs are appropriate for adding a benefactive and syntactic rules are not affected.

Asudeh (p. c. May 2016) and an anonymous reviewer of HeadLex16 pointed out to me that the rules in (26) and (27) can be generalized over if the arguments in (26) are made optional. (31) shows the rule in (26) with the DPs marked as optional by the brackets enclosing them.

(31) V′ → V (DP) (DP)
↑ = ↓ (↑ OBJ) = ↓ (↑ OBJ$_\theta$) = ↓
(@BENEFACTIVE)

Since both of the DPs are optional (31) is equivalent to a specification of four rules, namely (26) and the three versions of the rule in (32):

(32) a. V′ → V DP
↑ = ↓ (↑ OBJ$_\theta$) = ↓
(@BENEFACTIVE)

b. V′ → V DP
↑ = ↓ (↑ OBJ) = ↓
(@BENEFACTIVE)

c. V′ →   V
         ↑ = ↓
     (@BENEFACTIVE)

(32a) is the variant of (31) in which the OBJ is omitted (needed for (33a)), (32b) is the variant in which the OBJ$_\theta$ is omitted (needed for (33b)) and in (32c) both DPs are omitted (needed for (33c)).

(33) a. She had been prepared divine and elaborate meals.
b. What kind of picture did the kids draw the teacher?
c. Such divine and elaborate meals, she had never been prepared before, not even by her ex-husband who was a professional chef.

Hence, (31) can be used for V′'s containing two objects, for V′'s in the passive containing just one object, for V′ with the secondary object extraced and for V′ in the passive with the secondary object extracted. The template-based approach does not overgenerate since the benefactive template is specified such that it requires the verb it applies to to select for an ARG2. Since intransitives like *laugh* do not select for an ARG2 a benefactive cannot be added. So, in fact the actual configuration in the c-structure rule does only play a minor role: the account mainly relies on semantics and resource sensitivity. There is one piece of information that is contributed by the c-structure rule: it constrains the grammatical functions of ARG$_2$ and ARG$_3$, which are disjunctively specified in the template definitions for ARG$_2$ and ARG$_3$: ARG$_2$ can be realized as SUBJ or as OBJ. In the active case ARG$_1$ will be the SUBJ and because of function argument bi-uniqueness (Bresnan et al. 2015: 334) no other element can be the SUBJ and hence ARG$_2$ has to be an OBJ. ARG$_3$ can be either an OBJ or an OBJ$_\theta$. Since ARG$_2$ is an OBJ in the active, ARG$_3$ has to be an OBJ$_\theta$ in the active. In the passive case ARG$_1$ is suppressed or realized as OBL$_\theta$ (*by* PP). ARG$_2$ will be realized as SUBJ (since English requires a SUBJ to be realized) and ARG$_3$ could be realized as either OBJ or OBJ$_\theta$. This is not constrained by the template specifications so far. Because of the optionality in (31), either the OBJ or the OBJ$_\theta$ function could be chosen for ARG$_3$. This means that either Lexical Mapping Theory has to be revised or one has to make sure that the c-structure rule used in the passive of benefactives states the grammatical function of the object correctly. Hence one would need the c-structure rule in (27) and then there would be the missing generalization I pointed out above.

If one finds a way to set up the mappings to grammatical functions without reference to c-structures in lexical templates, this means that it is not the case that an argument is added by a certain configuration the verb enters in. Since any verb may enter (33) and since the only important thing is the interaction between the lexical specification of the verb and the benefactive template, the same structures would be licensed if the benefactive template were added to the lexical items of verbs directly. The actual configuration would not constrain anything. All (alleged) arguments from language acquisition and psycholinguistics (see Sections 21.6 and 21.7) for phrasal analyses would not apply to such a phrasal account.

If the actual c-structure configuration does not contribute any restrictions as to what arguments may be realized and what grammatical functions they get, the difference

21 Phrasal vs. lexical analyses

between the lexical use of the benefactive template and the phrasal introduction as executed in (31) is really minimal. However, there is one area in grammar where there is a difference: coordination. As Müller & Wechsler (2014a: Section 6.1) pointed out, it is possible to coordinate ditransitive verbs with verbs that appear together with a benefactive. (34) is one of their examples:

(34) She then offered and made me a wonderful espresso — nice.[27]

If the benefactive information is introduced at the lexical level the coordinated verbs basically have the same selectional requirements. If the benefactive information is introduced at the phrasal level *baked* and *gave* are coordinated and then the benefactive constraints are imposed on the result of the coordination by the c-structure rule. While it is clear that the lexical items that would be assumed in a lexical approach can be coordinated in a symmetric coordination, problems seem to arise for the phrasal approach. It is unclear how the asymmetric coordination of the mono- and ditransitive verbs can be accounted for and how the constraints of the benefactive template are distributed over the two conjuncts. The fact that the benefactive template is optional does not help here since the optionality means that the template is either called or it is not. The situation is depicted in Figure 21.3. The optionality of the template call in the top figure basically

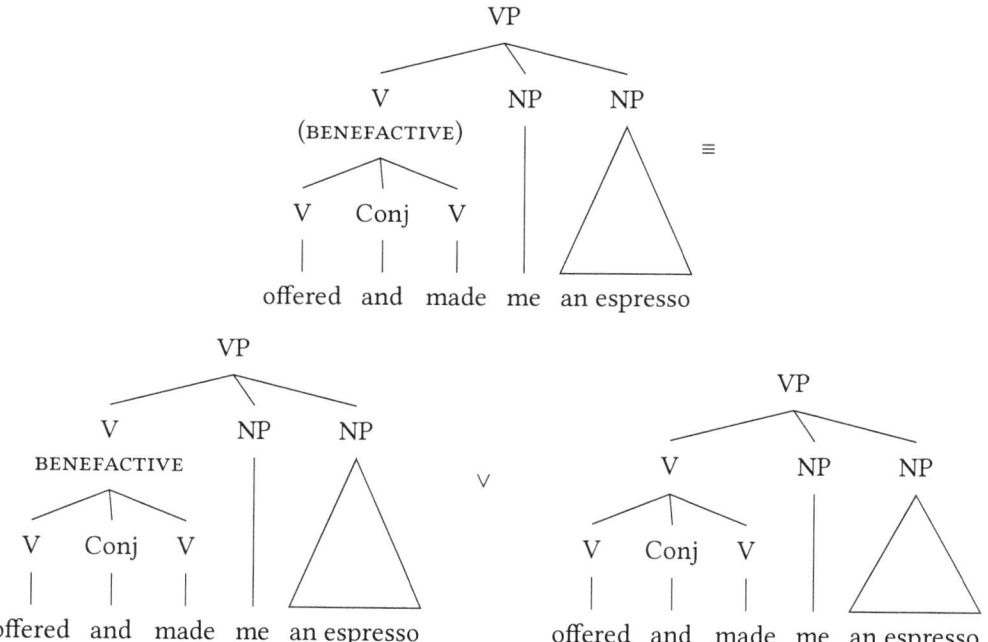

Figure 21.3: The optionality of a call of a template corresponds to a disjunction.

corresponds to the disjunction of the two trees in the lower part of the figure. The optionality does not allow for a distribution to one of the daughters in a coordination.

---

[27]http://www.thespinroom.com.au/?p=102 2012-07-07

Mary Dalrymple (p. c. 2016) pointed out that the coordination rule that coordinates two verbs can be annotated with two optional calls of the benefactive template.

(35) V →   V   Conj   V
              (@BENEFACTIVE)   (@BENEFACTIVE)

In an analysis of the examples in (34), the template in rule (26) would not be called but the respective templates in (35) would be called instead. While this does work technically, similar coordination rules would be needed for all other constructions that introduce arguments in c-structures. Furthermore, the benefactive would have to be introduced in several unrelated places in the grammar and finally the benefactive is introduced at nodes consisting of a single verb without any additional arguments being licensed, which means that one could have gone for the lexical approach right away.

Timm Lichte (p. c. 2016) pointed out an important consequence of a treatment of coordination via (35): since the result of the coordination behaves like a normal ditransitive verb it would enter the normal ditransitive construction. Toivonen's original motivation for a phrasal analysis was the observation that extraction out of and passivization of benefactive constructions is restricted for some speakers (Toivonen 2013: 416):

(36) a. The kids drew their teacher a picture.

   b. * Which teacher did the kids draw a picture?

(37) a. * My sister was carved a soap statue of Bugs Bunny (by a famous sculptor).

   b. My sister was given a soap statue of Bugs Bunny (by a famous sculptor).

The ungrammaticality of the passive in (37a) in comparison to the grammaticality of the passive with a normal ditransitive construction in (37b) would be accounted for by assuming a fixed phrasal configuration that is the only possibility to license benefactives in a grammar. But by having c-structure rules like (35) in the grammar there would be a way to circumvent the c-structure rule for benefactives. If sentences with coordinations can be analyzed by coordinating lexical verbs and then using the c-structure rule for ditransitives, it would be predicted that none of the constraints on passive and extraction that are formulated at the phrasal level would hold. This is contrary to the facts: by coordinating items with strong restrictions (imposed by the benefactive templates) with items with weaker restrictions, one gets a coordination structure that is at least as restrictive as the items that are coordinated. One does not get less restrictive by coordinating items. See Müller (2018a) for further discussion of ditransitives and benefactives and extraction and passivization.

In Müller & Wechsler (2014a) we argued that the approach to Swedish Caused-Motion Constructions in Asudeh et al. (2008; 2013) would not carry over to German since the German construction interacts with derivational morphology. Asudeh & Toivonen (2014) argued that Swedish is different from German and hence there would not be a problem. However, the situation is different with the benefactive constructions. Although English and German do differ in many respects, both languages have similar dative constructions:

(38) a. He baked her a cake.
b. Er buk   ihr   einen Kuchen.
   he baked her.DAT a.ACC cake

Now, the analysis of the free constituent order in German was explained by assuming binary branching structures in which a VP node is combined with one of its arguments or adjuncts (see Section 7.4). The c-structure rule is repeated in (39):

(39) VP →   NP   VP
           (↑ SUBJ |OBJ |OBJ$_\theta$) = ↓   ↑ = ↓

The dependent elements contribute to the f-structure of the verb and coherence/completeness ensure that all arguments of the verb are present. One could add the introduction of the benefactive argument to the VP node of the right-hand side of the rule. However, since the verb-final variant of (38b) would have the structure in (40), one would get spurious ambiguities, since the benefactive could be introduced at every node:

(40) weil   [$_{VP}$ er [$_{VP}$ ihr [$_{VP}$ einen Kuchen [$_{VP}$ [$_V$ buk]]]]]
     because   he   her   a   cake   baked

So the only option seems to be to introduce the benefactive at the rule that got the recursion going, namely the rule that projected the lexical verb to the VP level. The rule (39) from page 237 is repeated as (41) for convenience.

(41) VP →   (V)
              ↑ = ↓

Note also that benefactive datives appear in adjectival environments as in (42):

(42) a. der seiner   Frau einen Kuchen backende Mann
        the his.DAT wife a.ACC cake   baking   man
        'the man who is baking a cake for her'
     b. der einen Kuchen seiner   Frau backende Mann
        the a.ACC cake   his.DAT wife baking   man
        'the man who is baking a cake for her'

In order to account for these datives one would have to assume that the adjective-to-AP rule that would be parallel to (41) introduces the dative. The semantics of the benefactive template would have to somehow make sure that the benefactive argument is not added to intransitive verbs like *lachen* 'to laugh' or participles like *lachende* 'laughing'. While this may be possible, I find the overall approach unattractive. First it does not have anything to do with the original constructional proposal but just states that the benefactive may be introduced at several places in syntax, second the unary branching syntactic rule is applying to a lexical item and hence is very similar to a lexical rule and third the analysis does not capture cross-linguistic commonalities of the construction. In a lexical rule-based approach as the one that was suggested by Briscoe & Copestake (1999: Section 5), a benefactive argument is added to certain verbs and the lexical rule is parallel in all languages that have this phenomenon (Müller 2018a). The respective languages differ simply in the way the arguments are realized with respect to their heads. In languages that have adjectival participles, these are derived from the respective verbal stems. The morphological rule is the same independent of benefactive arguments and the syntactic rules for adjectival phrases do not have to mention benefactive arguments. I discuss the template-based approach in more detail in Müller (2018a). This book also contains a fully worked out analysis of the benefactive and the resultative constructions and their interactions in German and English in the framework of HPSG.

21.3 Radical underspecification: the end of argument structure?

21.3.1 Neo-Davidsonianism

In the last section we examined proposals that assume that verbs come with certain argument roles and are inserted into prespecified structures that may contribute additional arguments. While we showed that this is not without problems, there are even more radical proposals that the construction adds all agent arguments, or even all arguments. The notion that the agent argument should be severed from its verbs is put forth by Marantz (1984; 1997), Kratzer (1996), Embick (2004) and others. Others suggest that no arguments are selected by the verb. Borer (2003) calls such proposals *exoskeletal* since the structure of the clause is not determined by the predicate, that is, the verb does not project an inner "skeleton" of the clause. Counter to such proposals are *endoskeletal* approaches, in which the structure of the clause is determined by the predicate, that is, lexical proposals. The radical exoskeletal approaches are mainly proposed in Mainstream Generative Grammar (Borer 1994; 2003; 2005; Schein 1993; Hale & Keyser 1997; Lohndal 2012) but can also be found in HPSG (Haugereid 2009). We will not discuss these proposals in detail here, but we review the main issues insofar as they relate to the question of lexical argument structure.[28] We conclude that the available empirical evidence favors the lexical argument structure approach over such alternatives.

Exoskeletal approaches usually assume some version of Neo-Davidsonianism. Davidson (1967) argued for an event variable in the logical form of action sentences (43a). Dowty (1989) coined the term *neo-Davidsonian* for the variant in (43b), in which the verb translates to a property of events, and the subject and complement dependents are translated as arguments of secondary predicates such as *agent* and *theme*.[29] Kratzer (1996) further noted the possibility of mixed accounts such as (43c), in which the agent (subject) argument is severed from the *kill'* relation, but the theme (object) remains an argument of the *kill'* relation.[30]

---

[28] See Müller (2010a: Section 11.11.3) for a detailed discussion of Haugereid's approach.
[29] Dowty (1989) called the system in (43a) an *ordered argument system*.
[30] The event variable is shown as existentially bound, as in Davidson's original account. As discussed below, in Kratzer's version it must be bound by a lambda operator instead.

(43) a. *kill*: $\lambda y \lambda x \exists e[kill(e, x, y)]$ (Davidsonian)
   b. *kill*: $\lambda y \lambda x \exists e[kill(e) \wedge agent(e, x) \wedge theme(e, y)]$ (neo-Davidsonian)
   c. *kill*: $\lambda y \lambda x \exists e[kill(e, y) \wedge agent(e, x)]$ (mixed)

Kratzer (1996) observed that a distinction between Davidsonian, neo-Davidsonian and mixed can be made either "in the syntax" or "in the conceptual structure" (Kratzer 1996: 110–111). For example, on a lexical approach of the sort we advocate here, any of the three alternatives in (43) could be posited as the semantic content of the verb *kill*. A lexical entry for *kill* in the mixed model is given in (44).

(44) $\begin{bmatrix} \text{PHON} & \langle \textit{kill} \rangle \\ \text{ARG-ST} & \langle \text{NP}_x, \text{NP}_y \rangle \\ \text{CONTENT} & \textit{kill}(e, y) \wedge \textit{agent}(e, x) \end{bmatrix}$

In other words, the lexical approach is neutral on the question of the "conceptual structure" of eventualities, as noted already in a different connection in Section 21.1.4. For this reason, certain semantic arguments for the neo-Davidsonian approach, such as those put forth by Schein (1993: Chapter 4) and Lohndal (2012), do not directly bear upon the issue of lexicalism, as far as we can tell.

But Kratzer (1996), among others, has gone further and argued for an account that is neo-Davidsonian (or rather, mixed) "in the syntax". Kratzer's claim is that the verb specifies only the internal argument(s), as in (45a) or (45b), while the agent (external argument) role is assigned by the phrasal structure. On the "neo-Davidsonian in the syntax" view, the lexical representation of the verb has no arguments at all, except the event variable, as shown in (45c).

(45) a. *kill*: $\lambda y \lambda e[kill(e, y)]$ (agent is severed)
   b. *kill*: $\lambda y \lambda e[kill(e) \wedge theme(e, y)]$ (agent is severed)
   c. *kill*: $\lambda e[kill(e))]$ (all arguments severed)

On such accounts, the remaining dependents of the verb receive their semantic roles from silent secondary predicates, which are usually assumed to occupy the positions of functional heads in the phrase structure. An Event Identification rule identifies the event variables of the verb and the silent light verb (Kratzer 1996: 22); this is why the existential quantifiers in (43) have been replaced with lambda operators in (45). A standard term for the agent-assigning silent predicate is "little *v*" (see Section 4.1.4 on little *v*). These extra-lexical dependents are the analogs of the ones contributed by the constructions in Construction Grammar.

In the following subsections we address arguments that have been put forth in favor of the little *v* hypothesis, from idiom asymmetries (Section 21.3.2) and deverbal nominals (Section 21.3.3). We argue that the evidence actually favors the lexical view. Then we turn to problems for exoskeletal approaches, from idiosyncratic syntactic selection (Section 21.3.4) and expletives (Section 21.3.5). We conclude with a look at the treatment

21.3 Radical underspecification: the end of argument structure?

of idiosyncratic syntactic selection under Borer's exoskeletal theory (Section 21.3.7), and a summary (Section 21.3.8).

21.3.2 Little *v* and idiom asymmetries

Marantz (1984) and Kratzer (1996) argued for severing the agent from the argument structure as in (45a), on the basis of putative idiom asymmetries. Marantz (1984) observed that while English has many idioms and specialized meanings for verbs in which the internal argument is the fixed part of the idiom and the external argument is free, the reverse situation is considerably rarer. To put it differently, the nature of the role played by the subject argument often depends on the filler of the object position, but not vice versa. To take Kratzer's examples (Kratzer 1996: 114):

(46) a. kill a cockroach
 b. kill a conversation
 c. kill an evening watching TV
 d. kill a bottle (i.e. empty it)
 e. kill an audience (i.e., wow them)

On the other hand, one does not often find special meanings of a verb associated with the choice of subject, leaving the object position open (examples from Marantz (1984: 26)):

(47) a. Harry killed NP.
 b. Everyone is always killing NP.
 c. The drunk refused to kill NP.
 d. Silence certainly can kill NP.

Kratzer observes that a mixed representation of *kill* as in (48a) allows us to specify varying meanings that depend upon its sole NP argument.

(48) a. *kill*: $\lambda y \lambda e[kill(e, y)]$
 b. If a is a time interval, then $kill(e, a) = truth$ if e is an event of wasting a
 If a is animate, then $kill(e, a) = truth$ if e is an event in which a dies
 ... etc.

On the polyadic (Davidsonian) theory, the meaning could similarly be made to depend upon the filler of the agent role. On the polyadic view, "there is no technical obstacle" (Kratzer 1996: 116) to conditions like those in (48b), except reversed, so that it is the filler of the agent role instead of the theme role that affects the meaning. But, she writes, this could not be done if the agent is not an argument of the verb. According to Kratzer, the agent-severed representation (such as (48a)) disallows similar constraints on the meaning that depend upon the agent, thereby capturing the idiom asymmetry.

But as noted by Wechsler (2005), "there is no technical obstacle" to specifying agent-dependent meanings even if the Agent has been severed from the verb as Kratzer proposes. It is true that there is no variable for the agent in (48a). But there is an event variable e, and the language user must be able to identify the agent of e in order to interpret the sentence. So one could replace the variable a with "the agent of e" in the expressions in (48b), and thereby create verbs that violate the idiom asymmetry.

While this may seem to be a narrow technical or even pedantic point, it is nonetheless crucial. Suppose we try to repair Kratzer's argument with an additional assumption: that modulations in the meaning of a polysemous verb can only depend upon arguments of the *relation* denoted by that verb, and not on other participants in the event. Under that additional assumption, it makes no difference whether the agent is severed from the lexical entry or not. For example, consider the following (mixed) neo-Davidsonian representation of the semantic content in the lexical entry of *kill*:

(49)   kill: $\lambda y \lambda x \lambda e[kill(e, y) \wedge agent(e, x)]$

Assuming that sense modulations can only be affected by arguments of the *kill(e,y)* relation, we derive the idiom asymmetry, even if (49) is the lexical entry for *kill*. So suppose that we try to fix Kratzer's argument with a different assumption: that modulations in the meaning of a polysemous verb can only depend upon an argument of the lexically denoted function. Kratzer's "neo-Davidsonian in the syntax" lexical entry in (45a) lacks the agent argument, while the lexical entry in (49) clearly has one. But Kratzer's entry still fails to predict the asymmetry because, as noted above, it has the e argument and so the sense modulation can be conditioned on the "agent of e". As noted above, that event argument cannot be eliminated (for example through existential quantification) because it is needed in order to undergo event identification with the event argument of the silent light verb that introduces the agent (Kratzer 1996: 22).

Moreover, recasting Kratzer's account in lexicalist terms allows for verbs to vary. This is an important advantage, because the putative asymmetry is only a tendency. The following are examples in which the subject is a fixed part of the idiom and there are open slots for non-subjects:[31]

(50)   a. A little bird told X that S.

            'X heard the rumor that S.'

        b. The cat's got X's tongue.

            'X cannot speak.'

        c. What's eating X?

            'Why is X so galled?'

Further data and discussion of subject idioms in English and German can be found in Müller (2007a: Section 3.2.1).

---

[31] (50a) is from Nunberg, Sag & Wasow (1994: 526), (50b) from Bresnan (1982a: 349–350), and (50c) from Bresnan (1982a: 349–350).

21.3 Radical underspecification: the end of argument structure?

The tendency towards a subject-object asymmetry plausibly has an independent explanation. Nunberg, Sag & Wasow (1994) argue that the subject-object asymmetry is a side-effect of an animacy asymmetry. The open positions of idioms tend to be animate while the fixed positions tend to be inanimate. Nunberg et al. (1994) derive these animacy generalizations from the figurative and proverbial nature of the metaphorical transfers that give rise to idioms. If there is an independent explanation for this tendency, then a lexicalist grammar successfully encodes those patterns, perhaps with a mixed neo-Davidsonian lexical decomposition, as explained above (see Wechsler (2005) for such a lexical account of the verbs *buy* and *sell*). But the little *v* hypothesis rigidly predicts this asymmetry for all agentive verbs, and that prediction is not borne out.

21.3.3 Deverbal nominals

An influential argument against lexical argument structure involves English deverbal nominals and the causative alternation. It originates from a mention in Chomsky (1970), and is developed in detail by Marantz (1997); see also Pesetsky (1996) and Harley & Noyer (2000). The argument is often repeated, but it turns out that the empirical basis of the argument is incorrect, and the actual facts point in the opposite direction, in favor of lexical argument structure (Wechsler 2008b,a).

Certain English causative alternation verbs allow optional omission of the agent argument (51), while the cognate nominal disallows expression of the agent (52):

(51) a. that John grows tomatoes
     b. that tomatoes grow

(52) a. *John's growth of tomatoes
     b. the tomatoes' growth, the growth of the tomatoes

In contrast, nominals derived from obligatorily transitive verbs such as *destroy* allow expression of the agent, as shown in (54a):

(53) a. that the army destroyed the city
     b. *that the city destroyed

(54) a. the army's destruction of the city
     b. the city's destruction

Following a suggestion by Chomsky (1970), Marantz (1997) argued on the basis of these data that the agent role is lacking from lexical entries. In verbal projections like (51) and (53) the agent role is assigned in the syntax by little *v*. Nominal projections like (52) and (54) lack little *v*. Instead, pragmatics takes over to determine which agents can be expressed by the possessive phrase: the possessive can express "the sort of agent implied by an event with an external rather than an internal cause" because only the former can "easily be reconstructed" (quoted from Marantz (1997: 218)). The destruction of a city has a cause external to the city, while the growth of tomatoes is internally caused

625

by the tomatoes themselves (Smith 1970). Marantz points out that this explanation is unavailable if the noun is derived from a verb with an argument structure specifying its agent, since the deverbal nominal would inherit the agent of a causative alternation verb.

The empirical basis for this argument is the putative mismatch between the allowability of agent arguments, across some verb-noun cognate pairs: e.g., *grow* allows the agent but *growth* does not. But it turns out that the *grow/growth* pattern is rare. Most deverbal nominals precisely parallel the cognate verb: if the verb has an agent, so does the noun. Moreover, there is a ready explanation for the exceptional cases that exhibit the *grow/growth* pattern (Wechsler 2008a). First consider non-alternating theme-only intransitives (unaccusatives), as in (55) and non-alternating transitives as in (56). The pattern is clear: if the verb is agentless, then so is the noun:

(55) *arriv(al), disappear(ance), fall* etc.:
- a. A letter arrived.
- b. the arrival of the letter
- c. *The mailman arrived a letter.
- d. *the mailman's arrival of the letter

(56) *destroy/destruction, construct(ion), creat(ion), assign(ment)* etc.:
- a. The army is destroying the city.
- b. the army's destruction of the city

This favors the view that the noun inherits the lexical argument structure of the verb. For the anti-lexicalist, the badness of (55c) and (55d), respectively, would have to receive independent explanations. For example, on Harley and Noyer's 2000 proposal, (55c) is disallowed because a feature of the root ARRIVE prevents it from appearing in the context of *v*, but (55d) is instead ruled out because the cause of an event of arrival cannot be easily reconstructed from world knowledge. This exact duplication in two separate components of the linguistic system would have to be replicated across all non-alternating intransitive and transitive verbs, a situation that is highly implausible.

Turning to causative alternation verbs, Marantz's argument is based on the implicit generalization that noun cognates of causative alternation verbs (typically) lack the agent argument. But apart from the one example of *grow/growth*, there do not seem to be any clear cases of this pattern. Besides *grow(th)*, Chomsky (1970: examples (7c) and (8c)) cited two experiencer predicates, *amuse* and *interest*: *John amused (interested) the children with his stories* versus **John's amusement (interest) of the children with his stories*. But this was later shown by Rappaport (1983) and Dowty (1989) to have an independent aspectual explanation. Deverbal experiencer nouns like *amusement* and *interest* typically denote a mental state, where the corresponding verb denotes an event in which such a mental state comes about or is caused. These result nominals lack not only the agent but all the eventive arguments of the verb, because they do not refer to events. Exactly to the extent that such nouns can be construed as representing events, expression of the agent becomes acceptable.

21.3 Radical underspecification: the end of argument structure?

In a response to Chomsky (1970), Carlota Smith (1972) surveyed Webster's dictionary and found no support for Chomsky's claim that deverbal nominals do not inherit agent arguments from causative alternation verbs. She listed many counterexamples, including "*explode, divide, accelerate, expand, repeat, neutralize, conclude, unify*, and so on at length." (Smith 1972: 137). Harley and Noyer (2000) also noted many so-called "exceptions": *explode, accumulate, separate, unify, disperse, transform, dissolve/dissolution, detach(ment), disengage-(ment)*, and so on. The simple fact is that these are not exceptions because there is no generalization to which they can be exceptions. These long lists of verbs represent the norm, especially for suffix-derived nominals (in *-tion*, *-ment*, etc.). Many zero-derived nominals from alternating verbs also allow the agent, such as *change, release,* and *use*: *my constant change of mentors from 1992–1997; the frequent release of the prisoners by the governor; the frequent use of sharp tools by underage children* (examples from Borer (2003: fn. 13)).[32]

Like the experiencer nouns mentioned above, many zero-derived nominals lack event readings. Some reject all the arguments of the corresponding eventive verb, not just the agent: ** the freeze of the water, * the break of the window*, and so on. According to Stephen Wechsler, *his drop of the ball* is slightly odd, but *the drop of the ball* has exactly the same degree of oddness. The locution *a drop in temperature* matches the verbal one *The temperature dropped*, and both verbal and nominal forms disallow the agent: ** The storm dropped the temperature. * the storm's drop of the temperature*. In short, the facts seem to point in exactly the opposite direction from what has been assumed in this oft-repeated argument against lexical valence. Apart from the one isolated case of *grow/growth*, event-denoting deverbal nominals match their cognate verbs in their argument patterns.

Turning to *grow/growth* itself, we find a simple explanation for its unusual behavior (Wechsler 2008a). When the noun *growth* entered the English language, causative (transitive) *grow* did not exist. The OED provides these dates of the earliest attestations of *grow* and *growth*:

(57) a. intransitive *grow*:   c725   'be verdant' ... 'increase' (intransitive)
      b. the noun *growth*:   1587   'increase' (intransitive)
      c. transitive *grow*:   1774   'cultivate (crops)'

Thus *growth* entered the language at a time when transitive *grow* did not exist. The argument structure and meaning were inherited by the noun from its source verb, and then preserved into present-day English. This makes perfect sense if, as we claim, words have predicate argument structures. Nominalization by *-th* suffixation is not productive in English, so *growth* is listed in the lexicon. To explain why *growth* lacks the agent we need only assume that a lexical entry's predicate argument structure dictates whether it takes an agent argument or not. So even this one word provides evidence for lexical argument structure.

---

[32] Pesetsky (1996: 79, ex. (231)) assigns a star to *the thief's return of the money*, but it is acceptable to many speakers. The *Oxford English Dictionary* lists a transitive sense for the noun *return* (definition 11a), and corpus examples like *her return of the spoils* are not hard to find.

21 Phrasal vs. lexical analyses

21.3.4 Idiosyncratic syntactic selections

The notion of lexical valence structure immediately explains why the argument realization patterns are strongly correlated with the particular lexical heads selecting those arguments. It is not sufficient to have general lexical items without valence information and let the syntax and world knowledge decide about argument realizations, because not all realizational patterns are determined by the meaning. The form of the preposition of a prepositional object is sometimes loosely semantically motivated but in other cases arbitrary. For example, the valence structure of the English verb *depend* captures the fact that it selects an *on*-PP to express one of its semantic arguments:

(58) a. John depends on Mary. (*counts, relies,* etc.)
 b. John trusts (*on) Mary.
 c. $\begin{bmatrix} \text{PHON} & \langle \textit{depend} \rangle \\ \text{ARG-ST} & \langle \text{NP}_x, \text{PP}[on]_y \rangle \\ \text{CONTENT} & \textit{depend}(x,y) \end{bmatrix}$

Such idiosyncratic lexical selection is utterly pervasive in human language. The verb or other predicator often determines the choice between direct and oblique morphology, and for obliques, it determines the choice of adposition or oblique case. In some languages such as Icelandic even the subject case can be selected by the verb (Zaenen, Maling & Thráinsson 1985).

Selection is language-specific. English *wait* selects *for* (German *für*) while German *warten* selects *auf* 'on' with an accusative object:

(59) a. I am waiting for my man.
 b. Ich warte auf meinen Mann.
 I wait on my man.ACC

A learner has to acquire that *warten* has to be used with *auf* + accusative and not with other prepositions or other case. Similarly we have the verb *ergert* in Dutch that takes an *aan* PP while the German counterpart takes an *über* PP:

(60) a. Kim ergert zich aan Sandy.
 Kim annoys REFL to Sandy
 'Kim is/gets annoyed at Sandy.'
 b. Kim ärgert sich über Sandy.
 Kim annoys REFL above Sandy
 'Kim is/gets annoyed at Sandy.'

There are language-internal niches with the same type of prepositional objects. For instance, *freuen* 'to rejoice over/about' and *lachen* 'laugh at/about' take *über* as well. But there is no general way to predict on semantic grounds which preposition has to be taken.

21.3 Radical underspecification: the end of argument structure?

It is often impossible to find semantic motivation for case. In German there is a tendency to replace genitive (61a) with dative (61b) with no apparent semantic motivation:

(61) a. dass der Opfer gedacht werde
 that the victims.GEN remembered is
 'that the victims would be remembered'

 b. daß auch hier den Opfern des Faschismus gedacht werde [...]³³
 that also here the victims.DAT of.the fascism remembered is
 'that the victims of fascism would be remembered here too'

The synonyms *treffen* and *begegnen* 'to meet' govern different cases (example from Pollard & Sag (1987: 126)).

(62) a. Er traf den Mann.
 he.NOM met the.ACC man

 b. Er begegnete dem Mann.
 he.NOM met the.DAT man

One has to specify the case that the respective verbs require in the lexical items of the verbs.³⁴

A radical variant of the plugging approach is suggested by Haugereid (2009).³⁵ Haugereid (pages 12–13) assumes that the syntax combines a verb with an arbitrary combination of a subset of five different argument roles. Which arguments can be combined with a verb is not restricted by the lexical item of the verb.³⁶ A problem for such views is that the meaning of an ambiguous verb sometimes depends on which of its arguments are expressed. The German verb *borgen* has the two translations 'borrow' and 'lend', which basically are two different perspectives on the same event (see Kunze (1991; 1993) for an extensive discussion of verbs of exchange of possession). Interestingly, the dative object is obligatory only with the 'lend' reading (Müller 2010a: 403):

(63) a. Ich borge ihm das Eichhörnchen.
 I lend him the squirrel
 'I lend the squirrel to him.'

 b. Ich borge (mir) das Eichhörnchen.
 I borrow me the squirrel
 'I borrow the squirrel.'

---

[33] Frankfurter Rundschau, 07.11.1997, p. 6.

[34] Or at least mark the fact that *treffen* takes an object with the default case for objects and *begegnen* takes a dative object in German. See Haider (1985a), Heinz & Matiasek (1994), and Müller (2001) on structural and lexical case.

[35] Technical aspects of Haugereid's approach are discussed in Section 21.3.6.

[36] Haugereid has the possibility to impose valence restrictions on verbs, but he claims that he uses this possibility just in order to get a more efficient processing of his computer implementation (p. 13).

21 Phrasal vs. lexical analyses

If we omit it, we get only the 'borrow' reading. So the grammar must specify for specific verbs that certain arguments are necessary for a certain verb meaning or a certain perspective on an event.

Synonyms with differing valence specifications include the minimal triplet mentioned earlier: *dine* is obligatorily intransitive (or takes an *on*-PP), *devour* is transitive, and *eat* can be used either intransitively or transitively (Dowty 1989: 89–90). Many other examples are given in Levin (1993) and Levin & Rappaport Hovav (2005).

In a phrasal constructionist approach one would have to assume phrasal patterns with the preposition or case, into which the verb is inserted. For (59b), the pattern includes a prepositional object with *auf* and an accusative NP, plus an entry for *warten* specifying that it can be inserted into such a structure (see Kroch & Joshi (1985: Section 5.2) for such a proposal in the framework of TAG). Since there are generalizations regarding verbs with such valence representations, one would be forced to have two inheritance hierarchies: one for lexical entries with their valence properties and another one for specific phrasal patterns that are needed for the specific constructions in which these lexical items can be used.

More often, proponents of neo-constructionist approaches either make proposals that are difficult to distinguish from lexical valence structures (see Section 21.3.7 below) or simply decline to address the problem. For instance, Lohndal (2012) writes:

> An unanswered question on this story is how we ensure that the functional heads occur together with the relevant lexical items or roots. This is a general problem for the view that Case is assigned by functional heads, and I do not have anything to say about this issue here. (Lohndal 2012)

We think that getting case assignment right in simple sentences, without vast overgeneration of ill-formed word sequences, is a minimal requirement for a linguistic theory.

21.3.5 Expletives

A final example for the irreducibility of valence to semantics are verbs that select for expletives and reflexive arguments of inherently reflexive verbs in German:

(64) a. weil   es regnet
        because it rains

   b. weil   (es) mir   (vor   der Prüfung) graut
      because EXPL me.DAT before the exam   dreads
      'because I am dreading the exam'

   c. weil   er es   bis   zum Professor bringt
      because he EXPL until to.the professor brings
      'because he made it to professor'

   d. weil   es   sich um   den Montag handelt
      because EXPL REFL around the Monday trades
      'because it is about the Monday'

630

21.3 Radical underspecification: the end of argument structure?

e. weil   ich mich   (jetzt) erhole
   because I   myself   now   recreate
   'because I am relaxing now'

The lexical heads in (64) need to contain information about the expletive subjects/objects and/or reflexive pronouns that do not fill semantic roles. Note that German allows for subjectless predicates and hence the presence of expletive subjects cannot be claimed to follow from general principles. (64c) is an example with an expletive object. Explanations referring to the obligatory presence of a subject would fail on such examples in any case. Furthermore it has to be ensured that *erholen* is not realized in the [Sbj IntrVerb] construction for intransitive verbs or respective functional categories in a Minimalist setting although the relation *erholen′* (*relax′*) is a one-place predicate and hence *erholen* is semantically compatible with the construction.

21.3.6 An exoskeletal approach

In what follows I discuss Haugereid's proposal (2007) in more detail. His analysis has all the high-level problems that were mentioned in the previous subsections, but since it is worked out in detail it is interesting to see its predictions.

Haugereid (2007), working in the framework of HPSG, suggests an analysis along the lines of Borer (2005) where the meaning of an expression is defined as depending on the arguments that are present. He assumes that there are five argument slots that are assigned to semantic roles as follows:

- Arg1: agent or source
- Arg2: patient
- Arg3: benefactive or recipient
- Arg4: goal
- Arg5: antecedent

Here, antecedent is a more general role that stands for instrument, comitative, manner and source. The roles Arg1–Arg3 correspond to subject and objects. Arg4 is a resultative predicate of the end of a path. Arg4 can be realized by a PP, an AP or an NP. (65) gives examples for the realization of Arg4:

(65) a. John smashed the ball *out of the room.*
     b. John hammered the metal *flat.*
     c. He painted the car *a brilliant red.*

Whereas Arg4 follows the other participants in the causal chain of events, the antecedent precedes the patient in the order of events. It is realized as a PP. (66) is an example of the realization of Arg5:

631

21 Phrasal vs. lexical analyses

(66) John punctured the balloon *with a needle*.

Haugereid now assumes that argument frames consist of these roles. He provides the examples in (67):

(67) a. John smiles. (arg1-frame)
 b. John smashed the ball. (arg12-frame)
 c. The boat arrived. (arg2-frame)
 d. John gave Mary a book. (arg123-frame)
 e. John gave a book to Mary. (arg124-frame)
 f. John punctured the ball with a needle. (arg125-frame)

Haugereid points out that multiple verbs can occur in multiple argument frames. He provides the variants in (68) for the verb *drip*:

(68) a. The roof drips. (arg1-frame)
 b. The doctor drips into the eyes. (arg14-frame)
 c. The doctor drips with water. (arg15-frame)
 d. The doctor drips into the eyes with water. (arg145-frame)
 e. The roof drips water. (arg12-frame)
 f. The roof drips water into the bucket. (arg124-frame)
 g. The doctor dripped the eyes with water. (arg125-frame)
 h. The doctor dripped into the eyes with water. (arg145-frame)
 i. John dripped himself two drops of water. (arg123-frame)
 j. John dripped himself two drops of water into his eyes. (arg1234-frame)
 k. John dripped himself two drops of water into his eyes with a drop counter. (arg12345-frame)
 l. Water dripped. (arg2-frame)
 m. It drips. (arg0-frame)

He proposes the inheritance hierarchy in Figure 21.4 in order to represent all possible argument combinations. The Arg5 role is omitted due to space considerations.

Haugereid assumes binary-branching structures where arguments can be combined with a head in any order. There is a dominance schema for each argument role. The schema realizing the argument role 3 provides a link value *arg3+*. If the argument role 2 is provided by another schema, we arrive at the frame *arg23*. For unergative intransitive verbs, it is possible to determine that it has an argument frame of *arg1*. This frame is only compatible with the types *arg1+*, *arg2−*, *arg3−* and *arg4−*. Verbs that have an optional object are assigned to *arg1-12* according to Haugereid. This type allows for the following combinations: *arg1+*, *arg2−*, *arg3−* and *arg4−* such as *arg1+*, *arg2+*, *arg3−* and *arg4−*.

This approach comes very close to an idea by Goldberg: verbs are underspecified with regard to the sentence structures in which they occur and it is only the actual realization

21.3 Radical underspecification: the end of argument structure?

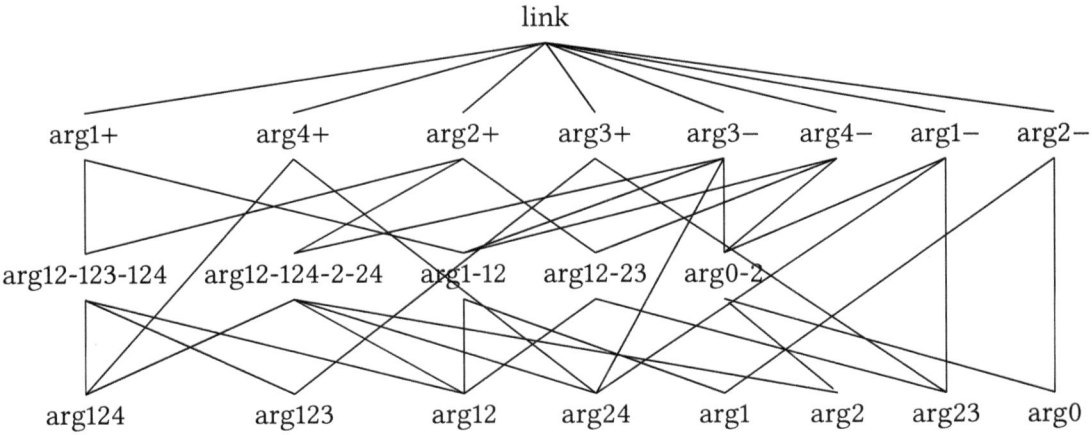

Figure 21.4: Hierarchy of argument frames following Haugereid (2007)

of arguments in the sentence that decides which combinations of arguments are realized. One should bear in mind that the hierarchy in Figure 21.4 corresponds to a considerable disjunction: it lists all possible realizations of arguments. If we say that *essen* 'to eat' has the type *arg1-12*, then this corresponds to the disjunction *arg1* ∨ *arg12*. In addition to the information in the hierarchy above, one also requires information about the syntactic properties of the arguments (case, the form of prepositions, verb forms in verbal complements). Since this information is in part specific to each verb (see Section 21.1), it cannot be present in the dominance schemata and must instead be listed in each individual lexical entry. For the lexical entry for *warten auf* 'wait for', there must be information about the fact that the subject has to be an NP and that the prepositional object is an *auf*-PP with accusative. The use of a type hierarchy then allows one to elegantly encode the fact that the prepositional object is optional. The difference to a disjunctively specified COMPS list with the form of (69) is just a matter of formalization.

(69) COMPS ⟨ NP[*str*] ⟩ ∨ ⟨ NP[*str*], PP[*auf*, *acc*] ⟩

Since Haugereid's structures are binary-branching, it is possible to derive all permutations of arguments (70a–b), and adjuncts can be attached to every branching node (70c–d).

(70) a. dass [$_{\text{arg1}}$ keiner [$_{\text{arg2}}$ Pizza isst]]
    that   nobody   pizza eats

    'that nobody eats pizza'

  b. dass [$_{\text{arg2}}$ Pizza [$_{\text{arg1}}$ keiner isst]]
    that   pizza   nobody eats

  c. dass [$_{\text{arg1}}$ keiner [gerne [$_{\text{arg2}}$ Pizza isst]]]
    that   nobody gladly   pizza eats

    'that nobody eats pizza gladly'

633

      d. dass [[hier [$_{\text{arg1}}$ keiner [$_{\text{arg2}}$ Pizza isst]]]
          that here   nobody   pizza eats
         'that nobody eats pizza here'

Haugereid has therefore found solutions for some of the problems in Goldberg's analysis that were pointed out in Müller (2006). Nevertheless, there are a number of other problems, which I will discuss in what follows. In Haugereid's approach, nothing is said about the composition of meaning. He follows the so-called Neo-Davidsonian approach. In this kind of semantic representation, arguments of the verb are not directly represented on the verb. Instead, the verb normally has an event argument and the argument roles belonging to the event in question are determined in a separate predication. (71) shows two alternative representations, where e stands for the event variable.

(71)   a. Der Mann isst eine Pizza.
         the man eats a pizza
       'The man is eating a pizza'
    b. *eat'*(e, x, y) ∧ *man'*(x) ∧ *pizza'*(y)
    c. *eat'*(e) ∧ *agent*(e,x) ∧ *theme*(e,y) ∧ *man'*(x) ∧ *pizza'*(y)

Haugereid adopts Minimal Recursion Semantics (MRS) as his semantic formalism (see also Section 9.1.6 and 19.3). The fact that arguments belong to a particular predicate is represented by the fact that the relevant predicates have the same handle. The representation in (71c) corresponds to (72):

(72)   h1:*essen'*(e), h1:*arg1*(x), h1:*arg2*(y), h2:*mann'*(x), h3:*pizza'*(y)

This analysis captures Goldberg's main idea: meaning arises from particular constituents being realized together with a head.

For the sentence in (73a), Haugereid (2007, p. c.) assumes the semantic representation in (73b):[37]

(73)   a. der Mann den Teich leer fischt
         the man the pond empty fishes
    b. h1:*mann'*(x), h2:*teich'*(y), h3:*leer'*(e),
       h4:*fischen'*(e2), h4:*arg1*(x), h4:*arg2*(y), h4:*arg4*(h3)

In (73b), the *arg1*, *arg2* and *arg4* relations have the same handle as *fischen'*. Following Haugereid's definitions, this means that *arg2* is the patient of the event. In the case of (73a), this makes incorrect predictions since the accusative element is not a semantic argument of the main verb. It is a semantic argument of the secondary predicate *leer* 'empty' and has been raised to the object of the resultative construction. Depending on

---

[37] See Haugereid (2009: 165) for an analysis of the Norwegian examples in (i).

  (i) Jon maler veggen rød.
     Jon paints wall.DEF red
     'Jon paints the wall red.'

21.3 Radical underspecification: the end of argument structure?

the exact analysis assumed, the accusative object is either a syntactic argument of the verb or of the adjective, however, it is never a semantic argument of the verb. In addition to this problem, the representation in (73b) does not capture the fact that *leer* 'empty' predicates over the object. Haugereid (2007, p.c.) suggests that this is implicit in the representation and follows from the fact that all *arg4*s predicate over all *arg2*s. Unlike Haugereid's analysis, analyses using lexical rules that relate a lexical item of a verb to another verbal item with a resultative meaning allow for a precise specification of the semantic representation that then captures the semantic relation between the predicates involved. In addition, the lexical rule-based analysis makes it possible to license lexical items that do not establish a semantic relation between the accusative object and the verb (Wechsler 1997; Wechsler & Noh 2001; Müller 2002a: Chapter 5).

Haugereid sketches an analysis of the syntax of the German clause and tackles active/passive alternations. However, certain aspects of the grammar are not elaborated on. In particular, it remains unclear how complex clauses containing AcI verbs such as *sehen* 'to see' and *lassen* 'to let' should be analyzed. Arguments of embedded and embedding verbs can be permuted in these constructions. Haugereid (2007, p. c.) assumes special rules that allow to saturate arguments of more deeply embedded verbs, for example, a special rule that combines an *arg2* argument of an argument with a verb. In order to combine *das Nilpferd* and *nicht füttern helfen lässt* in sentences such as (74), he is forced to assume a special grammatical rule that combines an argument of a doubly embedded verb with another verb:

(74) weil Hans Cecilia John das Nilpferd nicht füttern helfen lässt
because Hans Cecilia John the hippo not feed help let
'because Hans is not letting Cecilia help John feed the hippo.'

In Müller (2004d: 220), I have argued that embedding under complex-forming predicates is only constrained by performance factors (see also Section 12.6.3). In German, verbal complexes with more than four verbs are barely acceptable. Evers (1975: 58–59) has pointed out, however, that the situation in Dutch is different since Dutch verbal complexes have a different branching: in Dutch, verbal complexes with up to five verbs are possible. Evers attributes this difference to a greater processing load for German verbal complexes (see also Gibson 1998: Section 3.7). Haugereid would have to assume that there are more rules for Dutch than for German. In this way, he would give up the distinction between competence and performance and incorporate performance restrictions directly into the grammar. If he wanted to maintain a distinction between the two, then Haugereid would be forced to assume an infinite number of schemata or a schema with functional uncertainty since depth of embedding is only constrained by performance factors. Existing HPSG approaches to the analysis of verbal complexes do without functional uncertainty (Hinrichs & Nakazawa 1994). Since such raising analyses are required for object raising anyway (as discussed above), they should be given preference.

Summing up, it must be said that Haugereid's exoskeletal approach does account for different orderings of arguments, but it neither derives the correct semantic representations nor does it offer a solution for the problem of idiosyncratic selection of arguments and the selection of expletives.

21.3.7 Is there an alternative to lexical valence structure?

The question for theories denying the existence of valence structure is what replaces it to explain idiosyncratic lexical selection. In her exoskeletal approach, Borer (2005) explicitly rejects lexical valence structures. But she posits post-syntactic interpretive rules that are difficult to distinguish from them. To explain the correlation of *depend* with an *on*-PP, she posits the following interpretive rule (Borer 2005: Vol. II, p. 29):

(75)   MEANING $\Leftrightarrow \pi_9 + [\langle e^{on} \rangle]$

Borer refers to all such cases of idiosyncratic selection as idioms. In a rule such as (75), "MEANING is whatever the relevant idiom means" (Borer 2005: Vol. II, p. 27). In (75), π_9 is the "phonological index" of the verb *depend* and e^{on} "corresponds to an open value that must be assigned range by the f-morph *on*" (Borer 2005: Vol. II, p. 29), where f-morphs are function words or morphemes. Hence this rule brings together much the same information as the lexical valence structure in (58c). Discussing such "idiom" rules, Borer writes

> Although by assumption a listeme cannot be associated with any grammatical properties, one device used in this work has allowed us to get around the formidable restrictions placed on the grammar by such a constraint – the formation of idioms. [...] Such idiomatic specification could be utilized, potentially, not just for *arrive* and *depend on*, but also for obligatorily transitive verbs [...], for verbs such as *put*, with their obligatory locative, and for verbs which require a sentential complement.
>
> The reader may object that subcategorization, of sorts, is introduced here through the back door, with the introduction, in lieu of lexical syntactic annotation, of an articulated listed structure, called an *idiom*, which accomplishes, de facto, the same task. The objection of course has some validity, and at the present state of the art, the introduction of idioms may represent somewhat of a concession.
> (Borer 2005: Vol. II, p. 354–355)

Borer goes on to pose various questions for future research, related to constraining the class of possible idioms. With regard to that research program it should be noted that a major focus of lexicalist research has been narrowing the class of subcategorization and extricating derivable properties from idiosyncratic subcategorization. Those are the functions of HPSG lexical hierarchies, for example.

21.3.8 Summary

In Sections 21.3.2–21.3.5 we showed that the question of which arguments must be realized in a sentence cannot be reduced to semantics and world knowledge or to general facts about subjects. The consequence is that valence information has to be connected to lexical items. One therefore must either assume a connection between a lexical item and a certain phrasal configuration as in Croft's approach (2003) and in LTAG or assume our lexical variant. In a Minimalist setting the right set of features must be specified lexically to ensure the presence of the right case assigning functional heads. This is basically similar to the lexical valence structures we are proposing here, except that it needlessly introduces various problems discussed above, such as the problem of coordination raised in Section 21.2.1.

21.4 Relations between constructions

On the lexical rules approach, word forms are related by lexical rules: a verb stem can be related to a verb with finite inflection and to a passive verb form; verbs can be converted to adjectives or nouns; and so on. The lexical argument structure accompanies the word and can be manipulated by the lexical rule. In this section we consider what can replace such rules within a phrasal or ASC approach.

21.4.1 Inheritance hierarchies for constructions

For each valence structure that the lexicalist associates with a root lexeme (transitive, ditransitive, etc.), the phrasal approach requires multiple phrasal constructions, one to replace each lexical rule or combination of lexical rules that can apply to the word. Taking ditransitives, for example, the phrasal approach requires an active-ditransitive construction, a passive-ditransitive construction, and so on, to replace the output of every lexical rule or combination of lexical rules applied to a ditransitive verb. (Thus Bergen & Chang (2005: 169–170) assume an active-ditransitive and a passive-ditransitive construction and Kallmeyer & Osswald (2012: 171–172) assume active and passive variants of the transitive construction.) On that view some of the active voice constructions for German would be:

(76)   a. Nom V
       b. Nom Acc V
       c. Nom Dat V
       d. Nom Dat Acc V

The passive voice constructions corresponding to (76) would be:

(77)   a. V V-Aux
       b. Nom V V-Aux
       c. Dat V V-Aux
       d. Dat Nom V V-Aux

Merely listing all these constructions is not only uneconomical but fails to capture the obvious systematic relation between active and passive constructions. Since phrasalists reject both lexical rules and transformations, they need an alternative way to relate phrasal configurations and thereby explain the regular relation between active and passive. The only proposals to date involve the use of inheritance hierarchies, so let us examine them.

Researchers working in various frameworks, both with lexical and phrasal orientation, have tried to develop inheritance-based analyses that could capture the relation between valence patterns such as those in (76) and (77) (see for instance Kay & Fillmore 1999: 12; Michaelis & Ruppenhofer 2001: Chapter 4; Candito 1996; Clément & Kinyon 2003: 188; Kallmeyer & Osswald 2012: 171–172; Koenig 1999: Chapter 3; Davis & Koenig 2000; Kordoni 2001 for proposals in CxG, TAG, and HPSG). The idea is that a single representation (lexical or phrasal, depending on the theory) can inherit properties from multiple constructions. In a phrasal approach the description of the pattern in (76b) inherits from the transitive and the active construction and the description of (77b) inherits from both the transitive and the passive constructions. Figure 21.5 illustrates the inheritance-based lexical approach: a lexical entry for a verb such as *read* or *eat* is combined with either an active or passive representation. The respective representations for the active and passive are responsible for the expression of the arguments. As was already discussed in

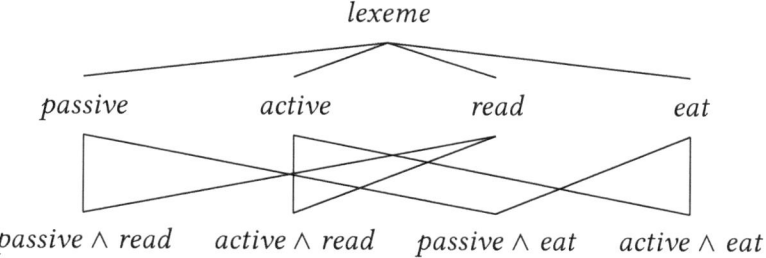

Figure 21.5: Inheritance Hierarchy for active and passive

Section 10.2, inheritance-based analyses cannot account for multiple changes in valence as for instance the combination of passive and impersonal construction that can be observed in languages like Lithuanian (Timberlake 1982: Section 5), Irish (Noonan 1994), and Turkish (Özkaragöz 1986). Özkaragöz's Turkish examples are repeated here with the original glossing as (78) for convenience:

(78) a. Bu şato-da   boğ-ul-un-ur.   (Turkish)
         this château-LOC strangle-PASS-PASS-AOR
         'One is strangled (by one) in this château.'

      b. Bu oda-da   döv-ül-ün-ür.
         this room-LOC hit-PASS-PASS-AOR
         'One is beaten (by one) in this room.'

      c. Harp-te   vur-ul-un-ur.
         war-LOC shoot-PASS-PASS-AOR
         'One is shot (by one) in war.'

Another example from Section 10.2 that cannot be handled with inheritance is multiple causativization in Turkish. Turkish allows double and even triple causativization (Lewis 1967: 146):

21.4 Relations between constructions

(79) Öl-dür-t-tür-t- (Turkish)
'to cause somebody to cause somebody to kill somebody'

An inheritance-based analysis would not work, since inheriting the same information several times does not add anything new. Krieger & Nerbonne (1993) make the same point with respect to derivational morphology in cases like *preprepreversion*: inheriting information about the prefix *pre-* twice or more often, does not add anything.

So assuming phrasal models, the only way to capture the generalization with regard to (76) and (77) seems to be to assume GPSG-like metarules that relate the constructions in (76) to the ones in (77). If the constructions are lexically linked as in LTAG, the respective mapping rules would be lexical rules. For approaches that combine LTAG with the Goldbergian plugging idea such as the one by Kallmeyer & Osswald (2012) one would have to have extended families of trees that reflect the possibility of having additional arguments and would have to make sure that the right morphological form is inserted into the respective trees. The morphological rules would be independent of the syntactic structures in which the derived verbal lexemes could be used. One would have to assume two independent types of rules: GPSG-like metarules that operate on trees and morphological rules that operate on stems and words. We believe that this is an unnecessary complication and apart from being complicated the morphological rules would not be acceptable as form-meaning pairs in the CxG sense since one aspect of the form namely that additional arguments are required is not captured in these morphological rules. If such morphological rules were accepted as proper constructions then there would not be any reason left to require that the arguments have to be present in a construction in order for it to be recognizable, and hence, the lexical approach would be accepted.[38]

Inheritance hierarchies are the main explanatory device in Croft's Radical Construction Grammar (Croft 2001). He also assumes phrasal constructions and suggests representing these in a taxonomic network (an inheritance hierarchy). He assumes that every idiosyncrasy of a linguistic expression is represented on its own node in this kind of network. Figure 21.6 shows part of the hierarchy he assumes for sentences. There are sentences with intransitive verbs and sentences with transitive verbs. Sentences with the form [Sbj kiss Obj] are special instances of the construction [Sbj TrVerb Obj]. The [Sbj kick Obj] construction also has further sub-constructions, namely the constructions [Sbj kick the bucket] and [Subj kick the habit]. Since constructions are always pairs of form and meaning, this gives rise to a problem: in a normal sentence with *kick*, there is a kicking relation between the subject and the object of *kick*. This is not the case for the idiomatic use of *kick* in (80):

(80) He kicked the bucket.

This means that there cannot be a normal inheritance relation between the [Sbj kick Obj] and the [Sbj kick the bucket] construction. Instead, only parts of the information may be inherited from the [Sbj kick Obj] construction. The other parts are redefined by the sub-construction. This kind of inheritance is referred to as *default inheritance*.

---

[38] Compare the discussion of *Totschießen* 'shoot dead' in example (94) below.

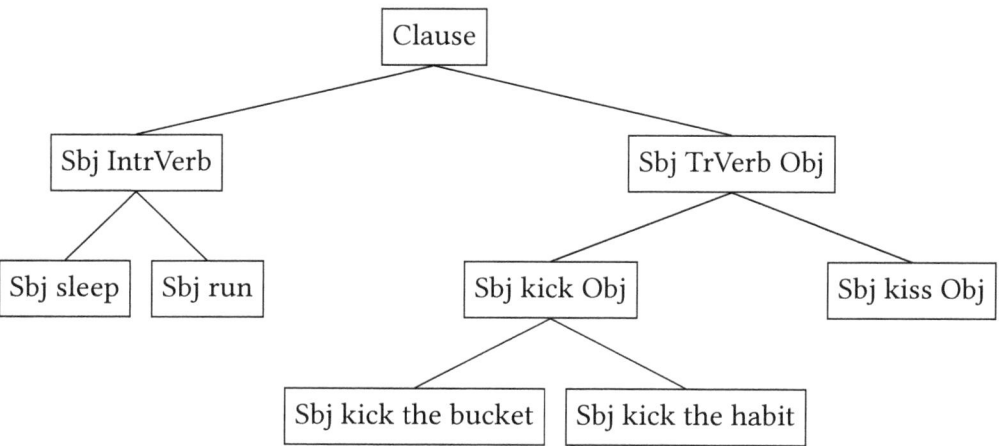

Figure 21.6: Classification of phrasal patterns in Croft (2001: 26)

kick the bucket is a rather fixed expression, that is, it is not possible to passivize it or front parts of it without losing the idiomatic reading (Nunberg, Sag & Wasow 1994: 508). However, this is not true for all idioms. As Nunberg, Sag & Wasow (1994: 510) have shown, there are idioms that can be passivized (81a) as well as realizations of idioms where parts of idioms occur outside of the clause (81b).

(81) a. The beans were spilled by Pat.
 b. The strings [that Pat pulled] got Chris the job.

The problem is now that one would have to assume two nodes in the inheritance hierarchy for idioms that can undergo passivization since the realization of the constituents is different in active and passive variants but the meaning is nevertheless idiosyncratic. The relation between the active and passive form would not be captured. Kay (2002) has proposed an algorithm for computing objects (Construction-like objects = CLOs) from hierarchies that then license active and passive variants. As I have shown in Müller (2006: Section 3), this algorithm does not deliver the desired results and it is far from straightforward to improve it to the point that it actually works. Even if one were to adopt the changes I proposed, there are still phenomena that cannot be described using inheritance hierarchies (see Section 10.2 in this book).

A further interesting point is that the verbs have to be explicitly listed in the constructions. This begs the question of how constructions should be represented where the verbs are used differently. If a new node in the taxonomic network is assumed for cases like (82), then Goldberg's criticism of lexical analyses that assume several lexical entries for a verb that can appear in various constructions[39] will be applicable here: one would have to assume constructions for every verb and every possible usage of that verb.

---

[39] Note the terminology: I used the word *lexical entry* rather than *lexical item*. The HPSG analysis uses lexical rules that correspond to Goldberg's templates. What Goldberg criticizes is lexical rules that relate lexical entries, not lexical rules that licence new lexical items, which may be stored or not. HPSG takes the latter approach to lexical rules. See Section 9.2.

21.4 Relations between constructions

(82) He kicked the bucket into the corner.

For sentences with negation, Croft assumes the hierarchy with multiple inheritance given in Figure 21.7. The problem with this kind of representation is that it remains

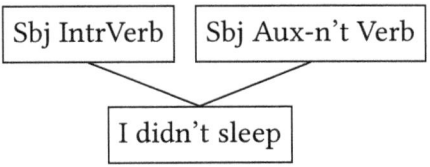

Figure 21.7: Interaction of phrasal patterns following Croft (2001: 26)

unclear as to how the semantic embedding of the verb meaning under negation can be represented. If all constructions are pairs of form and meaning, then there would have to be a semantic representation for [Sbj IntrVerb] (CONT value or SEM value). Similarly, there would have to be a meaning for [Sbj Aux-n't Verb]. The problem now arises that the meaning of [Sbj IntrVerb] has to be embedded under the meaning of the negation and this cannot be achieved directly using inheritance since X and not(X) are incompatible. There is a technical solution to this problem using auxiliary features. Since there are a number of interactions in grammars of natural languages, this kind of analysis is highly implausible if one claims that features are a direct reflection of observable properties of linguistic objects. For a more detailed discussion of approaches with classifications of phrasal patterns, see Müller (2010b) as well as Müller (2007a: Section 18.3.2.2) and for the use of auxiliary features in inheritance-based analyses of the lexicon, see Müller (2007a: Section 7.5.2.2).

Figure 21.8 shows Ziem & Lasch's hierarchy for German sentences with the verbs *lachen* 'laugh', *weinen* 'cry', *drücken* 'push', *mögen* 'like' that is similar to Croft's hierarchy in spirit (Ziem & Lasch 2013: 97). Things that I mentioned with respect to Croft's

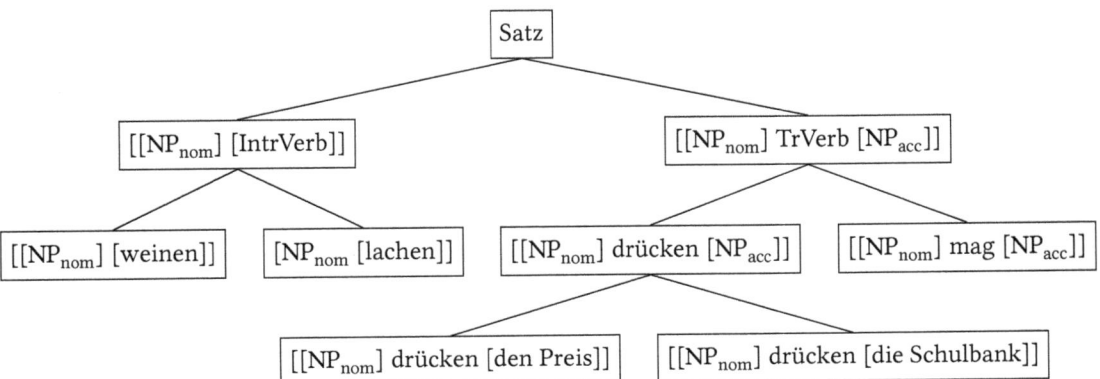

Figure 21.8: Inheritance hierarchy for clauses by Ziem & Lasch (2013: 97)

hierarchy also apply to this hierarchy for German and in fact they demonstrate the problems even more clearly. The idiomatic usages of *den Preis drücken* 'to beat down the price'

21 Phrasal vs. lexical analyses

and *die Schulbank drücken* 'to go to school' are not as fixed as the hierarchy seems to suggest. For example, *den Preis drücken* may appear with an indefinite article and there may be NP-internal modification:

(83)   a. Einen solch guten Preis kann man nur schwer weiter drücken.
          a   such good price can one only difficult further press
          'It is hardly possible to beat down such a good price even further.'
       b. So   kann man den schon recht guten Preis weiter drücken.
          this.way can one the yet   right good price further press
          'This way the rather good price can be reduced even further.'

Note also that it would be wrong to claim that all instances of the *den Preis drücken* involve the realization of an NP with nominative case.

(84)   Einen solchen Preis zu drücken ist nicht leicht.
       a   such   price to press is not easy
       'It is not easy to beat down such a good price.'

Since Construction Grammar does not use empty elements, (84) cannot be explained without the assumption of a separate phrasal construction, one without an NP[*nom*].

So what has to be said about the special usage of *drücken* 'to press' is that *drücken* has to cooccur with an NP (definite or indefinite) containing *Preis* 'price'. If one insists on a phrasal representation like the one in Figure 21.8, one has to explain how the clauses represented in this figure are related to other clauses in which the NP contains an adjective. One would be forced to assume relations between complex linguistic objects (basically something equivalent to transformations with the power that was assumed in the 50ies, see p. 86) or one would have to assume that *den Preis* 'the price' is not a more specific description of the NP[*acc*] but rather corresponds to some underspecified representation that allows the integration of adjectives between determiner and noun (see the discussion of the phrasal lexical item in (40) on p. 332. A third way to capture the relation between *den Preis drücken* 'reduce the price' and *den guten Preis drücken* 'reduce the good price' would be to assume a TAG-style grammar that can take a tree, break it up and insert an adjective in the middle. I never saw a discussion of these issues anywhere in the literature. Hierarchies like the ones in Figure 21.6 and Figure 21.8 seem to classify some attested examples but they do not say anything about general grammar. Note for instance, that (83a) differs from the representation in Figure 21.8 by having an additional modal verb and by having the NP containing *Preis* fronted. Such frontings can be nonlocal. How is this accounted for? If the assumption is that the elements in Figure 21.8 are not ordered, what would be left of the original constructional motivation? If the assumptions that elements of the phrasal constructions may be discontinuous, what are the restrictions on this (see Section 10.6.4.7 and Section 11.7.1)? The alternative to classifying (some of the) possible phrases is the hierarchy of lexical types given in Figure 21.9 on the facing page. The respective lexical items have valence specifications that allow them to be used in certain configurations: arguments can be scrambled, can be extracted, passivization lexical rules may apply and so on.

21.4 Relations between constructions

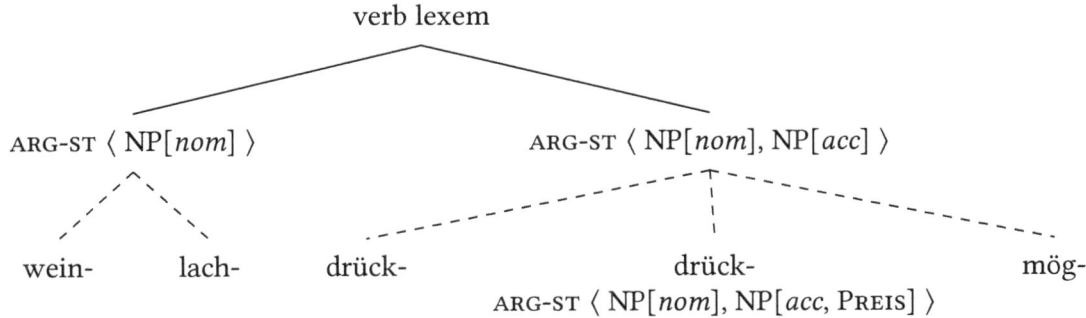

Figure 21.9: Lexical alternative to inheritance hierarchy in Figure 21.8

21.4.2 Mappings between different levels of representations

Culicover & Jackendoff (2005: Chapter 6.3) suggest that passive should be analyzed as one of several possible mappings from the Grammatical Function tier to the surface realization of arguments. Surface realizations of referential arguments can be NPs in a certain case, with certain agreement properties, or in a certain position. While such analyses that work by mapping elements with different properties onto different representations are common in theories like LFG and HPSG (Koenig 1999; Bouma, Malouf & Sag 2001), a general property of these analyses is that one needs one level of representation per interaction of phenomena (ARG-ST, SEM-ARG, ADD-ARG in Koenig's proposal, ARG-ST, DEPS, SPR, COMPS in Bouma, Malouf and Sag's proposal). This was discussed extensively in Müller (2007a: Section 7.5.2.2) with respect to extensions that would be needed for Koenig's analysis.

Since Culicover and Jackendoff argue for a phrasal model, we will discuss their proposal here. Culicover and Jackendoff assume a multilayered model in which semantic representations are linked to grammatical functions, which are linked to tree positions. Figure 21.10 shows an example for an active sentence. GF stands for Grammatical Func-

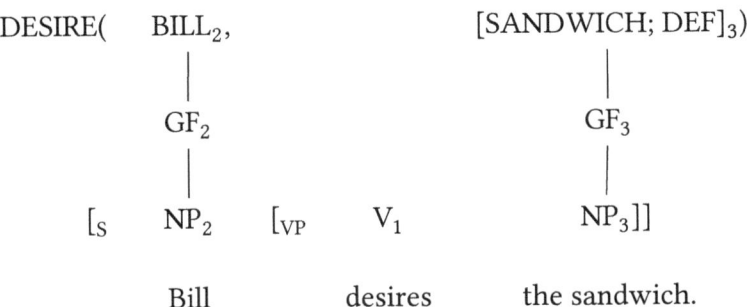

Figure 21.10: Linking grammatical functions to tree positions: active

tion. Culicover & Jackendoff (2005: 204) explicitly avoid names like Subject and Object since this is crucial for their analysis of the passive to work. They assume that the first

643

GF following a bracket is the subject of the clause the bracket corresponds to (p. 195–196) and hence has to be mapped to an appropriate tree position in English. Note that this view of grammatical functions and obliqueness does not account for subjectless sentences that are possible in some languages, for instance in German.[40]

Regarding the passive, the authors write:

> we wish to formulate the passive not as an operation that deletes or alters part of the argument structure, but rather as a piece of structure in its own right that can be unified with the other independent pieces of the sentence. The result of the unification is an alternative licensing relation between syntax and semantics. (Culicover & Jackendoff 2005: 203)

They suggest the following representation of the passive:

(85) $[GF_i > [GF \ldots]]_k \Leftrightarrow [\ldots V_k + \text{pass} \ldots (\text{by NP}_i) \ldots]_k$

The italicized parts are the normal structure of the sentence and the non-italicized parts are an overlay on the normal structure, that is, additional constraints that have to hold in passive sentences. Figure 21.11 shows the mapping of the example discussed above that corresponds to the passive.

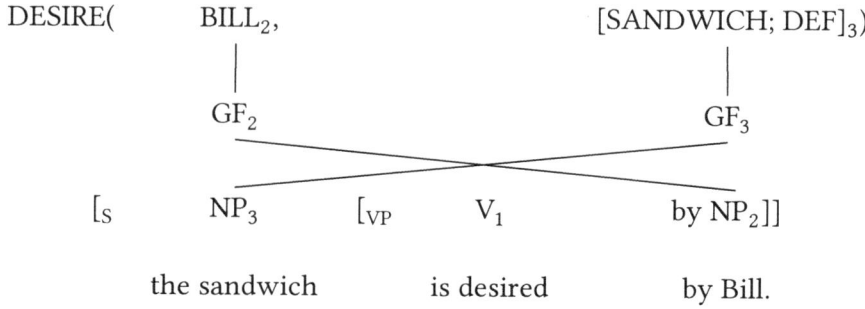

Figure 21.11: Linking grammatical functions to tree positions: passive

Although Culicover and Jackendoff emphasize the similarity between their approach and Relational Grammar (Perlmutter 1983), there is an important difference: in Relational Grammar additional levels (strata) can be stipulated if additional remappings are needed. In Culicover and Jackendoff's proposal there is no additional level. This causes problems for the analysis of languages which allow for multiple argument alternations. Examples from Turkish were provided in (78). Approaches that assume that the personal passive is the unification of a general structure with a passive-specific structure will not be able to capture this, since they committed to a certain structure too early. The problem for approaches that state syntactic structure for the passive is that such a structure, once stated, cannot be modified. Culicover and Jackendoff's proposal works in this respect

---

[40]Of course one could assume empty expletive subjects, as was suggested by Grewendorf (1993: 1311), but empty elements and especially those without meaning are generally avoided in the constructionist literature. See Müller (2010a: Section 3.4, Section 11.1.1.3) for further discussion.

21.4 Relations between constructions

since there are no strong constraints in the right-hand side of their constraint in (85). But there is a different problem: when passivization is applied the second time, it has to apply to the innermost bracket, that is, the result of applying (85) should be:

(86) $[GF_i > [GF_j \ldots]]_k \Leftrightarrow [\ldots V_k + \text{pass} \ldots (\text{by NP}_i) \ldots (\text{by NP}_j) \ldots]_k$

This cannot be done with unification, since unification checks for compatibility and since the first application of passive was possible it would be possible for the second time as well. Dots in representations are always dangerous and in the example at hand one would have to make sure that NP_i and NP_j are distinct, since the statement in (85) just says there has to be a *by*-PP somewhere. What is needed instead of unification would be something that takes a GF representation and searches for the outermost bracket and then places a bracket to the left of the next GF. But this is basically a rule that maps one representation onto another one, just like lexical rules do.

If Culicover and Jackendoff want to stick to a mapping analysis, the only option to analyze the data seems to be to assume an additional level for impersonal passives from which the mapping to phrase structure is done. In the case of Turkish sentences like (87), which is a personal passive, the mapping to this level would be the identity function.

(87)   Arkadaş-ım bu oda-da   döv-ül-dü.
       friend-my this room-LOC hit-PASS-AOR
       'My friend is beaten (by one) in this room.'

In the case of passivization + impersonal construction, the correct mappings would be implemented by two mappings between the three levels that finally result in a mapping as the one that is seen in (78b), repeated here as (88) for convenience.

(88)   Bu oda-da   döv-ül-ün-ür.
       this room-LOC hit-PASS-PASS-AOR
       'One is beaten (by one) in this room.'

Note that passivization + impersonal construction is also problematic for purely inheritance based approaches. What all these approaches can suggest though is that they just stipulate four different relations between argument structure and phrase structure: active, passive, impersonal construction, passive + impersonal construction. But this misses the fact that (88) is an impersonal variant of the passive in (87).

In contrast, the lexical rule-based approach suggested by Müller (2003b) does not have any problems with such multiple alternations: the application of the passivization lexical rule suppresses the least oblique argument and provides a lexical item with the argument structure of a personal passive. Then the impersonal lexical rule applies and suppresses the now least oblique argument (the object of the active clause). The result is impersonal constructions without any arguments as the one in (88).

21.4.3 Is there an alternative to lexical rules?

In this section we have reviewed the attempts to replace lexical rules with methods of relating constructions. These attempts have not been successful, in our assessment. We believe that the essential problem with them is that they fail to capture the derivational character of the relationship between certain word forms. Alternations signaled by passive voice and causative morphology are relatively simple and regular when formulated as operations on lexical valence structures that have been abstracted from their phrasal context. But non-transformational rules or systems formulated on the phrasal structures encounter serious problems that have not yet been solved.

21.5 Further problems for phrasal approaches

Müller (2006) discussed the problems shared by proposals that assume phrasal constructions to be a fixed configuration of adjacent material as for instance the one by Goldberg & Jackendoff (2004). I showed that many argument structure constructions allow great flexibility as far as the order of their parts is concerned. Back then I discussed resultative constructions in their interaction with free datives, passive and other valence changing phenomena and showed that for all these constructions licensed by such interactions the construction parts can be scrambled, the verb can appear in different positions, arguments can be extracted and so on. The following subsection discusses particle verbs, which pose similar problems for theories that assume a phrasal construction with fixed order of verb and particle.

21.5.1 Particle verbs and commitment to phrase structure configurations

A general problem of approaches that assume phrase structure configurations paired with meaning is that the construction may appear in different contexts: the construction parts may be involved in derivational morphology (as discussed in the previous subsection) or the construction parts may be involved in dislocations. A clear example of the latter type is the phrasal analysis of particle verbs that was suggested by Booij (2002: Section 2; 2012) and Blom (2005), working in the frameworks of Construction Grammar and LFG, respectively. The authors working on Dutch and German assume that particle verbs are licensed by phrasal constructions (pieces of phrase structure) in which the first slot is occupied by the particle.

(89) $[X [ ]_V]_{V'}$ where X = P, Adv, A, or N

Examples for specific Dutch constructions are:

(90) a. $[af [ ]_V]_{V'}$
      b. $[door [ ]_V]_{V'}$
      c. $[op [ ]_V]_{V'}$

This suggestion comes with the claim that particles cannot be fronted. This claim is made frequently in the literature, but it is based on introspection and wrong for languages like Dutch and German. On Dutch see Hoeksema (1991: 19), on German, Müller (2002a,c; 2003c; 2007c).[41] A German example is given in (91); several pages of attested

---

[41] Some more fundamental remarks on introspection and corpus data with relation to particle verbs can also be found in Müller (2007c) and Meurers & Müller (2009).

examples can be found in the cited references and some more complex examples will also be discussed in Section 21.7.3 on page 659.

(91) *Los* damit *geht* es schon am 15. April.⁴²
 PART there.with goes it already at.the 15 April

 'It already starts on April the 15th.'

Particle verbs are mini-idioms. So the conclusion is that idiomatic expressions that allow for a certain flexibility in order should not be represented as phrasal configurations describing adjacent elements. For some idioms, a lexical analysis along the lines of Sag (2007) seems to be required.⁴³ The issue of particle verbs will be taken up in Section 21.7.3 again, where we discuss evidence for/against phrasal analyses from neuroscience.

21.6 Arguments from language acquisition

The question whether language acquisition is pattern-based and hence can be seen as evidence for the phrasal approach has already been touched upon in the Sections 16.3 and 16.4. It was argued that constructions can be realized discontinuously in coordinations and hence it is the notion of dependency that has to be acquired; acquiring simple continuous patterns is not sufficient.

Since the present discussion about phrasal and lexical approaches deals with specific proposals, I would like to add two more special subsections: Section 21.6.1 deals with the recognizability of constructions and Section 21.6.2 discusses specific approaches to coordination in order to demonstrate how frameworks deal with the discontinuous realization of constructions.

21.6.1 Recognizability of constructions

I think that a purely pattern-based approach is weakened by the existence of examples like (92):

(92) a. John tried to sleep.
 b. John tried to be loved.

Although no argument of *sleep* is present in the phrase *to sleep* and neither a subject nor an object is realized in the phrase *to be loved*, both phrases are recognized as phrases containing an intransitive and a transitive verb, respectively.⁴⁴

The same applies to arguments that are supposed to be introduced/licensed by a phrasal construction: in (93) the resultative construction is passivized and then embedded under a control verb, resulting in a situation in which only the result predicate (*tot* 'dead')

---

⁴²taz, 01.03.2002, p. 8, see also Müller (2005c: 313).

⁴³Note also that the German example is best described as a clause with a complex internally structured constituent in front of the finite verb and it is doubtful whether linearization-based proposals like the ones in Kathol (1995: 244–248) or Wetta (2011) can capture this. See also the discussion of multiple frontings in connection to Dependency Grammar in Section 11.7.1.

⁴⁴Constructionist theories do not assume empty elements. Of course, in the GB framework the subject would be realized by an empty element. So it would be in the structure, although inaudible.

and the matrix verb (*geschossen* 'shot') are realized overtly within the local clause, bracketed here:

(93) Der kranke Mann wünschte sich, [totgeschossen zu werden].⁴⁵
 the sick man wished SELF dead.shot to be
 'The sick man wanted to be shot dead.'

Of course passivization and control are responsible for these occurrences, but the important point here is that arguments can remain unexpressed or implicit and nevertheless a meaning usually connected to some overt realization of arguments is present (Müller 2007b: Section 4). So, what has to be acquired by the language learner is that when a result predicate and a main verb are realized together, they contribute the resultative meaning. To take another example, NP arguments that are usually realized in active resultative constructions may remain implicit in nominalizations like the ones in (94):

(94) a. dann scheint uns das Totschießen mindestens ebensoviel Spaß zu machen⁴⁶
 then seems us the dead-shooting at.least as.much fun to make
 'then the shooting dead seems to us to be as least as much fun'

b. Wir lassen heut das Totgeschieße,
 we let today the annoying.repeated.shooting.dead
 Weil man sowas heut nicht tut.
 since one such.thing today not does
 Und wer einen Tag sich ausruht,
 and who a day SELF rests
 Der schießt morgen doppelt gut.⁴⁷
 this shoots tomorrow twice good
 'We do not shoot anybody today, since one does not do this today, and those who rest a day shoot twice as well tomorrow.'

The argument corresponding to the patient of the verb (the one who is shot) can remain unrealized, because of the syntax of nominalizations. The resultative meaning is still understood, which shows that it does not depend upon the presence of a resultative construction involving Subj V Obj and Obl.

21.6.2 Coordination and discontinuousness

The following subsection deals with analyses of coordination in some of the frameworks that were introduced in this book. The purpose of the section is to show that simple phrasal patterns have to be broken up in coordination structures. This was already mentioned in Section 16.3, but I think it is illuminative to have a look at concrete proposals.

---

⁴⁵Müller (2007b: 387).

⁴⁶https://www.elitepartner.de/forum/wie-gehen-die-maenner-mit-den-veraenderten-anspruechen-der-frauen-um-26421-6.html. 26.03.0212.

⁴⁷Gedicht für den Frieden, Oliver Kalkofe, http://www.golyr.de/oliver-kalkofe/songtext-gedicht-fuer-den-frieden-417329.html. 2018-02-20.

21.6 Arguments from language acquisition

In Categorial Grammar, there is a very elegant treatment of coordination (see Steedman 1991). A generalization with regard to so-called symmetric coordination is that two objects with the same syntactic properties are combined to an object with those properties. We have already encountered the relevant data in the discussion of the motivation for feature geometry in HPSG on page 273. Their English versions are repeated below as (95):

(95)   a. the man and the woman
       b. He knows and loves this record.
       c. He is dumb and arrogant.

Steedman (1991) analyzes examples such as those in (95) with a single rule:

(96)   X conj X $\Rightarrow$ X

This rule combines two categories of the same kind with a conjunction in between to form a category that has the same category as the conjuncts.[48] Figure 21.12 shows the analysis of (95a) and Figure 21.13 gives an analysis of the corresponding English example of (95b).

$$\begin{array}{ccccc} \textit{the} & \textit{man} & \textit{and} & \textit{the} & \textit{woman} \\ \hline np/n & n & conj & np/n & n \\ \hline \multicolumn{2}{c}{np} & & \multicolumn{2}{c}{np} \\ \hline \multicolumn{5}{c}{np} \end{array}$$

Figure 21.12: Coordination of two NPs in Categorial Grammar

$$\begin{array}{cccccc} \textit{he} & \textit{knows} & \textit{and} & \textit{loves} & \textit{this} & \textit{record} \\ \hline np & (s\backslash np)/np & conj & (s\backslash np)/np & n/np & n \end{array}$$

Figure 21.13: Coordination of two transitive verbs in Categorial Grammar

If we compare this analysis to the one that would have to be assumed in traditional phrase structure grammars, it becomes apparent what the advantages are: one rule was

---

[48] Alternatively, one could analyze all three examples using a single lexical entry for the conjunction *and*: *and* is a functor that takes a word or phrase of any category to its right and after this combination then needs to be combined with an element of the same category to its left in order to form the relevant category after combining with this second element. This means that the category for *und* would have the form (X\X)/X. This analysis does not require any coordination rules. If one wants to assume, as is common in GB/MP, that every structure has a head, then a headless analysis that assumes a special rule for coordination like the one in (96) would be ruled out.

649

required for the analysis of NP coordination where two NPs are coordinated to form an NP and another was required for the analysis of V coordination. This is not only undesirable from a technical point of view, neither does it capture the basic property of symmetric coordination: two symbols with the same syntactic category are combined with each other.

It is interesting to note that it is possible to analyze phrases such as (97) in this way:

(97) give George a book and Martha a record

In Section 1.3.2.4, we have seen that this kind of sentences is problematic for constituent tests. However, in Categorial Grammar, it is possible to analyze them without any problems if one adopts rules for type raising and composition as Dowty (1988) and Steedman (1991) do. In Section 8.5, we have already seen forward type raising as well as forward and backward composition. In order to analyze (97), one would require backward type raising repeated in (98) and backward composition repeated in (99):

(98) Backward type raising (< T)
X ⇒ T\(T/X)

(99) Backward composition (< B)
Y\Z * X\Y = X\Z

Dowty's analysis of (97) is given in Figure 21.14. vp stands for s\np.

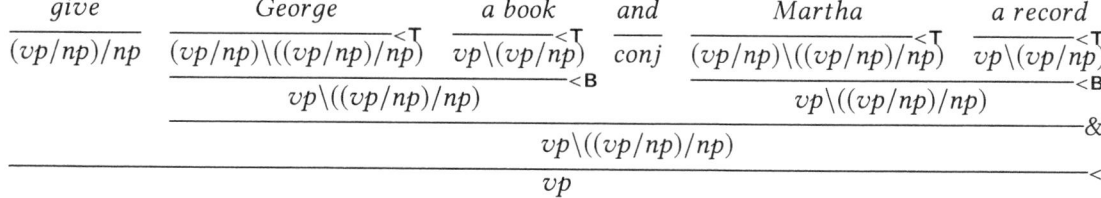

Figure 21.14: Gapping in Categorial Grammar

This kind of type-raising analysis was often criticized because raising categories leads to many different analytical possibilities for simple sentences. For example, one could first combine a type-raised subject with the verb and then combine the resulting constituent with the object. This would mean that we would have a [[S V] O] in addition to the standard [S [V O]] analysis. Steedman (1991) argues that both analyses differ in terms of information structure and it is therefore valid to assume different structures for the sentences in question.

I will not go into these points further here. However, I would like to compare Steedman's lexical approach to phrasal analyses: all approaches that assume that the ditransitive construction represents a continuous pattern encounter a serious problem with the examples discussed above. This can be best understood by considering the TAG analysis of coordination proposed by Sarkar & Joshi (1996). If one assumes that [Sbj TransVerb Obj] or [S [V O]] constitutes a fixed unit, then the trees in Figure 21.15 on the next page form the starting point for the analysis of coordination.

21.6 Arguments from language acquisition

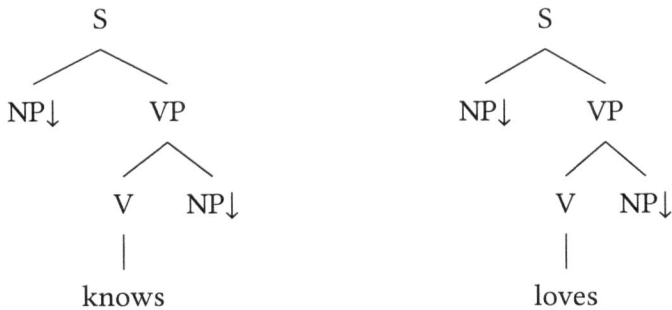

Figure 21.15: Elementary trees for *knows* and *loves*

If one wants to use these trees/constructions for the analysis of (100), there are in principle two possibilities: one assumes that two complete sentences are coordinated or alternatively, one assumes that some nodes are shared in a coordinated structure.

(100) He knows and loves this record.

Abeillé (2006) has shown that it is not possible to capture all the data if one assumes that cases of coordination such as those in (100) always involve the coordination of two complete clauses. It is also necessary to allow for lexical coordination of the kind we saw in Steedman's analysis (see also Section 4.6.3). Sarkar & Joshi (1996) develop a TAG analysis in which nodes are shared in coordinate structures. The analysis of (100) can be seen in Figure 21.16. The subject and object nodes are only present once in this figure.

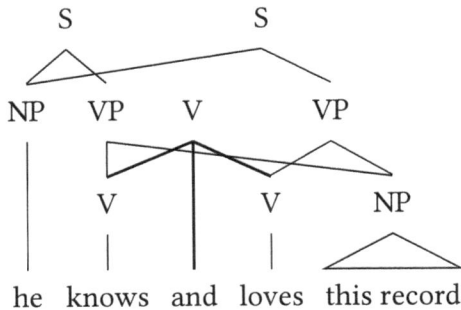

Figure 21.16: TAG analysis of *He knows and loves this record*.

The S nodes of both elementary trees both dominate the *he* NP. In the same way, the object NP node belongs to both VPs. The conjunction connects two verbs indicated by the thick lines. Sarkar and Joshi provide an algorithm that determines which nodes are to be shared. The structure may look strange at first, but for TAG purposes, it is not the derived tree but rather the derivation tree that is important, since this is the one that is used to compute the semantic interpretation. The authors show that the derivation trees

651

21 Phrasal vs. lexical analyses

for the example under discussion and even more complex examples can be constructed correctly.

In theories such as HPSG and LFG where structure building is, as in Categorial Grammar, driven by valence, the above sentence is unproblematic: both verbs are conjoined and then the combination behaves like a simple verb. The analysis of this is given in Figure 21.17. This analysis is similar to the Categorial Grammar analysis in Figure 21.13.[49] With Goldberg's plugging analysis one could also adopt this approach to coordination:

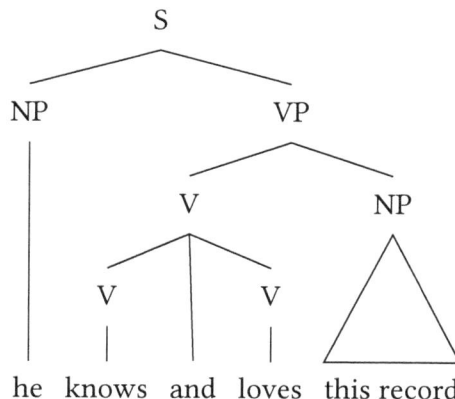

Figure 21.17: Selection-based analysis of *He knows and loves this record.* in tree notation

here, *knows* and *loves* would first be plugged into a coordination construction and the result would then be plugged into the transitive construction. Exactly how the semantics of *knows and loves* is combined with that of the transitive construction is unclear since the meaning of this phrase is something like *and'*(*know'*(x, y), *love'*(x, y)), that is, a complex event with at least two open argument slots x and y (and possibly additionally an event and a world variable depending on the semantic theory that is used). Goldberg would probably have to adopt an analysis such as the one in Figure 21.16 in order to maintain the plugging analysis.

Croft would definitely have to adopt the TAG analysis since the verb is already present in his constructions. For the example in (97), both Goldberg and Croft would have to draw from the TAG analysis in Figure 21.18 on the facing page.
The consequence of this is that one requires discontinuous constituents. Since coordination allows a considerable number of variants, there can be gaps between all arguments of constructions. An example with a ditransitive verb is given in (101):

(101) He gave George and sent Martha a record.

See Crysmann (2008) and Beavers & Sag (2004) for HPSG analyses that assume discontinuous constituents for particular coordination structures.

---

[49] A parallel analysis in Dependency Grammar is possible as well. Tesnière's original analysis was different though. See Section 11.6.2.1 for discussion.

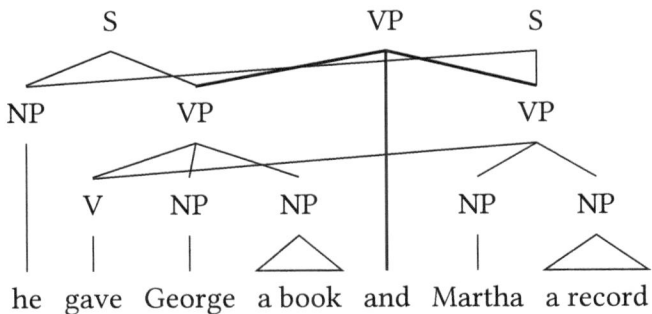

Figure 21.18: TAG analysis of *He gave George a book and Martha a record*.

The result of these considerations is that the argument that particular elements occur next to each other and that this occurrence is associated with a particular meaning is considerably weakened. What competent speakers do acquire is the knowledge that heads must occur with their arguments somewhere in the utterance and that all the requirements of the heads involved have to somehow be satisfied (θ-Criterion, coherence/completeness, empty SPR and COMPS list). The heads themselves need not necessarily occur directly adjacent to their arguments. See the discussion in Section 16.3 about pattern-based models of language acquisition.

The computation of the semantic contribution of complex structures such as those in Figure 21.18 is by no means trivial. In TAG, there is the derivation tree in addition to the derived tree that can then be used to compute the semantic contribution of a linguistic object. Construction Grammar does not have this separate level of representation. The question of how the meaning of the sentences discussed here is derived from their component parts still remains open for phrasal approaches.

Concluding the section on language acquisition, we assume that a valence representation is the result of language acquisition, since this is necessary for establishing the dependency relations in various possible configurations in an utterance. See also Behrens (2009: 439) for a similar conclusion.

21.7 Arguments from psycho- and neurolinguistics

This section has three parts: in the first part we compare approaches which assume that valence alternations are modeled by lexical rules, underspecification, or disjunctions with phrasal approaches. In Subsection 21.7.2 part we discuss approaches to light verb constructions and Subsection 21.7.3 is devoted to neurolinguistic findings.

21.7.1 Lexical rules vs. phrasal constructions

Goldberg (1995: Section 1.4.5) uses evidence from psycholinguistic experiments to argue against lexical approaches that use lexical rules to account for argument structure alternations: Carlson & Tanenhaus (1988) showed that sentences with true lexical ambiguity like those in (102) and sentences with two verbs with the same core meaning have different processing times.

(102) a. Bill set the alarm clock onto the shelf.
b. Bill set the alarm clock for six.

(103) a. Bill loaded the truck onto the ship.
b. Bill loaded the truck with bricks.

Errors due to lexical ambiguity cause a bigger increase in processing time than errors in the use of the same verb. Experiments showed that there was a bigger difference in processing times for the sentences in (102) than for the sentences in (103). The difference in processing times between (103a) and (103b) would be explained by different preferences for phrasal constructions. In a lexicon-based approach one could explain the difference by assuming that one lexical item is more basic, that is, stored in the mental dictionary and the other is derived from the stored one. The application of lexical rules would be time consuming, but since the lexical items are related, the overall time consumption is smaller than the time needed to process two unrelated items (Müller 2002a: 405).

Alternatively one could assume that the lexical items for both valence patterns are the result of lexical rule applications. As with the phrasal constructions, the lexical rules would have different preferences. This shows that the lexical approach can explain the experimental results as well, so that they do not force us to prefer phrasal approaches.

Goldberg (1995: 18) claims that lexical approaches have to assume two variants of *load* with different meaning and that this would predict that *load* alternations would behave like two verbs that really have absolutely different meanings. The experiments discussed above show that such predictions are wrong and hence lexical analyses would be falsified. However, as was shown in Müller (2010a: Section 11.11.8.2), the argumentation contains two flaws: let's assume that the construction meaning of the construction that licenses (103a) is C_1 and the construction meaning of the construction that licenses (103b) is C_2. Under such assumptions the semantic contribution of the two lexical items in the lexical analysis would be (104). load(…) is the contribution of the verb that would be assumed in phrasal analyses.

(104) a. load (onto): $C_1 \wedge$ load(…)
b. load (with): $C_2 \wedge$ load(…)

(104) shows that the lexical items partly share their semantic contribution. We hence predict that the processing of the dispreferred argument realization of *load* is simpler than the dispreferred meaning of *set*: in the latter case a completely new verb has to be activated while in the first case parts of the meaning are activated already.[50]

Goldberg (1995: 107) argues against lexical rule-based approaches for locative alternations like (105), since according to her such approaches have to assume that one of the verb forms has to be the more basic form.

---

[50] See also Croft (2003: 64–65) for a brief rejection of Goldberg's interpretation of the experiment that corresponds to what is said here.

21.7 Arguments from psycho- and neurolinguistics

(105) a. He loaded hay onto the wagon.
　　　b. He loaded the wagon with hay.

She remarks that this is problematic since we do not have clear intuitions about what the basic and what the derived forms are. She argues that the advantage of phrasal approaches is that various constructions can be related to each other without requiring the assumption that one of the constructions is more basic than the other. There are two phrasal patterns and the verb is used in one of the two patterns. This criticism can be addressed in two ways: first one could introduce two lexical types (for instance *onto-verb* and *with-verb*) into a type hierarchy. The two types correspond to two valence frames that are needed for the analysis of (105a) and (105b). These types can have a common supertype (*onto-with-verb*) which is relevant for all *spray/load* verbs. One of the subtypes or the respective lexical item of the verb is the preferred one. This corresponds to a disjunction in the lexicon, while the phrasal approach assumes a disjunction in the set of phrasal constructions.

A variant of this approach is to assume that the lexical description of *load* just contains the supertype describing all *spray/load* verbs. Since model theoretic approaches assume that all structures that are models of utterances contain only maximally specific types (see for instance King (1999) and Pollard & Sag (1994: 21)), it is sufficient to say about verbs like *load* that they are of type *onto-with-verb*. As this type has exactly two subtypes, *load* has to be either *onto-verb* or *with-verb* in an actual model.[51]

A second option is to stick with lexical rules and to assume a single representation for the root of a verb that is listed in the lexicon. In addition, one assumes two lexical rules that map this basic lexical item onto other items that can be used in syntax after being inflected. The two lexical rules can be described by types that are part of a type hierarchy and that have a common supertype. This would capture commonalities between the lexical rules. We therefore have the same situation as with phrasal constructions (two lexical rules vs. two phrasal constructions). The only difference is that the action is one level deeper in the lexical approach, namely in the lexicon (Müller 2002a: 405–406).

The argumentation with regard to the processing of resultative constructions like (106c) is parallel:

(106) a. He drinks.
　　　b. He drinks the milk.
　　　c. He drinks the pub empty.

When humans parse a sentence they build up structure incrementally. If one hears a word that is incompatible with the current hypothesis, the parsing process breaks down or the current hypothesis is revised. In (106c) *the pub* does not correspond to the normal transitive use of *drink*, so the respective hypothesis has to be revised. In the phrasal approach the resultative construction would have to be used instead of the transitive construction. In the lexical analysis the lexical item that is licensed by the resultative

---

[51]This analysis does not allow the specification of verb specific preferences for one of the realization patterns since the lexicon contains the general type only.

lexical rule would have to be used rather than the bivalent one. Building syntactic structure and lexicon access in general place different demands on our processing capacities. However, when (106c) is parsed, the lexical items for *drink* are active already, we only have to use a different one. It is currently unclear to us whether psycholinguistic experiments can differentiate between the two approaches, but it seems to be unlikely.

21.7.2 Light verbs

Wittenberg, Jackendoff, Kuperberg, Paczynski, Snedeker & Wiese (2014) report on a number of experiments that test predictions made by various approaches to light verb constructions. (107a) shows a typical light verb construction: *take* is a light verb that is combined with the nominal that provides the main predication.

(107) a. take a walk to the park
       b. walk to the park

Wittenberg & Piñango (2011) examined two psychologically plausible theories of light verb constructions. The phrasal approach assumes that light verb constructions are stored objects associated with semantics (Goldberg 2003b). The alternative compositional view assumes that the semantics is computed as a fusion of the semantics of the event noun and the semantics of the light verb (Grimshaw 1997; Butt 2003; Jackendoff 2002; Culicover & Jackendoff 2005; Müller 2010b; Beavers et al. 2008). Since light verb constructions are extremely frequent (Piñango, Mack & Jackendoff 2006; Wittenberg & Piñango 2011: 399), the phrasal approaches assuming that light verb constructions are stored items with the object and verb fixed predict that light verb constructions should be retrievable faster than non-light verb constructions like (108) (Wittenberg & Piñango 2011: 396).

(108) take a frisbee to the park

This is not the case. As Wittenberg and Piñango found, there is no difference in processing at the licensing condition (the noun in VO languages like English and the verb in OV languages like German).

However, Wittenberg & Piñango (2011) found an increased processing load 300ms *after* the light verb construction is processed. The authors explain this by assuming that semantic integration of the noun with the verbal meaning takes place after the syntactic combination. While the syntactic combination is rather fast, the semantic computation takes additional resources and this is measurable at 300ms. The verb contributes aspectual information and integrates the meaning of the nominal element. The semantic roles are fused. The resource consumption effect would not be expected if the complete light verb construction were a stored item that is retrieved together with the complete meaning (p. 404). We can conclude that Wittenberg and Piñango's results are compatible with the lexical proposal, but are incompatible with the phrasal view.

21.7.3 Arguments from neurolinguistics

Pulvermüller, Cappelle & Shtyrov (2013) discuss neurolinguistic facts and relate them to the CxG view of grammar theory. One important finding is that deviant words (lexical items) cause brain responses that differ in polarity from brain responses on incorrect strings of words, that is, syntactic combinations. This suggests that there is indeed an empirical basis for deciding the issue.

Concerning the standard example of the Caused-Motion Construction in (109) the authors write the following:

(109) She sneezed the foam off the cappuccino.[52]

> this constellation of brain activities may initially lead to the co-activation of the verb *sneeze* with the DCNAs for *blow* and thus to the sentence mentioned. Ultimately, such co-activation of a one-place verb and DCNAs associated with other verbs may result in the former one-place verb being subsumed into a three-place verb category and DCNA set, a process which arguably has been accomplished for the verb *laugh* as used in the sequence *laugh NP off the stage*. (Pulvermüller, Cappelle & Shtyrov 2013)

A DCNA is a discrete combinatorial neuronal assembly. Regarding the specifics of DCNAs the authors write that

> Apart from linking categories together, typical DCNAs establish a temporal order between the category members they bind to. DCNAs that do not impose temporal order (thus acting, in principle, as AND units for two constituents) are thought to join together constituents whose sequential order is free or allow for scrambling. (Pulvermüller, Cappelle & Shtyrov 2013: 404)

I believe that this view is entirely compatible with the lexical view outlined above: the lexical item or DCNA requires certain arguments to be present. A lexical rule that relates an intransitive verb to one that can be used in the Caused-Motion Construction is an explicit representation of what it means to activate the valence frame of *blow*.

The authors cite earlier work (Cappelle, Shtyrov & Pulvermüller 2010) and argue that particle verbs are lexical objects, admitting for a discontinuous realization despite their lexical status (p. 21). They restrict their claim to frequently occurring particle verbs. This claim is of course compatible with our assumptions here, but the differences in brain behavior are interesting when it comes to fully productive uses of particle verbs. For instance any semantically appropriate monovalent verb in German can be combined with the aspectual particle *los*: *lostanzen* 'start to dance', *loslachen* 'start to laugh', *lossingen* 'start to sing', ... Similarly, the combination of monovalent verbs with the particle *an* with the reading *directed-towards* is also productive: *anfahren* 'drive towards', *anlachen* 'laugh in the direction of', *ansegeln* 'sail towards', ... (see Stiebels (1996) on various productive patterns). The interesting question is how particle verbs behave that follow these

---
[52] Goldberg (2006: 42).

patterns but occur with low frequency. This is still an open question as far as the experimental evidence is concerned, but as I argue below lexical proposals to particle verbs as the one suggested by Müller (2003c) are compatible with both possible outcomes.

Summarizing the discussion so far, lexical approaches are compatible with the accumulated neurobiological evidence and as far as particle verbs are concerned they seem to be better suited than the phrasal proposals by Booij (2002: Section 2) and Blom (2005) (See Section 21.5.1 for discussion). However, in general, it remains an open question what it means to be a discontinuous lexical item. The idea of discontinuous words is pretty old (Wells 1947), but there have not been many formal accounts of this idea. Nunberg, Sag & Wasow (1994) suggest a representation in a linearization-based framework of the kind that was proposed by Reape (1994) and Kathol (1995: 244–248) and Crysmann (2002) worked out such analyses in detail. Kathol's lexical item for *aufwachen* 'to wake up' is given in (110):

(110) *aufwachen* (following Kathol 1995: 246):

$$\begin{bmatrix} \ldots|\text{HEAD}\ \boxed{1}\ \textit{verb} \\ \ldots|\text{VCOMP}\ \langle\rangle \\ \text{DOM}\ \left\langle \begin{bmatrix} \langle\ \textit{wachen}\ \rangle \\ \ldots|\text{HEAD}\ \boxed{1} \\ \ldots|\text{VCOMP}\ \langle\ \boxed{2}\ \rangle \end{bmatrix} \right\rangle \bigcirc \left\langle \begin{bmatrix} vc \\ \langle\ \textit{auf}\ \rangle \\ \text{SYNSEM}\ \boxed{2}\ \begin{bmatrix} \ldots|\text{HEAD} \begin{bmatrix} \textit{sepref} \\ \text{FLIP}\ - \end{bmatrix} \end{bmatrix} \end{bmatrix} \right\rangle \end{bmatrix}$$

The lexical representation contains the list-valued feature DOM that contains a description of the main verb and the particle (see Section 11.7.2.2 for details). The DOM list is a list that contains the dependents of a head. The dependents can be ordered in any order provided no linearization rule is violated (Reape 1994). The dependency between the particle and the main verb was characterized by the value of the VCOMP feature, which is a valence feature for the selection of arguments that form a complex predicate with their head. The shuffle operator ○ concatenates two lists without specifying an order between the elements of the two lists, that is, both *wachen, auf* and *auf, wachen* are possible. The little marking *vc* is an assignment to a topological field in the clause.

I criticized such linearization-based proposals since it is unclear how analyses that claim that the particle is just linearized in the domain of its verb can account for sentences like (111), in which complex syntactic structures are involved (Müller 2007b). German is a V2 language and the fronting of a constituent into the position before the finite verb is usually described as some sort of nonlocal dependency; that is, even authors who favor linearization-based analyses do not assume that the initial position is filled by simple reordering of material (Kathol 2000; Müller 1999b; 2002a; Bjerre 2006).[53]

---

[53]Kathol (1995: Section 6.3) working in HPSG suggested such an analysis for simple sentences, but later changed his view. Wetta (2011) also working in HPSG assumes a purely linearization-based approach. Similarly Groß & Osborne (2009) working in Dependency Grammar assume that there is a simple dependency structure in simple sentences while there are special mechanisms to account for extraction out of embedded clauses. I argue against such proposals in Müller (2017a) referring to the scope of adjuncts, coordination of simple with complex sentences and Across the Board Extraction and apparent multiple frontings. See also Section 11.7.1.

21.7 Arguments from psycho- and neurolinguistics

(111)   a.   [_vf_ [_mf_ Den Atem] [_vc_ an]]   hielt   die ganze Judenheit.[54]
               the breath   PART held   the whole Jewish.community
          'The whole Jewish community held their breath.'
   b.   [_vf_ [_mf_ Wieder] [_vc_ an]]   treten   auch   die beiden   Sozialdemokraten.[55]
              again   PART kick   also   the two   Social.Democrats
          'The two Social Democrats are also running for office again.'
   c.   [_vf_ [_vc_ Los] [_nf_ damit]]   geht es schon   am   15. April.[56]
              PART   there.with went it already at.the 15 April
          'It already starts on April the 15th.'

The conclusion that has to be drawn from examples like (111) is that particles interact in complex ways with the syntax of sentences. This is captured by the lexical treatment that was suggested in Müller (2002a: Chapter 6) and Müller (2003c): the main verb selects for the verbal particle. By assuming that *wachen* selects for *auf*, the tight connection between verb and particle is represented.[57] Such a lexical analysis provides an easy way to account for fully nontransparent particle verbs like *an-fangen* 'to begin'. However, I also argued for a lexical treatment of transparent particle verbs like *losfahren* 'to start to drive' and *jemanden/etwas anfahren* 'drive directed towards somebody/something'. The analysis involves a lexical rule that licenses a verbal item selecting for an adjunct particle. The particles *an* and *los* can modify verbs and contribute arguments (in the case of *an*) and the particle semantics. This analysis can be shown to be compatible with the neuro-mechanical findings: if it is the case that even transparent particle verb combinations with low frequency are stored, then the rather general lexical rule that I suggested in the works cited above is the generalization of the relation between a large amount of lexical particle verb items and their respective main verb. The individual particle verbs would be special instantiations that have the form of the particle specified as it is also the case for non-transparent particle verbs like *anfangen*. If it should turn out that productive combinations with particle verbs of low frequency cause syntactic reflexes in the brain, this could be explained as well: the lexical rule licenses an item that selects for an adverbial element. This selection would then be seen as parallel to the relation between the determiner and the noun in the NP *der Mut* 'the courage', which Cappelle et al. (2010: 191) discuss as an example of a syntactic combination. Note that this analysis is also compatible with another observation made by Shtyrov, Pihko & Pulvermüller (2005): morphological affixes also cause the lexical reflexes. In my analysis the stem of the main verb is related to another stem that selects for a particle. This stem can be combined with (derivational and inflectional) morphological affixes causing the lexical activation pattern in the brain. After this combination the verb is combined with the particle and the dependency can be either a lexical or a syntactic one, depending on

---

[54] Lion Feuchtwanger, *Jud Süß*, p. 276, quoted from Grubačić (1965: 56).
[55] taz, bremen, 24.05.2004, p. 21.
[56] taz, 01.03.2002, p. 8.
[57] Cappelle et al. (2010: 197) write: "the results provide neurophysiological evidence that phrasal verbs are lexical items. Indeed, the increased activation that we found for existing phrasal verbs, as compared to infelicitous combinations, suggests that a verb and its particle together form one single lexical representation, i. e. a single lexeme, and that a unified cortical memory circuit exists for it, similar to that encoding a single word". I believe that my analysis is compatible with this statement.

the results of the experiments to be carried out. The analysis is compatible with both results.

Note that my analysis allows the principle of lexical integrity to be maintained. I therefore do not follow Cappelle, Shtyrov & Pulvermüller (2010: 198), who claim that they "provide proof that potentially separable multi-word items can nonetheless be word-like themselves, and thus against the validity of a once well-established linguistic principle, the Lexical Integrity Principle". I agree that non-transparent particle verbs are multi-word lexemes, but the existence of multi-word lexemes does not show that syntax has access to the word-internal morphological structure. The parallel between particle verbs and clearly phrasal idioms was discussed in Müller (2002a,c) and it was concluded that idiom-status is irrelevant for the question of wordhood. Since the interaction of clearly phrasal idioms with derivational morphology as evidenced by examples like (112) did not force grammarians to give up on lexical integrity, it can be argued that particle verbs are not convincing evidence for giving up the Lexical Integrity Principle either.[58]

(112)   a. Er hat ins   Gras gebissen.
          he has in.the grass bit

         'He bit the dust.'

     b. „Heath Ledger" kann ich nicht einmal schreiben, ohne   dass mir sein ins
           Heath Ledger can I not even write   without that me his in.the
           Gras-Gebeiße wieder so wahnsinnig leid   tut[59]
           grass.biting again so crazy   sorrow does

         'I cannot even write "Heath Ledger" without being sad again about his biting the dust.'

The example in (112b) involves the discontinuous derivation with the circumfix *Ge- -e* (Lüdeling 2001: Section 3.4.3; Müller 2002a: 324–327, 372–377; Müller 2003c: Section 2.2.1, Section 5.2.1). Still the parts of the idiom *ins Gras beiß-* 'bite the dust' are present and with them the idiomatic reading. See Sag (2007) for a lexical analysis of idioms that can explain examples like (112).

So, while I think that it is impossible to distinguish phrasal and lexical approaches for phenomena where heads are used with different valence patterns (Section 21.7.1), there seem to be ways to test whether patterns with high frequency and strong collocations should be analyzed as one fixed chunk of material with a fixed form and a fixed meaning or whether they should be analyzed compositionally.

21.8 Arguments from statistical distribution

In this section, we want to look at arguments from statistics that have been claimed to support a phrasal view. We first look at data-oriented parsing, a technique that was successfully used by Bod (2009b) to model language acquisition and then we turn to the

---

[58]However, see Booij (2009) for some challenges to lexical integrity.
[59]http://www.coffee2watch.at/egala. 2012-03-23

21.8 Arguments from statistical distribution

collostructional analysis by Stefanowitsch & Gries (2009). Lastly, we argue that these distributional analyses cannot decide the question whether argument structure constructions are phrasal or lexical.

21.8.1 Unsupervised Data-Oriented Parsing

In Section 13.8.3, we saw Bod's approach to the structuring of natural language utterances (2009b). If one assumes that language is acquired from the input without innate knowledge, the structures that Bod extracts from the distribution of words would have to be the ones that children also learn (parts of speech, meaning, and context would also have to be included). These structures would then also have to be the ones assumed in linguistic theories. Since Bod does not have enough data, he carried out experiments under the assumption of binary-branching trees and, for this reason, it is not possible to draw any conclusions from his work about whether rules license flat or binary-branching structures. There will almost certainly be interesting answers to this question in the future. What can certainly not be determined in a distribution-based analysis is the exact node in the tree where meaning is introduced. Bod (2009a: 132) claims that his approach constitutes "a testable realization of CxG" in the Goldbergian sense, but the trees that he can construct do not help us to decide between phrasal or lexical analyses or analyses with empty heads. These alternative analyses are represented in Figure 21.19 on the next page.[60] The first figure stands for a complex construction that contributes the meaning as a whole. The second figure corresponds to the analysis with a lexical rule and the third corresponds to the analysis with an empty head. A distributional analysis cannot decide between these theoretical proposals. Distribution is computed with reference to words; what the words actually mean is not taken into account. As such, it is only possible to say that the word *fischt* 'fishes' occurs in a particular utterance, however it is not possible to see if this word contains resultative semantics or not. Similarly, a distributional analysis does not help to distinguish between theoretical analyses with or without a lexical head. The empty head is not perceptible in the signal. It is a theoretical construct and, as

---

[60] The discussion is perhaps easier to follow if one assumes flat structures rather than binary-branching ones.

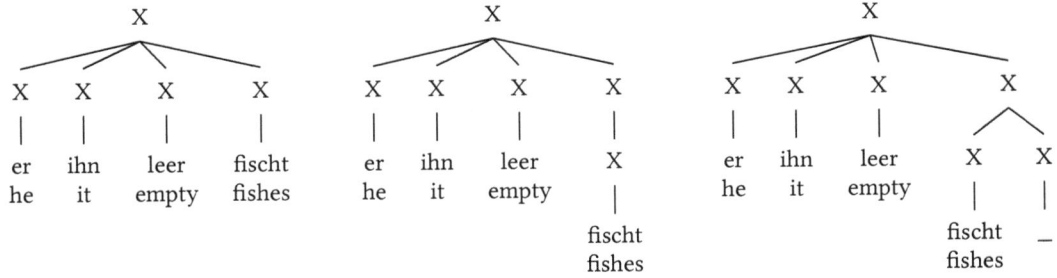

The first figure corresponds to the Goldbergian view of phrasal constructions where the verb is inserted into the construction and the meaning is present at the topmost node. In the second figure, there is a lexical rule that provides the resultative semantics and the corresponding valence information. In the third analysis, there is an empty head that combines with the verb and has ultimately the same effect as the lexical rule.

21 Phrasal vs. lexical analyses

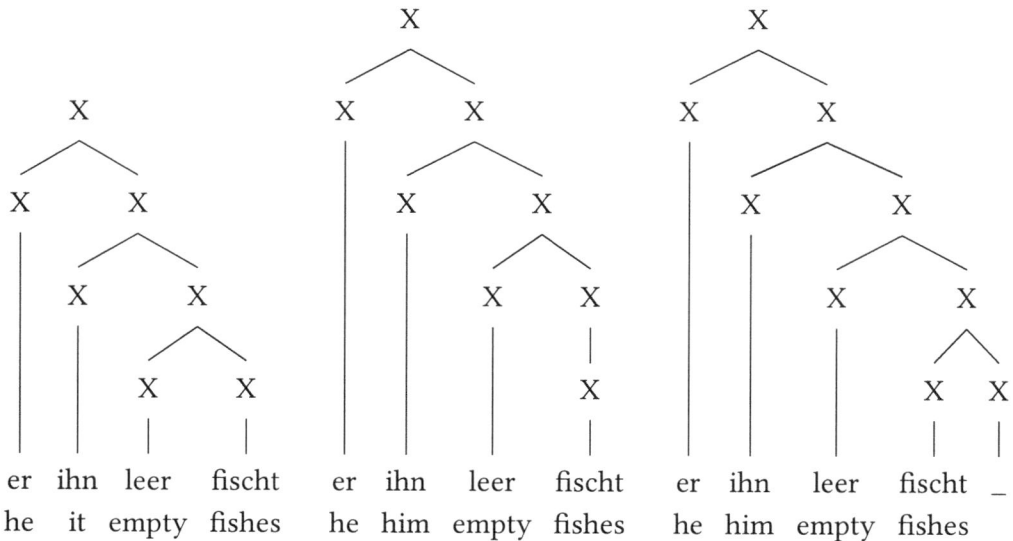

Figure 21.19: Three possible analyses for resultative construction: holistic construction, lexical rule, empty head

we have seen in Section 19.5, it is possible to translate an analysis using an empty head into one with a lexical rule. For the present example, any argumentation for a particular analysis will be purely theory-internal.

Although Unsupervised Data-Oriented Parsing (U-DOP) cannot help us to decide between analyses, there are areas of grammar for which these structures are of interest: under the assumption of binary-branching structures, there are different branching possibilities depending on whether one assumes an analysis with verb movement or not. This means that although one does not see an empty element in the input, there is a reflex in statistically-derived trees. The left tree in Figure 21.20 shows a structure that one would expect from an analysis following Steedman (2000: 159), see Section 8.3. The tree on the right shows a structure that would be expected from a GB-type verb movement analysis (see Section 3.2). But at present, there is no clear finding in this regard (Bod, p. c.

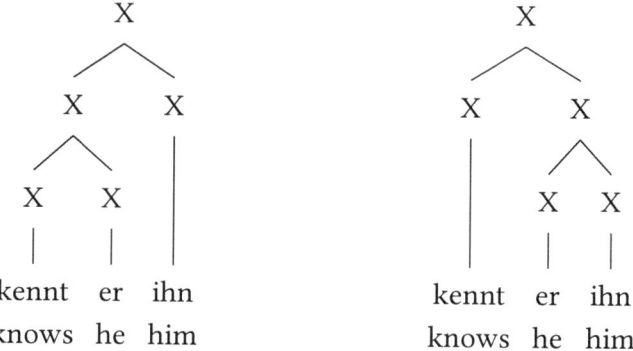

Figure 21.20: Structures corresponding to analyses with or without verb movement

662

21.8 Arguments from statistical distribution

2009). There is a great deal of variance in the U-DOP trees. The structure assigned to an utterance depends on the verb (Bod, referring to the Wall Street Journal). Here, it would be interesting to see if this changes with a larger data sample. In any case, it would be interesting to look at how all verbs as well as particular verb classes behave. The U-DOP procedure applies to trees containing at least one word each. If one makes use of parts of speech in addition, this results in structures that correspond to the ones we have seen in the preceding chapters. Sub-trees would then not have two Xs as their daughters but rather NP and V, for example. It is also possible to do statistic work with this kind of subtrees and use the part of speech symbols of words (the preterminal symbols) rather than the words themselves in the computation. For example, one would get trees for the symbol V instead of many trees for specific verbs. So instead of having three different trees for *küssen* 'kiss', *kennen* 'know' and *sehen* 'see', one would have three identical trees for the part of speech "verb" that corresponds to the trees that are needed for transitive verbs. The probability of the V tree is therefore higher than the probabilities of the trees for the individual verbs. Hence one would have a better set of data to compute structures for utterances such as those in Figure 21.20. I believe that there are further results in this area to be found in the years to come.

Concluding this subsection, we contend that Bod's paper is a milestone in the Poverty of the Stimulus debate, but it does not and cannot show that a particular version of constructionist theories, namely the phrasal one, is correct.

21.8.2 Collostructions

Stefanowitsch & Gries (2009: Section 5) assume a plugging analysis: "words occur in (slots provided by) a given construction if their meaning matches that of the construction". The authors claim that their *collostructional analysis has confirmed* [*the plugging analysis*] *from various perspectives*. Stefanowitsch and Gries are able to show that certain verbs occur more often than not in particular constructions, while other verbs never occur in the respective constructions. For instance, *give, tell, send, offer* and *show* are attracted by the Ditransitive Construction, while *make* and *do* are repelled by this construction, that is they occur significantly less often in this construction than what would be expected given the overall frequency of verbs in the corpus. Regarding this distribution the authors write:

> These results are typical for collexeme analysis in that they show two things. First, there are indeed significant associations between lexical items and grammatical structures. Second, these associations provide clear evidence for semantic coherence: the strongly attracted collexemes all involve a notion of 'transfer', either literally or metaphorically, which is the meaning typically posited for the ditransitive. This kind of result is typical enough to warrant a general claim that collostructional analysis can in fact be used to identify the meaning of a grammatical construction in the first place. (Stefanowitsch & Gries 2009: 943)

We hope that the preceding discussion has made clear that the distribution of words in a corpus cannot be seen as evidence for a phrasal analysis. The corpus study shows that *give* usually is used with three arguments in a certain pattern that is typical for English (Subject Verb Object1 Object2) and that this verb forms a cluster with other verbs that have a transfer component in their meaning. The corpus data do not show whether this meaning is contributed by a phrasal pattern or by lexical entries that are used in a certain configuration.

21.9 Conclusion

The essence of the lexical view is that a verb is stored with a valence structure indicating how it combines semantically and syntactically with its dependents. Crucially, that structure is abstracted from the actual syntactic context of particular tokens of the verb. Once abstracted, that valence structure can meet other fates besides licensing the phrasal structure that it most directly encodes: it can undergo lexical rules that manipulate that structure in systematic ways; it can be composed with the valence structure of another predicate; it can be coordinated with similar verbs; and so on. Such an abstraction allows for simple explanations of a wide range of robust, complex linguistic phenomena. We have surveyed the arguments against the lexical valence approach and in favor of a phrasal representation instead. We find the case for a phrasal representation of argument structure to be unconvincing: there are no compelling arguments in favor of such approaches, and they introduce a number of problems:

- They offer no account for the interaction of valence changing processes and derivational morphology.

- They offer no account for the interaction of valence changing processes and coordination of words.

- They offer no account for the iteration of valence changing processes.

- They overgenerate, unless a link between lexical items and phrasal constructions is assumed.

- They offer no account for distribution of arguments in partial fronting examples.

Assuming a lexical valence structure allows us to solve all the problems that arise with phrasal approaches.

21.10 Why (phrasal) constructions?

In previous sections, I have argued against assuming too much phrasality in grammatical descriptions. If one wishes to avoid transformations in order to derive alternative patterns from a single base structure, while still maintaining lexical integrity, then phrasal analyses become untenable for analyzing all those phenomena where changes in valence and derivational morphology interact. There are, however, some areas in which these

21.10 Why (phrasal) constructions?

two do not interact. In these cases, there is mostly a choice between analyses with silent heads and those with phrasal constructions. In this section, I will discuss some of these cases.

21.10.1 Verbless directives

Jacobs (2008) showed that there are linguistic phenomena where it does not make sense to assume that there is a head in a particular group of words. These configurations are best described as phrasal constructions, in which the adjacency of particular constituents leads to a complete meaning that goes beyond the sum of its parts. Examples of the phenomena that are discussed by Jacobs are phrasal templates such as those in (113) and verbless directives as in (118):

(113) Pro$_{+w,caus/purp}$ NP

    a. Wozu Konstruktionen?
       why   constructions
       'Why constructions?'

    b. Warum ich?
       why   I
       'Why me?'

(114) NP$_{acc}$ Y$_{PP/A/Adv}$
      Den Hut in der Hand (kam er ins   Zimmer).
      the hat in the hand came he into.the room
      '(He came into the room) hat in hand.'

In (113), we are dealing with abbreviated questions:

(115) a. Wozu   braucht man Konstruktionen? / Wozu   sollte   man Konstruktionen
        to.what needs   one constructions   to.what should one constructions
        annehmen?
        assume
        'Why do we need constructions?' / 'Why should we assume constructions?'

    b. Warum soll   ich das machen? / Warum wurde ich ausgewählt? / Warum
       why   should I   that do   why   was   I   chosen   why
      passiert mir sowas?
      happens me something.like.that
      'Why should I do that?' / 'Why was I chosen?' / 'Why do things like that happen to me?'

In (114), a participle has been omitted:

(116) Den Hut   in der Hand haltend kam er ins   Zimmer.
      the hat.ACC in the hand holding came he in.the room
      'He came into the room hat in hand.'

Cases such as (114) can be analyzed with an empty head that corresponds to *haltend* 'holding'. For (113), on the other hand, one would require either a syntactic structure with multiple empty elements, or an empty head that selects both parts of the construction and contributes the components of meaning that are present in (115). If one adopts the first approach with multiple silent elements, then one would have to explain why these elements cannot occur in other constructions. For example, it would be necessary to assume an empty element corresponding to *man* 'one'/'you'. But such an empty element could never occur in embedded clauses since subjects cannot simply be omitted there:

(117) * weil   dieses Buch gerne liest
         because this   book gladly reads

   Intended: 'because he/she/it likes to read this book'

If one were to follow the second approach, one would be forced to assume an empty head with particularly odd semantics.

The directives in (118) and (119) are similarly problematic (see also Jackendoff & Pinker (2005: 220) for parallel examples in English):

(118) a. Her mit dem Geld   / dem gestohlenen Geld!
          here with the money   the stolen   money

       'Hand over the (stolen) money!'

   b. Weg mit dem Krempel / dem alten Krempel!
      away with the junk   the old   junk

      'Get rid of this (old) junk!'

   c. Nieder mit   den Studiengebühren / den sozialfeindlichen Studiengebühren!
      down   with the tuition.fees   the antisocial   tuition.fees

      'Down with (antisocial) tuition fees!'

(119) a. In den Müll mit diesen Klamotten!
          in the trash with these clothes

      'Throw these clothes into the trash!'

   b. Zur   Hölle mit dieser Regierung!
      to.the hell with this   government

      'To hell with this government!'

Here, it is also not possible to simply identify an elided verb. It is, of course, possible to assume an empty head that selects an adverb or a *mit*-PP, but this would be *ad hoc*. Alternatively, it would be possible to assume that adverbs in (118) select the *mit*-PP. Here, one would have to disregard the fact that adverbs do not normally take any arguments. The same is true of Jacobs's examples in (119). For these, one would have to assume that *in* and *zur* 'to the' are the respective heads. Each of the prepositions would then have to select a noun phrase and a *mit*-PP. While this is technically possible, it is as unattractive as the multiple lexical entries that Categorial Grammar has to assume for pied-piping constructions (see Section 8.6).

21.10 Why (phrasal) constructions?

A considerably more complicated analysis has been proposed by G. Müller (2009a). Müller treats verbless directives as antipassive constructions. Antipassive constructions involve either the complete suppression of the direct object or its realization as an oblique element (PP). There can also be morphological marking on the verb. The subject is normally not affected by the antipassive but can, however, receive a different case in ergative case systems due to changes in the realization of the object. According to G. Müller, there is a relation between (120a) and (120b) that is similar to active-passive pairs:

(120) a. [dass] jemand   diese Klamotten in den Müll schmeißt
            that   somebody these clothes   in the trash throws
          'that somebody throws these clothes into the thrash'

       b. In den Müll mit   diesen Klamotten!
           in the trash with these   clothes
          'Throw these clothes into the trash!'

An empty passive morpheme absorbs the capability of the verb to assign accusative (see also Section 3.4 on the analysis of the passive in GB theory). The object therefore has to be realized as a PP or not at all. It follows from Burzio's Generalization that as the accusative object has been suppressed, there cannot be an external argument. G. Müller assumes, like proponents of Distributed Morphology (e.g., Marantz 1997), that lexical entries are inserted into complete trees post-syntactically. The antipassive morpheme creates a feature bundle in the relevant tree node that is not compatible with German verbs such as *schmeißen* 'throw' and this is why only a null verb with the corresponding specifications can be inserted. Movement of the directional PP is triggered by mechanisms that cannot be discussed further here. The antipassive morpheme forces an obligatory reordering of the verb in initial position (to C, see Section 3.2 and Section 4.2). By stipulation, filling the prefield is only possible in sentences where the C position is filled by a visible verb and this is why G. Müller's analysis does only derive V1 clauses. These are interpreted as imperatives or polar questions. Figure 21.21 on the next page gives the analysis of (120b). Budde (2010) and Maché (2010) note that the discussion of the data has neglected the fact that there are also interrogative variants of the construction:

(121) a. Wohin   mit den Klamotten?
          where.to with the clothes
          'Where should the clothes go?'

       b. Wohin   mit dem ganzen Geld?
          where.to with the entire   money
          'Where should all this money go?'

Since these questions correspond to V2 sentences, one does not require the constraint that the prefield can only be filled if the C position is filled.

One major advantage of this analysis is that it derives the different sentence types that are possible with this kind of construction: the V1-variants correspond to polar questions and imperatives, and the V2-variants with a question word correspond to *wh*-questions. A further consequence of the approach pointed out by G. Müller is that no

Figure 21.21: *In den Müll mit diesen Klamotten* 'in the trash with these clothes' as an antipassive following G. Müller (2009a)

further explanation is required for other interactions with the grammar. For example, the way in which the constructions interact with adverbs follows from the analysis:

(122)   a.   Schmeiß den Krempel weg!
             throw the junk away

       b.   Schmeiß den Krempel schnell weg!
             throw the junk quickly away

       c.   ?* Schmeiß den Krempel sorgfältig weg!
              throw the junk carefully away

(123)   a.   Weg mit dem Krempel!
             away with the junk

       b.   Schnell weg mit dem Krempel!
             quickly away with the junk

       c.   ?* Sorgfältig weg mit dem Krempel!
              carefully away with the junk

Nevertheless one should still bear the price of this analysis in mind: it assumes an empty antipassive morpheme that is otherwise not needed in German. It would only be used in constructions of the kind discussed here. This morpheme is not compatible with any verb and it also triggers obligatory verb movement, which is something that is not known from any other morpheme used to form verb diatheses.

21.10 Why (phrasal) constructions?

The costs of this analysis are, of course, less severe if one assumes that humans already have this antipassive morpheme anyway, that is, this morpheme is part of our innate Universal Grammar. But if one follows the argumentation from the earlier sections of this chapter, then one should only assume innate linguistic knowledge if there is no alternative explanation.

G. Müller's analysis can be translated into HPSG. The result is given in (124):

(124) $\begin{bmatrix} \textit{verb-initial-lr} \\ \text{RELS} \left\langle \begin{bmatrix} \textit{imperative-or-interrogative} \\ \text{EVENT } \boxed{2} \end{bmatrix} \right\rangle \oplus \square \\ \text{LEX-DTR} \begin{bmatrix} \text{PHON } \langle \rangle \\ \text{SS|LOC} \begin{bmatrix} \text{CAT} \begin{bmatrix} \text{HEAD|MOD } \textit{none} \\ \text{SPR } \langle \rangle \\ \text{COMPS } \langle \text{XP[MOD ... IND } \boxed{1}], (\text{PP}[\textit{mit}]_{\boxed{1}}) \rangle \end{bmatrix} \\ \text{CONT} \begin{bmatrix} \text{IND } \boxed{2} \\ \text{RELS } \left\langle \begin{bmatrix} \textit{directive} \\ \text{EVENT } \boxed{2} \\ \text{PATIENT } \boxed{1} \end{bmatrix} \right\rangle \end{bmatrix} \end{bmatrix} \end{bmatrix} \end{bmatrix}$

(124) contains a lexical entry for an empty verb in verb-initial position. *directive'* is a placeholder for a more general relation that should be viewed as a supertype of all possible meanings of this construction. These subsume both *schmeißen* 'to throw' and cases such as (125) that were pointed out to me by Monika Budde:

(125) Und mit dem Klavier ganz langsam durch die Tür!
and with the piano very slowly through the door
'Carry the piano very slowly through the door!'

Since only verb-initial and verb-second orders are possible in this construction, the application of the lexical rule for verb-initial position (see page 294) is obligatory. This can be achieved by writing the result of the application of this lexical rule into the lexicon, without having the object to which the rule should have applied actually being present in the lexicon itself. Koenig (1999: Section 3.4.2, 5.3) proposed something similar for English *rumored* 'it is rumored that ...' and *aggressive*. There is no active variant of the verb *rumored*, a fact that can be captured by the assumption that only the result of applying a passive lexical rule is present in the lexicon. The actual verb or verb stem from which the participle form has been derived exists only as the daughter of a lexical rule but not as an independent linguistic object. Similarly, the verb **aggress* only exists as the daughter of a (non-productive) adjective rule that licenses *aggressive* and a nominalization rule licensing *aggression*.

The optionality of the *mit*-PP is signaled by the brackets in (124). If one adds the information inherited from the type *verb-initial-lr* under SYNSEM, then the result is (126).

669

21 Phrasal vs. lexical analyses

(126)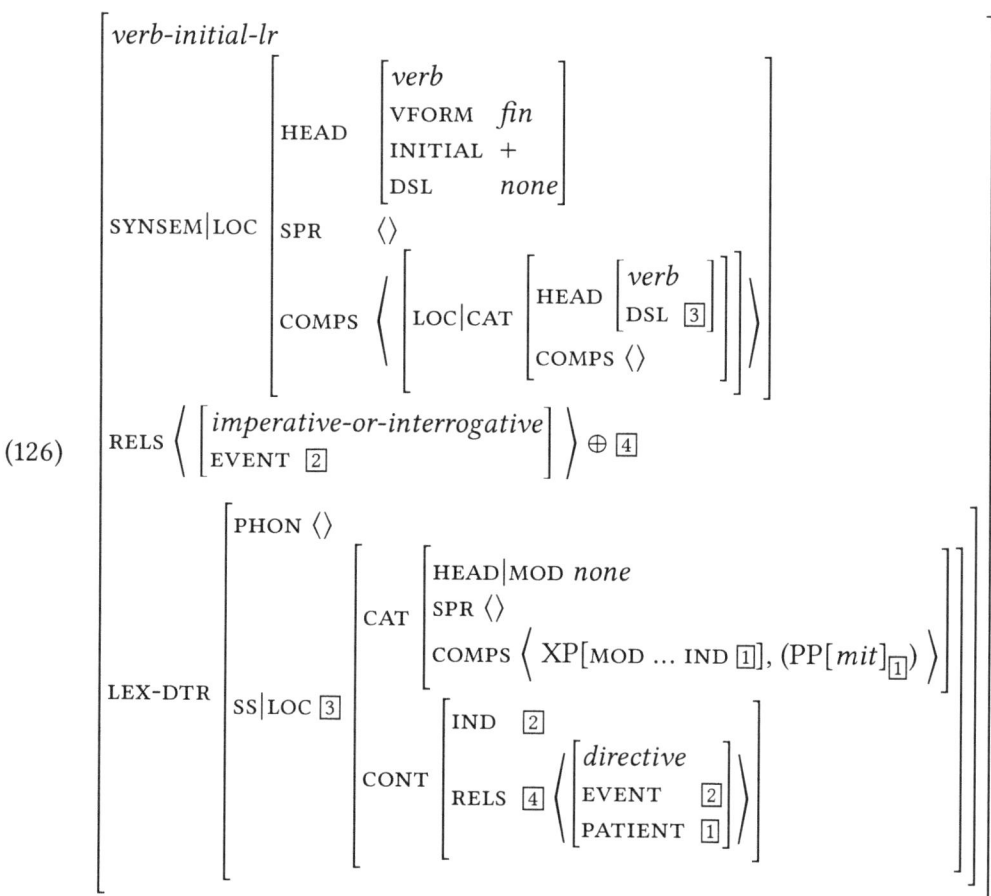

The valence properties of the empty verb in (126) are to a large extent determined by the lexical rule for verb-initial order: the V1-LR licenses a verbal head that requires a VP to its right that is missing a verb with the local properties of the LEX-DTR (3).

Semantic information dependent on sentence type (assertion, imperative or question) is determined inside the V1-LR depending on the morphological make-up of the verb and the SLASH value of the selected VP (see Müller 2007a: Section 10.3; 2016b; 2017a). Setting the semantics to *imperative-or-interrogative* rules out *assertion* as it occurs in V2-clauses. Whether this type is resolved in the direction of *imperative* or *interrogative* is ultimately decided by further properties of the utterance such as intonation or the use of interrogative pronouns.

The valence of the lexical daughters in (126) as well as the connection to the semantic role (the linking to the patient role) are simply stipulated. Every approach has to stipulate that an argument of the verb has to be expressed as a *mit*-PP. Since there is no antipassive in German, the effect that could be otherwise achieved by an antipassive lexical rule in (126) is simply written into the LEX-DTR of the verb movement rule.

The COMPS list of LEX-DTR contains a modifier (adverb, directional PP) and the *mit*-PP. This *mit*-PP is co-indexed with the patient of *directive′* and the modifier refers to the referent of the *mit*-PP. The agent of *directive′* is unspecified since it depends on the context (speaker, hearer, third person).

21.10 Why (phrasal) constructions?

This analysis is shown in Figure 21.22. Here, V[LOC [2]] corresponds to the LEX-DTR in

in den Müll   mit diesen Klamotten
in the trash   with these clothes

Figure 21.22: HPSG variant of the analysis of *In den Müll mit diesen Klamotten!/?*

(126). The V1-LR licenses an element that requires a maximal verb projection with that exact DSL value [2]. Since DSL is a head feature, the information is present along the head path. The DSL value is identified with the LOCAL value ([2] in Figure 21.22) in the verb movement trace (see page 295). This ensures that the empty element at the end of sentence has exactly the same local properties that the LEX-DTR in (126) has. Thus, both the correct syntactic and semantic information is present on the verb trace and structure building involving the verb trace follows the usual principles. The structures correspond to the structures that were assumed for German sentences in Chapter 9. Therefore, there are the usual possibilities for integrating adjuncts. The correct derivation of the semantics, in particular embedding under imperative or interrogative semantics, follows automatically (for the semantics of adjuncts in conjunction with verb position, see Müller (2007a: Section 9.4)). Also, the ordering variants with the *mit*-PP preceding the direction (125) and direction preceding the *mit*-PP (120b) follow from the usual mechanisms.

If one rejects the analyses discussed up to this point, then one is only really left with phrasal constructions or dominance schemata that connect parts of the construction and contribute the relevant semantics. Exactly how one can integrate adjuncts into the phrasal construction in a non-stipulative way remains an open question; however, there are already some initial results by Jakob Maché (2010) suggesting that directives can still be sensibly integrated into the entire grammar provided an appropriate phrasal schema is assumed.

21.10.2 Serial verbs

There are languages with so-called serial verbs. For example, it is possible to form sentences in Mandarin Chinese where there is only one subject and several verb phrases (Li & Thompson 1981: Chapter 21). There are multiple readings depending on the distribution of aspect marking inside the VP:[61] if the first VP contains a perfect marker, then we have the meaning 'VP1 in order to do/achieve VP2' (127a). If the second VP contains a perfect marker, then the entire construction means 'VP2 because VP1' (127b), and if the first VP contains a durative marker and the verb *hold* or *use*, then the entire construction means 'VP2 using VP1' (127c).

(127) a. Ta1 qu3   le qian2 qu4 guang1jie1.
        he withdraw PRF money go shop
        'He withdrew money to go shopping.'

   b. Ta1 chi1 pu2tao tu3 le   Pu2taopi2.
      he eat grape spit PRF grape.skin
      'He spat grape skins because he ate grapes.'

   c. Ta1 na2 zhe kuai4zi   chi1 fan4.
      he hold DUR chopsticks eat food
      'He eats with chopsticks.'

If we consider the sentences, we only see two adjacent VPs. The meanings of the entire sentences, however, contain parts of meaning that go beyond the meaning of the verb phrases. Depending on the kind of aspect marking, we arrive at different interpretations with regard to the semantic combination of verb phrases. As can be seen in the translations, English sometimes uses conjunctions in order to express relations between clauses or verb phrases.

There are three possible ways to capture these data:

1. One could claim that speakers of Chinese simply deduce the relation between the VPs from the context,

2. one could assume that there are empty heads in Chinese corresponding to *because* or *to*, or

3. one could assume a phrasal construction for serial verbs that contributes the correct semantics for the complete meaning depending on the aspect marking inside the VPs.

The first approach is unsatisfactory because the meaning does not vary arbitrarily. There are grammaticalized conventions that should be captured by a theory. The second solution has a stipulative character and thus, if one wishes to avoid empty elements, only the third solution remains. Müller & Lipenkova (2009) have presented a corresponding analysis.

---

[61]See Müller & Lipenkova (2009) for a detailed discussion and further references.

21.10.3 Relative and interrogative clauses

Sag (1997) develops a phrasal analysis of English relative clauses as have Ginzburg & Sag (2000) for interrogative clauses. Relative and interrogative clauses consist of a fronted phrase and a clause or a verb phrase missing the fronted phrase. The fronted phrase contains a relative or interrogative pronoun.

(128)   a. the man [who] sleeps
        b. the man [who] we know
        c. the man [whose mother] visited Kim
        d. a house [in which] to live

(129)   a. I wonder [who] you know.
        b. I want to know [why] you did this.

The GB analysis of relative clauses is given in Figure 21.23. In this analysis, an empty head is in the C position and an element from the IP is moved to the specifier position.

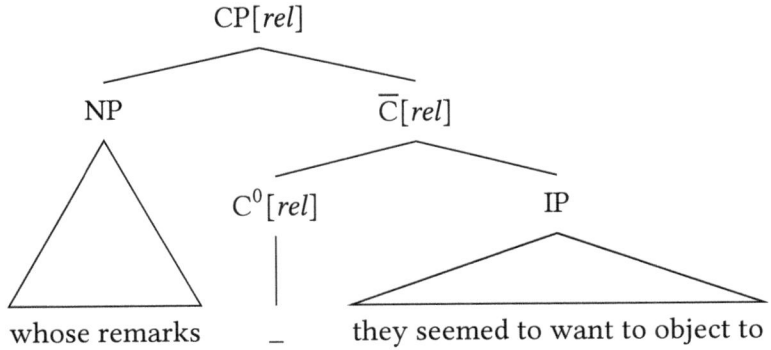

Figure 21.23: Analysis of relative clauses in GB theory

The alternative analysis shown in Figure 21.24 involves combining the subparts directly in order to form a relative clause. Borsley (2006) has shown that one would require

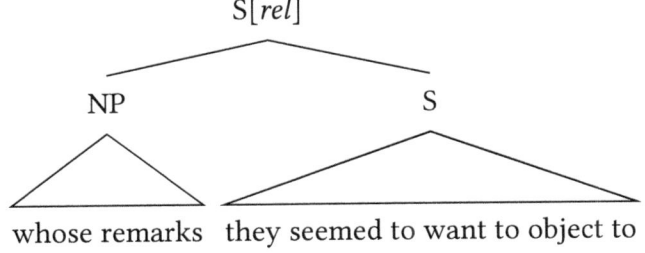

Figure 21.24: Analysis of relative clauses in HPSG following Sag (1997)

six empty heads in order to capture the various types of relative clauses possible in English if one wanted to analyze them lexically. These heads can be avoided and replaced by corresponding schemata (see Chapter 19 on empty elements). A parallel argument can also be found in Webelhuth (2011) for German: grammars of German would also have to assume six empty heads for the relevant types of relative clause.

Unlike the resultative constructions that were already discussed, there is no variability among interrogative and relative clauses with regard to the order of their parts. There are no changes in valence and no interaction with derivational morphology. Thus, nothing speaks against a phrasal analysis. If one wishes to avoid the assumption of empty heads, then one should opt for the analysis of relative clauses by Sag, or the variant in Müller (1999b: Chapter 10; 2007a: Chapter 11). The latter analysis does without a special schema for noun-relative clause combinations since the semantic content of the relative clause is provided by the relative clause schema.

Sag (2010) discusses long-distance dependencies in English that are subsumed under the term *wh*-movement in GB theory and the Minimalist Program. He shows that this is by no means a uniform phenomenon. He investigates *wh*-questions (130), *wh*-exclamatives (131), topicalization (132), *wh*-relative clauses (133) and *the*-clauses (134):

(130) a. How foolish is he?

　　　b. I wonder *how foolish he is.*

(131) a. What a fool he is!

　　　b. It's amazing *how odd it is.*

(132) The bagels, I like.

(133) a. I met the person *who they nominated.*

　　　b. I'm looking for a bank *in which to place my trust.*

(134) a. The more people I met, *the happier I became.*

　　　b. *The more people I met*, the happier I became.

These individual constructions vary in many respects. Sag lists the following questions that have to be answered for each construction:

- Is there a special *wh*-element in the filler daughter and, if so, what kind of element is it?

- Which syntactic categories can the filler daughters have?

- Can the head-daughter be inverted or finite? Is this obligatory?

- What is the semantic and/or syntactic category of the mother node?

- What is the semantic and/or syntactic category of the head-daughter?

- Is the sentence an island? Does it have to be an independent clause?

21.10 Why (phrasal) constructions?

The variation that exists in this domain has to be captured somehow by a theory of grammar. Sag develops an analysis with multiple schemata that ensure that the category and semantic contribution of the mother node correspond to the properties of both daughters. The constraints for both classes of constructions and specific constructions are represented in an inheritance hierarchy so that the similarities between the constructions can be accounted for. The analysis can of course also be formulated in a GB-style using empty heads. One would then have to find some way of capturing the generalizations pertaining to the construction. This is possible if one represents the constraints on empty heads in an inheritance hierarchy. Then, the approaches would simply be notational variants of one another. If one wishes to avoid empty elements in the grammar, then the phrasal approach would be preferable.

21.10.4 The N-P-N construction

Jackendoff (2008) discusses the English N-P-N construction. Examples of this construction are given in (135):

(135)   a. day by day, paragraph by paragraph, country by country
            b. dollar for dollar, student for student, point for point
            c. face to face, bumper to bumper
            d. term paper after term paper, picture after picture
            e. book upon book, argument upon argument

This construction is relatively restricted: articles and plural nouns are not allowed. The phonological content of the first noun has to correspond to that of the second. There are also similar constructions in German:

(136)   a. Er hat Buch um   Buch verschlungen.
              he has book around book swallowed
              'He binge-read book after book.'
            b. Zeile für Zeile[62]
              line   for line
              'line by line'

Determining the meaning contribution of this kind of N-P-N construction is by no means trivial. Jackendoff suggests the meaning *many Xs in succession* as an approximation.

Jackendoff points out that this construction is problematic from a syntactic perspective since it is not possible to determine a head in a straightforward way. It is also not clear what the structure of the remaining material is if one is working under assumptions of $\overline{\text{X}}$ theory. If the preposition *um* were the head in (136a), then one would expect that it is combined with an NP, however this is not possible:

---

[62] *Zwölf Städte*. Einstürzende Neubauten. Fünf auf der nach oben offenen Richterskala, 1987.

21 Phrasal vs. lexical analyses

(137) a. * Er hat dieses Buch um jenes Buch verschlungen.
       he has this book around this book swallowed
   b. * Er hat ein Buch um ein Buch verschlungen.
       he has a book around a book swallowed

For this kind of structures, it would be necessary to assume that a preposition selects a noun to its right and, if it find this, it then requires a second noun of this exact form to its left. For N-*um*-N and N-*für*-N, it is not entirely clear what the entire construction has to do with the individual prepositions. One could also try to develop a lexical analysis for this phenomenon, but the facts are different to those for resultative constructions: in resultative constructions, the semantics of simplex verbs clearly plays a role. Furthermore, unlike with the resultative construction, the order of the component parts of the construction is fixed in the N-P-N construction. It is not possible to extract a noun or place the preposition in front of both nouns. Syntactically, the N-P-N combination with some prepositions behaves like an NP (Jackendoff 2008: 9):

(138) Student after/upon/*by student flunked.

This is also strange if one wishes to view the preposition as the head of the construction.

Instead of a lexical analysis, Jackendoff proposes the following phrasal construction for N-*after*-N combinations:

(139) Meaning: MANY X$_i$s IN SUCCESSION [or however it is encoded]
   Syntax: [$_{NP}$ N$_i$ P$_j$ N$_i$]
   Phonology: Wd$_i$ after$_j$ Wd$_i$

The entire meaning as well as the fact that the N-P-N has the syntactic properties of an NP would be captured on the construction level.

I already discussed examples by Bargmann (2015) in Section 11.7.2.4 that show that N-P-N constructions may be extended by further P-N combinations:

(140) Day after day after day went by, but I never found the courage to talk to her.

So rather than an N-P-N pattern Bargmann suggests the pattern in (141), where '+' stands for at least one repetition of a sequence.

(141) N (P N)+

As was pointed out on page 411 this pattern is not easy to cover in selection-based approaches. One could assume that an N takes arbitrarily many P-N combinations, which would be very unusual for heads. Alternatively, one could assume recursion, so N would be combined with a P and with an N-P-N to yield N-P-N-P-N. But such an analysis would make it really difficult to enforce the restrictions regarding the identity of the nouns in the complete construction. In order to enforce such an identity the N that is combined with N-P-N would have to impose constraints regarding deeply embedded nouns inside the embedded N-P-N object (see also Section 18.2).

G. Müller (2011) proposes a lexical analysis of the N-P-N construction. He assumes that prepositions can have a feature REDUP. In the analysis of *Buch um Buch* 'book after

21.10 Why (phrasal) constructions?

book', the preposition is combined with the right noun *um Buch*. In the phonological component, reduplication of *Buch* is triggered by the REDUP feature, thereby yielding *Buch um Buch*. This analysis also suffers from the problems pointed out by Jackendoff: in order to derive the semantics of the construction, the semantics would have to be present in the lexical entry of the reduplicating preposition (or in a relevant subsequent component that interprets the syntax). Furthermore it is unclear how a reduplication analysis would deal with the Bargmann data.

22 Structure, potential structure and underspecification

The previous chapter extensively dealt with the question whether one should adopt a phrasal or a lexical analysis of valence alternations. This rather brief chapter deals with a related issue. I discuss the analysis of complex predicates consisting of a preverb and a light verb. Preverbs often have an argument structure of their own. They describe an event and the light verb can be used to realize either the full number of arguments or a reduced set of arguments. (1) provides the example from Hindi discussed by Ashwini, Rambow & Palmer (2019).

(1) a. logon=ne   pustak=kii tareef   k-ii
       people.M=ERG book.F=GEN praise.F do-PERF.F

   'People praised the book.' Lit: 'People did praise of the book.'

   b. pustak=kii   tareef   hu-ii
      book.F.SG=GEN praise.F be.PART-PERF.F.SG/be.PRES

   'The book got praised.' Lit: 'The praise of the book happened.'

tareef 'praise' is a noun that can be combined with the light verb *kar* 'do' to form an active sentence as in (1a) or with the light verb *ho* 'be' to form a passive sentence as in (1b). Similar examples can of course be found in other languages making heavy use of complex predicates (Müller 2010b).

In what follows I compare the analysis of Ashwini et al. (2019) in the framework of Lexicalized TAG with a an HPSG analysis. As the name specifies, LTAG is a lexicalized framework, something that was argued for in the previous chapter. However, TAG is similar to phrasal Construction Grammar in that it makes use of phrasal configurations to represent argument slots. This differs from Categorial Grammar and HPSG since the latter frameworks assume descriptions of arguments (head/functor representations in CG and valence lists in HPSG) rather than structures containing these arguments. So while TAG elementary trees contain actual structure, CG and HPSG lexical items contain potential structure. TAG structures can be taken appart and items can be inserted into the middle of an existing structure but usually the structure is not transformed into something else.[1] This is an interesting difference that becomes crucial when talking about the formation of complex predicates and in particular about certain active/passive alternations.

---

[1] One way to "delete" parts of the structure would be to assume empty elements that can be inserted into substitution nodes (see Chapter 19 for discussion).

22 Structure, potential structure and underspecification

Ashwini et al. (2019) assume that the structures for the examples in (1) are composed of elementary trees for *tareef* 'praise' and the respective light verbs. This is shown in Figure 22.1 and Figure 22.2 respectively. The TAG analysis is only sketched here. The

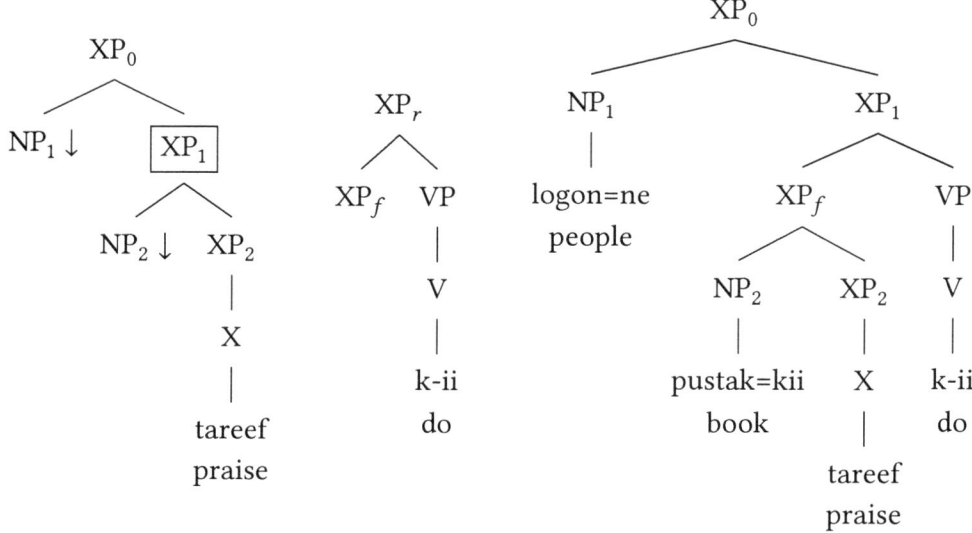

Figure 22.1: Analysis of *logon=ne pustak=kii tareef k-ii* 'People praised the book.' The tree of the light verb is adjoined into the tree of the preverb, into the XP_1 position

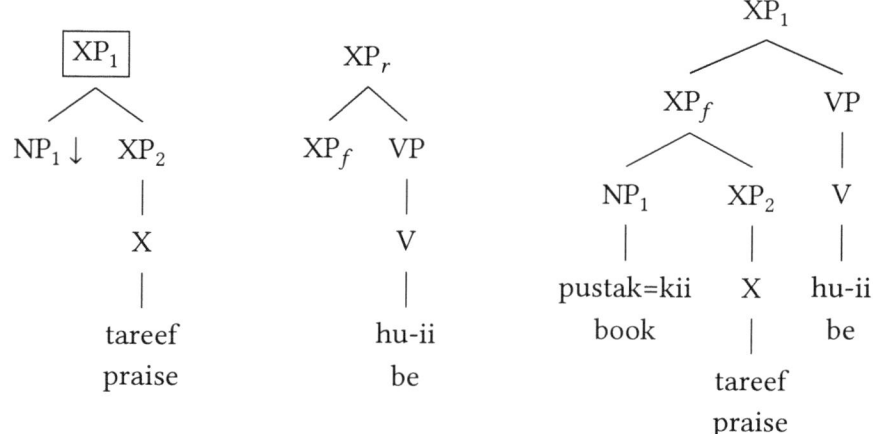

Figure 22.2: Analysis of *pustak=kii tareef hu-ii* 'The book got praised.'

authors use feature-based TAG, which makes it possible to enforce obligatory adjunction: the elementary tree for *tareef* is specified in a way that makes it necessary to take the tree apart and insert nodes of another tree (see page 428). This way it can be ensured that the preverb has to be augmented by a light verb. This results in XP_f being inserted at XP_1 in the figures above.

What the analysis clearly shows is that TAG assumes two lexical items for the preverb: one with two arguments for the active case and one with just one argument for the passive. In general one would say that *tareef* is a noun describing the praising event, that is, one person praises another one. Now this noun can be combined with a light verb and depending on which light verb is used we get an active sentence with both arguments realized or a passive sentence with the agent of the eventive noun suppressed. There is no morphological reflex of this active/passive alternation at the noun. It is just the same noun *tareef*: in an active sentence in (1a) and in a passive one in (1b).

And here we see a real difference between the frameworks: TAG is a framework in which structure is assembled: the basic operations are substitution and adjunction. The lexicon consists of ready-made building blocks that are combined to yield the trees we want to have in the end. This differs from Categorial Grammar and HPSG where lexical items do not encode real structure to be used in an analysis, but potential structure: lexical items come with a list of their arguments, that is, items that are required for the lexical element under consideration to project to a full phrase. However, lexical heads may enter relations with their valents and form NPs, APs, VPs, PPs or other phrases, but they do not have to. Geach (1970) developed a technique that is called functional composition or argument composition within the framework of Categorial Grammar and this was transferred to HPSG by Hinrichs & Nakazawa (1989b; 1994). Since the 90ies this technique is used for the analysis of complex predicates in HPSG for German (Hinrichs & Nakazawa 1989b; 1994; Kiss 1995; Meurers 1999a; Müller 1999b; Kathol 2000), Romance (Miller & Sag 1997: 600; Monachesi 1998; Abeillé & Godard 2002), Korean (Chung 1998), and Persian (Müller 2010b). See Godard & Samvelian (2019) for an overview. For instance Müller (2010b: 642) analyzes the light verbs *kardan* 'do' and *šodan* 'become' this way: both raise the subject of the embedded predicate and make it their own argument but *kardan* introduces an additional argument while *šodan* does not do so.

Applying the argument composition technique to our example, we get the following lexical item for *tareef*:

(2) Sketch of lexical item for *tareef* 'praise':
$$\begin{bmatrix} \text{HEAD} & \begin{bmatrix} noun \\ \text{SUBJ} \ \langle \boxed{1} \rangle \end{bmatrix} \\ \text{COMPS} & \langle \boxed{2}\,\text{NP} \rangle \\ \text{ARG-ST} & \langle \boxed{1}\,\text{NP}, \boxed{2}\,\text{NP} \rangle \end{bmatrix}$$

The ARG-ST list contains all arguments of a head. The arguments are linked to the semantic representation and are mapped to valence features like SPECIFIER and COMPLEMENTS. Depending on the langauge and the realizationability of subjects within projections, that subject may be mapped to a separate feature, which is a HEAD feature. HEAD features are projected along the head path but the features contained under HEAD do not license combinations with the head.

The lexical items for *kar* 'do' and *ho* 'be' are:

(3) a. Sketch of lexical item for *kar* 'do':
$$\begin{bmatrix} \text{HEAD} & verb \\ \text{ARG-ST} & \boxed{1} \oplus \boxed{2} \oplus \langle \text{N}[\text{SUBJ}\,\boxed{1},\,\text{COMPS}\,\boxed{2}] \rangle \end{bmatrix}$$

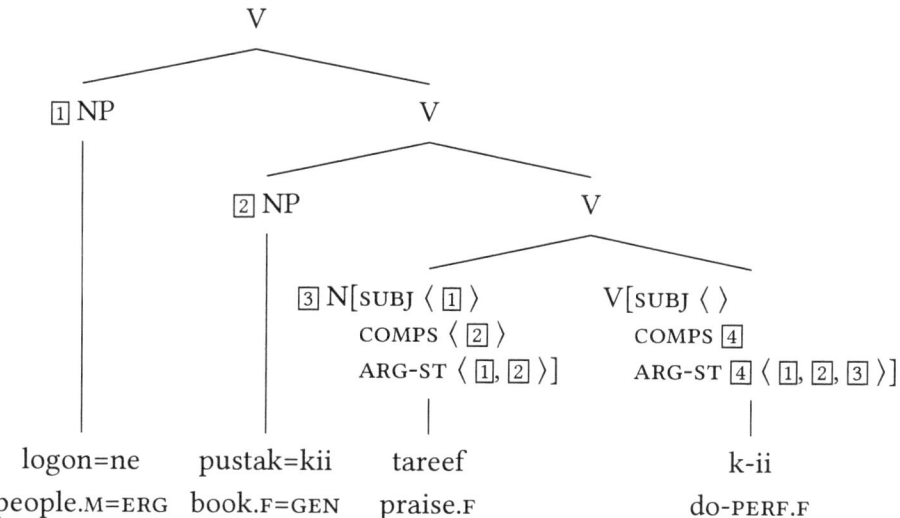

Figure 22.3: Analysis of *logon=ne pustak=kii tareef k-ii* 'People praised the book.' The arguments of the preverb are taken over by the light verb

b. Sketch of lexical item for *ho* 'be':
$$\begin{bmatrix} \text{HEAD} & verb \\ \text{ARG-ST} & \boxed{1} \oplus \langle \text{N}[\text{COMPS}\,\boxed{1}] \rangle \end{bmatrix}$$

The verb *kar* 'do' selects for a noun and takes whatever the subject of this noun is (☐) and concatenates the list of complements the noun takes (☐) with the value of SUBJ. The result is ☐ ⊕ ☐ and it is a prefix of the ARG-ST list of the light verb. The lexical item for *ho* 'be' is similar, the difference being that the subject of the embedded verb is not attracted to the higher ARG-ST list, only the complements (☐) are.

For finite verbs it is assumed that all arguments are mapped to the COMPS list of the verb, so the COMPS list is identical to the ARG-ST list. The analysis of our example sentences is shown in Figures 22.3 and 22.4.

The conclusion is that HPSG has a representation of potential structure. When light verbs are present, they can take over valents and "execute" them according to their own preferences. This is not possible in TAG since once structure is assembled it cannot be changed. We may insert items into the middle of an already assembled structure but we cannot take out arguments or reorder them. This is possible in Categorial Grammar and in HPSG: the governing head may choose which arguments to take order and in which order they should be represented in the valence repsresentations of the governing head.

LFG is somewhere in the middle between TAG and HPSG: the phrase structural configurations are not fully determined as in TAG since LFG does not store and manipulate phrase markers. But lexical items are associated with f-structures and these f-structures are responsible for which elements are realized in syntax. As complex predicates are assumed to be monoclausal it is not sufficient to embed the f-structure of the preverb

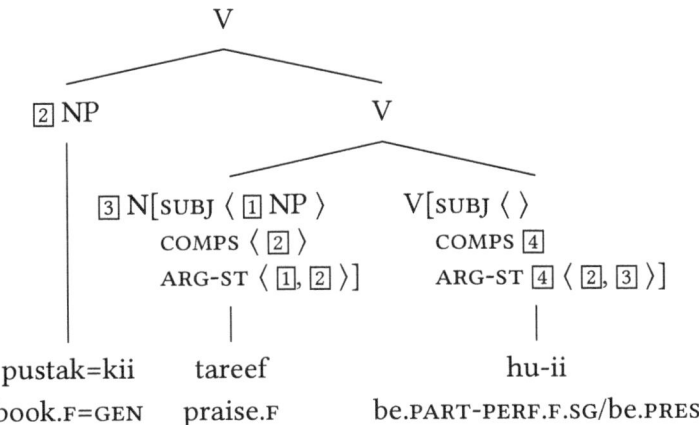

Figure 22.4: Analysis of *pustak=kii tareef hu-ii* 'The book got praised.'

within the f-structure of the light verb (Butt et al. 2003). Since the grammatical functions that are ultimately realized in the clause do not depend on the preverb alone the light verb may have to determine the grammatical functions contributed by the preverb. In order to be able to do this Butt et al. (2003) use the restriction operator (Kaplan & Wedekind 1993), which restricts out certain features or path equations provided by the preverb's and the light verb's f-structures. The statement of grammatical functions in f-structures is another instance of too strict specifications: once specified, it is difficult to get rid of it and special means like partial copying via restriction are needed. An alternative not relying on restriction was suggested by Butt (1997): embedding relations can be specified on the a-structure representation and then a mapping is defined that maps the complex a-structure to the desired f-structure. Mapping between several levels of representation is a general tool that is also used in HPSG: for instance, Bouma, Malouf & Sag (2001) used ARG-ST, DEPS, and COMPS in the treatment of nonlocal dependencies. See also Koenig (1999) on the introduction of arguments via additional auxiliary features. As I showed in Müller (2007a: Section 7.5.2.2), one would need an extra feature for every kind of argument alternation that is to be modeled this way. Recent versions of LFG use glue semantics to keep track of arguments (Dalrymple, Lamping & Saraswat 1993; Dalrymple 2001: Chapter 8). Glue semantics can be used to do argument extension and argument manipulation in general in ways that are parallel to argument attraction approaches. See for instance Asudeh, Dalrymple & Toivonen (2013) for a treatment of benefactive arguments.

Summing up, I showed that there are indeed differences between the frameworks that are due to the basic representational formalisms they assume. While TAG assumes that the lexicon contains trees with a certain structure, HPSG assumes that lexical items come with valence specifications, that is, they have descriptions of items that have to be combined with the lexical item. But the way in which the items have to be combined with the head is determined by dominance schemata (grammar rules) that are separate from the lexical items. So the valence specifications specify possible structures. Since valence representations can be composed by superordinate predicates there is enough flexibility to deal with various light verb phenomena. LFG is a bit more constrained due to the use of f-structures, but using a restriction operator unwanted information about grammatical functions can be keept out of f-structures of matrix predicates.

Further reading

This chapter is based on Müller (2018b).

23 Universal Grammar and doing comparative linguistics without an a priori assumption of a (strong) UG

The following two sections deal with the tools that I believe to be necessary to capture generalizations and the way one can derive such generalizations.

23.1 Formal tools for capturing generalizations

In Chapter 13, it was shown that all the evidence that has previously been brought forward in favor of innate linguistic knowledge is in fact controversial. In some cases, the facts are irrelevant to the discussion and in other cases, they could be explained in other ways. Sometimes, the chains of argumentation are not logically sound or the premises are not supported. In other cases, the argumentation is circular. As a result, the question of whether there is innate linguistic knowledge still remains unanswered. All theories that presuppose the existence of this kind of knowledge are making very strong assumptions. If one assumes, as Kayne (1994) for example, that all languages have the underlying structure [specifier [head complement]] and that movement is exclusively to the left, then these two basic assumptions must be part of innate linguistic knowledge since there is no evidence for the assumption that utterances in all natural languages have the structure that Kayne suggests. As an example, the reader may check Laenzlinger's proposal for German (2004: 224), which is depicted in Figure 4.20 on page 149. According to Laenzlinger, (1a) is derived from the underlying structure in (1b):

(1) a. weil   der Mann wahrscheinlich diese Sonate nicht oft   gut gespielt hat
       because the man   probably   this   sonata not often well played   has
       'because the man probably had not played this sonata well often'
   b. *weil   der Mann wahrscheinlich nicht oft   gut hat gespielt diese Sonate
       because the man   probably   not   often well has played   this sonata

(1b) is entirely unacceptable, so the respective structure cannot be acquired from input and hence the principles and rules that license it would have to be innate.

As we have seen, there are a number of alternative theories that are much more surface-oriented than most variants of Transformational Grammar. These alternative theories often differ with regard to particular assumptions that have been discussed in the preceding sections. For example, there are differences in the treatment of long-distance dependencies that have led to a proliferation of lexical items in Categorial Grammar (see Section 8.6). As has been shown by Jacobs (2008), Jackendoff (2008) and others, approaches such as Categorial Grammar that assume that every phrase must have a functor/head cannot explain certain constructions in a plausible way. Inheritance-based phrasal analyses that only list heads with a core meaning in the lexicon and have the constructions in which the heads occur determine the meaning of a complex expression turn out to have difficulties with derivational morphology and with accounting for alternative ways of argument realization (see Section 21.2.2, 21.4.1, and 21.4.2). We therefore need a theory that handles argument structure changing processes in the lexicon and still has some kind of phrase structure or relevant schemata. Some variants of GB/MP as well as LFG, HPSG, TAG and variants of CxG are examples of this kind of theory. Of these theories, only HPSG and some variants of CxG make use of the same descriptive tools ((typed) feature descriptions) for roots, stems, words, lexical rules and phrases. By using a uniform description for all these objects, it is possible to formulate generalizations over the relevant objects. It is therefore possible to capture what particular words have in common with lexical rules or phrases. For example, the -*bar* 'able' derivation corresponds to a complex passive construction with a modal verb. (2) illustrates.

(2) a. Das Rätsel ist lösbar.
   the puzzle is solvable
   b. Das Rätsel kann gelöst werden.
   the puzzle can solved be
   'The puzzle can be solved.'

By using the same descriptive inventory for syntax and morphology, it is possible to capture cross-linguistic generalizations: something that is inflection/derivation in one language can be syntax in another.

It is possible to formulate principles that hold for both words and phrases and furthermore, it is possible to capture cross-linguistic generalizations or generalizations that hold for certain groups of languages. For example, languages can be divided into those with fixed constituent order and those with more flexible or completely free constituent order. The corresponding types can be represented with their constraints in a type hierarchy. Different languages can use a particular part of the hierarchy and also formulate different constraints for each of the types (see Ackerman & Webelhuth 1998: Section 9.2). HPSG differs from theories such as LFG and TAG in that phrases are not ontologically different from words. This means that there are no special c-structures or tree structures. Descriptions of complex phrases simply have additional features that say something about their daughters. In this way, it is possible to formulate cross-linguistic generalizations about dominance schemata. In LFG, the c-structure rules are normally specified separately for each language. Another advantage of consistent description is that one can capture similarities between words and lexical rules, as well as between words and phrases. For example, a complementizer such as *dass* 'that' shares a number of properties with a simple verb or with coordinated verbs in initial position:

(3) a. [dass] Maria die Platte kennt und liebt
    that Maria the record knows and loves
    'that Maria knows and loves the record'

  b. [Kennt und liebt] Maria die Platte?
    knows and loves Maria the record
    'Does Maria know and love the record?'

The difference between the two linguistic objects mainly lies in the kind of phrase they select: the complementizer requires a sentence with a visible finite verb, whereas the verb in initial position requires a sentence without a visible finite verb.

In Section 9.1.5, a small part of an inheritance hierarchy was presented. This part contains types that probably play a role in the grammars of all natural languages: there are head-argument combinations in every language. Without this kind of combinatorial operation, it would not be possible to establish a relation between two concepts. The ability to create relations, however, is one of the basic properties of language.

In addition to more general types, the type hierarchy of a particular language contains language-specific types or those specific to a particular class of languages. All languages presumably have one and two-place predicates and for most languages (if not all), it makes sense to talk about verbs. It is then possible to talk about one and two-place verbs. Depending on the language, these can then be subdivided into intransitive and transitive. Constraints are formulated for the various types that can either hold generally or be language-specific. In English, verbs have to occur before their complements and therefore have the INITIAL value +, whereas verbs in German have the INITIAL value – and it is the lexical rule for initial position that licenses a verb with an INITIAL value +.

The differing settings of the INITIAL value for German and English is reminiscent of parameters from GB-Theory. There is one crucial difference, however: it is not assumed that a language learner sets the INITIAL value for all heads once and for all. The use of an INITIAL value is compatible with models of acquisition that assume that learners learn individual words with their positional properties. It is certainly possible for the respective words to exhibit different values for a particular feature. Generalizations about the position of entire word classes are only learned at a later point in the acquisition process.

A hierarchy analogous to the one proposed by Croft (see Section 21.4.1) is given in Figure 23.1 on the following page. For inflected words, the relevant roots are in the lexicon. Examples of this are *schlaf-* 'sleep', *lieb-* 'love' and *geb-* 'give'. In Figure 23.1, there are different subtypes of *root*, the general type for roots: e.g., *intrans-verb* for intransitive verbs and *trans-verb* for transitive verbs. Transitive verbs can be further subdivided into strictly transitive verbs (those with nominative and accusative arguments) and ditransitive verbs (those with nominative and both accusative and dative arguments). The hierarchy above would of course have to be refined considerably as there are even further sub-classes for both transitive and intransitive verbs. For example, one can divide intransitive verbs into unaccusative and unergative verbs and even strictly transitive verbs would have to be divided into further sub-classes (see Welke 2009: Section 2).

23 Universal Grammar and comparative linguistics without UG

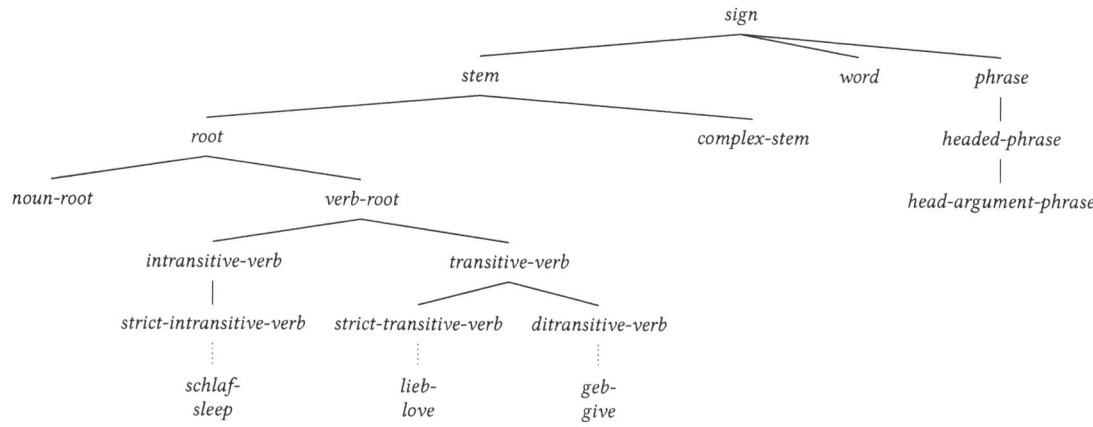

Figure 23.1: Section of an inheritance hierarchy with lexical entries and dominance schemata

In addition to a type for roots, the above figure contains types for stems and words. Complex stems are complex objects that are derived from simple roots but still have to be inflected (*lesbar-* 'readable', *besing-* 'to sing about'). Words are objects that do not inflect. Examples of these are the pronouns *er* 'he', *sie* 'she' etc. as well as prepositions. An inflected form can be formed from a verbal stem (*geliebt* 'loved', *besingt* 'sings about'). Relations between inflected words and (complex) stems can be formed again using derivation rules. In this way, *geliebt* 'loved' can be recategorized as an adjective stem that must then be combined with adjectival endings (*geliebt-e*). The relevant descriptions of complex stems/words are subtypes of *complex-stem* or *word*. These subtypes describe the form that complex words such as *geliebte* must have. For a technical implementation of this, see Müller (2002a: Section 3.2.7). Using dominance schemata, all words can be combined to form phrases. The hierarchy given here is of course by no means complete. There are a number of additional valence classes and one could also assume more general types that simply describe one, two and three-place predicates. Such types are probably plausible for the description of other languages. Here, we are only dealing with a small part of the type hierarchy in order to have a comparison to the Croftian hierarchy: in Figure 23.1, there are no types for sentence patterns with the form [Sbj IntrVerb], but rather types for lexical objects with a particular valence (V[COMPS ⟨ NP[*str*] ⟩]). Lexical rules can then be applied to the relevant lexical objects that license objects with another valence or introduce information about inflection. Complete words can be combined in the syntax with relatively general rules, for example in head-argument structures. The problems from which purely phrasal approaches suffer are thereby avoided. Nevertheless generalizations about lexeme classes and the utterances that can be formed can be captured in the hierarchy.

There are also principles in addition to inheritance hierarchies: the Semantics Principle presented in Section 9.1.6 holds for all languages. The Case Principle that we also saw is a constraint that only applies to a particular class of languages, namely nominative-accusative languages. Other languages have an ergative-absolutive system.

The assumption of innate linguistic knowledge is not necessary for the theory of language sketched here. As the discussion in Section 13 has shown, the question of whether this kind of knowledge exists has still not been answered conclusively. Should it turn out that this knowledge actually exists, the question arises of what exactly is innate. It would be a plausible assumption that the part of the inheritance hierarchy that is relevant for all languages is innate together with the relevant principles (e.g., the constraints on Head-Argument structures and the Semantics Principle). It could, however, also be the case that only a part of the more generally valid types and principles is innate since something being innate does not follow from the fact that it is present in all languages (see also Section 13.1.9).

In sum, one can say that theories that describe linguistic objects using a consistent descriptive inventory and make use of inheritance hierarchies to capture generalizations are the ones best suited to represent similarities between languages. Furthermore, this kind of theory is compatible with both a positive and a negative answer to the question of whether there is innate linguistic knowledge.

23.2 How to develop linguistic theories that capture cross-linguistic generalizations

In the previous section I argued for a uniform representation of linguistic knowledge at all descriptive levels and for type hierarchies as a good tool for representing generalizations. This section explores a way to develop grammars that are motivated by facts from several languages.

If one looks at the current practice in various linguistic schools one finds two extreme ways of approaching language. On the one hand, we have the Mainstream Generative Grammar (MGG) camp and, on the other hand, we have the Construction Grammar/Cognitive Grammar camp. I hasten to say that what I state here does not hold for all members of these groups, but for the extreme cases. The caricature of the MGG scientist is that he is looking for underlying structures. Since these have to be the same for all languages (poverty of the stimulus), it is sufficient to look at one language, say English. The result of this research strategy is that one ends up with models that were suggested by the most influential linguist for English and that others then try to find ways to accommodate other languages. Since English has an NP VP structure, all languages have to have it. Since English reorders constituents in passive sentences, passive is movement and all languages have to work this way. I discussed the respective analyses of German in more detail in Section 3.4.2 and in Chapter 20 and showed that the assumption that passive is movement makes unwanted predictions for German, since the subject of passives stays in the object position in German. Furthermore, this analysis requires the assumption of invisible expletives, that is, entities that cannot be seen and do not have any meaning.

On the other extreme of the spectrum we find people working in Construction Grammar or without any framework at all (see footnote 1 on page 1 for discussion) who claim that all languages are so different that we cannot even use the same vocabulary to analyze them. Moreover, within languages, we have so many different objects that it is impossible (or too early) to state any generalizations. Again, what I describe here are extreme positions and clichés.

In what follows, I sketch the procedure that we apply in the CoreGram project[1] (Müller 2013b; 2015b). In the CoreGram project we work on a set of typologically diverse languages in parallel:

- German (Müller 2007a; 2009c; 2012b; Müller & Ørsnes 2011; 2013a; Müller 2014b; 2017a)
- Danish (Ørsnes 2009b; Müller 2009c; 2012b; Müller & Ørsnes 2011; 2013a,b; 2015)
- Persian (Müller 2010b; Müller & Ghayoomi 2010)
- Maltese (Müller 2009b)
- Mandarin Chinese (Lipenkova 2009; Müller & Lipenkova 2009; 2013; 2016)
- Yiddish (Müller & Ørsnes 2011)
- English (Müller 2009c; 2012b; Müller & Ørsnes 2013a)
- Hindi
- Spanish (Machicao y Priemer 2015)
- French

These languages belong to diverse language families (Indo-European, Afro-Asiatic, Sino-Tibetan) and among the Indo-European languages the languages belong to different groups (Germanic, Romance, Indo-Iranian). Figure 23.2 provides an overview. We work out fully formalized, computer-processable grammar fragments in the framework of HPSG that have a semantics component. The details will not be discussed here, but the interested reader is referred to Müller (2015b).

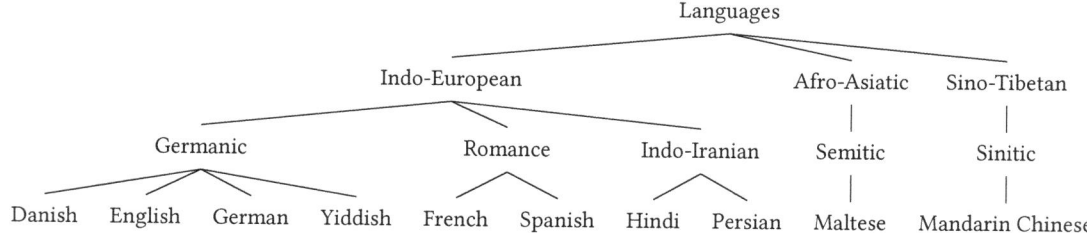

Figure 23.2: Language families and groups of the languages covered in the CoreGram project

---

[1]https://hpsg.hu-berlin.de/Projects/CoreGram.html, 15th August 2019.

23.2 How to develop linguistic theories that capture cross-linguistic generalizations

As was argued in previous sections, the assumption of innate language-specific knowledge should be kept to a minimum. This is also what Chomsky suggested in his Minimalist Program. There may even be no language-specific innate knowledge at all, a view taken in Construction Grammar/Cognitive Grammar. So, instead of imposing constraints from one language onto other languages, a bottom-up approach seems to be more appropriate: grammars for individual languages should be motivated language-internally. Grammars that share certain properties can be grouped in classes. This makes it possible to capture generalizations about groups of languages and natural language as such. Let us consider a few example languages: German, Dutch, Danish, English and French. If we start developing grammars for German and Dutch, we find that they share a lot of properties: for instance, both are SOV and V2 languages and both have a verbal complex. One main difference is the order of elements in the verbal complex. The situation can be depicted as in Figure 23.3. There are some properties that are shared

Figure 23.3: Shared properties of German and Dutch

between German and Dutch (Set 3). For instance, the argument structure of lexical items, a list containing descriptions of syntactic and semantic properties of arguments and the linking of these arguments to the meaning of the lexical items, is contained in Set 3. In addition to the constraints for SOV languages, the verb position and the fronting of a constituent in V2 clauses are contained in Set 3. The respective constraints are shared between the two grammars. Although these sets are arranged in a hierarchy in Figure 23.3 and the following figures this has nothing to do with the type hierarchies that have been discussed in the previous subsection. These type hierarchies are part of our linguistic theories and various parts of such hierarchies can be in different sets: those parts of the type hierarchy that concern more general aspects can be in Set 3 in Figure 23.3 and those that are specific to Dutch or German are in the respective other sets. When we add another language, say Danish, we get further differences. While German and Dutch are SOV, Danish is an SVO language. Figure 23.4 on the following page shows the resulting situation: the topmost node represents constraints that hold for all the languages considered so far (for instance the argument structure constraints, linking and V2) and the node below it (Set 4) contains constraints that hold for German and Dutch only.[2] For instance, Set 4 contains constraints regarding verbal complexes and SOV order. The union of Set 4 and Set 5 is Set 3 of Figure 23.3.

Figure 23.4: Shared properties of German, Dutch, and Danish

If we add further languages, further constraint sets will be distinguished. Figure 23.5 on the next page shows the situation that results when we add English and French. Again, the picture is not complete since there are constraints that are shared by Danish and English but not by French, but the general idea should be clear: by systematically working this way, we should arrive at constraint sets that directly correspond to those that have been established in the typological literature.

The interesting question is what will be the topmost set if we consider enough languages. At first glance, one would expect that all languages have valence representations and linkings between these and the semantics of lexical items (argument structure lists in the HPSG framework). However, Koenig & Michelson (2012) argue for an analysis of Oneida (a Northern Iroquoian language) that does not include a representation of syntactic valence. If this analysis is correct, syntactic argument structure would not be universal. It would, of course, be characteristic of a large number of languages, but it would not be part of the topmost set. So this leaves us with just one candidate for the topmost set from the area of syntax: the constraints that license the combination of two or more linguistic objects. This is basically Chomsky's External Merge without the binarity restriction[3]. In addition, the topmost set would, of course, contain the basic

---

[2]In principle, there could be constraints that hold for Dutch and Danish, but not for German or for German and Danish, but not for Dutch. These constraints would be removed from Set 1 and Set 2, respectively, and inserted into another constraint set higher up in the hierarchy. These sets are not illustrated in the figure and I keep the names Set 1 and Set 2 from Figure 23.3 for the constraint sets for German and Dutch.

[3]Note that binarity is more restrictive than flat structures: there is an additional constraint that there have to be exactly two daughters. As was argued in Section 21.10.4 one needs phrasal constructions with more than two constituents.

23.2 How to develop linguistic theories that capture cross-linguistic generalizations

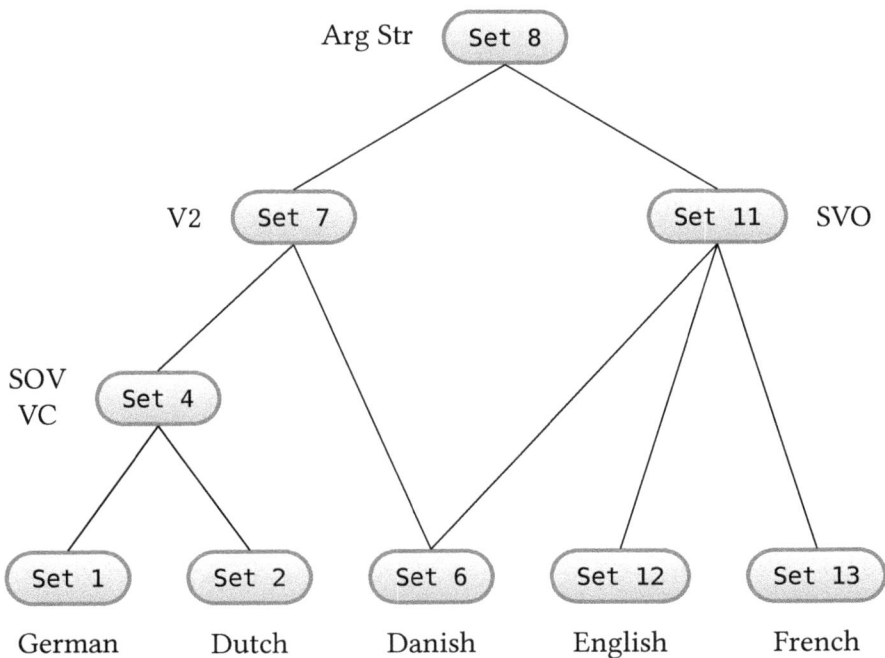

Figure 23.5: Languages and language classes

machinery for representing phonology and semantics.

It should be clear from what has been said so far that the goal of every scientist who works this way is to find generalizations and to describe a new language in a way that reuses theoretical constructs that have been found useful for a language that is already covered. However, as was explained above, the resulting grammars should be motivated by data of the respective languages and not by facts from other languages. In situations where more than one analysis would be compatible with a given dataset for language X, the evidence from language Y with similar constructs is most welcome and can be used as evidence in favor of one of the two analyses for language X. I call this approach the *bottom-up approach with cheating*: unless there is contradicting evidence, we can reuse analyses that have been developed for other languages.

Note that this approach is compatible with the rather agnostic view advocated by Haspelmath (2010a), Dryer (1997), Croft (2001: Section 1.4.2–1.4.3), and others, who argue that descriptive categories should be language-specific, that is, the notion of *subject* for Tagalog is different from the one for English, the category *noun* in English is different from the category *noun* in Persian and so on. Even if one follows such extreme positions, one can still derive generalizations regarding constituent structure, head-argument relations and so on. However, I believe that some categories can fruitfully be used cross-linguistically; if not universally, then at least for language classes. As Newmeyer (2010: 692) notes with regard to the notion of *subject*: calling two items *subject* in one language does not entail that they have identical properties. The same is true for two linguistic

693

items from different languages: calling a Persian linguistic item *subject* does not entail that it has exactly the same properties as an English linguistic item that is called *subject*. The same is, of course, true for all other categories and relations, for instance, parts of speech: Persian nouns do not share all properties with English nouns.[4] Haspelmath (2010c: 697) writes: "Generative linguists try to use as many crosslinguistic categories in the description of individual languages as possible, and this often leads to insurmountable problems." If the assumption of a category results in problems, they have to be solved. If this is not possible with the given set of categories/features, new ones have to be assumed. This is not a drawback of the methodology, quite the opposite is true: if we have found something that does not integrate nicely into what we already have, this is a sign that we have discovered something new and exciting. If we stick to language-particular categories and features, it is much harder to notice that a special phenomenon is involved, since all categories and features are specific to one language anyway. Note also that not all speakers of a language community have exactly the same categories. If one were to take the idea of language-particular category symbols to an extreme, one would end up with person specific category symbols like *Klaus-English-noun*.

After my talk at the MIT in 2013, members of the linguistics department objected to the approach taken in the CoreGram project and claimed that it would not make any predictions as far as possible/impossible languages are concerned. Regarding predictions two things must be said: firstly, predictions are being made on a language particular basis. As an example consider the following sentences from Netter (1991):

(4) a. [Versucht, zu lesen], hat er das Buch nicht.
tried to read has he.NOM the.ACC book not
'He did not try to read the book.'

b. [Versucht, einen Freund vorzustellen], hat er ihr noch nie.
tried a.ACC friend to.introduce has he.NOM her.DAT yet never
'He never before tried to introduce a friend to her.'

When I first read these sentences I had no idea about their structure. I switched on my computer and typed them in and within milliseconds I got an analysis of the sentences and by inspecting the result I realized that these sentences are combinations of partial verb phrase fronting and the so-called third construction (Müller 1999b: 439). I had previously implemented analyses of both phenomena but had never thought about

---

[4]Note that using labels like *Persian Noun* and *English Noun* (see for instance Haspelmath 2010a: Section 2 for such a suggestion regarding case, e.g., Russian Dative, Korean Dative, ...) is somehow strange since it implies that both Persian nouns and English nouns are somehow nouns. Instead of using the category *Persian Noun* one could assign objects of the respective class to the class *noun* and add a feature LANGUAGE with the value *persian*. This simple trick allows one to assign both objects of the type *Persian Noun* and objects of the type *English Noun* to the class *noun* and still maintain the fact that there are differences. Of course, no theoretical linguist would introduce the LANGUAGE feature to differentiate between Persian and English nouns, but nouns in the respective languages have other features that make them differ. So the part of speech classification as noun is a generalization over nouns in various languages and the categories *Persian Noun* and *English Noun* are feature bundles that contain further, language-specific information.

23.2 How to develop linguistic theories that capture cross-linguistic generalizations

the interaction of the two. The grammar predicted that examples like (4) are grammatical. Similarly the constraints of the grammar can interact to rule out certain structures. So predictions about ungrammaticality/impossible structures are in fact made as well.

Secondly, the topmost constraint set holds for all languages seen so far. It can be regarded as a hypothesis about properties that are shared by all languages. This constraint set contains constraints about the connection between syntax and information structure and such constraints allow for V2 languages but rule out languages with the verb in penultimate position (see Kayne 1994: 50 for the claim that such languages do not exist. Kayne develops a complicated syntactic system that predicts this). Of course, if a language is found that places the verb in penultimate position for the encoding of sentence types or some other communicative effect, a more general topmost set has to be defined. But this is parallel for Minimalist theories: if languages are found that are incompatible with basic assumptions, the basic assumptions have to be revised. As with the language particular constraints, the constraints in the topmost set make certain predictions about what can be and what cannot be found in languages.

Frequently discussed examples such as those languages that form questions by reversing the order of the words in a string (Haider 2015: 224; Musso et al. 2003) need not be ruled out by the grammar, since they are ruled out by language external constraints: we simply lack the working memory to do such complex computations.

A variant of this argument comes from David Pesetsky and was raised in Facebook discussions of an article by Paul Ibbotson and Michael Tomasello published in The Guardian[5]. Pesetsky claimed that Tomasello's theory of language acquisition could not explain why we find V2 languages but no V3 languages. First, I do not know of anything that blocks V3 languages in current Minimalist theories. So per se the fact that V3 languages may not exist cannot be used to support any of the competing approaches. Of course, the question could be asked whether the V3 pattern would be useful for reaching our communicative goals and whether it can be easily acquired. Now, with V2 as a pattern it is clear that we have exactly one position that can be used for special purposes in the V2 sentence (topic or focus). For monovalent and bivalent verbs we have an argument that can be placed in initial position. The situation is different for the hypothetical V3 languages, though: If we have monovalent verbs like *sleep*, there is nothing for the second position. As Pesetsky pointed out in the answer to my comment on a blog post, languages solve such problems by using expletives. For instance some languages insert an expletive to mark subject extraction in embedded interrogative sentences, since otherwise the fact that the subject is extracted would not be recognizable by the hearer. So the expletive helps to make the structure transparent. V2 languages also use expletives to fill the initial position if speakers want to avoid something in the special, designated position:

---

[5] *The roots of language: What makes us different from other animals?* Published 2015-11-05. http://www.theguardian.com/science/head-quarters/2015/nov/05/roots-language-what-makes-us-different-animals, 2018/04/25.

(5) Es   kamen drei Männer zum   Tor hinein.
    EXPL came   three man   to.the gate in
    'Three man came through the gate.'

In order to do the same in V3 languages one would have to put two expletives in front of the verb. So there seem to be many disadvantages of a V3 system that V2 systems do not have and hence one would expect that V3 systems are less likely to come into existence. If they existed, they would be expected to be subject to change in the course of time; e.g., omission of the expletive with intransitives, optional V2 with transitives and finally V2 in general. With the new modeling techniques for language acquisition and agent-based community simulation one can actually simulate such processes and I guess in the years to come, we will see exciting work in this area.

Cinque (1999: 106) suggested a cascade of functional projections to account for reoccurring orderings in the languages of the world. He assumes elaborate tree structures to play a role in the analysis of all sentences in all languages even if there is no evidence for respective morphosyntactic distinctions in a particular language (see also Cinque & Rizzi 2010: 55). In the latter case, Cinque assumes that the respective tree nodes are empty. Cinque's results could be incorporated in the model advocated here. We would define part of speech categories and morpho-syntactic features in the topmost set and state linearization constraints that enforce the order that Cinque encoded directly in his tree structure. In languages in which such categories are not manifested by lexical material, the constraints would never apply. Neither empty elements nor elaborate tree structures would be needed. Thus Cinque's data could be covered in a better way in an HPSG with a rich UG but I, nevertheless, refrain from introducing 400 categories (or features) into the theories of all languages and, again, I point out that such a rich and language-specific UG is implausible from a genetic point of view. Therefore, I wait for other, probably functional, explanations of the Cinque data.

Note also that implicational universals can be derived from hierarchically organized constraint sets as the ones proposed here. For instance, one can derive from Figure 23.5 the implicational statement that all SVO languages are V2 languages, since there is no language that has constraints from Set 4 that does not also have the constraints of Set 7. Of course, this implicational statement is wrong, since there are lots and lots of SOV languages and just exceptionally few V2 languages. So, as soon as we add other languages as for instance Persian or Japanese, the picture will change.

The methodology suggested here differs from what is done in MGG, since MGG stipulates the general constraints that are supposed to hold for all languages on the basis of general specualtions about language. In the best case, these general assumptions are fed by a lot of experience with different languages and grammars, in the worst case they are derived from insights gathered from one or more Indo-European languages. Quite often impressionistic data is used to motivate rather far-reaching fundamental design decisions (Fanselow 2009; Sternefeld & Richter 2012; Haider 2014). It is interesting to note that this is exactly what members of the MGG camp reproach typologists for. Evans & Levinson (2009a) pointed out that counterexamples can be found for many alleged universals. A frequent response to this is that unanalyzed data cannot refute grammatical

23.2 How to develop linguistic theories that capture cross-linguistic generalizations

hypotheses (see, for instance, Freidin 2009: 454). In the very same way it has to be said that unanalyzed data should not be used to build theories on (Fanselow 2009). In the CoreGram project, we aim to develop broad-coverage grammars of several languages, so those constraints that make it to the top node are motivated and not stipulated on the basis of intuitive implicit knowledge about language.

Since it is data-oriented and does not presuppose innate language-specific knowledge, this research strategy is compatible with work carried out in Construction Grammar (see Goldberg 2013b: 481 for an explicit statement to this end) and in any case it should also be compatible with the Minimalist world.

24 Conclusion

The analyses discussed in this book show a number of similarities. All frameworks use complex categories to describe linguistic objects. This is most obvious for GPSG, LFG, HPSG, CxG and FTAG, however, GB/Minimalism and Categorial Grammar also talk about NPs in third person singular and the relevant features for part of speech, person and number form part of a complex category. In GB, there are the feature N and V with binary values (Chomsky 1970: 199), Stabler (1992: 119) formalizes *Barriers* with feature-value pairs and Sauerland & Elbourne (2002: 290–291) argue for the use of feature-value pairs in a Minimalist theory. Also, see Veenstra (1998:) for a constraint-based formalization of a Minimalist analysis using typed feature descriptions. Dependency Grammar dialects like Hellwig's Dependency Unification Grammar also use feature-value pairs (Hellwig 2003: 612).

Furthermore, there is a consensus in all current frameworks (with the exception of Construction Grammar and Dependency Grammar) about how the sentence structure of German should be analyzed: German is an SOV and V2 language. Clauses with verb-initial order resemble verb-final ones in terms of structure. The finite verb is either moved (GB) or stands in a relation to an element in verb-final position (HPSG). Verb-second clauses consist of verb-initial clauses out of which one constituent has been extracted. It is also possible to see some convergence with regard to the analysis of the passive: some ideas originally formulated by Haider (1984; 1985a; 1986a) in the framework of GB have been adopted by HPSG. Some variants of Construction Grammar also make use of a specially marked 'designated argument' (Michaelis & Ruppenhofer 2001: 55–57).

If we consider new developments in the individual frameworks, it becomes clear that the nature of the proposed analyses can sometimes differ drastically. Whereas CG, LFG, HPSG and CxG are surface-oriented, sometimes very abstract structures are assumed in Minimalism and in some cases, one tries to trace all languages back to a common base structure (Universal Base Hypothesis).[1] This kind of approach only makes sense if one assumes that there is innate linguistic knowledge about this base structure common to all languages as well as about the operations necessary to derive the surface structures. As was shown in Chapter 13, all arguments for the assumption of innate linguistic knowledge are either not tenable or controversial at the very least. The acquisition of linguistic abilities can to a large extent receive an input-based explanation (Section 13.8.3, Section 16.3 and Section 16.4). Not all questions about acquisition have been settled once and for all, but input-based approaches are at least plausible enough for one to be very cautious about any assumption of innate linguistic knowledge.

---

[1] It should be noted that there are currently many subvariants and individual opinions in the Minimalist community so that it is only possible – as with CxG – to talk about tendencies.

24 Conclusion

Models such as LFG, CG, HPSG, CxG and TAG are compatible with performance data, something that is not true of certain transformation-based approaches, which are viewed as theories of competence that do not make any claims about performance. In MGG, it is assumed that there are other mechanisms for working with linguistic knowledge, for example, mechanisms that combine 'chunks' (fragments of linguistic material). If one wishes to make these assumptions, then it is necessary to explain how chunks and the processing of chunks are acquired and not how a complex system of transformations and transformation-comparing constraints is acquired. This means that the problem of language acquisition would be a very different one. If one assumes a chunk-based approach, then the innate knowledge about a universal transformational base would only be used to derive a surface-oriented grammar. This then poses the question of what exactly the evidence for transformations in a competence grammar is and if it would not be preferable to simply assume that the competence grammar is of the kind assumed by LFG, CG, HPSG, CxG or TAG. One can therefore conclude that constraint-based analyses and the kind of transformational approaches that allow a constraint-based reformulation are the only approaches that are compatible with the current facts, whereas all other analyses require additional assumptions.

A number of works in Minimalism differ from those in other frameworks in that they assume structures (sometimes also invisible structures) that can only be motivated by evidence from other languages. This can streamline the entire apparatus for deriving different structures, but the overall costs of the approach are not reduced: some amount of the cost is just transferred to the UG component. The abstract grammars that result cannot be learned from the input.

One can take from this discussion that only constraint-based, surface-oriented models are adequate and explanatory: they are also compatible with psycholinguistic facts and plausible from the point of view of acquisition.

If we now compare these approaches, we see that a number of analyses can be translated into one another. LFG (and some variants of CxG and DG) differ from all other theories in that grammatical functions such as subject and object are primitives of the theory. If one does not want this, then it is possible to replace these labels with Argument1, Argument2, etc. The numbering of arguments would correspond to their relative obliqueness. LFG would then move closer to HPSG. Alternatively, one could mark arguments in HPSG and CxG with regard to their grammatical function additionally. This is what is done for the analysis of the passive (DESIGNATED ARGUMENT).

LFG, HPSG, CxG and variants of Categorial Grammar (Moens et al. 1989; Briscoe 2000; Villavicencio 2002) possess means for the hierarchical organization of knowledge, which is important for capturing generalizations. It is, of course, possible to expand any other framework in this way, but this has never been done explicitly, except in computer implementations and inheritance hierarchies do not play an active role in theorizing in the other frameworks.

In HPSG and CxG, roots, stems, words, morphological and syntactic rules are all objects that can be described with the same means. This then allows one to make generalizations that affect very different objects (see Chapter 23). In LFG, c-structures are viewed as something fundamentally different, which is why this kind of generalization is not possible. In cross-linguistic work, there is an attempt to capture similarities in the f-structure, the c-structure is less important and is not even discussed in a number of works. Furthermore, its implementation from language to language can differ enormously. For this reason, my personal preference is for frameworks that describe all linguistic objects using the same means, that is, HPSG and CxG. Formally, nothing stands in the way of a description of the c-structure of an LFG grammar using feature-value pairs so that in years to come there could be even more convergence between the theories. For hybrid forms of HPSG and LFG, see Ackerman & Webelhuth (1998) and Hellan & Haugereid (2003), for example.

If one compares CxG and HPSG, it becomes apparent that the degree of formalization in CxG works is relatively low and a number of questions remain unanswered. The more formal approaches in CxG (with the exception of Fluid Construction Grammar) are variants of HPSG. There are relatively few precisely worked-out analyses in Construction Grammar and no description of German that would be comparable to the other approaches presented in this book. To be fair, it must be said that Construction Grammar is the youngest of the theories discussed here. Its most important contributions to linguistic theory have been integrated into frameworks such as HPSG and LFG.

The theories of the future will be a fusion of surface-oriented, constraint-based and model-theoretic approaches like CG, LFG, HPSG, Construction Grammar, equivalent variants of TAG and GB/Minimalist approaches that will be reformulated as constraint-based. (Variants of) Minimalism and (variants of) Construction Grammar are the most widely adopted approaches at present. I actually suspect the truth to lie somewhere in the middle. The linguistics of the future will be data-oriented. Introspection as the sole method of data collection has proven unreliable (Müller 2007c; Meurers & Müller 2009) and is being increasingly complemented by experimental and corpus-based analyses.

Statistical information and statistical processes play a very important role in machine translation and are becoming more important for linguistics in the narrow sense (Abney 1996). We have seen that statistical information is important in the acquisition process and Abney discusses cases of other areas of language such as language change, parsing preferences and gradience with grammaticality judgments. Following a heavy focus on statistical procedures, there is now a transition to hybrid forms in computational linguistics,[2] since it has been noticed that it is not possible to exceed certain levels of quality with statistical methods alone (Steedman 2011; Church 2011; Kay 2011). The same holds here as above: the truth is somewhere in between, that is, in combined systems. In order to have something to combine, the relevant linguistic theories first need to be developed. As Manfred Pinkal said: "It is not possible to build systems that understand language without understanding language."

---

[2]See Kaufmann & Pfister (2007) and Kaufmann (2009) for the combination of a speech recognizer with a HPSG grammar.

Appendix A: Solutions to the exercises

A.1 Introduction and basic terms

On (1c): theoretically, this could also be a case of extraposition of the relative clause to the postfield. Since *eine Frau, die Peter kennt* is a constituent, however, it is assumed that no reordering of the relative clause has taken place. Instead, we have a simpler structure with *eine Frau, die Peter kennt* as a complete NP in the middle field.

A Solutions to the exercises

A.2 Phrase structure grammars

1. For any grammar, it is possible to assume additional symbols and rules that create unnecessary structure or are simply never used because there are no words or phrases that could be used on the right-hand side of the rule. If we were to add the following rule to our grammar, for example, we would have a more complex grammar that can still analyze the same fragment of the language.

    (2) Tralala → Trulla Trololo

2. In general, it is assumed that the grammar with the fewest rules is the best one. Therefore, we can reject grammars that contain unnecessary rules such as (2).

    One should bear in mind what the aim of a theory of grammar is. If our goal is to describe the human language capacity, then a grammar with more rules could be better than other grammars with less rules. This is because psycholinguistic research has shown that highly-frequent units are simply stored in our brains and not built up from their individual parts each time, although we would of course be able to do this.

3. The problem here is the fact that it is possible to derive a completely empty noun phrase (see Figure A.1). This noun phrase could be inserted in all positions where

Figure A.1: Noun phrases without a visible determiner and noun

an otherwise filled NP would have to stay. Then, we would be able to analyze sequences of words such as (3), where the subject of *schläft* 'sleeps' is realized by an empty NP:

(3) * Ich glaube, dass schläft.
       I   believe that sleeps

This problem can be solved using a feature that determines whether the left periphery of the $\overline{\text{N}}$ is empty. Visible Ns and $\overline{\text{N}}$ with at least an adjective would have the value '−' and all others '+'. Empty determiners could then only be combined with $\overline{\text{N}}$s that have the value '−'. See Netter (1994).

4. If *Bücher* 'books' were an NP in the lexicon, then adjectives such as *interessant* 'interesting' would have to modify NPs in order for phrases such as (4) to be analyzed.

   (4) interessante Bücher
       interesting books

   If adjectives are combined with NPs, however, it still has to be explained why (5) is ungrammatical.

   (5) * interessante die Bücher
         interesting   the books

   For a detailed discussions of this topic, see Müller (2007a: Section 6.6.2).

5. This kind of rule cannot analyze noun phrases such as those in (6):

   (6) a. interessante [Aufsätze und Bücher]
          interesting essays   and books
       b. interessante [Aufsätze und Bücher aus Stuttgart]
          interesting essays   and books from Stuttgart

   Since adjectives can only be combined directly with nouns, these phrases cannot be analyzed. *Bücher* 'books' or *Bücher aus Stuttgart* 'books from Stuttgart' would be complete NPs. Since it is assumed that coordinated elements always have the same syntactic category, then *Aufsätze* 'essays' would have to be an NP. *Aufsätze und Bücher* and *Aufsätze und Bücher aus Stuttgart* would then also be NPs and it remains unexplained how an adjective can be combined with this NP. Because of (5), we must rule out analyses that assume that full NPs combine with adjectives.

   See Chapter 19 for a general discussion of empty elements.

6. If a specific determiner or just any determiner were to be combined with an adjective to form a complete NP, there would be no room for the integration of postnominal modifiers like modifying genitives, PPs and relative clauses. For PPs and relative clauses, analyses have been suggested in which these postnominal modifiers attach to complete NPs (Kiss 2005), but modifying genitives usually attach to smaller units. But even if one admits postnominal modifiers to attach to complete NPs, one cannot account for the iteration of adjectives and for arguments that depend on the elided noun.

   So, the simplest way to cope with the German data is the assumption of an empty noun. Alternatively one could assume that an adjective is directly projected to an $\overline{N}$. This $\overline{N}$ then can be modified by further adjectives or postnominal modifiers. The $\overline{N}$ is combined with a determiner to form a full NP. For phrases that involve elided relational nouns, one would have to assume the projection of an argument like *vom Gleimtunnel* 'of the Gleimtunnel' to $\overline{N}$. The $\overline{N}$ could be further modified or combined with a determiner directly.

A Solutions to the exercises

7. Adjective phrases such as those in (7) cannot be analyzed since the degree modifier occurs between the complement and the adjective:

(7) der auf seinen Sohn sehr stolze Vater
the on his son very proud father
'the father very proud of his son'

One would either have to allow for specifiers to be combined with their heads before complements or allow crossing lines in trees. Another assumption could be that German is like English, however then adjectival complements would have to be obligatorily reordered before their specifier. For a description of this kind of reordering, see Chapter 3. See Section 13.1.2 for a discussion of $\overline{\text{X}}$-Theory.

8. Write a phrase structure grammar that can analyze the sentences in (8), but does not allow the strings of words in (9).

(8) a. Der Mann hilft der Frau.
the.NOM man helps the.DAT woman
'The man helps the woman.'

b. Er gibt ihr das Buch.
he.NOM gives her.DAT the.ACC book
'He gives her the book.'

c. Er wartet auf ein Wunder.
he.NOM waits on a miracle.ACC
'He is waiting for a miracle.'

(9) a. * Der Mann hilft er.
the.NOM man helps he.NOM

b. * Er gibt ihr den Buch.
he.NOM gives her.DAT the.ACC book

In order to rule out the last two sentences, the grammar has to contain information about case. The following grammar will do the job:

(10) a. s → np(nom) v(nom_dat), np(dat)

b. s → np(nom), v(nom_dat_acc), np(dat), np(acc)

c. s → np(nom), v(nom_pp_auf), pp(auf,acc)

d. pp(Pform,Case) → p(Pform,Case), np(Case)

e. np(Case) → d(Case), n(Case)

f. v(nom_dat) → hilft

g. v(nom_dat_acc) → gibt

h. v(nom_pp_auf) → wartet
i. np(nom) → er
j. np(dat) → ihr
k. d(nom) → der
l. d(dat) → der
m. d(acc) → das
n. d(acc) → ein
o. n(nom) → Mann
p. n(dat) → Frau
q. n(acc) → Buch
r. n(acc) → Wunder
s. p(auf,acc) → auf

A.3 Transformational Grammar – Government & Binding

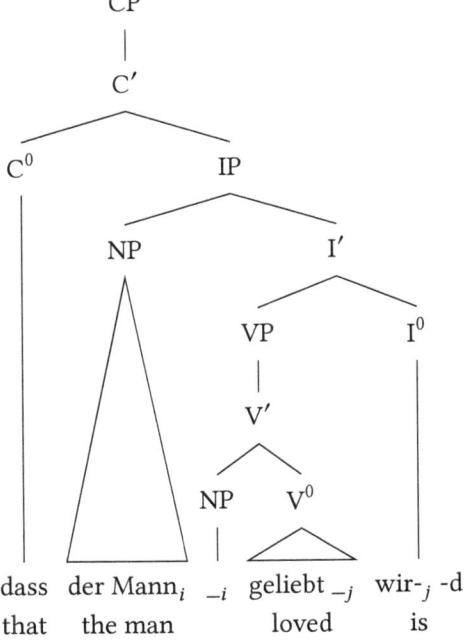

A Solutions to the exercises

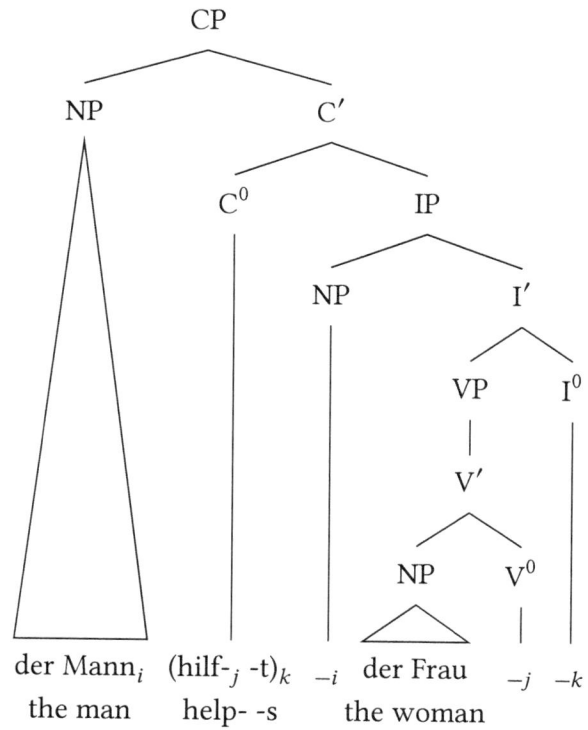

A.4 Generalized Phrase Structure Grammar

In order to analyze the sentences in (11), one requires a rule for transitive verbs and a metarule for the extraction of an element. Furthermore, rules for the combination of elements in the noun phrase are required.

(11)   a. [dass] der Mann ihn liest
            that   the man   it   reads

           'that the man reads it'

     b. [dass] ihn der Mann liest
            that   it   the man   reads

           'that the man reads it'

     c. Der Mann liest ihn.
        the man   reads it

        'The man reads it.'

It is possible to analyze the sentences in (11a,b) using the rules in (12) and the lexical entries in (13).

(12)   a. V3 → H[6], N2[CASE nom], N2[CASE acc]

     b. N2 → Det[CASE CAS], H1[CASE CAS]

     c. N1 → H[27]

(13)   a. Det[CASE nom] → der

     b. N[27] → Mann

     c. V[6, +FIN] → liest

     d. N2[CASE acc] → ihn

The rules (12b,c) correspond to $\overline{\text{X}}$-rules that we encountered in Section 2.4.1. They only differ from these rules in that the part of speech of the head is not given on the right-hand side of the rule. The part of speech is determined by the Head Feature Convention. The part of speech of the head is identical to that on the left-hand side of the rule, that is, it must be N in (12b,c). It also follows from the Head Feature Convention that the whole NP has the same case as the head and therefore does not have to be mentioned additionally in the rule above. 27 is the SUBCAT value. This number is arbitrary.

In order for the verb to appear in the correction position, we need linearization rules:

(14)   V[+MC] < X
       X   < V[−MC]

The fact that the determiner precedes the noun is ensured by the following LP-rule:

(15)   Det < X

A Solutions to the exercises

The Extraction Metarule in (16) is required in order to analyze (11c):

(16) V3 → W, X ↦
      V3/X → W

Among others, this metarule licenses the rule in (17) for (12a):

(17) V3/N2[CASE nom] → H[6], N2[CASE acc]

The rule in (18) is used to bind off long-distance dependencies.

(18) V3[+FIN] → X[+TOP], V3[+MC]/X

The following linearization rule ensures that the +TOP-constituent precedes the sentence in which it is missing:

(19) [+TOP] < X

Figure A.2 shows the structure licensed by the grammar. In sum, one can say that the

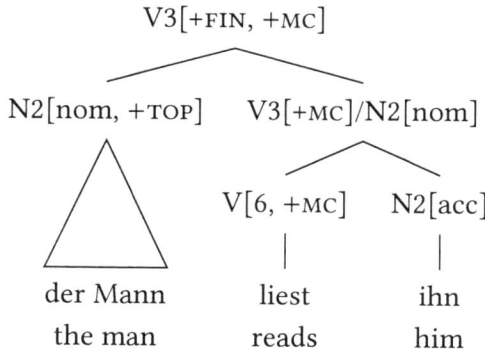

Figure A.2: Analysis of *Der Mann liest ihn.* 'The man reads it.'

grammar that licenses the sentences in (11) should have (at least) the following parts:

1. ID rules:

   (20) a. V3 → H[6], N2[CASE nom], N2[CASE acc]
         b. N2 → Det[CASE CAS], H1[CASE CAS]
         c. N1 → H[27]

2. LP rules:

   (21) V[+MC] < X
         X   < V[−MC]
         Det   < X
         [+TOP] < X

3. Metarules:

   (22) V3 → W, X ↦
         V3/X → W

4. Lexical entries

   (23) a. Det[CASE nom] → der
         b. N[27] → Mann
         c. V[6, +FIN] → liest
         d. N2[CASE acc] → ihn

A.5 Feature descriptions

1. For the class [+V], the type *verbal* is assumed with the subtypes *adjective* and *verb*. For the class [−V] there is the type *non-verbal* and its subtypes *noun* and *preposition*. This is analogous for the N values. The corresponding hierarchy is given in the following figure:

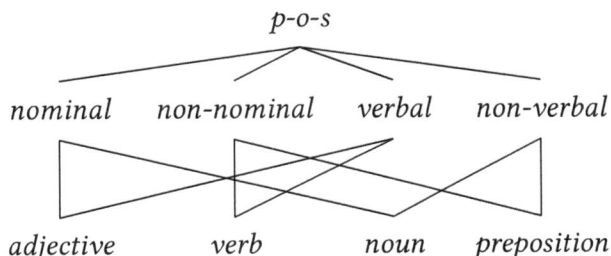

2. Lists can be described using recursive structures that consist of both a list beginning and a rest. The rest can either be a non-empty list (*ne_list*) or the empty list (*e_list*). The list ⟨ a, b, c ⟩ can be represented as follows:

$$
(24) \quad \begin{bmatrix} ne\_list \\ \text{FIRST} \ a \\ \text{REST} \ \begin{bmatrix} ne\_list \\ \text{FIRST} \ b \\ \text{REST} \ \begin{bmatrix} ne\_list \\ \text{FIRST} \ c \\ \text{REST} \ e\_list \end{bmatrix} \end{bmatrix} \end{bmatrix}
$$

A Solutions to the exercises

3. If we extend the data structure in (24) by two additional features, it is possible to do without *append*. The keyword is *difference list*. A difference list consists of a list and a pointer to the end of the list.

$$(25) \quad \begin{bmatrix} \textit{diff-list} \\ \text{LIST} \begin{bmatrix} \textit{ne\_list} \\ \text{FIRST} \ a \\ \text{REST} \begin{bmatrix} \textit{ne\_list} \\ \text{FIRST} \ b \\ \text{REST} \ \boxed{1} \ \textit{list} \end{bmatrix} \end{bmatrix} \\ \text{LAST} \ \boxed{1} \end{bmatrix}$$

Unlike the list representation in (24), the REST value of the end of the list is not *e_list*, but rather simply *list*. It is then possible to extend a list by adding another list to the point where it ends. The concatenation of (25) and (26a) is (26b).

$$(26) \quad \text{a.} \quad \begin{bmatrix} \textit{diff-list} \\ \text{LIST} \begin{bmatrix} \textit{ne\_list} \\ \text{FIRST} \ c \\ \text{REST} \ \boxed{2} \ \textit{list} \end{bmatrix} \\ \text{LAST} \ \boxed{2} \end{bmatrix}$$

$$\text{b.} \quad \begin{bmatrix} \textit{diff-list} \\ \text{LIST} \begin{bmatrix} \textit{ne\_list} \\ \text{FIRST} \ a \\ \text{REST} \begin{bmatrix} \textit{ne\_list} \\ \text{FIRST} \ b \\ \text{REST} \begin{bmatrix} \textit{ne\_list} \\ \text{FIRST} \ c \\ \text{REST} \ \boxed{2} \ \textit{list} \end{bmatrix} \end{bmatrix} \end{bmatrix} \\ \text{LAST} \ \boxed{2} \end{bmatrix}$$

In order to combine the lists, the LIST value of the second list has to be identified with the LAST value of the first list. The LAST value of the resulting list then corresponds to the LAST value of the second list (boxed 2 in the example.)

Information about the encoding of difference lists can be found by searching for the keywords *list*, *append*, and *feature structure*. In the search results, one can find pages on developing grammars that explain difference lists.

A.6 Lexical Functional Grammar

1. *kannte* 'knew' is a transitive verb:

    (27) *kannte*   V   ($\uparrow$ PRED) = 'KENNEN⟨SUBJ, OBJ⟩'
    ($\uparrow$ SUBJ AGR CAS = NOM)
    ($\uparrow$ OBJ AGR CAS = ACC)
    ($\uparrow$ TENSE) = PAST

2. In the sentence (28), the object of *hilft* 'helps' is in the prefield.

    (28) Dem   Kind hilft   Sandy.
    the.DAT child helps Sandy.NOM
    'Sandy helps the child.'

    The analysis is parallel to the analysis in Figure 7.5 on page 242. The difference is that the object is in the dative and not in the accusative. The respective grammatical function is OBJ$_\theta$ rather than OBJ.

    The necessary c-structure rules are given in (29):

    (29) a. VP $\rightarrow$ NP   VP
    ($\uparrow$SUBJ |OBJ |OBJ$_\theta$) = $\downarrow$ $\uparrow$ = $\downarrow$

    b. VP $\rightarrow$ (V)
    $\uparrow$ = $\downarrow$

    c. C' $\rightarrow$ C   VP
    $\uparrow$ = $\downarrow$ $\uparrow$ = $\downarrow$

    d. CP $\rightarrow$ XP   C'
    ($\uparrow$DF) = $\downarrow$ $\uparrow$=$\downarrow$
    ($\uparrow$DF) = ($\uparrow$COMP* GF)

    These rules allow two f-structures for the example in question: one in which the NP *dem Kind* 'the child' is the topic and another in which this NP is the focus. Figure A.3 shows the analysis with a topicalized constituent in the prefield.

A Solutions to the exercises

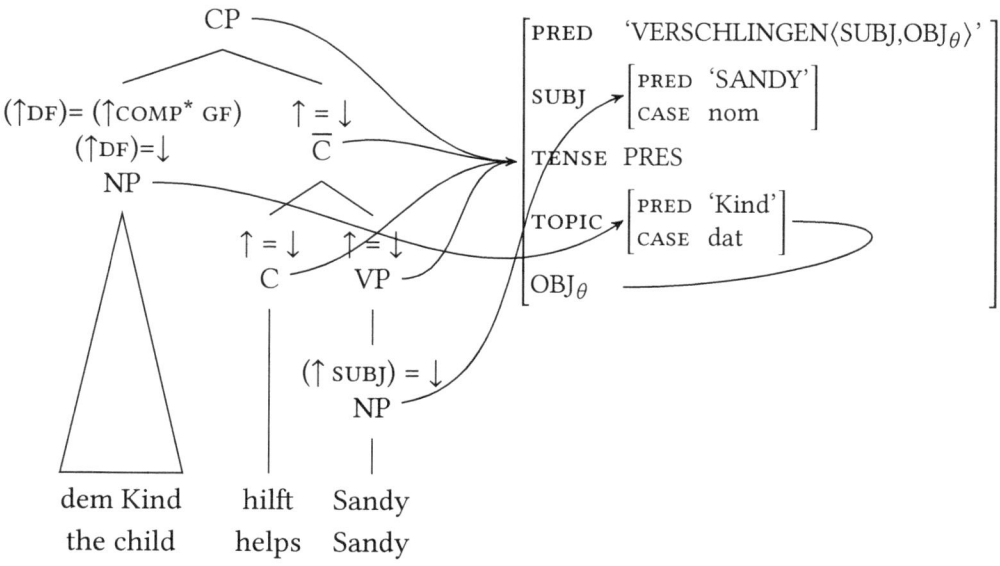

Figure A.3: Analysis of verb second

A.7 Categorial Grammar

1. The analysis of *The children in the room laugh loudly.* is given in Figure A.4.

$$
\begin{array}{ccccccc}
\underline{\textit{the}} & \underline{\textit{children}} & \underline{\textit{in}} & \underline{\textit{the}} & \underline{\textit{room}} & \underline{\textit{laugh}} & \underline{\textit{loudly}} \\
np/n & n & (n\backslash n)/np & np/n & n & s\backslash np & (s\backslash np)\backslash (s\backslash np)
\end{array}
$$

Figure A.4: Categorial Grammar analysis of *The children in the room laugh loudly.*

2. The analysis of *the picture of Mary* is given in Figure A.5. n/pp corresponds to N^0, n corresponds to $\overline{N}$ and np corresponds to NP.

$$
\begin{array}{cccc}
\underline{\textit{the}} & \underline{\textit{picture}} & \underline{\textit{of}} & \underline{\textit{Mary}} \\
np/n & n/pp & pp/np & np
\end{array}
$$

Figure A.5: Categorial Grammar analysis of *the picture of Mary*

714

A.8 Head-Driven Phrase Structure Grammar

1. The solution is:

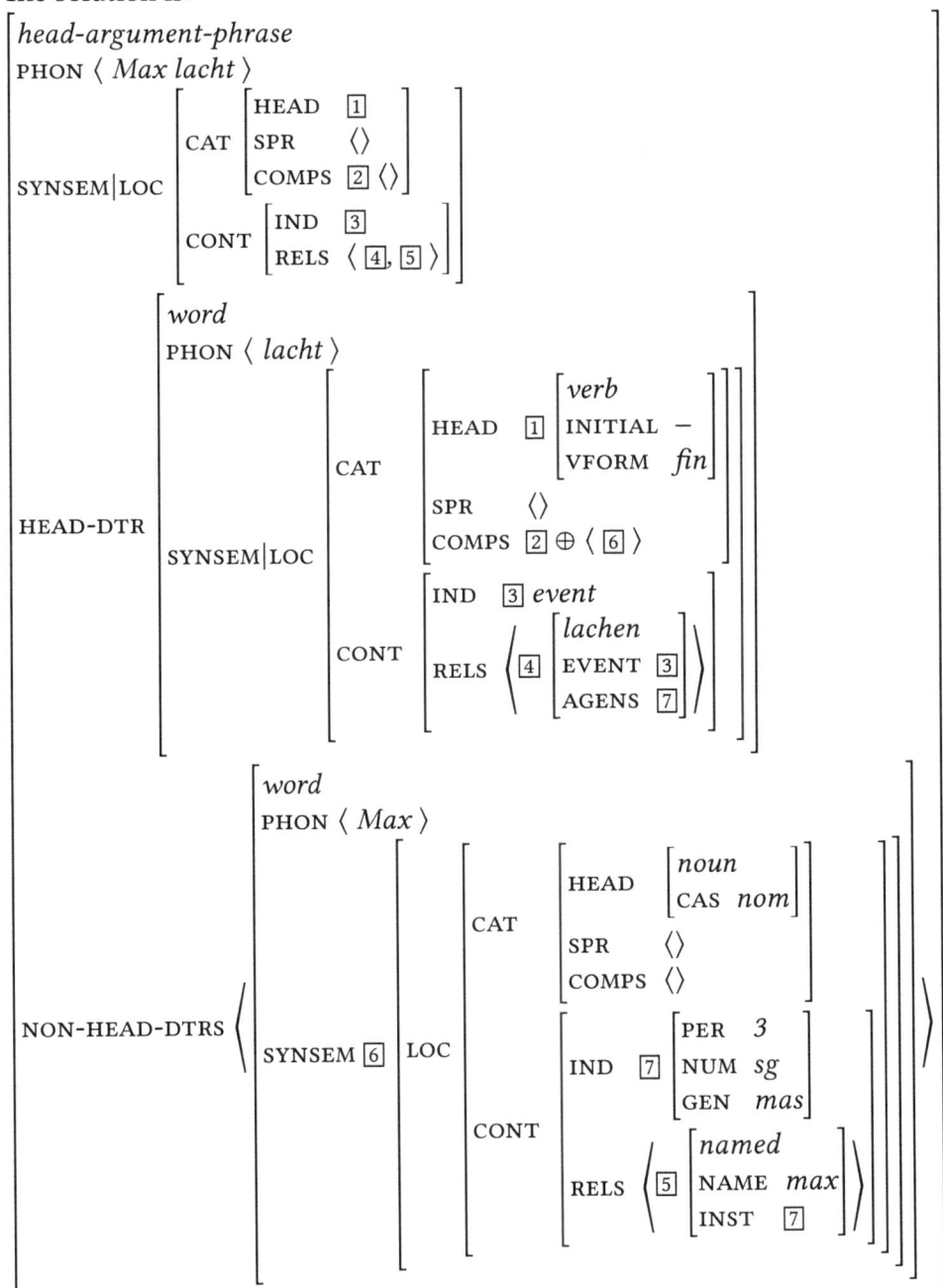

2. An analysis of the difference in (30) has to capture the fact that the case of the adjective has to agree with that of the noun. In (30a), the genitive form of *interessant* 'interesting' is used, whereas (30b) contains a form that is incompatible with the genitive singular.

(30) a. eines   interessanten Mannes
       one.GEN interesting.GEN man.GEN
    b. * eines   interessanter Mannes
       one.GEN interesting.NOM man.GEN

(31) shows the CAT value of *interessanten*.

(31) CAT value of *interessanten* 'interesting' with case information:

$$\begin{bmatrix} \text{HEAD} & \begin{bmatrix} adj \\ \text{MOD} & \overline{\text{N}}\,[\text{CASE}\,\boxed{1}] \\ \text{CASE} & \boxed{1}\,gen \end{bmatrix} \\ \text{SPR} & \langle\,\rangle \\ \text{COMPS} & \langle\,\rangle \end{bmatrix}$$

The structure sharing of the case value of the adjective with the case value of the $\overline{\text{N}}$ under MOD identifies the case values of the noun and the adjective. *interessanten* can therefore be combined with *Mannes*, but not with *Mann*. Similarly, *interessanter* can only be combined with the nominative *Mann*, but not with the genitive *Mannes*.

For a refinement of the analysis of agreement inside the noun phrase, see Müller (2007a: Abschnitt 13.2).

A.9 Construction Grammar

Idioms can be found by reading the newspaper carefully. The less exciting method is to look them up a dictionary of idioms such as the Free Dictionary of Idioms and Phrases[1].

---

[1] http://idioms.thefreedictionary.com/, 2018-02-20.

A.10 Dependency Grammar

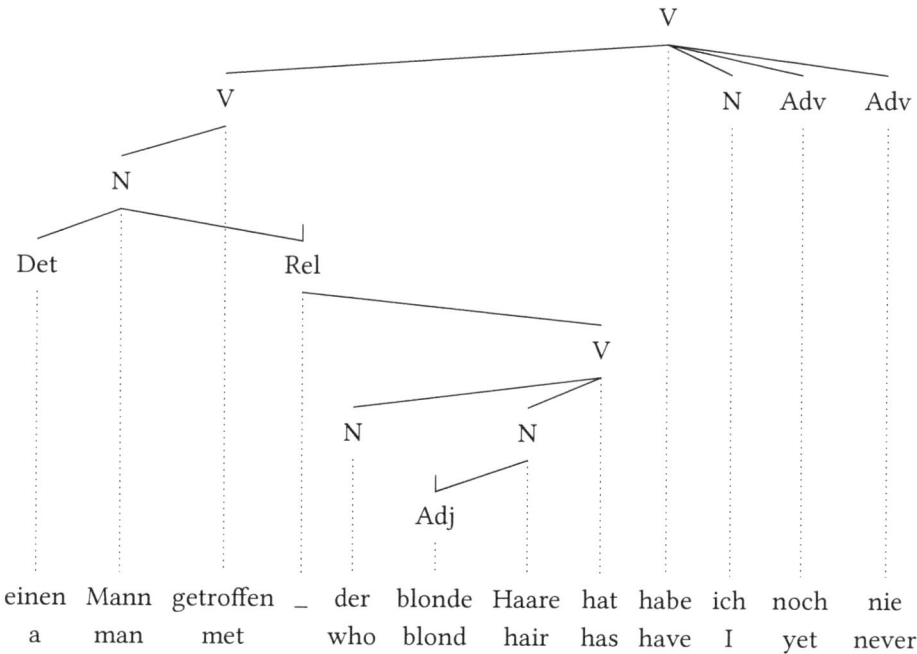

A.11 Tree Adjoining Grammar

The elementary trees in Figure A.6 are needed for the analysis of (32).

(32) der   dem   König treue Diener
     the.NOM the.DAT king loyal servant
     'the servant loyal to the king'

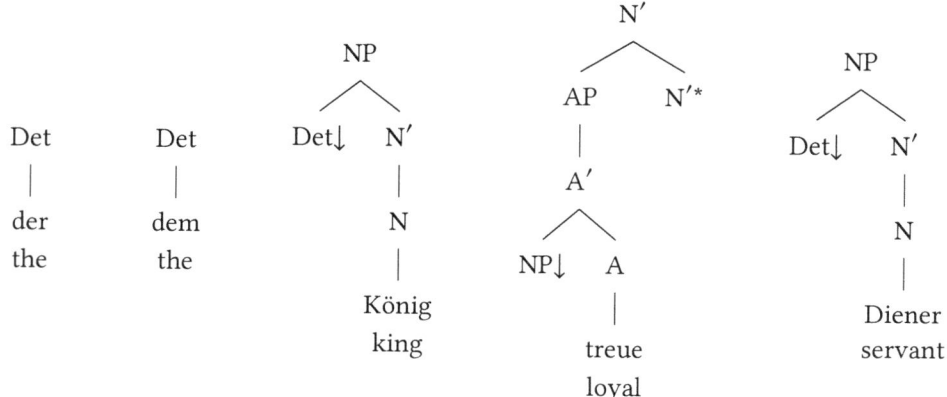

Figure A.6: Elementary trees for *der dem König treue Diener*

By substituting the tree for *dem* 'the' in the substitution node of *König* 'king', one then arrives at a full NP. This can then be inserted into the substitution node of *treue* 'loyal'.

A.11 Tree Adjoining Grammar

Similarly, the tree for *der* 'the' can be combined with the one for *Diener*. One then has both of the trees in Figure A.7.

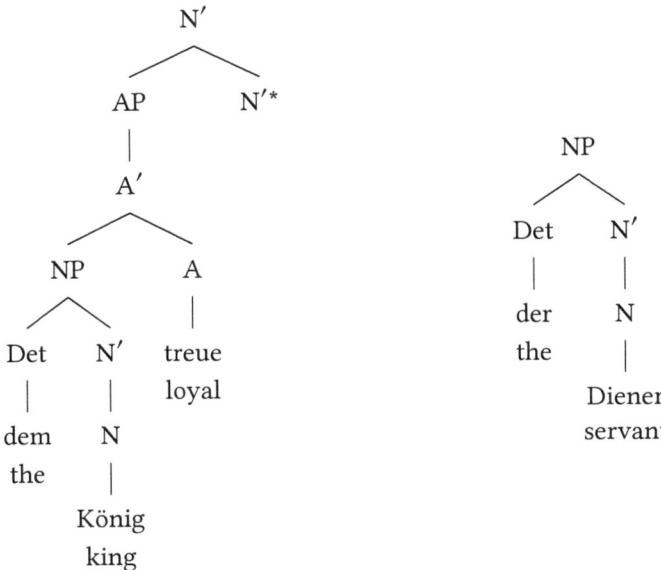

Figure A.7: Trees for *der dem König treue* and *der Diener* after substitution

The adjective tree can then be adjoined to the N'-node of *der Diener*, which yields the structure in Figure A.8 on the following page.

A Solutions to the exercises

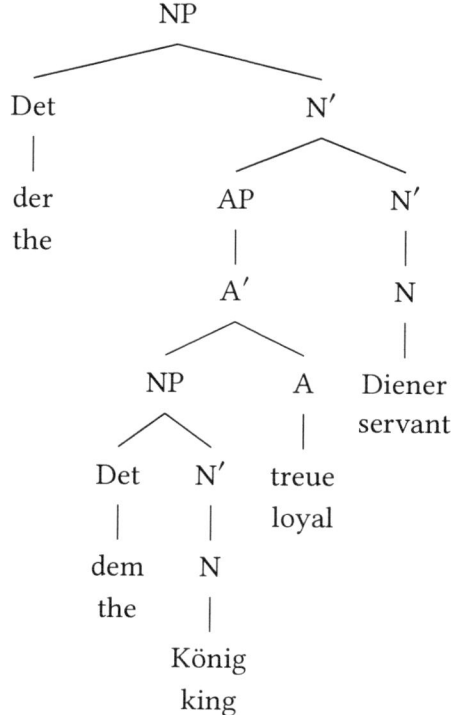

Figure A.8: Result of adjunction of the AP to the N′-node

References

Abbott, Barbara. 1976. Right node raising as a test for constituenthood. *Linguistic Inquiry* 7(4). 639–642.

Abeillé, Anne. 1988. Parsing French with Tree Adjoining Grammar: Some linguistic accounts. In Dénes Vargha (ed.), *Proceedings of COLING 88*, 7–12. University of Budapest: Association for Computational Linguistics. http://www.aclweb.org/anthology/C/C88/C88-1002.pdf, accessed 2018-2-25.

Abeillé, Anne. 2006. In defense of lexical coordination. In Olivier Bonami & Patricia Cabredo Hofherr (eds.), *Empirical issues in formal syntax and semantics*, vol. 6, 7–36. Paris: CNRS. http://www.cssp.cnrs.fr/eiss6/, accessed 2018-2-25.

Abeillé, Anne & Danièle Godard. 2002. The syntactic structure of French auxiliaries. *Language* 78(3). 404–452.

Abeillé, Anne & Owen Rambow (eds.). 2000. *Tree Adjoining Grammars: formalisms, linguistic analysis and processing* (CSLI Lecture Notes 156). Stanford, CA: CSLI Publications.

Abeillé, Anne & Yves Schabes. 1989. Parsing idioms in Lexicalized TAG. In Harold Somers & Mary McGee Wood (eds.), *Proceedings of the Fourth Conference of the European Chapter of the Association for Computational Linguistics*, 1–9. Manchester, England: Association for Computational Linguistics.

Abney, Steven P. 1987. *The English noun phrase in its sentential aspect*. Cambridge, MA: MIT dissertation. http://www.vinartus.net/spa/87a.pdf, accessed 2018-2-25.

Abney, Steven P. 1996. Statistical methods and linguistics. In Judith L. Klavans & Philip Resnik (eds.), *The balancing act: combining symbolic and statistical approaches to language* (Language, Speech, and Communication), 1–26. London, England/Cambridge, MA: MIT Press.

Abney, Steven P. & Jennifer Cole. 1986. A Government-Binding parser. In S. Berman, J-W. Choe & J. McDonough (eds.), *Proceedings of NELS 16*, 1–17. University of Massachusetts, Amherst: GLSA.

Abraham, Werner. 1995. *Deutsche Syntax im Sprachenvergleich: Grundlegung einer typologischen Syntax des Deutschen* (Studien zur deutschen Grammatik 41). Tübingen: Stauffenburg Verlag.

Abraham, Werner. 2003. The syntactic link between thema and rhema: The syntax-discourse interface. *Folia Linguistica* 37(1–2). 13–34.

Abraham, Werner. 2005. *Deutsche Syntax im Sprachenvergleich: Grundlegung einer typologischen Syntax des Deutschen*. 2nd edn. (Studien zur deutschen Grammatik 41). Tübingen: Stauffenburg Verlag.

References

Abzianidze, Lasha. 2011. *An HPSG-based formal grammar of a core fragment of Georgian implemented in TRALE.* Charles University in Prague MA thesis.

Ackerman, Farrell & Gert Webelhuth. 1998. *A theory of predicates* (CSLI Lecture Notes 76). Stanford, CA: CSLI Publications.

Adams, Marianne. 1984. Multiple interrogation in Italian. *The Linguistic Review* 4(1). 1–27.

Ades, Anthony E. & Mark J. Steedman. 1982. On the order of words. *Linguistics and Philosophy* 4(4). 517–558.

Adger, David. 2003. *Core syntax: A Minimalist approach* (Oxford Core Linguistics 1). Oxford: Oxford University Press.

Adger, David. 2010. A Minimalist theory of feature structure. In Anna Kibort & Greville G. Corbett (eds.), *Features: perspectives on a key notion in linguistics* (Oxford Linguistics), 185–218. Oxford: Oxford University Press.

Adger, David. 2013. Constructions and grammatical explanation: Comments on Goldberg. *Mind and Language* 28(4). 466–478.

Ágel, Vilmos. 2000. *Valenztheorie* (Narr Studienbücher). Tübingen: Gunter Narr Verlag.

Ágel, Vilmos, Ludwig M. Eichinger, Hans-Werner Eroms, Peter Hellwig, Hans Jürgen Heringer & Henning Lobin (eds.). 2003. *Dependenz und Valenz / Dependency and valency: Ein internationales Handbuch der zeitgenössischen Forschung / An international handbook of contemporary research.* Vol. 25.1 (Handbücher zur Sprach- und Kommunikationswissenschaft). Berlin: Walter de Gruyter.

Ágel, Vilmos, Ludwig M. Eichinger, Hans-Werner Eroms, Peter Hellwig, Hans Jürgen Heringer & Henning Lobin (eds.). 2006. *Dependenz und Valenz / Dependency and valency: Ein internationales Handbuch der zeitgenössischen Forschung / An international handbook of contemporary research.* Vol. 25.2 (Handbücher zur Sprach- und Kommunikationswissenschaft). Berlin: Walter de Gruyter.

Ágel, Vilmos & Klaus Fischer. 2010. 50 Jahre Valenztheorie und Dependenzgrammatik. *Zeitschrift für Germanistische Linguistik* 38(2). 249–290.

Ajdukiewicz, Kazimierz. 1935. Die syntaktische Konnexität. *Studia Philosophica* 1. 1–27.

Alqurashi, Abdulrahman & Robert D. Borsley. 2013. Arabic relative clauses in HPSG. In Stefan Müller (ed.), *Proceedings of the 20th International Conference on Head-Driven Phrase Structure Grammar, Freie Universität Berlin*, 25–43. Stanford, CA: CSLI Publications. http://csli-publications.stanford.edu/HPSG/2013/, accessed 2018-8-17.

Alsina, Alex. 1996. Resultatives: A joint operation of semantic and syntactic structures. In Miriam Butt & Tracy Holloway King (eds.), *Proceedings of the LFG '96 conference, Rank Xerox, Grenoble*. Stanford, CA: CSLI Publications. http://csli-publications.stanford.edu/LFG/1/, accessed 2018-2-25.

Alsina, Alex, KP Mohanan & Tara Mohanan. 2005. How to get rid of the COMP. In Miriam Butt & Tracy Holloway King (eds.), *Proceedings of the LFG 2005 conference.* Stanford, CA: CSLI Publications. http://csli-publications.stanford.edu/LFG/10/, accessed 2018-2-25.

Altmann, Hans & Ute Hofman. 2004. *Topologie fürs Examen: Verbstellung, Klammerstruktur, Stellungsfelder, Satzglied- und Wortstellung* (Linguistik fürs Examen 4). Wiesbaden: VS Verlag für Sozialwissenschaften/GWV Fachverlage GmbH.

Ambridge, Ben & Adele E. Goldberg. 2008. The island status of clausal complements: Evidence in favor of an information structure explanation. *Cognitive Linguistics* 19. 349–381.

Ambridge, Ben & Elena V. M. Lieven. 2011. *Child language acquisition: Contrasting theoretical approaches.* Cambridge, UK: Cambridge University Press.

Ambridge, Ben, Caroline F. Rowland & Julian M. Pine. 2008. Is structure dependence an innate constraint? New experimental evidence from children's complex-question production. *Cognitive Science: A Multidisciplinary Journal* 32(1). 222–255.

Anderson, John M. 1971. *The grammar of case: Towards a localistic theory.* Vol. 4 (Cambridge Studies in Linguistics). Cambridge, UK: Cambridge University Press.

Anderson, Stephen R. 1992. *A-morphous morphology* (Cambridge Studies in Linguistics 62). Cambridge: Cambridge University Press.

Aoun, Joseph & David W. Lightfoot. 1984. Government and contraction. *Linguistic Inquiry* 15(3). 465–473.

Aoun, Joseph & Dominique Sportiche. 1983. On the formal theory of government. *The Linguistic Review* 2(3). 211–236.

Arad Greshler, Tali, Livnat Herzig Sheinfux, Nurit Melnik & Shuly Wintner. 2015. Development of maximally reusable grammars: Parallel development of Hebrew and Arabic grammars. In Stefan Müller (ed.), *Proceedings of the 22nd International Conference on Head-Driven Phrase Structure Grammar, Nanyang Technological University (NTU), Singapore*, 27–40. Stanford, CA: CSLI Publications. http://csli-publications.stanford.edu/HPSG/2015/ahmw.pdf, accessed 2018-2-25.

Arends, Jacques. 2008. A demographic perspective on Creole formation. In Silvia Kouwenberg & John Victor Singler (eds.), *The handbook of pidgin and creole studies*, 309–331. Oxford/Cambridge: Blackwell Publishers Ltd.

Arka, I Wayan, Avery Andrews, Mary Dalrymple, Meladel Mistica & Jane Simpson. 2009. A linguistic and computational morphosyntactic analysis for the applicative -i in Indonesian. In Miriam Butt & Tracy Holloway King (eds.), *Proceedings of the LFG 2009 conference*, 85–105. Stanford, CA: CSLI Publications. http://csli-publications.stanford.edu/LFG/14/, accessed 2018-2-25.

Arnold, Doug & Andrew Spencer. 2015. A constructional analysis for the skeptical. In Stefan Müller (ed.), *Proceedings of the 22nd International Conference on Head-Driven Phrase Structure Grammar, Nanyang Technological University (NTU), Singapore*, 41–60. Stanford, CA: CSLI Publications. http://csli-publications.stanford.edu/HPSG/2015/arnold-spencer.pdf, accessed 2018-2-25.

Arnold, Jennifer E., Michael K. Tanenhaus, Rebecca J. Altmann & Maria Fagnano. 2004. The old and thee, uh, new. *Psychological Science* 15(9). 578–582.

Ashwini, Vaidya, Owen Rambow & Martha Palmer. 2019. Syntactic composition and selectional preferences in Hindi light verb constructions. *Linguistic Issues in Language Technology* 16(1).

References

Askedal, John Ole. 1986. Zur vergleichenden Stellungsfelderanalyse von Verbalsätzen und nichtverbalen Satzgliedern. *Deutsch als Fremdsprache* 23. 269–273 and 342–348.

Asudeh, Ash. 2004. *Resumption as resource management*. Stanford University dissertation.

Asudeh, Ash, Mary Dalrymple & Ida Toivonen. 2008. Constructions with lexical integrity: Templates as the lexicon-syntax interface. In Miriam Butt & Tracy Holloway King (eds.), *Proceedings of the LFG 2008 conference*. Stanford, CA: CSLI Publications. http://csli-publications.stanford.edu/LFG/13/, accessed 2018-2-25.

Asudeh, Ash, Mary Dalrymple & Ida Toivonen. 2013. Constructions with lexical integrity. *Journal of Language Modelling* 1(1). 1–54.

Asudeh, Ash, Gianluca Giorgolo & Ida Toivonen. 2014. Meaning and valency. In Miriam Butt & Tracy Holloway King (eds.), *Proceedings of the LFG 2014 conference*, 68–88. Stanford, CA: CSLI Publications.

Asudeh, Ash & Ida Toivonen. 2014. *With* lexical integrity. *Theoretical Linguistics* 40(1–2). 175–186.

Attardi, Giuseppe. 2006. Experiments with a multilanguage non-projective dependency parser. In *Proceedings of the 10th Conference on Computational Natural Language Learning (CoNLL-X)*, 166–170. Association for Computational Linguistics.

Attia, Mohammed A. 2008. *Handling Arabic morphological and syntactic ambiguity within the LFG framework with a view to machine translation*. School of Languages, Linguistics & Cultures, University of Manchester dissertation.

Avgustinova, Tania & Yi Zhang. 2009. Exploiting the Russian national corpus in the development of a Russian Resource Grammar. In Núria Bel, Erhard Hinrichs, Kiril Simov & Petya Osenova (eds.), *Adaptation of language resources and technology to new domains at the RANLP 2009 Conference, Borovets, Bulgaria*, 1–11. Shoumen, Bulgaria: INCOMA Ltd.

Bach, Emmon. 1962. The order of elements in a Transformational Grammar of German. *Language* 8(3). 263–269.

Bach, Emmon. 1976. An extension of classical Transformation Grammar. In *Problems in linguistic metatheory, Proceedings of the 1976 Conference at the Michigan State University*, 183–224.

Bahrani, Mohammad, Hossein Sameti & Mehdi Hafezi Manshadi. 2011. A computational grammar for Persian based on GPSG. *Language Resources and Evaluation* 45(4). 387–408.

Baker, Carl Lee. 1978. *Introduction to Generative-Transformational Syntax*. Englewood Cliffs, NJ: Prentice-Hall.

Baker, Mark C. 2003. Linguistic differences and language design. *Trends in Cognitive Sciences* 7(8). 349–353.

Baker, Mark C. 2009. Language universals: Abstract but not mythological. *The Behavioral and Brain Sciences* 32(5). 448–449.

Baldridge, Jason. 2002. *Lexically specified derivational control in Combinatory Categorial Grammar*. University of Edinburgh dissertation.

Baldridge, Jason, Sudipta Chatterjee, Alexis Palmer & Ben Wing. 2007. DotCCG and VisCCG: Wiki and programming paradigms for improved grammar engineering with OpenCCG. In Tracy Holloway King & Emily M. Bender (eds.), *Grammar Engineering across Frameworks 2007* (Studies in Computational Linguistics ONLINE), 5–25. Stanford, CA: CSLI Publications. http://csli-publications.stanford.edu/GEAF/2007/, accessed 2018-2-25.

Baldridge, Jason & Geert-Jan M. Kruijff. 2002. Coupling CCG and Hybrid Logic Dependency Semantics. In Pierre Isabelle (ed.), *40th Annual Meeting of the Association for Computational Linguistics: Proceedings of the conference*, 319–326. University of Pennsylvania, Philadelphia: Association for Computational Linguistics. http://www.aclweb.org/anthology/P02-1041, accessed 2018-2-25.

Ballweg, Joachim. 1997. Stellungsregularitäten in der Nominalphrase. In Hans-Werner Eroms, Gerhard Stickel & Gisela Zifonun (eds.), *Grammatik der deutschen Sprache*, vol. 7.3 (Schriften des Instituts für deutsche Sprache), 2062–2072. Berlin: Walter de Gruyter.

Baltin, Mark. 1981. Strict bounding. In Carl Lee Baker & John J. McCarthy (eds.), *The logical problem of language acquisition*, 257–295. Cambridge, MA: MIT Press.

Baltin, Mark. 2004. Remarks on the relation between language typology and Universal Grammar: Commentary on Newmeyer. *Studies in Language* 28(3). 549–553.

Baltin, Mark. 2017. Extraposition. In Martin Everaert & Henk van Riemsdijk (eds.), *The Blackwell companion to syntax*, 2nd edn. (Blackwell Handbooks in Linguistics), 237–271. Oxford: Blackwell Publishers Ltd. DOI:10.1002/9781118358733

Bangalore, Srinivas, Aravind K. Joshi & Owen Rambow. 2003. Dependency and valency in other theories: Tree Adjoining Grammar. In Vilmos Ágel, Ludwig M. Eichinger, Hans-Werner Eroms, Peter Hellwig, Hans Jürgen Heringer & Henning Lobin (eds.), *Dependenz und Valenz / Dependency and valency: Ein internationales Handbuch der zeitgenössischen Forschung / An international handbook of contemporary research*, vol. 25.1 (Handbücher zur Sprach- und Kommunikationswissenschaft), 669–678. Berlin: Walter de Gruyter.

Bannard, Colin, Elena Lieven & Michael Tomasello. 2009. Modeling children's early grammatical knowledge. *Proceedings of the National Academy of Sciences* 106(41). 17284–17289.

Bargmann, Sascha. 2015. *Syntactically flexible VP-idioms and the N-after-N Construction*. Poster presentation at the 5th General Meeting of PARSEME, Iasi, 23–24 September 2015.

Bar-Hillel, Yehoshua, Micha A. Perles & Eliahu Shamir. 1961. On formal properties of simple phrase-structure grammars. *Zeitschrift für Phonetik, Sprachwissenschaft und Kommunikationsforschung* 14(2). 143–172.

Bartsch, Renate & Theo Vennemann. 1972. *Semantic structures: A study in the relation between semantics and syntax* (Athenäum-Skripten Linguistik 9). Frankfurt/Main: Athenäum.

Barwise, Jon & John Perry. 1983. *Situations and attitudes*. Cambridge, MA: MIT Press.

References

Barwise, Jon & John Perry. 1987. *Situationen und Einstellungen – Grundlagen der Situationssemantik*. Berlin, New York: de Gruyter.

Baschung, K., G. G. Bes, A. Corluy & T. Guillotin. 1987. Auxiliaries and clitics in French UCG grammar. In Bente Maegaard (ed.), *Proceedings of the Third Conference of the European Chapter of the Association for Computational Linguistics*, 173–178. Copenhagen, Denmark: Association for Computational Linguistics.

Bates, Elizabeth A. 1984. Bioprograms and the innateness hypothesis. *The Behavioral and Brain Sciences* 7(2). 188–190.

Baumgärtner, Klaus. 1965. Spracherklärung mit den Mitteln der Abhängigkeitsstruktur. *Beiträge zur Sprachkunde und Informationsverarbeitung* 5. 31–53.

Baumgärtner, Klaus. 1970. Konstituenz und Dependenz: Zur Integration beider grammatischer Prinzipien. In Hugo Steger (ed.), *Vorschläge für eine strukturelle Grammatik des Deutschen* (Wege der Forschung 144), 52–77. Darmstadt: Wissenschaftliche Buchgesellschaft.

Bausewein, Karin. 1990. Haben kopflose Relativsätze tatsächlich keine Köpfe? In Gisbert Fanselow & Sascha W. Felix (eds.), *Strukturen und Merkmale syntaktischer Kategorien* (Studien zur deutschen Grammatik 39), 144–158. Tübingen: originally Gunter Narr Verlag now Stauffenburg Verlag.

Bayer, Josef & Jaklin Kornfilt. 1989. *Restructuring effects in German*. DYANA Report. University of Edinburgh.

Beavers, John. 2003. *A CCG implementation for the LKB*. LinGO Working Paper 2002-08. Stanford, CA: CSLI Stanford. http://lingo.stanford.edu/pubs/WP-2002-08.ps.gz, accessed 2018-2-25.

Beavers, John. 2004. Type-inheritance Combinatory Categorial Grammar. In *Proceedings of COLING 2004*, 57–63. Geneva, Switzerland: Association for Computational Linguistics.

Beavers, John, Elias Ponvert & Stephen Mark Wechsler. 2008. Possession of a controlled substantive. In T. Friedman & S. Ito (eds.), *Proceedings of Semantics and Linguistic Theory (SALT) XVIII*, 108–125. Ithaca, NY: Cornell University.

Beavers, John & Ivan A. Sag. 2004. Coordinate ellipsis and apparent non-constituent coordination. In Stefan Müller (ed.), *Proceedings of the 11th International Conference on Head-Driven Phrase Structure Grammar, Center for Computational Linguistics, Katholieke Universiteit Leuven*, 48–69. Stanford, CA: CSLI Publications. http://cslipublications.stanford.edu/HPSG/2004/, accessed 2018-2-25.

Bech, Gunnar. 1955. *Studien über das deutsche Verbum infinitum* (Linguistische Arbeiten 139). Tübingen: Max Niemeyer Verlag. 2nd unchanged edition 1983.

Becker, Tilman, Aravind K. Joshi & Owen Rambow. 1991. Long-distance scrambling and Tree Adjoining Grammars. In *Fifth Conference of the European Chapter of the Association for Computational Linguistics. Proceedings of the conference*, 21–26. Berlin: Association for Computational Linguistics. http://www.aclweb.org/anthology/E91-1005.pdf, accessed 2018-2-25.

Beermann, Dorothee & Lars Hellan. 2004. A treatment of directionals in two implemented HPSG grammars. In Stefan Müller (ed.), *Proceedings of the 11th International*

Conference on Head-Driven Phrase Structure Grammar, Center for Computational Linguistics, Katholieke Universiteit Leuven, 357–377. Stanford, CA: CSLI Publications. http://csli-publications.stanford.edu/HPSG/2004/, accessed 2018-2-25.

Beghelli, Filippo & Timothy Stowell. 1997. Distributivity and negation: The syntax of *each* and *every*. In Anna Szabolcsi (ed.), *Ways of scope taking*, 71–107. Dordrecht: Kluwer Academic Publishers.

Behaghel, Otto. 1909. Beziehung zwischen Umfang und Reihenfolge von Satzgliedern. *Indogermanische Forschungen* 25. 110–142.

Behaghel, Otto. 1930. Von deutscher Wortstellung. *Zeitschrift für Deutschkunde* 44. 81–89.

Behrens, Heike. 2009. Konstruktionen im Spracherwerb. *Zeitschrift für Germanistische Linguistik* 37(3). 427–444.

Bellugi, Ursula, Liz Lichtenberger, Wendy Jones, Zona Lai & Marie St. George. 2000. The neurocognitive profile of Williams Syndrome: A complex pattern of strengths and weaknesses. *Journal of Cognitive Neuroscience* 12. 7–29.

Bender, Emily M. 2000. *Syntactic variation and linguistic competence: The case of AAVE copula absence*. Stanford University dissertation. http://faculty.washington.edu/ebender/dissertation/, accessed 2018-2-25.

Bender, Emily M. 2008a. Evaluating a crosslinguistic grammar resource: A case study of Wambaya. In Johanna D. Moore, Simone Teufel, James Allan & Sadaoki Furui (eds.), *Proceedings of the 46th Annual Meeting of the Association for Computational Linguistics: Human Language Technologies*, 977–985. Columbus, Ohio: Association for Computational Linguistics. http://aclweb.org/anthology/P08-1111, accessed 2018-2-25.

Bender, Emily M. 2008b. Grammar engineering for linguistic hypothesis testing. In Nicholas Gaylord, Alexis Palmer & Elias Ponvert (eds.), *Proceedings of the Texas Linguistics Society X Conference: Computational linguistics for less-studied languages*, 16–36. Stanford CA: CSLI Publications ONLINE.

Bender, Emily M. 2008c. Radical non-configurationality without shuffle operators: An analysis of Wambaya. In Stefan Müller (ed.), *Proceedings of the 15th International Conference on Head-Driven Phrase Structure Grammar*, 6–24. Stanford, CA: CSLI Publications. http://csli-publications.stanford.edu/HPSG/2008/, accessed 2018-2-25.

Bender, Emily M. 2010. Reweaving a grammar for Wambaya: A case study in grammar engineering for linguistic hypothesis testing. *Linguistic Issues in Language Technology – LiLT* 3(3). 1–34. http://journals.linguisticsociety.org/elanguage/lilt/article/view/662/523.html, accessed 2018-2-25.

Bender, Emily M., Daniel P. Flickinger & Stephan Oepen. 2002. The Grammar Matrix: An open-source starter-kit for the rapid development of cross-linguistically consistent broad-coverage precision grammars. In John Carroll, Nelleke Oostdijk & Richard Sutcliffe (eds.), *Proceedings of the Workshop on Grammar Engineering and Evaluation at the 19th International Conference on Computational Linguistics*, 8–14. Taipei, Taiwan.

Bender, Emily M. & Melanie Siegel. 2005. Implementing the syntax of Japanese numeral classifiers. In Keh-Yih Su, Oi Yee Kwong, Jn'ichi Tsujii & Jong-Hyeok Lee (eds.), *Natural language processing IJCNLP 2004* (Lecture Notes in Artificial Intelligence 3248), 626–635. Berlin: Springer Verlag.

Bender, Emily & Daniel P. Flickinger. 1999. Peripheral constructions and core phenomena: Agreement in tag questions. In Gert Webelhuth, Jean-Pierre Koenig & Andreas Kathol (eds.), *Lexical and Constructional aspects of linguistic explanation* (Studies in Constraint-Based Lexicalism 1), 199–214. Stanford, CA: CSLI Publications.

Bergen, Benjamin K. & Nancy Chang. 2005. Embodied Construction Grammar in simulation-based language understanding. In Jan-Ola Östman & Mirjam Fried (eds.), *Construction Grammars: Cognitive grounding and theoretical extensions*, 147–190. Amsterdam: John Benjamins Publishing Co.

Berman, Judith. 1996. Eine LFG-Grammatik des Deutschen. In *Deutsche und französische Syntax im Formalismus der LFG* (Linguistische Arbeiten 344), 11–96. Tübingen: Max Niemeyer Verlag.

Berman, Judith. 1999. Does German satisfy the Subject Condition? In Miriam Butt & Tracy Holloway King (eds.), *Proceedings of the LFG '99 conference, University of Manchester*. Stanford, CA: CSLI Publications. http://csli-publications.stanford.edu/LFG/4/, accessed 2018-2-25.

Berman, Judith. 2003a. *Clausal syntax of German* (Studies in Constraint-Based Lexicalism). Stanford, CA: CSLI Publications.

Berman, Judith. 2003b. Zum Einfluss der strukturellen Position auf die syntaktische Funktion der Komplementsätze. *Deutsche Sprache* 3. 263–286.

Berman, Judith. 2007. Functional identification of complement clauses in German and the specification of COMP. In Annie Zaenen, Jane Simpson, Tracy Holloway King, Jane Grimshaw, Joan Maling & Chris Manning (eds.), *Architectures, rules, and preferences: Variations on themes by Joan W. Bresnan*, 69–83. Stanford, CA: CSLI Publications.

Berwick, Robert C. 1982. Computational complexity and Lexical-Functional Grammar. *American Journal of Computational Linguistics* 8(3–4). 97–109.

Berwick, Robert C. & Samuel David Epstein. 1995. On the convergence of 'Minimalist' Syntax and Categorial Grammar. In Anton Nijholt, Giuseppe Scollo & Rene Steetskamp (eds.), *Algebraic methods in language processing*, 143–148. Enschede: University of Twente. http://eprints.eemcs.utwente.nl/9555/01/twlt10.pdf, accessed 2018-9-25.

Berwick, Robert C. & Partha Niyogi. 1996. Learning from triggers. *Linguistic Inquiry* 27. 605–622.

Berwick, Robert C., Paul Pietroski, Beracah Yankama & Noam Chomsky. 2011. Poverty of the Stimulus revisited. *Cognitive Science* 35(7). 1207–1242.

Bick, Eckhard. 2001. En Constraint Grammar parser for dansk. In Peter Widell & Mette Kunøe (eds.), *8. Møde om Udforskningen af Dansk Sprog, 12.–13. October 2000*, vol. 8, 40–50. Århus: Århus University.

Bick, Eckhard. 2003. A Constraint Grammar-based question answering system for Portuguese. In Fernando Moura Pires & Salvador Abreu (eds.), *Progress in artificial intelligence: 11th Protuguese Conference on Artificial Intelligence, EPIA 2003, Beja, Portugal, December 4–7, 2003, proceedings* (Lecture Notes in Computer Science 2902), 414–418. Berlin: Springer Verlag.

Bick, Eckhard. 2006. A Constraint Grammar parser for Spanish. In *Proceedings of TIL 2006 – 4th Workshop on Information and Human Language Technology (Ribeirão Preto, October 27–28, 2006)*, 3–10. http://www.nilc.icmc.usp.br/til/til2006/, accessed 2015-12-23.

Bick, Eckhard. 2009. A Dependency Constraint Grammar for Esperanto. In Eckhard Bick, Kristin Hagen, Kaili Müürisep & Trond Trosterud (eds.), *Constraint Grammar and robust parsing: Proceedings of the NODALIDA 2009 workshop* (NEALT Proceedings Series 8), 8–12. Tartu: Tartu University Library.

Bick, Eckhard. 2010. FrAG: A hybrid Constraint Grammar parser for French. In Nicoletta Calzolari, Khalid Choukri, Bente Maegaard, Joseph Mariani, Jan Odijk, Stelios Piperidis, Mike Rosner & Daniel Tapias (eds.), *Proceedings of the Seventh International Conference on Language Resources and Evaluation (LREC'10)*, 794–798. Valletta, Malta: European Language Resources Association (ELRA).

Bick, Eckhard & Lars Nygaard. 2007. Using Danish as a CG interlingua: A wide-coverage Norwegian-English machine translation system. In Joakim Nivre, Heiki-Jaan Kaalep, Kadri Muischnek & Mare Koit (eds.), *Proceedings of the 16th Nordic Conference of Computational Linguistics*, 21–28. Forlag uden navn.

Bickerton, Derek. 1984a. Creol is still king. *The Behavioral and Brain Sciences* 7(2). 212–218.

Bickerton, Derek. 1984b. The Language Bioprogram Hypothesis. *The Behavioral and Brain Sciences* 7(2). 173–188.

Bickerton, Derek. 1997. How to acquire language without positive evidence: What acquisitionists can learn from Creoles. In Michel DeGraff (ed.), *Language creation and language change: creolization, diachrony, and development* (Learning, Development, and Conceptual Change), 49–74. Cambridge, MA: MIT Press.

Bierwisch, Manfred. 1963. *Grammatik des deutschen Verbs* (studia grammatica 2). Berlin: Akademie Verlag.

Bierwisch, Manfred. 1966. Strukturalismus: Geschichte, Probleme und Methoden. *Kursbuch* 5. 77–152.

Bierwisch, Manfred. 1992. Grammatikforschung in der DDR: Auch ein Rückblick. *Linguistische Berichte* 139. 169–181.

Bildhauer, Felix. 2008. *Representing information structure in an HPSG grammar of Spanish*. Universität Bremen Dissertation.

Bildhauer, Felix. 2011. Mehrfache Vorfeldbesetzung und Informationsstruktur: Eine Bestandsaufnahme. *Deutsche Sprache* 39(4). 362–379.

Bildhauer, Felix. 2014. Head-Driven Phrase Structure Grammar. In Andrew Carnie, Yosuke Sato & Dan Siddiqi (eds.), *The Routledge handbook of syntax*, 526–555. Oxford: Routledge.

Bildhauer, Felix & Philippa Cook. 2010. German multiple fronting and expected topichood. In Stefan Müller (ed.), *Proceedings of the 17th International Conference on Head-Driven Phrase Structure Grammar, Université Paris Diderot*, 68–79. Stanford, CA: CSLI Publications. http://csli-publications.stanford.edu/HPSG/2010/, accessed 2018-2-25.

References

Bird, Steven & Ewan Klein. 1994. Phonological analysis in typed feature systems. *Computational Linguistics* 20(3). 455–491.

Bishop, Dorothy V. M. 2002. Putting language genes in perspective. *TRENDS in Genetics* 18(2). 57–59.

Bjerre, Tavs. 2006. *Object positions in a topological sentence model for Danish: A linearization-based HPSG approach*. http://www.hum.au.dk/engelsk/engsv/objectpositions/workshop/Bjerre.pdf, accessed 2018-2-25. Presentation at Ph.D.-Course at Sandbjerg, Denmark.

Blackburn, Patrick & Johan Bos. 2005. *Representation and inference for natural language: A first course in computational semantics*. Stanford, CA: CSLI Publications.

Blackburn, Patrick, Claire Gardent & Wilfried Meyer-Viol. 1993. Talking about trees. In Steven Krauwer, Michael Moortgat & Louis des Tombe (eds.), *Sixth Conference of the European Chapter of the Association for Computational Linguistics. Proceedings of the conference*, 21–29. Uetrecht: Association for Computational Linguistics.

Błaszczak, Joanna & Hans-Martin Gärtner. 2005. Intonational phrasing, discontinuity, and the scope of negation. *Syntax* 8(1). 1–22.

Blevins, James P. 2003. Passives and impersonals. *Journal of Linguistics* 39(3). 473–520.

Block, Hans-Ulrich & Rudolf Hunze. 1986. Incremental construction of c- and f-structure in a LFG-parser. In Makoto Nagao (ed.), *Proceedings of COLING 86*, 490–493. University of Bonn: Association for Computational Linguistics.

Blom, Corrien. 2005. *Complex predicates in Dutch: Synchrony and diachrony* (LOT Dissertation Series 111). Utrecht: Utrecht University.

Bloom, Paul. 1993. Grammatical continuity in language development: The case of subjectless sentences. *Linguistic Inquiry* 24(4). 721–734.

Boas, Hans C. 2003. *A Constructional approach to resultatives* (Stanford Monographs in Linguistics). Stanford, CA: CSLI Publications.

Boas, Hans C. 2014. Lexical approaches to argument structure: Two sides of the same coin. *Theoretical Linguistics* 40(1–2). 89–112.

Bobaljik, Jonathan. 1999. Adverbs: The hierarchy paradox. *Glot International* 4(9/10). 27–28.

Bod, Rens. 2009a. Constructions at work or at rest? *Cognitive Linguistics* 20(1). 129–134.

Bod, Rens. 2009b. From exemplar to grammar: Integrating analogy and probability in language learning. *Cognitive Science* 33(4). 752–793. DOI:10.1111/j.1551-6709.2009.01031.x

Bögel, Tina, Miriam Butt & Sebastian Sulger. 2008. Urdu ezafe and the morphology-syntax interface. In Miriam Butt & Tracy Holloway King (eds.), *Proceedings of the LFG 2008 conference*, 129–149. Stanford, CA: CSLI Publications. http://csli-publications.stanford.edu/LFG/13/, accessed 2018-2-25.

Bohnet, Bernd. 2010. Very high accuracy and fast Dependency Parsing is not a contradiction. In Chu-Ren Huang & Dan Jurafsky (eds.), *Proceedings of the 23rd International Conference on Computational Linguistics*, 89–97. Stroudsburg, PA, USA: Association for Computational Linguistics.

Bolc, Leonard, Krzysztof Czuba, Anna Kupść, Małgorzata Marciniak, Agnieszka Mykowiecka & Adam Przepiórkowski. 1996. *A survey of systems for implementing

HPSG grammars. Tech. rep. 814. Warsaw, Poland: Institute of Computer Science, Polish Academy of Sciences. http://www.cs.cmu.edu/~kczuba/systems-wide.ps.gz, accessed 2018-2-25.

Booij, Geert E. 2002. Separable complex verbs in Dutch: A case of periphrastic word formation. In Nicole Dehé, Ray S. Jackendoff, Andrew McIntyre & Silke Urban (eds.), *Verb-particle explorations* (Interface Explorations 1), 21–41. Berlin: Mouton de Gruyter.

Booij, Geert E. 2005. Construction-Dependent Morphology. *Lingue e linguaggio* 4. 31–46.

Booij, Geert E. 2009. Lexical integrity as a formal universal: A Constructionist view. In Sergio Scalise, Elisabetta Magni & Antonietta Bisetto (eds.), *Universals of language today* (Studies in Natural Language and Linguistic Theory 76), 83–100. Berlin: Springer Verlag.

Booij, Geert E. 2010. Construction morphology. *Language and Linguistics Compass* 4(7). 543–555. DOI:10.1111/j.1749-818X.2010.00213.x

Booij, Geert E. 2012. Construction morphology. Ms. Leiden University.

Borer, Hagit. 1994. The projection of arguments. In E. Benedicto & J. Runner (eds.), *Functional projections* (UMass Occasional Papers in Linguistics (UMOP) 17), 19–47. Massachusetts: University of Massachusetts Graduate Linguistic Student Association.

Borer, Hagit. 2003. Exo-skeletal vs. endo-skeletal explanations: Syntactic projections and the lexicon. In John Moore & Maria Polinsky (eds.), *The nature of explanation in linguistic theory*, 31–67. Stanford, CA: CSLI Publications.

Borer, Hagit. 2005. *Structuring sense: In name only*. Vol. 1. Oxford: Oxford University Press.

Borsley, Robert D. 1987. *Subjects and complements in HPSG*. Report No. CSLI-87-107. Stanford, CA: Center for the Study of Language & Information.

Borsley, Robert D. 1989. Phrase-Structure Grammar and the Barriers conception of clause structure. *Linguistics* 27(5). 843–863.

Borsley, Robert D. 1991. *Syntactic theory: A unified approach*. London: Edward Arnold.

Borsley, Robert D. 1999a. Mutation and constituent structure in Welsh. *Lingua* 109(4). 267–300. DOI:10.1016/S0024-3841(99)00019-4

Borsley, Robert D. 1999b. *Syntactic theory: A unified approach*. 2nd edn. London: Edward Arnold.

Borsley, Robert D. 2005. Against ConjP. *Lingua* 115(4). 461–482.

Borsley, Robert D. 2006. *Syntactic and lexical approaches to unbounded dependencies*. Essex Research Reports in Linguistics 49. University of Essex. 31–57. http://core.ac.uk/download/pdf/4187949.pdf#page=35, accessed 2018-2-25.

Borsley, Robert D. 2007. Hang on again! Are we 'on the right track'? In Andrew Radford (ed.), *Martin Atkinson – the Minimalist muse* (Essex Research Reports in Linguistics 53), 43–69. Essex: Department of Language & Linguistics, University of Essex.

Borsley, Robert D. 2009. On the superficiality of Welsh agreement. *Natural Language and Linguistic Theory* 27(2). 225–265.

Borsley, Robert D. 2012. Don't move! *Iberia: An International Journal of Theoretical Linguistics* 4(1). 110–139.

References

Borsley, Robert D. 2013. On the nature of Welsh unbounded dependencies. *Lingua* 133. 1–29. DOI:10.1016/j.lingua.2013.03.005

Borsley, Robert D. & Stefan Müller. 2019. Minimalism. In Stefan Müller, Anne Abeillé, Robert D. Borsley & Jean-Pierre Koenig (eds.), *Head-Driven Phrase Structure Grammar: The handbook* (Empirically Oriented Theoretical Morphology and Syntax). Berlin: Language Science Press. To appear.

Bos, Johan. 1996. Predicate logic unplugged. In Paul J. E. Dekker & M. Stokhof (eds.), *Proceedings of the Tenth Amsterdam Colloquium*, 133–143. Amsterdam: ILLC/Department of Philosophy, University of Amsterdam.

Bosse, Solveig & Benjamin Bruening. 2011. Benefactive versus experiencer datives. In Mary Byram Washburn, Katherine McKinney-Bock, Erika Varis, Ann Sawyer & Barbara Tomaszewicz (eds.), *Proceedings of the 28th West Coast Conference on Formal Linguistics*, 69–77. Somerville, MA: Cascadilla Press.

Boukedi, Sirine & Kais Haddar. 2014. HPSG grammar treating of different forms of Arabic coordination. *Research in Computing Science* 86: Advances in Computational Linguistics and Intelligent Decision Making. 25–41.

Boullier, Pierre & Benoît Sagot. 2005a. Analyse syntaxique profonde à grande échelle: SxLfg. *Traitement Automatique des Langues (T.A.L.)* 46(2). 65–89.

Boullier, Pierre & Benoît Sagot. 2005b. Efficient and robust LFG parsing: SxLfg. In *Proceedings of IWPT 2005*, 1–10. Vancouver, Canada: Association for Computational Linguistics.

Boullier, Pierre, Benoît Sagot & Lionel Clément. 2005. Un analyseur LFG efficace pour le français: SxLfg. In *Actes de TALN 05*, 403–408. Dourdan, France.

Bouma, Gosse. 1996. Extraposition as a nonlocal dependency. In Geert-Jan Kruijff, Glynn V. Morrill & Dick Oehrle (eds.), *Proceedings of Formal Grammar 96*, 1–14. Prag. http://www.let.rug.nl/gosse/papers.html, accessed 2018-2-25.

Bouma, Gosse, Robert Malouf & Ivan A. Sag. 2001. Satisfying constraints on extraction and adjunction. *Natural Language and Linguistic Theory* 19(1). 1–65.

Bouma, Gosse & Gertjan van Noord. 1994. Constraint-based Categorial Grammar. In James Pustejovsky (ed.), *32th Annual Meeting of the Association for Computational Linguistics. Proceedings of the conference*, 147–154. Las Cruces: Association for Computational Linguistics.

Bouma, Gosse & Gertjan van Noord. 1998. Word order constraints on verb clusters in German and Dutch. In Erhard W. Hinrichs, Andreas Kathol & Tsuneko Nakazawa (eds.), *Complex predicates in nonderivational syntax* (Syntax and Semantics 30), 43–72. San Diego: Academic Press.

Bouma, Gosse, Gertjan van Noord & Robert Malouf. 2001. Alpino: wide-coverage computational analysis of Dutch. In Walter Daelemans, Khalil Sima'an, Jorn Veenstra & Jakub Zavrel (eds.), *Computational linguistics in the Netherlands 2000: Selected papers from the Eleventh CLIN Meeting* (Language and Computers 37). Amsterdam/New York, NY: Rodopi.

Braine, Martin D. S. 1987. What is learned in acquiring word classes—A step toward an acquisition theory. In Brian MacWhinny (ed.), *Mechanisms of language acquisition*, 65–87. Hillsdale, NJ: Lawrence Erlbaum Associates, Publishers.

Branco, António & Francisco Costa. 2008a. *A computational grammar for deep linguistic processing of Portuguese: LXGram, version A.4.1*. Tech. rep. TR-2008-17. Universidade de Lisboa, Faculdade de Ciências, Departamento de Informática.

Branco, António & Francisco Costa. 2008b. LXGram in the shared task 'comparing semantic representations' of STEP 2008. In Johan Bos & Rodolfo Delmonte (eds.), *Semantics in text processing: STEP 2008 conference proceedings*, vol. 1 (Research in Computational Semantics), 299–314. London: College Publications. http://www.aclweb.org/anthology/W08-2224, accessed 2018-2-25.

Branco, António & Francisco Costa. 2010. LXGram: A deep linguistic processing grammar for Portuguese. In Thiago A.S. Pardo (ed.), *Computational processing of the Portuguese language: 9th International Conference, PROPOR 2010, Porto Alegre, RS, Brazil, April 27–30, 2010. Proceedings* (Lecture Notes in Artificial Intelligence 6001), 86–89. Berlin: Springer Verlag.

Brants, Sabine, Stefanie Dipper, Peter Eisenberg, Silvia Hansen-Schirra, Esther König, Wolfgang Lezius, Christian Rohrer, George Smith & Hans Uszkoreit. 2004. TIGER: Linguistic interpretation of a German corpus. *Research on Language and Computation* 2(4). 597–620.

Bresnan, Joan. 1974. The position of certain clause-particles in phrase structure. *Linguistic Inquiry* 5(4). 614–619.

Bresnan, Joan. 1978. A realistic Transformational Grammar. In Morris Halle, Joan Bresnan & George A. Miller (eds.), *Linguistic theory and psychological reality*, 1–59. Cambridge, MA: MIT Press.

Bresnan, Joan. 1982a. Control and complementation. *Linguistic Inquiry* 13(3). 343–434.

Bresnan, Joan. 1982b. The passive in lexical theory. In Joan Bresnan (ed.), *The mental representation of grammatical relations* (MIT Press Series on Cognitive Theory and Mental Representation), 3–86. Cambridge, MA/London: MIT Press.

Bresnan, Joan. 2001. *Lexical-Functional Syntax*. Oxford: Blackwell Publishers Ltd.

Bresnan, Joan, Ash Asudeh, Ida Toivonen & Stephen Mark Wechsler. 2015. *Lexical-functional syntax*. 2nd edn. Oxford: Blackwell Publishers Ltd. DOI:10.1002/9781119105664

Bresnan, Joan & Jane Grimshaw. 1978. The syntax of free relatives in English. *Linguistic Inquiry* 9. 331–392.

Bresnan, Joan & Jonni M. Kanerva. 1989. Locative inversion in Chichewa: A case study of factorization in grammar. *Linguistic Inquiry* 20(1). 1–50.

Bresnan, Joan & Ronald M. Kaplan. 1982. Introduction: grammars as mental representations of language. In Joan Bresnan (ed.), *The mental representation of grammatical relations* (MIT Press Series on Cognitive Theory and Mental Representation), xvii–lii. Cambridge, MA/London: MIT Press.

Bresnan, Joan & Sam A. Mchombo. 1995. The Lexical Integrity Principle: Evidence from Bantu. *Natural Language and Linguistic Theory* 13. 181–254.

References

Bresnan, Joan & Annie Zaenen. 1990. Deep unaccusativity in LFG. In Katarzyna Dziwirek, Patrick Farrell & Errapel Mejías-Bikandi (eds.), *Grammatical relations: A crosstheoretical perspective*, 45–57. Stanford, CA: CSLI Publications.

Brew, Chris. 1995. Stochastic HPSG. In Steven P. Abney & Erhard W. Hinrichs (eds.), *Proceedings of the Seventh Conference of the European Chapter of the Association for Computational Linguistics*, 83–89. Dublin: Association for Computational Linguistics.

Briscoe, Ted J. 1997. Review of Edward P. Stabler, Jr., The logical approach to syntax: Foundations, specifications, and implementations of theories of Government and Binding. *Journal of Linguistics* 33(1). 223–225.

Briscoe, Ted J. 2000. Grammatical acquisition: inductive bias and coevolution of language and the language acquisition device. *Language* 76(2). 245–296.

Briscoe, Ted J. & Ann Copestake. 1999. Lexical rules in constraint-based grammar. *Computational Linguistics* 25(4). 487–526. http://www.aclweb.org/anthology/J99-4002, accessed 2018-10-7.

Bröker, Norbert. 2003. Formal foundations of Dependency Grammar. In Vilmos Ágel, Ludwig M. Eichinger, Hans-Werner Eroms, Peter Hellwig, Hans Jürgen Heringer & Henning Lobin (eds.), *Dependenz und Valenz / Dependency and valency: Ein internationales Handbuch der zeitgenössischen Forschung / An international handbook of contemporary research*, vol. 25.1 (Handbücher zur Sprach- und Kommunikationswissenschaft), 294–310. Berlin: Walter de Gruyter.

Brosziewski, Ulf. 2003. *Syntactic derivations: A nontransformational view* (Linguistische Arbeiten 470). Tübingen: Max Niemeyer Verlag.

Brown, Roger & Camille Hanlon. 1970. Derivational complexity and order of acquisition in child speech. In John R. Hayes (ed.), *Cognition and the development of language*, 11–53. New York: John Wiley & Sons, Inc.

Bruening, Benjamin. 2009. Selectional asymmetries between CP and DP suggest that the DP hypothesis is wrong. In Laurel MacKenzie (ed.), *Proceedings of the 32th Annual Penn Linguistics Colloquium* (Penn Working Papers in Linguistics 15.1), 26–35. Philadelphia.

Bruening, Benjamin. 2018. The lexicalist hypothesis: Both wrong and superfluous. *Language* 94(1). 1–42. DOI:10.1353/lan.2018.0000

Bryant, John. 2003. *Constructional analysis*. University of Califorma at Berkeley MA thesis. http://www.icsi.berkeley.edu/~jbryant/old-analyzer.html, accessed 2018-2-25.

Budde, Monika. 2010. *Konstruktionen integrativ: Topik-Konstruktionen als rein-syntaktisches Pendant zu den lexikalisch verankerten Komplement-Konstruktionen*. Vortrag auf der Tagung Konstruktionsgrammatik: Neue Perspektiven zur Untersuchung des Deutschen und Englischen. Internationale Fachtagung an der Christian-Albrechts-Universität zu Kiel vom 18. bis 20. Februar 2010.

Bungeroth, Jan. 2002. *A formal description of Sign Language using HPSG*. Karlsruhe: Department of Computer Science, University of Stellenbosch, Lehrstuhl Informatik für Ingenieure und Naturwissenschaftler, Universität Karlsruhe (TH) Diploma Thesis. http://www-i6.informatik.rwth-aachen.de/~bungeroth/diplarb.pdf, accessed 2018-2-25.

Burzio, Luigi. 1981. *Intransitive verbs and Italian auxiliaries*. MIT dissertation.

Burzio, Luigi. 1986. *Italian syntax: A Government-Binding approach* (Studies in Natural Language and Linguistic Theory 1). Dordrecht: D. Reidel Publishing Company.

Busemann, Stephan. 1992. *Generierung natürlicher Sprache mit generalisierten Phrasenstrukturgrammatiken*. Vol. 313 (Informatik-Fachberichte). Berlin: Springer Verlag.

Bußmann, Hadumod (ed.). 1983. *Lexikon der Sprachwissenschaft* (Kröners Taschenausgabe 452). Stuttgart: Alfred Kröner Verlag.

Bußmann, Hadumod (ed.). 1990. *Lexikon der Sprachwissenschaft*. 2nd edn. (Kröners Taschenausgabe 452). Stuttgart: Alfred Kröner Verlag.

Butt, Miriam. 1997. Complex predicates in Urdu. In Alex Alsina, Joan Bresnan & Peter Sells (eds.), *Complex predicates* (CSLI Lecture Notes 64), 107–149. Stanford, CA: CSLI Publications.

Butt, Miriam. 2003. The light verb jungle. In C. Quinn, C. Bowern & G. Aygen (eds.), *Papers from the Harvard/Dudley House light verb workshop* (Harvard Working Papers in Linguistics 9), 1–49. Harvard University, Department of Linguistics.

Butt, Miriam, Stefanie Dipper, Anette Frank & Tracy Holloway King. 1999. Writing large-scale parallel grammars for English, French and German. In Miriam Butt & Tracy Holloway King (eds.), *Proceedings of the LFG '99 conference, University of Manchester*. Stanford, CA: CSLI Publications. http://csli-publications.stanford.edu/LFG/4/, accessed 2018-2-25.

Butt, Miriam, Helge Dyvik, Tracy Holloway King, Hiroshi Masuichi & Christian Rohrer. 2002. The Parallel Grammar Project. In *Proceedings of COLING-2002 Workshop on Grammar Engineering and Evaluation*, 1–7.

Butt, Miriam, Tracy Holloway King & John T. Maxwell III. 2003. Complex predication via restriction. In Miriam Butt & Tracy Holloway King (eds.), *Proceedings of the LFG 2003 conference*, 92–104. Stanford, CA: CSLI Publications.

Butt, Miriam, Tracy Holloway King, María-Eugenia Niño & Frédérique Segond. 1999. *A grammar writer's cookbook* (CSLI Lecture Notes 95). Stanford, CA: CSLI Publications.

Butt, Miriam, Tracy Holloway King & Sebastian Roth. 2007. Urdu correlatives: Theoretical and implementational issues. In Miriam Butt & Tracy Holloway King (eds.), *Proceedings of the LFG 2007 conference*, 107–127. Stanford, CA: CSLI Publications. http://csli-publications.stanford.edu/LFG/12/, accessed 2018-2-25.

Cahill, Aoife, Michael Burke, Martin Forst, Ruth O'Donovan, Christian Rohrer, Josef van Genabith & Andy Way. 2005. Treebank-based acquisition of multilingual unification grammar resources. *Research on Language and Computation* 3(2). 247–279.

Cahill, Aoife, Michael Burke, Ruth O'Donovan, Stefan Riezler, Josef van Genabith & Andy Way. 2008. Wide-coverage deep statistical parsing using automatic dependency structure annotation. *Computational Linguistics* 34(1). 81–124.

Calder, Jonathan, Ewan Klein & Henk Zeevat. 1988. Unification Categorial Grammar: A concise, extendable grammar for natural language processing. In Dénes Vargha (ed.), *Proceedings of COLING 88*, 83–86. University of Budapest: Association for Computational Linguistics. https://aclanthology.info/pdf/C/C88/C88-1018.pdf, accessed 2018-3-20.

References

Callmeier, Ulrich. 2000. PET—A platform for experimentation with efficient HPSG processing techniques. *Journal of Natural Language Engineering* 1(6). 99–108. (Special Issue on Efficient Processing with HPSG: Methods, Systems, Evaluation).

Candito, Marie-Hélène. 1996. A principle-based hierarchical representation of LTAGs. In Jun-ichi Tsuji (ed.), *Proceedings of COLING-96. 16th International Conference on Computational Linguistics (COLING96). Copenhagen, Denmark, August 5–9, 1996*, 194–199. Copenhagen, Denmark: Association for Computational Linguistics.

Candito, Marie-Hélène. 1998. Building parallel LTAG for French and Italian. In *Proceedings of the 36th Annual Meeting of the Association for Computational Linguistics and 17th International Conference on Computational Linguistics*, 211–217. Montreal, Quebec, Canada: Association for Computational Linguistics.

Candito, Marie-Hélène. 1999. *Organisation modulaire et paramétrable de grammaires électroniques lexicalisées. Application au français et à l'italien*. Université Paris 7 dissertation.

Candito, Marie-Hélène & Sylvain Kahane. 1998. Can the TAG derivation tree represent a semantic graph? An answer in the light of Meaning-Text Theory. In *TAG+4*, 25–28.

Cappelle, Bert. 2006. Particle placement and the case for "allostructions". *Constructions online* 1(7). 1–28.

Cappelle, Bert, Yury Shtyrov & Friedemann Pulvermüller. 2010. *Heating up* or *cooling up* the brain? MEG evidence that phrasal verbs are lexical units. *Brain and Language* 115. 189–201.

Carlson, Gregory N. & Michael K. Tanenhaus. 1988. Thematic roles and language comprehension. In Wendy Wilkins (ed.), *Thematic relations* (Syntax and Semantics 21), 263–289. San Diego: Academic Press.

Carnie, Andrew. 2013. *Syntax: A generative introduction*. 3rd edn. (Introducing Linguistics 20). Wiley-Blackwell.

Carpenter, Bob. 1992. *The logic of typed feature structures* (Tracts in Theoretical Computer Science). Cambridge: Cambridge University Press.

Carpenter, Bob. 1994. *A natural deduction theorem prover for type-theoretic Categorial Grammars*. Tech. rep. Carnegie Mellon Laboratory for Computational Linguistics. http://www.essex.ac.uk/linguistics/external/clmt/papers/cg/carp_cgparser_doc.ps, accessed 2018-2-25.

Carpenter, Bob. 1998. *Type-logical semantics*. Cambridge, MA: MIT Press.

Carpenter, Bob & Gerald Penn. 1996. Efficient parsing of compiled typed attribute value logic grammars. In Harry Bunt & Masaru Tomita (eds.), *Recent advances in parsing technology* (Text, Speech and Language Technology 1), 145–168. Dordrecht: Kluwer Academic Publishers.

Çetinoğlu, Özlem & Kemal Oflazer. 2006. Morphology-syntax interface for Turkish LFG. In Nicoletta Calzolari, Claire Cardie & Pierre Isabelle (eds.), *Proceedings of the 21st International Conference on Computational Linguistics and 44th Annual Meeting of the Association for Computational Linguistics*, 153–160. Sydney, Australia: Association for Computational Linguistics.

Chang, Nancy Chih-Lin. 2008. *Constructing grammar: A computational model of the emergence of early constructions*. Technical Report UCB/EECS-2009-24. Electrical Engineering & Computer Sciences, University of California at Berkeley.

Chaves, Rui P. 2009. Construction-based cumulation and adjunct extraction. In Stefan Müller (ed.), *Proceedings of the 16th International Conference on Head-Driven Phrase Structure Grammar, University of Göttingen, Germany*, 47–67. Stanford, CA: CSLI Publications. http://csli-publications.stanford.edu/HPSG/2009/, accessed 2018-2-25.

Chesi, Cristiano. 2015. On directionality of phrase structure building. *Journal of Psycholinguistic Research* 44(1). 65–89. DOI:10.1007/s10936-014-9330-6

Choi, Hye-Won. 1999. *Optimizing structure in scrambling: Scrambling and information structure* (Dissertations in Linguistics). Stanford, CA: CSLI Publications.

Chomsky, Noam. 1956. Three models for the description of language. *IRE Transactions on Information Theory* 2. 113–124.

Chomsky, Noam. 1957. *Syntactic structures* (Janua Linguarum / Series Minor 4). The Hague/Paris: Mouton.

Chomsky, Noam. 1959. On certain formal properties of grammars. *Information and Control* 2(2). 137–167.

Chomsky, Noam. 1964a. *Current issues in linguistic theory* (Janua Linguarum / Series Minor 38). The Hague/Paris: Mouton.

Chomsky, Noam. 1964b. Degrees of grammaticalness. In Jerry A. Fodor & Jerrold J. Katz (eds.), *The structure of language*, 384–389. Englewood Cliffs, NJ: Prentice-Hall.

Chomsky, Noam. 1965. *Aspects of the theory of syntax*. Cambridge, MA: MIT Press.

Chomsky, Noam. 1968. Language and the mind. *Psychology Today* 1(9). 48–68. Reprint as: Chomsky (1976a).

Chomsky, Noam. 1970. Remarks on nominalization. In Roderick A. Jacobs & Peter S. Rosenbaum (eds.), *Readings in English Transformational Grammar*, chap. 12, 184–221. Waltham, MA/Toronto/London: Ginn & Company.

Chomsky, Noam. 1971. *Problems of knowledge and freedom*. London: Fontana.

Chomsky, Noam. 1973. Conditions on transformations. In Stephen R. Anderson & Paul Kiparsky (eds.), *A festschrift for Morris Halle*, 232–286. New York: Holt, Rinehart & Winston.

Chomsky, Noam. 1975. *The logical structure of linguistic theory*. New York: Plenum Press.

Chomsky, Noam. 1976a. Language and the mind. In Diane D. Borstein (ed.), *Readings in the theory of grammar: from the 17th to the 20th century*, 241–251. Cambridge, MA: Winthrop. Reprint from: Chomsky (1968).

Chomsky, Noam. 1976b. *Reflections on language*. New York: Pantheon Books.

Chomsky, Noam. 1977. *Essays on form and interpretation*. New York: North Holland.

Chomsky, Noam. 1980. *Rules and representations*. Oxford: Basil Blackwell.

Chomsky, Noam. 1981a. *Lectures on government and binding*. Dordrecht: Foris Publications.

Chomsky, Noam. 1981b. Reply to comments of Thompson. *Philosophical Transactions of the Royal Society of London. Series B, Biological Sciences* 295(1077). 277–281.

References

Chomsky, Noam. 1982. *Some concepts and consequences of the theory of Government and Binding* (Linguistic Inquiry Monographs 5). Cambridge, MA: MIT Press.

Chomsky, Noam. 1986a. *Barriers* (Linguistic Inquiry Monographs 13). Cambridge, MA: MIT Press.

Chomsky, Noam. 1986b. *Knowledge of language: Its nature, origin, and use* (Convergence). New York/Westport, Connecticut/London: Praeger.

Chomsky, Noam. 1988. *Language and problems of knowledge: The Managua lectures* (Current Studies in Linguistics 16). Cambridge, MA: MIT Press.

Chomsky, Noam. 1989. Some notes on economy of derivation and representation. In I. Laka & Anoop Mahajan (eds.), *Functional heads and clause structure* (MIT Working Papers in Linguistics 10), 43–74. Cambridge, MA: Department of Linguistics & Philosophy.

Chomsky, Noam. 1990. On formalization and formal linguistics. *Natural Language and Linguistic Theory* 8(1). 143–147.

Chomsky, Noam. 1991. Some notes on economy of derivation and representation. In Robert Freidin (ed.), *Principles and parameters in Generative Grammar*, 417–454. Cambridge, MA: MIT Press. Reprint as: Chomsky (1995b: 129–166).

Chomsky, Noam. 1993. A Minimalist Program for linguistic theory. In Kenneth Hale & Samuel Jay Keyser (eds.), *The view from building 20: Essays in linguistics in honor of Sylvain Bromberger* (Current Studies in Linguistics 24), 1–52. Cambridge, MA/London: MIT Press.

Chomsky, Noam. 1995a. Bare phrase structure. In Hector Campos & Paula Kempchinsky (eds.), *Evolution and revolution in linguistic theory: Essays in honor of Carlos Otero*, 51–109. Washington, DC: Georgetown U Press.

Chomsky, Noam. 1995b. *The Minimalist Program* (Current Studies in Linguistics 28). Cambridge, MA: MIT Press.

Chomsky, Noam. 1998. Noam Chomsky's Minimalist Program and the philosophy of mind: An interview [with] Camilo J. Cela-Conde and Gisde Marty. *Syntax* 1(1). 19–36.

Chomsky, Noam. 1999. *Derivation by phase*. MIT Occasional Papers in Linguistics 18. MIT. Reprint in: Michael Kenstowicz, ed. 2001. Ken Hale. A Life in Language. Cambridge, MA: MIT Press, 1–52.

Chomsky, Noam. 2000. *New horizons in the study of language and mind*. Cambridge, UK: Cambridge University Press.

Chomsky, Noam. 2001. Derivation by phase. In Michael Kenstowicz (ed.), *Ken Hale: A life in language*, 1–52. Cambridge, MA: MIT Press.

Chomsky, Noam. 2002. *On nature and language*. Cambridge, UK: Cambridge University Press.

Chomsky, Noam. 2005. Three factors in language design. *Linguistic Inquiry* 36(1). 1–22.

Chomsky, Noam. 2007. Approaching UG from below. In Uli Sauerland & Hans-Martin Gärtner (eds.), *Interfaces + recursion = language? Chomsky's Minimalism and the view from syntax-semantics* (Studies in Generative Grammar 89), 1–29. Berlin: Mouton de Gruyter.

Chomsky, Noam. 2008. On phases. In Robert Freidin, Carlos P. Otero & Maria Luisa Zubizarreta (eds.), *Foundational issues in linguistic theory: Essays in honor of Jean-Roger Vergnaud*, 133–166. Cambridge, MA: MIT Press.

Chomsky, Noam. 2010. *Restricting stipulations: consequences and challenges*. Talk given in Stuttgart.

Chomsky, Noam. 2013. Problems of projection. *Lingua* 130. 33–49. DOI:10.1016/j.lingua.2012.12.003

Chomsky, Noam. 2014. Minimal recursion: Exploring the prospects. In Tom Roeper & Margaret Speas (eds.), *Recursion: Complexity in cognition*, vol. 43 (Studies in Theoretical Psycholinguistics), 1–15. Springer Verlag.

Chomsky, Noam & George A. Miller. 1963. Introduction to the formal analysis of natural languages. In R. Duncan Luce, Robert R. Bush & Eugene Galanter (eds.), *Handbook of mathematical psychology*, vol. 2, 269–321. New York: John Wiley & Sons, Inc.

Chouinard, Michelle M. & Eve V. Clark. 2003. Adult reformulations of child errors as negative evidence. *Journal of Child Language* 30. 637–669.

Chrupala, Grzegorz & Josef van Genabith. 2006. Using machine-learning to assign function labels to parser output for Spanish. In Nicoletta Calzolari, Claire Cardie & Pierre Isabelle (eds.), *Proceedings of the 21st International Conference on Computational Linguistics and 44th Annual Meeting of the Association for Computational Linguistics*, 136–143. Sydney, Australia: Association for Computational Linguistics.

Chung, Chan. 1998. Argument composition and long-distance scrambling in Korean. In Erhard W. Hinrichs, Andreas Kathol & Tsuneko Nakazawa (eds.), *Complex predicates in nonderivational syntax* (Syntax and Semantics 30), 159–220. San Diego: Academic Press.

Chung, Sandra & James McCloskey. 1983. On the interpretation of certain island facts in GPSG. *Linguistic Inquiry* 14. 704–713.

Church, Kenneth. 2011. A pendulum swung too far. *Linguistic Issues in Language Technology* 6(5). 1–27. http://journals.linguisticsociety.org/elanguage/lilt/article/view/2581.html, accessed 2018-2-25. Special Issue on Interaction of Linguistics and Computational Linguistics.

Cinque, Guglielmo. 1994. On the evidence for partial N movement in the Romance DP. In Guglielmo Cinque, Jan Koster, Jean-Yves Pollock, Luigi Rizzi & Raffaella Zanuttini (eds.), *Paths towards Universal Grammar: Studies in honor of Richard S. Kayne*, 85–110. Washington, D.C.: Georgetown University Press.

Cinque, Guglielmo. 1999. *Adverbs and functional heads: A cross-linguistic perspective*. New York, Oxford: Oxford University Press.

Cinque, Guglielmo & Luigi Rizzi. 2010. The cartography of syntactic structures. In Bernd Heine & Heiko Narrog (eds.), *The Oxford handbook of linguistic analysis*, 51–65. Oxford: Oxford University Press.

Citko, Barbara. 2008. Missing labels. *Lingua* 118(7). 907–944.

Clark, Alexander. 2000. Inducing syntactic categories by context distribution clustering. In *Proceedings CoNLL 2000*, 91–94. Stroudsburg, PA: Association for Computational Linguistics.

References

Clark, Herbert H. & Jean E. Fox Tree. 2002. Using *uh* and *um* in spontaneous speaking. *Cognition* 84(1). 73–111.

Clark, Herbert H. & Thomas Wasow. 1998. Repeating words in spontaneous speech. *Cognitive Psychology* 37(3). 201–242.

Clark, Stephen & James Curran. 2007. Wide-coverage efficient statistical parsing with CCG and log-linear models. *Computational Linguistics* 33(4). 493–552.

Clark, Stephen, Julia Hockenmaier & Mark J. Steedman. 2002. Building deep dependency structures with a wide-coverage CCG parser. In Pierre Isabelle (ed.), *40th Annual Meeting of the Association for Computational Linguistics: Proceedings of the conference*, 327–334. University of Pennsylvania, Philadelphia: Association for Computational Linguistics. http://aclweb.org/anthology/P02-1042, accessed 2018-2-25.

Clément, Lionel. 2009. *XLFG5 documentation*. http://www.xlfg.org/, accessed 2018-2-25. Translated from French by Olivier Bonami.

Clément, Lionel & Alexandra Kinyon. 2001. XLFG—An LFG parsing scheme for French. In Miriam Butt & Tracy Holloway King (eds.), *Proceedings of the LFG 2001 conference*. Stanford, CA: CSLI Publications. http://csli-publications.stanford.edu/LFG/6/, accessed 2018-2-25.

Clément, Lionel & Alexandra Kinyon. 2003. Generating parallel multilingual LFG-TAG grammars from a MetaGrammar. In Erhard Hinrichs & Dan Roth (eds.), *Proceedings of the 41st Annual Meeting of the Association for Computational Linguistics*, 184–191. Sapporo, Japan: Association for Computational Linguistics.

Clifton, Charles Jr. & Penelope Odom. 1966. Similarity relations among certain English sentence constructions. *Psychological Monographs: General and Applied* 80(5). 1–35.

Coch, Jose. 1996. Overview of AlethGen. In *Demonstrations and posters of the Eighth International Natural Language Generation Workshop (INLG'96)*, 25–28.

Cook, Philippa. 2006. The datives that aren't born equal: Beneficiaries and the dative passive. In Daniel Hole, André Meinunger & Werner Abraham (eds.), *Datives and similar cases: Between argument structure and event structure*, 141–184. Amsterdam: John Benjamins Publishing Co.

Cook, Philippa Helen. 2001. *Coherence in German: An information structure approach*. Departments of Linguistics & German, University of Manchester dissertation.

Cooper, Robin, Kuniaki Mukai & John Perry (eds.). 1990. *Situation Theory and its applications*. Vol. 1 (CSLI Lecture Notes 22). Stanford, CA: CSLI Publications.

Coopmans, Peter. 1989. Where stylistic and syntactic processes meet: Locative inversion in English. *Language* 65(4). 728–751.

Copestake, Ann. 2002. *Implementing typed feature structure grammars* (CSLI Lecture Notes 110). Stanford, CA: CSLI Publications.

Copestake, Ann. 2007. Applying robust semantics. In *Proceedings of the 10th Conference of the Pacific Assocation for Computational Linguistics (PACLING)*, 1–12.

Copestake, Ann & Ted Briscoe. 1995. Semi-productive polysemy and sense extension. *Journal of Semantics* 12(1). 15–67.

Copestake, Ann & Ted J. Briscoe. 1992. Lexical operations in a unification based framework. In James Pustejovsky & Sabine Bergler (eds.), *Lexical semantics and knowledge representation* (Lecture Notes in Artificial Intelligence 627), 101–119. Berlin: Springer Verlag.

Copestake, Ann & Daniel P. Flickinger. 2000. An open-source grammar development environment and broad-coverage English grammar using HPSG. In *Proceedings of the second Linguistic Resources and Evaluation Conference*, 591–600. Athens, Greece.

Copestake, Ann, Daniel P. Flickinger, Carl J. Pollard & Ivan A. Sag. 2005. Minimal Recursion Semantics: An introduction. *Research on Language and Computation* 3(2–3). 281–332. DOI:10.1007/s11168-006-6327-9

Correa, Nelson. 1987. An Attribute-Grammar implementation of Government-Binding Theory. In Candy Sidner (ed.), *25th Annual Meeting of the Association for Computational Linguistics*, 45–51. Stanford, CA: Association for Computational Linguistics.

Covington, Michael A. 1990. Parsing discontinuous constituents in Dependency Grammar. *Computational Linguistics* 16(4). 234–236.

Crabbé, Benoit. 2005. *Représentation informatique de grammaires d'arbres fortement lexicalisées: le cas de la grammaire d'arbres adjoints*. Université Nancy 2 dissertation.

Crain, Stephen, Drew Khlentzos & Rosalind Thornton. 2010. Universal Grammar versus language diversity. *Lingua* 120(12). 2668–2672.

Crain, Stephen & Mineharu Nakayama. 1987. Structure dependence in grammar formation. *Language* 63(3). 522–543.

Crain, Stephen & Mark J. Steedman. 1985. On not being led up the garden path: The use of context by the psychological syntax processor. In David R. Dowty, Lauri Karttunen & Arnold M. Zwicky (eds.), *Natural language processing*, 320–358. Cambridge, UK: Cambridge University Press.

Crain, Stephen, Rosalind Thornton & Drew Khlentzos. 2009. The case of the missing generalizations. *Cognitive Linguistics* 20(1). 145–155.

Cramer, Bart & Yi Zhang. 2009. Construction of a German HPSG grammar from a detailed treebank. In Tracy Holloway King & Marianne Santaholma (eds.), *Proceedings of the 2009 Workshop on Grammar Engineering Across Frameworks (GEAF 2009)*, 37–45. Suntec, Singapore: Association for Computational Linguistics. http://www.aclweb.org/anthology/W/W09/#2600, accessed 2018-2-25.

Crocker, Matthew Walter & Ian Lewin. 1992. Parsing as deduction: Rules versus principles. In Bernd Neumann (ed.), *ECAI 92. 10th European Conference on Artificial Intelligence*, 508–512. John Wiley & Sons, Inc.

Croft, William. 2001. *Radical Construction Grammar: Syntactic theory in typological perspective*. Oxford: Oxford University Press.

Croft, William. 2003. Lexical rules vs. constructions: A false dichotomy. In Hubert Cuyckens, Thomas Berg, René Dirven & Klaus-Uwe Panther (eds.), *Motivation in language: Studies in honour of Günter Radden* (Current Issues in Linguistic Theory 243), 49–68. Amsterdam: John Benjamins Publishing Co. DOI:10.1075/cilt.243.07cro

Croft, William. 2009. Syntax is more diverse, and evolutionary linguistics is already here. *The Behavioral and Brain Sciences* 32(5). 457–458.

References

Crysmann, Berthold. 2001. Clitics and coordination in linear structure. In Birgit Gerlach & Janet Grijzenhout (eds.), *Clitics in phonology, morphology and syntax* (Linguistik Aktuell/Linguistics Today 36), 121–159. Amsterdam: John Benjamins Publishing Co.

Crysmann, Berthold. 2002. *Constraint-based co-analysis: Portuguese cliticisation and morphology-syntax interaction in HPSG* (Saarbrücken Dissertations in Computational Linguistics and Language Technology 15). Saarbrücken: Deutsches Forschungszentrum für Künstliche Intelligenz und Universität des Saarlandes.

Crysmann, Berthold. 2003. On the efficient implementation of German verb placement in HPSG. In *Proceedings of RANLP 2003*, 112–116. Borovets, Bulgaria.

Crysmann, Berthold. 2004. Underspecification of intersective modifier attachment: Some arguments from German. In Stefan Müller (ed.), *Proceedings of the 11th International Conference on Head-Driven Phrase Structure Grammar, Center for Computational Linguistics, Katholieke Universiteit Leuven*, 378–392. Stanford, CA: CSLI Publications. http://csli-publications.stanford.edu/HPSG/2004/, accessed 2018-2-25.

Crysmann, Berthold. 2005a. An inflectional approach to Hausa final vowel shortening. In Geert Booij & Jaap van Marle (eds.), *Yearbook of morphology 2004*, 73–112. Dordrecht: Kluwer Academic Publishers.

Crysmann, Berthold. 2005b. Relative clause extraposition in German: An efficient and portable implementation. *Research on Language and Computation* 1(3). 61–82.

Crysmann, Berthold. 2005c. Syncretism in German: A unified approach to underspecification, indeterminacy, and likeness of case. In Stefan Müller (ed.), *Proceedings of the 12th International Conference on Head-Driven Phrase Structure Grammar, Department of Informatics, University of Lisbon*, 91–107. Stanford, CA: CSLI Publications. http://csli-publications.stanford.edu/HPSG/2005/, accessed 2018-2-25.

Crysmann, Berthold. 2008. An asymmetric theory of peripheral sharing in HPSG: Conjunction reduction and coordination of unlikes. In Gerhard Jäger, Paola Monachesi, Gerald Penn & Shuly Wintner (eds.), *Proceedings of Formal Grammar 2003, Vienna, Austria*, 47–62. Stanford, CA: CSLI Publications.

Crysmann, Berthold. 2009. Autosegmental representations in an HPSG of Hausa. In Tracy Holloway King & Marianne Santaholma (eds.), *Proceedings of the 2009 Workshop on Grammar Engineering Across Frameworks (GEAF 2009)*, 28–36. Suntec, Singapore: Association for Computational Linguistics. http://www.aclweb.org/anthology/W/W09/#2600, accessed 2018-2-25.

Crysmann, Berthold. 2011. A unified account of Hausa genitive constructions. In Philippe de Groote, Markus Egg & Laura Kallmeyer (eds.), *Formal Grammar: 14th International Conference, FG 2009, Bordeaux, France, July 25–26, 2009, revised selected papers* (Lecture Notes in Artificial Intelligence 5591), 102–117. Berlin: Springer Verlag.

Crysmann, Berthold. 2012. HaG: A computational grammar of Hausa. In Michael R. Marlo, Nikki B. Adams, Christopher R. Green, Michelle Morrison & Tristan M. Purvis (eds.), *Selected proceedings of the 42nd Annual Conference on African Linguistics (ACAL 42)*, 321–337. Somerville, MA: Cascadilla Press. http://www.lingref.com/cpp/acal/42/paper2780.pdf, accessed 2018-2-25.

Crysmann, Berthold. 2013. On the locality of complement clause and relative clause extraposition. In Gert Webelhuth, Manfred Sailer & Heike Walker (eds.), *Rightward movement in a comparative perspective* (Linguistik Aktuell/Linguistics Today 200), 369–396. Amsterdam: John Benjamins Publishing Co.

Crysmann, Berthold. 2016. Representing morphological tone in a computational grammar of Hausa. *Journal of Language Modelling* 3(2). 463–512.

Culicover, Peter W. 1999. *Syntactic nuts: Hard cases, syntactic theory, and language acquisition. foundations of syntax*. Vol. 1 (Oxford Linguistics). Oxford: Oxford University Press.

Culicover, Peter W. & Ray S. Jackendoff. 2005. *Simpler Syntax*. Oxford: Oxford University Press.

Culy, Christopher. 1985. The complexity of the vocabulary of Bambara. *Linguistics and Philosophy* 8(3). 345–351. DOI:10.1007/BF00630918

Curtiss, Susan. 1977. *Genie: A psycholinguistic study of a modern-day "wild child"*. New York: Academic Press.

Dąbrowska, Ewa. 2001. From formula to schema: The acquisition of English questions. *Cognitive Linguistics* 11(1–2). 83–102.

Dąbrowska, Ewa. 2004. *Language, mind and brain: Some psychological and neurological constraints on theories of grammar*. Washington, D.C.: Georgetown University Press.

Dahl, Östen. 1980. Some arguments for higher nodes in syntax: A reply to Hudson's 'constituency and dependency'. *Linguistics* 18(5–6). 485–488. DOI:10.1515/ling.1980.18.5-6.485

Dahl, Östen & Viveka Velupillai. 2013a. Perfective/imperfective aspect. In Matthew S. Dryer & Martin Haspelmath (eds.), *The world atlas of language structures online*. Leipzig: Max Planck Institute for Evolutionary Anthropology. http://wals.info/chapter/65, accessed 2018-2-25.

Dahl, Östen & Viveka Velupillai. 2013b. The past tense. In Matthew S. Dryer & Martin Haspelmath (eds.), *The world atlas of language structures online*. Leipzig: Max Planck Institute for Evolutionary Anthropology. http://wals.info/chapter/66, accessed 2018-2-25.

Dahllöf, Mats. 2002. Token dependency semantics and the paratactic analysis of intensional constructions. *Journal of Semantics* 19(4). 333–368.

Dahllöf, Mats. 2003. *Two reports on computational syntax and semantics*. Reports from Uppsala University (RUUL) 36. Department of Linguistics. http://stp.ling.uu.se/~matsd/pub/ruul36.pdf, accessed 2018-2-25.

Dalrymple, Mary. 1993. *The syntax of anaphoric binding* (CSLI Lecture Notes 36). Stanford, CA: CSLI Publications.

Dalrymple, Mary (ed.). 1999. *Semantics and syntax in Lexical Functional Grammar: The Resource Logic approach* (Language, Speech, and Communication). Cambridge, MA: MIT Press.

Dalrymple, Mary. 2001. *Lexical Functional Grammar* (Syntax and Semantics 34). New York, NY: Academic Press.

References

Dalrymple, Mary. 2006. Lexical Functional Grammar. In Keith Brown (ed.), *The encyclopedia of language and linguistics*, 2nd edn., 82–94. Oxford: Elsevier Science Publisher B.V. (North-Holland).

Dalrymple, Mary, Ronald M. Kaplan & Tracy Holloway King. 2001. Weak crossover and the absence of traces. In Miriam Butt & Tracy Holloway King (eds.), *Proceedings of the LFG 2001 conference*, 66–82. Stanford, CA: CSLI Publications. http://csli-publications.stanford.edu/LFG/6/, accessed 2018-2-25.

Dalrymple, Mary, Ronald M. Kaplan & Tracy Holloway King. 2004. Linguistic generalizations over descriptions. In Miriam Butt & Tracy Holloway King (eds.), *Proceedings of the LFG 2004 conference*, 199–208. Stanford, CA: CSLI Publications. http://csli-publications.stanford.edu/LFG/9/, accessed 2018-2-25.

Dalrymple, Mary, Ronald M. Kaplan, John T. Maxwell III & Annie Zaenen (eds.). 1995. *Formal issues in Lexical-Functional Grammar* (CSLI Lecture Notes 47). Stanford, CA: CSLI Publications.

Dalrymple, Mary, John Lamping & Vijay Saraswat. 1993. LFG semantics via constraints. In Steven Krauwer, Michael Moortgat & Louis des Tombe (eds.), *Sixth Conference of the European Chapter of the Association for Computational Linguistics. Proceedings of the conference*, 97–105. Uetrecht: Association for Computational Linguistics. DOI:10.3115/976744.976757

Dalrymple, Mary, Maria Liakata & Lisa Mackie. 2006. Tokenization and morphological analysis for Malagasy. *Computational Linguistics and Chinese Language Processing* 11(4). 315–332.

Dalrymple, Mary & Helge Lødrup. 2000. The grammatical functions of complement clauses. In Miriam Butt & Tracy Holloway King (eds.), *Proceedings of the LFG 2000 conference*. Stanford, CA: CSLI Publications. http://csli-publications.stanford.edu/LFG/5/pdfs/lfg00dalrympl-lodrup.pdf, accessed 2018-2-25.

Davidson, Donald. 1967. The logical form of action sentences. In Nicholas Rescher (ed.), *The logic of decision and action*, 81–95. Pittsburg: Pittsburg University Press.

Davis, Anthony R. 1996. *Lexical semantics and linking in the hierarchical lexicon*. Stanford University dissertation.

Davis, Anthony R. & Jean-Pierre Koenig. 2000. Linking as constraints on word classes in a hierarchical lexicon. *Language* 76(1). 56–91.

De Kuthy, Kordula. 2000. *Discontinuous NPs in German — A case study of the interaction of syntax, semantics and pragmatics*. Saarbrücken: Universität des Saarlandes dissertation.

De Kuthy, Kordula. 2001. Splitting PPs from NPs. In Walt Detmar Meurers & Tibor Kiss (eds.), *Constraint-based approaches to Germanic syntax* (Studies in Constraint-Based Lexicalism 7), 31–76. Stanford, CA: CSLI Publications.

De Kuthy, Kordula. 2002. *Discontinuous NPs in German* (Studies in Constraint-Based Lexicalism 14). Stanford, CA: CSLI Publications.

De Kuthy, Kordula, Vanessa Metcalf & Walt Detmar Meurers. 2004. *Documentation of the implementation of the Milca English Resource Grammar in the Trale system*. Ohio State University, ms.

De Kuthy, Kordula & Walt Detmar Meurers. 2001. On partial constituent fronting in German. *Journal of Comparative Germanic Linguistics* 3(3). 143–205.

De Kuthy, Kordula & Walt Detmar Meurers. 2003a. Dealing with optional complements in HPSG-based grammar implementations. In Stefan Müller (ed.), *Proceedings of the 10th International Conference on Head-Driven Phrase Structure Grammar, Michigan State University, East Lansing*, 88–96. Stanford, CA: CSLI Publications. http://csli-publications.stanford.edu/HPSG/2003/, accessed 2018-2-25.

De Kuthy, Kordula & Walt Detmar Meurers. 2003b. The secret life of focus exponents, and what it tells us about fronted verbal projections. In Stefan Müller (ed.), *Proceedings of the 10th International Conference on Head-Driven Phrase Structure Grammar, Michigan State University, East Lansing*, 97–110. Stanford, CA: CSLI Publications. http://csli-publications.stanford.edu/HPSG/2003/, accessed 2018-2-25.

de Saussure, Ferdinand. 1916a. *Cours de linguistique générale* (Bibliothèque Scientifique Payot). Paris: Payot. Edited by Charles Bally and Albert Sechehaye.

de Saussure, Ferdinand. 1916b. *Grundfragen der allgemeinen Sprachwissenschaft*. Berlin: Walter de Gruyter & Co. 2nd edition 1967.

de Alencar, Leonel. 2004. Complementos verbais oracionais – uma análise léxico-funcional. *Lingua(gem)* 1(1). 173–218.

de Alencar, Leonel. 2013. BrGram: uma gramática computacional de um fragmento do português brasileiro no formalismo da LFG. In *Proceedings of the 9th Brazilian Symposium in Information and Human Language Technology. Fortaleza, Ceará, Brazil, October 20–24*, 183–188. Fortaleza, Ceará: Sociedade Brasileira de Computação. http://www.aclweb.org/anthology/W13-4823, accessed 2018-2-25.

de Alencar, Leonel Figueiredo. 2015. A Passiva em português como construção predicativa adjetival: evidência morfológica e implementação computacional em LFG/XLE [passive as adjective predicative construction in Portuguese: Morphological evidence and implementation in LFG/XLE]. *Estudos da Língua(gem)* 13(2). 35–57. http://www.estudosdalinguagem.org/index.php/estudosdalinguagem/article/view/471, accessed 2018-2-28.

de Alencar, Leonel Figueiredo. 2017. A computational implementation of periphrastic verb constructions in French. *Alfa: Revista de Linguística (São José do Rio Preto)* 61(2). 437–466. http://seer.fclar.unesp.br/alfa/article/view/8537/6749, accessed 2018-2-28.

Delmonte, Rodolfo. 1990. Semantic parsing with an LFG-based lexicon and conceptual representations. *Computers and the Humanities* 24(5–6). 461–488.

Demberg, Vera & Frank Keller. 2008. A psycholinguistically motivated version of TAG. In *Proceedings of the 9th International Workshop on Tree Adjoining Grammars and Related Formalisms TAG+9*, 25–32. Tübingen.

Demske, Ulrike. 2001. *Merkmale und Relationen: Diachrone Studien zur Nominalphrase des Deutschen* (Studia Linguistica Germanica 56). Berlin: Walter de Gruyter Verlag.

den Besten, Hans. 1983. On the interaction of root transformations and lexical deletive rules. In Werner Abraham (ed.), *On the formal syntax of the Westgermania: Papers from the 3rd Groningen Grammar Talks, Groningen, January 1981* (Linguistik Aktuell/Linguistics Today 3), 47–131. Amsterdam: John Benjamins Publishing Co.

References

den Besten, Hans. 1985. Some remarks on the Ergative Hypothesis. In Werner Abraham (ed.), *Erklärende Syntax des Deutschen* (Studien zur deutschen Grammatik 25), 53–74. Tübingen: originally Gunter Narr Verlag now Stauffenburg Verlag.

Deppermann, Arnulf. 2006. Construction Grammar – eine Grammatik für die Interaktion? In Arnulf Deppermann, Reinhard Fiehler & Thomas Spranz-Fogasy (eds.), *Grammatik und Interaktion*, 43–65. Radolfzell: Verlag für Gesprächsforschung.

Derbyshire, Desmond C. 1979. *Hixkaryana* (Lingua Descriptive Series 1). Amsterdam: North Holland.

Devlin, Keith. 1992. *Logic and information*. Cambridge: Cambridge University Press.

Dhonnchadha, E. Uí & Josef van Genabith. 2006. A part-of-speech tagger for Irish using finite-state morphology and Constraint Grammar disambiguation. In *Proceedings of lrec'06*, 2241–2244.

Diesing, Molly. 1992. *Indefinites*. Cambridge, MA: MIT Press.

Dione, Cheikh Mouhamadou Bamba. 2013. Handling Wolof Clitics in LFG. In Christine Meklenborg Salvesen & Hans Petter Helland (eds.), *Challenging clitics* (Linguistik Aktuell/Linguistics Today 206), 87–118. Amsterdam: John Benjamins Publishing Co.

Dione, Cheikh Mouhamadou Bamba. 2014. An LFG approach to Wolof cleft constructions. In Miriam Butt & Tracy Holloway King (eds.), *Proceedings of the LFG 2014 conference*, 157–176. Stanford, CA: CSLI Publications.

Dipper, Stefanie. 2003. *Implementing and documenting large-scale grammars – German LFG*. IMS, University of Stuttgart dissertation. Arbeitspapiere des Instituts für Maschinelle Sprachverarbeitung (AIMS), Volume 9, Number 1.

Donati, Caterina. 2006. On *wh*-head-movement. In Lisa Lai-Shen Cheng & Norbert Corver (eds.), Wh-*movement: Moving on* (Current Studies in Linguistics 42), 21–46. Cambridge, MA: MIT Press.

Donohue, Cathryn & Ivan A. Sag. 1999. Domains in Warlpiri. In *Sixth International Conference on HPSG–Abstracts. 04–06 August 1999*, 101–106. Edinburgh.

Doran, Christine, Beth Ann Hockey, Anoop Sarkar, Bangalore Srinivas & Fei Xia. 2000. Evolution of the XTAG system. In Anne Abeillé & Owen Rambow (eds.), *Tree Adjoining Grammars: formalisms, linguistic analysis and processing* (CSLI Lecture Notes 156), 371–403. Stanford, CA: CSLI Publications.

Dörre, Jochen & Michael Dorna. 1993. *CUF: A formalism for linguistic knowledge representation*. DYANA 2 deliverable R.1.2A. Stuttgart, Germany: IMS.

Dörre, Jochen & Roland Seiffert. 1991. A formalism for natural language – STUF. In Otthein Herzog & Claus-Rainer Rollinger (eds.), *Text understanding in LILOG* (Lecture Notes in Artificial Intelligence 546), 29–38. Berlin: Springer Verlag.

Dowty, David. 1997. Non-constituent coordination, wrapping, and Multimodal Categorial Grammars: Syntactic form as logical form. In Maria Luisa Dalla Chiara, Kees Doets, Daniele Mundici & Johan Van Benthem (eds.), *Structures and norms in science* (Synthese Library 260), 347–368. Springer.

Dowty, David R. 1978. Governed transformations as lexical rules in a Montague Grammar. *Linguistic Inquiry* 9(3). 393–426.

Dowty, David R. 1979. *Word meaning and Montague Grammar* (Synthese Language Library 7). Dordrecht: D. Reidel Publishing Company.

Dowty, David R. 1988. Type raising, functional composition, and nonconstituent coordination. In Richard Oehrle, Emmon Bach & Deirdre Wheeler (eds.), *Categorial Grammars and natural language structures*, 153–198. Dordrecht: D. Reidel Publishing Company.

Dowty, David R. 1989. On the semantic content of the notion 'thematic role'. In Gennaro Chierchia, Barbara H. Partee & Raymond Turner (eds.), *Properties, types and meaning*, vol. 2 (Studies in Linguistics and Philosophy), 69–130. Dordrecht: Kluwer Academic Publishers.

Dowty, David R. 1991. Thematic proto-roles and argument selection. *Language* 67(3). 547–619.

Dowty, David R. 2003. The dual analysis of adjuncts and complements in Categorial Grammar. In Ewald Lang, Claudia Maienborn & Cathrine Fabricius-Hansen (eds.), *Modifying adjuncts* (Interface Explorations 4), 33–66. Berlin: Mouton de Gruyter.

Dras, Mark, François Lareau, Benjamin Börschinger, Robert Dale, Yasaman Motazedi, Owen Rambow, Myfany Turpin & Morgan Ulinski. 2012. Complex predicates in Arrernte. In Miriam Butt & Tracy Holloway King (eds.), *Proceedings of the LFG 2012 conference*, 177–197. Stanford, CA: CSLI Publications.

Drellishak, Scott. 2009. *Widespread but not universal: Improving the typological coverage of the Grammar Matrix*. University of Washington Doctoral dissertation.

Drosdowski, Günther. 1984. *Duden: Grammatik der deutschen Gegenwartssprache*. 4th edn. Vol. 4. Mannheim, Wien, Zürich: Dudenverlag.

Drosdowski, Günther. 1995. *Duden: Die Grammatik*. 5th edn. Vol. 4. Mannheim, Leipzig, Wien, Zürich: Dudenverlag.

Dryer, Matthew S. 1992. The Greenbergian word order correlations. *Language* 68(1). 81–138.

Dryer, Matthew S. 1997. Are grammatical relations universal? In Joan Bybee, John Haiman & Sandra Thompson (eds.), *Essays on language function and language type: Dedicated to T. Givon*, 115–143. Amsterdam: John Benjamins Publishing Co.

Dryer, Matthew S. 2013a. Order of adposition and noun phrase. In Matthew S. Dryer & Martin Haspelmath (eds.), *The world atlas of language structures online*. Leipzig: Max Planck Institute for Evolutionary Anthropology. http://wals.info/chapter/85, accessed 2018-2-25.

Dryer, Matthew S. 2013b. Order of object and verb. In Matthew S. Dryer & Martin Haspelmath (eds.), *The world atlas of language structures online*. Leipzig: Max Planck Institute for Evolutionary Anthropology. http://wals.info/chapter/83, accessed 2018-2-25.

Dryer, Matthew S. 2013c. Order of subject, object and verb. In Matthew S. Dryer & Martin Haspelmath (eds.), *The world atlas of language structures online*. Leipzig: Max Planck Institute for Evolutionary Anthropology. http://wals.info/chapter/81, accessed 2018-2-25.

Dürscheid, Christa. 1989. *Zur Vorfeldbesetzung in deutschen Verbzweit-Strukturen* (FOKUS 1). Trier: Wissenschaftlicher Verlag.

References

Dürscheid, Christa. 2003. *Syntax: Grundlagen und Theorien.* 2nd edn. (Studienbücher zur Linguistik 3). Westdeutscher Verlag.

Dyvik, Helge, Paul Meurer & Victoria Rosén. 2005. *LFG, Minimal Recursion Semantics and translation.* Paper presented at the LFG conference 2005.

Egg, Markus. 1999. Derivation and resolution of ambiguities in *wieder*-sentences. In Paul J. E. Dekker (ed.), *Proceedings of the 12th Amsterdam Colloquium*, 109–114.

Eisele, Andreas & Jochen Dörre. 1986. A Lexical Functional Grammar system in Prolog. In Makoto Nagao (ed.), *Proceedings of COLING 86*, 551–553. University of Bonn: Association for Computational Linguistics. https://www.aclweb.org/anthology/C86-1129, accessed 2019-8-14.

Eisenberg, Peter. 1992. Platos Problem und die Lernbarkeit der Syntax. In Peter Suchsland (ed.), *Biologische und soziale Grundlagen der Sprache* (Linguistische Arbeiten 280), 371–378. Tübingen: Max Niemeyer Verlag.

Eisenberg, Peter. 1994a. German. In Ekkehard König & Johan van der Auwera (eds.), *The Germanic languages* (Routledge Language Family Descriptions), 349–387. London: Routledge.

Eisenberg, Peter. 1994b. *Grundriß der deutschen Grammatik.* 3rd edn. Stuttgart, Weimar: Verlag J. B. Metzler.

Eisenberg, Peter. 2004. *Grundriß der deutschen Grammatik.* 2nd edn. Vol. 2. Der Satz. Stuttgart, Weimar: Verlag J. B. Metzler.

Eisenberg, Peter, Jörg Peters, Peter Gallmann, Cathrine Fabricius-Hansen, Damaris Nübling, Irmhild Barz, Thomas A. Fritz & Reinhard Fiehler. 2005. *Duden: Die Grammatik.* 7th edn. Vol. 4. Mannheim, Leipzig, Wien, Zürich: Dudenverlag.

Ellefson, Michelle R. & Morten Christiansen. 2000. Subjacency constraints without Universal Grammar: Evidence from artificial language learning and connectionist modeling. In *Proceedings of the 22nd Annual Conference of the Cognitive Science Society*, 645–650. Mahwah, NJ: Lawrence Erlbaum Associates.

Elman, Jeffrey L. 1993. Learning and development in neural networks: The importance of starting small. *Cognition* 48(1). 71–99.

Elman, Jeffrey L., Elizabeth A. Bates, Mark H. Johnson, Annette Karmiloff-Smith, Domenico Parisi & Kim Plunkett. 1996. *Rethinking innateness: A connectionist perspective on development.* Cambridge, MA: Bradford Books/MIT Press.

Embick, David. 2004. On the structure of resultative participles in English. *Linguistic Inquiry* 35(3). 355–392.

Emirkanian, Louisette, Lyne Da Sylva & Lorne H. Bouchard. 1996. The implementation of a computational grammar of French using the Grammar Development Environment. In Jun-ichi Tsuji (ed.), *Proceedings of COLING-96. 16th International Conference on Computational Linguistics (COLING96). Copenhagen, Denmark, August 5–9, 1996*, 1024–1027. Copenhagen, Denmark: Association for Computational Linguistics.

Engdahl, Elisabet & Enric Vallduví. 1996. Information packaging in HPSG. In Claire Grover & Enric Vallduví (eds.), *Edinburgh Working Papers in Cognitive Science, vol. 12: Studies in HPSG*, chap. 1, 1–32. Edinburgh: Centre for Cognitive Science, University of Edinburgh. ftp://ftp.cogsci.ed.ac.uk/pub/CCS-WPs/wp-12.ps.gz, accessed 2018-3-20.

Engel, Ulrich. 1970. *Regeln zur Wortstellung*. Forschungsberichte des Instituts für deutsche Sprache 5. Mannheim: Institut für deutsche Sprache. 3–148.

Engel, Ulrich. 1977. *Syntax der deutschen Gegenwartssprache*. Vol. 22 (Grundlagen der Germanistik). Berlin: Erich Schmidt Verlag.

Engel, Ulrich. 1996. Tesnière mißverstanden. In Gertrud Gréciano & Helmut Schumacher (eds.), *Lucien Tesnière – Syntaxe Structurale et Opèrations Mentales. Akten des deutsch-französischen Kolloquiums anläßlich der 100. Wiederkehr seines Geburtstages. Strasbourg 1993* (Linguistische Arbeiten 348), 53–61. Tübingen: Max Niemeyer Verlag.

Engel, Ulrich. 2014. Die dependenzielle Verbgrammatik (DVG). In Jörg Hagemann & Sven Staffeldt (eds.), *Syntaxtheorien: Analysen im Vergleich* (Stauffenburg Einführungen 28), 43–62. Tübingen: Stauffenburg Verlag.

Erbach, Gregor. 1995. ProFIT: prolog with features, inheritance and templates. In Steven P. Abney & Erhard W. Hinrichs (eds.), *Proceedings of the Seventh Conference of the European Chapter of the Association for Computational Linguistics*, 180–187. Dublin: Association for Computational Linguistics.

Ernst, Thomas. 1992. The phrase structure of English negation. *The Linguistic Review* 9(2). 109–144.

Eroms, Hans-Werner. 1985. Eine reine Dependenzgrammatik für das Deutsche. *Deutsche Sprache* 13. 306–326.

Eroms, Hans-Werner. 1987. Passiv und Passivfunktionen im Rahmen einer Dependenzgrammatik. In Centre de Recherche en Linguistique Germanique (Nice) (ed.), *Das Passiv im Deutschen* (Linguistische Arbeiten 183), 73–95. Tübingen: Max Niemeyer Verlag.

Eroms, Hans-Werner. 2000. *Syntax der deutschen Sprache* (de Gruyter Studienbuch). Berlin: Walter de Gruyter Verlag.

Eroms, Hans-Werner & Hans Jürgen Heringer. 2003. Dependenz und lineare Ordnung. In Vilmos Ágel, Ludwig M. Eichinger, Hans-Werner Eroms, Peter Hellwig, Hans Jürgen Heringer & Henning Lobin (eds.), *Dependenz und Valenz / Dependency and valency: Ein internationales Handbuch der zeitgenössischen Forschung / An international handbook of contemporary research*, vol. 25.1 (Handbücher zur Sprach- und Kommunikationswissenschaft), 247–263. Berlin: Walter de Gruyter.

Eroms, Hans-Werner, Gerhard Stickel & Gisela Zifonun (eds.). 1997. *Grammatik der deutschen Sprache*. Vol. 7 (Schriften des Instituts für deutsche Sprache). Berlin: Walter de Gruyter.

Erteschik-Shir, Nomi. 1973. *On the nature of island constraints*. Cambridge, MA: MIT dissertation.

Erteschik-Shir, Nomi. 1981. More on extractability from quasi-NPs. *Linguistic Inquiry* 12(4). 665–670.

Erteschik-Shir, Nomi & Shalom Lappin. 1979. Dominance and the functional explanation of island phenomena. *Theoretical Linguistics* 6(1–3). 41–86.

Estigarribia, Bruno. 2009. Facilitation by variation: right-to-left learning of English yes/no questions. *Cognitive Science* 34(1). 68–93.

References

Evans, Nicholas & Stephen C. Levinson. 2009a. The myth of language universals: Language diversity and its importance for cognitive science. *The Behavioral and Brain Sciences* 32(5). 429–448.

Evans, Nicholas & Stephen C. Levinson. 2009b. With diversity in mind: freeing the language sciences from Universal Grammar. *The Behavioral and Brain Sciences* 32(5). 472–492.

Evans, Roger. 1985. ProGram: A development tool for GPSG grammars. *Linguistics* 23(2). 213–244.

Everett, Daniel L. 2005. Cultural constraints on grammar and cognition in Pirahã. *Current Anthropology* 46(4). 621–646.

Everett, Daniel L. 2009. Pirahã culture and grammar: A response to some criticisms. *Language* 85(2). 405–442.

Everett, Daniel L. 2012. What does Pirahã grammar have to teach us about human language and the mind? *Cognitive Science* 3(6). 555–563. DOI:10.1002/wcs.1195

Evers, Arnold. 1975. *The transformational cycle in Dutch and German.* University of Utrecht dissertation.

Faaß, Gertrud. 2010. *A morphosyntactic description of Northern Sotho as a basis for an automated translation from Northern Sotho into English.* Pretoria, South Africa: University of Pretoria dissertation. http://hdl.handle.net/2263/28569, accessed 2018-2-25.

Fabregas, Antonio, Tom Stroik & Michael Putnam. 2016. *Is simplest merge too simple?* Ms. Penn State University.

Falk, Yehuda N. 1984. The English auxiliary system: A Lexical-Functional analysis. *Language* 60(3). 483–509.

Fan, Zhenzhen, Sanghoun Song & Francis Bond. 2015. An HPSG-based shared-grammar for the Chinese languages: ZHONG [|]. In Emily M. Bender, Lori Levin, Stefan Müller, Yannick Parmentier & Aarne Ranta (eds.), *Proceedings of the Grammar Engineering Across Frameworks (GEAF) Workshop*, 17–24. The Association for Computational Linguistics.

Fang, Ji & Tracy Holloway King. 2007. An LFG Chinese grammar for machine use. In Tracy Holloway King & Emily M. Bender (eds.), *Grammar Engineering across Frameworks 2007* (Studies in Computational Linguistics ONLINE), 144–160. Stanford, CA: CSLI Publications. http://csli-publications.stanford.edu/GEAF/2007/, accessed 2018-2-25.

Fanselow, Gisbert. 1981. *Zur Syntax und Semantik der Nominalkomposition* (Linguistische Arbeiten 107). Tübingen: Max Niemeyer Verlag.

Fanselow, Gisbert. 1987. *Konfigurationalität* (Studien zur deutschen Grammatik 29). Tübingen: originally Gunter Narr Verlag now Stauffenburg Verlag.

Fanselow, Gisbert. 1988. Aufspaltung von NPn und das Problem der ‚freien' Wortstellung. *Linguistische Berichte* 114. 91–113.

Fanselow, Gisbert. 1990. Scrambling as NP-movement. In Günther Grewendorf & Wolfgang Sternefeld (eds.), *Scrambling and Barriers* (Linguistik Aktuell/Linguistics Today 5), 113–140. Amsterdam: John Benjamins Publishing Co.

Fanselow, Gisbert. 1992a. „ERGATIVE" VERBEN UND DIE STRUKTUR DES DEUTSCHEN MITTELFELDS. In Ludger Hoffmann (ed.), *Deutsche Syntax: Ansichten und Aussichten* (Institut für deutsche Sprache, Jahrbuch 1991), 276–303. Berlin: de Gruyter.

Fanselow, Gisbert. 1992b. Zur biologischen Autonomie der Grammatik. In Peter Suchsland (ed.), *Biologische und soziale Grundlagen der Sprache* (Linguistische Arbeiten 280), 335–356. Tübingen: Max Niemeyer Verlag.

Fanselow, Gisbert. 1993. Die Rückkehr der Basisgenerierer. *Groninger Arbeiten zur Germanistischen Linguistik* 36. 1–74.

Fanselow, Gisbert. 2000a. Does constituent length predict German word order in the Middle Field? In Josef Bayer & Christine Römer (eds.), *Von der Philologie zur Grammatiktheorie: Peter Suchsland zum 65. Geburtstag*, 63–77. Tübingen: Max Niemeyer Verlag.

Fanselow, Gisbert. 2000b. Optimal exceptions. In Barbara Stiebels & Dieter Wunderlich (eds.), *The lexicon in focus* (studia grammatica 45), 173–209. Berlin: Akademie Verlag.

Fanselow, Gisbert. 2001. Features, θ-roles, and free constituent order. *Linguistic Inquiry* 32(3). 405–437.

Fanselow, Gisbert. 2002. Against remnant VP-movement. In Artemis Alexiadou, Elena Anagnostopoulou, Sjef Barbiers & Hans-Martin Gärtner (eds.), *Dimensions of movement: From features to remnants* (Linguistik Aktuell/Linguistics Today 48), 91–127. Amsterdam: John Benjamins Publishing Co.

Fanselow, Gisbert. 2003a. Free constituent order: A Minimalist interface account. *Folia Linguistica* 37(1–2). 191–231.

Fanselow, Gisbert. 2003b. Münchhausen-style head movement and the analysis of verb second. In Anoop Mahajan (ed.), *Proceedings of the workshop on head movement* (UCLA Working Papers in Linguistics 10). Los Angeles: UCLA, Linguistics Department.

Fanselow, Gisbert. 2003c. Zur Generierung der Abfolge der Satzglieder im Deutschen. *Neue Beiträge zur Germanistik* 112. 3–47.

Fanselow, Gisbert. 2004a. Cyclic phonology-syntax-interaction: PPT Movement in German (and other languages). In Shinichiro Ishihara, Michaela Schmitz & Anne Schwarz (eds.), *Interdisciplinary studies on information structure* (Working Papers of the SFB 632 1), 1–42. Potsdam: Universitätsverlag.

Fanselow, Gisbert. 2004b. Fakten, Fakten, Fakten! *Linguistische Berichte* 200. 481–493.

Fanselow, Gisbert. 2004c. Münchhausen-style head movement and the analysis of verb second. In Ralf Vogel (ed.), *Three papers on German verb movement* (Linguistics in Potsdam 22), 9–49. Universität Potsdam.

Fanselow, Gisbert. 2006. On pure syntax (uncontaminated by information structure). In Patrick Brandt & Eric Fuss (eds.), *Form, structure and grammar: A festschrift presented to Günther Grewendorf on occasion of his 60th birthday* (Studia grammatica 63), 137–157. Berlin: Akademie Verlag.

Fanselow, Gisbert. 2009. Die (generative) Syntax in den Zeiten der Empiriediskussion. *Zeitschrift für Sprachwissenschaft* 28(1). 133–139.

Fanselow, Gisbert & Sascha W. Felix. 1987. *Sprachtheorie 2. Die Rektions- und Bindungstheorie* (UTB für Wissenschaft: Uni-Taschenbücher 1442). Tübingen: A. Francke Verlag GmbH.

References

Fanselow, Gisbert, Matthias Schlesewsky, Damir Cavar & Reinhold Kliegl. 1999. *Optimal parsing, syntactic parsing preferences, and Optimality Theory*. Rutgers Optimality Archive (ROA) 367. Universität Potsdam. http://roa.rutgers.edu/view.php3?roa=367, accessed 2018-2-25.

Feldhaus, Anke. 1997. *Eine HPSG-Analyse ausgewählter Phänomene des deutschen w-Fragesatzes*. Working Papers of the Institute for Logic and Linguistics 27. IBM Scientific Center Heidelberg: Institute for Logic & Linguistics.

Feldman, Jerome. 1972. Some decidability results on grammatical inference and complexity. *Information and Control* 20(3). 244–262.

Fillmore, Charles J. 1968. The case for case. In Emmon Bach & Robert T. Harms (eds.), *Universals of linguistic theory*, 1–88. New York: Holt, Rinehart, & Winston.

Fillmore, Charles J. 1971. Plädoyer für Kasus. In Werner Abraham (ed.), *Kasustheorie* (Schwerpunkte Linguistik und Kommunikationswissenschaft 2), 1–118. Frankfurt/Main: Athenäum.

Fillmore, Charles J. 1988. The mechanisms of "Construction Grammar". In Shelley Axmaker, Annie Jaisser & Helen Singmaster (eds.), *Proceedings of the 14th Annual Meeting of the Berkeley Linguistics Society*, 35–55. Berkeley, CA: Berkeley Linguistics Society.

Fillmore, Charles J. 1999. Inversion and Constructional inheritance. In Gert Webelhuth, Jean-Pierre Koenig & Andreas Kathol (eds.), *Lexical and Constructional aspects of linguistic explanation* (Studies in Constraint-Based Lexicalism 1), 113–128. Stanford, CA: CSLI Publications.

Fillmore, Charles J., Paul Kay & Mary Catherine O'Connor. 1988. Regularity and idiomaticity in grammatical constructions: The case of *let alone*. *Language* 64(3). 501–538.

Fillmore, Charles J., Russell R. Lee-Goldmann & Russell Rhomieux. 2012. The FrameNet constructicon. In Hans C. Boas & Ivan A. Sag (eds.), *Sign-Based Construction Grammar* (CSLI Lecture Notes 193), 309–372. Stanford, CA: CSLI Publications.

Fischer, Ingrid & Martina Keil. 1996. Parsing decomposable idioms. In Jun-ichi Tsuji (ed.), *Proceedings of COLING-96. 16th International Conference on Computational Linguistics (COLING96). Copenhagen, Denmark, August 5–9, 1996*, 388–393. Copenhagen, Denmark: Association for Computational Linguistics.

Fischer, Kerstin & Anatol Stefanowitsch (eds.). 2006. *Konstruktionsgrammatik: Von der Anwendung zur Theorie* (Stauffenburg Linguistik 40). Tübingen: Stauffenburg Verlag.

Fisher, Simon E. & Gary F. Marcus. 2005. The eloquent ape: genes, brains and the evolution of language. *Nature Reviews Genetics* 7(1). 9–20.

Fisher, Simon E., Faraneh Vargha-Khadem, Kate E. Watkins, Anthony P. Monaco & Marcus E. Pembrey. 1998. Localisation of a gene implicated in a severe speech and language disorder. *Nature Genetics* 18(2). 168–170.

Fitch, W. Tecumseh. 2010. Three meanings of "recursion": key distinctions for biolinguistics. In Richard K. Larson, Viviane Déprez & Hiroko Yamakido (eds.), *The evolution of human language: biolinguistic perspectives* (Approaches to the Evolution of Language 2), 73–90. Cambridge, UK: Cambridge University Press.

Fitch, W. Tecumseh, Marc D. Hauser & Noam Chomsky. 2005. The evolution of the language faculty: clarifications and implications. *Cognition* 97(2). 179–210.

Flickinger, Daniel P. 1983. Lexical heads and phrasal gaps. In *Proceedings of the West Coast Conference on Formal Linguistics*, vol. 2. Stanford University Linguistics Dept.

Flickinger, Daniel P. 1987. *Lexical rules in the hierarchical lexicon*. Stanford University dissertation.

Flickinger, Daniel P. 2000. On building a more efficient grammar by exploiting types. *Natural Language Engineering* 6(1). 15–28. Special Issue on Efficient Processing with HPSG: Methods, Systems, Evaluation.

Flickinger, Daniel P. 2008. Transparent heads. In Stefan Müller (ed.), *Proceedings of the 15th International Conference on Head-Driven Phrase Structure Grammar*, 87–94. Stanford, CA: CSLI Publications. http://csli-publications.stanford.edu/HPSG/2008/abstr-flickinger.shtml, accessed 2018-2-25.

Flickinger, Daniel P. & Emily M. Bender. 2003. Compositional semantics in a multilingual grammar resource. In Emily M. Bender, Daniel P. Flickinger, Frederik Fouvry & Melanie Siegel (eds.), *Proceedings of the ESSLLI 2003 Workshop "Ideas and Strategies for Multilingual Grammar Development"*, 33–42. Vienna, Austria.

Flickinger, Daniel P., Ann Copestake & Ivan A. Sag. 2000. HPSG analysis of English. In Wolfgang Wahlster (ed.), *Verbmobil: Foundations of speech-to-speech translation* (Artificial Intelligence), 254–263. Berlin: Springer Verlag.

Flickinger, Daniel P., Carl J. Pollard & Thomas Wasow. 1985. Structure-sharing in lexical representation. In William C. Mann (ed.), *Proceedings of the Twenty-Third Annual Meeting of the Association for Computational Linguistics*, 262–267. Chicago, IL.

Fodor, Janet Dean. 1998a. Parsing to learn. *Journal of Psycholinguistic Research* 27(3). 339–374.

Fodor, Janet Dean. 1998b. Unambiguous triggers. *Linguistic Inquiry* 29(1). 1–36.

Fodor, Janet Dean. 2001. Parameters and the periphery: reflections on *syntactic nuts*. *Journal of Linguistics* 37. 367–392.

Fodor, Jerry A., Thomas G. Bever & Merrill F. Garrett. 1974. *The psychology of language: An introduction to psycholinguistics and Generative Grammar*. New York: McGraw-Hill Book Co.

Fokkens, Antske. 2011. Metagrammar engineering: Towards systematic exploration of implemented grammars. In *Proceedings of the 49th Annual Meeting of the Association for Computational Linguistics: Human Language Technologies*, 1066–1076. Portland, Oregon, USA: Association for Computational Linguistics. http://www.aclweb.org/anthology/P11-1107, accessed 2018-2-20.

Fokkens, Antske, Laurie Poulson & Emily M. Bender. 2009. Inflectional morphology in Turkish VP coordination. In Stefan Müller (ed.), *Proceedings of the 16th International Conference on Head-Driven Phrase Structure Grammar, University of Göttingen, Germany*, 110–130. Stanford, CA: CSLI Publications. http://csli-publications.stanford.edu/HPSG/2009/, accessed 2018-2-25.

Fong, Sandiway. 1991. *Computational properties of principle-based grammatical theories*. MIT Artificial Intelligence Lab dissertation.

References

Fong, Sandiway. 2014. Unification and efficient computation in the Minimalist Program. In L. Francis & L. Laurent (eds.), *Language and recursion*, 129–138. Berlin: Springer Verlag.

Fong, Sandiway & Jason Ginsburg. 2012. Computation with doubling constituents: Pronouns and antecedents in Phase Theory. In Anna Maria Di Sciullo (ed.), *Towards a Biolinguistic understanding of grammar: Essays on interfaces* (Linguistik Aktuell/Linguistics Today 194), 303–338. Amsterdam: John Benjamins Publishing Co.

Fordham, Andrew & Matthew Walter Crocker. 1994. Parsing with principles and probabilities. In Judith L. Klavans Philip Resnik (ed.), *The balancing act: combining symbolic and statistical approaches to language*. Las Cruces, New Mexico, USA: Association for Computational Linguistics.

Forst, Martin. 2006. COMP in (parallel) grammar writing. In Miriam Butt & Tracy Holloway King (eds.), *Proceedings of the LFG 2006 conference*. Stanford, CA: CSLI Publications. http://csli-publications.stanford.edu/LFG/11/pdfs/lfg06forst.pdf, accessed 2018-2-25.

Forst, Martin & Christian Rohrer. 2009. Problems of German VP coordination. In Miriam Butt & Tracy Holloway King (eds.), *Proceedings of the LFG 2009 conference*, 297–316. Stanford, CA: CSLI Publications. http://csli-publications.stanford.edu/LFG/14/, accessed 2018-2-25.

Fortmann, Christian. 1996. *Konstituentenbewegung in der DP-Struktur: Zur funktionalen Analyse der Nominalphrase im Deutschen* (Linguistische Arbeiten 347). Tübingen: Max Niemeyer Verlag.

Fourquet, Jean. 1957. Review of: Heinz Anstock: Deutsche Syntax – Lehr- und Übungsbuch. *Wirkendes Wort* 8. 120–122.

Fourquet, Jean. 1970. *Prolegomena zu einer deutschen Grammatik* (Sprache der Gegenwart – Schriften des Instituts für deutsche Sprache in Mannheim 7). Düsseldorf: Pädagogischer Verlag Schwann.

Fouvry, Frederik. 2003. Lexicon acquisition with a large-coverage unification-based grammar. In *Proceedings of EACL 03, 10th Conference of the European Chapter of the Association for Computational Linguistics, research notes and demos, April 12–17, 2003, Budapest, Hungary*, 87–90.

Fraj, Fériel Ben, Chiraz Zribi & Mohamed Ben Ahmed. 2008. ArabTAG: A Tree Adjoining Grammar for Arabic syntactic structures. In *Proceedings of the International Arab Conference on Information Technology*. Sfax, Tunisia.

Frank, Anette. 1994. *Verb second by lexical rule or by underspecification*. Arbeitspapiere des SFB 340 No. 43. Heidelberg: IBM Deutschland GmbH. ftp://ftp.ims.uni-stuttgart.de/pub/papers/anette/v2-usp.ps.gz, accessed 2018-3-20.

Frank, Anette. 1996. Eine LFG-Grammatik des Französischen. In *Deutsche und französische Syntax im Formalismus der LFG* (Linguistische Arbeiten 344), 97–244. Tübingen: Max Niemeyer Verlag.

Frank, Anette. 2006. (Discourse-) functional analysis of asymmetric coordination. In Miriam Butt, Mary Dalrymple & Tracy Holloway King (eds.), *Intelligent linguistic ar-*

chitectures: Variations on themes by Ronald M. Kaplan, 259–285. Stanford, CA: CSLI Publications.

Frank, Anette & Uwe Reyle. 1995. Principle based semantics for HPSG. In Steven P. Abney & Erhard W. Hinrichs (eds.), *Proceedings of the Seventh Conference of the European Chapter of the Association for Computational Linguistics*, 9–16. Dublin: Association for Computational Linguistics.

Frank, Anette & Annie Zaenen. 2002. Tense in LFG: Syntax and morphology. In Hans Kamp & Uwe Reyle (eds.), *How we say when it happens: Contributions to the theory of temporal reference in natural language*, 17–52. Tübingen: Max Niemeyer Verlag. Reprint as: Frank & Zaenen (2004).

Frank, Anette & Annie Zaenen. 2004. Tense in LFG: Syntax and morphology. In Louisa Sadler & Andrew Spencer (eds.), *Projecting morphology*, 23–66. Stanford, CA: CSLI Publications.

Frank, Robert. 2002. *Phrase structure composition and syntactic dependencies* (Current Studies in Linguistics 38). Cambridge, MA/London: MIT Press.

Franks, Steven. 1995. *Parameters in Slavic morphosyntax*. New York, Oxford: Oxford University Press.

Frazier, Lyn. 1985. Syntactic complexity. In David R. Dowty, Lauri Karttunen & Arnold M. Zwicky (eds.), *Natural language processing*, 129–189. Cambridge, UK: Cambridge University Press.

Frazier, Lyn & Charles Jr. Clifton. 1996. *Construal*. Cambridge, MA: MIT Press.

Freidin, Robert. 1975. The analysis of passives. *Language* 51(2). 384–405.

Freidin, Robert. 1997. Review article: The Minimalist Program. *Language* 73(3). 571–582.

Freidin, Robert. 2009. A note on methodology in linguistics. *The Behavioral and Brain Sciences* 32(5). 454–455.

Freudenthal, Daniel, Julian M. Pine, Javier Aguado-Orea & Fernand Gobet. 2007. Modeling the developmental patterning of finiteness marking in English, Dutch, German, and Spanish using MOSAIC. *Cognitive Science* 31(2). 311–341. DOI:10.1080/15326900701221454

Freudenthal, Daniel, Julian M. Pine & Fernand Gobet. 2006. Modeling the development of children's use of optional infinitives in Dutch and English using MOSAIC. *Cognitive Science* 30(2). 277–310. DOI:10.1207/s15516709cog0000_47

Freudenthal, Daniel, Julian M. Pine & Fernand Gobet. 2009. Simulating the referential properties of Dutch, German, and English root infinitives in MOSAIC. *Language Learning and Development* 5(1). 1–29. DOI:10.1080/15475440802502437

Frey, Werner. 1993. *Syntaktische Bedingungen für die semantische Interpretation: Über Bindung, implizite Argumente und Skopus* (studia grammatica 35). Berlin: Akademie Verlag.

Frey, Werner. 2000. Über die syntaktische Position der Satztopiks im Deutschen. In Ewald Lang, Marzena Rochon, Kerstin Schwabe & Oliver Teuber (eds.), *Issues on topics* (ZAS Papers in Linguistics 20), 137–172. Berlin: ZAS, Humboldt-Universität zu Berlin.

References

Frey, Werner. 2001. About the whereabouts of indefinites. *Theoretical Linguistics* 27(2/3). 137–161. Special Issue: NP Interpretation and Information Structure, Edited by Klaus von Heusinger and Kerstin Schwabe. DOI:10.1515/thli.2001.27.2-3.137

Frey, Werner. 2004a. A medial topic position for German. *Linguistische Berichte* 198. 153–190.

Frey, Werner. 2004b. *The grammar-pragmatics interface and the German prefield*. Forschungsprogramm Sprache und Pragmatik 52. Germanistisches Institut der Universität Lund. 1–39.

Frey, Werner. 2005. Pragmatic properties of certain German and English left peripheral constructions. *Linguistics* 43(1). 89–129.

Frey, Werner & Hans-Martin Gärtner. 2002. On the treatment of scrambling and adjunction in Minimalist Grammars. In Gerhard Jäger, Paola Monachesi, Gerald Penn & Shuly Wintner (eds.), *Proceedings of Formal Grammar 2002*, 41–52. Trento.

Frey, Werner & Uwe Reyle. 1983a. A Prolog implementation of Lexical Functional Grammar as a base for a natural language processing system. In Antonio Zampolli (ed.), *First Conference of the European Chapter of the Association for Computational Linguistics: Proceedings of the conference*, 52–57. Pisa, Italy: Association for Computational Linguistics. http://aclweb.org/anthology/E/E83/, accessed 2018-2-25.

Frey, Werner & Uwe Reyle. 1983b. Lexical Functional Grammar und Diskursrepräsentationstheorie als Grundlagen eines sprachverarbeitenden Systems. *Linguistische Berichte* 88. 79–100.

Fried, Mirjam. 2013. Principles of constructional change. In Thomas Hoffmann & Graeme Trousdale (eds.), *The Oxford handbook of Construction Grammar* (Oxford Handbooks), 419–437. Oxford: Oxford University Press.

Fried, Mirjam. 2015. Construction Grammar. In Tibor Kiss & Artemis Alexiadou (eds.), *Syntax – theory and analysis: An international handbook*, vol. 42.3 (Handbooks of Linguistics and Communication Science), 974–1003. Berlin: Mouton de Gruyter. DOI:10.1515/9783110363685

Friederici, Angela D. 2009. Pathways to language: fiber tracts in the human brain. *Trends in Cognitive Sciences* 13(4). 175–181.

Friedman, Joyce. 1969. Applications of a computer system for Transformational Grammar. In Research Group for Quantitative Linguistics (ed.), *Proceedings of COLING 69*, 1–27.

Friedman, Joyce, Thomas H. Bredt, Robert W. Doran, Bary W. Pollack & Theodore S. Martner. 1971. *A computer model of Transformational Grammar* (Mathematical Linguistics and Automatic Language Processing 9). New York: Elsevier.

Fries, Norbert. 1988. *Über das Null-Topik im Deutschen*. Forschungsprogramm Sprache und Pragmatik 3. Germanistisches Institut der Universität Lund. 19–49.

Fukui, Naoki & Margaret Speas. 1986. Specifiers and projection. In N. Fukui, T. R. Rapoport & E. Sagey (eds.), *Papers in theoretical linguistics* (MIT Working Papers 8), 128–172. Cambridge, MA: MIT.

Futrell, Richard, Laura Stearns, Daniel L. Everett, Steven T. Piantadosi & Edward Gibson. 2016. A corpus investigation of syntactic embedding in pirahã. *PLoS ONE* 11(3). 1–20. DOI:10.1371/journal.pone.0145289

Gaifman, Haim. 1965. Dependency systems and phrase-structure systems. *Information and Control* 8(3). 304–397. DOI:10.1016/S0019-9958(65)90232-9

Gallmann, Peter. 2003. *Grundlagen der deutschen Grammatik*. Lecture notes Friedrich-Schiller-Universität Jena. http://www.syntax-theorie.de, accessed 2018-2-25.

Gardner, R. Allen. 1957. Probability-learning with two and three choices. *The American Journal of Psychology* 70(2). 174–185.

Gärtner, Hans-Martin & Jens Michaelis. 2007. Some remarks on locality conditions and Minimalist Grammars. In Uli Sauerland & Hans-Martin Gärtner (eds.), *Interfaces + recursion = language? Chomsky's Minimalism and the view from syntax-semantics* (Studies in Generative Grammar 89), 161–195. Berlin: Mouton de Gruyter.

Gärtner, Hans-Martin & Markus Steinbach. 1997. Anmerkungen zur Vorfeldphobie pronominaler Elemente. In Franz-Josef d'Avis & Uli Lutz (eds.), *Zur Satzstruktur im Deutschen* (Arbeitspapiere des SFB 340 No. 90), 1–30. Tübingen: Eberhard-Karls-Universität Tübingen.

Gazdar, Gerald. 1981a. On syntactic categories. *Philosophical Transactions of the Royal Society of London. Series B, Biological Sciences* 295(1077). 267–283.

Gazdar, Gerald. 1981b. Unbounded dependencies and coordinate structure. *Linguistic Inquiry* 12. 155–184.

Gazdar, Gerald, Ewan Klein, Geoffrey K. Pullum & Ivan A. Sag. 1985. *Generalized Phrase Structure Grammar*. Cambridge, MA: Harvard University Press.

Gazdar, Gerald, Geoffrey K. Pullum, Bob Carpenter, Ewan Klein, Thomas E. Hukari & Robert D. Levine. 1988. Category structures. *Computational Linguistics* 14(1). 1–19.

Geach, Peter Thomas. 1970. A program for syntax. *Synthese* 22. 3–17.

Geißler, Stefan & Tibor Kiss. 1994. *Erläuterungen zur Umsetzung einer HPSG im Basisformalismus STUF III*. Tech. rep. 19. Heidelberg: IBM Informationssysteme GmbH – Institut für Logik und Linguistik (Verbundvorhaben Verbmobil).

Gerdes, Kim. 2002a. DTAG? In *Proceedings of the Sixth International Workshop on Tree Adjoining Grammar and Related Frameworks (TAG+6)*, 242–251. Università di Venezia.

Gerdes, Kim. 2002b. *Topologie et grammaires formelles de l'allemand*. Ecole doctorale Science du langage, UFR de linguistique, Université Paris 7 dissertation.

Gerdes, Kim & Sylvain Kahane. 2001. Word order in German: A formal Dependency Grammar using a topological hierarchy. In *Proceedings of the 39th Annual Meeting on Association for Computational Linguistics*, 220–227. Toulouse, France: Association for Computational Linguistics. DOI:10.3115/1073012.1073041

Gerken, LouAnn. 1991. The metrical basis for children's subjectless sentences. *Journal of Memory and Language* 30. 431–451.

Gibson, Edward. 1998. Linguistic complexity: Locality of syntactic dependencies. *Cognition* 68(1). 1–76.

References

Gibson, Edward & James Thomas. 1999. Memory limitations and structural forgetting: The perception of complex ungrammatical sentences as grammatical. *Language and Cognitive Processes* 14(3). 225–248.

Gibson, Edward & Kenneth Wexler. 1994. Triggers. *Linguistic Inquiry* 25(3). 407–454.

Ginzburg, Jonathan & Ivan A. Sag. 2000. *Interrogative investigations: The form, meaning, and use of English interrogatives* (CSLI Lecture Notes 123). Stanford, CA: CSLI Publications.

Godard, Danièle & Pollet Samvelian. 2019. Complex predicates. In Stefan Müller, Anne Abeillé, Robert D. Borsley & Jean-Pierre Koenig (eds.), *Head-Driven Phrase Structure Grammar: The handbook* (Empirically Oriented Theoretical Morphology and Syntax), 233–268. Berlin: Language Science Press. To appear. DOI:??

Gold, Mark E. 1967. Language identification in the limit. *Information and Control* 10(5). 447–474.

Goldberg, Adele E. 1995. *Constructions: A Construction Grammar approach to argument structure* (Cognitive Theory of Language and Culture). Chicago/London: The University of Chicago Press.

Goldberg, Adele E. 2003a. Constructions: A new theoretical approach to language. *Trends in Cognitive Sciences* 7(5). 219–224.

Goldberg, Adele E. 2003b. Words by default: The Persian Complex Predicate Construction. In Elaine J. Francis & Laura A. Michaelis (eds.), *Mismatch: form-function incongruity and the architecture of grammar* (CSLI Lecture Notes 163), 117–146. Stanford, CA: CSLI Publications.

Goldberg, Adele E. 2006. *Constructions at work: The nature of generalization in language* (Oxford Linguistics). Oxford: Oxford University Press.

Goldberg, Adele E. 2009. Constructions work. [response]. *Cognitive Linguistics* 20(1). 201–224.

Goldberg, Adele E. 2013a. Argument structure Constructions vs. lexical rules or derivational verb templates. *Mind and Language* 28(4). 435–465. DOI:10.1111/mila.12026

Goldberg, Adele E. 2013b. Explanation and Constructions: Response to Adger. *Mind and Language* 28(4). 479–491. DOI:10.1111/mila.12028

Goldberg, Adele E. 2014. Fitting a slim dime between the verb template and argument structure construction approaches. *Theoretical Linguistics* 40(1–2). 113–135.

Goldberg, Adele E., Devin Casenhiser & Nitya Sethuraman. 2004. Learning argument structure generalizations. *Cognitive Linguistics* 15(3). 289–316.

Goldberg, Adele E. & Ray S. Jackendoff. 2004. The English resultative as a family of Constructions. *Language* 80(3). 532–568.

Gopnik, Myrna & Martha B. Cargo. 1991. Familial aggregation of a developmental language disorder. *Cognition* 39(1). 1–50.

Gordon, Peter. 1985. Level ordering in lexical development. *Cognition* 21(2). 73–93. DOI:10.1016/0010-0277(85)90046-0

Gosch, Angela, Gabriele Städing & Rainer Pankau. 1994. Linguistic abilities in children with Williams-Beuren Syndrome. *American Journal of Medical Genetics* 52(3). 291–296.

Götz, Thilo, Walt Detmar Meurers & Dale Gerdemann. 1997. *The ConTroll manual: (ConTroll v.1.0 beta, XTroll v.5.0 beta)*. User's Manual. Universität Tübingen: Seminar für Sprachwissenschaft. http://www.sfs.uni-tuebingen.de/controll/code.html, accessed 2018-2-25.

Grebe, Paul & Helmut Gipper. 1966. *Duden: Grammatik der deutschen Gegenwartssprache*. 2nd edn. Vol. 4. Mannheim, Wien, Zürich: Dudenverlag.

Green, Georgia M. 2011. Modelling grammar growth: Universal Grammar without innate principles or parameters. In Robert D. Borsley & Kersti Börjars (eds.), *Non-transformational syntax: Formal and explicit models of grammar: A guide to current models*, 378–403. Oxford, UK/Cambridge, MA: Blackwell Publishers Ltd.

Grewendorf, Günther. 1983. Reflexivierungen in deutschen A.c.I.-Konstruktionen – kein transformationsgrammatisches Dilemma mehr. *Groninger Arbeiten zur Germanistischen Linguistik* 23. 120–196.

Grewendorf, Günther. 1985. Anaphern bei Objekt-Koreferenz im Deutschen: Ein Problem für die Rektions-Bindungs-Theorie. In Werner Abraham (ed.), *Erklärende Syntax des Deutschen* (Studien zur deutschen Grammatik 25), 137–171. Tübingen: originally Gunter Narr Verlag now Stauffenburg Verlag.

Grewendorf, Günther. 1987. Kohärenz und Restrukturierung: Zu verbalen Komplexen im Deutschen. In Brigitte Asbach-Schnitker & Johannes Roggenhofer (eds.), *Neuere Forschungen zur Wortbildung und Histographie: Festgabe für Herbert E. Brekle zum 50. Geburtstag* (Tübinger Beiträge zur Linguistik 284), 123–144. Tübingen: Gunter Narr Verlag.

Grewendorf, Günther. 1988. *Aspekte der deutschen Syntax: Eine Rektions-Bindungs-Analyse* (Studien zur deutschen Grammatik 33). Tübingen: originally Gunter Narr Verlag now Stauffenburg Verlag.

Grewendorf, Günther. 1989. *Ergativity in German* (Studies in Generative Grammar 35). Dordrecht: Foris Publications. DOI:10.1515/9783110859256

Grewendorf, Günther. 1993. German: A grammatical sketch. In Joachim Jacobs, Arnim von Stechow, Wolfgang Sternefeld & Theo Vennemann (eds.), *Syntax – Ein internationales Handbuch zeitgenössischer Forschung*, vol. 9.2 (Handbücher zur Sprach- und Kommunikationswissenschaft), 1288–1319. Berlin: Walter de Gruyter Verlag. DOI:10.1515/9783110095869.1

Grewendorf, Günther. 2002. *Minimalistische Syntax* (UTB für Wissenschaft: Uni-Taschenbücher 2313). Tübingen, Basel: A. Francke Verlag GmbH.

Grewendorf, Günther. 2009. The left clausal periphery: Clitic left dislocation in Italian and left dislocation in German. In Benjamin Shear, Philippa Helen Cook, Werner Frey & Claudia Maienborn (eds.), *Dislocated elements in discourse: Syntactic, semantic, and pragmatic perspectives* (Routledge Studies in Germanic Linguistics), 49–94. New York: Routledge.

Grimshaw, Jane. 1986. Subjacency and the S/S' Parameter. *Linguistic Inquiry* 17(2). 364–369.

Grimshaw, Jane. 1997. Projections, heads, and optimality. *Linguistic Inquiry* 28. 373–422.

References

Grinberg, Dennis, John D. Lafferty & Daniel Dominic Sleator. 1995. A robust parsing algorithm for Link Grammars. In *Proceedings of the Fourth International Workshop on Parsing Technologies*. http://arxiv.org/abs/cmp-lg/9508003, accessed 2018-2-25. Also as Carnegie Mellon University Computer Science Technical Report CMU-CS-95-125.

Groos, Anneke & Henk van Riemsdijk. 1981. Matching effects in free relatives: A parameter of core grammar. In A. Belletti, L. Brandi & L. Rizzi (eds.), *Theory of markedness in Generative Grammar*, 171–216. Pisa: Scuola Normale Superiore.

Groß, Thomas M. & Timothy Osborne. 2009. Toward a practical Dependency Grammar theory of discontinuities. *SKY Journal of Linguistics* 22. 43–90.

Groß, Thomas Michael. 2003. Dependency Grammar's limits – and ways of extending them. In Vilmos Ágel, Ludwig M. Eichinger, Hans-Werner Eroms, Peter Hellwig, Hans Jürgen Heringer & Henning Lobin (eds.), *Dependenz und Valenz / Dependency and valency: Ein internationales Handbuch der zeitgenössischen Forschung / An international handbook of contemporary research*, vol. 25.1 (Handbücher zur Sprach- und Kommunikationswissenschaft), 331–351. Berlin: Walter de Gruyter.

Grosu, Alexander. 1973. On the status of the so-called Right Roof Constraint. *Language* 49(2). 294–311.

Grover, Claire, John Carroll & Ted J. Briscoe. 1993. *The Alvey Natural Language Tools grammar (4th release)*. Technical Report 284. Computer Laboratory, Cambridge University, UK.

Grubačić, Emilija. 1965. *Untersuchungen zur Frage der Wortstellung in der deutschen Prosadichtung der letzten Jahrzehnte*. Zagreb: Philosophische Fakultät dissertation.

Gruber, Jeffrey. 1965. *Studies in lexical relations*. MIT dissertation.

Gunji, Takao. 1986. Subcategorization and word order. In William J. Poser (ed.), *Papers from the Second International Workshop on Japanese Syntax*, 1–21. Stanford, CA: CSLI Publications.

Günther, Carsten, Claudia Maienborn & Andrea Schopp. 1999. The processing of information structure. In Peter Bosch & Rob van der Sandt (eds.), *Focus: Linguistic, cognitive, and computational perspectives* (Studies in Natural Language Processing), 18–42. Cambridge, UK: Cambridge University Press. Rev. papers orig. presented at a conference held 1994, Schloss Wolfsbrunnen, Germany.

Guo, Yuqing, Haifeng Wang & Josef van Genabith. 2007. Recovering non-local dependencies for Chinese. In *Proceedings of the Joint Conference on Empirical Methods in Natural Language Processing and Natural Language Learning, (EMNLP-CoNLL 2007)*, 257–266. Prague, Czech Republic: Association for Computational Linguistics.

Guzmán Naranjo, Matías. 2015. Unifying everything: Integrating quantitative effects into formal models of grammar. In *Proceedings of the 6th Conference on Quantitative Investigations in Theoretical Linguistics*. Tübingen. DOI:10.15496/publikation-8636

Haddar, Kais, Sirine Boukedi & Ines Zalila. 2010. Construction of an HPSG grammar for the Arabic language and its specification in TDL. *International Journal on Information and Communication Technologies* 3(3). 52–64.

Haegeman, Liliane. 1994. *Introduction to Government and Binding Theory*. 2nd edn. (Blackwell Textbooks in Linguistics 1). Oxford: Blackwell Publishers Ltd.

Haegeman, Liliane. 1995. *The syntax of negation*. Cambridge, UK: Cambridge University Press.

Haftka, Brigitta. 1995. Syntactic positions for topic and contrastive focus in the German middlefield. In Inga Kohlhof, Susanne Winkler & Hans-Bernhard Drubig (eds.), *Proceedings of the Göttingen Focus Workshop, 17 DGfS, March 1–3* (Arbeitspapiere des SFB 340 No. 69), 137–157. Eberhard-Karls-Universität Tübingen.

Haftka, Brigitta. 1996. Deutsch ist eine V/2-Sprache mit Verbendstellung und freier Wortfolge. In Ewald Lang & Gisela Zifonun (eds.), *Deutsch – typologisch* (Institut für deutsche Sprache, Jahrbuch 1995), 121–141. Berlin: Walter de Gruyter.

Hagen, Kristin, Janne Bondi Johannessen & Anders Nøklestad. 2000. A constraint-based tagger for Norwegian. In C.-E. Lindberg & S. N. Lund (eds.), *17th Scandinavian Conference of Linguistic, Odense*, vol. I (Odense Working Papers in Language and Communication 19), 1–15.

Hahn, Michael. 2011. Null conjuncts and bound pronouns in Arabic. In Stefan Müller (ed.), *Proceedings of the 18th International Conference on Head-Driven Phrase Structure Grammar, University of Washington*, 60–80. Stanford, CA: CSLI Publications. http://csli-publications.stanford.edu/HPSG/2011/, accessed 2018-2-25.

Haider, Hubert. 1982. Dependenzen und Konfigurationen: Zur deutschen V-Projektion. *Groninger Arbeiten zur Germanistischen Linguistik* 21. 1–60.

Haider, Hubert. 1984. Was zu haben ist und was zu sein hat – Bemerkungen zum Infinitiv. *Papiere zur Linguistik* 30(1). 23–36.

Haider, Hubert. 1985a. The case of German. In Jindřich Toman (ed.), *Studies in German grammar* (Studies in Generative Grammar 21), 23–64. Dordrecht: Foris Publications.

Haider, Hubert. 1985b. Über *sein* oder nicht *sein*: Zur Grammatik des Pronomens *sich*. In Werner Abraham (ed.), *Erklärende Syntax des Deutschen* (Studien zur deutschen Grammatik 25), 223–254. Tübingen: originally Gunter Narr Verlag now Stauffenburg Verlag.

Haider, Hubert. 1986a. Fehlende Argumente: Vom Passiv zu kohärenten Infinitiven. *Linguistische Berichte* 101. 3–33.

Haider, Hubert. 1986b. Nicht-sententiale Infinitive. *Groninger Arbeiten zur Germanistischen Linguistik* 28. 73–114.

Haider, Hubert. 1990a. Pro-bleme? In Gisbert Fanselow & Sascha W. Felix (eds.), *Strukturen und Merkmale syntaktischer Kategorien* (Studien zur deutschen Grammatik 39), 121–143. Tübingen: originally Gunter Narr Verlag now Stauffenburg Verlag.

Haider, Hubert. 1990b. Topicalization and other puzzles of German syntax. In Günther Grewendorf & Wolfgang Sternefeld (eds.), *Scrambling and Barriers* (Linguistik Aktuell/Linguistics Today 5), 93–112. Amsterdam: John Benjamins Publishing Co. DOI:10.1075/la.5.06hai

Haider, Hubert. 1991. *Fakultativ kohärente Infinitivkonstruktionen im Deutschen*. Arbeitspapiere des SFB 340 No. 17. Heidelberg: IBM Deutschland GmbH.

Haider, Hubert. 1993. *Deutsche Syntax – generativ: Vorstudien zur Theorie einer projektiven Grammatik* (Tübinger Beiträge zur Linguistik 325). Tübingen: Gunter Narr Verlag.

References

Haider, Hubert. 1994. (Un-)heimliche Subjekte: Anmerkungen zur Pro-drop Causa, im Anschluß an die Lektüre von Osvaldo Jaeggli & Kenneth J. Safir, eds., The Null Subject Parameter. *Linguistische Berichte* 153. 372–385.

Haider, Hubert. 1995. *Studies on phrase structure and economy*. Arbeitspapiere des SFB 340 No. 70. Stuttgart: Universität Stuttgart.

Haider, Hubert. 1997a. Projective economy: On the minimal functional structure of the German clause. In Werner Abraham & Elly van Gelderen (eds.), *German: Syntactic problems—Problematic syntax* (Linguistische Arbeiten 374), 83–103. Tübingen: Max Niemeyer Verlag.

Haider, Hubert. 1997b. Typological implications of a directionality constraint on projections. In Artemis Alexiadou & T. Alan Hall (eds.), *Studies on Universal Grammar and typological variation* (Linguistik Aktuell/Linguistics Today 13), 17–33. Amsterdam: John Benjamins Publishing Co.

Haider, Hubert. 1999. The license to license: Structural case plus economy yields Burzio's Generalization. In Eric Reuland (ed.), *Arguments and case: Explaining Burzio's Generalization* (Linguistik Aktuell/Linguistics Today 34), 31–55. Amsterdam: John Benjamins Publishing Co.

Haider, Hubert. 2000. OV is more basic than VO. In Peter Svenonius (ed.), *The derivation of VO and OV*, 45–67. Amsterdam: John Benjamins Publishing Co.

Haider, Hubert. 2001. Parametrisierung in der Generativen Grammatik. In Martin Haspelmath, Ekkehard König, Wulf Oesterreicher & Wolfgang Raible (eds.), *Sprachtypologie und sprachliche Universalien – Language typology and language universals: Ein internationales Handbuch – An international handbook*, 283–294. Berlin: Mouton de Gruyter.

Haider, Hubert. 2014. *Scientific ideology in grammar theory*. Ms. Universität Salzburg, Dept. of Linguistics and Centre for Cognitive Neuroscience.

Haider, Hubert. 2015. "intelligent design" of grammars – a result of cognitive evolution. In *Variation in language: System- and usage-based approaches* (linguae & litterae 50), 203–238. de Gruyter. DOI:10.1515/9783110346855-009

Haider, Hubert. 2016. *On predicting resultative adjective constructions*. Ms. Universität Salzburg.

Hajičová, Eva & Petr Sgall. 2003. Dependency Syntax in Functional Generative Description. In Vilmos Ágel, Ludwig M. Eichinger, Hans-Werner Eroms, Peter Hellwig, Hans Jürgen Heringer & Henning Lobin (eds.), *Dependenz und Valenz / Dependency and valency: Ein internationales Handbuch der zeitgenössischen Forschung / An international handbook of contemporary research*, vol. 25.1 (Handbücher zur Sprach- und Kommunikationswissenschaft), 570–592. Berlin: Walter de Gruyter.

Hakuta, Kenji, Ellen Bialystok & Edward Wiley. 2003. Critical evidence: A test of the Critical-Period Hypothesis for second-language acquisition. *Psychological Science* 14(1). 31–38.

Hale, Kenneth. 1976. The adjoined relative clause in Australia. In R.M.W. Dixon (ed.), *Grammatical catgeories of Australian languages* (Linguistic Series 22), 78–105. New Jersey: Humanities Press.

Hale, Kenneth & Samuel Jay Keyser. 1993. On argument structure and the lexical expression of syntactic relations. In Kenneth Hale & Samuel Jay Keyser (eds.), *The view from building 20: Essays in linguistics in honor of Sylvain Bromberger* (Current Studies in Linguistics 24), 53–109. Cambridge, MA/London: MIT Press.

Hale, Kenneth & Samuel Jay Keyser. 1997. On the complex nature of simple predicators. In Alex Alsina, Joan Bresnan & Peter Sells (eds.), *Complex predicates* (CSLI Lecture Notes 64), 29–65. Stanford, CA: CSLI Publications.

Han, Chung-hye, Juntae Yoon, Nari Kim & Martha Palmer. 2000. *A feature-based Lexicalized Tree Adjoining Grammar for Korean*. Technical Report IRCS-00-04. University of Pennsylvania Institute for Research in Cognitive Science. https://repository.upenn.edu/ircs_reports/35/, accessed 2018-2-25.

Harbour, Daniel. 2011. Mythomania? Methods and morals from 'The myth of language universals'. *Lingua* 121(12). 1820–1830.

Harley, Heidi & Rolf Noyer. 2000. Formal versus encyclopedic properties of vocabulary: Evidence from nominalizations. In Bert Peeters (ed.), *The lexicon–encyclopedia interface*, 349–374. Amsterdam: Elsevier.

Harman, Gilbert. 1963. Generative grammars without transformation rules: A defence of phrase structure. *Language* 39. 597–616.

Harris, Zellig S. 1957. Co-occurrence and transformation in linguistic structure. *Language* 33(3). 283–340.

Haspelmath, Martin. 2008. Parametric versus functional explanations of syntactic universals. In T. Biberauer (ed.), *The limits of syntactic variation*, 75–107. Amsterdam: John Benjamins Publishing Co.

Haspelmath, Martin. 2009. The best-supported language universals refer to scalar patterns deriving from processing costs. *The Behavioral and Brain Sciences* 32(5). 457–458.

Haspelmath, Martin. 2010a. Comparative concepts and descriptive categories in crosslinguistic studies. *Language* 86(3). 663–687.

Haspelmath, Martin. 2010b. Framework-free grammatical theory. In Bernd Heine & Heiko Narrog (eds.), *The Oxford handbook of grammatical analysis*, 341–365. Oxford: Oxford University Press.

Haspelmath, Martin. 2010c. The interplay between comparative concepts and descriptive categories (reply to Newmeyer). *Language* 86(3). 696–699.

Haugereid, Petter. 2007. Decomposed phrasal constructions. In Stefan Müller (ed.), *Proceedings of the 14th International Conference on Head-Driven Phrase Structure Grammar*, 120–129. Stanford, CA: CSLI Publications. http://csli-publications.stanford.edu/HPSG/2007/, accessed 2018-2-25.

Haugereid, Petter. 2009. *Phrasal subconstructions: A Constructionalist grammar design, exemplified with Norwegian and English*. Norwegian University of Science & Technology, Trondheim dissertation.

Haugereid, Petter. 2017. Increasing grammar coverage through fine-grained lexical distinctions. In Victoria Rosén & Koenraad De Smedt (eds.), *The very model of a modern linguist — in honor of Helge Dyvik* (Bergen Language and Linguistics Studies (BeLLS) 8), 97–111. University of Bergen. DOI:10.15845/bells.v8i1

Haugereid, Petter, Nurit Melnik & Shuly Wintner. 2013. Nonverbal predicates in Modern Hebrew. In Stefan Müller (ed.), *Proceedings of the 20th International Conference on Head-Driven Phrase Structure Grammar, Freie Universität Berlin*, 69–89. Stanford, CA: CSLI Publications. http://csli-publications.stanford.edu/HPSG/2013/hmw.pdf, accessed 2018-2-25.

Hauser, Marc D., Noam Chomsky & W. Tecumseh Fitch. 2002. The faculty of language: What is it, who has it, and how did it evolve? *Science* 298(5598). 1569–1579. DOI:10.1126/science.298.5598.1569

Hausser, Roland. 1992. Complexity in left-associative grammar. *Theoretical Computer Science* 106(2). 283–308.

Hawkins, John A. 1999. Processing complexity and filler-gap dependencies across grammars. *Language* 75(2). 244–285.

Hawkins, John A. 2004. *Efficiency and complexity in grammars*. Oxford: Oxford University Press.

Hays, David G. 1964. Dependency Theory: A formalism and some observations. *Language* 40(4). 511–525.

Hays, David G. & T. W. Ziehe. 1960. *Studies in machine translation: 10–Russian sentence-structure determination*. Tech. rep. Rand Corporation.

Heinecke, Johannes, Jürgen Kunze, Wolfgang Menzel & Ingo Schröder. 1998. Eliminative parsing with graded constraints. In Pierre Isabelle (ed.), *Proceedings of the 36th Annual Meeting of the Association for Computational Linguistics and 17th International Conference on Computational Linguistics*, 526–530. Montreal, Quebec, Canada: Association for Computational Linguistics. DOI:10.3115/980845.980953

Heinz, Wolfgang & Johannes Matiasek. 1994. Argument structure and case assignment in German. In John Nerbonne, Klaus Netter & Carl J. Pollard (eds.), *German in Head-Driven Phrase Structure Grammar* (CSLI Lecture Notes 46), 199–236. Stanford, CA: CSLI Publications.

Helbig, Gerhard & Joachim Buscha. 1969. *Deutsche Grammatik: Ein Handbuch für den Ausländerunterricht*. Leipzig: VEB Verlag Enzyklopädie.

Helbig, Gerhard & Joachim Buscha. 1998. *Deutsche Grammatik: Ein Handbuch für den Ausländerunterricht*. 18th edn. Leipzig Berlin München: Langenscheidt Verlag Enzyklopädie.

Helbig, Gerhard & Wolfgang Schenkel. 1969. *Wörterbuch zur Valenz und Distribution deutscher Verben*. Leipzig: VEB Bibliographisches Institut Leipzig.

Hellan, Lars. 1986. The headedness of NPs in Norwegian. In Peter Muysken & Henk van Riemsdijk (eds.), *Features and projections*, 89–122. Dordrecht/Cinnaminson, U.S.A.: Foris Publications.

Hellan, Lars. 2007. On 'deep evaluation' for individual computational grammars and for cross-framework comparison. In Tracy Holloway King & Emily M. Bender (eds.), *Grammar Engineering across Frameworks 2007* (Studies in Computational Linguistics

ONLINE), 161–181. Stanford, CA: CSLI Publications. http://csli-publications.stanford.edu/GEAF/2007/, accessed 2018-2-25.

Hellan, Lars & Dorothee Beermann. 2006. The 'specifier' in an HPSG grammar implementation of Norwegian. In S. Werner (ed.), *Proceedings of the 15th NODALIDA Conference, Joensuu 2005* (Ling@JoY: University of Joensuu electronic publications in linguistics and language technology 1), 57–64. Joensuu: University of Joensuu.

Hellan, Lars & Petter Haugereid. 2003. Norsource – An excercise in the Matrix Grammar building design. In Emily M. Bender, Daniel P. Flickinger, Frederik Fouvry & Melanie Siegel (eds.), *Proceedings of the ESSLLI 2003 Workshop "Ideas and Strategies for Multilingual Grammar Development"*. Vienna, Austria.

Hellwig, Peter. 1978. PLAIN – Ein Programmsystem zur Sprachbeschreibung und maschinellen Sprachbearbeitung. *Sprache und Datenverarbeitung* 1(2). 16–31.

Hellwig, Peter. 1986. Dependency Unification Grammar. In Makoto Nagao (ed.), *Proceedings of COLING 86*, 195–198. University of Bonn: Association for Computational Linguistics.

Hellwig, Peter. 2003. Dependency Unification Grammar. In Vilmos Ágel, Ludwig M. Eichinger, Hans-Werner Eroms, Peter Hellwig, Hans Jürgen Heringer & Henning Lobin (eds.), *Dependenz und Valenz / Dependency and valency: Ein internationales Handbuch der zeitgenössischen Forschung / An international handbook of contemporary research*, vol. 25.1 (Handbücher zur Sprach- und Kommunikationswissenschaft), 593–635. Berlin: Walter de Gruyter.

Hellwig, Peter. 2006. Parsing with Dependency Grammars. In Vilmos Ágel, Ludwig M. Eichinger, Hans-Werner Eroms, Peter Hellwig, Hans Jürgen Heringer & Henning Lobin (eds.), *Dependenz und Valenz / Dependency and valency: Ein internationales Handbuch der zeitgenössischen Forschung / An international handbook of contemporary research*, vol. 25.2 (Handbücher zur Sprach- und Kommunikationswissenschaft), 1081–1109. Berlin: Walter de Gruyter.

Her, One-Soon, Dan Higinbotham & Joseph Pentheroudakis. 1991. An LFG-based machine translation system. *Computer Processing of Chinese and Oriental Languages* 5(3–4). 285–297.

Heringer, Hans-Jürgen. 1996. *Deutsche Syntax dependentiell* (Stauffenburg Linguistik). Tübingen: Stauffenburg Verlag.

Herring, Joshua. 2016. *Grammar construction in the Minimalist Program*. Indiana University dissertation.

Higginbotham, James. 1985. On semantics. *Linguistic Inquiry* 16(4). 547–593.

Hinrichs, Erhard W., Walt Detmar Meurers, Frank Richter, Manfred Sailer & Heike Winhart (eds.). 1997. *Ein HPSG-Fragment des Deutschen. Teil 1: Theorie*. Vol. No. 95 (Arbeitspapiere des SFB 340). Tübingen: Eberhard-Karls-Universität Tübingen.

Hinrichs, Erhard W. & Tsuneko Nakazawa. 1989a. Flipped out: AUX in German. In *Aspects of German VP structure* (SfS-Report-01-93). Tübingen: Eberhard-Karls-Universität Tübingen.

References

Hinrichs, Erhard W. & Tsuneko Nakazawa. 1989b. Subcategorization and VP structure in German. In *Aspects of German VP structure* (SfS-Report-01-93). Tübingen: Eberhard-Karls-Universität Tübingen.

Hinrichs, Erhard W. & Tsuneko Nakazawa. 1994. Linearizing AUXs in German verbal complexes. In John Nerbonne, Klaus Netter & Carl J. Pollard (eds.), *German in Head-Driven Phrase Structure Grammar* (CSLI Lecture Notes 46), 11–38. Stanford, CA: CSLI Publications.

Hinterhölzel, Roland. 2004. Language change versus grammar change: What diachronic data reveal about the interaction between core grammar and periphery. In Carola Trips & Eric Fuß (eds.), *Diachronic clues to synchronic grammar*, 131–160. Amsterdam: John Benjamins Publishing Co.

Hoberg, Ursula. 1981. *Die Wortstellung in der geschriebenen deutschen Gegenwartssprache* (Heutiges Deutsch. Linguistische Grundlagen. Forschungen des Instituts für deutsche Sprache 10). München: Max Hueber Verlag.

Hockett, Charles F. 1960. The origin of speech. *Scientific American* 203. 88–96.

Hoeksema, Jack. 1991. Theoretische Aspekten van Partikelvooropplaatsing. *TABU Bulletin voor Taalwetenschap* 21(1). 18–26.

Hoekstra, Teun. 1987. *Transitivity: grammatical relations in Government-Binding Theory*. Dordrecht: Foris Publications.

Hoffman, Beryl Ann. 1995. *The computational analysis of the syntax and interpretation of "free" word order in Turkish*. University of Pennsylvania dissertation.

Höhle, Tilman N. 1978. *Lexikalische Syntax: Die Aktiv-Passiv-Relation und andere Infinitkonstruktionen im Deutschen* (Linguistische Arbeiten 67). Tübingen: Max Niemeyer Verlag.

Höhle, Tilman N. 1982. Explikationen für „normale Betonung" und „normale Wortstellung". In Werner Abraham (ed.), *Satzglieder im Deutschen – Vorschläge zur syntaktischen, semantischen und pragmatischen Fundierung* (Studien zur deutschen Grammatik 15), 75–153. Tübingen: originally Gunter Narr Verlag now Stauffenburg Verlag. Republished as Höhle (2018c).

Höhle, Tilman N. 1983. Topologische Felder. Köln, ms, Published as Höhle (2018f).

Höhle, Tilman N. 1986. Der Begriff „Mittelfeld": Anmerkungen über die Theorie der topologischen Felder. In Walter Weiss, Herbert Ernst Wiegand & Marga Reis (eds.), *Akten des VII. Kongresses der Internationalen Vereinigung für germanische Sprach- und Literaturwissenschaft. Göttingen 1985. Band 3. Textlinguistik contra Stilistik? – Wortschatz und Wörterbuch – Grammatische oder pragmatische Organisation von Rede?* (Kontroversen, alte und neue 4), 329–340. Tübingen: Max Niemeyer Verlag. Republished as Höhle (2018b).

Höhle, Tilman N. 1988. *Verum-Fokus*. Netzwerk Sprache und Pragmatik 5. Lund: Universität Lund, Germanistisches Institut. Republished as Höhle (2018g).

Höhle, Tilman N. 1991a. On reconstruction and coordination. In Hubert Haider & Klaus Netter (eds.), *Representation and derivation in the theory of grammar* (Studies in Natural Language and Linguistic Theory 22), 139–197. Dordrecht: Kluwer Academic Publishers. Republished as Höhle (2018d).

Höhle, Tilman N. 1991b. Projektionsstufen bei V-Projektionen: Bemerkungen zu F/T. Ms. Published as Höhle (2018e).

Höhle, Tilman N. 1997. Vorangestellte Verben und Komplementierer sind eine natürliche Klasse. In Christa Dürscheid, Karl Heinz Ramers & Monika Schwarz (eds.), *Sprache im Fokus: Festschrift für Heinz Vater zum 65. Geburtstag*, 107–120. Tübingen: Max Niemeyer Verlag. Republished as Höhle (2018h).

Höhle, Tilman N. 1999. An architecture for phonology. In Robert D. Borsley & Adam Przepiórkowski (eds.), *Slavic in Head-Driven Phrase Structure Grammar*, 61–90. Stanford, CA: CSLI Publications. Republished as Höhle (2018a).

Höhle, Tilman N. 2018a. An architecture for phonology. In Stefan Müller, Marga Reis & Frank Richter (eds.), *Beiträge zur Grammatik des Deutschen: Gesammelte Schriften von Tilman N. Höhle* (Classics in Linguistics 5), 571–607. Berlin: Language Science Press. Originally published as Höhle (1999). DOI:10.5281/zenodo.1145680

Höhle, Tilman N. 2018b. Der Begriff „Mittelfeld": Anmerkungen über die Theorie der topologischen Felder. In Stefan Müller, Marga Reis & Frank Richter (eds.), *Beiträge zur Grammatik des Deutschen: Gesammelte Schriften von Tilman N. Höhle* (Classics in Linguistics 5), 279–294. Berlin: Language Science Press. First published as Höhle (1986). DOI:10.5281/zenodo.1145680

Höhle, Tilman N. 2018c. Explikationen für „normale Betonung" und „normale Wortstellung". In Stefan Müller, Marga Reis & Frank Richter (eds.), *Beiträge zur Grammatik des Deutschen: Gesammelte Schriften von Tilman N. Höhle* (Classics in Linguistics 5), 107–191. Berlin: Language Science Press. DOI:10.5281/zenodo.1145680

Höhle, Tilman N. 2018d. On reconstruction and coordination. In Stefan Müller, Marga Reis & Frank Richter (eds.), *Beiträge zur Grammatik des Deutschen: Gesammelte Schriften von Tilman N. Höhle* (Classics in Linguistics 5), 311–368. Berlin: Language Science Press. DOI:10.5281/zenodo.1145680

Höhle, Tilman N. 2018e. Projektionsstufen bei V-Projektionen: Bemerkungen zu F/T. In Stefan Müller, Marga Reis & Frank Richter (eds.), *Beiträge zur Grammatik des Deutschen: Gesammelte Schriften von Tilman N. Höhle* (Classics in Linguistics 5), 369–379. Berlin: Language Science Press. First circulated in 1991. DOI:10.5281/zenodo.1145680

Höhle, Tilman N. 2018f. Topologische Felder. In Stefan Müller, Marga Reis & Frank Richter (eds.), *Beiträge zur Grammatik des Deutschen: Gesammelte Schriften von Tilman N. Höhle* (Classics in Linguistics 5), 7–89. Berlin: Language Science Press. First circulated as draft in 1983. DOI:10.5281/zenodo.1145680

Höhle, Tilman N. 2018g. Über Verum-Fokus im Deutschen. In Stefan Müller, Marga Reis & Frank Richter (eds.), *Beiträge zur Grammatik des Deutschen: Gesammelte Schriften von Tilman N. Höhle* (Classics in Linguistics 5), 381–416. Berlin: Language Science Press. Originally published as Höhle (1988). DOI:10.5281/zenodo.1145680

Höhle, Tilman N. 2018h. Vorangestellte Verben und Komplementierer sind eine natürliche Klasse. In Stefan Müller, Marga Reis & Frank Richter (eds.), *Beiträge zur Grammatik des Deutschen: Gesammelte Schriften von Tilman N. Höhle* (Classics in Linguistics 5), 417–433. Berlin: Language Science Press. First published as Höhle (1997). DOI:10.5281/zenodo.1145680

References

Holler, Anke. 2005. *Weiterführende Relativsätze: Empirische und theoretische Aspekte* (studia grammatica 60). Berlin: Akademie Verlag.

Hornstein, Norbert. 2013. Three grades of grammatical involvement: Syntax from a Minimalist perspective. *Mind and Language* 28(4). 392–420.

Hornstein, Norbert, Jairo Nunes & Kleantes K. Grohmann. 2005. *Understanding Minimalism* (Cambridge Textbooks in Linguistics). Cambridge, UK: Cambridge University Press. DOI:10.1017/CBO9780511840678

Hudson Kam, Carla L. & Elissa L. Newport. 2005. Regularizing unpredictable variation: The roles of adult and child learners in language formation and change. *Language Learning and Development* 1. 151–195.

Hudson, Carla L. & Elissa L. Newport. 1999. Creolization: could adults really have done it all? In Annabel Greenhill, Heather Littlefield & Cheryl Tano (eds.), *Proceedings of the Boston University Conference on Language Development*, vol. 23, 265–276. Somerville, MA: Cascadilla Press.

Hudson, Dick. 2019. HPSG and Dependency Grammar. In Stefan Müller, Anne Abeillé, Robert D. Borsley & Jean-Pierre Koenig (eds.), *Head-Driven Phrase Structure Grammar: The handbook* (Empirically Oriented Theoretical Morphology and Syntax). Berlin: Language Science Press. To appear.

Hudson, Richard. 1980. Constituency and dependency. *Linguistics* 18. 179–198.

Hudson, Richard. 1984. *Word grammar*. Oxford: Basil Blackwell.

Hudson, Richard. 1988. Coordination and grammatical relations. *Journal of Linguistics* 24(2). 303–342.

Hudson, Richard. 1989. Towards a computer-testable Word Grammar of English. *UCL Working Papers in Linguistics* 1. 321–339.

Hudson, Richard. 1990. *English Word Grammar*. Oxford: Basil Blackwell.

Hudson, Richard. 1991. *English Word Grammar*. Oxford: Basil Blackwell.

Hudson, Richard. 1997. *German partial VP fronting*. Ms. University College London. http://dickhudson.com/papers/, accessed 2018-2-20.

Hudson, Richard. 2000. Discontinuity. *Dependency Grammars, TAL* 41(1). 15–56.

Hudson, Richard. 2003. Mismatches in default inheritance. In Elaine J. Francis & Laura A. Michaelis (eds.), *Mismatch: form-function incongruity and the architecture of grammar* (CSLI Lecture Notes 163), 355–402. Stanford, CA: CSLI Publications.

Hudson, Richard. 2004. Are determiners heads? *Functions of Language* 11(1). 7–42.

Hudson, Richard. 2007. *Language networks: The new Word Grammar*. Oxford: Oxford University Press.

Hudson, Richard. 2010a. *An introduction to Word Grammar* (Cambridge Textbooks in Linguistics). Cambridge, UK: Cambridge University Press.

Hudson, Richard. 2010b. Reaction to: "The myth of language universals and cognitive science": On the choice between phrase structure and dependency structure. *Lingua* 120(12). 2676–2679.

Hudson, Richard. 2017. Pied piping in cognition. *Journal of Linguistics* 54(1). 85–138. DOI:10.1017/S0022226717000056

Humboldt, Wilhelm von. 1988. *Gesammelte Werke*. Berlin, New York: Walter de Gruyter.

Hurford, James R. 2002. Expression/induction models of language evolution: dimensions and issues. In Ted J. Briscoe (ed.), *Linguistic evolution through language acquisition*, 301–344. Cambridge, UK: Cambridge University Press.

Hurskainen, Arvi. 2006. Constraint Grammar in unconventional use: Handling complex Swahili idioms and proverbs. *Suominen, Mickael et.al.: A Man of Measure: Festschrift in Honour of Fred Karlsson on his 60th Birthday. Special Supplement to SKY Jounal of Linguistics* 19. 397–406.

Imrényi, András. 2013. Constituency or dependency? Notes on Sámuel Brassai's syntactic model of Hungarian. In Péter Szigetvári (ed.), *Papers presented to László Varga on his 70th birthday*, 167–182. Budapest: Tinta.

Ingram, David & William Thompson. 1996. Early syntactic acquisition in German: Evidence for the modal hypothesis. *Language* 72(1). 97–120.

Iordanskaja, L., M. Kim, R. Kittredge, B. Lavoie & A. Polguère. 1992. Generation of extended bilingual statistical reports. In Antonio Zampolli (ed.), *14th International Conference on Computational Linguistics (COLING '92), August 23–28*, vol. 3, 1019–1023. Nantes, France: Association for Computational Linguistics.

Islam, Md. Asfaqul, K. M. Azharul Hasan & Md. Mizanur Rahman. 2012. Basic HPSG structure for Bangla grammar. In *15th International Conference on Computer and Information Technology (ICCIT)*, 185–189. Curran Associates. DOI:10.1109/ICCITechn.2012.6509749

Jackendoff, Ray S. 1972. *Semantic interpretation in Generative Grammar*. Cambridge, MA: MIT Press.

Jackendoff, Ray S. 1975. Morphological and semantic regularities in the lexikon. *Language* 51(3). 639–671.

Jackendoff, Ray S. 1977. *$\overline{X}$ syntax: A study of phrase structure*. Cambridge, MA: MIT Press.

Jackendoff, Ray S. 1997. *The architecture of the language faculty* (Linguistic Inquiry Monographs 28). Cambridge, MA/London: MIT Press.

Jackendoff, Ray S. 2000. Fodorian modularity and representational modularity. In Yosef Grodzinsky, Lewis P. Shapiro & David Swinney (eds.), *Language and the brain: Representation and processing* (Foundations of Neuropsychology), 3–30. San Diego: Academic Press.

Jackendoff, Ray S. 2002. *Foundations of language*. Oxford: Oxford University Press.

Jackendoff, Ray S. 2007. A parallel architecture perspective on language processing. *Brain Research* 1146. 2–22.

Jackendoff, Ray S. 2008. Construction after Construction and its theoretical challenges. *Language* 84(1). 8–28.

Jackendoff, Ray S. 2011. What is the human language faculty? Two views. *Language* 87(3). 586–624.

Jackendoff, Ray S. & Steven Pinker. 2005. The nature of the language faculty and its implications for evolution of language (reply to Fitch, Hauser, and Chomsky). *Cognition* 97(2). 211–225.

Jackendoff, Ray S. & Steven Pinker. 2009. The reality of a universal language faculty. *The Behavioral and Brain Sciences* 32(5). 465–466.

References

Jacobs, Joachim. 1986. The syntax of focus and adverbials in German. In Werner Abraham & S. de Meij (eds.), *Topic, focus, and configurationality: Papers from the 6th Groningen Grammar Talks, Groningen, 1984* (Linguistik Aktuell/Linguistics Today 4), 103–127. Amsterdam: John Benjamins Publishing Co.

Jacobs, Joachim. 1991. *Bewegung als Valenztransfer*. SFB 282: Theorie des Lexikons 1. Düsseldorf/Wuppertal: Heinrich Heine Uni/BUGH.

Jacobs, Joachim. 2008. Wozu Konstruktionen? *Linguistische Berichte* 213. 3–44.

Jacobson, Pauline. 1987a. Phrase structure, grammatical relations, and discontinuous constituents. In Geoffrey J. Huck & Almerindo E. Ojeda (eds.), *Discontinuous constituency* (Syntax and Semantics 20), 27–69. New York: Academic Press.

Jacobson, Pauline. 1987b. Review of Generalized Phrase Structure Grammar. *Linguistics and Philosophy* 10(3). 389–426.

Jaeggli, Osvaldo A. 1986. Passive. *Linguistic Inquiry* 17(4). 587–622.

Jäger, Gerhard & Reinhard Blutner. 2003. Competition and interpretation: The German adverb *wieder* 'again'. In Ewald Lang, Claudia Maienborn & Cathrine Fabricius-Hansen (eds.), *Modifying adjuncts* (Interface Explorations 4), 393–416. Berlin: Mouton de Gruyter.

Jäppinen, H., Aarno Lehtola & K. Valkonen. 1986. Functional structures for parsing dependency constraints. In Makoto Nagao (ed.), *Proceedings of COLING 86*, 461–463. Bonn, Germany: Association for Computational Linguistics. DOI:10.3115/991365.991501

Johnson, David E. & Shalom Lappin. 1997. A critique of the Minimalist Programm. *Linguistics and Philosophy* 20(3). 273–333.

Johnson, David E. & Shalom Lappin. 1999. *Local constraints vs. economy* (Stanford Monographs in Linguistics). Stanford, CA: CSLI Publications.

Johnson, David E. & Paul M. Postal. 1980. *Arc Pair Grammar*. Princeton, NJ: Princeton University Press.

Johnson, Jacqueline S. & Elissa L. Newport. 1989. Critical period effects in second language learning: The influence of maturational state on the acquisition of English as a second language. *Cognitive Psychology* 21(1). 60–99.

Johnson, Kent. 2004. Gold's theorem and cognitive science. *Philosophy of Science* 71(4). 571–592.

Johnson, Mark. 1986. A GPSG account of VP structure in German. *Linguistics* 24(5). 871–882.

Johnson, Mark. 1988. *Attribute-value logic and the theory of grammar* (CSLI Lecture Notes 16). Stanford, CA: CSLI Publications.

Johnson, Mark. 1989. Parsing as deduction: The use of knowledge of language. *Journal of Psycholinguistic Research* 18(1). 105–128.

Johnson, Mark, Stuart Geman, Stephen Canon, Zhiyi Chi & Stefan Riezler. 1999. Estimators for stochastic "unification-based" grammars. In Robert Dale & Ken Church (eds.), *Proceedings of the Thirty-Seventh Annual Meeting of the ACL*, 535–541.

Joshi, Aravind K. 1985. Tree Adjoining Grammars: How much context-sensitivity is required to provide reasonable structural descriptions? In David Dowty, Lauri Karttunen

& Arnold Zwicky (eds.), *Natural language parsing*, 206–250. Cambridge University Press.

Joshi, Aravind K. 1987a. Introduction to Tree Adjoining Grammar. In Alexis Manaster-Ramer (ed.), *The mathematics of language*, 87–114. Amsterdam: John Benjamins Publishing Co.

Joshi, Aravind K. 1987b. Word-order variation in natural language generation. In *AAAI 87, Sixth National Conference on Artificial Intelligence*, 550–555. Seattle.

Joshi, Aravind K., Tilman Becker & Owen Rambow. 2000. Complexity of scrambling: A new twist to the competence-performance distinction. In Anne Abeillé & Owen Rambow (eds.), *Tree Adjoining Grammars: formalisms, linguistic analysis and processing* (CSLI Lecture Notes 156), 167–181. Stanford, CA: CSLI Publications.

Joshi, Aravind K., Leon S. Levy & Masako Takahashi. 1975. Tree Adjunct Grammar. *Journal of Computer and System Science* 10(2). 136–163.

Joshi, Aravind K. & Yves Schabes. 1997. Tree-Adjoining Grammars. In G. Rozenberg & A. Salomaa (eds.), *Handbook of formal languages*, 69–123. Berlin: Springer Verlag.

Joshi, Aravind K., K. Vijay-Shanker & David Weir. 1990. *The convergence of mildly context-sensitive grammar formalisms*. Tech. rep. MS-CIS-90-01. Department of Computer & Information Science, University of Pennsylvania. https://repository.upenn.edu/cis_reports/539/, accessed 2018-2-25.

Jungen, Oliver & Horst Lohnstein. 2006. *Einführung in die Grammatiktheorie* (UTB 2676). München: Wilhelm Fink Verlag.

Jurafsky, Daniel. 1996. A probabilistic model of lexical and syntactic access and disambiguation. *Cognitive Science* 20(2). 137–194.

Kahane, Sylvain. 1997. Bubble trees and syntactic representations. In Tilman Becker & Hans-Ulrich Krieger (eds.), *Proceedings of Mathematics of Language (MOL5) Meeting*, 70–76. Saarbrücken.

Kahane, Sylvain. 2003. The Meaning-Text Theory. In Vilmos Ágel, Ludwig M. Eichinger, Hans-Werner Eroms, Peter Hellwig, Hans Jürgen Heringer & Henning Lobin (eds.), *Dependenz und Valenz / Dependency and valency: Ein internationales Handbuch der zeitgenössischen Forschung / An international handbook of contemporary research*, vol. 25.1 (Handbücher zur Sprach- und Kommunikationswissenschaft), 546–570. Berlin: Walter de Gruyter.

Kahane, Sylvain. 2009. On the status of phrases in Head-Driven Phrase Structure Grammar: Illustration by a fully lexical treatment of extraction. In Alain Polguère & Igor A. Mel'čuk (eds.), *Dependency in linguistic description* (Studies in Language Companion Series 111), 111–150. Amsterdam: John Benjamins Publishing Co.

Kahane, Sylvain, Alexis Nasr & Owen Rambow. 1998. Pseudo-projectivity: A polynomially parsable non-projective Dependency Grammar. In Pierre Isabelle (ed.), *Proceedings of the 36th Annual Meeting of the Association for Computational Linguistics and 17th International Conference on Computational Linguistics*, 646–652. Montreal, Quebec, Canada: Association for Computational Linguistics. http://www.aclweb.org/anthology/P98-1106, accessed 2018-2-25. DOI:10.3115/980845.980953

References

Kahane, Sylvain & Timothy Osborne. 2015. Translators' introduction. In *Elements of structural syntax*, xxix–lxxiii. Amsterdam: John Benjamins Publishing Co. Translated by Timothy Osborne and Sylvain Kahane.

Kallmeyer, Laura. 2005. Tree-local Multicomponent Tree Adjoining Grammars with shared nodes. *Computational Linguistics* 31(2). 187–225.

Kallmeyer, Laura & Aravind K. Joshi. 2003. Factoring predicate argument and scope semantics: underspecified semantics with LTAG. *Research on Language and Computation* 1(1–2). 3–58. DOI:10.1023/A:1024564228892

Kallmeyer, Laura, Timm Lichte, Wolfgang Maier, Yannick Parmentier, Johannes Dellert & Kilian Evang. 2008. TuLiPA: Towards a multi-formalism parsing environment for grammar engineering. In Stephen Clark & Tracy Holloway King (eds.), *Coling 2008: Proceedings of the Workshop on Grammar Engineering Across Frameworks*, 1–8. Manchester, England: Association for Computational Linguistics.

Kallmeyer, Laura & Rainer Osswald. 2012. A frame-based semantics of the dative alternation in Lexicalized Tree Adjoining Grammars. In Christopher Piñón (ed.), *Empirical issues in syntax and semantics*, vol. 9, 167–184. Paris: CNRS.

Kallmeyer, Laura & Maribel Romero. 2008. Scope and situation binding in LTAG using semantic unification. *Research on Language and Computation* 6(1). 3–52.

Kallmeyer, Laura & SinWon Yoon. 2004. Tree-local MCTAG with shared nodes: An analysis of word order variation in German and Korean. *Traitement automatique des langues TAL* 45(3). 49–69.

Kamp, Hans & Uwe Reyle. 1993. *From discourse to logic: Introduction to modeltheoretic semantics of natural language, formal logic and Discourse Representation Theory* (Studies in Linguistics and Philosophy 42). Dordrecht: Kluwer Academic Publishers.

Kaplan, Ronald M. 1995. The formal architecture of Lexical-Functional Grammar. In Mary Dalrymple, Ronald M. Kaplan, John T. Maxwell III & Annie Zaenen (eds.), *Formal issues in Lexical-Functional Grammar* (CSLI Lecture Notes 47), 7–27. Stanford, CA: CSLI Publications.

Kaplan, Ronald M. & Joan Bresnan. 1982. Lexical-Functional Grammar: A formal system for grammatical representation. In Joan Bresnan (ed.), *The mental representation of grammatical relations* (MIT Press Series on Cognitive Theory and Mental Representation), 173–281. Cambridge, MA/London: MIT Press. Reprint in: Dalrymple, Kaplan, Maxwell III & Zaenen (1995: 29–130).

Kaplan, Ronald M. & John T. Maxwell III. 1996. *LFG grammar writer's workbench*. Tech. rep. Xerox PARC.

Kaplan, Ronald M., Stefan Riezler, Tracy Holloway King, John T. Maxwell III, Alexander Vasserman & Richard Crouch. 2004. Speed and accuracy in shallow and deep stochastic parsing. In *Proceedings of the Human Language Technology Conference and the 4th Annual Meeting of the North American Chapter of the Association for Computational Linguistics (HLT-NAACL '04)*. Boston, MA: Association for Computational Linguistics.

Kaplan, Ronald M. & Jürgen Wedekind. 1993. Restriction and correspondence-based translation. In *Proceedings of the 31st Annual Meeting of the Association for Compu-

tational Linguistics, 193–202. Columbus, Ohio, USA: Association for Computational Linguistics.

Kaplan, Ronald M. & Annie Zaenen. 1989. Long-distance dependencies, constituent structure and functional uncertainty. In Mark R. Baltin & Anthony S. Kroch (eds.), *Alternative conceptions of phrase structure*, 17–42. Chicago/London: The University of Chicago Press.

Karimi, Simin. 2005. *A Minimalist approach to scrambling: Evidence from Persian* (Studies in Generative Grammar 76). Berlin, New York: Mouton de Gruyter.

Karimi-Doostan, Gholamhossein. 2005. Light verbs and structural case. *Lingua* 115(12). 1737–1756.

Karlsson, Fred. 1990. Constraint Grammar as a framework for parsing running text. In Hans Karlgren (ed.), *COLING-90: Papers presented to the 13th International Conference on Computational Linguistics*, 168–173. Helsinki: Association for Computational Linguistics.

Karmiloff-Smith, Annette. 1998. Development itself is the key to understanding developmental disorders. *Trends in Cognitive Sciences* 2(10). 389–398.

Karmiloff-Smith, Annette, Julia Grant, Ioanna Berthoud, Mark Davies, Patricia Howlin & Orlee Udwin. 1997. Language in Williams Syndrome: How intact is 'intact'? *Child Development* 68(2). 246–262.

Karttunen, Lauri. 1986. *Radical lexicalism*. Report No. CSLI-86-68. Center for the Study of Language & Information.

Karttunen, Lauri. 1989. Radical lexicalism. In Mark R. Baltin & Anthony S. Kroch (eds.), *Alternative conceptions of phrase structure*, 43–65. Chicago/London: The University of Chicago Press.

Kasper, Robert T. 1994. Adjuncts in the Mittelfeld. In John Nerbonne, Klaus Netter & Carl J. Pollard (eds.), *German in Head-Driven Phrase Structure Grammar* (CSLI Lecture Notes 46), 39–70. Stanford, CA: CSLI Publications.

Kasper, Robert T., Bernd Kiefer, Klaus Netter & K. Vijay-Shanker. 1995. Compilation of HPSG to TAG. In Hans Uszkoreit (ed.), *33rd Annual Meeting of the Association for Computational Linguistics. Proceedings of the conference*, 92–99. Cambridge, MA: Association for Computational Linguistics.

Kathol, Andreas. 1995. *Linearization-based German syntax*. Ohio State University dissertation.

Kathol, Andreas. 2000. *Linear syntax*. New York, Oxford: Oxford University Press.

Kathol, Andreas. 2001. Positional effects in a monostratal grammar of German. *Journal of Linguistics* 37(1). 35–66.

Kathol, Andreas & Carl J. Pollard. 1995. Extraposition via complex domain formation. In Hans Uszkoreit (ed.), *33rd Annual Meeting of the Association for Computational Linguistics. Proceedings of the conference*, 174–180. Cambridge, MA: Association for Computational Linguistics.

Kaufmann, Ingrid & Dieter Wunderlich. 1998. *Cross-linguistic patterns of resultatives*. SFB 282: Theorie des Lexikons 109. Düsseldorf: Heinrich Heine Uni/BUGH.

References

Kaufmann, Tobias. 2009. *A rule-based language model for speech recognition*. Computer Engineering & Networks Laboratory, ETH Zürich dissertation.

Kaufmann, Tobias & Beat Pfister. 2007. Applying licenser rules to a grammar with continuous constituents. In Stefan Müller (ed.), *Proceedings of the 14th International Conference on Head-Driven Phrase Structure Grammar*, 150–162. Stanford, CA: CSLI Publications. http://csli-publications.stanford.edu/HPSG/2007/, accessed 2018-2-25.

Kaufmann, Tobias & Beat Pfister. 2008. Applying a grammar-based language model to a broadcast-news transcription task. In Johanna D. Moore, Simone Teufel, James Allan & Sadaoki Furui (eds.), *Proceedings of the 46th Annual Meeting of the Association for Computational Linguistics: Human Language Technologies*, 106–113. Columbus, Ohio: Association for Computational Linguistics. http://www.aclweb.org/anthology/P08-1013, accessed 2018-2-25.

Kay, Martin. 1967. Experiments with a powerful parser. In *Proceedings of Conference Internationale Sur Le Traitement Automatique Des Langues (COLING 1967)*. Grenoble. http://aclweb.org/anthology/C67-1009, accessed 2018-2-25.

Kay, Martin. 2000. David G. Hays. In William J. Hutchins (ed.), *Early years in machine translation* (Amsterdam Studies in the Theory and History of Linguistics Science Series 3), 165–170. Amsterdam: John Benjamins Publishing Co.

Kay, Martin. 2011. Zipf's law and *L'Arbitraire du Signe*. *Linguistic Issues in Language Technology* 6(8). 1–25. http://journals.linguisticsociety.org/elanguage/lilt/article/view/2584.html, accessed 2018-2-25. Special Issue on Interaction of Linguistics and Computational Linguistics.

Kay, Paul. 2002. An informal sketch of a formal architecture for Construction Grammar. *Grammars* 5(1). 1–19.

Kay, Paul. 2005. Argument structure constructions and the argument-adjunct distinction. In Mirjam Fried & Hans C. Boas (eds.), *Grammatical constructions: Back to the roots* (Constructional Approaches to Language 4), 71–98. Amsterdam: John Benjamins Publishing Co.

Kay, Paul & Charles J. Fillmore. 1999. Grammatical constructions and linguistic generalizations: The What's X Doing Y? Construction. *Language* 75(1). 1–33.

Kay, Paul, Ivan A. Sag & Daniel P. Flickinger. 2015. *A lexical theory of phrasal idioms*. Ms. CSLI Stanford.

Kayne, Richard S. 1994. *The antisymmetry of syntax* (Linguistic Inquiry Monographs 25). Cambridge, MA: MIT Press.

Kayne, Richard S. 2011. Why are there no directionality parameters? In Mary Byram Washburn, Katherine McKinney-Bock, Erika Varis, Ann Sawyer & Barbara Tomaszewicz (eds.), *Proceedings of the 28th West Coast Conference on Formal Linguistics*, 1–23. Somerville, MA: Cascadilla Press.

Keenan, Edward L. & Bernard Comrie. 1977. Noun phrase accessibility and Universal Grammar. *Linguistic Inquiry* 8(1). 63–99.

Keller, Frank. 1994. *German functional HPSG – An experimental CUF encoding*. Tech. rep. Stuttgart: Institut für Maschinelle Sprachverarbeitung.

Keller, Frank. 1995. Towards an account of extraposition in HPSG. In Steven P. Abney & Erhard W. Hinrichs (eds.), *Proceedings of the Seventh Conference of the European Chapter of the Association for Computational Linguistics*, 301–306. Dublin: Association for Computational Linguistics.

Kern, Franz. 1884. *Grundriß der Deutschen Satzlehre*. Berlin: Nicolaische Verlags-Buchhandlung.

Kettunen, Kimmo. 1986. On modelling dependency-oriented parsing. In Fred Karlsson (ed.), *Papers from the Fifth Scandinavian Conference of Computational Linguistics*, 113–120. Helsinki.

Kibort, Anna. 2008. On the syntax of ditransitive constructions. In Miriam Butt & Tracy Holloway King (eds.), *Proceedings of the LFG 2008 conference*, 312–332. Stanford, CA: CSLI Publications. http://csli-publications.stanford.edu/LFG/13/, accessed 2018-2-25.

Kiefer, Bernd, Hans-Ulrich Krieger & Mark-Jan Nederhof. 2000. Efficient and robust parsing of word hypotheses graphs. In Wolfgang Wahlster (ed.), *Verbmobil: Foundations of speech-to-speech translation* (Artificial Intelligence), 280–295. Berlin: Springer Verlag.

Kifle, Nazareth Amlesom. 2012. *Tigrinya applicatives in Lexical-Functional Grammar*. University of Bergen dissertation. http://hdl.handle.net/1956/5730, accessed 2018-2-25.

Kim, Jong-Bok. 2016. *The syntactic structures of Korean: A Construction Grammar perspective*. Cambridge, UK: Cambridge University Press.

Kim, Jong-Bok & Peter Sells. 2008. *English syntax: An introduction* (CSLI Lecture Notes 185). Stanford, CA: CSLI Publications.

Kim, Jong-Bok, Peter Sells & Jaehyung Yang. 2007. Parsing two types of multiple nominative constructions: A Constructional approach. *Language and Information* 11(1). 25–37.

Kim, Jong-Bok & Jaehyung Yang. 2003. Korean phrase structure grammar and its implementations into the LKB system. In Dong Hong Ji & Kim Teng Lua (eds.), *Proceedings of the 17th Pacific Asia Conference on Language, Information and Computation*, 88–97. National University of Singapore: COLIPS Publications.

Kim, Jong-Bok & Jaehyung Yang. 2004. Projections from morphology to syntax in the Korean Resource Grammar: implementing typed feature structures. In Alexander Gelbukh (ed.), *Computational linguistics and intelligent text processing: 5th International Conference, CICLing 2004, Seoul, Korea, February 15-21, 2004, Proceedings* (Lecture Notes in Computer Science 2945), 13–24. Berlin: Springer Verlag.

Kim, Jong-Bok & Jaehyung Yang. 2006. Coordination structures in a typed feature structure grammar: formalization and implementation. In Tapio Salakoski, Filip Ginter, Sampo Pyysalo & Tapio Pahikkala (eds.), *Advances in natural language processing: 5th International Conference, FinTAL 2006 Turku, Finland, August 23-25, 2006 proceedings* (Lecture Notes in Artificial Intelligence 4139), 194–205. Berlin: Springer Verlag.

Kim, Jong-Bok & Jaehyung Yang. 2009. Processing three types of Korean cleft constructions in a typed feature structure grammar. *Korean Journal of Cognitive Science* 20(1). 1–28.

References

Kim, Jong-Bok, Jaehyung Yang, Sanghoun Song & Francis Bond. 2011. Deep processing of Korean and the development of the Korean Resource Grammar. *Linguistic Research* 28(3). 635–672.

Kimball, John P. 1973. *The formal theory of grammar* (Foundations of Modern Linguistics). Englewood Cliffs, NJ: Prentice-Hall.

King, Paul. 1994. *An expanded logical formalism for Head-Driven Phrase Structure Grammar*. Arbeitspapiere des SFB 340 No. 59. Tübingen: Eberhard-Karls-Universität. http://www.sfs.uni-tuebingen.de/sfb/reports/berichte/59/59abs.html, accessed 2018-2-25.

King, Paul. 1999. Towards truth in Head-Driven Phrase Structure Grammar. In Valia Kordoni (ed.), *Tübingen studies in Head-Driven Phrase Structure Grammar* (Arbeitsberichte des SFB 340 No. 132), 301–352. Tübingen: Universität Tübingen. http://www.sfs.uni-tuebingen.de/sfb/reports/berichte/132/132abs.html, accessed 2018-2-25.

King, Tracy Holloway & John T. Maxwell III. 2007. Overlay mechanisms for multi-level deep processing applications. In Tracy Holloway King & Emily M. Bender (eds.), *Grammar Engineering across Frameworks 2007* (Studies in Computational Linguistics ONLINE), 182–202. Stanford, CA: CSLI Publications. http://csli-publications.stanford.edu/GEAF/2007/, accessed 2018-2-25.

Kinyon, Alexandra, Owen Rambow, Tatjana Scheffler, SinWon Yoon & Aravind K. Joshi. 2006. The Metagrammar goes multilingual: A cross-linguistic look at the V2-phenomenon. In Laura Kallmeyer & Tilman Becker (eds.), *TAG+8: The Eighth International Workshop on Tree Adjoining Grammar and Related Formalisms: Proceedings of the workshop*, 17–24. Sydney, Australia: Association for Computational Linguistics.

Kiparsky, Paul. 1987. *Morphology and grammatical relations*. unpublished paper, Stanford University, Stanford.

Kiparsky, Paul. 1988. *Agreement and linking theory*. unpublished paper, Stanford University, Stanford.

Kiparsky, Paul & Carol Kiparsky. 1970. Fact. In Manfred Bierwisch & Karl Erich Heidolph (eds.), *Progress in linguistics*, 143–173. The Hague/Paris: Mouton.

Kiss, Katalin E. 2003. Argument scrambling, focus movement and topic movement in Hungarian. In Simin Karimi (ed.), *Word order and scrambling*, 22–43. London: Blackwell.

Kiss, Tibor. 1991. The grammars of LILOG. In Otthein Herzog & Claus-Rainer Rollinger (eds.), *Text understanding in LILOG* (Lecture Notes in Artificial Intelligence 546), 183–199. Berlin: Springer Verlag.

Kiss, Tibor. 1992. Variable Subkategorisierung: Eine Theorie unpersönlicher Einbettungen im Deutschen. *Linguistische Berichte* 140. 256–293.

Kiss, Tibor. 1993. *Infinite Komplementation – Neue Studien zum deutschen Verbum infinitum*. Arbeiten des SFB 282 No. 42. Bergische Universität Gesamthochschule Wuppertal.

Kiss, Tibor. 1995. *Infinite Komplementation: Neue Studien zum deutschen Verbum infinitum* (Linguistische Arbeiten 333). Tübingen: Max Niemeyer Verlag.

Kiss, Tibor. 2001. Configurational and relational scope determination in German. In Walt Detmar Meurers & Tibor Kiss (eds.), *Constraint-based approaches to Germanic syntax* (Studies in Constraint-Based Lexicalism 7), 141–175. Stanford, CA: CSLI Publications.

Kiss, Tibor. 2005. Semantic constraints on relative clause extraposition. *Natural Language and Linguistic Theory* 23(2). 281–334. DOI:10.1007/s11049-003-1838-7

Kiss, Tibor & Birgit Wesche. 1991. Verb order and head movement. In Otthein Herzog & Claus-Rainer Rollinger (eds.), *Text understanding in LILOG* (Lecture Notes in Artificial Intelligence 546), 216–242. Berlin: Springer Verlag.

Klann-Delius, Gisela. 2008. *Spracherwerb*. 2nd edn. Stuttgart: J.B. Metzler–Verlag.

Klein, Wolfgang. 1971. *Parsing: Studien zur maschinellen Satzanalyse mit Abhängigkeitsgrammatiken und Transformationsgrammatiken*. Vol. 2. Frankfurt a. M.: Athenäum Verlag.

Klein, Wolfgang. 1985. Ellipse, Fokusgliederung und thematischer Stand. In Reinhard Meyer-Hermann & Hannes Rieser (eds.), *Ellipsen und fragmentarische Ausdrücke*, 1–24. Tübingen: Max Niemeyer Verlag.

Klein, Wolfgang. 1986. *Second language acquisition* (Cambridge Textbooks in Linguistics). Cambridge, UK: Cambridge University Press.

Klein, Wolfgang. 2009. Finiteness, Universal Grammar and the language faculty. In Jiansheng Guo, Elena Lieven, Nancy Budwig, Susan Ervin-Tripp, Keiko Nakamura & Seyda Ozcaliskan (eds.), *Cross-linguistic approaches to the study of language: Research in the tradition of Dan Isaac Slobin* (Psychology Press Festschrift Series), 333–344. New York: Psychology Press.

Klenk, Ursula. 2003. *Generative Syntax* (Narr Studienbücher). Tübingen: Gunter Narr Verlag.

Kluender, Robert. 1992. Deriving island constraints from principles of predication. In Helen Goodluck & Michael Rochemont (eds.), *Island constraints: Theory, acquisition, and processing*, 223–258. Dordrecht: Kluwer Academic Publishers.

Kluender, Robert & Marta Kutas. 1993. Subjacency as a processing phenomenon. *Language and Cognitive Processes* 8(4). 573–633.

Knecht, Laura. 1985. *Subject and object in Turkish*. M.I.T. dissertation.

Kobele, Gregory M. 2008. Across-the-board extraction in Minimalist Grammars. In *Proceedings of the Ninth International Workshop on Tree Adjoining Grammar and Related Formalisms (TAG+9)*, 113–128.

Koenig, Jean-Pierre. 1999. *Lexical relations* (Stanford Monographs in Linguistics). Stanford, CA: CSLI Publications.

Koenig, Jean-Pierre & Karin Michelson. 2010. Argument structure of Oneida kinship terms. *International Journal of American Linguistics* 76(2). 169–205.

Koenig, Jean-Pierre & Karin Michelson. 2012. The (non)universality of syntactic selection and functional application. In Christopher Piñón (ed.), *Empirical issues in syntax and semantics*, vol. 9, 185–205. Paris: CNRS.

Kohl, Dieter. 1992. Generation from under- and overspecified structures. In Antonio Zampolli (ed.), *14th International Conference on Computational Linguistics (COLING '92), August 23–28*, 686–692. Nantes, France: Association for Computational Linguistics.

References

Kohl, Dieter, Claire Gardent, Agnes Plainfossé, Mike Reape & Stefan Momma. 1992. Text generation from semantic representation. In Gabriel G. Bes & Thierry Guillotin (eds.), *The construction of a natural language and graphic interface: Results and perspectives from the ACORD project*, 94–161. Berlin: Springer Verlag.

Kohl, Karen T. 1999. *An analysis of finite parameter learning in linguistic spaces*. Massachusetts Institute of Technology MA thesis. http://karentkohl.org/papers/SM.pdf, accessed 2018-2-25.

Kohl, Karen T. 2000. Language learning in large parameter spaces. In *Proceedings of the Seventeenth National Conference on Artificial Intelligence and Twelfth Conference on Innovative Applications of Artificial Intelligence*, 1080. AAAI Press / The MIT Press.

Kolb, Hans-Peter. 1997. *GB blues: Two essays on procedures and structures in Generative Syntax*. Arbeitspapiere des SFB 340 No. 110. Tübingen: Eberhard-Karls-Universität.

Kolb, Hans-Peter & Craig L. Thiersch. 1991. Levels and empty categories in a Principles and Parameters based approach to parsing. In Hubert Haider & Klaus Netter (eds.), *Representation and derivation in the theory of grammar* (Studies in Natural Language and Linguistic Theory 22), 251–301. Dordrecht: Kluwer Academic Publishers.

Koller, Alexander. 2017. A feature structure algebra for FTAG. In *Proceedings of the 13th International Workshop on Tree Adjoining Grammars and Related Formalisms (TAG+13)*. Umea. http://www.coli.uni-saarland.de/~koller/papers/ftag-irtg-17.pdf, accessed 2018-2-28.

Konieczny, Lars. 1996. *Human sentence processing: A semantics-oriented parsing approach*. Universität Freiburg Dissertation. IIG-Berichte 3/96.

König, Esther. 1999. LexGram: A practical Categorial Grammar formalism. *Journal of Language and Computation* 1(1). 33–52.

Koopman, Hilda & Dominique Sportiche. 1991. The position of subjects. *Lingua* 85(2–3). 211–258.

Kordoni, Valia (ed.). 1999. *Tübingen studies in Head-Driven Phrase Structure Grammar* (Arbeitspapiere des SFB 340, No. 132, Volume 1). Tübingen: Eberhard-Karls-Universität Tübingen.

Kordoni, Valia. 2001. Linking experiencer-subject psych verb constructions in Modern Greek. In Daniel P. Flickinger & Andreas Kathol (eds.), *Proceedings of the HPSG-2000 Conference, University of California, Berkeley*, 198–213. CSLI Publications. http://csli-publications.stanford.edu/HPSG/1/, accessed 2018-2-25.

Kordoni, Valia & Julia Neu. 2005. Deep analysis of Modern Greek. In Keh-Yih Su, Oi Yee Kwong, Jn'ichi Tsujii & Jong-Hyeok Lee (eds.), *Natural language processing IJCNLP 2004* (Lecture Notes in Artificial Intelligence 3248), 674–683. Berlin: Springer Verlag.

Kornai, András & Geoffrey K. Pullum. 1990. The X-bar Theory of phrase structure. *Language* 66(1). 24–50.

Koster, Jan. 1975. Dutch as an SOV language. *Linguistic Analysis* 1(2). 111–136. http://www.dbnl.org/tekst/kost007dutc01_01/kost007dutc01_01.pdf, accessed 2018-2-25.

Koster, Jan. 1978. *Locality principles in syntax*. Dordrecht: Foris Publications.

Koster, Jan. 1986. The relation between pro-drop, scrambling, and verb movements. *Groningen Papers in Theoretical and Applied Linguistics* 1. 1–43.

Koster, Jan. 1987. *Domains and dynasties: The radical autonomy of syntax*. Dordrecht: Foris Publications.

Kratzer, Angelika. 1984. On deriving syntactic differences between German and English. TU Berlin, ms.

Kratzer, Angelika. 1996. Severing the external argument from its verb. In Johan Rooryck & Laurie Zaring (eds.), *Phrase structure and the lexicon*, 109–137. Dordrecht: Kluwer Academic Publishers.

Krieger, Hans-Ulrich & John Nerbonne. 1993. Feature-based inheritance networks for computational lexicons. In Ted Briscoe, Ann Copestake & Valeria de Paiva (eds.), *Inheritance, defaults, and the lexicon*, 90–136. Cambridge, UK: Cambridge University Press. A version of this paper is available as DFKI Research Report RR-91-31. Also published in: Proceedings of the ACQUILEX Workshop on Default Inheritance in the Lexicon, Technical Report No. 238, University of Cambridge, Computer Laboratory, October 1991.

Kroch, Anthony S. 1987. Unbounded dependencies and subjacency in a Tree Adjoining Grammar. In Alexis Manaster-Ramer (ed.), *Mathematics of language*, 143–172. Amsterdam: John Benjamins Publishing Co.

Kroch, Anthony S. & Aravind K. Joshi. 1985. *The linguistic relevance of Tree Adjoining Grammar*. Tech. rep. MS-CIS-85-16. University of Pennsylvania. http://repository.upenn.edu/cis_reports/671/, accessed 2018-2-25.

Kroch, Anthony S. & Aravind K. Joshi. 1987. Analyzing extraposition in a Tree Adjoining Grammar. In Geoffrey J. Huck & Almerindo E. Ojeda (eds.), *Discontinuous constituency* (Syntax and Semantics 20), 107–149. New York: Academic Press.

Kropp Dakubu, Mary Esther, Lars Hellan & Dorothee Beermann. 2007. Verb sequencing constraints in Ga: Serial verb constructions and the extended verb complex. In Stefan Müller (ed.), *Proceedings of the 14th International Conference on Head-Driven Phrase Structure Grammar*, 99–119. Stanford, CA: CSLI Publications. http://csli-publications.stanford.edu/HPSG/2007/, accessed 2018-2-25.

Kruijff-Korbayová, Ivana & Mark J. Steedman. 2003. Discourse and information structure. *Journal of Logic, Language and Information: Special Issue on Discourse and Information Structure* 12(3). 249–259.

Kübler, Sandra, Ryan McDonald & Joakim Nivre. 2009. *Dependency Parsing* (Synthesis Lectures on Human Language Technologies 2). San Rafael, U.S.A: Morgan & Claypool Publishers. 1–127.

Kuhn, Jonas. 1995. *Information packaging in German: Some motivation from HPSG-based translation*. ftp://ftp.ims.uni-stuttgart.de/pub/papers/kuhn/Info-Pack.pdf, accessed 2018-3-20. Universität Stuttgert, ms.

Kuhn, Jonas. 1996. An underspecified HPSG representation for information structure. In Jun-ichi Tsuji (ed.), *Proceedings of COLING-96. 16th International Conference on Computational Linguistics (COLING96). Copenhagen, Denmark, August 5–9, 1996*, 670–675. Copenhagen, Denmark: Association for Computational Linguistics.

References

Kuhn, Jonas. 2007. Interfaces in constraint-based theories of grammar. In Gillian Ramchand & Charles Reiss (eds.), *The Oxford handbook of linguistic interfaces*, 613–650. Oxford: Oxford University Press. DOI:10.1093/oxfordhb/9780199247455.013.0020

Kuhn, Jonas & Christian Rohrer. 1997. Approaching ambiguity in real-life sentences: The application of an Optimality Theory-inspired constraint ranking in a large-scale LFG grammar. In *Proceedings of DGfS/CL 97*. Heidelberg.

Kuhns, Robert J. 1986. A PROLOG implementation of Government-Binding Theory. In Alan W. Biermann (ed.), *Proceedings of the Twenty-Fourth Annual Meeting of the Association for Computational Linguistics*, 546–550. Columbia University, New York.

Kunze, Jürgen. 1968. The treatment of non-projective structures in the syntactic analysis and synthesis of English and German. *Computational Linguistics* 7. 67–77.

Kunze, Jürgen. 1975. *Abhängigkeitsgrammatik* (studia grammatica 12). Berlin: Akademie Verlag.

Kunze, Jürgen. 1991. *Kasusrelationen und semantische Emphase* (studia grammatica XXXII). Berlin: Akademie Verlag.

Kunze, Jürgen. 1993. *Sememstrukturen und Feldstrukturen* (studia grammatica 36). Berlin: Akademie Verlag. unter Mitarbeit von Beate Firzlaff.

Labelle, Marie. 2007. Biolinguistics, the Minimalist Program, and psycholinguistic reality. *Snippets* 14. 6–7. http://www.ledonline.it/snippets/allegati/snippets14002.pdf, accessed 2018-2-25.

Laczkó, Tibor, György Rákosi & Ágoston Tóth. 2010. HunGram vs. EngGram in ParGram: On the comparison of Hungarian and English in an international computational linguistics project. In Irén Hegedűs & Sándor Martsa (eds.), *Selected papers in linguistics from the 9th HUSSE Conference*, vol. 1, 81–95. Pécs: Institute of English Studies, Faculty of Humanities, University of Pécs.

Laenzlinger, Christoph. 2004. A feature-based theory of adverb syntax. In Jennifer R. Austin, Stefan Engelberg & Gisa Rauh (eds.), *Adverbials: The interplay between meaning, context, and syntactic structure* (Linguistik Aktuell/Linguistics Today 70), 205–252. Amsterdam: John Benjamins Publishing Co.

Lai, Cecilia S. L., Simon E. Fisher, Jane A. Hurst, Faraneh Vargha-Khadem & Anthony P. Monaco. 2001. A forkhead-domain gene is mutated in a severe speech and language disorder. *Nature* 413(6855). 519–523. DOI:10.1038/35097076

Lakoff, George. 1987. *Women, fire, and dangerous things: What categories reveal about the mind*. Chicago: The University of Chicago Press.

Langacker, Ronald W. 1987. *Foundations of Cognitive Grammar*. Vol. 1. Stanford, CA: Stanford University Press.

Langacker, Ronald W. 2000. A dynamic usage-based model. In Michael Barlow & Suzanne Kemmer (eds.), *Usage-based models of language*, 1–63. Stanford, CA: CSLI Publications.

Langacker, Ronald W. 2008. *Cognitive Grammar: A basic introduction*. Oxford: Oxford University Press.

Langacker, Ronald W. 2009. Cognitive (Construction) Grammar. *Cognitive Linguistics* 20(1). 167–176.

Lappin, Shalom, Robert D. Levine & David E. Johnson. 2000a. The revolution confused: A response to our critics. *Natural Language and Linguistic Theory* 18(4). 873–890.

Lappin, Shalom, Robert D. Levine & David E. Johnson. 2000b. The structure of unscientific revolutions. *Natural Language and Linguistic Theory* 18(3). 665–671.

Lappin, Shalom, Robert D. Levine & David E. Johnson. 2001. The revolution maximally confused. *Natural Language and Linguistic Theory* 19(4). 901–919.

Larson, Richard K. 1988. On the double object construction. *Linguistic Inquiry* 19(3). 335–391.

Lascarides, Alex & Ann Copestake. 1999. Default representation in constraint-based frameworks. *Computational Linguistics* 25(1). 55–105.

Lasnik, Howard & Mamoru Saito. 1992. *Move α: conditions on its application and output* (Current Studies in Linguistics 22). Cambridge, MA: MIT Press.

Lasnik, Howard & Juan Uriagereka. 2002. On the poverty of the challenge. *The Linguistic Review* 19(1–2). 147–150.

Lavoie, Benoit & Owen Rambow. 1997. RealPro–A fast, portable sentence realizer. In *Proceedings of the Conference on Applied Natural Language Processing (ANLP'97)*.

Le, Hong Phuong, Thi Minh Huyen Nguyen & Azim Roussanaly. 2008. Metagrammar for Vietnamese LTAG. In *Proceedings of the Ninth International Workshop on Tree Adjoining Grammars and Related Formalisms (TAG+9)*, 129–132. Tübingen.

Legate, Julie & Charles D. Yang. 2002. Empirical re-assessment of stimulus poverty arguments. *The Linguistic Review* 19(1–2). 151–162. DOI:10.1515/tlir.19.1-2.151

Lehtola, Aarno. 1986. DPL: A computational method for describing grammars and modelling parsers. In Fred Karlsson (ed.), *Papers from the Fifth Scandinavian Conference of Computational Linguistics*, 151–159. Helsinki.

Leiss, Elisabeth. 2003. Empirische Argumente für Dependenz. In Vilmos Ágel, Ludwig M. Eichinger, Hans-Werner Eroms, Peter Hellwig, Hans Jürgen Heringer & Henning Lobin (eds.), *Dependenz und Valenz / Dependency and valency: Ein internationales Handbuch der zeitgenössischen Forschung / An international handbook of contemporary research*, vol. 25.1 (Handbücher zur Sprach- und Kommunikationswissenschaft), 311–324. Berlin: Walter de Gruyter.

Leiss, Elisabeth. 2009. *Sprachphilosophie* (de Gruyter Studienbuch). Berlin: Walter de Gruyter.

Lenerz, Jürgen. 1977. *Zur Abfolge nominaler Satzglieder im Deutschen* (Studien zur deutschen Grammatik 5). Tübingen: originally Gunter Narr Verlag now Stauffenburg Verlag.

Lenerz, Jürgen. 1994. Pronomenprobleme. In Brigitta Haftka (ed.), *Was determiniert Wortstellungsvariation? Studien zu einem Interaktionsfeld von Grammatik, Pragmatik und Sprachtypologie*, 161–174. Opladen: Westdeutscher Verlag.

Lenneberg, Eric H. 1964. The capacity for language acquisition. In Jerry A. Fodor & Jerrold J. Katz (eds.), *The structure of language*, 579–603. Englewood Cliffs, NJ: Prentice-Hall.

Lenneberg, Eric H. 1967. *Biological foundations of language*. New York: John Wiley & Sons, Inc.

References

Levelt, Willem J. M. 1989. *Speaking: from intonation to articulation* (ACL-MIT Press Series in Natural Language Processing). Cambridge, MA: MIT Press.

Levin, Beth. 1993. *English verb classes and alternations: A preliminary investigation.* Chicago, Illinois: University of Chicago Press.

Levin, Beth & Malka Rappaport Hovav. 2005. *Argument realization.* Cambridge University Press.

Levine, Robert D. 2003. Adjunct valents, cumulative scopings and impossible descriptions. In Jongbok Kim & Stephen Mark Wechsler (eds.), *The proceedings of the 9th International Conference on Head-Driven Phrase Structure Grammar*, 209–232. Stanford, CA: CSLI Publications. http://csli-publications.stanford.edu/HPSG/3/, accessed 2018-9-25.

Levine, Robert D. & Thomas E. Hukari. 2006. *The unity of unbounded dependency constructions* (CSLI Lecture Notes 166). Stanford, CA: CSLI Publications.

Levine, Robert D. & Walt Detmar Meurers. 2006. Head-Driven Phrase Structure Grammar: Linguistic approach, formal foundations, and computational realization. In Keith Brown (ed.), *The encyclopedia of language and linguistics*, 2nd edn., 237–252. Oxford: Elsevier Science Publisher B.V. (North-Holland).

Lewis, Geoffrey L. 1967. *Turkish grammar.* Oxford: Clarendon Press.

Lewis, John D. & Jeffrey L. Elman. 2001. Learnability and the statistical structure of language: Poverty of Stimulus arguments revisited. In Barbora Skarabela, Sarah Fish & Anna H.-J. Do (eds.), *Proceedings of the 26th Annual Boston University Conference on Language Development*, 359–370. http://crl.ucsd.edu/~elman/Papers/BU2001.pdf, accessed 2018-2-25.

Li, Charles N. & Sandra A. Thompson. 1981. *Mandarin Chinese: A functional reference grammar.* Berkeley & Los Angeles: University of California Press.

Li, Wei. 1996. *Esperanto inflection and its interface in HPSG.* Working Papers of the Linguistics Circle. University of Victoria. 71–80.

Lichte, Timm. 2007. An MCTAG with tuples for coherent constructions in German. In Laura Kallmeyer, Paola Monachesi, Gerald Penn & Giorgio Satta (eds.), *Proceedings of the 12th Conference on Formal Grammar 2007.* Dublin, Ireland.

Lichte, Timm & Laura Kallmeyer. 2017. Tree-Adjoining Grammar: A tree-based constructionist grammar framework for natural language understanding. In *Proceedings of the AAAI 2017 Spring Symposium on Computational Construction Grammar and Natural Language Understanding* (Technical Report SS-17-02). Association for the Advancement of Artificial Intelligence.

Lieb, Hans-Heinrich. 1983. *Integrational linguistics: Vol. I.: General outline* (Current Issues in Linguistic Theory 17). Amsterdam: John Benjamins Publishing Co.

Lightfoot, David W. 1997. Catastrophic change and learning theory. *Lingua* 100(1). 171–192.

Lin, Dekang. 1993. Principle-based parsing without overgeneration. In *Proceedings of the 31st Annual Meeting of the Association for Computational Linguistics*, 112–120. Columbus, Ohio, USA: Association for Computational Linguistics. DOI:10.3115/981574.981590

Link, Godehard. 1984. Hydras: On the logic of relative constructions with multiple heads. In Fred Landmann & Frank Veltman (eds.), *Varieties of formal semantics*, 245–257. Dordrecht: Foris Publications.

Lipenkova, Janna. 2009. *Serienverbkonstruktionen im Chinesischen und ihre Analyse im Rahmen von HPSG*. Institut für Sinologie, Freie Universität Berlin MA thesis.

Liu, Gang. 1997. *Eine unifikations-basierte Grammatik für das moderne Chinesisch – dargestellt in der HPSG*. FG Sprachwissenschaft, Universität Konstanz dissertation. http://nbn-resolving.de/urn:nbn:de:bsz:352-opus-1917, accessed 2018-2-25.

Liu, Haitao. 2009. *Dependency Grammar: From theory to practice*. Beijing: Science Press.

Liu, Haitao & Wei Huang. 2006. Chinese Dependency Syntax for treebanking. In *Proceedings of the Twentieth Pacific Asia Conference on Language, Information and Computation*, 126–133. Beijing: Tsinghua University Press.

Lloré, F. Xavier. 1995. *Un Método de 'Parsing' para Gramáticas Categoriales Multimodales*. I.C.E. de la Universidad Politécnica de Catalunya dissertation.

Lobin, Henning. 1993. *Koordinationssyntax als strukturales Phänomen* (Studien zur Grammatik 46). Tübingen: Gunter Narr Verlag.

Lobin, Henning. 2003. Dependenzgrammatik und Kategorialgrammatik. In Vilmos Ágel, Ludwig M. Eichinger, Hans-Werner Eroms, Peter Hellwig, Hans Jürgen Heringer & Henning Lobin (eds.), *Dependenz und Valenz / Dependency and valency: Ein internationales Handbuch der zeitgenössischen Forschung / An international handbook of contemporary research*, vol. 25.1 (Handbücher zur Sprach- und Kommunikationswissenschaft), 325–330. Berlin: Walter de Gruyter.

Löbner, Sebastian. 1986. In Sachen Nullartikel. *Linguistische Berichte* 101. 64–65.

Lohndal, Terje. 2012. Toward the end of argument structure. In María Cristina Cuervo & Yves Roberge (eds.), *The end of argument structure?*, vol. 38 (Syntax and Semantics), 155–184. Bingley, UK: Emerald Group Publishing.

Lohnstein, Horst. 1993. *Projektion und Linking: Ein prinzipienbasierter Parser fürs Deutsche* (Linguistische Arbeiten 287). Tübingen: Max Niemeyer Verlag.

Lohnstein, Horst. 2014. Artenvielfalt in freier Wildbahn: Generative Grammatik. In Jörg Hagemann & Sven Staffeldt (eds.), *Syntaxtheorien: Analysen im Vergleich* (Stauffenburg Einführungen 28), 165–185. Tübingen: Stauffenburg Verlag.

Longobardi, Giuseppe & Ian Roberts. 2010. Universals, diversity and change in the science of language: Reaction to "The myth of language universals and cognitive science". *Lingua* 120(12). 2699–2703.

Lorenz, Konrad. 1970. *Studies in human and animal behavior*. Vol. I. Cambridge, MA: Harvard University Press.

Lötscher, Andreas. 1985. Syntaktische Bedingungen der Topikalisierung. *Deutsche Sprache* 13(3). 207–229.

Loukam, Mourad, Amar Balla & Mohamed Tayeb Laskri. 2015. Towards an open platform based on HPSG formalism for the Standard Arabic language. *International Journal of Speech Technology*. DOI:10.1007/s10772-015-9314-4

Lüdeling, Anke. 2001. *On particle verbs and similar constructions in German* (Dissertations in Linguistics). Stanford, CA: CSLI Publications.

References

Luuk, Erkki & Hendrik Luuk. 2011. The redundancy of recursion and infinity for natural language. *Cognitive Processing* 12(1). 1–11.

Maas, Heinz Dieter. 1977. The Saarbrücken Automatic Translation System (SUSY). In Eric James Coates (ed.), *Proceedings of the Third European Congress on Information Systems and Networks: Overcoming the Language Barrier*, vol. 1, 585–592. München: Verlag Dokumentation.

Maché, Jakob. 2010. *Towards a compositional analysis of verbless directives in German*. Paper presented at the HPSG 2010 Conference.

Machicao y Priemer, Antonio. 2015. *SpaGram: An implemented grammar fragment of Spanish*. Ms. Humboldt Universität zu Berlin. In Preparation.

MacWhinney, Brian. 1995. *The CHILDES project: Tools for analyzing talk*. 2nd edn. Hillsdale, NJ: Erlbaum.

Maess, Burkhard, Stefan Koelsch, Thomas C. Gunter & Angela D. Friederici. 2001. Musical syntax is processed in Broca's area: An MEG study. *Nature Neuroscience* 4(5). 540–545.

Marantz, Alec. 1984. *On the nature of grammatical relations* (Linguistic Inquiry Monographs 10). Cambridge, MA: MIT Press.

Marantz, Alec. 1997. No escape from syntax: Don't try morphological analysis in the privacy of your own lexicon. *U. Penn Working Papers in Linguistics* 4(2). 201–225. http://www.ling.upenn.edu/papers/v4.2-contents.html, accessed 2018-2-25.

Marantz, Alec. 2005. Generative linguistics within the cognitive neuroscience of language. *The Linguistic Review* 22(2–4). 429–445.

Marcus, Gary F. 1993. Negative evidence in language acquisition. *Cognition* 46(1). 53–85.

Marcus, Gary F. & Simon E. Fisher. 2003. FOXP2 in focus: What can genes tell us about speech and language? *TRENDS in Cognitive Sciences* 7(6). 257–262.

Marcus, Mitchell P. 1980. *A theory of syntactic recognition for natural language*. London, England/Cambridge, MA: MIT Press.

Marimon, Montserrat. 2013. The Spanish DELPH-IN grammar. *Language Resources and Evaluation* 47(2). 371–397. DOI:10.1007/s10579-012-9199-7

Marshall, Ian & Éva Sáfár. 2004. Sign Language generation in an ALE HPSG. In Stefan Müller (ed.), *Proceedings of the 11th International Conference on Head-Driven Phrase Structure Grammar, Center for Computational Linguistics, Katholieke Universiteit Leuven*, 189–201. Stanford, CA: CSLI Publications. http://csli-publications.stanford.edu/HPSG/2004/, accessed 2018-2-25.

Marslen-Wilson, William D. 1975. Sentence perception as an interactive parallel process. *Science* 189(4198). 226–228. DOI:10.1126/science.189.4198.226

Martorell, Jordi. 2018. Merging generative linguistics and psycholinguistics. *Frontiers in Psychology* 9(2283). 1–5. DOI:10.3389/fpsyg.2018.02283

Masuichi, Hiroshi & Tomoko Ohkuma. 2003. Constructing a practical Japanese parser based on Lexical-Functional Grammar. *Journal of Natural Language Processing* 10. 79–109. in Japanese.

Masum, Mahmudul Hasan, Muhammad Sadiqul Islam, M. Sohel Rahman & Reaz Ahmed. 2012. HPSG analysis of type-based Arabic nominal declension. In *The 13th International Arab Conference*, 272–279.

Mayo, Bruce. 1997. *Die Konstanzer LFG-Umgebung*. Arbeitspapier 82 des Fachbereichs Sprachwissenschaft der Universität Konstanz. Universität Konstanz.

Mayo, Bruce. 1999. *A computational model of derivational morphology*. Universität Hamburg dissertation. http://www.sub.uni-hamburg.de/opus/volltexte/1999/386/, accessed 2018-2-25.

McCawley, James D. 1981. The syntax and semantics of English relative clauses. *Lingua* 53(2). 99–149. http://www.sciencedirect.com/science/article/pii/0024384181900140. DOI:10.1016/0024-3841(81)90014-0

Meinunger, André. 2000. *Syntactic aspects of topic and comment* (Linguistik Aktuell/Linguistics Today 38). Amsterdam: John Benjamins Publishing Co.

Meisel, Jürgen. 1995. Parameters in acquisition. In Paul Fletcher & Brian MacWhinny (eds.), *The handbook of child language*, 10–35. Oxford: Blackwell Publishers Ltd. DOI:10.1111/b.9780631203124.1996.00002.x

Meisel, Jürgen M. 2013. Sensitive phases in successive language acquisition: The critical period hypothesis revisited. In *The Cambridge handbook of Biolinguistics* (Cambridge Handbooks in Language and Linguistics), 69–85. Cambridge, UK: Cambridge University Press. DOI:10.1017/CBO9780511980435

Mel'čuk, Igor A. 1964. *Avtomatičeskij sintaksičeskij analiz*. Vol. 1. Novosibirsk: Izdatel'stvo SO AN SSSR.

Mel'čuk, Igor A. 1981. Meaning-Text Models: A recent trend in Soviet linguistics. *Annual Review of Anthropology* 10. 27–62.

Mel'čuk, Igor A. 1988. *Dependency Syntax: Theory and practice* (SUNY Series in Linguistics). Albany, NY: SUNY Press.

Mel'čuk, Igor A. 2003. Levels of dependency description: Concepts and problems. In Vilmos Ágel, Ludwig M. Eichinger, Hans-Werner Eroms, Peter Hellwig, Hans Jürgen Heringer & Henning Lobin (eds.), *Dependenz und Valenz / Dependency and valency: Ein internationales Handbuch der zeitgenössischen Forschung / An international handbook of contemporary research*, vol. 25.1 (Handbücher zur Sprach- und Kommunikationswissenschaft), 188–230. Berlin: Walter de Gruyter.

Melnik, Nurit. 2007. From "hand-written" to computationally implemented HPSG theories. *Research on Language and Computation* 5(2). 199–236.

Mensching, Guido & Eva-Maria Remberger. 2011. Syntactic variation and change in Romance: A Minimalist approach. In Peter Siemund (ed.), *Linguistic universals and language variation* (Trends in Linguistics. Studies and Monographs 231), 361–403. Berlin: Mouton de Gruyter.

Menzel, Wolfgang. 1998. Constraint satisfaction for robust parsing of spoken language. *Journal of Experimental & Theoretical Artificial Intelligence* 10(1). 77–89.

Menzel, Wolfgang & Ingo Schröder. 1998a. Constraint-based diagnosis for intelligent language tutoring systems. In *Proceedings of the ITF & KNOWS Conference at the 1FIP '98 Congress*. Wien/Budapest.

References

Menzel, Wolfgang & Ingo Schröder. 1998b. Decision procedures for Dependency Parsing using graded constraints. In Alain Polguère & Sylvain Kahane (eds.), *Processing of dependency-based grammars: Proceedings of the workshop at COLING-ACL'98*, 78–87. Association for Computational Linguistics. http://www.aclweb.org/anthology/W98-0509, accessed 2018-2-25.

Meurer, Paul. 2009. A computational grammar for Georgian. In Peter Bosch, David Gabelaia & Jérôme Lang (eds.), *Logic, language, and computation: 7th International Tbilisi Symposium on Logic, Language, and Computation, TbiLLC 2007, Tbilisi, Georgia, October 2007, revised selected papers* (Lecture Notes in Artificial Intelligence 5422), 1–15. Berlin: Springer Verlag.

Meurers, Walt Detmar. 1994. On implementing an HPSG theory. In Erhard W. Hinrichs, Walt Detmar Meurers & Tsuneko Nakazawa (eds.), *Partial-VP and split-NP topicalization in German – An HPSG analysis and its implementation* (Arbeitspapiere des SFB 340 No. 58), 47–155. Tübingen: Eberhard-Karls-Universität. http://www.sfs.uni-tuebingen.de/~dm/papers/on-implementing.html, accessed 2018-2-25.

Meurers, Walt Detmar. 1999a. German partial-VP fronting revisited. In Gert Webelhuth, Jean-Pierre Koenig & Andreas Kathol (eds.), *Lexical and Constructional aspects of linguistic explanation* (Studies in Constraint-Based Lexicalism 1), 129–144. Stanford, CA: CSLI Publications.

Meurers, Walt Detmar. 1999b. *Lexical generalizations in the syntax of German non-finite constructions*. Tübingen: Eberhard-Karls-Universität dissertation.

Meurers, Walt Detmar. 1999c. Raising spirits (and assigning them case). *Groninger Arbeiten zur Germanistischen Linguistik (GAGL)* 43. 173–226. http://www.sfs.uni-tuebingen.de/~dm/papers/gagl99.html, accessed 2018-2-25.

Meurers, Walt Detmar. 2000. *Lexical generalizations in the syntax of German non-finite constructions*. Arbeitspapiere des SFB 340 No. 145. Tübingen: Eberhard-Karls-Universität. http://www.sfs.uni-tuebingen.de/~dm/papers/diss.html, accessed 2018-2-25.

Meurers, Walt Detmar. 2001. On expressing lexical generalizations in HPSG. *Nordic Journal of Linguistics* 24(2). 161–217.

Meurers, Walt Detmar, Kordula De Kuthy & Vanessa Metcalf. 2003. Modularity of grammatical constraints in HPSG-based grammar implementations. In Emily M. Bender, Daniel P. Flickinger, Frederik Fouvry & Melanie Siegel (eds.), *Proceedings of the ESSLLI 2003 Workshop "Ideas and Strategies for Multilingual Grammar Development"*, 83–90. Vienna, Austria. http://www.sfs.uni-tuebingen.de/~dm/papers/meurers-dekuthy-metcalf-03.html, accessed 2008-2-22.

Meurers, Walt Detmar & Stefan Müller. 2009. Corpora and syntax. In Anke Lüdeling & Merja Kytö (eds.), *Corpus linguistics: An international handbook*, vol. 29 (Handbücher zur Sprach- und Kommunikationswissenschaft), chap. 42, 920–933. Berlin: Mouton de Gruyter.

Meurers, Walt Detmar, Gerald Penn & Frank Richter. 2002. A web-based instructional platform for constraint-based grammar formalisms and parsing. In Dragomir Radev & Chris Brew (eds.), *Effective tools and methodologies for teaching NLP and CL*, 18–25.

Association for Computational Linguistics. Proceedings of the Workshop held at 40th Annual Meeting of the Association for Computational Linguistics. Philadelphia, PA.

Micelli, Vanessa. 2012. Field topology and information structure: A case study for German constituent order. In Luc Steels (ed.), *Computational issues in Fluid Construction Grammar* (Lecture Notes in Computer Science 7249), 178–211. Berlin: Springer Verlag.

Michaelis, Laura A. 2006. Construction Grammar. In Keith Brown (ed.), *The encyclopedia of language and linguistics*, 2nd edn., 73–84. Oxford: Elsevier Science Publisher B.V. (North-Holland).

Michaelis, Laura A. & Josef Ruppenhofer. 2001. *Beyond alternations: A Constructional model of the German applicative pattern* (Stanford Monographs in Linguistics). Stanford, CA: CSLI Publications.

Michaelis, Jens. 2001. *On formal properties of Minimalist Grammars*. Universität Potsdam dissertation.

Miller, George A. & Kathryn Ojemann McKean. 1964. A chronometric study of some relations between sentences. *Quarterly Journal of Experimental Psychology* 16(4). 297–308.

Miller, Philip H. & Ivan A. Sag. 1997. French clitic movement without clitics or movement. *Natural Language and Linguistic Theory* 15(3). 573–639.

Mittendorf, Ingo & Louisa Sadler. 2005. Numerals, nouns and number in Welsh NPs. In Miriam Butt & Tracy Holloway King (eds.), *Proceedings of the LFG 2005 conference*, 294–312. Stanford, CA: CSLI Publications. http://csli-publications.stanford.edu/LFG/10/, accessed 2018-2-25.

Miyao, Yusuke, Takashi Ninomiya & Jun'ichi Tsujii. 2005. Corpus-oriented grammar development for acquiring a Head-Driven Phrase Structure Grammar from the Penn Treebank. In Keh-Yih Su, Oi Yee Kwong, Jn'ichi Tsujii & Jong-Hyeok Lee (eds.), *Natural language processing IJCNLP 2004* (Lecture Notes in Artificial Intelligence 3248), 684–693. Berlin: Springer Verlag.

Miyao, Yusuke & Jun'ichi Tsujii. 2008. Feature forest models for probabilistic HPSG parsing. *Computational Linguistics* 34(1). 35–80.

Moeljadi, David, Francis Bond & Sanghoun Song. 2015. Building an HPSG-based Indonesian resource grammar. In Emily M. Bender, Lori Levin, Stefan Müller, Yannick Parmentier & Aarne Ranta (eds.), *Proceedings of the Grammar Engineering Across Frameworks (GEAF) Workshop*, 9–16. The Association for Computational Linguistics.

Moens, Marc, Jo Calder, Ewan Klein, Mike Reape & Henk Zeevat. 1989. Expressing generalizations in unification-based grammar formalisms. In Harold Somers & Mary McGee Wood (eds.), *Proceedings of the Fourth Conference of the European Chapter of the Association for Computational Linguistics*, 174–181. Manchester, England: Association for Computational Linguistics.

Monachesi, Paola. 1998. Italian restructuring verbs: A lexical analysis. In Erhard W. Hinrichs, Andreas Kathol & Tsuneko Nakazawa (eds.), *Complex predicates in nonderivational syntax* (Syntax and Semantics 30), 313–368. San Diego: Academic Press.

Montague, Richard. 1974. *Formal philosophy*. New Haven: Yale University Press.

References

Moortgat, Michael. 1989. *Categorical investigations: Logical and linguistic aspects of the Lambek Calculus* (Groningen Amsterdam Studies in Semantics 9). Dordrecht/Cinnaminson, U.S.A.: Foris Publications.

Moortgat, Michael. 2011. Categorial type logics. In Johan F. A. K. van Benthem & G. B. Alice ter Meulen (eds.), *Handbook of logic and language*, 2nd edn., 95–179. Amsterdam: Elsevier.

Moot, Richard. 2002. *Proof nets for linguistic analysis*. University of Utrecht dissertation.

Morgan, James L. 1989. Learnability considerations and the nature of trigger experiences in language acquisition. *Behavioral and Brain Sciences* 12(2). 352–353.

Morin, Yves Ch. 1973. A computer tested Transformational Grammar of French. *Linguistics* 116(11). 49–114.

Morrill, Glyn. 1995. Discontinuity in Categorial Grammar. *Linguistics and Philosophy* 18(2). 175–219.

Morrill, Glyn. 2012. CatLog: A Categorial parser/theorem-prover. In *Logical aspects of computational linguistics: System demonstrations*, 13–16. Nantes, France: University of Nantes.

Morrill, Glyn. 2017. Parsing Logical Grammar: CatLog3. In Roussanka Loukanova & Kristina Liefke (eds.), *Proceedings of the workshop on logic and algorithms in computational linguistics 2017, LACompLing2017, DiVA*, 107–131. Stockholm: Stockholm University.

Morrill, Glyn V. 1994. *Type Logical Grammars: Categorial logic of signs*. Dordrecht: Kluwer Academic Publishers.

Müller, Gereon. 1996a. A constraint on remnant movement. *Natural Language and Linguistic Theory* 14(2). 355–407.

Müller, Gereon. 1996b. On extraposition and successive cyclicity. In Uli Lutz & Jürgen Pafel (eds.), *On extraction and extraposition in German* (Linguistik Aktuell/Linguistics Today 11), 213–243. Amsterdam: John Benjamins Publishing Co.

Müller, Gereon. 1998. *Incomplete category fronting: A derivational approach to remnant movement in German* (Studies in Natural Language and Linguistic Theory 42). Dordrecht: Kluwer Academic Publishers.

Müller, Gereon. 2000. *Elemente der optimalitätstheoretischen Syntax* (Stauffenburg Linguistik 20). Tübingen: Stauffenburg Verlag.

Müller, Gereon. 2009a. *There are no Constructions*. https://hpsg.hu-berlin.de/Events/Ring2009/gmueller.pdf, accessed 2019-6-30. Handout Ringvorlesung: *Algorithmen und Muster: Strukturen in der Sprache*. Freie Universität Berlin, 20. Mai.

Müller, Gereon. 2011. Regeln oder Konstruktionen? Von verblosen Direktiven zur sequentiellen Nominalreduplikation. In Stefan Engelberg, Anke Holler & Kristel Proost (eds.), *Sprachliches Wissen zwischen Lexikon und Grammatik* (Institut für Deutsche Sprache, Jahrbuch 2010), 211–249. Berlin: de Gruyter.

Müller, Gereon. 2014a. *Syntactic buffers*. Linguistische Arbeitsberichte 91. Institut für Linguistic Universität Leipzig. http://www.uni-leipzig.de/~muellerg/mu765.pdf, accessed 2018-2-25.

Müller, Natascha & Beate Riemer. 1998. *Generative Syntax der romanischen Sprachen: Französisch, Italienisch, Portugiesisch, Spanisch* (Stauffenburg Einführungen 17). Tübingen: Stauffenburg Verlag.

Müller, Stefan. 1995. Scrambling in German – Extraction into the *Mittelfeld*. In Benjamin K. T'sou & Tom Bong Yeung Lai (eds.), *Proceedings of the Tenth Pacific Asia Conference on Language, Information and Computation*, 79–83. City University of Hong Kong.

Müller, Stefan. 1996c. The Babel-System: An HPSG fragment for German, a parser, and a dialogue component. In *Proceedings of the Fourth International Conference on the Practical Application of Prolog*, 263–277. London.

Müller, Stefan. 1996d. Yet another paper about partial verb phrase fronting in German. In Jun-ichi Tsuji (ed.), *Proceedings of COLING-96: 16th International Conference on Computational Linguistics (COLING96). Copenhagen, Denmark, August 5–9, 1996*, 800–805. Copenhagen, Denmark: Association for Computational Linguistics.

Müller, Stefan. 1999a. An HPSG-analysis for free relative clauses in German. *Grammars* 2(1). 53–105.

Müller, Stefan. 1999b. *Deutsche Syntax deklarativ: Head-Driven Phrase Structure Grammar für das Deutsche* (Linguistische Arbeiten 394). Tübingen: Max Niemeyer Verlag.

Müller, Stefan. 1999c. Parsing of an HPSG grammar for German: word order domains and discontinuous constituents. In Jost Gippert & Peter Olivier (eds.), *Multilinguale Corpora: Codierung, Strukturierung, Analyse. 11. Jahrestagung der Gesellschaft für Linguistische Datenverarbeitung*, 292–303. Prag: enigma corporation.

Müller, Stefan. 1999d. Restricting discontinuity. In *Proceedings of the 5th Natural Language Processing Pacific Rim Symposium 1999 (NLPRS'99)*, 85–90. Peking.

Müller, Stefan. 2001. Case in German – towards an HPSG analysis. In Walt Detmar Meurers & Tibor Kiss (eds.), *Constraint-based approaches to Germanic syntax* (Studies in Constraint-Based Lexicalism 7), 217–255. Stanford, CA: CSLI Publications.

Müller, Stefan. 2002a. *Complex predicates: Verbal complexes, resultative constructions, and particle verbs in German* (Studies in Constraint-Based Lexicalism 13). Stanford, CA: CSLI Publications.

Müller, Stefan. 2002b. Multiple frontings in German. In Gerhard Jäger, Paola Monachesi, Gerald Penn & Shuly Wintner (eds.), *Proceedings of Formal Grammar 2002*, 113–124. Trento.

Müller, Stefan. 2002c. Syntax or morphology: German particle verbs revisited. In Nicole Dehé, Ray S. Jackendoff, Andrew McIntyre & Silke Urban (eds.), *Verb-particle explorations* (Interface Explorations 1), 119–139. Berlin: Mouton de Gruyter.

Müller, Stefan. 2003a. Mehrfache Vorfeldbesetzung. *Deutsche Sprache* 31(1). 29–62.

Müller, Stefan. 2003b. Object-to-subject-raising and lexical rule: An analysis of the German passive. In Stefan Müller (ed.), *Proceedings of the 10th International Conference on Head-Driven Phrase Structure Grammar, Michigan State University, East Lansing*, 278–297. Stanford, CA: CSLI Publications.

Müller, Stefan. 2003c. Solving the bracketing paradox: An analysis of the morphology of German particle verbs. *Journal of Linguistics* 39(2). 275–325. DOI:10.1017/S0022226703002032

References

Müller, Stefan. 2004a. An analysis of depictive secondary predicates in German without discontinuous constituents. In Stefan Müller (ed.), *Proceedings of the 11th International Conference on Head-Driven Phrase Structure Grammar, Center for Computational Linguistics, Katholieke Universiteit Leuven*, 202–222. Stanford, CA: CSLI Publications.

Müller, Stefan. 2004b. An HPSG analysis of German depictive secondary predicates. In Lawrence S. Moss & Richard T. Oehrle (eds.), *Proceedings of the joint meeting of the 6th Conference on Formal Grammar and the 7th Conference on Mathematics of Language* (Electronic Notes in Theoretical Computer Science 53), 233–245. Helsinki: Elsevier Science Publisher B.V. (North-Holland). DOI:10.1016/S1571-0661(05)82585-X

Müller, Stefan. 2004c. Complex NPs, subjacency, and extraposition. *Snippets* 8. 10–11.

Müller, Stefan. 2004d. Continuous or discontinuous constituents? A comparison between syntactic analyses for constituent order and their processing systems. *Research on Language and Computation, Special Issue on Linguistic Theory and Grammar Implementation* 2(2). 209–257.

Müller, Stefan. 2005a. Resultative Constructions: Syntax, world knowledge, and collocational restrictions: Review of Hans C. Boas: A Constructional approach to resultatives. *Studies in Language* 29(3). 651–681.

Müller, Stefan. 2005b. Zur Analyse der deutschen Satzstruktur. *Linguistische Berichte* 201. 3–39.

Müller, Stefan. 2005c. Zur Analyse der scheinbar mehrfachen Vorfeldbesetzung. *Linguistische Berichte* 203. 297–330.

Müller, Stefan. 2006. Phrasal or lexical Constructions? *Language* 82(4). 850–883. DOI:10.1353/lan.2006.0213

Müller, Stefan. 2007a. *Head-Driven Phrase Structure Grammar: Eine Einführung.* 1st edn. (Stauffenburg Einführungen 17). Tübingen: Stauffenburg Verlag.

Müller, Stefan. 2007b. Phrasal or lexical Constructions: Some comments on underspecification of constituent order, compositionality, and control. In Stefan Müller (ed.), *Proceedings of the 14th International Conference on Head-Driven Phrase Structure Grammar*, 373–393. Stanford, CA: CSLI Publications.

Müller, Stefan. 2007c. Qualitative Korpusanalyse für die Grammatiktheorie: Introspektion vs. Korpus. In Gisela Zifonun & Werner Kallmeyer (eds.), *Sprachkorpora – Datenmengen und Erkenntnisfortschritt* (Institut für Deutsche Sprache Jahrbuch 2006), 70–90. Berlin: Walter de Gruyter.

Müller, Stefan. 2007d. The Grammix CD Rom: A software collection for developing typed feature structure grammars. In Tracy Holloway King & Emily M. Bender (eds.), *Grammar Engineering across Frameworks 2007* (Studies in Computational Linguistics ONLINE), 259–266. Stanford, CA: CSLI Publications. http://csli-publications.stanford.edu/GEAF/2007/, accessed 2018-2-25.

Müller, Stefan. 2008. Depictive secondary predicates in German and English. In Christoph Schroeder, Gerd Hentschel & Winfried Boeder (eds.), *Secondary predicates in Eastern European languages and beyond* (Studia Slavica Oldenburgensia 16), 255–273. Oldenburg: BIS-Verlag.

Müller, Stefan. 2009b. A Head-Driven Phrase Structure Grammar for Maltese. In Bernard Comrie, Ray Fabri, Beth Hume, Manwel Mifsud, Thomas Stolz & Martine Vanhove (eds.), *Introducing Maltese linguistics: Papers from the 1st International Conference on Maltese Linguistics (Bremen/Germany, 18–20 October, 2007)* (Studies in Language Companion Series 113), 83–112. Amsterdam: John Benjamins Publishing Co.

Müller, Stefan. 2009c. On predication. In Stefan Müller (ed.), *Proceedings of the 16th International Conference on Head-Driven Phrase Structure Grammar, University of Göttingen, Germany*, 213–233. Stanford, CA: CSLI Publications.

Müller, Stefan. 2010a. *Grammatiktheorie* (Stauffenburg Einführungen 20). Tübingen: Stauffenburg Verlag.

Müller, Stefan. 2010b. Persian complex predicates and the limits of inheritance-based analyses. *Journal of Linguistics* 46(3). 601–655. DOI:10.1017/S0022226709990284

Müller, Stefan. 2012a. A personal note on open access in linguistics. *Journal of Language Modelling* 0(1). 9–39. DOI:10.15398/jlm.v0i1.52

Müller, Stefan. 2012b. *On the copula, specificational constructions and type shifting*. Ms. Freie Universität Berlin.

Müller, Stefan. 2013a. *Grammatiktheorie*. 2nd edn. (Stauffenburg Einführungen 20). Tübingen: Stauffenburg Verlag.

Müller, Stefan. 2013b. The CoreGram project: A brief overview and motivation. In Denys Duchier & Yannick Parmentier (eds.), *Proceedings of the workshop on high-level methodologies for grammar engineering (HMGE 2013), Düsseldorf*, 93–104.

Müller, Stefan. 2013c. Unifying everything: Some remarks on Simpler Syntax, Construction Grammar, Minimalism and HPSG. *Language* 89(4). 920–950. DOI:10.1353/lan.2013.0061

Müller, Stefan. 2014b. Artenvielfalt und Head-Driven Phrase Structure Grammar. In Jörg Hagemann & Sven Staffeldt (eds.), *Syntaxtheorien: Analysen im Vergleich* (Stauffenburg Einführungen 28), 187–233. Tübingen: Stauffenburg Verlag.

Müller, Stefan. 2014c. Elliptical constructions, multiple frontings, and surface-based syntax. In Paola Monachesi, Gerhard Jäger, Gerald Penn & Shuly Wintner (eds.), *Proceedings of Formal Grammar 2004, Nancy*, 91–109. Stanford, CA: CSLI Publications.

Müller, Stefan. 2014d. Kernigkeit: Anmerkungen zur Kern-Peripherie-Unterscheidung. In Antonio Machicao y Priemer, Andreas Nolda & Athina Sioupi (eds.), *Zwischen Kern und Peripherie* (studia grammatica 76), 25–39. Berlin: de Gruyter.

Müller, Stefan. 2015a. HPSG – A synopsis. In Tibor Kiss & Artemis Alexiadou (eds.), *Syntax – Theory and analysis: An international handbook* (Handbooks of Linguistics and Communication Science 42.2), 937–973. Berlin: Walter de Gruyter. DOI:10.1515/9783110363708-004

Müller, Stefan. 2015b. The CoreGram project: Theoretical linguistics, theory development and verification. *Journal of Language Modelling* 3(1). 21–86. DOI:10.15398/jlm.v3i1.91

Müller, Stefan. 2016a. *Grammatical Theory: From Transformational Grammar to Constraint-Based Approaches* (Textbooks in Language Sciences 1). Berlin: Language Science Press. DOI:10.17169/langsci.b25.167

References

Müller, Stefan. 2016b. Satztypen: Lexikalisch oder/und phrasal. In Rita Finkbeiner & Jörg Meibauer (eds.), *Satztypen und Konstruktionen im Deutschen* (Linguistik – Impulse & Tendenzen 65), 72–105. Berlin: de Gruyter.

Müller, Stefan. 2017a. *German sentence structure: An analysis with special consideration of so-called multiple fronting* (Empirically Oriented Theoretical Morphology and Syntax). Berlin: Language Science Press. Revise and resubmit.

Müller, Stefan. 2017b. Head-Driven Phrase Structure Grammar, Sign-Based Construction Grammar, and Fluid Construction Grammar: Commonalities and differences. *Constructions and Frames* 9(1). 139–174. DOI:10.1075/cf.9.1.05mul

Müller, Stefan. 2018a. *A lexicalist account of argument structure: Template-based phrasal LFG approaches and a lexical HPSG alternative* (Conceptual Foundations of Language Science 2). Berlin: Language Science Press. DOI:10.5281/zenodo.1441351

Müller, Stefan. 2018b. Complex predicates: Structure, potential structure and underspecification. *Linguistic Issues in Language Technology*. To appear.

Müller, Stefan. 2018c. The end of lexicalism as we know it? *Language* 94(1). e54–e66. DOI:10.1353/lan.2018.0014

Müller, Stefan. 2019a. Evaluating theories: Counting nodes and the question of constituency. *Language Under Discussion* 5(1). 52–67. http://ludjournal.org/index.php?journal=LUD&page=article&op=view&path%5B%5D=65&path%5B%5D=34, accessed 2019-5-2.

Müller, Stefan. 2019b. *Germanic syntax*. Ms. Humboldt Universität zu Berlin, to be submitted to Language Science Press. Berlin. https://hpsg.hu-berlin.de/~stefan/Pub/germanic.html, accessed 2019-6-30.

Müller, Stefan. 2019c. HPSG and Construction Grammar. In Stefan Müller, Anne Abeillé, Robert D. Borsley & Jean-Pierre Koenig (eds.), *Head-Driven Phrase Structure Grammar: The handbook* (Empirically Oriented Theoretical Morphology and Syntax). Berlin: Language Science Press. To appear.

Müller, Stefan & Masood Ghayoomi. 2010. PerGram: A TRALE implementation of an HPSG fragment of Persian. In *Proceedings of 2010 IEEE International Multiconference on Computer Science and Information Technology – Computational Linguistics Applications (CLA'10). Wisła, Poland, 18–20 October 2010*, vol. 5, 461–467. Polnish Information Processing Society.

Müller, Stefan & Martin Haspelmath. 2013. *Language Science Press: A publication model for open-access books in linguistics*. Grant Proposal to the DFG.

Müller, Stefan & Walter Kasper. 2000. HPSG analysis of German. In Wolfgang Wahlster (ed.), *Verbmobil: foundations of speech-to-speech translation* (Artificial Intelligence), 238–253. Berlin: Springer Verlag.

Müller, Stefan & Janna Lipenkova. 2009. Serial verb constructions in Chinese: An HPSG account. In Stefan Müller (ed.), *Proceedings of the 16th International Conference on Head-Driven Phrase Structure Grammar, University of Göttingen, Germany*, 234–254. Stanford, CA: CSLI Publications.

Müller, Stefan & Janna Lipenkova. 2013. ChinGram: A TRALE implementation of an HPSG fragment of Mandarin Chinese. In Huei-ling Lai & Kawai Chui (eds.),

Proceedings of the 27th Pacific Asia Conference on Language, Information, and Computation (PACLIC 27), 240–249. Taipei, Taiwan: Department of English, National Chengchi University.

Müller, Stefan & Janna Lipenkova. 2016. *Mandarin Chinese in Head-Driven Phrase Structure Grammar* (Empirically Oriented Theoretical Morphology and Syntax). Berlin: Language Science Press. In Preparation.

Müller, Stefan & Antonio Machicao y Priemer. 2019. Head-Driven Phrase Structure Grammar. In András Kertész, Edith Moravcsik & Csilla Rákosi (eds.), *Current approaches to syntax: A comparative handbook* (Comparative Handbooks of Linguistics 3). Berlin: Mouton de Gruyter. DOI:10.1515/9783110540253-012

Müller, Stefan & Bjarne Ørsnes. 2011. Positional expletives in Danish, German, and Yiddish. In Stefan Müller (ed.), *Proceedings of the 18th International Conference on Head-Driven Phrase Structure Grammar, University of Washington, U.S.A.* 167–187. Stanford, CA: CSLI Publications.

Müller, Stefan & Bjarne Ørsnes. 2013a. Passive in Danish, English, and German. In Stefan Müller (ed.), *Proceedings of the 20th International Conference on Head-Driven Phrase Structure Grammar, Freie Universität Berlin*, 140–160. Stanford, CA: CSLI Publications.

Müller, Stefan & Bjarne Ørsnes. 2013b. Towards an HPSG analysis of object shift in Danish. In Glyn Morrill & Mark-Jan Nederhof (eds.), *Formal Grammar: 17th and 18th International Conferences, FG 2012, Opole, Poland, August 2012, revised selected papers, FG 2013, Düsseldorf, Germany, August 2013: Proceedings* (Lecture Notes in Computer Science 8036), 69–89. Berlin: Springer Verlag.

Müller, Stefan & Bjarne Ørsnes. 2015. *Danish in Head-Driven Phrase Structure Grammar* (Empirically Oriented Theoretical Morphology and Syntax). Berlin: Language Science Press. In Preparation.

Müller, Stefan & Stephen Mark Wechsler. 2014a. Lexical approaches to argument structure. *Theoretical Linguistics* 40(1–2). 1–76. DOI:10.1515/tl-2014-0001

Müller, Stefan & Stephen Mark Wechsler. 2014b. Two sides of the same slim Boojum: Further arguments for a lexical approach to argument structure. *Theoretical Linguistics* 40(1–2). 187–224. DOI:10.1515/tl-2014-0009

Muraki, Kazunori, Shunji Ichiyama & Yasutomo Fukumochi. 1985. Augmented Dependency Grammar: A simple interface between the grammar rule and the knowledge. In Maghi King (ed.), *Proceedings of the 2nd European Meeting of the Association for Computational Linguistics*, 198–204. Geneva: Association for Computational Linguistics. http://aclweb.org/anthology/E85-1029.pdf, accessed 2018-2-25.

Musso, Mariacristina, Andrea Moro, Volkmar Glauche, Michel Rijntjes, Jürgen Reichenbach, Christian Büchel & Cornelius Weiller. 2003. Broca's area and the language instinct. *Nature Neuroscience* 6(7). 774–781. DOI:10.1038/nn1077

Müürisep, Kaili. 1999. Determination of syntactic functions in Estonian Constraint Grammar. In Henry S. Thompson & Alex Lascarides (eds.), *Ninth conference of the European Chapter of the Association for Computational Linguistics*, 291–292. Bergen, Norway.

References

Müürisep, Kaili, Tiina Puolakainen, Kadri Muischnek, Mare Koit, Tiit Roosmaa & Heli Uibo. 2003. A new language for Constraint Grammar: Estonian. In *International Conference Recent Advances in Natural Language Processing*, 304–310.

Muysken, Pieter. 1982. Parametrizing the notion of "head". *Journal of Linguistic Research* 2. 57–75.

Mykowiecka, Agnieszka, Małgorzata Marciniak, Adam Przepiórkowski & Anna Kupść. 2003. An implementation of a Generative Grammar of Polish. In Peter Kosta, Joanna Błaszczak, Jens Frasek, Ljudmila Geist & Marzena Żygis (eds.), *Investigations into formal slavic linguistics: Contributions of the Fourth European Conference on Formal Description of Slavic Languages – FDSL IV held at Potsdam University, November 28–30, 2001*, 271–285. Frankfurt am Main: Peter Lang.

Naumann, Sven. 1987. Ein einfacher Parser für generalisierte Phrasenstrukturgrammatiken. *Zeitschrift für Sprachwissenschaft* 6(2). 206–226.

Naumann, Sven. 1988. *Generalisierte Phrasenstrukturgrammatik: Parsingstrategien, Regelorganisation und Unifikation* (Linguistische Arbeiten 212). Tübingen: Max Niemeyer Verlag.

Neeleman, Ad. 1994. *Complex predicates*. Utrecht: Onderzoeksinstituut voor Taal en Spraak (OTS) dissertation.

Nelimarkka, Esa, Harri Jäppinen & Aarno Lehtola. 1984. Two-way finite automata and Dependency Grammar: A parsing method for inflectional free word order languages. In Yorick Wilks (ed.), *Proceedings of the 10th International Conference on Computational Linguistics and 22nd Annual Meeting of the Association for Computational Linguistics*, 389–392. Stanford University, California: Association for Computational Linguistics.

Nerbonne, John. 1986a. A phrase-structure grammar for German passives. *Linguistics* 24(5). 907–938.

Nerbonne, John. 1986b. 'Phantoms' and German fronting: Poltergeist constituents? *Linguistics* 24(5). 857–870. DOI:10.1515/ling.1986.24.5.857

Nerbonne, John. 1993. A feature-based syntax/semantics interface. *Annals of Mathematics and Artificial Intelligence* 8(1–2). 107–132. Special issue on Mathematics of Language edited by Alexis Manaster-Ramer and Wlodek Zadrozsny, selected from the 2nd Conference on Mathematics of Language. Also published as DFKI Research Report RR-92-42.

Nerbonne, John, Klaus Netter & Carl J. Pollard (eds.). 1994. *German in Head-Driven Phrase Structure Grammar* (CSLI Lecture Notes 46). Stanford, CA: CSLI Publications.

Netter, Klaus. 1991. *Clause union phenomena and complex predicates in German*. DYANA Report, Deliverable R1.1.B. University of Edinburgh.

Netter, Klaus. 1992. On non-head non-movement: An HPSG treatment of finite verb position in German. In Günther Görz (ed.), *Konvens 92. 1. Konferenz „Verarbeitung natürlicher Sprache". Nürnberg 7.–9. Oktober 1992* (Informatik aktuell), 218–227. Berlin: Springer Verlag.

Netter, Klaus. 1993. Architecture and coverage of the DISCO Grammar. In Stephan Busemann & Karin Harbusch (eds.), *DFKI Workshop on Natural Language Systems: Re-*

Usability and Modularity, October 23 (DFKI Document D-93-03), 1–10. Saarbrücken, Germany: DFKI.

Netter, Klaus. 1994. Towards a theory of functional heads: German nominal phrases. In John Nerbonne, Klaus Netter & Carl J. Pollard (eds.), *German in Head-Driven Phrase Structure Grammar* (CSLI Lecture Notes 46), 297–340. Stanford, CA: CSLI Publications.

Netter, Klaus. 1996. *Functional categories in an HPSG for German.* Saarbrücken: Universität des Saarlandes Dissertation.

Netter, Klaus. 1998. *Functional categories in an HPSG for German* (Saarbrücken Dissertations in Computational Linguistics and Language Technology 3). Saarbrücken: Deutsches Forschungszentrum für Künstliche Intelligenz and Universität des Saarlandes.

Neville, Anne & Patrizia Paggio. 2004. Developing a Danish grammar in the GRASP project: A construction-based approach to topology and extraction in Danish. In Lawrence S. Moss & Richard T. Oehrle (eds.), *Proceedings of the joint meeting of the 6th Conference on Formal Grammar and the 7th Conference on Mathematics of Language* (Electronic Notes in Theoretical Computer Science 53), 246–259. Helsinki: Elsevier Science Publisher B.V. (North-Holland).

Nevins, Andrew Ira, David Pesetsky & Cilene Rodrigues. 2009. Pirahã exceptionality: A reassessment. *Language* 85(2). 355–404. DOI:10.1353/lan.0.0107

Newmeyer, Frederick J. 2004a. Against a parameter-setting approach to language variation. *Linguistic Variation Yearbook* 4. 181–234.

Newmeyer, Frederick J. 2004b. Typological evidence and Universal Grammar. *Studies in Language* 28(3). 527–548.

Newmeyer, Frederick J. 2005. *Possible and probable languages: A Generative perspective on linguistic typology.* Oxford: Oxford University Press.

Newmeyer, Frederick J. 2010. On comparative concepts and descriptive categories: A reply to Haspelmath. *Language* 86(3). 688–695.

Newport, Elissa L. 1990. Maturational constraints on language learning. *Cognitive Science* 14(1). 11–28.

Ng, Say Kiat. 1997. *A double-specifier account of Chinese NPs using Head-Driven Phrase Structure Grammar.* University of Edinburgh, Department of Linguistics MSc Speech and Language Processing.

Nivre, Joakim. 2003. An efficient algorithm for projective dependency parsing. In Gertjan van Noord (ed.), *Proceedings of the 8th International Workshop on Parsing Technologies (IWPT 03)*. Nancy.

Nolda, Andreas. 2007. *Die Thema-Integration: Syntax und Semantik der gespaltenen Topikalisierung im Deutschen* (Studien zur deutschen Grammatik 72). Tübingen: Stauffenburg Verlag.

Noonan, Michael. 1994. A tale of two passives in Irish. In Barbara Fox & Paul J. Hopper (eds.), *Voice: form and function* (Typological Studies in Language 27), 279–311. Amsterdam: John Benjamins Publishing Co.

References

Nordgård, Torbjørn. 1994. E-Parser: An implementation of a deterministic GB-related parsing system. *Computers and the Humanities* 28(4–5). 259–272.

Nordlinger, Rachel. 1998. *Constructive case: Evidence from Australia* (Dissertations in Linguistics). Stanford, CA: CSLI Publications.

Nowak, Martin A., Natalia L. Komarova & Partha Niyogi. 2001. Evolution of Universal Grammar. *Science* 291(5501). 114–118.

Nozohoor-Farshi, R. 1986. On formalizations of Marcus' parser. In Makoto Nagao (ed.), *Proceedings of COLING 86*, 533–535. University of Bonn: Association for Computational Linguistics.

Nozohoor-Farshi, R. 1987. Context-freeness of the language accepted by Marcus' parser. In Candy Sidner (ed.), *25th Annual Meeting of the Association for Computational Linguistics*, 117–122. Stanford, CA: Association for Computational Linguistics.

Nunberg, Geoffrey. 1995. Transfers of meaning. *Journal of Semantics* 12(2). 109–132.

Nunberg, Geoffrey, Ivan A. Sag & Thomas Wasow. 1994. Idioms. *Language* 70(3). 491–538.

Nunes, Jairo. 2004. *Linearization of chains and Sideward Movement* (Linguistic Inquiry Monographs 43). Cambridge, MA: MIT Press.

Nykiel, Joanna & Jong-Bok Kim. 2019. Ellipsis. In Stefan Müller, Anne Abeillé, Robert D. Borsley & Jean-Pierre Koenig (eds.), *Head-Driven Phrase Structure Grammar: The handbook* (Empirically Oriented Theoretical Morphology and Syntax). Berlin: Language Science Press. To appear.

Ochs, Elinor. 1982. Talking to children in Western Samoa. *Language and Society* 11(1). 77–104.

Ochs, Elinor & Bambi B. Schieffelin. 1985. Language acquisition and socialization: Three developmental stories. In Richard A. Shweder & Robert A. LeVine (eds.), *Culture theory: Essays in mind, self and emotion*, 276–320. Cambridge, UK: Cambridge University Press.

O'Donovan, Ruth, Michael Burke, Aoife Cahill, Josef van Genabith & Andy Way. 2005. Large-scale induction and evaluation of lexical resources from the Penn-II and Penn-III Treebanks. *Computational Linguistics* 31(3). 328–365.

Oepen, Stephan & Daniel P. Flickinger. 1998. Towards systematic grammar profiling: Test suite technology ten years after. *Journal of Computer Speech and Language* 12(4). 411–436. http://www.delph-in.net/itsdb/publications/profiling.ps.gz, accessed 2018-2-25. (Special Issue on Evaluation).

Oliva, Karel. 1992. *Word order constraints in binary branching syntactic structures*. CLAUS-Report 20. Saarbrücken: Universität des Saarlandes.

Oliva, Karel. 2003. Dependency, valency and Head-Driven Phrase-Structure Grammar. In Vilmos Ágel, Ludwig M. Eichinger, Hans-Werner Eroms, Peter Hellwig, Hans Jürgen Heringer & Henning Lobin (eds.), *Dependenz und Valenz / Dependency and valency: Ein internationales Handbuch der zeitgenössischen Forschung / An international handbook of contemporary research*, vol. 25.1 (Handbücher zur Sprach- und Kommunikationswissenschaft), 660–668. Berlin: Walter de Gruyter.

O'Neill, Michael & Randall Wood. 2012. *The grammar of happiness*. Essential Media & Entertainment / Smithsonian Networks. https://www.youtube.com/watch?v=fcOuBggle4Y#t=1519, accessed 2018-2-25.

Oppenrieder, Wilhelm. 1991. *Von Subjekten, Sätzen und Subjektsätzen* (Linguisitische Arbeiten 241). Tübingen: Max Niemeyer Verlag.

Orgun, Cemil Orhan. 1996. *Sign-based morphology and phonology*. University of California, Berkeley dissertation.

Ørsnes, Bjarne. 1995. *The derivation and compounding of complex event nominals in Modern Danish: An HPSG approach with an implementation in Prolog*. University of Copenhagen dissertation.

Ørsnes, Bjarne. 2002. Case marking and subject extraction in Danish. In Miriam Butt & Tracy Holloway King (eds.), *Proceedings of the LFG 2002 conference*, 333–353. Stanford, CA: CSLI Publications. http://csli-publications.stanford.edu/LFG/7/, accessed 2018-2-25.

Ørsnes, Bjarne. 2009a. Das Verbalfeldmodell: Ein Stellungsfeldermodell für den kontrastiven DaF-Unterricht. *Deutsch als Fremdsprache* 46(3). 143–149.

Ørsnes, Bjarne. 2009b. Preposed negation in Danish. In Stefan Müller (ed.), *Proceedings of the 16th International Conference on Head-Driven Phrase Structure Grammar, University of Göttingen, Germany*, 255–275. Stanford, CA: CSLI Publications. http://csli-publications.stanford.edu/HPSG/2009/, accessed 2018-2-25.

Ørsnes, Bjarne & Jürgen Wedekind. 2003. Paralelle datamatiske grammatikker for Norsk og Dansk [parallel computational grammars for Norwegian and Danish]. In Henrik Holmboe (ed.), *Årbog for nordisk sprogteknologisk forskningsprogram 2000–2004*, 113–130. Kopenhagen: Museum Tusculanums Forlag.

Ørsnes, Bjarne & Jürgen Wedekind. 2004. Paralelle datamatiske grammatikker for Norsk og Dansk: Analyse og disambiguering af modalverber [parallel computational grammars for Norwegian and Danish: Analysis and disambiguation of modal verbs]. In Henrik Holmboe (ed.), *Årbog for Nordisk Sprogteknologisk forskningsprogram 2000–2004*, 165–182. Kopenhagen: Museum Tusculanums Forlag.

Osborne, Miles & Ted J. Briscoe. 1997. Learning Stochastic Categorial Grammars. In T. Mark Ellison (ed.), *CoNLL97: Computational Natural Language Learning: Proceedings of the 1997 meeting of the ACL Special Interest Group in Natural Language Learning*, 80–87. Madrid: Association for Computational Linguistics. http://www.aclweb.org/anthology/W97-1010, accessed 2018-2-25.

Osborne, Timothy. 2014. Dependency Grammar. In Andrew Carnie, Yosuke Sato & Dan Siddiqi (eds.), *The Routledge handbook of syntax*, 604–626. Oxford: Routledge.

Osborne, Timothy. 2018a. Ellipsis in Dependency Grammar. In Jeroen van Craenenbrok (ed.), *Oxford handbook of ellipsis*. Oxford: Oxford University Press. To appear.

Osborne, Timothy. 2018b. Tests for constituents: What they really reveal about the nature of syntactic structure. *Language Under Discussion* 5(1). 1–41. http://www.ludjournal.org/index.php?journal=LUD&page=article&op=view&path%5B%5D=59.

Osborne, Timothy. 2019. In defense of the simplicity and accuracy of Dependency Syntax: A reply to the discussion notes. *Language Under Discussion*. To appear.

References

Osborne, Timothy & Thomas M. Groß. 2012. Constructions are catenae: Construction Grammar meets Dependency Grammar. *Cognitive Linguistics* 23(1). 165–216.

Osborne, Timothy & Thomas Michael Groß. 2016. The *Do-So*-Diagnostic: Against finite VPs and for flat non-finite VPs. *Folia Linguistica* 50(1). 97–135. DOI:10.1515/flin-2016-0004

Osborne, Timothy, Michael Putnam & Thomas M. Groß. 2011. Bare Phrase Structure, label-less trees, and specifier-less syntax: Is Minimalism becoming a Dependency Grammar? *The Linguistic Review* 28(3). 315–364.

Osenova, Petya. 2010a. *Bulgarian Resource Grammar – efficient and realistic (BURGER)*. Tech. rep. LingoLab, CSLI Stanford. http://www.bultreebank.org/BURGER/BURGER3.pdf, accessed 2018-2-25.

Osenova, Petya. 2010b. *Bulgarian Resource Grammar: modeling Bulgarian in HPSG*. Saarbrücken: VDM Verlag Dr. Müller.

Osenova, Petya. 2011. Localizing a core HPSG-based grammar for Bulgarian. In Hanna Hedeland, Thomas Schmidt & Kai Wörner (eds.), *Multilingual resources and multilingual applications: Proceedings of the Conference of the German Society for Computational Linguistics and Language Technology (GSCL) 2011* (Arbeiten zur Mehrsprachigkeit/Working Papers in Multilingualism, Folge B/Series B 96), 175–182. Hamburg: Universitat Hamburg.

Ott, Dennis. 2011. A note on free relative clauses in the theory of Phases. *Linguistic Inquiry* 42(1). 183–192.

Özkaragöz, İnci. 1986. Monoclausal double passives in Turkish. In Dan I. Slobin & Karl Zimmer (eds.), *Studies in Turkish linguistics* (Typological Studies in Language 8), 77–91. Amsterdam: John Benjamins Publishing Co.

Packard, Woodley. 2015. *Full forest treebanking*. University of Washington MA thesis.

Pafel, Jürgen. 1993. Ein Überblick über die Extraktion aus Nominalphrasen im Deutschen. In Franz-Josef d'Avis, Sigrid Beck, Uli Lutz, Jürgen Pafel & Susanne Trissler (eds.), *Extraktion im Deutschen I* (Arbeitspapiere des SFB 340 No. 34), 191–245. Tübingen: Eberhard-Karls-Universität Tübingen.

Pafel, Jürgen. 2011. *Einführung in die Syntax: Grundlagen – Strukturen – Theorien*. Stuttgart, Weimar: Verlag J. B. Metzler.

Paggio, Patrizia. 2005. Representing information structure in a formal grammar of Danish. In Takashi Washio, Akito Sakurai, Katsuto Nakajima, Hideaki Takeda, Satoshi Tojo & Makoto Yokoo (eds.), *New frontiers in artificial intelligence: Joint JSAI 2005 Workshop post-proceedings* (Lecture Notes in Computer Science 4012), 93–102. Berlin: Springer Verlag. DOI:10.1007/11780496

Parmentier, Yannick, Laura Kallmeyer, Wolfgang Maier, Timm Lichte & Johannes Dellert. 2008. TuLiPA: A syntax-semantics parsing environment for mildly context-sensitive formalisms. In *Proceedings of the Ninth International Workshop on Tree Adjoining Grammars and Related Formalisms (TAG+9)*, 121–128. Tübingen. http://www.sfs.uni-tuebingen.de/~lk/papers/tag+9-parmentier-et-al.pdf, accessed 2018-2-25.

Partee, Barbara H. 1987. Noun phrase interpretation and type-shifting principles. In Jeroen A. G. Groenendijk, Dick de Jongh & Martin J. B. Stokhof (eds.), *Studies in*

Discourse Representation Theory and the theory of generalized quantifiers (Groningen-Amsterdam Studies in Semantics 8), 115–143. Dordrecht: Foris Publications.

Patejuk, Agnieszka & Adam Przepiórkowski. 2012. Towards an LFG parser for Polish: An exercise in parasitic grammar development. In *Proceedings of the Eighth International Conference on Language Resources and Evaluation, LREC 2012*, 3849–3852. Istanbul, Turkey.

Paul, Hermann. 1919. *Deutsche Grammatik. Teil IV: Syntax*. Vol. 3. Halle an der Saale: Max Niemeyer Verlag. 2nd unchanged edition 1968, Tübingen: Max Niemeyer Verlag.

Paul, Soma. 2004. *An HPSG account of Bangla compound verbs with LKB implementation*. Hyderabad, India: CALTS, University of Hyderabad, India dissertation.

Penn, Gerald. 2019. Balancing clarity and efficiency in typed feature logic through delaying. In, 239–246.

Penn, Gerald & Bob Carpenter. 1999. ALE for speech: A translation prototype. In Géza Gordos (ed.), *Proceedings of the 6th Conference on Speech Communication and Technology (EUROSPEECH)*. Budapest, Hungary.

Perlmutter, David M. 1978. Impersonal passives and the Unaccusative Hypothesis. In *Proceedings of the 4th Annual Meeting of the Berkeley Linguistics Society*, 157–189. Berkeley Linguistic Society. https://escholarship.org/uc/item/73h0s91v, accessed 2018-4-26.

Perlmutter, David M. (ed.). 1983. *Studies in relational grammar*. Vol. 1. Chicago: The University of Chicago Press.

Perlmutter, David M. (ed.). 1984. *Studies in relational grammar*. Vol. 2. Chicago: The University of Chicago Press.

Perlmutter, David M. & John Robert Ross. 1970. Relative clauses with split antecedents. *Linguistic Inquiry* 1(3). 350.

Pesetsky, David. 1996. *Zero syntax: Experiencers and cascades*. Cambridge, MA: MIT Press.

Peters, Stanley & R. W. Ritchie. 1973. On the generative power of Transformational Grammar. *Information Sciences* 6(C). 49–83. DOI:10.1016/0020-0255(73)90027-3

Petrick, Stanley Roy. 1965. *A recognition procedure for Transformational Grammars*. Massachusetts Institute of Technology. Dept. of Modern Languages dissertation. http://hdl.handle.net/1721.1/13013, accessed 2018-2-25.

Phillips, Colin. 2003. Linear order and constituency. *Linguistic Inquiry* 34(1). 37–90. DOI:10.1162/002438903763255922

Phillips, John D. 1992. A computational representation for Generalised Phrase Structure Grammars. *Linguistics and Philosophy* 15(3). 255–287.

Phillips, John D. & Henry S. Thompson. 1985. GPSGP – A parser for Generalized Phrase Structure Grammar. *Linguistics* 23(2). 245–261.

Piattelli-Palmarini, Massimo (ed.). 1980. *Language and learning: The debate between Jean Piaget and Noam Chomsky*. Cambridge: Harvard University Press.

Pickering, Martin & Guy Barry. 1993. Dependency Categorial Grammar and coordination. *Linguistics* 31(5). 855–902.

References

Pienemann, Manfred. 2005. An introduction to Processability Theory. In Manfred Pienemann (ed.), *Cross-linguistic aspects of processablity theory*, 1–60. Amsterdam: John Benjamins Publishing Co.

Piñango, Maria Mercedes, Jennifer Mack & Ray S. Jackendoff. 2006. Semantic combinatorial processes in argument structure: evidence from light-verbs. In *Proceedings of the 32nd Annual Meeting of the Berkeley Linguistics Society: Theoretical approaches to argument structure*, vol. 32. Berkeley, CA: BLS.

Pineda, Luis Alberto & Iván V. Meza. 2005a. A computational model of the Spanish clitic system. In Alexander Gelbkuh (ed.), *Computational linguistics and intelligent language processing*, 73–82. Berlin: Springer Verlag.

Pineda, Luis Alberto & Iván V. Meza. 2005b. The Spanish pronominal clitic system. *Procesamiento del Lenguaje Natural* 34. 67–103.

Pinker, Steven. 1984. *Learnability and cognition: The acquisition of argument structure.* London/Cambridge, MA: MIT Press.

Pinker, Steven. 1994. *The language instinct: How the mind creates language.* New York: William Morrow.

Pinker, Steven & Ray S. Jackendoff. 2005. The faculty of language: What's special about it? *Cognition* 95(2). 201–236.

Pittner, Karin. 1995. Regeln für die Bildung von freien Relativsätzen: Eine Antwort an Oddleif Leirbukt. *Deutsch als Fremdsprache* 32(4). 195–200.

Plank, Frans & Elena Filimonova. 2000. The universals archive: A brief introduction for prospective users. *Sprachtypologie und Universalienforschung* 53(1). 109–123.

Plath, Warren J. 1973. Transformational Grammar and transformational parsing in the Request System. In A. Zampolli & N. Calzolari (eds.), *COLING 1973: computational and mathematical linguistics: proceedings of the international conference on computational linguistics*, vol. 2. https://www.aclweb.org/anthology/C73-2028.

Poletto, Cecilia. 2000. *The higher functional field: Evidence from Northern Italian Dialects.* Oxford: Oxford University Press.

Pollard, Carl J. 1984. *Generalized Phrase Structure Grammars, Head Grammars, and natural language.* Stanford University dissertation.

Pollard, Carl J. 1988. Categorial Grammar and Phrase Structure Grammar: An excursion on the syntax-semantics frontier. In Richard Oehrle, Emmon Bach & Deirdre Wheeler (eds.), *Categorial Grammars and natural language structures*, 391–415. Dordrecht: D. Reidel Publishing Company.

Pollard, Carl J. 1994. Toward a unified account of passive in German. In John Nerbonne, Klaus Netter & Carl J. Pollard (eds.), *German in Head-Driven Phrase Structure Grammar* (CSLI Lecture Notes 46), 273–296. Stanford, CA: CSLI Publications.

Pollard, Carl J. 1996a. On head non-movement. In Harry Bunt & Arthur van Horck (eds.), *Discontinuous constituency* (Natural Language Processing 6), 279–305. Berlin: Mouton de Gruyter. Published version of a Ms. dated January 1990.

Pollard, Carl J. 1996b. *The nature of constraint-based grammar.* http://lingo.stanford.edu/sag/L221a/pollard-96.txt, accessed 2018-2-25. Paper presented at the Pacific

Asia Conference on Language, Information, and Computation, Kyung Hee University, Seoul, Korea.

Pollard, Carl J. 1999. Strong generative capacity in HPSG. In Gert Webelhuth, Jean-Pierre Koenig & Andreas Kathol (eds.), *Lexical and Constructional aspects of linguistic explanation* (Studies in Constraint-Based Lexicalism 1), 281–298. Stanford, CA: CSLI Publications.

Pollard, Carl J. & Andrew M. Moshier. 1990. Unifying partial descriptions of sets. In Philip P. Hanson (ed.), *Information, language and cognition* (Vancouver Studies in Cognitive Science 1), 285–322. Vancouver: University of British Columbia Press.

Pollard, Carl J. & Ivan A. Sag. 1987. *Information-based syntax and semantics* (CSLI Lecture Notes 13). Stanford, CA: CSLI Publications.

Pollard, Carl J. & Ivan A. Sag. 1992. Anaphors in English and the scope of Binding Theory. *Linguistic Inquiry* 23(2). 261–303.

Pollard, Carl J. & Ivan A. Sag. 1994. *Head-Driven Phrase Structure Grammar* (Studies in Contemporary Linguistics). Chicago: The University of Chicago Press.

Pollock, Jean-Yves. 1989. Verb movement, Universal Grammar and the structure of IP. *Linguistic Inquiry* 20(3). 365–424.

Popowich, Fred & Carl Vogel. 1991. A logic based implementation of Head-Driven Phrase Structure Grammar. In Charles Grant Brown & Gregers Koch (eds.), *Natural Language Understanding and Logic Programming, III. The 3rd International Workshop, Stockholm, Sweden, 23–25 Jan., 1991*, 227–246. Amsterdam: Elsevier, North-Holland.

Porzel, Robert, Vanessa Micelli, Hidir Aras & Hans-Peter Zorn. 2006. Tying the knot: Ground entities, descriptions and information objects for Construction-based information extraction. In *Proceedings of the OntoLex Workshop at LREC, May 2006. Genoa, Italy*, 35–40.

Postal, Paul M. 2004. *Skeptical linguistic essays*. Oxford: Oxford University Press.

Postal, Paul M. 2009. The incoherence of Chomsky's 'Biolinguistic' ontology. *Biolinguistics* 3(1). 104–123.

Postal, Paul M. & Geoffrey K. Pullum. 1986. Misgovernment. *Linguistic Inquiry* 17(1). 104–110.

Prince, Alan & Paul Smolensky. 1993. *Optimality Theory: Constraint interaction in Generative Grammar*. RuCCS Technical Report 2. Center for Cognitive Science, Rutgers University, Piscataway, N.J., & Computer Science Department, University of Colorado, Boulder. http://roa.rutgers.edu/files/537-0802/537-0802-PRINCE-0-0.PDF, accessed 2018-2-25.

Przepiórkowski, Adam. 1999a. *Case assignment and the complement-adjunct dichotomy: A non-configurational constraint-based approach*. Eberhard-Karls-Universität Tübingen dissertation. https://publikationen.uni-tuebingen.de/xmlui/handle/10900/46147, accessed 2018-2-25.

Przepiórkowski, Adam. 1999b. On case assignment and "adjuncts as complements". In Gert Webelhuth, Jean-Pierre Koenig & Andreas Kathol (eds.), *Lexical and Constructional aspects of linguistic explanation* (Studies in Constraint-Based Lexicalism 1), 231–245. Stanford, CA: CSLI Publications.

References

Przepiórkowski, Adam & Anna Kupść. 2006. HPSG for Slavicists. *Glossos* 8. 1–68.

Przepiórkowski, Adam, Anna Kupść, Małgorzata Marciniak & Agnieszka Mykowiecka. 2002. *Formalny opis języka polskiego: Teoria i implementacja*. Warsaw: Akademicka Oficyna Wydawnicza EXIT.

Pullum, Geoffrey K. 1977. Word order universals and grammatical relations. In Peter Cole & Jerrold M. Sadock (eds.), *Grammatical relations* (Syntax and Semantics 8), 249–277. New York, San Francisco, London: Academic Press.

Pullum, Geoffrey K. 1982. Free word order and phrase structure rules. In James Pustejovsky & Peter Sells (eds.), *Proceedings of the 12th Anual Meeting of the Northeast Linguistic Society*, 209–220. Amherst: Graduate Linguistics Student Association.

Pullum, Geoffrey K. 1983. How many possible human languages are there? *Linguistic Inquiry* 14(3). 447–467.

Pullum, Geoffrey K. 1984. Stalking the perfect journal. *Natural Language and Linguistic Theory* 2(2). 261–267.

Pullum, Geoffrey K. 1985. Assuming some version of X-bar Theory. In *Papers from the 21st Annual Meeting of the Chicago Linguistic Society*, 323–353.

Pullum, Geoffrey K. 1986. Footloose and context-free. *Natural Language and Linguistic Theory* 4(3). 409–414.

Pullum, Geoffrey K. 1988. Citation etiquette beyond thunderdome. *Natural Language and Linguistic Theory* 6(4). 579–588.

Pullum, Geoffrey K. 1989a. Formal linguistics meets the Boojum. *Natural Language and Linguistic Theory* 7(1). 137–143. DOI:10.1007/BF00141350

Pullum, Geoffrey K. 1989b. The incident of the node vortex problem. *Natural Language and Linguistic Theory* 7(3). 473–479.

Pullum, Geoffrey K. 1991. *The great Eskimo vocabulary hoax and other irreverent essays on the study of language*. Chicago: The University of Chicago Press.

Pullum, Geoffrey K. 1996. Learnability, hyperlearning, and the Poverty of the Stimulus. In J. Johnson, M. L. Juge & J. L. Moxley (eds.), *Proceedings of the 22nd Annual Meeting of the Berkeley Linguistics Society: General session and parasession on the role of learnability in grammatical theory*, 498–513. Berkeley, CA: Berkeley Linguistic Society. https://journals.linguisticsociety.org/proceedings/index.php/BLS/article/viewFile/1336/1120, accessed 2018-2-25.

Pullum, Geoffrey K. 2003. Learnability: Mathematical aspects. In William J. Frawley (ed.), *Oxford international encyclopedia of linguistics*, 2nd edn., 431–434. Oxford: Oxford University Press.

Pullum, Geoffrey K. 2007. The evolution of model-theoretic frameworks in linguistics. In James Rogers & Stephan Kepser (eds.), *Model-theoretic syntax at 10 – Proceedings of the ESSLLI 2007 MTS@10 Workshop, August 13–17*, 1–10. Dublin: Trinity College Dublin.

Pullum, Geoffrey K. 2009. Response to Anderson. *Language* 85(2). 245–247.

Pullum, Geoffrey K. 2013. The central question in comparative syntactic metatheory. *Mind and Language* 28(4). 492–521.

Pullum, Geoffrey K. & Kyle Rawlins. 2007. Argument or no argument? *Linguistics and Philosophy* 30(2). 277–287.

Pullum, Geoffrey K. & Barbara C. Scholz. 2001. On the distinction between generative-enumerative and model-theoretic syntactic frameworks. In Philippe de Groote, Glyn Morrill & Christian Retor (eds.), *Logical Aspects of Computational Linguistics: 4th International Conference* (Lecture Notes in Computer Science 2099), 17–43. Berlin: Springer Verlag.

Pullum, Geoffrey K. & Barbara C. Scholz. 2002. Empirical assessment of stimulus poverty arguments. *The Linguistic Review* 19(1–2). 9–50. DOI:10.1515/tlir.19.1-2.9

Pullum, Geoffrey K. & Barbara C. Scholz. 2010. Recursion and the infinitude claim. In Harry van der Hulst (ed.), *Recursion in human language* (Studies in Generative Grammar 104), 113–138. Berlin: Mouton de Gruyter.

Pulman, Stephen G. 1985. A parser that doesn't. In Maghi King (ed.), *Proceedings of the 2nd European Meeting of the Association for Computational Linguistics*, 128–135. Geneva: Association for Computational Linguistics. http://aclweb.org/anthology/E/E85/, accessed 2018-2-25.

Pulvermüller, Friedemann. 2003. *The neuroscience of language: On brain circuits of words and serial order*. Cambridge, UK: Cambridge University Press.

Pulvermüller, Friedemann. 2010. Brain embodiment of syntax and grammar: discrete combinatorial mechanisms spelt out in neuronal circuits. *Brain & Language* 112(3). 167–179.

Pulvermüller, Friedemann, Bert Cappelle & Yury Shtyrov. 2013. Brain basis of meaning, words, constructions, and grammar. In Thomas Hoffmann & Graeme Trousdale (eds.), *The Oxford handbook of Construction Grammar* (Oxford Handbooks), 397–416. Oxford: Oxford University Press.

Quaglia, Stefano. 2014. On the syntax of some apparent spatial particles in Italian. In Miriam Butt & Tracy Holloway King (eds.), *Proceedings of the LFG 2014 conference*, 503–523. Stanford, CA: CSLI Publications.

Radford, Andrew. 1990. *Syntactic theory and the acquisition of English syntax*. Cambridge, MA: Blackwell Publishers Ltd.

Radford, Andrew. 1997. *Syntactic theory and the structure of English: A Minimalist approach* (Cambridge Textbooks in Linguistics). Cambridge, UK: Cambridge University Press.

Rákosi, György, Tibor Laczkó & Gábor Csernyi. 2011. On English phrasal verbs and their Hungarian counterparts: From the perspective of a computational linguistic project. *Argumentum* 7. 80–89.

Rambow, Owen. 1994. *Formal and computational aspects of natural language syntax*. University of Pennsylvania dissertation.

Ramchand, Gillian. 2005. Post-Davidsonianism. *Theoretical Linguistics* 31(3). 359–373. DOI:10.1515/thli.2005.31.3.359

Randriamasimanana, Charles. 2006. Simple sentences in Malagasy. In Henry Y. Chang, Lillian M. Huang & Dah-ah Ho (eds.), *Streams converging into an ocean: Festschrift in honor of Professor Paul Jen-kuei Li on his 70th birthday*, 71–96. Taipei, Taiwan: Institute of Linguistics, Academia Sinica.

References

Raposo, Eduardo & Juan Uriagereka. 1990. Long-distance case assignment. *Linguistic Inquiry* 21(4). 505–537.

Rappaport, Malka. 1983. On the nature of derived nominals. In Lori S. Levin, Malka Rappaport & Annie Zaenen (eds.), *Papers in Lexical Functional Grammar*, 113–42. Indiana: Indiana University Linguistics Club.

Rauh, Gisa. 2016. Linguistic categories and the syntax-semantics interface: Evaluating competing approaches. In Jens Fleischhauer, Anja Latrouite & Rainer Osswald (eds.), *Explorations of the syntax-semantics interface* (Studies in Language and Cognition 3), 15–55. Düsseldorf: düsseldorf university press.

Reape, Mike. 1991. *Word order variation in Germanic and parsing*. DYANA Report Deliverable R1.1.C. University of Edinburgh.

Reape, Mike. 1992. *A formal theory of word order: A case study in West Germanic*. University of Edinburgh dissertation.

Reape, Mike. 1994. Domain union and word order variation in German. In John Nerbonne, Klaus Netter & Carl J. Pollard (eds.), *German in Head-Driven Phrase Structure Grammar* (CSLI Lecture Notes 46), 151–198. Stanford, CA: CSLI Publications.

Reape, Mike. 2000. *Formalisation and abstraction in linguistic theory II: Toward a radical Linearisation Theory of German*. unpublished paper.

Redington, Martin, Nick Chater & Steven Finch. 1998. Distributional information: A powerful cue for acquiring syntactic categories. *Cognitive Science* 22(4). 425–469.

Reis, Marga. 1974. Syntaktische Hauptsatzprivilegien und das Problem der deutschen Wortstellung. *Zeitschrift für Germanistische Linguistik* 2(3). 299–327.

Reis, Marga. 1980. On justifying topological frames: 'Positional field' and the order of nonverbal constituents in German. *Documentation et Recherche en Linguistique Allemande Contemporaine. Revue de Linguistique* 22/23. 59–85.

Reis, Marga. 1982. Zum Subjektbegriff im Deutschen. In Werner Abraham (ed.), *Satzglieder im Deutschen – Vorschläge zur syntaktischen, semantischen und pragmatischen Fundierung* (Studien zur deutschen Grammatik 15), 171–211. Tübingen: originally Gunter Narr Verlag now Stauffenburg Verlag.

Remberger, Eva-Maria. 2009. Null subjects, expletives and locatives in Sardinian. In Georg A. Kaiser & Eva-Maria Remberger (eds.), *Proceedings of the workshop Null-Subjects, Expletives, and Locatives in Romance* (Arbeitspapier 123), 231–261. Konstanz: Fachbereich Sprachwissenschaft, Universität Konstanz.

Resnik, Philip. 1992. Probabilistic Tree-Adjoining Grammar as a framework for statistical natural language processing. In Antonio Zampolli (ed.), *14th International Conference on Computational Linguistics (COLING '92), August 23–28*, 418–424. Nantes, France: Association for Computational Linguistics.

Reyle, Uwe. 1993. Dealing with ambiguities by underspecification: Construction, representation and deduction. *Jounal of Semantics* 10(2). 123–179.

Richards, Marc. 2015. Minimalism. In Tibor Kiss & Artemis Alexiadou (eds.), *Syntax – theory and analysis: An international handbook*, vol. 42.3 (Handbooks of Linguistics and Communication Science), 803–839. Berlin: Mouton de Gruyter. DOI:10.1515/9783110363685

Richter, Frank. 2004. *A mathematical formalism for linguistic theories with an application in Head-Driven Phrase Structure Grammar*. Universität Tübingen Phil. Dissertation (2000). https://publikationen.uni-tuebingen.de/xmlui/handle/10900/46230, accessed 2018-2-25.

Richter, Frank. 2007. Closer to the truth: A new model theory for HPSG. In James Rogers & Stephan Kepser (eds.), *Model-theoretic syntax at 10 – Proceedings of the ESSLLI 2007 MTS@10 Workshop, August 13–17*, 101–110. Dublin: Trinity College Dublin.

Richter, Frank & Manfred Sailer. 1999a. A lexicalist collocation analysis of sentential negation in French. In Valia Kordoni (ed.), *Tübingen studies in Head-Driven Phrase Structure Grammar* (Arbeitspapiere des SFB 340, No. 132, Volume 1), 231–300. Tübingen: Eberhard-Karls-Universität Tübingen.

Richter, Frank & Manfred Sailer. 1999b. Lexicalizing the left periphery of German finite sentences. In Valia Kordoni (ed.), *Tübingen studies in Head-Driven Phrase Structure Grammar* (Arbeitspapiere des SFB 340, No. 132, Volume 1), 116–154. Tübingen: Eberhard-Karls-Universität Tübingen.

Richter, Frank & Manfred Sailer. 2004. Basic concepts of lexical resource semantics. In Arnold Beckmann & Norbert Preining (eds.), *ESSLLI 2003 – Course material I* (Collegium Logicum 5), 87–143. Wien: Kurt Gödel Society.

Richter, Frank & Manfred Sailer. 2009. Phraseological clauses as Constructions in HPSG. In Stefan Müller (ed.), *Proceedings of the 16th International Conference on Head-Driven Phrase Structure Grammar, University of Göttingen, Germany*, 297–317. Stanford, CA: CSLI Publications. http://csli-publications.stanford.edu/HPSG/2009/, accessed 2018-2-25.

Riehemann, Susanne. 1993. *Word formation in lexical type hierarchies: A case study of bar-adjectives in German*. Eberhard-Karls-Universität Tübingen MA thesis. Also published as SfS-Report-02-93, Seminar für Sprachwissenschaft, University of Tübingen.

Riehemann, Susanne Z. 1998. Type-based derivational morphology. *Journal of Comparative Germanic Linguistics* 2(1). 49–77. DOI:10.1023/A:1009746617055

Riemsdijk, Henk van. 1978. *A case study in syntactic markedness: The binding nature of prepositional phrases*. Lisse: The Peter de Ridder Press.

Riezler, Stefan, Tracy Holloway King, Ronald M. Kaplan, Richard Crouch, John T. Maxwell III & Mark Johnson. 2002. Parsing the Wall Street Journal using a Lexical-Functional Grammar and discriminative estimation techniques. In Pierre Isabelle (ed.), *40th Annual Meeting of the Association for Computational Linguistics: Proceedings of the conference*, 271–278. University of Pennsylvania, Philadelphia: Association for Computational Linguistics. http://aclweb.org/anthology/P/P02/, accessed 2018-2-25.

Rizzi, Luigi. 1982. Violations of the *wh* island constraint and the Subjacency Condition. In Luigi Rizzi (ed.), *Issues in Italian syntax* (Studies in Generative Grammar 11), 49–76. Dordrecht: Foris Publications.

Rizzi, Luigi. 1986. Null objects in Italian and the theory of *pro*. *Linguistic Inquiry* 17(3). 501–577.

Rizzi, Luigi. 1997. The fine structure of the left periphery. In Liliane Haegeman (ed.), *Elements of grammar*, 281–337. Dordrecht: Kluwer Academic Publishers.

Rizzi, Luigi. 2009a. Language variation and universals: Some notes on N. Evans and S. C. Levinson (2009) "The myth of language universals: Language diversity and its importance for cognitive science". In Paola Cotticelli-Kurras & Alessandra Tomaselli (eds.), *La Grammatica tra storia e teoria. Studi in onore di Giorgio Graffi*, 153–162. Alessandra: Edizioni dell'Orso.

Rizzi, Luigi. 2009b. The discovery of language invariance and variation, and its relevance for the cognitive sciences. *The Behavioral and Brain Sciences* 32(5). 467–468.

Rizzi, Luigi. 2014. Syntactic Cartography and the Syntacticisation of Scope-Discourse Semantics. In Anne Reboul (ed.), *Mind, Values, and Metaphysics: Philosophical Essays in Honor of Kevin Mulligan*, vol. 2, 517–533. Cham: Springer International Publishing. DOI:10.1007/978-3-319-05146-8_30

Roberts, Ian F. & Anders Holmberg. 2005. On the role of parameters in Universal Grammar: A reply to Newmeyer. In Hans Broekhuis, N. Corver, Riny Huybregts, Ursula Kleinhenz & Jan Koster (eds.), *Organizing grammar: Linguistic studies in honor of Henk van Riemsdijk* (Studies in Generative Grammar 86), 538–553. Berlin: Mouton de Gruyter. DOI:10.1515/9783110892994.538

Robins, Robert Henry. 1997. *A short history of linguistics*. 4th edn. (Longman Linguistics Library). London: Routledge.

Rogers, James. 1994. Obtaining trees from their descriptions: An application to Tree-Adjoining Grammars. *Computational Intelligence* 10(4). 401–421.

Rogers, James. 1997. "Grammarless" Phrase Structure Grammar. *Linguistics and Philosophy* 20. 721–746.

Rogers, James. 1998. *A descriptive approach to language-theoretic complexity* (Studies in Logic, Language and Information). Stanford, CA: CSLI Publications.

Rohrer, Christian. 1996. Fakultativ kohärente Infinitkonstruktionen im Deutschen und deren Behandlung in der Lexikalisch Funktionalen Grammatik. In Gisela Harras & Manfred Bierwisch (eds.), *Wenn die Semantik arbeitet: Klaus Baumgärtner zum 65. Geburtstag*, 89–108. Tübingen: Max Niemeyer Verlag.

Rohrer, Christian & Martin Forst. 2006. Improving coverage and parsing quality of a large-scale LFG for German. In *Proceedings of the Language Resources and Evaluation Conference (LREC-2006)*. Genoa, Italy.

Ross, John Robert. 1967. *Constraints on variables in syntax*. MIT dissertation. http://files.eric.ed.gov/fulltext/ED016965.pdf, accessed 2018-2-25. Reproduced by the Indiana University Linguistics Club and later published as Ross (1986).

Ross, John Robert. 1986. *Infinite syntax!* (Language and Being 5). Norwood, New Jersey: Ablex Publishing Corporation.

Rothkegel, Annely. 1976. *Valenzgrammatik* (Linguistische Arbeiten 19). Saarbrücken, Germany: Sonderforschungsbereich Elektronische Sprachforschung, Universität des Saarlandes.

Sabel, Joachim. 1999. Das Passiv im Deutschen: Derivationale Ökonomie vs. optionale Bewegung. *Linguistische Berichte* 177. 87–112.

Sáfár, Éva & John Glauert. 2010. Sign Language HPSG. In *Proceedings of the 4th Workshop on the Representation and Processing of Sign Languages: Corpora and Sign Language Technologies, LREC 2010, 22–23 May 2010, Malta*, 204–207.

Sáfár, Éva & Ian Marshall. 2002. Sign language translation via DRT and HPSG. In Alexander Gelbukh (ed.), *Computational linguistics and intelligent text processing: Third International Conference, CICLing 2002 Mexico City, Mexico, February 17–23, 2002 Proceedings* (Lecture Notes in Computer Science 2276), 58–68. Berlin: Springer Verlag.

Safir, Kenneth J. 1985. Missing subjects in German. In Jindřich Toman (ed.), *Studies in German grammar* (Studies in Generative Grammar 21), 193–229. Dordrecht: Foris Publications.

Sag, Ivan A. 1997. English relative clause constructions. *Journal of Linguistics* 33(2). 431–484.

Sag, Ivan A. 2000. *Another argument against* Wh-*trace*. http://ling.ucsc.edu/Jorge/sag.html, accessed 2018-2-25. Jorge Hankamer Webfest.

Sag, Ivan A. 2007. Remarks on locality. In Stefan Müller (ed.), *Proceedings of the 14th International Conference on Head-Driven Phrase Structure Grammar*, 394–414. Stanford, CA: CSLI Publications. http://csli-publications.stanford.edu/HPSG/2007/, accessed 2018-2-25.

Sag, Ivan A. 2010. English filler-gap constructions. *Language* 86(3). 486–545.

Sag, Ivan A. 2012. Sign-Based Construction Grammar: An informal synopsis. In Hans C. Boas & Ivan A. Sag (eds.), *Sign-Based Construction Grammar* (CSLI Lecture Notes 193), 69–202. Stanford, CA: CSLI Publications.

Sag, Ivan A. 2013. *Lessons from the English auxiliary system*. Ms. Stanford University.

Sag, Ivan A., Hans C. Boas & Paul Kay. 2012. Introducing Sign-Based Construction Grammar. In Hans C. Boas & Ivan A. Sag (eds.), *Sign-Based Construction Grammar* (CSLI Lecture Notes 193), 1–29. Stanford, CA: CSLI Publications.

Sag, Ivan A., Philip Hofmeister & Neal Snider. 2007. Processing complexity in subjacency violations: The Complex Noun Phrase Constraint. In Malcolm Elliott, James Kirby, Osamu Sawada, Eleni Staraki & Suwon Yoon (eds.), *Proceedings of the 43rd Annual Meeting of the Chicago Linguistic Society*, 215–229. Chicago: Chicago Linguistic Society.

Sag, Ivan A. & Carl J. Pollard. 1991. An integrated theory of complement control. *Language* 67(1). 63–113.

Sag, Ivan A. & Thomas Wasow. 2011. Performance-compatible competence grammar. In Robert D. Borsley & Kersti Börjars (eds.), *Non-transformational syntax: Formal and explicit models of grammar: A guide to current models*, 359–377. Oxford, UK/Cambridge, MA: Blackwell Publishers Ltd.

Sag, Ivan A. & Thomas Wasow. 2015. Flexible processing and the design of grammar. *Journal of Psycholinguistic Research* 44(1). 47–63.

Sag, Ivan A., Thomas Wasow & Emily M. Bender. 2003. *Syntactic theory: A formal introduction*. 2nd edn. (CSLI Lecture Notes 152). Stanford, CA: CSLI Publications.

Sailer, Manfred. 2000. *Combinatorial semantics and idiomatic expressions in Head-Driven Phrase Structure Grammar*. Eberhard-Karls-Universität Tübingen Dissertation. https://publikationen.uni-tuebingen.de/xmlui/handle/10900/46191, accessed 2018-2-25.

References

Samarin, William J. 1984. Socioprogrammed linguistics. *The Behavioral and Brain Sciences* 7(2). 206–207.

Sampson, Geoffrey. 1989. Language acquisition: growth or learning? *Philosophical Papers* 18(3). 203–240.

Samvelian, Pollet. 2007. A (phrasal) affix analysis of the Persian Ezafe. *Journal of Linguistics* 43. 605–645.

Sarkar, Anoop & Aravind K. Joshi. 1996. Coordination in Tree Adjoining Grammars: formalization and implementation. In Jun-ichi Tsuji (ed.), *Proceedings of COLING-96. 16th International Conference on Computational Linguistics (COLING96). Copenhagen, Denmark, August 5–9, 1996*, 610–615. Copenhagen, Denmark: Association for Computational Linguistics.

Sato, Yo. 2006. Constrained free word order parsing with Lexicalised Linearisation Grammar. In *Proceedings of 9th Annual CLUK Research Colloquium*. Open University, UK.

Sato, Yo. 2008. *Implementing Head-Driven Linearisation Grammar*. King's College London dissertation.

Sauerland, Uli & Paul Elbourne. 2002. Total reconstruction, PF movement, and derivational order. *Linguistic Inquiry* 33(2). 283–319.

Savin, Harris B. & Ellen Perchonock. 1965. Grammatical structure and the immediate recall of English sentences. *Journal of Verbal Learning and Verbal Behavior* 4(5). 348–353.

Schabes, Yves, Anne Abeillé & Aravind K. Joshi. 1988. *Parsing strategies with 'lexicalized' grammars: Application to Tree Adjoining Grammars*. Technical Report MS-CIS-88-65. University of Pennsylvania Department of Computer & Information Science.

Schein, Barry. 1993. *Plurals and events* (Current Studies in Linguistics 23). Cambridge, MA: MIT Press.

Scherpenisse, Wim. 1986. *The connection between base structure and linearization restrictions in German and Dutch* (Europäische Hochschulschriften, Reihe XXI, Linguistik 47). Frankfurt/M.: Peter Lang.

Schluter, Natalie & Josef van Genabith. 2009. Dependency parsing resources for French: Converting acquired Lexical Functional Grammar f-structure annotations and parsing f-structures directly. In Kristiina Jokinen & Eckhard Bick (eds.), *Nodalida 2009 conference proceedings*, 166–173.

Schmidt, Paul, Sibylle Rieder & Axel Theofilidis. 1996. *Final documentation of the German LS-GRAM lingware*. Deliverable DC-WP6e (German). Saarbrücken: IAI.

Schmidt, Paul, Axel Theofilidis, Sibylle Rieder & Thierry Declerck. 1996. Lean formalisms, linguistic theory, and applications: grammar development in ALEP. In Jun-ichi Tsuji (ed.), *Proceedings of COLING-96. 16th International Conference on Computational Linguistics (COLING96). Copenhagen, Denmark, August 5–9, 1996*, 286–291. Copenhagen, Denmark: Association for Computational Linguistics. DOI:10.3115/992628.992679

Scholz, Barbara C. & Geoffrey K. Pullum. 2002. Searching for arguments to support linguistic nativism. *The Linguistic Review* 19(1–2). 185–223. DOI:10.1515/tlir.19.1-2.185

Schubert, K. 1987. *Metataxis: Contrastive Dependency Syntax for machine translation*. Dordrecht: Foris Publications.

Schumacher, Helmut, Jacqueline Kubczak, Renate Schmidt & Vera de Ruiter. 2004. *VALBU – Valenzwörterbuch deutscher Verben*. Tübingen: Gunter Narr Verlag.

Schütz, Jörg. 1996. *The ALEP formalism in a nutshell*. Tech. rep. Saarbrücken: IAI.

Schwarze, Christoph & Leonel de Alencar. 2016. *Lexikalisch-funktionale Grammatik: Eine Einführung am Beispiel des Französischen, mit computerlinguistischer Implementierung* (Stauffenburg Einführungen 30). Tübingen: Stauffenburg Verlag.

Seiss, Melanie & Rachel Nordlinger. 2012. An electronic dictionary and translation system for Murrinh-Patha. *The EUROCALL Review: Proceedings of the EUROCALL 2011 Conference* 20(1). 135–138.

Sengupta, Probal & B. B. Chaudhuri. 1997. A delayed syntactic-encoding-based LFG parsing strategy for an Indian language—Bangla. *Computational Linguistics* 23(2). 345–351.

Seuren, Pieter A. M. 1984. The Bioprogram Hypothesis: facts and fancy. *The Behavioral and Brain Sciences* 7(2). 208–209.

Seuren, Pieter A. M. 2004. *Chomsky's Minimalism*. Oxford: Oxford University Press.

Shieber, Stuart M. 1985. Evidence against the context-freeness of natural language. *Linguistics and Philosophy* 8(3). 333–343.

Shieber, Stuart M. 1986. *An introduction to unification-based approaches to grammar* (CSLI Lecture Notes 4). Stanford, CA: CSLI Publications.

Shieber, Stuart M. & Mark Johnson. 1993. Variations on incremental interpretation. *Journal of Psycholinguistic Research* 22(2). 287–318.

Shieber, Stuart M., Hans Uszkoreit, Fernando Pereira, Jane Robinson & Mabry Tyson. 1983. The formalism and implementation of PATR-II. In *Research on interactive acquisition and use of knowledge*, 39–79. Menlo Park, CA: Artificial Intelligence Center, SRI International.

Shtyrov, Yury, Elina Pihko & Friedemann Pulvermüller. 2005. Determinants of dominance: is language laterality explained by physical or linguistic features of speech? *Neuroimage* 27(1). 37–47. DOI:10.1016/j.neuroimage.2005.02.003

Siegel, Melanie. 2000. HPSG analysis of Japanese. In Wolfgang Wahlster (ed.), *Verbmobil: Foundations of speech-to-speech translation* (Artificial Intelligence), 264–279. Berlin: Springer Verlag.

Siegel, Melanie & Emily M. Bender. 2002. Efficient deep processing of Japanese. In *Proceedings of the 3rd Workshop on Asian Language Resources and International Standardization at the 19th International Conference on Computational Linguistics*. Taipei, Taiwan. http://www.aclweb.org/anthology/W02-1210, accessed 2018-2-25.

Siegel, Melanie, Emily M. Bender & Francis Bond. 2016. *Jacy: An implemented grammar of Japanese* (CSLI Studies in Computational Linguistics). Stanford, CA: CSLI Publications.

Simov, Kiril, Petya Osenova, Alexander Simov & Milen Kouylekov. 2004. Design and implementation of the Bulgarian HPSG-based treebank. *Research on Language and Computation* 2(4). 495–522.

Simpson, Jane. 1983. Resultatives. In Lori S. Levin, Malka Rappaport & Annie Zaenen (eds.), *Papers in Lexical Functional Grammar*, 143–157. Indiana: Indiana University Linguistics Club. Reprint: Simpson (2005b).

References

Simpson, Jane. 2005a. Depictives in English and Warlpiri. In Nikolaus P. Himmelmann & Eva Schultze-Berndt (eds.), *Secondary predication and adverbial modification: The typology of depictives*, 69–106. Oxford: Oxford University Press.

Simpson, Jane. 2005b. Resultatives. In Miriam Butt & Tracy Holloway King (eds.), *Lexical semantics in LFG*, 149–161. Stanford, CA: CSLI Publications.

Singleton, Jenny L. & Elissa L. Newport. 2004. When learners surpass their models: The acquisition of American Sign Language from inconsistent input. *Cognitive Psychology* 49(4). 370–407.

Slayden, Glenn C. 2012. *Array TFS storage for unification grammars*. University of Washington MA thesis.

Sleator, Daniel D. K. & Davy Temperley. 1991. *Parsing English with a Link Grammar*. CMU-CS-TR-91-126. School of Computer Science, Carnegie Mellon University.

Smith, Carlota S. 1970. Jespersen's "move and change" class and causative verbs in English. In Bert Peeters (ed.), *The lexicon–encyclopedia interface*, 101–109. Amsterdam: Elsevier.

Smith, Carlota S. 1972. On causative verbs and derived nominals in English. *Linguistic Inquiry* 3(1). 136–138.

Snyder, William. 2001. On the nature of syntactic variation: Evidence from complex predicates and complex word-formation. *Language* 77(2). 324–342.

Soehn, Jan-Philipp & Manfred Sailer. 2008. At first blush on tenterhooks: About selectional restrictions imposed by nonheads. In Gerhard Jäger, Paola Monachesi, Gerald Penn & Shuly Wintner (eds.), *Proceedings of Formal Grammar 2003, Vienna, Austria*, 149–161. Stanford, CA: CSLI Publications. http://csli-publications.stanford.edu/FG/2003/soehn.pdf, accessed 2018-2-25.

Son, Minjeong. 2007. Directionality and resultativity: The cross-linguistic correlation revisited. *Tromsø University Working Papers on Language & Linguistics* 34. 126–164. http://hdl.handle.net/10037/3191, accessed 2018-2-25.

Son, Minjeong & Peter Svenonius. 2008. Microparameters of cross-linguistic variation: Directed motion and resultatives. In Natasha Abner & Jason Bishop (eds.), *Proceedings of the 26th West Coast Conference on Formal Linguistics*, 388–396. Somerville, MA: Cascadilla Proceedings Project.

Song, Sanghoun, Jong-Bok Kim, Francis Bond & Jaehyung Yang. 2010. Development of the Korean Resource Grammar: Towards grammar customization. In *Proceedings of the 8th Workshop on Asian Language Resources, Beijing, China, 21–22 August 2010*, 144–152. Asian Federation for Natural Language Processing.

Sorace, Antonella. 2003. Near-nativeness. In Catherine J. Doughty & Michael H. Long (eds.), *The handbook of second language acquisition* (Blackwell Handbooks in Linguistics), 130–151. Oxford: Blackwell Publishers Ltd.

Sorace, Antonella & Frank Keller. 2005. Gradience in linguistic data. *Lingua* 115(11). 1497–1524. DOI:10.1016/j.lingua.2004.07.002

Sportiche, Dominique, Hilda Koopman & Edward Stabler. 2013. *An introduction to syntactic analysis and theory*. Wiley-Blackwell.

Stabler, Edward P. 1987. Restricting logic grammars with Government-Binding Theory. *Computational Linguistics* 13(1–2). 1–10.

Stabler, Edward P. 1991. Avoid the pedestrian's paradox. In Robert C. Berwick, Steven P. Abney & Carol Tenny (eds.), *Principle-based parsing: computation and psycholinguistics*, 199–237. Dordrecht: Kluwer Academic Publishers.

Stabler, Edward P. 1992. *The logical approach to syntax: Foundations, specifications, and implementations of theories of Government and Binding* (ACL-MIT Press Series in Natural Language Processing). Cambridge, MA: MIT Press.

Stabler, Edward P. 2001. Minimalist Grammars and recognition. In Christian Rohrer, Antje Rossdeutscher & Hans Kamp (eds.), *Linguistic form and its computation* (Studies in Computational Linguistics 1), 327–352. Stanford, CA: CSLI Publications.

Stabler, Edward P. 2011a. After Governement and Binding Theory. In Johan F. A. K. van Benthem & G. B. Alice ter Meulen (eds.), *Handbook of logic and language*, 2nd edn., 395–414. Amsterdam: Elsevier.

Stabler, Edward P. 2011b. Computational perspectives on Minimalism. In Cedric Boeckx (ed.), *The Oxford handbook of linguistic Minimalism* (Oxford Handbooks in Linguistics), chap. 27, 616–641. Oxford: Oxford University Press.

Starosta, Stanley. 1988. *The case for Lexicase* (Open Linguistics Series). London: Pinter Publishers.

Starosta, Stanley & Hirosato Nomura. 1986. Lexicase parsing: A lexicon-driven approach to syntactic analysis. In Makoto Nagao (ed.), *Proceedings of COLING 86*, 127–132. Bonn, Germany: Association for Computational Linguistics. DOI:10.3115/991365.991400

Steedman, Mark J. 1985. Dependency and coordination in the grammar of Dutch and English. *Language* 61(3). 523–568.

Steedman, Mark J. 1989. Constituency and coordination in a Combinatory Grammar. In Mark R. Baltin & Anthony S. Kroch (eds.), *Alternative conceptions of phrase structure*, 201–231. Chicago/London: The University of Chicago Press.

Steedman, Mark J. 1991. Structure and intonation. *Language* 67(2). 260–296.

Steedman, Mark J. 1997. *Surface structure and interpretation* (Linguistic Inquiry Monographs 30). Cambridge, MA: MIT Press.

Steedman, Mark J. 2000. *The syntactic process* (Language, Speech, and Communication). Cambridge, MA: MIT Press.

Steedman, Mark J. 2011. Romantics and revolutionaries. *Linguistic Issues in Language Technology* 6(11). 1–20. http://journals.linguisticsociety.org/elanguage/lilt/article/view/2587.html, accessed 2018-2-25. Special Issue on Interaction of Linguistics and Computational Linguistics.

Steedman, Mark J. & Jason Baldridge. 2006. Combinatory Categorial Grammar. In Keith Brown (ed.), *Encyclopedia of language and linguistics*, 2nd edn., 610–621. Oxford: Elsevier.

Steels, Luc. 2003. Evolving grounded communication for robots. *Trends in Cognitive Science* 7(7). 308–312.

Steels, Luc (ed.). 2011. *Design patterns in Fluid Construction Grammar* (Constructional Approaches to Language 11). Amsterdam: John Benjamins Publishing Co.

References

Steels, Luc (ed.). 2012. *Computational issues in Fluid Construction Grammar* (Lecture Notes in Computer Science 7249). Berlin: Springer Verlag.

Steels, Luc. 2013. Fluid Construction Grammar. In Thomas Hoffmann & Graeme Trousdale (eds.), *The Oxford handbook of Construction Grammar* (Oxford Handbooks), 153–167. Oxford: Oxford University Press.

Steels, Luc. 2015. *The Talking Heads experiment: Origins of words and meanings* (Computational Models of Language Evolution 1). Berlin: Language Science Press.

Steels, Luc & Joachim De Beule. 2006. *A (very) brief introduction to Fluid Construction Grammar*. Paper presented at the Third International Workshop on Scalable Natural Language Understanding (ScaNaLU 2006) June 8, 2006, following HLT/NAACL, New York City.

Steels, Luc & Remi van Trijp. 2011. How to make Construction Grammars fluid and robust. In Luc Steels (ed.), *Design patterns in Fluid Construction Grammar* (Constructional Approaches to Language 11), 301–330. Amsterdam: John Benjamins Publishing Co. DOI:10.1075/cal.11

Stefanowitsch, Anatol. 2008. Negative entrenchment: A usage-based approach to negative evidence. *Cognitive Linguistics* 19(3). 513–531.

Stefanowitsch, Anatol & Kerstin Fischer (eds.). 2008. *Konstruktionsgrammatik II: Von der Konstruktion zur Grammatik* (Stauffenburg Linguistik 47). Tübingen: Stauffenburg Verlag.

Stefanowitsch, Anatol & Stephan Th. Gries. 2009. Corpora and grammar. In Anke Lüdeling & Merja Kytö (eds.), *Corpus linguistics: An international handbook*, vol. 29 (Handbücher zur Sprach- und Kommunikationswissenschaft), chap. 43, 933–952. Berlin: Mouton de Gruyter.

Sternefeld, Wolfgang. 1985a. Deutsch ohne grammatische Funktionen: Ein Beitrag zur Rektions- und Bindungstheorie. *Linguistische Berichte* 99. 394–439.

Sternefeld, Wolfgang. 1985b. On case and binding theory. In Jindřich Toman (ed.), *Studies in German grammar* (Studies in Generative Grammar 21), 231–285. Dordrecht: Foris Publications.

Sternefeld, Wolfgang. 1995. Voice phrases and their specifiers. *FAS Papers in Linguistics* 3. 48–85.

Sternefeld, Wolfgang. 2006. *Syntax: Eine morphologisch motivierte generative Beschreibung des Deutschen* (Stauffenburg Linguistik 31). Tübingen: Stauffenburg Verlag.

Sternefeld, Wolfgang & Frank Richter. 2012. Wo stehen wir in der Grammatiktheorie? — Bemerkungen anläßlich eines Buchs von Stefan Müller. *Zeitschrift für Sprachwissenschaft* 31(2). 263–291. DOI:10.1515/zfs-2012-0010

Stiebels, Barbara. 1996. *Lexikalische Argumente und Adjunkte: Zum semantischen Beitrag verbaler Präfixe und Partikeln* (studia grammatica 39). Berlin: Akademie Verlag.

Stowell, Timothy. 1981. *Origins of phrase structure*. MIT dissertation. http://hdl.handle.net/1721.1/15626, accessed 2018-2-25.

Strunk, Jan & Neal Snider. 2013. Subclausal locality constraints on relative clause extraposition. In Gert Webelhuth, Manfred Sailer & Heike Walker (eds.), *Rightward move-*

ment in a comparative perspective (Linguistik Aktuell/Linguistics Today 200), 99–143. Amsterdam: John Benjamins Publishing Co.

Suchsland, Peter. 1997. *Syntax-Theorie: Ein zusammengefaßter Zugang* (Konzepte der Sprach- und Literaturwissenschaft 55). Tübingen: Max Niemeyer Verlag. Deutsche Bearbeitung von Borsley (1991) durch Peter Suchsland.

Sulger, Sebastian. 2009. Irish clefting and information-structure. In Miriam Butt & Tracy Holloway King (eds.), *Proceedings of the LFG 2009 conference*, 562–582. Stanford, CA: CSLI Publications. http://csli-publications.stanford.edu/LFG/14/, accessed 2018-2-25.

Sulger, Sebastian. 2010. Analytic and synthetic verb forms in Irish – An agreement-based implementation in LFG. In Manfred Pinkal, Ines Rehbein, Sabine Schulte im Walde & Angelika Storrer (eds.), *Semantic approaches in natural language processing: Proceedings of the Conference on Natural Language Processing 2010*, 169–173. Saarbrücken: Saarland University Press (universaar).

Svenonius, Peter. 2004. Slavic prefixes inside and outside VP. *Nordlyd. Special Issue on Slavic Prefixes* 32(2). 205–253.

Takami, Ken-ichi. 1988. Preposition stranding: Arguments against syntactic analyses and an alternative functional explanation. *Lingua* 76(4). 299–335.

Tanenhaus, Michael K., Michael J. Spivey-Knowlton, Kathleen M. Eberhard & Julie C. Sedivy. 1995. Integration of visual and linguistic information in spoken language comprehension. *Science* 268(5217). 1632–1634. DOI:10.1126/science.7777863

Tanenhaus, Michael K., Michael J. Spivey-Knowlton, Kathleen M. Eberhard & Julie C. Sedivy. 1996. Using eye movements to study spoken language comprehension: Evidence for visually mediated incremental interpretation. In Toshio Inui & James L. McClelland (eds.), *Information integration in perception and communication* (Attention and Performance XVI), 457–478. Cambridge, MA: MIT Press.

ten Hacken, Pius. 2007. *Chomskyan linguistics and its competitors*. London: Equinox Publishing Ltd.

Tesnière, Lucien. 1959. *Eléments de syntaxe structurale*. Paris: Librairie C. Klincksieck.

Tesnière, Lucien. 1980. *Grundzüge der strukturalen Syntax*. Stuttgart: Klett-Cotta. Translated by Ulrich Engel.

Tesnière, Lucien. 2015. *Elements of structural syntax*. Amsterdam: John Benjamins Publishing Co. Translated by Timothy Osborne and Sylvain Kahane.

Thiersch, Craig L. 1978. *Topics in German syntax*. M.I.T. Dissertation. http://hdl.handle.net/1721.1/16327, accessed 2018-2-25.

Thompson, Henry S. 1982. *Handling metarules in a parser for GPSG*. D.A.I. Research 175. University of Edinburgh.

Timberlake, Alan. 1982. The impersonal passive in Lithuanian. In Monica Macaulay, Orin D. Gensler, Claudia Brugmann, Inese Čivkulis, Amy Dahlstrom, Katherine Krile & Rob Sturm (eds.), *Proceedings of the Eighth Annual Meeting of the Berkeley Linguistics Society*, 508–524. Berkeley: University of California.

Toivonen, Ida. 2013. English benefactive NPs. In Miriam Butt & Tracy Holloway King (eds.), *Proceedings of the LFG 2013 conference*, 503–523. Stanford, CA: CSLI Publications.

References

Tomasello, Michael. 1995. Language is not an instinct. *Cognitive Development* 10(1). 131–156.

Tomasello, Michael. 2000. Do young children have adult syntactic competence? *Cognition* 74(3). 209–253.

Tomasello, Michael. 2003. *Constructing a language: A usage-based theory of language acquisition*. Cambridge, MA: Harvard University Press.

Tomasello, Michael. 2005. Beyond formalities: The case of language acquisition. *The Linguistic Review* 22(2–4). 183–197.

Tomasello, Michael. 2006a. Acquiring linguistic constructions. In Deanna Kuhn & Robert Siegler (eds.), *Handbook of child psychology*, 6th edn., vol. 2. New York: John Wiley & Sons, Inc.

Tomasello, Michael. 2006b. Construction Grammar for kids. *Constructions* Special Volume 1. https://journals.linguisticsociety.org/elanguage/constructions/article/view/26.html, accessed 2018-2-25.

Tomasello, Michael. 2006c. Konstruktionsgrammatik und früher Erstspracherwerb. In Kerstin Fischer & Anatol Stefanowitsch (eds.), *Konstruktionsgrammatik: Von der Anwendung zur Theorie* (Stauffenburg Linguistik 40), 19–37. Tübingen: Stauffenburg Verlag.

Tomasello, Michael. 2009. Universal Grammar is dead. *The Behavioral and Brain Sciences* 32(5). 470–471.

Tomasello, Michael, Nameera Akhtar, Kelly Dodsen & Laura Rekau. 1997. Differential productivity in young children's use of nouns and verbs. *Journal of Child Language* 24(2). 373–387.

Tomasello, Michael, Malinda Carpenter, Josep Call, Tanya Behne & Henrike Moll. 2005. Understanding and sharing intentions: The origins of cultural cognition. *The Behavioral and Brain Sciences* 28(5). 675–735.

Travis, Lisa. 1984. *Parameters and effects of word order variation*. Cambridge, MA: M.I.T. Dissertation.

Trinh, Tue H. 2011. *Edges and linearization*. Massachusetts Institute of Technology dissertation. https://dspace.mit.edu/handle/1721.1/68523, accessed 2019-5-9.

Trosterud, Trond. 2009. A Constraint Grammar for Faroese. In Eckhard Bick, Kristin Hagen, Kaili Müürisep & Trond Trosterud (eds.), *Constraint Grammar and robust parsing: Proceedings of the NODALIDA 2009 workshop*, vol. 8 (NEALT Proceedings Series 8), 1–7. Tartu: Tartu University Library.

Tseng, Jesse (ed.). 2000. *Aspekte eines HPSG-Fragments des Deutschen* (Arbeitspapiere des SFB 340 No. 156). Tübingen: Eberhard-Karls-Universität Tübingen. http://www.sfs.uni-tuebingen.de/sfb/reports/berichte/156/156abs.html, accessed 2018-2-25.

Tseng, Jesse L. 2003. LKB grammar implementation: French and beyond. In Emily M. Bender, Daniel P. Flickinger, Frederik Fouvry & Melanie Siegel (eds.), *Proceedings of the ESSLLI 2003 Workshop "Ideas and Strategies for Multilingual Grammar Development"*, 91–97. Vienna, Austria. https://hal.inria.fr/inria-00099472/document, accessed 2018-2-25.

Tseng, Jesse L. 2007. English prepositional passive constructions. In Stefan Müller (ed.), *Proceedings of the 14th International Conference on Head-Driven Phrase Structure Grammar*, 271–286. Stanford, CA: CSLI Publications. http://csli-publications.stanford.edu/HPSG/2007/, accessed 2018-2-25.

Umemoto, Hiroshi. 2006. Implementing a Japanese semantic parser based on glue approach. In *Proceedings of The 20th Pacific Asia Conference on Language, Information and Computation*, 418–425. www.aclweb.org/anthology/Y06-1061, accessed 2018-2-25.

Uszkoreit, Hans. 1986a. Categorial Unification Grammars. In Makoto Nagao (ed.), *Proceedings of COLING 86*, 187–194. University of Bonn: Association for Computational Linguistics. http://aclweb.org/anthology/C86-1045, accessed 2018-2-25.

Uszkoreit, Hans. 1986b. *Linear precedence in discontinuous constituents: complex fronting in German*. Report No. CSLI-86-47. Stanford, CA: Center for the Study of Language & Information.

Uszkoreit, Hans. 1987. *Word order and constituent structure in German* (CSLI Lecture Notes 8). Stanford, CA: CSLI Publications.

Uszkoreit, Hans. 1990. Extraposition and adjunct attachment in Categorial Unification Grammar. In Werner Bahner, Joachim Schildt & Dieter Viehweger (eds.), *Proceedings of the Fourteenth International Congress of Linguists, Berlin/GDR, August 10–15, 1987*, vol. 3, 2331–2336. Berlin: Akademie Verlag.

Uszkoreit, Hans, Rolf Backofen, Stephan Busemann, Abdel Kader Diagne, Elizabeth A. Hinkelman, Walter Kasper, Bernd Kiefer, Hans-Ulrich Krieger, Klaus Netter, Günter Neumann, Stephan Oepen & Stephen P. Spackman. 1994. DISCO—An HPSG-based NLP system and its application for appointment scheduling. In Makoto Nagao (ed.), *Proceedings of COLING 94*, 436–440. Kyoto, Japan: Association for Computational Linguistics.

Uszkoreit, Hans, Rolf Backofen, Jo Calder, Joanne Capstick, Luca Dini, Jochen Dörre, Gregor Erbach, Dominique Estival, Suresh Manandhar, Anne-Marie Mineur & Stephan Oepen. 1996. *The EAGLES formalisms working group: Final report Expert Advisory Group on Language Engineering Standards*. http://www.coli.uni-sb.de/publikationen/softcopies/Uszkoreit:1996:EFW.pdf, accessed 2018-2-25. Technical Report LRE 61–100.

Valian, Virginia. 1991. Syntactic subjects in the early speech of American and Italian children. *Cognition* 40(1–2). 21–81.

Van Eynde, Frank. 2015. Sign-Based Construction Grammar: A guided tour. *Journal of Linguistics*. DOI:10.1017/S0022226715000341

Van Langendonck, Willy. 1994. Determiners as heads? *Cognitive Linguistics* 5. 243–259.

Van Valin, Robert D. Jr. (ed.). 1993. *Advances in Role and Reference Grammar*. Amsterdam: John Benjamins Publishing Co.

Van Valin, Robert D. Jr. 1998. The acquisition of *wh*-questions and the mechanisms of language acquisition. In Michael Tomasello (ed.), *The new psychology of language: Cognitive and functional approaches to language structure*, 221–249. Hillsdale, NJ: Lawrence Erlbaum.

References

van Noord, Gertjan & Gosse Bouma. 1994. The scope of adjuncts and the processing of lexical rules. In Makoto Nagao (ed.), *Proceedings of COLING 94*, 250–256. Kyoto, Japan: Association for Computational Linguistics.

van Trijp, Remi. 2011. A design pattern for argument structure constructions. In Luc Steels (ed.), *Design patterns in Fluid Construction Grammar* (Constructional Approaches to Language 11), 115–145. Amsterdam: John Benjamins Publishing Co. DOI:10.1075/cal.11.07tri

van Trijp, Remi. 2013. A comparison between Fluid Construction Grammar and Sign-Based Construction Grammar. *Constructions and Frames* 5(1). 88–116.

van Trijp, Remi. 2014. Long-distance dependencies without filler–gaps: A cognitive-functional alternative in Fluid Construction Grammar. *Language and Cognition* 6(2). 242–270.

Vancoppenolle, Jean, Eric Tabbert, Gerlof Bouma & Manfred Stede. 2011. A German grammar for generation in Open CCG. In Hanna Hedeland, Thomas Schmidt & Kai Wörner (eds.), *Multilingual resources and multilingual applications: Proceedings of the Conference of the German Society for Computational Linguistics and Language Technology (GSCL) 2011* (Arbeiten zur Mehrsprachigkeit/Working Papers in Multilingualism, Folge B/Series B 96), 145–150. Hamburg: Universität Hamburg.

Vargha-Khadem, Faraneh, Kate E. Watkins, Katie Alcock, Paul Fletcher & Richard Passingham. 1995. Praxic and nonverbal cognitive deficits in a large family with a genetically transmitted speech and language disorder. In *Proceedings of the National Academy of Sciences of the United States of America*, vol. 92, 930–933.

Vasishth, Shravan & Richard L. Lewis. 2006. Human language processing: Symbolic models. In Keith Brown (ed.), *The encyclopedia of language and linguistics*, 2nd edn., vol. 5, 410–419. Oxford: Elsevier Science Publisher B.V. (North-Holland).

Vasishth, Shravan, Katja Suckow, Richard L. Lewis & Sabine Kern. 2010. Short-term forgetting in sentence comprehension: Crosslinguistic evidence from verb-final structures. *Language and Cognitive Processes* 25(4). 533–567.

Vater, Heinz. 2010. Strukturalismus und generative Grammatik in Deutschland. In Hans-Harald Müller, Marcel Lepper & Andreas Gardt (eds.), *Strukturalismus in Deutschland: Literatur- und Sprachwissenschaft 1910–1975* (Marbacher Schriften. Neue Folge 5), 125–160. Göttingen: Wallstein Verlag.

Veenstra, Mettina Jolanda Arnoldina. 1998. *Formalizing the Minimalist Program*. Rijksuniversiteit Groningen Ph.D. thesis.

Vennemann, Theo & Ray Harlow. 1977. Categorial Grammar and consistent basic VX serialization. *Theoretical Linguistics* 4(1–3). 227–254. DOI:10.1515/thli.1977.4.1-3.227

Verhagen, Arie. 2010. What do you think is the proper place of recursion? Conceptual and empirical issues. In Harry van der Hulst (ed.), *Recursion in human language* (Studies in Generative Grammar 104), 93–110. Berlin: Mouton de Gruyter.

Verspoor, Cornelia Maria. 1997. *Contextually-dependent lexical semantics*. University of Edinburgh dissertation.

Vierhuff, Tilman, Bernd Hildebrandt & Hans-Jürgen Eikmeyer. 2003. Effiziente Verarbeitung deutscher Konstituentenstellung mit der Combinatorial Categorial Grammar. *Linguistische Berichte* 194. 213–237.

Vijay-Shanker, K. & Aravind K. Joshi. 1988. Feature structures based Tree Adjoining Grammars. In Dénes Vargha (ed.), *Proceedings of COLING 88*, vol. 1, 714–719. University of Budapest: Association for Computational Linguistics. http://www.aclweb.org/anthology/C88-2147, accessed 2018-2-25.

Villavicencio, Aline. 2002. *The acquisition of a unification-based Generalised Categorial Grammar*. UCAM-CL-TR-533. University of Cambridge Computer Laboratory.

Vogel, Ralf. 2001. Case conflict in German free relative constructions: An Optimality Theoretic treatment. In Gereon Müller & Wolfgang Sternefeld (eds.), *Competition in syntax*, 341–375. Berlin: Mouton de Gruyter.

Vogel, Ralf & Markus Steinbach. 1998. The dative – An oblique case. *Linguistische Berichte* 173. 65–91.

Volk, Martin. 1988. *Parsing German with GPSG: The problem of separable-prefix verbs*. University of Georgia MA thesis.

von Stechow, Arnim. 1979. Deutsche Wortstellung und Montague-Grammatik. In Jürgen M. Meisel & Martin D. Pam (eds.), *Linear order and Generative theory*, 317–490. Amsterdam: John Benjamins Publishing Co.

von Stechow, Arnim. 1989. Distinguo: Eine Antwort auf Dieter Wunderlich. *Linguistische Berichte* 122. 330–339.

von Stechow, Arnim. 1996. The different readings of *wieder* 'again': A structural account. *Journal of Semantics* 13(2). 87–138.

von Stechow, Arnim & Wolfgang Sternefeld. 1988. *Bausteine syntaktischen Wissens: Ein Lehrbuch der Generativen Grammatik*. Opladen/Wiesbaden: Westdeutscher Verlag.

Voutilainen, Atro, Juha Heikkilä & Arto Anttila. 1992. *Constraint Grammar of English: A performance-oriented introduction* (Publications of the Department of General Linguistics 21). Helsinki: University of Helsinki.

Wada, Hajime & Nicholas Asher. 1986. BUILDRS: An implementation of DR Theory and LFG. In Makoto Nagao (ed.), *Proceedings of COLING 86*, 540–545. University of Bonn: Association for Computational Linguistics.

Wahlster, Wolfgang (ed.). 2000. *Verbmobil: Foundations of speech-to-speech translation* (Artificial Intelligence). Berlin: Springer Verlag.

Walther, Markus. 1999. *Deklarative prosodische Morphologie: Constraint-basierte Analysen und Computermodelle zum Finnischen und Tigrinya* (Linguistische Arbeiten 399). Tübingen: Max Niemeyer Verlag.

Webelhuth, Gert. 1985. German is configurational. *The Linguistic Review* 4(3). 203–246.

Webelhuth, Gert. 1990. Diagnostics for structure. In Günther Grewendorf & Wolfgang Sternefeld (eds.), *Scrambling and Barriers* (Linguistik Aktuell/Linguistics Today 5), 41–75. Amsterdam: John Benjamins Publishing Co.

Webelhuth, Gert. 1995. X-bar Theory and Case Theory. In Gert Webelhuth (ed.), *Government and Binding Theory and the Minimalist Program: Principles and Parameters in syntactic theory* (Generative Syntax), 15–95. Oxford, UK & Cambrigde, USA: Blackwell Publishers Ltd.

Webelhuth, Gert. 2011. Paradigmenwechsel rückwärts: Die Renaissance der grammatischen Konstruktion. In Stefan Engelberg, Anke Holler & Kristel Proost (eds.), *Sprachliches Wissen zwischen Lexikon und Grammatik* (Institut für Deutsche Sprache, Jahrbuch 2010), 149–180. Berlin: de Gruyter.

Weber, Heinz J. 1997. *Dependenzgrammatik: Ein interaktives Arbeitsbuch*. 2nd edn. (Narr Studienbücher). Tübingen: Gunter Narr Verlag.

Wechsler, Stephen Mark. 1991. *Argument structure and linking*. Stanford University dissertation.

Wechsler, Stephen Mark. 1995. *The semantic basis of argument structure* (Dissertations in Linguistics). Stanford, CA: CSLI Publications.

Wechsler, Stephen Mark. 1997. Resultative predicates and control. In Ralph C. Blight & Michelle J. Moosally (eds.), *Texas Linguistic Forum 38: The syntax and semantics of predication: Proceedings of the 1997 Texas Linguistics Society Conference*, 307–321. Austin, Texas: University of Texas, Department of Linguistics.

Wechsler, Stephen Mark. 2005. What is right and wrong about little v. In *Grammar and beyond—Essays in honour of Lars Hellan*, 179–195. Oslo, Norway: Novus Press.

Wechsler, Stephen Mark. 2008a. A diachronic account of English deverbal nominals. In Charles B. Chang & Hannah J. Haynie (eds.), *Proceedings of the 26th West Coast Conference on Formal Linguistics*, 498–506. Somerville, MA: Cascadilla Proceedings Project.

Wechsler, Stephen Mark. 2008b. Dualist syntax. In Stefan Müller (ed.), *Proceedings of the 15th International Conference on Head-Driven Phrase Structure Grammar*, 294–304. Stanford, CA: CSLI Publications. http://csli-publications.stanford.edu/HPSG/2008/, accessed 2018-2-25.

Wechsler, Stephen Mark & Bokyung Noh. 2001. On resultative predicates and clauses: Parallels between Korean and English. *Language Sciences* 23(4). 391–423.

Wegener, Heide. 1985. *Der Dativ im heutigen Deutsch* (Studien zur deutschen Grammatik 28). Tübingen: originally Gunter Narr Verlag now Stauffenburg Verlag.

Weir, Morton W. 1964. Developmental changes in problem-solving strategies. *Psychological Review* 71(6). 473–490.

Weissgerber, Monika. 1983. *Valenz und Kongruenzbeziehungen: Ein Modell zur Vereindeutigung von Verben in der maschinellen Analyse und Übersetzung*. Frankfurt a. M.: Peter Lang.

Weisweber, Wilhelm. 1987. *Ein Dominanz-Chart-Parser für generalisierte Phrasenstrukturgrammatiken*. KIT-Report 45. Berlin: Technische Universität Berlin.

Weisweber, Wilhelm & Susanne Preuss. 1992. Direct parsing with metarules. In Antonio Zampolli (ed.), *14th International Conference on Computational Linguistics (COLING '92), August 23–28*, 1111–1115. Nantes, France: Association for Computational Linguistics.

Welke, Klaus. 1988. *Einführung in die Valenz- und Kasustheorie*. Leipzig: Bibliographisches Institut.

Welke, Klaus. 2009. Konstruktionsvererbung, Valenzvererbung und die Reichweite von Konstruktionen. *Zeitschrift für Germanistische Linguistik* 37(3). 514–543.

Welke, Klaus. 2011. *Valenzgrammatik des Deutschen: Eine Einführung* (De Gruyter Studium). Berlin: de Gruyter.

Welke, Klaus. 2019. *Konstruktionsgrammatik des Deutschen: Ein sprachgebrauchsbezogener Ansatz* (Linguistik – Impulse & Tendenzen 77). Berlin: de Gruyter.

Wells, Rulon S. 1947. Immediate constituents. *Language* 23(2). 81–117.

Werner, Edeltraud. 1993. *Translationstheorie und Dependenzmodell: Kritik und Reinterpretation des Ansatzes von Lucien Tesnière* (Kultur und Erkenntnis: Schriften der Philosophischen Fakultät der Heinrich-Heine-Universität Düsseldorf 10). Tübingen: Francke Verlag.

Wetta, Andrew C. 2011. A Construction-based cross-linguistic analysis of V2 word order. In Stefan Müller (ed.), *Proceedings of the 18th International Conference on Head-Driven Phrase Structure Grammar, University of Washington*, 248–268. Stanford, CA: CSLI Publications. http://csli-publications.stanford.edu/HPSG/2011/, accessed 2018-2-25.

Wexler, Kenneth. 1998. Very early parameter setting and the unique checking constraint: A new explanation of the optional infinitive stage. *Lingua* 106(1–4). 23–79.

Wexler, Kenneth & Peter W. Culicover. 1980. *Formal principles of language acquisition*. Cambridge, MA/London: MIT Press.

Weydt, Harald. 1972. „UNENDLICHER GEBRAUCH VON ENDLICHEN MITTELN": MIßVERSTÄNDNISSE UM EIN LINGUISTISCHES THEOREM. *Poetica* 5(3/4). 249–267.

Wharton, R. M. 1974. Approximate language identification. *Information and Control* 26(3). 236–255.

White, Mike & Jason Baldridge. 2003. Adapting chart realization to CCG. In Ehud Reiter, Helmut Horacek & Kees van Deemter (eds.), *Proceedings of the 9th European Workshop on Natural Language Generation (ENLG-2003) at EACL 2003*, 119–126.

Wijnen, Frank, Masja Kempen & Steven Gillis. 2001. Root infinitives in Dutch early child language: An effect of input? *Journal of Child Language* 28(3). 629–660.

Wiklund, Anna-Lena, Gunnar Hrafn Hrafnbjargarson, Kristine Bentzen & Þorbjörg Hróarsdóttir. 2007. Rethinking Scandinavian verb movement. *Journal of Comparative Germanic Linguistics* 10(3). 203–233.

Wilcock, Graham. 2001. Towards a discourse-oriented representation of information structure in HPSG. In *13th Nordic Conference on Computational Linguistics, Uppsala, Sweden*. http://www.ling.helsinki.fi/~gwilcock/Pubs/2001/Nodalida-01.pdf, accessed 2018-2-25.

Wilcock, Graham. 2005. Information structure and Minimal Recursion Semantics. In Antti Arppe, Lauri Carlson, Krister Lindén, Jussi Piitulainen, Mickael Suominen, Martti Vainio, Hanna Westerlund & Anssi Yli-Jyrä (eds.), *Inquiries into words, constraints and contexts: Festschrift for Kimmo Koskenniemi on his 60th birthday* (CSLI Studies in Computational Linguistics ONLINE), 268–277. Stanford, CA: CSLI Publications.

References

Wilder, Chris. 1991. Small clauses and related objects. *Groninger Arbeiten zur Germanistischen Linguistik* 34. 215–236.

Williams, Edwin. 1984. Grammatical relations. *Linguistic Inquiry* 15(4). 639–673.

Winkler, Susanne. 1997. *Focus and secondary predication* (Studies in Generative Grammar 43). Berlin, New York: Mouton de Gruyter.

Wittenberg, Eva, Ray S. Jackendoff, Gina Kuperberg, Martin Paczynski, Jesse Snedeker & Heike Wiese. 2014. The processing and representation of light verb constructions. In Asaf Bachrach, Isabelle Roy & Linnaea Stockall (eds.), *Structuring the argument* (Language Faculty and Beyond 10), 61–80. Amsterdam: John Benjamins Publishing Co.

Wittenberg, Eva & Maria Mercedes Piñango. 2011. Processing light verb constructions. *The Mental Lexicon* 6(3). 393–413. DOI:10.1075/ml.6.3.03wit

Wöllstein, Angelika. 2010. *Topologisches Satzmodell* (Kurze Einführungen in die Germanistische Linguistik 8). Heidelberg: Universitätsverlag Winter.

Wunderlich, Dieter. 1987. Vermeide Pronomen – Vermeide leere Kategorien. *Studium Linguistik* 21. 36–44.

Wunderlich, Dieter. 1989. Arnim von Stechow, das Nichts und die Lexikalisten. *Linguistische Berichte* 122. 321–333.

Wunderlich, Dieter. 1992. *CAUSE and the structure of verbs*. Arbeiten des SFB 282 No. 36. Düsseldorf/Wuppertal: Heinrich Heine Uni/BUGH.

Wunderlich, Dieter. 1997. Argument extension by lexical adjunction. *Journal of Semantics* 14(2). 95–142. DOI:10.1093/jos/14.2.95

Wunderlich, Dieter. 2004. Why assume UG? *Studies in Language* 28(3). 615–641.

Wunderlich, Dieter. 2008. Spekulationen zum Anfang von Sprache. *Zeitschrift für Sprachwissenschaft* 27(2). 229–265.

Wurmbrand, Susanne. 2003a. *Infinitives: Restructuring and clause structure* (Studies in Generative Grammar 55). Berlin: Mouton de Gruyter.

Wurmbrand, Susanne. 2003b. *Long passive (corpus search results)*. Ms. University of Connecticut.

XTAG Research Group. 2001. *A lexicalized Tree Adjoining Grammar for English*. Tech. rep. Philadelphia: Institute for Research in Cognitive Science. ftp://ftp.cis.upenn.edu/pub/xtag/release-2.24.2001/tech-report.pdf, accessed 2015-12-23.

Yamada, Hiroyasu & Yuji Matsumoto. 2003. Statistical dependency analysis with support vector machines. In Gertjan van Noord (ed.), *Proceedings of the 8th International Workshop on Parsing Technologies (IWPT 03)*. Nancy.

Yamada, Jeni. 1981. *Evidence for the independence of language and cognition: case study of a "hyperlinguistic" adolescent*. UCLA Working Papers in Cognitive Linguistics 3. University of California, Los Angeles. 121–160.

Yampol, Todd & Lauri Karttunen. 1990. An efficient implementation of PATR for Categorial Unification Grammar. In Hans Karlgren (ed.), *COLING-90: Papers presented to the 13th International Conference on Computational Linguistics*, 419–424. Helsinki: Association for Computational Linguistics.

Yang, Charles D. 2004. Universal Grammar, statistics or both? *Trends in Cognitive Sciences* 8(10). 451–456. DOI:10.1016/j.tics.2004.08.006

Yang, Chunlei & Dan Flickinger. 2014. ManGO: Grammar engineering for deep linguistic processing. *New Technology of Library and Information Service* 30(3). 57–64.

Yasukawa, Hidekl. 1984. LFG System in Prolog. In Yorick Wilks (ed.), *Proceedings of the 10th International Conference on Computational Linguistics and 22nd Annual Meeting of the Association for Computational Linguistics*, 358–361. Stanford University, California: Association for Computational Linguistics.

Yip, Moira, Joan Maling & Ray S. Jackendoff. 1987. Case in tiers. *Language* 63(2). 217–250. DOI:10.2307/415655

Yoshinaga, Naoki, Yusuke Miyao, Kentaro Torisawa & Jun'ichi Tsujii. 2001. Resource sharing amongst HPSG and LTAG communities by a method of grammar conversion between FB-LTAG and HPSG. In *Proceedings of ACL/EACL workshop on Sharing Tools and Resources for Research and Education*, 39–46. Toulouse, France.

Zaenen, Annie & Ronald M. Kaplan. 1995. Formal devices for linguistic generalizations: West Germanic word order in LFG. In Mary Dalrymple, Ronald M. Kaplan, John T. Maxwell III & Annie Zaenen (eds.), *Formal issues in Lexical-Functional Grammar* (CSLI Lecture Notes 47), 215–239. Stanford, CA: CSLI Publications.

Zaenen, Annie & Ronald M. Kaplan. 2002. Subsumption and equality: German partial fronting in LFG. In Miriam Butt & Tracy Holloway King (eds.), *Proceedings of the LFG 2002 conference*. Stanford, CA: CSLI Publications. http://csli-publications.stanford.edu/LFG/7/, accessed 2018-2-25.

Zaenen, Annie, Joan Maling & Höskuldur Thráinsson. 1985. Case and grammatical functions: The Icelandic passive. *Natural Language and Linguistic Theory* 3(4). 441–483.

Zappa, Frank. 1986. *Does humor belong in music?* EMI Music Germany GmbH & Co. KG.

Ziem, Alexander & Alexander Lasch. 2013. *Konstruktionsgrammatik: Konzepte und Grundlagen gebrauchsbasierter Ansätze* (Germanistische Arbeitshefte 44). de Gruyter.

Zucchi, Alessandro. 1993. *The language of propositions and events: issues in the syntax and the semantics of nominalization* (Studies in Linguistics and Philosophy 51). Berlin: Springer Verlag.

Zwart, C. Jan-Wouter. 1994. Dutch is head-initial. *The Linguistic Review* 11(3–4). 377–406.

Zweigenbaum, Pierre. 1991. Un analyseur pour grammaires lexicales-fonctionnelles. *TA Informations* 32(2). 19–34.

Zwicky, Arnold M., Joyce Friedman, Barbara C. Hall & Donald E. Walker. 1965. The MITRE syntactic analysis procedure for Transformational Grammars. In *Proceedings – FALL Joint Computer Conference*, 317–326. DOI:10.1109/AFIPS.1965.108

Name index

Abbott, Barbara, 606
Abeillé, Anne, 121, 162, 163, 415, 416, 561, 562, 651, 681
Abney, Steven P., 29, 118–120, 128, 487, 502, 519, 539, 701
Abraham, Werner, 12, 153
Abzianidze, Lasha, 264
Ackerman, Farrell, 118, 536, 686, 701
Adams, Marianne, 465
Ades, Anthony E., 524
Adger, David, xvi, xxii, 127, 132–134, 136, 138–142, 148, 166, 173, 178, 558, 589, 591
Ágel, Vilmos, 365, 413
Aguado-Orea, Javier, 495, 540
Ahmed, Mohamed Ben, 415
Ahmed, Reaz, 263
Ajdukiewicz, Kazimierz, 160, 163, 245
Alqurashi, Abdulrahman, 568
Alsina, Alex, 38, 312, 454, 597, 602, 609
Altmann, Hans, 48
Ambridge, Ben, 463–465, 490, 494, 501, 546
Anderson, John M., 365
Anderson, Stephen R., 231
Andrews, Avery, 222
Aoun, Joseph, 120
Arad Greshler, Tali, 263, 264
Arends, Jacques, 479
Arka, I Wayan, 222
Arnold, Doug, 567
Arnold, Jennifer E., 523
Asher, Nicholas, 221
Ashwini, Vaidya, 679, 680
Askedal, John Ole, 43
Asudeh, Ash, xxi, 230, 242, 306, 312, 597, 609–612, 615, 619, 683
Attardi, Giuseppe, 366
Attia, Mohammed A., 221
Avgustinova, Tania, 265

Bach, Emmon, 62, 103
Backofen, Rolf, 263
Bahrani, Mohammad, 181
Baker, Carl Lee, 482, 488
Baker, Mark C., 450, 454, 458, 530
Baldridge, Jason, xvi, 163, 245, 246, 251[5], 253, 257, 261, 298, 576
Balla, Amar, 263
Ballweg, Joachim, 548
Baltin, Mark, 458, 459
Bangalore, Srinivas, 413
Bannard, Colin, 313, 566
Bar-Hillel, Yehoshua, 567, 569
Bargmann, Sascha, 411, 676
Barry, Guy, 261
Bartsch, Renate, 104, 161
Barwise, Jon, 280
Baschung, K., 245
Bates, Elizabeth A., 475, 477, 505
Baumgärtner, Klaus, 365, 369, 399
Bausewein, Karin, 157, 158, 286
Bayer, Josef, 101, 117
Beavers, John, 162, 163, 245, 304, 339, 652, 656
Bech, Gunnar, 47, 421, 434
Becker, Tilman, 96, 421, 423, 432
Beermann, Dorothee, 264
Beghelli, Filippo, 146
Behrens, Heike, 363, 475, 544, 653
Bellugi, Ursula, 481
Bender, Emily M., xvi, 6, 27, 119, 264, 265, 281, 307, 327, 328, 331, 334, 525, 560, 563, 568
Bentzen, Kristine, 146
Bergen, Benjamin K., 96, 311, 322, 323, 338, 340, 341, 542, 615, 637
Berman, Judith, 38, 75, 101, 103, 221, 233–236, 238, 241, 244, 431, 454, 456
Berwick, Robert C., 160, 172, 176, 489, 531, 532, 547

Name index

Bes, G. G., 245
Bever, Thomas G., 520
Bialystok, Ellen, 477
Bick, Eckhard, 367
Bickerton, Derek, 478
Bierwisch, Manfred, 6, 83, 103, 117, 119, 469
Bildhauer, Felix, xvi, 17, 148, 154, 265, 266, 309, 323, 347, 395
Bird, Steven, 266, 334
Bishop, Dorothy V. M., 480–482
Bjerre, Tavs, 658
Blackburn, Patrick, 81, 509, 576
Błaszczak, Joanna, 146, 178
Blevins, James P., 319
Block, Hans-Ulrich, 221
Blom, Corrien, 646, 658
Bloom, Paul, 118, 531, 533
Blutner, Reinhard, 575
Boas, Hans C., 327, 353, 362, 598
Bobaljik, Jonathan, 148
Bod, Rens, 489, 495, 496, 660, 661
Bögel, Tina, 222
Bohnet, Bernd, 366
Bolc, Leonard, 263
Bond, Francis, 263, 264
Booij, Geert E., 612, 658, 660
Borer, Hagit, 155, 604, 621, 627, 631, 636
Börschinger, Benjamin, 221
Borsley, Robert D., 123, 125, 148, 161, 162, 172, 178, 269, 293, 336, 362, 402, 568, 673, 813
Bos, Johan, 81, 576
Bosse, Solveig, 147
Bouchard, Lorne H., 181
Boukedi, Sirine, 263
Boullier, Pierre, 221
Bouma, Gerlof, 245
Bouma, Gosse, 168, 170, 172, 245, 264, 284, 296, 303, 322, 349, 381, 386, 509, 567, 568, 582, 592, 643, 683
Braine, Martin D. S., 466, 502
Branco, António, 264
Brants, Sabine, 461
Bredt, Thomas H., 120
Bresnan, Joan, 101, 125, 157, 162, 172, 221, 224, 226, 231, 232, 234, 236, 244, 319, 348, 451, 454, 547, 559, 564, 568, 581, 606, 610, 616, 617, 624
Brew, Chris, 265, 359
Briscoe, Ted, 123, 181, 246, 253, 261, 359, 466, 583, 601, 620, 700
Bröker, Norbert, 373
Brosziewski, Ulf, 132
Brown, Roger, 503
Bruening, Benjamin, 29, 147, 174, 613
Bryant, John, 312
Budde, Monika, xvi, 667
Bühler, Karl, 468[25]
Bungeroth, Jan, 265
Burzio, Luigi, 93, 113
Buscha, Joachim, 365
Busemann, Stephan, 203, 263
Bußmann, Hadumod, 13
Butt, Miriam, 221, 222, 656, 683

Cahill, Aoife, 222
Calder, Jo, 263
Calder, Jonathan, 245
Callmeier, Ulrich, 263
Candito, Marie-Hélène, 316, 415, 416, 418, 426, 638
Cappelle, Bert, 322, 345, 615, 657, 659, 660
Capstick, Joanne, 263
Cargo, Martha B., 481
Carlson, Gregory N., 654
Carnie, Andrew, 100
Carpenter, Bob, 205, 219, 245, 263
Carroll, John, 181
Cavar, Damir, 519
Çetinoğlu, Özlem, 222
Chang, Nancy, 96, 311, 312, 322, 323, 338, 340, 341, 542, 615, 637
Chatterjee, Sudipta, 245, 246
Chaudhuri, B. B., 221
Chaves, Rui P., 387, 568
Chesi, Cristiano, 4
Choi, Hye-Won, 234, 235
Chomsky, Noam, 4, 6, 75, 83–86, 89, 92–94, 96, 97, 100, 110, 112, 118, 120, 122, 127, 129, 134, 144, 145, 154–162, 165, 170–172, 175–179, 181, 268, 311, 319, 355, 432, 443, 447, 449, 450, 452, 454, 456, 458, 466–469, 471, 473–475, 478, 480, 482, 486,

487, 489, 502, 503, 517, 520, 523, 525, 526, 529, 535, 537–539, 547, 554, 568, 608, 616, 625–627, 699, 737, 738
Chouinard, Michelle M., 503
Christiansen, Morten, 465
Chrupala, Grzegorz, 222
Chung, Chan, 681
Chung, Sandra, 465
Church, Kenneth, 701
Cinque, Guglielmo, 145, 147, 150, 152, 175, 466, 467, 473, 696
Citko, Barbara, 157, 159
Clark, Alexander, 502
Clark, Eve V., 503
Clark, Herbert H., 522
Clark, Stephen, 245, 246
Clément, Lionel, 221, 316, 638
Clifton, Charles Jr., 519, 526
Coch, Jose, 367
Cole, Jennifer, 120, 519
Comrie, Bernard, 158, 163, 286
Cook, Philippa, xvi, 17, 39, 154, 221, 347, 395, 464
Cooper, Robin, 280
Coopmans, Peter, 567
Copestake, Ann, 177, 263, 264, 272, 282, 315, 327, 356, 359, 361, 420, 576, 583, 601, 620
Corluy, A., 245
Correa, Nelson, 120
Costa, Francisco, 264
Covington, Michael A., 367, 398
Crabbé, Benoit, 415
Crain, Stephen, 456, 457, 465, 494, 501, 524
Cramer, Bart, 265
Crocker, Matthew Walter, 120, 122, 123
Croft, William, 311, 312, 454, 467, 542, 597, 598, 603, 639–641, 654, 693
Crouch, Richard, 221
Crysmann, Berthold, 17, 104, 162, 163, 264, 266, 304, 339, 353, 652, 658
Csernyi, Gábor, 222
Culicover, Peter W., 83, 161, 166, 456, 474, 521, 538, 569, 597, 643, 644, 656
Culy, Christopher, 201, 415, 473, 547
Curran, James, 245

Curtiss, Susan, 477
Da Sylva, Lyne, 181
Dąbrowska, Ewa, 311, 363, 480, 482, 493, 541, 597
Dahl, Östen, 399, 407, 466
Dahllöf, Mats, 263, 264
Dale, Robert, 221
Dalrymple, Mary, 38, 101, 222, 223, 227–230, 234, 242, 244, 306, 312, 373, 454, 457, 554, 568, 574, 609, 683, 772
Davidson, Donald, 621
Davis, Anthony R., 282, 316, 638
De Alencar, Leonel, 221, 222, 244
De Beule, Joachim, 312
De Kuthy, Kordula, 15, 17, 119, 171, 264, 323, 347, 464, 548, 549
de Saussure, Ferdinand, 3, 469
Declerck, Thierry, 263
Dellert, Johannes, 415
Delmonte, Rodolfo, 221, 222
Demberg, Vera, 355
Demske, Ulrike, 29
den Besten, Hans, 117, 161
Deppermann, Arnulf, 362, 483, 612
Derbyshire, Desmond C., 471
Devlin, Keith, 280
Dhonnchadha, E. Uí, 367
Diagne, Abdel Kader, 263
Diesing, Molly, 102
Dini, Luca, 263
Dione, Cheikh Mouhamadou Bamba, 222
Dipper, Stefanie, 221
Donati, Caterina, 156
Donohue, Cathryn, 304
Doran, Christine, 415
Doran, Robert W., 120
Dorna, Michael, 263
Dörre, Jochen, 221, 263
Dowty, David, 6, 92, 161, 246, 249, 345, 575, 581, 604, 610, 621, 626, 630, 650
Dras, Mark, 221
Drellishak, Scott, 265
Drosdowski, Günther, 25, 41
Dryer, Matthew S., 103, 450, 451, 693
Dürscheid, Christa, 48, 117, 548
Dyvik, Helge, xvii, 222

Name index

Egg, Markus, 575, 577
Eichinger, Ludwig M., 413
Eikmeyer, Hans-Jürgen, 245
Eisele, Andreas, 221
Eisenberg, Peter, xvi, 13, 23–26, 28, 33, 35, 37, 42, 48, 49, 64, 72, 161, 268, 486
Elbourne, Paul, 116, 176, 527, 699
Ellefson, Michelle R., 465
Elman, Jeffrey L., 477, 479, 480, 490, 493, 494, 505
Embick, David, 621
Emirkanian, Louisette, 181
Engdahl, Elisabet, 347
Engel, Ulrich, 365, 368, 370, 371, 373, 374, 379, 403, 413, 549, 568
Epstein, Samuel David, 160, 172
Erbach, Gregor, 263
Ernst, Thomas, 152, 153
Eroms, Hans-Werner, 96, 245, 365, 370, 373–375, 377–379, 385, 391, 392, 410, 413, 568
Erteschik-Shir, Nomi, 462–465
Estigarribia, Bruno, 495
Estival, Dominique, 263
Evang, Kilian, 415
Evans, Nicholas, 451, 454, 457, 466, 467, 473, 696
Evans, Roger, 181
Everett, Daniel L., 470, 472
Evers, Arnold, 117, 119, 635
Evert, Stefan, xvi

Faaß, Gertrud, 222
Fabregas, Antonio, 159
Falk, Yehuda N., 122
Fan, Zhenzhen, 263, 264
Fang, Ji, 222
Fanselow, Gisbert, xvi, 83, 100, 110, 115–117, 119, 120, 125, 153, 170, 171, 245, 253, 297, 299, 396, 436, 454, 457, 464, 478, 519, 548, 593, 696, 697
Feldhaus, Anke, 103
Feldman, Jerome, 484
Felix, Sascha W., 83, 100, 110, 125
Filimonova, Elena, 449
Fillmore, Charles J., 68, 79, 122, 172, 311–315, 323–326, 338, 493, 562, 569, 601, 603, 638
Fischer, Ingrid, 561
Fischer, Kerstin, 362
Fischer, Klaus, 365
Fisher, Simon E., 480–482
Fitch, W. Tecumseh, 86, 145, 443, 458, 467, 469–471, 473, 474, 480, 482, 502
Flickinger, Dan, 119, 177, 210, 264, 265, 272, 282, 307, 315, 327, 331, 334, 345, 420, 560, 576, 584, 614
Fodor, Janet Dean, 518^2, 530, 531, 535, 536, 538
Fodor, Jerry A., 520
Fokkens, Antske, 264, 265
Fong, Sandiway, xvi, 120, 176
Fordham, Andrew, 120, 122, 123
Forst, Martin, 38, 221, 454
Fortmann, Christian, 548
Fourquet, Jean, 103
Fouvry, Frederik, 265
Fox Tree, Jean E., 522
Fraj, Fériel Ben, 415
Frank, Anette, 103, 221, 576, 755
Frank, Robert, 415
Franks, Steven, 492, 529
Frazier, Lyn, 518, 526
Freidin, Robert, 120, 181, 458, 697
Freudenthal, Daniel, 495, 539–541
Frey, Werner, 114, 115, 117, 123, 153, 160, 167, 221, 227, 306, 548
Fried, Mirjam, 311, 313
Friederici, Angela D., 477, 480
Friedman, Joyce, 120
Fries, Norbert, 286
Fukui, Naoki, 102
Fukumochi, Yasutomo, 367
Futrell, Richard, 470

Gaifman, Haim, 369, 398, 399
Gallmann, Peter, xviii, 125
Gardent, Claire, 221
Gardner, R. Allen, 479
Garrett, Merrill F., 520
Gärtner, Hans-Martin, xvi, 12, 146, 160, 167, 178, 548
Gazdar, Gerald, 120, 122, 123, 125, 163, 171, 181, 182, 184, 188, 189, 193–195,

199, 203, 307, 319, 350, 507, 509, 568
Geach, Peter Thomas, 171, 201, 681
Geißler, Stefan, 264
George, Marie St., 481
Gerdemann, Dale, 263
Gerdes, Kim, xvi, 367, 372, 415
Gerken, LouAnn, 533
Ghayoomi, Masood, 264, 690
Gibson, Edward, 297, 432, 450, 465, 470, 518, 519, 530–532, 635
Gillis, Steven, 539, 540
Ginsburg, Jason, 120, 176
Ginzburg, Jonathan, xxii, 122, 163, 169, 172, 272, 280, 305, 399, 408, 483, 493, 495, 538, 673
Giorgolo, Gianluca, xxi, 615
Gipper, Helmut, 41
Glauert, John, 265
Gobet, Fernand, 495, 539–541
Godard, Danièle, 681
Gold, Mark E., 483
Goldberg, Adele E., xvi, 311–313, 322, 343, 345, 362, 363, 463–465, 503, 505, 539, 542, 546, 566, 569, 597–601, 603, 604, 609, 612, 646, 653, 654, 656, 657, 697
Gopnik, Myrna, 481
Gordon, Peter, 482, 486
Gosch, Angela, 481
Götz, Thilo, 263
Grebe, Paul, 41
Green, Georgia M., 544
Grewendorf, Günther, 83, 93, 94, 98, 100, 105, 109, 113, 117, 119, 125, 127, 145, 178, 286, 455, 548, 567, 644
Gries, Stephan Th., 661, 663
Grimshaw, Jane, xvi, 157, 465, 656
Grinberg, Dennis, 366
Grohmann, Kleantes K., 151, 178, 469, 470
Groos, Anneke, 158
Groß, Thomas M., xvi, 158, 197, 374, 377, 379, 380, 390, 395, 407, 413, 569, 593, 594, 658
Groß, Thomas Michael, 35, 409
Grosu, Alexander, 465
Grover, Claire, 181

Grubačić, Emilija, 659
Guillotin, T., 245
Gunji, Takao, 593
Günther, Carsten, 347
Guo, Yuqing, 222
Guzmán Naranjo, Matías, 359

Haddar, Kais, 263
Haegeman, Liliane, 97, 98, 100, 125, 148, 553, 557, 588
Haftka, Brigitta, 94, 153
Hagen, Kristin, 367
Hahn, Michael, 263
Haider, Hubert, 75, 83, 100, 101, 103, 110, 113, 117, 118, 123, 148, 151, 152, 171, 234, 243, 286, 288, 290, 297, 306, 346, 426, 454, 455, 460, 529, 548, 563, 567, 593, 629, 695, 696, 699
Hajičová, Eva, 365
Hakuta, Kenji, 476, 477
Hale, Kenneth, 133, 471, 621
Hall, Barbara C., 120
Han, Chung-hye, 416
Hanlon, Camille, 503
Harley, Heidi, 625
Harlow, Ray, 29
Harman, Gilbert, 81, 181
Harris, Zellig S., 4
Hasan, K. M. Azharul, 263
Haspelmath, Martin, xvi, xix, 95[7], 447, 467, 530, 693, 694
Haugereid, Petter, 264, 285, 305, 621, 629, 631, 633, 634, 701
Hauser, Marc D., 86, 145, 443, 458, 467, 469, 473, 474, 480, 482, 502
Hausser, Roland, 524
Hawkins, John A., 297, 451, 462, 465
Hays, David G., 366, 367, 369, 399
Heinecke, Johannes, 367
Heinz, Wolfgang, 109, 243, 629
Helbig, Gerhard, 365
Hellan, Lars, 29, 264, 701
Hellwig, Peter, 365, 367, 372, 373, 398, 405, 407, 413, 547, 699
Her, One-Soon, 221, 222
Heringer, Hans Jürgen, 375, 378, 379, 413
Heringer, Hans-Jürgen, 96, 366, 369, 378, 399

Name index

Herring, Joshua, 176
Herzig Sheinfux, Livnat, 263, 264
Higginbotham, James, 307, 564
Higinbotham, Dan, 221, 222
Hildebrandt, Bernd, 245
Hinkelman, Elizabeth A., 263
Hinrichs, Erhard W., 119, 171, 264, 289, 307, 375, 433, 583, 592, 595, 635, 681
Hinterhölzel, Roland, 153
Hoberg, Ursula, 434, 591
Hockenmaier, Julia, 245, 246
Hockett, Charles F., 471
Hockey, Beth Ann, 415
Hoeksema, Jack, 646
Hoekstra, Teun, 268
Hoffman, Beryl Ann, 245, 253, 298
Hofman, Ute, 48
Hofmeister, Philip, 465
Höhle, Tilman N., 43, 52, 101, 103, 114, 253, 266, 292, 513, 592, 766, 767
Holler, Anke, 272
Holmberg, Anders, 530
Hornstein, Norbert, 128, 151, 175, 178, 466, 469, 470, 475
Hrafnbjargarson, Gunnar Hrafn, 146
Hróarsdóttir, Þorbjörg, 146
Huang, Wei, 367
Hudson Kam, Carla L., 479
Hudson, Carla L., 479
Hudson, Dick, 365
Hudson, Richard, xvi, 29, 365–369, 373–375, 379–382, 385, 390, 403, 405, 406, 408, 409, 475
Hukari, Thomas E., 567, 568
Humboldt, Wilhelm von, 468
Hunze, Rudolf, 221
Hurford, James R., 475, 494
Hurskainen, Arvi, 367

Ibbotson, Paul, 695
Ichiyama, Shunji, 367
Imrényi, András, 365
Ingram, David, 541
Iordanskaja, L., 367
Islam, Md. Asfaqul, 263
Islam, Muhammad Sadiqul, 263

Jackendoff, Ray S., 75, 83, 94, 96, 119, 144, 161, 163, 166, 288, 312, 355, 363, 411, 451, 456, 467, 474, 494, 521, 525, 527, 528, 538, 569, 583, 597, 609, 643, 644, 646, 656, 666, 675, 676, 686
Jacobs, Joachim, 103, 194, 252, 362, 665, 686
Jacobson, Pauline, 194, 203, 293
Jaeggli, Osvaldo A., 588
Jäger, Gerhard, 575
Jäppinen, H., 367
Jäppinen, Harri, 367
Johannessen, Janne Bondi, 367
Johnson, David E., 144
Johnson, Jacqueline S., 476, 477
Johnson, Kent, 485, 486
Johnson, Mark, 122, 198, 200, 205, 219, 221, 222, 355, 439, 524–526, 547
Johnson, Mark H., 477, 505
Jones, Wendy, 481
Joshi, Aravind K., 96, 339, 413, 415, 416, 418, 420, 421, 423, 425–427, 432–434, 437–439, 630, 650, 651
Jungen, Oliver, xvi
Jurafsky, Daniel, 313, 566

Kahane, Sylvain, xvi, 365, 367, 370, 372, 379, 385, 389, 390, 399, 410, 418
Kallmeyer, Laura, xvi, 313, 316, 415, 416, 418, 420, 437, 439, 568, 637–639
Kamp, Hans, 227
Kanerva, Jonni M., 232
Kaplan, Ronald M., 123, 125, 221, 222, 226, 231, 234, 235, 238, 240, 242, 306, 324, 454, 470, 509, 547, 568, 581, 683, 772
Karimi-Doostan, Gholamhossein, 148
Karimi, Simin, 148
Karmiloff-Smith, Annette, 477, 481, 482, 505
Karttunen, Lauri, 236, 245
Kasper, Robert T., 104, 191, 296, 322, 399, 438, 555
Kasper, Walter, 177, 263, 264, 359
Kathol, Andreas, 48, 197, 289, 296, 304, 339, 347, 354, 397, 402, 647, 658, 681
Kaufmann, Ingrid, 610
Kaufmann, Tobias, 263, 264, 701

Name index

Kay, Martin, 120, 122, 366, 701
Kay, Paul, xvi, 311–315, 323–327, 331, 338, 362, 493, 562, 601, 610, 614, 638, 640
Kayne, Richard S., 147, 161, 162, 175, 297, 685, 695
Keenan, Edward L., 158, 163, 286
Keil, Martina, 561
Keller, Frank, 172, 264, 353, 355, 510
Kempen, Masja, 539, 540
Kern, Franz, 365
Kern, Sabine, 519
Kettunen, Kimmo, 367
Keyser, Samuel Jay, 133, 621
Khlentzos, Drew, 456, 457, 465
Kibort, Anna, 615
Kiefer, Bernd, 263, 361, 438
Kifle, Nazareth Amlesom, 222
Kim, Jong-Bok, 4, 125, 264, 298, 468, 469, 483
Kim, Nari, 416
Kimball, John P., 482, 487
King, Paul, 205, 219, 266, 470, 509, 655
King, Tracy Holloway, 221, 222, 242, 306
Kinyon, Alexandra, 221, 316, 416, 426, 638
Kiparsky, Carol, 464
Kiparsky, Paul, 464
Kiss, Katalin E., 148
Kiss, Tibor, xvi, 81, 103, 115, 116, 119, 253, 264, 286, 453, 460, 593, 681, 705
Klann-Delius, Gisela, xvi, 546
Klein, Ewan, 120, 163, 181, 182, 184, 188, 189, 193, 203, 245, 266, 319, 334, 507, 511, 568
Klein, Wolfgang, 161, 286, 366, 383, 475, 476, 486
Klenk, Ursula, 85, 86
Kliegl, Reinhold, 519
Kluender, Robert, 465, 475
Knecht, Laura, 319
Kobele, Gregory M., 171
Koenig, Jean-Pierre, 282, 316, 318, 360, 638, 643, 669, 683, 692
Kohl, Dieter, 221
Kohl, Karen T., 532
Koit, Mare, 367
Kolb, Hans-Peter, 120, 122, 123, 144
Koller, Alexander, 415

Komarova, Natalia L., 4, 468, 530
Konieczny, Lars, 351, 355
König, Esther, 245, 568
Koopman, Hilda, 100, 102
Kordoni, Valia, 264, 316, 638
Kornai, András, 77, 120, 452
Kornai, András, 470
Kornfilt, Jaklin, 101, 117
Koster, Jan, 103, 104, 113, 114, 117, 306, 459, 460
Kouylekov, Milen, 263
Kratzer, Angelika, 117, 548, 558, 621–624
Krieger, Hans-Ulrich, 263, 320, 361, 612, 639
Krifka, Manfred, 475
Kroch, Anthony S., 415, 425, 439, 568, 630
Kropp Dakubu, Mary Esther, 264
Kruijff, Geert-Jan M., 576
Kruijff-Korbayová, Ivana, 223
Kübler, Sandra, 366
Kuhn, Jonas, xvi, 125, 178, 221, 231, 232, 243, 347, 527, 528, 538
Kuhns, Robert J., 120
Kunze, Jürgen, 366, 379, 390, 629
Kuperberg, Gina, 656
Kupść, Anna, 264, 309
Kutas, Marta, 465

Labelle, Marie, 520
Laczkó, Tibor, 222
Laenzlinger, Christoph, 142, 143, 147, 149, 153, 297
Lai, Cecilia S. L., 481
Lai, Zona, 481
Lakoff, George, 311, 508
Lamping, John, 227, 373, 683
Langacker, Ronald W., 311, 341, 597, 598
Lappin, Shalom, 120, 144, 462–464
Lareau, François, 221
Larson, Richard K., 111, 133, 160, 166, 567, 587
Lascarides, Alex, 583
Lasch, Alexander, 641
Laskri, Mohamed Tayeb, 263
Lasnik, Howard, 490, 526
Lavoie, Benoit, 367
Le, Hong Phuong, 416
Lee-Goldmann, Russell R., 79
Legate, Julie, 490–492

829

Name index

Lehtola, Aarno, 367
Leiss, Elisabeth, 4, 403, 517, 565
Lenerz, Jürgen, 12, 112, 117, 119, 142, 591
Lenneberg, Eric H., 476, 477
Levelt, Willem J. M., 244
Levin, Beth, 630
Levine, Robert D., xvi, 144, 309, 355, 356, 359, 386, 567, 568
Levinson, Stephen C., 451, 454, 457, 466, 467, 473, 696
Levy, Leon S., 415, 439
Lewin, Ian, 120, 122
Lewis, Geoffrey L., 319, 638
Lewis, John D., 490, 493
Lewis, Richard L., 519
Li, Charles N., 672
Li, Wei, 264
Liakata, Maria, 222
Lichte, Timm, xvi, 313, 415, 423, 437
Lichtenberger, Liz, 481
Lieb, Hans-Heinrich, xvi
Lieven, Elena, 313, 546, 566
Lightfoot, David W., 120, 539
Lin, Dekang, 120, 122, 123
Link, Godehard, 453
Lipenkova, Janna, 264, 362, 672, 690
Liu, Gang, 264
Liu, Haitao, xvi, 367
Lloré, F. Xavier, 245
Lobin, Henning, 261, 366, 413
Löbner, Sebastian, 567
Lødrup, Helge, 38, 454
Lohndal, Terje, 621, 622, 630
Lohnstein, Horst, xvi, 97, 113, 120, 123, 125, 520, 567, 588
Longobardi, Giuseppe, 475
Lorenz, Konrad, 476
Lötscher, Andreas, 563
Loukam, Mourad, 263
Lüdeling, Anke, xvi, 660
Luuk, Erkki, 469, 470, 474
Luuk, Hendrik, 469, 470, 474

Maas, Heinz Dieter, 367
Maché, Jakob, 667, 671
Machicao y Priemer, Antonio, 264, 309, 690
Maché, Jakob, xvi

Mack, Jennifer, 656
Mackie, Lisa, 222
MacWhinney, Brian, 488
Maess, Burkhard, 480
Maier, Wolfgang, 415
Maling, Joan, 119, 191, 233, 288, 628
Malouf, Robert, 170, 264, 284, 303, 322, 349, 381, 386, 567, 568, 582, 643, 683
Manandhar, Suresh, 263
Manshadi, Mehdi Hafezi, 181
Marantz, Alec, 155, 520, 523, 621, 623, 625, 667
Marciniak, Małgorzata, 264
Marcus, Gary F., 480–482, 503
Marcus, Mitchell P., 120, 121
Marimon, Montserrat, 265
Marshall, Ian, 265
Marslen-Wilson, William D., 522
Martinet, André, 468[25]
Martner, Theodore S., 120
Martorell, Jordi, 4
Masuichi, Hiroshi, 222
Masum, Mahmudul Hasan, 263
Matiasek, Johannes, 109, 243, 629
Matsumoto, Yuji, 366
Maxwell III, John T., 221, 772
Mayo, Bruce, 221, 222
McCawley, James D., 465
McCloskey, James, 465
Mchombo, Sam A., 231, 610
McIntyre, Andrew, xvi
McKean, Kathryn Ojemann, 519
Meinunger, André, 97, 117, 142, 146, 581
Meisel, Jürgen, 451, 478, 529, 546
Meisel, Jürgen M., 476
Mel'čuk, Igor A., 365–367, 373, 406
Melnik, Nurit, 263, 264
Mensching, Guido, xvi, xviii, 537
Menzel, Wolfgang, 367
Metcalf, Vanessa, 264
Meurer, Paul, 221, 222
Meurers, Walt Detmar, 17, 103, 119, 171, 263, 264, 288, 289, 295, 307, 309, 345, 355, 356, 359, 402, 434, 461, 560, 563, 583, 646, 681, 701
Meza, Iván V., 265
Micelli, Vanessa, 313, 320

Name index

Michaelis, Jens, xvi, 164, 167, 547, 548
Michaelis, Laura A., xvi, 243, 312, 316, 326, 327, 362, 569, 638, 699
Michelson, Karin, 360, 692
Miller, George A., 432, 517, 519
Miller, Philip H., 681
Mineur, Anne-Marie, 263
Mistica, Meladel, 222
Mittendorf, Ingo, 222
Miyao, Yusuke, 265, 438
Moeljadi, David, 264
Moens, Marc, 700
Mohanan, KP, 38, 454
Mohanan, Tara, 38, 454
Mok, Eva, 312
Momma, Stefan, 221
Monachesi, Paola, 681
Montague, Richard, 188
Moortgat, Michael, 246
Moot, Richard, 245
Morgan, James L., 485
Morin, Yves Ch., 120
Morrill, Glyn, 245, 246, 259
Moshier, Andrew M., 318
Motazedi, Yasaman, 221
Muischnek, Kadri, 367
Mukai, Kuniaki, 280
Müller, Gereon, xvi, 94, 117, 119, 143, 171, 174, 415, 667–669, 676
Müller, Max, 474
Müller, Natascha, 476
Müller, Stefan, xv, xix, xxi–xxiii, 6, 15, 29, 35, 42, 103, 110, 119, 148, 155, 157, 158, 160, 163, 164, 167, 168, 170–173, 177, 178, 180, 219, 231, 243, 251, 263–265, 271, 274, 281, 285, 286, 288–290, 294, 296, 304–307, 309, 311–313, 318–320, 324, 329, 334, 336, 337, 342–344, 347, 353, 354, 356, 359–363, 395–397, 402, 409, 410, 426, 433, 436, 447, 454, 457, 459, 461, 469, 473, 514, 515, 542, 548, 560, 563, 567, 581–584, 592, 598, 600, 603, 606, 610–613, 615, 618, 619, 621, 624, 629, 634, 635, 640, 641, 643–648, 654–656, 658–660, 671, 672, 679, 681, 683, 684, 688, 690, 694, 701, 705, 716
Muraki, Kazunori, 366, 367
Musso, Mariacristina, 480, 695
Müürisep, Kaili, 367
Muysken, Pieter, 76, 162
Mykowiecka, Agnieszka, 264

Nakayama, Mineharu, 494, 501
Nakazawa, Tsuneko, 119, 171, 289, 307, 375, 433, 583, 592, 595, 635, 681
Nasr, Alexis, 390
Naumann, Sven, 181
Nederhof, Mark-Jan, 361
Neeleman, Ad, 312
Nelimarkka, Esa, 367
Nerbonne, John, 198, 200, 280, 305, 320, 454, 576, 612, 639
Netter, Klaus, 29, 81, 103, 251, 252, 263, 264, 305, 433, 438, 694, 704
Neu, Julia, 264
Neumann, Günter, 263
Neville, Anne, 263
Nevins, Andrew Ira, 470
Newmeyer, Frederick J., 451, 452, 458, 467, 475, 530, 538, 539, 567, 693
Newport, Elissa L., 476, 477, 479
Ng, Say Kiat, 264
Nguyen, Thi Minh Huyen, 416
Niño, María-Eugenia, 222
Nivre, Joakim, 366
Niyogi, Partha, 4, 468, 530–532
Noh, Bokyung, 583, 610, 635
Nøklestad, Anders, 367
Nolda, Andreas, xvi
Nomura, Hirosato, 367
Noonan, Michael, 319, 638
Nordgård, Torbjørn, xvii, 120
Nordhoff, Sebastian, xvi, xx, 613
Nordlinger, Rachel, 222, 307
Nowak, Martin A., 4, 468, 530
Noyer, Rolf, 625
Nozohoor-Farshi, R., 121
Nunberg, Geoffrey, 538, 601, 624, 625, 640, 658
Nunes, Jairo, 151, 171, 178, 469, 470
Nygaard, Lars, 367
Nykiel, Joanna, 483

831

Name index

O'Connor, Mary Catherine, 311
O'Donovan, Ruth, 222
O'Neill, Michael, 4, 469
Ochs, Elinor, 494, 503
Odom, Penelope, 519
Oepen, Stephan, 119, 263, 265
Ørsnes, Bjarne, xvi
Oflazer, Kemal, 222
Ohkuma, Tomoko, 222
Oliva, Karel, 103, 293, 398, 406, 413
Oppenrieder, Wilhelm, 117, 592
Orgun, Cemil Orhan, 266
Ørsnes, Bjarne, 104, 107, 164, 171, 221, 263, 265, 690
Osborne, Miles, 246
Osborne, Timothy, xvi, xxiii, 158, 197, 374, 377, 379, 380, 389, 390, 395, 407, 409, 410, 413, 569, 593, 594, 658
Osenova, Petya, 263
Osswald, Rainer, 316, 637–639
Ott, Dennis, 158
Özkaragöz, İnci, 319, 638

Packard, Woodley, 263
Paczynski, Martin, 656
Pafel, Jürgen, 48, 548
Paggio, Patrizia, 263, 347
Palmer, Alexis, 245, 246
Palmer, Martha, 416, 679
Pankau, Andreas, xvi, xviii
Pankau, Rainer, 481
Parisi, Domenico, 477, 505
Parmentier, Yannick, 415
Partee, Barbara H., 584
Patejuk, Agnieszka, 222
Paul, Hermann, 46
Paul, Soma, 263
Penn, Gerald, 263, 356
Pentheroudakis, Joseph, 221, 222
Perchonock, Ellen, 519
Pereira, Fernando, 338
Perles, Micha A., 567, 569
Perlmutter, David M., xvi, 93, 119, 140, 286, 453, 644
Perry, John, 280
Pesetsky, David, 470, 625, 627, 695
Peters, Stanley, 86

Petrick, Stanley Roy, 120
Pfister, Beat, 264, 701
Phillips, Colin, 355, 519, 525
Phillips, John D., 181
Piantadosi, Steven T., 470
Piattelli-Palmarini, Massimo, 489
Pickering, Martin, 261
Pienemann, Manfred, 244
Pietroski, Paul, 176, 489
Pietsch, Christian, xvi
Pihko, Elina, 659
Piñango, Maria Mercedes, 656
Pine, Julian M., 494, 495, 501, 539–541
Pineda, Luis Alberto, 265
Pinker, Steven, 86, 144, 244, 449–451, 454, 466, 467, 469, 474, 480, 666
Pittner, Karin, 286
Plainfossé, Agnes, 221
Plank, Frans, 449, 449[4]
Plath, Warren J., 120, 122
Plunkett, Kim, 477, 505
Poletto, Cecilia, 146, 153
Pollack, Bary W., 120
Pollard, Carl J., 29, 35, 156, 170, 171, 203, 205, 210, 256–259, 263, 265, 268, 269, 272, 274, 280–282, 284, 289, 297, 300, 305, 307, 315, 318, 319, 327, 328, 334, 336, 337, 354, 397, 410, 420, 470, 527, 536, 547, 554, 559, 560, 562, 563, 568, 574, 576, 582, 629, 655
Pollock, Jean-Yves, 100, 145, 148, 231
Popowich, Fred, 263
Porzel, Robert, 338
Postal, Paul M., 120, 470, 567
Poulson, Laurie, 265
Preuss, Susanne, 181, 191, 193
Prince, Alan, xvi
Przepiórkowski, Adam, 119, 222, 264, 288, 307, 309, 560, 563
Pullum, Geoffrey K., xvi, xix, 4, 77, 86, 93, 120, 158, 163, 181, 182, 184, 185, 188, 189, 193, 201, 203, 286, 319, 415, 452, 469–471, 473, 482, 484–489, 492, 495, 496, 503, 505, 507–511, 529, 568
Pulman, Stephen G., 524

Pulvermüller, Friedemann, 4, 494, 505, 657, 659, 660
Puolakainen, Tiina, 367
Putnam, Michael, 158, 413

Quaglia, Stefano, 222

Radford, Andrew, 150, 178, 539
Rahman, M. Sohel, 263
Rahman, Md. Mizanur, 263
Rákosi, György, 222
Rambow, Owen, 96, 221, 367, 390, 413, 415, 416, 421, 423, 426, 427, 430–432, 436, 437, 439, 568, 679
Ramchand, Gillian, 584
Randriamasimanana, Charles, 222
Raposo, Eduardo, 492, 529
Rappaport Hovav, Malka, 626, 630
Rauh, Gisa, 155
Rawlins, Kyle, 473
Reape, Mike, 96, 221, 296, 303, 304, 323, 339, 347, 354, 361, 548, 658
Redington, Martin, 502
Reis, Marga, 35, 36, 43, 49, 52, 103, 104, 117, 455
Remberger, Eva-Maria, 492, 537
Resnik, Philip, 416
Reyle, Uwe, 221, 227, 576
Rhomieux, Russell, 79
Richards, Marc, 129, 144, 520, 523
Richter, Frank, xvi, xvii, 178, 205, 219, 263, 280, 304, 329, 331, 333, 337, 356, 358, 390, 470, 560, 564, 696
Rieder, Sibylle, 263
Riemer, Beate, 476
Riemsdijk, Henk van, 95, 467
Riezler, Stefan, 221, 222
Ritchie, R. W., 86
Rizzi, Luigi, 145, 146, 148, 150, 153, 175, 456, 458, 466, 467, 473, 529, 696
Roberts, Ian, 475, 530
Robins, Robert Henry, xvi
Robinson, Jane, 338
Rodrigues, Cilene, 470
Rogers, James, 123, 470, 509
Rohrer, Christian, 221, 222
Romero, Maribel, 439
Roosmaa, Tiit, 367

Rosén, Victoria, 222
Ross, John Robert, 119, 199, 258, 350, 453, 458, 462, 806
Roth, Sebastian, 222
Rothkegel, Annely, 366
Roussanaly, Azim, 416
Rowland, Caroline F., 494, 501
Ruppenhofer, Josef, 243, 312, 316, 326, 569, 638, 699

Sabel, Joachim, 548
Sadler, Louisa, 222
Sáfár, Éva, 265
Safir, Kenneth J., 567
Sag, Ivan A., xvi, xxi–xxiii, 27, 29, 120, 122, 153, 156, 162, 163, 169–172, 177, 181, 182, 184, 188, 189, 193, 203, 205, 210, 258, 263, 264, 267–269, 272, 274, 280–282, 284, 297, 300, 303–305, 312, 315, 318, 319, 322, 327, 328, 334–339, 347, 349, 355, 358, 361, 362, 381, 386, 399, 408, 410, 420, 465, 483, 493, 495, 507, 519, 522, 524, 525, 527, 528, 536, 538, 554, 559, 560, 562, 563, 567, 568, 576, 582, 610, 614, 624, 625, 629, 640, 643, 647, 652, 655, 658, 660, 673, 674, 681, 683
Sagot, Benoît, 221
Sailer, Manfred, 280, 304, 329, 331, 337, 560, 561, 564
Saito, Mamoru, 526
Samarin, William J., 479
Sameti, Hossein, 181
Sampson, Geoffrey, 475, 476, 490
Samvelian, Pollet, 453, 681
Saraswat, Vijay, 227, 373, 683
Sarkar, Anoop, 339, 415, 650, 651
Sato, Yo, 263, 304
Sauerland, Uli, xvi, 116, 176, 527, 699
Savin, Harris B., 519
Schabes, Yves, 416, 439, 561, 562
Schäfer, Roland, xvi, xviii, 250[4]
Scheffler, Tatjana, 416, 426
Schein, Barry, 621, 622
Schenkel, Wolfgang, 365
Scherpenisse, Wim, 108, 117, 197, 377

Name index

Schieffelin, Bambi B., 494, 503
Schlesewsky, Matthias, 519
Schluter, Natalie, 222
Schmidt, Paul, 263
Scholz, Barbara C., 4, 86, 469–471, 482, 485–489, 492, 495, 496, 503, 505, 508–511, 529
Schröder, Ingo, 367
Schubert, K., 366
Schumacher, Helmut, 365
Schütz, Jörg, 263
Schwarze, Christoph, xvi, 221, 244
Segond, Frédérique, 222
Seiffert, Roland, 263
Seiss, Melanie, 222
Sells, Peter, 4, 125, 264, 468, 469
Sengupta, Probal, 221
Seuren, Pieter A. M., 144, 479
Sgall, Petr, 365
Shamir, Eliahu, 567, 569
Shieber, Stuart M., 201, 205, 219, 338, 355, 415, 439, 473, 524, 525, 547
Shtyrov, Yury, 657, 659, 660
Siegel, Melanie, 177, 264
Simov, Alexander, 263
Simov, Kiril, 263
Simpson, Jane, 222, 312, 563, 610, 809
Singleton, Jenny L., 479
Slayden, Glenn C., 263
Sleator, Daniel D. K., 366, 367
Smith, Carlota S., 626, 627
Smolensky, Paul, xvi
Snedeker, Jesse, 656
Snider, Neal, 462, 465
Snyder, William, 529
Soehn, Jan-Philipp, 337
Son, Minjeong, 530, 537
Song, Sanghoun, 263, 264
Sorace, Antonella, 510
Spackman, Stephen P., 263
Speas, Margaret, 102
Spencer, Andrew, 567
Sportiche, Dominique, 100, 102, 120
Srinivas, Bangalore, 415
Stabler, Edward, 100, 120, 121, 145, 164, 165, 167, 175–177, 308, 456, 524, 526, 527, 547, 564, 699

Städing, Gabriele, 481
Stark, Elisabeth, xviii
Starosta, Stanley, 367, 568
Stearns, Laura, 470
Stede, Manfred, 245
Steedman, Mark J., 160, 161, 163, 168, 223, 245–247, 251, 253–258, 261, 298, 321, 511, 524, 527, 649, 650, 662, 701
Steels, Luc, 312, 313, 342, 345, 346, 361
Stefanowitsch, Anatol, 362, 504, 661, 663
Steinbach, Markus, 12, 117, 548
Sternefeld, Wolfgang, xvii, 83, 98, 101, 117, 125, 145, 150, 151, 178, 234, 390, 454, 523, 567, 696
Stickel, Gerhard, 245
Stiebels, Barbara, 657
Stowell, Timothy, 146, 463
Strunk, Jan, xvi, 462
Suchsland, Peter, 548
Suckow, Katja, 519
Sulger, Sebastian, 222
Svenonius, Peter, 148, 530, 537

Tabbert, Eric, 245
Takahashi, Masako, 415, 439
Takami, Ken-ichi, 464
Tanenhaus, Michael K., 522, 523, 654
Temperley, Davy, 366, 367
Ten Hacken, Pius, 123, 512
Tesnière, Lucien, 31, 365, 372, 382, 383, 389, 410, 413
Theofilidis, Axel, 263
Thiersch, Craig L., 103, 117, 120, 122, 123
Thomas, James, 518
Thompson, Henry S., 125, 181, 190
Thompson, Sandra A., 672
Thompson, William, 541
Thornton, Rosalind, 456, 457, 465
Thráinsson, Höskuldur, 191, 233, 628
Timberlake, Alan, 319, 638
Toivonen, Ida, xxi, 242, 306, 312, 609–611, 615, 616, 619, 683
Tomasello, Michael, 86, 118, 313, 363, 449, 467, 473, 478, 481, 486, 503, 505, 539, 541, 542, 546, 566, 597–600, 603, 695

Torisawa, Kentaro, 438
Tóth, Ágoston, 222
Travis, Lisa, 451
Trinh, Tue H., 520
Trosterud, Trond, 367
Tseng, Jesse, 264, 285
Tsujii, Jun'ichi, 265, 438
Turpin, Myfany, 221
Tyson, Mabry, 338

Uibo, Heli, 367
Ulinski, Morgan, 221
Umemoto, Hiroshi, 222
Uriagereka, Juan, 490, 492, 529
Uszkoreit, Hans, 96, 182, 190, 194, 201, 203, 245, 253, 263, 338, 420, 432, 461, 518, 568

Valian, Virginia, 533–535
Valkonen, K., 367
Vallduví, Enric, 347
Van Eynde, Frank, 337
Van Genabith, Josef, 222, 367
Van Langendonck, Willy, 29, 368
Van Noord, Gertjan, 168, 245, 264, 296, 322, 509, 592
Van Riemsdijk, Henk, 158
Van Trijp, Remi, xvi, 342–349, 351, 353–356, 361, 615
Van Valin, Robert D. Jr., xvi, 464
Vancoppenolle, Jean, 245
Vargha-Khadem, Faraneh, 481
Vasishth, Shravan, xvi, 519
Vater, Heinz, 83
Veenstra, Mettina Jolanda Arnoldina, 120, 123, 166, 176, 205, 456, 509, 568, 699
Velupillai, Viveka, 466
Vennemann, Theo, 29, 104, 161
Verhagen, Arie, 565
Verspoor, Cornelia Maria, 583, 610
Vierhuff, Tilman, 245
Vijay-Shanker, K., 421, 427, 438
Villavicencio, Aline, 245, 246, 253, 261, 467, 493, 700
Vogel, Carl, 263
Vogel, Ralf, 117, 158, 548
Volk, Martin, 181

Von Stechow, Arnim, 83, 98, 117, 125, 146, 245, 567, 575, 581
Voutilainen, Atro, 367

Wada, Hajime, 221
Wahlster, Wolfgang, 177, 265
Walker, Donald E., 120
Walther, Markus, 266, 334
Wasow, Thomas, xvi, 27, 210, 263, 265, 281, 307, 327, 328, 355, 519, 522, 524, 525, 528, 538, 568, 624, 625, 640, 658
Webelhuth, Gert, 113, 117, 118, 146, 536, 674, 686, 701
Weber, Heinz J., 366, 383, 388
Wechsler, Stephen Mark, xvi, 155, 160, 167, 282, 312, 320, 343, 353, 363, 542, 583, 598, 608–611, 618, 619, 624–627, 635
Wedekind, Jürgen, 221, 683
Wegener, Heide, 435
Weir, David, 421
Weir, Morton W., 479
Weissgerber, Monika, 366
Weisweber, Wilhelm, 181, 191, 193
Welke, Klaus, xxiii, 320, 321, 366, 368, 687
Wells, Rulon S., 339, 658
Werner, Edeltraud, 366
Wesche, Birgit, 103, 253
Wetta, Andrew C., 197, 304, 647, 658
Wexler, Kenneth, 161, 450, 530–532, 539
Weydt, Harald, 468
Wharton, R. M., 484
White, Mike, 245
Wiese, Heike, 656
Wijnen, Frank, 539, 540
Wiklund, Anna-Lena, 146
Wilcock, Graham, 347
Wilder, Chris, 117
Wiley, Edward, 477
Williams, Edwin, 242, 243, 454
Wing, Ben, 245, 246
Winkler, Susanne, 117, 307, 346, 564
Wintner, Shuly, 263, 264
Wittenberg, Eva, xvi, 656
Wöllstein, Angelika, 43, 48
Wood, Randall, 4, 469

Name index

Wunderlich, Dieter, 86, 312, 466, 567, 569, 610
Wurmbrand, Susanne, 174, 592

Xia, Fei, 415

Yamada, Hiroyasu, 366
Yamada, Jeni, 481
Yampol, Todd, 245
Yang, Charles D., 490–492, 532, 537
Yang, Chunlei, 264
Yang, Jaehyung, 264
Yankama, Beracah, 176, 489
Yasukawa, Hidekl, 221
Yatsushiro, Kazuko, 116
Yip, Moira, 119, 288
Yoon, Juntae, 416
Yoon, SinWon, 415, 416, 426
Yoshinaga, Naoki, 438

Zaenen, Annie, 37, 191, 221, 231, 233, 234, 238, 240, 324, 568, 628, 755, 772
Zalila, Ines, 263
Zappa, Frank, 448[3]
Zeevat, Henk, 245
Zhang, Yi, 265
Ziehe, T. W., 366, 367
Ziem, Alexander, 641
Zifonun, Gisela, 245
Živanović, Sašo, xviii, xxi
Zribi, Chiraz, 415
Zucchi, Alessandro, 608
Zwart, C. Jan-Wouter, 148
Zweigenbaum, Pierre, 221
Zwicky, Arnold M., 120, 122

Language index

Abaza, 457
Akan, 462
Akkadian, 471
Arabic, 103, 221, 246, 263, 415, 568
Arrernte, 221

Bambara, 473
Basque, 368, 530, 575, 581
Bengali, 221, 263
Bulgarian, 263

Cantonese, 263
Catalan, 368
Chamorro, 303
Czech, 530

Danish, 103, 104, 221, 263, 265, 366, 367, 462, 465, 492
Dutch, 113[21], 114, 148, 174, 245, 251, 264, 366, 459[13], 539–541, 592, 628, 635, 646
Dyirbal, 451, 471

English, 3, 27, 68[10], 74, 85, 87, 98, 103, 112, 114, 118, 152, 177, 189, 193, 221, 227, 231, 245, 253, 264, 293[17], 297, 307[26], 313, 331, 366, 367, 402[31], 405, 410, 415, 426, 450, 457, 459, 465, 477, 486–495, 501, 503, 504, 531, 533, 536, 539–541, 560, 563, 566, 567, 581, 590, 621, 649, 666, 669, 673–675, 687, 690
Esperanto, 264, 366, 367, 382
Estonian, 367
Ewe, 303

Faroese, 367
Finnish, 236[10], 245, 367, 368
French, 27, 103, 221, 244, 245, 264, 265, 303, 366, 367, 387, 415, 503, 690

Ga, 264

Galician, 492, 529[1]
Georgian, 221, 264
German, 177, 265, 366–368, 501, 541, 689, 690
Germanic, 100
Greek, 264
Guugu Yimidhirr, 457

Hausa, 264
Hawaiian Creole English, 479
Hebrew, 264, 530
Hindi, 222, 679
Hixkaryána, 471
Hungarian, 151, 222, 451

Icelandic, 37, 303, 592
Indonesian, 222, 264
Irish, 222, 303, 367, 638
Italian, 147, 153, 222, 366, 368, 415, 480, 492, 529[1], 533, 533

Jakaltek, 451
Japanese, 87, 116, 116[25], 118, 174, 177, 222, 253, 264, 298, 366, 367, 450, 462, 480, 530
Javanese, 530
Jiwarli, 451

Kikuyu, 303
Korean, 222, 264, 267, 298, 416, 462, 530

Latin, 3, 253, 367
Lithuanian, 638

Malagasy, 222
Malayalam, 451, 530
Maltese, 264, 265, 690
Mandarin Chinese, 222, 264, 265, 367, 466, 477, 501, 533, 672, 690
Moore, 303
Murrinh-Patha, 222

Language index

Norwegian, 222, 264, 366, 367, 462, 492

Old Icelandic, 367
Oneida, 692

Palauan, 303
Persian, 264, 265, 450, 681, 690
Pirahã, 470
Polish, 222, 264
Portuguese, 222, 264, 366, 367
Proto-Uralic, 471

Romance, 681
Russian, 236^{10}, 265, 366, 367

Sahaptin, 265
Sami, 368
sign language, 478–479
    American (ASL), 477, 530
    British, 265
    French, 265
    German, 265
    Greek, 265
    South African, 265
Slavic, 365
Sorbian
    Lower, 492, 529^{1}
    Upper, 492, 529^{1}
Sotho, Northern, 222
Spanish, 154, 222, 265, 303, 323, 366, 367, 477,
    540–541, 690
Straits Salish, 466
Swahili, 367
Swedish, 366, 368, 462, 610^{20}, 619
Swiss German, 473

Tagalog, 245, 253, 451
Tamil, 462
Thompson Salish, 303
Tigrinya, 222
Turkish, 222, 245, 253, 265, 320, 638

Urdu, 222, 679

Vietnamese, 416

Wambaya, 265, 307, 451, 562
Warlpiri, 451, 471

Welsh, 103, 222, 265, 402^{31}, 568
Wolof, 222

Yiddish, 265, 303, 416, 690

Subject index

!, 336
+, 411, 676
\, 247, 253
◯, 400
↓, 227, 259, 416
∃, 91
∀, 91
λ-calculus, 60
⊕, 273
→, 53
↑, 227, 255, 259
↑↑, 257
∨, 211
|, 237, 253
*, 9^2, 64, 75, 135, 190, 234, 240, 416
/, 195, 246–247, 253
#, 9^2
§, 9^2
⇒, 273, 278
─◦, 228

a-structure, 233
accent, 266
accomplishment, 602
acquisition, 5, 476–477, 482–504, 527, 529–545, 687
    second language, 476
    speed, 475–476
Across the Board Extraction, 171, 199, 350, 658^{53}
actant, 31, 370
activity, 602
adjacency, 55
adjective, 18–19, 21, 23, 93, 283, 466
    depictive, 41
    predicative, 41
adjunct, 30–35, 63–65, 75, 92, 102, 154, 189–191, 231, 249, 274, 283–285, 315, 416–417, 463, 555
    head, 76

adjunction, 417
    ban, 562
    obligatory, 426, 428–430
adjuncts, 230
adposition, 22, 466
adverb, 18, 22, 94
    pronominal-, 24
    relative, 25
adverbial, 34^{15}, 40–41
adverbs, 22
affix hopping, 100
agent, 31, 92, 232
Agree, 130–131, 152, 153, 176, 558, 591^1
agreement, 5, 35, 56–58, 151, 152, 176, 211, 374, 385
    object, 145, 575, 581
ambiguity, 433, 434
    spurious, 71, 76, 515, 620
analogy, 501
animacy, 92
antipassive, 667–670
apparent multiple fronting, 197^{14}
Arc Pair Grammar, 470
argument, 30–35, 91, 246, 281, 463
    designated, 243, 285, 316^5, 699
    external, 92, 101, 243
    internal, 92, 243
    position, 92
argument attraction, 681
argument composition, 681
argument structure, 91
article, 18, 53
aspect, 602
attribute-value matrix (AVM), 205
attribute-value structure, 205
automaton
    finite, 502
auxiliary inversion, 97, 98, 121, 172, 293^{17}, 489–503, 539

Subject index

back-formation, 103
backward application, 168, 247
base generation, 116
benefactive, 615–621, 683
beneficiary, 92, 233, 234
β-reduction, 61, 248
bias, 539
binary, 55
Binding Theory, 90, 144, 281, 286^{15}, 456–458, 554, 555, 567
Biolinguistics, 355
bit vector, 361
blocking, 503
bounding node, 458
branching, 55
    binary, 55, 160, 471^{27}, 496, 502, 553–556, 632, 692
    unary, 55
Broca's area, 479
Burzio's Generalization, 113, 667

c-command, 138, 297^{21}, 456
c-structure, 191^2, 223, 227
capacity
    generative, 164, 190, 201, 438, 547–551
cartography, 145^8, 466
case, 20, 23, 33, 58, 243, 280, 307, 434
    absolutive, 688
    accusative, 20, 38, 40, 43, 110, 688
    agreement, 42, 109^{18}
    dative, 20, 110
    ergative, 688
    filter, 111
    genitive, 20, 110, 289
    lexical, 109–233
    nominative, 20, 35, 110, 688
    semantic, 40
    structural, 109–454
Case Theory, 144, 243
Categorial Grammar (CG), 164–173, 177, 194, 201, 203, 245–260, 267, 290, 293^{17}, 304, 306, 307, 312, 315, 365, 375, 433, 439, 453, 454, 471, 493, 507, 509, 511, 519, 523, 525, 527^{14}, 554, 568, 576, 581, 584^5, 679, 701
category
    functional, 93, 145, 154, 175, 466

−Pol, 146
μ, 146
+Pol, 146
%Pol, 146
Adverb, 146, 152
Agr, 232
AgrA, 146
AgrIO, 146, 454
AgrN, 146
AgrO, 145, 146, 454, 575, 581
AgrS, 145, 146, 454, 575
AgrV, 146
Asp, 147, 148
Aux, 146
Benefactive, 147
C, 95, 466
Clitic Voices, 146
Color, 147^{11}
D, 95
Dist, 146, 148
Fin, 145
Foc, 145, 153
Force, 145
Gender, 146
Hearer, 147, 153
Honorific, 146
I, 95, 97–101, 110, 466
Intra, 148
Kontr, 153
Mod, 147
Mood, 147
Nationality, 147^{11}
Neg, 145, 146, 148, 232, 391
Number, 146
Obj, 148
OuterTop, 146
Pass, 589
Passive, 141
PassP, 587
PathP, 148
Perf, 589
Perfect(?), 147
Person, 146
PlaceP, 148
Predicate, 146
Quality, 147^{11}
Shape, 147^{11}

Share, 146
Size, 147[11]
Speaker, 147, 153
Subj, 148
T, 95, 147, 232, 575
Tense, 134, 146
Top, 145, 148, 153
Tra, 148
v, 132–134, 587, 622–625
Voice, 147, 558, 575
Z, 146
lexical, 27, 93, 466
syntactic, 27
causative construction, 320
CAUSE, 575
change of state, 602
CHILDES, 488–490, 490[36], 492, 501
chimpanzee, 477
classifier, 467
clitic, 540
CoGETI, 265
Cognitive Grammar, 311, 448, 493, 541, 569
coherence, 235, 239, 242
coindexation, 280
Colocant, 409
comparative, 21, 23
competence, 354–355, 432–437, 469, 517–528, 533, 544
complement, 35, 75, 92, 160–165, 274
complementizer, 105, 253, 292
completeness, 235, 239, 242
Complex NP Constraint, 458, 462
complexity class, 85, 415, 502, 547–551
composition, 254–255, 486
backward, 254, 650
forward, 254
compositionality, 282, 475
computer science, 120
configurationality, 117
conjunction, 22, 53, 155[16]
constituent, 7, 13
discontinuous, 44, 96, 322–323, 339, 652
constituent order, 117, 186, 235, 237, 253–298, 323, 420–423
fixed, 253, 297
free, 253, 297

constituent position, 296
Constraint Language for Lambda-Structures (CLLS), 575
constraint-based grammar, 83[1], 116[25], 122, 125, 177, 178, 241, 470, 495, 507–515, 519, 520[4], 525, 525[11], 526, 526[13], 699–701
construction
Active Ditransitive, 340
Caused-Motion, 345, 347, 604, 609, 619, 657
Determiner Noun, 338
linking, 315
N-P-N, 411–412, 415[2], 675–677
passive, 316
resultative, 312, 566, 583–584, 611–635
subject, 316
transitive, 316
verb phrase, 314
Construction Grammar (CxG), 96, 117, 155, 172, 173, 176[40], 194, 200, 201, 236[10], 242, 243, 267, 279, 282, 285[12], 306, 311–363, 415, 448, 493, 519[3], 525, 527[14], 541–544, 554, 562, 565, 569, 589, 598, 612[23], 646, 677, 699, 701
Fluid, 320, 405
Sign-Based, 338, 354–361
Construction Grammar(CxG), 639
context, 494
context-free grammar, 201, 415, 483, 484, 547
probabilistic (PCFG), 313, 566
context-sensitive grammar, 415, 484, 485, 547
context-free grammar, 85
contraction, 90
contrast, 523
control, 35, 224
Control Theory, 91, 144
conversion, 27
cooperativeness, 433
coordination, 16–17, 48[23], 66, 79, 122, 167–168, 197[14], 257, 273, 339[25], 471, 525[12], 543
-test, 10–11, 16
copula, 45, 568
Copy Theory of Movement, 154[15], 156, 172,

841

176[43]
core grammar, 93, 311, 529, 537
CoreGram, 265
corpus, 6
corpus annotation, 366
corpus linguistics, 504, 701
coverb, 451, 467
creole language, 478–479
critical period, 476–477
cycle
    in feature description, 213, 294, 341, 401
    transformational, 463, 521, 557

D-structure, 87, 144, 306
declarative clause, 106
Deep Structure, see D-Structure, 307
Definite Clause Grammar (DCG), 81, 219
deletion, 520
DELPH-IN, 263
dependency, 475
Dependency Categorial Grammar, 261
Dependency Grammar (DG), 96, 117, 173, 194, 197[14], 439, 517[1], 652[49], 658[53]
Dependency Unification Grammar (DUG), 407, 547, 699
depictive predicate, 286[15], 307[26], 563–565
derivation, 27, 123, 320, 688
derivation tree, 418
Derivational Theory of Complexity (DTC), 519[3], 519–522
descriptive adequacy, 447
determiner, 23, 53
    as head, 29
directive, 665
disjunction, 210–211, 237
Distributed Morphology, 667
do-Support, 541
dominance, 54
    immediate, 54, 185, 267, 322

economy
    transderivational, 144
elementary tree, 416
ellipsis, 286[15], 483[31], 520, 525[12], 553, 567, 666
empty element, 15[8], 68, 113, 154, 160, 166, 170, 295, 305, 312, 323, 422, 432, 437, 452, 455, 456, 554, 567–584, 661, 673

PRO, see PRO
empty head, 666, 675
endocentricity, 96
entity, 188
epsilon, 569
epsilon production, 68
escape hatch, 460
event, 281
evidence
    negative
        indirect, 503
evokes operator, 341
Exceptional Case Marking (ECM), 558
experiencer, 31, 92, 233
explanatory adequacy, 447
Extended Projection Principle (EPP), 454, 535
external argument, 93
extraction, 386, 458, 462–465, 568, 619
    from adjuncts, 548
    from specifier, 548
    island, 462
    subject, 529
extraction path marking, 303, 349, 381
extraposition, 104[13], 147[12], 172, 397, 433, 458, 462
Extraposition, 458

f-structure, 191[2], 223, 227, 554, 557, 562
Faculty of Language
    in the Broad Sense (FLB), 474
    in the Narrow Sense (FLN), 475
feature
    ADJ, 224, 230
    ARG-ST, 270, 554, 582
    COMPS, 268, 328
    COMP, 224
    CONT, 641
    DAUGHTERS, 169
    DF, 241
    DSL, 291, 293, 300
    EVOKES, 341
    FOCUS, 224, 239
    GEN, 280
    HEAD-DTR, 271
    HEAD, 276, 336–337
    INITIAL, 274

LEX-DTR, 288
MC, 186
MOD, 283
MOTHER, 327
NON-HEAD-DTRS, 271
NUM, 280
OBJ, 224
OBL, 224
PER, 280
PRED, 223
QUE, 300
REL, 300
SEM, 641
SLASH, 300
SPECIFIED, 334*
SPR, 268
SUBJ, 224
SYNSEM, 328
TOPIC, 224, 239
VAL, 315
XARG, 330, 334*, 560
XCOMP, 224
    checking, 129
    deletion, 130
    strong, 127
    weak, 127
feature checking, 144
feature description, 205–217
feature structure, 215–217
feature-value structure, 205
feral child, 477
field
    middle-, 44, 101
    post-, 44
    pre-, 44, 101
filler, 196, 314
focus, 107, 145, 153–154, 223–224, 239, 464
Foot Feature Principle, 198
foot node, 428
formal language, 496
formalization, 6, 312, 542
forward application, 168, 246
FoxP2, 481–482
fronting, 10, 13–16
    apparent multiple, 17^9, 154, 171, 395, 396, 647^{43}, 658^{53}
function composition, 267, 307, 681

functional application, 188
functional uncertainty, 240, 324, 562, 635
functor, 246, 544
future, 20, 540

gap, 89
gender, 20, 23, 58, 280, 307, 512–515, 557
gene, 481–482, 696
Generalized Phrase Structure Grammar (GPSG), 75, 103^{11}, 123, 125, 219, 235^8, 237, 246, 260, 267, 274, 276, 290, 296, 304, 306, 323, 327, 340, 381, 399^{29}, 415, 417, 421, 439, 470, 507, 509, 519, 525, 527^{14}, 568, 699
Generative Grammar, 54, 83, 470, 507
genitive, 38, 565
Gesetz der wachsenden Glieder, 557
glue language, 228
glue semantics, 227–230, 373, 683
goal, 233
government, 33, 120
Government and Binding (GB), xviii, 75, 84, 86, 87, 89, 90, 102, 108, 122, 192, 194^5, 223, 225, 226, 228, 234, 235, 246, 249, 252, 253, 260, 267, 290, 306, 312, 395, 417, 422, 433, 454, 456, 489, 519, 519^3, 521, 554, 557, 560, 564, 567, 575, 649^{48}, 667, 673, 674, 701
gradability, 509–510
Grammar Matrix, 265
grammatical function, 148, 231, 286, 314, 454–456, 700
    governable, 223
Greediness Constraint, 531, 532, 532^2

head, 28–30, 227, 274
head domain
    extended, 235, 307
head feature, 30
Head Feature Convention (HFC), 182, 276
Head-Driven Phrase Structure Grammar (HPSG), 75, 96, 101^{10}, 116^{25}, 123, 125, 145^8, 154, 155, 162, 168, 173, 191^2, 194, 197^{14}, 201, 242, 243, 252^6, 253, 263–308, 312, 315, 316, 328, 339, 340, 354–361, 375, 381, 382, 386, 395, 397, 410, 415, 426,

439, 454, 457, 470, 483[31], 493, 509, 512, 519, 521, 525, 527[14], 528, 536, 547, 554–556, 559, 560, 563, 568, 570, 576, 581, 584[5], 621, 652, 658[53], 679, 686, 690, 699, 701
    Constructional, 334
Heavy-NP-Shift, 323
Hole Semantics, 576
hydra clause, 453
hypotenuse, 341

iambus, 533
Icelandic, 288[16]
ID/LP grammar, 185, 235[8], 267, 420
identification in the limit, 483–486
ideophone, 467
idiom, 338, 537, 560–565, 614[25], 639
imperative, 20, 35
implication, 273, 278
index, 154
indicative, 20
inflection, 19–22, 27, 88, 688
    -paradigm, 20
inflectional class, 21, 58
information structure, 107, 153–154, 223, 347, 465, 612[22]
inheritance, 242, 282, 314, 315, 320, 612, 639–641, 675, 700
    default, 123, 407, 639
    multiple, 210, 426
instrument, 233
Integrational Linguistics, xvi
interface, 355
interjection, 22, 23
interrogative clause, 48–49, 272, 673–675
intervention, 138
introspection, 701
inversion, 567
IQ, 481

Kleene star, 190, 234

label, 154–160, 169
λ-abstraction, 61
λ-conversion, 61
language
    formal, 120, 482

language acquisition, 118, 134, 246, 312, 447, 458[11], 553
language evolution, 312
learnability, 485
learning theory, 496
left associativity, 247
lexeme, 27
Lexical Decomposition Grammar, 312
Lexical Functional Grammar (LFG), 38, 39, 75, 101[10], 125, 154, 173, 177, 178, 191[2], 194, 200, 219, 290, 304–307, 312, 323, 373, 382, 431, 454, 455, 470, 507, 509, 519, 519[3], 525, 527[14], 528, 547, 554, 555, 559, 560, 562, 568, 572, 574, 602, 612[23], 646, 652, 686, 699, 701
lexical integrity, 231, 312, 610, 613, 660
Lexical Mapping Theory (LMT), 232–234, 290
Lexical Resource Semantics (LRS), 280[9]
lexical rule, 193, 251, 285–584
    verb-initial position, 294–295
lexicon, 88–279
linear logic, 228
linear precedence, 185, 267, 322
Linear Precedence Rule, 186
linearization rule, 170, 231, 340
Linguistic Knowledge Builder (LKB), 263
Link Grammar, 366
linking, 93, 232–234, 270, 281–282, 315–320, 372
list, 207, 711
    difference, 712
local maximum, 532
locality, 153, 272, 327–334, 338, 418, 438, 556–565
    of matching, 138
locative alternation, 654
Logical Form (LF), 88, 90–91, 306, 439
long-distance dependency, 106–109, 195–198, 237–241, 257, 293[17], 298–304, 323–324, 327, 426
long-Distance dependency, 254–382
lowering, 100
LP-rule, 186

macaque, 477

Subject index

machine translation, 366
macro, 242, 306
Mainstream Generative Grammar, 83
Mandarin Chinese, 451, 486
Markov model, 502
matryoshka, 4, 7
maturation, 532
Meaning–Text Theory (MTT), 365, 366^2, 373, 406^{35}
meaning constructor, 228
memory, 520^4
Merge, 144, 154, 453, 467^{23}, 471^{27}, 478
    External, 144, 692
    Internal, 144
metarule, 186–188, 193–194, 556
metrical grid, 266
metrics, 533
Middle Construction, 318, 320
middle field, *see* field
mildly context-sensitive grammar
    context-sensitive grammar, 415, 438, 473, 547, 551
Minimal Recursion Semantics (MRS), 272, 280, 284^{11}, 315, 327, 420, 576, 634
Minimalist Grammar (MG), 145^8, 164–172, 176, 308, 547, 548
Minimalist Program (MP), 127–174, 192, 355, 391, 452, 453, 471, 509, 511, 523, 584^5, 649^{48}, 674, 699, 701
Missing VP effect, 518
MITRE, 122
model, 215–217
model-theoretic grammar, 83, 266, 470, 507–515
modifier, 34, 92
modularity, 523
module, 527
modus ponens, 229
mood, 20
morphology, 88, 176, 231–686
Move, 144
movement
    altruistic, 153, 170
    covert, 151
    feature-driven, 153
    permutation, 13
movement test, 9–10

Move α, 89
Multi-Component TAG, 420, 421, 423
music, 474, 480

nativism, 448
negative evidence, 484, 488, 491, 503–504
Neo-Davidsonian semantics, 634
neural network, 493–494
neutral order, 114
New Prague School, 365
Nirvana, 534
No Tampering Condition (NTC), 355^{34}, 525^{12}
node, 54
    daughter, 55
    mother, 55
    sister, 55
nominalization, 110, 503
Non-Tangling Condition, 96
nonlocal dependency, 321
noun, 18, 20, 23, 53, 68, 93, 466
    common, 338
    mass, 69
    relational, 66
NP-split, 14
nucleus, 368
number, 20, 56, 58, 280, 307
numeration, 128, 176

o-command, 297^{21}
object, 306, 454–456
    direct, 38, 39
    indirect, 38, 39
obliqueness, 286^{15}, 454
Obliqueness, 297^{21}
observational adequacy, 447
Off-Line Parsability, 547
Optimality Theory (OT), xvi, 519^3
optional infinitive, 539
optionality, 32, 34
order
    unmarked, 114
organ, 480

paradigm, 27
parameter, 86, 458^{11}, 478, 529–537, 687
    default value, 531, 532, 535
    head direction, 450–451

head position, 86
pro-drop, 492, 492, 529, 533–535
subjacency, 465, 529
subject article drop, 533
SV, 530
topic drop, 533
V2, 530, 532
parser, 548
Parsing as Deduction, 122
partial verb phrase fronting, 200–201, 694
participle
adjectival, 140
particle, 22, 23
passive, 109, 110, 114, 140–142, 191–194, 231–234, 249–251, 285–320, 326, 373–375, 425–426, 520, 561, 581, 612[22], 617, 619, 686
impersonal, 110, 113, 193, 194, 289, 567
long, 306[25], 309
remote, 592
path, 206
path equation, 338
patient, 31, 92, 233
PATR-II, 219, 338
performance, 313, 354–355, 432–437, 463, 465, 469, 517–528, 533, 544, 635, 695
periphery, 93[4], 311, 537
permutation test, 9–10
person, 20, 56
Person, 280
phase, 129, 355, 523
phenomenon, 215
Phenomenon, 217
Phonetic Form (PF), 88–90
phonology, 267
phrase, 7
phrase structure grammar, 53–59, 246, 267, 271, 507, 567
pidgin language, 478
pied-piping, 258, 410[38]
pivot schema, 541
plural, 20, 69
Polish, 560
polygraph, 389–390
positional, 467
postfield, *see* field

postposition, 22
Poverty of the Stimulus, 457, 458[11], 478, 482–504
predicate, 91
predicate logic, 30
predicate-argument structure, 475
predicative, 41–42
prefield, *see* field
ellipsis, 286[15]
preposition, 18, 22, 71–73, 94
present, 20
presupposition, 464
preterite, 20
PrinciParse, 122
principle
case, 688
Case, 288–290
Generalized Head Feature, 408
Head Feature, 276, 336–337
NONLOC-, 301
Semantics, 282, 688
Sign, 328[15]
Subject-Mapping, 233
Principles & Parameters, 86–87, 529–537
PRO, 422
Probability Matching, 479
progressive, 541
projection, 29, 96
maximal, 29, 77, 96
of features, 30
projectivity, 372, 377, 392, 400–405, 421, 593
pronominalization test, 8
pronoun, 24–688
expletive, 11–12, 26, 31, 107, 113, 455, 492, 534, 567
reflexive, 280, 555
relative, 568
prosody, 257, 511, 523

quantification, 230
quantifier
existential, 91
universal, 91, 189
question tag, 560

raising, 288[16], 425, 559, 634–635
Random Step, 532
Rangprobe, 47

recursion, xvii, 4^1, 49–50, 65, 437, 502, 517, 517^1, 565–566
recursively enumerable language, 484
reference, 11, 12
regular language, 484, 547
relation, 556
    ◯, 400
    append, 219, 273, 297
    shuffle, 400
Relational Grammar, xvi, 508
relative clause, 32, 47–49, 272, 380, 410, 465, 517, 673–675
    free, 157–158, 286^{15}
remote passive, 374^{11}
repetitive, 575
representational model, 123
REQUEST, 122
restitutive, 575
resultative construction, 530, 583
rewrite grammar, 483
Right Roof Constraint, 458
right to left elaboration, 495
Right-Node-Raising, 162
rising, 379, 593
Role and Reference Grammar, xvi, 155
root, 687
root Infinitive, 539
rule-to-rule hypothesis, 62, 189

S-structure, 87, 144, 306
S-Structure, 439
satellite, 368
Satzglied, 13^4
schema
    Filler-Head, 302
    head-adjunct, 284
    Head-Complement, 273
scope, 104–116, 197^{14}, 231, 323, 420, 567, 658^{53}
segmentation, 539
selection, 31
    restriction, 434
self-embedding, 468^{25}, 517, 565, 566
semantic role, 31, 92, 232–234, 281, 315, 373, 631
semantics, 176, 282
sentence bracket, 44, 101

sentence symbol, 279
set, 207, 324–326
sexus, 513
Shortest Move Constraint (SMC), 165^{32}, 548
sideward movement, 171
sign language, 479
    American (ASL), 479
signature, 215
Single Value Constraint, 531, 532
singular, 20
Situation Semantics, 280^9
specifier, 75, 97, 160–165, 548
statistics, 222, 246, 313, 416, 494, 496–502, 504, 661
stem, 688
strength, 127
Structure Preservation, 525^{12}
structure sharing, 211–213, 269, 290, 338, 381, 521
subcategorization, 91, 182, 268
subcategorization frame, 91
subjacency, 458–466, 529
Subjacency, 144
subject, 35–38, 97, 110, 306, 314, 454–456, 560
Subject Condition, 454
subjunctive, 20
substitution, 416
substitution test, 7, 8
subsumption, 325
superlative, 21
Surface Structure, *see* S-structure
SVO, 531
symbol
    non-terminal, 483
    terminal, 483
syntax-semantics interface, 60

T model, 87–89
TAG
    Free Order (FO-TAG), 421
Tamagotchi, 476
tense, 20, 23
text, 471^{26}
that-t, 529
the-clause, 674
thematic grid, 91
theme, 92, 233

Subject index

theory, 215–217
Theta-Criterion, 92, 144, 226, 243
θ-grid, 91, 223
θ-role, 92
θ-Theory, 122, 243, 526
third construction, 694
Tiger corpus, 461
topic, 145, 153–154, 223–224, 239
Topic Drop, 286[15]
topicalization, 107, 255, 257, 674
topology, 43–50, 101, 321
trace, 89
    extraction trace, 301, 303
    verb, 15[8], 293, 295
TRALE, 263, 356
transderivational constraint, 158, 174, 176
transformation, 84–86, 312, 437, 439, 493, 519–522, 525, 581–584
    fact-Deletion, 464
Transformational Grammar, 517[1], 83–517
Tree Adjoining Grammar (TAG), 96, 164, 167, 173, 194[5], 306, 313, 316, 339[25], 415–439, 507, 509, 525, 527[14], 536, 547, 565, 568, 581, 650, 651, 653, 679, 686, 699, 701
    Feature Structure-Based (FTAG), 427, 680
    Synchronous (STAG), 439
    Feature Structure-Based (FTAG), 427–430
    Multi-Component (MC-TAG), 421–423
    Tree Tuple MC-TAG (TT-MC-TAG), 423, 437
    Vector (V-TAG), 423, 430–432, 437, 439, 568
trigger, 537
trochee, 533
truth value, 188
type, 208–211
    atomic, 209
    head-adjunct-phrase, 284
    head-argument-phrase, 402
    head-comp-cx, 328, 337
    head-complement-phrase, 273
    head-filler-phrase, 302
    headcomplement-phrase, 296
    headed-phrase, 169, 277

type hierarchy, 209–210, 282
type raising, 254, 254, 568, 584[5]
    backward, 650

unary, 55
underspecification, 575
Underspecified Discourse Representation Theory (UDRT), 576
unification, 213–215, 248, 325
uniformity, 456, 567
universal, 449–475
    implicational, 449[4]
    implicative, 696
Universal Base Hypothesis, 699
Universal Grammar (UG), 145, 147, 246, 448, 591, 669
    as a toolkit, 467
    falsifiability, 465[19], 467, 473
unrestricted grammars, 547
Unsupervised Data-Oriented Parsing (U-DOP), 496–502, 661–663

valence, 31–35, 57, 182, 223, 246–247, 267–268, 281, 416
    change, 674
    classes, 88
valence frame, 91
verb, 18–19, 23, 53, 93, 466, 687
    -final, 43
    -first, 43
    -second, 43
    AcI, 109
    auxiliary, 487
    bivalent, 43
    ditransitive, 42, 111[20], 530
    ergative, 93[3]
    inherent reflexives, 16, 31
    intransitive, 42
    modal, 487, 541
    monovalent, 166–167
    particle, 520, 530
    perception, 109[19]
    serial, 672
    subjectless, 325
    transitive, 42, 286[13]
    unaccusative, 93, 117, 140, 234, 286[13], 626, 687
    unergative, 286[13], 687

verb position, 106, 195, 234, 251–253, 290–323, 425, 667, 669
  -second-, 106
Verb position, 194
verb-final language, 105, 235
verb-second language, 107
verb-particle, 5
verbal complex, 119, 635
Verb*mobil*, 177, 265, 359^{37}
visual perception, 474
Vorfeld, 17^9

Wernicke's area, 479
wh-exclamative, 674
Williams Syndrome, 481
word, 688
Word Grammar (WG), 366, 369, 374^{11}, 375^{12}, 380, 381, 406^{35}
word sequence, 7

$\overline{\text{X}}$ theory, 73–77, 80, 84, 93–96, 118, 122, 123, 127, 131, 144, 155, 160–164, 170, 249^3, 283, 451–453, 526, 553, 554, 557, 675
XP, 75

www.ingramcontent.com/pod-product-compliance
Ingram Content Group UK Ltd.
Pitfield, Milton Keynes, MK11 3LW, UK
UKHW050937280426
12129UKWH00013B/890